Dear Reader,

We are delighted to present the 2018 edition of the MICHELIN Main Cities of Europe guide.

The guide caters for every type of visitor, from business traveller to families on holiday, and lists the best establishments across all categories of comfort and price - from cosy bistros and intimate townhouses to celebrated restaurants and luxurious hotels. So, whether you're visiting for work or pleasure, you'll find something that's right for you.

All of the establishments in the guide have been selected by our team of famous Michelin inspectors, who are the eyes and ears of our readers. Each year, they search for new establishments to add to the guide - and only the best make it through. Once the annual selection has been made, the "best of the best" are then recognised with distinctions.

Regular readers will notice that the guide has a different look this year. The most significant change is that the restaurants - our readers' favourite part - now appear at the front of each locality, with the hotels following afterwards. Restaurants are also now ordered according to the quality of their food, with the awards that you already know and love (Stars ❀ and Bib Gourmands ⊛) being placed at the top. The rest of the restaurants in our selection are then identified by a new symbol: The Michelin Plate ⅼ◯. Being chosen by the Michelin Inspectors for inclusion in the guide is a guarantee of quality in itself and the plate symbol highlights restaurants where you will have a good meal.

The presentation of the guide may have changed but our mission is still the same: to help you find the best restaurants and hotels on your travels.

We trust you will enjoy travelling with the 2018 edition of the Main Cities of Europe guide.

3

The MICHELIN Guide's Commitments

Experienced in quality!

Whether they are in Japan, the USA, China or Europe, our inspectors apply the same criteria to judge the quality of each and every restaurant and hotel that they visit. The MICHELIN guide commands a worldwide reputation thanks to the commitments we make to our readers – and we reiterate these below:

ANONYMOUS INSPECTIONS

Our inspectors make regular and anonymous visits to hotels and restaurants to gauge the quality of products and services offered to an ordinary customer. They settle their own bill and may then introduce themselves and ask for more information about the establishment. Our readers' comments are also a valuable source of information, which we can follow up with a visit of our own.

INDEPENDENCE

To remain totally objective for our readers, the selection is made with complete independence. Entry into the guide is free. All decisions are discussed with the Editor and our highest awards are considered at a European level.

SELECTION AND CHOICE

The guide offers a selection of the best restaurants and hotels in every category of comfort and price. This is only possible because all the inspectors rigorously apply the same methods.

ANNUAL UPDATES

All the practical information, classifications and awards are revised and updated every year to give the most reliable information possible.

CONSISTENCY

The criteria for the classifications are the same in every country covered by the MICHELIN guide.

The sole intention of Michelin is to make your travels safe and enjoyable.

The
MICHELIN Distinctions

To help you select the best establishment for every occasion, we award several distinctions:

✿✿✿ **Three Stars: Exceptional cuisine, worth a special journey!**
Our highest award is given for the superlative cooking of chefs at the peak of their profession. The ingredients are exemplary, the cooking is elevated to an art form and their dishes are often destined to become classics.

✿✿ **Two Stars: Excellent cooking, worth a detour!**
The personality and talent of the chef and their team is evident in the expertly crafted dishes, which are refined, inspired and sometimes original.

✿ **One Star: High quality cooking, worth a stop!**
Using top quality ingredients, dishes with distinct flavours are carefully prepared to a consistently high standard.

☺ **Bib Gourmand: Good quality, good value cooking**
'Bibs' are awarded for simple yet skilful cooking.

⭐ **Plate: Good cooking**
Fresh ingredients, capably prepared: simply a good meal.

Our famous one ✿, two ✿✿ and three ✿✿✿ stars identify establishments serving the highest quality cuisine – taking into account the quality of ingredients, the mastery of techniques and flavours, the levels of creativity and, of course, consistency.

Contents

Consult the MICHELIN guide at: www.ViaMichelin.com
and write to us at: themichelinguide-europe@michelin.com

Countries

How to use this Guide

RESTAURANTS

Restaurants are listed by distinction.
Within each distinction category, they
are ordered by comfort.
Within each comfort category, they are
then ordered alphabetically.

Distinctions:

❀❀❀ Three Stars: Exceptional cuisine
❀❀ Two Stars: Excellent cooking
❀ One Star: High quality cooking
⊛ Bib Gourmand: Good quality, good value cooking
⑩ Plate: Good cooking

Comfort:

Level of comfort from XxXxX to X,
followed by ⑨/ for tapas bars and ⑤
for pubs.
Red: our most delightful places.

RESTAURANTS & HOTELS

The country is indicated by the
coloured strip down the side of the
page: dark for restaurants, light for
hotels.

HOTELS

Hotels are listed by comfort from ⋒⋒⋒
to ⋒, followed by ⋒ for guesthouses.
Within each comfort category, they are
ordered alphabetically.
Red: our most delightful places.

MONTMARTRE – PIGALLE

❀❀ **Les Trois Maisons**
151bis rue Marcadet (18th) – Ⓜ Lamar
– ☏ 01 42 57 71 22 – www.troismaison
– Menu 47 € – Carte 55/85 €
• Mediterranean • Rustic •
This restaurant's intimate setting high
sculptures on display. The fine cont
produce, including game in season
choice of champagnes.
→ Encornets farcis aux oignons do
filet d'agneau des Pyrénées rôtis, j
lante aux fruits de saison parfumé

❀ **Les Bancs publics**
151bis rue Marcadet (18th) – Ⓜ
– ☏ 01 42 57 71 22 – www.lesba
Menu 42 € ⑨ – Carte 45/80€
• Rustic • Friendly •
A charming pavilion (1850) ju
Cascade) in the Bois de Boulo
majestic rotunda or on the de
→ Tourteau de Bretagne au r
du pays d'Oc, tomates et pru

⊛ **Caillebotte**
83 rue Lepic (18th) – Ⓜ Ab
– www.caillebotte.fr – clo
Menu 36 € – Carte 45/55
• Classic • Trendy •
Two young enthusiasti
inviting vintage bistro w
nofrills dishes pay tribu
contrasting seasonings

⋒⋒⋒ **Hôtel Le Tertre**
12 rue J. de Maistre (1
– www.reservationle
85 rm ⋤ – ∮ 210/2
• Family • Cosy •
At the foot of Sacré
upper floors on th
beautiful fireplace
❀ **La Terrasse** –

⋒ **Paris-Montm**
1 rue Caulainco
– www.mercure
305 rm – ∮∮ 1
• Chain ho
The hotel is n
the rooms on

⋒ **Hôtel Anv**
55 bd Roche
– www.hot
111 rm ⋤
• Traditi
This estab
of Paris. C

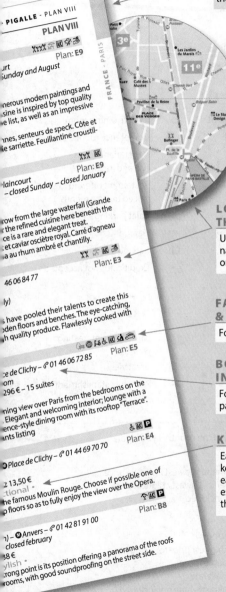

PLAN VIII

XxxX 🛋 🖼 🌸 🍃
Plan: **E9**

urt
unday and August

nerous modern paintings and
uisine is inspired by top quality
e list, as well as an impressive

nnes, senteurs de speck. Côte et
e sarriette. Feuillantine croustil-

XxX 🖼
Plan: **E9**

laincourt
– closed Sunday – closed January

row from the large waterfall (Grande
r the refined cuisine here beneath the
ce is a rare and elegant treat. Carré d'agneau
et caviar osciètre royal. Carré d'agneau
a au rhum ambré et chantilly.

XX 🛋 🖼 🗻
Plan: **E3**

46 06 84 77

ly)

s have pooled their talents to create this
oden floors and benches. The eye-catching,
h quality produce. Flawlessly cooked with

🍴⭐🖼 Ɫ⬆🖼 🛋 🚗
Plan: **E5**

te de Clichy – ☎ 01 46 06 72 85
om
296 € – 15 suites

ning view over Paris from the bedrooms on the
. Elegant and welcoming interior; lounge with a
ence-style dining room with its rooftop "Terrace".
nts listing

♿ 🖼 🅿
Plan: **E4**

Place de Clichy – ☎ 01 44 69 70 70

z 13,50 €
tional –
he famous Moulin Rouge. Choose if possible one of
p floors so as to fully enjoy the view over the Opera.

⬆🖼 🅿
Plan: **B8**

) – Ⓜ Anvers – ☎ 01 42 81 91 00
closed february

8 €
ylish •
trong point is its position offering a panorama of the roofs
ooms, with good soundproofing on the street side.

LOCATION

The country, the town,
the district and the map.

LOCATING
THE ESTABLISHMENT

Use the references and coordi-
nates to locate establishments
on the city plans.

FACILITIES
& SERVICES

For more details see page 10.

BOOKING
INFORMATION

For more details on prices see
page 10.

KEY WORDS

Each entry comes with two
keywords, making it quick and
easy to identify the type of
establishment and/or the food
that it serves.

The Symbols

City Plan Key

● Restaurants
▲ Hotels

SIGHTS

▭ Place of interest   ⛪ Interesting place of worship

ROADS

═══ Motorway   ❶ Junctions: complete

─── Dual carriageway   ❶ Junctions: limited

Pedestrian street   🚉 Station and railway

VARIOUS SIGNS

🅸 Tourist Information Centre   ✈ Airport

▨▨ Mosque   ✚ Hospital

▨▨ Synagogue   ✉ Covered market

⚘⚘ Ruins   ▭ Public buildings:

Garden, Park, Wood   H Town Hall

🚌 Coach station   R Town Hall (Germany)

Ⓜ Metro station   M Museum

⊖ Underground station (UK)   U University

11

Selection
by Country

VIENNA ●

● Salzburg

AUSTRIA
ÖSTERREICH

adisa/iStock

VIENNA
WIEN

badahos/iStock

VIENNA IN...

→ **ONE DAY**
A tram ride round the Ringstrasse, St Stephen's Cathedral, a section of the Hofburg Palace, cakes in a café.

→ **TWO DAYS**
MuseumsQuartier, Spittelberg, Hundertwasserhaus, Prater.

→ **THREE DAYS**
A day at the Belvedere, a night at the opera.

Beethoven, Brahms, Mozart, Haydn, Strauss...not a bad list of former residents, by any stretch of the imagination. One and all, they succumbed to the opulent aura of Vienna, a city where an appreciation of the arts is as conspicuous as its famed cakes. Sumptuous architecture and a refined air reflect the city's historic position as the seat of the powerful Habsburg dynasty and former epicentre of the Austro-Hungarian Empire.

Despite its grand image, Vienna has propelled itself into the 21C with a handful of innovative hotspots, most notably the MuseumsQuartier cultural complex, a stone's throw from the mighty Hofburg Imperial

Palace. This is not a big city, although its vivid image gives that impression. The compact centre teems with elegant shops, fashionable coffee-houses and grand avenues, and the empire's awesome 19C remnants keep visitors' eyes fixed forever upwards. Many towns and cities are defined by their ring roads, but Vienna can boast a truly upmarket version: the Ringstrasse, a showpiece boulevard that cradles the inner city and the riches that lie therein. Just outside, to the southwest are the districts of Neubau and Spittelberg, both of which have taken on a quirky, modernistic feel. To the east lies Prater, the green lung of Vienna and further out lies the suburban area enhanced by the grandeur of the Schönbrunn palace.

EATING OUT

Vienna is the spiritual home of the café and Austrians drink nearly twice as much coffee as beer. It is also a city with a sweet tooth: cream cakes enhance the window displays of most eateries and is there a visitor to Vienna who hasn't succumbed to the sponge of the Sachertorte? Viennese food is essentially the food of Bohemia, which means that meat has a strong presence on the plate. Expect beef, veal and pork, alongside potatoes, dumplings or cabbage - be sure to try traditional boiled beef and the ubiquitous Wiener Schnitzel (deep-fried breaded veal). Also worth experiencing are the Heurigen, traditional Austrian wine taverns which are found in Grinzing, Heiligenstadt, Neustift and Nussdorf. You'll find plenty of snug cafés and bars too. If you want to snack, the place to go is Naschmarkt, Vienna's best market, where the stalls spill over into the vibrant little restaurants. When it comes to tipping, if you're in the more relaxed local pubs and wine taverns, just round up the bill, otherwise add on ten per cent.

AUSTRIA - VIENNA

❀❀ **Silvio Nickol Gourmet Restaurant** – Hotel Palais Coburg Residenz
Coburgbastei 4 ✉ *1010* – ⓜ *Stubentor*   XxxX 🐝 🏡 & 🅰🅒 ⇆ 🚗
– ℰ *(01) 51 81 81 30*   Plan: **E2**
– *www.palais-coburg.com*
– *Closed 21 January-8 February and Sunday-Monday*
Menu 109/188 €
– Carte 109/153 € – *(dinner only) (booking advisable)*
• Modern cuisine • Elegant • Luxury •
The culinary creations served at Silvio Nickol are modern, highly elaborate, considered right down to the smallest detail, and made from nothing but the finest produce and ingredients. Whatever you do, don't forget to take a good look at the wine list as it contains some genuine rarities.
➔ Entenleber, Ananas, Ingwer, Mohn. Kalbsschulterscherzel, Aubergine, Erdnuss, Federkohl. Wilde Blaubeere, Nussbutter, Fichte, weiße Schokolade.

❀❀ **Steirereck im Stadtpark** (Heinz Reitbauer)   XxxX 🐝 🏡 & 🅰🅒
Am Heumarkt 2a ✉ *1030* – ⓜ *Stadtpark*   ⇆
– ℰ *(01) 7 13 31 68*   Plan: **F2**
– *www.steirereck.at*
– *Closed Saturday-Sunday and Bank Holidays*
Menu 95 € (lunch)/152 €
– Carte 69/117 € – *(booking essential)*
• Creative • Design • Chic •
All the ingredients used here are excellent, including produce from the restaurant's long-standing local suppliers and herbs from its own roof garden. The food is creative but never fussy, strong on regional and national influences and full of intense, finely balanced flavours. The service is professional yet relaxed.
➔ Saibling im Bienenwachs mit gelber Rübe, Pollen und Rahm. Rehragout mit Schrot, Brokkoli und Schwarznessel. Java Kaffee mit gelben Datteln, Zwetschken und Zimtblüten.
🍴 **Meierei im Stadtpark** – See restaurant listing

❀❀ **Konstantin Filippou**   XX 🐝 🏡
Dominikanerbastei 17 ✉ *1010* – ⓜ *Stubentor*   Plan: **E2**
– ℰ *(01) 5 12 22 29*
– *www.konstantinfilippou.com*
– *Closed Saturday-Sunday and Bank Holidays*
Menu 46 € (lunch)/139 € (dinner) – *(booking advisable)*
• Modern cuisine • Minimalist • Romantic •
Creative, modern and fashionably informal describe both the interior and the cuisine on offer here. Find attractive wooden tables, a cooking station in the dining room and small windows offering views of the busy chefs at work in the kitchen. Good accompanying wines.
➔ Langostino, Kalbszunge, Cochayuyo, Zitrus. Brandade, Black Cod, Saiblingskaviar. Miéral Taube "Marokko".
🍴 **O boufés** – See restaurant listing

❀ **Edvard** – Hotel Palais Hansen Kempinski   XxX 🏡 🅰🅒
Schottenring 24 ✉ *1010* – ⓜ *Schottenring*   Plan: **D1**
– ℰ *(01) 2 36 10 00 80 82* – *www.kempinski.com/wien*
– *Closed 8-14 January, August, Sunday-Monday and Bank Holidays*
Menu 89/129 €
– Carte 45/78 €
• Modern cuisine • Elegant • Luxury •
This elegant gourmet restaurant offers a successful marriage of the modern and classic, both in its sophisticated aromatic cuisine and the accomplished, pleasantly informal service. The excellent wine suggestions and good wines by the glass are also worth a mention.
➔ Sot l'y laisse, Bio Ei, Karfiol Nüsse. Rind, Wacholder, Paradeiser. Traube, Bahibé, Pekannuss.

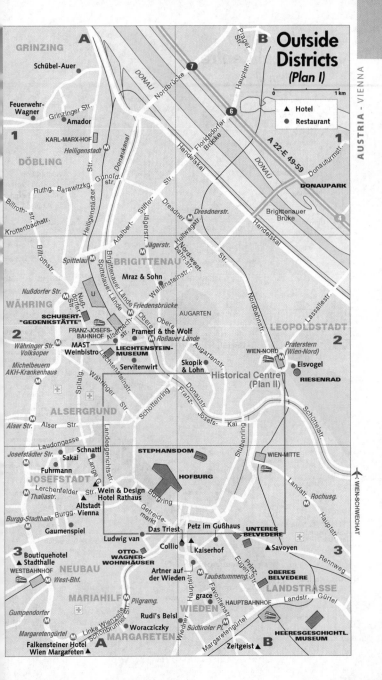

Outside Districts (Plan I)

Legend:
▲ Hotel
● Restaurant

0 — 1 km

Labels on map

GRINZING

Schübel-Auer

Feuerwehr-Wagner

Grinzinger Str.

Amador

KARL-MARX-HOF

Heiligenstadt

DÖBLING

Ruthg. Barawitzkg.

Billroth-str.

Krottenbachstr.

Billrothstr.

Spittelau

Nußdorfer Str.

WÄHRING

Nußdorfer Str.

SCHUBERT-"GEDENKSTÄTTE"

FRANZ-JOSEFS-BAHNHOF

MAST Weinbistro

Währinger Str. Volksoper

Michelbeuern AKH-Krankenhaus

ALSERGRUND

Alser Str. Alser Str.

Laudongasse

Josefstädter Str.

Schnattl

Sakai

Fuhrmann

JOSEFSTADT

Lerchenfelder Str.

Thaliastr.

Burgg.

Altstadt Vienna

Burgg-Stadthalle

Gaumenspiel

Boutiquehotel ▲ Stadthalle

WESTBAHNHOF

West-Bhf.

NEUBAU

Gumpendorfer Str.

MARIAHILF

Margaretengürtel

Falkensteiner Hotel Wien Margareten ▲

MARGARETEN

BRIGITTENAU

Mraz & Sohn

Brigittenauer Lände Spittelauer Lände

Friedensbrücke

AUGARTEN

Prameri & the Wolf

Roßauer Lände

LIECHTENSTEIN-MUSEUM

Servitenwirt

Skopik & Lohn

Schottenring

Schottenring Franz-Josefs-Kai

Landesgerichtsstr. Lange G.

STEPHANSDOM

HOFBURG

Wein & Design Hotel Rathaus

Getreide-markt

Das Triest

Ludwig van

OTTO-WAGNER-WOHNHÄUSER

Collio

Artner auf der Wieden

Pilgramg.

Rudi's Beisl

Woracziczky

Linke Wienzeile Schönbrunner Str.

WIEDEN

Wiednr

Südtiroler Pl.

Margaretengürtel

GRINZING

DONAU

Nordbrücke

Prater Str.

Haupstr.

Floridsdorfer Brücke

DONAU

A 22-E 49-59

Donauturmstr.

DONAUPARK

Handelskai

Dresdnerstr.

Brigittenauer Brüke

Handelskai

LEOPOLDSTADT

Nordbahnstr.

Lassallestr.

Praterstern (Wien-Nord)

WIEN-NORD

Eisvogel

RIESENRAD

Historical Centre (Plan II)

Stubenring

WIEN-MITTE

Landstr. Rochusg.

UNTERES BELVEDERE

Petz im Gußhaus

Kaiserhof

Savoyen

OBERES BELVEDERE

LANDSTRASSE

Rennweg

Landstr. Gürtel

grace

HAUPTBAHNHOF

Prinz-Eugen-Str.

Faulstr.

Taubstummeng.

HEERESGESCHICHTL. MUSEUM

Zeitgeist ▲

WIEN-SCHWECHAT

19

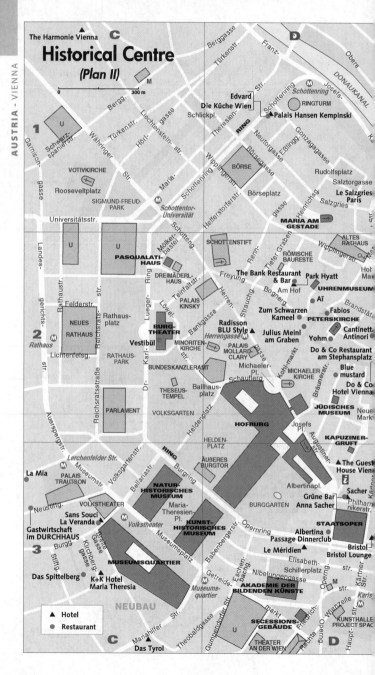

Historical Centre
(Plan II)

The Harmonie Vienna ▲ **C**

M

0   300 m

AUSTRIA - VIENNA

Berggasse

Türkenstr.

Franz-

D

Obere

DONAUKANAL

Edvard
Die Küche Wien
Schlickpl.

Str.

Schottenring

M Schottenring

Josefs-

RINGTURM

Theresien-

RING

Neutorgasse

Gonzagagasse

▲ Palais Hansen Kempinski

Berg-

Lichtenstein-

gasse

Wipplingerstr.

Börsegasse

Eßling-

str.

Kai

Türkenstr.

Hörl-

BÖRSE

Rudolfsplatz

Maria-

Salztorgasse

Le Salzgries
Paris

VOTIVKIRCHE

Str.

Schottenring

Börseplatz

gasse

Heinrichsg.

Salzgries

Rooseveltplatz

Helferstorferstr.

Wippling-

**MARIA AM
GESTADE**

Währinger

Schottenring

ALTES
RATHAUS

SIGMUND-FREUD-
PARK

M

Schottentor-
Universität

Wipplingerstr.

Universitätsstr.

Landes-

gerichts-

U

U

Mölker-
bastei

SCHOTTENSTIFT

Renn-

Tiefer Graben

RÖMISCHE
BAURESTE

Hoh

Ma

**PASQUALATI-
HAUS**

gasse

Ring

DREIMÄDERL-
HAUS

Teinfalt-str.

Freyung

Bognerg.

**The Bank Restaurant
& Bar**
Am Hof

Park Hyatt

UHRENMUSEUM

Felderstr.

Lueger-

Löwel-

PALAIS
KINSKY

Herren-

Strauchg.

Brandstät

AT

PETERSKIRCHE

Fabios

Rathaus-

str.

Bankgasse

**Zum Schwarzen
Kameel**

Cantinett
Antinori

NEUES
RATHAUS

Rathaus-
platz

Reichsrats-

**BURG-
THEATER**

Radisson
BLU Style ▲

Julius Meinl
am Graben

Yohm

M Rathaus

Lichtenfelsg.

Vestibül

MINORITEN-
KIRCHE

Herrengasse

Kohlmarkt

Do & Co Restaurant
am Stephansplatz

Reichsratsstraße

RATHAUS-
PARK

Karl-

str.

PALAIS
MOLLARD-
CLARY

Bräunerstr.

Blue
mustard

Dr.-

BUNDESKANZLERAMT

Michaeler-
Pl.

**MICHAELER
KIRCHE**

Do & Co
Hotel Vienna

Auersperg

THESEUS-
TEMPEL

Ballhaus-
platz

Schauflerg.

Heidenplatz

**JÜDISCHES
MUSEUM**

Neue

PARLAMENT

VOLKSGARTEN

HOFBURG

Josefs
Pl.

Mark

**KAPUZINER-
GRUFT**

HELDEN-
PLATZ

ÄUSSERES
BURGTOR

Augustiner-

▲ The Guest
House Vien

Lerchenfelder Str.

RING

i

Sacher

La Mia

Museumstr.

PALAIS
TRAUTSON

Bellariastr.

Burgring

Albertinapl.

Grüne Bar

BURGGARTEN

Anna Sacher

Philhar

nikerstr.

Neustiftg.

VOLKSTHEATER

**NATUR-
HISTORISCHES
MUSEUM**

Maria-
Theresien-
Pl.

**KUNST-
HISTORISCHES
MUSEUM**

Opernring

Albertina
Passage Dinnerclub

STAATSOPER

Sans Souci
La Veranda

M Volkstheater

Museumsplatz

Babenbergerstr.

Le Méridien ▲

Bristol
Bristol Lounge

Gastwirtschaft
im DURCHHAUS

Burgg.

Kirchberg-

gasse

Stiftg.

MUSEUMSQUARTIER

Eschen-

bach-

Nibelungengasse

Elisabeth-
Schillerplatz

str.

Opern-

M

Kärtner

Das Spittelberg ●

K+K Hotel
Maria Theresia

Museums-
quartier

Getreide-

**AKADEMIE DER
BILDENDEN KÜNSTE**

Karls

NEUBAU

Str.

**SECESSIONS-
GEBÄUDE**

markt

Friedrich-

Wienzeile

**KUNSTHALLE
PROJECT SPAC**

▲ Hotel

● Restaurant

Mariahilfer

Theobaldgasse

Gumpendorfer Str.

C

Das Tyrol

U

Rechte

Linke

**THEATER
AN DER WIEN**

D

20

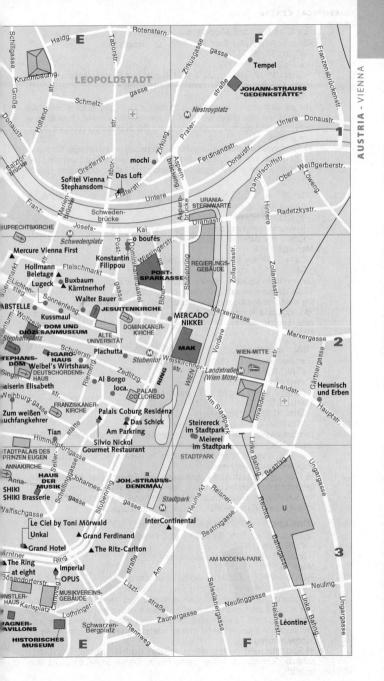

LEOPOLDSTADT

Tempel

JOHANN-STRAUSS "GEDENKSTÄTTE"

Nestroyplatz

mochi

Das Loft

Sofitel Vienna Stephansdom

URANIA-STERNWARTE

RUPRECHTSKIRCHE

Schwedenplatz

o boufés

Mercure Vienna First

Konstantin Filippou

Hollmann Beletage

Fleischmarkt

Buxbaum

Lugeck

Kärntnerhof

POST-SPARKASSE

Walter Bauer

ABSTELLE

JESUITENKIRCHE

Sonnenfelsg.

MERCADO NIKKEI

Kussmaul

DOMINIKANER-KIRCHE

DOM UND DIÖZESANMUSEUM

MAK

Stephansplatz

ALTE UNIVERSITÄT

Plachutta

WIEN-MITTE

FIGARO HAUS

STEPHANS-DOM

Weibel's Wirtshaus

DEUTSCHORDENS-HAUS

Stubentor

WIEN Landstraße (Wien Mitte)

Al Borgo loca.

Heunisch und Erben

Kaiserin Elisabeth

PALAIS COLLOREDO

FRANZISKANER-KIRCHE

Zum weißen Rauchfangkehrer

Palais Coburg Residenz

Das Schick

Tian

Am Parkring

Silvio Nickol Gourmet Restaurant

Steirereck im Stadtpark

Meierei im Stadtpark

STADTPARK

TADTPALAIS DES PRINZEN EUGEN

ANNAKIRCHE

HAUS DER MUSIK

JOH.-STRAUSS-DENKMAL

SHIKI

SHIKI Brasserie

Stadtpark

Le Ciel by Toni Mörwald

Unkai

InterContinental

Grand Ferdinand

Grand Hotel

The Ritz-Carlton

AM MODENA-PARK

The Ring

at eight

Imperial

OPUS

MUSIKVEREINS-GEBÄUDE

Karlsplatz

KÜNSTLER-HAUS

Léontine

WAGNER-PAVILLONS

HISTORISCHES MUSEUM

Schwarzen-Bergplatz

Rennweg

AUSTRIA - VIENNA

Le Ciel by Toni Mörwald – Grand Hotel XxX 🛋 🕭 & ⚠ ⟳

Kärntner Ring 9 (7th floor) ✉ *1010 –* ⓜ *Karlsplatz* 🚗
– ✆ (01) 5 15 80 91 00 Plan: **E3**
– www.leciel.at
– Closed 16-19 February, 22 July-20 August and Sunday-Monday
Menu 45 € (lunch)/111 € (dinner) – Carte 67/92 €
• Classic cuisine • Elegant •

The atmosphere up on the seventh floor is classically elegant and, quite naturally, the best tables are those on the roof terrace. The kitchens serve distinctive and creative food made using the best quality produce. Attentive service.

→ Taschenkrebssalat mit gegrilltem Junglauch und Avocado, Kräutersalat, Emulsion von Knoblauch und Olivenöl. Beinfleisch mit saurem Spargel, Haferwurzel und Roggen. Mandarine mit Safran, Kokos und Gewürzen.

OPUS – Hotel Imperial XxX & ⚠

Kärntner Ring 16 ✉ *1015 –* ⓜ *Karlsplatz* Plan: **E3**
– ✆ (01) 50 11 03 89
– www.imperialvienna.com
– Closed mid July-mid August and Monday
Menu 69/124 €
– Carte 59/98 € – *(dinner only) (booking advisable)*
• Modern cuisine • Elegant • Luxury •

Located in an attractive, classical building, OPUS is decorated in the style of a 1930s Viennese workshop, in elegant grey tones with chandeliers and art on the walls. The ambitious cuisine is creative and regionally inspired.

→ Langustino - Paprikasud, Mango - Koriandersalat, Passe-Pierre. Entrecôte, Eierschwammerl, Erdäpfel, Lauch. Mara des Bois Erdbeere, Burrata, Melisse.

Blue mustard XX ⚠

Dorotheergasse 6 ✉ *1010 –* ⓜ *Stephansplatz* Plan: **D2**
– ✆ (01) 9 34 67 05
– www.bluemustard.at
– Closed 3 weeks August and Sunday-Monday
Menu 55/65 €
– Carte 51/66 € – *(dinner only)*
• Modern cuisine • Fashionable •

This fashionable address is close to St Stephen's Cathedral. It offers an eclectic mix of dishes – traditional, modern and exotic – all made from good, fresh produce and served in original surroundings. In summer it also operates a food truck serving takeaway meals.

→ Kurz gegarte Lachsforelle, gepoppter Reis, Erbsencrème, Brunnenkresse, Bergamott-Gel, Kokos-Currysauce. Sous-vide gegarte Hühnerbrust, sautierter Steinpilz, confierter Erdapfel, Most-Quitten-Kübelspeck. Zartbitterschokolade-Ingwer-Flan, gerösteter Sesam, Joghurtschaum.

Das Loft – Hotel Sofitel Vienna Stephansdom XX ❀ ≼ ⚠ 🚙

Praterstr. 1 (18th floor) ✉ *1020 –* ⓜ *Schwedenplatz* Plan: **E1**
– ✆ (01) 9 06 16 81 10
– www.sofitel-vienna-stephansdom.com
Menu 32/99 €
– Carte 60/98 € – *(bookings advisable at dinner)*
• International • Design • Fashionable •

The spectacular location and view of Vienna here are topped only by the sophisticated, modern and thoroughly delicious cuisine prepared by the motivated young team. Excellent wine selection and professional service. The reduced lunchtime menu is paired with an interesting set lunch. Brunch only on Sunday mornings.

→ Rindstatar und Auster, salzige Kräuter, Rettich. Saibling, Dashibutter, Kohlrabi, Schnittlauch. Toffee Crème Brûlée, Granny Smith, Basilikum, Buttermilch.

AUSTRIA - VIENNA

SHIKI   XX ⅙ ⅿⅽ ⇔

Krugerstr. 3 ✉ *1010 –* Ⓜ *Karlsplatz –* ✆ *(01) 5 12 73 97*   Plan: **E3**
– www.shiki.at – Closed 1 week January, 2 weeks August, Sunday-Monday
and Bank Holidays
Menu 86/122 € – *(booking advisable)*
• Japanese • Fashionable • Design •
SHIKI offers fine dining Japanese-style in the heart of Vienna, close to the Opera. The
elegant restaurant decorated in dark tones offers a perfect marriage of tradition and
modernity. It serves ambitious, seasonal cuisine ('Shiki' means the four seasons).
➜ Hummer- und Langustenstücke im Wagyu-Dotter-Schaum und Krusten-
tierfond mit Norialgen. Variation vom Kalb mit Sellerie-Miso und Karamell-
Yuzu. Karotte und Wachauer Marille.
🍴 **SHIKI Brasserie** – See restaurant listing

Tian   XX ⅜ ⇔

Himmelpfortgasse 23 ✉ *1010 –* Ⓜ *Stephansplatz*   Plan: **E2**
– ✆ *(01) 8 90 46 65 – www.tian-restaurant.com – Closed 2 weeks January,*
3 weeks mid July-mid August, during Christmas and Sunday-Monday
Menu 37 € (lunch)/143 € (dinner)
• Vegetarian • Elegant • Fashionable •
Punchy and rich in contrast yet full of finesse, Tian serves excellent vegetarian
and vegan cuisine. The colourful, beautifully presented food is well matched by
the relaxed yet professional service and the modern interior. Diners can choose
between the light and airy restaurant with its stucco ceiling or the more intimate basement dining room.
➜ Fisser Gerste, Fichte, Ei. Eierschwammerl, Erbse, Zitrone. Berry Trail, Cru
Virunga, Beeren, Paradeiser.

Walter Bauer   XX ⅜ ⅿⅽ

Sonnenfelsgasse 17 ✉ *1010 –* Ⓜ *Stubentor*   Plan: **E2**
– ✆ *(01) 5 12 98 71 – Closed 23 July-18 August*
and Saturday-Monday lunch
Carte 50/74 € – *(booking advisable)*
• Classic cuisine • Cosy • Family •
This listed building in the centre of the old town has oodles of Viennese charm,
as well as a wonderful vaulted ceiling in the restaurant. The owners place great
importance on providing attentive and personal service, as well as classic cuisine without frills. There is also an excellent wine list.
➜ Gänseleber mit Brioche. Geschmortes Rindsbackerl mit Püree. Topfen-
knöderln mit Marillen Röster.

Vestibül   XX ⅜ ⅷ ⅙

Universitätsring 2 (at Burgtheater) ✉ *1010*   Plan: **C2**
– Ⓜ *Herrengasse –* ✆ *(01) 5 32 49 99 – www.vestibuel.at – Closed*
1-7 January, 21 July-15 August, Saturday lunch, Sunday and
Bank Holidays
Menu 55/69 € (dinner) – Carte 37/81 € – *(booking advisable)*
• International • Classic décor • Brasserie •
Though the chef sets great store by using high quality Austrian ingre-
dients, there is nothing that quite matches the lobster in Vestibül's highly prized
Szegediner lobster with cabbage. The unusual location – in the famous and
charming Burgtheater – is another selling point. Don't miss the excellent
wines, some of which are available as magnums.

Eisvogel   XX ⅷ ⅙ ⅿⅽ ⇔ 🅿

Riesenradplatz 5 (Prater) ✉ *1020 –* Ⓜ *Praterstern*   Plan I: **B2**
– ✆ *(01) 9 08 11 87 – www.stadtgasthaus-eisvogel.at*
Menu 36/49 € – Carte 28/63 € – *(bookings advisable at dinner)*
• Austrian • Elegant • Friendly •
Set in the pulsating heart of Vienna next to the giant Riesenrad Ferris wheel at
the entrance to the Prater, Eisvogel is a great place for an aperitif with a view (by
reservation only). The excellent classic Austrian fare on offer includes Beuschel
(veal lung ragout), Wiener Schnitzel and goulash. There is a small, sheltered terrace facing the Prater.

23

Meierei im Stadtpark – Restaurant Steirereck X 🕏 ᢕ 📠

Am Heumarkt 2a ⊠ *1030 –* ❻ *Stadtpark*   Plan: **F2**
– ℰ *(01) 7 13 31 68 – www.steirereck.at – Closed Bank Holidays*
Menu 47/57 € (dinner) – Carte 27/57 €
• Country • Friendly •

The Reitbauer family's latest upmarket culinary venture, Meierei serves such seasonal delights as mixed cucumbers braised and marinated with six-row barley, coconut and tartare of Arctic char alongside Austrian classics (including the inevitable Wiener Schnitzel). The interior is light and modern, the service attentive.

Heunisch und Erben   X 🕏 🕏 📠

Landstrasser Hauptstr. 17 / Seidlgasse 36 ⊠ *1030*   Plan: **F2**
– ❻ *Landstraße (Wien-Mitte) –* ℰ *(01) 2 86 85 63 – www.heunisch.at*
– Closed Sunday-Monday and Bank Holidays
Menu 37/79 € – Carte 25/53 €
• Country • Fashionable • Neighbourhood •

In an interesting mix of modern wine bar and restaurant, Heunisch und Erben offers some 100 different wines to accompany its ambitious, market-fresh food. Menu options range from mountain trout with pumpkin, salt-baked beetroot and Uhudler wine to creamy veal goulash. Shorter, simpler lunchtime menu.

Kussmaul   X 📠 ⇔

Bäckerstr. 5 ⊠ *1010 –* ❻ *Stubentor –* ℰ *(01) 2 86 11 17*   Plan: **E2**
– www.kussmaul-vienna.com – Closed mid July-mid August and Sunday
Carte 21/79 € – *(dinner only)*
• International • Chic • Fashionable •

Kussmaul promises a relaxed atmosphere in a fresh, stylish interior – complete with bar and vaulted cellar – in which to sample its fine international cuisine (many of the dishes come as good-value set menu servings). Alternatively try one of the "Big Cuts" – a whole fish, for example.

LABSTELLE   X 🕏 ⇔

Lugeck 6 ⊠ *1010 –* ❻ *Stephansplatz*   Plan: **E2**
– ℰ *(01) 2 36 21 22 – www.labstelle.at – Closed Sunday and Bank Holidays*
Menu 48/58 € (dinner) – Carte 32/59 € – *(booking advisable)*
• Country • Design • Bistro •

Labstelle offers an attractive, upmarket bistro atmosphere with a relaxed bar area. It serves ambitious seasonal, regional fare including Arctic char, Marschfeld artichoke, parsnips and parsley. There is also a reduced lunchtime menu and a pretty interior courtyard.

Lugeck   X 📠 ⇔

Lugeck 4 ⊠ *1010 –* ❻ *Stephansplatz*   Plan: **E2**
– ℰ *(01) 5 12 50 60 – www.lugeck.com*
Carte 24/57 €
• Austrian • Contemporary décor • Rustic •

Located in Vienna's striking and history-filled Regensburger Hof building close to St Stephen's cathedral, Lugeck serves contemporary re-interpretations of traditional Viennese dishes such as Tafelspitz (boiled topside of veal) and Wiener schnitzel, alongside some appealing international cuisine.

Mochi   X 📠 🍽

Praterstr. 15 ⊠ *1020 –* ❻ *Nestroyplatz*   Plan: **E1**
– ℰ *(01) 9 25 13 80 – www.mochi.at – Closed 23 December-2 January, Sunday and Bank Holidays*
Carte 19/47 € – *(booking essential at dinner)*
• Japanese • Trendy • Fashionable •

This is a lively, informal restaurant serving authentic Japanese cuisine with the occasional modern twist at very moderate prices. You can watch the chefs at work as they prepare their rolls, gyoza soup and gyu tataki. At lunchtimes the food is served in simple bowls, in the evenings the presentation is a little more elaborate. Bookings start at 3pm.

AUSTRIA - VIENNA

O boufés – Restaurant Konstantin Filippou   ✗ 🏠 🏠

Dominikanerbastei 17 ✉ *1010* – **Ⓜ** *Stubentor* Plan: **E2**
– 📞 *(01) 5 12 22 29 10* – *www.konstantinfilippou.com* – *Closed Sunday and Bank Holidays*
Carte 34/52 € – *(dinner only) (booking advisable)*
• Mediterranean cuisine • Bistro •

Located just next door to its gourmet counterpart, this relaxed restaurant with its bare walls, high ceilings and minimalist decor, serves a varied menu. It ranges from a charcuterie plate to *keftedes* (meatballs) with *hilopites* (small green pasta squares), as well as black pudding ravioli with cuttlefish, shellfish and peas. The food is accompanied by a choice of natural wines.

Petz im Gußhaus   ✗ 🏠 ♿

Gußhausstr. 23 ✉ *1040* – **Ⓜ** *Taubstummeng.* Plan I: **B3**
– 📞 *(01) 5 04 47 50* – *www.gusshaus.at* – *Closed 1 week early February, 3 weeks August and Sunday-Monday*
Carte 31/57 € – *(dinner only) (booking advisable)*
• Austrian • Cosy •

Located not far from the Karlsplatz, this restaurant promises excellent, fully flavoured cuisine with international influences, as well as Austrian dishes. Try the fried chicken with potato and cucumber salad, the lemon and veal ragout with bone marrow dumplings, or the octopus in fennel and curry stock with risotto balls. All served in a smart dining room.

Grüne Bar – Hotel Sacher   ✗✗✗✗ 🏠 ♿ 🅰🅲 🚗

Philharmonikerstr. 4 ✉ *1010* – **Ⓜ** *Karlsplatz* Plan: **D3**
– 📞 *(01) 5 14 46 10 01* – *www.sacher.com*
Menu 79/109 € – Carte 55/79 € – *(dinner only) (booking advisable)*
• Classic cuisine • Luxury •

The Hotel Sacher's fine dining restaurant with its upmarket green and wood interior features a number of original paintings by Viennese impressionist Anton Faistauer. The ambitious re-interpreted classics on offer have a strong Viennese flavour, as evidenced by the Mangalitza pigs' cheeks with calf's heart und turnips.

Bristol Lounge – Hotel Bristol   ✗✗✗ 🏠 ♿ 🅰🅲

Kärntner Ring 1 ✉ *1010* – **Ⓜ** *Karlsplatz* Plan: **D3**
– 📞 *(01) 51 51 65 53* – *www.bristolvienna.com*
Menu 28 € (lunch)/82 € – Carte 36/91 €
• Classic cuisine • Classic décor • Chic •

Bristol Lounge combines minimalist-style elegance and historical charm with some pleasing details, including the original wood panelling, open fire and striking crystal chandeliers, which give the room atmosphere. Austrian cuisine.

Albertina Passage Dinnerclub   ✗✗ 🅰🅲

Opernring 4/1/12 (corner Operngasse) ✉ *1010* Plan: **D3**
– **Ⓜ** *Karlsplatz* – 📞 *(01) 5 12 08 13* – *www.albertinapassage.at*
– *Closed mid June-mid September and Sunday-Monday*
Menu 52/59 € – Carte 35/54 € – *(dinner only) (booking advisable)*
• Modern cuisine • Trendy •

If you are looking for something special, this restaurant – a mix of music venue and sophisticated restaurant – is both stylish and upmarket. It offers a lounge-like atmosphere (dimmed lights, bar area, live music), professional and attentive service and elaborate, ambitious cuisine full of contrasts.

Rote Bar – Hotel Sacher   ✗✗ ♿ 🅰🅲 🚗

Philharmonikerstr. 4 ✉ *1010* – **Ⓜ** *Karlsplatz* Plan: **D3**
– 📞 *(01) 5 14 56 10 02* – *www.sacher.com*
Menu 60/67 € – Carte 42/83 €
• Austrian • Elegant • Traditional décor •

A mainstay of the Hotel Sacher, which epitomises the charm of this great Viennese establishment, Rote Bar is also a champion of Austrian cuisine. Treat yourself to a Wiener schnitzel or traditional rump of beef and soak up the atmosphere!

Zum Schwarzen Kameel   XX 🕮 🍴 AC ⇔

Bognergasse 5 ✉ 1010 – Ⓜ *Herrengasse*   Plan: **D2**
– ☎ *(01) 5 33 81 25 – www.kameel.at*
Menu 69/89 € – Carte 38/78 € – *(booking essential)*
• Traditional cuisine • Friendly • Cosy •
One of Vienna's oldest restaurants (1618), fitted out in the much admired Viennese Art Nouveau style in 1901/02. Guests are offered international and regional cuisine. The restaurant's own delicatessen and patisserie are great for buying gifts.

Aï   XX AC

Seitzergasse 6/1 ✉ 1010 – Ⓜ *Stephansplatz*   Plan: **D2**
– ☎ *(01) 5 32 29 00 – www.airestaurant.co*
Menu 39 € (lunch)/145 € (dinner) – Carte 21/117 € – *(booking essential)*
• Asian • Design • Chic •
A really fun place to eat, Aï promises an informal atmosphere, a smart interior with bar, open kitchen and robata grill and – last but not least – a menu full of "innovative Asian cuisine" including sushi and sashimi.

Al Borgo   XX 🍴 AC

An der Hülben 1 ✉ 1010 – Ⓜ *Stubentor*   Plan: **E2**
– ☎ *(01) 5 12 85 59 – www.alborgo.at – Closed Saturday lunch, Sunday and Bank Holidays*
Carte 28/47 €
• Italian • Friendly •
Al Borgo enjoys a very central and yet secluded location in the heart of Vienna's 1st district. It serves classic Italian cuisine and a range of excellent seasonal dishes. Regular themed weeks.

at eight – The Ring   XX 🍴 & AC 🚗

Kärntner Ring 8 ✉ 1010 – Ⓜ *Karlsplatz*   Plan: **E3**
– ☎ *(01) 2 21 22 39 30 – www.ateight-restaurant.com*
Menu 45/75 € – Carte 49/74 €
• Traditional cuisine • Fashionable •
Simple lines set the tone here in this light and airy restaurant, where the attentive front-of-house team serve up modern cuisine alongside Viennese classics. The attractive terrace overlooks the Ring.

Cantinetta Antinori   XX 🍴 AC ⇔

Jasomirgottstr. 3 ✉ 1010 – Ⓜ *Stephansplatz*   Plan: **D2**
– ☎ *(01) 5 33 77 22 10 – www.cantinettaantinori-vienna.at*
Carte 42/79 € – *(booking advisable)*
• Italian • Friendly • Cosy •
The Viennese offshoot of the original Florentine restaurant serves primarily Tuscan cuisine, including succulent braised rabbit. It has a lively but stylish atmosphere. Wide selection of high quality Antinori wines (available by the glass).

Collio – Hotel Das Triest   XX 🍴 & AC

Wiedner Hauptstr. 12 ✉ 1040 – Ⓜ *Karlsplatz*   Plan: I: **B3**
– ☎ *(01) 58 91 80 – www.dastriest.at – Closed Saturday lunch, Sunday and Bank Holidays*
Carte 33/56 €
• Italian • Chic •
Collio offers a modern interior and a wonderful terrace in the gloriously green inner courtyard. The food on offer is Italian, focusing particularly on the cuisine of northern Italy. There's a less expensive lunchtime menu.

Das Schick – Hotel Am Parkring   XX ≤ AC 🚗

Parkring 12 ✉ 1010 – Ⓜ *Stubentor –* ☎ *(01)*   Plan: **E2**
51 48 04 17 – www.schick-hotels.com – Closed Saturday lunch, Sunday lunch and Bank Holidays lunch
Menu 59/87 € – Carte 49/80 €
• Mediterranean cuisine • Fashionable • Elegant •
Das Schick offers a friendly atmosphere, seasonal cuisine with an upmarket touch and a phenomenal view! That is the recipe that brings diners up here to the 12th floor.

‖○   **Die Küche Wien** – Hotel Palais Hansen Kempinski   XX 🅰️🅲️
Schottenring 24 ✉ *1010 –* ⓜ *Schottenring*   Plan: **D1**
– ℰ (01) 2 36 80 80 – www.kempinski.com/wien
Carte 31/55 €
• Country • Friendly •
The Palais Hansen's second restaurant focuses on new interpretations of Viennese cuisine including dishes such as veal ragout and Wienerwald beef sirloin. The Wohnzimmer, Wintergarten and Küche dining rooms offer their own special atmosphere.

‖○   **Do & Co Restaurant am Stephansplatz** – Do & Co Hotel Vienna
Stephansplatz 12 (7th floor) ✉ *1010*   XX ⪡ 🏠 🏡 ⅙ 🅰️🅲️ ⇧ 🚗
*– * ⓜ *Stephansplatz – ℰ (01) 5 35 39 69*   Plan: **D2**
– www.doco.com
Carte 40/62 € – *(booking essential)*
• Asian • Trendy • Design •
An ultra-modern restaurant on the seventh floor with a great terrace and view of St Stephen's Cathedral. Southeast Asian dishes include chicken kaow soy and sushi alongside Austrian classics such as braised calves' cheeks and goose liver.

‖○   **Fabios**   XX 🏡 🅰️🅲️
Tuchlauben 6 ✉ *1010 –* ⓜ *Stephansplatz*   Plan: **D2**
– ℰ (01) 5 32 22 22 – www.fabios.at – Closed Sunday
Carte 49/82 € – *(booking essential)*
• Italian • Trendy •
A veritable Who's Who of Vienna! The Italian cuisine served in this fashionable city restaurant is just as modern and minimalist as the interior design – two equally good reasons to give it a try! The bar also serves a range of snacks.

‖○   **Gaumenspiel**   XX 🏡
Zieglergasse 54 ✉ *1070 –* ⓜ *Burgg-Stadthalle*   Plan I: **A3**
– ℰ (01) 5 26 11 08 – www.gaumenspiel.at – Closed Sunday
Menu 38/58 € – *(dinner only)*
• International • Friendly •
A friendly restaurant which has long since become a culinary institution in Vienna's 7th District. The interior is warm and welcoming with wooden floors and red walls, while the interior courtyard is particularly inviting in summer. The menu includes turbot fried in miso with Jerusalem artichokes and hazelnuts.

‖○   **Julius Meinl am Graben**   XX 🕸️ 🅰️🅲️
Graben 19 (1st floor) ✉ *1010 –* ⓜ *Stephansplatz*   Plan: **D2**
– ℰ (01) 5 32 33 34 60 00 – www.meinlamgraben.at – Closed 3 weeks
August, Sunday and Bank Holidays
Menu 39 € (lunch)/93 € – Carte 43/88 € – *(booking essential)*
• Classic cuisine • Chic • Cosy •
This restaurant and its sister delicatessen (housed in the same building) come to life early in the morning. Ambitious food is served using the finest quality ingredients from breakfast through to dinner (make sure you try the stuffed quail with greengages) complete with a view over Vienna's pedestrian zone.

‖○   **La Veranda** – Hotel Sans Souci   XX 🏡 ⅙ 🅰️🅲️ ⇧
Burggasse 2 ✉ *1070 –* ⓜ *Volkstheater*   Plan: **C3**
– ℰ (01) 5 22 25 20 19 4 – www.laveranda-wien.com
Menu 25/69 € (dinner) – Carte 30/70 €
• International • Fashionable •
This elegant, modern restaurant sets great store by fresh regional and seasonal produce. The menu options include breast of organic chicken with a duo of pumpkins, almonds and dill, as well as Wiener Schnitzel with multi-coloured salad and parsley potatoes. Pavement terrace in front of the restaurant.

AUSTRIA - VIENNA

Plachutta ⅞○ XX 🍴 AC ⇔

Wollzeile 38 ✉ *1010 –* Ⓜ *Stubentor – ℰ (01) 5 12 15 77* — Plan: **E2**
– www.plachutta.at
Carte 31/52 € *– (booking advisable)*
• Austrian • Traditional décor • Inn •

For years, the Plachutta family has been committed to Viennese tradition. They serve beef in many forms in the green panelled dining room or on the large terrace.

Skopik & Lohn ⅞○ XX 🍴

Leopoldsgasse 17 ✉ *1020 –* Ⓜ *Taborstrasse* — Plan I: **B2**
– ℰ (01) 2 19 89 77 – www.skopikundlohn.at – Closed Sunday-Monday
Menu 34 € – Carte 27/49 € *– (dinner only)*
• Austrian • Friendly • Family •

The first thing you'll notice here is the wonderful painted ceiling, the work of artist Otto Zitko. The service is friendly and attentive, the food flavoursome and the Austrian classics on the menu include Wiener schnitzel with cucumber, potato and sour cream salad and, for dessert, perhaps an île flottante?

The Bank Brasserie & Bar – Hotel Park Hyatt ⅞○ XX � ⇔ 🚗

Bognergasse 4 ✉ *1010 –* Ⓜ *Herrengasse* — Plan: **D2**
– ℰ (01) 2 27 40 12 36 – www.restaurant-thebank.com
Carte 31/80 €
• International • Classic décor •

If you are looking to eat out in an unusual setting, try the period lobby in this former bank with its imposing high ceilings and marble columns. The menu offers French brasserie-style dishes that are prepared in the open show kitchen. The Am Hof café is also popular.

Unkai – Grand Hotel ⅞○ XX ♿ AC 🚗

Kärntner Ring 9 (7th floor) ✉ *1010 –* Ⓜ *Karlsplatz* — Plan: **E3**
– ℰ (01) 5 15 80 91 10 – www.grandhotelwien.com – Closed Monday lunch
Menu 35 € (lunch)/120 € – Carte 24/75 €
• Japanese • Minimalist •

A pleasantly light and modern restaurant where you can eat either at authentic teppanyaki grill tables or more conventionally. You will also find the Unkai sushi bar on the ground floor serving a sushi brunch on Saturdays, Sundays and public holidays.

Zum weissen Rauchfangkehrer ⅞○ XX 🍴 AC

Weihburggasse 4 ✉ *1010 –* Ⓜ *Stephansplatz* — Plan: **E2**
– ℰ (01) 5 12 34 71 – www.weisser-rauchfangkehrer.at
Menu 30/50 € (dinner) – Carte 38/60 € *– (booking advisable)*
• Austrian • Traditional décor • Chic •

The Viennese cuisine includes seasonal dishes such as duo of Schneebergland duck and specials like calf's head brawn. These are served throughout the day in comfortable, traditional dining rooms. There's also a wide range of wines and digestifs.

Artner auf der Wieden ⅞○ X 🍴

Floragasse 6 ✉ *1040 –* Ⓜ *Taubstummengasse* — Plan I: **B3**
– ℰ (01) 5 03 50 33 – www.artner.co.at – Closed Saturday lunch, Sunday lunch and Bank Holidays lunch
Menu 13 € (lunch)/65 € – Carte 31/64 €
• International • Fashionable • Design •

Regional and modern, the flavoursome fare on offer includes Wiener Schnitzel with parsley potatoes and Mühlbachtaler salmon trout with pan-fried citrus peel and crispy polenta, not to mention a range of grilled dishes. The interior is attractive and minimalist in style and the service is relaxed. Good value lunch-time menu.

AUSTRIA - VIENNA

Buxbaum ✕ 🏠 🅐🅚 ⇔

Grashofgasse 3 ✉ 1010 – Ⓜ *Schwedenplatz*   Plan: **E2**
– ✆ (01) 2 76 82 26 – www.buxbaum.restaurant – Closed Sunday and
Bank Holidays
Menu 50/62 € – Carte 36/69 €
• Market cuisine • Cosy • Chic •
This comfortable, stylishly rustic restaurant lies a little out of the way in the Heiligenkreuzerhof. At midday it serves a quick business lunch, in the evenings international and regional set menus alongside the à la carte offerings. Attractive terrace.

Das Spittelberg ✕ 🏠 🅐🅚 ⇔

Spittelbergstr. 12 ✉ 1070 – Ⓜ *Volkstheater*   Plan: **C3**
– ✆ (01) 5 87 76 28 – www.das-spittelberg.at – Closed Sunday-Monday
Menu 49/59 € – Carte 32/58 € – *(dinner only)*
• Austrian • Brasserie • Classic décor •
This friendly and welcoming restaurant located in the charming Spittelberg district revolves around the rotisserie grill in the open kitchen, where the matured Simmentaler beef is a speciality. The Austrian fare is accompanied by a range of good Austrian wines, including some magnums.

Gastwirtschaft im DURCHHAUS ✕ 🏠 ⇔

Neustiftgasse 16 ✉ 1070 – Ⓜ *Lerchenfelder Str.*   Plan: **C3**
– ✆ (01) 5 26 94 48 – www.durchhaus.at – Closed Monday
Carte 24/42 € – *(dinner only)*
• Country • Cosy •
Though somewhat unprepossessing from the outside, this restaurant close to the Volkstheater has a pretty interior courtyard with a terrace. Couples should ask for the little alcove booth – perfect for a tête-à-tête! The regional fare includes pink roast sirloin steak with wild mushrooms and herb and mustard brioche.

La Mia ✕ 🏠 ⊞

Lerchenfelder Str. 13 ✉ 1070 – Ⓜ *Lerchenfelder Str.*   Plan: **C3**
– ✆ (01) 5 22 42 21 – www.lamia.at
Carte 31/45 €
• Italian • Bistro • Rustic •
This lively friendly bistro with its covered interior courtyard serves pizzas and pasta dishes – try the excellent spaghetti frutti di mare – alongside grilled specialities including gamberoni alla diavola and tagliata di manzo. Just around the corner the same team offers traditional Viennese cuisine.

Léontine ✕ 🏠

Reisnerstrasse 39 ✉ 1030 – Ⓜ *Stadtpark*   Plan: **F3**
– ✆ (01) 7 12 54 30 – www.leontine.at – Closed 1 week February, 1 week
during Easter, 2 weeks July-August, 2 weeks end December-early January
and Sunday-Monday, Tuesday dinner, Wednesday dinner
Menu 54 € (dinner) – Carte 45/57 €
• Modern French • Bistro •
If you enjoy a bistro atmosphere, you will love this charming restaurant set in a quiet residential district close to the Stadtpark. It serves modern French cuisine with menu options including turbot with carrots, olives and macadamia nuts.

loca. ✕ 🏠 🅐🅚

Stubenbastei 10 ✉ 1010 – Ⓜ *Stubentor*   Plan: **E2**
– ✆ (01) 5 12 11 72 – www.bettereatbetter.com
Menu 36/48 € – Carte 38/47 € – *(dinner only) (booking advisable)*
• Country • Cosy •
"Better eat better" is the slogan of this friendly little restaurant close to the Stadtpark. The menu includes dishes such as zander served with two sorts of pumpkin and speck. Don't be afraid to ask for the special theatre menus.

AUSTRIA - VIENNA

Ludwig van   X

Laimgrubengasse 22 ⊠ 1060 – Ⓜ Museumsquartier   Plan I: **A3**
– ℰ (01) 5 87 13 20 – www.ludwigvan.wien – Closed 4 weeks July-August,
Saturday-Sunday, Monday dinner and Bank Holidays
Menu 47/64 € (dinner) – Carte 42/56 €
• Country • Rustic • Cosy •

The ground floor of this house where Beethoven once lived is now home to a warm and welcoming, rustic dining room with a charming front-of-house team serving contemporary takes on regional fare. Made using top-quality ingredients, the food is pleasingly simple, refined and rich in flavour.

MERCADO NIKKEI   X 🛋 ✿

Stubenring 18 ⊠ 1010 – Ⓜ Stubentor   Plan: **E2**
– ℰ (01) 5 12 25 05 – www.mercado.at – Closed Saturday lunch, Sunday
lunch and Bank Holidays lunch
Menu 29/46 € (dinner) – Carte 24/48 €
• World cuisine • Exotic décor • Cosy •

The ideal restaurant for those who like it hot! Mercado serves "Latin inspired market cuisine" in a relaxed, Latin American atmosphere. Don't miss the panfried octopus with potatoes and tamarind barbecue sauce – served à la carte or "family-style".

Sakai   X

Florianigasse 36 ⊠ 1080 – Ⓜ Josefstädter Str.   Plan I: **A3**
– ℰ (01) 7 29 65 41 – www.sakai.co.at – Closed 30 July-21 August,
Monday-Tuesday and Bank Holidays
Menu 30 € (lunch)/79 € – Carte 17/60 €
• Japanese • Minimalist •

Hiroshi Sakai, no stranger in Vienna, set up his own restaurant after 10 years at Unkai. He serves seasonally influenced, traditional Japanese cuisine. Take a seat in the authentically simple surroundings and enjoy some sushi and sashimi or better still, one of his sophisticated set Kaiseki menus.

Le Salzgries Paris   X 🛋 🄰🄲

Marc-Aurel-Str. 6 ⊠ 1010 – Ⓜ Schwedenplatz   Plan: **D1**
– ℰ (01) 5 33 40 30 – www.le-salzgries.at – Closed 1-9 January, 27 March-
3 April, 29 July-16 August, Saturday-Sunday and Bank Holidays
Menu 48/86 € (dinner) – Carte 43/66 €
• Classic French • Brasserie • Fashionable •

This exuberant, lively bistro is decorated in warm colours and has a modern bar, which is a real eye-catcher. The tried and tested French cuisine offers classic dishes including entrecote.

Schnattl   X 🛋

Lange Gasse 40 ⊠ 1080 – Ⓜ Rathaus   Plan I: **A3**
– ℰ (01) 4 05 34 00 – www.schnattl.com – Closed 1 week Easter, 3 weeks
August, during Christmas, New Year, Saturday-Sunday and Bank Holidays
Menu 18 € (lunch)/56 € (dinner)
– Carte 33/57 € – (lunch only, except Friday)
• Country • Cosy •

This friendly, personally-run restaurant is set a little out of the way but remains popular with regulars and theatregoers, who appreciate the classic cuisine and warm, friendly atmosphere.

Servitenwirt   X 🛋 ✿

Servitengasse 7 ⊠ 1090 – Ⓜ Roßauer Lände   Plan I: **A2**
– ℰ (01) 3 15 23 87 – www.servitenwirt.at
Menu 47/67 € (dinner) – Carte 28/53 €
• Austrian • Friendly • Cosy •

If you're looking for some typical, fresh Viennese fare, you'll find it in this quiet square by the church. Try the lights cooked in Riesling, the fried breaded chicken and the Topfenschmarrn, a sort of sweet quark-based pancake. Alternatively, go for the entrecote. The garden is inviting in fine weather.

🍴⃝ **SHIKI Brasserie** – Restaurant SHIKI   🗙 🏠 ⅙ 🄰🄲
Krugerstr. 3 ✉ *1010 –* Ⓜ *Karlsplatz –* ☎ *(01) 5 12 73 97*   Plan: **E3**
– www.shiki.at – Closed 1 week January, 2 weeks August, Sunday-Monday
and Bank Holidays
Carte 30/89 €
• Japanese • Brasserie • Design •
This minimalist-style brasserie with its large terrace is SHIKI's less formal eatery. It offers a wider range of dishes from miso soup to tempura and sushi – the latter prepared before you as you sit at the sushi bar.

🍴⃝ **Tempel**   🗙 🏠
Praterstr. 56 ✉ *1020 –* Ⓜ *Nestroyplatz*   Plan: **F1**
– ☎ *(01) 2 14 01 79 – www.restaurant-tempel.at – Closed 23 December-*
9 January and Saturday lunch, Sunday-Monday
Menu 18 € (lunch)/56 € – Carte 27/49 €
• Country • Bistro •
You may have to search for the slightly concealed entrance to the interior courtyard and lovely terrace that lead to this friendly restaurant. It serves flavoursome, contemporary Mediterranean cuisine and offers a good value lunchtime menu.

🍴⃝ **Weibel's Wirtshaus**   🗙 🏠
Kumpfgasse 2 ✉ *1010 –* Ⓜ *Stubentor*   Plan: **E2**
– ☎ *(01) 5 12 39 86 – www.weibel.at*
Menu 39 € (dinner) – Carte 26/53 € – *(booking advisable)*
• Austrian • Friendly •
Just a few minutes' walk from St Stephen's Cathedral, Weibel's Wirtshaus is the archetypal Viennese restaurant – warm and friendly, rustic and snug! It also has a charming garden in the small alleyway. The food is traditional and Viennese.

🍴⃝ **Yohm**   🗙 🏠
Petersplatz 3 ✉ *1010 –* Ⓜ *Stephansplatz*   Plan: **D2**
– ☎ *(01) 5 33 29 00 – www.yohm.at*
Menu 49/69 € – Carte 32/60 €
• Asian • Fashionable • Neighbourhood •
A pleasant modern restaurant with striking orange decor, occupying two floors. The open kitchen serves up contemporary twists on Southeast Asian cuisine that borrows liberally from around the globe. Good wine selection.

🏛⃝ **Imperial**   🕏 🖧 🕸 🄰🄲 🕭
Kärntner Ring 16 ✉ *1015 –* Ⓜ *Karlsplatz*   Plan: **E3**
– ☎ *(01) 50 11 00 – www.imperialvienna.com*
138 rm – 🛏400/819 € 🛏🛏400/819 € – ⌑41 € – 31 suites
• Palace • Grand Luxury • Historic •
This grand hotel was opened in 1873 to celebrate Vienna's World Expo, and still promises all the majesty of the Austrian Empire in its splendid interior. The lobby is stylish and the rooms and suites are lavish and elegant. Don't miss the fascinating 'Course of History'. The restaurant is decidedly upmarket, while the Café Imperial has the feel of a classic Viennese coffee house.
❀ **OPUS** – See restaurant listing

🏛⃝ **Palais Coburg Residenz**   🕏 🖴 🕸 🖵 ⅙ 🄰🄲 🕭 �
Coburgbastei 4 ✉ *1010 –* Ⓜ *Stubentor*   Plan: **E2**
– ☎ *(01) 51 81 81 30 – www.palais-coburg.com*
34 suites ⌑ – 🛏795/2695 € 🛏🛏795/2695 €
• Grand Luxury • Historic • Contemporary •
This magnificent, classic building was built in 1840. It offers guests an imposing hotel setting that is more than matched by the luxurious, largely duplex suites and the excellent service. The Clementine restaurant serves international fare, has a winter garden feel and boasts an attractive terrace.
❀❀ **Silvio Nickol Gourmet Restaurant** – See restaurant listing

AUSTRIA - VIENNA

Palais Hansen Kempinski

Schottenring 24 ⊠ *1010* – **Ⓜ** *Schottenring*   Plan: **D1**
– ℰ *(01) 2 36 80 00* – *www.kempinski.com/wien*
116 rm – 🛏350/435 € 🛏🛏350/475 € – ⊊ 42 € – 36 suites
• Grand Luxury • Historic • Elegant •
This hotel is housed in the listed Palais Hansen, which was built in 1873 close to the stock exchange. It offers luxurious yet tasteful rooms and suites with all the latest technology (including your own iPad). There's an elegant Lobby, an attractive bar area, a modern spa and exclusive events rooms.
❀ **Edvard** • 🍽 **Die Küche Wien** – See restaurant listing

Park Hyatt

Am Hof 2 ⊠ *1010* – **Ⓜ** *Herrengasse*   Plan: **D2**
– ℰ *(01) 2 27 40 12 34* – *www.parkhyattvienna.com*
143 rm – 🛏450/520 € 🛏🛏450/520 € – ⊊ 37 € – 35 suites
• Historic • Luxury • Elegant •
Dating back to 1915, this former bank combines stylish period architecture, modern design and the latest technology. This creates an impressive luxury hotel with an upmarket Arany Spa – the old vaults now house a gold-plated pool!
🍽 **The Bank Brasserie & Bar** – See restaurant listing

Sacher

Philharmonikerstr. 4 ⊠ *1010* – **Ⓜ** *Karlsplatz*   Plan: **D3**
– ℰ *(01) 51 45 60* – *www.sacher.com*
149 rm – 🛏440/650 € 🛏🛏440/650 € – ⊊ 41 € – 21 suites
• Grand Luxury • Classic • Personalised •
Established in 1876, the Sacher is surely one of the most famous hotels in the world. Despite its long tradition, it nevertheless keeps up with the times – not least in its elegant rooms. Just add the old-school Viennese charm of the exceptional front-of-house team and the picture is complete. And then, of course, there's the cult Café Sacher with its eponymous cake! Plus, the new Sacher Eck pavement cafe.
🍽 **Grüne Bar** • 🍽 **Rote Bar** – See restaurant listing

Grand Hotel

Kärntner Ring 9 ⊠ *1010* – **Ⓜ** *Karlsplatz*   Plan: **E3**
– ℰ *(01) 51 58 00* – *www.grandhotelwien.com*
205 rm – 🛏460/558 € 🛏🛏460/558 € – ⊊ 36 € – 11 suites
• Grand Luxury • Classic •
A classic grand hotel with an imposing lobby, sumptuous furnishings in a period setting and a superb spa. The comfortable rooms exude real Viennese charm. Don't miss the house speciality: 'Guglhupf' – a delicious ring-shaped cake. The Grand Brasserie serves traditional cuisine. There's also a pleasant pavement terrace.
❀ **Le Ciel by Toni Mörwald** • 🍽 **Unkai** – See restaurant listing

The Ritz-Carlton

Schubertring 5 ⊠ *1010* – **Ⓜ** *Karlsplatz* – ℰ *(01) 3 11 88*   Plan: **E3**
– *www.ritzcarlton.com/vienna*
202 rm – 🛏365/625 € 🛏🛏365/625 € – ⊊ 36 € – 19 suites
• Business • Grand Luxury • Contemporary •
This luxury hotel is created from four individual buildings and set right on Vienna's Ringstraße. It offers a restrained and tasteful modern interior that is never ostentatious and has lots of period detail (the comfortable lobby was once a bank vault). There is an exclusive Guerlain Spa and impeccable service of the sort you would expect in a Ritz-Carlton. The Distrikt restaurant serves international cuisine and various cuts of steak.

Bristol

Plan: **D3**

Kärntner Ring 1 ✉ 1010 – Ⓜ Karlsplatz – ✆ (01) 5 15 60 – www.bristolvienna.com

150 rm – †290/650 € ††290/650 € – ☕ 36 € – 16 suites

• Luxury • Traditional • Classic •

The traditional-style Bristol is run with great commitment and Viennese charm. Its period lounge and saloon areas set the tone for the lovely interior. The Opera suites look out on the Staatsoper and the Prince of Wales suite is genuinely imposing.

Bristol Lounge – See restaurant listing

InterContinental

Plan: **E3**

Johannesgasse 28 ✉ 1030 – Ⓜ Stadtpark – ✆ (01) 71 12 20 – www.vienna.intercontinental.com

459 rm – †199/499 € ††199/499 € – ☕ 33 € – 15 suites

• Chain • Business • Classic •

This business hotel on the edge of the Stadtpark boasts a tasteful, elegant lobby and a wide range of conference facilities. If you are looking for something special, the Presidential Suite on the 12th floor promises 140m² of luxury with a view over the city thrown in! They serve champagne brunch every Sunday.

Le Méridien

Plan: **D3**

Robert-Stolz-Platz 1 ✉ 1010 – Ⓜ Karlsplatz – ✆ (01) 58 89 00 – www.lemeridienvienna.com

294 rm – †189/495 € ††189/495 € – ☕ 32 € – 17 suites

• Chain • Design •

The classic façade belies the modern design, artwork and custom-designed lighting system that you will find inside. See and be seen is the order of the day in Le Moët bar, which serves choice snacks and champagne from breakfast to dinner. The YOU restaurant offers a small selection of sharing plates and an evening DJ.

Savoyen

Plan I: **B3**

Rennweg 16 ✉ 1030 – Ⓜ Karlsplatz – ✆ (01) 20 63 30 – www.austria-trend.at

309 rm ☕ – †150/190 € ††170/210 € – 43 suites

• Luxury • Contemporary •

The most imposing building of the former government printing works. An impressive atrium-style lobby and good conference facilities (including the largest venue in Vienna at 1 100 m²), provide modern style in a historic setting. The rooms on the seventh and eighth floors have balconies. The restaurant serves international cuisine.

Sofitel Vienna Stephansdom

Plan: **E1**

Praterstr. 1 ✉ 1020 – Ⓜ Schwedenplatz – ✆ (01) 90 61 60 – www.sofitel-vienna-stephansdom.com

182 rm – †241/574 € ††261/594 € – ☕ 32 € – 26 suites

• Luxury • Business • Design •

This hotel is the work of French architect Jean Nouvel. It offers a harmonious blend of ultra-modern urban elements both inside and out. Its minimalist design includes lots of glass, classic whites, greys and blacks, and it provides a unique view of Vienna.

✿ **Das Loft** – See restaurant listing

Sans Souci

Plan: **C3**

Burggasse 2 ✉ 1070 – Ⓜ Volkstheater – ✆ (01) 5 22 25 20 – www.sanssouci-wien.com

65 rm ☕ – †299/450 € ††339/490 €

• Townhouse • Traditional • Personalised •

A high class boutique hotel and an epitome of urban lifestyle, located in the Spittelberg artists' quarter, opposite the Volkstheater and close to the major museums. Artwork includes originals by Roy Lichtenstein, Allen Jones and Steve Kaufman.

La Veranda – See restaurant listing

Radisson BLU Style ⭐ 🕭 🎵 ⅏ 🆊 🛬

Herrengasse 12 ✉ *1010 –* Ⓜ *Herrengasse* Plan: **D2**
– 𝒞 (01) 22 78 00 – www.radissonblu.com/stylehotel-vienna
78 rm – 🛏149/619 € 🛏🛏149/619 € – ⬮ 24 €
• Townhouse • Historic • Design •
The use of high quality materials right up into the eaves and a cosmopolitan style characterise this former bank building; even the old vault doors in the gym have been retained! If you like international cuisine, try the Sapori restaurant.

The Ring 🕭 🎵 ⅏ 🆊 🛬

Kärntner Ring 8 ✉ *1010 –* Ⓜ *Karlsplatz* Plan: **E3**
– 𝒞 (01) 2 21 22 – www.theringhotel.com
68 rm – 🛏229/459 € 🛏🛏229/459 € – ⬮ 32 € – 8 suites
• Townhouse • Contemporary • Contemporary •
This modern, well-run business hotel is housed in a historic townhouse. It has a luxurious touch and a pleasant, informal atmosphere. The heritage protected lift is not to be missed.
🍴 **at eight** – See restaurant listing

Das Triest 🕭 🎵 🆊 🛁

Wiedner Hauptstr. 12 ✉ *1040 –* Ⓜ *Karlsplatz* Plan I: **B3**
– 𝒞 (01) 58 91 80 – www.dastriest.at - (extention by 50 rooms tll summer)
71 rm – 🛏269/369 € 🛏🛏269/369 € – ⬮ 26 € – 2 suites
• Business • Design •
The light, simple and elegant decor in this designer hotel is the work of Sir Terence Conran. Something of a home-from-home for its many regulars, it was once a posting house on the Vienna-Trieste route. It also has a smart bar.
🍴 **Collio** – See restaurant listing

Altstadt Vienna 🆊 🛁

Kirchengasse 41 ✉ *1070 –* Ⓜ *Volkstheater* Plan I: **A3**
– 𝒞 (01) 5 22 66 66 – www.altstadt.at
45 rm ⬮ – 🛏109/239 € 🛏🛏149/259 € – 8 suites
• Historic • Design • Personalised •
From the outside you would never guess the tasteful and original combination of art, design and charm that awaits you behind the attractive old façade of this period hotel. The lovely high-ceilinged rooms are all different and genuinely individual. Central location close to all the major sights.

Do & Co Hotel Vienna 🥢 🛎 🆊 🛬

Stephansplatz 12 ✉ *1010 –* Ⓜ *Stephansplatz* Plan: **D2**
– 𝒞 (01) 2 41 88 – www.doco.com
43 rm – 🛏249/299 € 🛏🛏249/299 € – ⬮ 29 € – 2 suites
• Business • Design • Grand luxury •
The ultra-modern exterior of this hotel provides a real contrast to the other buildings around St Stephen's Cathedral. A very special designer hotel - fashionable and upmarket. The bar serves Euro-Asian fusion food from the show kitchen before transforming itself into a trendy club in the evening!
🍴 **Do & Co Restaurant am Stephansplatz** – See restaurant listing

Hollmann Beletage 🎵 🆊

Köllnerhofgasse 6 (2nd floor) ✉ *1010* Plan: **E2**
– Ⓜ *Stephansplatz – 𝒞 (01) 9 61 19 60 – www.hollmann-beletage.at*
26 rm ⬮ – 🛏149/199 € 🛏🛏159/239 € – 1 suite
• Townhouse • Design • Contemporary •
This hotel with its fine 19C architecture boasts a number of attractive features. These include a relaxed, modern atmosphere, a beautifully planted interior courtyard, a small cinema (complete with popcorn machine!), and afternoon delicacies served for hotel guests. Not to mention the use of an iPad for the duration of your stay! The highlight is the 95m² Séparée Suite.

Hotel Rathaus - Wein & Design

Lange Gasse 13 ✉ *1080 –* Ⓜ *Rathaus*   Plan I: **A3**
– ☏ *(01) 4 00 11 22 – www.hotel-rathaus-wien.at*
– *Closed 23-26 December*
40 rm – ♦130/160 € ♦♦170/220 € – 立 18 € – 1 suite
• Townhouse • Historic • Design •

The atmosphere is relaxing and homely thanks to the wonderful service and the charming building with its historical façade and modern interior. Breakfast is an impressively generous buffet, which can be enjoyed in the pretty interior courtyard. The wine bar offers a selection of some 450 Austrian wines.

Kaiserhof

Frankenberggasse 10 ✉ *1040 –* Ⓜ *Karlsplatz*   Plan I: **B3**
– ☏ *(01) 5 05 17 01 – www.hotel-kaiserhof.at*
74 rm 立 – ♦113/303 € ♦♦148/377 € – 4 suites
• Traditional • Art déco • Contemporary •

Remarkable, friendly service, Viennese charm, and a tasteful juxtaposition of modern and classic features characterise this beautiful 1896 hotel. There is a lovely breakfast room with a buffet service and they serve a snack menu in the bar.

The Guest House Vienna

Führichgasse 10 ✉ *1010 –* Ⓜ *Herrengasse*   Plan: **D3**
– ☏ *(01) 5 12 13 20 – www.theguesthouse.at*
39 rm – ♦195/325 € ♦♦262/325 € – 立 9 € – 3 suites
• Luxury • Townhouse • Contemporary •

Are you looking for understated, modern comfort and a discreet atmosphere? This boutique hotel behind the Albertina museum and the Opera offers high quality rooms in a Terence Conran designed interior. Food is excellent, from the great All Day Breakfast (bread and pastry baked on the premises) to dinner.

The Harmonie Vienna

Harmoniegasse 5 ✉ *1090 –* Ⓜ *Schottentor*   Plan: **C1**
– ☏ *(01) 3 17 66 04 – www.harmonie-vienna.at*
66 rm 立 – ♦123/173 € ♦♦143/193 €
• Boutique hotel • Elegant • Contemporary •

Set in a fine building dating back to the 19C, Harmonie is close to the Palais Liechtenstein and easily accessible by tram (Line D). A well-run hotel, it offers comfortable, upmarket rooms decorated in tasteful colours. It also has charming service, a good, fresh breakfast and delicious afternoon coffee and cakes. The bistro serves a small selection of regional dishes.

Am Parkring

Parkring 12 ✉ *1010 –* Ⓜ *Stubentor*   Plan: **E2**
– ☏ *(01) 51 48 00 – www.schick-hotels.com*
55 rm – ♦112/225 € ♦♦154/320 € – 立 19 € – 4 suites
• Business • Functional •

Am Parkring is located opposite the Stadtpark, on the upper floors of Vienna's high-rise Gartenbauhochhaus. It offers modern rooms with great views over Vienna, some with balconies. Be sure to ask for a room on the 13th floor.
⇞○ **Das Schick** – See restaurant listing

Grand Ferdinand

Schubertring 10 ✉ *1010 –* Ⓜ *Karlsplatz*   Plan: **E3**
– ☏ *(01) 91 88 00 – www.grandferdinand.com*
186 rm – ♦200/320 € ♦♦200/320 € – 立 29 € – 1 suite
• Boutique hotel • Elegant •

The chic designer rooms with their fashionable baroque touch are not the only highlight at this stylish, modern hotel. The breakfast room on the first floor affords a great view over the city and the Grand Ferdinand Restaurant serves regional cuisine. Gulasch & Champagne offers a small menu of good plain fare.

Kaiserin Elisabeth   AK

Weihburggasse 3 ⊠ 1010 – ⓜ Stephansplatz   Plan: E2
– ℰ (01) 5 15 26 – www.kaiserinelisabeth.at
63 rm ⌂ – ♦133/148 € ♦♦205/228 €
• Traditional • Classic •

The 400-year-old history of the hotel is reflected in the classic decor including paintings by Elisabeth and Kaiser Franz in the stylish lobby. Particularly
comfortable superior rooms. Try some of the delicious Kaiserschmarrn for
breakfast!

K+K Hotel Maria Theresia   ⍟ AK ⌘ ⌂

Kirchberggasse 6 ⊠ 1070 – ⓜ Volkstheater   Plan: C3
– ℰ (01) 5 21 23 – www.kkhotels.com
132 rm ⌂ – ♦165/450 € ♦♦165/450 €
• Business • Functional •

Located in arty Spittelberg, this hotel offers functional rooms. Ask for one with a
view over the city. The spacious lobby has a bar that serves a small menu.

Mercure Vienna First   ⚐ AK

Desider Friedmann Platz 2 ⊠ 1010 – ⓜ Stephansplatz   Plan: E2
– ℰ (01) 9 05 82 80 – www.mercure.com
49 rm – ♦109 € ♦♦299 € – ⌂ 20 € – 1 suite
• Chain • Design • Contemporary •

Enjoying a great city-centre location, this functional and attractive hotel offers
stylish design with a Viennese theme. The My Room category rooms, in particular, have their own individual character. The modern restaurant serves regional
and international fare.

Das Tyrol   ⍟ AK ⌂

Mariahilfer Str. 15 ⊠ 1060 – ⓜ Museumsquartier   Plan: C3
*– ℰ (01) 5 87 54 15 – www.das-tyrol.at - (from May till September2018:
reconstruction works)*
30 rm ⌂ – ♦109/229 € ♦♦149/358 €
• Boutique hotel • Personalised •

A beautifully restored corner building offering attractive, timelessly furnished
rooms, an excellent breakfast and a small sauna decorated in gold tones. Contemporary art hangs on the walls throughout the hotel. Close to the museum
quarter.

Kärntnerhof

Grashofgasse 4 ⊠ 1010 – ⓜ Stephansplatz   Plan: E2
– ℰ (01) 5 12 19 23 – www.karntnerhof.com
44 rm ⌂ – ♦85/135 € ♦♦109/269 € – 3 suites
• Traditional • Historic • Cosy •

Kärntnerhof boasts a stylish and timeless designer interior that sits perfectly in
the period setting of this fine 19C building. It has a number of attractive features
including the parquet flooring, antiques and paintings.

OUTER DISTRICTS   PLAN I

❁❁ ### Amador   XXX ⌘ ⍟

Grinzingerstr. 86 ⊠ 1190 – ⓜ Heiligenstadt   Plan: A1
– ℰ (0660) 9 07 05 00 – www.restaurant-amador.com
– Closed 2 weeks February, 2 weeks mid-end July and Sunday-Monday
Menu 175/195 € – *(dinner only) (booking essential)*
• Creative • Chic • Elegant •

Michelin-starred chef Amador is starting to make a name for himself in this elegant vaulted wine cellar in Vienna. His team combine intensive flavours and
high-quality ingredients to create sophisticated food that is strong on detail. A
glass wall affords diners a fascinating view of the wine barrels stored in another
part of the cellar.

→ Kabeljau, Miso, Shiitake, Cecina de Leon. Miéral Taube, Mango, Cocos,
Purple Curry. Brick in the Wall, Marille, Lorbeer, Edelweiss.

Mraz & Sohn XX 🏵 🅿

Wallensteinstr. 59 ✉ *1200* – Ⓜ *Friedensbrücke*   Plan: **A2**
– ℰ *(01) 3 30 45 94 – www.mrazundsohn.at – Closed 24 December-*
8 January, Saturday-Sunday and Bank Holidays
Menu 78/129 € – *(dinner only) (booking advisable)*
• Creative • Fashionable • Chic •

In the 20th district on the outskirts of Vienna, Mraz & Sohn offers some of the most creative cuisine to be found in the city, serving punchy food that is full of flavour in a distinctive, modern setting. The excellent service and first-class wine recommendations add the final touch to this culinary experience.
➜ Kaviar, Mandelmilch, Curry. Steinpilz, Kombu. Huhn, Trüffel, Soja.

Pramerl & the Wolf (Wolfgang Zankl-Sertl) X

Pramergasse 21 ✉ *1090* – Ⓜ *Roßauer Lände*   Plan: **A2**
– ℰ *(01) 9 46 41 39 – www.pramerlandthewolf.com – Closed 8-30 January,*
26 March-3 April, 13-28 August and Sunday-Tuesday
Menu 57/68 € – *(dinner only) (booking essential)*
• Creative • Bistro • Neighbourhood •

This former bar in Vienna's 9th district is simple and pleasantly unpretentious, its surprise menu promising inexpensive yet sophisticated fare that is full of contrast. No unnecessary frills here, just excellent produce and great value for money! The best way to reach it is on the U4 underground line.
➜ Kukuruz, Hendl, Sonnenblumenkerne. Schwein, Grünkohl, Apfel, Senf. Heidelbeeren, Tanne, Zitronenthymian.

Freyenstein X 🏠 ✿

Thimiggasse 11 (by Währinger Straße A2) ✉ *1180* – ℰ *(0664) 4 39 08 37*
– www.freyenstein.at – Closed February and Sunday-Monday
Menu 38/52 € – *(dinner only) (booking advisable)*
• Traditional cuisine • Family •

This restaurant promises a warm and friendly, family ambience and attentive, pleasantly informal service. However, attention focuses on the set menu, which offers two small dishes per course, and all are flavoursome and aromatic. Demand for tables here is correspondingly high!

MAST Weinbistro X 🏵 🆎

Porzellangasse 53 ✉ *1090* – Ⓜ *Friedensbrücke*   Plan: **A2**
– ℰ *(01) 9 22 66 79 – www.mast.wine – Closed 8-23 January, 1-14 August*
and Monday-Tuesday, Saturday lunch, Sunday lunch
Menu 43/57 € – Carte 30/34 €
• Austrian • Winstub • Rustic •

No wonder MAST is so popular – the atmosphere is friendly, the decor rustic yet modern and the excellent food offers great value for money! Try the braised Jerusalem artichokes, marinated fillet steak of venison and porcini.

Woracziczky X 🏠 ✉

Spengergasse 52 ✉ *1050* – Ⓜ *Pilgramgasse*   Plan: **A3**
– ℰ *(0699) 11 22 95 30 – www.woracziczky.at – Closed 24 December-*
14 January, 6-26 August, Saturday-Sunday and Bank Holidays
Carte 23/47 €
• Austrian • Neighbourhood • Family •

The chef reserves a warm personal welcome for diners in this friendly, pleasantly informal inn (pronounced 'Vorashitkzy'). It is particularly popular for its casual atmosphere and local Viennese cuisine.

⫯○ **57** – Hotel Meliá XX ≼ & 🆎 🚗

Donau City Str. 7 (by A 22 **B1**) ✉ *1220* – ℰ *(01) 9 01 04*
– www.57melia.com – Closed 8-14 January, 6-19 August and Saturday
lunch, Sunday dinner
Menu 29 € (lunch)/68 € (dinner) – Carte 50/68 €
• Mediterranean cuisine • Design •

The spectacular view from 57 – set on 57th floor of the Meliá Hotel – is completed by the smart designer interior and, of course, the menu, which contains such offerings as saddle of lamb with courgettes, mushrooms and spinach brioche.

AUSTRIA - VIENNA

⊓⊙ **Eckel** XX 🍴 ✿

Sieveringer Str. 46 (by Billrothstraße **A1**) ✉ *1190 – ℰ (01) 3 20 32 18*
– www.restauranteckel.at – Closed 5-20 August and Sunday-Monday
Carte 27/63 €
• Country • Family • Traditional décor •

This family-run restaurant in the attractive 19th district attracts plenty of regulars who come to sample its fresh cuisine. Menu options include such classics as breaded veal sweetbreads with potato and lamb's lettuce salad. The cosy atmosphere and attractive dining rooms are equally appealing, as is the magnificent garden terrace.

⊓⊙ **grace** XX 🍴

Danhausergasse 3 ✉ *1040 –* Ⓜ *Taubstummengasse* Plan: **B3**
– ℰ (01) 5 03 10 22 – www.grace-restaurant.at – Closed 2 weeks summer,
1 week winter and Sunday-Monday
Menu 49/86 € – Carte 45/56 € – *(Tuesday to Friday dinner only)*
• Creative • Cosy •

A café in a previous incarnation, grace has now been converted into a pretty, modern restaurant with a quiet, secluded terrace. You will still find the original wood panelling and tiled floor in one of the rooms. The cuisine is creative.

⊓⊙ **Feuerwehr-Wagner** X 🍴

Grinzingerstr. 53 (Heiligenstadt) ✉ *1190* Plan: **A1**
– ℰ (01) 3 20 24 42 – www.feuerwehrwagner.at
Carte 16/32 € – *(open from 16:00)*
• Country • Wine bar • Rustic •

This typical, traditional Austrian wine tavern is greatly appreciated by regulars. You'll find a cosy, rustic interior with dark wood and simple tables. The terraced garden is particularly nice.

⊓⊙ **Fuhrmann** X 🍴

Fuhrmanngasse 9 ✉ *1080 – ℰ (01) 9444324* Plan: **A3**
– www.restaurantfuhrmann.com – Closed 1-6 January, Saturday-Sunday
and Bank Holidays
Carte 28/50 €
• Austrian • Family • Friendly •

If you're after some top-of-the-range Austrian cuisine, you need look no further than this comfortable, well-run restaurant, where you might try the Donauland lamb with marinated tomatoes, puntarelle and polenta. Pretty rear courtyard terrace.

⊓⊙ **Kutschker 44** X 🍴

Kutschergasse 44 (by Währinger Straße **A2**) ✉ *1180 – ℰ (01) 4 70 20 47*
– www.kutschker44.at – Closed Sunday-Monday and Bank Holidays
Carte 27/63 € – *(dinner only)*
• Traditional cuisine • Fashionable •

This relaxed and friendly, modern restaurant is very popular with locals, and no wonder given the delicious fare on offer. Menu options include chanterelle terrine with walnuts, lamb's lettuce and bresaola as well as Viennese specialities such as veal lights and Black Angus rib eye steak. Terrace onto the pedestrian zone.

⊓⊙ **Rudi's Beisl** X 🍴 ⊟

Wiedner Hauptstr. 88 ✉ *1050 –* Ⓜ *Taubstummengasse* Plan: **B3**
– ℰ (01) 5 44 51 02 – www.rudisbeisl.at – Closed Saturday-Sunday and
Bank Holidays
Carte 16/49 € – *(booking advisable)*
• Country • Bourgeois • Neighbourhood •

Always busy and bustling, Rudi's Beisl is a down-to-earth eatery with lots of decoration on the walls – small, simple and snug! The friendly owner does the cooking himself: traditional fare such as schnitzel, boiled beef and pancakes.

Schübel-Auer

Kahlenberger Str. 22/Zahnradbahnstr. 17 (Döbling)   Plan: **A1**
✉ *1190 – ℰ (01) 3 70 22 22 – www.schuebel-auer.at – Closed 15 October-15 March and Monday, mid March-end April: Monday-Tuesday*
Carte 17/33 € – (open from 15:30, Sunday open from 14:00)
• Country • Wine bar • Cosy •

Today the carefully refurbished former Auerhof (built in 1642 as a wine-grower's house) with its quiet interior courtyard makes a lovely restaurant. Located at the end of tramline D, it is easy to reach from the city centre.

Falkensteiner Hotel Wien Margareten

Margaretengürtel 142 ✉ *1050 –* ◍ *Margaretengürtel*
– ℰ (01) 509 911 30 00 – www.falkensteiner.com   Plan: **A3**
195 rm – ♦99/199 € ♦♦99/199 € – 🖵 22 € – 2 suites
• Business • Chain • Contemporary •

This business hotel is set between Schönbrunn Castle and the city. It offers good conference facilities, easy connections into Vienna and an appealing mix of modern design and Biedermeier style. The seventh floor houses a leisure area complete with terrace for rest and relaxation.

Meliá

Donau City Str. 7 (by A 22 **B1***)* ✉ *1220 – ℰ (01) 9 01 04 – www.melia.com*
253 rm – ♦165/390 € ♦♦165/390 € – 🖵 26 € – 5 suites
• Chain • Business • Design •

The Meliá is located in the modern DC Tower, just a short U-Bahn trip to the city centre. The rooms, too, are impressive: upmarket and functional with state-of-the-art technology and floor-to-ceiling panoramic windows. The bar on the 58th floor boasts a great view and a small terrace.
♨ **57** – See restaurant listing

Boutiquehotel Stadthalle

Hackengasse 20 ✉ *1150 –* ◍ *Westbahnhof*   Plan: **A1**
– ℰ (01) 9 82 42 72 – www.hotelstadthalle.at
79 rm 🖵 – ♦88/258 € ♦♦98/268 €
• Townhouse • Personalised • Contemporary •

Organic food and sustainability take centre stage in this attractive hotel not far from the Stadthalle. The rooms offer an individual mix of classic and modern styling. The garden rooms, which look out onto the beautifully planted interior courtyard (where breakfast is served in summer) are particularly quiet.

Zeitgeist

Sonnwendgasse 15 ✉ *1100 –* ◍ *Hauptbahnhof*   Plan: **B3**
– ℰ (01) 90 26 50 – www.zeitgeist-vienna.com
254 rm – ♦85/250 € ♦♦100/270 € – 🖵 17 €
• Business • Functional •

Located not far from the main railway station, Zeitgeist offers a variety of different room categories. These include Urban, Prestige (with a view and a terrace) and Zeitgeist Suite, which are all fashionable, minimalist in style and have the latest technology. The Pergola bistro serves international fare and there's also a sauna and a courtyard garden.

AT THE AIRPORT

NH Vienna Airport

Einfahrtsstr. 1 ✉ *1300 – ℰ (01) 70 15 10 – www.nh-hotels.com*
499 rm – ♦139/359 € ♦♦139/359 € – 🖵 25 €
• Business • Contemporary • Classic •

The lobby, bar and restaurant area are spacious, the rooms well equipped and the hotel enjoys a convenient location close to the airport arrivals hall. All in all an ideal destination for the business traveller. The restaurant serves international cuisine alongside Austrian classics.

SALZBURG
SALZBURG

oriedmouse/iStock

SALZBURG IN...

→ **ONE DAY**
Festung Hohensalzburg,
Museum der Moderne, Cathedral,
Residenzplatz.

→ **TWO DAYS**
Mozart's birthplace, Nonntal,
Kapuzinerberg, Mirabell Gardens,
concert at Mozarteum.

→ **THREE DAYS**
Mozart's residence, Hangar 7,
Hellbrunn Palace, concert at
Landestheater.

Small but perfectly formed, Salzburg is a chocolate-box treasure, gift-wrapped in stunning Alpine surroundings. It's immortalised as the birthplace and inspiration of one of classical music's greatest stars, and shows itself off as northern Europe's grandest exhibitor of baroque style. Little wonder that in summer its population rockets, as the sound of music wafts from hotel rooms and festival hall windows during rehearsals for the Festspiele. In quieter times of the year, Salzburgers enjoy a leisurely and relaxed pace of life. Their love of music and the arts is renowned; and they enjoy the

outdoors, too, making the most of the mountains and lakes, and the paths which run along the river Salzach and zig-zag through the woods and the grounds of Hellbrunn. The dramatic natural setting of Salzburg means you're never likely to get lost. Rising above the left bank (the Old Town) is the Mönchsberg Mountain and its fortress, the Festung Hohensalzburg, while the right bank (the New Town, this being a relative term) is guarded by the even taller Kapuzinerberg. In the New Town stands the Mozart family home, while the graceful gardens of the Schloss Mirabell draw the right bank crowds. The Altstadt (Old Town) is a UNESCO World Heritage Site and its star turn is its Cathedral. To the east is the quiet Nonntal area overlooked by the Nuns' Mountain.

EATING OUT

Salzburg's cuisine takes much of its influence from the days of the Austro-Hungarian Empire, with Bavarian elements added to the mix. Over the centuries it was characterised by substantial pastry and egg dishes to fill the stomachs of local salt mine workers; it's still hearty and meaty and is typified by dumplings and broths. In the city's top restaurants, a regional emphasis is still very important but the cooking has a lighter, more modern touch. Beyond the city are picturesque inns and tranquil beer gardens, many idyllically set by lakes. Do try the dumplings: Pinzgauer Nocken are made of potato pastry and filled with minced pork; another favourite is Gröstl, a filling meal of 'leftovers', including potatoes, dumplings, sausages and smoked meat roasted in a pan. If you want a snack, then Jausen is for you – cold meals with bread and sausage, cheese, dumplings, bacon etc, followed by an Obstler, made from distilled fruit. Salzburg's sweet tooth is evident in the Salzburger Nockerl, a rich soufflé omelette made with fruit and soft meringue.

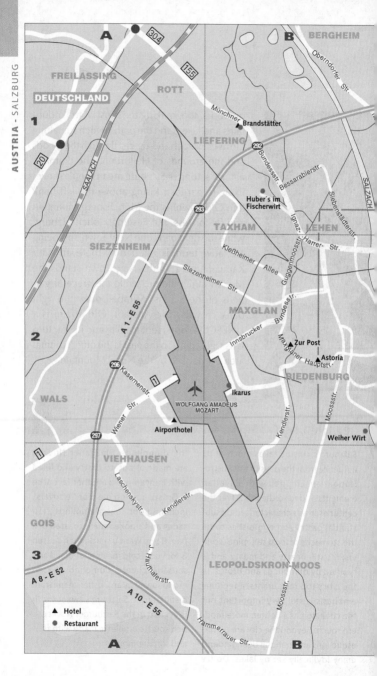

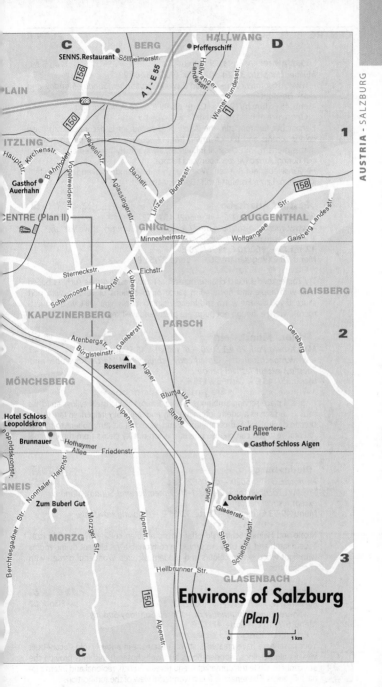

Environs of Salzburg
(Plan I)

0   1 km

AUSTRIA - SALZBURG

✿ Esszimmer (Andreas Kaiblinger)   XxX 🏠 AK
Müllner Hauptstr. 33 ✉ 5020 – ☏ (0662) 87 08 99   Plan: **E1**
– www.esszimmer.com – Closed 2 weeks September, Sunday-Monday and Bank Holidays
Menu 45 € (lunch)/126 € – Carte 68/99 € – *(booking advisable)*
• Creative • Fashionable • Elegant •
Elegant but far from stiff, the Kaiblinger's restaurant is decorated with lively colour accents and the charming front-of-house team serve punchy cuisine that is modern with classical influences, always finely balanced and anything but boring! Attractive rear courtyard terrace.
→ Gänseleber auf 3 Arten. Wolfsbarsch mit Koriandergurken und Räucherkartoffeln. Lammkotelette mit Bohnencassoulet.

☺ Gasthof Auerhahn   XX ⇦ 🏠 ⇄ P
Bahnhofstr. 15 ✉ 5020 – ☏ (0662) 45 10 52   Plan I: **C1**
– www.auerhahn-salzburg.at – Closed 1 week January, 3 weeks July, 1 week September and Sunday dinner-Tuesday
12 rm ☲ – †60/70 € ††98/120 €
Menu 28 € (Vegetarian)/56 € – Carte 27/51 €
• Country • Friendly • Cosy •
Try Topfenknödel (curd cheese dumplings) and classic dishes such as boiled beef with apple and horseradish sauce or medallions of venison with port sauce. If you like the warm and friendly dining rooms, you will love the guestrooms, which although not huge, are pretty and well kept.

🍴○ Schloss Mönchstein   XxX ⩽ 🍴 🏠 AK P
Mönchsberg Park 26 ✉ 5020 – ☏ (0662) 8 48 55 50   Plan: **E1**
– www.monchstein.at – Closed early February-mid March, November and Tuesday, except festival period
Menu 55/145 € – Carte 59/118 €
• Classic cuisine • Elegant • Classic décor •
A special place serving ambitious cuisine, Schloss Mönchstein enjoys an idyllic setting and serves modern, internationally and regionally influenced fare that is prepared with skill and commitment and served in an atmosphere to match. Alternatively, you can choose one of the top-quality steaks from the charcoal grill.

🍴○ Riedenburg   XX 🏠 P
Neutorstr. 31 ✉ 5020 – ☏ (0662) 83 08 15   Plan: **E2**
– www.riedenburg.at – Closed 1-10 September and Sunday-Monday, except festival period
Menu 49/73 € (dinner) – Carte 32/66 € – *(booking advisable)*
• Classic cuisine • Cosy •
Nicole and Helmut Schinwald offer classic Austrian cuisine. Wiener Schnitzel, Tauern lamb and sea bass are served in comfortable yet elegant dining rooms with light wood, warm colours and modern pictures. Wonderful garden with chestnut trees.

🍴○ Brunnauer   XX 🍸 🏠 ⅙
Fürstenallee 5 ✉ 5020 – ☏ (0662) 25 10 10   Plan I: **C2**
– www.restaurant-brunnauer.at – Closed Saturday-Sunday
Menu 67/110 € – Carte 47/77 €
• French • Elegant • Friendly •
Your hosts here have created a stylish restaurant in a lovely, old Ceconi-built villa. Its high ceilings, wooden floors and well-chosen furnishings provide the atmosphere, while the upmarket menu reveals French, regional and international influences. The terrace offers a wonderful view of the fortifications.

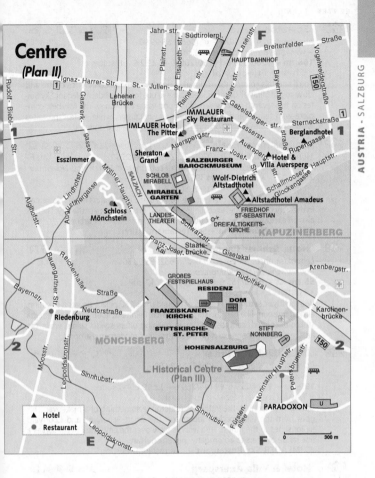

Centre
(Plan II)

▲ Hotel
● Restaurant

0   300 m

‖○   **IMLAUER Sky Restaurant** – IMLAUER Hotel Pitter   ✗ 斉 🆎

Rainerstr. 6 (6th floor) ✉ 5020   ⇔
– ℰ (0662) 88 97 86 66 – www.imlauer.com   Plan: **F1**
Carte 33/70 €

• International • Fashionable •

Enjoying a great location on the 6th floor of the Imlauer Hotel, Sky offers guests some great views of Salzburg as well as international and regional cuisine from steak and pasta to the classics.

‖○   **Weiher Wirt**   ✗ 斉

König Ludwig Str. 2 ✉ 5020   Plan I: **B2**
– ℰ (0662) 82 93 24 – www.weiherwirt.com – Closed January and Monday
Carte 26/54 €

• Austrian • Inn •

This restaurant is wonderfully located on the banks of Leopoldskroner Lake. It serves regional dishes such as Szegediner pork goulash with boiled potatoes. Warm colours and modern notes provide a pleasant feel; outside is a lovely garden.

45

Sheraton Grand

Auerspergstr. 4 ✉ *5020 –* ℰ *(0662) 88 99 90* Plan: **E1**
– www.sheratongrandsalzburg.com
166 rm – ♦200/650 € ♦♦250/700 € – ⬜ 32 € – 8 suites
• Chain • Functional •

You'll find this comfortable, upmarket hotel next to the conference centre and close to the Mirabell Gardens. Keep an eye out for the modern, elegant Sky Suites on the seventh floor, which offer good value for money. The Mirabell, complete with terrace and garden, serves classic cuisine, while 'taste.it' promises Italian specialities with a focus on home-made pasta and antipasti.

Schloss Mönchstein

Mönchsberg Park 26 ✉ *5020 –* ℰ *(0662) 8 48 55 50* Plan: **E1**
– www.monchstein.at – Closed early February-mid March and November
24 rm ⬜ – ♦316/460 € ♦♦395/680 € – 3 suites
• Historic • Personalised •

This hotel is set in a 14C castle at the "top of Salzburg". It offers rooms decorated in the very best of taste, excellent service and great views over the city. There is also an exclusive spa and an outdoor pool set in 3½ acres of grounds.
⑩ **Schloss Mönchstein** – See restaurant listing

Hotel Schloss Leopoldskron

Leopoldskronstr. 56 ✉ *5020 –* ℰ *(0662) 83 98 30* Plan I: **C1**
– www.schloss-leopoldskron.com
55 rm ⬜ – ♦135/155 € ♦♦165/280 € – 12 suites
• Historic • Historic •

With an idyllic setting in 17 acres of grounds, this 18C palace boasts a stunning, almost museum-like hall, the sumptuous Max Reinhardt library and a wonderful stucco-decorated staircase. The main building offers stylish suites, while the adjacent Meierhof annexe is home to attractive, modern guestrooms.

IMLAUER Hotel Pitter

Rainerstr. 6 ✉ *5020 –* ℰ *(0662) 88 97 80* Plan: **F1**
– www.imlauer.com
190 rm – ♦124/229 € ♦♦144/269 € – ⬜ 19 € – 8 suites
• Townhouse • Cosy • Elegant •

Dating back to 1864, the Pitter has undergone something of a makeover. This goes from the ultra-modern lobby and the smart Panorama and Courtyard junior suites to the fitness area with its view over the city. Pitter Keller serves a fine range of beers to accompany the regional fare.
⑩ **IMLAUER Sky Restaurant** – See restaurant listing

Hotel & Villa Auersperg

Auerspergstr. 61 ✉ *5020 –* ℰ *(0662) 88 94 40* Plan: **F1**
– www.auersperg.at
55 rm ⬜ – ♦145/195 € ♦♦155/305 € – 2 suites
• Townhouse • Contemporary • Elegant •

A veritable oasis in the midst of the city, the Auersperg offers spacious, upmarket rooms with lots of little extras, a charming garden, committed staff and a great bar that serves snacks until late into the evening. Don't miss the wonderful sauna with its impressive roof terrace!

Astoria

Maxglaner Hauptstr. 7 ✉ *5020 –* ℰ *(0662) 83 42 77* Plan I: **B2**
– www.salzburgastoria.com
29 rm ⬜ – ♦85/115 € ♦♦95/175 €
• Family • Functional • Contemporary •

With its warm welcome, personal service and location just a 15-minute walk from the centre, the Astoria provides contemporary rooms (including family rooms) decorated in warm tones and a good breakfast buffet including freshly cooked eggs in a variety of styles. The added extra: the artwork dotted around the hotel.

Wolf-Dietrich Altstadthotel 🏠 🗔

Wolf-Dietrich-Str. 7 ✉ 5020 – ℰ (0662) 87 12 75
– www.wolf-dietrich.at   Plan: **F1**
40 rm ☞ – ♦73/148 € ♦♦113/262 €
• Townhouse • Cosy •

This hotel in the old town is regularly maintained to ensure everything is in perfect working order. The rooms are well appointed and classic in style. There is also a pretty indoor pool complete with sauna in the former wine cellar.

Zur Post 🏠 ⅙ 🅿

Maxglaner Hauptstr. 45 ✉ 5020 – ℰ (0662) 8 32 33 90
– www.hotelzurpost.info – Closed 20-27 December   Plan I: **B2**
30 rm – ♦60/73 € ♦♦86/110 € – ☞ 15 €
• Inn • Functional •

At Zur Post you can look forward to attractive rooms, a good breakfast and committed family management. The main building, the Garten Haus, the Bürger Haus and the Villa Ceconi (200m away) offer a range of accommodation from classic to modern.

Altstadthotel Amadeus 🏠

Linzer Gasse 43 ✉ 5020 – ℰ (0662) 87 14 01
– www.hotelamadeus.at   Plan: **F1**
20 rm – ♦120/195 € ♦♦140/280 € – ☞ 20 €
• Historic • Townhouse • Personalised •

This centuries' old hotel is not only very central but also contemporary and tasteful. It boasts a pretty and welcoming breakfast room with a white vaulted ceiling, as well as an Italian restaurant.

Berglandhotel 🅿

Rupertgasse 15 ✉ 5020 – ℰ (0662) 87 23 18
– www.berglandhotel.at – Closed 17-27 December   Plan: **F1**
18 rm – ♦69/85 € ♦♦89/155 € – ☞ 5 €
• Family • Personalised • Functional •

What distinguishes the Berglandhotel from many other city hotels is its warm and friendly welcome. The owners set great store by personal service and the beautifully kept rooms all have an individual touch.

HISTORICAL CENTRE   PLAN III

✿ Carpe Diem XX 🆔

Getreidegasse 50 (1st floor) ✉ 5020   Plan: **G1**
– ℰ (0662) 84 88 00 – www.carpediemfinestfingerfood.com – Closed
5-20 February and Sunday
Menu 75/115 € – Carte 61/102 €
• Market cuisine • Fashionable • Design •

You can sample Carpe Diem's famous "cones" throughout the restaurant and its classically based cuisine with modern, international influences made using only the finest ingredients on the first floor. The service is friendly and professional. Look out for the great value lunchtime menu.
➜ Beef Tatar mit Kartoffelpüree im Cone. Huchen, Hollerblüte, Stangensellerie und Bergamotte. Rehrücken, Topfenserviettenknödel, Spitzkraut und Kirschen.

🙂 Goldgasse – Hotel Goldgasse X 🍴

Goldgasse 10 ✉ 5020 – ℰ (0662) 84 56 22   Plan: **H1**
– www.hotelgoldgasse.at
Carte 27/68 €
• Traditional cuisine • Cosy • Friendly •

The speciality here is new interpretations of old Salzburg recipes taken from a cookbook published in 1719! The food is a perfect match for the period setting with modern touches and the lively atmosphere – the charming service is the icing on the cake! Try the fried breaded chicken with potato and cucumber salad and cranberries and the apple strudel with vanilla sauce.

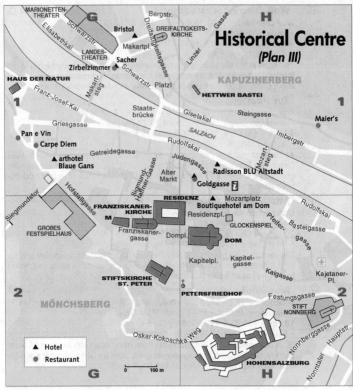

Historical Centre
(Plan III)

▲ Hotel
● Restaurant

0 — 100 m

🍴 **Pan e Vin**   XX

Gstättengasse 1 (1st floor) ☒ *5020 –* ✆ *(0662) 84 46 66*   Plan: **G1**
– www.panevin.at – Closed 1-10 September and Sunday, except festival period

Menu 48/89 € (dinner) – Carte 42/79 €

• **Mediterranean cuisine • Cosy •**

Pan e Vin is set in a 600 year-old building with an interior decorated in warm tones. It serves food with a distinctly Mediterranean feel alongside a well-stocked international wine list. The Azzuro on the ground floor is also a good option.

🍴 **Zirbelzimmer** – Hotel Sacher   XX 😊 よ 🆒 🚗

Schwarzstr. 5 ☒ *5020 –* ✆ *(0662) 88 97 70*   Plan: **G1**
– www.sacher.com

Menu 49/66 € – Carte 47/69 €

• **Market cuisine • Elegant •**

Sacher's culinary flagship offers a wide and varied menu ranging from poached langoustine to Styrian fried chicken, all served in a warm, friendly and typically Austrian setting. There is also an attractive balcony overlooking the River Salzach.

48

†○ **Maier's** ✗
Steingasse 61 ✉ *5020 –* ☎ *(0662) 87 93 79* Plan: **H1**
– www.maiers-salzburg.at – Closed Sunday-Monday
Carte 35/56 € – (dinner only) (booking advisable)
• International • Friendly • Cosy •
Many regulars visit this restaurant in an old alleyway to enjoy classic fare inclu-
ding steaks and Szegediner goulash. The feel is welcoming, the service friendly
and you can park in the multi-storey car park right opposite the restaurant.

†○ **PARADOXON** ✗ 🏠 📫
Zugallistr. 7 ✉ *5020 –* ☎ *(0664) 1 61 61 91* Plan: **F2**
– www.restaurant-paradoxon.com – closed Sunday-Monday
Carte 41/59 € – (dinner only)
• International • Chic • Friendly •
Those who like a restaurant with a difference will find both the interior and the
cuisine here unpretentious, unconventional and anything but staid. The one
thing you can always be sure of is the quality of the food.

🏨 **Sacher**
Schwarzstr. 5 ✉ *5020 –* ☎ *(0662) 88 97 70* Plan: **G1**
– www.sacher.com
109 rm – †350/750 € ††350/750 € – ☲ 35 € – 5 suites
• Traditional • Historic • Classic •
The flagship of the Salzburg hotel world, Sacher really is a top international
hotel. It offers classically designed, tasteful and luxurious rooms and suites.
Alongside the Grill restaurant, don't miss the Café Sacher, the epitome of Vien-
nese coffee house style.
†○ **Zirbelzimmer** – See restaurant listing

🏨 **Bristol** ☆ Ⓜ ﹩ ⇔
Makartplatz 4 ✉ *5020 –* ☎ *(0662) 87 35 57* Plan: **G1**
– www.bristol-salzburg.at – Closed February-March
60 rm ☲ – †260/450 € ††285/480 € – 6 suites
• Traditional • Classic •
The stylish decor in the high-ceilinged rooms hint at the history of this hotel,
built in 1619 and run as a hotel since 1892. Individually designed rooms come
with stucco work, crystal chandeliers, antiques, sumptuous fabrics and paintings. The restaurant serves classic cuisine with traditional influences.

🏨 **Radisson BLU Altstadt** ☆ Ⓜ ﹩
Rudolfskai 26 (Judengasse 15) ✉ *5020* Plan: **H1**
– ☎ *(0662) 8 48 57 10 – www.radissonblu.com/hotel-salzburg*
49 rm – †136 € ††165 € – ☲ 26 € – 13 suites
• Townhouse • Elegant • Classic •
Close to the Mozartplatz, the Altstadt's historical exterior conceals attractive
rooms in a classically elegant style, the executive suites and suites being the
most spacious. The restaurant with a winter garden overlooking the River Salzach and the terrace in the courtyard both serve international fare. Alternatively,
there is the modern Café Altstadt.

🏠 **arthotel Blaue Gans** ☆ Ⓜ ﹩
Getreidegasse 41 ✉ *5020 –* ☎ *(0662) 8 42 49 10* Plan: **G1**
– www.blauegans.at – Closed April
35 rm ☲ – †135/277 € ††177/387 € – 3 suites
• Townhouse • Contemporary • Personalised •
At 650 years old, Blaue Gans is Salzburg's oldest hotel. Today it offers a successful mix of chic modern design and contemporary art in a fine period setting. If
you're looking for somewhere special to stay, try the Maisonette Suite. The restaurant serves regional cuisine in its pretty vaulted dining room and on the
attractive terrace.

🏠 Boutiquehotel am Dom   [AC]

Goldgasse 17 ✉ *5020 – ℰ (0662) 84 27 65*   Plan: **H2**
– www.hotelamdom.at
15 rm ⌂ – †109/229 € ††119/389 €
• Townhouse • Contemporary •

It is hard to imagine that this out of the way little hotel would conceal such generous rooms. They offer smart modern design, beautifully appointed bathrooms and immaculate cleanliness. Use the underground car park in the old town.

🏠 Goldgasse

Goldgasse 10 ✉ *5020 – ℰ (0662) 84 56 22*   Plan: **H1**
– www.hotelgoldgasse.at
16 rm – †160/220 € ††200/350 € – ⌂ 25 € – 1 suite
• Townhouse • Historic • Personalised •

This is a real picture-postcard boutique hotel dating back 700 years. Goldgasse simply oozes history, though the rooms (mostly junior suites) are modern and individually designed. The restaurant serves traditional Austrian cuisine.
🍴 **Goldgasse** – See restaurant listing

ENVIRONS OF SALZBURG AND AIRPORT   PLAN I

✿✿ Ikarus   XxxX 🏵 ⪡ 🛋 & [AC] ⇦ [P]

Wilhelm-Spazier-Str. 7a (Hangar 7) ✉ *5020*   Plan: **B2**
– ℰ (0662) 2 19 70 – www.hangar-7.com – closed end December-early January
Menu 58 € (lunch)/180 €
– Carte 65/127 € – *(Monday to Wednesday dinner only) (booking essential)*
• Creative • Fashionable • Elegant •

An unusual concept, the architecturally impressive Hangar-7 is both a Red Bull exhibition space and an ultra-modern luxury restaurant serving top quality creative cuisine. Choose from a menu devised by the international guest chef of the month or the restaurant's own Ikarus selection.
➙ Texturen Fourme d'Ambert mit Dattelcrème, Erdnuss und Perigord Trüffel. Gebratener bretonischer Hummer mit gerösteten Mandeln. Filet vom japanischen Wagyu mit Pont Neuf Kartoffeln und geschmorter Zwiebel.

✿✿ SENNS.Restaurant   XxX [P]

Söllheimerstr. 16 (at Gusswerk - Object 6c) ✉ *5020*   Plan: **C1**
– ℰ (0664) 4 54 02 32 – www.senns.restaurant – Closed 23 December-7 January and Sunday-Monday, except festival period
Menu 118/179 € – Carte 66/104 € – *(booking advisable)*
• Creative • Fashionable • Friendly •

There's plenty to look at in this former foundry with its stylish urban look and industrial charm, but as soon as the friendly yet discreet front-of-house team has served the first course, you'll find that Andreas Senn and Christian Geisler's creative, fully flavoured, modern cuisine made using the very best ingredients demands your full attention.
➙ Rote Garnele, Aubergine, junge Kokosnuss, Erbse, Kaffirlimette. Black Cod, Miso, Dashi, Puntarelle. Iberisches Schwein, Tomate, Mais.

🍴 Brandstätter – Hotel Brandstätter   XX 🍴 🛋 [P]

Münchner Bundesstr. 69 ✉ *5020 – ℰ (0662) 43 45 35*   Plan: **B1**
– www.hotel-brandstaetter.com – Closed 23-27 December and Sunday, except festival period and Advent
Carte 33/79 € – *(booking advisable)*
• Country • Cosy •

Try the creamy veal goulash and the local venison, and dont' miss the Mohr im Hemd (chocolate hazelnut pudding with an exquisite chocolate sauce!). Pretty, cosy dining rooms – the Swiss pine room with its tiled oven has its own charm.

Huber's im Fischerwirt   XX 🏡

Peter Pfenninger Str. 8 ✉ 5020 – ℰ (0662) 42 40 59   Plan: **B1**
– www.fischerwirt-liefering.at
– Closed 12 February-7 March, 4-27 July and Tuesday-Wednesday
Menu 39/80 € – Carte 27/92 €
• Austrian • Cosy • Rural •

The Hubers serve regional classics and international fare in their charming restaurant. Dishes include Viennese fried chicken with lamb's lettuce and potato salad, and game stew with bread dumplings. There is also a small shop selling jams, chocolate and caviar.

Zum Buberl Gut   XX 🏡 ✿ **P**

Gneiser Str. 31 ✉ 5020 – ℰ (0662) 82 68 66   Plan: **C3**
– www.buberlgut.at – Closed 1 week March, 1 week June, 1 week
September and Tuesday, festival period: Tuesday lunch
Menu 26 € (lunch)/78 € (dinner) – Carte 43/75 € – *(booking advisable)*
• Traditional cuisine • Cosy • Rustic •

This pretty 17C manor house offers more than just an attractive setting. The food served in the splendid, elegant dining rooms and lovely garden is delicious. It includes dishes such as tuna fish tartare with avocado and mango and paprika chutney, as well as ossobuco with creamed Jerusalem artichokes and gremolata.

Gasthof Schloss Aigen   XX 🏡 ✿ **P**

Schwarzenbergpromenade 37 ✉ 5026   Plan: **D2**
– ℰ (0662) 62 12 84 – www.schloss-aigen.at
– Closed Monday-Wednesday, except festival period
Menu 36 € (lunch)/64 € – Carte 30/71 €
• Austrian • Inn • Friendly •

Dating back to 1402, Schloss Aigen serves traditional Austrian cuisine with modern influences. Try the boiled beef, which comes in a range of different preparations. There is also a charming interior courtyard terrace set beneath sweet chestnut trees.

Rosenvilla   **P**

Höfelgasse 4 ✉ 5020 – ℰ (0662) 62 17 65   Plan: **C2**
– www.rosenvilla.com – Closed 2 weeks end December-early January
14 rm – †70/90 € ††120/140 € – ⊊ 14 €
• Family • Contemporary • Cosy •

Stefanie Fleischhaker is a born hostess and you are always sure of a warm welcome. Enjoy the great service, tasteful decor and lovely terrace, as well as the excellent breakfasts which are popular even with non-residents. The single rooms are compact.

Airporthotel   🕊 ᵫ 🐾 ☐ ⚒ 🚗

Dr.-Matthias-Laireiter-Str. 9 ✉ 5020 Salzburg-Loig   Plan: **A2**
– ℰ (0662) 85 00 20 – www.airporthotel.at
36 rm ⊊ – †105/165 € ††145/199 €
• Inn • Cosy •

This hotel is across from the airport, and consists of two connected hotel buildings, which are typical of the region. Functional rooms, some with air-conditioning.

Brandstätter   ⇦ ᵫ ☐ ⚒ **P**

Münchner Bundesstr. 69 ✉ 5020 – ℰ (0662) 43 45 35   Plan: **B1**
– www.hotel-brandstaetter.com – Closed 23-26 December
35 rm ⊊ – †95/130 € ††145/165 €
• Family • Cosy •

The hotel's proximity to the main street and the motorway is more than compensated for by the hospitality of the Brandstätter family and their staff. Some of the lovely country house style rooms face out onto the garden.
🍴 **Brandstätter** – See restaurant listing

51

AUSTRIA - SALZBURG

Doktorwirt

🏠 ⚘ 🛏 ♨ 🎱 🐕 📶 P

Glaserstr. 9 ✉ *5026 – ℰ (0662) 6 22 97 30*   Plan: **D3**
– www.doktorwirt.at – Closed 3-28 February, 15 October- 24 November
41 rm ⌷ – †80/135 € ††130/170 €
• Inn • Traditional • Cosy •

The comfortable accommodation here in this 12C guesthouse includes some attractive tower rooms with small bow-fronted windows. The Doktorwirt also boasts a spacious pool area, serves its own honey and there is a meadow behind the hotel where you pick fruit. The comfortable dining rooms and terrace serve regional food.

AT ELIXHAUSEN   North: 7,5 km by Vogelweiderstraße **C1**

Gmachl

🏠 🛏 ♨ ⚘ 🎱 🐕 📶 & 🅰 ⟳ 🚗

Dorfstr. 14 ✉ *5161 – ℰ (0662) 48 02 12 – www.gmachl.com*
76 rm ⌷ – †122/208 € ††198/328 €
• Country house • Family • Cosy •

Now in its 23rd generation, the dedicated Hirnböck-Gmachl family has been at the helm here for over 675 years. Its tasteful rooms split between the old Gasthof and the newer Klosterhof buildings, the hotel also boasts a lovely spa with a panoramic view and a restaurant comprising various cosy dining rooms serving regional fare.

AT HALLWANG

⛺ Pfefferschiff (Jürgen Vigné)

XX ⚘ 🍴 P

Söllheim 3 ✉ *5300 – ℰ (0662) 66 12 42*   Plan: **D1**
– www.pfefferschiff.at – Closed 2 weeks mid June-early July and Sunday-Monday, except festival period
Menu 78 € (Vegetarian)/98 € (dinner)
– Carte 63/90 € – (Tuesday to Friday dinner only, except festival period) (booking essential)
• Classic cuisine • Elegant • Cosy •

Standing at the gates of Salzburg, this top gourmet restaurant is located in a lovely 17C former parish house. The owner Jürgen Vigné's flavoursome and distinctive cuisine is matched by the charming front-of-house team managed by his wife. The dining rooms are delightful and the terrace is wonderful.
➙ Marinierte Gänseleber mit Wachauer Marille und Fenchel. Rosa gebratener Rehrücken mit Sellerie, Mandel und Kirsche. Heidelbeerdatschi, Sauerrahmschaum und Schmandeis.

AT HOF BEI SALZBURG   North-East: 18 km by Wolfgangsee Straße **D1**

🍴 Schloss Restaurant – Hotel Schloss Fuschl

XxX ⚘ 🍴 🅰 🚗

Schloss Str. 19 ✉ *5322 – ℰ (06229) 2 25 30*
– www.schlossfuschlsalzburg.com
Menu 65/129 € – Carte 50/98 € – *(dinner only)*
• Classic cuisine • Romantic • Elegant •

Where else could you enjoy ambitious cuisine in such an elegant setting with a lovely lake view? The food here is a mix of classic and international, the fish comes from the restaurant's own farm and the cellar provides over 1 000 different wines to accompany the Fuschlsee whitefish, mousseline of baby leeks, porcini and beurre noisette or the Mieral pigeon with mango, purple curry and coconut.

Schloss Fuschl

🏖 ← 🛏 ♨ ⚘ 🐕 🎱 🔲 🅿 & 🅰 🛎 🚗

Schloss Str. 19 ✉ *5322 – ℰ (06229) 2 25 30*
– www.schlossfuschlsalzburg.com
110 rm ⌷ – †245/750 € ††295/800 € – 13 suites
• Luxury • Classic •

This magnificent property on a small peninsula extending into the lake (where the famous "Sissi" films starring Romy Schneider were filmed in the 1950s) makes an ideal wedding venue. Alongside stylishly elegant rooms, a remarkable collection of paintings and its warm and welcoming staff, the hotel also boasts a bathing beach with jetty, motor boats, its own fish smokery and shop and a Rolls Royce you can hire!
🍴 **Schloss Restaurant** – See restaurant listing

Antwerp

BRUSSELS

BELGIUM
BELGIË - BELGIQUE

MarioGuti/iStock

BRUSSELS
BRUXELLES/BRUSSEL

sedmak/iStock

BRUSSELS IN...

→ **ONE DAY**
Grand Place, Musées Royaux des Beaux-Arts,
Place Ste-Catherine.

→ **TWO DAYS**
Marolles, Place du Grand Sablon,
Musical Instrument Museum,
concert at Palais des Beaux-Arts.

→ **THREE DAYS**
Parc du Cinquantenaire, Horta's
house, tour St Gilles and Ixelles.

There aren't many cities where you can use a 16C century map and accurately navigate your way around; or where there are enough restaurants to dine somewhere different every day for five years; or where you'll find a museum dedicated to the comic strip – but then every city isn't Brussels. It was tagged a 'grey' capital because of its EU associations but those who've spent time here know it to be, by contrast, a buzzing town. It's the home of art nouveau, it features a wonderful maze of medieval alleys and places to eat, and it's warm and friendly, with an outgoing, cosmopolitan feel – due in no small

part to its turbulent history, which has seen it under frequent occupation. Generally speaking, the Bruxellois believe that you shouldn't take things too seriously: they have a soft spot for puppets and Tintin, street music and majorettes; and they do their laundry in communal places like the Wash Club.

The area where all visitors wend is the Lower Town and the Grand Place but the northwest and southern quarters (Ste-Catherine and The Marolles) are also of particular interest. To the east, higher up an escarpment, lies the Upper Town – this is the traditional home of the aristocracy and encircles the landmark Parc de Bruxelles. Two suburbs of interest are St Gilles, to the southwest, and Ixelles, to the southeast, where trendy bars and art nouveau are the order of the day.

EATING OUT

As long as your appetite hasn't been sated at the chocolatiers, or with a cone of frites from a street stall, you'll relish the dining experience in Brussels. As long as you stay off the main tourist drag (i.e. Rue des Bouchers), you're guaranteed somewhere good to eat within a short strolling distance. There are lots of places to enjoy Belgian dishes such as moules frites, Ostend lobster, eels with green herbs, or waterzooi (chicken or fish stew with vegetables). Wherever you're eating, at whatever price range, food is invariably well cooked and often bursting with innovative touches. As a rule of thumb, the Lower Town has the best places, with the Ste-Catherine quarter's seafood establishments the pick of the bunch; you'll also find a mini Chinatown here. Because of the city's cosmopolitan character there are dozens of international restaurants - ranging from French and Italian to more unusual Moroccan, Tunisian and Congolese destinations. Belgium beers are famous the world over and are served in specially designed glasses.

 සිස සිස **Sea Grill** (Yves Mattagne) – Hôtel Radisson Blu Royal XxxX 錦 よ
rue du Fossé aux Loups 47 ⊠ *1000* ⚑ ⇔ ⬢
– ✆ *0 2 212 08 00 – www.seagrill.be* Plan: **N1**
– *closed 2-8 April, 29 April-1 Mai, 21 July-15 August, 1-4 November,*
1-7 January, Bank Holidays, Saturday lunch and Sunday
Menu 65 € (lunch), 150/205 €
– Carte 128/193 €
• Seafood • Elegant • Luxury •
The classy appeal of the Sea Grill lies in the details, including its stylish artwork
and the separate dining rooms which offer a high level of discretion. Chef Mattagne delights guests with sublime classics, which take the taste of the sea to
new heights. His delicious flavour combinations are arresting.
→ Langoustines cuites sur galet et flambées, émulsion de châtaigne, truffe
et artichaut. Homard bleu breton à la presse. Fraises gariguette au poivron,
crémeux à la pistache et gel vanillé.

සිස සිස **Comme Chez Soi** (Lionel Rigolet) XxX ⚑ ⇔ ⬢
place Rouppe 23 ⊠ *1000* Plan: **L2**
– ✆ *0 2 512 29 21 – www.commechezsoi.be*
– *closed 3, 4, 10 and 11 April, 15 July-15 August, 30 and 31 October,*
24 December-8 January, 13 February, Tuesday lunch, Wednesday lunch,
Sunday and Monday
Menu 60 € (lunch), 99/227 € – Carte 94/377 € – *(pre-book)*
• Creative French • Elegant •
This Brussels institution was founded in 1926. The menu features specialities
that have held their own over four generations, complemented by new creations by Lionel Rigolet. It has all the comfort of a bistro, Horta-inspired decor
and comfortable tables in the kitchen itself, from where you can watch the
chefs in action.
→ Duo de haricots en salade croquante à la truffe d'été et foie gras de
canard. Suprêmes de pigeonneau, morilles, asperges blanches et fèves
des marais. Déclinaison de fraises et rhubarbe au yuzu, citron vert et
violette.

සිස **L'Écailler du Palais Royal** XxX ⚑ ⇔ ⬢
rue Bodenbroek 18 ⊠ *1000* Plan: **N3**
– ✆ *0 2 512 87 51 – www.lecaillerdupalaisroyal.be*
– *closed 23 December-2 January and August*
Menu 60 € (lunch), 125/220 € ☉ – Carte 76/180 €
• Seafood • Traditional décor •
Since 1967, this luxurious institution has been pampering its discerning clientele. The house specialty, seafood, is remarkable. The chef assembles premium
produce into generous recipes that reveal the full depth and flavour of each
ingredient. A classic!
→ Fraîcheur de homard et déclinaison d'artichaut. Sole Thermidor. Crêpe
Normande et glace à la vanille tournée minute.

සිස **San Daniele** (Franco Spinelli) XxX 錦 ⚑ ⇔
avenue Charles-Quint 6 ⊠ *1083* Plan: **A2**
– ✆ *0 2 426 79 23 – www.san-daniele.be*
– *closed 1 week Easter, mid July-mid August, late December, Carnival*
holiday, Bank Holidays, Sunday and Monday
Menu 50 € (lunch)/110 € – Carte 62/95 €
• Italian • Intimate •
Welcome to the Spinelli family's fiefdom – they have made the San Daniele a
blue-chip culinary establishment since 1983. The revamped interior is stylish
and the food fervently upholds Italian tradition. Seabass in a salt crust, carved
and filleted at the table. Depth of taste is the house signature.
→ Tartare, vitello et émulsion de thon rouge au foie gras, citron confit,
céleri vert et câpre de Pantelleria. Bar de ligne et ragoût de fèves, carottes
confites et mousse de céleri. Composition d'ananas, crème brûlée à la réglisse et mascarpone, sorbet à l'orange sanguine.

senzanome (Giovanni Bruno) ☆☆☆ 🕸 🏧 ⇔

place du Petit Sablon 1 ✉ 1000 — Plan: **N3**
– ℰ 02 223 16 17 – www.senzanome.be – closed 1 week at Easter, mid July-mid August, Christmas-New Year, Bank Holidays, Saturday lunch and Sunday
Menu 50 € (lunch), 90/145 € – Carte 88/137 €
• Italian • Design •
All the flavours and aromas of rich Italian, particularly Sicilian, culinary traditions are showcased at senzanome. The talented chef rustles up beautifully prepared and presented dishes of flawless harmony. A prestigious establishment, entirely in keeping with the neighbourhood.
➔ Tartare de crevette rouge au concombre, citron vert et huile d'olive fumée, purée de pommes de terre au vinaigre de thon. Filet et ris de veau à la sauce grappa aux épices. Baba au fruit de la passion et caviar de limoncello et crème à la vanille.

Bozar Brasserie X 🕸 ⇔

rue Baron Horta 3 ✉ 1000 — Plan: **N2**
– ℰ 02 503 00 00 – www.bozarbrasserie.be – closed late July-August, Saturday lunch, Sunday and Monday
Menu 39 € (lunch), 54/89 € – Carte 76/138 €
• Modern French • Fashionable • Brasserie •
Chef Torosyan's pork pie, the house speciality, is emblematic of his cuisine which subtly reinterprets traditional recipes. Do not expect pointlessly complicated dishes – the emphasis is on fine, generously served food.
➔ Quenelles de sandre à la lyonnaise, sauce Nantua. Agneau de lait rôti au sautoir, coco de Paimpol, houmous et coriandre. Millefeuille à la vanille.

JB XX 🕸 🏧 ⇔

rue du Grand Cerf 24 ✉ 1000 – ℰ 02 512 04 84 — Plan: **M3**
– www.restaurantjb.com – closed August, 23-27 December, Bank Holidays, Monday lunch, Saturday lunch and Sunday
Menu 37/50 € – Carte 49/76 €
• Traditional cuisine • Friendly • Family •
Despite being located close to the Place Louise, this family-run restaurant remains discreet. The regulars all have their favourites, be it Flemish asparagus or grilled veal sweetbreads. Flavours are pronounced and the menu represents good value for money.

Les Petits Oignons X 🏧 ⇔

rue de la Régence 25 ✉ 1000 – ℰ 02 511 76 15 — Plan: **M3**
– www.lespetitsoignons.be – closed 2 April, 24 and 25 December and 1 January
Menu 17 € (lunch)/37 € – Carte 40/58 €
• Classic cuisine • Brasserie •
The visitor is of course charmed by the timeless decor and the lively atmosphere in this restaurant, but the delicious brasserie dishes are the real hit! Good quality produce, carefully prepared and simply presented dishes and an excellent wine list – you are in for VIP treatment!

Bocconi – Hôtel Amigo XXX & 🏧 ⇔ 🍽

rue de l'Amigo 1 ✉ 1000 – ℰ 02 547 47 15 — Plan: **M2**
– www.roccofortehotels.com
Menu 18 € (lunch), 42/55 € – Carte 43/65 €
• Italian • Elegant •
This renowned Italian restaurant occupies a luxury hotel near the Grand Place. Modern brasserie-style decor provides the backdrop for enticing Italian cuisine.

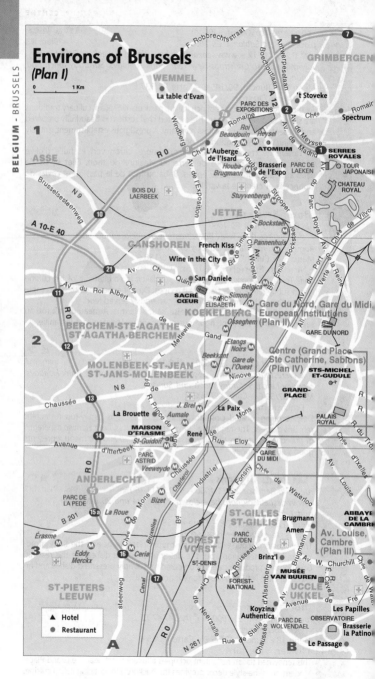

Environs of Brussels
(Plan I)

0   1 Km

WEMMEL

La table d'Evan

PARC DES EXPOSITIONS

Romaine

Roi Baudouin   Heysel

ATOMIUM

L'Auberge de l'Isard

Houba-Brugmann

Brasserie de l'Expo

A 12

't Stoveke

Chée de Meysse

Av. de Madrid

Romain

Spectrum

GRIMBERGEN

F. Robbrechtsstraat

Boechoutlaan   Antwerpselaan

Av. de Meysse

SERRES ROYALES

TOUR JAPONAISE

PARC DE LAEKEN

CHATEAU ROYAL

ASSE

Brusselsesteenweg

N 9

A 10-E 40

R 0

Av. de l'Exposition

BOIS DU LAERBEEK

Stuyvenbergh

Strooper

JETTE

Bockstael

Parc Royal

Chée de Vilvor

GANSHOREN

French Kiss

Wine in the City

Quint   San Daniele

SACRÉ CŒUR

PARC ELISABETH

KOEKELBERG

Osseghem

Pannenhuis

Emile Bockstael

Av. Wooste

Belgica

Simonis

Verte de la Reine

Av. du Port de la Reine

Ch. Smet de Naeyer

Bd

Gare du Nord, Gare du Midi, European Institutions (Plan II)

GARE DU NORD

Centre (Grand Place, Ste Catherine, Sablons) (Plan IV)

STS-MICHEL-ET-GUDULE

Av. du Roi Albert

R 0

BERCHEM-STE-AGATHE ST-AGATHA-BERCHEM

Gand

L. Mettewie

de

Etangs Noirs

Beekkant

Gare de l'Ouest

Ninove

MOLENBEEK-ST-JEAN ST-JANS-MOLENBEEK

N 8

Chaussée

R. Prince de Liège

J. Brel

Aumale

La Brouette

MAISON D'ERASME

St-Guidon

René

Rue

Eloy

La Paix

Mons

GRAND-PLACE

PALAIS ROYAL

R.

R.

R. du Trôr

Av. d'Ixelles

Avenue

d'Itterbeek

PARC ASTRID

Veeweyde

Chée de Mons

Chatterij

Industriel

Av. Fonsny

Chée de

GARE DU MIDI

Av. Louise

ANDERLECHT

PARC DE LA PEDE

La Roue

B 201

Chée de Mons

Bruxelles

Bizet

Ch. de Neerstalle

Waterloo

ST-GILLES ST-GILLIS

Brugmann

Amen

ABBAYE DE LA CAMBRE

Av. Louise, Cambre (Plan III)

Érasme

Eddy Merckx

Ceria

Canal

FOREST VORST

ST-DENIS

PARC DUDEN

Brinz'l

Av. V. Rousseau

FOREST-NATIONAL

Brugmann

W. Churchill

Chée de Wate

Fré

ST-PIETERS LEEUW

steenweg

R 0

Av. d'Alsemberg

MUSÉE VAN BUUREN

UCCLE UKKEL

Av. de Fré

Les Papilles

Koyzina Authentica

PARC DE WOLVENDAEL

OBSERVATOIRE

Brasserie la Patino

N 261

Rue de Stalle

Chaussée

Le Passage

▲ Hotel

● Restaurant

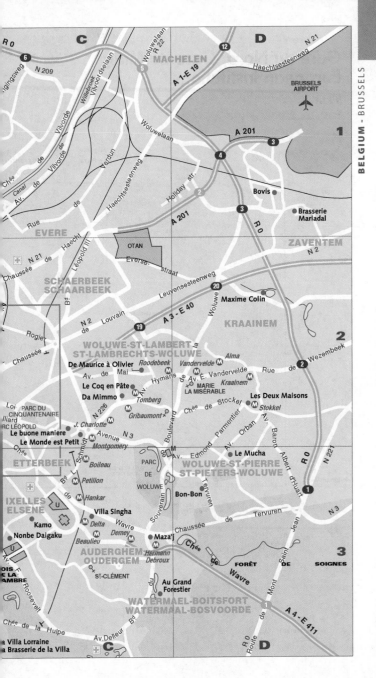

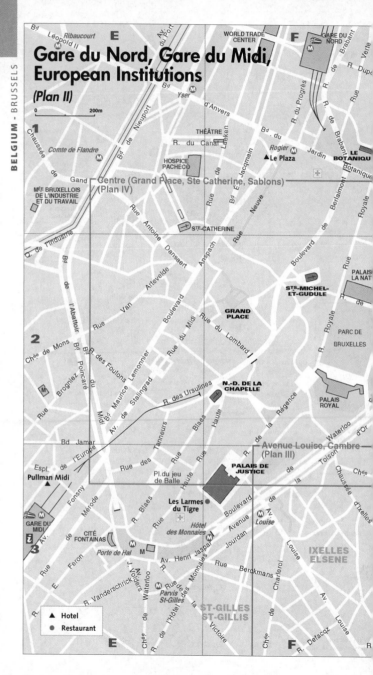

Gare du Nord, Gare du Midi, European Institutions

(Plan II)

0 ——— 200m

BELGIUM - BRUSSELS

▲ Hotel
● Restaurant

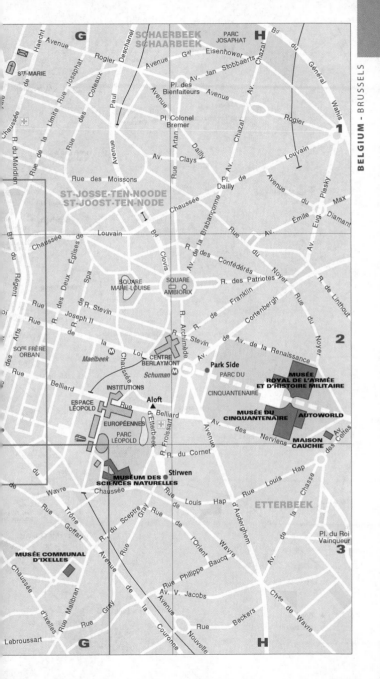

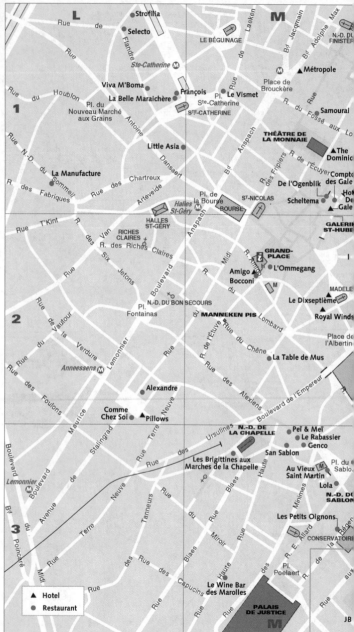

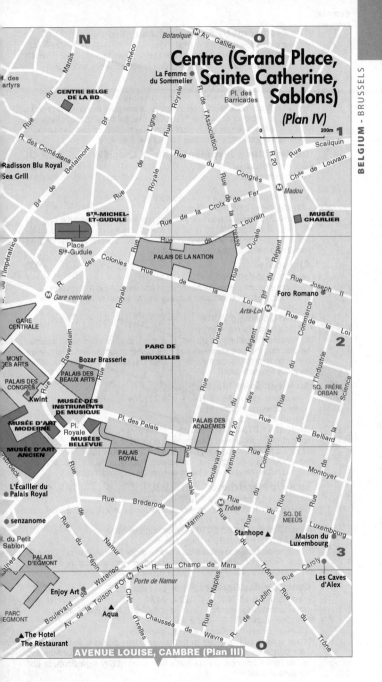

Centre (Grand Place, Sainte Catherine, Sablons)

(Plan IV)

0   200m

Botanique Ⓜ Av. Galilée

N

I. des Martyrs

Rue du Marais

Pachéco

CENTRE BELGE DE LA BD

La Femme du Sommelier

Rue Royale

Pl. des Barricades

Rue de l'Association

Ligne

R. des Comédiens

Bd de Berlaimont

Rue de Royale

Rue du Congrès

R 20

Rue Scailquin

Chée de Louvain

Ⓜ Madou

Radisson Blu Royal Sea Grill

STS-MICHEL-ET-GUDULE

Rue de la Croix de Fer

Rue de la Presse

Rue de Louvain

MUSÉE CHARLIER

Place Ste-Gudule

Rue des Colonies

Rue de la

PALAIS DE LA NATION

Rue Ducale

Rue du Régent

Rue Joseph II

l'Impératrice

Ⓜ Gare centrale

Rue Royale

Loi Ⓜ Arts-Loi

Foro Romano

Rue de la Loi

Rue de Commerce

GARE CENTRALE

Ravenstein

Bozar Brasserie

PARC DE BRUXELLES

Rue Ducale

Rue du Régent

Rue des Arts

Rue de l'Industrie

SQ. FRÈRE ORBAN

Science

MONT DES ARTS

PALAIS DES BEAUX ARTS

PALAIS DES CONGRÈS

Kwint

MUSÉE DES INSTRUMENTS DE MUSIQUE

Pl. des Palais

PALAIS DES ACADÉMIES

R 20

Rue de Commerce

Rue de la

Belliard

MUSÉE D'ART MODERNE

Pl. Royale

MUSÉES BELLEVUE

Rue Ducale

Boulevard

Avenue

Rue de

Montoyer

MUSÉE D'ART ANCIEN

PALAIS ROYAL

Rue Brederode

Rue Marnix

Rue du

SQ. DE MEEÛS

L'Écailler du Palais Royal

senzanome

Stanhope ▲

Maison du Luxembourg

Luxembourg

I. du Petit Sablon

PALAIS D'EGMONT

Rue du Pépin

Rue de Namur

Av. R. du Champ de Mars

Rue de Naples

Trône

Rue Caroly

Les Caves d'Alex

Enjoy Art

PARC EGMONT

Boulevard de Waterloo

Av. de la Toison d'Or

Ⓜ Porte de Namur

Chée d'Ixelles

Aqua ▲

Chaussée de Wavre

Rue de Dublin

Rue du Trône

▲ The Hotel The Restaurant

AVENUE LOUISE, CAMBRE (Plan III)

⇃○ **The Restaurant by Pierre Balthazar** – The Hotel XxX ⟨
boulevard de Waterloo 38 ⊠ *1000* ♿ 🅰🅲 ⇄ 🥘 🚗
– ☎ *02 504 13 33* – *www.therestaurant.be* – *closed mid* Plan: **L3**
July-mid August, Bank Holidays, Monday lunch, Saturday lunch and
Sunday
Menu 35 € (lunch), 55/65 € – Carte 52/71 €
• Modern cuisine • Chic • Fashionable •
Trendy bar food, made-to-measure cocktails, an inventive menu concept and a
sexy lounge ambience depict The Restaurant. Chef Balthazar changes the menu
weekly to allow free rein to his inspiration. The result is an enticing range of
dishes with ingredients and recipes from all over the world.

⇃○ **Les Brigittines Aux Marches de la Chapelle** XX ⇄
place de la Chapelle 5 ⊠ *1000* – ☎ *02 512 68 91* 🥘
– *www.lesbrigittines.com* – *closed Saturday lunch and* Plan: **M3**
Sunday
Menu 35 € (lunch), 48/55 € – Carte 45/83 €
• Traditional cuisine • Vintage •
This lavish Art Nouveau brasserie will, first and foremost, delight the eye! You
will also find it impossible to resist the mouthwatering recipes rustled up by
chef Dirk Myny. He is a genuine Brusselian, whose exuberant personality gives
character to his traditional market fresh dishes.

⇃○ **Alexandre** XX
rue du Midi 164 ⊠ *1000* – ☎ *02 502 40 55* Plan: **L2**
– *www.restaurant-alexandre.be* – *closed last week August-first week*
September, first week January, Tuesday lunch, Saturday lunch, Sunday
and Monday
Menu 45 € (lunch), 65/130 €
• Modern cuisine • Intimate •
The restaurant's name gives no hint as to the restaurant's feminine character.
The charming manageress greets and takes care of guests, while the female kitchen brigade prepares creative dishes. Their compositions are elegant with a
deliciously feminine touch.

⇃○ **Au Vieux Saint Martin** XX 🍴
pl. du Grand Sablon 38 ⊠ *1000* – ☎ *02 512 64 76* Plan: **L2**
– *www.auvieuxsaintmartin.be*
Carte 46/68 € – *(open until midnight)*
• Belgian • Brasserie • Classic décor •
The spirit of the well-heeled Sablons neighbourhood is visible in both the interior
(colourful artwork) and the terrace. The brasserie is frequently packed to the seams,
always proof of a good restaurant. The generous helpings of Brussels' specialties and
other exquisitely prepared dishes (based on eggs) are truly mouthwatering.

⇃○ **La Belle Maraîchère** XX 🅰🅲 ⇄ 🅿
place Sainte-Catherine 11 ⊠ *1000* – ☎ *02 512 97 59* Plan: **L1**
– *www.labellemaraichere.com* – *closed mid July-early August, 2 weeks at*
Carnival, Wednesday and Thursday
Menu 42/65 € – Carte 55/110 € – *(booking advisable)*
• Seafood • Friendly • Elegant •
This welcoming, family-run restaurant is a popular choice for locals, with its charmingly
nostalgic decor. Enticing, traditional cuisine includes fish, shellfish and game depending
on the season, as well as high quality sauces. Appealing set menus.

⇃○ **Comptoir des Galeries** – Hôtel des Galeries XX 🍴
Galerie du Roi 6 ⊠ *1000* – ☎ *02 213 74 74* Plan: **M1**
– *www.comptoirdesgaleries.be* – *closed Bank Holidays, Sunday and Monday*
Menu 26 € (lunch)/31 € – Carte 48/70 €
• Classic French • Brasserie • Friendly •
Vintage accents add character to this contemporary brasserie, in the heart of
which stands a somewhat incongruous medal press! Pleasant establishment,
ideal to savour brasserie classics made with good quality ingredients, or just
for a glass of good wine.

Lola

XX AC

place du Grand Sablon 33 ✉ *1000 –* ☎ *0 2 514 24 60*   Plan: **M3**
*– www.restolola.be – closed 2 weeks in August and dinner 24 and
31 December*
Carte 43/66 € – *(open until 11pm)*
• Mediterranean cuisine • Brasserie •

A friendly brasserie with contemporary decor, serving Italian dishes based on
the freshest ingredients. The pleasant counter is perfect for a meal on the hoof.

L'Ommegang

XX AC P

Grand-Place 9 ✉ *1000 –* ☎ *0 25 11 82 44*   Plan: **M2**
*– www.brasseriedelommegang.be – closed 23 July-15 August, Bank
Holidays and Sunday*
Menu 15 € (lunch) – Carte 36/59 €
• Traditional cuisine • Classic décor • Elegant •

The Ommegang and its iconic terrace is the best restaurant on the Grand-Place
of Brussels. The staff's inimitable Brussels' sense of humour, the classical dining
room with high ceilings and wainscoting and Belgian classics set the scene.
Authentic Belgium!

Le Rabassier

XX

rue de Rollebeek 23 ✉ *1000 –* ☎ *0 2 502 04 00*   Plan: **L2**
*– www.lerabassier.be – closed 2 weeks in July, 2 weeks in January and
Monday*
Menu 69/145 € – Carte 90/139 € – *(dinner only except Sunday)*
• Classic cuisine • Elegant • Chic •

Whether black or white, from January to December the truffle is the star of this
pocket-handkerchief restaurant. The chef is a past master in the art of extracting
the full flavour of this noble ingredient. Fine French wines, attractive menus and
delightful manageress.

Kwint

X ⇐ 斎 AC

Mont des Arts 1 ✉ *1000 –* ☎ *0 25 05 95 95*   Plan: **N2**
– www.kwintbrussels.com
Menu 19 € (lunch), 28/46 € – Carte 36/62 € – *(open until 11 pm)*
• Modern French • Brasserie •

An amazing sculpture by artist Arne Quinze adds cachet to this elegant brasserie. It serves a tasty up-to-the-minute menu in which fine quality produce takes
pride of place. The view of the city from the Mont des Arts is breathtaking. A
great way to see another side of Brussels.

Enjoy

X AC ⟷

boulevard de Waterloo 22 ✉ *1000 –* ☎ *0 2 641 57 90*   Plan: **N3**
– www.enjoybrussels.be – closed Bank Holidays and Sunday
Menu 23 € (lunch)/39 € – Carte 37/70 €
• Creative French • Fashionable •

Diners can choose from the BMW showroom on the left or the trendy restaurant
on the right, which serves brasserie fare amidst modern art. The fresh, flavourful
ingredients are a hit with gourmets.

La Femme du Sommelier

X 器

rue de l'Association 9 ✉ *1000 –* ☎ *0 476 45 02 10*   Plan: **10M1**
– closed Saturday and Sunday
Menu 37 € – *(lunch only) (tasting menu only)*
• Classic cuisine • Wine bar • Neighbourhood •

As the name suggests, this bistro is in the capable hands of a sommelier and his
spouse. He advises guests on the choice of wine, while she prepares classic recipes, using only the best ingredients.

67

BELGIUM - BRUSSELS

Genco ✗

rue Joseph Stevens 28 ✉ *1000 –* ✆ *0 2 511 34 44* Plan: **9L3**
– closed 21 July-21 August, Sunday dinner and Monday
Carte 31/67 €
• Italian • Traditional décor • Bourgeois •
You will be welcomed into this Italian restaurant like a long-lost friend. Sit down to sample the chef's concoctions, whose generosity is equalled only by their flawless classicism. It is not difficult to understand why Genco has such a faithful clientele!

Les Larmes du Tigre ✗ 🎐 ✿

rue de Wynants 21 ✉ *1000 –* ✆ *0 2 512 18 77* Plan: **F3**
– www.leslarmesdutigre.be – closed Saturday lunch and Monday
Menu 16 € (lunch), 45/65 € – Carte 30/47 €
• Thai • Exotic décor •
A real voyage for the taste buds! They have been serving authentic Thai food here for over 30 years, and the enjoyment for money ratio is excellent. Buffet at lunch and Sunday evenings.

Little Asia ✗ 🅰🅒 ✿

rue Sainte-Catherine 8 ✉ *1000 –* ✆ *0 2 502 88 36* Plan: **L1**
– www.littleasia.be – closed 15 July-15 August, Monday, Tuesday, Wednesday and Sunday
Menu 25 € (lunch), 45/69 € – Carte 49/73 €
• Vietnamese • Fashionable • Exotic décor •
The trendy restaurant of TV personality Truong Thi Quyên is a pleasant place for an intimate meal. The chef prepares authentic Vietnamese fare, respecting natural ingredients and creating a good balance between fresh, intense and spicy flavours. If you're not a fan of meat, the vegetarian menu has some great alternatives.

La Manufacture ✗ 🎐 ✿ 🍽

rue Notre-Dame du Sommeil 12 ✉ *1000* Plan: **L1**
– ✆ *0 2 502 25 25 – www.manufacture.be – closed 21 July-6 August, 24 December-2 January, Bank Holidays, Saturday lunch and Sunday*
Menu 16 € (lunch), 28/70 € 🍷 – Carte 40/60 €
• Belgian • Brasserie • Trendy •
Delvaux once had a leather workshop here and, today, leather is combined with wood and metal in the decor of this lively brasserie. The menu is equally up-to-the-minute, with its contemporary interpretations of well-known dishes and some occasional Asian influences.

De l'Ogenblik ✗ 🎐 ✿

Galerie des Princes 1 ✉ *1000 –* ✆ *0 2 511 61 51* Plan: **M1**
– www.ogenblik.be – closed 1-15 August, lunch on Bank Holidays and Sunday
Menu 48/60 € – Carte 47/74 € *– (open until midnight)*
• Classic cuisine • Bistro • Simple •
Lovers of tradition will immediately feel at home in this former café. It opened its doors in 1969 and has lost none of its authentic charm. The chef knows his classic cuisine and offers well-known favourites alongside some regularly changing specials too.

Peï & Meï ✗ 🎐

rue de Rollebeek 15 ✉ *1000 –* ✆ *0 2 880 53 39* Plan: **M3**
– www.peietmei.be – closed first week January, Saturday lunch and Sunday
Menu 21 € (lunch), 42/60 € – Carte 60/70 €
• Classic cuisine • Friendly • Minimalist •
One glimpse of the huge, somewhat battered red brick wall inside is all it takes to understand that this establishment is far from run of the mill. This first impression is confirmed when you sample the creative dishes of 'Peï' Gauthier, which mingle classicism with a hint of originality, and are served by the smiling 'Meï' (Mélissa).

Samourai 🗙 🖭 ⇔

rue du Fossé aux Loups 28 ⊠ 1000 – ℰ 02 217 56 39   Plan: **M1**
*– www.samourai-bruxelles.be – closed 16 July-15 August, Sunday and
Monday*
Menu 27 € (lunch), 69/99 € – Carte 49/139 €
• Japanese • Intimate • Minimalist •

A Japanese restaurant which opened in 1975 near the Théâtre de la Monnaie.
Dining rooms on three floors with a decorative Japanese theme. Top-notch cuisine based around quality products and adapted to Western tastes.

San Sablon 🗙

rue Joseph Stevens 12 ⊠ 1000 – ℰ 02 512 42 12   Plan: **L3**
*– www.sansablon.be – closed 1 week Easter, 2 weeks in August, late
December-early January, Sunday and Monday*
Menu 28 € (lunch)/55 € – *(tasting menu only)*
• Creative • Bistro •

In keeping with the cosmopolitan Sablons district, the San Sablon is urbane and
suave. Subtle, delicate flavours served in its hallmark bowls. The quirky, relaxed
interior perfectly matches the establishment.

Scheltema 🗙 🕍 🖭 ⇔

rue des Dominicains 7 ⊠ 1000 – ℰ 02 512 20 84   Plan: **M1**
– www.scheltema.be – closed 2 weeks in August and Sunday
Menu 20 € (lunch)/33 € – Carte 42/83 € – *(open until 11.30pm)*
• Seafood • Brasserie •

An attractive old brasserie located in the city's Ilot Sacré district. It has a lively
atmosphere and pleasant retro-style wooden furnishings. Traditional dishes
and daily specials with seafood specialities.

Selecto 🗙 🕸

rue de Flandre 95 ⊠ 1000 – ℰ 02 511 40 95   Plan: **L1**
– www.le-selecto.com – closed Sunday and Monday
Menu 15 € (lunch)/42 €
• Modern French • Friendly •

In the heart of the lively Ste Catherine neighbourhood, Selecto leads Belgium's
vanguard of bistronomic (bistro + gastronomic) culture. Good food, a great
atmosphere and reasonable prices!

Strofilia 🗙 🕸 ⇔

rue du Marché aux Porcs 11 ⊠ 1000 – ℰ 02 512 32 93   Plan: **L1**
– www.strofilia.be – closed Saturday lunch and Sunday
Menu 22 € (lunch), 35/55 € – Carte 29/47 € – *(open until 11pm)*
• Greek • Trendy •

A modern, airy interior and a relaxed ambience. Strofilia specialises in Greek and
Byzantine delicacies, both in the glass and on the plate. The chef is a consummate culinary artist, whose cuisine borders on the contemporary despite his
classical training.

La Table de Mus 🗙

place de la Vieille Halle aux Blés 31 ⊠ 1000   Plan: **L2**
*– ℰ 02 511 05 86 – www.latabledemus.be – closed 1 week Easter, last
week July-first 2 weeks August, first week January, Wednesday and Sunday*
Menu 30 € (lunch), 36/75 €
• Modern cuisine • Friendly •

The experienced Mustafa Ducan is a charismatic man – you'll notice that immediately – and he ensures that you will enjoy the chef's delicious cooking in a
pleasant ambience. In every dish you'll find original touches which add fun
and punch to the flavours.

BELGIUM - BRUSSELS

Le Vismet
X 𝄞

place Sainte-Catherine 23 ⊠ 1000 – ℰ 02 218 85 45   Plan: **9L1**
– www.levismet.be – closed Sunday and Monday
Menu 22 € (lunch)/65 € ♆ – Carte 46/71 €
• Seafood • Traditional décor •
The Vismet (Brussels' fish market) is a stone's throw from this traditional restaurant, as quickly becomes apparent. The ambience is relaxed, the service typical of Brussels and the food scrumptious. Fish and shellfish take pride of place in dishes with an emphasis on fresh, generous portions.

Viva M'Boma
X 𝄞 AC ⇔

rue de Flandre 17 ⊠ 1000 – ℰ 02 512 15 93   Plan: **L1**
– www.vivamboma.be – closed first week April, 25 July-7 August, first week January and Bank Holidays
Carte 29/38 €
• Country • Bistro •
This elegant canteen-style restaurant has closely packed tables and tiled walls reminiscent of a Parisian métro station. It is popular with fans of offal and old Brussels specialities (cow's udder, *choesels* (sweetbreads), marrowbone, ox cheek).

Le Wine Bar des Marolles
X 𝄞

rue Haute 198 ⊠ 1000 – ℰ 02 503 62 50   Plan: **M3**
– www.winebarsablon.be – closed mid July-mid August, 22 December-4 January, Monday, Tuesday and Wednesday
Menu 15 € (lunch)
– Carte 36/68 € – (dinner only except Saturday and Sunday, open until 11pm)
• Country • Wine bar •
Are you a fan of dishes that draw on local specialities, redolent of the terroir? If so, don't miss Le Wine Bar! Known only to insiders, this restaurant installed in the heart of the Marolles offers hearty cuisine and a good choice of wines.

The Hotel
⩽ ⅙ 🕉 ⅖ AC 🛁 🚗

boulevard de Waterloo 38 ⊠ 1000 – ℰ 02 504 11 11   Plan: **N3**
– www.thehotel.be
420 rm ⊊ – ♦150/250 € ♦♦170/270 € – 5 suites
• Townhouse • Grand Luxury • Design •
Enjoy the breathtaking view of Brussels and the hidden charms of the city in this well-preserved district. This establishment is also ideal for exploring the shops along Avenue Louise. Shopaholics take note!
iO **The Restaurant by Pierre Balthazar** – See restaurant listing

Amigo
⅙ AC 🛁 🚗

rue de l'Amigo 1 ⊠ 1000 – ℰ 02 547 47 47   Plan: **M2**
– www.roccofortehotels.com
154 rm – ♦197/660 € ♦♦197/660 € – ⊊ 19 € – 19 suites
• Grand Luxury • Townhouse • Personalised •
A real institution, and one of the best hotels in Brussels! Its assets? Its central location (behind the Grand Place), luxurious rooms, impeccable service and refined charm. You may even run into a celebrity here.
iO **Bocconi** – See restaurant listing

Métropole
𝄞 ⅙ ⅖ AC 🛁 🚗

place de Brouckère 31 ⊠ 1000 – ℰ 02 217 23 00   Plan: **M1**
– www.metropolehotel.com
263 rm ⊊ – ♦125/459 € ♦♦125/519 € – 5 suites
• Grand Luxury • Historic • Personalised •
This sumptuous hotel has been a reference point in Brussels since 1895. The authentic soul of the building has been preserved and the luxurious décor has been attractively modernised. Café Métropole serves brasserie dishes which you can enjoy on one of the most famous terraces of the capital, overlooking the Place De Brouckère.

Le Plaza   🏠 ⛴ 🅰🅲 ♨ 🚗

boulevard Adolphe Max 118 ✉ *1000 –* ☎ *02 278 01 00*   Plan: **F1**
– www.leplaza-brussels.be
184 rm – 🛏120/495 € 🛏🛏140/495 € – ⛷29 € – 6 suites
• Palace • Grand Luxury • Elegant •
A 1930s building imitating the George V hotel in Paris. Classic public areas, large cosy guestrooms and a superb Baroque theatre used for receptions and events. An elegant bar and restaurant beneath an attractive dome painted with a trompe l'œil sky.

Radisson Blu Royal   🏠 ⛴ 🎐 & 🅰🅲 ♨ 🚗

rue du Fossé aux Loups 47 ✉ *1000 –* ☎ *02 219 28 28*   Plan: **N1**
– www.radissonblu.com/royalhotel-brussels
269 rm – 🛏150/400 € 🛏🛏150/400 € – ⛷15 € – 12 suites
• Luxury • Chain • Contemporary •
Impressive modern glass atrium, remains of the city's fortifications, and extremely comfortable suites and guestrooms. Breakfast room adorned with wooden railway sleepers. A contemporary style brasserie illuminated by natural light through the glass roof.

Royal Windsor   🏠 ⛴ 🎐 🅰🅲 ♨ 🚗

rue Duquesnoy 5 ✉ *1000 –* ☎ *02 505 55 55*   Plan: **M2**
– www.warwickhotels.com/brussels
260 rm – 🛏134/700 € 🛏🛏134/700 € – ⛷24 € – 7 suites
• Luxury • Personalised •
Royal – what better word to describe a stay in this luxury hotel? The historic city centre is a stone's throw from this establishment, which has faultless service. The elegant, comfortable rooms have a nostalgic British flavour.

Le Dixseptième   ⛱ ⛴ 🎐 🅰🅲 ♨

rue de la Madeleine 25 ✉ *1000 –* ☎ *02 517 17 17*   Plan: **M2**
– www.ledixseptieme.be
35 rm – 🛏120/200 € 🛏🛏140/220 € – ⛷15 € – 2 suites
• Luxury • Grand luxury •
This townhouse dating from the 17C was once the official residence of the Spanish ambassador in the city. Elegant lounges, attractive inner courtyard, and guestrooms embellished with furniture of varying styles.

The Dominican   🏠 ⛴ 🎐 & 🅰🅲 ♨

rue Léopold 9 ✉ *1000 –* ☎ *02 203 08 08*   Plan: **M1**
– www.thedominican.be
147 rm – 🛏140/450 € 🛏🛏140/450 € – ⛷27 € – 3 suites
• Historic building • Grand townhouse • Elegant •
A designer-inspired luxury hotel on the site of a former Dominican convent. Open spaces, elegant furniture and modern comforts which benefit from maximum attention to detail. The Grand Lounge takes full advantage of the natural light from the patio. A modern menu and non-stop service.

Hôtel des Galeries   🏠 ⛴

rue des Bouchers 38 ✉ *1000 –* ☎ *02 213 74 70*   Plan: **M1**
– www.hoteldesgaleries.be
23 rm – 🛏130/290 € 🛏🛏130/290 € – ⛷19 € – 3 suites
• Luxury • Contemporary • Elegant •
This boutique hotel in a classical edifice enjoys a premium location on the corner of Rue des Bouchers and the King's Gallery. The luxury setting combines vintage touches with a contemporary interior, whose attention to detail extends as far as the ceramic tiles in the washrooms. Perfectly located for a stay in Brussels.
🍴 **Comptoir des Galeries** – See restaurant listing

Pillows ♿ 🅺 🛁

place Rouppe 17 ✉ *1000 –* ☎ *0 2 204 00 40* Plan: **L2**
– www.pillowshotels.com
43 rm 🛏 – 🛉119/525 € 🛉🛉119/525 €
• Luxury • Contemporary •

Black and white dominate this handsome manor house on Place Rouppe, a few steps from the town centre. The warm, inviting rooms offer all the facilities one has come to expect from a good hotel.

QUARTIER LOUISE-CAMBRE

✿✿ Le Chalet de la Forêt (Pascal Devalkeneer) XxxX 🏵 🍴 ⇔ 🅿

drêve de Lorraine 43 ✉ *1180 –* ☎ *0 2 374 54 16*
*– www.lechaletdelaforet.be – closed last week December-first
week January, Saturday and Sunday*
Menu 64 € (lunch), 145/185 € – Carte 132/197 €
• Creative • Elegant •

This chalet with its lovely terrace, set on the edge of the Sonian Forest, combines elegance and sophistication. The food has a certain cachet, with its consummate combination of classicism and creativity, finesse and generosity. Intense sensations are guaranteed.

➜ Tartare d'huîtres ' Régis Borde ' au caviar osciètre et fleurs de brocoli en parmentier. Homard breton et ris de veau croustillant, candele farcis et citron confit. Chaud-froid au chocolat.

✿✿ La Villa in the Sky (Alexandre Dionisio) XX 🏵 ⪕ 🍴 🛥

avenue Louise 480 (25th floor) ✉ *1050* Plan: **K3**
– ☎ *0 2 644 69 14 – www.lavillainthesky.be – closed 30 March-9 April, 5-
27 August, 25 and 30 December-8 January, Saturday lunch, Sunday and
Monday*
Menu 135 € 🍷 (lunch), 155/210 € – (booking essential)
• Creative • Design • Minimalist •

Dining in this glass cube is a real experience. Not only because of the unique location – more than 120 metres above ground level and with a stunning view of Brussels – but because of the playful cuisine of Alexandre Dionisio. His technique is infallible, his creativity on-point, and he uses only a couple of top ingredients to create a memorable feast of flavours!

➜ Risotto à l'encre de seiche, calamar, textures de chorizo et crème de persil. Coquelet rôti, crémeux de pommes de terre et morilles, cromesquis de maïs et écume au vin jaune. Fraises belges, granité de wasabi et crémeux vanillé.

✿ La Villa Lorraine XxxX 🏵 🍴 🅺 ⇔ 🛥 🅿

avenue du Vivier d'Oie 75 ✉ *1000 –* ☎ *0 23 74 31 63* Plan: **C3**
*– www.villalorraine.be – closed 1-9 April, 5-20 August, 25 December, 1-
10 January, Sunday and Monday*
Menu 56 € (lunch), 130/170 € – Carte 111/167 €
• Creative • Elegant •

Since 1953, this grande dame of the Brussels gastronomic scene has been a popular meeting place for gourmets. The grand, luxurious interior commands respect, as does the cooking. Classical dishes come with modern touches and are packed with flavour. There's also a charming terrace for warmer days.

➜ Œuf de poule cuit en blanc-manger, asperges blanches, beurre blanc au caviar et mouillette végétale. Saint-pierre de petit bateau au citron confit et gingembre, tagliatelle de seiche, sauce fenouil et curry vert. Le café : crémeux café blanc, biscuit nougatine, dulce de leche et glace au café.

☺ **La Brasserie de la Villa** – See restaurant listing

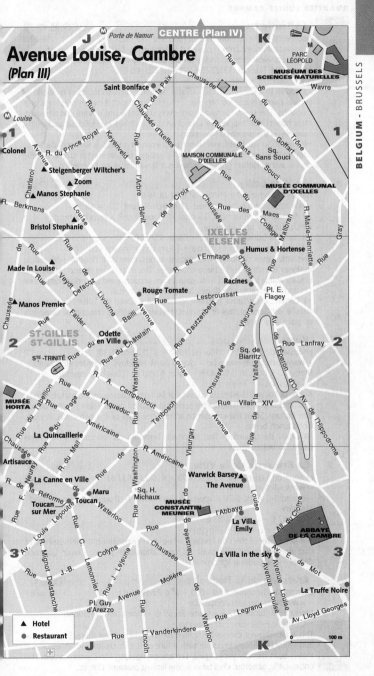

Avenue Louise, Cambre
(Plan III)

Hotel ▲
Restaurant ●

0   100 m

La Truffe Noire   XxX 🐿 🅰 ⇧ 🍽

boulevard de la Cambre 12 ✉ *1000 – ☏ 0 2 640 44 22*   Plan: **K3**
*– www.truffenoire.com – closed 1 week Easter, first 2 weeks August,
Christmas-New Year, Monday lunch, Saturday lunch and Sunday*
Menu 50 € (lunch), 135/225 € – Carte 82/146 €
• Italian • Elegant •

As you sit in a restaurant that radiates nostalgic class, surrounded by works of
art and purple hues, you can watch the charismatic chef-owner prepare a beef
carpaccio. This spectacle takes place every day at La Truffe Noire and demonstrates how classic recipes are valued here. The dishes are delicious and truffle,
naturally, is the preferred seasoning.
➜ Carpaccio de bœuf aux vieux parmesan et truffes à la façon de Luigi.
Saint-pierre farci de truffes cuit à la vapeur et son nectar truffé. Soufflé
chaud aux noisettes grillées, sabayon à la vanille et au Frangelico.

La Villa Emily   XX 🐚 🅰 ⇧ 🍽

rue de l'Abbaye 4 ✉ *1000 – ☏ 0 23 18 18 58*   Plan: **K3**
*– www.lavillaemily.be – closed 31 March-9 April, 10-14 Mai, 5-
20 August, 1-5 November, 25 and 31 December-8 January, Saturday
lunch, Sunday and Monday*
Menu 52 € (lunch), 79/115 € – Carte 75/97 €
• Mediterranean cuisine • Elegant • Intimate •

This little jewel combines the elegant atmosphere of a boudoir with subtle
designer elements and a huge chandelier. This impressive balance of styles is
equally visible in the food. Main courses are accompanied by sophisticated sauces and impeccable side dishes. It's splendidly classical.
➜ Carpaccio de bœuf Holstein, girolles et velouté de laitue. Suprême de
volaille du Gers, blettes et morilles. Fraises marinées, croustillant bruxellois
et glace à la vanille.

Kamo (Tomoyasu Kamo)   X

chaussée de Waterloo 550a ✉ *1050 – ☏ 0 2 648 78 48*   Plan: **C3**
– www.restaurant-kamo.be – closed Bank Holidays, Saturday and Sunday
Menu 25 € (lunch), 50/120 € – Carte 67/98 € – *(booking essential)*
• Japanese • Trendy •

A slice of Tokyo in Ixelles: the classics of Japanese cuisine and remarkable combinations with bold flavours are served in a pared-down setting with a trendy
atmosphere. Sit at the counter to admire the skills of the two chefs at work.
Good lunch bento.
➜ Tataki de canard et flan japonais. Tempura de langouste et bouillon
dashi. Sorbet au yuzu.

La Brasserie de la Villa   XX 🐚 🛋 🍽 🅿

avenue du Vivier d'Oie 75 ✉ *1000 – ☏ 0 23 74 31 63*   Plan: **C3**
– www.villalorraine.be
*– closed 1-9 April, 5-20 August, 25 December, 1-10 January, Sunday and
Monday*
Menu 37 € – Carte 52/88 €
• Classic cuisine • Elegant •

The little sister of the Villa Lorraine where you can soak up the atmosphere of
that prestigious establishment at more affordable prices. Classic brasserie
dishes and appetising light meals.

Brasserie de la Patinoire   XX 🛋 ⇧

chemin du Gymnase 1 ✉ *1000 – ☏ 0 2 649 70 02*   Plan: **12R3**
– www.brasseriedelapatinoire.be
Menu 16 € (lunch)/37 € – Carte 36/59 € – *(open until 11.30pm)*
• Classic French • Brasserie •

This establishment cannot be faulted for its stylish, classy allure. Book a table
and enjoy this luxury brasserie with a hint of British charm and an ambience
that is both friendly yet elegant. Terrace overlooking the Cambre wood. The
enthusiastic, generous chef takes a new look at brasserie classics.

BELGIUM - BRUSSELS

Maza'j
XX

boulevard du Souverain 145 ⊠ 1160 – ℰ 02 675 55 10   Plan: C3
– www.mazaj.be – closed Saturday lunch and Sunday
Menu 20 € (lunch), 37/75 € – Carte 31/55 € – (bar lunch)
• Lebanese • Friendly •
If you feel like exploring a new culinary horizon, why not book a table at Maza'j? Don't be misled by the bright contemporary interior, this establishment is a champion of traditional Lebanese culture and cuisine. All the dishes are laid centrally on the table for everyone to sample and the atmosphere is friendly and relaxed.

Toucan
XX

avenue Louis Lepoutre 1 ⊠ 1050 – ℰ 02 345 30 17   Plan: J3
– www.toucanbrasserie.com – closed dinner 24 and 31 December
Menu 20 € (lunch)/37 €
– Carte 33/68 € – (open until 11pm) (booking advisable)
• Modern cuisine • Bistro • Design •
The plumage of this toucan adds the finishing touch to a lovely classical brasserie, embellished with the occasional modern design twist. The ambience is one of the highlights of the establishment, as is the seamless service. The chef uses only the best quality produce and has no qualms about piling the plates high with tasty fare.

Saint Boniface
X

rue Saint-Boniface 9 ⊠ 1050 – ℰ 02 511 53 66   Plan: J1
– www.saintboniface.be – closed first 3 weeks September, Bank Holidays, Saturday lunch, Sunday and Monday
Menu 25 € (lunch) – Carte 37/56 €
• Cuisine from South West France • Bistro •
Tightly packed tables, posters on the walls and a collection of biscuit tins characterise this extremely welcoming bistro. The locals flock here to sample its Basquaise, Lyonnaise and specialities from Southwest France. Cooking is generous and delicious!

Maru
X

chaussée de Waterloo 510 ⊠ 1050 – ℰ 02 346 11 11   Plan: J3
– closed 17 July-16 August, 24 December-1 January and Monday
Menu 18 € (lunch) – Carte 31/81 €
• Korean • Minimalist •
If your mouth is already watering at the prospect of crunchy deep-fried pancakes or sweet and sour tangsuyuk, head straight for this 'urban-style' Korean restaurant whose fresh ingredients are equalled by the authentic cooking methods. Even better, the wine list is full of pleasant surprises.

Villa Singha
X AC

rue des Trois Ponts 22 ⊠ 1160 – ℰ 02 675 67 34   Plan: C3
– www.singha.be – closed 2-31 July, 25 December-2 January, Bank Holidays, Saturday lunch and Sunday
Menu 19 € (lunch)/25 € – Carte 25/40 €
• Thai • Exotic décor •
Singha, the mythological lion, watches over this pleasant Thai restaurant, where fresh produce and authentic flavours enhance the traditional Thai cuisine. One such dish is Kha Nom Jeep, delicious steamed dumplings of chopped pork and Thai spices. The welcome and service are equally charming.

Brugmann
XxX

avenue Brugmann 52 ⊠ 1190 – ℰ 02 880 55 54   Plan: B3
– www.brugmann.com – closed Saturday lunch and Monday
Menu 24 € (lunch)/86 € – Carte 51/87 €
• Modern cuisine • Elegant •
Brugmann is a picture of elegance. The interior is adorned with fine modern art and the rear terrace is superb. What is more the chef's cuisine is equally stylish, combining ingredients and techniques in dishes that are as modern as the decor. A first-class establishment.

⬤

Rouge Tomate
XX 🏠 ⟳

avenue Louise 190 ✉ *1050 – ℰ 02 647 70 44*   Plan: **J2**
– www.rougetomate.be – closed Bank Holidays, Saturday lunch and Sunday
Menu 35 € (lunch), 55/75 € – Carte 55/79 €
• Creative • Trendy •
Forgo the bustle of Avenue Louise and venture into this elegant, modern mansion, and perhaps to the lovely terrace at the back or the cocktail bar on the first floor. The same harmony is present in the dishes, all of which demonstrate the young chef's desire to experiment with creative, yet balanced recipes.

⬤

Amen
XX 🏠 AC 🍽

rue Franz Merjay 165 ✉ *1050 – ℰ 02 217 10 19*   Plan: **11Q2**
– www.amen.restaurant – closed Sunday and Monday
Menu 19 € (lunch)/54 € – Carte 51/79 € – (open until 11pm)
• Market cuisine • Friendly •
Two-star chef Pascal Devalkeneer (Le Chalet de la Fôret) has a knack for picking the best produce. From the contemporary dishes and intense flavours to the range of textures, his dishes are masterpieces of culinary art. Amen!

⬤

Artisauce
XX 🏠

chaussée de Waterloo 421 ✉ *1050 – ℰ 0 483 65 65 16*   Plan: **11Q2**
– www.artisauce.com – closed 21 July-15 August, Saturday lunch, Sunday and Monday
Menu 17 € (lunch)/48 €
• Classic cuisine • Friendly •
Dad Frédéric greets guests and seats them in the dining room or on the pretty terrace. His son, Christopher, is hard at work in the kitchen creating classic dishes, liberally sprinkled with worldwide flavours.

⬤

Brinz'l
XX 🍽

rue des Carmélites 93 ✉ *1180 – ℰ 02 218 23 32*   Plan: **11P2**
– www.brinzl.be – closed Wednesday lunch, Saturday lunch, Sunday and Monday
Menu 30 € 🍷 (lunch)/49 € – Carte 62/89 €
• Modern French • Contemporary décor • Bistro •
While Brinzelle (Creole for aubergine) may evoke the chef's Mauritian roots, her cuisine is nonetheless firmly French! After learning her trade in several Starred restaurants, she now excels in flavoursome, carefully assembled meals that, above all, seek to enhance the quality of the ingredients.

⬤

Colonel
XX 🏠

rue Jean Stas 24 ✉ *1060 – ℰ 02 538 57 36*   Plan: **J1**
– www.colonelbrussels.com – closed Sunday and Monday
Menu 24 € (lunch) – Carte 46/72 €
• Meats and grills • Brasserie • Fashionable •
Generous cuts of meat greet you as you enter this brasserie, making the house speciality blatantly clear. The quality of the charcuterie, perfectly cooked red meat, French fries and delicious sauces are quite stunning. A Paradise for carnivores!

⬤

Le Passage
XX 🏠 P

avenue Jean et Pierre Carsoel 17 ✉ *1180*   Plan: **B3**
– ℰ 02 374 66 94 – www.lepassage.be – closed 2 weeks in July, Saturday lunch and Sunday
Menu 35 € (lunch), 55/75 € – Carte 51/83 €
• Classic cuisine • Cosy •
Most diners have high expectations when they book a table here, such is the chef's reputation for creativity and flair, as he mingles tradition with modernity. You will not be disappointed by his distinctive cuisine, rich in unforgettable flavours.

La Canne en Ville   X 🏠 ♻

rue de la Réforme 22 ⊠ *1050* – ☎ *0 2 347 29 26*   Plan: **J3**
– www.lacanneenville.be – closed first 2 weeks September, late December-early January, Saturday lunch and Sunday
Menu 18 € (lunch) – Carte 51/61 €
• Classic cuisine • Family • Neighbourhood •
This friendly, long-standing bistro sits within in a old butcher's shop, as the tiles and the occasional decorative feature bear witness. The chef treats diners to a repertoire of succulent, classical dishes, while the lady of the house graciously welcomes one and all.

Les Caves d'Alex   X 🏠

rue Caroly 37 ⊠ *1050* – ☎ *0 2 540 89 37*   Plan: **N3**
– www.lescavesdalex.be – closed 10-17 April, 21 July-13 August, 26 December-1 January, Saturday, Sunday and Monday
Menu 19 € (lunch), 24/38 € – Carte 41/98 €
• Classic French • Bistro • Neighbourhood •
Most of the wines in the cellar of Alex Cardoso, the owner, come from the Côtes du Rhône and Languedoc regions of France. The food is free of unnecessary frills, offering classical dishes prepared with enthusiasm and know-how – a genuine treat!

Koyzina Authentica   X 🏠

avenue Brugmann 519 ⊠ *1180* – ☎ *0 2 346 14 38*   Plan: **11P3**
– www.koyzinaauthentica.be – closed late August-first 2 weeks September, late December, Sunday and Monday
Menu 15 € (lunch) – Carte 30/47 €
• Greek • Mediterranean décor • Neighbourhood •
Greek cuisine has far more to offer than the hackneyed *gyros* and *souvlaki*, as this friendly, if sometimes packed, restaurant proves. The traditional dishes are modern in flavour while remaining authentic.

Nonbe Daigaku   X

avenue Adolphe Buyl 31 ⊠ *1050* – ☎ *0 2 649 21 49*   Plan: **C3**
– closed 1 week Easter, 21 July-15 August, 25 December-4 January, Sunday and Monday
Menu 18 € (lunch) – Carte 31/65 € – *(bookings advisable at dinner)*
• Japanese • Minimalist • Traditional décor •
If you like eating Japanese, you shouldn't miss this modest venue. The very experienced chef has mastered the subtlety and nuances that are typical of the cuisine of his home country. You can see him at work behind the sushi bar, driven and precise, creating a delicious variety of flavours and textures.

Les Papilles   X 🏠

chaussée de Waterloo 782 ⊠ *1180* – ☎ *0 2 374 69 66*   Plan: **B3**
– www.lespapilles.mobi – closed Bank Holidays, Monday dinner and Sunday
Menu 22 € (lunch)/39 € – Carte 41/62 €
• Traditional cuisine • Wine bar •
Your taste buds will definitely start tingling when you enter this delightful establishment. It specialises in distinctive and characteristic brasserie fare, and has a sushi bar in the evening. Before sitting down for your meal, pick yourself a bottle of wine directly from the shelves. Friendly and relaxed.

La Quincaillerie   X 🏠 🅰 ♻ 🅿

rue du Page 45 ⊠ *1050* – ☎ *0 2 533 98 33*   Plan: **J2**
– www.quincaillerie.be – closed Sunday lunch
Menu 18 € (lunch), 36/47 € – Carte 39/74 €
• Classic cuisine • Brasserie •
A meal at this lively brasserie with an oyster bar is a must. It's housed in a former hardware store (dating from 1903) and its art nouveau décor is worth a visit in itself. The environment is fabulous, with authentic cabinets and shelves, and the unfussy French/Belgian classics are very tasty.

BELGIUM - BRUSSELS

Toucan sur Mer

avenue Louis Lepoutre 17 ✉ *1050 –* ☎ *0 2 340 07 40* — Plan: **J3**
– www.toucanbrasserie.com – closed dinner 24 and 31 December
Menu 20 € (lunch) – Carte 45/62 € – *(booking advisable)*
• Seafood • Bistro •
The impeccable quality and freshness of the fish and shellfish of the Toucan sur Mer are more than comparable with seafood restaurants on the coast. This pleasant bistro will certainly appeal to seafood lovers.

Steigenberger Wiltcher's

avenue Louise 71 ✉ *1050 –* ☎ *0 2 542 42 42* — Plan: **J1**
– www.wiltchers.com
267 rm ⌒ – †190/350 € ††190/350 € – 14 suites
• Chain • Palace • Classic •
The Steigenberger offers modern luxury within the walls of a historic building dating from 1918. Attractive and stylish guestrooms, excellent leisure and spa options, as well as extensive conference facilities.

Bristol Stephanie

avenue Louise 91 ✉ *1050 –* ☎ *0 25 43 33 11* — Plan: **J1**
– www.thonhotels.com/bristolstephanie
142 rm – †130/350 € ††140/360 € – ⌒ 27 € – 2 suites
• Luxury • Business • Personalised •
This luxury hotel is the perfect place to unwind. It sits in a superb spot on Avenue Louise and has spacious rooms with retro-modern décor. Not only is it a great place to stay but its brasserie is a pleasant place to dine. If you really want to try to escape, book in for a game at the nearby 'escape rooms'.

Manos Premier

chaussée de Charleroi 102 ✉ *1060 –* ☎ *0 2 537 96 82* — Plan: **J2**
– www.manoshotel.com
47 rm ⌒ – †109/349 € ††129/389 € – 3 suites
• Grand townhouse • Business • Elegant •
The chic, elegant Manos Premier has the grace of a late-19C townhouse with its rich Louis XV and Louis XVI furnishings; if possible, book a room overlooking the garden. It has a charming patio and an authentic Oriental hammam in the basement, along with a stylish restaurant, veranda and lounge bar.

Manos Stéphanie

chaussée de Charleroi 28 ✉ *1060 –* ☎ *0 2 539 02 50* — Plan: **J1**
– www.manosstephanie.com
55 rm ⌒ – †100/250 € ††120/270 €
• Manor house • Business • Classic •
A townhouse with warm, classically styled guestrooms with a contemporary feel and light wood furnishings. Cupola above the breakfast room.

Warwick Barsey

avenue Louise 381 ✉ *1050 –* ☎ *0 2 641 51 11* — Plan: **K3**
– www.warwickbarsey.com
94 rm – †100/475 € ††100/475 € – ⌒ 24 € – 5 suites
• Luxury • Business • Personalised •
This magnificent Second Empire style hotel is home to characterful guestrooms, making it the darling of artists and cinema crews. Breakfast is served in a neoclassical, extravagantly glamorous lounge.

Aqua

rue de Stassart 43 ✉ *1050 –* ☎ *0 2 213 01 01* — Plan: **N3**
– www.aqua-hotel-brussels.com
97 rm ⌒ – †85/350 € ††95/350 €
• Business • Design •
Minimalist decor embellished with a blue wood 'wave' sculpture, created by contemporary artist Arne Quinze. It offers pared-down rooms with walls painted white and blue and parquet flooring. A calm environment.

🏠 **Made in Louise** 　　　　　　　　　🛏 ♿

rue Veydt 40 ✉ 1050 – ☏ 0 2 537 40 33　　Plan: **11Q1**
– www.madeinlouise.com
48 rm – 🛏89/329 € 🛏🛏89/329 € – ☕ 10 €
• Manor house • Family • Contemporary •

This large mansion has no lack of welcoming, hospitable nooks and crannies for the comfort of guests. The stylish, vintage inspired bedrooms extend an invitation to relax and rest. A charming hotel fully in keeping with its smart neighbourhood.

🏠 **Zoom**

rue de la Concorde 59 ✉ 1000 – ☏ 0 2 515 00 60　　Plan: **11Q1**
– www.zoomhotel.be
37 rm – 🛏75/200 € 🛏🛏95/220 € – ☕ 15 €
• Boutique hotel • Vintage •

Photography is the byword of this boutique hotel. All the vintage inspired bedrooms are graced with photos of Brussels, and the same theme is visible in the welcoming lobby. Fine selection of beers at the bar.

EUROPEAN INSTITUTIONS

✿✿ **Bon-Bon** (Christophe Hardiquest) 　　　　XxX 🏠 🌳 🍴

avenue de Tervueren 453 ✉ 1150 – ☏ 0 2 346 66 15　　Plan: **D3**
– www.bonbon.restaurant – closed 31 March-16 April, 21 July-13 August, 23 December-8 January, Bank Holidays, Saturday, Sunday and Monday
Menu 185/235 € – Carte 93/265 €
• Creative • Elegant •

Christophe Hardiquest invites you on an adventure. A quest for culinary harmony, first-class ingredients, inventive recipes and rich flavours … This chef combines flair and subtlety. Take a seat in the contemporary elegant interior and order with complete confidence.
➜ Bijoux d'huître, chantilly à la livèche et gelée de vodka. Canard aux spéculoos. Fontainebleau aux herbes du jardin.

✿ **Da Mimmo** 　　　　　　　　XxX 🏠 🌳 🅰🅺

avenue du Roi Chevalier 24 ✉ 1200 – ☏ 0 2 771 58 60　　Plan: **D2**
– www.da-mimmo.be – closed 20 July-10 August, late December-early January, Saturday lunch and Sunday
Menu 45 € (lunch), 95/125 € – Carte 83/106 €
• Italian • Cosy •

This elegant Italian restaurant speaks one language: that of good produce. Do not expect complex, oversophisticated dishes; they are, on the contrary, an expression of precision, bearing frank, generous flavours. This is Italian cuisine at its best... accompanied by fine wines.
➜ Oeuf 63°, duo d'asperges et mousse de parmesan. Ris de veau, langoustine et truffe en parfaite harmonie. Raviole d'ananas au fromage blanc et carvi, sorbet à la coriandre.

✿ **Le Monde est Petit** (Loïc Villers) 　　　　X 🌳 ♻

rue des Bataves 65 ✉ 1040 – ☏ 0 2 732 44 34　　Plan: **D2**
– www.lemondeestpetit.be – closed last week July-first 2 weeks August, late December-early January, Bank Holidays, Saturday and Sunday
Menu 25 € (lunch) – Carte 55/74 €
• Creative French • Friendly • Family •

It's a small world we live in, as this pleasant little restaurant proves. The chef sources excellent ingredients from all over the world and knows how to combine them with local delicacies. It results in dishes with great depth of flavour, which can be described in one word: delicious!
➜ Tartare de veau, glace tonnato, gauffre aux olives noires et mayonnaise au basilic. Magret de caneton et poêlée de cerises, radis et shiitakes, gâteau de navet et jus des sucs. Millefeuille d'aubergine, espuma de banane, sorbet mangue et yuzu.

Les Deux Maisons   XX 🍴 🅰🅲

Val des Seigneurs 81 ✉ *1150 –* ☏ *02 771 14 47*   Plan: **D2**
*– www.lesdeuxmaisons.be – closed 1 week Easter, first 3 weeks August,
late December, Bank Holidays, Sunday and Monday*
Menu 22 € (lunch), 37/65 € – Carte 55/84 €
• Classic French • Classic décor • Romantic •

Two houses have merged to create this elegant restaurant, where a classically
trained chef rustles up tempting dishes using excellent ingredients. The 'Tradition' menu with its luscious selection of desserts is highly recommended. There's also a fine wine cellar.

Maison du Luxembourg   XX ✿

rue du Luxembourg 37 ✉ *1050 –* ☏ *02 511 99 95*   Plan: **N3**
*– www.maisonduluxembourg.be – closed 1-19 August, 22 December-
2 January, Bank Holidays, Friday dinner, Saturday and Sunday*
Menu 32 € (lunch)/37 € – Carte 48/70 €
• Regional cuisine • Friendly •

Country cooking from the Luxembourg region moves to Brussels. This contemporary restaurant offers well-presented classical fare, highlighting produce sourced from the French-speaking province of Luxembourg. The ingredients are
superlatively fresh and the vegetable side dishes are delicious. A great adverti-
sement for the region.

Park Side   XX 🍴 ⚐ 🅰🅲 ✿

avenue de la Joyeuse Entrée 24 ✉ *1040*   Plan: **H2**
– ☏ *02 238 08 08 – www.restoparkside.be – closed 3 weeks in August,
Bank Holidays, Saturday and Sunday*
Menu 37/55 € – Carte 37/59 €
• Modern cuisine • Fashionable • Brasserie •

Park Side sits in a great location besides the Jubilee Park (parc du Cinquantenaire). Inside it's equally appealing, with chic decor and ultra-modern design features – the main light in particular is a talking point! Modern brasserie specialities feature on the à la carte menu.

Le Coq en Pâte   X 🍴 🅰🅲 ✿

Tomberg 259 ✉ *1200 –* ☏ *02 762 19 71*   Plan: **C2**
– www.lecoqenpate.be – closed Monday
Menu 18 € (lunch), 35/49 € 🍷 – Carte 36/49 €
• Italian • Neighbourhood •

This family-run restaurant has been regaling diners since 1972. Its secret lies first
and foremost in the owner-chef's know-how, born out of his experience, creativity and dedication to Italian cuisine. However, the excellent value for money
and comfortable decor are also much appreciated.

De Maurice à Olivier   X 🅰🅲

chaussée de Roodebeek 246 ✉ *1200 –* ☏ *02 771 33 98*   Plan: **C2**
*– www.demauriceaolivier.be – closed 2-18 April, 16 July-
17 August, Monday dinner and Sunday*
Menu 22 € (lunch), 35/55 € – Carte 42/58 €
• Classic cuisine • Vintage •

Maurice, the father, has passed the business onto his son Olivier. He has also
bequeathed a rich culinary heritage of French cuisine enriched in Mediterranean influences; the dishes are beautifully presented. Amusingly, the restaurant
is also a newsagents.

Le Mucha   X 🍴 ✿

avenue Jules Du Jardin 23 ✉ *1150 –* ☏ *02 770 24 14*   Plan: **D3**
*– www.lemucha.be – closed last week August-first week September,
Sunday dinner and Monday*
Menu 17 € (lunch)/37 € – Carte 41/79 €
• Classic cuisine • Neighbourhood • Cosy •

The interior of Le Mucha is reminiscent of Parisian brasseries in the 1900s, even
down to the waiters! It's an ideal place to sample traditional French cuisine from
a fine choice of classical dishes, without forgetting a few Italian favourites.

Odette en Ville
XX ⇔ 🏠 🍴

rue du Châtelain 25 ✉ 1050 – ☏ 02 640 26 26
Plan: **R1**
– www.odetteenville.be
– closed 5-27 August, 24 and 25 December, 1-8 January, Sunday and Monday
8 rm – ▮155/375 € – ▮▮155/375 € – ⬮ 25 €
Carte 34/79 € – *(open until midnight)*
• Creative French • Trendy •

Odette is depicted by an ultra-trendy interior set in a handsome town house. Add to this a contemporary bistro and luxurious guestrooms. The establishment is in the heart of a fashionable district, which has rubbed off onto the menu of tasty, international dishes.

Au Grand Forestier
XX 🏠

avenue du Grand Forestier 2 ✉ 1170 – ☏ 02 672 57 79
Plan: **7G6**
– www.augrandforestier.be – closed dinner 24 and 31 December and
Sunday dinner
Carte 37/66 € – *(open until 11pm)*
• Belgian • Contemporary décor •

Pure luxury is essentially a question of detail, as this delightful brasserie so admirably illustrates! A flawless welcome and personalised service set the scene to make you feel at home. The same attention to detail can be tasted in the immaculately cooked meat, served with delicious sauces – a princely treat for your taste buds!

Le Buone Maniere
XX 🏠 ⇔

avenue de Tervueren 59 ✉ 1040 – ☏ 02 762 61 05
Plan: **D2**
– www.buonemaniere.be – closed 10 August-10 September, 23 December-
3 January, Saturday lunch and Sunday
Menu 40 € (lunch)/65 € – Carte 53/85 €
• Italian • Classic décor •

Maurizio Zizza's manners are impeccable! He has chosen to share his love of Italian art de vivre in this stylish and elegant town house, which boasts a terrace to the front and the rear. Simple, tasty dishes, which sometimes surprise, transport the diner to southern Europe.

Stirwen
XX ⇔

chaussée Saint-Pierre 15 ✉ 1040 – ☏ 02 640 85 41
Plan: **G3**
– www.stirwen.be – closed 26 Mai, August, 24-26 December, 2 and
3 January, Bank Holidays, Saturday and Sunday
Menu 40 € (lunch), 60/80 € – Carte 70/109 €
• Modern French • Bourgeois •

This renowned restaurant is today in the capable hands of an ambitious duo. David is in charge of the service, while François-Xavier takes a new look at French classics. First-class ingredients are used such as Noirmoutier sole, Lozère lamb and Corrèze veal.

Foro Romano
X ⇔

rue Joseph II 19 ✉ 1000 – ☏ 02 280 29 76 – closed Bank
Plan: **N2**
Holidays, Saturday and Sunday
Menu 30 € (lunch), 35/50 € – Carte approx. 45 €
• Italian • Neighbourhood •

Foro Romano is a cosy, convivial Italian restaurant. Dishes from the region of Puglia are a hit with the international clientele, even more so because the chef is generous with his flavours and portions. Owner Gianfranco is a gregarious man, which you will see when he presents the interesting wine list.

Humus x Hortense
X

rue de Vergnies 2 ✉ 1050 – ☏ 0 474 65 37 06
Plan: **R1**
– www.humusrestaurant.be – closed Sunday and Monday
Menu 23 € (lunch), 36/52 € – *(booking advisable) (tasting menu only)*
• Creative • Vintage •

The encounter between vegetables and an inspired and inventive chef could not fail but produce something special! Light years from culinary tradition, get ready to enjoy surprising, attractive and varied flavours and contrasts, washed down with equally intriguing cocktails, all under the watchful eyes of the angels on the ceiling.

Racines

chaussée d'Ixelles 353 ✉ 1050 – ✆ 02 642 95 90 Plan: **R1**
– www.racinesbruxelles.com – closed 21 July-15 August, first week February, Saturday lunch and Sunday
Menu 36/70 € – Carte 44/79 €
• Italian • Trattoria • Trendy •

Francesco and Ugo are proud of their Italian heritage. One of them pulls up a chair to walk you through the menu, rich in delicious specialties from their homeland, prepared creatively and masterfully. Organic biodynamic wines figure prominently on the wine list, which is definitely worth a close look.

Stanhope

rue du Commerce 9 ✉ 1000 – ✆ 02 506 91 11 Plan: **N3**
– www.thonhotels.com/stanhope – closed 22-26 December
125 rm – †109/475 € ††134/500 € – ☕ 30 € – 9 suites
• Grand Luxury • Traditional • Elegant •

The splendours of the Victorian era are brought to life in this British-style townhouse. It offers varying categories of rooms, including superb suites and duplexes. The elegant dining room has a classic feel and a menu to match, and there's also a pretty courtyard terrace.

Aloft

place Jean Rey 3 ✉ 1040 – ✆ 02 800 08 88 Plan: **G2**
– www.aloftbrussels.com
150 rm – †89/249 € ††89/249 € – ☕ 15 €
• Business • Functional •

A 'loft' spirit reigns throughout this hotel, which is located on the doorstep of the European Institutions. The spacious, comfortable and practical rooms are popular with civil servants and business travellers.

GARE DU MIDI

La Paix (David Martin)

rue Ropsy-Chaudron 49 (opposite abattoirs) ✉ 1070 Plan: **B2**
– ✆ 02 523 09 58 – www.lapaix.eu – closed July, Christmas-New Year, Bank Holidays, Saturday and Sunday
Menu 70/135 € – Carte 119/193 € – *(lunch only except Friday)*
• Asian influences • Fashionable • Friendly •

This characterful restaurant is a perfect example of multicultural Brussels. In the kitchen, chef David Martin deploys the sophistication required for Japanese cuisine. He works with impeccable ingredients such as his own home-grown vegetables or Norwegian King crab, fresh out of the tank. His creative recipes will linger on in your memory.

→ Rouget barbet et jus à la pulpe de moules de bouchot crues. Volaille de Bresse cuit en cocotte aux sarments de vignes. Millefeuille inversé, miso et vanille.

La Brouette

boulevard Prince de Liège 61 ✉ 1070 – ✆ 02 522 51 69 Plan: **A2**
– www.labrouette.be
– closed 1 week Easter, August, 23 September, 5-8 January, Carnival holiday, Tuesday dinner, Saturday lunch, Sunday dinner and Monday
Menu 28 € (lunch), 37/55 € – Carte 51/66 €
• Creative French • Friendly •

Herman Dedapper welcomes you with open arms to his neighbourhood restaurant, decorated in warm colours and hung with pictures he has taken himself. He is an excellent sommelier, who loves to share his passion for wine with his guests. The chef's generous, French-inspired dishes highlight the quality of these wines.

⅋○ **René**   X 🍴 AC

place de la Résistance 14 ⊠ 1070 – ℰ 0 2 523 28 76   Plan: **A2**
– closed last week June, July, Monday and Tuesday
Carte 27/58 €
• Belgian • Family •

This former chippy has been turned into a delightful vintage-style bistro by René, who takes us back in time to an era when cooking was simple and unfussy. Mussels, steak and nourishing stews are all served with generous portions of french fries – a treat for lovers of down-to-earth, wholesome food.

🏨 **Pullman Midi**   🏠 ƒ⅋ 🕭 & AC ⅘

place Victor Horta 1 ⊠ 1060 – ℰ 0 2 528 98 00   Plan: **E3**
– www.pullmanhotels.com/7431
237 rm – ♦95/400 € ♦♦95/400 € – ⊊ 26 € – 2 suites
• Townhouse • Business • Contemporary •

Just a stone's throw from Brussels-South railway station, this hotel transports you to another world. Trendy decor and modern comforts go hand in hand with elegant, designer inspired guestrooms. Alternatively, you can drop in and enjoy a good meal.

ATOMIUM QUARTER

❀ **'t Stoveke** (Daniel Antuna)   XX 🍴 ⇔

Jetsestraat 52 ⊠ 1853 Strombeek-Bever   Plan: **B1**
– ℰ 0 22 67 67 25 – www.tstoveke.be – closed late July-early August, late December-early January, Saturday lunch, Sunday dinner, Tuesday and Wednesday
Menu 36 € (lunch)/67 €
– Carte 68/87 € – *(number of covers limited, pre-book)*
• Modern cuisine • Cosy • Design •

The chef of 't Stoveke follows in the footsteps of some of the best-known chefs in the world, but has added his own personal touch. This has ensured that his cuisine remains resolutely up to date. The dishes reveal an explosion of flavours that are as much a delight to the eye as to the palate.
➔ Gemarineerde makreel met eendenlever, rode biet en truffelmayonaise. Gebakken zeebaars met asperges, paksoi en een aardappelespuma. Aardbeien en chocolade met een citruscrumble en roomijs van matchathee.

❀ **Wine in the City** (Eddy Münster)   X ⅋⅋ 🍴 AC

place Reine Astrid 34 ⊠ 1090 – ℰ 0 24 20 09 20   Plan: **B2**
– www.wineinthecity.be – closed 2-10 April, 16-31 July, 1-9 January, Sunday, Monday and Tuesday
Menu 45 € (lunch), 60/85 € – *(lunch only except Friday and Saturday)*
(booking essential)
• Creative • Wine bar •

In this restaurant-wine bar, amid rows and rows of bottles, sample the wholesome fare of an enthusiastic and creative chef whose dishes frequently surprise. Excellent produce, faultless combinations and of course a magnificent wine list!
➔ Mosaïque de foie gras et anguille fumée à l'émulsion de poire. Presa iberique et poitrine laquée, poivron et croquette au jambon belotta. Kadaïf aux fruits rouges et sirop au miel.

⅋ **L'Auberge de l'Isard**   XX 🍴 ⇔ P

Romeinsesteenweg 964 ⊠ 1780 Wemmel   Plan: **B1**
– ℰ 0 2 479 85 64 – www.isard.be – closed dinner on Bank Holidays, Sunday dinner, Monday and Tuesday
Menu 29 € (lunch), 37/55 € – Carte 46/65 €
• Classic French • Friendly •

To escape the bustle of Heysel and Brussels' ring road, head for the elegant villa of Roland Taildeman, who opened his restaurant in 1989. Guests are particularly taken with the extensive set menu. There is a wide and varied choice with one constant byword – taste.

La Brasserie de la Gare
X 🕮 AC

chaussée de Gand 1430 ⊠ 1082 – ℰ 02 469 10 09 Plan: **A2**
– www.brasseriedelagare.be – closed Saturday lunch and Sunday
Menu 16 € (lunch)/37 € – Carte 37/55 €
• Belgian • Brasserie • Neighbourhood •

For a typical Brussels experience, come and discover this old café, which has retained all of its retro charm. The chef's cooking honours tradition by having a pleasing simplicity and you enjoy succulent boar in season or a timeless steak tartare and chips... This is one of life's certainties!

Brasserie de l'Expo
X 🕮

avenue Houba de Strooper 188 ⊠ 1020 Plan: **B1**
– ℰ 02 476 99 70 – www.brasseriedelexpo.be – closed dinner 24 and 31 December
Menu 16 € (lunch)/35 € – Carte 43/65 €
• Seafood • Brasserie •

The memory of the 1958 Expo continues to linger in this delightful vintage brasserie opposite Heysel stadium. Right from the word go, the seafood bar leaves you in no doubt that fresh, quality ingredients take pride of place in the chef's cuisine. Brasserie fare at its best!

French Kiss
X 🕮 🕮 AC

rue Léopold I 470 ⊠ 1090 – ℰ 02 425 22 93 Plan: **B2**
– www.restaurantfrenchkiss.com – closed 22 July-16 August, 24 and 31 December, 1 January and Monday
Menu 29/37 € – Carte 38/57 €
• Meats and grills • Friendly •

A pleasant restaurant renowned for its excellent grilled dishes and impressive wine list. Dining area with a low ceiling and bright paintings adding colour to the brick walls.

Spectrum
X 🕮

Romeinsesteenweg 220 ⊠ 1800 Vilvoorde Plan: **B1**
– ℰ 02 267 00 45 – www.restospectrum.be – closed Monday dinner, Saturday lunch and Sunday
Menu 35 € – Carte 38/59 €
• Market cuisine • Brasserie •

Could it be better food? And at a better price? On the contrary, the quality to price ratio at Spectrum is among the best in Brussels and the surrounding area. Classic cuisine, copious portions and modest prices – what more could you ask for?

La table d'Evan
XX 🕮 ⇔ P

Brusselsesteenweg 21 ⊠ 1780 Wemmel Plan: **A1**
– ℰ 02 460 52 39 – www.evanrestaurants.be – closed Saturday lunch and Sunday
Menu 35 € (lunch), 55/110 € – Carte 72/100 €
• Mediterranean cuisine • Brasserie • Trendy •

Chef Evan's restaurant is modern, comfortable and free of unnecessary frills. On a constant quest for fine produce, he deploys his talent and experience to create delicious dishes. 'Quality before all else' is his motto – much to the delight of our taste buds!

AIRPORT & NATO

Maxime Colin
XX < 🕮 🕮 ⇔

Pastoorkesweg 1 ⊠ 1950 Kraainem – ℰ 02 720 63 46 Plan: **D2**
– www.maximecolin.be – closed 31 July-13 August, 30 October-5 November, 13-19 February, Sunday and Monday
Menu 32 € (lunch), 57/79 € – (tasting menu only)
• Creative French • Romantic • Friendly •

When you first enter chef Colin's establishment you will want to admire the setting. Located in the gardens of Jourdain Castle, the restaurant has a romantic interior and a handsome terrace beside a pond. The modern cuisine uses a wide variety of good quality produce.

iO **Bovis** ✗ Ⓐ

Heldenplein 16 ✉ *1930 Zaventem –* ✆ *0 2 308 83 43* Plan: **D1**
– www.bovis-zaventem.be – closed Bank Holidays, Saturday and Sunday
Carte 47/75 €
• Meats and grills • Brasserie •
The strapline of this restaurant is 'simply meat'; it uses only the very best quality
and ensures that each cut is aged until it reaches perfect maturity. All are served
with handcut chips fried in beef fat, and can be accompanied by some interesting wines.

iO **Brasserie Mariadal** ✗ 🖢 🏡 Ⓐ ⇔ 🅿

Kouterweg 2 ✉ *1930 Zaventem –* ✆ *0 2 720 59 30* Plan: **D1**
– www.brasseriemariadal.be
Menu 38 € – Carte 26/66 €
• Modern French • Brasserie •
Imagine a handsome castle surrounded by a moat, sporting an unusual interior
decor. There is also a menu that can hold its own with the best brasseries with a
few more personal creations, all of which is in the grounds of an airport complex. You will understand why the Mariadal leaves no one indifferent! Fine
choice on the menu and good value for money.

ANTWERP
ANTWERPEN/ANVERS

RossHelen/iStock

ANTWERP IN...

➡ **ONE DAY**
Grote Markt, Our Lady's Cathedral, MoMu, Het Zuid.

➡ **TWO DAYS**
Rubens' House, Royal Museum of Fine Arts, a stroll to the Left Bank via the Sint-Anna tunnel.

➡ **THREE DAYS**
Het Eilandje and MAS, a river trip, Kloosterstraat, Nationalestraat.

Antwerp calls itself the pocketsize metropolis, and with good reason. Although it's Europe's second largest port, it still retains a compact intimacy, defined by bustling squares and narrow streets. It's a place with many facets, not least its marked link to Rubens, the diamond trade and, in later years, the fashion collective The Antwerp Six. The city's centre teems with ornate gabled guild-houses, and in summer, open-air cafés line the area beneath the towering cathedral, giving the place a festive, almost bohemian air. It's a fantastic place to shop: besides clothing boutiques, there are antiques emporiums and diamond stores – to say nothing of

the chocolate shops with their appealing window displays. Bold regeneration projects have transformed the skyline and the waterfront's decrepit warehouses have started new lives as ritzy storerooms of 21C commerce. The nightlife here is the best in Belgium, while the beer is savoured the way others might treat a vintage wine.

The Old Town is defined by Grote Markt, Groenplaats and The Meir shopping street – these are a kind of dividing line between Antwerp's north and south. North of the centre is Het Eilandje, the hip former warehouse area; to the east is the Diamond District. Antique and bric-a-brac shops are in abundance in the 'designer heart' Het Zuid, south of the centre, which is also home to the best museums and art galleries.

EATING OUT

The menus of Flanders are heavily influenced by the lush meadows, the canals swarming with eels and the proximity of the North Sea – but the eating culture in Antwerp offers more than just seafood. With its centuries old connection to more exotic climes, there's no shortage of fragrant spices such as cinnamon in their dishes, especially in the rich stews so beloved by the locals. If you want to eat with the chic, hang around the Het Eilandje dockside or the rejuvenated ancient warehouses south of Grote Markt. For early risers, the grand cafés are a popular port of call, ideal for a slow coffee and a trawl through the papers. Overall the city boasts the same tempting Belgian specialities as Brussels (stewed eel in chervil sauce; mussels; dishes containing rabbit; beef stew and chicory), but also with a focus on more contemporary cuisine. Don't miss out on the local chocolate (shaped like a hand in keeping with the legend which gave Antwerp its name), and be sure to try their De Koninck beer, served in a glass designed like an open bowl.

CENTRE (Old Town and Main Station)

✿✿ **'t Zilte** (Viki Geunes)

Hanzestedenplaats 5 ✉ 2000 – ✆ 0 3 283 40 40 Plan: **B1**
– www.tzilte.be – closed 1 week Easter, 2 weeks in July, Autumn break, late December, Saturday, Sunday and after 8.30pm
Menu 68 € (lunch), 130/180 € – Carte 160/193 €
• Creative • Design •

Savour the view of Antwerp at your feet as you sample sophisticated dishes. 't Zilte is wonderfully located on the top floor of the Museum Aan de Stroom. Viki Geunes' joyful cooking is depicted by diverse textures and flavours, a whirlwind of international ingredients and desserts of which the chef is particularly proud.
➜ Toro tonijn en noordzeekrab met kombu en koolrabi. Wagyu met aubergine, gepofte ui, artisjok en miso. Geitenyoghurt met zuring, ananas en sorbet van cedraat.

✿✿ **The Jane** (Nick Bril)

Paradeplein 1 ✉ 2018 – ✆ 0 3 808 44 65 Plan: **H1**
– www.thejaneantwerp.com – closed late March-early April, late June-early July, late September-early October, 23 December-3 January, Sunday and Monday
Menu 110/130 € – *(booking essential) (tasting menu only)*
• Creative • Fashionable • Design •

This striking chapel, now a trend-setting temple, is unique in Belgium! Chef Nick Bril can be relied upon to introduce diners to mind-blowing flavours. His food is both sophisticated and simple, steeped in powerful flavours and yet amazingly harmonious. The Upper Room Bar serves cocktails.
➜ Gepocheerde kreeft en hamachi in ceviche, curry en avocado. Gebakken duif met smaken uit Dubai. Matcha, lychee, basilicum en sorbet van sakura.

✿ **'t Fornuis** (Johan Segers)

Reyndersstraat 24 ✉ 2000 – ✆ 0 3 233 62 70 Plan: **D2**
– closed 16 July-15 August, late December, Bank Holidays, Saturday and Sunday
Carte 75/120 €
• Classic cuisine • Romantic • Classic décor •

Fine classic cuisine and quality wines are served in this rustic restaurant housed in an old building. The owner/chef has been running the show since 1976 and was awarded his first Michelin star in 1986. Miniature stoves exhibited downstairs.
➜ Cassoulet van varkenspoot en kreeft. Wilde eend met spruitjes en gebraiseerd witloof. Cappuccino frappé.

✿ **Het Gebaar** (Roger van Damme)

Leopoldstraat 24 ✉ 2000 – ✆ 0 3 232 37 10 Plan: **D2**
– www.hetgebaar.be – closed Bank Holidays, Saturday and Sunday
Carte 69/102 € – *(lunch only) (booking essential)*
• Creative • Cosy •

This restaurant is located in an elegant building on the edge of the botanical park. Luxury tea room cuisine, which the chef enriches with modern twists; mouthwatering desserts! Non-stop service until 6pm.
➜ Tartaar van tonijn met rode biet en avocado. Tarbot met fijne lente-groenten, mosseltjes en een jus van schaal- en schelpdieren. Appeltaartje met pistacheroomijs, amandel, noten en een vanillesaus.

✿ **Bistrot du Nord** (Michael Rewers)

Lange Dijkstraat 36 ✉ 2060 – ✆ 0 3 233 45 49 Plan: **B1**
– www.bistrotdunord.be – closed 24 December-3 January, Bank Holidays, Wednesday, Saturday and Sunday
Carte 50/102 €
• Traditional cuisine • Bourgeois • Intimate •

A lesson in tradition! The chef, an authentic craftsman, knows how to get the best out of fine produce. He admits to a weakness for tripe, but diners need have no fears - whatever your choice, your taste buds will be delighted.
➜ Lamstong met doperwtjes en mosterdvinaigrette. Bombe van ossestaart met truffel. Bavarois van witte chocolade met ananas, munt en kokossorbet.

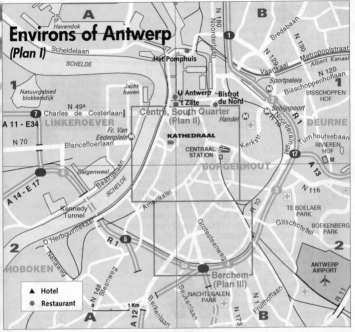

Dôme (Frédéric Chabbert)   XX � AC ⬦
Plan: **G2**
Grote Hondstraat 2 ✉ *2018 – ☏ 03 239 90 03*
– www.domeweb.be – closed Sunday and Monday
Menu 35 € (lunch)/75 € – Carte 84/106 €
• Classic French • Elegant • Romantic •

The memory of a meal beneath the dome of this elegant restaurant will linger long after the last bite! The experienced chef, Frédéric Chabbert (who learned the trade in Hong Kong among others), will treat you to fine, classical fare using techniques that have fallen by the wayside. Top quality produce and rich flavours define the Dôme.

→ Gebakken coquilles met een slaatje van belugalinzen, brunoise van eekhoorntjesbrood en algen. Pladijs op de graat gepocheerd met rode kool, cranberries en boterjus met azijn. Hindefilet met een puree van rode biet met sinaaszeste, spätzle en champignons.

Bij Lam & Yin (Lap Yee Lam)   X AC
Plan: **D2**
Reynderstraat 17 ✉ *2000 – ☏ 03 232 88 38 – lam-en-*
yin.be – closed Easter holiday, late December, Monday and Tuesday
Carte 51/71 € – (dinner only) (booking essential)
• Chinese • Minimalist • Exotic décor •

Lam & Yin is definitely not a run-of-the-mill Asian restaurant. Don't expect a menu as long as the Great Wall of China or paper lanterns! This is the place for delicate, subtle Cantonese cuisine, depicted by fresh, original flavours and a quest for authenticity before all else. Genuine saké in the Gang Bei!

→ Stoommandje met dimsum. Gestoomde zeebaars met gember en pijpajuin. Gebakken lam met szechuanpeper.

89

The Butcher's son (Bert-Jan Michielsen) ✗

Boomgaardstraat 1 ⊠ 2018 – ℰ 03 230 16 38   Plan: **F3**
*– www.thebutchersson.be – closed 2 weeks in August, late December,
Saturday and Sunday*
Menu 30 € (lunch) – Carte 52/83 €
• Traditional cuisine • Trendy •

De Koninck brasserie is the perfect blend of smart, urban design. Red meat
showcased like artwork in display cabinets reminds the visitor that meat is the
star of the show here. Traditionally prepared by the chef and served with delicious side dishes. Balanced flavour above all else at the Butcher's son.
→ Open ravioli met asperges en morieljes, Simmenthal en merg. Vol-au-
vent met kalfszwezerik, botersla en frietjes. Banaan, moka en chocolade.

B 23 ✗

Brouwersvliet 23 ⊠ 2000 – ℰ 03 345 15 14   Plan: **D1**
*– www.brouwersvliet23.be – closed 29 July-15 August, 1-
10 January, Saturday lunch, Sunday and Wednesday*
Menu 17 € (lunch), 37/56 € – Carte 53/100 €
• Modern cuisine • Brasserie • Wine bar •

Step into this wine bar at N°23 Brouwersvliet and you will find a lively brasserie
to the rear. The menu can hold its own with the best, and the fine produce is
enhanced by modern techniques and combinations. B 23 brings the promise of
an explosion of flavours.

Brasserie Dock's ✗ 🛖 🅐🅒 ✿ 🐖

Jordaenskaai 7 ⊠ 2000 – ℰ 03 226 63 30   Plan: **D1**
– www.docks.be – closed Bank Holidays and Sunday
Menu 18 € (lunch), 30/37 € – Carte 36/77 €
• Seafood • Fashionable • Brasserie •

Since 1994, this upmarket brasserie has been a favourite venue in the hip docklands
district. Jules Vernes must have had a hand in the interior decoration! The establishment
is famous for its excellent house specialties (such as Bresse chicken) and flavoursome
seafood (delicious oysters). All the ingredients for a delicious culinary journey!

Bún ✗

Sint-Jorispoort 22 ⊠ 2000 – ℰ 03 234 04 16   Plan: **D3**
*– www.bunantwerp.be – closed 17-28 April, 17-21 July, 2-6 October, 9-
13 January, Sunday and Monday*
Carte 29/39 € – *(booking essential)*
• Vietnamese • Simple •

A fresco on the wall depicts a cockerel fight, transporting you right to the midst
of a Vietnamese street! This modest bistro will take you on an amazing gourmet
journey from East to West. Vietnamese cooking at its best.

InVINcible ✗ 🏦 🛖 🅐🅒

Haarstraat 9 ⊠ 2000 – ℰ 03 231 32 07   Plan: **C1**
*– www.invincible.be – closed 1-8 January, Bank Holidays, Saturday and
Sunday*
Menu 25 € 🍷 (lunch), 37/57 €
• Modern cuisine • Trendy •

A glass of wine from the impressive selection, accompanied by a flawlessly cooked
French dish… talk about an invincible combination! The menu is small but the choice
is not easy because the chef beautifully interweaves flavours and really makes the
dishes his own. Tip: a seat at the counter will complete your experience.

Schnitzel ✗ 🛖

Paardenmarkt 53 ⊠ 2000 – ℰ 03 256 63 86   Plan: **K1**
– www.schnitzelantwerpen.be – closed Saturday and Sunday
Carte 26/41 € – *(dinner only)*
• Classic cuisine • Neighbourhood • Traditional décor •

Simple but good is the motto of this establishment. The experienced chef
deploys his talents to prepare delicious cooked meats and *beuling*, a sort of
black pudding. He rustles up these ingredients into dishes designed to be shared. Refreshingly down to earth and wholesome!

BELGIUM - ANTWERP

Lux

XxX ≤ AC ⇔

Plan: **D1**

Adriaan Brouwerstraat 13 ⊠ 2000 – ℰ 03 233 30 30
– www.luxantwerp.com – closed 9-24 July, 1 January, lunch on Bank
Holidays, Saturday lunch, Sunday and Monday
Menu 33 € (lunch), 45/75 € – Carte 66/78 €
• Classic cuisine • Chic •

This restaurant occupies the house of a former ship owner, and has a terrace that overlooks the port. There is a profusion of marble (columns, fireplaces), a wine and cocktail bar, à la carte options, plus an attractive lunch menu.

Ardent

XX 🍴

Plan: **F3**

Dageraadplaats 3 ⊠ 2018 – ℰ 03 336 32 99
– www.resto-ardent.be – closed Saturday lunch, Monday, Tuesday and
after 8.30pm
Menu 29 € (lunch), 49/69 € – Carte 57/73 €
• Modern cuisine • Minimalist •

Passion is often said to be the distinctive character trait of great chefs. Wouter Van Steenwinkel is no exception to this rule and his tasteful restaurant will give you an insight into his many talents. You can expect well-thought out and balanced meals with perfectly blended flavours.

DIM

XX

Plan: **J2**

Vrijdagmarkt 7 ⊠ 2000 – ℰ 03 226 26 70
– www.dimdining.be – closed 30 August-26 September, Tuesday and
Wednesday
Menu 45 € – Carte 47/138 €
• Asian influences • Design • Elegant •

DIM's luminous interior suits the minimalist approach of Japanese cuisine. Dimitri Proost prepares the sushi on the counter and the meticulously crafted main ingredient is served with delicious sauces and not overloaded with side dishes. Subtle, rich in flavour and aroma.

Graanmarkt 13

XX 🍴 AC ⇔

Plan: **E2**

Graanmarkt 13 ⊠ 2000 – ℰ 03 337 79 91
– www.graanmarkt13.be – closed Sunday and Monday
Menu 35 € (lunch)/45 € – *(tasting menu only)*
• Organic • Minimalist • Trendy •

The days are long past when vegetables were little more than bland anonymous extras on the plate. Seppe Nobels proves that they are fully capable of taking the star role and he brilliantly and skilfully incorporates them into contemporary recipes rich in powerful flavours. Each dish is a new discovery! Buffet on Sundays.

Marcel

XX 🍴 ⇔

Plan: **D1**

Van Schoonbekeplein 13 ⊠ 2000 – ℰ 03 336 33 02
– www.restaurantmarcel.be – closed late December and Sunday
Menu 30 € (lunch), 50/75 € – Carte 49/70 €
• Classic French • Brasserie • Vintage •

Welcome to Marcel's – a vintage bistro with a distinctly French feel. The culinary repertory mingles traditional recipes with touches of modernity, resulting in cuisine steeped in wholesome flavours. Terrace overlooking the MAS.

Món

XX 🍴

Plan: **D1**

Sint-Aldegondiskaai 30 ⊠ 2000 – ℰ 03 345 67 89
– www.monantwerp.com
Carte 36/64 €
• Meats and grills • Brasserie • Trendy •

The sculpture of a bull's head immediately gives you a foretaste of the menu, in which red meat takes pride of place. In fact, not just any meat but home raised Limousine beef prepared in a Josper charcoal fire. The cooking and accompaniments are a treat for your taste buds.

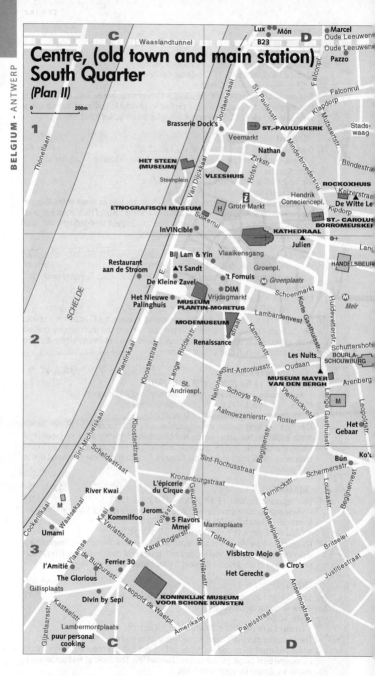

Centre, (old town and main station) South Quarter
(Plan II)

0   200m

BELGIUM - ANTWERP

C   Waaslandtunnel   D

Lux   Món
B23   Marcel
Oude Leeuwen
Oude Leeuwen
Pazzo

Falconrui

Falconpl.

Klapdorp

Stads-
waag

St.-Paulusstr.

Brasserie Dock's

Veemarkt

ST.-PAULUSKERK

Nathan

Zirkstr.

Minderbroedersrui

Minderbroedersstr.

Musserstr.

Blindestra

HET STEEN
(MUSEUM)

Hofstr.

Steenplein

VLEESHUIS

ROCKOXHUIS

Keizerstraa

Van Dijckkaai

De Witte Le

Hendrik
Consciencepll.

Kipdorp

ETNOGRAFISCH MUSEUM

Suikerrui

H   Grote Markt

i

ST.-CAROLUS
BORROMEUSKER

InVINcible

KATHEDRAAL

Vlaaikensgang

Julien

Lang

Bij Lam & Yin

Groenpl.

HANDELSBEUR

Restaurant
aan de Stroom

▲'t Sandt

De Kleine Zavel

't Fornuis

M Groenplaats

Schoenmarkt

Korte Gasthuisstr.

M

Meir

Het Nieuwe
Palinghuis

DIM

Vrijdagmarkt

MUSEUM
PLANTIN-MORETUS

Lambardenvest

Huidevettersstr.

Schuttershof

SCHELDE

Plantinkaai

Kloosterstraat

Lange   Ridderstr.

Kammenstr.

MODEMUSEUM

Renaissance

Nationalestraat

Sint-Antoniusstr.

Les Nuits

Oudaan

BOURLA-
SCHOUWBURG

MUSEUM MAYER
VAN DEN BERGH

Arenberg

St.
Andriespl.

Schoyte Str.

Vleminckveld

Lange Gasthuisstr.

M

Leopoldstr.

Aalmoezenierstr.

Rosier

Het
Gebaar

Ko'u

Sint-Michielskaai

Scheldestraat

Kloosterstraat

Sint-Rochusstraat

Begijnenstr.

Terninckstr.

Schermersstr.

Bún

Cockerillkaai

Waalsekaai

M

River Kwai

Kronenburgstraat

L'épicerie
du Cirque

Gouzensstr.

Kasteelpleinstr.

Louizastr.

Begijnenvest

Britseler

Justitiestraat

Umami

Kaai

Vlaamse de Burburstr.

Kommilfoo

Verlatstraat

Jerom.

Volkstr.

5 Flavors
Mmei

Marnixplaats

de Vrierestr.

Tolstraat

Marnixplaats

Karel Rogiersstr.

l'Amitié

Ferrier 30

Visbistro Mojo

Ciro's

The Glorious

Het Gerecht

Gillisplaats

Divin by Sepi

Leopold de Waelpl.

KONINKLIJK MUSEUM
VOOR SCHONE KUNSTEN

Anselmostraat

Gizelaarsstr.

Kasteelstr.

Lambermontplaats

puur personal
cooking

Amerikalei

Paleisstraat

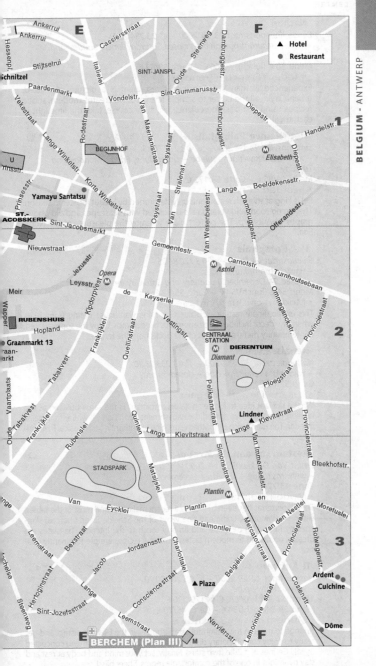

Nathan   XX

Lange Koepoortstraat 13 ⊠ *2000 –* ✆ *03 284 28 13*   Plan: **J1**
*– www.restaurant-nathan.be – closed Saturday lunch, Sunday and
Monday*
Menu 30 € (lunch), 46/66 € – Carte 58/82 €
• Modern French • Trendy •
Experienced Nathan Van Echelpoel's restaurant is a picture of relaxed,
urbane style, all the better to sample fine food. He creates modern, subtle
recipes using first-class ingredients, which, of course, take the limelight in
each meal.

Het Nieuwe Palinghuis   XX AC

Sint-Jansvliet 14 ⊠ *2000 –* ✆ *03 231 74 45*   Plan: **C2**
*– www.hetnieuwepalinghuis.be – closed June, Friday, Monday and
Tuesday*
Menu 44/85 € – Carte 58/172 €
• Seafood • Friendly •
Eel is king at this fish restaurant, only dethroned by Escaut lobster in season.
The dining room and veranda are decorated with seascapes and old photo-
graphs of Antwerp. The perfect place to enjoy the pleasures of the North
Sea.

Het Pomphuis   XX ⩽ 🛋 ✿ P

Siberiastraat ⊠ *2030 –* ✆ *03 770 86 25*   Plan: **B1**
– www.hetpomphuis.be
– closed 24 December, 1 January and Saturday lunch
Menu 34 € (lunch)/54 € – Carte 55/83 €
• Modern cuisine • Vintage •
This extraordinary restaurant occupies a huge warehouse dating from 1920,
where the decor includes three enormous bilge pumps. Enjoy the sophisticated,
contemporary menu and views of the docks from the terrace.

Renaissance   XX 🛋

Nationalestraat 32 ⊠ *2000 –* ✆ *03 233 93 90*   Plan: **D2**
– www.resto-renaissance.be – closed Sunday
Carte 52/63 €
• Italian • Design • Elegant •
What a brilliant idea to locate an Italian restaurant in the same building as the
fashion museum! This splendid establishment sports an all-white, minimalist
interior. The menu, rich in southern sunshine, is authentic and classical in its origins.

Restaurant aan de Stroom   XX ⩽ 🛋 ✿

Ernest Van Dijckkaai 37 ⊠ *2000 –* ✆ *03 234 12 75*   Plan: **F1**
– www.ras.today – closed 24 December
Carte 43/72 €
• Modern cuisine • Elegant • Trendy •
The Zuiderterras has been treated to a recent makeover and most of the tables,
set in bay windows, command fine views of the Schelde River. Charcoal sketches by Rinus Van de Velde add an arty touch to the interior. The plates are
dressed according to modern tastes, while the recipes are predominantly classic.

U Antwerp   XX 🛋

Nassaustraat 42 ⊠ *2000 –* ✆ *03 201 90 70*   Plan: **F1**
– www.u-antwerp.be
15 rm ⊡ – †170/220 € ††170/220 €
Menu 29 € (lunch)/34 € – Carte 45/70 €
• Modern cuisine • Trendy •
Arrange to meet in this delightful establishment in the Eilandje district and get
ready to enjoy contemporary dishes from a modern, attractive menu concocted
by Viki Geunes of 't Zilte (two stars). Finally, set your mind and body at rest and
stay overnight in one of the comfortable rooms. Sheer bliss!

Cuichine
X 🎐

Draakstraat 13 ✉ 2018 — Plan: **F3**
– ☎ 03 289 92 45 – www.cuichine.be
– closed 2-9 April, first 2 weeks September, 24, 25 and 26 December, 1 and 2 January, Saturday lunch, Sunday and Monday
Menu 23 € (lunch)/40 € – Carte 44/62 €
• Chinese • Friendly •

Two childhood friends, both sons of restaurant owners, created Cuichine with the idea of serving dishes they used to eat at home. Their Cantonese recipes are well prepared from fresh produce and without fussy frills. Even better, the à la carte menu is well priced and the lunch menu unbeatable.

De Kleine Zavel
X 🎐 AC

Stoofstraat 2 ✉ 2000 — Plan: **C1**
– ☎ 03 231 96 91 – www.dkz-group.be
– closed Monday and Tuesday
Menu 39 € (lunch), 60/95 € – Carte 48/58 €
• Modern cuisine • Bistro •

De Kleine Zavel is a Belgian version of a gastropub: good food served in a friendly, vintage setting. The menu demonstrates that the chef has the ambition and talent to back it up, with a modern, attractive and faultlessly executed repertory.

Ko'uzi
X 🎐

Leopoldplaats 12 ✉ 2000 — Plan: **D3**
– ☎ 03 232 24 88 – www.kouzi.be
– closed 2 weeks in August, Bank Holidays, Sunday, Monday and after 8pm
Carte 23/63 €
• Japanese • Minimalist • Design •

The interior design is as hip and minimalist as the food. Sushi and sashimi classics rub shoulders with other more inventive recipes. Enjoy delicious fare and the chance to sample different teas in the tasting lounge. The chef Kawada also organises sushi classes that are all the rage.

Pazzo
X 🕸 AC ✿

Oude Leeuwenrui 12 ✉ 2000 — Plan: **D1**
– ☎ 03 232 86 82 – www.pazzo.be
– closed 20 July-20 August, late December-early January, Bank Holidays, Saturday and Sunday
Menu 22 € (lunch) – Carte 41/66 €
• Modern cuisine • Friendly •

This trendy brasserie with a lively atmosphere occupies a former warehouse near the docks. Enjoy Mediterranean- and Asian-inspired bistro cuisine and excellent wines.

Yamayu Santatsu
X AC ✿

Ossenmarkt 19 ✉ 2000 — Plan: **E1**
– ☎ 03 234 09 49 – www.santatsu.be
– closed Sunday lunch and Monday
Menu 16 € (lunch), 23/50 €
– Carte 32/59 €
• Japanese • Simple •

A lively and authentic Japanese restaurant that only uses the best hand picked ingredients, and prepares sushi in full view of diners. Assorted à la carte options with four different menus for two people.

De Witte Lelie 🐾 🎨 🕭 🚗

Keizerstraat 16 ✉ 2000   Plan: **D1**
– ☎ 0 32 26 19 66 – www.dewittelelie.be
10 rm – ♦255/495 € ♦♦295/635 € – ☲ 30 € – 1 suite
• Historic • Personalised •
This historic abode fully justifies its reputation for poised sophistication and graceful hospitality. The 17C walls, tasteful decor down to the tiniest detail, and its precious peace and quiet in the city centre explain the appeal of this luxury boutique hotel.

Julien 🕭 🕭 🎨 🕭

Korte Nieuwstraat 24 ✉ 2000   Plan: **D2**
– ☎ 0 3 229 06 00 – www.hotel-julien.com
21 rm – ♦150/179 € ♦♦179/219 € – ☲ 23 €
• Luxury • Grand luxury • Design •
Hidden behind its carriage entrance this hotel is a real gem. It boasts a warm welcome, cosy atmosphere and very refined Scandinavian-style rooms. Don't miss the spa built in the 16C cellar. From the roof terrace there is a breathtaking view of the cathedral.

Lindner 🕭 🎨 🕭 🕭 🎨 🕭 🚗

Lange Kievitstraat 125 ✉ 2018   Plan: **F2**
– ☎ 0 3 227 77 00 – www.lindnerhotels.be
173 rm – ♦99/219 € ♦♦109/249 € – ☲ 22 € – 4 suites
• Townhouse • Modern •
This modern, almost futuristic hotel was cleverly built near the new station. A good starting point for your trip, whether it is for business or pleasure. Spacious rooms.

Les Nuits 🎨 🎨

Lange Gasthuisstraat 12 ✉ 2000   Plan: **D2**
– ☎ 0 3 225 02 04 – www.hotellesnuits.be
25 rm – ♦129/149 € ♦♦139/159 € – ☲ 19 €
• Luxury • Cosy • Modern •
Looking for a hip place in town? This boutique hotel offers a nice contrast between the dark colours of the night (la nuit) and lighter shades. Its interior design is really charming.

't Sandt 🎨 🕭 🚗

Zand 17 ✉ 2000   Plan: **C2**
– ☎ 0 3 232 93 90 – www.hotel-sandt.be
29 rm ☲ – ♦160/240 € ♦♦180/260 € – 2 suites
• Luxury • Classic •
This establishment is in an attractive building with a fine Rococo façade near the banks of the Escaut. It offers attentive service, bedrooms full of character, meeting rooms, a patio and a roof terrace.

SOUTH QUARTER AND BERCHEM

❄ Kommilfoo (Olivier de Vinck de Winnezeele) 🍴🍴 🎨 🅿

Vlaamse Kaai 17 ✉ 2000   Plan: **C3**
– ☎ 0 3 237 30 00 – www.restaurantkommilfoo.be
– closed first 3 weeks July, 25 December, Saturday lunch, Sunday and Monday
Menu 40 € (lunch), 45/85 € – Carte 82/108 €
• Creative • Cosy •
Smart yet casual, Kommilfoo will acquaint you with the creative and inventive talent of a dedicated chef. The dishes are both amusing and imaginative, with a clear desire to render contrasting tastes harmonious. Pyrenean goat, the house speciality, is on the menu all year long.
➜ Gebakken langoustines, soepje van eekhoorntjesbrood en gepocheerd kwartelei. Hazenrug met rode biet, knolselderij en blauwe bessen. Banaantaartje.

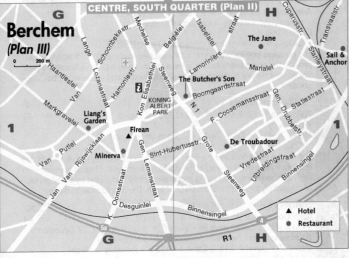

The Glorious

❀

X ⇦ 錨 🏠 **AK**
Plan: **C3**

De Burburestraat 4a ✉ *2000 – ℰ 03 237 06 13*
– www.theglorious.be – closed 3-11 April, 17 July-1 August, 25 and
26 December, Sunday and Monday
Menu 39 € (lunch), 65/95 € – Carte 72/106 €
· **Modern French · Wine bar · Chic ·**

This former warehouse now houses a chic, well-designed restaurant. The sommelier, Jurgen, is in charge of the renowned wine selection and the chef, Johan, tempts you with his cooking, which elevates classic dishes to a whole new level. Enjoy this glorious adventure surrounded by original baroque and art deco features.

➜ Taartje van burrata, cevenne-ui en zachte pepers. Op karkas gebakken wilde patrijs met pommes pont-neuf, eekhoorntjesbrood en compote van veenbessen. Gepocheerde peer met pistache, chocoladeroomijs en sabayon met marsala.

De Troubadour

❀

XX **AK** ⇦ **P**
Plan: **H1**

Driekoningenstraat 72 ✉ *2600 Berchem*
– ℰ 03 239 39 16 – www.detroubadour.be – closed first 3 weeks August,
Sunday and Monday
Menu 26 € (lunch), 37/54 € – Carte approx. 45 €
· **Modern cuisine · Trendy ·**

Out-going, sociable Johan Verbeeck welcomes diners with his inimitable style and fun-loving personality. Popular with gourmets since 1990, the establishment is depicted by a trendy vintage style. The menu and dishes seek to enhance and exalt the excellent seasonal ingredients and produce.

Ciro's

X 帝 AC

Amerikalei 6 ☒ 2018 – ℰ 03 238 11 47 – www.ciros.be — Plan: **D3**
– closed July, Saturday lunch and Monday
Carte 36/58 €

• Belgian • Neighbourhood • Traditional décor •

The nostalgic interior, working class atmosphere and traditional Belgian fare will provide the opportunity to turn a meal at Ciro's into a taste of Antwerp's past. Vol-au-vent deluxe is the star of the show. Book ahead – you won't be disappointed!

5 Flavors Mmei

X

Volkstraat 37 ☒ 2000 – ℰ 03 281 30 37 – closed — Plan: **F2**
Wednesday
Menu 35/45 € – Carte 24/42 € – *(open until 11pm)*

• Chinese • Simple •

The most well-known and the most obvious can sometimes surprise – and this restaurant is a perfect example. The chef pays homage to Chinese tradition with fresh and sometimes surprising preparations, which put paid to many prejudices regarding the cuisine of his place of birth. The dim sum are to die for!

Minerva – Hotel Firean

XXX AC

Karel Oomsstraat 36 ☒ 2018 – ℰ 03 216 00 55 — Plan: **G1**
– www.restaurantminerva.be – closed 16 July-16 August, 24 December-10 January, Bank Holidays, Saturday and Sunday
Menu 39 € (lunch)/60 € – Carte 55/103 € – *(booking advisable)*

• Classic cuisine • Elegant •

Minerva was also the name of the legendary Belgian luxury car, the repair workshops of which were located here. The site is now that of a well-oiled restaurant, serving good quality, traditional fare. You might be interested to know that all the meat is sliced in front of you!

Ferrier 30

XX 帝 AC ⇔

Leopold de Waelplaats 30 ☒ 2000 – ℰ 03 216 50 62 — Plan: **C3**
– www.ferrier-30.be – closed Wednesday
Carte 38/65 € – *(open until 11pm)*

• Italian • Design •

The best Italian restaurant in the area is doubtless Ferrier 30. The meat, fish and pasta dishes (lasagne al ragu, taglioni con prosciutto) are all steeped in authentic Italian flavours and are further enhanced by wines brought back by the owner in person.

Het Gerecht

XX 帝 ⇔

Amerikalei 20 ☒ 2000 – ℰ 03 248 79 28 — Plan: **D3**
– www.hetgerecht.be – closed 31 March-16 April, 15 July-6 August, 24 December-8 January, 12-19 February, Wednesday dinner, Saturday lunch, Sunday and Monday
Menu 30 € (lunch), 56/68 €
– Carte 62/77 € – (set menu only at weekends)

• Market cuisine • Cosy •

This restaurant is full of character. Peggy pampers her customers while Wim treats their taste buds to his talented creations. The photos adorning the walls are Wim's handiwork, as is the French inspired cuisine, which follows the seasons. The lunch menu is great.

Jerom.

XX 帝

Graaf van Egmontstraat 39a ☒ 2000 – ℰ 0 487 70 70 70 — Plan: **E2**
– www.restaurantjerom.be – closed 9-16 April, 2-23 July, 23 December-3 January, Saturday lunch, Sunday and Monday
Menu 32 € (lunch), 39/85 € – Carte 76/93 €

• Modern French • Trendy •

Spacious and contemporary, rough yet elegant. This restaurant is both a great place to eat and eminently welcoming. Masterfully sourced ingredients, distinctive, up-to-the-minute, combinations and flawlessly balanced flavours.

BELGIUM - ANTWERP

Liang's Garden
XX 🔠 ⇔

Generaal Lemanstraat 54 ✉ *2000 –* ☎ *03 237 22 22*
Plan: **G1**
– www.liangsgarden.eu – closed Sunday
Menu 27 € (lunch), 37/72 € – Carte 33/85 €
• Chinese • Traditional décor • Classic décor •

A stalwart of Chinese cuisine in the city! A spacious restaurant where the authentic menu covers specialities from Canton (dim sum), Peking (duck) and Szechuan (fondue).

puur personal cooking
X 🔛

Edward Pecherstraat 51 ✉ *2000 –* ☎ *0 495 83 24 87*
Plan: **C3**
– www.puurpersonalcooking.be – closed last 2 weeks July, late December, Monday lunch, Saturday and Sunday
Menu 40 € (lunch)/60 € – (booking essential)
• Modern cuisine • Bistro • Intimate •

One man and his AGA oven occupy the heart of this cosy bistro. The chef develops a personal version of contemporary cuisine, focused on unadulterated flavours. A menu in which quality and passion take pride of place.

l'Amitié
X 🔛

Vlaamse Kaai 43 ✉ *2000 –* ☎ *03 257 50 05*
Plan: **C3**
– www.lamitie.net – closed 31 December-4 January, Saturday lunch, Sunday and Monday
Menu 30 € (lunch) – Carte 38/65 €
• Modern cuisine • Fashionable •

When you arrive in this fully renovated bistro, it won't be friendship, but something more akin to love that you will feel. Fish takes pride of place and the first class ingredients are prepared according to modern techniques and served in small dishes. Scrumptious!

Divin by Sepi
X 🥢 🔛

Verschansingstraat 5 ✉ *2000 –* ☎ *03 284 07 40*
Plan: **E2**
– www.divinbysepi.be – closed Saturday lunch, Tuesday and Wednesday
Menu 29 € (lunch) – Carte 57/67 €
• Mediterranean cuisine • Wine bar • Fashionable •

Sepideh Sedaghatnia first earned a name for herself as a sommelier and this wine bar is the result of her expertise! The excellent selection features a number of surprising organic vintages. The menu takes you on a whirlwind world tour of finger food and more classical dishes. Taste without pretentious frills is the guiding principle here.

L'épicerie du Cirque
X 🔠

Volkstraat 23 ✉ *2000 –* ☎ *0 32 38 05 71*
Plan: **C3**
– www.lepicerieducirque.be – closed 24 and 25 December, 2 weeks in January, Sunday and Monday
Menu 33 € (lunch), 49/95 € – Carte 62/99 €
• Creative • Fashionable • Bistro •

This 'circus grocery store' is depicted by a pure Scandinavian-inspired interior and no-frills food. The chef's creativity results in unexpected, flavoursome dishes, devoid of complex superfluity. Take some home with you by stopping off at the delicatessen store a few houses down the street.

River Kwai
X 🥢 🔠 ⇔

Vlaamse Kaai 14 ✉ *2000 –* ☎ *03 237 46 51*
Plan: **C3**
– www.riverkwai.be – closed Monday
Menu 25/49 € 🍷
– Carte 35/47 € – (dinner only except Thursday and Friday)
• Thai • Exotic décor •

This reliable restaurant has been serving authentic Thai cuisine for over 25 years. Find an attractive retro façade, dining rooms on separate floors with a typical decor, an elegant lounge and a front terrace.

Sail & Anchor ✗

Guldenvliesstraat 60 ✉ *2600 Berchem* – ✆ *0 3 430 40 04* Plan: **G3**
– www.sailandanchor.be – closed Sunday dinner, Monday and Tuesday
Menu 65/100 € *– (dinner only except Sunday) (tasting menu only)*
• Modern British • Vintage •

Forget any preconceptions you may have about British cuisine! Chef Yates of this urbane establishment works with classical ingredients (mustard, lemon), combining them into creative masterpieces. Food whose sophisticated blend of tastes and colours will both surprise and delight.

Umami ✗ 🛋 �&

Luikstraat 6 ✉ *2000* – ✆ *0 3 237 39 78* Plan: **C3**
– www.umami-antwerp.be – closed Monday and Tuesday
Menu 45/59 € – Carte 32/55 € *– (dinner only except Sunday)*
• Asian • Exotic décor •

Asian wood and lounge furniture happily rub shoulders beneath a well of light in this handsome establishment. The menu respects the house's motto - contemporary Asian cuisine. Oriental traditions with an ingenious modern twist.

Visbistro Mojo ✗ 🛋

Kasteelpleinstraat 56 ✉ *2000* – ✆ *0 3 237 49 00* Plan: **F2**
– www.visbistro-mojo.be – closed Saturday lunch, Sunday and Monday
Menu 21 € (lunch)/33 € – Carte 39/53 €
• Seafood • Bistro • Simple •

Fresh fish and shellfish are attractively displayed on the counter, bringing the promise of succulent fare. Chef Johan and his sister Nuria are determined to provide diners with excellent quality produce at reasonable prices. No frills, good wholesome food!

Firean ⊗ 🅰🅲 🚗

Karel Oomsstraat 6 ✉ *2018* – ✆ *0 3 237 02 60* Plan: **G1**
– www.hotelfirean.com
9 rm – ❗155/165 € ❗❗155/225 € – ☲ 18 €
• Luxury • Personalised •

This property full of charm occupies an Art Deco-style building (1929). It features public rooms in the style of the period, a flower-filled patio, and personalised guestrooms with antique furnishings. Impeccable service.

⃝ **Minerva** – See restaurant listing

Erik Wijstock

PRAGUE

CZECH REPUBLIC
ČESKÁ REPUBLIKA

MarekKijevsky/iStock

PRAGUE
PRAHA

satariel/iStock

PRAGUE IN...

→ **ONE DAY**
Old Town Square, the astronomical clock, Charles Bridge, Prague Castle, Petřín Hill.

→ **TWO DAYS**
Josefov, the National Theatre, Golden Lane.

→ **THREE DAYS**
Wenceslas Square, the National Museum, cross the bridge to look round Malá Strana.

Prague's history stretches back to the Dark Ages. In the ninth century a princely seat comprising a simple walled-in compound was built where the castle now stands; in the tenth century the first bridge over the Vltava arrived; and by the 13C the enchanting cobbled alley-ways below the castle were complete. But Prague has come of age and Europe's most perfectly preserved capital now proffers consumer choice as well as medieval marvels. Its state-of-the-art shopping malls and pulsing nightlife bear testament to its popularity with tourists – the iron glove of communism long since having given way to western consumerism. These days there are practically two

versions of Prague: the lively, youthful, 'stag party capital', and the sedate, enchanting 'city of a hundred spires'.

The four main zones of Prague were originally independent towns in their own right. The river Vltava winds its way through their heart and is spanned by the iconic Charles Bridge. On the west side lie Hradcany – the castle quarter, built on a rock spur – and Malá Strana, Prague's most perfectly preserved district, located at the bottom of the castle hill. Over the river are Staré Město, the old town with its vibrant medieval square and outer boulevards, and Nové Město, the new town, which is the city's commercial heart and where you'll find Wenceslas Square and Prague's young partygoers.

EATING OUT

Since the late 1980s, Prague has undergone a bit of a foodie revolution. Global menus have become common currency and the heavy, traditional Czech cuisine is now often served – in the better establishments – with a creative flair and an international touch. Lunch is the main meal of the Czech day and many restaurants close well before midnight. Prague was and still is, to an extent, famous for its infinite variety of dumplings – these were the glutinous staple that saw locals through the long years of stark Communist rule. The favoured local dish is still pork, pickled cabbage and dumplings, and those on a budget can also mix the likes of schnitzel, beer and ginger cake for a ridiculously cheap outlay. Some restaurants include a tip in your final bill, so check closely to make sure you don't tip twice. Czechs consume more beer than anyone else in the world and there are some excellent microbrewery tipples to be had.

La Degustation Bohême Bourgeoise (Oldřich Sahajdák)

Haštalská 18 ⊠ 110 00 – ⓜ Náměsti Republiky   XX ❀ ⓚ ⅙
– ☏ 222 311 234 – www.ladegustation.cz – Closed   Plan: **G1**
1 week January, 24 December and Monday
Menu 3450 CZK – (dinner only) (booking essential) (tasting menu only)
• Modern cuisine • Intimate • Fashionable •
It might be set in a historic building at the end of a narrow lane, but this restaurant is surprisingly stylish, with bespoke chandeliers hung above tables inlaid with slices of oak. Marie B Svobodová's 19C cookery school provides the inspiration for creative modern dishes which stimulate the taste buds.
→ Cauliflower, parsley mayonnaise and potatoes. Catfish, fermented vegetables and almonds. Yoghurt, potatoes and berries.

Field (Radek Kašpárek)   XX ⓚ ⅙

U Milosrdných 12 ⊠ 110 00 – ⓜ Staroměstská   Plan: **G1**
– ☏ 222 316 999 – www.fieldrestaurant.cz – Closed 24-26 December and
1 January
Menu 3200 CZK – Carte 1160/1230 CZK – (booking essential)
• Modern cuisine • Design • Friendly •
Two friends run this stylishly understated restaurant, which has a warm, intimate feel. An eye-catching mural is projected overhead and the well-balanced Scandinavian cooking is equally stimulating. Alongside wine pairings are non-alcoholic drink matches, such as tomato, cucumber and chilli juice.
→ Cod, artichoke, cucumber and seaweed. Heifer, kohlrabi, shallot and mustard. Strawberry, straw, rose and elderflower.

Divinis   XX ⓚ ⅙

Týnská 21 ⊠ 110 00 – ⓜ Náměsti Republiky   Plan: **G1**
– ☏ 222 325 440 – www.divinis.cz – Closed 2 weeks August, 24-
26 December and Sunday
Carte 865/1435 CZK – (dinner only) (booking essential)
• Italian • Friendly •
You'll find this intimate, homely restaurant tucked away on a side street; it's run with great passion and has a friendly feel. Rustic, seasonal Italian dishes have original touches and are cooked with flair. The perfect accompaniment comes in the form of a large collection of wines from Italian growers.

Bistrōt 104   X ⌂ ⓚ

Korunni 104 ⊠ 10100 – ⓜ Jiřiho z Poděbrad   Plan I: **C2**
– ☏ 272 660 837 – www.bistrot.cz – Closed Sunday and Monday
Menu 350/990 CZK – Carte 395/715 CZK
• Modern cuisine • Minimalist • Design •
A vast, quasi-industrial former retail unit dominated by a large open kitchen and run with considerable passion. The cooking is influenced by the New Nordic kitchen; produce is well-sourced and dishes uncluttered. It offers exceptional value.

Eska   X ⌂ ⓚ ⅙ ☷

Pernerova 49, Karlín ⊠ 186 00 – ⓜ Křižíkova   Plan I: **C1**
– ☏ 731 140 884 – www.eska.ambi.cz – Closed 24 December
Carte 385/1151 CZK
• Czech • Design • Fashionable •
A café, bakery and restaurant in a converted fabric factory. The dining room has a stark, industrial feel with exposed bricks, pipework and girders, and the open kitchen adds to the buzz. Old family favourites are given modern makeovers; much use is made of traditional techniques like marinating and fermenting.

Sansho
X ⌂ 🏵

Petrská 25 ⊠ 110 00 – ⓜ Florenc – ℰ 222 317 425
– www.sansho.cz – Closed Christmas, 31 December, Saturday lunch,
Sunday and Monday
Menu 1100 CZK (dinner) – Carte 510/890 CZK – *(booking essential at dinner)*
• Asian • Neighbourhood • Simple •

A fun neighbourhood eatery that uses organic and free range ingredients from the owner's butcher's shop. Dishes have an Asian base and could include the likes of soft shell crab sliders or dry sweet pork with coconut rice and papaya; at dinner, they serve a 6 course tasting menu. Some tables are for sharing.

Maso A Kobliha
🏠 ⌂

Petrská 23 ⊠ 110 00 – ⓜ Florenc – ℰ 224 815 056
– www.masoakobliha.cz – Closed Christmas, Sunday and Monday
Carte 305/475 CZK
• Traditional British • Neighbourhood • Pub •

Behind the butcher's counter of "Meat and Doughnuts" is a bright, fashionable bar. Try a local beer from the 'kegerator' alongside a gutsy, classical dish smoked on-site; the scotch eggs and custard-filled doughnuts are must-tries. Stop at the counter on your way out to buy some fresh free range meat.

Alcron – Radisson Blu Alcron Hotel
XxX ⴵ 🏵 ⇿ 🅿

Štepánská 40 ⊠ 110 00 – ⓜ Muzeum – ℰ 222 820 000
– www.alcron.cz – Closed Saturday lunch and Sunday
Menu 1500/2600 CZK – *(booking essential)*
• Modern cuisine • Intimate • Vintage •

An intimate, semi-circular restaurant dominated by an art deco mural of dancing couples by Tamara de Lempicka. Choose 'hot' or 'cold' dishes from an elaborate international menu. There's a good choice of wines and staff are attentive.

Aromi
XX 🏵 ⌂ 🏵 ⇿ 🐾

Náměstí Míru 6 ⊠ 120 00 – ⓜ Náměstí Míru
– ℰ 222 713 222 – www.aromi.lacollezione.cz
Menu 345 CZK (weekday lunch) – Carte 995/1155 CZK
• Italian • Brasserie • Neighbourhood •

A friendly team welcomes you to this bright modern restaurant. Simply prepared, classically based Italian dishes are given modern touches; the fresh fish display demonstrates the owners' commitment to sourcing good quality produce.

Bellevue
XX ⩽ 🏵 🏵 ⇿ ⇿

Smetanovo Nábreží 18 ⊠ 110 00 – ⓜ Staroměstská
– ℰ 222 221 443 – www.bellevuerestaurant.cz – Closed 24 December
Menu 1680 CZK – Carte 1245/1885 CZK – *(booking essential at dinner)*
• Modern cuisine • Chic • Contemporary décor •

Sit on the pleasant terrace or in the contemporary, pastel-hued dining room of this elegant 19C townhouse and take in the view over Charles Bridge and the river. Ambitious, original modern dishes consist of many different elements.

Café Imperial – Hotel Imperial
XX 🏵 ⇿

Na Porící 15 ⊠ 110 00 – ⓜ Náměsti Republiky
– ℰ 246 011 440 – www.cafeimperial.cz
Carte 579/863 CZK – *(booking essential)*
• Traditional cuisine • Grand café • Vintage •

The Imperial hotel's restaurant is an impressive room, with a high ceiling and colourful mosaic-tiled walls and pillars. Menus list robust Czech dishes. It was the place to be seen in the 1920s and, as they say, Kafka's spirit lives on...

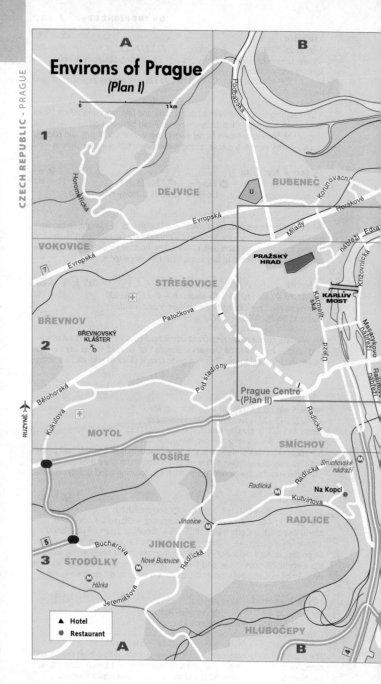

Environs of Prague
(Plan I)

0   1 km

RUZYNĚ ➤

DEJVICE

BUBENEČ

Podbabská

Korunovacní

Horoměřická

Evropská

Hotákové

VOKOVICE

Evropská

7

STŘEŠOVICE

Mlady

PRAŽSKÝ HRAD

nábřeží Edva

Křižovnická

Karmelit-ská

KARLŮV MOST

BŘEVNOV

Patočkova

Masarykovo nábřeží

U

BŘEVNOVSKÝ KLÁŠTER

2

pzeľn

Rašínovo nábřeží

Bělohorská

Pod stadiony

Kukulova

Prague Centre (Plan II)

Radlická

MOTOL

SMÍCHOV

KOŠÍŘE

Smíchovské nádraží

Radlická

Radlická

Na Kopci

Jinonice

Kutvirtova

RADLICE

Bucharova

5

JINONICE

Radlická

3

STODŮLKY

Nové Butovice

Hůrka

Jeremiášova

HLUBOČEPY

▲ Hotel

● Restaurant

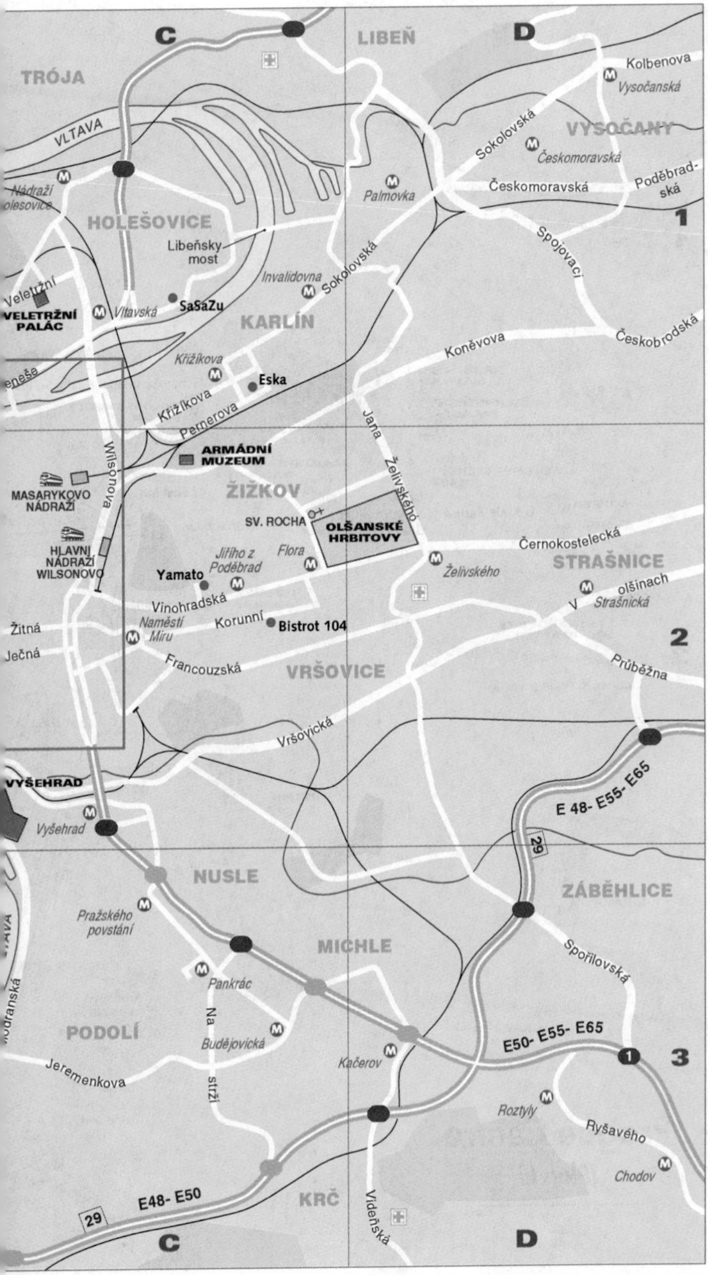
C
D
LIBEŇ
TRÓJA
VLTAVA
Kolbenova
Vysočanská
VYSOČANY
Sokolovská
Českomoravská
Českomoravská
Poděbrad-
ská
Palmovka
Nádraží
Holešovice
HOLEŠOVICE
Libeňsky
most
Spojovací
1
Invalidovna
Sokolovská
Veletržní
VELETRŽNÍ
PALÁC
Vltavská
SaSaZu
KARLÍN
Českobrodská
Koněvova
Křižíkova
Eska
Křižíkova
Pernerova
Jana
Želivského
Wilsonova
ARMÁDNÍ
MUZEUM
MASARYKOVO
NÁDRAŽÍ
ŽIŽKOV
SV. ROCHA
OLŠANSKÉ
HRBITOVY
HLAVNÍ
NÁDRAŽÍ
WILSONOVO
Jiřího z
Poděbrad
Flora
Černokostelecká
STRAŠNICE
Želivského
Yamato
V olšinach
Strašnická
Vinohradská
Žitná
Naměstí
Míru
Korunní
Bistrot 104
2
Ječná
Francouzská
VRŠOVICE
Průběžna
Vršovická
VYŠEHRAD
E 48- E55- E65
Vyšehrad
29
NUSLE
ZÁBĚHLICE
Pražského
povstání
MICHLE
Spořilovská
Pankrác
Na
strži
PODOLÍ
Budějovická
E50- E55- E65
1
3
Jeremenkova
Kačerov
Roztyly
Ryšavého
Chodov
29
E48- E50
KRČ
Vídeňská
C
D

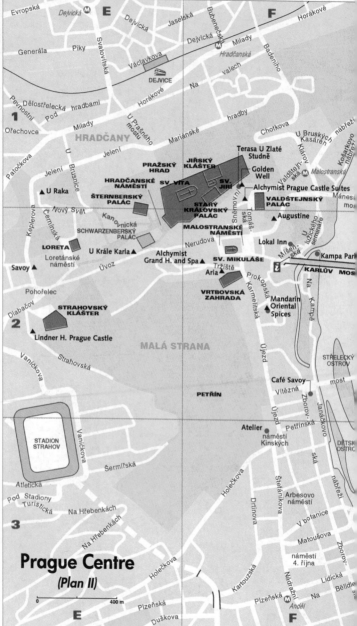

Evropská Dejvická Ⓜ **E** Dejvická Jaselská **F** Horákové

Generála Piky Svatovítská Dejvická Milady
Bubenečská Ⓜ Baderiho
Václavkova Hradčanská
🚉 DEJVICE Na valech

Pevnostní Dělostřelecká hradbami Horákové hradby

Ořechovce Pod Milady U Prašného mostu Mariánské Chotkova

Patočkova **HRADČANY** U Brusských Kasáren nábřeží
Jelení Klárov Kosárkovo
nábřeží

Jelení **PRAŽSKÝ** **JIŘSKÝ** Terasa U Zlaté
Brusnice **HRAD** **KLÁŠTER** Studně
▲ U Raka **HRADČANSKÉ** **SV. VÍTA** **SV.** Golden
Keplerova **NÁMĚSTÍ** **JIŘÍ** Well
Nový Svět **ŠTERNBERSKÝ** Alchymist Prague Castle Suites
Černínská **PALÁC** **STARÝ** **VALDŠTEJNSKÝ** Mánes
Kanovnická **KRÁLOVSKÝ** **PALÁC** mos
SCHWARZENBERSKÝ **PALÁC**
PALÁC **MALOSTRANSKÉ** ▲ Augustine
NÁMĚSTÍ
LORETA U Krále Karla ▲ Nerudova Lokal Inn
Loretánské Alchymist Míšeňská Kampa Park
Savoy ▲ náměstí Úvoz **Grand H. and Spa** ▲ **SV. MIKULÁŠE** Ž **KARLŮV MOS**
Tržiště
Aria ▲ Prokopská Na Kampě Mandarin Oriental Spices

Pohořelec **VRTBOVSKÁ**
Dlabačov **ZAHRADA** Karmelitská
STRAHOVSKÝ
KLÁŠTER

▲ Lindner H. Prague Castle **MALÁ STRANA**

Vaníčkova Strahovská STŘELECKÝ
OSTROV
Café Savoy most
PETŘÍN Vítězná
Újezd Zborov- Janáčkovo

STADION Atelier Petřínská DĚTSKÍ
STRAHOV náměstí ská OSTRO
Kinských
Šermířská Štefánikova nábřeží

Atletická Holečkova Arbesovo
Pod Stadiony náměstí
Turistická Na Hřebenkách Drtinova V botanice
Na Hřebenkách Matoušova
Kartouzská náměstí Zborov-
4. října
Prague Centre Holečkova Lidická
(Plan II) Plzeňská Ⓜ Na Bělidle
0 ——— 400 m Plzeňská Anděl
E Duškova **F**

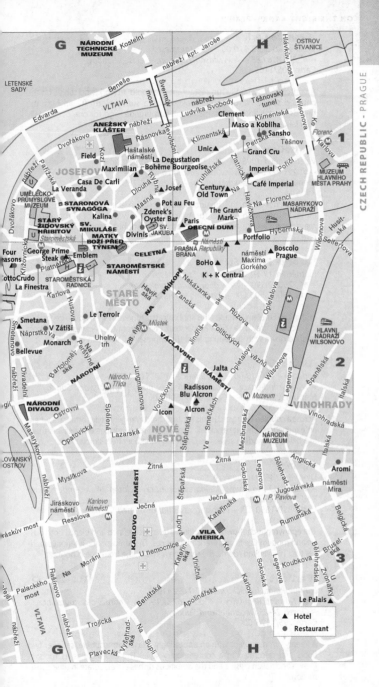

Hotel
Restaurant

CZECH REPUBLIC - PRAGUE

†○ **Casa De Carli** XX 斎 🗚 ⇆ ⇄
Vezenskská 5 ✉ *110 00 –* Ⓜ *Staroměstská* Plan: **G1**
– ☏ 224 816 688 – www.casadecarli.com – Closed Sunday
Carte 505/1165 CZK
• Italian • Friendly • Neighbourhood •
A contemporary family-run restaurant with bold artwork, and tables on the
cobbled street. Flavoursome cooking has a subtle North Italian bias; the
breads, pastas and ice creams are all homemade – go for one of the daily
specials.

†○ **CottoCrudo** – Four Seasons Hotel XX 斎 �&. 🗚 ⇄
Veleslavínova 1098/2A ✉ *110 00 –* Ⓜ *Staroměstská* Plan: **G2**
– ☏ 221 427 000 – www.fourseasons.com/prague
Menu 380 CZK (weekday lunch) – Carte 920/1800 CZK
• Italian • Elegant • Design •
Enjoy a cocktail in this luxurious hotel's stylish bar before taking a seat
either at the Crudo counter for Asian-inspired raw dishes, or in the elegant
main room, where an attentive team serve sophisticated, modern Italian
fare.

†○ **George Prime Steak** – Emblem Hotel XX 舒 &. 🗚 ⇄
Platnéřská 19 ✉ *110 00 –* Ⓜ *Staroměstská* Plan: **G2**
– ☏ 226 202 599 – www.georgeprimesteak.com
Carte 1500/3500 CZK – *(booking essential at dinner)*
• Meats and grills • Fashionable •
Within the Emblem hotel sits this sophisticated American steakhouse decorated
in black and grey. The USDA Prime steak comes from the Midwest and is best
washed down with something from the impressive Californian wine list.

†○ **Grand Cru** XX 舒 斎 &. 🗚 ⇄
Lodecká 4 ✉ *110 00 –* Ⓜ *Florenc – ☏ 775 044 076* Plan: **H1**
– www.grand-cru.cz – Closed 24-26 December, 1 January and Sunday
Menu 450/1300 CZK – Carte 900/1500 CZK
• Modern cuisine • Fashionable • Elegant •
Across a cobbled courtyard is this sophisticated orangery-style restaurant where
an experienced chef takes classic Czech and French recipes and delivers them
in a balanced modern style. The charming wine bar offers simpler fare.

†○ **Kalina** XX 🗚 ⇄
Dlouhá 12 ✉ *110 00 –* Ⓜ *Staroměstská* Plan: **G1**
*– ☏ 222 317 715 – www.kalinarestaurant.cz – Closed 24 December dinner
and 25 December*
Carte 850/1850 CZK – *(booking essential at dinner)*
• Modern cuisine • Intimate •
The eponymous chef-owner's cooking is gutsy yet refined and blends both classic and modern Czech and French influences. The atmospheric interior comprises two 16C vaulted rooms: the rear one is cosier, the front one is brighter.

†○ **Portfolio** XX 舒 🗚 ⇆ ⇄
Lannův Palác, Havlíčkova 1030/1 ✉ *110 00* Plan: **H1**
– Ⓜ *Náměsti Republiky – ☏ 224 267 579 – www.portfolio-restaurant.cz*
– Closed 24-25 December and Sunday
Carte 795/1175 CZK
• Modern cuisine • Contemporary décor • Design •
A keenly run restaurant with an appealingly relaxed atmosphere, set over two
floors and decorated in a contemporary style. The cooking has its roots in
French and Italian cuisine and the ambitious dishes are elaborate in their const-
ruction.

CZECH REPUBLIC - PRAGUE

𝐢○ **Pot au Feu** XX AC ⇔
Plan: **G1**
Rybná 13 ⊠ 110 00 – Ⓜ *Náměstí Republiky
–* 𝒫 *739 654 884 – www.potaufeu.cz – Closed Christmas, Easter, Saturday lunch and Sunday*
Menu 495/995 CZK (weekdays) – Carte 615/1235 CZK – *(bookings advisable at dinner)*
• French • Intimate •
The chef-owner's cooking is inspired by the French classics but also by his travels. The intimate interior comes with striking artwork and shelves packed with directly sourced French wines. Service is relaxed yet clued-up.

𝐢○ **Le Terroir** XX 𝄢 🏠 AC ⇔
Plan: **G2**
*Vejvodova 1 (Entrance from Jilskà Street) ⊠ 110 00
–* Ⓜ *Můstek –* 𝒫 *602 889 118 – www.leterroir.cz – Closed Sunday and Monday*
Menu 395/1495 CZK – Carte 635/1035 CZK
• French • Romantic • Intimate •
An intimate, atmospheric 12C cellar with a vaulted ceiling. The kitchen takes classic French dishes like frogs' legs, snails, beef Bourguignon and coq au vin and adds its own contemporary touches. The French wine list is excellent.

𝐢○ **La Veranda** XX AC ⇔
Plan: **G1**
Elišky Krásnohorské 2 ⊠ 110 00 – Ⓜ *Staroměstská
–* 𝒫 *224 814 733 – www.laveranda.cz – Closed 24 December and Sunday*
Carte 585/1155 CZK
• Mediterranean cuisine • Cosy • Friendly •
Sit surrounded by books in the colourfully decorated main room or head down to the intimate basement. Cooking takes its inspiration from the Med, with Italy playing a big part. Staff are friendly and welcoming.

𝐢○ **V Zátiši** XX AC ⇔
Plan: **G2**
Liliová 1, Betlémské Nám. ⊠ 110 00 – Ⓜ *Můstek
–* 𝒫 *222 221 155 – www.zatisi.cz – Closed 24 December*
Menu 990/1190 CZK – *(booking essential at dinner)*
• Modern cuisine • Cosy • Contemporary décor •
This modern city centre restaurant is a popular spot. Its name means 'timeless' and with its clever blend of modern Czech and Indian dishes, well-judged spicing and attractive presentation, it looks set to stand up to its name.

𝐢○ **Yamato** XX AC
Plan I: **C2**
U Kanálky 14 ⊠ 120 00 – Ⓜ *Jiřiho z Poděbrad
–* 𝒫 *222 212 617 – www.yamato.cz – Closed Christmas, Saturday lunch and Sunday*
Menu 1390 CZK (dinner) – Carte 505/4000 CZK – *(booking essential at dinner)*
• Japanese • Elegant • Friendly •
The chef is a local but he trained in Japan, so alongside an array of authentic dishes you'll find some original creations. A selection of Japanese beers and whiskies complement the cooking, and the place is run with real passion.

𝐢○ **La Finestra** X 𝄢 AC ⇔
Plan: **G2**
Platnérská 13 ⊠ 110 00 – Ⓜ *Staroměstská
–* 𝒫 *222 325 325 – www.lafinestra.cz*
Carte 985/1145 CZK – *(booking essential at dinner)*
• Italian • Rustic • Cosy •
You'd never guess but from 1918-1945, this lovely restaurant with its red-brick vaulted ceiling was an Alfa Romeo showroom! Expect rustic Italian dishes and fine Italian wines, and be sure to stop-off at their neighbouring shop.

113

CZECH REPUBLIC - PRAGUE

‖○ **Monarch** 🍴 🎋 AC ⟷

Na Perštýně 15 ✉ *110 00 –* Ⓜ *Můstek –* 𝒞 *224 239 602*   Plan: **G2**
– www.monarch.cz – Closed 24-26 December and 1 January
Menu 150/1200 CZK – Carte 465/1555 CZK
• Czech • Traditional décor • Friendly •

The baby sister of Grand Cru has a relaxed, pub-like atmosphere, a large bar and liberal use of black in its decoration. The kitchen, visible through a large hatch, focuses on traditional Czech cooking, with steaks a speciality.

‖○ **Zdenek's Oyster Bar** 🍴 🎋 AC

Malá Štupartská 5 ✉ *110 00 –* Ⓜ *Náměsti Republiky*   Plan: **G1**
– 𝒞 *725 946 250 – www.oysterbar.cz – Closed 24-25 December*
Carte 1685/2855 CZK
• Seafood • Bistro • Wine bar •

Deep in the heart of the city is this atmospheric, dimly lit restaurant with a pretty pavement terrace. Menus include tapas, caviar, elaborate seafood platters, dishes from the Josper grill and, of course, 8 different types of oyster.

🏨 **Four Seasons**   🛁 ⊕ 🛠 🕭 AC ⟷ 🛎

Veleslavínova 1098/2A ✉ *101 00 –* Ⓜ *Staroměstská*   Plan: **G2**
– 𝒞 *221 427 777 – www.fourseasons.com/prague*
157 rm – ♦7600/13600 CZK ♦♦7600/13600 CZK – ⊡ 960 CZK – 19 suites
• Grand Luxury • Contemporary • Elegant •

This characterful waterside hotel has an understated elegance which sits well with its baroque and Renaissance features. Luxurious bedrooms are designed by Pierre-Yves Rochon; the best are duplex suites with river and castle views. Be sure to find time to unwind in the smart riverside spa.
‖○ **CottoCrudo** – See restaurant listing

🏨 **Boscolo Prague** 🕸 🛁 ⊕ 🛠 ◫ AC ⟷ 🛎 🚗

Senovážné Nám. 13 ✉ *110 00 –* Ⓜ *Náměsti Republiky*   Plan: **H2**
– 𝒞 *224 593 111 – www.boscolohotels.com*
152 rm ⊡ **–** ♦3270/8830 CZK ♦♦3815/9420 CZK – 6 suites
• Grand Luxury • Historic • Elegant •

This impressive former bank features neo-Renaissance style pillars, a stunning marble lobby and a smart Roman spa and pool. Each of the luxurious bedrooms is unique in shape and style; those in the older building are the biggest. The elegant Salon restaurant serves a mix of Czech and international dishes.

🏨 **Le Palais** 🕸 🛁 ⊕ 🛠 🕭 AC ⟷ 🛎 🚗

U Zvonarky 1 ✉ *120 00 –* Ⓜ *I. P. Pavlova*   Plan: **H3**
– 𝒞 *234 634 111 – www.lepalaishotel.eu*
72 rm ⊡ **–** ♦3180/6750 CZK ♦♦3915/8640 CZK – 8 suites
• Townhouse • Luxury • Elegant •

The stylish bedrooms of this 19C mansion come with luxurious pink marble bathrooms and the terrace of the classical dining room has a wonderful outlook. The hotel has one of the largest private collections of Le Corbusier lithographs, along with works by Czech artists Miloš Reindl and Pavel Skalnik.

🏨 **Radisson Blu Alcron** 🕸 🛁 🛠 🕭 AC ⟷ 🛎 🚗

Štepánská 40 ✉ *110 00 –* Ⓜ *Muzeum –* 𝒞 *222 820 000*   Plan: **H2**
– www.radissonblu.com/en/hotel-prague
204 rm ⊡ **–** ♦4100/7200 CZK ♦♦4700/7800 CZK – 12 suites
• Luxury • Business • Elegant •

The art deco features of this imposing 1930s building are superb and its original white and green marble floor has been meticulously maintained. Bedrooms are warmly decorated and well-equipped. La Rotonde has a pleasant summer terrace and serves international and Czech cuisine; Alcron offers modern tasting dishes.
‖○ **Alcron** – See restaurant listing

BoHo

Senovázná 4 ✉ *110 00* – **Ⓜ** *Náměsti Republiky*
– 𝒞 *234 622 600* – www.hotelbohoprague.com
57 rm ☐ – **†**3105/5715 CZK **††**3627/7803 CZK
• Boutique hotel • Luxury • Design •

Its original staircase and mosaic floors are still on display but this former newspaper office now has an understated designer feel. Spanish-inspired bedrooms feature luxurious glass cube bathrooms. The well-stocked library and chic wellness centre make the perfect oases. Light dishes are served in the evening.

Century Old Town

Na Porící 7 ✉ *110 00* – **Ⓜ** *Náměsti Republiky*
– 𝒞 *221 800 800* – www.accorhotels.com
169 rm – **†**2200/6800 CZK **††**2200/6800 CZK – ☐ 485 CZK – 2 suites
• Business • Historic • Contemporary •

Franz Kafka's spirit can be felt throughout this appealing business hotel, which was formerly the Workmen's Accident Insurance Institute HQ – Kafka's place of work from 1908 to 1922. Contemporary bedrooms have compact, shower-only bathrooms. Dine in the courtyard, from an international menu.

The Grand Mark

Hybernská 12 ✉ *110 00* – **Ⓜ** *Náměsti Republiky*
– 𝒞 *226 226 135* – www.grandmark.cz
75 rm – **†**6700/13300 CZK **††**6700/13300 CZK – ☐ 690 CZK – 62 suites
• Historic • Grand luxury • Contemporary •

A striking 200 year old listed building with a glass-topped atrium, a baroque archway and lovely courtyard gardens. Pass the top-hatted doorman into the sleek, modern interior filled with contemporary art. Many of the bedrooms are suites with kitchenettes. The restaurant has a cool, elegant feel and a modern menu.

Imperial

Na Porící 15 ✉ *110 00* – **Ⓜ** *Náměsti Republiky*
– 𝒞 *246 011 600* – www.hotel-imperial.cz
126 rm ☐ – **†**2610/7830 CZK **††**2610/7830 CZK – 1 suite
• Business • Vintage • Historic •

The cubist-style façade dates from 1914 and the characterful interior features exquisite art deco mosaics (the building is a listed Czech National Monument). Dark wood furnished bedrooms combine retro styling with modern comforts.
ⓘ⃝ **Café Imperial** – See restaurant listing

Jalta

Václavské Nám. 45 ✉ *110 00* – **Ⓜ** *Muzeum*
– 𝒞 *222 822 111* – www.hoteljalta.com
94 rm ☐ – **†**2750/9250 CZK **††**2750/9250 CZK – 5 suites
• Business • Historic • Elegant •

There's a real sense of history here, from the original staircase and doors leading out onto the balcony which overlooks Wenceslas Square, to the UNESCO listed façade and the nuclear bunker in the basement, which is now a museum! The chic restaurant unusually blends Mediterranean dishes with sushi.

Paris

U Obecního domu 1 ✉ *110 00* – **Ⓜ** *Náměsti Republiky*
– 𝒞 *222 195 195* – www.hotel-paris.cz
86 rm ☐ – **†**4600/11000 CZK **††**4600/11000 CZK – 3 suites
• Historic building • Elegant • Art déco •

The Paris hotel is an impressive neo-gothic building with art nouveau styling and plenty of characterful original features. Pieces from the family-owners' art collection line the corridors, and the Tower Suite has a fantastic 360° view. Dine in the Parisian café or amongst mosaic pillars in the restaurant.

Plan: **H2**

Plan: **H1**

Plan: **H2**

Plan: **H1**

Plan: **H2**

Plan: **H1**

Emblem

Platnéřská 19 ⊠ *110 00 –* Ⓜ *Staroměstská*   Plan: **G2**
– ℰ 226 202 500 – www.emblemprague.com
59 rm � *–* ♟4700/7000 CZK ♟♟5200/7800 CZK – 2 suites
• Boutique hotel • Design • Contemporary •
It might be housed within a 1907 property but inside you'll find a stylish designer hotel with a private members club in the basement. Head to the lounge to check in, then up to one of the sleek, modern bedrooms with oak flooring and walnut desks. Specially commissioned abstract art hangs in the hallways.
🍴 **George Prime Steak** – See restaurant listing

Icon

V Jámě 6 ⊠ *110 00 Praha –* Ⓜ *Můstek*   Plan: **G2**
– ℰ 221 634 100 – www.iconhotel.eu
31 rm ⊒ *–* ♟2000/6000 CZK ♟♟2000/8000 CZK – 2 suites
• Business • Modern • Design •
This centrally located hotel has a relaxed feel and is run by a friendly, helpful team. The 'chill-out' lounge is hung with contemporary Czech art and stylish bedrooms feature Hästens beds and biometric safes. An international vibe comes courtesy of a tapas bar and a small Thai massage centre.

Josef

Rybná 20 ⊠ *110 00 –* Ⓜ *Náměsti Republiky*   Plan: **G1**
– ℰ 221 700 111 – www.hoteljosef.com
109 rm ⊒ *–* ♟3300/16500 CZK ♟♟3300/16500 CZK
• Townhouse • Design • Minimalist •
A modern boutique hotel comprising two buildings linked by a courtyard garden. Bedrooms are smart and design-led, and there's an attractive rooftop gym and sauna. The in-house bakery means that breakfast is a real treat.

K + K Central

Hybernská 10 ⊠ *110 00 –* Ⓜ *Náměsti Republiky*   Plan: **H2**
– ℰ 225 022 000 – www.kkhotels.com
127 rm ⊒ *–* ♟2800/5800 CZK ♟♟2800/5800 CZK – 1 suite
• Business • Historic • Contemporary •
A smart hotel with a wonderful art nouveau façade dating from 1901, a glass conference room occupying what was once a theatre, and a spa featuring bas-relief Asian-themed imagery, as it's located in the theatre's old Orient Bar.

Maximilian

Haštalská 14 ⊠ *110 00 –* Ⓜ *Náměsti Republiky*   Plan: **G1**
– ℰ 225 303 111 – www.maximilianhotel.com
71 rm ⊒ *–* ♟3500/8700 CZK ♟♟4000/9300 CZK – 1 suite
• Business • Modern • Minimalist •
Maximilian is set in a peaceful area and comes with an Asian massage studio, comfy contemporary bedrooms and two brightly furnished lounges – one with an honesty bar. Unusually, you can request a goldfish for the duration of your stay!

Smetana

20 Smetanovo Nabrezi ⊠ *110 00 –* Ⓜ *Staroměstská*   Plan: **G2**
– ℰ 234 705 111 – www.smetanahotel.com
48 rm *–* ♟5875/10250 CZK ♟♟7450/11800 CZK *–* ⊒ 590 CZK – 28 suites
• Townhouse • Historic building • Elegant •
Formerly called Pachtuv Palace, this beautiful 18C residence sits by the river and has a charming baroque style. Most of the spacious, elegant bedrooms are suites with antique furnishings and mosaic-tiled bathrooms; ask for one with a view. Elegant Atelier Kalina serves modern French cuisine.

🏨 **Unic**   ☆ 🕭 📾 ⇜
Soukenická 25 ⊠ 110 00 – ⓜ *Náměstí Republiky*   Plan: **H1**
– ℰ 222 312 521 – www.hotel-unic.cz
90 rm ⬚ – **i**2325/6560 CZK **ii**2600/6835 CZK – 8 suites
• Business • Contemporary • Grand luxury •

This 19C townhouse conceals a stylish design hotel with subtle Spanish influences. Relax in the library-lounge or bright, laid-back bar, then enjoy modern versions of classic Czech dishes in the spacious restaurant. The smartly restored staircase leads up to sleek, contemporary bedrooms.

🏠 **Clement**   🕭 📾 ⇜ ♨
Klimentská 30 ⊠ 110 00 – ⓜ *Náměstí Republiky*   Plan: **H1**
– ℰ 222 314 350 – www.hotelclement.cz
76 rm ⬚ – **i**2050/4550 CZK **ii**2250/4700 CZK – 1 suite
• Business • Traditional • Functional •

This former office building is close to the river and the city centre. Bedrooms are modern and functional; the Superior rooms with their bold red and black colour schemes are worth paying extra for – some also have panoramic windows.

ON THE LEFT BANK   **PLAN II**

☺ **Na Kopci**   ❌ 🕭 📾 ⇜ **P**
K Závěrce 2774/20 ⊠ 150 00 – ⓜ *Smíchovské Nádraží*   Plan I: **B3**
– ℰ 251 553 102 – www.nakopci.com – Closed Christmas
Carte 535/805 CZK – *(booking essential)*
• Traditional cuisine • Bistro • Simple •

Leave the city behind and escape to this buzzy bistro, whose name means 'on the hill'. The wallpaper is a montage of pictures of the owner's family, and the atmosphere is warm and welcoming. You can't book for lunch and by 12pm it's packed. Flavoursome Czech and French dishes are accompanied by local beers.

🍽 **Terasa U Zlaté Studně** – Golden Well Hotel   ❌❌ ≼ 🕭 📾 ⇜
U Zlaté Studně 166/4 ⊠ 118 00 – ⓜ *Malostranská*   Plan: **F1**
– ℰ 257 533 322 – www.terasauzlatestudne.cz – Closed 10-19 January
Menu 790/1500 CZK – Carte 1120/2460 CZK – *(booking essential)*
• Classic cuisine • Cosy • Elegant •

This long-standing restaurant opened in 1901 and, in fact, predates the hotel it sits atop. The intimate room has blue and gold walls and a picture window, while above is a heated terrace with a stunning panoramic view. The classic international menu displays influences ranging from the Med through to Asia.

🍽 **Kampa Park**   ❌❌ ≼ 🕭 📾 ⇜
Na Kampe 8b, Malá Strana ⊠ 118 00   Plan: **F2**
– ⓜ *Malostranská – ℰ 257 532 685 – www.kampagroup.com – Closed lunch 25 December and 1 January*
Carte 1515/1915 CZK – *(booking essential at dinner)*
• Modern cuisine • Fashionable • Design •

Kampa Park is stunningly located by the water's edge, next to Charles Bridge. Choose from several dining areas: the best spots are the Winter Garden and the riverside terrace. The décor is contemporary, as is the interesting menu.

🍽 **SaSaZu**   ❌❌ 📾 **P**
Bubenské nábř. 306 ⊠ 170 04 – ⓜ *Vltavská*   Plan I: **C1**
– ℰ 284 097 455 – www.sasazu.com – Closed 24-25 December and lunch 1 January
Carte 615/960 CZK – *(booking essential at dinner)*
• Asian • Exotic décor • Fashionable •

You'll find this chic restaurant and bar inside a cavernous warehouse in Prague Market. The extensive menu lists dishes under their cooking techniques, with all the sweet, sour, spicy and salty flavours of Southeast Asia present.

Spices – Mandarin Oriental Hotel
XX 😋 🕏 AK ⇔

Nebovidská 459/1 ☒ 118 00 – ⓜ *Malostranská*   Plan: **F2**
– ℰ 233 088 777 – www.mandarinoriental.com/prague
Carte 795/1465 CZK – *(dinner only)*
• Asian • Intimate • Fashionable •
Softly backlit dark wood panels and decorative Chinoiserie items set the tone in this chic hotel restaurant. The pan-Asian menu is divided into three regions – Northeast, Southeast and Southwest – and there's a separate sushi list too.

Atelier
X 🕃 🕏 AK ⇔

Rošických 4 ☒ 150 00 – ⓜ *Anděl – ℰ 257 218 277*   Plan: **F3**
– www.atelieratelier.cz – Closed Sunday and Monday lunch
Menu 190 CZK (weekday lunch) – Carte 500/820 CZK
• Modern cuisine • Wine bar • Friendly •
This bright, keenly run wine-bar-cum-bistro is hidden away off the beaten track. Wines play a key role – with over 130 on offer – and the unfussy, fiercely seasonal cooking comes with clearly defined flavours and modern twists.

Café Savoy
X AK 🖢

Vítězná 5 ☒ 150 00 – ⓜ *Anděl – ℰ 257 311 562*   Plan: **F2**
– www.cafesavoy.ambi.cz – Closed 24 December
Carte 561/1345 CZK – *(booking essential)*
• Traditional cuisine • Elegant • Grand café •
This atmospheric grand café with its superb neo-renaissance ceiling has been open since 1893. Come for coffee and a cake from their patisserie, the daily lunch special and a beer, or generously sized Czech and French classics.

Lokal Inn
🕮 ⇦ 😋 🖢

Míšeňská 12 ☒ 118 00 – ⓜ *Malostranská*   Plan: **F2**
– ℰ 257 014 800 – www.lokalinn.cz – Closed Christmas
14 rm ⬓ – †1800/3600 CZK ††2000/4000 CZK   Carte 230/550 CZK
• Traditional cuisine • Pub • Rustic •
'Lokal' is the perfect name for this inn, which is set within an 18C house and offers the simple combination of Czech beer (from big steel tanks under the bar) and hearty, traditional Czech cuisine. At night they open up the atmospheric vaulted cellars, while above, large, simply furnished bedrooms await.

Mandarin Oriental
🚑 ⅙ 🕙 🕏 AK 🖢 🔧 🚗

Nebovidská 459/1 ☒ 118 00 – ⓜ *Malostranská*   Plan: **F2**
– ℰ 233 088 888 – www.mandarinoriental.com/prague
99 rm ⬓ – †6700/20500 CZK ††6700/20500 CZK – 20 suites
• Grand Luxury • Historic • Elegant •
A former monastery dating from the 14C provides the charming setting for this luxurious hotel. Chic, tastefully decorated bedrooms have goose down bedding and an Asian feel courtesy of silk bedspreads and potted orchids. Relax on the terraces or in the delightful spa which occupies the old chapel.
🖢 **Spices** – See restaurant listing

Aria
🏠 ⅙ 🕙 🕏 AK 🖢 🔧 🚗

Tržiště 9 ☒ 118 00 – ⓜ *Malostranská – ℰ 225 334 111*   Plan: **F2**
– www.ariahotel.net
51 rm ⬓ – †6350/10350 CZK ††6350/10350 CZK – 4 suites
• Luxury • Design • Themed •
A musical motif features throughout, from the mosaic music notes in the lobby and the collection of 5,000 CDs and DVDs in the music room, to the bedrooms, which are themed around composers or styles of music. The restaurant boasts a superb rooftop terrace with castle views and the piano is played nightly.

CZECH REPUBLIC - PRAGUE

Augustine

Letenská 12/33 ⊠ 118 00 – **Ⓜ** Malostranská
– ℰ 266 112 280 – www.augustinehotel.com   Plan: **F2**
101 rm – ♦8250/14200 CZK ♦♦8250/14200 CZK – ☲ 1050 CZK – 7 suites
• Historic • Grand Luxury • Design •
An impressive hotel set over 7 different buildings, including a 13C monastery. Original frescoes and vaulted ceilings remain, yet it has a contemporary look and feel. The bar occupies the old refectory and serves a custom microbrew based on the monks' original recipe. The chic restaurant serves a modern menu.

Alchymist Grand H. and Spa

Tržiště 19 ⊠ 118 00 – **Ⓜ** Malostranská – ℰ 257 286 011   Plan: **F2**
– www.alchymisthotel.com
45 rm ☲ – ♦5500/9000 CZK ♦♦5500/9000 CZK – 9 suites
• Historic • Luxury • Historic •
The Alchymist is a magnificent baroque townhouse characterised by sumptuous gilt furnishings and ostentatious styling. Bedrooms come in rich reds or blues, picked out with gold. Relax in the atmospheric Indonesian spa with its mosaic-tiled pool, then enjoy modern international dishes on the terrace.

Lindner H. Prague Castle

Strahovská 128 ⊠ 118 00 – ℰ 226 080 000   Plan: **E2**
– www.lindnerhotels.cz
138 rm – ♦2054/4940 CZK ♦♦2054/4940 CZK – ☲ 494 CZK – 3 suites
• Business • Historic • Functional •
This modern hotel is set within the UNESCO protected grounds of the Strahov Monastery and its spacious lobby-lounge was once the stables. Bedrooms feature art deco paintings; those located in the 16C part have characterful timbered ceilings. Summer BBQs use seasonings made from herbs grown in the grounds.

Savoy

Keplerova 6 ⊠ 118 00 – ℰ 224 302 430   Plan: **E2**
– www.hotelsavoyprague.com
56 rm ☲ – ♦4900/5550 CZK ♦♦4900/6250 CZK – 2 suites
• Luxury • Traditional • Elegant •
An imposing period property with professional service and a distinctly British feel, located at the top of the hill. The marble lobby leads to a clubby tartan bar and an elegant restaurant with a retractable roof and an international menu. Bedrooms are warmly decorated; each floor has a different colour scheme.

Golden Well

U Zlaté Studně 166/4 ⊠ 118 00 – **Ⓜ** Malostranská   Plan: **F1**
– ℰ 257 011 213 – www.goldenwell.cz – Closed 10-31 January
19 rm – ♦5200/10400 CZK ♦♦5200/10400 CZK – ☲ 1000 CZK – 2 suites
• Historic • Townhouse • Elegant •
A charming, intimate hotel, tucked away in a quiet cobbled street close to the Royal Gardens and Charles Bridge. Understated bedrooms have a classical style and come with antique furnishings, modern touches and fresh fruit. The roof terrace offers outstanding views over the castle and city.
⑩ **Terasa U Zlaté Studně** – See restaurant listing

Alchymist Prague Castle Suites

Sněmovní 8 ⊠ 118 00 – **Ⓜ** Malostranká   Plan: **F1**
– ℰ 257 286 960 – www.alchymistpraguecastle.com
8 rm ☲ – ♦5500/10000 CZK ♦♦5500/10000 CZK – 1 suite
• Townhouse • Elegant • Historic •
A delightful 15C house in a quiet square beneath the castle; its former owners include the architect Fanta and painter Brandl. Lavish decoration takes in chandeliers, gilt furnishings and hand-painted ceilings and wallpapers. All 8 bedrooms have butler service and dinner can be taken at the Alchymist Grand.

⌂ U Raka   ⌾ 🆎 ♿ 🅿

Cernínská 10 ✉ 118 00 – ☏ 220 511 100   Plan: **E1**
– www.hoteluraka.cz
6 rm ⌷ – †2345/2800 CZK ††3520/6250 CZK
• Family • Cosy • Traditional •

You enter through this peaceful hotel's charming cobbled terrace – which is a great spot for breakfast come summer. It's a hugely characterful place, with rustic bedrooms featuring exposed stone, tile and wood; they are decorated with old millstones and one even has its own well, along with a garden terrace.

⌂ U Krále Karla   ♿

Nerudova-Úvoz 4 ✉ 118 00 – ☏ 257 531 211   Plan: **E2**
– www.hotelukralekarla.cz
19 rm ⌷ – †1300/4000 CZK ††2345/4000 CZK
• Historic • Classic • Cosy •

Close to the castle is this Gothic-style townhouse, which was once home to a Benedictine order. Antique-furnished bedrooms are reached via an impressive stone staircase; many feature ornately painted ceilings and stained glass windows.

Aarhus

COPENHAGEN

DENMARK
DANMARK

Westersoe/iStock

COPENHAGEN
KØBENHAVN

AleksandarGeorgiev/IStock

Some cities overwhelm you, and give the impression that there's too much of them to take in. Not Copenhagen. Most of its key sights are neatly compressed within its central Slotsholmen 'island', an area that enjoyed its first golden age in the early seventeenth century in the reign of Christian IV, when it became a harbour of great consequence. It has canals on three sides and opposite the harbour is the area of Christianshavn, home of the legendary freewheeling 'free-town' community of Christiania. Further up from the centre are Nyhavn, the much-photographed canalside with brightly coloured buildings where the sightseeing cruises leave from, and the elegant

Frederiksstaden, whose wide streets contain palaces and museums. West of the centre is where Copenhageners love to hang out: the Tivoli Gardens, a kind of magical fairyland. Slightly more down-to-earth are the western suburbs of Vesterbro and Nørrebro, which were run-down areas given a street credible spit and polish for the 21C, and are now two of the trendiest districts.

Once you've idled away some time in the Danish capital, you'll wonder why anyone might ever want to leave. With its waterfronts, quirky shops and cafés, the city presents a modern, user-friendly ambience – but it also boasts world class art collections, museums, and impressive parks, gardens and lakes, all of which bear the mark of an earlier time.

EATING OUT

Fresh regional ingredients have revolutionized the menus of Copenhagen's hip restaurants and its reputation for food just keeps getting bigger. The city's dining establishments manage to marry Danish dining traditions such as herring or frikkadeller meatballs with global influences to impressive effect. So impressive that in recent times the city has earned itself more Michelin Stars, for its crisp and precise cooking, than any other in Scandinavia. Many good restaurants blend French methods and dishes with regional ingredients and innovative touches and there is a trend towards fixed price, no choice menus involving several courses, which means that dinner can be a pleasingly drawn-out affair, stretching over three or four hours. There's no need to tip, as it should be included in the cost of the meal. Danes, though, have a very good reputation as cheerful, helpful waiting staff, so you might feel like adding a bit extra. But be warned, many restaurants – and even hotels – charge between 2.5% and 5% for using a foreign credit card.

Geranium (Rasmus Kofoed) XxXX 段 ≤ & 🔟 ⇔

*Per Henrik Lings Allé 4 (8th Fl), Parken National Stadium (3 km via Dag
Hammaraskjölds Allé C1)* ✉ *2100 Ø*
*– ℰ 69 96 00 20 – www.geranium.dk – Closed 2 weeks Christmas, 2 weeks
summer and Sunday-Tuesday*
Menu 2000 DKK *– (booking essential) (surprise menu only)*
• Creative • Design • Elegant •

It might be unusually located on the 8th floor of the National Football Stadium, but with its panoramic park views, this luxurious restaurant feels as if
it is inviting the outside in. Modern techniques and the finest organic and
biodynamic ingredients are used to create beautiful, pure and balanced
dishes.

→ Lobster, fermented carrot juice & sea buckthorn. Salted hake, parsley stems
and caviar in buttermilk. Beeswax and pollen ice cream with rhubarb.

a|o|c (Søren Selin) XxX 段 ⇔

Dronningens Tvaergade 2 ✉ *1302 K*   Plan: **D2**
– Ⓜ Kongens Nytorv – ℰ 33 11 11 45 – www.restaurantaoc.dk
– Closed Christmas, 1 week February, July, Sunday and Monday
Menu 1500/1800 DKK *– (dinner only) (tasting menu only)*
• Modern cuisine • Elegant • Romantic •

A spacious, simply decorated restaurant in the vaults of an eye-catching
17C building close to Nyhavn harbour; owned and run by an experienced
sommelier. Skilful, well-judged and, at times, playful cooking has a Danish
heart and shows great originality, as well as a keen eye for detail, flavour
and texture.

→ Onion with caviar and elderflower. Roe deer with ramson butter.
Burnt artichoke with hazelnuts and caramel ice cream.

Kadeau Copenhagen (Nicolai Nørregaard) XxX

Wildersgade 10B ✉ *1408 K – Ⓜ Christianshavn*   Plan: **D3**
*– ℰ 33 25 22 23 – www.kadeau.dk – Closed 5 weeks July-
August, 1 week Christmas and Sunday-Tuesday*
Menu 1850 DKK *– (dinner only and Saturday lunch) (booking essential)
(tasting menu only)*
• Modern cuisine • Design • Fashionable •

You'll receive a warm welcome at this delightful restaurant, where the open
kitchen adds a sense of occasion to the sophisticated room. The chefs have
an innate understanding of how best to match fresh and aged produce,
and use their experience in preserving and fermenting to add many elements to each dish.

→ Garden vegetable terrine with tomato broth and cherry oil. Peas
with mint and roasted nasturtium. Smoked celeriac, white asparagus
and woodruff.

Kong Hans Kælder XxX 段 ⇔

Vingaardsstræde 6 ✉ *1070 K – Ⓜ Kongens Nytorv*   Plan: **C2**
*– ℰ 33 11 68 68 – www.konghans.dk – Closed 13-27 February, 11-
12 April, 24 July-14 August, 24-28 December, 31 December and
Sunday-Tuesday*
Menu 1700 DKK *– Carte 1115/2215 DKK – (dinner only) (booking
essential)*
• Classic French • Elegant • Intimate •

An intimate, historic restaurant in a beautiful vaulted Gothic cellar in the
heart of the city. Richly flavoured, classic French cooking uses luxury ingredients – signature dishes could include Danish Black lobster. There's a 5
course tasting menu and Gueridon trolleys add a theatrical element to proceedings.

→ Turbot with olive blanquette and black truffle. Black lobster 'à la
nage', 'thermidor' and 'à l'américaine'. Chocolate soufflé and vanilla ice
cream.

DENMARK - COPENHAGEN

Era Ora
XxX 🏵 🛋

Overgaden Neden Vandet 33B ✉ *1414 K* — Plan: **D3**
– **Ⓜ** *Christianshavn* – ✆ *32 54 06 93* – *www.era-ora.dk* – *Closed 24-26 December, 1 January, Easter Monday and Sunday*
Menu 598/1250 DKK – *(booking essential) (tasting menu only)*
• Italian • Elegant • Intimate •

Set on a quaint cobbled street by the canal, a grand, long-standing restaurant with an enclosed rear terrace and a formal air. Complex, innovative dishes feature lots of different ingredients (many imported from Italy) and are often explorative in their approach. The wine cellar boasts over 90,000 bottles.
→ Pasta with porcini and hazelnuts. Braised beef cheek, potato purée and dragon kale. Sweet plin ravioli, black tea and orange broth.

Kiin Kiin
XX 🆉 ⇔ 🕾

Guldbergsgade 21 ✉ *2200 N* – ✆ *35 35 75 55* — Plan: **A1**
– *www.kiin.dk* – *Closed Christmas and Sunday*
Menu 495/975 DKK – *(dinner only) (booking essential) (tasting menu only)*
• Thai • Exotic décor • Intimate •

A charming restaurant, whose name means 'come and eat'. Start with refined versions of street food in the moody lounge, then head for the tasteful dining room decorated with golden Buddhas and fresh flowers. Menus offer modern, personal interpretations of Thai dishes, which have vibrant flavour combinations.
→ Frozen red curry with baby lobster and coriander. Quail in coconut milk with lemongrass. Lemon and lime foam with holy basil sorbet.

Clou (Jonathan Berntsen)
XX

Øster Farimagsgade 8 ✉ *2100 K* – **Ⓜ** *Nørreport* — Plan: **C2**
– ✆ *91 92 72 30* – *www.restaurant-clou.dk* – *Closed Sunday-Tuesday*
Menu 1600 DKK – *(dinner only) (booking essential) (tasting menu only)*
• Modern cuisine • Intimate • Neighbourhood •

An intimate, suburban restaurant where you can see into the basement kitchen from the street. The tasting 'journey' of 20 dishes is designed to match 6 carefully chosen, top quality wines. Creative dishes stimulate the senses with their intense natural flavours and well-balanced contrasts in texture and taste.
→ Sea urchin and Oscietra caviar. Boudin noir with truffle and blackcurrant. Pickled fruits and cow's milk sorbet.

formel B (Kristian Arpe-Møller)
XX 🏵 🆉

Vesterbrogade 182-184, Frederiksberg (2 km on Vesterbrogade A3)
✉ *1800 C* – ✆ *33 25 10 66* – *www.formelb.dk* – *Closed 24-26 December and Sunday*
Menu 850 DKK – Carte 615/895 DKK – *(dinner only) (booking essential)*
• Modern cuisine • Fashionable • Design •

The friendly staff help to create a relaxed environment at this appealing modern restaurant, with its tree pictures and dark wood branches; ask for a table on the lower level by the kitchen if you want to get close to the action. Complex, original small plates are crafted with an assured and confident touch.
→ Langoustine 'à la nage' with Danish vegetables. Sweetbread, kale, rhubarb, horseradish and acidified cream. Sea buckthorn 'en surprise'.

Kokkeriet
XX ⇔

Kronprinsessegade 64 ✉ *1306 K* – ✆ *33 15 27 77* — Plan: **C1**
– *www.kokkeriet.dk* – *Closed 24-26 December, 1 January and Sunday*
Menu 900/1200 DKK – *(dinner only) (booking essential) (tasting menu only)*
• Modern cuisine • Intimate • Design •

A discreet, elegant corner restaurant with two narrow, atmospheric rooms decorated in black and grey and hung with a collection of contemporary art. Modern dishes keep their focus firmly on nature, while the traditional Danish flavours will evoke memories of childhood; the midweek 'test' menus are good value.
→ Scallops, green strawberries, almonds and mussel sauce. Quail with squid tart, garlic and parsley. Ice cream with apple, and brown sugar sauce.

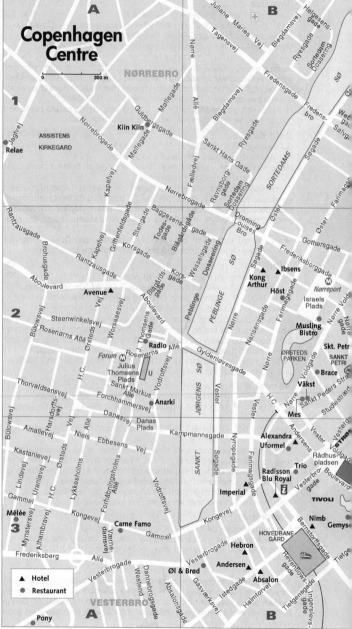

Copenhagen Centre

0   300 m

NØRREBRO

ASSISTENS KIRKEGARD

Kiin Kiin

Relae

Juliane Maries Vej

Tagensvej

Blegdamsvej

Helgesens- gade

Ryesgade

Sortedam Dossering

Fredensgade

Nørre Allé

Blegdamsvej

Ryesgade

Fredens- bro

Wei gad

Søvg.

Guldbergsgade

Møllegade

Nørrebrogade

Møllegade

Sankt Hans Gade

Fælledvej

Kapelvej

Nørrebrogade

Ramsborg- gade

Sortedam Dossering

Østergade

SORTEDAMS SØ

Øster Farimags

Rantzausgade

Brohusgade

Griffenfeldsgade

Stengade

Todes- gade

Baggesensgade

Bjelkes- gade

Dronning Louises Bro

Gothersgade

Aboulevard

Kapelvej

Rantzausgade

Korsgade

Blådsgårds gade

Wessel sgade

Dossering

PEBLINGE SØ

Søgade

Frederiksborggade

Ibsens

Kong Arthur

Øster Farimagsgade

Nørreport

Israels Plads

Nørre Vold

Avenue

Steenwinkelsvej

Bülowsvej

Rosenørns Allé

H.C. Ørsteds Vej

Worsaaesvej

J. Thomsens Gade

Åboulevard

Blågårds- gade

Korsgade

Peblinge

Nørre Søgade

Nansensgade

Høst

Musling Bistro

Nørre Voldgade

Nørre gade

Skt. Petr

Radio

Rosenørns Allé

Vodroffsvej

Gyldenløvesgade

ØRSTEDS PARKEN

SANKT PETRI

Brace

Forum

Julius Thomsens Plads

Sankt Markus Allé

Forchhammersvej

Anarki

U

Väkst

Sankt Peders Stræ

Studiestræt

Thorvaldsensvej

Harsdorffs- vej

Danasvej

Vester Søgade

H.C. Andersens

Vester Voldgade

Mes

Amalievej

Niels Ebbesens Vej

Danas Plads

Kampmanngsgade

Nyropsgade

Farimagsgade

Alexandra

Uformel

STRØ

Bülowsvej

Kastanievej

Lindevej

Uraniavej

H.C. Ørsteds

Lykkesholms Allé

Forhåbningsholms Allé

Vodroffsvej

SANKT JØRGENS SØ

Sankt Søgade

Radisson Blu Royal

Trio

Rådhus pladsen

Vesterbro gade

Vesterbro Boulevard

Mêlée

Mynstersvej

Alhambravej

Værne damsvej

Kongevej

Carne Famo

Gammel

Imperial

TIVOLI

Nimb

Gemys

Frederiksberg

Allé

Vesterbrogade

Gammel Kongevej

Vester damsvej

Hebron

HOVEDBANE GÅRD

Bernstorffsgade

Pony

VESTERBRO

Vesterbrogade

Dannebrogsgade

Westend

Øl & Brød

Gasværksvej

Absalonsvej

Istedgade

Andersen

Absalon

Haimtorvet

Tietgensgade

Ingerslevs-

Reventlowsgade

Halmtorvet

▲ Hotel

● Restaurant

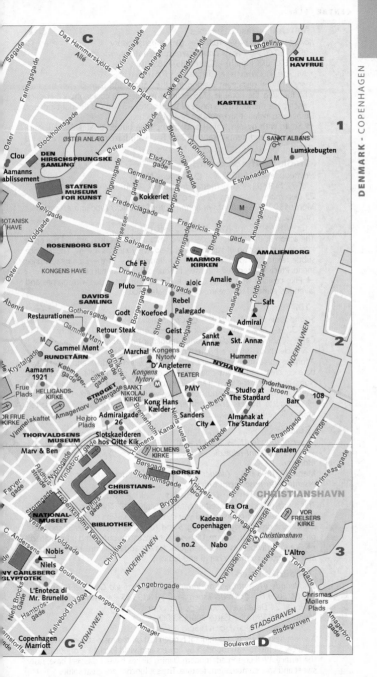

C

D

Langelinie

DEN LILLE
HAVFRUE

Dag Hammarskjölds
Allé

Kristianiagade

Østbanegade

Folke Bernadottes Allé

KASTELLET

Sogade

Farimagsgade

Stockholmsgade

Oslo Plads

Øster

ØSTER ANLÆG

Øster

Voldgade

Store Kongensgade

Grønningen

SANKT ALBANS

M

Lumskebugten

Clou

DEN
HIRSCHSPRUNGSKE
SAMLING

Aamanns
ablissement

Elsdyrs-
gade

Esplanaden

Gemersgade

gade

STATENS
MUSEUM
FOR KUNST

Rigensgade

Kokkeriet

Fredericiagade

Borgergade

Amaliegade

M

BOTANISK
HAVE

Voldgade

Sølvgade

Kronprinsesse-

Sølvgade

Fredericia-
gade

Bredgade

gade

Øster

ROSENBORG SLOT

AMALIENBORG

KONGENS HAVE

Ché Fè

MARMOR-
KIRKEN

Abenrå

Dronningens Tværgade

alolc

Amalie

Toldbodgade

Pluto

DAVIDS
SAMLING

Rebel

Salt

Gothersgade

Godt

Koefoed

Palægade

Amaliegade

Restaurationen

Borgergade

Admiral

Gammel Mont

Retour Steak

Store

Geist

Sankt
Annæ

Skt. Annæ

INDERHAVNEN

M

Gammel Mont

Marchal

Kongens
Nytorv

Bredgade

Hummer

RUNDETÅRN

Krystalgade

Aamanns
1921

Købmager-
gade

D'Angleterre

NYHAVN

Inderhavns-
broen

Frue
Plads

HELLIGÅNDS-
KIRKE

Silke-
gade

STRØGET

Bernikows
Gade

Kongens
Nytorv

TEATER

PMY

Studio at
The Standard

108

Barr

OR FRUE
KIRKE

Amagertorv

Østergade

M

SANKT
NIKOLAJ
KIRKE

Kong Hans
Kælder

Holbergsgade

Vimmelskaftet

Højbro
Plads

Admiralgade

Sanders

Almanak at
The Standard

Strandgade

THORVALDSENS
MUSEUM

Niels Juels Gade

City

Havnegade

Marv & Ben

Slotskælderen
hos Gitte Kik

Nybrogade

Bremerholm

Holmens Kanal

Kanalen

Farver-
gade

Vindebro-
gade

Rådhus-
stræde

Holmens
gade

HOLMENS
KIRKE

Overgaden oven Vandet

Prinsessegade

Børsgade

BØRSEN

Slotsholmsgade

CHRISTIANSHAVN

Stormgade

CHRISTIANS-
BORG

Knippels-
bro

Strandgade

Era Ora

VOR
FRELSERS
KIRKE

Frederiksholms Kanal

Tøjhus-
gade

Brygge

Kadeau
Copenhagen

Torvegade

Christianshavn

NATIONAL-
MUSEET

BIBLIOTHEK

M

Overgaden oven Vandet

Vester

Christians

INDERHAVNEN

no.2

Nabo

L'Altro

C. Andersens

Voldgade

Torvegade

Nobis

Brygge

Chrismas
Møllers
Plads

Niels

NY CARLSBERG
GLYPTOTEK

Boulevard

Langebro

Amagerbro-
gade

Niels Brocks

L'Enoteca di
Mr. Brunello

Kalvebod Brygge

Langebrogade

Amager

STADSGRAVEN

Stadsgraven

Hambros-
gade

SYDHAVNEN

Copenhagen
Marriott

Boulevard

C

D

1

2

3

❀ **Marchal** – D'Angleterre Hotel   XX 🌸 🈴 ⅗ **AC**

Kongens Nytorv 34 ✉ *1050 K –* Ⓜ *Kongens Nytorv*   Plan: **C2**
– ☎ 33 12 00 94 – www.dangleterre.com/en/dining/marchal
Menu 525 DKK (lunch) – Carte 585/1185 DKK
• Modern cuisine • Elegant • Romantic •

A stylish hotel restaurant overlooking the Square and named after the man who founded the hotel in 1755. Refined, Nordic-style cooking has a classical French base; menus offer a range of small plates – 3 is about the right amount. Dinner also includes an extensive caviar collection.
➜ Squid with oysters, caviar and champagne butter. Chateaubriand, smoked marrow and pepper sauce. "Gold Bar" with hazelnuts and calvados ice cream.

❀ **Stud!o at The Standard**   XX ⩽ **AC**

Havnegade 44 ✉ *1058 K –* Ⓜ *Kongens Nytorv*   Plan: **D2**
– ☎ 72 14 88 08 – www.thestandardcph.dk – Closed 8-30 July,
23 December-3 January, 17-25 February, Sunday and Monday
Menu 1300 DKK – *(dinner only and Saturday lunch) (booking essential) (surprise menu only)*
• Creative • Fashionable • Design •

The action at this stylishly understated restaurant is focused around the open kitchen, with seating of varying heights so everyone has a view. You'll notice subtle references to Chile – the chef's homeland – in the 7 course surprise menu. Precisely prepared, intensely flavoured dishes are full of creativity.
➜ Pike ceviche with sweet onion and whitecurrant. Duck with grapes and lavender. Almond ice cream, cep and balsamico.

❀ **108** (Kristian Baumann)   X ⩽

Strandgade 108 ✉ *1401 K –* Ⓜ *Christianshavn*   Plan: **D2**
– ☎ 32 96 32 92 – www.108.dk – Closed Christmas and 1 January
Carte 405/970 DKK – *(dinner only) (booking advisable)*
• Modern cuisine • Neighbourhood • Design •

A former whale meat warehouse with floor-to-ceiling windows and water views; bare concrete and a semi-open kitchen give it a cool Nordic style. There's a Noma alumnus in the kitchen and plenty of pickled, cured and fermented ingredients on the 'no rules' menu, from which you pick as many dishes as you like.
➜ Courgette flowers and summer greens. Glazed pork belly with salted apples. Rose hips with sea buckthorn.

❀ **Relæ**   X

Jægersborggade 41 ✉ *2200 N – ☎ 36 96 66 09*   Plan: **A1**
– www.restaurant-relae.dk – Closed Christmas-New Year, Sunday and Monday
Menu 475/895 DKK – *(dinner only and lunch Friday- Saturday) (booking essential) (surprise menu only)*
• Modern cuisine • Minimalist • Fashionable •

This modern, understated restaurant never stands still. The open kitchen provides a real sense of occasion and you can feel the passion of the chefs as they explain the dishes they are serving. 5 and 10 course surprise menus showcase produce grown on their farm. Dishes are intensely flavoured and unrestrained.
➜ Green strawberries and marigold. Havervadgård lamb, romaine salad and tarragon. Yoghurt, chervil and lemon.

☺ **Frederiks Have**   XX 🈴

Smallegade 41, (entrance on Virginiavej) (1.5 km. via Gammel Kongevej A3) ✉ *2000 F –* Ⓜ *Frederiksberg – ☎ 38 88 33 35 – www.frederikshave.dk – Closed 24 December-1 January, Easter and Sunday*
Menu 295/535 DKK – Carte 340/530 DKK
• Danish • Neighbourhood • Family •

A sweet neighbourhood restaurant hidden just off the main street in a residential area. Sit inside – surrounded by flowers and vivid local art – or outside, on the terrace. Well-presented, modern Danish dishes have a classical base; tasty sweet and sour combinations feature. The set lunches are great value.

L'Altro
X AC

Torvegade 62 ⊠ 1400 K – Ⓜ Christianshavn   Plan: **D3**
*– ℰ 32 54 54 06 – www.laltro.dk – Closed Easter, 1-15 January, Tuesday
and Wednesday*
*Menu 340/450 DKK – (dinner only) (booking essential) (tasting menu
only)*
• Italian • Intimate • Traditional décor •
A cosy, long-standing restaurant with a warm, rustic style; it celebrates 'la
cucina de la casa' – the homely Italian spirit of "mama's kitchen". Regularly
changing set menus feature tasty family recipes from Umbria and Tuscany;
dishes are appealing and rely on good quality ingredients imported from
Italy.

Anarki
X 🏵

Vodroffsvej 47 ⊠ 1900 C – Ⓜ Forum   Plan: **A2**
*– ℰ 22 13 11 34 – www.restaurant-anarki.dk – Closed July,
Christmas, Easter and Monday*
Menu 395 DKK – Carte 275/435 DKK – (dinner only)
• Traditional cuisine • Neighbourhood • Bistro •
An unassuming and proudly run neighbourhood bistro, set just over the
water in Frederiksberg. The interesting menu of gutsy, flavourful dishes
draws inspiration from all over the world, so expect to see words like cevi-
che, paella and burrata as well as bakskuld – with plenty of offal and some
great wines.

Enomania
X 🏵 ⇔

Vesterbrogade 187 (2.5 km via Vesterbrogade A3) ⊠ 1800 C
*– ℰ 33 23 60 80 – www.enomania.dk – Closed 22 December-
2 January, 9-18 February, 29 March-2 April, 18-22 April, 7 July-
6 August, 13-22 October, Saturday-Monday and bank holidays*
*Menu 390 DKK – Carte 260/380 DKK – (dinner only and lunch Thurs-
day-Friday) (booking essential)*
• Italian • Wine bar • Simple •
A simple, bistro-style restaurant near Frederiksberg Park – its name means
'Wine Mania'. The wine cellar comes with a table for tasting and there's an
excellent list of over 600 bins, mostly from Piedmont and Burgundy. These
are complemented by straightforward, tasty Italian dishes from a daily 4
course menu.

Kødbyens Fiskebar
X 🛆 P

*Den Hvide Kødby, Flæsketorvet 100 (1 km via Halmtorvet B3)
⊠ 1711 V – ℰ 32 15 56 56 – www.fiskebaren.dk – Closed 24-
26 December and lunch Monday to Thursday*
Menu 295 DKK (lunch) – Carte 290/565 DKK
• Seafood • Simple • Fashionable •
This buzzy, industrial-style restaurant is set, somewhat incongruously, in a
former butcher's shop in a commercial meat market. Menus feature freshly
prepared 'hot' and 'cold' seafood dishes which are based around the latest
catch and oysters are a speciality. The terrace is a popular spot come summer.

Marv & Ben
X

Snaregade 4 ⊠ 1205 K – Ⓜ Kongens Nytorv   Plan: **C2/3**
– ℰ 33 91 01 91 – www.marvogben.dk – Closed Christmas and Sunday
*Menu 400/600 DKK – Carte 305/355 DKK – (dinner only) (booking
advisable)*
• Modern cuisine • Friendly • Romantic •
The young owners bring plenty of enthusiasm to this little restaurant, where
dining is split over two dimly lit floors. Organic produce features in seasonal
dishes which display purity and depth of flavour. Choose 'Four Favourites' (4
courses), 'Almost Everything' (6 courses) or from the à la carte.

DENMARK - COPENHAGEN

Mêlée   ✗

Martensens Allé 16 ✉ 1828 C – **Ⓜ** *Frederiksberg*   Plan: **A3**
*– ℰ 35 13 11 34 – www.melee.dk – Closed Christmas-New Year,
Easter and Sunday*
Menu 395 DKK – Carte 325/430 DKK – *(dinner only) (booking essential)*
• French • Friendly • Bistro •

A bustling neighbourhood bistro with a friendly, laid-back atmosphere; run by an experienced team. Modern, country-style cooking is French-based but has Danish influences; menus might be concise but portions are generous and flavours are bold. An excellent range of wines from the Rhône Valley accompany.

Musling Bistro   ✗ AC

Linnésgade 14 ✉ 1361 K – ℰ 34 10 56 56   Plan: **B1**
– www.musling.net – Closed 24-25 December, Sunday and Monday
Carte 360/480 DKK
• Seafood • Bistro • Fashionable •

A relaxed bar-cum-bistro next to the Nørrebro food market – find a space at the black ash counter, grab your cutlery from one of the pots, and choose from the list of modern craft beers and unusual wines. Fantastic fresh seafood is to the fore on the concise menu, and service is swift and efficient.

Pluto   ✗ 🍽

Borgergade 16 ✉ 1300 K – **Ⓜ** *Kongens Nytorv*   Plan: **C2**
*– ℰ 33 16 00 16 – www.restaurantpluto.dk – Closed 24-25 December and
1 January*
Menu 475 DKK – Carte 235/410 DKK – *(dinner only)*
• Mediterranean cuisine • Bistro • Rustic •

An appealing restaurant in a residential area, with concrete pillars and an intentionally 'unfinished' feel – sit at wooden tables, at the long metal bar or at communal marble-topped tables. An enticing menu of small plates includes 'cheese' and 'sweets' sections; cooking is rustic, unfussy and flavoursome.

PMY   ✗

Tordenskjoldsgade 11 ✉ 1055 K – **Ⓜ** *Kongens Nytorv – ℰ 50 81 00 02
– www.restaurant-pmy.com – Closed July, Christmas, 1 week January,
Monday and Tuesday*
Menu 375/495 DKK – *(dinner only) (booking essential)*
• South American • Friendly • Trendy •

Start with some snacks and a cocktail at this fun, laid-back restaurant, before moving on to fresh, zingy dishes bursting with Latin American flavours. Potato, maize and yuca feature highly on the small menu, which lists tasty, good value dishes from Peru, Mexico and Venezuela.

Rebel   ✗ 🍴

Store Kongensgade 52 ✉ 1264 K   Plan: **C/D2**
– **Ⓜ** *Kongens Nytorv – ℰ 33 32 32 09 – www.restaurantrebel.dk – Closed
23 July-6 August, 2 weeks Christmas, Sunday and Monday*
Carte 335/565 DKK – *(dinner only)*
• Modern cuisine • Bistro • Fashionable •

Located in a busy part of the city; a simply decorated, split-level restaurant with closely set tables and a buzzy vibe. Choose 3 or 4 dishes from the list of 12 starter-sized options; cooking is modern and refined, and relies largely on Danish produce. The atmospheric lower floor is often used for parties.

⍥ Mielcke & Hurtigkarl   ✗✗

*Runddel 1 (2 km via Veseterbrogade and Frederiksberg Allé A 3) ✉ 2000 C
– ℰ 38 34 84 36 – www.mhcph.com – Closed 3 weeks Christmas, Sunday
and Monday*
Menu 800/1100 DKK – *(dinner only) (booking essential)*
• Creative • Elegant • Exotic décor •

A charming 1744 orangery with a fire-lit terrace, set in a delightful spot in Frederiksberg Gardens. The walls are painted with garden scenes and dishes use an amazing array of herbs which come from the garden. Dishes originate from around the globe but Asian influences are kept to the fore.

Aamanns 1921

XX

Plan: C2

Niels Hemmingsens Gade 19-21 ✉ 1153 K – Ⓜ Kongens Nytorv – ☎ 20 80 52 04 – www.aamanns.dk – Closed 25-26 December, 31 December, 1 January and dinner Sunday-Monday

Menu 325/390 DKK – Carte 265/475 DKK – *(booking advisable)*

• Modern cuisine • Brasserie • Design •

An appealing restaurant with original stone arches. Lunch sees traditional smørrebrød, while dinner focuses on modern dishes. They grind and mill their own flours, marinate their herring for 6-12 months and gather the herbs for their snaps.

Amass

XX

Refshalevej 153 (3 km via Torvgade and Prinsessgade D3) ✉ 1432 K – ☎ 43 58 43 30 – www.amassrestaurant.com – Closed 1 week Summer, Christmas, February, Sunday and Monday

Menu 695/895 DKK – *(dinner only and lunch Friday-Saturday) (booking essential)*

• Danish • Minimalist • Friendly •

A large restaurant just outside the city. It has an urban, industrial feel courtesy of graffitied concrete walls and huge windows overlooking the old docks. Prices and the authenticity of ingredients are key; cooking is modern Danish.

Brace

XX

Plan: B2

Teglgårdstræde 8a ✉ 1452 K – Ⓜ København Hovedbane Gård – ☎ 28 88 20 01 – www.restaurantbrace.dk – Closed 24-26 December, 2-22 January, Sunday and Monday

Menu 350/775 DKK – *(dinner only) (booking essential)*

• Italian • Elegant • Fashionable •

The name of this smart restaurant, set in the heart of the city, refers to the building's external structure and to the solidarity of the tight-knit team. Dishes are a fusion of Danish and Italian, and come with colourful modern twists.

L' Enoteca di Mr. Brunello

XX

Plan: C3

Rysensteensgade 16 ✉ 1564 K – ☎ 33 11 47 20 – www.lenoteca.dk – Closed Easter,1 July-8 August, 23 December-2 January, Sunday and bank holidays

Menu 495/695 DKK – Carte 530/560 DKK – *(dinner only)*

• Italian • Elegant • Neighbourhood •

Tucked away near the Tivoli Gardens and run by passionate, experienced owners. Refined, classic Italian cooking uses good quality produce imported from Italy. The good value Italian wine list has over 150 different Brunello di Montalcinos.

Gammel Mønt

XX

Plan: C2

Gammel Mønt 41 ✉ 1117 K – Ⓜ Kongens Nytorv – ☎ 33 15 10 60 – www.glmoent.dk – Closed July, Christmas, Easter, Sunday, Monday and bank holidays

Carte 455/685 DKK – *(lunch only and dinner Wednesday-Friday)*

• Traditional cuisine • Cosy • Friendly •

A part-timbered house in the heart of the city; it dates back to 1739 and sports a striking shade of deep terracotta. The menu celebrates Danish flavours and dishes are gutsy and reassuringly traditional – try the pickled herrings.

Geist

XX

Plan: C2

Kongens Nytorv 8 ✉ 1050 K – Ⓜ Kongens Nytorv – ☎ 33133713 – www.restaurantgeist.dk – Closed 23-26 December and 1 January

Carte 385/840 DKK – *(dinner only)*

• Modern cuisine • Design • Trendy •

A lively, fashionable restaurant with an open kitchen and a sexy nightclub vibe, set in a striking red-brick property with floor to ceiling windows overlooking the square. Cleverly crafted dishes display a light touch; 4 should suffice.

‖○ **Godt**   XX

Gothersgade 38 ⊠ 1123 K – Ⓜ Kongens Nytorv   Plan: **C2**
– 𝒞 33 15 21 22 – www.restaurant-godt.dk – Closed mid July to mid
August, Christmas-New Year, Easter, Sunday, Monday and bank holidays
Menu 600/680 DKK – *(dinner only) (tasting menu only)*
• Classic cuisine • Friendly • Family •

A stylish restaurant seating just 20; the service here is particularly friendly. Traditional French and European daily menus – of 4 and 5 courses – are formed around the latest market produce. Old WWII shells act as candle holders.

‖○ **Kiin Kiin VeVe**   XX

Dampfærgevej 7-9 (North 2.5 km by Store Kongensgade and Folke
Bernadottes Allé) ⊠ 2100 Ø – 𝒞 51 22 59 55 – www.veve.dk – Closed
Sunday-Tuesday
Menu 750 DKK – *(dinner only) (booking essential) (tasting menu only)*
• Vegetarian • Design • Contemporary décor •

A former bread factory houses this chic restaurant which serves sophisticated vegetarian cuisine. The 6 course tasting menu revolves around the seasons and offers some imaginative combinations. Wine and juice pairings accompany.

‖○ **Koefoed**   XX 🏠 🍴

Landgreven 3 ⊠ 1301 K – Ⓜ Kongens Nytorv   Plan: **C2**
– 𝒞 56 48 22 24 – www.restaurant-koefoed.dk – Closed 22 December-
4 January and Sunday-Tuesday
Menu 295/495 DKK – Carte 425/510 DKK – *(booking essential at dinner)*
• Modern cuisine • Intimate • Romantic •

An intimate collection of rooms in an old coal cellar, where everything from the produce to the glassware celebrates Bornholm island. Modern cooking is accompanied by an impressive range of bordeaux wines. Lunch sees reinvented smørrebrød.

‖○ **Lumskebugten**   XX 🍴 ⇔

Esplanaden 21 ⊠ 1263 K – 𝒞 33 15 60 29   Plan: **D1**
– www.lumskebugten.dk – Closed 3 weeks July, Christmas, Easter, Sunday
and bank holidays
Menu 325/475 DKK – Carte 450/700 DKK
• Traditional cuisine • Cosy • Classic décor •

A restored quayside pavilion dating from 1854; the Royal Family occasionally dine here. A series of small rooms are adorned with maritime memorabilia and paintings. Local menus offer a wide selection of traditional fish dishes.

‖○ **Niels** – Nobis Hotel   XX 🍴 ⌨ 🅰 ⇔

Niels Brocks Gade 1 ⊠ 1574 V   Plan: **C3**
– Ⓜ København Hovedbane Gård – 𝒞 78 74 14 00 – www.nobishotel.dk
Menu 200/645 DKK – Carte 515/755 DKK
• Modern cuisine • Design • Chic •

Lots of glass and mirrors give this contemporary hotel restaurant an airy feel. Well-presented, satisfying modern Scandinavian cooking gives a nod to France and has plenty of texture and flavour contrasts. In summer, head for the terrace.

‖○ **Palægade**   XX 🍴

Palægade 8 ⊠ 1261 K – Ⓜ Kongens Nytorv   Plan: **C/D2**
– 𝒞 70 82 82 88 – www.palaegade.dk – Closed 24-27 December, 1 week
January, dinner 16 July-5 August and Sunday dinner
Menu 495 DKK – Carte 285/620 DKK
• Smørrebrød • Friendly • Simple •

More than 40 classic smørrebrød are available at lunch – with plenty of local beers and snaps to accompany them. Things become more formal in the evenings, when they serve highly seasonal dishes in a traditional Northern European style.

Restaurationen XX ⌘
Plan: **C2**
Møntergade 19 ⌧ 1116 K – Ⓜ Kongens Nytorv
– ℰ 33 14 94 95 – www.restaurationen.com – Closed July-28 August,
22 December-8 January, 25 March-2 April, Sunday and Monday
Menu 605 DKK – *(dinner only)*
• Classic cuisine • Chic • Romantic •
This restaurant celebrated 25 years in 2016, and is run by a well-known chef who also owns the next door wine bar. Modern Danish dishes are created with quality local produce. The dining room displays some impressive vibrant modern art.

Salt – Admiral Hotel XX 🕾 🅿
Plan: **D2**
Toldbodgade 24-28 ⌧ 1253 K – Ⓜ Kongens Nytorv
– ℰ 33 74 14 44 – www.salt.dk
Menu 395/445 DKK – Carte 430/540 DKK
• Modern cuisine • Design • Fashionable •
A bright, airy hotel restaurant; its vast old timber beams are a reminder of the building's previous life as a granary and its harbourside terrace is a great spot in the summer. Extensive menus offer interesting modern cooking.

Trio XX ≤ & 🎰 ⟷
Plan: **B3**
Axel Towers (9th Floor), Jernbanegade 11 ⌧ 1608 V
– Ⓜ København Hovedbane Gård – ℰ 44 22 74 74
– www.restauranttrio.dk – Closed Christmas, Easter, 1 January and Sunday
Menu 350/675 DKK – Carte 320/540 DKK
• Modern cuisine • Design • Fashionable •
The highest restaurant in the city is located on floors 9 and 10 of the striking Axel Towers building; enjoy a cocktail while taking in the view. Accomplished dishes take their influences from both classic French and modern Nordic cuisine.

Barr X ≤
Plan: **D2**
Strandgade 93 ⌧ 1401 K – Ⓜ Christianshavn
– ℰ 32 96 32 93 – www.restaurantbarr.com – Closed 1 November and
22 December-3 January
Carte 325/455 DKK – *(dinner only and lunch Friday-Sunday) (booking essential)*
• Modern cuisine • Trendy • Rustic •
A laid-back quayside restaurant with wood-clad walls. Its name means 'Barley' and it offers an amazing array of cask and bottled beers – some custom-brewed – and beer pairings to match the food. Intensely flavoured, rustic dishes have classic Nordic roots but are taken to new heights; the sweet cake is a must.

Gemyse – Nimb Hotel X 🕾 ⟷
Plan: **B3**
Tivoli Gardens, Bernstoffsgade 5 ⌧ 1572 V
– Ⓜ København Hovedbane Gård – ℰ 88 70 00 80 – www.nimb.dk
Menu 250/600 DKK – Carte 215/275 DKK
• Modern cuisine • Rustic • Romantic •
Part of the Nimb hotel, Gemyse is a delightful, vegetable-orientated restaurant set in the heart of Tivoli Gardens, and comes complete with a greenhouse and raised beds where they grow much of their produce. Dishes are well-prepared, attractively presented and very tasty. The daily set menu is a good choice.

Kanalen X ≤ 🕾 ⟷ 🅿
Plan: **D3**
Wilders Plads 1-3 ⌧ 1403 K – Ⓜ Christianshavn
– ℰ 32 95 13 30 – www.restaurant-kanalen.dk – Closed Christmas, New Years Eve, Easter, Sunday and bank holidays
Menu 300/400 DKK – Carte 335/555 DKK – *(booking essential)*
• Danish • Bistro • Cosy •
Find a spot on the delightful canalside terrace of this quaint, shack-like building – formerly the Harbour Police office – and watch the boats bobbing up and down as you eat. Alongside classic Danish flavours you'll find some light French and Asian touches; for dessert, the 'flødeboller' is a must.

〒◯ ### Aamanns Etablissement   ✗

Øster Farimagsgade 12 ☒ 2100 Ø – ⓜ Nørreport   Plan: **C1**
– 𝒞 20 80 52 02 – www.aamanns.dk – Closed July, Christmas-New Year
and dinner Sunday-Tuesday
Carte 325/460 DKK – (booking advisable)
• Danish • Bistro • Cosy •
A cosy, contemporary restaurant with cheery service and an informal atmo-
sphere. Concise, seasonal menus blend traditional smørrebrød with more
modern 'small plates'. Two dishes per person plus dessert is about right.

〒◯ ### Admiralgade 26   ✗ ⅋

Admiralgade 26 ☒ 1066 K – ⓜ Kongens Nytorv   Plan: **C2**
– 𝒞 33 33 79 73 – www.admiralgade26.dk
– Closed Christmas, 31 December-2 January and Sunday
Menu 550 DKK – Carte 305/425 DKK
• Modern cuisine • Intimate • Cosy •
This historic house dates from 1796 and sits in one of the oldest parts of the city.
It's a relaxed place – a mix of wine bar, café and bistro – and, alongside an
appealing modern menu, offers around 4,000 frequently changing wines.

〒◯ ### Almanak at The Standard   ✗ 〒

Havnegade 44 ☒ 1058 K – ⓜ Kongens Nytorv   Plan: **D2**
– 𝒞 72 14 88 08 – www.thestandardcph.dk – Closed 24-25 December and
Monday
Menu 575 DKK (dinner) – Carte 265/500 DKK – (bookings advisable at
dinner)
• Modern cuisine • Fashionable • Chic •
A chic restaurant on the ground floor of an impressive art deco customs buil-
ding on the waterfront. At lunch, it's all about smørrebrød, while dinner sees a
concise menu of updated Danish classics. An open kitchen adds to the theatre.
❀ **Studio at The Standard** – See restaurant listing

〒◯ ### Ché Fè   ✗

Borgergade 17a ☒ 1300 K – ⓜ Kongens Nytorv   Plan: **C2**
– 𝒞 33 11 17 21 – www.chefe.dk – Closed 1 week Christmas, 1 January
and Sunday
Menu 385/495 DKK – Carte 425/485 DKK – (dinner only) (booking essential)
• Italian • Simple • Neighbourhood •
An unassuming façade conceals an appealing trattoria with pastel hues and coffee sack curtains. Menus offer authentic Italian classics, including homemade
pastas; virtually all ingredients are imported from small, organic producers.

〒◯ ### 56°   ✗ 〒 ✿

Krudtløbsvej 8 (2.5 km. via Torvgade, Prinsessgade and Refshalevej D3)
☒ 1439 K – 𝒞 31 16 32 05 – www.restaurant56grader.dk – Closed
Christmas, lunch Tuesday-Thursday in winter, Sunday dinner and Monday
Menu 275/400 DKK
• Danish • Rustic • Romantic •
A sweet, rustic restaurant, unusually set within the 1.5m thick walls of a 17C
gunpowder store. Flavoursome Danish cooking mixes modern and traditional
elements and keeps Nordic produce to the fore. The large garden is a hit.

〒◯ ### Gorilla   ✗ 〒

Flæsketorvet 63 (1 km via Halmtorvet) ☒ 1711 V – 𝒞 33 33 83 30
– www.restaurantgorilla.dk – Closed 24-25 December, 1 January, Sunday
and bank holidays
Menu 375/475 DKK – Carte 135/860 DKK – (dinner only)
• Modern cuisine • Brasserie • Simple •
A buzzy, canteen-style restaurant in the meatpacking district; the stone floor,
zinc ducting and large windows create an industrial feel. The menu offers something for everyone; dishes are well-presented, tasty and designed for sharing.

‖○ **Höst**   ✗ ⇔
Nørre Farimagsgade 41 ⊠ 1364 K – Ⓜ Nørreport   Plan: **B2**
– ℰ 89 93 84 09 – www.cofoco.dk/restauranter/hoest
– Closed 24 December, 1 January and lunch Sunday-Wednesday
Menu 350/895 DKK
• Modern cuisine • Friendly • Rustic •
A busy neighbourhood bistro with fun staff and a lively atmosphere; sit in the
Garden Room. The great value monthly set menu comprises 3 courses but
comes with lots of extras. Modern Nordic cooking is seasonal and boldly flavou-
red.

‖○ **Hummer**   ✗ ≤ 斎
Nyhavn 63A ⊠ 1051 K – Ⓜ Kongens Nytorv   Plan: **D2**
– ℰ 33 33 03 39 – www.restauranthummer.dk – Closed 23-27 December
and Monday-Tuesday October-April
Menu 395 DKK – Carte 280/610 DKK
• Seafood • Friendly • Simple •
Lobster is the mainstay of the menu at this restaurant, situated among the
brightly coloured buildings on the famous Nyhavn strip. Enjoy a meal on the
sunny terrace or in the modish, nautically styled dining room.

‖○ **Mes**   ✗
Jarmers Plads 1 ⊠ 1551 V   Plan: **B2**
– Ⓜ København Hovedbane Gård – ℰ 25 36 51 81
– www.restaurant-mes.dk – Closed 24-30 December and Sunday
Menu 350 DKK – *(dinner only) (booking essential) (tasting menu only)*
• Danish • Intimate • Friendly •
A sweet little restaurant run by a tight-knit team. The frequently changing set
menu lists classic dishes – some of which are pepped up with modern techni-
ques. A 120 year old German cooling cabinet plays host to the wines.

‖○ **Nabo**   ✗ ⇔
Wildersgade 10a ⊠ 1408 K – Ⓜ Christianhavn   Plan: **D3**
– ℰ 33 22 10 02 – www.nabonabo.dk – Closed Christmas, Monday dinner
and Sunday
Carte 320/435 DKK
• Danish • Cosy • Neighbourhood •
This laid-back restaurant – sister to neighbouring Kadeau – is open from mor-
ning 'til night, for everything from coffee to a 3 course meal. Sit surrounded by
preserving jars and Danish pottery. The rustic cooking really hits the spot.

‖○ **no.2**   ✗ ≤ 斎 🅰🅲
Nicolai Eigtveds Gade 32 ⊠ 1402 C   Plan: **D3**
– Ⓜ Christianshaven – ℰ 33 11 11 68 – www.nummer2.dk – Closed
Christmas, Easter, 2 weeks in July, Saturday lunch and Sunday
Menu 325/475 DKK – Carte 275/525 DKK
• Modern cuisine • Design • Fashionable •
Set among smart offices and apartments on the edge of the dock is this elegant
restaurant; a sister to a|o|c. Fresh, flavoursome dishes focus on quality Danish
ingredients – highlights include the cured hams, cheeses and ice creams.

‖○ **Øl & Brød**   ✗
Viktoriagade 6 ⊠ 1620 V   Plan: **B3**
– Ⓜ København Hovedbane Gård – ℰ 33 31 44 22 – www.ologbrod.com
– Closed Monday and dinner Tuesday-Wednesday
Menu 500 DKK (dinner) – Carte lunch 280/440 DKK – *(booking essential)*
• Modern cuisine • Neighbourhood • Cosy •
A cosy, hip neighbourhood restaurant where the emphasis is as much on aqua-
vit and craft beers as it is on the refined and flavourful modern food. Lunch sees
smørrebrød taken to a new level, while dinner offers a choice of 3 or 6 courses.

DENMARK - COPENHAGEN

DENMARK - COPENHAGEN

Pony Ⅹ

Vesterbrogade 135 ⊠ 1620 V – ℰ 33 22 10 00   Plan: **A3**
– www.ponykbh.dk – Closed July-August, 1 week Christmas and Monday
Menu 425/485 DKK – *(dinner only) (booking essential)*
• Danish • Bistro • Neighbourhood •

A buzzy restaurant with chatty service: sit on high stools by the kitchen or in the retro dining room. Choose from the fixed price menu or try the more adventurous 4 course 'Pony Kick'. Refined, modern cooking has a 'nose-to-tail' approach.

Radio Ⅹ

Julius Thomsens Gade 12 ⊠ 1632 V – Ⓜ Forum   Plan: **A2**
– ℰ 25102733 – www.restaurantradio.dk – Closed 3 weeks summer,
2 weeks Christmas-New Year, Sunday and Monday
Menu 350/435 DKK – *(dinner only and lunch Friday-Saturday) (booking essential) (tasting menu only)*
• Modern cuisine • Minimalist • Neighbourhood •

An informal restaurant with an unfussy urban style, wood-clad walls and cool anglepoise lighting. Oft-changing set menus feature full-flavoured, good value dishes and use organic ingredients grown in the chefs' nearby fields.

Retour Steak Ⅹ

Ny Østergade 21 ⊠ 1101 K – Ⓜ Kongens Nytorv   Plan: **C2**
– ℰ 33 16 17 19 – www.retoursteak.dk – Closed 24-25 December and 1 January
Carte 240/595 DKK – *(dinner only) (booking essential)*
• Meats and grills • Bistro • Friendly •

A relaxed, informal restaurant with a stark white interior and contrasting black furnishings. A small menu offers simply prepared grills, good quality American rib-eye steaks and an affordable selection of wines.

Uformel Ⅹ 🆊 ⇔

Studiestraede 69 ⊠ 1554 K   Plan: **B3**
– Ⓜ København Hovedbane Gård – ℰ 70 99 91 11 – www.uformel.dk
– Closed Christmas-New Year
Menu 800 DKK – Carte 440/660 DKK – *(dinner only) (booking essential)*
• Modern cuisine • Fashionable • Trendy •

The informal sister of Formel B, with gold table-tops, black cutlery, a smart open kitchen and a cocktail bar (a lively spot at the weekend!) Dishes are tasting plates and all are the same price; 4-6 is about the right amount.

Väkst Ⅹ 🍴 ♿ 🆊

Sankt Peders Stræde 34 ⊠ 1453 K – Ⓜ Nørreport   Plan: **B2**
– ℰ 38 41 27 27 – www.hostvakst.dk/vakst/restaurant/ – Closed Sunday lunch
Menu 325/425 DKK
• Modern cuisine • Rustic • Trendy •

Dining outside 'inside' is the theme here, and you'll find plants, garden furniture and a full-sized greenhouse at the centre of the room. Interesting Danish cooking follows the seasons and is light, stimulating and full of flavour.

D'Angleterre 🆊 🕸 🌙 🗔 ♿ 🆊 🏊

Kongens Nytorv 34 ⊠ 1050 K – Ⓜ Kongens Nytorv   Plan: **C2**
– ℰ 33 12 00 95 – www.dangleterre.com
92 rm – †2750/4750 DKK ††2750/4750 DKK – ⌸ 325 DKK – 30 suites
• Luxury • Historic • Contemporary •

A smartly refurbished landmark hotel dating back over 250 years. Well-equipped bedrooms come in various shapes and sizes; it's worth paying the extra for a Royal Square view. Unwind in the basement spa or the chic champagne bar.

❀ **Marchal** – See restaurant listing

Copenhagen Marriott 　　　　⇗ ⇐ ♨ ⚅ ⚄ ⚄ 🅿

Kalvebod Brygge 5 ✉ *1560 V* – ☎ *88 33 99 00* 　Plan: **C3**
– www.copenhagenmarriott.dk
402 rm – 🛉1900/5000 DKK 🛉🛉1900/5000 DKK – ☲ 230 DKK – 9 suites
• Luxury • Business • Modern •

A striking waterfront hotel; take in the views from the terrace or from the lounge-bar's floor to ceiling windows. Bright, spacious bedrooms are handsomely appointed and afford canal or city views. The popular American grill restaurant offers steaks, chops and seafood, and has a lively open kitchen.

Skt. Petri 　　　　　　　　⇗ ♨ ⚅ ⚄

Krystalgade 22 ✉ *1172 K* – Ⓜ Nørreport 　Plan: **B2**
– ☎ *33 45 91 00* – www.sktpetri.com
288 rm – 🛉1200/2000 DKK 🛉🛉1200/2000 DKK – ☲ 195 DKK – 9 suites
• Business • Boutique hotel • Modern •

Much of this 7-storey building is listed but it's been stylishly fitted out and displays modern Danish art. The basement restaurant P Eatery serves international cuisine and there's a nice garden courtyard with a wood-burning stove. Bedrooms are state-of-the-art and some have views over the city spires.

Nimb 　　　　　　　　　　⇗ ♨ ⚄ ⚄

Bernstorffsgade 5 ✉ *1577 V* 　Plan: **B3**
– Ⓜ København Hovedbane Gård – ☎ *88 70 00 00* – www.nimb.dk
38 rm – 🛉2800/3000 DKK 🛉🛉3900/5400 DKK – ☲ 255 DKK – 12 suites
• Luxury • Design • Romantic •

An ornate, Moorish-style building dating from 1909, situated in Tivoli Gardens. Smart bedrooms are sympathetically designed and well-equipped – most overlook the gardens. Eat in the lively bar and grill, the formal brasserie or vegetable-orientated Gemyse. The rustic wine bar offers over 2,000 bottles – and you can enjoy Danish open sandwiches and snaps in Fru Nimb.

Admiral 　　　　　　　　⇐ ♨ ⚄ 🅿

Toldbodgade 24-28 ✉ *1253 K* – Ⓜ Kongens Nytorv 　Plan: **D2**
– ☎ *33 74 14 14* – www.admiralhotel.dk
366 rm – 🛉1335/1825 DKK 🛉🛉2275/2925 DKK – ☲ 150 DKK
• Business • Historic • Modern •

An impressive 1787 former grain-drying warehouse, with an appealing maritime theme running throughout. Bedrooms feature vintage beams and bespoke wood furniture and have city or harbour views; opt for one of the duplex suites.
⑩ **Salt** – See restaurant listing

Imperial 　　　　　　　⇗ ⚄ ⚅ ⚄ 🚗

Vester Farimagsgade 9 ✉ *1606 V* 　Plan: **B3**
– Ⓜ København Hovedbane Gård – ☎ *33 12 80 00*
– www.imperialhotel.dk
304 rm – 🛉1300/2300 DKK 🛉🛉1600/2800 DKK – ☲ 185 DKK – 1 suite
• Business • Traditional • Modern •

A well-known hotel, geared up for conferences and centrally located on a wide city thoroughfare. Bedrooms are particularly spacious and have a subtle Danish style. The contemporary restaurant features a brightly coloured Italian theme wall and serves Italian dishes to match.

Island 　　　　　　　⇗ ⇐ ♨ ⚅ ⚄ ⚄ 🅿

Kalvebod Brygge 53 (via Kalvebod Brygge C3) ✉ *1560 V* – ☎ *33 38 96 00*
– www.copenhagenisland.dk
326 rm – 🛉895/3450 DKK 🛉🛉995/5650 DKK – ☲ 185 DKK
• Business • Chain • Modern •

A contemporary glass and steel hotel set just outside the city, on a man-made island in the harbour. Bedrooms are well-equipped – some are allergy friendly and some have balconies; choose a water view over a city view. The stylish multi-level lounge-bar and restaurant serves a wide-ranging international menu.

Kong Arthur
ᵻ⅃ 🌐 🍴 ♨ 🅿

Nørre Søgade 11 ✉ *1370 K*
Plan: **B2**
– Ⓜ Nørreport
– 🕾 *33 11 12 12 – www.arthurhotels.dk*
155 rm – ♦800/1895 DKK ♦♦1100/2300 DKK – ☷ 175 DKK
• Townhouse • Traditional • Classic •

Four 1882 buildings set around a courtyard, in an elegant residential avenue close to Peblinge Lake. Well-equipped bedrooms have a high level of facilities. Relax in the smart Thai spa and enjoy complimentary drinks from 5-6pm.

Nobis
🍴 ⅄ 🄰🄺 🚗

Neils Brocks Gade 1 ✉ *1574 V*
Plan: **C3**
– Ⓜ København Hovedbane Gård
– 🕾 *78 74 14 00 – www.nobishotel.dk*
77 rm ☷ – ♦2500/3500 DKK ♦♦2800/3800 DKK – 1 suite
• Historic building • Luxury • Design •

The impressive former music academy building sits close to Tivoli Gardens. Other than an impressive staircase, little of its 20C history remains; instead it's a cool, stylish and understated space with modern Danish furnishings.
⅃○ **Niels** – See restaurant listing

Radisson Blu Royal
🏋 ≤ ᵻ⅃ 🍴 ⅄ 🄰🄺 ♨ 🚗

Hammerichsgade 1 ✉ *1611 V*
Plan: **B3**
– Ⓜ København Hovedbane Gård
– 🕾 *33 42 60 00 – www.radissonblu.com/royalhotel-copenhagen*
261 rm – ♦1195/6995 DKK ♦♦1495/7495 DKK – ☷ 195 DKK – 2 suites
• Business • Design •

A spacious hotel designed by Arne Jacobson, with extensive conference and fitness facilities. Bedrooms have a Scandic style – the largest are the double-aspect corner rooms; Number 606 still has its original furnishings. All-day Café Royal has a designer feel and offers afternoon tea and weekend brunches.

Sanders
🏋 ⅄ 🄰🄺

Tordenskjoldsgade 15 ✉ *1055 K*
Plan: **D2**
– Ⓜ Kongens Nytorv
– 🕾 *46 40 00 40 – www.hotelsanders.com*
54 rm ☷ – ♦2400/2600 DKK ♦♦3100/6600 DKK – 6 suites
• Townhouse • Elegant • Design •

Set in a residential area close to Nyhavn and the theatre is this neoclassical Jugendstil-style townhouse. It is intimate, homely and elegant, from the cosy open-fired living room, atmospheric cocktail bar and small all-day brasserie to the sophisticated bedrooms where no detail is overlooked. A charming young team provide friendly, attentive and personalised service.

Absalon
⅄

Helgolandsgade 15 ✉ *1653 V*
Plan: **B3**
– Ⓜ København Hovedbane Gård
– 🕾 *33 31 43 44 – www.absalon-hotel.dk*
161 rm ☷ – ♦1100/2250 DKK ♦♦1200/2350 DKK – 2 suites
• Family • Design • Grand luxury •

A family-run hotel located close to the railway station and furnished with vibrantly coloured fabrics. Elegant, comfortable bedrooms feature an 'art-box' on the wall which celebrates an aspect of Danish design such as Lego or porcelain.

DENMARK - COPENHAGEN

🏠 Alexandra

H.C. Andersens Boulevard 8 ✉ 1553 V
Plan: **B3**
– Ⓜ København Hovedbane Gård – 𝒞 33 74 44 44
– www.hotelalexandra.dk – Closed Christmas
61 rm – ♦695/1875 DKK ♦♦795/2075 DKK – ♺ 142 DKK
• Boutique hotel • Business • Design •
A well-run, late Victorian hotel in the city centre, with a contrastingly modern interior. Bedrooms are individually styled and there's an entire 'allergy friendly' floor; the 12 'Design' rooms are styled by famous Danish designers.

🏠 Andersen

Helgolandsgade 12 ✉ 1653 V
Plan: **B3**
– Ⓜ København Hovedbane Gård – 𝒞 33 31 46 10
– www.andersen-hotel.dk – Closed 22-25 December
69 rm ♺ – ♦1245/2195 DKK ♦♦1445/2795 DKK
• Family • Design • Contemporary •
Bright, funky styling marks out this boutique hotel, where the bedrooms are classified as 'Cool', 'Brilliant', 'Wonderful' and 'Amazing'. There's an honesty bar in reception and you can enjoy a complimentary glass of wine from 5–6pm.

🏠 Avenue
🔥 🅿

Åboulevard 29 ✉ 1960 C – Ⓜ Forum – 𝒞 35 37 31 11
Plan: **A2**
– www.brochner-hotels.dk
68 rm – ♦795/4000 DKK ♦♦795/4000 DKK – ♺ 160 DKK
• Business • Family • Modern •
A well-maintained, family-run hotel dating back to 1899. Relax around the central bar in the smart modern lounge or out on the courtyard patio. Bedrooms have a bright, crisp style and feature striking Philippe Starck lights.

🏠 City
🔥

Peder Skrams Gade 24 ✉ 1054 K – Ⓜ Kongens Nytorv
Plan: **D2**
– 𝒞 33 13 06 66 – www.hotelcity.dk
81 rm ♺ – ♦1045/2745 DKK ♦♦1145/2845 DKK
• Business • Traditional • Grand luxury •
A modern hotel in a quiet street between the city and the docks. Bedrooms boast monochrome Jan Persson jazz photos and Jacobsen armchairs. Designer furniture features throughout and there's an eye-catching water feature in the lobby.

🏠 Skt. Annæ

Sankt Annæ Plads 18-20 ✉ 1250 K
Plan: **D2**
– Ⓜ Kongens Nytorv – 𝒞 33 96 20 00 – www.hotelsanktannae.dk
154 rm – ♦1000/4000 DKK ♦♦1500/4500 DKK – ♺ 175 DKK – 1 suite
• Business • Townhouse • Cosy •
Three Victorian townhouses not far from the bustling harbourside of Nyhavn. Ask for a 'Superior' bedroom for more space and quiet; Room 601 is the best – it's accessed via the roof terrace and has its own balcony overlooking the rooftops. Dine on modern small plates in the restaurant.

🏠 Hebron
🔥

Helgolandsgade 4 ✉ 1653 V
Plan: **B3**
– Ⓜ København Hovedbane Gård – 𝒞 33 31 69 06 – www.hebron.dk
– Closed 22 December-2 January
99 rm ♺ – ♦700/1900 DKK ♦♦900/2100 DKK – 2 suites
• Traditional • Family • Functional •
A smart hotel behind a Victorian façade – this was one of the city's biggest when it opened in 1899 and some original features still remain. There's a comfy lounge and a grand breakfast room; well-kept bedrooms range in shape and size.

141

⌂ **Ibsens** P

Vendersgade 23 ✉ *1363 K –* Ⓜ *Nørreport* Plan: **B2**
– ☎ *33 13 19 13 – www.arthurhotels.dk*
118 rm ☒ *–* ♛880/2445 DKK ♛♛1230/2820 DKK
• Historic • Family • Personalised •

The little sister to Kong Arthur is this simple, brightly furnished hotel with a relaxed, bohemian feel. The small bar serves breakfast, as well as complimentary drinks from 5-6pm. Bedrooms are well-kept – 'Tiny' really are compact.

SMØRREBRØD *The following list of simpler restaurants and cafés/bars specialise in Danish open sandwiches and are generally open from 10.00am to 4.00pm.*

🍴 **Amalie** X

Amaliegade 11 ✉ *1256 K –* Ⓜ *Kongens Nytorv* Plan: **D2**
– ☎ *33 12 88 10 – www.restaurantamalie.dk – Closed 3 weeks July, 24 December-3 January, Easter, Sunday and bank holidays*
Menu 279 DKK – Carte 230/350 DKK *– (lunch only) (booking essential)*
• Smørrebrød • Intimate • Rustic •

A charming 18C townhouse by Amalienborg Palace, with two tiny, cosy rooms filled with old paintings and elegant porcelain. The Danish menu offers a large choice of smørrebrød, herring, salmon and salads. Service is warm and welcoming.

🍴 **Sankt Annæ** X 🏤 ✿

Sankt Annæ Plads 12 ✉ *1250 K –* Ⓜ *Kongens Nytorv* Plan: **D2**
– ☎ *33 12 54 97 – www.restaurantsanktannae.dk – Closed July-August, Sunday and bank holidays*
Carte 220/395 DKK *– (lunch only) (booking essential)*
• Smørrebrød • Cosy • Classic décor •

An attractive terraced building with a traditional, rather quaint interior. There's a seasonal à la carte and a daily blackboard menu: prices can vary so check before ordering. The lobster and shrimp – fresh from local fjords – are a hit.

🍴 **Slotskælderen hos Gitte Kik** X

Fortunstræde 4 ✉ *1065 K –* Ⓜ *Kongens Nytorv* Plan: **C2**
– ☎ *33 11 15 37 – www.slotskaelderen.dk – Closed July, Sunday, Monday and bank holidays*
Carte 205/340 DKK *– (lunch only) (booking essential)*
• Smørrebrød • Family • Traditional décor •

Set in a 1797 building and family-run since 1910, this established restaurant sets the benchmark for this type of cuisine. The rustic inner is filled with portraits and city scenes. Go to the counter to see the full selection of smørrebrød.

ENVIRONS OF COPENHAGEN

AT NORDHAVN North : 3 km by Østbanegade and Road 2

🍴 **Paustian** XX ≤ 🏤 P

Kalkbrænderiløbskaj 2 ✉ *2100 Ø –* ☎ *39 18 55 01 – www.paustian.com*
– Closed July, 23 December-14 January and Sunday
Carte 420/435 DKK *– (lunch only) (booking advisable)*
• Danish • Fashionable • Design •

A friendly, informal restaurant set in an impressive harbourside building designed by renowned architect Jørn Utzon. Traditional Danish cooking has French touches; watch the chefs at work in the open kitchen.

DENMARK - COPENHAGEN

❀ **Jordnær** (Eric Kragh Vildgaard)   XX ✿ P

Gentofte Hotel, Gentoftegade 29 ⊠ 2820 – ✆ 22 40 80 20
– www.restaurantjordnaer.dk – Closed 24-30 December, Sunday and
Monday
Menu 500/750 DKK *– (dinner only) (booking essential) (tasting menu only)*
• Danish • Romantic • Intimate •

The passionately run 'Down to earth' is housed within an unassuming suburban hotel. The building dates from 1666 and the rustic modern room comes with grey painted timbers. The daily menu offer 3, 5 or 7 courses; knowledgeably prepared dishes feature ingredients foraged by the chef and flavours are harmonious.
→ Scallops, white currants and aromatic herbs. Duck with beetroot and truffle. Blackberry, sheep's milk and verbena

AT SØLLERØD   North : 20 km by Tagensvej (take the train to Holte then taxi)
- ⊠ 2840 Holte

❀ **Søllerød Kro**   XXX 🍴 ☂ ✿ P

Søllerødvej 35 ⊠ 2840 – ✆ 45 80 25 05 – www.soelleroed-kro.dk – Closed
3 weeks July, 1 week February, Easter, Sunday dinner, Monday and
Tuesday
Menu 395/1095 DKK *– Carte 910/1410 DKK*
• Modern cuisine • Inn • Elegant •

A characterful 17C thatched inn by a pond in a picturesque village, with a delightful courtyard terrace and three elegant, intimate rooms. In keeping with the surroundings, cooking has a classical heart but is presented in a modern style. Dishes have deceptive depth and the wine list is a tome of beauty.
→ Oscietra caviar 'en surprise'. Black lobster, vin jaune and creamed morels. Gourmandise desserts.

Aarhus
AARHUS

Uniliux/iStock

AARHUS IN...

→ **ONE DAY**
ARoS Art Museum, the Viking Museum, Aarhus Cathedral, stroll around the Latin Quarter.

→ **TWO DAYS**
Den Gamle By (open air 'living' museum), hire a bike and ride into the country.

→ **THREE DAYS**
Marselisborg Palace (summer residence of the Royal family), Moesgaard Museum.

Known as the world's smallest big city, Denmark's second city is a vibrant, versatile place, yet has the charm of a small town. It was originally founded by the Vikings in the 8th century and has been an important trading centre ever since. It's set on the Eastern edge of Jutland and is the country's main port; lush forests surround it, and there are beautiful beaches to the north and south. It's easy to enjoy the great outdoors, while also benefiting from the advantages of urban life.

There's plenty to see and do, and most of it is within walking distance: the city centre is awash with shops – from big chains to

quirky boutiques – as well as museums, bars and restaurants, and the student population contributes to its youthful feel. The most buzzing area is Aboulevarden; a pedestrianized street which runs alongside the river, lined with clubs and cafés. Cultural activities are also high on the agenda of the European Capital of Culture 2017: visit the 12th century Cathedral and the ARoS Art Museum with its colourful rooftop panorama; witness the 2000 year old Grauballe man on display at the Moesgaard prehistoric museum; or step back in time at Den Gamle By. This is not a place that stands still and bold redevelopment projects are reshaping the cityscape, with shiny new apartment and office blocks springing up around the harbour.

EATING OUT

Being a student city, Aarhus hums with café culture all year round. You'll find cosy coffee shops on almost every street, offering breakfasts, cakes, sandwiches and light lunches – some are also popular places to enjoy an evening drink, especially in the lively Aboulevarden area. Eating out is something the Danes excel at and restaurants range from friendly bistros to elegant fine dining establishments. Most offer food with a Danish heart but influences come from around the globe. Local produce includes freshly caught fish landed at the harbour and vegetables from the island of Samso. Restaurants tend to offer set menus of between 3 and 7 courses and these are great way to sample a varied selection of dishes. They tend to open early – at around 6pm – while the bars and clubs stay open late, and often offer live music. Not to be overlooked are the city's classic Danish smørrebørd restaurants, where satisfying and wonderfully tasty open sandwiches are served, often along with a tempting selection of cakes and pastries. Tipping is not expected, but obviously greatly appreciated.

✿ **Frederikshøj** (Wassim Hallal)　　　　　XxX 錚 ≤ ⌂ AC

Oddervej 19-21 (South: 3.5 km by Spanien and Strandvejen) ✉ *8000*
– 𝒞 86 14 22 80 – www.frederikshoj.com – Closed 4 weeks midsummer,
1 week October, Christmas-New Year and Sunday-Tuesday
Menu 995 DKK – *(dinner only) (booking essential) (tasting menu only)*
• Creative • Elegant • Luxury •
Set in the former staff lodge to the Royal Palace, this restaurant is smart, luxurious and contemporary with edgy artwork, iPad menus and floor to ceiling windows affording views over the gardens and out to sea. Dishes are elaborate, creative and visually impressive. Service is professional and knowledgeable.
→ Bresse chicken with peas and chanterelles. Danish lamb with textures of onions. Rhubarb with chocolate and caramel.

✿ **Domestic** (Morten Rastad and Christoffer Norton)　　　XX 斎 & ⇔

Mejlgade 35B ✉ *8000 – 𝒞 6143 7010*　　　　　　　Plan: **B2**
– www.restaurantdomestic.dk – Closed Christmas-New Year, Easter,
Sunday and Monday
Menu 550/950 DKK – *(dinner only) (booking essential) (tasting menu only)*
• Modern cuisine • Fashionable • Minimalist •
The hottest ticket in town is this elegant rustic restaurant where 4 friends work together to serve skilfully cooked, feel-good food with pure, natural flavours – using only Danish ingredients. Hanging hams, pickling jars and cookbooks feature. Menus offer 4 or 8 set courses; the fish dishes are a highlight.
→ Lobster with burnt cream and chanterelles. Pork with black garlic and onion. Buttermilk, herbs and fermented honey.

✿ **Gastromé** (William Jørgensen)　　　　　　　　　XX ⇔

Rosensgade 28 ✉ *8000 – 𝒞 28 78 16 17*　　　　　Plan: **B2**
– www.gastrome.dk – Closed 25-26 December, Sunday and Monday
Menu 600/1000 DKK – *(dinner only) (tasting menu only)*
• Modern cuisine • Fashionable • Intimate •
This intimate Latin Quarter restaurant features a semi open plan kitchen and stark white walls punctuated with contemporary art. The menu is divided into a 'half throttle' of 4 courses and a 'full throttle' of 8, with wines to match. Complex cooking showcases modern techniques. Service is informative.
→ Halibut, Jerusalem artichoke and watercress. Quail with chanterelles and onions. Elderflower, white chocolate and bee pollen.

✿ **Substans** (René Mammen)　　　　　　　　　　XX AC

Frederiksgade 74 ✉ *8000 – 𝒞 86 23 04 01*　　　　Plan: **A2**
– www.restaurantsubstans.dk – Closed Sunday-Tuesday
Carte 700/1000 DKK – *(dinner only) (tasting menu only)*
• Modern cuisine • Friendly • Simple •
Classically Scandic in style, with a fresh, uncluttered feel, Pondus' older, more adventurous sister is run by the same experienced husband and wife team. Creative, contemporary cooking uses top quality, mostly organic, ingredients. Dishes have unfussy touches, distinct flavours and stimulating combinations.
→ Brown crab, caviar and rose hip. Organic pork with wild onions, brown butter and herbs. Raspberries with caramel, sour cream and hazelnut.

㊚ **Hærværk**　　　　　　　　　　　　　　　X & AC

Frederiks Allé 105 ✉ *8000 – 𝒞 50 51 26 51*　　　　Plan: **A2**
– www.restaurant-haervaerk.dk – Closed Sunday-Tuesday
Menu 450 DKK – *(dinner only) (tasting menu only)*
• Danish • Intimate • Fashionable •
A lively place set in two converted shops and run by four enthusiastic friends. It has industrial-chic styling courtesy of a concrete floor, stark white décor and a glass-fronted fridge of hanging meats. Well-crafted Danish dishes have a rustic style and a refined touch. The daily set menu is great value.

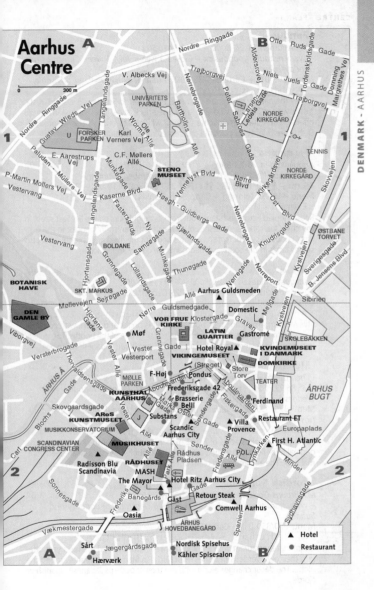

Aarhus Centre

0 — 300 m

A

V. Albecks Vej
Nordre Ringgade
Trøjborgvej
Nørrebrogade

B
Otte Ruds Gade
Aldersrovej
Niels Juels Gade
Tordenskjoldsgade
Donning Margrethes Vej
Trøjborgvej
Peter Sabroes Gade
Larsens Gade
NORDE KIRKEGÅRD

Nordre Ringgade
Gustav Wieds Vej
Langelandsgade
Ole Worms Allé
Bartholins Allé
UNIVERITETS PARKEN
Karl Verners Vej
FORSKER PARKEN
U
1

E. Aarestrups Vej
Paludan - Müllers Vej
P-Martin Mollers Vej
Vestervang
C.F. Møllers Allé
Ny Munkegade
Kaserne Blvd.
Høegh - Vennelyst Bvld
STENO MUSEET
Nørre Blvd
Kirkegårdsvej
Øst Blvd
TENNIS
NORDE KIRKEGÅRD
Skovvejen

Vestervang
Langelandsgade
Fastergade
Ny Munkegade
Samsøgade
Sjællandsgade
Høegh - Guldbergs Gade
Nørrebrogade
Knudrisgade
Nørregade
ØSTBANE TORVET
Sverigesgade

BOLDANE
Hjortensgade
Grønnegade
Lollandsgade
Thunøgade
Allé Aarhus Guldsmeden ▲
Nørreport
Kystvejen
B. Jensens Blvd
Sibirien

BOTANISK HAVE
SKT. MARKUS
Møllevejen
Sejrøgade
Nørre Guldsmedgade
Guldsmedgade
Klostergade
Domestic ●
Graven
Meijgade
SKOLEBÆKKEN

DEN GAMLE BY
Hortens Gade
Vester Allé
Grønnegade
Vesterport
VOR FRUE KIRKE
Gastromé ●
KVINDEMUSEET I DANMARK ▲

Viborgvej
Versterbrogade
Thorvaldsensgade
Møf ●
Vester Vesterport Gade
LATIN QUARTIER
Hotel Royal ▲
DOMKIRKE

ÅRHUS Å
Blochs Gade
MØLLE PARKEN
VIKINGEMUSEET
(Strøget)
Store Torv
TEATER
ÅRHUS BUGT

Skovgaardsgade
KUNSTHAL AARHUS
Vester
F-Høj ●
Åboulevarden
Pondus ●
Frederiksgade 42
Fiskergade
Ferdinand ●
Sønder Gade

ARoS KUNSTMUSEET
J
Substans ●
Brasserie Belli ●
Øster Gade
Gråbrødre Gade
Villa Provence ▲
Restaurant ET ●

MUSIKKONSERVATORIUM
Scandic Aarhus City ▲
Europaplads
First H. Atlantic ▲

SCANDINAVIAN CONGRESS CENTER
MUSIKHUSET
Park Allé
Sønder Allé
Fredensgade
Dynkarken
Mindet

Carl Blochs Gade
Radisson Blu Scandinavia ▲
RÅDHUSET
Rådhus Pladsen
POL.

2

Sønnesgade
MASH ●
The Mayor ▲
Hotel Ritz Aarhus City ▲
Sydhavnsgade

Vækmestergade
Frederiks Banegårds Gade
Gäst ●
Retour Steak ●
Comwell Aarhus ▲

Oasia ●
ÅRHUS HOVEDBANEGÅRD
Spanien

A
Sårt ●
Jægergårdsgade
Nordisk Spisehus ●
Kähler Spisesalon ●
B

Hærværk ●

▲ Hotel
● Restaurant

DENMARK - AARHUS

(😊) **Pondus** ✗

Åboulevarden 51 ✉ *8000* – ✆ *28 77 18 50*　　　　Plan: **B2**
– www.restaurantpondus.dk – Closed 3 weeks July, 1 week Christmas and Sunday-Tuesday
Menu 295 DKK – Carte 315/355 DKK – *(dinner only) (booking advisable)*
• Danish • Bistro • Rustic •

Set by the narrow city centre canal, the little sister to Substans is a small, rustic bistro with a friendly vibe and a stripped-back style. The blackboard menu offers great value, flavoursome cooking which uses organic Danish produce. Dishes are bright and colourful and represent great value.

🍴 **Ferdinand** ✗✗ ⇦ 🛁 🎍 🅰🅲

Åboulevarden 28 ✉ *8000* – ✆ *87 32 14 44*　　　　Plan: **B2**
– www.hotelferdinand.dk – Closed 23 December-4 January
19 rm – 🛏950/1150 DKK 🛏🛏1150/1350 DKK – ⌷ 110 DKK – 8 suites
Menu 445 DKK (dinner) – Carte 345/435 DKK
• French • Brasserie • Fashionable •

Red-canopied Ferdinand stands out from its neighbours on the liveliest street in the city. Classic brasserie dishes mix French and Danish influences; in the evening, choose a selection of small plates or go for the fixed price menu. A bar also serves tapas in the courtyard. Bedrooms are comfy and spacious.

🍴 **MASH** ✗✗ 🛁 🎍 🅰🅲

Banegaardspladsen 12 ✉ *8000* – ✆ *33 13 93 00*　　　　Plan: **A2**
– www.mashsteak.dk – Closed 24-25 December and 1 January
Carte 365/700 DKK
• Meats and grills • Fashionable • Friendly •

This Modern American Steak House (MASH) is bright and smart, with colourful cow ornaments and red leather banquettes; sit in one of the booths. Top quality imported USDA steaks are listed alongside Danish and Japanese Kobe beef.

🍴 **Mejeriet** ✗✗ 🛁 🍽 ⇔ 🅿

Vilhelmsborg, Bedervej 101, Mårslet (South : 11 km by 451) ✉ *8320*
– ✆ 86 93 71 95 – www.restaurant-mejeriet.dk – Closed Monday-Wednesday and Sunday dinner
Menu 375/695 DKK – *(dinner only and Sunday lunch) (booking essential)* *(tasting menu only)*
• Modern cuisine • Design • Rustic •

Set within the old stables of a 19C manor in the heart of the countryside; the original brick floor and arched ceilings remain but it now has a clean-lined minimal look. The accomplished team offer beautifully presented, creative dishes.

🍴 **Nordisk Spisehus** ✗✗ 🅰🅲

M.P.Bruuns Gade 31 ✉ *8000* – ✆ *86 17 70 99*　　　　Plan: **A/B2**
– www.nordiskspisehus.dk – Closed 24-26 December, 1 January and Sunday
Menu 270/850 DKK – Carte 500/850 DKK
• Modern cuisine • Neighbourhood • Fashionable •

An intimate restaurant with a unique concept: four themed menus a year offering their own versions of dishes from Michelin Starred restaurants around the globe. The décor changes along with the theme: perhaps Japanese, Spanish or Nordic.

🍴 **Restaurant ET** ✗✗ 🛁 🎍 ♿ 🅰🅲 ⇔

Åboulevarden 7 ✉ *8000* – ✆ *86 13 88 00*　　　　Plan: **B2**
– www.restaurant-et.dk – Closed Christmas and Sunday
Menu 360 DKK – Carte 375/515 DKK
• French • Design • Fashionable •

You'll find charming service, modern brasserie styling and a central kitchen at this well-run restaurant. Classic Gallic dishes are full of flavour and some come with a Danish twist. There's also a superb choice of French wines.

iO **Brasserie Belli** X 🛱

Frederiksgade 54 ⊠ 8000 – 𝒞 86 12 07 60 Plan: **B2**
– www.belli.dk – Closed 1 week July, Easter, Christmas, Sunday and bank holidays
Menu 250 DKK – Carte 290/500 DKK
• Classic French • Brasserie • Traditional décor •

A long-standing, family-owned restaurant set on a pedestrianised city centre street. It offers good value, satisfying French brasserie classics and service is polite and friendly. Check out the owner's costumes from her circus days.

iO **Frederiksgade 42** X

Frederiksgade 42 ⊠ 8000 – 𝒞 606 89 606 Plan: **B2**
– www.frederiksgade42.dk – Closed 22-25 December, Sunday and Monday
Menu 220/530 DKK – *(dinner only) (tasting menu only)*
• Danish • Neighbourhood • Bistro •

The experienced owner extends a warm welcome to customers at this delightful restaurant in the heart of the city. The focus is on vegetarian dishes, with seasonal menus of well-priced small plates designed for sharing.

iO **GÄST** – The Mayor Hotel X 🅿

Banegårdspladsen 14 ⊠ 8000 – 𝒞 87 32 01 67 Plan: **A2**
– www.restaurant-gaest.dk – Closed 23 December-8 January and Sunday
Menu 400 DKK – Carte 330/435 DKK
• Italian • Bistro • Fashionable •

This spacious, relaxed Italian restaurant, set on the ground floor of The Mayor Hotel, serves a seasonal, modern menu. Carefully cooked dishes are full of flavour; everything is prepared in-house and the pasta is the highlight.

iO **Møf** X

Vesterport 10 ⊠ 8000 – 𝒞 61 73 33 33 Plan: **A2**
– www.restaurantmoef.com – Closed 24 December, 1-2 January, Tuesday and Wednesday
Menu 325 DKK (dinner) – Carte 380/505 DKK – *(booking essential)*
• Danish • Neighbourhood • Trendy •

Ask for a seat at the counter to watch the young chef-owners cook in the open kitchen. Lunch sees a selection of smørrebrød and tarteletter, while dinner has a more modern style – dishes are Danish at heart and made with local produce.

iO **Retour Steak** X 🛱

Banegårdspladsen 4 ⊠ 8000 – 𝒞 88 63 02 90 Plan: **B2**
– www.retoursteakaarhus.dk – Closed 24-25 December and 1 January
Carte 240/595 DKK – *(dinner only)*
• Meats and grills • Fashionable • Bistro •

A busy restaurant close to station: the latest outpost of the famed steak group. They serve some simple starters and puddings but the main focus is on meat, with tasty Danish rib-eye in various sizes accompanied by fluffy homemade chips.

iO **Sårt** X

Jægergårdsgade 6 ⊠ 8000 – 𝒞 86 12 00 70 Plan: **A2**
– www.saart.dk – Closed 19-26 December, Sunday lunch and Monday
Menu 250/350 DKK – Carte 200/375 DKK
• Danish • Tapas bar • Rustic •

A simple but serious restaurant with its own deli: the first thing you see is a chiller filled with cured meats and preserved legs of ham; they also import whole cheeses, make their own pasta and have fresh bread delivered daily.

DENMARK - AARHUS

DENMARK - AARHUS

SMØRREBRØD The following simpler restaurants and cafés specialize in Danish open sandwiches

⫶○ ### F-Høj X 🛋

Grønnegade 2 ✉ 8000 – www.fhoj.dk Plan: A2
– Closed 4 weeks midsummer, 1 week October, Christmas-New Year, Sunday and Monday
Carte 275/395 DKK *– (lunch only) (bookings not accepted)*
• Smørrebrød • Neighbourhood • Friendly •
A bright, busy café with a pavement terrace; fridges and cabinets display a tempting selection of desserts, cakes, biscuits and drinks. There are six fresh, flavoursome classics on the smørrebrød menu; two plus dessert should suffice.

⫶○ ### Kähler Spisesalon X 🛋

M.P. Bruuns Gade 33 ✉ 8000 – ✆ 86 12 20 53 Plan: A/B2
– www.spisesalon.dk – Closed 24-26 December and 1 January
Menu 200/410 DKK *– (bookings not accepted)*
• Smørrebrød • Neighbourhood • Traditional décor •
An informal smørrebrød café, popular with shoppers and open in the evening. They offer soups, salads, smørrebrød and pastries, as well as organic juices and top-notch teas and coffees. Monochrome pictures of Aarhus add to the charm.

Comwell Aarhus ✿ ⪕ 🏖 & 🆔 🛁 🚗

Værkmestergade 2 ✉ 8000 – ✆ 86 72 80 00 Plan: B2
– www.comwellaarhus.dk
240 rm ☲ – †1100/1900 DKK ††1300/2500 DKK
• Business • Modern • Design •
A stylish, modern hotel set over 12 floors of a tower block. With 19 meeting rooms, it's aimed at businesspeople; the largest has space for 475. Bedrooms are bright and contemporary with monsoon showers; choose a corner Business Class room for super city views. Guest areas include a bar and buzzy bistro.

Radisson Blu Scandinavia ✿ 🏖 & 🆔 🛁 🚗

Margrethepladsen 1 ✉ 8000 – ✆ 86 12 86 65 Plan: A2
– www.radissonblu.com/hotel-aarhus
234 rm – †895/3245 DKK ††995/3345 DKK – ☲ 175 DKK – 5 suites
• Business • Chain • Modern •
A conference-orientated hotel close to the ARoS Museum. Spacious, contemporary bedrooms offer all the facilities a modern traveller would expect. Business Class rooms and suites on the top two floors offer the best views along with extra touches. International dishes are served in the informal restaurant.

Scandic Aarhus City ✿ 🏖 & 🆔 🛁 🚗

Østergade 10 ✉ 8000 – ✆ 89 31 81 00 Plan: B2
– www.scandichotels.com/aarhus
228 rm ☲ – †700/2600 DKK ††800/2800 DKK – 8 suites
• Business • Chain • Modern •
Behind the 19C façade of a Viennese Renaissance café lies a smart, modern hotel with an open-plan lobby, lounge and bar. Bright bedrooms feature photos of city scenes and the suites come with balconies. Solar panels supply electricity and rooftop hives provide honey. The Grill restaurant has an open kitchen.

Villa Provence 🛗 🅿

Fredens Torv 10-12 ✉ 8000 – ✆ 86 18 24 00 Plan: B2
– www.villaprovence.dk – Closed 20 December-4 January
39 rm ☲ – †1295/1695 DKK ††1395/3300 DKK
• Townhouse • Traditional • Personalised •
This charming townhouse is proudly run by an amiable couple and brings a little bit of Provence to Aarhus. Enter through the archway into a lovely cobbled garden designed by Tage Anderson, then head inside to be surrounded by books and French antiques. Bedrooms are individually styled; some have four-posters.

🏠 **First H. Atlantic** ⚐ ⇆ ⟨ **P**
Europaplads 10 ⊠ 8000 – ℰ 86 13 11 11 Plan: **B2**
– www.firsthotels.dk
102 rm ⌑ – ♦995/1895 DKK ♦♦1095/2195 DKK
· Business · Chain · Modern ·
Although its exterior can hardly be deemed charming, its rooms are spacious and modern with good facilities, a balcony and a vista of either the city or the sea. Enjoy breakfast with a view on the top floor. Classic Italian dishes are served in the smart restaurant. Gym membership is available at the adjacent fitness club.

🏠 **Hotel Ritz Aarhus City**
Banegårdspladsen 12 ⊠ 8000 – ℰ 86 13 44 44 Plan: **A2**
– www.hotelritz.dk – Closed 24-25 December
67 rm ⌑ – ♦1000/1150 DKK ♦♦1150/1350 DKK
· Historic · Traditional · Art déco ·
An iconic 1932 hotel in distinctive yellow brick, situated opposite the railway station. It's friendly and welcoming with an appealing art deco style and neat, modern bedrooms in warm colours; most rooms have a shower only.

🏠 **Hotel Royal** ⚐ ⅃♨ ⁂ 🆊 🛁
Store Torv 4 ⊠ 8000 – ℰ 86 12 00 11 Plan: **B2**
– www.hotelroyal.dk
63 rm – ♦995/1895 DKK ♦♦1195/2095 DKK – ⌑ 95 DKK – 5 suites
· Historic · Traditional · Classic ·
Beside the cathedral is the city's oldest hotel; 2018 marks its 180th birthday and it has a wonderfully classical feel – enhanced by paintings depicting Denmark's Kings and Queens. Very spacious bedrooms combine antique furniture and modern facilities. The informal restaurant serves international dishes.

🏠 **The Mayor** 🛁 **P**
Banegårdspladsen 14 ⊠ 8000 – ℰ 87 32 01 00 Plan: **A2**
– www.themayor.dk
162 rm ⌑ – ♦795/1995 DKK ♦♦1045/2095 DKK
· Family · Townhouse · Modern ·
Recently refurbished in a contemporary style, this hotel is situated close to the train station and has been owned by the same family for over twenty years. Cosy bedrooms have a modern industrial feel.
⇋○ **GÄST** – See restaurant listing

🏠 **Aarhus Guldsmeden**
Guldsmedgade 40 ⊠ 8000 – ℰ 86 13 45 50 Plan: **B1**
– www.guldsmedenhotels.com
22 rm ⌑ – ♦945/1345 DKK ♦♦1075/1475 DKK
· Townhouse · Traditional · Personalised ·
A relaxed hotel with an eco/organic ethos and a friendly atmosphere. Simply decorated bedrooms vary in shape and size; some feature antique furniture and the larger ones have four-posters. They offer complimentary tea, coffee and juice.

🏠 **Oasia** **P**
Kriegersvej 27-31 ⊠ 8000 – ℰ 87 32 37 15 Plan: **A2**
– www.hoteloasia.com – Closed 23-26 December
65 rm ⌑ – ♦900/1400 DKK ♦♦1000/1650 DKK
· Townhouse · Traditional · Design ·
After a day's sightseeing or shopping, you will be happy to head back to this hotel in a quieter area of the city. Bright, uncluttered bedrooms offer good facilities; go for one of the suites with their modern four-posters.

HELSINKI

FINLAND
SUOMI

scanrail/iStock

153

HELSINKI
HELSINGFORS

petriarttturiasikainen/iStock

Cool, clean and chic, the 'Daughter of the Baltic' sits prettily on a peninsula, jutting out between the landmasses of its historical overlords, Sweden and Russia. Surrounded on three sides by water, Helsinki is a busy port, but that only tells a small part of the story: forests grow in abundance around here and trees reach down to the lapping shores. This is a striking city to look at: it was rebuilt in the 19C after a fire, and many of the buildings have a handsome neoclassical or art nouveau façade. Shoppers can browse the picturesque outdoor food and tourist markets stretching along the main harbour, where island-hopping ferries ply their trade.

In a country with over 200,000 lakes it would be pretty hard to escape a green sensibility, and the Finnish capital has made sure that concrete and stone have never taken priority over its distinctive features of trees, water and open space. There are bridges at every turn connecting the city's varied array of small islands, and a ten kilometre strip of parkland acts as a spine running vertically up from the centre. Renowned as a city of cool, it's some-where that also revels in a hot nightlife and even hotter saunas – this is where they were invented. And if your blast of dry heat has left you wanting a refreshing dip, there's always a freezing lake close at hand.

EATING OUT

Local - and we mean local - ingredients are very much to the fore in the kitchens of Helsinki's restaurants. Produce is sourced from the country's abundant lakes, forests and seas, so your menu will assuredly be laden with the likes of smoked reindeer, reindeer's tongue, elk in aspic, lampreys, Arctic char, Baltic herring, snow grouse and cloudberries. Generally speaking, complicated, fussy preparations are overlooked for those that let the natural flavours shine through. In the autumn, markets are piled high with woodland mushrooms, often from Lapland, and chefs make the most of this bounty. Local alcoholic drinks include schnapps, vodka and liqueurs made from local berries: lakka (made from cloudberries) and mesimarja (brambleberries) are definitely worth discovering – you may not find them in any other European city. You'd find coffee anywhere in Europe, but not to the same extent as here: Finns are among the world's biggest coffee drinkers. In the gastronomic restaurants, lunch is a simpler affair, often with limited choice.

155

❀ **Ask** (Filip Langhoff)   XX 🗚

Vironkatu 8 ✉ *00170*   Plan: **C1**
– Ⓜ *Kaisaniemi*
– 𝒞 *(040) 581 8100 – www.restaurantask.com*
– *Closed Easter, Christmas, Sunday-Tuesday and bank holidays*
Menu 50/110 € – *(dinner only and lunch Friday-Saturday) (tasting menu only)*
• Modern cuisine • Intimate • Cosy •

It may be hidden away but this welcoming restaurant is well-known. It's a charming place, run by a delightful, experienced couple, who offer modern Nordic cooking crafted almost entirely from organic ingredients. Dishes are light and original, produce is top quality and flavours are clearly defined.
→ Smoked reindeer tartare and hazelnut. Pike-perch with brown butter and caviar. Pancakes, spruce and caramel.

❀ **Demo** (Tommi Tuominen)   XX

Uudenmaankatu 9-11 ✉ *00120*   Plan: **C2**
– Ⓜ *Rautatientori* – 𝒞 *(09) 228 90 840 – www.restaurantdemo.fi*
– *Closed 3 weeks July-August, 2 weeks Christmas, Easter, midsummer, Sunday and Monday*
Menu 60/105 € – *(dinner only) (booking essential) (tasting menu only)*
• Modern cuisine • Intimate •

An unassuming-looking restaurant decorated in neutral tones and hung with huge cotton pendant lights. Classically based cooking combines French and Finnish influences to produce robust, satisfying dishes with a subtle modern edge. Choose 4-7 courses; the menu is presented verbally and changes almost daily.
→ Black Angus carpaccio with oyster emulsion. Duck breast with chanterelle porridge. Caramelised brioche, fermented strawberry and crème brûlée ice cream.

❀ **Olo** (Jari Vesivalo)   XX & 🗚 ⇕

Pohjoisesplanadi 5 ✉ *00170*   Plan: **C2**
– Ⓜ *Kaisaniemi*
– 𝒞 *(010) 3206 250 – www.olo-ravintola.fi*
– *Closed Easter, midsummer, Christmas, Sunday and Monday*
Menu 65/120 € – *(dinner only) (booking essential) (tasting menu only)*
• Modern cuisine • Design • Contemporary décor •

An attractive harbourside townhouse plays host to this cool, minimalist restaurant, whose four rooms have a delightfully understated feel. Lunch is 4 courses, while dinner arrives in up to 18 servings. Local meats such as moose and elk feature in exciting, innovative dishes which are packed with flavour.
→ Pike-perch with horseradish mousse. Reindeer, salt-baked celeriac and mushrooms. Aerated honey parfait with sea buckthorn.

❀ **Grön** (Toni Kostian)   X

Albertinkatu 36 ✉ *00180*   Plan: **B2**
– Ⓜ *Kammpi*
– 𝒞 *(050) 3289181 – www.restaurantgron.com*
– *Closed Sunday and Monday*
Menu 49 €
– *Carte 47/53 € – (dinner only) (booking essential)*
• Finnish • Neighbourhood • Intimate •

A warmly run restaurant where the open kitchen is the focal point and the chefs bring the dishes to the table to explain them. Cooking has a satisfying earthiness and clever use is made of both fresh and fermented ingredients, with vegetables given equal billing as meat or fish. Natural wines are well-chosen.
→ Aged beef, chickweed and smoked bone marrow. New potatoes with summer onions and herring butter. Wild strawberries with fennel leaves and milk.

Ora (Sasu Laukkonen) 🟇 Plan: C3

Huvilakatu 28A ⊠ 00150 – ℰ (40) 0959 440
– www.orarestaurant.fi – Closed 22 June-24 July, 10 days Christmas-New Year, 1 week March, Easter and Sunday-Tuesday
Menu 85 € – (dinner only and lunch Friday-Saturday) (booking essential) (tasting menu only)
• Modern cuisine • Chic • Cosy •

This small, intimate restaurant is run by chef-owner Sasu Laukkonen. The cooking focuses on local ingredients and uses modern techniques to enhance classic Finnish flavours. Dishes are served and explained by the chefs themselves.
➔ Pumpkin and zucchini tart with sea buckthorn. Whitefish from Inari with nasturtium. Blueberries with Douglas fir.

Boulevard Social 🟇 🛱 & 🄰🄲 Plan: C2

Bulevardi 6 ⊠ 00120 – Ⓜ Rautatientori – ℰ (010) 3229387 – www.boulevardsocial.fi – Closed Christmas, midsummer, Saturday lunch and Sunday
Menu 30/65 € – Carte 35/50 €
• Mediterranean cuisine • Fashionable •

Owned by the same people as next door Gaijin, this lively, informal restaurant offers an accessible range of authentic North African, Turkish and Eastern Mediterranean dishes; try the set or tasting menus to experience a cross-section of them all. If they're fully booked, ask for a seat at the counter.

Emo 🟇 & 🄰🄲 ⇔ Plan: C2

Kluuvikatu 2 ⊠ 00100 – Ⓜ Rautatientori – ℰ (010) 505 0900 – www.emo-ravintola.fi – Closed Christmas, New Year, Easter, midsummer, Saturday lunch and Sunday
Menu 39/54 € – Carte 50/76 €
• Modern cuisine • Fashionable • Intimate •

A laid-back restaurant with an adjoining bar, run by a friendly team. The menu is easy-going too, offering around 10 regularly changing dishes that can be taken either as starters or main courses. Good quality ingredients feature in flavoursome, unfussy preparations which come with a contemporary touch.

Farang 🟇 & 🄰🄲 ⇔ Plan: B2

Ainonkatu 3 (inside the Kunsthalle) ⊠ 00100 – Ⓜ Kamppi – ℰ (010) 322 9385 – www.farang.fi – Closed Christmas, midsummer, Easter, last 3 weeks July, Saturday lunch, Sunday and Monday
Menu 32/64 € – Carte 30/65 €
• South East Asian • Simple • Intimate •

This stylish, modern restaurant is housed in the Kunsthalle art centre. One room is decorated with large photos of Thai scenes and has communal tables; the other is more intimate and furnished in red, black and grey. Zesty, harmonious dishes take their influences from Vietnam, Thailand and Malaysia.

Gaijin 🟇 🛱 & 🄰🄲 Plan: C2

Bulevardi 6 ⊠ 00120 – Ⓜ Rautatientori – ℰ (010) 3229386 – www.gaijin.fi – Closed Christmas, midsummer and lunch Saturday-Monday
Menu 39/64 € – Carte 39/74 € – (booking essential)
• Asian • Fashionable •

Gaijin comes with dark, contemporary décor, a buzzing atmosphere, attentive service and an emphasis on sharing. Its experienced owners offer boldly flavoured, skilfully presented modern takes on Japanese, Korean and Northern Chinese recipes. The tasting menus are a great way to sample the different cuisines.

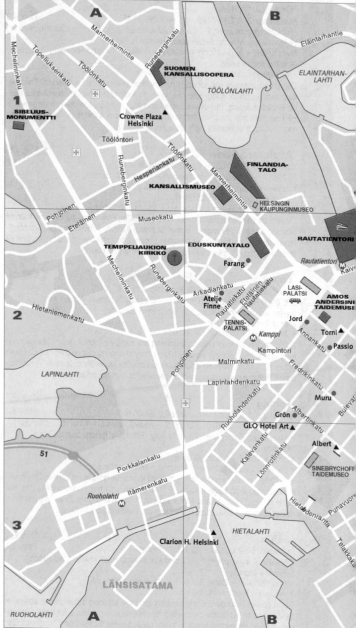

FINLAND - HELSINKI

A

B

Mannerheimintie

Mechelininkatu

Topeliuksenkatu

Töölönkatu

Runeberginkatu

Eläintarhantie

ELÄINTARHAN-LAHTI

SUOMEN KANSALLISOOPERA

TÖÖLÖNLAHTI

1

SIBELIUS-MONUMENTTI

Crowne Plaza Helsinki

Töölöntori

Runeberginkatu

Hesperiankatu

Töölönkatu

Mannerheimintie

FINLANDIA-TALO

KANSALLISMUSEO

HELSINGIN KAUPUNGINMUSEO

Pohjoinen

Eteläinen

Museokatu

TEMPPELIAUKION KIRKKO

EDUSKUNTATALO

RAUTATIENTORI

Mechelininkatu

Runeberginkatu

Rautatientori

Kaiv

Farang

Hietaniemenkatu

Arkadiankatu

Eteläinen Rautatiekatu

Rautatiekatu

LASI-PALATSI

AMOS ANDERSINI TAIDEMUSE

2

Atelje Finne

TENNIS-PALATSI

Jord

Torni

Annankatu

Passio

Kamppi

LAPINLAHTI

Pohjoinen

Kampintori

Malminkatu

Lapinlahdenkatu

Fredrikinkatu

Muru

Grön

Albertinkatu

GLO Hotel Art

Ruoholahdenkatu

Bulev

Albert

51

Porkkalankatu

Kalevankatu

Lönnrotinkatu

SINEBRYCHOFF TAIDEMUSEO

Ruoholahti

Itämerenkatu

Hietalahdentaranta

Punavuor

3

Clarion H. Helsinki

HIETALAHTI

Telakka

LÄNSISATAMA

RUOHOLAHTI

A

B

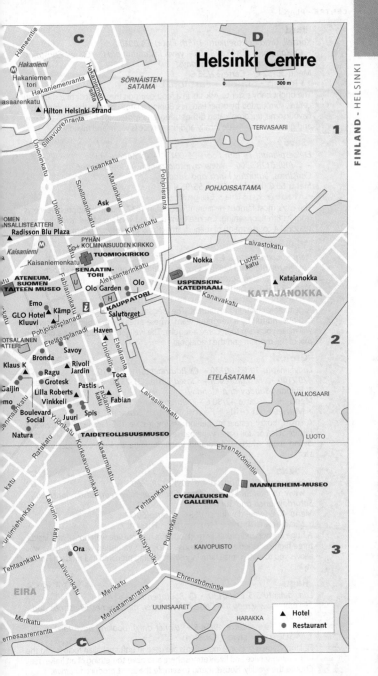

Helsinki Centre

0   300 m

C

Hakaniemi

Hakaniemen tori

Hakaniemenranta

Hakaniemen Silta

asaarenkatu

▲ Hilton Helsinki Strand

Sillavuorenranta

Liisankatu

Unioninkatu

Snellmaninkatu

Maliankatu

Ask ●

Kirkkokatu

SÖRNÄISTEN SATAMA

D

TERVASAARI

1

POHJOISSATAMA

SUOMEN KANSALLISTEATTERI

Radisson Blu Plaza ▲

Kaisaniemi Ⓜ

PYHÄN KOLMINAISUUDEN KIRKKO

Kaisaniemenkatu

TUOMIOKIRKKO ✚

SENAATIN-TORI

Fabianinkatu

Aleksanterinkatu

Olo ●

Laivastokatu

Nokka ●

Luotsi-katu

▲ Katajanokka

ATENEUM, SUOMEN TAITEEN MUSEO

Olo Garden ●

USPENSKIN-KATEDRAALI ■

KATAJANOKKA

Kanavakatu

Emo ●

GLO Hotel Kluuvi ▲ ● **Kämp**

ⓘ

KAUPPATORI Ⓗ

Pohjoisesplanadi

Salutorget ●

Eteläesplanadi

Haven ●

OTSALAINEN ATTERI

Savoy ●

Bronda ●

Klaus K ▲

Ragu ●

▲ **Rivoli Jardin**

Unioninkatu

Eteläranta

2

ETELÄSATAMA

VALKOSAARI

Gaijin ●

Grotesk ●

Toca ●

Lilla Roberts ▲ Pastis ●

Fabianinkatu

mo

Vinkkeli ●

● Fabian

LUOTO

Boulevard Social ●

Juuri ● Spis ●

Yrjönkatu

Natura ●

Ratakatu

TAIDETEOLLISUUSMUSEO

Kasarmikatu

Ehrenströmintie

Korkeavuorenkatu

katu

Laivurin-katu

ursimiehenkatu

Tehtaankatu

Puistokatu

Neitsytpolku

CYGNAEUKSEN GALLERIA

■ **MANNERHEIM-MUSEO**

3

KAIVOPUISTO

Ora ●

Laivurinkatu

Merikatu

Merisatamanranta

UUNISAARET

Ehrenströmintie

EIRA

Merikatu

ernesaarenranta

HARAKKA

▲ Hotel

● Restaurant

C

D

FINLAND - HELSINKI

(43) **Jord** ✗ ᴀᴄ

Kortteli, Urho Kekkosenkatu 1 (5th Floor) ✉ *00100*   Plan: **B2**
– Ⓜ *Kamppi –* ℰ *405 828 100 – www.restaurantjord.fi – Closed Christmas,*
Easter, Sunday and bank holidays
Menu 35/52 € – Carte 32/53 €
• Finnish • Simple • Fashionable •

The bright baby sister to Ask sits in a food court on the 5th floor of a shopping
centre, surrounded by other eateries. Behind a large counter, the chefs prepare
flavoursome, uncomplicated dishes using largely organic produce. The crockery
and glassware are made locally and the service is warm and friendly.

⑪◯ **Savoy** ✗✗✗ ⊛ ⇐ ⇌ ⴴ ᴀᴄ ⇦

Eteläesplanadi 14 (8th floor) ✉ *00130 –* Ⓜ *Kaisaniemi*   Plan: **C2**
– ℰ *(09) 6128 5300 – www.ravintolasavoy.fi – Closed Easter,*
Christmas, Saturday lunch and Sunday
Menu 65 € (lunch) – Carte 55/95 €
• Modern cuisine • Elegant •

The city's most famous restaurant opened in 1937 and offers impressive views
from its 8th floor setting. Choose from updated versions of old favourites or a
seasonal 4 course menu of refined, attractively presented modern dishes.

⑪◯ **Vinkkeli** ✗✗ ᴀᴄ

Pieni Roobertinkatu 8 ✉ *00130 –* ℰ *(29) 1800 222*   Plan: **C2**
– www.ravintolavinkkeli.fi – Closed 25 June-21 August, 22 December-
9 January, Easter, Saturday lunch, Sunday and Monday
Menu 29/54 € – Carte dinner 45/52 €
• Classic cuisine • Elegant • Romantic •

A genuinely charming restaurant. The elegant, high-ceilinged room is smartly
laid out and run by a delightful team, whose attentive and personable service
will make you want to become a regular. The well-judged cooking is a pleasing
mix of the modern and the traditional.

⑪◯ **Grotesk** ✗✗ ⇌ ᴀᴄ ⇦

Ludviginkatu 10 ✉ *00130 –* Ⓜ *Rautatientori –* ℰ *(010)*   Plan: **C2**
470 2100 – www.grotesk.fi – Closed Easter, 21-23 June, 24-26 December,
1 January, Sunday and Monday
Menu 59 € – Carte 42/80 € – *(dinner only)*
• Meats and grills • Fashionable • Brasserie •

A smart, buzzy restaurant behind an impressive 19C façade. It comprises a
fashionable cocktail bar, a wine bar serving interesting small plates, and a chic
dining room which is decorated in black, white and red and specialises in
steaks.

⑪◯ **Nokka** ✗✗ ⇌ ᴀᴄ ⇦

Kanavaranta 7F ✉ *00160 –* ℰ *(09) 6128 5600*   Plan: **D2**
– www.ravintolanokka.fi – Closed Christmas-New Year, Easter, lunch July,
Saturday lunch and Sunday
Menu 47 € (weekday lunch)/58 € – Carte 50/72 €
• Modern cuisine • Romantic • Rustic •

A huge anchor and propeller mark out this harbourside warehouse and inside,
three high-ceilinged rooms juxtapose brick with varnished wood. A glass wall
allows you to watch small farm ingredients being prepared in a modern Finnish
style.

⑪◯ **Ragu** ✗✗ ⴴ ᴀᴄ ⇦

Ludviginkatu 3-5 ✉ *00130 –* Ⓜ *Rautatientori –* ℰ *(09)*   Plan: **C2**
596 659 – www.ragu.fi – Closed July, Easter, midsummer, Christmas and
Sunday
Menu 45/59 € – Carte 49/54 € – *(dinner only) (booking advisable)*
• Modern cuisine • Design • Chic •

Finland's famed seasonal ingredients are used in unfussy Italian recipes and the
welcoming service and lively atmosphere also have something of an Italian feel.
Choose the weekly 'House' menu to sample the latest produce to arrive.

FINLAND - HELSINKI

Salutorget
XX & AC

Pohjoisesplanadi 15 ✉ *00170* – Ⓜ *Kaisaniemi* – ✆ *(09)*
Plan: **C2**
6128 5950 – *www.salutorget.fi* – *Closed Easter, Christmas, midsummer,*
Sunday and Bank holidays
Menu 35 € (weekday lunch)/45 € – Carte 30/60 €
• **International** • **Brasserie** • **Elegant** •

An old bank, located on the esplanade; now an elegant restaurant with impressive columns and attractive stained glass. The classic, brasserie-style menu has global influences. Enjoy afternoon tea in the plush cocktail bar.

Muru
X 🕸 AC

Fredrikinkatu 41 ✉ *00120* – Ⓜ *Kamppi* – ✆ *(300)*
Plan: **B2**
472 335 – *www.murudining.fi* – *Closed Christmas, New Year, Easter,*
1 May, midsummer, Sunday, Monday and bank holidays
Menu 46/52 € – Carte 46/52 € – *(dinner only) (booking essential)*
• **Modern cuisine** • **Neighbourhood** • **Trendy** •

The charming team really enhance your experience at this cosy little bistro. It's a quirky place, with a wine bottle chandelier, a bar made from old wine boxes and a high level wine cellar. A blackboard lists snacks and around 7 main dishes but most diners choose the 4 course daily menu with a Gallic base.

Ateljé Finne
X AC

Arkadiankatu 14 ✉ *00100* – Ⓜ *Kamppi* – ✆ *(010)*
Plan: **B2**
281 8242 – *www.ateljefinne.fi* – *Closed Christmas, Easter, midsummer,*
weekends in July, Sunday and Monday
Menu 44 € – Carte 46/63 € – *(dinner only) (booking advisable)*
• **Modern cuisine** • **Bistro** • **Family** •

This is the old studio of sculptor Gunnar Finne, who worked here for over 30 years. Local art decorates the small bistro-style dining rooms set over three levels. Regional dishes are given subtle modern and international twists.

Bronda
X & AC ⟷

Eteläesplanadi 20 ✉ *00130* – Ⓜ *Rautatientori*
Plan: **C2**
– ✆ *(010) 322 9383* – *www.ravintolabronda.fi* – *Closed Christmas,*
midsummer and Sunday
Menu 29/57 € – Carte 36/70 €
• **Modern cuisine** • **Fashionable** • **Brasserie** •

The floor to ceiling windows of this old furniture showroom flood it with light. Have cocktails and snacks at the bar or comforting, boldly flavoured, Mediterranean sharing plates in the brasserie. Each dish arrives as it's ready.

Juuri
X

Korkeavuorenkatu 27 ✉ *00130* – ✆ *(09) 635 732*
Plan: **C2**
– *www.juuri.fi* – *Closed midsummer and 24-26 December*
Carte 38/63 €
• **Traditional cuisine** • **Bistro** • **Intimate** •

A friendly bistro with colourful décor and a rustic feel. The focus here is on sharing: small, tapas-style plates showcase organic produce and classic Finish recipes are given a modern makeover. They brew their own beer in the cellar.

Natura
X

Iso Roobertinkatu 11 ✉ *00120* – ✆ *(040) 6891 111*
Plan: **C2**
– *www.restaurantnatura.com* – *Closed July, Christmas, midsummer,*
Monday and Tuesday
Menu 39/89 € – Carte 25/45 € – *(dinner only) (booking essential)*
• **Finnish** • **Neighbourhood** • **Design** •

Carefully chosen ingredients are bound together in appealing seasonal small plates at this intimate restaurant. Techniques mix the old and the new and dishes are full of colour. Go for the 'Classic' menu, accompanied by a pure wine.

⊪⃝ ### Olo Garden ✗ 🅰️Ⅽ

Pohjoisesplanadi 5 (Entrance on Helenankatu 2) Plan: **C2**
✉ 00170 – ☏ (010) 320 6250 – www.olo-ravintola.fi – *Closed Christmas, July, Sunday and Monday*
Menu 57/75 € – Carte 52/72 € – *(dinner only) (booking essential)*
• **Modern cuisine • Simple •**
The casual addendum to Olo occupies a glass-roofed inner courtyard and has a feeling of openness. The menu has a light, modern style and some occasional Asian notes; some dishes are designed for sharing. The cocktails are popular.

⊪⃝ ### Passio ✗ 🅰️Ⅽ

Kalevankatu 13 ✉ 00100 – Ⓜ *Kamppi* – ☏ (020) Plan: **B2**
7352 040 – www.passiodining.fi – *Closed Christmas, midsummer and lunch Saturday-Sunday*
Menu 29/50 € – *(booking advisable)*
• **Modern cuisine • Friendly • Neighbourhood •**
Exposed ducts, dimly lit lamps and leather-topped tables give Passio a faux industrial feel. Modern cooking showcases regional ingredients and flavours are well-defined. It's run by a local brewer, so be sure to try the artisan beers.

⊪⃝ ### Pastis ✗ 🅰️Ⅽ

Pieni Roobertinkatu 2 ✉ 00130 – ☏ (030) 04 72 336 Plan: **C2**
– www.pastis.fi – *Closed Easter, 4 November, 6 December, 22 December-8 January, 22-24 June, Sunday and bank holidays*
Menu 29 € – Carte 40/54 € – *(booking essential)*
• **Classic French • Bistro • Neighbourhood •**
The clue is in the name: they serve classic French dishes, alongside several different brands of pastis. It's a popular place, so there's always a lively atmosphere. Come for Saturday brunch or have a private meal in Petit Pastis.

⊪⃝ ### Spis ✗

Kasarmikatu 26 ✉ 00130 – ☏ (045) 305 1211 Plan: **C2**
– www.spis.fi – *Closed Sunday, Monday and bank holidays*
Menu 50/77 € – *(dinner only) (booking essential) (tasting menu only)*
• **Modern cuisine • Neighbourhood • Bistro •**
An intimate restaurant seating just 18; the décor is 'faux derelict', with exposed brick and plaster walls. Creative, flavoursome cooking features Nordic flavours in attractive, imaginative combinations. Most dishes are vegetable-based.

⊪⃝ ### Toca ✗

Unioninkatu 18 ✉ 00130 – ☏ (044) 2379922 Plan: **C2**
– www.toca.fi – *Closed 22 June-31 July, 22 December-8 January, Sunday and Monday*
Menu 25 € (lunch)/65 € – *(booking essential)*
• **Modern cuisine • Trendy •**
A modest little bistro with an unfinished look. At lunch they serve just two dishes – aimed at local workers – while dinner offers a 3 or 5 set course menu. Cooking is an original mix of Italian simplicity and Finnish modernity.

🏨 ### Kämp ✿ 🛎 🌐 🎐 ⅋ 🅰️Ⅽ 🧖 🚗

Pohjoisesplanadi 29 ✉ 00100 – Ⓜ *Kaisaniemi* – ☏ (09) Plan: **C2**
576 111 – www.hotelkamp.com
179 rm – 🛏220/620 € 🛏🛏220/620 € – � 32 € – 7 suites
• **Grand Luxury • Classic • Historic •**
The grand façade, columned interior and impressive staircase point back to this luxurious hotel's 19C roots and the classically furnished bedrooms follow suit; the superb spa, meanwhile, adds a modern touch. The chic bar serves an excellent selection of champagne and cocktails, while for dining, there's a bustling brasserie with an appealing globally inspired menu.

FINLAND - HELSINKI

Crowne Plaza Helsinki ⋔ ₤₈ 🏧 ⋙ 📺 ₠ 🎴 🚗
Mannerheimintie 50 ⊠ 00260 – ℰ (09) 2521 0000 Plan: **A1**
– www.crowneplaza-helsinki.fi
349 rm ⊊ – †145/500 € ††145/500 € – 4 suites
• Business • Chain • Contemporary •
A spacious hotel specialising in conferences. Comfy, up-to-date bedrooms have good facilities and city or lake views; the higher the floor, the better the grade. Pay a visit to the huge basement fitness club and spa, then make for the warm, welcoming restaurant which serves Mediterranean cuisine.

Hilton Helsinki Strand ⋔ ≤ ₤₈ ⋙ 📺 ₠ 🎴 🚗
John Stenbergin Ranta 4 ⊠ 00530 – ⓜ Hakaniemi Plan: **C1**
– ℰ (09) 393 51 – www.hilton.com
190 rm – †130/360 € ††165/395 € – ⊊ 22 € – 7 suites
• Business • Luxury • Classic •
This spacious waterfront hotel has a classical 1980s design, an impressive atrium and an 8th floor fitness and relaxation centre; take in the view from the gym or pool. Smartly kept bedrooms boast marble bathrooms – ask for a room overlooking the water. The restaurant offers global classics and local specialities.

Clarion H.Helsinki ⋔ ₤₈ 🏧 ⋙ 📺 ₠ 🎴 🚗
Tyynenmerenkatu 2 ⊠ 00220 – ⓜ Ruoholahti Plan: **B3**
– ℰ (010) 850 3820 – www.nordichoicehotel.com
425 rm ⊊ – †100/150 € ††120/350 € – 16 suites
• Chain • Business • Design •
This smart skyscraper sits to the west of the city – take in the stunning view from the cool modern bedrooms or the 16th floor gym, outdoor swimming pool or Sky Bar. Meeting rooms are housed within a warehouse dating from 1937. The stylish ground floor bistro has a subtle American theme.

GLO Hotel Kluuvi ⋔ ₤₈ 🏧 ⋙ ₠ 🎴 🚗 ♢
Kluuvikatu 4 ⊠ 00100 – ⓜ Kaisaniemi – ℰ (010) Plan: **C2**
3444 400 – www.glohotels.fi
184 rm ⊊ – †125/370 € ††230/380 € – 6 suites
• Luxury • Modern • Design •
A stylish hotel on a fashionable shopping street; a boutique sister to next door Kämp, whose spa it shares. Spacious bedrooms have a contemporary look and come with smart glass shower rooms. There's also a lively bar-lounge and a fashionable restaurant serving cuisine from around the globe.

Haven ⋔ ₤₈ ₠ 📺 🎴
Unioninkatu 17 ⊠ 00130 – ℰ (09) 681930 Plan: **C2**
– www.hotelhaven.fi
137 rm ⊊ – †160/300 € ††180/320 €
• Business • Luxury • Modern •
A former city centre office block is home to this elegant hotel. Colourful modern bedrooms come with high ceilings, top quality furnishings and a plush feel. Extensive breakfasts are served in an impressive room. Snacks and light dishes are offered in the two cosy bars and they also have a great rum selection.

Klaus K ⋔ ₤₈ ⋙ 📺 🎴
Bulevardi 2/4 ⊠ 00120 – ⓜ Rautatientori – ℰ (020) Plan: **C2**
770 4703 – www.klauskhotel.com
171 rm ⊊ – †120/320 € ††140/640 €
• Luxury • Design • Personalised •
The Kalevala – a 19C work of poetry based on Finnish folklore – leads the design at this striking hotel, from the mosaic fish in the bar to the graffiti panelled corridors and stylish bedrooms. The Sky Loft rooms are particularly sumptuous.

FINLAND - HELSINKI

Lilla Roberts ⚘ 🛗 & 🄰🄲

Pieni Roobertinkatu 1-3 ✉ *00130* – ☏ *(09) 689 9880*   Plan: **C2**
– www.lillaroberts.fi
130 rm ⬛ – **†**150/210 € **††**170/220 € – 1 suite
• Business • Design • Personalised •

This building was designed in 1908 by one of Finland's top architects and was originally head office for the city's energy works. The smart, designer interior uses dark colours and is centred around the concept of 'hygge' (enjoying the simple things in life). The elegant restaurant serves an appealing menu.

Radisson Blu Plaza ⚘ 🛗 🏡 & 🄰🄲 🛁

Mikonkatu 23 ✉ *00100* – Ⓜ *Kaisaniemi* – ☏ *(020)*   Plan: **C2**
1234 703 – www.radissonblu.com/plazahotel-helsinki
302 rm – **†**120/389 € **††**135/405 € – ⬛ 25 € – 1 suite
• Business • Chain • Contemporary •

An elegant 20C building set close to the station and completed by a more modern wing. Well-equipped bedrooms come in a choice of modern or classic styles and many have 3D TVs. The bar is a fashionable spot and the large restaurant – unusually set over several rooms – offers five different types of cuisine.

Torni ⚘ 🄰🄲 🛁

Yrjönkatu 26 ✉ *00100* – Ⓜ *Rautatientori* – ☏ *(020)*   Plan: **B2**
1234 604 – www.sokoshoteltorni.fi
152 rm ⬛ – **†**180/280 € **††**180/280 € – 6 suites
• Business • Art déco • Elegant •

A delightful early 20C hotel with a palpable sense of history. Bedrooms come in 'Art Deco', 'Art Nouveau' and 'Functionalist' styles – the latter, in the 11 storey tower, have glass-walled bathrooms. The top floor bar has a terrace and superb city views; the restaurant offers traditional Finnish cuisine.

Fabian 🏡 & 🄰🄲

Fabiankatu 7 ✉ *00130* – ☏ *(09) 6128 2000*   Plan: **C2**
– www.hotelfabian.fi
58 rm – **†**120/350 € **††**140/450 € – ⬛ 22 €
• Townhouse • Contemporary • Modern •

A charming boutique hotel close to the harbour. Bedrooms have stylish black & white themes and smart bathrooms with heated floors. Have breakfast in the central courtyard in summer – ingredients are organic or from small producers.

GLO Hotel Art ⚘ 🏡 & 🄰🄲 🛁 🚗

Lönnrotinkatu 29 ✉ *00180* – Ⓜ *Kamppi* – ☏ *(010)*   Plan: **B3**
3444 100 – www.glohotels.fi
171 rm ⬛ – **†**150/300 € **††**165/365 €
• Townhouse • Business • Modern •

Sited in the heart of the lively Design District, a 1903 art nouveau castle with modern extensions and its own art collection. Chic bedrooms were styled by Finnish designers and come in three sizes. You can borrow everything from bicycles to paints and brushes. A Nordic grill menu is served in the old cellars.

Katajanokka ⚘ 🛗 🏡 & 🄰🄲 🛁 🅿

Merikasarminkatu 1A ✉ *00160* – ☏ *(09) 686 450*   Plan: **D2**
– www.hotelkatajanokka.fi
106 rm ⬛ – **†**90/250 € **††**100/400 €
• Historic • Personalised • Vintage •

A pleasantly restored, late 19C prison where they have retained the original staircases and high ceilinged corridors. The old cells are now comfortable, well-equipped bedrooms with modern bathrooms. The traditional cellar restaurant features a preserved prison cell and serves traditional Finnish cuisine.

Albert
⚑ 𝔪 ⚐ AC

Albertinkatu 30 ✉ 00180 – ☎ (020) 1234 638
Plan: **B3**
– www.sokoshotels.fi – Closed Christmas
95 rm ⚏ – 🛈129/185 € 🛈🛈144/200 €
• Business • Contemporary • Personalised •

An unassuming 19C building with a contrastingly cosy interior. Good-sized contemporary bedrooms are well-equipped and come with Nordic furnishings and up-to-date bathrooms. Have drinks in the welcoming open-plan lounge-bar, then head to the trattoria-style restaurant for a selection of Italian classics.

Rivoli Jardin
𝔪 ⚐

Kasarmikatu 40 ✉ 00130 – ☎ (09) 681 500
Plan: **C2**
– www.rivoli.fi – Closed Christmas
55 rm ⚏ – 🛈100/240 € 🛈🛈120/260 €
• Townhouse • Cosy • Personalised •

A small, city centre oasis hidden away off a courtyard, with an intimate conservatory lounge, and a sauna and meeting room tucked away in the cellar. Bedrooms are cosy and individually decorated; the top floor rooms have terraces.

AT HELSINKI-VANTAA AIRPORT

Hilton Helsinki Airport
⚑ ☐ 𝔪 ⚐ AC ⊬ ⚒ P

Lentàjànkuja 1 ✉ 01530 – ☎ (09) 732 20 – www.hilton.com
330 rm – 🛈99/370 € 🛈🛈109/400 € – ⚏ 27 € – 5 suites
• Business • Chain • Modern •

3mins from the international terminal (T2); a spacious glass hotel with a relaxed ambience and a large conference capacity. Well-soundproofed bedrooms boast locally designed furniture, good facilities and large bathrooms – some have saunas. The stylish restaurant serves Finnish and international cuisine.

PARIS ●

● Lyons

FRANCE
FRANCE

Jerome_Correia/iStock

PARIS
PARIS

MaxOzerov/iStock

PARIS IN...

➜ **ONE DAY**
Eiffel Tower, Notre-Dame Cathedral, a café on Boulevard St Germain, Musée d'Orsay, Montmartre.

➜ **TWO DAYS**
The Louvre, Musée du Quai Branly.

➜ **THREE DAYS**
Canal Saint-Martin, Centre Pompidou, Picasso Museum and the Marais.

The French capital is one of the truly great cities of the world, a metropolis that eternally satisfies the desires of its beguiled visitors. With its harmonious layout, typified by the grand geometric boulevards radiating from the Arc de Triomphe like the spokes of a wheel, Paris is designed to enrapture. Despite its ever-widening tentacles, most of the things worth seeing are contained within the city's ring road. Paris wouldn't be Paris sans its Left and Right Banks: the Right Bank comprises the north and west; the Left Bank takes in the city south of the Seine. A stroll along the Left Bank conjures

images of Doisneau's magical monochrome photographs, while the narrow, cobbled streets of Montmartre vividly call up the colourful cool of Toulouse-Lautrec.

The Ile de la Cité is the nucleus around which the city grew and the oldest quarters around this site are the 1st, 2nd, 3rd, 4th arrondissements on the Right Bank and 5th and 6th on the Left Bank. Landmarks are universally known: the Eiffel Tower and the Arc de Triomphe to the west, the Sacré-Coeur to the north, Montparnasse Tower to the south, and, of course, Notre-Dame Cathedral in the middle. But Paris is not resting on its laurels. New buildings and new cultural sensations are never far away: Les Grands Travaux are forever in the wings, waiting to inspire.

EATING OUT

Food plays such an important role in Gallic life that eating well is deemed a citizen's birth-right. Parisians are intensely knowledgeable about their food and wine - simply stroll around any part of the capital and you'll come across lavish looking shops offering perfectly presented treats. Restaurants, bistros and brasseries too can call on the best available bounty around: there are close to a hundred city-wide markets teeming with fresh produce. As Charles De Gaulle said: "How can you govern a country which has 246 varieties of cheese?" Whether you want to linger in a legendary café or dine in a grand salon, you'll find the choice is endless. The city's respect for its proud culinary heritage is palpable but it is not resting on its laurels. Just as other European cities with vibrant restaurant scenes started to play catch-up, so young chefs here took up the cudgels. By breaking away from formulaic regimes and adopting more contemporary styles of cooking, they have ensured that the reputation of the city remains undimmed.

FRANCE – PARIS

CHAMPS-ÉLYSÉES – ÉTOILE – PALAIS DES CONGRÈS PLAN II

Alain Ducasse au Plaza Athénée – Hôtel Plaza Athénée

25 av. Montaigne (8th) – ⓜ *Alma Marceau*
– ☏ 01 53 67 65 00 – www.alain-ducasse.com   Plan: **G3**
– Closed 20 July-27 August, 21 to 30 december, Monday lunch, Tuesday lunch, Wednesday lunch, Saturday and Sunday
Menu 210 € 🍷 (lunch)/390 €
– Carte 245/395 € – *(booking advisable)*
• Creative • Luxury • Design •

Alain Ducasse has rethought his entire restaurant along the lines of 'naturality' – his culinary Holy Grail is to uncover the truth of each ingredient. Based on the trilogy fish-vegetables-cereals (here too, a respect for nature prevails), the dishes are really outstanding, and the setting is magnificent!
→ Lentilles vertes du Puy et caviar, délicate gelée d'anguille fumée. Homard du Cotentin, les œufs émulsionnés, courgette grillée et cassis. Fontainebleau de lait de soja, cacahouètes des Hautes-Pyrénées.

Alléno Paris au Pavillon Ledoyen (Yannick Alléno)

8 av. Dutuit (carré Champs-Elysees) (8th)
– ⓜ Champs-Elysées Clemenceau – ☏ 01 53 05 10 00   Plan: **H3**
– www.yannick-alleno.com
– Closed 2 weeks in August, Saturday lunch and Sunday
Menu 145 € (lunch), 340/580 €
– Carte 190/385 €
• Modern cuisine • Luxury •

Taken over by Yannick Alléno, this Parisian institution – in an elegant Second Empire pavilion in the Jardins des Champs Elysées – has embarked on a new chapter in its history. The chef produces a tour de force, immediately stamping his hallmark on dishes. He manages with all his mastery to put a new spin on haute cuisine, magnifying for example jus and sauces through clever extractions. Prepare to be impressed!
→ Asperges vertes rôties à l'huile fumée, papaye au safran, olives de Kalamata et sauce au poivre. Pigeon de Pornic, consommé double au poivre noir fermenté et saucisson de béatilles. Meringue au charbon de bois et cardamome, glace fleur d'oranger.

Le Cinq – Hôtel Four Seasons George V

31 av. George V (8th) – ⓜ *George V* – ☏ *01 49 52 71 54*   Plan: **G3**
– www.restaurant-lecinq.com
Menu 145 € (lunch), 210/330 €
– Carte 250/450 €
• Modern cuisine • Luxury • Elegant •

After the fabulous years at Ledoyen, Christian Le Squer is now at the helm of this renowned establishment. The majesty of the Grand Trianon inspired decor remains intact, waiters in uniform still perform their dizzying ballet, and the expertise of the chef does the rest, keeping the finest tradition alive!
→ Langoustines bretonnes raidies, mayonnaise tiède. Bar de ligne au caviar et lait ribot. Croquant de pamplemousse confit et cru.

Épicure – Hôtel Bristol

112 r. du Faubourg-St-Honoré (8th) – ⓜ *Miromesnil*   Plan: **H2**
– ☏ 01 53 43 43 40 – www.lebristolparis.com
Menu 145 € (lunch)/340 € – Carte 170/380 €
• Modern cuisine • Luxury • Classic décor •

The Bristol's restaurant with its bright dining room overlooking the gardens boasts a restrained, distinguished elegance in which the glamour of the 18C shines forth. The virtuosity of Éric Fréchon's classic cuisine bears witness to his freedom of expression with regard to great tradition. He creates dishes that are fresh and endowed with the finest flavours!
→ Macaronis farcis, truffe noire, artichaut et foie gras gratinés au vieux parmesan. Poularde de Bresse en vessie, suprêmes au vin jaune, écrevisses et girolles. Citron de Menton givré au limoncello et citron confit, aux saveurs de poire.

FRANCE - PARIS

Pierre Gagnaire   XxxX 🕸 ♿ 📷 ⇔ 🍽

6 r. Balzac (8th) – Ⓜ *George V* – 𝒞 *01 58 36 12 50*   Plan: **G2**
– *www.pierregagnaire.com* – *Closed 2 weeks in August, 1 week Christmas
Holidays, Saturday and Sunday*
Menu 90 € (lunch), 155/310 € – Carte 320/400 €
• Creative • Elegant • Chic •

The restaurant's chic and restrained contemporary decor is in complete contrast
to the renowned inventiveness of this famous chef.
→ Le jardin marin. Canard de Challans au chocolat. Le grand dessert de
Pierre Gagnaire.

Le Taillevent   XxXxX 🕸 📷 ⇔ 🍽

15 r. Lamennais (8th) – Ⓜ *Charles de Gaulle-Etoile*   Plan: **G2**
– 𝒞 *01 44 95 15 01* – *www.taillevent.com* – *Closed 28 July-27 August,
Saturday, Sunday and Bank Holidays*
Menu 104 € 🍷 (lunch)/198 € – Carte 160/250 €
• Classic cuisine • Luxury • Elegant •

Wainscoting and works of art adorn this former private residence dating from
the 19C. It was once home to the Duke of Morny, and is now a guardian of
French haute cuisine. Exquisite dishes and a magnificent wine list.
→ Boudin de homard bleu "tradition Taillevent". Bar de ligne cuit à l'étuvée, poireaux, champagne et caviar osciètre. Crêpes Suzette flambées.

L'Abeille – Hôtel Shangri-La   XxxX 🕸 ♿ 📷 🍽

10 av. d'Iéna (16th) – Ⓜ *Iéna* – 𝒞 *01 53 67 19 90*   Plan: **F3**
– *www.shangri-la.com* – *Closed 29 July-27 August, 23 to 30 December,
Sunday, Monday and lunch*
Menu 230 € – Carte 150/230 €
• Modern cuisine • Luxury • Elegant •

The Shangri-La Hotel's 'French restaurant' has a name that gives a nod to the
Napoleonic emblem of the bee. As you might expect, France's grand culinary
tradition is honoured here under the auspices of a team that has inherited the
best expertise. The menu promotes fine classicism and noble ingredients.
→ Araignée de mer rafraîchie à la tomate et au gingembre, sabayon
coraillé. Homard et coque d'amande en cocotte lutée, pêche au parfum
de sangria. Miel du maquis corse givré aux parfums de citron et d'eucalyp-
tus.

Le Clarence   XxxX 🕸 ♿ 📷 ⇔ 🍽

31 av. F.-D.-Roosevelt (8th) – Ⓜ *Franklin D. Roosevelt*   Plan: **H3**
– 𝒞 *01 82 82 10 10* – *www.le-clarence.paris* – *Closed Tuesday lunch,
Sunday and Monday*
Menu 90 € (lunch), 190/320 € – *(booking advisable)*
• Modern cuisine • Luxury • Historic •

This superb 1884 mansion located close to the Champs-Elysées hosts the
remarkable talent of Christophe Pelé (former chef of La Bigarrade, in Paris). He
is an artist when it comes to marrying produce from land and sea. As for the
sumptuous wine list, it is enough to make you dizzy before you have even had a
glass!
→ Bar de ligne. Saint-pierre et ris de veau. Desserts du Clarence.

Le Gabriel – Hôtel La Réserve   XxxX 🕸 🍴 ♿ 📷 🍽

42 av. Gabriel (8th) – Ⓜ *Champs Elysées Clemenceau*   Plan: **H3**
– 𝒞 *01 58 36 60 50* – *www.lareserve-paris.com* – *Closed Saturday lunch*
Menu 95 € (weekday lunch), 180/250 € – Carte 160/240 €
• Modern cuisine • Elegant • Luxury •

The restaurant is nestled in the elegant setting of La Réserve and features Versailles wooden flooring and Cordovan leather with a gold patina. Chef Jérôme
Banctel, no stranger to Paris' *grandes maisons*, cooks his own superb take on
the classics, with a smattering of Asian touches and executed in the proper way. A
success!
→ Cœur d'artichaut de Macau en impression de sakura et de coriandre
fraîche. Pigeon de Vendée, cacao et sarrasin croustillant. Grains de café
meringués, crème glacée au sirop de merisier.

177

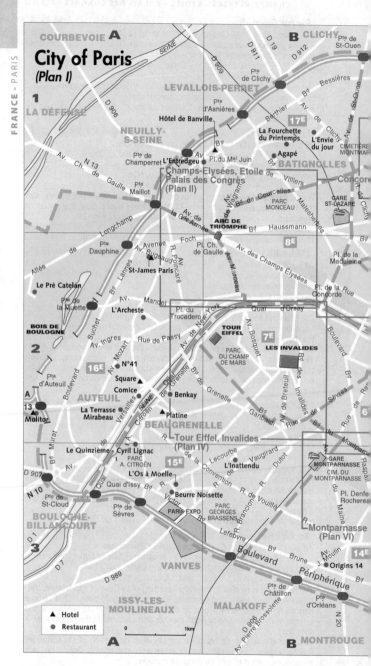

City of Paris
(Plan I)

COURBEVOIE **A**

B CLICHY Pte de St-Ouen

SEINE

D 19 D 911 D 912

Pte de Clichy

LEVALLOIS-PERRET

Bessières

Av. de Clichy

1

LA DÉFENSE

D 906

Pte d'Asnières

Barthier

17E

Hôtel de Banville

NEUILLY-S-SEINE

Pl. du Mal Juin

La Fourchette du Printemps

L'Envie du jour

CIMETIÈRE MONTMAR

Pte de Champerret L'Entredgeu

Agapé

BATIGNOLLES

Av.

N 13

Pte Maillot

Av. Ch. de Gaulle

Champs-Elysées, Etoile, Palais des Congrès (Plan II)

Villiers

Concor

GARE ST-LAZARE

Av. de la Gde Armée

Bd de Courcelles

PARC MONCEAU

Malesherbes

Av. Wagram

ARC DE TRIOMPHE

Bd

Haussmann

8E

Longchamp

Pte Dauphine

Avenue

Av. Bugeaud

Foch

Pl. Ch. de Gaulle

Av. des Champs Elysées

Pl. de la Madeleine

Br Lannes

St-James Paris

R. Poincaré

Av. Marceau

Le Pré Catelan

Mandel

Pl. de la Rue Concorde

Pte de la Muette

L'Archeste

Pl. du Trocadéro

Quai d'Orsay

BOIS DE BOULOGNE

Av. Ingres

Rue de Passy

TOUR EIFFEL

7E

LES INVALIDES

Av. Mozart

N°41

PARC DU CHAMP DE MARS

Av. de New York

Av. Bosquet

Boulevard

2

16E

Square

Comice

Benkay

AUTEUIL

SEINE

Platine

Av. de Breteuil

Invalides

Sèvres

A

13

Molitor

La Terrasse Mirabeau

Quai Citroën

BEAUGRENELLE

Bd Garibaldi

Rue de

de

6

Murat

Tour Eiffel, Invalides (Plan IV)

GARE MONTPARNASSE

Le Quinzième - Cyril Lignac

PARC A. CITROËN

R. de la Convention

Vaugirard

Dutot

CIM. DU MONTPARNASSE

D 907

L'Os à Moelle

15E

L'Inattendu

Pl. Denfert Rocheres

Pte de St-Cloud

Quai d'Issy

Beurre Noisette

R. de Vouillé

Maine

N 10

BOULOGNE-BILLANCOURT

Victor

PARIS-EXPO

PARC GEORGES BRASSENS

R. Brancion

Montparnasse (Plan VI)

D 1

Pte de Sèvres

Lefebvre

14E

D 7

Bd

Brune

Origins 14

Av. J. Moulin

D 989

VANVES

Boulevard

Périphérique

Bd

3

Pte de Châtillon

Pte d'Orléans

N 20

ISSY-LES-MOULINEAUX

MALAKOFF

D 906 Av. Pierre Brossolette

A

B MONTROUGE

▲ Hotel
● Restaurant

0   1km

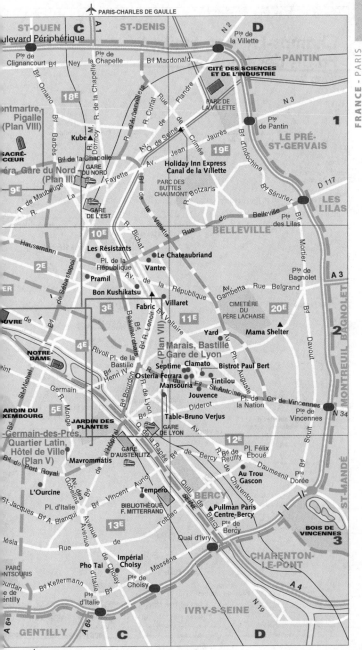

PARIS-CHARLES DE GAULLE

ST-OUEN **C** ST-DENIS **D**
ulevard Périphérique N 2 Pte de la Villette
PANTIN
Pte de Clignancourt Bd Ney Pte de la Chapelle Bd Macdonald
CITÉ DES SCIENCES ET DE L'INDUSTRIE
ntmartre, Pigalle (Plan VIII) **18E** PARC DE LA VILLETTE N 3
Kube Pte de Pantin **1** LE PRÉ-ST-GERVAIS
SACRÉ-CŒUR **19E**
éra, Gare du Nord (Plan III) GARE DU NORD Holiday Inn Express Canal de la Villette LES LILAS
9E GARE DE L'EST PARC DES BUTTES CHAUMONT Belleville Pte des Lilas D 117
Haussmann **10E** BELLEVILLE
Les Résistants Le Chateaubriand
2E Pl. de la République Vantre Pte de Bagnolet A 3
ER Pramil Av. de la République Rue Belgrand
Bon Kushikatsu Av. Gambetta
Fabric Villaret CIMETIÈRE DU PÈRE LACHAISE **20E**
3E **11E** (Plan VII)
UVRE **4E** Rivoli Pl. de la Bastille Yard Mama Shelter
NOTRE-DAME Marais, Bastille, Gare de Lyon Ph.
Septime Clamato Bistrot Paul Bert
Osteria Ferrara Tintilou
ARDIN DU XEMBOURG **5E** Mansouria Jouvence St-Antoine Pl. de la Nation Crs de Vincennes Pte de Vincennes N 34
Germain-des-Prés, Quartier Latin, Hôtel de Ville (Plan V) Diderot Table-Bruno Verjus
Mavrommátis GARE DE LYON **12E** Pl. Félix Éboué
L'Ourcine Tempero Au Trou Gascon Pte Dorée
BIBLIOTHÈQUE F. MITTERRAND BERCY Pullman Paris Centre-Bercy Pte de Bercy BOIS DE VINCENNES **3**
13E
Quai d'Ivry
Pho Tai Impérial Choisy Masséna CHARENTON-LE-PONT A 4
Pte de Choisy
PARC NTSOURIS Bd Kellermann Pte d'Italie IVRY-S-SEINE N 19
GENTILLY **C** **D**

PARIS-ORLY

179

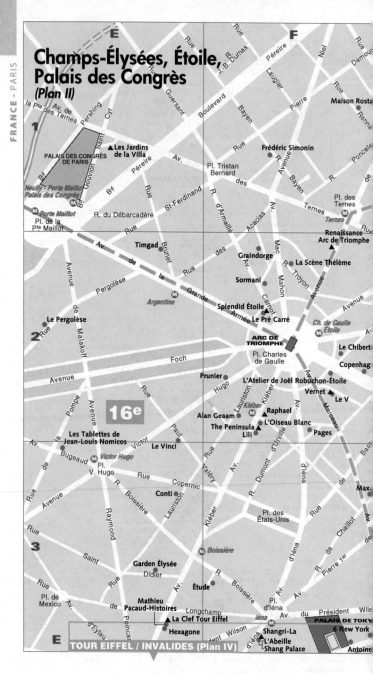

Champs-Élysées, Étoile, Palais des Congrès
(Plan II)

▲ Hotel
● Restaurant

G

Av.
d'Abbanes Wagram
Rue
Jouffroy
R.
Wagram
de
Cardinet
de
Prony
Rue

17e

Courcelles
R. T. Ribot
Courcelles
Daru
Boulevard
Rue
M Courcelles
Rue
Hoche

PARC
MONCEAU

M Monceau

Ba
H
Malesherbes
Pl. du Gal
Catroux
Rue
de
Malesherbes
Villiers
Malesherbes
Courcelles
M Villiers
R. du Rocher

1

Rue
Boulevard
Monceau
de
de
Lisbonne
Malesherbes

Rue
Av.
de
R.
Treilhard
Dominique Bouchet
Messine

Le Royal
Monceau
Matsuhisa
Carpaccio
du
Les 110 de Taillevent
Helen
Boulevard
Faubourg
Berri
Courcelles
Haussmann
Pomze
8e
La Boétie

2

de
Friedland
Le Taillevent
Washington
Penati al Baretto
Champs-Élysées
Plaza ▲
Apicius
L'Arôme
Rue
M
Miromesnil
Miromesnil

Pierre
Gagnaire
R.
Rue
d'Artois
Saint
St-Philippe
du Roule
114, Faubourg
Le Bristol
Épicure

Av.
George V
M
▲ Fouquet's Barrière
Rue
La Boétie
de
Franklin
Ponthieu
Jean
Mermoz
Matignon
La Pagode de Cos
Le Gabriel
La Réserve
Honoré
PALAIS
DE L'ÉLYSÉE

Prince de Galles
La Scène
Le 39V
DES
R.
Pierre
Charon
Marbeuf
Franklin D.
Roosevelt
Kisin
Av.
Rd-Pt des
Champs-Élysée
Marcel Dassault
NoLita
Gabriel
Laurent

Av. George V
erbie
Four Seasons George V
Le Cinq
Le George
L'Orangerie
ôtel de Sers
Alain Ducasse
au Plaza Athénée
La Cour Jardin
François 1er
Montaigne
Delano
Le Clarence
CHAMPS
Champs-Élysées
Clemenceau
M
Churchill
ÉLYSÉES

Le Relais Plaza
Maison Blanche
Plaza Athénée
Manko
Av.
Goulon
Lasserre
Roosevelt
Jean
GRAND
PALAIS
PALAIS
DE LA
DÉCOUVERTE
Av. W. Churchill
PETIT
PALAIS
Alléno Paris
Pavillon
Ledoyen

Shirvan
Marius et Janette
Rue
Cours
Albert 1er
Cours
Mini Palais
la
Reine

Alma
arceau
G
H
Pont
Inval
Pont
dre III
0   200 m
SEINE

CONCORDE / OPÉRA / GARE DU NORD (Plan III)

FRANCE - PARIS

🕸🕸 **Mathieu Pacaud - Histoires** XxxX 🕸 🔣 ⇔ 🚳

85 av. Kléber (16th) – Ⓜ Trocadéro – ☎ 01 70 98 16 35 Plan: **E3**
– www.histoires-paris.fr – Closed August, Tuesday lunch, Saturday lunch,
Sunday and Monday
Menu 95 € (lunch), 240/350 € – Carte 205/455 € – *(booking advisable)*
• Creative • Elegant • Luxury •
Mathieu Pacaud and his team explore countless combinations here, with a view
to generating an original and well-sculpted menu. The chef draws on numerous
techniques – infusion, maceration, deglazing, marinade – and invites us to a real
cavalcade in pursuit of taste, in which each dish is an experience in itself.
→ Ceviche de langoustines royales, pain léger et croustillant, réduction
pomme-fenouil. Turbot sauvage, sabayon et segments maltais, cocos de
Paimpol à la moutarde de Charroux. Grande valse brillante.

🕸🕸 **Maison Rostang** XxxX 🕸 🔣 ⇔ 🚳

20 r. Rennequin (17th) – Ⓜ Ternes – ☎ 01 47 63 40 77 Plan: **F1**
– www.maisonrostang.com – Closed 3 weeks in August, Monday lunch,
Saturday lunch and Sunday
Menu 90 € (lunch), 185/225 € – Carte 150/225 €
• Classic cuisine • Elegant • Luxury •
Wood panelling, Robj figurines, works by Lalique and an Art Deco stained-glass
window make up the interior, which is at once luxurious and unusual. The fine
and superbly classical food is by Nicolas Beaumann, formerly Yannick Alleno's
sous-chef at Le Meurice. His remarkable compositions are enhanced by a magnificent wine list.
→ Tourteau au gingembre, crémeux de courgettes en impression de caviar. Noix
de ris de veau croustillante, navets farcis et petits pois étuvés, crème d'écrevisses.
Cigare croustillant au tabac Havane et mousseline Cognac

🕸 **Laurent** XxxxX 🕸 🛱 ⇔ 🚳

41 av. Gabriel (8th) – Ⓜ Champs Elysées Clemenceau Plan: **H3**
– ☎ 01 42 25 00 39 – www.le-laurent.com Closed 23 December-3 January,
Saturday lunch, Sunday and Bank Holidays
Menu 95/159 € – Carte 155/245 €
• Classic cuisine • Elegant • Luxury •
A stone's throw from the Champs Élysées, this former hunting lodge belonging
to Louis XIV with its elegant shaded terraces has a loyal following. Traditional
cuisine and a good wine list.
→ Araignée de mer, ses sucs en gelée, et crème de fenouil. Turbot nacré à l'huile
d'olive, bardes et légumes verts dans une fleurette iodée. Glace vanille minute.

🕸 **Apicius** XxxX 🕸 🛒 🔣 ⇔ 🚳 🅿

20 r. d'Artois (8th) – Ⓜ St-Philippe du Roule Plan: **G2**
– ☎ 01 43 80 19 66 – www.restaurant-apicius.com – Closed August,
Saturday, Sunday and Bank Holidays
Menu 140 € (lunch), 180/220 € – Carte 125/215 €
• Classic cuisine • Elegant • Luxury •
Restaurant on the ground floor of a listed town house with a garden. There is a
succession of fine rooms in a chic mix of classic, rococo and modern styles. Up-
to-date cuisine; superb wine list.
→ Foie gras de canard poêlé et grillé en aigre-doux. Ris de veau rôti, feuil-
les et jeunes pousses. Soufflé au chocolat guanaja, chantilly sans sucre.

🕸 **Lasserre** XxxX 🕸 🔣 ⇔ 🚳

17 av. F.-D.-Roosevelt (8th) – Ⓜ Franklin D. Roosevelt Plan: **H3**
– ☎ 01 43 59 02 13 – www.restaurant-lasserre.com – Closed August,
Tuesday lunch, Wednesday lunch, Saturday lunch, Sunday and Monday
Menu 60 € (lunch), 190/340 € 🍷 – Carte 165/275 €
• Classic cuisine • Luxury • Chic •
One of the temples of Parisian gastronomy. The elegance of the interior (columns, dra-
peries, tassels etc), the tableware, the quality of the service – it all comes together to
magnify haute cuisine! Fashions come and go, Lasserre remains.
→ Macaroni, truffe noire et foie gras de canard. Canard de Challans, pêche
de vigne farcie et rôtie, jus d'une sangria. Crêpes Suzette.

FRANCE - PARIS

Le George – Hôtel Four Seasons George V

31 av. George-V (8th) – **Ⓜ** *George V* – ℰ *01 49 52 72 09*
– *www.legeorge.com*   Plan: **G3**
Menu 110 € – Carte 50/95 €

• Italian • Elegant • Cosy •

In the kitchens of the George since September 2016, Simone Zanoni has made an impression with his light, Italian-inspired cooking, often served in tasting-size portions. Superb dining room or conservatory in the courtyard.

→ Tarte Tatin d'oignon, glace au parmesan. Cabri de 36 heures. Déclinaison de noisettes et de citron.

Il Carpaccio – Hôtel Le Royal Monceau

37 av. Hoche (8th) – **Ⓜ** *Charles de Gaulle-Etoile*
– ℰ *01 42 99 88 12* – *www.leroyalmonceau.com* – *Closed 1 to 21 August, Sunday and Monday*   Plan: **G2**
Menu 120/145 € – Carte 95/135 €

• Italian • Elegant •

You reach the restaurant via a remarkable corridor decorated with thousands of shells. The restaurant decor, reminiscent of a winter garden, is also delightful. The menu is unapologetically simple and in the great tradition of Italian home cooking.

→ Poulpe grillé et en carpaccio. Noix de veau cuite en calzone au foin. Tiramisu.

La Scène – Hôtel Prince de Galles

33 av. George V (8th) – **Ⓜ** *George V* – ℰ *01 53 23 78 50*
– *www.restaurant-la-scene.fr* – *Closed August, Sunday, Monday and lunch*   Plan: **G3**
Menu 125/185 € – Carte 125/165 €

• Modern cuisine • Elegant • Luxury •

Within the elegant Prince de Galles Hotel, La Scène shines the spotlight on the kitchens, which are separated from the dining area by just a white marble counter. They are the realm of Stéphanie Le Quellec, no stranger to the limelight since winning France's 'Top Chef' TV show in 2011. Imaginative, harmonious and precise dishes.

→ Caviar osciètre, pain mi-perdu et mi-soufflé, pomme Pompadour. Pigeon des Costières rôti, figues, noix et légèreté de pomme de terre ratte. Vanille en crème glacée, esprit d'une omelette norvégienne.

Shang Palace – Hôtel Shangri-La

10 av. d'Iéna (16th) – **Ⓜ** *Iéna* – ℰ *01 53 67 19 92*
– *www.shangri-la.com* – *Closed 20 February-7 March, 10 July-1 August, Tuesday and Wednesday*   Plan: **F3**
Menu 48 € (lunch), 98/128 € – Carte 65/170 €

• Chinese • Exotic décor •

The Shang Palace occupies one of the lower floors of the Shangri-La hotel. It gracefully recreates the decor of a luxury Chinese restaurant with its jade columns, sculpted screens and crystal chandeliers. The menu pays homage to the full flavours and authenticity of Cantonese gastronomy.

→ Saumon Lo Hei. Canard laqué façon pékinoise en deux services. Crème de mangue, pomélo et perles de sagou.

Antoine

10 av. de New-York (16th) – **Ⓜ** *Alma Marceau*
– ℰ *01 40 70 19 28* – *www.antoine-paris.fr* – *Closed 3 weeks in August, 1 week Christmas Holidays, Sunday and Monday*   Plan: **F3**
Menu 48 € (weekday lunch), 90/165 € – Carte 120/150 €

• Seafood • Elegant •

Under the aegis of chef Thibault Sombardier, this is one of Paris's top seafood restaurants (also serving other dishes). The menu changes daily to offer the best fresh fish and seafood, sourced directly from ports in Brittany, the Basque Country or Mediterranean; everything is made with savoir faire and inspiration. The contemporary decor is elegant. In short: don't miss this place.

→ Pain soufflé de homard, pistache et bouillon aux champignons de Paris. Saint-pierre, cresson grillé et girolles clous. Galet mirabelle et noisette.

FRANCE - PARIS

L'Arôme

XxX ⌘ 🄰🄲 ⅏ ⇔ ☕

3 r. St-Philippe-du-Roule (8th)   Plan: **G-H2**
– ⓜ St-Philippe-du-Roule – ☎ 01 42 25 55 98 – www.larome.fr
– Closed 1 week in February, 3 weeks in August, Saturday and Sunday
Menu 59 € (lunch), 79/159 € – Carte 65/105 €
• Modern cuisine • Chic • Romantic •

Attractive restaurant run by Eric Martins (front of house) and Thomas Boullault (in the kitchen). Comfortable dining room with a warm atmosphere and an open kitchen. Modern cuisine.
→ Pressé de tourteau breton, avocat, riz koshihikari et eau de tomate. Onglet de bœuf Black Angus rôti aux herbes, aubergine fumée et jus épicé. Pannacotta aux framboises et parfumée à la rose, aloe vera et sorbet litchi.

Le Chiberta

XxX 🄰🄲 ⇔ ☕

3 r. Arsène-Houssaye (8th) – ⓜ Charles de Gaulle-Etoile   Plan: **F2**
– ☎ 01 53 53 42 00 – www.lechiberta.com
– Closed 3 weeks in August, Saturday lunch and Sunday
Menu 49 € (lunch), 110/165 € 🍷 – Carte 90/140 €
• Creative • Minimalist •

Find a serene atmosphere, soft lighting and simple decor designed by J M Wilmotte (dark colours and unusual wine bottle walls). This provides the setting for inventive cuisine supervised by Guy Savoy.
→ Salade de homard, vinaigrette de corail. Filet de bœuf charolais à la truffe, girolles et pommes noisette, jus truffé. Terrine d'orange et de pamplemousse au thé earl grey.

Copenhague

XxX 🍴 � 🄰🄲

142 av. des Champs-Élysées (Maison du Danemark - 1st   Plan: **F2**
floor) (8th) – ⓜ George V – ☎ 01 44 13 86 26
– www.restaurant-copenhague-paris.fr
– Closed August, Saturday, Sunday and Bank Holidays
Menu 55 € (lunch)/115 € – Carte 55/70 €
• Danish • Contemporary décor • Minimalist •

The Maison du Danemark on the Champs Élysées has long been a culinary ambassador of the food of the Great North. A tasteful, low-key interior ideally showcases its gourmet ambitions. Cod in a frothy sauce of grey shrimp and smoked reindeer are some of the iconic dishes of Scandinavia served here.
→ Maquereau, concombre et raifort. Poulet, ramslog et moule. Topinambour, poire et chocolat blanc.

Étude (Keisuke Yamagishi)

XxX ⌘ 🄰🄲

14 r. Bouquet-de-Longchamp (16th) – ⓜ Boissière   Plan: **E3**
– ☎ 01 45 05 11 41 – www.restaurant-etude.fr
– Closed Saturday lunch, Sunday and Monday
Menu 45 € (lunch), 58/80 € – (booking advisable)
• Modern cuisine • Elegant •

Nourished by his meetings with small-scale producers, by the discovery of ingredients from afar – pepper from Taiwan with citrus notes, Iranian berries – the chef, Keisuke Yamagishi, cooks here like a tightrope walker, offering set menus named "Symphonie", "Ballade", "Prélude" in homage to Chopin. Each dish is a masterclass in harmony.
→ Cuisine du marché.

Helen

XxX 🄰🄲 ⇔

3 r. Berryer (8th) – ⓜ George V – ☎ 01 40 76 01 40   Plan: **G2**
– www.helenrestaurant.com – Closed 3 weeks in August, 24 December-
2 January, Saturday lunch, Sunday and Monday
Menu 48 € (lunch)/138 € – Carte 76/162 €
• Seafood • Elegant • Design •

Founded in 2012, Helen has already made its mark among the fish restaurants of Paris' chic neighbourhoods. If you love fish, you will be bowled over: from the quality of the ingredients (only wild fish sourced from fishermen who bring in the catch of the day on small boats) to the care taken over the recipes. Sober and elegant decor.
→ Carpaccio de daurade royale au citron caviar. Bar de ligne aux olives taggiasche. Saint-honoré.

❀ **Penati al Baretto** (Alberico Penati)   XxX 🕸 🅰️

9 r. Balzac (8th) – Ⓜ George V   Plan: **G2**
– ✆ 01 42 99 80 00 – www.penatialbaretto.eu – Closed Saturday lunch and
Sunday
Menu 49 € (lunch) – Carte 75/120 €
• Italian • Classic décor • Elegant •

Alberico Penati's Italian restaurant, opened mid-2014, right away imposed itself
as one of the best in the city! In accordance with the finest Italian tradition,
generosity and refinement distinguish each recipe. The dishes are brimming
with flavour as they explore all the regions of the peninsula. A succulent voyage.
➜ Purée de potiron de Mantoue aux fruits de mer, sauce salmoriglio. Thon
rouge de Méditerranée aux tomates sautées, sauce aux câpres. Cassata sicilienne.

❀ **Le Pergolèse** (Stéphane Gaborieau)   XxX 🕸 🅰️ ⇔ 🍽️

40 r. Pergolèse (16th) – Ⓜ Porte Maillot   Plan: **E2**
– ✆ 01 45 00 21 40 – www.lepergolese.com – Closed 3 weeks in August,
Saturday lunch and Sunday
Menu 64 € 🍷 (lunch), 85/135 € – Carte 85/125 €
• Traditional cuisine • Elegant •

Sun-drenched cuisine given a nice new spin by a *Meilleur Ouvrier de France* chef,
and served in a pared-down and elegant decor.
➜ Moelleux de sardines, compotée de poivrons basquaise, sorbet tomate.
Sole meunière farcie d'une duxelles de champignons. Soufflé chaud aux
saveurs du moment.

❀ **Les Tablettes de Jean-Louis Nomicos**   XxX ⅙ 🅰️ 🍽️

16 av. Bugeaud (16th) – Ⓜ Victor Hugo   Plan: **E3**
– ✆ 01 56 28 16 16 – www.lestablettesjeanlouisnomicos.com
Menu 42 € (lunch), 85 € 🍷/150 € – Carte 110/160 €
• Modern cuisine • Elegant •

Having manned the kitchens at Lasserre, Jean-Louis Nomicos pursues his solo
career on the premises formerly occupied by Joël Robuchon's La Table. Savour
his fine, Mediterranean-inspired cuisine to a backdrop of original and contemporary decor.
➜ Macaroni gratiné au parmesan, truffe noire, foie gras de canard et jus de
veau truffé. Carabineros grillés à la plancha, riz noir façon risotto aux encornets. Granité à la Chartreuse verte, glace à l'eau de rose.

❀ **114, Faubourg** – Hôtel Bristol   XX ⅙ 🅰️

114 r. du Faubourg-St-Honoré (8th) – Ⓜ Miromesnil   Plan: **H2**
– ✆ 01 53 43 44 44 – www.lebristolparis.com – Closed August, lunch
Saturday and Sunday
Menu 114 € (lunch) – Carte 80/165 €
• Modern cuisine • Elegant •

This chic brasserie within the premises of Le Bristol has a lavish interior with gilded columns, floral motifs and a grand staircase. Savour dishes from the menu
of fine brasserie classics cooked with care and lots of taste.
➜ Œuf king-crab, mayonnaise au gingembre et citron. Ris de veau braisé au
bâton de cannelle. Soufflé au chocolat guanaja, crème glacée au cognac.

❀ **Hexagone**   XX 🕸 🅰️ ⇔ 🍽️

85 av. Kléber (16th) – Ⓜ Trocadéro – ✆ 01 42 25 98 85   Plan: **E3**
– www.hexagone-paris.fr
Menu 49 € (weekday lunch), 90/135 € – Carte 100/140 €
• Modern cuisine • Trendy • Design •

After many years working with his father Bernard at L'Ambroisie, Mathieu
Pacaud has embarked on his own gourmet adventure. Here he brilliantly concocts his own version of French culinary classics, whilst preserving a unity of
technique, flavour and sauce. Inspiring!
➜ Œuf de poule mollet, fine ratatouille et crème glacée de céleri. Sole à la
viennoise, poêlée de girolles, amandes fraîches et sauce au vin jaune.
Ganache bayano, glace au miel, croquant à la noisette, sarrasin glacé et
soufflé.

FRANCE - PARIS

L'Orangerie – Hôtel Four Seasons George V   XX 賤 🛖 🖭

31 av. George-V (8th)   Plan: **G3**
– Ⓜ George V
– 𝒞 01 49 52 72 24 – www.lorangerieparis.com
Menu 95/125 €
– Carte 100/145 € – (booking advisable)
· Modern cuisine · Elegant ·

This tiny restaurant (18 seats only) is between La Galerie restaurant and the handsome courtyard of the Four Seasons George V hotel. It features a concise, seasonal menu in which tradition is updated thanks to elegant, perfumed notes and a delicate blend of flavours.
→ Langoustines à la nage, tartare d'algues et crémeux de noisettes torréfiées. Pigeon en croûte de son, navet, olives noires et truffe. Fleur de vacherin, framboises et menthe poivrée.

La Scène Thélème   XX & 🖭 🎲

18 r. Troyon (17th) – Ⓜ Charles de Gaulle - Étoile   Plan: **F2**
– 𝒞 01 77 37 60 99 – www.lascenetheleme.fr
– Closed 30 July-19 August, Saturday lunch, Sunday and Monday
Menu 49 € (lunch), 95/169 €
– Carte 120/160 €
· Modern cuisine · Contemporary décor · Cosy ·

An unusual restaurant, where theatre and gastronomy come together. Some evenings, you can attend a theatrical show before being seated at your table. A wonderful idea! The generous and tasty ingredient focused cuisine, created by a young chef who is perfectly at ease in his role, also works a treat. The scene is set for a memorable culinary intermission.
→ Transparence de langoustines aux effluves de feuilles de shiso. Canard de Challans aux prunes. Chocolat du Guatemala, glace pain grillé.

Le 39V (Frédéric Vardon)   XX 🖭

39 av. George V (6th floor - entrance at 17 r. Quentin-Bauchart) (8th) – Ⓜ George V   Plan: **G3**
– 𝒞 01 56 62 39 05 – www.le39v.com
– Closed August, Saturday and Sunday
Menu 95/195 € 🍷
– Carte 95/155 €
· Modern cuisine · Design · Friendly ·

The temperature is rising at 39, avenue George V! On the 6th floor of this impressive Haussmann-style building overlooking the rooftops of Paris, diners can enjoy the chef's refined cuisine in a stylish setting. Dishes are based around a classic repertoire, top quality ingredients and fine flavours.
→ Œuf bio cuit mollet, royale et émulsion de champignons, mouillettes. Macaronis gratinés, ragoût de truffe melanosporum. Soufflé au chocolat, sauce au piment d'Espelette.

Agapé   XX 賤 🖭 🎲

51 r. Jouffroy-D'Abbans (17th) – Ⓜ Wagram   Plan I: **B1**
– 𝒞 01 42 27 20 18 – www.agape-paris.fr – Closed Saturday and Sunday
Menu 44 € (lunch), 99/139 €
– Carte 120/160 €
· Modern cuisine · Elegant · Friendly ·

Agápe meant unconditional love of another in Ancient Greece. Here, you do indeed feel the love, as you taste this good quality food, which cultivates classicism and sometimes takes liberties – such as the Caesar salad made with calf sweetbreads and crayfish! The finesse of the flavours and the precision of the cooking makes it a sure-fire winner.
→ Tartare de noix de veau fumée au foin. Carré d'agneau de lait de Corrèze. Chocolat grand cru guanaja.

Alan Geaam XX 🅰

19 r. Lauriston (16th) – Ⓜ Charles de Gaulle-Etoile Plan: **F2**
– ℰ 01 45 01 72 97 – www.alangeaam.fr – Closed 3 weeks in
August, 1 week Christmas Holidays, Sunday and Monday
Menu 40 € (lunch), 60/80 € – *(booking advisable)*
• Creative • Elegant •

Everyone has heard of the American dream, but Alan Geaam prefers the French version! Moving to Paris at the age of 24, he has climbed the rungs of the ladder of gastronomy. His original recipes combine France's rich culinary heritage with touches from his native Lebanon and his commitment and passion can be sampled in each creation.
→ Cuisine du marché.

Dominique Bouchet XX ✧

11 r. Treilhard (8th) – Ⓜ Miromesnil – ℰ 01 45 61 09 46 Plan: **H2**
– www.dominique-bouchet.com – Closed 2 weeks in August, Saturday and
Sunday
Menu 60 € (lunch) – Carte 77/116 € – *(booking advisable)*
• Classic cuisine • Elegant •

This is the sort of place that you want to recommend to your friends: a nicely refurbished contemporary interior with an intimate atmosphere, tasty and well put-together market cuisine, and alert service.
→ Charlotte de king crab, pastèque, avocat et mangue. Parmentier de homard, beurre blanc au caviar. Soufflé au Grand Marnier.

Frédéric Simonin XX 🅰

25 r. Bayen (17th) – Ⓜ Ternes – ℰ 01 45 74 74 74 Plan: **F1**
– www.fredericsimonin.com – Closed 5 to 29 August, Sunday and Monday
Menu 55 € (lunch), 98/155 € – Carte 95/180 €
• Modern cuisine • Cosy • Elegant •

Black-and-white decor forms the backdrop to this chic restaurant close to Place des Ternes. Fine, delicate cuisine from a chef with quite a career behind him already.
→ Pomme délicatesse de l'Ardèche fondante et fumée au bois de hêtre et caviar. Saint-pierre étuvé au beurre de yuzu, langues de coques à la cardamome. Pêches blanches et jaunes rafraîchies à la verveine et mousse de lait.

Pages (Ryuji Teshima) XX

4 r. Auguste-Vacquerie (16th) Plan: **F2**
– Ⓜ Charles de Gaulle-Étoile – ℰ 01 47 20 74 94 – www.restaurantpages.fr
– Closed February Holidays, 3 weeks in August, Sunday and Monday
Menu 50 € (lunch), 75/90 € – *(booking advisable)*
• Creative • Minimalist • Elegant •

Ryuji Teshima, aka Teshi, worked in some top establishments, before deciding to deploy his own contemporary and personal vision of French food. His "surprise" menus create incredible associations of flavours that seem most unlikely on paper but that taste somehow undisputable when in the mouth. You can even put your head into the kitchen for a closer look!
→ Cuisine du marché.

L'Atelier de Joël Robuchon - Étoile X 🅰 ✧ 🍴

133 av. des Champs-Élysées (Publicis Drugstore Plan: **F2**
basement) (8th) – Ⓜ Charles de Gaulle-Étoile – ℰ 01 47 23 75 75
– www.joel-robuchon.com
Menu 49 € (lunch), 99/199 € – Carte 100/210 €
• Creative • Design • Minimalist •

Paris, London, Las Vegas, Tokyo, Taipei, Hong Kong, Singapore and back to Paris: the destiny of these Ateliers, in tune with the times, has been an international one. The chef has come up with a great concept: serving dishes drawing on France, Spain and Asia cooked with precision, on a long counter with bar stools and a red and black colour scheme.
→ Langoustine en ravioli truffé à l'étuvée de chou vert. Côtelettes d'agneau de lait à la fleur de thym. Chocolat tendance, crémeux onctueux au chocolat araguani, sorbet cacao et biscuit Oréo.

Graindorge   XX

15 r. Arc-de-Triomphe (17th)   Plan: **F2**
– **Ⓜ** *Charles de Gaulle-Étoile* – ✆ *01 47 54 00 28* – *www.le-graindorge.fr*
– *Closed 2 weeks in August, Monday lunch, Saturday lunch and Sunday*
Menu 32 € (lunch), 37/50 € – Carte 45/65 €
• Flemish • Vintage • Friendly •

Potjevlesch (potted meat), bintje farcie (stuffed potatoes), waterzoï (a stew with Ostend grey prawns) and kippers from Boulogne are just some of the hearty Northern dishes on offer in the Graindorge's attractive Art Deco setting, washed down with some delicious traditional beers.

Pomze   XX 🄰🄲 ⇔

109 bd Haussmann (1ˢᵗ floor) (8th) – **Ⓜ** *St-Augustin*   Plan: **H2**
– ✆ *01 42 65 65 83* – *www.pomze.com* – *Closed 22 December-2 January, Saturday except dinner from September-June and Sunday*
Menu 36 € – Carte 48/62 €
• Modern cuisine • Minimalist •

The unusual concept behind Pomze is to take the humble apple as a starting point for a culinary voyage! From the food shop (where you will find cider and calvados) to the restaurant, this 'forbidden fruit' provides the central theme. Creative and intrepid dishes offer excellent value for money.

Kisin   X 🄰🄲

9 r. de Ponthieu (8th) – **Ⓜ** *Franklin D. Roosevelt*   Plan: **H3**
– ✆ *01 71 26 77 28* – *www.udon-kisin.fr* – *Closed 2 weeks in August and Sunday*
Menu 30/45 € – Carte 28/36 €
• Japanese • Simple •

When a bib gourmand chef from Tokyo arrives in Paris, the first thing he does is open a restaurant, tantalising and bewitching our senses. Diners will sample Japanese produce and genuine udon, made in front of the diner. Natural, additive-free ingredients, most of which are imported direct from the land of the rising sun. Healthy, wholesome and succulent.

La Cour Jardin – Hôtel Plaza Athénée   XxX 🕭 🄰🄲 🍴

25 av. Montaigne (8th) – **Ⓜ** *Alma Marceau*   Plan: **G3**
– ✆ *01 53 67 66 65*
– *www.dorchestercollection.com/paris/hotel-plaza-athenee* – *Open mid-may to mid-september*
Carte 76/124 € – *(booking advisable)*
• Mediterranean cuisine • Elegant • Romantic •

First comes delight at finding such a ravishing, flower-filled courtyard, planted with trees and with ivy, Virginia creeper and geraniums scaling its walls... And then the food: created by Alain Ducasse, it is summery, light and aromatic. The ingredients are exceedingly fresh and the flavours speak for themselves. Impeccable service.

Maison Blanche   XxX 🕭 ≤ 🕭 🄰🄲 🍴

15 av. Montaigne (8th) – **Ⓜ** *Alma Marceau*   Plan: **G3**
– ✆ *01 47 23 55 99* – *www.maison-blanche.fr* – *Closed Lunch Saturday and Sunday*
Menu 69/125 € – Carte 78/132 €
• Modern cuisine • Design • Friendly •

Majestically located on the rooftop of the Champs Elysées Theatre, this immense two-floor loft overlooks the Eiffel Tower and a big chunk of Paris! The contemporary cuisine with Mediterranean accents bears witness to the chef's international background.

Prunier ☆☆☆ 🍴 🅰🅺 ⇔ 🐎

16 av. Victor-Hugo (16th) – Ⓜ Charles de Gaulle-Etoile — Plan: **F2**
– ☏ 01 44 17 35 85 – www.prunier.com – Closed August, Saturday lunch,
Sunday and Bank Holidays
Menu 47 € (weekday lunch), 85/175 € – Carte 64/202 €
• Seafood • Elegant •

Top-notch seafood (with, in particular, caviar produced by Prunier in the South-West), a fine wine list with a good choice of Burgundy whites, not to mention a superb setting, dreamed up by the greatest mosaic artists, engravers and sculptors of the Art Deco era... Fans of the style will be in seventh heaven!

Lili – Hôtel Peninsula ☆☆☆ & 🅰🅺 ⇔

19 av. Kléber (16th) – Ⓜ Kléber – ☏ 01 58 12 67 50 — Plan: **F2**
– www.peninsula.com/fr/ – Closed 22 to 28 February and 13 to 30 August
Menu 58 € (lunch), 68/138 € – Carte 55/188 €
• Chinese • Elegant • Exotic décor •

Opened by the Hong Kong luxury hotel group of the same name, the already famous Peninsula Hotel is the rightful home of Asian restaurant, Lili. It is named after a famous Chinese singer of the 1920s. In a very theatrical setting, the long menu unveils a wide range of Chinese specialties. A real embassy!

Sormani ☆☆☆ 🕸 🅰🅺 ⇔ 🐎

4 r. Gén.-Lanrezac (17th) – Ⓜ Charles de Gaulle-Étoile — Plan: **F2**
– ☏ 01 43 80 13 91 – www.restaurantsormani.fr – Closed 3 weeks in
August, Saturday, Sunday and Bank Holidays
Carte 70/140 €
• Italian • Romantic • Elegant •

Fabric wallpaper, Murano glass chandeliers, mouldings and mirrors: all the elegance of Italy comes to the fore in this chic and hushed restaurant. The cooking of Pascal Fayet (grandson of a Florentine cabinet maker) pays a subtle homage to Italian cuisine. From the lobster ravioli and veal with ceps to the remarkable dessert, the "gigantesco".

Le V – Hôtel Vernet ☆☆☆ 🅰🅺 ⇔

25 r. Vernet (8th) – Ⓜ Charles de Gaulle-Etoile — Plan: **F2**
– ☏ 01 44 31 98 00 – www.hotelvernet.com – Closed August, Saturday
lunch and Sunday
Menu 39 € (lunch), 50/95 € – Carte 68/95 €
• Modern cuisine • Elegant •

The stunning dining room of the Hôtel Vernet is crowned by a large, Eiffel-designed glass canopy and embellished with pilasters and drapes. The perfect setting for a special occasion, where the refined cuisine encompasses a classic repertoire with new combinations of flavours.

Les 110 de Taillevent ☆☆ 🕸 & 🅰🅺 🐎

195 r. du Faubourg-St-Honoré (8th) — Plan: **G2**
– Ⓜ Charles de Gaulle-Etoile – ☏ 01 40 74 20 20
– www.les-110-taillevent-paris.com – Closed 5 to 27 August
Menu 44 € – Carte 52/92 €
• Traditional cuisine • Cosy •

Under the aegis of the prestigious Taillevent name, this ultra-chic brasserie puts the onus on food and wine pairings. The concept is a success, with its remarkable choice of 110 wines by the glass, and nicely done traditional food (pâté en croûte, bavette steak with a peppercorn sauce etc). Elegant and inviting decor.

Matsuhisa – Hôtel Le Royal Monceau ☆☆ 🕸 🍴 & 🅰🅺 🐎

37 av. Hoche (8th) – Ⓜ Charles de Gaulle-Etoile — Plan: **G2**
– ☏ 01 42 99 98 80 – www.leroyalmonceau.com – Closed lunch Saturday and Sunday
Carte 60/350 €
• Japanese • Design • Chic •

The chef Nobu Matsuhisa is known as being the inventor of the Peruvian-Japanese style. He entrusts sushi master Hideki Endo with the task of sublimating Japanese – but also French – ingredients, such as crunchy oysters with caviar, wasabi and aioli sauce. In all the sumptuous setting of the Royal Monceau.

L'Oiseau Blanc – Hôtel Peninsula
XX 🛋 &. AC
19 av. Kléber (16th) – Ⓜ *Kléber* – ☏ *01 58 12 67 30*   Plan: **F2**
– www.peninsula.com/fr/
Menu 69 € (lunch), 109/129 € – Carte 80/140 €
• Modern cuisine • Design • Elegant •
This is the Peninsula's rooftop restaurant for 'contemporary French gastronomy'. Part of the luxury hotel that opened in 2014 near the Arc de Triomphe, the restaurant is presided over by a replica of the White Bird (in homage to the plane in which Nungesser and Coli attempted to cross the Atlantic in 1927) and offers stunning views.

La Pagode de Cos – Hôtel La Réserve
XX 🛋 &. AC 🍽
42 av. Gabriel (8th) – Ⓜ *Champ Elysées Clemenceau*   Plan: **H3**
– ☏ 01 58 36 60 50 – www.lareserve-paris.com
Menu 67 € (lunch) – Carte 80/140 €
• Classic cuisine • Elegant • Bourgeois •
The restaurant's name is a tribute to the Cos d'Estournel, one of the first Bordeaux wineries to export its production to the Far East, explaining why the chateau-winery is adorned with pagodas! The meticulous cooking is French and showcases premium quality ingredients: ravioles of crayfish with coriander dressing, duckling à la bordelaise…

Le Relais Plaza – Hôtel Plaza Athénée
XX AC
21 av. Montaigne (8th) – Ⓜ *Alma Marceau*   Plan: **G3**
– ☏ 01 53 67 64 00
– www.dorchestercollection.com/paris/hotel-plaza-athenee – Closed end-July to end-August
Menu 64 € – Carte 80/135 €
• Classic cuisine • Elegant • Brasserie •
Within the Plaza Athénée is this chic and exclusive brasserie, popular with regulars from the fashion houses nearby. It is impossible to resist the charm of the lovely 1930s decor inspired by the liner SS Normandie. A unique atmosphere for food that has a pronounced sense of tradition. As Parisian as it gets.

Timgad
XX AC 🍽
21 r. Brunel (17th) – Ⓜ *Argentine* – ☏ *01 45 74 23 70*   Plan: **E2**
– www.timgad.fr
Carte 40/100 €
• North African • Oriental décor • Exotic décor •
Experience the historic splendour of the city of Timgad in this elegant Moroccan restaurant adorned with fine stuccowork. Fragrant North African cuisine, including couscous and tagines.

Conti
XX AC 🍽
72 r. Lauriston (16th) – Ⓜ *Boissière* – ☏ *01 47 27 74 67*   Plan: **E3**
– www.leconti.fr – Closed 31 July-20 August, 24 December-1 January, Sunday, Monday and Bank Holidays
Menu 39 € (lunch) – Carte 55/82 €
• Italian • Intimate • Cosy •
Stendhal would no doubt have appreciated this restaurant where the food celebrates his much-loved Italy and the decor is scarlet and black. Two Frenchmen reinterpret Italian recipes adding their own personal touches, bringing together influences from the two countries. The result is quality cuisine that is appreciated by the many regulars.

Marius et Janette
XX 🛋 AC 🍽
4 av. George-V (8th) – Ⓜ *Alma Marceau*   Plan: **G3**
– ☏ 01 47 23 41 88 – www.mariusjanette.com
Menu 68 € – Carte 91/180 €
• Seafood • Mediterranean décor • Friendly •
This seafood restaurant's name recalls Marseille's Estaque district. It has an elegant nautical decor and a pleasant street terrace in summertime.

FRANCE - PARIS

Maxan   XX AK ⇔

3 r. Quentin-Bauchart (8th) – Ⓜ George V   Plan: F3
– ℰ 01 40 70 04 78 – www.rest-maxan.com – Closed 2 weeks in August,
Saturday lunch and Sunday
Menu 40 € – Carte 48/82 €
• Modern cuisine • Elegant •

So this is the spot, a stone's throw from Avenue George V, where Maxan (previously near Miromesnil) is now to be found. Its new decor is elegant and discreet, in a palette of greys, and it is not without pleasure that we reacquaint ourselves with their flavoursome market-based cuisine.

Mini Palais   XX 🛋 ⴳ ⇔ 🍴

Au Grand Palais - 3 av. Winston-Churchill (8th)   Plan: H3
– Ⓜ Champs-Elysées Clemenceau – ℰ 01 42 56 42 42
– www.minipalais.com
Carte 35/75 €
• Modern cuisine • Fashionable • Brasserie •

Concealed within the Grand Palais, the Mini Palace is dedicated to the full pleasures of the palate, with a focus on generosity, abundance and the finest ingredients. The snack menu is available from midday to midnight. Tea room and an exquisite terrace.

Nolita   XX 🏛 AK

1 av. Matignon (Motor Village - 2nd floor) (8th)   Plan: H3
– Ⓜ Franklin D. Roosevelt – ℰ 01 53 75 78 78 – www.nolitaparis.fr
– Closed 2 weeks in August, Saturday lunch and Sunday dinner
Menu 39 € (weekday lunch) – Carte 58/85 €
• Italian • Design •

A chic restaurant within MotorVillage (the showroom of a major Italian car manufacturer). The chef draws on the great Italian tradition, composing a menu to make your mouth water. Try linguine with sardines, risotto with Italian ham and mushrooms, Venetian-style calf's liver and onions, and an excellent tiramisu!

Le Pré Carré – Hôtel Splendid Étoile   XX AK

1 bis av. Carnot (17th) – Ⓜ Charles de Gaulle-Étoile   Plan: F2
– ℰ 01 46 22 57 35 – www.restaurant-le-pre-carre.com – Closed 3 weeks in
August, 1 week Christmas Holidays, Saturday lunch and Sunday
Menu 41 € (dinner) – Carte 42/79 €
• Traditional cuisine • Fashionable • Elegant •

In the dining room, two mirrors facing each other reflect Le Pré Carré's infinite elegance and welcoming decor. Aromatic herbs and spices add a gentle touch to the gourmet cuisine, which is very much in keeping with the times.

6 New York   XX AK 🍴

6 av. de New-York (16th) – Ⓜ Alma Marceau   Plan: F3
– ℰ 01 40 70 03 30 – www.6newyork.fr – Closed August, Saturday lunch
and Sunday
Menu 45 € (weekday lunch)/70 € – Carte 54/70 €
• Modern cuisine • Elegant •

Although the name gives away the address – on Avenue de New York – the restaurant couldn't be further from a typical American restaurant. Well-defined, honest flavours and a respect for the seasons are behind cuisine in perfect harmony with the elegant and contemporary setting.

Le Vinci   XX AK 🍴

23 r. Paul-Valéry (16th) – Ⓜ Victor Hugo   Plan: E2-3
– ℰ 01 45 01 68 18 – www.restaurantlevinci.fr – Closed August, Saturday
and Sunday
Menu 39 € – Carte 52/87 €
• Italian • Friendly •

The pleasing interior design and friendly service make Le Vinci a very popular choice a stone's throw from avenue Victor-Hugo. The impressive selection of pastas and risottos, as well as the à la carte meat and fish dishes vary according to the seasons.

Manko
X ⓂC ⇔

15 av. Montaigne (8th) – Ⓜ *Alma Marceau* Plan: **G3**
– ℰ 01 82 28 00 15 – www.manko-paris.com
– Closed Saturday lunch and Sunday
Menu 65 €
– Carte 40/80 €
• Peruvian • Elegant • Exotic décor •

Star chef, Peruvian Gaston Acurio, and singer Garou are the driving force behind Manko. This restaurant, lounge and cabaret bar in the Théâtre des Champs-Elysées basement proposes Peruvian recipes peppered with Asian and African touches. The food is nicely done and ideal for sharing.

Shirvan
X 🍴 ⅙ ⓂC

5 pl. de l'Alma (8th) – Ⓜ *Alma Marceau* Plan: **G3**
– ℰ 01 47 23 09 48 – www.shirvancafemetisse.fr
Menu 32 € (weekday lunch)
– Carte 41/87 €
• Modern cuisine • Contemporary décor • Vintage •

This renovated restaurant near the Alma Bridge is the brainchild of Akrame Benallal. Starched white linen has given way to designer cutlery, earthenware goblets and a menu inspired by the Silk Road with spices and flavours picked up on a journey from Morocco to India, via Azerbaijan. A delicious melting pot of culinary influences. Professional service, open almost all-day long.

L'Entredgeu
X

83 r. Laugier (17th) – Ⓜ *Porte de Champerret* Plan I: **AB1**
– ℰ 01 40 54 97 24 – Closed Sunday
Menu 38/45 €
• Traditional cuisine • Bistro • Friendly •

L'Entredgeu has had a facelift. With the arrival of a young chef-patron, a graduate of some prestigious establishments, the quality of this traditional cuisine, attentive to the seasons and the market, is perpetuated. A lively atmosphere and good food guaranteed in this neighbourhood bistro that is popular with the regulars... and the others!

Le Bristol
 ⬅ ♨ ⊗ 🔲 ⓂC 🛁 🚗

112 r. du Faubourg-St-Honoré (8th) – Ⓜ *Miromesnil* Plan: **H2**
– ℰ 01 53 43 43 00 – www.lebristolparis.com
148 rm – ♦950/1300 € ♦♦950/1300 € – ⊡ 65 € – 42 suites
• Palace • Grand luxury •

This luxury hotel, built in 1925 and boasting a new wing added in 2009, is arranged around a magnificent garden. Sumptuous guestrooms decorated in Louis XV or Louis XVI style, as well as a stunning swimming pool, reminiscent of a 19C yacht, on the top floor.
❀❀❀ **Épicure** • ❀ **114, Faubourg** – See restaurant listing

Four Seasons George V
✿ ♨ ⊗ 🔲 ⅙ ⓂC 🛁

31 av. George-V (8th) – Ⓜ *George V* Plan: **G3**
– ℰ 01 49 52 70 00 – www.fourseasons.com/paris
185 rm – ♦1090/1350 € ♦♦1090/1350 € – ⊡ 59 € – 59 suites
• Palace • Historic • Elegant •

This mythical luxury hotel, founded in 1928, has an interior design that reflects the splendours and refinement of the 18C. Its sumptuous and spacious guestrooms, art collections, superb spa and lovely interior courtyard – not to mention its gastronomic history – make this a truly exceptional place!
❀❀❀ **Le Cinq** • ❀ **Le George** • ❀ **L'Orangerie** – See restaurant listing

FRANCE - PARIS

The Peninsula

19 av. Kléber (16th) – **Ⓜ** *Kléber* – ✆ *01 58 12 28 88*
– *www.peninsula.com/fr/*
Plan: **F2**

166 rm – ♦750/1750 € ♦♦750/1750 € – ⌑ 42 € – 34 suites
• Palace • Historic • Elegant •

So it is with this hotel that the Hong Kong Peninsula group arrived in Paris in 2014. A master stroke! Just minutes from the Arc de Triomphe, in a beautiful Belle Epoque building, the hotel has the greatest of everything. Find luxurious interiors, hi-tech equipment and top of the range amenities. 'Tis a rock, a peak, a cape… no, a peninsula!
❍ **L'Oiseau Blanc** • ❍ **Lili** – See restaurant listing

Plaza Athénée

25 av. Montaigne (8th) – **Ⓜ** *Alma Marceau*
– ✆ *01 53 67 66 65*
Plan: **G3**

– *www.dorchestercollection.com/paris/hotel-plaza-athenee*
154 rm – ♦990/2150 € ♦♦990/2150 € – ⌑ 60 € – 54 suites
• Palace • Grand Luxury • Classic •

The Parisian luxury hotel par excellence: inaugurated in 1911, the Plaza Athénée is wearing the passing years wonderfully well. Nothing alters the establishment's primacy, which is at the zenith of French-style luxury and elegance. Brilliant classicism, exceptional amenities, including the fabulous Christian Dior Spa. The legend lives on.
❀❀❀ **Alain Ducasse au Plaza Athénée** • ❍ **La Cour Jardin** • ❍ **Le Relais Plaza** – See restaurant listing

La Réserve

42 av. Gabriel (8th) – **Ⓜ** *Champs Elysées Clemenceau*
– ✆ *01 58 36 60 50* – *www.lareserve-paris.com*
Plan: **H3**

14 rm – ♦1000/1500 € ♦♦1900/16700 € – ⌑ 56 € – 26 suites
• Palace • Grand Luxury • Elegant •

Handsome wooden floors, inviting sofas and gold-plated cornices are a few of the exclusive details that set the Belle Epoque scene in this handsome 19C Parisian mansion, revamped by Jacques Garcia. The suites enjoy views over the Elysée palace gardens, the Grand Palais or the Eiffel Tower. The quintessence of luxury.
❀❀ **Le Gabriel** • ❍ **La Pagode de Cos** – See restaurant listing

Le Royal Monceau

37 av. Hoche (8th) – **Ⓜ** *Charles de Gaulle-Etoile*
– ✆ *01 42 99 88 12* – *www.leroyalmonceau.com*
Plan: **G2**

108 rm – ♦850/1400 € ♦♦1500/2500 € – ⌑ 58 € – 41 suites
• Palace • Grand Luxury • Design •

This 21C luxury hotel, decorated by Philippe Starck, plays with current expectations. There is an art gallery, a bookshop, a hi-tech cinema and a superb spa.
❀ **Il Carpaccio** • ❍ **Matsuhisa** – See restaurant listing

Shangri-La

10 av. d'Iéna (16th) – **Ⓜ** *Iéna* – ✆ *01 53 67 19 98*
– *www.shangri-la.com*
Plan: **F3**

75 rm – ♦795/1675 € ♦♦795/1675 € – ⌑ 58 € – 25 suites
• Palace • Historic • Grand Luxury •

The hallmark of this palatial hotel, opened in 2011, is its fusion of French Empire and Asian styles. Occupying the former home of Prince Roland Bonaparte (1896), its classic architecture encompasses grandiose lounges, opulent luxury and dining options for every taste. A true sense of exclusivity!
❀❀ **L'Abeille** • ❀ **Shang Palace** – See restaurant listing

Champs-Élysées Plaza

35 r. de Berri (8th) – **Ⓜ** *George V* – ✆ *01 53 53 20 20*
– *www.champselyseesplaza.com*
Plan: **G2**

39 rm – ♦290/490 € ♦♦290/490 € – ⌑ 32 € – 10 suites
• Townhouse • Personalised • Elegant •

With its elegance and space, its harmony of colours, its fusion of styles and its attentive service, this hotel is the epitome of luxury. Fitness centre.

FRANCE - PARIS

Fouquet's Barrière

46 av. George-V (8th) – Ⓜ *George V* – ☏ *01 40 69 60 00*
Plan: **G2**
– *www.lefouquets-paris.com*
48 rm – ♦630/2100 € ♦♦630/2100 € – ☑ 49 € – 33 suites
• Luxury • Art déco • Elegant •

Born in the wake of the iconic brasserie, this luxury hotel appointed by Jacques Garcia sports a mixture of Empire and Art deco, and is depicted by a binge of mahogany, silk and velvet, all of which accompanied by hi-tech gadgets and a stunning spa. Pierre Gagnaire signs the famous brasserie's menu. Quintessential Paris.

Prince de Galles

33 av. George-V (8th) – Ⓜ *George V* – ☏ *01 53 23 77 77*
Plan: **G3**
– *www.hotelprincedegalles.fr*
115 rm – ♦650/1020 € ♦♦950/1950 € – ☑ 38 € – 44 suites
• Grand Luxury • Art déco • Historic •

This legendary jewel of Parisian Art Deco is a beacon of elegance on Avenue George V. Built in 1928 and exuding a new freshness, the charm of the place remains intact; from the luxurious and refined guestrooms to the "Les Heures" bar, where time stands still, opposite the listed patio.
✿ **La Scène** – See restaurant listing

Raphael

17 av. Kléber (16th) – Ⓜ *Kléber* – ☏ *01 53 64 32 00*
Plan: **F2**
– *www.raphael-hotel.com*
46 rm – ♦600/1050 € ♦♦600/1050 € – ☑ 40 € – 37 suites
• Luxury • Classic •

A magnificent entrance gallery with woodwork, very elegant rooms (some with views over Paris), a gourmet restaurant and an undeniably elegant English bar: such are the treasures of the Raphael. Founded in 1925, and a stone's throw from the Arc de Triomphe, it is a legend among Parisian hotels.

Vernet

25 r. Vernet (8th) – Ⓜ *Charles de Gaulle-Etoile*
Plan: **F2**
– ☏ *01 44 31 98 00* – *www.hotelvernet.com*
41 rm – ♦690/2200 € ♦♦690/2200 € – ☑ 25 € – 9 suites
• Historic • Townhouse • Elegant •

This building, which dates back to the Roaring Twenties, is in a small street set slightly back from the Champs-Élysees and home to a brand new hotel. It has been completely refurbished and exudes a very Parisian 'je ne sais quoi', from the bright lobby to the elegant and refined guestrooms.
⊙ **Le V** – See restaurant listing

La Clef Tour Eiffel

83 av. Kléber (16th) – Ⓜ *Trocadéro* – ☏ *01 44 05 75 75*
Plan: **E3**
– *www.the-ascott.com*
94 rm – ♦220/620 € ♦♦220/620 € – ☑ 25 € – 18 suites
• Luxury • Personalised •

Not far from Trocadéro, the elegant Haussmann façade hides a contemporary interior designed by Ricardo Bofill. The alchemy works and it all appeals: from the vast lobby to the patio complete with trees, from the inviting guestrooms to the apartments with all mod cons. A top-notch offer.

Renaissance Arc de Triomphe

39 av. Wagram (17th) – Ⓜ *Ternes* – ☏ *01 55 37 55 37*
Plan: **F2**
– *www.marriott.fr*
118 rm – ♦260/729 € ♦♦260/729 € – ☑ 30 € – 5 suites
• Luxury • Chain • Design •

You can't miss the impressive façade of this hotel designed by Christian de Portzamparc, which stands close to Place de l'Étoile. Originality and contemporary style are also the name of the game inside, from the elegant guestrooms to the vast lobby. Try the Sunday brunch.

FRANCE - PARIS

Hôtel de Sers   ✿ 𝄃ᴓ ₺ 𝔸�ℂ 🔊 ➭

41 av. Pierre-1ᵉʳ-de-Serbie (8th) – 🄼 *George V*   Plan: **G3**
– 𝒞 *01 53 23 75 75* – *www.hoteldesers.com*
45 rm – 🛏350/690 € 🛏🛏500/800 € – ☷ 30 € – 7 suites
· Grand townhouse · Historic · Elegant ·
The Marquis de Sers would fail to recognise his late-19C property! The mix of
styles is, however, a success. While the entrance hall has preserved its original
character, the guestrooms are resolutely contemporary. An elegant address.

Marignan Champs-Elysées   ✿ ₺ 𝔸�ℂ 🔊

12 r. de Marignan (8th) – 🄼 *Franklin D. Roosevelt*   Plan: **G3**
– 𝒞 *01 40 76 34 56* – *www.hotelmarignanelyseesparis.com*
45 rm – 🛏270/880 € 🛏🛏270/880 € – ☷ 40 € – 5 suites
· Luxury · Townhouse · Contemporary ·
This hotel in a former townhouse, just off the Champs-Élysées, offers a discreet take on
luxury. All of the guestrooms are done out in an elegant and sleek style with oak floorboards, chic 1950s and 1960s furniture and large beds. Style and subtlety.

Garden Élysée   ⊗ 𝄃ᴓ 𝔸�ℂ

12 r. St-Didier (16th) – 🄼 *Boissière* – 𝒞 *01 47 55 01 11*   Plan: **E3**
– *www.paris-hotel-gardenelysee.com*
46 rm – 🛏170/390 € 🛏🛏175/570 € – ☷ 22 €
· Business · Contemporary ·
This hotel's main advantage has to be the peace and quiet. Although within a
stone's throw of Trocadéro, it stands in a verdant courtyard, which is a delight in
summer. As for the completely refurbished guestrooms, they are pleasant and
nicely fitted out.

Splendid Étoile   𝔸�ℂ 🔊

1bis av. Carnot (17th) – 🄼 *Charles de Gaulle-Étoile*   Plan: **F2**
– 𝒞 *01 45 72 72 00* – *www.hsplendid.com*
55 rm – 🛏156/650 € 🛏🛏156/650 € – ☷ 25 € – 2 suites
· Traditional · Business · Personalised ·
The Splendid Étoile is recognisable by its attractive stone façade and wrought-
iron balconies. It offers large guestrooms (some with views of the Arc de
Triomphe), which owe their character to the Louis XV inspired furniture and
heavy drapes. Overall, a very pleasant, elegant style.
⏀ **Le Pré Carré** – See restaurant listing

Les Jardins de la Villa   𝄃ᴓ 🍃 ₺ 𝔸�ℂ 🔊

5 r. Bélidor (17th) – 🄼 *Porte Maillot* – 𝒞 *01 53 81 01 10*   Plan: **E1**
– *www.jardinsdelavilla.com*
33 rm – 🛏155/400 € 🛏🛏155/400 € – ☷ 19 €
· Boutique hotel · Luxury · Design ·
Fashionistas will be thrilled by this small boutique hotel with numerous references to
the fashion world, along with black, shocking pink and grey tones. It also boasts a spa
with fitness facilities, a sauna and a hammam. Original, chic and comfortable!

❁❁   ### Le Meurice Alain Ducasse – Hôtel Le Meurice   XxXxX ⊗⊗ 𝔸�ℂ

228 r. de Rivoli (1st) – 🄼 *Tuileries* – 𝒞 *01 44 58 10 55*   ➭ 🍴
– *www.alainducasse-meurice.com/fr* – *Closed*   Plan: **J-K3**
17 February-5 March, 28 July-27 August, Saturday and Sunday
Menu 110 € (lunch), 130/380 € – Carte 250/345 €
· Modern cuisine · Luxury · Romantic ·
In the heart of the iconic luxury hotel, the restaurant is the epitome of a great
French restaurant. Its lavish interior, inspired by the royal apartments of Versailles Palace, has been tastefully updated by Philippe Starck. Under the watchful eye of Alain Ducasse, executive chef Jocelyn Herland signs a menu that celebrates top quality produce. Stylish flair.
➜ Langoustines croustillantes, fenouil et citron. Bar de ligne à l'écaille, artichaut et
riquette. Chocolat de notre manufacture, grué de cacao et coriandre.

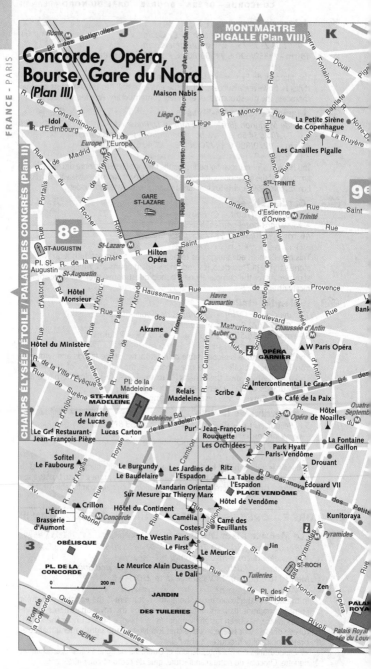

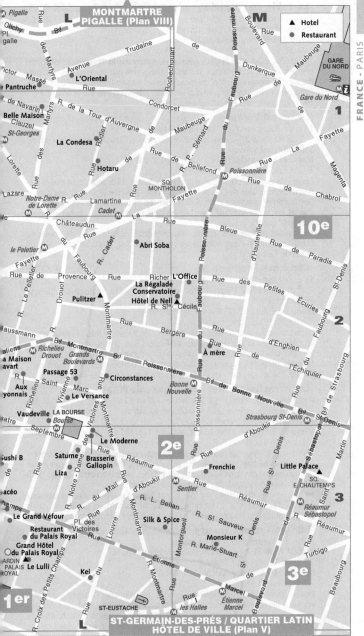

MONTMARTRE
PIGALLE (Plan VIII)

▲ Hotel
● Restaurant

GARE
DU NORD

Gare du Nord

1

10e

L'Oriental

Pantruche

Belle Maison

La Condesa

Hotaru

Notre-Dame
de Lorette

Abri Soba

Richer L'Office
La Régalade
Conservatoire
Hôtel de Nell
R. Ste Cécile

Pulitzer

2

À mère

le Peletier

Montmartre
a Maison Richelieu Grands
avart   Drouot   Boulevards

Passage 53   Circonstances

Aux
yonnais   Le Versance
Vaudeville LA BOURSE
Bourse

Bonne
Nouvelle

Strasbourg St-Denis

Septembre

Le Moderne

2e

Sushi B   Saturne Brasserie
                     Gallopin
           Liza   Frenchie   Little Palace

                                                    SQ.
                                                    E. CHAUTEMPS

acéo   Réaumur
amps   Sébastopol
    Le Grand Véfour
                                                    3
         Restaurant   Silk & Spice
         du Palais Royal
    Grand Hôtel   Monsieur K
    du Palais Royal
ARDIN   Le Lulli
PALAIS
OYAL   3e
                      Kei

1er   Marcel
                              Étienne
              ST-EUSTACHE   Marcel

les Halles

ST-GERMAIN-DES-PRÉS / QUARTIER LATIN
HÔTEL DE VILLE (Plan V)

197

✿✿   **La Table de l'Espadon** – Hôtel Ritz   ХХХхХ ⌖ & 🆔 ⇔ 🍴

15 pl. Vendôme (1st) – ⓜ *Opéra* – 𝒞 *01 43 16 33 74*   Plan: **K3**
– www.ritzparis.com – Closed lunch
Menu 195/340 € – Carte 200/420 €
• Modern cuisine • Elegant • Luxury •

The interior, submerged in golds and drapes, is stunning. In this magical setting, the precise cuisine of young Nicolas Sale shines. Choose the bait, then the line, and finally the bite: the announcement of the meals is packed with nods to fishing and swordfish. Taste, personality, intensity: a wind of modernity is blowing over the Ritz. Superb!
➔ La langoustine. Le homard bleu. Le miel.

✿✿   **Le Grand Véfour** (Guy Martin)   ХххХ ⌖ 🆔 ⇔ 🍴

17 r. de Beaujolais (1st) – ⓜ *Palais Royal*   Plan: **L3**
– 𝒞 01 42 96 56 27 – www.grand-vefour.com – Closed 3 weeks in August, Saturday and Sunday
Menu 115 € (lunch)/315 € – Carte 230/320 €
• Creative • Classic décor •

Bonaparte and Joséphine, Lamartine, Hugo, Sartre… For more than two centuries, the former Café de Chartres has been cultivating the legend. Nowadays it is Guy Martin who maintains the aura. Influenced by travel and painting – colours, shapes, textures – the chef 'sketches' his dishes like an artist… between invention and history.
➔ Ravioles de foie gras, crème foisonnée truffée. Parmentier de queue de bœuf aux truffes. Palet noisette et chocolat au lait, glace au caramel brun et sel de Guérande.

✿✿   **Carré des Feuillants** (Alain Dutournier)   ХххХ ⌖ 🆔 ⇔ 🍴

14 r. de Castiglione (1st) – ⓜ *Tuileries*   Plan: **K3**
– 𝒞 01 42 86 82 82 – www.carredesfeuillants.fr – Closed August, Saturday and Sunday
Menu 68 € (lunch)/198 € – Carte 130/160 €
• Modern cuisine • Elegant •

Elegant and minimalist contemporary restaurant on the site of the old Feuillants convent. Modern menu with strong Gascony influences. Superb wines and Armagnacs.
➔ Pâté croûte de caille des prés façon Rossini, tapenade de truffe et crumble noisettes. Agneau de lait, cousinage de légumes et ris cuits dans l'argile. Fraises des bois en pavlova, sorbet à la rose, gelée de litchis.

✿✿   **Le Grand Restaurant - Jean-François Piège**   ХхХ ⌖ &

7 r. d'Aguesseau (8th) – ⓜ *Madeleine* – 𝒞 *01 53 05 00 00*   🆔
– www.jeanfrancoispiege.com – Closed 30 July-   Plan: **J2**
21 August, Saturday and Sunday
Menu 85 € (lunch), 216/616 € 🍷 – Carte 175/285 € – *(booking advisable)*
• Modern cuisine • Elegant • Design •

Jean-François Piège has found the perfect setting to showcase the great laboratory kitchen he had been dreaming of for so long. The lucky few to get a seat (25 maximum) can sample delicate, light dishes whose emotion can be both tasted and experienced. The quintessence of talent!
➔ Ma version du gâteau de foie blond façon Lucien Tendret, sauce aux queues d'écrevisses et truffe noire. Mijoté de homard en feuilles de cassis sur les carapaces, concentré des baies et foie gras. Blanc à manger.

✿✿   **Sur Mesure par Thierry Marx** – Hôtel Mandarin Oriental

251 r. St-Honoré (1st) – ⓜ *Concorde*   ХхХ ⌖ & 🆔
– 𝒞 01 70 98 71 25 – www.mandarinoriental.fr/paris   Plan: **J3**
– Closed Sunday and Monday
Menu 85 € (weekday lunch), 190/250 €
• Creative • Design • Elegant •

Precise 'tailor-made' (sur mesure) cuisine is the hallmark of Thierry Marx, who confirms his talent as a master culinary craftsman at the Mandarin Oriental's showcase restaurant. Every dish reveals his tireless scientific approach, which is sometimes teasing but always exacting. An experience in itself, aided by the stunning, immaculate and ethereal decor.
➔ Risotto de soja. Bœuf wasabi. Saint-honoré

FRANCE - PARIS

❀❀ **Kei** (Kei Kobayashi) XxX Ⓐ
5 r. du Coq-Héron (1st) Plan: **L3**
– Ⓜ *Louvre Rivoli*
– ℰ *01 42 33 14 74 – www.restaurant-kei.fr*
– *Closed Easter Holidays, 3 weeks in August, Christmas Holidays, Thursday lunch, Sunday and Monday*
Menu 58 € (lunch), 105/199 €
• Modern cuisine • Elegant • Minimalist •
Japanese-born Kei Kobayashi's discovery of French gastronomy on TV was a revelation to him. So much so that as soon as he was old enough he headed to France to train in some of the country's best restaurants. His career now sees him branching out on his own. He offers fine cuisine that reflects his twin influences and the passion for his work.
➔ Jardin de légumes croquants, saumon fumé d'Écosse, émulsion de citron et crumble d'olives. Bar de ligne en écaille croustillante, réduction de vin rouge épicée et anguille fumée. Vacherin aux agrumes et au basilic.

❀❀ **Passage 53** (Shinichi Sato) XX ❀ Ⓐ
53 passage des Panoramas (2nd) Plan: **L2**
– Ⓜ *Grands Boulevards*
– ℰ *01 42 33 04 35 – www.passage53.com*
– *Closed 2 weeks in August, Sunday and Monday*
Menu 60 € (lunch), 120/160 €
• Creative • Intimate • Design •
In an authentic covered passage, this restaurant has a minimalist decor and offers a fine panorama of contemporary cuisine. Using market-fresh produce, the young Japanese chef – trained at L'Astrance – turns out irrefutably precise compositions that are cooked to perfection.
➔ Langoustines, crème et gelée de kombu, lamelles de radis. Turbot et déclinaison de cèpes. Dessert autour du citron.

❀ **L'Écrin** – Hôtel Crillon XxXX ❀ ♿ Ⓐ ♨
10 pl. de la Concorde (8th) Plan: **J3**
– Ⓜ *Concorde*
– ℰ *01 44 71 15 30 – www.rosewoodhotels.com/fr/hotel-de-crillon*
– *Closed Tuesday, Wednesday and lunch*
Menu 195/260 €
• Modern cuisine • Elegant • Contemporary décor •
The dining room of the legendary, 18C Hôtel de Crillon is exclusive, almost secretive and its timeless style expresses the epitome of table art. Christopher Hache's menu aims at legibility, seasonality and flavour. The subtle, succulent dishes are fully worthy of their prestigious setting.
➔ Tomate bavaroise. "Tourtatouille" moderne. Meringue pépite.

❀ **Les Jardins de l'Espadon** – Hôtel Ritz XxX ❀ ♿ ♨ ♿ ♨
15 pl. Vendôme (1st) Plan: **K3**
– Ⓜ *Opéra*
– ℰ *01 43 16 33 74 – www.ritzparis.com*
– *Closed Saturday, Sunday and dinner*
Menu 120/145 €
• Modern cuisine • Romantic •
This retractable conservatory, lined in greenery and entered by a flower-decked, gilt-edged gallery, is one of the main new features of the revamped Ritz. It serves as a setting for Nicolas Salle's inspired cuisine: langoustine cannelloni, spiky green cabbage and Meursault sauce or roast breast of pigeon. A concise menu, inventive dishes, flawless service – Bravo!
➔ Cannelloni de langoustine, chou pointu et sauce au vin de Meursault. Merlan de ligne et crème de charlotte grenobloise. Chocolat de Madagascar, textures de meringue et sauce chocolat frappé.

FRANCE - PARIS

Lucas Carton   XxX 舒 █ ✿

9 pl. de la Madeleine (8th) – **M** *Madeleine*   Plan: **J2**
– ℰ 01 42 65 22 90 – www.lucascarton.com – Closed 3 weeks in August,
Sunday and Monday
Menu 89 € (weekdays), 142/175 € – Carte 135/225 €
• Modern cuisine • Historic • Chic •

The rebirth of Lucas Carton... Symbolising its prestigious past, the intact decor of Art Nouveau wood panelling still works its magic, while cohabiting with futuristic furnishings. This famous place on the Place de la Madeleine is writing a new page in its gastronomic history.

→ Chou-fleur croustillant. Sarrasin et merlan croustillant. Pomme verte et cardamome.

Pur' - Jean-François Rouquette – Hôtel Park Hyatt Paris-Vendôme

5 r. de la Paix (2nd) – **M** *Opéra* – ℰ 01 58 71 10 60   XxX & █ 🍴
– www.paris-restaurant-pur.fr – Closed August and   Plan: **K3**
lunch
Menu 145/275 € ♟ – Carte 95/245 €
• Creative • Elegant •

Enjoy a sense of pure enjoyment as you dine in this restaurant. The highly elegant contemporary decor and creative dishes are carefully conjured by the chef using the finest ingredients. Attractive, delicious and refined.

→ Ormeaux dorés au beurre d'algues, artichaut poivrade, vadouvan et tobiko. Ris de veau croustillant, sauce blanquette aux baies de genièvre. Déclinaison aux trois chocolats dans l'esprit d'une feuille de cacaoyer.

Le Baudelaire – Hôtel Le Burgundy   XxX █ 🍴

6-8 r. Duphot (1st) – **M** *Madeleine* – ℰ 01 71 19 49 11   Plan: **J3**
– www.leburgundy.com – Closed lunch in August, Saturday lunch and
Sunday
Menu 58 € (lunch), 105/210 € ♟ – Carte 93/122 €
• Modern cuisine • Elegant •

This restaurant is within the luxurious Hotel Burgundy. It is a quality, gourmet establishment, where the food reveals finesse and lightness. There is a lovely atmosphere around the inner patio.

→ Escargots en "casse-croûte" glacés au jus, gnocchettis de pomme de terre à l'ail doux. Ris de veau croustillant parfumé à la bruyère de Sologne, girolles aux abricots. Chocolat Macaé, meringue cacao.

Restaurant du Palais Royal   XX 舒 & █ ✿ 🍴

110 galerie de Valois (1st) – **M** *Palais Royal*   Plan: **L3**
– ℰ 01 40 20 00 27 – www.restaurantdupalaisroyal.com – Closed
18 February-5 March, Sunday and Monday
Menu 55 € (lunch)/148 € – Carte 100/160 €
• Creative • Elegant •

Magnificently located beneath the arcades of the Palais Royal, this elegant restaurant is now the playground of young chef Philip Chronopoulos, formerly of the Atelier Etoile de Joël Robuchon. Philip concocts creative, striking meals, such as flash-fried scampi with girolle mushrooms and fresh almonds.

→ Poulpe au piment fumé, pommes grenaille caramélisées. Cabillaud confit à l'huile d'argan, citron rôti et pousses d'épinard. Baba au rhum, chantilly et glace au gingembre.

Akrame (Akrame Benallal)   XX 舒

7 r. Tronchet (8th) – **M** *Madeleine* – ℰ 01 40 67 11 16   Plan: **J2**
– www.akrame.com – Closed 2 weeks in August, 1 week Christmas
Holidays, Saturday and Sunday
Menu 65 € (lunch), 130/160 €
• Creative • Design •

Akrame Benallal now dons his chef's hat in this restaurant tucked away behind a heavy *porte cochère* (coach gateway). With a single, well put-together set menu, he unleashes great inventiveness to capitalise on excellent quality ingredients. The dishes are meticulously prepared. Needless to say, it's a hit!

→ Cuisine du marché.

Saturne (Sven Chartier) XX 🕸 AC

17 r. N.-D.-des-Victoires (2nd) – Ⓜ Bourse
Plan: **L3**
– ✆ 01 42 60 31 90 – www.saturne-paris.fr – Closed Christmas Holidays,
Saturday and Sunday
Menu 45 € (lunch)/85 €
· Creative · Trendy ·

The young chef at this restaurant named after Saturn (the god of agriculture)
offers a single menu with an emphasis on excellent ingredients and naturally
produced wines. A typically Scandinavian loft-style atmosphere (with pale
wood and polished concrete).
→ Cuisine du marché.

Jin X AC ⇔

6 r. de la Sourdière (1st) – Ⓜ Tuileries
Plan: **K3**
– ✆ 01 42 61 60 71 – Closed 2 weeks in August,
Christmas Holidays, Sunday and Monday
Menu 95 € (lunch), 145/195 €
· Japanese · Elegant · Design ·

A new showcase for Japanese cuisine, right in the heart of Paris! Jin is first and
foremost the know-how of Takuya Watanabe, the chef, who comes from
Sapporo. Before your eyes, he creates delicious sushi and sashimi, using fish
sourced from Brittany, Oléron and Spain. The whole menu is a treat.
→ Cuisine du marché.

Sushi B X AC

5 r. Rameau (2nd) – Ⓜ Bourse – ✆ 01 40 26 52 87
Plan: **L3**
– www.sushi-b-fr.com – Closed 2 weeks in August and Tuesday
Menu 58 € (weekday lunch), 95/160 €
· Japanese · Minimalist ·

It is enjoyable to linger in this tiny restaurant (with just seven places) on the
edge of the pleasant Square Louvois for its sleek, soothing interior, of course...
but particularly to witness for oneself the chef's great talent. Like an excellent
artisan, he uses only the freshest top-notch ingredients, which he handles with
surgical precision.
→ Cuisine du marché.

Abri Soba X

10 r. Saulnier (9th) – Ⓜ Cadet – ✆ 01 45 23 51 68
Plan: **L2**
– Closed 3 weeks in August, 24 to 30 December, Sunday lunch and
Monday
Menu 38 € – Carte 25/40 €
· Japanese · Bistro ·

You may have heard of soba, Japanese pasta made with buckwheat, the reputation of which is currently snowballing around the planet. The chef of this restaurant has made soba his house speciality and serves it lunch and evening in
an amazing variety of preparations: hot, cold, in stock or with finely sliced duck.
Simply flavoursome – get out your chopsticks!

Les Canailles Pigalle X

25 r. La Bruyère (9th) – Ⓜ St-Georges
Plan: **K1**
– ✆ 01 48 74 10 48 – www.restaurantlescanailles.fr – Closed 3 weeks in
August, Saturday and Sunday
Menu 35 € – Carte 54/63 €
· Modern cuisine · Bistro · Friendly ·

This pleasant restaurant was created in 2012 by two Bretons with impressive
culinary backgrounds. They slip into the bistronomy (gastro bistro), serving
bistro and seasonal dishes. Specialities: ox tongue carpaccio and sauce ravigote,
and rum baba with vanilla whipped cream... Tuck in!

FRANCE - PARIS

Circonstances

X 🍴 (dinner)

174 r. Montmartre (2nd) – Ⓜ Grands Boulevards   Plan: **L2**
– ℰ 01 42 36 17 05 – www.circonstances.fr – Closed 3 weeks in August,
Monday dinner, Tuesday dinner, Saturday and Sunday
Menu 36/45 €
• Traditional cuisine • Friendly •

On the doorstep of the Grands Boulevards metro station, this bistro was founded by two old hands determined to uphold the tradition of good market-fresh
cuisine and fine produce. Ravioles of shrimps with "coriander mint", salt cod and
potato mash with coconut milk and olive oil, or dark chocolate mousse. We take
our hats off!

L'Office

X 🆔

3 r. Richer (9th) – Ⓜ Poissonnière – ℰ 01 47 70 67 31   Plan: **M2**
– www.office-resto.com – Closed 3 weeks in August, 1 week Christmas
Holidays, Saturday and Sunday
Menu 27 € – Carte 37/54 €
• Modern cuisine • Bistro • Friendly •

A tiny bistro a stone's throw from Les Folies Bergère. Seated at tightly packed
tables, diners dig into food that changes with the seasons. Precise, flavoursome
dishes are accompanied by a well-selected wine list - all at reasonable prices.

Le Pantruche

X

3 r. Victor-Massé (9th) – Ⓜ Pigalle – ℰ 01 48 78 55 60   Plan: **L1**
– Closed 1 week Easter Holidays, 3 weeks in August, 1 week Christmas
Holidays, Saturday and Sunday
Menu 36 € – Carte 39/50 €
• Modern cuisine • Bistro •

'Pantruche' is slang for Paris... an apt name for this bistro with its chic retro
decor, which happily cultivates a 1940s-1950s atmosphere. As for the food, the
chef and his small team put together lovely seasonal dishes in keeping with current culinary trends.

Zen

X 🍵 🆔

8 r. de L'Échelle (1st) – Ⓜ Palais Royal   Plan: **K3**
– ℰ 01 42 61 93 99 – www.restaurantzenparis.fr – Closed 3 weeks in
August and 31 December-5 January
Menu 20 € (weekday lunch), 35/55 € – Carte 19/58 €
• Japanese • Minimalist •

This enticing restaurant combines a refreshing contemporary interior design
and authentic Japanese cooking. The menu is well-rounded and faithful to the
classic sushi, grilled dishes and tempura, with house specialities of gyoza and
chirashi. Ideal for a quick lunch or a relaxing 'zen' dinner.

Drouant

XxX 🕸 🍵 🆔 ⇔ 🍴

16 pl. Gaillon (2nd) – Ⓜ Quatre Septembre   Plan: **K3**
– ℰ 01 42 65 15 16 – www.drouant.com
Menu 45 € (weekday lunch) – Carte 70/100 €
• Traditional cuisine • Elegant •

A legendary restaurant where the Prix Goncourt has been awarded since 1914.
With Antoine Westermann at the helm, it serves traditional cuisine with a
modern touch. Elegant, richly decorated interior.

Macéo

XxX 🕸 🆔 ⇔

15 r. Petits-Champs (1st) – Ⓜ Bourse – ℰ 01 42 97 53 85   Plan: **L3**
– www.maceorestaurant.com – Closed Saturday lunch and Sunday
Menu 35 € (lunch)/45 € – Carte 50/58 €
• Modern cuisine • Classic décor •

Macéo is first a tribute by the owner to Maceo Parker, a great American saxo-
phonist who played with James Brown. It also has a Second Empire interior
and serves seasonal recipes that invariably delight. Roast duckling and miniature vegetables with a Spanish twist or slow-cooked beef ravioli, for example.
Vegetarian menu and international wine list.

FRANCE - PARIS

🍴 **Le Versance** XxX 🏵 🅰🅲
Plan: **L2**

16 r. Feydeau (2nd) – Ⓜ Bourse – 𝒞 01 45 08 00 08
– www.leversance.fr – Closed 1 to 22 August, 22 December-3 January,
Saturday lunch, Sunday and Monday
Menu 43 € (lunch) – Carte 75/90 €
• Modern cuisine • Elegant •

A minimalist stage enhanced by beams, stained glass and designer furnishings. The globetrotting chef's cuisine is equally ambitious: ceviche of tuna, chicken broth, lemon verbena and combawa. Opposite, a delicatessen grocery proposes homemade sandwiches and carefully selected produce.

🍴 **Brasserie d'Aumont** – Hôtel Crillon XX 🅰🅲 🏵
Plan: **J3**

10 pl. de la Concorde (8th) – Ⓜ Concorde
– 𝒞 01 44 71 15 15 – www.rosewoodhotels.com/fr/hotel-de-crillon
Carte 65/120 €
• Modern cuisine • Brasserie • Luxury •

The Brasserie d'Aumont sports a handsome Art deco interior, whose two connecting dining rooms are flanked by a shellfish counter with bar seats. Simply-laid tables and top-quality brasserie classics with a modern touch. Concise wine list and fine choice by the glass. Pleasant terrace. Smart and succulent.

🍴 **Le Café de la Paix** – Hôtel Intercontinental Le Grand XX 🅰🅲
Plan: **K2**

2 r. Scribe (9th) – Ⓜ Opéra – 𝒞 01 40 07 32 32
– www.paris.intercontinental.com
Menu 55 € – Carte 90/110 €
• Classic cuisine • Elegant •

Frescoes, gilded wainscotting and furniture inspired by the Napoleon-III style: this luxurious, legendary restaurant, open from 7am to midnight, remains the haunt of well-heeled Parisians. It stands to reason: the pâté en croûte is wonderful, and it is a joy to delve into the layers of the vanilla mille-feuille. Fine brasserie cuisine.

🍴 **Camélia** – Hôtel Mandarin Oriental XX 🏵 🅰🅲
Plan: **J3**

251 r. St-Honoré (1st) – Ⓜ Concorde – 𝒞 01 70 98 74 00
– www.mandarinoriental.fr/paris
Menu 65 € (weekday lunch)/98 € – Carte 80/115 €
• Modern cuisine • Elegant • Design •

Keep it simple, concentrate on the flavour of the top-notch ingredients, draw inspiration from France's gastronomical classics and enhance them with Asian touches. This is the approach of Thierry Marx at Camélia; an elegant, soothing, zen place. An unequivocal success.

🍴 **Le Dalí** – Hôtel Le Meurice XX 🅰🅲
Plan: **J-K3**

228 r. de Rivoli (1st) – Ⓜ Tuileries – 𝒞 01 44 58 10 44
– www.dorchestercollection.com/fr/paris/le-meurice/
Menu 84 € 🍷 – Carte 60/130 €
• Mediterranean cuisine • Chic • Romantic •

The Number 2 restaurant of the Meurice Hotel, in the heart of its luxury parent, paints a stylish tribute to its surrealist namesake, once a regular guest, with a handsome classical interior (pilasters, mirrors and lighting). Flawlessly executed dishes, whose seasonal ingredients have a distinct Mediterranean accent, without forgetting the classics associated with luxury hotels.

🍴 **Le Lulli** – Grand Hôtel du Palais Royal XX 🅰🅲
Plan: **L3**

4 r. de Valois (1st) – Ⓜ Palais Royal – 𝒞 01 42 96 72 20
– www.grandhoteldupalaisroyal.com – Closed 31 July-27 August,
Saturday, Sunday, Bank Holidays and dinner
Menu 38 € – Carte 44/74 €
• Modern cuisine • Elegant • Romantic •

Plant-motif decoration and contemporary paintings: the lovely interior is propitious to enjoying the moment! The chef, Jean-Baptiste Orieux, proposes refined contemporary cuisine, made with local and seasonal ingredients. As for the service, friendly and professional, it seals the deal.

FRANCE - PARIS

Les Orchidées – Hôtel Park Hyatt Paris-Vendôme   XX 🍴 ♿ 🅰🅲
5 r. de la Paix (2nd) – Ⓜ *Opéra –* ☎ *01 58 71 10 60*   Plan: **K3**
– www.parisvendome.park.hyatt.com
Carte 67/120 €
• Modern cuisine • Elegant •
On the famous rue de la Paix, a stone's throw from Place Vendôme, Jean-François Rouquette (Crillon, Taillevent) creates inspired cuisine, based on ingredients selected with irreproachable rigour. Eat beneath the glass roof or on the terrace in the summer season... surrounded by orchids.

Brasserie Gallopin   XX ♿ 🅰🅲 ♻
40 r. N.-D.-des-Victoires (2nd) – Ⓜ *Bourse*   Plan: **L3**
– ☎ *01 42 36 45 38 – www.gallopin.com*
Menu 29 € – Carte 35/71 €
• Traditional cuisine • Brasserie •
This brasserie, set opposite Palais Brongniart, is a genuine institution founded in 1876 by a Mr Gallopin. Parisians and tourists are attracted by its handsome Victorian interior of mahogany, its turn of the 20C conservatory and its bourgeois bistro classics: calf's head, Noirmoutier turbot, baked Alaska with raspberry liqueur.

Le First – Hôtel The Westin Paris   XX 🍴 🅰🅲
234 r. de Rivoli (1st) – Ⓜ *Tuileries –* ☎ *01 44 77 10 40*   Plan: **J3**
– www.lefirstrestaurant.com/fr/
Menu 54 € 🍷 – Carte 58/71 €
• Modern cuisine • Elegant • Vintage •
A stone's throw from the Tuileries, in The Westin, a lovely setting with soft lighting – the stamp of Jacques Garcia –, where the food respectfully revisits tradition. In summer, head for the terrace nestled in the courtyard and oh so peaceful.

La Fontaine Gaillon   XX 🍴 🅰🅲 ♻ 🍽
pl. Gaillon (2nd) – Ⓜ *Quatre Septembre*   Plan: **K2-3**
– ☎ *01 47 42 63 22 – www.restaurant-la-fontaine-gaillon.com – Closed Saturday lunch and Sunday*
Menu 55 € (lunch) – Carte 67/86 €
• Seafood • Elegant •
Beautiful 17C townhouse supervised by Gérard Depardieu with a hushed setting and terrace around a fountain. Spotlight on seafood, accompanied by a pleasant selection of wines.

Le Marché du Lucas – Restaurant Lucas Carton   XX 🅰🅲
9 pl. de la Madeleine (8th) – Ⓜ *Madeleine*   Plan: **J2**
– ☎ *01 42 65 56 66 – www.lucascarton.com – Closed 3 weeks in August, Sunday and Monday*
Menu 45 €
• Traditional cuisine • Classic décor • Cosy •
Above Lucas Carton, in a pleasant Art Nouveau setting, chef Julien Dumas plumps for simplicity and generosity with a daily-changing spoken menu. Free-range pork chop with black olives and black pudding….hearty cooking!

Vaudeville   XX 🍴
29 r. Vivienne (2nd) – Ⓜ *Bourse –* ☎ *01 40 20 04 62*   Plan: **L2**
– www.vaudevilleparis.com
Menu 32 € – Carte 35/50 €
• Traditional cuisine • Brasserie • Vintage •
A grand Art Deco brasserie in the pure Parisian tradition. Seafood, fresh tagliatelle with morels and Beaufort, calf's head with ravigote sauce, andouillette and braised sauerkraut are on the menu. By day, a regular lunchtime spot for journalists and in the evening, a haunt for theatre-goers after the show.

FRANCE - PARIS

La Condesa ✗

17 r. Rodier (9th) – Ⓜ Notre-Dame de Lorette — Plan: **L1**
*– ℰ 09 67 19 94 90 – www.lacondesa-paris.com – Closed 3 weeks in
August, Saturday lunch, Sunday and Monday*
Menu 30 € (lunch), 48/68 €
• Creative • Cosy • Chic •

Condesa is a district of Mexico City as well as the restaurant of Indra Carillo, who came
from Mexico to study at the Paul Bocuse institute. He composes a high-flying culinary
score with disconcerting ease, featuring a variety of cultures and influences. An excellent restaurant, further enhanced by the professional attentive personnel.

À mère ✗

49 r. de l'Échiquier (10th) – Ⓜ Bonne Nouvelle — Plan: **M2**
*– ℰ 01 48 00 08 28 – www.amere.fr – Closed August, 24 December-
6 January, Saturday and Sunday*
Menu 35 € (lunch), 45/65 €
• Creative • Fashionable • Trendy •

Maurizio Zillo, an Italian-Brazilian chef who has had a dazzling career (Bocuse,
Alléno, Atala in São Paulo...), has put together a dream team (including a sommelier from the George V) to create this trendy bistro. His dishes are packed
with flavour, and his inventiveness hits the nail on the head every time. What a
lovely surprise!

Aux Lyonnais ✗ 🅰🅲 ⇔

32 r. St-Marc (2nd) – Ⓜ Richelieu Drouot — Plan: **L2**
*– ℰ 01 42 96 65 04 – www.auxlyonnais.com – Closed August, Saturday
lunch, Sunday and Monday*
Menu 35 € – Carte 42/60 €
• Lyonnaise • Bistro • Vintage •

This bistro, founded in 1890, serves delicious cuisine which explores the gastronomic history of the city. Deliciously retro decor, featuring a zinc counter, banquettes, bevelled mirrors and moulded fixtures and fittings.

Belle Maison ✗

4 r. de Navarin (9th) – Ⓜ Saint-Georges — Plan: **L1**
*– ℰ 01 42 81 11 00 – www.restaurant-bellemaison.com – Closed 2 weeks
in August, 1 week Christmas Holidays, Sunday and Monday*
Carte 41/58 €
• Seafood • Bistro • Trendy •

The three associates of Pantruche and Caillebotte are back behind the wheel in
this Belle Maison, named after a beach on the Island of Yeu where they used to
spend their holidays. The chef rustles up seafood-inspired dishes with disconcerting expertise: crab ravioles and gazpacho; line caught croaker, peas and
girolles – a tantalising experience awaits!

Frenchie ✗ 🅰🅲

5 r. du Nil (2nd) – Ⓜ Sentier – ℰ 01 40 39 96 19 — Plan: **M3**
*– www.frenchie-restaurant.com – Closed 6 to 21 August, 25 December-3 January,
Monday lunch, Tuesday lunch, Wednesday lunch, Saturday and Sunday*
Menu 45 € (lunch)/74 €
• Modern cuisine • Friendly • Fashionable •

Near the Sentier metro station, this small, loft-style restaurant has exposed
brickwork, stones and beams. It specialises in contemporary-style cuisine created by a young chef with an international CV.

Hotaru ✗

18 r. Rodier (9th) – Ⓜ Notre-Dame de Lorette — Plan: **L1**
*– ℰ 01 48 78 33 74 – Closed 3 weeks in August,
Christmas Holidays, Sunday and Monday*
Menu 24 € (lunch) – Carte 26/53 €
• Japanese • Rustic •

A welcoming Japanese restaurant with a young chef who produces traditional,
family cuisine with an emphasis on fish. Enjoy sushi, maki and sashimi, as well as
a selection of cooked and fried dishes.

⑩ **Kunitoraya** X AK ⇔

5 r. Villedo (1st) – Ⓜ Pyramides – ℰ 01 47 03 07 74 Plan: **K3**
– www.kunitoraya.com – Closed 2 weeks in August, Christmas Holidays,
Sunday dinner and Monday
Menu 32 € (weekday lunch)/52 € – Carte approx. 40 €
• Japanese • Vintage • Minimalist •

With its old zinc counter, mirrors and Métro-style tiling, Kunitoraya has the feel
of a late-night Parisian restaurant from the early 1900s. Refined Japanese cuisine
is based around "udon", a thick homemade noodle prepared with wholemeal
flour imported from Japan.

⑩ **Liza** X AK

14 r. de la Banque (2nd) – Ⓜ Bourse – ℰ 01 55 35 00 66 Plan: **L3**
– www.restaurant-liza.com – Closed Sunday dinner
Menu 38 € (dinner)/48 € – Carte 35/65 €
• Lebanese • Oriental décor •

Originally from Beirut, Liza Asseily gives pride of place to her country's cuisine.
In a contemporary interior dotted with Middle Eastern touches, opt for the shish
taouk or mechoui kafta (lamb, hummus and tomato preserves). Dishes are meticulously prepared using fresh ingredients. A real treat!

⑩ **Le Moderne** X 🍴 AK

40 r. N.-D.-des-Victoires (2nd) – Ⓜ Bourse Plan: **L3**
– ℰ 01 53 40 84 10 – www.le-moderne.fr – Closed 3 weeks in August,
Saturday and Sunday
Menu 32/45 € – Carte 45/61 €
• Modern cuisine • Friendly •

Close to the Palais Brongniart, now stripped of its vocation as the Bourse de
Paris, the Café Moderne plunges you into the still bustling atmosphere of the
neighbourhood. At lunchtime, the place is packed to the rafters, while in the
evening it has an intimate feel. On the menu are good, fresh ingredients, cooked with taste.

⑩ **Monsieur K** X

10 r. Marie-Stuart (2nd) – Ⓜ Sentier – ℰ 01 42 36 01 09 Plan: **M3**
– www.kapunkaparis.com – Closed 1 week in August and Sunday
Menu 27 € (lunch), 30/39 € – Carte 30/55 €
• Thai • Friendly •

The chef is a true Asia enthusiast. He has travelled the length and breadth of
Thailand 16 times to sample its many cuisines and to reproduce a replica of
the best dishes. He is a perfectionist fighting for the good cause, and makes a
mean Pad Thai.

⑩ **La Petite Sirène de Copenhague** X

47 r. Notre-Dame-de-Lorette (9th) – Ⓜ St-Georges Plan: **K1**
– ℰ 01 45 26 66 66 – www.lapetitesireneparis.com – Closed August,
23 December-2 January, Saturday lunch, Sunday and Monday
Menu 35 € (lunch)/41 € – Carte 50/82 €
• Danish • Bistro •

The Danish flag flying above the entrance provides a strong clue to the gourmet offerings inside. There is a daily menu chalked up on a slate board, as well
as a more expensive à la carte, from which guests can feast on Danish specialities such as herrings.

⑩ **La Régalade Conservatoire** – Hôtel de Nell X & AK ⇔ 🥢

7-9 r. du Conservatoire (9th) – Ⓜ Bonne Nouvelle Plan: **M2**
– ℰ 01 44 83 83 60 – www.charmandmore.com
Menu 37 €
• Modern cuisine • Fashionable • Friendly •

After his Régalades in the 14th and 1st arrondissements, Bruno Doucet has
opened a third, this time close to Grands Boulevards inside the luxurious Hôtel
de Nell. Here bistro-style goes chic, and the chef's cooking is as well-executed,
generous and tasty as ever.

🍴 **Silk & Spice**   ✗ & 🗚 ↔
6 r. Mandar (2nd) – Ⓜ *Sentier* – ℰ *01 44 88 21 91*   Plan: **L3**
– www.silkandspice.fr – Closed Saturday lunch and Sunday
Menu 32/48 € – Carte 28/50 €
• Thai • Exotic décor •
Hushed atmosphere and delicious Thai-inspired cuisine. The signature dishes
here are king prawns and shrimps in a lemon grass reduction, and green beef
curry.

🏨🏨 **Crillon**   ℉ 🌐 🗋 & 🗚 🏊
10 pl. de la Concorde (8th) – Ⓜ *Concorde*   Plan: **J3**
– ℰ 01 44 71 15 00 – www.rosewoodhotels.com/fr/hotel-de-crillon
124 rm – ♦1350/2500 € ♦♦1350/2500 € – � 60 € – 43 suites
• Palace • Grand luxury •
We take our hat off to this masterpiece of 18C architecture, whose iconic façade
graces the prestigious Place de la Concorde and which has lost none of its lavish
ornamentation. Luxurious bedrooms and themed apartments (one of which is
the work of Karl Lagerfeld). French art de vivre in all its timeless splendour. A
mythical luxury hotel.
✿ **L'Écrin** • 🍴 **Brasserie d'Aumont** – See restaurant listing

🏨🏨 **Mandarin Oriental**   ℉ 🌐 🗋 & 🗚 🏊
251 r. St-Honoré (1st) – Ⓜ *Concorde* – ℰ *01 70 98 78 88*   Plan: **J3**
– www.mandarinoriental.fr/paris
98 rm – ♦995/1500 € ♦♦995/1500 € – ⊻ 47 € – 40 suites
• Palace • Elegant •
Faithful to the principles of this Hong Kong group, the property is the height of
refinement. It combines French elegance with the delicate touches of Asia and
features sleek lines, lots of space and peace and quiet. A capital address in the
heart of the French capital!
✿✿ **Sur Mesure par Thierry Marx** • 🍴 **Camélia** – See restaurant listing

🏨🏨 **Le Meurice**   ℉ 🌐 & 🗚 🏊
228 r. de Rivoli (1st) – Ⓜ *Tuileries* – ℰ *01 44 58 10 10*   Plan: **J-K3**
– www.dorchestercollection.com/fr/paris/le-meurice/
136 rm – ♦695/4000 € ♦♦695/4000 € – ⊻ 58 € – 24 suites
• Palace • Grand Luxury • Historic •
Opened in 1835, the Meurice was one of the first luxury hotels in Paris. Overlooking the leafy Tuileries Gardens, the opulent establishment is supremely classical, with the occasional modern detail added by cult designer Philippe Starck.
Luxurious spa, exclusive, club-style bar, Le Meurice is the epitome of gracious
art de vivre.
✿✿ **Le Meurice Alain Ducasse** • 🍴 **Le Dalí** – See restaurant listing

🏨🏨 **Ritz**   ℉ 🛏 ℉ 🌐 🗋 & 🗚 🏊
15 pl. Vendôme (1st) – Ⓜ *Opéra* – ℰ *01 43 16 33 74*   Plan: **K3**
– www.ritzparis.com
71 rm – ♦1300/3100 € ♦♦1300/3100 € – ⊻ 60 € – 71 suites
• Grand Luxury • Historic • Historic •
The mythical hotel has reopened after four years of refurbishment and is as
luxurious as ever. On legendary Place Vendôme, César Ritz opened the "perfect
hotel" in 1898. Proust, Hemingway and Coco Chanel were a few of its illustrious
patrons, enticed by the incomparable sophistication of a 28 000m²/92 000ft²
luxury hotel. Everything is lavish from the Hemingway Bar and the 1 500m²/
5 000ft² spa to the Mansard suite, whose huge terrace overlooks Place Vendôme and reveals a 360° panorama over Paris. The legend continues.
✿✿ **La Table de l'Espadon** • ✿ **Les Jardins de l'Espadon** – See restaurant listing

FRANCE - PARIS

Intercontinental Le Grand

2 r. Scribe (9th) – Ⓜ *Opéra* – ☏ *01 40 07 32 32*
Plan: **K2**
– www.paris.intercontinental.com
442 rm – ♦335/950 € ♦♦335/950 € – ☑ 45 € – 28 suites
• Historic • Grand luxury •
Opened in 1862, the Intercontinental stands on the Place de l'Opéra in the heart of Haussmann's Paris. With its superbly decorated Café de la Paix, its interior courtyard with a Proustian ambience and its Second Empire-style guestrooms, this is a real Parisian landmark.
🍴 **Le Café de la Paix** – See restaurant listing

Park Hyatt Paris-Vendôme – Hôtel Park Hyatt

5 r. de la Paix (2nd) – Ⓜ *Opéra* – ☏ *01 58 71 12 34*
– www.parisvendome.park.hyatt.com
Plan: **K3**
110 rm – ♦830/1400 € ♦♦830/1400 € – ☑ 38 € – 43 suites
• Luxury • Elegant •
Ed Tuttle designed his dream hotel, which stands on the famous rue de la Paix. It has a collection of contemporary art and French-style classicism with a subtle blend of Louis XVI-style and 1930s furnishings. There is a spa and hi-tech equipment, as well as restaurants for all tastes. An authentic palace.
❀ **Pur' - Jean-François Rouquette** • 🍴 **Les Orchidées** – See restaurant listing

Le Burgundy

6-8 r. Duphot (1st) – Ⓜ *Madeleine* – ☏ *01 42 60 34 12*
Plan: **J3**
– www.leburgundy.com
51 rm ☑ – ♦350/940 € ♦♦350/940 € – 8 suites
• Grand Luxury • Design • Personalised •
In this luxury hotel, the wood panelling combines harmoniously with the coloured fabrics, designer furniture and contemporary art to provide a hushed, arty atmosphere.
❀ **Le Baudelaire** – See restaurant listing

Costes

239 r. St-Honoré (1st) – Ⓜ *Concorde* – ☏ *01 42 44 50 00*
Plan: **K3**
– www.hotelcostes.com
84 rm – ♦500/700 € ♦♦500/700 € – ☑ 35 € – 2 suites
• Luxury • Personalised • Cosy •
This extremely chic and plush palace remains a firm favourite with the jet set. There are nooks and crannies everywhere, and it is furnished with squat armchairs and benches made from pear wood. The guestrooms are refined down to the smallest details: purple and gold colour scheme, monogrammed linen etc.

Hilton Opéra

108 r. St-Lazare (8th) – Ⓜ *Saint-Lazare*
Plan: **J2**
– ☏ *01 40 08 44 44* – www.parisopera.hilton.com
257 rm – ♦229/500 € ♦♦400/1000 € – ☑ 29 € – 11 suites
• Chain • Contemporary •
Completely refurbished in 2015, this hotel is in touch with its Belle Époque past: a lobby with marble columns and a ceiling crafted with gold leaf, a large majestic lounge, with a glass roof and frescoes... the bright and contemporary guestrooms are very comfortable.

Hôtel de Vendôme

1 pl. Vendôme (1st) – Ⓜ *Opéra* – ☏ *01 55 04 55 00*
Plan: **K3**
– www.hoteldevendome.com
29 rm – ♦380/590 € ♦♦580/920 € – ☑ 29 € – 9 suites
• Luxury • Palace • Grand luxury •
Period furnishings and marble rub shoulders with modern, comfortable fixtures and fittings in this glittering noble 18C edifice. The emphasis is on discreet classicism. The restaurant seeks to create the ambience of an exclusive Parisian salon, into which only friends and acquaintances are invited.

FRANCE - PARIS

Scribe

1 r. Scribe (9th) – Ⓜ Opéra – ℰ 01 44 71 24 24
Plan: **K2**
– www.hotel-scribe.com
204 rm – 🛏300/690 € 🛏🛏300/1400 € – � 35 € – 9 suites
• Luxury • Personalised • Classic •
Fall under the charm of this chic, very Parisian hotel occupying a Haussmann-style building close to the Opéra, where the hushed atmosphere is almost secretive in feel. It was here, in 1895, that the Lumière brothers hosted their very first cinema screening. A legendary address with a discreet elegance all of its own.

Sofitel le Faubourg

15 r. Boissy-d'Anglas (8th) – Ⓜ Concorde
Plan: **J3**
– ℰ 01 44 94 14 14 – www.sofitel-paris-lefaubourg.com
120 rm – 🛏336/950 € 🛏🛏336/950 € – ⊑ 36 € – 29 suites
• Luxury • Contemporary • Personalised •
This elegant hotel occupies two 18C and 19C residences. It offers attractive suites in a contemporary style, as well as elegant guestrooms. There is also a lounge crowned with a glass roof, a fitness centre and a hammam.

The Westin Paris

3 r. de Castiglione (1st) – Ⓜ Tuileries – ℰ 01 44 77 11 11
Plan: **J3**
– www.thewestinparis.fr
348 rm ⊑ – 🛏300/850 € 🛏🛏300/850 € – 80 suites
• Luxury • Personalised •
This hotel built in 1878 combines old-world charm (Napoleon III lounges) and elegant contemporary touches. Some guestrooms boast views across the Tuileries gardens. The designer Jacques Garcia has brought his chic and opulent modern boudoir style to the interior of Le First. Peaceful accommodation on the courtyard side at La Terrasse.
🍴 **Le First** – See restaurant listing

W Paris Opéra

4 r. Meyerbeer (9th) – Ⓜ Chaussée d'Antin
Plan: **K2**
– ℰ 01 77 48 94 94 – www.wparisopera.fr
89 rm – 🛏370/2200 € 🛏🛏370/2200 € – ⊑ 39 € – 2 suites
• Luxury • Design • Contemporary •
You would be hard-pressed to be more at the heart of Haussmann's Paris than in this fine building from 1870 adjacent to Opéra. If this hotel, opened in 2012, has opted for Parisian chic, its version is in a resolutely designer vein, at once luxurious and easygoing. View over the Palais Garnier opera house. Trendy and appealing.

Banke

20 r. Lafayette (9th) – Ⓜ Chaussée d'Antin
Plan: **K2**
– ℰ 01 55 33 22 22 – www.derbyhotels.com
91 rm – 🛏250/530 € 🛏🛏270/650 € – ⊑ 24 €
• Luxury • Design •
Situated in the heart of the Belle Epoque business district between the Bourse and the Opera, this former bank building was converted into a unique luxury hotel in 2009. The opulent lobby, crowned by a glass ceiling, is highly striking, while the guestrooms have a warm, welcoming feel.

Édouard VII

39 av. de l'Opéra (2nd) – Ⓜ Opéra – ℰ 01 42 61 86 11
Plan: **K3**
– www.edouard7hotel.com
59 rm ⊑ – 🛏230/550 € 🛏🛏350/1360 € – 10 suites
• Luxury • Personalised • Cosy •
Shimmering fabrics and refined decor in the Couture rooms, while the mood in the Edouard VII rooms is more understated. The hotel exudes elegance and the suites are superb. Cosy bar and light meals in a very pleasant contemporary setting.

FRANCE - PARIS

Hôtel de Nell
👤 🅰🄲 ♿

7-9 r. du Conservatoire (9th) – 🚇 *Bonne Nouvelle*   Plan: **M2**
– 𝒞 01 44 83 83 60 – www.charmandmore.com
33 rm – 🛏220/1200 € 🛏🛏220/1200 € – ☲ 21 €
• Luxury • Townhouse • Design •

A very fine hotel, housed in a Haussmann building next to the Conservatoire
National Supérieur d'Art Dramatique. You can't find fault with its fittings, in a
confident style designed by Jean-Michel Wilmotte. Untreated wood, pale
tones, clean lines... in keeping with the spirit of contemporary luxury.
🍽 **La Régalade Conservatoire** – See restaurant listing

Grand Hôtel du Palais Royal
🔊 ♿ 🅰🄲

4 r. de Valois (1st) – 🚇 *Palais Royal* – 𝒞 01 42 96 15 35   Plan: **L3**
– www.grandhoteldupalaisroyal.com
64 rm – 🛏390/1200 € 🛏🛏390/1200 € – ☲ 34 € – 4 suites
• Luxury • Contemporary • Elegant •

Set next to the Palais Royal, the Ministry of Culture and the Conseil d'État, this
18C building boasts an impeccable location! Inside, the place is elegant but
without pomp. The guestrooms are sober and decorated with contemporary
furnishings and white walls. Although very central, the neighbourhood is quiet.
🍽 **Le Lulli** – See restaurant listing

Hôtel du Ministère
🔊 ♿ 🅰🄲 ♿

31 r. de Surène (8th) – 🚇 *Madeleine* – 𝒞 01 42 66 21 43   Plan: **J2**
– www.ministerehotel.com
42 rm – 🛏170/576 € 🛏🛏190/576 € – ☲ 19 € – 5 suites
• Boutique hotel • Luxury • Personalised •

This hotel is a stone's throw from the French Home Office, the Palais de l'Élysée,
and Faubourg St Honoré. The comfortable and very functional guestrooms pay
tribute to the 1970s, which won't fail to please fans of the era, nor those who are
feeling nostalgic. Charming service.

La Maison Favart
🔊 ♿ 🅰🄲

5 r. Marivaux (2nd) – 🚇 *Richelieu Drouot*   Plan: **L2**
– 𝒞 01 42 97 59 83 – www.lamaisonfavart.com
39 rm – 🛏499/1900 € 🛏🛏499/1900 € – ☲ 24 € – 6 suites
• Luxury • Townhouse • Elegant •

A timeless atmosphere reigns in this hotel (1824), where painter Francisco de
Goya once stayed. The guestrooms – some facing the Opéra Comique – are
very pleasant. This is a charming hotel, full of romanticism and poetry.

Maison Nabis
♿ 🅰🄲

7 r. de Parme (9th) – 🚇 *Liège* – 𝒞 01 55 31 60 00   Plan: **JK-1**
– www.maison-nabis.com
30 rm – 🛏180/300 € 🛏🛏180/320 € – ☲ 15 €
• Business • Cosy •

Located in a quiet street, this hotel has a restrained yet elegant decor and a hushed ambience. It has small but intimate rooms featuring wood furnishings and
warm tones. The all-inclusive package of breakfast, teatime buffet and Wi-Fi is a
particular plus.

Hôtel de Noailles
🅰🄲 ♿

9 r. de la Michodière (2nd) – 🚇 *Quatre Septembre*   Plan: **K2**
– 𝒞 01 47 42 92 90 – www.hotelnoailles.com
56 rm – 🛏180/600 € 🛏🛏200/600 € – ☲ 20 € – 5 suites
• Townhouse • Contemporary • Cosy •

Hip, contemporary elegance behind a pretty 1900 façade. Sleek, minimalist
rooms, most of which open on to the patio (with a balcony on the 5th and 6th
floors).

FRANCE - PARIS

Hôtel Monsieur 🛏 & AC

62 r. des Mathurins (8th) – Ⓜ *Havre-Caumartin* Plan: **J2**
– ℰ 01 43 87 17 11 – www.hotelmonsieur.com
29 rm – ♦189/320 € ♦♦189/320 € – ⌷ 20 € – 2 suites
• Townhouse • Personalised •
A stone's throw from the Théâtre des Mathurins, this recent hotel pays a discreet homage to the world of the theatre and one of its prominent figures, Sacha Guitry. The guestrooms are comfortable and truly inviting, some even have a terrace. Small fitness space.

Little Palace & AC

4 r. Salomon-de-Caus (3rd) Plan: **M3**
– Ⓜ Réaumur-Sébastopol – ℰ 01 42 72 08 15 – www.littlepalacehotel.com
49 rm – ♦165/265 € ♦♦195/390 € – ⌷ 15 € – 4 suites
• Townhouse • Functional • Elegant •
The charming Little Palace is a successful fusion of Belle Époque and contemporary styles. Welcoming guestrooms with those on the 6th and 7th floors (with a balcony and views of Paris) preferable.

Pulitzer & AC

23 r. du Faubourg-Montmartre (9th) Plan: **L2**
– Ⓜ Grands Boulevards – ℰ 01 53 34 98 10 – www.hotelpulitzer.com
44 rm – ♦110/400 € ♦♦120/650 € – ⌷ 18 €
• Business • Industrial •
The charm of a British library (comfy Chesterfield armchairs) and the contemporary elegance of industrial-style come together at this hotel. It is located in the heart of the city's theatres and department stores. This Pulitzer would be a worthy winner of a prize for originality.

Hôtel du Continent AC

30 r. Mont-Thabor (1st) – Ⓜ *Tuileries* – ℰ 01 42 60 75 32 Plan: **J3**
– www.hotelcontinent.com
25 rm – ♦160/400 € ♦♦220/400 € – ⌷ 12 €
• Traditional • Townhouse • Elegant •
Set near the Tuileries, this hotel is run with a personal touch and was completely redesigned in 2013 by Christian Lacroix. The six continents are the theme for the decor. Elegance, interplay of colours and overall character – it is a pleasure to venture into this new territory.

Idol & AC

16 r. d'Édimbourg (8th) – Ⓜ *Europe* – ℰ 01 45 22 14 31 Plan: **J1**
– www.idolhotel-paris.com
32 rm – ♦120/200 € ♦♦150/399 € – ⌷ 17 €
• Townhouse • Personalised • Design •
Vintage 1970s furniture and a "jazzy" theme adorn this hotel, refurbished in 2014 near the station Gare Saint-Lazare. The style is in keeping with this music orientated area with more than its fair share of stringed instrument shops. The guestrooms have names like Lady Soul and Light My Fire. A real music box.

Relais Madeleine & AC

11 bis r. Godot-de-Mauroy (9th) – Ⓜ *Havre Caumartin* Plan: **J2**
– ℰ 01 47 42 22 40 – www.relaismadeleine.fr
23 rm – ♦209/549 € ♦♦209/549 € – ⌷ 15 €
• Traditional • Personalised • Classic •
Staying at this small hotel is a bit like spending time in a family home, but right in the centre of Paris! It has undeniable charm with carefully chosen furniture, sparkling colours and delightful fabrics - not to mention the attentive service.

FRANCE - PARIS

✿✿✿ Arpège (Alain Passard)   XxX 🅰🅲 ⇔

84 r. de Varenne (7th) – Ⓜ *Varenne – ℰ 01 47 05 09 06*   Plan: **Q2**
– www.alain-passard.com – Closed Saturday and Sunday
Menu 175 € (lunch), 320/380 € – Carte 225/305 €
• Creative • Elegant •

Precious woods and a Lalique crystal decor provide the backdrop for the dazzling, vegetable-inspired cuisine of this culinary genius. He creates his astonishing dishes from organic produce grown in his three vegetable gardens!
➜ Fines ravioles potagères multicolores, consommé aux légumes. Corps-à-corps de volaille haute couture. Tarte aux pommes bouquet de roses.

✿✿✿ Astrance (Pascal Barbot)   XxX 🍸 🅰🅲

4 r. Beethoven (16th) – Ⓜ *Passy – ℰ 01 40 50 84 40*   Plan: **N1**
– www.astrancerestaurant.com – Closed August, Christmas Holidays,
Saturday, Sunday, Monday and Bank Holidays
Menu 75 € (lunch), 170/370 € 🍷 – *(booking advisable)*
• Creative • Minimalist • Elegant •

No menu or à la carte choices in this restaurant, where chef Pascal Barbot produces a different 'surprise menu' at each sitting. Sample the inventive cuisine of a chef at the height of his art, who focuses on excellent ingredients and creative flair. An unforgettable culinary experience.
➜ Crevettes dorées, pâte de satay. Canard de Challans, purée de griotte. Tartelette aux agrumes.

✿✿ Sylvestre   XxX 🍸 🅰🅲 ⇔

79 r. St-Dominique (1st floor) (7th)   Plan: **P1**
– Ⓜ *La Tour Maubourg – ℰ 01 47 05 79 00 – www.thoumieux.fr – Closed*
August, Sunday, Monday and lunch
Menu 175/250 € – Carte 155/200 € – *(booking advisable)*
• Modern cuisine • Elegant • Intimate •

It took aplomb, and even courage, to step into the shoes of media star Jean-François Piège at the Thoumieux Hotel. Yet Sylvestre Wahid has done it! This multicultural chef concocts magical, and above all seasonal recipes like cucumber water and vegetable cannelloni or three preparations of cèpes in tribute to autumn.
➜ Fenouil bulbe aux algues cuit à la braise, anchois et ricotta. Pigeon des Costières au raisin muscat, blettes et chia. Citron de Menton, coque de meringue à la laitue de mer.

✿ Le Jules Verne   XxX 🍸 ≤ 🅰🅲 🥢

2nd floor Eiffel Tower (Private lift, South pillar) (7th)   Plan: **O1**
– Ⓜ *Bir-Hakeim – ℰ 01 45 55 61 44 – www.lejulesverne-paris.com*
Menu 105 € (weekday lunch), 190/230 €
• Modern cuisine • Design • Chic •

The designer decor on the second floor of the Eiffel Tower lives up to expectations, with a magical view as a bonus! French culinary heritage is the focus here, where classic dishes are accompanied by some excellent wines.
➜ Foie gras de canard confit, melon et poivre. Homard au four, petit épeautre aux courgettes. Écrou croustillant au chocolat de notre manufacture à Paris.

✿ Divellec   XX 🍸 ♿ 🅰🅲 ⇔ 🥢

18 r. Fabert (7th) – Ⓜ *Invalides – ℰ 01 45 51 91 96*   Plan: **P-Q1**
– www.divellec-paris.fr
Menu 49 € (weekday lunch), 90/210 € – Carte 85/160 €
• Seafood • Chic • Elegant •

The famous restaurant of Jacques Le Divellec has treated itself to a makeover. At the helm is the starred chef Mathieu Pacaud (Hexagone and Histoires in Paris), who channels his considerable talent into impeccable fish and seafood cuisine. The delicacies come thick and fast. Le Divellec is back with a vengeance!
➜ Calque de bar, bonbons de pomme verte et baies roses. Navarin de homard, minestrone de basilic, vuletta croustillante. Soufflé au chocolat.

Auguste (Gaël Orieux)   XX 🅰🅒

54 r. de Bourgogne (7th) – 🚇 *Varenne*   Plan: **Q2**
*– ✆ 01 45 51 61 09 – www.restaurantauguste.fr – Closed 1 to 15 August,
Saturday and Sunday*
Menu 38 € (lunch), 88/154 € 🍷 – Carte 100/120 € – *(booking advisable)*
• Modern cuisine • Elegant •

Intimate atmosphere, mirrors, white walls and pretty armchairs... Auguste is perfectly tailored to the cuisine of Gaël Orieux, a chef who is passionate about food
and ingredients. His dishes? A quest for harmony and inventiveness, finely wea-
ving together ingredients from land and sea. Affordable prices at lunch; they
pull out all the stops at dinner.
→ Huîtres creuses en gelée d'eau de mer, mousse raifort et poire comice.
Ris de veau croustillant, cacahouètes caramélisées, girolles, abricots secs et
vin jaune. Millefeuille parfumé à la fève tonka.

David Toutain   XX 🅰🅒 ⇔

29 r. Surcouf (7th) – 🚇 *Invalides – ✆ 01 45 50 11 10*   Plan: **P1**
– www.davidtoutain.com – Closed 6 to 19 August, Saturday and Sunday
Menu 55 € (lunch), 80/140 €
• Modern cuisine • Design • Fashionable •

Having made a name for himself at some renowned establishments (L'Arpège, Agapé
Substance), David Toutain has opened his own restaurant. All this experience is chan-
nelled into his cooking. While riding the wave of culinary trends, its finesse, creativity
and palette of expressions reveal insight and singularity – a great balance!
→ Cuisine du marché.

Garance (Guillaume Iskandar)   XX 🕸 🅰🅒 ⇔

34 r. St-Dominique (7th) – 🚇 *Invalides*   Plan: **Q1**
*– ✆ 01 45 55 27 56 – www.garance-saintdominique.fr – Closed Saturday
and Sunday*
Menu 39 € (lunch), 68/90 € – Carte 75/90 € – *(booking advisable)*
• Creative • Design • Elegant •

Guillaume Muller and Guillaume Iskandar (both formerly of L'Arpège) have teamed up to open this contemporary bistro in an old building near Invalides. The
recipes are very contemporary and always highlight the ingredients (celery cooked in hay and Italian bacon, lamb two ways). Success guaranteed!
→ Cuisine du marché.

Loiseau rive Gauche   XX 🕸 🅰🅒 ⇔

5 r. Bourgogne (7th) – 🚇 *Assemblée Nationale*   Plan: **Q1**
*– ✆ 01 45 51 79 42 – www.bernard-loiseau.com – Closed 2 weeks in
August, Sunday and Monday*
Menu 42 € (lunch), 70/90 € – Carte 80/100 €
• Traditional cuisine • Elegant •

A stone's throw from the Palais Bourbon, traditional cuisine that harks back
(notably) to fine Burgundian roots. Vegetarians are also catered to here, thanks
to the "Légumes en fête" set menu, devised by chef Maxime Laurenson. Wood
panelling, Louis XV chairs and astonishing table design: the atmosphere feels
resolutely luxurious.
→ Huître perle blanche, jus de kiwi et laitue de mer. Cabillaud de nos
côtes, jus à l'oursin violet et jeunes carottes. Fraîcheur au jasmin, mûres.

Nakatani (Shinsuke Nakatani)   XX 🅰🅒

27 r. Pierre-Leroux (7th) – 🚇 *Vaneau – ✆ 01 47 34 94 14*   Plan: **Q3**
*– www.restaurant-nakatani.com – Closed 3 weeks in August, Sunday and
Monday*
Menu 40 € (lunch), 68/135 € – *(tasting menu only)*
• Modern cuisine • Intimate • Romantic •

Japanese chef Shinsuke Nakatani (formerly at Hélène Darroze) is now standing
on his own two feet. With a keen sense of seasoning, technique and the aesthetics of the dishes, he cooks fabulous French cuisine using seasonal ingredients.
All this is served by discreet and efficient staff. Impeccable!
→ Consommé de légumes. Bœuf Wagyu. Sorbet ananas et banane, écume
de thym citron, fruits de la passion.

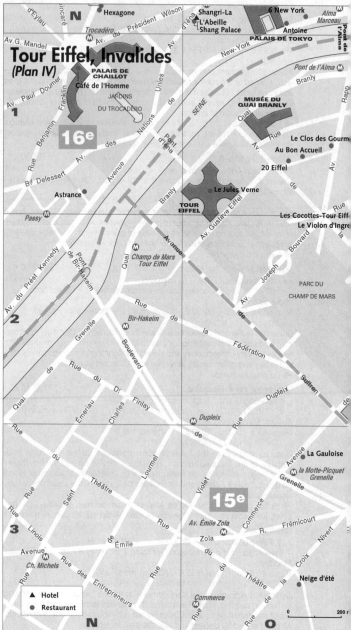

Tour Eiffel, Invalides
(Plan IV)

16e

15e

PALAIS DE CHAILLOT
Café de l'Homme
JARDINS DU TROCADÉRO

Hexagone
Trocadéro
Av. G. Mandel
Av. du Président Wilson
d'Eylau
Poincaré
Av. Paul Doumer
Rue Benjamin Franklin
Bd Delessert
Astrance
Passy

Shangri-La
L'Abeille
Shang Palace
Antoine
PALAIS DE TOKYO
6 New York
Alma Marceau
Pont de l'Alma
New-York
Pont de l'Alma
Branly
MUSÉE DU QUAI BRANLY
Rapp
Le Clos des Gourm
Au Bon Accueil
20 Eiffel
Le Jules Verne
TOUR EIFFEL
Les Cocottes-Tour Eiff
Le Violon d'Ingre
Av. Gustave Eiffel
Bouvard
Joseph
PARC DU CHAMP DE MARS

Champ de Mars Tour Eiffel
Pont de Bir-Hakeim
Av. du Prést Kennedy
Quai
Rue Bir-Hakeim
Boulevard de Grenelle
Rue du Dr Finlay
Charles
Émeriau
Quai
Suffren
Dupleix
Av. de la Fédération

La Gauloise
la Motte-Picquet Grenelle
Violet
Commerce
Av. Émile Zola
Zola
Rue du
Commerce
Frémicourt
Nivert
Croix
Neige d'été
Théâtre
Théâtre
Saint
Lourmel
Rue
Rue Linois
Avenue Ch. Michels
Rue des Entrepreneurs
Émile
Rue de

▲ Hotel
● Restaurant

0   200 r

214

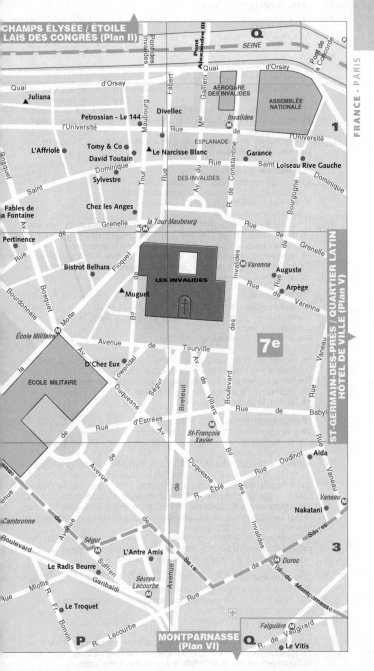

CHAMPS ÉLYSÉE / ÉTOILE
PALAIS DES CONGRÈS (Plan II)

SEINE

Pont Alexandre III

Pont de la Concorde

Quai d'Orsay

Quai d'Orsay

▲ Juliana

Fabert

Galliéni

AÉROGARE DES INVALIDES

ASSEMBLÉE NATIONALE

Petrossian - Le 144

Maubourg

Divellec

Mal

Ⓜ Invalides

de

1

l'Université

Rue

L'Affriolé

Tomy & Co

▲ Le Narcisse Blanc

ESPLANADE

Garance

l'Université

David Toutain

Tour

Rue

Rue

Constantine

Saint Loiseau Rive Gauche

Dominique

Sylvestre

Rue

R. de

DES INVALIDES

Bourgogne

Saint

Dominique

Fables de la Fontaine

Chez les Anges

la Tour Maubourg

Rue

de

Grenelle

Grenelle

Av. de

Ⓜ

La

Pertinence

Rue

Picquet

Ⓜ Varenne

Bistrot Belhara

LES INVALIDES

Invalides

Auguste

Rue

Rue

de

Arpège

▲ Muguet

Bourdonnais

Bosquet

Motte

de

Varenne

des

7e

École Militaire

Av.

Avenue

de

Tourville

Lowendal

D'Chez Eux

Boulevard

ÉCOLE MILITAIRE

Ségur

Duquesne

Breteuil

de

Villars

Rue

de

Babyl

d'Estrées

Av.

St-François Xavier

Bd

de

Rue

Oudinot

des

Aida

Duquesne

R. Éblé

Invalides

Vaneau

Nakatani

Vaneau Ⓜ

Cambronne

Avenue

de

Sèvres

Boulevard

Ségur

Ⓜ

L'Antre Amis

Saxe

Ⓜ Duroc

3

Le Radis Beurre

Suffren

Garibaldi

Sèvres Lecourbe

Ⓜ

Avenue

Rue

Bd. du Montparnasse

Miollis

R. Fr.

Le Troquet

Bonvin

Lecourbe

P

R.

MONTPARNASSE
(Plan VI)

Q

Falguière Ⓜ

R. de Vaugirard

Le Vitis

Neige d'Été (Hideki Nishi)   XX

12 r. de l'Amiral-Roussin (15th) – ⓜ *Avenue Émile Zola*   Plan: **O3**
– ✆ *01 42 73 66 66* – *www.neigedete.fr* – *Closed 2 weeks in August, 1 week
Christmas Holidays, Sunday and Monday*
Menu 45 € (weekday lunch), 60/100 €
• Modern cuisine • Minimalist •

The name (meaning 'Summer Snow') is poetically Japanese, and that is no coin-
cidence. This restaurant was opened in mid-2014 by a young Japanese chef,
Hideki Nishi, who used to be at the George V. It also hints at the contrasts and
minimalism that are the hallmarks of his work, which is always spot-on and full
of counterpoints.

➔ Déclinaison de tomates. Canard de Challans grillé au charbon de bois
japonais. Millefeuille aux fruits exotiques.

Le Violon d'Ingres (Christian Constant)   XX 🅰🅲

135 r. St-Dominique (7th) – ⓜ *École Militaire*   Plan: **O1**
– ✆ *01 45 55 15 05* – *www.maisonconstant.com*
Menu 49 € (weekday lunch)/120 € – Carte 76/90 €
• Traditional cuisine • Elegant •

Diners are fighting each other off for a spot at Christian Constant's restaurant!
His recipes reveal the soul of an authentic cook, firmly in line with the finest tradition. Their execution shows off the know-how of a talented team.

➔ Fine gelée d'araignée de mer, crémeux de tourteau à l'infusion d'herbes.
Ris de veau braisé au vin jaune, poêlée de girolles. Traditionnel millefeuille,
crème légère à la vanille.

Aida (Koji Aida)   X 🕸 🅰🅲 ⇔

1 r. Pierre-Leroux (7th) – ⓜ *Vaneau* – ✆ *01 43 06 14 18*   Plan: **Q3**
– *www.aida-paris.net* – *Closed 1 week in March, 3 weeks in August,
Monday and lunch*
Menu 160/280 € – *(booking advisable)*
• Japanese • Elegant • Minimalist •

Be transported to the Land of the Rising Sun in this restaurant. It breathes
authenticity and purity through its delicious Japanese cuisine full of finesse.
The fish, presented alive and then prepared in front of you, couldn't be fresher.
The art of simplicity and transparency at its best!

➔ Sashimi. Teppanyaki. Wagashi.

Pertinence (Kwen Liew et Ryunosuke Naito)   X

29 r. de l'Exposition (7th) – ⓜ *École Militaire*   Plan: **P2**
– ✆ *01 45 55 20 96* – *www.restaurantpertinence.com* – *Closed August,
Sunday and Monday*
Menu 38 € (weekday lunch)/85 € – Carte 65/120 € – *(booking advisable)*
• Modern cuisine • Design • Fashionable •

This minimalist interior, depicted by light wood Knoll chairs, near the Champs
Elysees is the fief of Japanese Ryu and Malaysian Kwen. Ryu carefully and
expertly nurtures and coaxes market-fresh ingredients into succulent classical
French dishes, brushing off the cobwebs of tradition on the way. We expect to
hear much more from this quarter!

➔ Coquillages à l'étuvée parfumés au gingembre, amandes de mer,
coques et couteaux. Bar rôti, mousseline de pomme de terre et sauce au
vin jaune. Tarte à la mangue et fruits de la passion.

Au Bon Accueil   XX 🅰🅲

14 r. Monttessuy (7th) – ⓜ *Alma Marceau*   Plan: **O1**
– ✆ *01 47 05 46 11* – *www.aubonaccueilparis.com* – *Closed 3 weeks in
August, Saturday and Sunday*
Menu 36/55 € – Carte 63/84 €
• Modern cuisine • Bistro • Cosy •

In the shadow of the Eiffel Tower in a quiet street, this shy, but smart bistro serves appetising, market-fresh cuisine that mirror the seasons. Grilled squid, crus-
hed potatoes and aioli; roast saddle and confit shoulder of lamb…

Chez les Anges   XX ⚜ AC ⇔ 🎣

54 bd de la Tour-Maubourg (7th) — **Plan: P1**
– Ⓜ La Tour Maubourg – ℰ 01 47 05 89 86 – www.chezlesanges.com
– Closed 3 weeks in August, Saturday and Sunday
Menu 36/55 € – Carte 61/83 €
• Classic cuisine • Elegant • Neighbourhood •

A stylish interior provides the setting for authentic, appetising food, poised between tradition and modernity. Joël Thiébault vegetables in lemon sauce, farm-bred guinea fowl, aubergines in orange and spelt curry or Venezuelan dark chocolate tart. Splendid wine and whisky list.

L'Antre Amis   X 🍽 AC

9 r. Bouchut (15th) – Ⓜ Ségur – ℰ 01 45 67 15 65 — **Plan: P3**
– www.lantreamis.com – Closed August, Saturday and Sunday
Menu 35/75 € 🍷 – Carte approx. 46 €
• Modern cuisine • Contemporary décor •

The chef-patron at L'Antre Amis brings passion to his cooking. Using excellent produce sourced from Rungis Market (meat, fish, shellfish etc), he composes scrupulous dishes, precisely made and organised into a very short menu. To be accompanied by your choice from a fine wine list – around 150 sorts.

Le Clos des Gourmets   X ⚜ ⇔

16 av. Rapp (7th) – Ⓜ Alma Marceau — **Plan: O1**
– ℰ 01 45 51 75 61 – www.closdesgourmets.com – Closed 1 to 25 August,
Sunday and Monday
Menu 30 € (lunch), 35/42 € – Carte 43/69 €
• Modern cuisine • Fashionable •

Sleek and welcoming modern bistro where the chef loves good food and cares enough to do it well. Asparagus crème brûlée, fennel slow cooked with mellow spices: the cuisine is honest and full of delicious flavours.

Les Cocottes - Tour Eiffel   X

135 r. St-Dominique (7th) – Ⓜ École Militaire — **Plan: O1**
– ℰ 01 45 50 10 28 – www.maisonconstant.com
Menu 28 € (weekday lunch) – Carte 34/59 €
• Traditional cuisine • Fashionable •

The concept in this friendly eatery is based around bistro cuisine with a modern touch cooked in cast-iron casserole pots (cocottes), and includes popular dishes such as country paté, roast veal etc. No advance booking.

Le Radis Beurre   X

51 bd Garibaldi (15th) – Ⓜ Sèvres Lecourbe — **Plan: P3**
– ℰ 01 40 33 99 26 – www.restaurantleradisbeurre.com – Closed 3 weeks
in August, Saturday and Sunday
Menu 35 € – Carte 35/44 €
• Traditional cuisine • Bistro •

It was in 2015 on Boulevard Garibaldi in Paris that chef Jérôme Bonnet found the perfect site for his restaurant. He prepares tasty, carefully created food that bears the hallmark of his southern upbringing. An example? Pig's trotters with duck foie gras and meat juices. You may even get to nibble on a few radishes with butter while you wait.

Le Troquet   X

21 r. François-Bonvin (15th) – Ⓜ Cambronne — **Plan: P3**
– ℰ 01 45 66 89 00 – www.restaurantletroquet.fr – Closed 1 week in May,
3 weeks in August, 1 week in December, Sunday and Monday
Menu 33 € (lunch), 35/41 €
• Traditional cuisine • Bistro • Vintage •

A typical Parisian 'troquet' (café-bar) in all its splendour! Although Christian Etchebest is no longer at the helm, a young promising chef is working with the same team. He has the same reliance on ultra-fresh ingredients and the same culinary focus on southwest France.

FRANCE - PARIS

20 Eiffel
X AC

20 r. de Monttessuy (7th) – Ⓜ *Alma Marceau*
Plan: **O1**
– ℰ 01 47 05 14 20 – www.restaurant20eiffel.fr – Closed 2 weeks in August and Sunday
Menu 32 € – Carte 47/55 €
• Traditional cuisine • Classic décor •

In a quiet street a stone's throw from the Eiffel Tower, this restaurant offers a understated interior full of light. On the menu, you can choose from a range of updated dishes, prepared by two chefs, all of which place the focus on flavour and taste. For example, a delicious fillet of wild pollack with squash.

Petrossian - Le 144
XxX AC ⇔ 🍽

144 r. de l'Université (7th) – Ⓜ *Invalides*
Plan: **P1**
– ℰ 01 44 11 32 32 – www.petrossian.fr – Closed August and Sunday
Menu 39 € (lunch), 95/170 € – Carte 55/95 €
• Seafood • Chic • Elegant •

The Petrossians have been serving Parisians with caviar from the Caspian Sea since 1920. Enjoy fish and seafood in the elegant dining room above the boutique.

Café de l'Homme
XX 🍽 & AC ⇔

17 pl. du Trocadéro (16th) – Ⓜ *Trocadéro*
Plan: **N1**
– ℰ 01 44 05 30 15 – www.cafedelhomme.com
Carte 50/80 €
• Modern cuisine • Elegant • Fashionable •

On the rooftop of the Palais de Chaillot, the huge 330m² terrace of the Café de l'Homme commands a matchless view of the nearby Eiffel Tower, guaranteed to leave you with unforgettable memories. Classical recipes (beef fillet and pepper sauce) rub shoulders with exotic creations (tataki of red tuna with yuzu and wasabi), each dish is a talented mix of creative culinary dedication.

D'Chez Eux
XX 🍽 AC

2 av. Lowendal (7th) – Ⓜ *École Militaire*
Plan: **P2**
– ℰ 01 47 05 52 55 – www.chezeux.com
Menu 34 € (weekday lunch) – Carte 42/93 €
• Cuisine from South West France • Rustic • Friendly •

This restaurant has had a winning formula for over 40 years – and the place shows no sign of ageing! Sample the generous portions of dishes inspired by the southwest of France. These are made with quality ingredients and served by waiters in old-fashioned aprons in a provincial inn ambience.

La Gauloise
XX 🍽 ⇔

59 av. La Motte-Picquet (15th)
Plan: **O3**
– Ⓜ *La Motte Picquet Grenelle – ℰ 01 47 34 11 64 – Closed 2 weeks in August*
Menu 31 € – Carte 35/68 €
• Traditional cuisine • Elegant • Vintage •

This Belle Epoque brasserie boasts the delightful air of Parisian life from yesteryear. It has a menu that features dishes such as poached eggs and vegetable pot-au-feu, pork crepinettes, turbot with a Béarnaise sauce, and onion soup. La Gauloise's attractive terrace is also much appreciated by diners.

L'Affriolé
X AC

17 r. Malar (7th) – Ⓜ *Invalides – ℰ 01 44 18 31 33*
Plan: **P1**
– www.laffriole.fr – Closed 3 weeks in August, Sunday and Monday
Menu 25 € (lunch)/39 € – Carte approx. 47 €
• Modern cuisine • Fashionable •

Daily selection chalked up on a slate and a monthly menu illustrate the chef's dedication to market availability. The warm, contemporary interior is quite striking. Lunchtime menu caters to busy working men and women.

Bistrot Belhara

🍴

23 r. Duvivier (7th) – Ⓜ *École Militaire*
Plan: **P2**
– ☏ *01 45 51 41 77* – www.bistrotbelhara.com
– *Closed 1 week in February, 3 weeks in August, Sunday and Monday*
Menu 34 € (lunch), 38/52 € – Carte 40/65 €
• Traditional cuisine • Bistro •

Belhara is a site that is famous for its superb waves on the Basque coast - and this is the chef's nod to his origins. It is a tough call to summarise his impressive career path (Guérard, Loiseau, Ducasse etc). A convert to the bistro mode, Thierry Dufroux works wonders as he revisits the classics – the chef is definitely on the crest of the wave!

Les Fables de La Fontaine

🍴 ☂ 🆎

131 r. St-Dominique (7th) – Ⓜ *École Militaire*
Plan: **P1**
– ☏ *01 44 18 37 55* – www.lesfablesdelafontaine.net
Menu 75 €
– Carte 50/75 € – *(booking advisable)*
• Modern cuisine • Bistro • Friendly •

The former sous-chef of Les Fables has slipped effortlessly into the role of chef. He composes modern cuisine that is fragrant and bursting with colours, demonstrating an impressive maturity and undeniable talent. Relish your meal in a sleek, light and elegant bistro decor.

Tomy & Co

🍴 🆎

22 r. Surcouf (7th) – Ⓜ *Invalides*
Plan: **P1**
– ☏ *01 45 51 46 93*
– *Closed 1 week in February, August, 23 to 30 December, Saturday and Sunday*
Menu 47/68 €
• Modern cuisine • Friendly • Bistro •

This establishment bears the hallmark of the unabashed talent of Tomy Gousset (ex-Meurice and Taillevent). Tomy plays a gourmet-bistro score whose modern notes reveal a deceptively simple melody. The establishment is determined to consume locally (organic veggies from Essonne). Booking would be a good idea!

Juliana

🛁 🕸 ᵹ 🆎

10-12 r. Cognacq-Jay (7th) – Ⓜ *Alma-Marceau*
Plan: **P1**
– ☏ *01 44 05 70 00* – www.hoteljuliana.paris
45 rm ☲ – ✦350/800 € ✦✦450/900 € – 5 suites
• Luxury • Elegant • Contemporary •

The superlative elegance of this hotel is undeniable. Find chandeliers, extravagant mirrors, sculptures and mother-of-pearl furnishings. The rooms satisfy the two-fold demand for good taste and optimum comfort (Japanese toilets). Attractive, flower-decked façade come summertime.

Le Narcisse Blanc

⚘ 🌐 🕸 ◻ ᵹ 🆎 ᵴ

19 bd de la Tour-Maubourg (7th)
Plan: **P1**
– Ⓜ *La Tour Maubourg*
– ☏ *01 40 60 44 32* – www.lenarcisseblanc.com
34 rm – ✦250/1000 € ✦✦250/1000 € – ☲ 38 € – 3 suites
• Luxury • Grand townhouse • Contemporary •

An attractive conversion for this former army administrative building, now a refined hotel. The Art Nouveau decoration pays homage to Cléo de Mérode, Belle Epoque dancer and icon, nicknamed "pretty little narcissus". She inspired Nadar, Lautrec, Proust... and now this charming establishment. Pleasant spa.

FRANCE - PARIS

Platine   ⛔ 📺 ♊

20 r. de l'Ingénieur-Robert-Keller (15th)   Plan I: **A2**
– **Ⓜ** *Charles Michels* – ☏ *01 45 71 15 15 – www.platinehotel.fr*
46 rm – 🚹129/315 € 🚹🚹139/415 € – 🍵 15 €
• Townhouse • Personalised •

Platine or platinum blonde – like Marilyn Monroe – to whom this hotel pays homage. The guestrooms are comfortable and well kept. Go for one of those with a round bed for optimum glamour and to channel your inner star! There is a pleasant relaxation suite in the basement.

Muguet   ⛔ 📺

11 r. Chevert (7th) – **Ⓜ** *École Militaire*   Plan: **P2**
– ☏ *01 47 05 05 93 – www.hotelparismuguet.com*
40 rm – 🚹100/190 € 🚹🚹120/290 € – 🍵 14 €
• Family • Classic •

In a quiet street a stone's throw from Les Invalides, this hotel has been refurbished in a classic style. Attractively maintained guestrooms; those overlooking the small flower-decked garden are generally quieter.

SAINT-GERMAIN DES PRES – QUARTIER LATIN – HOTEL DE VILLE   PLAN V

✺✺✺ Guy Savoy   XxxX ˆ ⛔ 📺 ⇅ Ž

11 quai de Conti (6th) – **Ⓜ** *St-Michel* – ☏ *01 43 80 40 61*   Plan: **S1**
– *www.guysavoy.com – Closed August, Christmas Holidays, Saturday lunch, Sunday and Monday*
Menu 395 € – Carte 210/335 €
• Creative • Luxury • Romantic •

Guy Savoy, act II, in the Hôtel de la Monnaie, on the bank of the Seine. The setting is sumptuous – six rooms adorned with contemporary works lent by François Pinault –, and the host, true to himself: sincere and passionate, inventive without excess, unfailing generosity. Irresistible!

→ Soupe d'artichaut à la truffe noire, brioche feuilletée aux champignons et aux truffes. Paleron maturé et basse côte persillée de bœuf Wagyu en "bœuf-aubergines". Abricot et jasmin, sablé au muesli.

✺✺ L'Atelier de Joël Robuchon - St-Germain   X ˆ 📺 ⇅

5 r. de Montalembert (7th) – **Ⓜ** *Rue du Bac*   Ž
– ☏ *01 42 22 56 56 – www.joel-robuchon.net – Open*   Plan: **R1**
from 11.30am to 3.30pm and 6.30pm to midnight. Reservations at certain times only: please enquire.
Menu 189 € – Carte 80/170 €
• Creative • Design • Minimalist •

This contemporary Atelier by Joël Robuchon – the first in a long line – is a must! Find the long counter flanked by high stools, a small, intimate dining area, and a red and black colour scheme. The studied half-light is directed onto the stunning food, prepared with a watchmaker's precision.

→ Caviar sur un œuf de poule mollet et friand au saumon fumé. Merlan frit Colbert avec un beurre aux herbes. Soufflé passion, fraicheur d'ananas et sorbet piña colada.

✺ Tour d'Argent   XxxxX ˆ < ⛔ 📺 ⇅ Ž

15 quai de la Tournelle (5th) – **Ⓜ** *Maubert Mutualité*   Plan: **U2**
– ☏ *01 43 54 23 31 – www.tourdargent.com – Closed 3 weeks in August, Sunday and Monday*
Menu 105 € (lunch), 350/360 € – Carte 185/330 €
• Modern cuisine • Luxury • Elegant •

This institution dating back to 1582 is undergoing a velvet revolution! Chef Philippe Labbé serves modern, vivacious dishes, whose updated classicism continues to bear his inspired hallmark. The service is impeccable and the wine cellar boasts some 400,000 bottles. Tradition hand in hand with modernity.

→ Quenelle de brochet André Terrail, hommage au grand-père. Caneton de Challans Mazarine. Crêpes "mademoiselle".

FRANCE - PARIS

Hélène Darroze ✿ ❀❀❀ 🅺 ⇔ 📖

4 r. d'Assas (6th)
Plan: **R2**
– Ⓜ Sèvres Babylone
– ℰ 01 42 22 00 11 – www.helenedarroze.com
– Closed Sunday and Monday
Menu 58 € (lunch), 98/185 €
• Modern cuisine • Contemporary décor • Elegant •

Hélène Darroze, the descendent of a family of cooks from southwest France (Aquitaine, Landes, Basque country), finds the raw ingredients for her cuisine in her homeland. To this heritage, she has added her experience, insatiable curiosity and own distinctive blend of talent and intuition.
→ Huître, caviar et haricots maïs du Béarn. Homard tandoori, carotte, agrumes et coriandre fraîche. Baba au bas-armagnac, framboises, poivres de Tasmanie et de Sarawak.

Relais Louis XIII (Manuel Martinez) ❀❀❀ 🆎 🅺 ⇔ 📖

8 r. des Grands-Augustins (6th)
Plan: **T2**
– Ⓜ Odéon – ℰ 01 43 26 75 96 – www.relaislouis13.com
– Closed 1 week in May, August, 1 week in January, Sunday and Monday
Menu 65 € (lunch), 95/145 €
– Carte approx. 130 €
• Classic cuisine • Elegant • Bourgeois •

Very close to the Seine, this old house located in historical Paris takes us back to Louis XIII's day. The decor is full of character with exposed beams, stonework and stained-glass windows. This forms an elegant backdrop for Manuel Martinez's cooking, which is in line with French culinary classicism. Good value lunch menu.
→ Quenelle de bar, mousseline de champignons et glaçage au champagne. Canard challandais rôti aux épices et tourte au foie gras. Millefeuille à la vanille de Taithi.

Les Climats ❀❀ 🆎 🈁 🅺 ❧ 📖 (dinner)

41 r. de Lille (7th)
Plan: **R1**
– Ⓜ Rue du Bac
– ℰ 01 58 62 10 08 – www.lesclimats.fr
– Closed 3 weeks in August, 1 to 15 January, Sunday and Monday
Menu 45 € (lunch)/130 €
– Carte 110/130 €
• Modern cuisine • Vintage • Elegant •

A restaurant in the unusual setting of the former Maison des Dames des Postes, which housed postal and telecommunications service operators from 1905. The French cuisine is spiced up with modern touches. The mosaic floors, antique brass light fittings and vert d'Estours marble gives character to the decor.
→ Homard bleu en deux services, purée d'abricot au vin de Viré-Clessé, girolles et thé vert. Ris de veau doré au sautoir crousti-fondant, boulgour au jus de veau relevé d'Angostura. Pavlova aux fruits rouges.

La Dame de Pic ❀❀ 👤 🅺 ⇔

20 r. du Louvre (1st) – Ⓜ Louvre Rivoli
Plan: **T1**
– ℰ 01 42 60 40 40 – www.anne-sophie-pic.com
– Closed 11 to 19 August
Menu 59 € (weekday lunch), 105/135 €
• Creative • Design • Elegant •

Anne-Sophie Pic's Parisian restaurant, depicted by a soft feminine interior, is 2 minutes from the Louvre. A fine blend of flavours, precise creations and the ability to mix unexpected ingredients are the hallmarks of this talented chef, embodied by her frogs' legs in Lapsang Souchong tea or roast lamb chartreuse with spring vegetables.
→ Berlingots au coulant de brillat-savarin fumé, champignons des bois à la fève tonka. Saint-pierre rôti meunière aux baies de la passion, tomates anciennes et sauge. Chocolat aux arômes de citron et glace moelleuse.

221

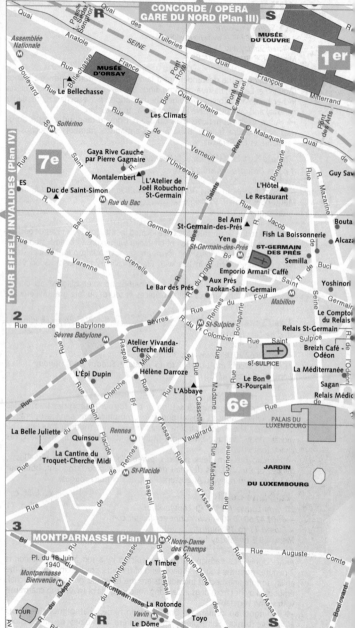

CONCORDE / OPÉRA
GARE DU NORD (Plan III)

1er

7e

6e

MONTPARNASSE (Plan VI)

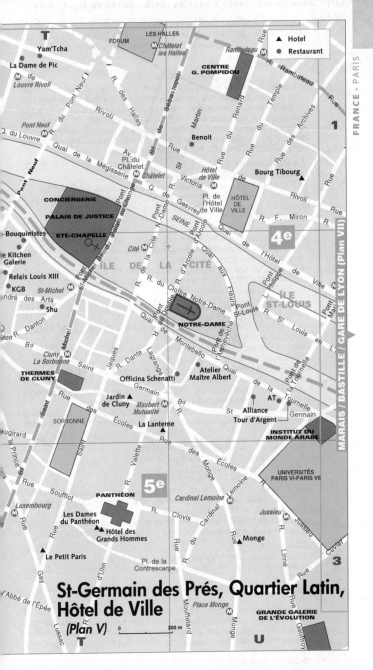

St-Germain des Prés, Quartier Latin, Hôtel de Ville
(Plan V) 0 200 m

FRANCE - PARIS

Emporio Armani Caffè   XX & AC

149 bd St-Germain (6th) – Ⓜ St-Germain des Prés   Plan: **S2**
– ℰ 01 45 48 62 15 – www.mori.paris – Closed 6 to 20 August
Menu 50/90 €
– Carte 79/110 €
• **Italian** • Contemporary décor • **Chic** •

On the first floor of the boutique in the heart of this chic Left Bank neighbourhood, this Caffè turns out to be an excellent surprise. The chef, former sous-chef at Casadelmar in Porto-Vecchio, cooks lovely Italian cuisine using very fine ingredients. It is fresh, tasty and skilfully done. Excellent work.
→ Bagna verde di carciofini violetti, verdurine, cuore di bottarga sarda. Mezzo maniche alla crema di zucca mantovana, fonduta di parmigiano e menta. Gelato all'amaretto con crumble alla vaniglia.

Le Restaurant – Hôtel L'Hôtel   XX AC

13 r. des Beaux-Arts (6th) – Ⓜ St-Germain des Prés   Plan: **S1**
– ℰ 01 44 41 99 01 – www.l-hotel.com – Closed August, 24 December-
7 January, Tuesday lunch, Wednesday lunch, Sunday and Monday
Menu 55 € (lunch), 110/190 € 𝟵
– Carte 40/47 €
• **Modern cuisine** • Elegant • **Romantic** •

Le Restaurant is part of L'Hôtel, with a decor also created by Jacques Garcia. The chef revisits classic French gastronomy with creative dishes based around evocative flavours and superb ingredients.
→ Tourteau de Loctudy, mousse avocat et yuzu. Ris de veau "crousti-moelleux" et petits pois à la française. Meringue italienne, biscuit craquant, crémeux et zeste de citron.

Alliance (Toshitaka Omiya)   XX AC

5 r. de Poissy (5th) – Ⓜ Maubert Mutualité   Plan: **U2**
– ℰ 01 75 51 57 54 – www.restaurant-alliance.fr – Closed 6 to 24 August,
1 to 7 January, Saturday and Sunday
Menu 46 € (lunch), 90/110 € – Carte 75/105 € – (booking advisable)
• **Modern cuisine** • Contemporary décor • **Minimalist** •

Alliance brings together two alumni of the restaurant Agapé Substance as partners in this adventure. A starter of oyster, onion and lemon; foie gras, vegetable pot-au-feu and Corsican broth... The chef's dishes are flashes of simplicity, at once subtle and well executed. We will be going back for more.
→ Pommes de terre "Allians", échalote et champignons. Rouget des côtes vendéennes, chou rouge et betterave fumée. Parfait aux noisettes et citron.

Benoit   XX 🎋 AC ⟷

20 r. St-Martin (4th) – Ⓜ Châtelet-Les Halles   Plan: **U1**
– ℰ 01 42 72 25 76 – www.benoit-paris.com
Menu 39 € (lunch) – Carte 70/115 €
• **Classic cuisine** • Bistro • **Classic décor** •

Alain Ducasse supervises this chic and lively bistro, one of the oldest in Paris. The classic food is prepared in time-honoured tradition, and respects the soul of this authentic and fine establishment.
→ Langue de bœuf Lucullus, cœur de romaine à la crème moutardée. Filet de sole Nantua, épinards crémés. Savarin à l'armagnac, chantilly.

ES (Takayuki Honjo)   XX AC

91 r. de Grenelle (7th) – Ⓜ Solférino – ℰ 01 45 51 25 74   Plan: **R1**
– www.es-restaurant.fr – Closed 3 weeks in August, Tuesday lunch, Sunday
and Monday
Menu 42 € (lunch)/105 € – (booking advisable)
• **Modern cuisine** • Minimalist •

A restaurant run by Takayuki Honjo, a young Japanese chef who is a fan of French cuisine. From the first mouthful, his talent jumps out at you. Foie gras and sea urchins, pigeon and cacao: all the pairings work, with never a wrong note; he masters the flavours and always has in mind the bigger picture. Clarity and harmony.
→ Cuisine du marché.

Yam'Tcha (Adeline Grattard) XX

121 r. St-Honoré (1st) – Ⓜ *Louvre Rivoli* — Plan: **T1**
– ℰ *01 40 26 08 07* – *www.yamtcha.com* – *Closed August, Christmas
Holidays, Sunday, Monday and Tuesday*
Menu 70 € (weekday lunch)/150 €
• Creative • Elegant •

Adeline Grattard has a remarkable feel for ingredients with simple and striking
associations – influences of France and Asia – devised to be paired with a selection of excellent teas. This young chef, trained at L'Astrance and in Hong Kong,
cultivates clarity with style.
➜ Homard rôti, jus de crustacés et pâtisson. Bar de ligne cuit vapeur, tétra-
gone et sauce aux agrumes. Variation de pêche et de fleur d'oranger,
soupe d'oseille et sorbet orgeat.

Gaya Rive Gauche par Pierre Gagnaire X AC

44 r. du Bac (7th) – Ⓜ *Rue du Bac* – ℰ *01 45 44 73 73* — Plan: **R1**
– *www.pierre-gagnaire.com* – *Closed 3 weeks in August, Christmas
Holidays, Sunday and Monday*
Menu 65 € (lunch) – Carte 75/110 €
• Seafood • Cosy • Elegant •

Under the influence of designer Violaine Jeantet, this restaurant (Pierre Gagnaire's second in Paris) has become cosier and more refined, thanks in particular to
the sapele wall panelling. As for the food, it still celebrates fish and seafood in
original ways but without excess. Delicious!
➜ Carpaccio de daurade royale et râpée de poivrade. Fricassée de homard
bleu à la verveine, côtes de blette , fregola et abricot. "Paley-Guimet", compote de rhubarbe, groseille et grenade.

Quinsou (Antonin Bonnet) X 🕸 ໕

33 r. de l'Abbé-Grégoire (6th) – Ⓜ *St-Placide* — Plan: **R3**
– ℰ *01 42 22 66 09* – *Closed August, Christmas Holidays,
Sunday and Monday*
Menu 35 € (lunch), 48/65 €
• Creative • Fashionable • Trendy •

Opposite Ferrandi, the French School of Culinary Arts, Quinsou - "chaffinch" in
langue d'oc – cooks up a storm, relished by the fine palates of the 6th *arrondissement* and beyond, with, for instance, monkfish, Hokkaido squash and curry
sauce: Antonin Bonnet, former chef from Le Sergent Recruteur, brings the ingredients to life. A really great place.
➜ Cuisine du marché.

Ze Kitchen Galerie (William Ledeuil) X AC 🍽

4 r. des Grands-Augustins (6th) – Ⓜ *St-Michel* — Plan: **T2**
– ℰ *01 44 32 00 32* – *www.zekitchengalerie.fr* – *Closed 3 weeks in August,
1 week in January, Saturday and Sunday*
Menu 48 € (lunch), 85/98 €
• Creative • Contemporary décor •

William Ledeuil has breathed his love of Southeast Asian flavours (Thailand,
Vietnam and Japan) that inspire his creations into this establishment. Galanga,
ka-chaï, curcuma, wasabi and ginger – herbs, roots, spices and condiments from
all over the world at the service of French classics.
➜ Thon rouge, vinaigrette sésame, grenade et griotte. Agneau de pré salé,
condiment miso-harissa. Glace chocolat blanc , wasabi, fraise et pistache.

La Méditerranée XX AC 🔄 🍽

2 pl. Odéon (6th) – Ⓜ *Odéon* – ℰ *01 43 26 02 30* — Plan: **S-T2**
– *www.la-mediterranee.com* – *Closed 24 to 31 December*
Menu 36 € – Carte 57/71 €
• Seafood • Mediterranean décor • Colourful •

The frescoes evoke the Mediterranean in this restaurant opposite the Théâtre
de l'Odéon. The maritime inspired cuisine, in which particular attention is paid
to the best ingredients, is influenced by the accents of the south. In summer
dine beneath the azure blue awning.

FRANCE - PARIS

Alcazar
XX ⅋ AC ⇔

62 r. Mazarine (6th) – Ⓜ *Odéon* – ℰ *01 53 10 19 99*   Plan: **S2**
– www.alcazar.fr
Menu 34 € (lunch) – Carte 55/65 €
• Modern cuisine • Brasserie • Fashionable •

Alcazar's interior was designed by the architect and decorator Lola Gonzalez. Plants have the upper hand, endowing the space with the timeless elegance of a grand winter garden. The kitchen never fails to turn out an appetising menu of contemporary brasserie dishes, such as the excellent roasted free-range chicken and home-made chips, or the confit shoulder of lamb. Brunch on Sundays.

Atelier Maître Albert
XX AC ⇔ 🍴

1 r. Maître-Albert (5th) – Ⓜ *Maubert Mutualité*   Plan: **U2**
– ℰ 01 56 81 30 01 – www.ateliermaitrealbert.com – Closed 2 weeks in August, Christmas Holidays, Saturday lunch and Sunday lunch
Menu 35/70 € – Carte 40/60 €
• Traditional cuisine • Friendly • Chic •

An attractive medieval fireplace and roasting spits take pride of place in this handsome interior designed by Jean-Michel Wilmotte. Guy Savoy is responsible for the mouthwatering menu.

Les Bouquinistes
XX ⅋ AC 🍴

53 quai des Grands-Augustins (6th) – Ⓜ *St-Michel*   Plan: **T1**
– ℰ 01 43 25 45 94 – www.lesbouquinistes.com – Closed 2 weeks in August and Christmas Holidays
Menu 36 € (lunch), 44/78 € – Carte 50/66 €
• Modern cuisine • Contemporary décor •

Looking out over the *bouquinistes* – the booksellers lining the banks of the Seine – this restaurant set up by Guy Savoy has a trendy modern decor that calls to mind a New York loft. Discuss literature over chicory in remoulade dressing with *œuf parfait* and Mimolette cheese, confit suckling pig with slow-cooked lentils, or hazelnut floating islands.

Boutary
XX ⅋ AC ⇔

25 r. Mazarine (6th) – Ⓜ *Odéon* – ℰ *01 43 43 69 10*   Plan: **S2**
– www.boutary-restaurant.com – Closed August, Saturday lunch, Sunday and Monday
Menu 35 € (lunch)/79 € – Carte 60/74 € – *(booking advisable)*
• Modern cuisine • Chic • Intimate •

In the middle of rue Mazarine, this old building hosts a Japanese-Korean chef with a fine track record. Armed with magnificent ingredients, he proposes fine and tasty recipes that pop with colours and brim with ideas. Taste has come home to roost here: a pleasant dining experience, not least as the bill won't break the bank.

AT
X AC ⇔

4 r. Cardinal-Lemoine (5th) – Ⓜ *Cardinal Lemoine*   Plan: **U2**
– ℰ 01 56 81 94 08 – www.atushitanaka.com – Closed Monday lunch and Sunday
Menu 55 € (lunch)/105 € – *(booking advisable)*
• Creative • Design • Minimalist •

A stone's throw from the banks of the Seine and the Tour d'Argent, the minimalist interior of this small restaurant embodies the quintessence of Japan. Chef Tanaka, formerly with Pierre Gagnaire, loves fresh ingredients and precise cooking and is forever surprising us with his creative recipes. Vaulted basement.

Atelier Vivanda - Cherche Midi
X AC

20 r. du Cherche-Midi (6th) – Ⓜ *Sèvres Babylone*   Plan: **R2**
– ℰ 01 45 44 50 44 – www.ateliervivanda.com – Closed Sunday and Monday
Menu 39 € – Carte 32/47 €
• Meats and grills • Bistro • Friendly •

Welcome to this bistrot à viande run by Akrame Benallal. Superb pieces of meat are of course on the menu: Black Angus beef (flank and marbled cuts), chicken supreme and Iberian pork chop, all lovingly prepared and accompanied by gratin dauphinois or homemade fries. Wildly good.

Aux Prés ✗ AK

27 r. du Dragon (6th) – Ⓜ *St-Germain des Prés*
Plan: **S2**
– ℰ 01 45 48 29 68 – www.restaurantauxpres.com
Menu 38 € (weekday lunch)/49 €
• Modern cuisine • Bistro • Vintage •

Cyril Lignac is clearly not short of a project or two! After changing the name and concept of his St Germain establishment, he now serves international, decidedly creative and spontaneous cuisine, without losing sight of French country roots. The Sunday brunch is a great success.

Le Bar des Prés ✗ & AK

25 r. du Dragon (6th) – Ⓜ *St-Germain des Prés*
Plan: **S2**
– ℰ 01 43 25 87 67 – www.lebardespres.com
Menu 40 € – Carte 42/65 €
• Modern cuisine • Design • Contemporary décor •

Cyril Lignac has placed a Japanese chef with a strong track record in the kitchens of Le Bar des Prés, next door to his restaurant Aux Prés. On the menu, extremely fresh sushi and sashimi, but also a few contemporary dishes: tartare of sea bream and petits pois with menthol; *galette craquante* and crab with Madras curry. Cocktails courtesy of a mixologist.

Le Bon Saint-Pourçain ✗ ⌂

10 bis r. Servandoni (6th) – Ⓜ *Mabillon*
Plan: **S2**
– ℰ 01 42 01 78 24 – Closed 3 weeks in August, 1 week
Christmas Holidays, Sunday and Monday
Carte 47/67 € – *(booking advisable)*
• Modern cuisine • Bistro • Vintage •

Tucked away behind St-Sulpice church in the heart of the high-brow Saint-Germain-des-Prés district, this restaurant honours bistro traditions with a modern twist. Delicious food – doubtless due to the high quality fresh produce. Booking advisable!

Breizh Café - Odéon ✗ ⌂ &

1 r. de l'Odéon (6th) – Ⓜ *Odéon – ℰ 01 42 49 34 73*
Plan: **S-T2**
– www.breizhcafe.com
Carte 26/52 €
• Breton • Contemporary décor • Friendly •

The location, for a start, couldn't be better: a freestone building right on the Carrefour de l'Odéon is home to the youngest of Bertrand Larcher's crêperies. This Brittany-born chef spent time in Japan before settling down in France. Tuck into savoury *galettes* and sweet *crêpes*, made with organic flour and artisanal ingredients and accompanied by quality ciders and sakes.

La Cantine du Troquet - Cherche Midi ✗

79 r. du Cherche-Midi (6th) – Ⓜ *St Placide*
Plan: **R3**
– ℰ 01 43 27 70 06 – www.lacantinedutroquet.com – Closed 2 weeks in
August, Saturday and Sunday
Carte 29/50 €
• Traditional cuisine • Bistro •

La Cantine du Troquet mark 4 on Paris's Left Bank shares the osmosis of its predecessors between decoration (brick walls and exposed stonework, tightly packed tables) and cuisine that is a fine celebration of tradition. Razor clams a la plancha, *onglet de bœuf* steak with a red wine sauce... This is generous, neat and tasty fare. Now, *à table*!

Le Comptoir du Relais – Hôtel Relais St-Germain ✗ ⌂ AK

5 carr. de l'Odéon (6th) – Ⓜ *Odéon – ℰ 01 44 27 07 50*
Plan: **S2**
– www.hotelrsg.com
Menu 60 € (weekday dinner) – Carte 29/65 €
• Traditional cuisine • Bistro • Friendly •

In this pocket-sized 1930s bistro, chef Yves Camdeborde delights customers with his copious traditional cuisine. Brasserie dishes are to the fore at lunchtime, with a more refined single menu available in the evening.

FRANCE - PARIS

L'Épi Dupin
𝕏 ⌂

11 r. Dupin (6th) – Ⓜ *Sèvres Babylone*
Plan: **R2**
– 𝒞 01 42 22 64 56 – www.epidupin.com – Closed 1 to 24 August,
Saturday, Sunday and Monday
Menu 42 €

• Modern cuisine • Friendly •

True to his beliefs, chef François Pasteau runs an eco-friendly establishment. He buys his fruit and vegetables locally, recycles organic waste, filters the drinking water on site, etc. This respect for the health of our planet and bodies can be tasted in his recipes, which provide an appetising tribute to French country traditions.

Fish La Boissonnerie
𝕏 ⌂ 🅰🅲

69 r. de Seine (6th) – Ⓜ *Odéon* – 𝒞 *01 43 54 34 69*
Plan: **S2**
– www.laboissonnerie.com – Closed August and 23 December-2 January
Menu 29 € (lunch) – Carte 37/57 €

• Modern cuisine • Bistro • Friendly •

For almost 20 years this restaurant has been paying a fine tribute to the wine god Bacchus: 300 sorts of wine (Burgundy, Champagne, Côtes du Rhône appellations) accompany appealingly contemporary market-based cooking: broccoli soup with burrata and mint; pork chop with new potatoes and roasted onions.

KGB
𝕏 🅰🅲 🎴

25 r. des Grands-Augustins (6th) – Ⓜ *St-Michel* – 𝒞 *01 46 33 00 85*
Plan: **T2**
– www.zekitchengalerie.fr – Closed 1 to 20 August, Sunday and Monday
Menu 36 € (lunch), 55/66 € – Carte 51/72 €

• Modern cuisine • Contemporary décor • Colourful •

KGB stands for Kitchen Galerie Bis, 'bis' referring to the fact that is the second William Ledeuil address in Paris. A cross between an art gallery and a less than conventional restaurant, it has the same feel as its elder sibling. The original cuisine explores sweet and sour associations, flavoured with the spices of Asia.

Officina Schenatti
𝕏 ⌷

15 r. Frédéric-Sauton (5th) – Ⓜ *Maubert Mutualité*
Plan: **U2**
– 𝒞 01 46 34 08 91 – www.officinaschenatti.com – Closed 3 weeks in
August, 24 to 28 December, Monday lunch and Sunday
Menu 35/69 € – Carte 45/68 €

• Italian • Contemporary décor • Friendly •

Ivan Schenatti, who comes from Lombardy, chose this street near the Seine to set up his 'officina' (studio) with a decor blending stone and designer furniture. He creates tasty cuisine from Italy's regions, such as homemade ravioli stuffed with chanterelles, and pairs them with good Italian wines.

Sagan
𝕏 ⌂

8 r. Casimir-Delavigne (6th) – Ⓜ *Odéon*
Plan: **T2**
– 𝒞 06 69 37 82 19 – Closed 3 weeks in August,
Christmas Holidays, Sunday, Monday and lunch
Carte 30/60 € – (booking advisable)

• Japanese • Minimalist • Intimate •

Near to Odéon, a tiny restaurant (15 covers) from the owner of Lengué in the 5th *arrondissement*. In an unadorned, hushed and intimate interior, diners sample inventive and often surprising Japanese food, such as Japanese-style ratatouille, tuna tataki, horsemeat sashimi and squab with Japanese pepper. Fine wine list.

Semilla
𝕏 🅰🅲

54 r. de Seine (6th) – Ⓜ *Odéon* – 𝒞 *01 43 54 34 50*
Plan: **S2**
– www.semillaparis.com – Closed 2 weeks in August and 23 December-2 January
Carte 51/77 €

• Modern cuisine • Trendy • Friendly •

This bistro – a good "seed" (*semilla* in Spanish) – was founded in 2012 on the initiative of the owners of Fish La Boissonnerie, which is just opposite. Find a convivial atmosphere, trendy decor and, in the kitchens, a young and passionate team, who work exclusively with hand-picked suppliers. Delicious and well done!

FRANCE - PARIS

Shu   X

8 r. Suger (6th) – Ⓜ St-Michel – ☏ 01 46 34 25 88   Plan: **T2**
*– www.restaurant-shu.com – Closed Easter Holidays, 3 weeks in August,
Sunday and lunch*
Menu 42/68 € – *(booking advisable)*
• Japanese • Minimalist • Friendly •

You have to stoop to get through the doorway that leads to this 17C cellar. In a minimalist decor, discover authentic and finely executed Japanese cuisine, in which the freshness of the ingredients works its magic in kushiage, sushi and sashimi.

Taokan - St-Germain   X & AC

8 r. du Sabot (6th) – Ⓜ St-Germain des Prés   Plan: **S2**
*– ☏ 01 42 84 18 36 – www.taokan.fr – Closed 4 to 18 August and Sunday
lunch*
Menu 24 € (lunch)/70 € – Carte 43/66 €
• Chinese • Trendy • Contemporary décor •

Come inside this pretty restaurant, in the heart of St-Germain des Prés, to enjoy Chinese cuisine. Cantonese specialities feature; for example dim sum, steamed fish, duck breast with honey, and caramelised sliced chicken. Beautiful presentation and good ingredients: this is a real ambassador for Chinese food!

Yen   X AC

22 r. St-Benoît (6th) – Ⓜ St-Germain-des-Prés   Plan: **S2**
*– ☏ 01 45 44 11 18 – www.yen-paris.fr – Closed 2 weeks in August and
Sunday*
Menu 90 € (dinner) – Carte 40/90 €
• Japanese • Minimalist • Contemporary décor •

The highly refined Japanese decor in this restaurant will appeal to fans of the minimalist look. The menu showcases the chef's speciality, soba – buckwheat noodles served hot or cold and prepared in front of you.

Yoshinori   X

18 r. Grégoire-de-Tours (6th) – Ⓜ Odéon   Plan: **S2**
*– ☏ 09 84 19 76 05 – Closed 1 week in February, 3 weeks
in August, 1 week early January, Sunday and Monday*
Menu 50 € (lunch)/70 €
• Modern cuisine • Intimate • Contemporary décor •

Yoshinori Morié's latest where the Japanese chef regales us with his refined, vegetable-based, aesthetic cuisine, presented as a seasonal menu. For instance, tartare of milk-fed Corrèze veal with cauliflower, Utah Beach cockles. So many unabashed odes to elegance and our taste buds. Pleasant lunch set menu. A real winner.

L'Abbaye   🌿 AC

10 r. Cassette (6th) – Ⓜ St-Sulpice – ☏ 01 45 44 38 11   Plan: **S2**
– www.hotel-abbaye.com
40 rm – ♦200/600 € ♦♦200/600 € – � 18 € – 4 suites
• Luxury • Historic • Classic •

A hotel with a rare charm occupying a former 17C abbey. It features highly refined guestrooms, which are both bright and classically styled, as well as a peaceful and leafy courtyard where the only noise is from the bubbling fountain. Thoughtful and attentive staff.

L'Hôtel   ⓦ AC

13 r. des Beaux-Arts (6th) – Ⓜ St-Germain des Prés   Plan: **S1**
– ☏ 01 44 41 99 00 – www.l-hotel.com
20 rm ⊆ – ♦305/1150 € ♦♦305/1150 €
• Boutique hotel • Luxury • Personalised •

It was at L'Hôtel that the great Oscar Wilde died in 1900. The atypical, aesthetic decor, updated by Jacques Garcia, still manages to pay homage to artistic pomp and splendour. There is a nod to Baroque, Empire and Oriental styles.
❀ **Le Restaurant** – See restaurant listing

FRANCE - PARIS

Relais St-Germain

9 carr. de l'Odéon (6th) – Ⓜ Odéon – ℰ 01 44 27 07 97
– www.hotelrsg.com   Plan: **S2**
22 rm ⌗ – ♦295/460 € ♦♦295/460 €
• Grand townhouse • Traditional • Personalised •
Life never seems to stand still at the Carrefour de l'Odéon – a good reason for
taking refuge in this refined hotel. The painted wood beams, shimmering fabrics and antique furniture bestow a unique character on the guestrooms, which
are perfect for literary inspiration!
⊩○ **Le Comptoir du Relais** – See restaurant listing

Bel Ami St-Germain-des-Prés

7 r. St-Benoit (6th) – Ⓜ St-Germain des Prés
– ℰ 01 42 61 8717 – www.hotel-bel-ami.com   Plan: **S2**
108 rm – ♦229/660 € ♦♦229/660 € – ⌗ 29 € – 7 suites
• Townhouse • Contemporary •
A former printing works, where the first copy of Bel Ami, Maupassant's famous
novel, was produced. Now a hotel for chic urbanites, complete with a trendy bar
and guestrooms done out in a revisited 1970s style. Spa with gym and treatment rooms. Brunch at weekends.

Montalembert

3 r. Montalembert (7th) – Ⓜ Rue du Bac
– ℰ 01 45 49 68 68 – www.hotelmontalembert-paris.fr   Plan: **R1**
44 rm ⌗ – ♦340/1390 € ♦♦340/1390 € – 6 suites
• Historic • Personalised • Design •
This handsome Belle Époque (1926) edifice is strategically located between the
Seine, the Orsay Museum and St Germain des Prés and its terrace rubs shoul-
ders with the next-door Gallimard publishing house. Smart, modern interior,
stylish, well-equipped rooms. Entirely renovated in 2016 by interior decorator
Pascal Allaman.

Le Bellechasse

8 r. de Bellechasse (7th) – Ⓜ Musée d'Orsay
– ℰ 01 45 50 22 31 – www.lebellechasse.com   Plan: **R1**
33 rm – ♦159/470 € ♦♦159/470 € – ⌗ 21 €
• Luxury • Personalised • Design •
A lovely hotel that has been entirely decorated by Christian Lacroix. The fashion
house has created designer guestrooms with splashes of colour. They have old
or contemporary details that often have a dreamlike quality. It makes for a 'journey within a journey' – fashionable and full of character!

La Belle Juliette

92 r. du Cherche-Midi (6th) – Ⓜ Vaneau
– ℰ 01 42 22 97 40 – www.labellejuliette.com   Plan: **R3**
39 rm – ♦190/520 € ♦♦190/600 € – ⌗ 22 € – 6 suites
• Boutique hotel • Elegant • Personalised •
Each floor of the hotel is decorated on a different theme: Madame Récamier on
the first floor (the famous Juliette), Italy on the second, Chateaubriand on the
third etc. The decor combines the old and the new, and remains inviting. A
place with character.

Bourg Tibourg

19 r. du Bourg-Tibourg (4th) – Ⓜ Hôtel de Ville
– ℰ 01 42 78 47 39 – www.bourgtibourg.com   Plan: **U1**
30 rm – ♦220/320 € ♦♦290/400 € – ⌗ 20 € – 1 suite
• Luxury • Townhouse • Cosy •
Hotel entirely styled by Jacques Garcia. Each room has its own individual decor
(neo-Gothic, Baroque, Eastern etc) and exudes luxury and refinement. A little
gem in the heart of the Marais district.

FRANCE - PARIS

Les Dames du Panthéon

19 pl. du Panthéon (5th) – **M** *Luxembourg*
– ℰ 01 43 54 32 95 – www.hoteldupantheon.com
35 rm – †200/450 € ††200/450 € – ☑ 18 €
• Boutique hotel • Cosy • Personalised •

Plan: **T3**

The Panthéon, the Sorbonne, the Luxembourg Gardens... no doubt about it, we are in the heart of the Latin Quarter! Facing the Panthéon, this hotel has guestrooms with decor inspired by French women who have left their mark on history: Marguerite Duras, Juliette Gréco, George Sand and Édith Piaf. A romantic and elegant hotel.

Hôtel des Grands Hommes

17 pl. du Panthéon (5th) – **M** *Luxembourg*
– ℰ 01 46 34 19 60 – www.hoteldesgrandshommes.com
30 rm – †185/340 € ††195/450 € – ☑ 14 €
• Boutique hotel • Classic • Elegant •

Plan: **T3**

This charming hotel enjoys a fine location near the Panthéon. The well-maintained guestrooms are furnished in Directoire-style and have plenty of character. Superb views from the balconies and terraces on the fifth and sixth floors.

La Lanterne

12 r. de la Montagne-Ste-Geneviève (5th)
*– **M** Maubert Mutualité – ℰ 01 53 19 88 39 – www.hotel-la-lanterne.com*
26 rm – †210/620 € ††210/620 € – ☑ 19 € – 1 suite
• Boutique hotel • Cosy • Elegant •

Plan: **T2**

In the heart of the Latin Quarter, between Notre-Dame and the Pantheon, this oh-so-chic boutique hotel has comfortable guestrooms (including four in a little interior garden). The bonus? The relaxation suite with pool, hammam and sensory shower, which is a rarity in the area.

Monge

55 r. Monge (5th) – **M** *Place Monge* – ℰ 01 43 54 55 55
– www.hotelmonge.com
30 rm – †196/350 € ††196/350 € – ☑ 18 €
• Boutique hotel • Luxury • Cosy •

Plan: **U3**

This charming hotel is situated in the Latin Quarter, in front of the Arènes de Lutèce. It has retained the charm of 19C mansions (interconnecting rooms, moulding, floorboards etc). The decoration of the guestrooms features wildlife wallpaper in a nod to the nearby Jardin des Plantes. Parisian-style elegance all the way.

Jardin de Cluny

9 r. du Sommerard (5th) – **M** *Maubert Mutualité*
– ℰ 01 43 54 22 66 – www.hoteljardindecluny.com
39 rm – †130/250 € ††220/360 € – ☑ 17 €
• Townhouse • Business • Personalised •

Plan: **T2**

Environmentally conscious travellers will enjoy staying at this Écolabel-certified hotel, where the elegance and comfort in the guestrooms has not been sacrificed one bit. The vaulted room where breakfast is served has lots of charm.

Le Petit Paris

214 r. St-Jacques (5th) – **M** *Luxembourg*
– ℰ 01 53 10 29 29 – www.hotelpetitparis.com
20 rm – †180/420 € ††240/500 € – ☑ 16 €
• Boutique hotel • Townhouse • Personalised •

Plan: **T3**

With their elegant yet fun and colourful decor, the guestrooms in this hotel evoke the style of the Middle Ages, the 1920s, 1970s, or the Louis VX and Napoleon III periods.

231

FRANCE - PARIS

☸

Cobéa (Philippe Bélissent) XxX ⚬ AC
11 r. Raymond-Losserand (14th) – Ⓜ *Gaité* Plan: **V2**
– ☎ 01 43 20 21 39 – www.cobea.fr – Closed 1 week Easter Holidays,
August, 1 week Christmas Holidays, Sunday and Monday
Menu 50 € (lunch), 70/120 €
• Modern cuisine • Elegant •

Co, as in Jérôme Cobou, in the restaurant, Bé, as in Philippe Bélissent, in the kitchens, and A for Associates. Cobéa is the venture of two passionate young profes-
sionals, who have created a place in their image, that is, guided by the taste
for good things! A feel for ingredients, harmony and strength of flavours and
finesse. A delicious restaurant.
➜ Tortellinis de homard breton. Quasi de veau français à la plancha. Pêche
et dragées.

☸

Montée (Takayuki Nameura) X AC
9 r. Léopold-Robert (14th) Plan: **W1**
– Ⓜ Notre-Dame-des-Champs – ☎ 01 43 25 57 63
– www.restaurant-montee.fr – Closed Sunday and Monday
Menu 32 € (weekday lunch)/80 €
• Modern cuisine • Elegant • Cosy •

A Japanese chef (from Kobe in this case) shares his love of French food in this
establishment. His graphic, meticulously crafted dishes are rich in distinctive flavours, revealing his undisputed skill, know-how and personality. Finally, the
stripped-back décor further enhances and amplifies to the culinary experience.
➜ Cuisine du marché.

☺

Bistrotters X AC
9 r. Decrès (14th) – Ⓜ *Plaisance* – ☎ 01 45 45 58 59 Plan: **V2**
– www.bistrotters.com – Closed 24 December-2 January
Menu 23 € (weekday lunch), 32/36 €
• Modern cuisine • Bistro • Simple •

A very lovely find in the southern reaches of the 14th *arrondissement*, close to
Métro Plaisance. The values of *bistronomie* and Epicureanism are at the fore
with hearty, elaborate fare made from fine ingredients (small producers from
the Île-de-France area are preferred). Bistro interior and laid-back service.

☺

Le Timbre X
3 r. Ste-Beuve (6th) – Ⓜ *Notre-Dame des Champs* Plan: **W1**
– ☎ 01 45 49 10 40 – www.restaurantletimbre.com – Closed August, 1 to
6 January, Tuesday lunch, Sunday and Monday
Menu 28 € (lunch), 36/54 €
• Modern cuisine • Bistro • Friendly •

A young chef with a varied career path (Australia, Belgium) is at the helm of this
charming bistro – wooden tables, banquette seating, small open kitchen – where
you can enjoy an informal dining experience. He proposes original and tasty
market-sourced cuisine, accompanied by well-chosen wines, most of which
are organic or natural.

☺

Le Vitis X AC ⟷
8 r. Falguière (15th) – Ⓜ *Falguière* – ☎ 01 42 73 07 02 Plan: **V1**
– www.levitis.fr – Closed Sunday dinner and Monday
Menu 36 € – Carte 40/48 €
• Traditional cuisine • Bistro •

The Delacourcelle brothers, first encountered at Le Pré Verre (in the 5th *arrondissement*), are at the helm of this tiny bistro. Their recipes give diners well-made,
bold and flavoursome dishes: pan-fried razor shells, tender suckling pig with
mild spices... Excellent!

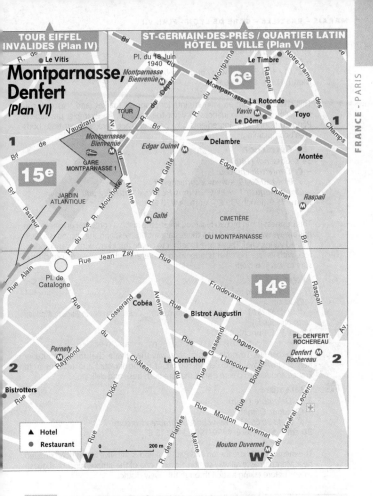

TOUR EIFFEL
INVALIDES (Plan IV)

ST-GERMAIN-DES-PRÉS / QUARTIER LATIN
HÔTEL DE VILLE (Plan V)

Montparnasse, Denfert
(Plan VI)

Le Vitis

Pl. du 18 Juin 1940

Montparnasse Bienvenüe

Le Timbre

6e

TOUR

La Rotonde

Vavin

Le Dôme

Toyo

Vaugirard

Montparnasse Bienvenüe

GARE MONTPARNASSE 1

Edgar Quinet

Delambre

Montée

1

15e

Edgar

Quinet

Raspail

JARDIN ATLANTIQUE

R. de la Gaîté

Gaîté

CIMETIÈRE DU MONTPARNASSE

Rue Jean Zay

Rue

Pl. de Catalogne

Froidevaux

14e

Cobéa

Bistrot Augustin

Pernety

Raymond

Château

Daguerre

Liancourt

PL. DENFERT ROCHEREAU

Denfert Rochereau

2

Le Cornichon

Rue Mouton Duvernet

Bistrotters

Mouton Duvernet

▲ Hotel
● Restaurant

0   200 m

V   W

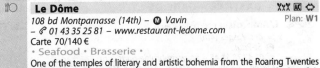

🍽️ **Le Dôme**   XxX Ⓐ ⟷
                                   Plan: **W1**
108 bd Montparnasse (14th) – Ⓜ Vavin
– ☎ 01 43 35 25 81 – www.restaurant-ledome.com
Carte 70/140 €
• Seafood • Brasserie •
One of the temples of literary and artistic bohemia from the Roaring Twenties with a legendary Art Deco setting. Le Dôme continues to serve the freshest fish and seafood in the best time-honoured fashion.

🍽️ **La Rotonde**   XX 🌧 Ⓐ ⟷
                                   Plan: **W1**
105 bd Montparnasse (6th) – Ⓜ Vavin
– ☎ 01 43 26 68 84 – www.rotondemontparnasse.com
Menu 46 € – Carte 29/83 €
• Traditional cuisine • Brasserie • Friendly •
A stone's throw from the theatres of the Rue de la Gaîté, La Rotonde has been the incarnation of the very essence of the Parisian brasserie for over a century. The decor is typical – very 1930s – all brass fittings and red banquettes, and the dishes are brasserie classics, such as Salers beef and oyster platters. Plus, it is open until 2am!

FRANCE - PARIS

Bistrot Augustin
✗ ⌂ 🖴 ৬ 🆔

79 r. Daguerre (14th)
Plan: **W2**
– Ⓜ Gaîté
– ☎ 01 43 21 92 29 – www.augustin-bistrot.fr – Closed Sunday
Menu 41 € – Carte 46/67 €
• Traditional cuisine • Bistro • Friendly •

This chic bistro with an intimate interior proposes market (and seasonal) cuisine with southern influences to whet the appetite. An example: the superb Périgord pork chop... Ingredients take pride of place here, and our taste buds aren't complaining!

Le Cornichon
✗

34 r. Gassendi (14th)
Plan: **W2**
– Ⓜ Denfert Rochereau
– ☎ 01 43 20 40 19 – www.lecornichon.fr
– Closed August, 1 week Christmas Holidays, Saturday and Sunday
Menu 35 € (lunch)/39 € – Carte 44/70 €
• Modern cuisine • Bistro • Friendly •

This business is run by two real food lovers: the first is a computer engineer who has always wanted to get into the restaurant business and the second is a well-trained young chef. They came together to create this bistro with a very modern feel. With its fine ingredients, appealing dishes and full flavours, Le Cornichon is sure to win you over!

Toyo
✗ 🆔 ⇄

17 r. Jules-Chaplain (6th)
Plan: **W1**
– Ⓜ Vavin
– ☎ 01 43 54 28 03 – www.restaurant-toyo.com – Closed 3 weeks in August, Monday lunch and Sunday
Menu 39 € (lunch), 49/99 €
• Creative • Minimalist • Contemporary décor •

In a former life, Toyomitsu Nakayama was the private chef for the couturier Kenzo. Nowadays, he excels in the art of fusing flavours and textures from France and Asia to create dishes that are both fresh and delicate.

Delambre
৬ 🆔

35 r. Delambre (14th)
Plan: **W1**
– Ⓜ Edgar Quinet
– ☎ 01 43 20 66 31 – www.hoteldelambreparis.com
30 rm – ♦99/199 € ♦♦99/199 € – ☲ 13 €
• Traditional • Functional •

The memory of André Breton and Paul Gauguin is still alive in this hotel situated near Montparnasse railway station. Relax in one of the simple, functional guestrooms before taking a stroll through this lively district.

MARAIS – BASTILLE – GARE DE LYON
PLAN VII

❀❀❀ ### L'Ambroisie (Bernard Pacaud)
✗✗✗✗ 🆔 🍽

9 pl. des Vosges (4th)
Plan: **X2**
– Ⓜ St-Paul
– ☎ 01 42 78 51 45 – www.ambroisie-paris.com
– Closed 18 February-5 March, 29 April-6 May, 5 to 26 August, Sunday and Monday
Carte 210/340 € – (booking advisable)
• Classic cuisine • Luxury • Elegant •

Ambrosia was the food of the gods on Mount Olympus. Without question, the cuisine of Bernard Pacaud reaches similar heights, with its explosion of flavours, its scientific approach and its perfect execution. Incomparable classicism and an immortal feast for the senses in the regal setting of a townhouse on Place des Vosges.
➜ Feuillantine de langoustines aux graines de sésame, sauce au curry. Escalopines de bar à l'émincé d'artichaut, nage réduite au caviar. Tarte fine sablée au cacao amer, glace à la vanille Bourbon.

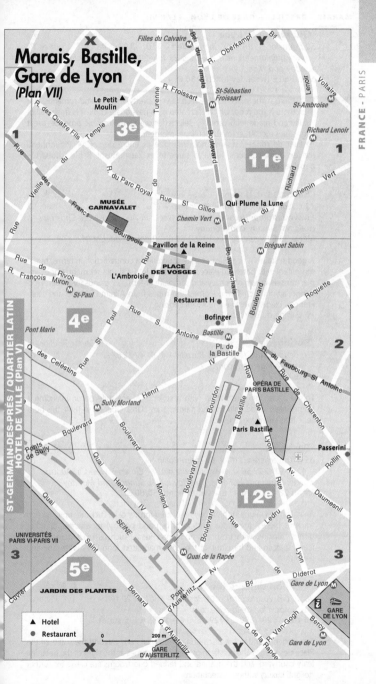

Marais, Bastille, Gare de Lyon
(Plan VII)

Le Petit Moulin ▲

3e

11e

MUSÉE CARNAVALET

Qui Plume la Lune ●

Pavillon de la Reine ▲

PLACE DES VOSGES

L'Ambroisie ●

Restaurant H ●

Bofinger ●

4e

St-Paul Ⓜ

Pont Marie

Bastille Ⓜ

Pl. de la Bastille

OPÉRA DE PARIS BASTILLE

Paris Bastille ▲

Passerini ●

Sully Morland Ⓜ

12e

Quai de la Rapée Ⓜ

5e

UNIVERSITÉS PARIS VI-PARIS VII

JARDIN DES PLANTES

SEINE

Pont d'Austerlitz

Gare de Lyon Ⓜ

GARE DE LYON

Gare de Lyon Ⓜ

GARE D'AUSTERLITZ

▲ Hotel
● Restaurant

0   200 m

ST-GERMAIN-DES-PRÉS / QUARTIER LATIN / HÔTEL DE VILLE (Plan V)

235

FRANCE - PARIS

Qui plume la Lune

50 r. Amelot (11th) – Ⓜ *Chemin Vert –* ✆ *01 48 07 45 48*　Plan: **Y1**
*– www.quiplumelalune.fr – Closed 29 July-20 August, 1 to 8 January,
Sunday and Monday*
Menu 60 € (weekday lunch)/130 €
• Modern cuisine • Cosy •

First, there is the place itself, which is very pretty, inviting and romantic and then there is the food, which is created by a passionate cook. It is fresh, full of vitality and made with carefully selected ingredients (organic produce, great vegetables etc). An enjoyable culinary moment.
→ Filet de rouget, sésame noir, mangue et encre de seiche. Pigeonneau rôti en deux cuissons, jus à la sarriette et katsuobushi. Sable "rhubarba-papa" et lavande.

Restaurant H (Hubert Duchenne)

13 r. Jean-Beausire (4th) – Ⓜ *Bastille –* ✆ *01 43 48 80 96*　Plan: **Y2**
*– www.restauranth.com – Closed 3 weeks in August, 1 week Christmas
Holidays, Sunday and Monday*
Menu 36 € (weekday lunch), 60/80 € – *(booking advisable)*
• Creative • Cosy • Intimate •

A good restaurant near Bastille may sound like a contradiction in terms, but at this eatery with barely 20 places, diners tuck into a single set menu (for example: mussels, cream of parsley and samphire greens). "H" stands for Hubert Duchenne, a young chef who learned the ropes from Akrame Benallal and Jean-François Piège. Inventive and skilful cooking.
→ Cuisine du marché.

Bofinger

5 r. de la Bastille (4th) – Ⓜ *Bastille –* ✆ *01 42 72 87 82*　Plan: **Y2**
– www.bofingerparis.com
Carte 41/77 €
• Traditional cuisine • Brasserie • Historic •

This is a real Paris institution with a striking, Alsace-style decor, including a dome, inlaid wood, mirrors, and paintings by Hansi. Opened in 1864, this brasserie is as charming as ever.

Passerini

65 r. Traversière (12th) – Ⓜ *Ledru Rollin*　Plan: **Y3**
– ✆ *01 43 42 27 56 – www.passerini.paris – Closed 3 weeks in August,
1 week Christmas Holidays, Tuesday lunch, Sunday and Monday*
Menu 28 € (lunch)/48 € – Carte dinner 50/80 €
• Italian • Contemporary décor • Friendly •

An Italian feel reigns in this nicely renovated former café. Tuck into aptly named "grosses pièces" (generous platters of fish and poultry) for sharing, or other dishes bursting with freshness and good ideas, such as roast guinea fowl, leeks, spinach and hazelnut, or tagliolini, marinated John Dory with sage and lemon.

Pavillon de la Reine

28 pl. des Vosges (3rd) – Ⓜ *Bastille –* ✆ *01 40 29 19 19*　Plan: **Y2**
– www.pavillon-de-la-reine.com
56 rm – 🚹297/890 € 🚹🚹297/890 € – ☲ 35 € – 5 suites
• Luxury • Historic • Personalised •

The elegance and noble discretion of historical Paris. Beyond the vaults of the Place des Vosges, the first flash of inspiration comes at the sight of the beautiful leafy courtyard, and the hushed and refined guestrooms are cause for further delight. Luxury without ostentation!

Le Petit Moulin   AK

29 r. du Poitou (3rd)   Plan: **X1**
– Ⓜ *St-Sébastien Froissart*
– ✆ *01 42 74 10 10 – www.hoteldupetitmoulin.com*
17 rm – ♦185/495 € ♦♦185/495 € – ☲ 16 €
• Luxury • Personalised •

Christian Lacroix is behind the unique and refined decor in this hotel in the Marais, which plays on the contrasts between the traditional and the modern. Every bedroom is a delight, with vibrant tones and free-standing bathtubs.

Paris Bastille   &. AK ṡ♣

67 r. de Lyon (12th) – Ⓜ *Bastille*   Plan: **Y2**
– ✆ *01 40 01 07 17 – www.hotelparisbastille.com*
37 rm ☲ – ♦95/219 € ♦♦99/224 €
• Business • Functional • Contemporary •

Fine fabrics, exotic woods and selected hues characterise the bedrooms and the breakfast room in this comfortable modern hotel opposite Opera Bastille.

MONTMARTRE – PIGALLE   PLAN VIII

La Table d'Eugène (Geoffroy Maillard)   XX

18 r. Eugène-Sue (18th)   Plan: **AA 1**
– Ⓜ *Jules Joffrin*
– ✆ *01 42 55 61 64 – www.latabledeugene.com*
– *Closed 22 to 30 April, 5 to 27 August, 1 to 8 January, Sunday and Monday*
Menu 42 € (lunch), 89/120 € – *(booking advisable)*
• Modern cuisine • Elegant •

Without any difficulty, Geoffroy Maillard – whose CV includes Frechon – will have raised his charming place to the ranks of the best. Good news for the 18th *arrondissement* and all foodies! He creates very fresh cuisine, full of colours and aromas. Let the "carte blanche" menu transport you, with marriages of dishes and wines. Strength and finesse.
→ Cuisine du marché.

Ken Kawasaki   X

15 r. Caulaincourt (18th)   Plan: **Z1**
– Ⓜ *Blanche* – ✆ *09 70 95 98 32 – www.restaurantkenkawasaki.fr*
– *Closed August, 1 week in December, Wednesday lunch, Thursday lunch and Sunday*
Menu 30 € (lunch)/70 € – *(booking advisable) (tasting menu only)*
• Creative • Minimalist •

This establishment invites you to celebrate a splendid marriage between Japanese and French cuisine. Japanese chef Ken Kawasaki has put together a fine team, who together prepare exquisitely graphic dishes, full of unusual flavours using market-fresh ingredients. Simply excellent.
→ Cuisine du marché.

L'Arcane (Laurent Magnin)   X

39 r. Lamarck (18th) – Ⓜ *Lamarck Caulaincourt*   Plan: **AA1**
– ✆ *01 46 06 86 00 – www.restaurantlarcane.com*
– *Closed August, 1 week Christmas Holidays, Tuesday lunch, Sunday and Monday*
Menu 49/80 €
• Modern cuisine • Cosy •

Let's try to get to the bottom of the secrets of this restaurant behind Sacré Cœur. The chef offers his take on tradition, and it has to be said that the pleasant surprises come thick and fast over the course of the meal: prawns three ways, skate wing *à la grenobloise* etc. An appealing place, the charms of which are liable to radiate well beyond Montmartre.
→ Cuisine du marché.

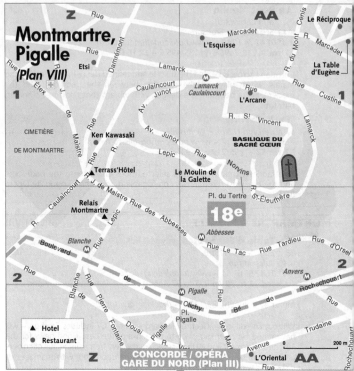

Montmartre, Pigalle
(Plan VIII)

Map legend:
- ▲ Hotel
- ● Restaurant

CONCORDE / OPÉRA
GARE DU NORD (Plan III)

18e

0   200 m

(☺) **L'Esquisse** ✕
Plan: **AA1**

151 bis r. Marcadet (18th) – Ⓜ Lamarck-Caulaincourt
– ℰ 01 53 41 63 04 – Closed 3 weeks in August,
Sunday and Monday
Menu 23 € (weekday lunch) – Carte 34/46 €
• Modern cuisine • Bistro •

Two young enthusiastic food lovers have pooled their talents to create this inviting vintage bistro with solid wooden floors and benches. The eye-catching, no-
frills dishes pay tribute to the high quality produce. Flawlessly cooked with contrasting seasonings. Delicious!

(☺) **Etsi** ✕
Plan: **Z1**

23 r. Eugène-Carrière (18th) – Ⓜ Place de Clichy
– ℰ 01 71 50 00 80 – www.etsi-paris.fr – Closed 3 weeks in August, Sunday
dinner, Monday and weekday lunch
Carte 28/40 €
• Greek • Tavern •

The intense blue of the façade draws the eye. This is the story of a young chef of
Greek origin, who turned her focus to the cooking of her homeland after cutting
her teeth with some well-known French names (Michel Rostang, Cyril Lignac).
Here, she proposes mezze that are strikingly fresh and littered with bold touches. Her father, who still lives in Greece, sends her ingredients that can't be
found anywhere else! A real winner.

FRANCE - PARIS

Le Réciproque
14 r. Ferdinand-Flocon (18th) Plan: **AA1**
– **Ⓜ** *Jules Joffrin*
– *℡ 09 86 37 80 77 – www.lereciproque.com*
– *Closed mid-July to end-August, 23 December-1 January, Sunday and Monday*
Menu 23 € (lunch), 37/84 € 🍷 – *(booking advisable)*
• Traditional cuisine • Contemporary décor •

Tucked away in a small side street behind the 18th town hall, this restaurant is the work of two youthful partners, each of whom boasts an impressive résumé. One is in the kitchen where he excels at cooking traditional, flavoursome recipes, while the other is in charge of the friendly, courteous service. Reasonable prices to boot!

Le Moulin de la Galette
83 r. Lepic (18th) Plan: **AA1**
– **Ⓜ** *Abbesses*
– *℡ 01 46 06 84 77 – www.lemoulindelagalette.fr*
– *Closed Monday and Tuesday*
Menu 39 € (weekday lunch)
– Carte 42/58 €
• Traditional cuisine • Elegant •

Le Moulin de la Galette is back, since two business associates took over this historical Montmartre building in late 2015. They propose fresh, well-composed cuisine. The fine meats braised over charcoals alone justify a visit. As for the service, the young, efficient team does sterling work.

L'Oriental
47 av. Trudaine (9th) Plan: **AA2**
– **Ⓜ** *Pigalle*
– *℡ 01 42 64 39 80 – www.loriental-restaurant.com*
Menu 33 € – Carte 35/50 €
• North African • Exotic décor •

Sit on the pleasant outdoor terrace or in the welcoming and comfortable dining room with its oriental decor. Evocatively flavoured Moroccan cuisine includes signature couscous dishes.

Terrass' Hôtel
12 r. J.-de-Maistre (18th) Plan: **Z1**
– **Ⓜ** *Place de Clichy*
– *℡ 01 46 06 72 85 – www.terrass-hotel.com*
92 rm – †160/450 € ††200/500 € – ⊆ 25 € – 6 suites
• Boutique hotel • Contemporary •

Not far from Montmartre Cemetery, this hotel is reminiscent of an artist's studio, with guestrooms inspired by the neighbourhood's bohemian feel. What is more, this fine establishment reveals an uninterrupted view over Paris, to admire from the panoramic restaurant on the seventh floor.

Relais Montmartre
6 r. Constance (18th) – **Ⓜ** *Abbesses* Plan: **Z2**
– *℡ 01 70 64 25 25 – www.relaismontmartre.fr*
26 rm – †119/249 € ††119/249 € – ⊆ 15 €
• Traditional • Cosy •

Not far from the shops of rue Lepic, this small characterful hotel – an unexpected find in such a lively neighbourhood – has the charm of a bourgeois house. With their period furniture and exposed beams, the guestrooms are extremely stylish. And such peace and quiet.

FRANCE - PARIS

Le Pré Catelan ✿✿✿ XxXxX ⌂ ⌂ 🔥 Ⓜ ↔ 🐖 🅿

au Bois de Boulogne - rte de Suresnes (16th) Plan: **A2**
– ℰ 01 44 14 41 14 – www.precatelanparis.com
– *Closed 18 February-5 March, 29 July-20 August, 21 to 29 October,
Sunday and Monday*
Menu 130 € (lunch), 220/280 €
– Carte 250/315 €
• Creative • Luxury • Elegant •

Set within the Bois de Boulogne, the superb Napoleon-III pavilion installed here since 1905 is easily recognisable. In this dream location, Frédéric Anton works wonders: the precision and rigour passed on by his
mentors (who include Robuchon) are his signature, along with his taste
for original pairings. Topped off by a prestigious wine cellar and perfect
service.
➜ Crabe, crème légère à l'aneth, caviar de France et soupe au parfum
de fenouil. Cabillaud aux algues, beurre aux zestes de citron vert.
Pomme soufflée croustillante, crème glacée au caramel, cidre et sucre
pétillant.

La Grande Cascade ✿ XxXxX ⌂ ⌂ ↔ 🐖 🅿

au Bois de Boulogne - allée de Longchamp (16th)
– ℰ 01 45 27 33 51 – www.restaurantsparisiens.com
– *Closed 22 December-20 January*
Menu 89/192 € – Carte 170/220 €
• Modern cuisine • Classic décor • Elegant •

A charming pavilion (1850) just a stone's throw from the large waterfall
(Grande Cascade) in the Bois de Boulogne. To savour the refined cuisine
here beneath the majestic rotunda or on the delightful terrace is a rare
and elegant treat.
➜ Tourteau de Bretagne au naturel, neige au citron et caviar oscietre royal.
Turbot cuit au goémon, variation d'artichaut, émulsion pistache. Mille gauf-
res, crème légère à la vanille.

St-James Paris – Hôtel St-James Paris ✿ XxX ⌂ 🔥 Ⓜ ↔ 🅿

43 av. Bugeaud (16th) – Ⓜ *Porte Dauphine* Plan: **A2**
– ℰ 01 44 05 81 88 – www.saint-james-paris.com
– *Closed Sunday dinner and lunch*
Menu 140 € – Carte 105/160 €
• Modern cuisine • Classic décor • Elegant •

An exclusive hotel with the atmosphere of an English member's-only club. The
setting is superb, as chic as it is elegant with its wood panelling, golden brown
fabrics, high, trompe-l'oeil ceiling and very secret garden. The food is in keeping
with the rest: delicate, precise and nicely composed. A place with plenty of
good taste!
➜ Huîtres et caviar, longuet de volaille toasté. Homard juste saisi, bouillon
de corail aux aromates et légumes comme un risotto. Fraîcheur de fruits de
saison au parfum de verveine.

Le Quinzième - Cyril Lignac ✿ XxX Ⓜ ↔ 🐖

14 r. Cauchy (15th) – Ⓜ *Javel* Plan: **A2-3**
– ℰ 01 45 54 43 43 – www.restaurantlequinzieme.com
– *Closed 3 weeks in August, Saturday and Sunday*
Menu 69 € (lunch), 140/250 € 🍷
• Modern cuisine • Elegant •

Cyril Lignac has definitely perfected the art of creating distinctive cuisine. Not
only are they visually striking, the combination of unusual, complimentary flavours is heavenly. An example: three super-fresh, juicy scallops served with a
purée of carrot and Corsican clementines.
➜ Langoustine dorée, tartare et fraises de Plougastel, vinaigre de fruits
rouges. Homard breton confit au beurre de corail, gnocchis de pomme
de terre. Chocolat Équateur, mousse légère alpaco et crémeux chocolat
au lait.

FRANCE - PARIS

❀ **L'Archeste** (Yoshiaki Ito)   XX 占 🅰️

79 r. de la Tour (16th) – Ⓜ *Rue de la Pompe*   Plan: **A2**
– ☏ 01 40 71 69 68 – www.archeste.com – Closed Saturday lunch, Sunday and Monday
Menu 48 € (weekday lunch), 68/98 € – *(booking advisable)*
• Creative • Minimalist • Contemporary décor •

Yoshiaki Ito, former chef at Hiramatsu, astounds in this restaurant with a pared-down interior... in keeping with his work. The set menus (three or five courses at lunch, seven at dinner) are models of creativity and precision, espousing the seasons and always giving the best of excellent ingredients. Fine recipes from a repertoire of contemporary French cuisine, which have already garnered quite a following.
→ Cuisine du marché.

❀ **Au Trou Gascon**   XX 🕸️ 🅰️

40 r. Taine (12th) – Ⓜ *Daumesnil* – ☏ 01 43 44 34 26   Plan: **D3**
– www.autrougascon.fr – Closed August, 1 to 7 January, Saturday and Sunday
Menu 42 € (lunch)/78 € – Carte 65/80 €
• Cuisine from South West France • Elegant •

This institution, dedicated to the cuisine of Southwest France, transports diners to the area between the River Adour and the ocean. It has earned the loyalty of many long-standing regulars with its pâté en croûte with duck foie gras, lièvre à la royale (hare), and warm and crusty tourtière - not to mention the ever-popular cassoulet.
→ Escalope de foie gras de canard des Landes poêlée, gâteau truffé de topinambour. Ris de veau doré au sautoir, barigoule d'artichaut violet. Figues caramélisées au gingembre confit, glace aux noix et riz au lait.

❀ **Comice** (Noam Gedalof)   XX 🅰️

31 av. de Versailles (16th) – Ⓜ *Mirabeau*   Plan: **A2**
– ☏ 01 42 15 55 70 – www.comice.paris – Closed 2 weeks in April, in August and in January, Tuesday lunch, Wednesday lunch, Sunday and Monday
Menu 80 € (weekday lunch)/120 € – Carte 60/100 €
• Modern cuisine • Elegant •

A Canadian couple had the excellent idea to open their first restaurant in Paris: the chef, Noam, draws inspiration from the foundations of French cuisine, which he gives a modern tweak. Etheliya manages the service and wine. From their complicity a vibrant array of flavours is born; for you to sample in an elegant, intimate interior. A success!
→ Carpaccio de bar de ligne, radis, concombre, poivron et petit lait. Filet de veau, pancetta, pommes de terre confites, jus de veau. Soufflé au chocolat, glace à la vanille

❀ **Mavrommatis**   XX 🍴 🅰️ ⇦

42 r. Daubenton (5th) – Ⓜ *Censier Daubenton*   Plan: **C3**
– ☏ 01 43 31 17 17 – www.mavrommatis.com – Closed August, Tuesday lunch, Wednesday lunch, Sunday and Monday
Menu 42 € (weekday dinner)/79 € – Carte 55/79 €
• Greek • Elegant • Classic décor •

A different vision of Greek food in Paris! The setting is elegant and the chef cooks up a lovely interpretation of Greek gastronomy. Enjoy lamb, octopus, Mediterranean vegetables and Retsina wine. High quality dishes.
→ Découverte des mézédés. Encornets farcis, crevettes obsiblues grillées, fenouil au curcuma. Tarte vanille et châtaigne.

❀ **Table - Bruno Verjus**   ✗ 🕸️ ⇦

3 r. de Prague (12th) – Ⓜ *Ledru Rollin* – ☏ 01 43 43 12 26   Plan: **C2**
– www.tablerestaurant.fr – Closed 4 to 25 August, Saturday lunch and Sunday
Menu 29 € (weekday lunch) – Carte 57/101 € – *(booking advisable)*
• Modern cuisine • Design • Trendy •

Choosing the finest ingredients and cooking them humbly is the way of Bruno Verjus – a remarkable character, entrepreneur, blogger and food critic... turned chef! His dishes are full of energy and flavour, and reveal a rich interplay of textures, hinting at the chef's sincere and contagious passion.
→ Cuisine du marché.

⌘

Le Chateaubriand (Inaki Aizpitarte)   ✗ 🕸

129 av. Parmentier (11th) – Ⓜ *Goncourt*   Plan: **C2**
– ☏ 01 43 57 45 95 – www.lechateaubriand.net – Closed 25 December to
1 January, Sunday, Monday and lunch
Menu 70/135 € ♑
• Modern cuisine • Minimalist • Bistro •

The high profile chef at this in vogue restaurant offers a unique menu that changes with his inspiration and the seasons. Well worth a visit for the presentation
alone!
→ Cuisine du marché.

⌘

La Fourchette du Printemps (Nicolas Mouton)   ✗ 🄰🄲

30 r. du Printemps (17th) – Ⓜ *Wagram*   Plan: **B1**
– ☏ 01 42 27 26 97 – www.lafourchetteduprintemps.com – Closed August,
Sunday and Monday
Menu 32 € (weekday lunch), 57/77 € – Carte approx. 65 €
• Modern cuisine • Bistro • Friendly •

Whatever the season, this contemporary bistro stands out from the crowd. The
young chef, an alumnus of some top restaurants, hones ingredients to reveal
lovely flavours - surrounded by unpretentious decor that matches the laid-
back service. Here, taste goes hand in hand with simplicity.
→ Raviole ouverte de tourteau, mangue, pomme verte, avocat et crumble
de fruits secs. Saint-pierre poêlé aux olives taggiasche, risotto crémeux et
jus de coques monté au beurre. Sphère citron et verveine.

⌘

Septime (Bertrand Grébaut)   ✗

80 r. de Charonne (11th) – Ⓜ *Charonne*   Plan: **D2**
– ☏ 01 43 67 38 29 – www.septime-charonne.fr – Closed 3 weeks in
August, Monday lunch, Saturday and Sunday
Menu 42 € (lunch)/80 € – *(booking advisable)*
• Modern cuisine • Contemporary décor •

Since May 2011, when this restaurant first opened, word of mouth has spread
through the local neighbourhood. The key to its success? The neo-industrial
decor, resolutely seasonal cuisine and high quality ingredients. Professionalism
and simplicity all in one!
→ Cuisine du marché.

☻

La Terrasse Mirabeau   ✗✗ 🛋 🍴

5 pl. de Barcelone (16th) – Ⓜ *Mirabeau*   Plan: **A2**
– ☏ 01 42 24 41 51 – www.terrasse-mirabeau.com – Closed 3 weeks in
August, 1 week in December, Saturday and Sunday
Menu 36/75 € ♑ – Carte approx. 45 €
• Traditional cuisine • Contemporary décor •

Pierre Négrevergne, trained under Michel Rostang, is one of those cooks who
knows the French classics like the back of his hand. His recipes are traditional
and work like a charm, and the flavours are bold and agreeable; to be sampled
in a discreetly contemporary interior. And the terrace, shaded by plane trees, is
pleasant.

☻

Clamato   ✗ 🄰🄲

80 r. de Charonne (11th) – Ⓜ *Charonne*   Plan: **D2**
– ☏ 01 43 72 74 53 – www.clamato-charonne.fr – Closed 3 weeks in
August, Wednesday lunch, Thursday lunch, Friday lunch, Monday and
Tuesday
Carte 35/50 € – *(bookings not accepted)*
• Seafood • Fashionable •

The Septime's little sister is becoming something of a bistronomic hit, thanks to
its fashionable interior and concise menu focused on seafood and vegetables.
Each ingredient is selected carefully and meals are served in a genuinely
friendly atmosphere. No bookings are taken – it's first come, first served!

FRANCE - PARIS

L'Envie du Jour
X AK

106 r. Nollet (17th) – Ⓜ Brochant – ℰ 01 42 26 01 02   Plan: **B1**
– www.lenviedujour.com – Closed August, Sunday and Monday
Menu 32/44 €
• Modern cuisine • Friendly • Fashionable •

This restaurant is the brainchild of enthusiastic young chef Sergio Dias Lino. All eyes are on the kitchens, which open out onto the small dining room. The cook's movements are the focus, as he carefully prepares his lovely ingredients to bring out their best in the form of colourful and fragrant dishes.

Impérial Choisy
X AK

32 av. de Choisy (13th) – Ⓜ Porte de Choisy   Plan: **C3**
– ℰ 0145864240
Carte 20/45 €
• Chinese • Simple •

A genuine Chinese restaurant frequented by many local Chinese people who use it as their lunchtime canteen. Hardly surprising given the delicious Cantonese specials on offer!

Jouvence
X AK

172 bis r. du Faubourg-St-Antoine (12th)   Plan: **D2**
– Ⓜ Faidherbe-Chaligny – ℰ 01 56 58 04 73 – www.jouvence.paris
– Closed August, Sunday and Monday
Menu 24 € (weekday lunch) – Carte 36/49 € – (booking advisable)
• Modern cuisine • Vintage • Fashionable •

Situated on the corner of rue de Cîteaux, this former apothecary-style shop from the 1900s does not merely rest on its decorative laurels. They serve contemporary cuisine, replete with quality ingredients, such as prawn tempura, cucumber kimchi and celery juice. The young chef, formerly with Dutournier (Pinxo restaurant), certainly has talent.

N° 41
X ⅖ AK

41 av. Mozart (16th) – Ⓜ Ranelagh – ℰ 01 45 03 65 16   Plan: **A2**
– www.n41.fr – Closed 2 weeks in August
Carte 27/59 € – (booking advisable)
• Traditional cuisine • Bistro •

This pleasant industrial-style bistro serves tasty, quality cuisine, such as eggs baked in ramekins and cream of foie gras. The restaurant has a modern feel and is run by a couple of restaurateurs who are passionate about what they do.

Origins 14
X ⅜ AK

49 r. Jean-Moulin (14th) – Ⓜ Porte d'Orléans   Plan: **B3**
– ℰ 01 45 45 68 58 – www.laregalade14.com – Closed Monday lunch,
Saturday and Sunday
Menu 37 €
• Traditional cuisine • Friendly •

After sharpening his skills under the masterful eye of Bruno Doucet, young Cornish-born chef Ollie Clarke has taken the plunge in the ex-Régalade, now Origins 14. Inspired by his love of French cuisine, he scrupulously sources and assembles fine ingredients accompanied with equally well-chosen wines.

L'Os à Moelle
X

3 r. Vasco-de-Gama (15th) – Ⓜ Lourmel   Plan: **A3**
– ℰ 01 45 57 27 27 – Closed 3 weeks in August, 1 week
Christmas Holidays, Saturday lunch, Sunday and Monday
Menu 35/42 € – Carte 35/47 €
• Traditional cuisine • Friendly • Bistro •

Thierry Faucher is still at the commands of L'Os à Moelle, where, in the early 2000s, he secured his position as one of the precursors of the *bistronomie* movement. Oysters and leeks in vinaigrette, calf's liver, swede mash with ginger, marrowbone, soup of the day... It's simple, delicious fare and truly enjoyable!

FRANCE - PARIS

Pho Tai
X AC ⅍
13 r. Philibert-Lucot (13th) – Ⓜ *Maison Blanche*   Plan: **C3**
– ℰ *01 45 85 97 36* – Closed August and Monday
Carte 25/35 €
• Vietnamese • Simple •

In a quiet street in the Asian quarter, this small Vietnamese restaurant stands out from the crowd. All credit to the chef, Mr Te, who arrived in France in 1968 and is a magnificent ambassador for Vietnamese cuisine. Dumplings, crispy chicken with fresh ginger, bo bun and phô soups: everything is full of flavour.

Les Résistants
X & AC
16-18 r. du Château-d'Eau (10th) – Ⓜ *République*   Plan: **C2**
– ℰ *01 42 06 43 74* – www.lesresistants.fr – Closed August, Sunday and Monday
Menu 19 € (weekday lunch) – Carte approx. 35 €
• Modern cuisine • Friendly • Fashionable •

These résistants believe that taste and traceability should be the backbone of all food. Indeed, the credo of owner, Florent Piard, is none other than "good food that respects natural cycles!" and he amply proves his case in this cheerful establishment. The concise menu changes daily in keeping with market availability and the prices are never outlandish. Natural wines bien sûr!

Tempero
X
5 r. Clisson (13th) – Ⓜ *Chevaleret* – ℰ *09 54 17 48 88*   Plan: **C3**
– www.tempero.fr – Closed August, 1 week Christmas Holidays, Monday dinner, Tuesday dinner, Wednesday dinner, Saturday and Sunday
Menu 21 € (lunch) – Carte dinner 32/45 € – (booking advisable)
• Creative • Bistro • Friendly •

A friendly little bistro, which is rather like its chef, Alessandra Montagne. Originally from Brazil, she worked at some fine Parisian establishments before opening her own place. Here she cooks with market-fresh ingredients, creating invigorating and reasonably priced dishes that draw on French, Brazilian and Asian cooking. A lovely fusion!

Villaret
X 🍴 AC 🥂 (dinner)
13 r. Ternaux (11th) – Ⓜ *Parmentier* – ℰ *01 43 57 75 56*   Plan: **C2**
– Closed 2 weeks in August, Saturday lunch and Sunday
Menu 27 € (lunch), 35/55 € – Carte 45/59 €
• Traditional cuisine • Friendly • Bistro •

From the moment you arrive, cooking aromas will entice you! This convivial bistro serves appealing seasonal fare: baked eggs with foie gras, salted monkfish, and chocolate biscuits. Good choice of wines.

Yard
X 🍴
6 r. Mont-Louis (11th) – Ⓜ *Philippe Auguste*   Plan: **D2**
– ℰ *01 40 09 70 30* – Closed August, 24 to 31 December, Saturday and Sunday
Menu 19 € (lunch) – Carte dinner 33/50 €
• Modern cuisine • Bistro •

The restaurant is very much of its time with a pretty little façade, an inviting bistro interior and laid-back service. The young British chef produces uninhibited cuisine according to the inspiration of the moment, with dishes such as homemade rabbit ravioli. There's also a friendly tapas bar and a lively pavement terrace.

Benkay
XxX ≤ & AC ⇔ 🥂
61 quai de Grenelle (15th) – Ⓜ *Bir-Hakeim*   Plan: **A2**
– ℰ *01 40 58 21 26* – www.restaurant-benkay.com – Closed August
Menu 100/160 € – Carte 47/146 €
• Japanese • Elegant • Elegant •

On the banks of the Seine, with a view over the river, the elegant Benkay artfully honours Japanese gastronomy. You can opt for the teppanyaki (the hot plate where the dishes are cooked in front of you) or the 'washoku' (table service) - not to mention the sushi counter, which is simply divine.

ﾎﾄ○ **L'Inattendu** XX 🅰️

99 r. Blomet (15th) – Ⓜ Vaugirard – ☎ 01 55 76 93 12 Plan: **B3**
– www.restaurant-inattendu.fr – Closed Sunday and Monday
Menu 25 € (weekdays), 38/47 €
• Traditional cuisine • Cosy •

This small, elegantly decorated restaurant is run by two experienced partners
who have opened a fishmonger's next door – a real guarantee of fresh produce!
Reliable, well-presented cuisine with the occasional unexpected surprise.

ﾎﾄ○ **Bon Kushikatsu** X ♿ 🅰️

24 r. Jean-Pierre-Timbaud (11th) – Ⓜ Oberkampf Plan: **C2**
– ☎ 01 43 38 82 27 – www.kushikatsubon.fr – Closed Sunday
Menu 58 €
• Japanese • Intimate • Elegant •

This restaurant is an express trip to Osaka to discover the city's culinary speciality of *kushikatsu* (meat, vegetables or seafood skewers coated with breadc-
rumbs and deep-fried). Dish after dish reveals fine flavours, such as: beef san-
cho, peppered foie gras, and shiitake mushrooms. The courteous service
transports you to Japan.

ﾎﾄ○ **Molitor** – Hôtel Molitor X 🏠 🅰️ ⇔ 🛏️

2 av. de la Porte-Molitor (16th) Plan: **A2**
– Ⓜ Michel Ange Molitor – ☎ 01 56 07 08 50 – www.mltr.fr
Menu 35 € – Carte 40/62 €
• Modern cuisine • Design • Elegant •

The Hotel Molitor needed a fittingly vibrant restaurant, strongly attached to
modernity, a reflection of itself: the result is this pleasant "urban brasserie". In
an interior blending modernity with a homage to history – like the original ceiling, with its Art Deco mouldings –, enjoy precise and immaculate dishes, faultlessly cooked and focused on flavours.

ﾎﾄ○ **Beurre Noisette** X

68 r. Vasco-de-Gama (15th) – Ⓜ Lourmel Plan: **A3**
*– ☎ 01 48 56 82 49 – www.restaurantbeurrenoisette.com – Closed 2 weeks
in August, Sunday and Monday*
Menu 32 € (lunch), 38/56 €
• Traditional cuisine • Friendly •

A tasty bistro, with a following of regulars. Thierry Blanqui draws his inspiration
from the market: blood pudding ravioli, chorizo; caramelised pork belly; rum
baba, and good old, down-to-earth *canaille* dishes. Straddling the traditional
and the new: most enjoyable. Always a good bet.

ﾎﾄ○ **Bistrot Paul Bert** X 🏠 🛏️

18 r. Paul-Bert (11th) – Ⓜ Faidherbe Chaligny Plan: **D2**
– ☎ 01 43 72 24 01 – Closed Sunday and Monday
Menu 19 € (weekday lunch)/41 €
• Traditional cuisine • Vintage • Bistro •

The façade of this pleasant bistro promises "cuisine familiale". Translate this as:
feuilleté of calf sweetbreads with mushrooms, and roast venison with cranberries and celeriac purée. Generous, tasty dishes are prepared without frills. You
will be asking for more but be sure to save some room for the rum baba!

ﾎﾄ○ **Mansouria** X 🅰️

11 r. Faidherbe (11th) – Ⓜ Faidherbe-Chaligny Plan: **D2**
*– ☎ 01 43 71 00 16 – www.mansouria.fr – Closed 13 to 19 August, Monday
lunch and Sunday*
Menu 28/36 € – Carte 33/53 €
• North African • Oriental décor •

Tajines, couscous, and crème à la fleur d'oranger are among the aromatic dishes
prepared by the talented female chefs here under the baton of Fatema Hal, an
ethnologist, writer and leading figure in North African gastronomy.

FRANCE - PARIS

FRANCE - PARIS

Osteria Ferrara ✗ 🏠 ✿

7 r. du Dahomey (11th) – Ⓜ *Faidherbe Chaligny*　　Plan: **D2**
– ☎ 01 43 71 67 69 – Closed 3 weeks in August,
Saturday and Sunday
Carte 32/52 €
• Italian • Friendly •

Gourmets come here, safe in the knowledge they have found sanctuary in this elegant interior. The Sicilian chef whips up mouth-watering Italian recipes based on excellent ingredients. Loin of veal à la Milanese with stir-fried spinach leaf. This Osteria has soul and a fine wine list to boot!

L'Ourcine ✗

92 r. Broca (13th) – Ⓜ *Les Gobelins* – ☎ 01 47 07 13 65　　Plan: **C3**
– www.restaurant-lourcine.fr – Closed 3 weeks in August, Sunday and Monday
Menu 38 €
• Traditional cuisine • Bistro • Friendly •

Quality and modesty summarise nicely the spirit of L'Ourcine, a pleasant little bistro which offers inspired, seasonal cuisine. The menu du jour and the 'coups de cœur' set menu on the blackboard offer an array of great suggestions.

Pramil ✗ 🄰🄲

9 r. Vertbois (3rd) – Ⓜ *Temple* – ☎ 01 42 72 03 60　　Plan: **C2**
– www.pramil.fr – Closed 1 to 4 May, 13 to 27 August, 24 to 28 December, Sunday lunch and Monday
Menu 33 € – Carte 38/48 €
• Modern cuisine • Bistro •

The elegant yet restrained decor helps focus the senses on the attractive and honest seasonal cuisine conjured up by Alain Pramil. He is a self-taught chef passionate about food who, in another life, was a physics teacher!

Tintilou ✗ ✿

37 bis r. de Montreuil (11th) – Ⓜ *Faidherbe-Chaligny*　　Plan: **D2**
– ☎ 01 43 72 42 32 – www.letintilou.fr – Closed 3 weeks in August, 1 week in January, Monday lunch, Saturday lunch and Sunday
Menu 25 € (lunch), 36/49 € – Carte 48/60 €
• Modern cuisine • Cosy •

This 16C former relais de mousquetaires – frequented by Louis XIII's guards – is elegant and original. The flavoursome cuisine served here evokes travel. The menu is short and changes every month, presenting dishes with enigmatic marriages of flavour: salmon, pumpkin, fennel, botargo; wild duck and cocoa. Tasty simplicity!

Vantre ✗ 🕸 🄰🄲

19 r. de la Fontaine-au-Roi (11th) – Ⓜ *Goncourt*　　Plan: **C2**
– ☎ 01 48 06 16 96 – www.vantre.fr – Closed 3 weeks in August, 1 week in January, Saturday and Sunday
Carte 40/64 €
• Modern cuisine • Bistro •

In the Middle Ages, the "vantre" was a "place of enjoyment". A play on words, it also means "stomach" in modern French (ventre). Two cohorts have joined forces to tease and tempt our taste buds, a chef (ex-Saturne) and wine waiter (ex-Bristol and Taillevent). The food features carefully sourced ingredients and over 1000 wines on the wine list. Well-deserved success.

St-James Paris ॐ 🍴 🄻🄰 🄰🄲 ✤ 🅿

43 av. Bugeaud (16th) – Ⓜ *Porte Dauphine*　　Plan: **A2**
– ☎ 01 44 05 81 81 – www.saint-james-paris.com
36 rm – ♦390/1080 € ♦♦390/1080 € – ⧠ 36 € – 13 suites
• Historic • Luxury • Personalised •

This superb late-19C mansion has been given a new look by designer Bambi Sloan. Napoleon-III style flirts with a very British brand of originality and includes lovely materials and shimmering prints. There is a delightful library, a majestic staircase and some fabulous collections of books. The blueprint for a unique place.
🕸 **St-James Paris** – See restaurant listing

Pullman Paris Centre-Bercy ☆ 📠 ᵹ 🌆 🏊

1 r. de Libourne (12th) – Ⓜ Cour St-Émilion
– ℰ 01 44 67 34 71 – www.pullmanhotels.com
396 rm ⌿ – ♦179/1500 € ♦♦179/1500 € – 20 suites
• Business • Chain • Contemporary •

Between Bercy village (home to shops, cinemas and restaurants) and the Seine, this huge glass edifice can be seen from all around! The rooms are very comfortable and those on the upper floors command a fine view of Paris.

Molitor 🌐 ⊐ ⊡ ᵹ 🌆 🏊

2 av. de la Porte-Molitor (16th)
– Ⓜ Michel Ange Molitor – ℰ 01 56 07 08 50 – www.mltr.fr
117 rm ⌿ – ♦270/700 € ♦♦270/700 € – 7 suites
• Luxury • Townhouse • Design •

A true emblem of western Paris since the 1920s, the Piscine Molitor was resurrected in 2014 and has been converted into a gorgeous luxury hotel. There are nods to its history with the blue and yellow façade around the pool and the restaurant's decoration, along with ultra-modern minimalism in the guestrooms.
🍴 **Molitor** – See restaurant listing

Square ☆ 🌐 ᵹ 🌆 🏊 🚗

3 r. Boulainvilliers (16th) – Ⓜ Mirabeau
– ℰ 01 44 14 91 90 – www.hotelsquare.com
22 rm – ♦200/420 € ♦♦380/660 € – ⌿ 25 €
• Luxury • Design •

This contemporary hotel is located just opposite the Maison de la Radio. It has guestrooms that are spacious and quiet, thanks to the excellent soundproofing. The hi-tech facilities and modern art collection underline the Square's boutique hotel image.

Kube ☆ 📠 ᵹ 🌆 🏊 🛁 🚗

1-5 passage Ruelle (18th) – Ⓜ La Chapelle
– ℰ 01 42 05 20 00 – www.kubehotel-paris.com
39 rm – ♦159/449 € ♦♦159/449 € – ⌿ 18 €
• Townhouse • Design • Minimalist •

Although not located in one of the city's most attractive districts, this resolutely 21C hotel with its designer look and hi-tech gadgetry, will appeal to a more contemporary clientele. Transparent glass, clean white lines and loft-style guestrooms provide the decor in this cutting-edge property. It has a restaurant, as well as two bars, including the Ice Kube (-10°C, warm clothing provided!).

Fabric 📠 ᵹ 🌆

31 r. de la Folie-Méricourt (11th) – Ⓜ Saint-Ambroise
– ℰ 01 43 57 27 00 – www.hotelfabric.com
33 rm – ♦180/340 € ♦♦180/340 € – ⌿ 18 €
• Townhouse • Design • Contemporary •

In a former textile factory, lying halfway between République and Bastille, this beautiful hotel has retained some of its industrial heritage. Find elegant, designer guestrooms, as well as iron light fixtures, beams, antique furniture and a palette of grey tones.

Hôtel de Banville 🌆

166 bd Berthier (17th) – Ⓜ Porte de Champerret
– ℰ 01 42 67 70 16 – www.hotelbanville.fr
38 rm ⌿ – ♦125/350 € ♦♦125/350 €
• Luxury • Boutique hotel • Personalised •

This charming boutique hotel is decorated with great taste, and guestrooms are embellished with shiny wood and opulent detail. Jazz evenings in the piano-bar every Tuesday.

Holiday Inn Express Canal de la Villette ⟨≤ ⟩ 点 🎦 🛅

68 quai de Seine (19th) – **ⓜ** *Crimée* – *𝒞 01 44 65 01 01*
– *www.holidayinnexpress.com/paris-canal*
144 rm 🛏 – **†**89/299 € **††**89/299 €
Plan: **D1**
• Business • Chain • Contemporary •

Those who enjoy a stroll around the Bassin de la Villette know this building well: its twin (a warehouse dating from 1853) still stands on the opposite bank. The hotel, rebuilt in 2008, is striking for its unusual metal cladding and has a warm, friendly atmosphere. Some of the spacious guestrooms overlook the water.

Mama Shelter 🛖 点 🎦 🛅 🚗

109 r. de Bagnolet (20th) – **ⓜ** *Gambetta*
– *𝒞 01 43 48 48 48* – *www.mamashelter.com*
Plan: **D2**
172 rm – **†**79/239 € **††**89/249 € – 🛏 17 € – 1 suite
• Townhouse • Unique •

Philippe Starck is behind the refined, fantasy decor in this huge hotel, which is at the cutting edge of contemporary design. It is characterised by a young and slightly bohemian atmosphere in keeping with this district, which is enjoying an urban revival.

LA DÉFENSE   PLAN I

Hilton La Défense 🛖 🛗 点 🎦 🛅

2 pl. de la Défense ✉ *92053* – **ⓜ** *La Défense* – *𝒞 01 46 92 10 10*
– *www.hiltonparisladefense.com*
153 rm – **†**169/299 € **††**179/399 € – 🛏 26 € – 4 suites
• Business • Chain • Contemporary •

Hotel situated within the CNIT complex. Some of the rooms have been particularly designed with the business traveller in mind: work, rest, relaxation and Jacuzzi tubs in the bathrooms. At Côté Parvis, modern cuisine and a fine view of the Arch of La Défense.

Sofitel Paris La Défense 🛖 点 🎦 🛅 🚗

34 cours Michelet (on the ring road, exit La Défense 4) ✉ *92060 Puteaux*
– **ⓜ** *Esplanade de la Défense* – *𝒞 01 47 76 44 43*
– *www.sofitel-paris-ladefense.com*
151 rm – **†**180/435 € **††**180/435 € – 🛏 27 €
• Luxury • Chain • Personalised •

This business hotel not far from the CNIT and Grande Arche blends in perfectly with the high-rise buildings of the Défense district. Spacious, well-equipped guestrooms, as well as a restaurant (Mediterranean cuisine) and a small fitness suite.

PARIS AIRPORT ROISSY

At Roissypole

Hilton 🛖 🛗 🖥 点 🎦 🛅 🚗

Roissypôle – *𝒞 01 49 19 77 77* – *www.hiltonhotels.com*
392 rm – **†**179/809 € **††**179/809 € – 🛏 25 €
• Chain • Business • Personalised •

There reigns a certain excess in this top-class hotel, which is a veritable modern town within the airport perimeter. It has a huge lobby with a vertiginous glass roof, particularly spacious guestrooms, and many amenities including restaurants, a swimming pool, meeting rooms etc.

Pullman Airport 🛖 🛗 🧖 🖥 点 🎦 🛅 🚗

3 bis r. de la Haye – *𝒞 01 70 03 11 63* – *www.pullmanhotels.com*
294 rm – **†**169/450 € **††**169/450 € – 🛏 26 € – 11 suites
• Business • Contemporary • Design •

A modern and contemporary complex, which is the perfect addition to the hotels on offer around the airport. The guestrooms are elegant and well-appointed with wifi, safe, iron, flat screen TV etc. On the lower floors, there is a sauna, a hammam and a large fitness centre.

LYONS
LYON

matteo69/iStock

Lyons is a city that needs a second look, because the first one may be to its disadvantage: from the outlying autoroute, drivers get a vision of the petrochemical industry. But strip away that industrial façade and look what lies within: the gastronomic epicentre of France; a wonderfully characterful old town of medieval and Renaissance buildings with a World Heritage Site stamp of approval; and the peaceful flow of two mighty rivers. Lyons largely came of age in the 16C thanks to its silk industry; many of the city's finest buildings were erected by Italian merchants who flocked here at the time. What they left behind was the largest Renaissance quarter in France, with glorious architecture and an imposing cathedral.

Nowadays it's an energised city whose modern industries give it a 21C feel but that hasn't pervaded the three-hour lunch ethos of the older quarters. The rivers Saône and Rhône provide the liquid heart of the city. Modern Lyons in the shape of the new Villeurbanne and La Part Dieu districts are to the east of the Rhône. The medieval sector, the old town, is west of the Saône. Between the two rivers is a peninsula, the Presqu'ile, which is indeed almost an island. This area is renowned for its red-roofed 16C and 17C houses. Just north of here on a hill is the old silk-weavers' district, La Croix-Rousse.

EATING OUT

Lyons is a great place for food. In the old town virtually every square metre is occupied by a restaurant but if you want a real encounter with the city, step inside a Lyonnais bouchon. These provide the true gastronomic heartbeat of the city - authentic little establishments where the cuisine revolves around the sort of thing the silk workers ate all those years ago: tripe, pigs' trotters, calf's head; fish lovers go for quenelles. For the most atmospheric example of the bouchon, try one in a tunnel-like recess inside a medieval building in the old town. Lyons also has plenty of restaurants serving dishes from every region in France and is a city that loves its wine: it's said that Lyons is kept afloat on three rivers: the Saône, the Rhône and the Beaujolais. Furthermore, the locals still enthusiastically embrace the true concept of lunch and so, unlike in many cities, you can enjoy a midday meal that continues for quite a few hours. With the reputation the city has for its restaurants, it's usually advisable to book ahead.

FRANCE - LYONS

❀ **Les Loges** – Hôtel Cour des Loges ✗✗✗ 🆊

6 r. du Bœuf ✉ *69005 –* Ⓜ *Vieux Lyon –* ☏ *04 72 77 44 44* Plan: **E2**
– www.courdesloges.com – Closed August and lunch except Sunday
Menu 105/135 € – Carte 90/175 € – *(booking advisable)*
• Modern cuisine • Romantic • Elegant •

Time seems to have stood still in this enchanting and romantic setting. Find a Florentine courtyard ringed by three floors of galleries and crowned by a contemporary glass ceiling. Savour the refined and inventive cuisine with flickering candlelight adding a final touch.

→ Escalope de foie gras de canard et racines confites dans une orange lutée. Pigeonneau, pain croustillant de champignons et fruit épicé. Grands crus de cacao, parfums de sous-bois.

❀ **Les Terrasses de Lyon** – Hôtel Villa Florentine ✗✗✗ 🏵 ≤ ☂

25 montée St-Barthélémy ✉ *69005 –* Ⓜ *Fourvière* ♿ 🆊 🅿
– ☏ *04 72 56 56 02 – www.villaflorentine.com – Closed* Plan: **E2**
Sunday and Monday
Menu 49 € *(weekday lunch)*, 89/115 € – Carte 105/130 €
• Classic cuisine • Elegant • Luxury •

In the heights of Fourvière; an elegant restaurant with a splendid view of the city. Classical cooking which places the emphasis on quality regional produce.
→ Foie gras de canard, muesli aux framboises et au green masala. Médaillons de homard rôtis, cappuccino de cocos de Paimpol et coppa. Soufflé chaud au chocolat kalapaia et crème glacée à la fève tonka.

❀ **Têtedoie** (Christian Têtedoie) ✗✗✗ 🏵 ≤ ♿ 🆊 ⇔ 🍸 🅿

4 r. Professeur-Pierre-Marion (montée du Chemin-Neuf) Plan: **E2**
✉ *69005 –* Ⓜ *Minimes –* ☏ *04 78 29 40 10 – www.tetedoie.com*
Menu 45 € *(weekday lunch)*, 68/140 € – Carte 84/110 €
• Modern cuisine • Design • Chic •

Perched on Fourvière hill, this restaurant, with its ultra-contemporary design, is a vantage point over the city. Christian Têtedoie applies his talent to exploring French tradition. His signature dish, casseroled lobster and calf's head cromesquis, is quite simply exquisite. At La Terrasse de l'Antiquaille, the Mediterranean has the place of honour.
→ Grenouilles, panure légère à l'ail, asperges vertes, citron caviar et sarriette. Homard bleu rôti en cocotte, chou-rave et tête de veau braisée. Soufflé à la faisselle, crème glacée à l'huile d'olive noire, rhubarbe et hibiscus.

❀ **Au 14 Février** (Tsuyoshi Arai) ✗✗ 🆊

36 r. du Bœuf – Ⓜ *Vieux Lyon –* ☏ *04 78 92 91 39* Plan: **E2**
– www.au14fevrier.com – Closed 3 weeks in August, 2 weeks in January,
Sunday, Monday and lunch except Saturday
Menu 92 € – *(booking advisable) (tasting menu only)*
• Creative • Elegant • Cosy •

The '14 février' has moved to Rue du Bœuf in the heart of historic Lyon. Talented, imaginative chef, Tsuyoshi Arai, continues to exalt outstanding produce (young pigeon from the Masse house, marbled Wagyu beef) with his hallmark blend of textures and flavours. The restaurant's delightful staff are as gracious and welcoming as ever.
→ Menu surprise.

❀ **Jérémy Galvan** ✗ 🆊

29 r. du Bœuf ✉ *69005 –* Ⓜ *Vieux-Lyon* Plan: **E2**
– ☏ *04 72 40 91 47 – www.jeremygalvanrestaurant.com – Closed 1 week*
in April, 3 weeks in August, 1 week Christmas Holidays, Wednesday lunch,
Saturday lunch, Sunday and Monday
Menu 33 € *(lunch)*, 65/85 € – Carte 70/90 €
• Creative • Cosy • Contemporary décor •

Cuisine based on instinct is what is promised here, with menus labelled "Interlude", "Let go" and "Perfume" setting the tone for the dishes. These are original, creative and playful; deviating from well-trodden paths but always respecting the seasons and nature.
→ Cuisine du marché.

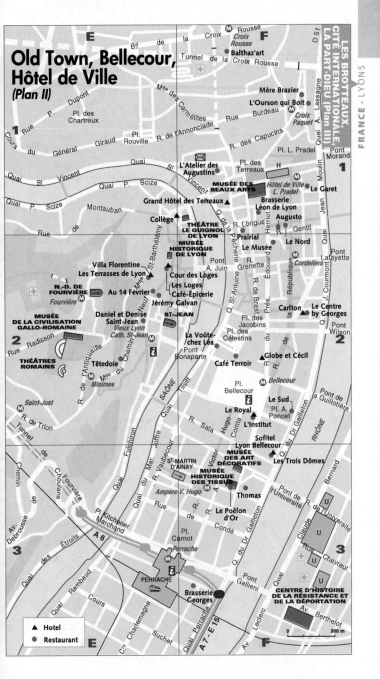

Old Town, Bellecour,
Hôtel de Ville
(Plan II)

▲ Hotel
● Restaurant

0   300 m

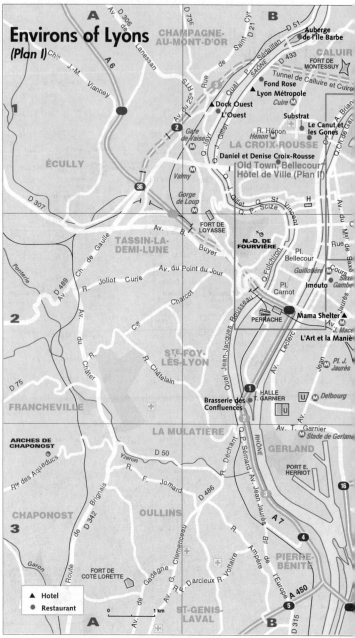

Environs of Lyons
(Plan I)

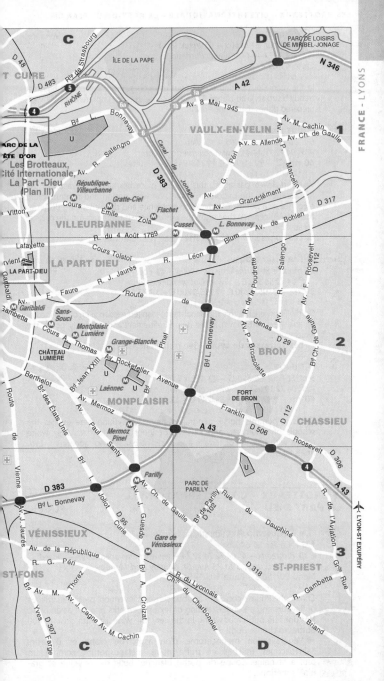

Café-Épicerie – Hôtel Cour des Loges ⚕ 🛜 AC

2 r. du Bœuf ⊠ 69005 – Ⓜ *Vieux Lyon* — Plan: **E2**
– ☎ 04 72 77 44 44 – www.courdesloges.com
Carte 41/62 €
• Modern cuisine • Trendy • Friendly •

In the marvellous setting of the Cour des Loges, this Café-Épicerie boasts a trendy bistro-style ambience. The locals come to enjoy unpretentious yet well-prepared dishes that change daily.

Cour des Loges 🦢 ʃₓ 🌀 AC ʂΔ 🅿

6 r. du Bœuf ⊠ 69005 – Ⓜ *Vieux Lyon* — Plan: **E2**
– ☎ 04 72 77 44 44 – www.courdesloges.com
60 rm 🍽 – †224/924 € ††248/948 € – 4 suites
• Luxury • Historic • Personalised •

Vaults, galleries, passages... this magical place has all the character of the Renaissance in the middle of Vieux-Lyon with design and contemporary elegance as a bonus. Trendy bistro ambience and daily changing dishes at the Café-Épicerie. At the Loges, the atmosphere is romantic and the cuisine, creative.

❀ **Les Loges** • ⚕ **Café-Épicerie** – See restaurant listing

Villa Florentine 🦢 ≤ 🏠 ʃₓ 🌀 🛁 🕭 AC ʂΔ 🚗

25 montée St-Barthélémy ⊠ 69005 – Ⓜ *Fourvière* — Plan: **E2**
– ☎ 04 72 56 56 56 – www.villaflorentine.com
30 rm – †195/1200 € ††195/1200 € – 🍽 25 €
• Historic • Luxury • Romantic •

On the Fourvière hill, this 18C Renaissance-inspired residence enjoys an incomparable view of the town. In the rooms, refinement and classic styling are the watchwords.

❀ **Les Terrasses de Lyon** – See restaurant listing

Collège 🕭 AC ʂΔ 🚗

5 pl. St-Paul ⊠ 69005 – Ⓜ *Vieux Lyon* — Plan: **E-F1**
– ☎ 04 72 10 05 05 – www.college-hotel.com
40 rm – †89/249 € ††89/249 € – 🍽 16 €
• Business • Townhouse • Personalised •

Desks, a pommel horse, geography maps: everything here evokes the schools of yesteryear, and all in a designer style. Immaculately white rooms with balcony or terrace and pleasant bar serving 'gôneries' – Lyonnais tapas!

LES BROTTEAUX – CITÉ INTERNATIONALE – LA PART-DIEU

PLAN III

❀❀ Le Neuvième Art (Christophe Roure) XxX 🏵 🕭 AC

173 r. Cuvier ⊠ 69006 — Plan: **H2**
– Ⓜ *Brotteaux* – ☎ 04 72 74 12 74 – www.leneuviemeart.com – Closed 11 to 26 February, 5 to 28 August, Sunday and Monday
Menu 90/150 € – Carte 105/145 €
• Creative • Design • Contemporary décor •

Christophe Roure's cooking - a subtle sense of invention, precise marriages of flavours and an understanding of textures - marks him out as an artist. Nor does he put a foot wrong in the very fine wine list, with close to 400 bottles to choose from!

➜ Végétalisation monochrome d'un aspic de crabe et d'oursin. Saint-Jacques fraîches et truffe noire melanosporum comme un œuf à la neige. Soupe de pêche blanche, bulle de verveine et granité sphérique.

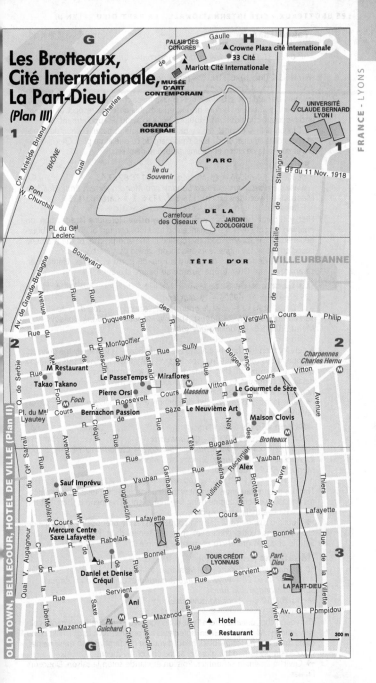

Les Brotteaux,
Cité Internationale,
La Part-Dieu
(Plan III)

PALAIS DES CONGRÈS
Gaulle

▲ Crowne Plaza cité internationale
● 33 Cité
Mariott Cité Internationale

MUSÉE D'ART CONTEMPORAIN

de

Charles

RHÔNE

Quai

GRANDE ROSERAIE

UNIVERSITÉ CLAUDE BERNARD LYON I

Bd du 11 Nov. 1918

Stalingrad

de

Île du Souvenir

PARC

Cⁱˢ Aristide Briand

Pont W. Churchill

Pl. du Gᵉˡ Leclerc

Carrefour des Oiseaux

DE LA JARDIN ZOOLOGIQUE

la Bataille

de

TÊTE   D'OR   VILLEURBANNE

Boulevard

Av. de Grande-Bretagne

Rue

Rue

des

Duquesne

Rue

R.

Av.

Bd A. France

Verguin

Cours   A.   Philip

Rue du

Rue

de Serbie

Mᵃˡ

Rue

Foch

M Restaurant

Takao Takano

Foch

Pl. du Mᵃˡ Lyautey

Duguesclin

Sully

R. Duguesclin
Montgolfier

Garibaldi

Rue

Sully

Le PasseTemps   Miraflores

Pierre Orsi

Roosevelt

F.

Bernachon Passion

de

Cours

Cours   Masséna

Sèze

Vitton

Belges

Bd

Cours   Vitton

Charpennes
Charles Hernu

Ⓜ

Le Gourmet de Sèze

Le Neuvième Art

Ney

Bd

des

Maison Clovis

Brotteaux

Avenue

R. Créqui

Rue

Avenue

Bugeaud

Masséna

Juliette

R.

Tête

d'Or

Récamier

Brotteaux

Vauban

Alex

Quai du Gᵉˡ Sarrail

Rue

Rue

Sauf Imprévu

Molière

Rue

Duguesclin

Vauban

Garibaldi

Ney

Bd J. Favre

Thiers

Lafayette

Cours

Mᵃˡ

Mercure Centre
Saxe Lafayette

R.

de

Rabelais

Lafayette

Cours

de

Bonnel

Rue   de   la   Villette

Quai V. Augagneur

Daniel et Denise
Créqui

Bonnel

Rue

TOUR CRÉDIT LYONNAIS Ⓜ

Part-Dieu

Ⓜ

R.

de

Servient

Rue

Servient

LA PART-DIEU

Ani

Pl. Guichard

R. Duguesclin

Créqui

Mazenod

Garibaldi

Av. Gᵉˡ Pompidou

Vivier Merle

Quai de la

Rue

Liberté

R.

Saxe

Mazenod

▲ Hotel
● Restaurant

0   300 m

G   H

FRANCE - LYONS

Takao Takano ❀❀ XX & AC

33 r. Malesherbes ✉ *69006 –* Ⓜ *Foch* Plan: **G2**
*– ℰ 04 82 31 43 39 – www.takaotakano.com – Closed 3 weeks in August,
Saturday and Sunday*
Menu 35 € (lunch), 65/100 € *– (booking advisable)*
• Creative • Design • Elegant •

It would be hard not to be won over by Japanese chef Takao Takano's sense of precision, his humility before his ingredients, his absolute respect of flavours and his subtle compositions. Exquisite. Book to avoid disappointment.
➔ Langoustines bretonnes saisies, œuf fermier fumé et battu. Cochon du Cantal et cèpes cuits au charbon de bois, condiment de l'oreille et du pied. Chocolat noir cru et cuit, pâte de citron et caramel au beurre demi-sel..

Pierre Orsi ❀ XXXX 🕮 🖙 & AC ✿ 🗷

3 pl. Kléber ✉ *69006 –* Ⓜ *Masséna – ℰ 04 78 89 57 68* Plan: **G2**
– www.pierreorsi.com – Closed Sunday and Monday except Bank Holidays
Menu 60 € (weekday lunch), 115 € 🍷/135 € 🍷 – Carte 85/175 €
• Classic cuisine • Bourgeois • Romantic •

First, you come face to face with the lovely ochre Florentine façade, then, on entering, you discover the elegance and luxurious comfort of an opulent bourgeois house. As for the food: the cuisine is fine and precise, of the moment, based on top-notch ingredients and accompanied by superb wines.
➔ Ravioles de foie gras de canard au jus de porto et truffes. Homard en carapace "Pierre Orsi". Crêpe Suzette au beurre d'orange.

Le Gourmet de Sèze ❀ (Bernard Mariller) XXX & AC ✿

125 r. de Sèze ✉ *69006 –* Ⓜ *Masséna* Plan: **H2**
*– ℰ 04 78 24 23 42 – www.le-gourmet-de-seze.com – Closed 15 to
18 February, 29 July-24 August, Sunday, Monday and Bank Holidays*
Menu 58/125 € *– (booking advisable)*
• Classic cuisine • Elegant • Cosy •

A new location – a short hop along the rue de Sèze – is thankfully the only real change at this restaurant! In a spacious but cosy interior, diners can still enjoy dishes that show off chef Bernard Mariller's inventiveness and attention to detail. He continues to pay a fitting tribute to his mentors, who include Joël Robuchon and Philippe Chavent.
➔ Saint-Jacques d'Erquy. Pied de cochon à la lyonnaise retravaillé. Citron revisité.

Maison Clovis ❀ (Clovis Khoury) X AC

19 bd Brotteaux ✉ *69006 –* Ⓜ *Brotteaux* Plan: **H2**
*– ℰ 04 72 74 44 61 – www.maisonclovis.com – Closed 6 to 14 May, 5 to
27 August, 1 to 7 January, Sunday and Monday*
Menu 59/95 € – Carte 60/110 €
• Modern cuisine • Contemporary décor • Trendy •

This designer restaurant is elegant without being uptight. Clovis Khoury prepares delicious seasonal cuisine using fine ingredients. The menu is short, but the choice is nevertheless impossible.
➔ Oursin d'Islande servi dans sa coque, cuisses de grenouilles et raviole de champignons. Lotte confite et marinée servie dans l'esprit d'un tajine. Soufflé chocolat grand cru et menthe poivrée.

Miraflores ❀ (Carlos Camino) X

60 r. Garibaldi ✉ *69006 –* Ⓜ *Massena* Plan: **G2**
*– ℰ 04 37 43 61 26 – www.restaurant-miraflores.com – Closed August,
Sunday, Monday and lunch*
Menu 70/110 € *– (booking advisable)*
• Peruvian • Intimate • Elegant •

The young chef, originally from Peru, takes you on a joyful, French-Peruvian culinary journey. All of the Peruvian ingredients are organic, such as *aji* (chilli), *camu camu* (fruit) and *huacatay* (black mint). If you are not familiar with these names, you can simply turn to the glossary at the end of the menu.
➔ Ceviche liménien saisonnier. Poisson et viande selon la saison. Douceurs finales.

FRANCE - LYONS

❀ **Le Passe Temps** (Younghoon Lee) 🕸 ☒ 𝔸𝔺
52 r. Tronchet ⊠ 69006 – Ⓜ *Masséna* Plan: **G2**
*– 𝒞 04 72 82 90 14 – www.lepassetemps-restaurant.com – Closed 3 weeks
in August, Sunday, Monday and Bank Holidays*
Menu 33 € (weekday lunch), 60/85 € *– (booking advisable)*
• Creative • Minimalist • Design •
Mr Lee, originally from Seoul, has brought a little of his native country to the
Brotteaux neighbourhood. With a sharp sense of aestheticism and flavours, he
reinterprets French cuisine by adding Korean touches. His speciality, foie gras
with root and other vegetables in a soya broth, is quite simply delicious!
➔ Cuisine du marché.

😊 **Ani** ☒ 𝔸𝔺
199 r. de Créqui ⊠ 69003 – Ⓜ *Place Guichard* Plan: **G3**
– 𝒞 09 67 23 51 33 – Closed Sunday and Monday
Menu 32 € – Carte 83/106 € *– (booking advisable)*
• Creative • Trendy • Fashionable •
Located between La Part-Dieu and the banks of the Rhône, the third Lyon restaurant to be opened by chef-patron Gaby Didonna is bound to win you over:
open kitchen, with the option of eating at the bar, industrial loft interior and
creative, well-made and flavoursome dishes that lay the emphasis squarely on
seafood. A success story.

😊 **M Restaurant** ☒ 𝒓 𝔸𝔺
47 av. Foch ⊠ 69006 – Ⓜ *Foch – 𝒞 04 78 89 55 19* Plan: **G2**
*– www.mrestaurant.fr – Closed 1 week in February, 3 weeks in August,
Saturday and Sunday*
Menu 27/37 € – Carte 43/51 €
• Market cuisine • Trendy • Friendly •
The charming and fashionable M serves delicious gourmet cuisine which is full
of flavour. The decor is slightly psychedelic.

😊 **Sauf Imprévu** ☒ ✧
40 r. Pierre-Corneille ⊠ 69006 – Ⓜ *Foch* Plan: **G3**
*– 𝒞 04 78 52 16 35 – Closed 3 weeks in August,
Saturday, Sunday and dinner except Thursday*
Menu 26 € – Carte approx. 34 €
• Traditional cuisine • Simple • Family •
"Marguerite" terrine in homage to his great-grandmother, coco de Paimpol
beans with shellfish, grilled prime rib of beef with homemade chips... With his
focus firmly on tradition, Félix Gagnaire proposes delicious and copious dishes.
Everything is fresh, homemade and spot on, and the prices are also fair!

😊 **33 Cité** ☒ 𝟾𝟾 𝒓 ⅙ 𝔸𝔺 ✧
33 quai Charles-de-Gaulle ⊠ 69006 – 𝒞 04 37 45 45 45 Plan: **H1**
– www.33cite.com – Closed 3 weeks in August
Menu 27 € – Carte 33/58 €
• Traditional cuisine • Brasserie • Contemporary décor •
Three talented chefs – Mathieu Viannay (Meilleur Ouvrier de France), Christophe
Marguin and Frédéric Berthod (alumnus of Bocuse) – joined forces to create this
chic brasserie. It opens onto the Tête-d'Or Park. On the menu find great brasserie specialities.

🍴 **Bernachon Passion** ☒ 𝔸𝔺
42 cours Franklin-Roosevelt ⊠ 69006 – Ⓜ *Foch* Plan: **G2**
*– 𝒞 04 78 52 23 65 – www.bernachon.com – Closed 23 July-22 August,
Sunday, Monday, Bank Holidays and dinner*
Menu 30 € – Carte 36/54 € *– (booking advisable)*
• Traditional cuisine • Simple • Intimate •
The famous Lyon-based chocolatier of Bernachon needs no introduction. The
son of the founder married the eldest daughter of Paul Bocuse and it is the
grandchildren of the great chef who are at the reins here! On the menu find
good traditional recipes (such as pike quenelles and pâté en croûte) and pastries... made by Bernachon, of course.

Marriott Cité Internationale
70 quai Charles-de-Gaulle ⊠ *69006*   Plan: **H1**
– ℰ 04 78 17 50 50 – www.marriottlyon.com
199 rm – †90/600 € ††90/600 € – ⊊ 24 € – 5 suites
• Chain • Business • Contemporary •

Between the Rhône and the Tête d'Or park, this impressive red-brick and glass structure now bears the Marriott hallmark. The rooms are just as well equipped, spacious and contemporary in style. Guests also appreciate the large meeting rooms and fitness facilities.

Crowne Plaza Cité Internationale
22 quai Charles-de-Gaulle ⊠ *69006*   Plan: **H1**
– ℰ 04 78 17 86 86 – www.crownplaza.com/lyonciteintl
156 rm – †79/440 € ††79/440 € – ⊊ 22 € – 7 suites
• Chain • Business • Contemporary •

Recently constructed building designed by Renzo Piano. It has bright rooms overlooking the Tête-d'Or park or the Rhône. Traditional French cuisine and regional ingredients in the restaurant, as well as a pleasant terrace.

Mercure Centre Saxe Lafayette
29 r. Bonnel ⊠ *69003*   Plan: **G3**
– Ⓜ Place Guichard – ℰ 04 72 61 90 90
– www.mercure-lyon-saxe-lafayette.com
156 rm – †115/300 € ††115/300 € – ⊊ 17 €
• Chain • Business • Contemporary •

This former garage, built in 1932, is conveniently located between the Gare de la Part-Dieu (railway station) neighbourhood and the quays of the Rhône. The guestrooms are spacious and elegant. There is a small indoor pool and fitness facilities in the basement.

TOWN CENTRE   PLAN II

✸✸ Mère Brazier (Mathieu Viannay)
12 r. Royale ⊠ *69001*   Plan: **F1**
– Ⓜ Hôtel de Ville
– ℰ 04 78 23 17 20 – www.lamerebrazier.fr
– Closed 10 to 18 February, 3 to 26 August, Saturday and Sunday
Menu 100/160 €
– Carte 140/180 €
• Modern cuisine • Elegant • Chic •

The guardian of Lyon cuisine, Eugénie Brazier (1895-1977) is without doubt looking down on Mathieu Viannay – winner of the Meilleur Ouvrier de France award – with pride. An emblematic restaurant where high-powered classics and creativity continue to be served.
➜ Artichaut et foie gras. Pain de brochet croustillant aux écrevisses. Soufflé au Grand-Marnier.

✸ Les Trois Dômes – Hôtel Sofitel Lyon Bellecour
20 quai Gailleton (8th floor) ⊠ *69002*   Plan: **F3**
– Ⓜ Bellecour
– ℰ 04 72 41 20 97 – www.les-3-domes.com
– Closed August, Sunday and Monday
Menu 47 € (lunch), 81/125 €
– Carte 100/180 €
• Modern cuisine • Contemporary décor • Minimalist •

On the top floor of the hotel; high-level cooking with the accent on delicious food and wine pairings. From a terrine of pot au feu with foie gras to leg of Limousin lamb, the classics are skillfully reworked. Magical views of the city from the elegant and contemporary dining room.
➜ Quenelles de brochet, sauce écrevisse et pousses d'épinard. Filet de bœuf Salers, foie gras chaud, artichauts violets et sauce au vin rouge. Macaron au chocolat nyangbo, glace au safran.

❀ **Prairial** (Gaëtan Gentil)   X AC

11 r. Chavanne ✉ *69001 –* Ⓜ *Cordeliers*   Plan: **F1**
– ☏ 04 78 27 86 93 – www.prairial-restaurant.com – Closed 6 to 12 March,
1 to 7 May, 28 August-17 September, Sunday and Monday
Menu 34 € (weekday lunch), 53/88 € – *(booking advisable)*
• Modern cuisine • Minimalist • Contemporary décor •

Gaëtan Gentil took over this restaurant in the city's Presqu'île district in the
spring of 2015. In this pleasant setting, complete with a vertical garden, he creates his *"gastronomy décomplexée"*: contemporary cuisine, resolutely creative, with vegetables at its core.
➜ Cuisine du marché.

🙂 **Augusto**   X 🛋 AC

6 r. Neuve ✉ *69002 –* Ⓜ *Cordelier – ☏ 04 72 19 44 29*   Plan: **F1**
– augusto-restaurant-lyon.fr – Closed 3 weeks in August, Sunday and
Monday
Menu 19 € (lunch), 26/29 € – Carte dinner 33/46 € – *(booking advisable)*
• Italian • Cosy •

Difficult not to rave about the work of Augusto, the very committed young Brazilian chef at the helm of this Italian restaurant. Fine ingredients, deployed with
great precision, dishes brimming with flavour and colour – just as it should be.
The place is delightful down to the last detail, not to mention the charming service.

🙂 **Balthaz'art**   X ⇔

7 r. des Pierres-Plantées ✉ *69001 –* Ⓜ *Croix-Rousse*   Plan: **F1**
– ☏ 04 72 07 08 88 – www.restaurantbalthazart.com – Closed 2 weeks in
August, 24 December-1 January, Tuesday lunch, Wednesday lunch, Sunday
and Monday
Menu 17 € (weekday lunch), 29/34 € – Carte 33/46 €
• Modern cuisine • Bistro • Friendly •

You have to earn your meal at this restaurant located near the top of La Croix-
Rousse! Housed in the former French Communist Party HQ, red dominates the
interior, and Picasso and Modigliani prints hang on the walls. The imagination
and beauty found in the decoration are also present in the dishes, which are
paired with well-chosen wines.

🙂 **L'Ourson qui Boit**   X AC

23 r. Royale ✉ *69001 –* Ⓜ *Croix-Paquet*   Plan: **F1**
– ☏ 04 78 27 23 37 – Closed 4 weeks in July-August,
2 weeks in December, Saturday dinner, Wednesday, Sunday and Bank
Holidays
Menu 32 €
• Modern cuisine • Friendly • Bistro •

The Japanese chef at this contemporary bistro has worked in some of the finest
restaurants. His cuisine blends the subtle flavours of yuzu and ginger with traditional French ingredients – all at reasonable prices. Not to be missed!

🍽️ **Brasserie Léon de Lyon**   XX 🍴 🛋 & AC ⇔

1 r. Pleney (corner of r. du Plâtre) ✉ *69001*   Plan: **F1**
– Ⓜ *Hôtel de Ville – ☏ 04 72 10 11 12 – www.leondelyon.com*
Menu 29 € – Carte 43/55 €
• Traditional cuisine • Elegant • Brasserie •

This Lyon institution, founded in 1904, has kept its affluent setting and its convivial atmosphere. Excellent ingredients combine to produce hearty gourmet
dishes.

🍽️ **Brasserie Georges**   XX 🛋 & ⇔

30 cours de Verdun ✉ *69002 –* Ⓜ *Perrache*   Plan: **F3**
– ☏ 04 72 56 54 54 – www.brasseriegeorges.com
Menu 23/28 € – Carte 30/51 €
• Traditional cuisine • Brasserie • Vintage •

'Good beer and good cheer since 1836' in the jealously guarded Art Deco setting of this brasserie that is a veritable institution. Lively atmosphere.

FRANCE - LYONS

⏐◯ **L'Institut** – Hôtel Le Royal   X & AC ⇔
*20 pl. Bellecour ⊠ 69002 – **M** Bellecour*   Plan: **F2**
– 𝒞 04 78 37 23 02 – www.institutpaulbocuse.com – Closed 6 to
28 August, 24 December-8 January, Sunday and Monday
Carte approx. 51 € – *(booking advisable)*
• Modern cuisine • Elegant • Contemporary décor •
On Place Bellecour, the training restaurant of the Paul Bocuse Institute feels
nothing like a school! In a contemporary decor designed by Pierre-Yves
Rochon, with open kitchens giving onto the restaurant, the students deliver
a high standard of service. The dishes are extremely well made and deserve
a high mark.

⏐◯ **L'Atelier des Augustins**   X AC
*11 r. des Augustins ⊠ 69001 – **M** Hôtel de Ville*   Plan: **F1**
– 𝒞 04 72 00 88 01 – www.latelierdesaugustins.com – Closed 1 week in
May, 2 weeks in August, 1 week Christmas Holidays, Saturday lunch,
Sunday and Monday
Menu 41 € (dinner) – Carte 42/61 €
• Modern cuisine • Contemporary décor • Minimalist •
After stints in some fine establishments, the former chef of the embassies of
France in London and Bamako, Nicolas Guilloton, left the world of diplomatic
missions to open this refined Atelier. Here food remains an important matter.
He creates lovely recipes that are full of colour and flavour, and are nicely
modern!

⏐◯ **Café Terroir**   X 𝕬 🍴 AC
*14 r. d'Amboise ⊠ 69002 – **M** Bellecour*   Plan: **F2**
– 𝒞 09 53 36 08 11 – www.cafeterroir.fr – Closed Sunday except dinner
from September-April and Monday
Menu 21 € (weekday lunch) – Carte 29/40 €
• Country • Friendly • Bistro •
The philosophy of the two young owners of the Café Terroir, near
the Célestins Theatre, is to source the best of the region's produce
to create mouthwatering dishes. The house classics include shepherd's pie with farm reared Ain poultry, hot pistachio sausages,
and Lyonnaise cream cheese dip.

⏐◯ **Le Centre by Georges**   X 𝕬 🍴 & AC ⇔
*14 r. Grolée ⊠ 69002 – **M** Cordeliers – 𝒞 04 72 04 44 44*   Plan: **F2**
– www.lespritblanc.com
Menu 24 € (weekday lunch)/32 € – Carte 40/75 €
• Meats and grills • Brasserie • Contemporary décor •
Georges Blanc, the famous chef from the restaurant in Vonnas, is the master-
mind behind this contemporary brasserie. It is dedicated to meat – and fine
meats at that. Find Charolais, Wagyu beef, Aveyron lamb and Bresse chicken
served with a large choice of accompaniments and sauces. Calling all carnivores!

⏐◯ **Le Nord**   X & AC ⇔
*18 r. Neuve ⊠ 69002 – **M** Hôtel de Ville*   Plan: **F1**
– 𝒞 04 72 10 69 69 – www.nordsudbrasseries.com
Menu 27 € (weekdays)/33 € – Carte 36/62 €
• Traditional cuisine • Brasserie • Historic •
The smallest of the Bocuse brasseries, with a veranda giving onto the street and
private lounges on the first floor. The kitchen team are well trained: the use of
fresh ingredients is a dogma, and tradition goes hand in hand with generosity
and flavour. *Salade lyonnaise, saucisson chaud pistaché en brioche* (brioche sausage roll), Burgundy snails etc: a reliable option.

FRANCE - LYONS

○↑○ **Le Sud**   ✗ ⌂ ᗦ ᴀᴄ ⇆
11 pl. Antonin-Poncet ⊠ 69002 – ⓜ Bellecour   Plan: **F2**
– ℰ 04 72 77 80 00 – www.brasseries-bocuse.com
Menu 27 € (weekday lunch) – Carte 35/60 €
• Mediterranean cuisine • Brasserie • Mediterranean décor •
There is an elegant Greek feel to the white and blue decor of this Bocuse brasserie situated a hop, skip and a jump from Place Bellecour. The name is no coinci-
dence: here, it's the South – chicken pastilla with cinnamon and coriander;
shank of lamb with couscous; fresh cod with aioli – and even more so in summer, on the terrace!

○↑○ **Thomas**   ✗ ⌂ ᴀᴄ
6 r. Laurencin ⊠ 69002 – ⓜ Bellecour   Plan: **F3**
– ℰ 04 72 56 04 76 – www.restaurant-thomas.com
– Closed 24 December-2 January, Saturday and Sunday
Menu 22 € (lunch), 36/47 €
• Traditional cuisine • Bistro • Friendly •
This cosy, modern bistro is under the auspices of a young chef who communi-
cates his passion for delicious, refined cuisine (on a monthly changing menu).
Game is a feature, as is one of the house classic desserts, pain perdu (French
toast).

○↑○ **La Voûte - Chez Léa**   ✗ ᴀᴄ
11 pl. Antonin-Gourju ⊠ 69002 – ⓜ Bellecour   Plan: **F2**
– ℰ 04 78 42 01 33 – www.lavoutechezlea.com
– Closed 2 weeks in August and Sunday
Menu 21 € (weekday lunch)/30 € – Carte 37/61 €
• Lyonnaise • Traditional décor • Friendly •
One of the oldest restaurants in Lyon: in a welcoming atmosphere, tradition
carries on with verve. A fine menu with tasty regional dishes and game in
autumn.

BOUCHONS *Regional wine tasting and local cuisine in a typical
Lyonnaise atmosphere*

☺ **Daniel et Denise Croix-Rousse**   ✗ ⌂ ᴀᴄ
8 r. de Cuire ⊠ 69004 – ⓜ Croix-Rousse   Plan: **F1**
– ℰ 04 78 28 27 44 – www.daniel-et-denise.fr
– Closed Sunday and Monday
Menu 33/50 € ☗ – Carte 38/51 €
• Lyonnaise • Lyonnaise bistro • Bistro •
This Daniel and Denise (the third in the story, after Rue de Créqui and the St
Jean district) enjoys the same success as its elder sisters. It must be said that
Joseph Viola is unparalleled in the art of fresh, tasty Lyonnaise classics. There is
also a delightful vintage decor.

☺ **Daniel et Denise Saint-Jean**   ✗ ᴀᴄ ⇆
32 r. Tramassac ⊠ 69005 – ⓜ Vieux Lyon   Plan: **E2**
– ℰ 04 78 42 24 62 – www.daniel-et-denise.fr
– Closed 30 December-4 January, Sunday and Monday
Menu 33/50 € ☗ – Carte 35/54 €
• Lyonnaise • Lyonnaise bistro • Friendly •
A stone's throw from Cathédrale St-Jean, this bouchon in the picturesque Old
Town is run by chef Joseph Viola (Meilleur Ouvrier de France). Like the two
other branches (Créqui and the Croix-Rousse), the menu offers Lyonnaise cui-
sine that is hearty and tasty.

Daniel et Denise Créqui X 🍴 AK

156 r. de Créqui ⊠ 69003 – **Ⓜ** *Place Guichard* Plan: **G3**
– ℰ 04 78 60 66 53 – www.daniel-et-denise.fr – Closed Saturday and Sunday
Menu 33/50 € 🍷 – Carte 39/52 € – *(booking advisable)*
• Lyonnaise • Lyonnaise bistro • Friendly •

A dyed-in-the-wool 'bouchon', smooth with the patina of age, serving tasty, generous cuisine with excellent ingredients. Unsurprisingly, typical dishes take pride of place.

Le Garet X AK

7 r. du Garet ⊠ 69001 – **Ⓜ** *Hôtel de Ville* Plan: **F1**
– ℰ 04 78 28 16 94 – Closed 28 July-28 August, Saturday and Sunday
Menu 20 € (lunch)/28 € – Carte 25/43 € – *(booking advisable)*
• Lyonnaise • Lyonnaise bistro • Friendly •

This veritable institution is well known among aficionados of Lyonnais cuisine. Calf's head, tripe, dumplings and andouillette sausages are served in a convivial atmosphere and in a typical setting.

Le Musée X

2 r. des Forces ⊠ 69002 – **Ⓜ** *Cordeliers* Plan: **F2**
– ℰ 04 78 37 71 54 – Closed August, 24 December-2 January, Saturday dinner, Sunday and Monday
Menu 24 € (lunch)/29 € – Carte approx. 31 € – *(booking advisable)*
• Lyonnaise • Lyonnaise bistro • Friendly •

A sincere and authentic bouchon with a decor of checked tablecloths, closely packed tables and a buzzing atmosphere. In the kitchen, the young chef creates the classics with real know-how, such as Lyonnaise pork, foie de veau persillé (calf's liver), trotters and brawn salad.

Le Poêlon d'or X AK ⇔

29 r. des Remparts-d'Ainay ⊠ 69002 – **Ⓜ** *Ampère* Plan: **F3**
– ℰ 04 78 37 65 60 – www.lepoelondor-restaurant.fr – Closed 4 to 26 August, Saturday and Sunday
Menu 20 € (lunch), 27/34 € – Carte 27/50 € – *(booking advisable)*
• Lyonnaise • Bistro • Friendly •

It's hard to say whether or not the chef does actually use a golden saucepan (poêlon d'or), but he must have a secret weapon – he revisits Lyon's terroir so well and creates food that is as tasty as it is perfectly put together - from the gâteau de foie de volaille (chicken liver) with tomato coulis, to the pike quenelle gratin with béchamel sauce. A must!

Sofitel Lyon Bellecour ☆ ≤ ⅃ゟ �🍴 ⅃ AK ⚙ 🚗

20 quai Gailleton ⊠ 69002 – **Ⓜ** *Bellecour* Plan: **F3**
– ℰ 04 72 41 20 20 – www.sofitel.com
135 rm – ♥205/1200 € ♥♥205/1200 € – 🖃 26 € – 29 suites
• Chain • Luxury • Contemporary •

A luxurious and elegant Sofitel in a contemporary building with futuristic facilities. Bill Clinton stayed in the presidential suite here. There are two options for dinner: the beautiful Trois Dômes restaurant (see restaurants) or Le Silk restaurant (an international menu in a sleek setting).
❀ **Les Trois Dômes** – See restaurant listing

Carlton ゟ ⅃ AK ⚙

4 r. Jussieu ⊠ 69002 – **Ⓜ** *Cordeliers – ℰ 04 78 42 56 51* Plan: **F2**
– www.mgallery.com
80 rm – ♥155/530 € ♥♥155/530 € – 🖃 25 €
• Business • Chain • Elegant •

This illustrious establishment was completely refurbished in 2013. It transports guests back in time to a 1930s ambience with an interior in predominantly red tones. The guestrooms are spacious and well appointed, and the period lift is magnificent. A marriage of comfort and charm.

Le Royal
≤ 🏿 🅰🅺 🏩 🚗

20 pl. Bellecour ✉ 69002 – **Ⓜ** *Bellecour*
– ℰ 04 78 37 57 31 – www.sofitel.com
Plan: **F2**

72 rm – ♦140/500 € ♦♦160/500 € – � 25 € – 5 suites
• Luxury • Historic • Elegant •

Established in 1912, Le Royal wins over hotel guests with its blend of comfort and refinement. A century on, the institution has lost none of its charm and style. Cornices, Toiles de Jouy fabrics, traditional old furniture… it is quite simply elegant.

⏉○ **L'Institut** – See restaurant listing

Globe et Cécil
🏿 🅰🅺 🏩

21 r. Gasparin ✉ 69002 – **Ⓜ** *Bellecour*
– ℰ 04 78 42 58 95 – www.globeetcecilhotel.com
Plan: **F2**

60 rm – ♦116/220 € ♦♦126/270 € – ⊒ 18 €
• Traditional • Personalised • Classic •

This hotel, dating back to the end of the 19C, is located a stone's throw from Place Bellecour. It has pretty and immaculately kept guestrooms (some have floorboards and fireplaces). The foyer and lounge offer first-rate amenities.

Grand Hôtel des Terreaux
🔲 🅰🅺

16 r. Lanterne ✉ 69001 – **Ⓜ** *Hôtel de Ville*
– ℰ 04 78 27 04 10 – www.hotel-lyon-grandhoteldesterreaux.fr
Plan: **F1**

53 rm – ♦95/175 € ♦♦115/275 € – ⊒ 17 €
• Traditional • Cosy • Personalised •

This 19C post house is conducive to relaxing in the centre of town. Find tastefully decorated rooms, a small indoor pool and attentive service.

AROUND THE CENTRE

❀ **Auberge de l'Île Barbe** (Jean-Christophe Ansanay-Alex)   XxX

pl. Notre-Dame (on Barbe Island) ✉ 69009   ❀ ⇄ 🍽 (dinner) 🅿
– ℰ 04 78 83 99 49 – www.aubergedelile.com – Closed   Plan: **B1**
6 to 21 August, 2 to 16 January, Sunday dinner, Tuesday lunch and Monday
Menu 98 € (lunch), 128/158 €
• Classic cuisine • Romantic • Elegant •

A country feel in the heart of the leafy Île Barbe, an island in the Saône. The walls date from 1601 and there is a softly intimate atmosphere. The refined cuisine has remarkable flavour associations and creative flights of fancy.
➜ Velouté de cèpe comme un cappuccino, vapeur de foie gras. Selle d'agneau servie comme au dîner de gala du patrimoine mondial de l'Unesco. Glace à la réglisse.

😊 **L'Art et la Manière**   X 🅰🅺 ⇄

102 Gde-Rue de la Guillotière ✉ 69007   Plan: **B-C2**
– **Ⓜ** *Saxe-Gambetta* – ℰ 04 37 27 05 83 – www.art-et-la-maniere.fr
– Closed 3 weeks in August, Saturday and Sunday
Menu 31 € – Carte 37/46 € – (booking advisable)
• Traditional cuisine • Bistro • Friendly •

A contemporary bistro that champions conviviality, seasonal cuisine and enticing, reasonably priced wines. It is also a great excuse for discovering the La Guillotière district. As it has a loyal local following, you are best advised to book ahead.

😊 **Le Canut et les Gones**   X 🏮

29 r. Belfort ✉ 69004 – **Ⓜ** *Croix-Rousse*   Plan: **B1**
– ℰ 04 78 29 17 23 – www.lecanutetlesgones.com
– Closed Sunday and Monday
Menu 21 € (weekday lunch)/32 €
• Modern cuisine • Bistro • Vintage •

A unique atmosphere, somewhere between bistro and secondhand shop – formica bar, wooden floorboards, vintage tapestry, collection of old clocks on the walls –, modern cuisine in tune with the seasons, a wine list boasting over 300 types... In a little-frequented area of La Croix-Rousse, this is definitely one to try out.

☺ Imouto   X AC

21 r. Pasteur ✉ 69007 – Ⓜ Guillotière   Plan: **B2**
– ℰ 04 72 76 99 53 – Closed Sunday and Monday
Menu 32 € – *(booking advisable)*
• Fusion • Design • Simple •

Originally from Vietnam, Gaby Didonna has opened Imouto ("little sister" in Japanese) in a working class district of Lyon. He is part of a team of two, along with Guy Kendell, his Australian second-in-command. The result is delicious fusion cuisine combining French tradition and Japanese influences. Tasty and always very impressive!

☺ Substrat   X ⅙ AC

7 r. Pailleron ✉ 69004 – Ⓜ Hénon – ℰ 04 78 29 14 93   Plan: **B1**
– www.substrat-restaurant.com – Closed 1 week in March, 3 weeks in August and Sunday
Menu 22 € (weekday lunch), 33/44 € – Carte approx. 40 € – *(booking advisable)*
• Modern cuisine • Bistro • Friendly •

This restaurant that feels like a cross between a country house and an artisan's workshop promises "produce of the harvest and wines for drinking". The promise is kept: wild garlic, cranberries, ceps and bilberries accompany tasty dishes bursting with nature, accompanied by good wines. A real treat!

🍽 Brasserie des Confluences   X ⅙ P

86 quai Perrache (at the Confluences museum) ✉ 69002   Plan: **B2**
– ℰ 04 72 41 12 34 – www.museedesconfluences-restauration.com
– Closed Sunday dinner and Monday
Menu 49 € – Carte 40/60 €
• Modern cuisine • Contemporary décor • Brasserie •

This contemporary brasserie, which opened its doors in 2015, is also that of the Musée des Confluences, with modern architecture using glass, concrete and stainless steel. The food, meanwhile, is a tasty new spin on tradition, with dishes such as pâté en croûte, foie gras and chicken, and vol-au-vent with sauce Nantua.

🍽 Fond Rose   X 🍴 🍴 ⅙ AC ⇔ P

23 chemin de Fond-Rose ✉ 69300 Caluire-et-Cuire   Plan: **B1**
– ℰ 04 78 29 34 61 – www.brasseries-bocuse.fr
Menu 31 € (weekday lunch) – Carte 40/70 €
• Traditional cuisine • Brasserie • Elegant •

A 1920s mansion transformed into a chic brasserie by the Bocuse group. With its terrace surrounded by 100 year-old trees, it is the epitome of peace and quiet. The food is tasty and generous and squarely in the tradition of the areas around the River Saône, with frogs' legs and quenelles etc.

🍽 L'Ouest   X 🍴 AC P

1 quai du Commerce ✉ 69009 – Ⓜ Gare de Vaise   Plan: **B1**
– ℰ 04 37 64 64 64 – www.brasseries-bocuse.com
Menu 27 € (weekdays) – Carte 35/67 €
• Traditional cuisine • Brasserie • Contemporary décor •

Another of Paul Bocuse's brasseries, but this one is quite simply huge! The menu pays homage to the tradition that made a name for this great chef. Dishes include calf's liver with onions (foie de veau à la lyonnaise), spit-roast Bresse chicken, and sole meunière. It has a designer interior and a pretty terrace by the Saône.

COLLONGES-AU-MONT-D'OR

✿✿✿ Paul Bocuse   XXXXX ✿ ⅙ AC ⇔ 🍸 P

40 quai de la Plage – ℰ 04 72 42 90 90 – www.bocuse.fr
Menu 170/275 € – Carte 152/251 €
• Classic cuisine • Elegant • Luxury •

A high temple of tradition and old-style service, which is oblivious to passing culinary trends. Paul Bocuse is still offering the same "presidential" truffle soup first served in 1975, and has had three Michelin stars since 1965!
➜ Soupe aux truffes V.G.E. Rouget en écailles de pommes de terre. Baba au rhum.

La Rotonde ❀ XxxX 🕸 🍴 ⚐ 🆒 ⇔ 🚭 🅿

20 av. du Casino (At the Lyon Vert casino) ✉ *69260 La Tour de Salvagny*
– ☎ 04 78 87 00 97 – www.restaurant-rotonde.com – Closed 30 July-
23 August, Tuesday lunch, Saturday lunch, Sunday and Monday
Menu 45 € (lunch), 78/135 € – Carte 95/125 €
• Modern cuisine • Elegant • Luxury •
In this pleasantly leafy area on the outskirts of town: a fine legacy of the Art
Deco period which also houses the casino Le Lyon Vert. The menu is in a classic
French vein and combines timeless dishes with new influences - not forgetting
the great repertoire of Lyon cuisine.
➜ Pâté en croûte "Champion du Monde 2013". Lotte de petit bateau aux
coquillages, émulsion marinière. Finger praliné au citron, noisettes et crème
glacée au chocolat gianduja.

Le Pavillon de la Rotonde 🚿 🍴 🛁 🌐 📺 ⚐ 🆒 🛁 🅿

3 av. Georges-Bassinet – ☎ 04 78 87 79 79 – www.pavillon-rotonde.com
– Closed 30 July-23 August
16 rm – ▪150/570 € ▪▪150/570 € – ⊇ 22 €
• Luxury • Spa and wellness • Elegant •
A stone's throw from the casino and set in wooded parkland, this luxury hotel
blends the modern with discreet touches of Art Deco. Some of the guestrooms
have a hammam and a terrace. A very fine establishment on the outskirts of
Lyons.
❀ **La Rotonde** – See restaurant listing

Lyon Métropole ⚲ 🛁 🌐 🏊 📺 🍴 ⇄ ⚐ 🆒 🛁 🚗

85 quai Joseph Gillet ✉ *69004 – ☎ 04 72 10 44 44*   Plan: **B1**
– www.lyonmetropole.com
174 rm – ▪129/300 € ▪▪129/300 € – ⊇ 20 €
• Business • Spa and wellness • Functional •
A hotel popular for its Olympic size swimming pool and its sports facilities: a
superb spa, a gym, tennis and squash courts, etc. In the restaurant, seafood
and fish are to the fore.

Dock Ouest ⚐ 🆒 🚗

39 r. des Docks ✉ *69009 – Ⓜ Gare de Vaise*   Plan: **B1**
– ☎ 04 78 22 34 34 – www.dockouest.com
43 rm – ▪75/242 € ▪▪75/242 € – ⊇ 13 €
• Townhouse • Business • Contemporary •
Dock Ouest is located in an up-and-coming district of Lyon, just opposite Paul
Bocuse's fast food outlet. The guestrooms are comfortable and decorated in a
restrained style, with the added bonus of a kitchenette. Gourmet breakfasts.

Mama Shelter ⚲ ⚐ 🆒 🛁 🚗

13 r. Domer ✉ *69007 – Ⓜ Jean Macé*   Plan: **B2**
– ☎ 04 78 02 58 58 – www.mamashelter.com
156 rm – ▪69/269 € ▪▪69/269 € – ⊇ 17 €
• Business • Townhouse • Design •
After Paris and Marseille, Mama Shelter has landed in Lyons, to the delight of
locals! The decor is as trendy as ever (raw concrete, designer flourishes, offbeat
touches), guestrooms are modern and public transport is close by. Splendid.

Hamburg

BERLIN ●

Munich

GERMANY
DEUTSCHLAND

BERLIN
BERLIN

TomasSereda/iStock

Berlin's parliament faces an intriguing dilemma when it comes to where to call its heart, as, although they are homogeneous in many other ways, the east and the west of the city still lay claim to separate centres after 40 years of partition. Following the tempestuous 1990s, Berlin sought to resolve its new identity, and it now stands proud as one of the most dynamic and forward thinking cities in the world. Alongside its idea of tomorrow, it's never lost sight of its bohemian past, and many parts of the city retain the arty sense of adventure that characterised downtown Berlin during the 1920s: turn any corner and you might find a modernist art gallery, a tiny cinema or a cutting-edge club.

The eastern side of the River Spree, around Nikolaiviertel, is the historic heart of the city, dating back to the 13C. Meanwhile, way over to the west of the centre lie Kurfürstendamm and Charlottenburg; smart districts which came to the fore after World War II as the heart of West Berlin. Between the two lie imposing areas which swarm with visitors: Tiergarten is the green lung of the city, and just to its east is the great boulevard of Unter den Linden. Continuing eastward, the self-explanatory Museum Island sits snugly and securely in the tributaries of the Spree. The most southerly of Berlin's sprawling districts is Kreuzberg, renowned for its bohemian, alternative character.

EATING OUT

Many of Berlin's best restaurants are found within the grand hotels and you only have to go to Savignyplatz near Ku'damm to realise how smart dining has taken off. Dinner is the most popular meal and you can invariably eat late, as lots of places stay open until 2 or 3am. Berlin also has a reputation for simple, hearty dishes, inspired by the long, hard winter and, when temperatures drop, the city's comfort food has an irresistible allure – there's pork knuckle, Schnitzel, Bratwurst in mustard, chunky dumplings... and the real Berlin favourite, Currywurst. Bread and potatoes are ubiquitous but since reunification, many dishes have also incorporated a more global influence, so produce from the local forests, rivers and lakes may well be given an Asian or Mediterranean twist (Berlin now claims a wider range of restaurants than any other German city). Service is included in the price of your meal but it's customary to round up the bill. Be sure to try the local 'Berliner Weisse mit Schuss' – a light beer with a dash of raspberry or woodruff.

❄❄ **Lorenz Adlon Esszimmer** – Hotel Adlon Kempinski ✗✗✗ ⊛
Unter den Linden 77 ✉ *10117* ⵛ 🅰🅲 ⇆ ⌂
– Ⓜ *Brandenburger Tor* – ℰ *(030) 22 61 19 60* Plan: **G1**
– *www.lorenzadlon-esszimmer.de* – *Closed Sunday-Tuesday*
Menu 145/205 € – *(dinner only) (booking essential)*
• Creative • Luxury • Elegant •
Eminently elegant and luxurious, this restaurant pays tribute to the hotel's foun-
der Lorenz Adlon. You can eat in the dining room with its fine wood panelling
and open fire, or in the library. Sample either of Hendrik Otto's two menus to
find out just how skilfully he combines classic dishes and contemporary elements.
➜ Langoustino, Krustentierfond, Fenchel, Pastiskaviar, Avocado, Basilikum.
Bretonischer Steinbutt, Périgord Trüffel, Risotto à la Romana. Reh, Pfeffer-
sauce, geschmorte Zwiebel, Pumpernickel, gedörrte Beeren, Holunder,
Miere.

❄❄ **FACIL** – Hotel THE MANDALA ✗✗✗ ⊛ 🍃 ⵛ 🅰🅲 ⇆ ⌂
Potsdamer Str. 3 (5th floor) ✉ *10785* Plan: **F2**
– Ⓜ *Potsdamer Platz* – ℰ *(030) 5 90 05 12 34* – *www.facil.de* – *Closed
2 weeks early January, 3 weeks July - August and Saturday-Sunday*
Menu 96/190 € – Carte 111/134 € – *(booking advisable)*
• Creative • Chic •
FACIL is an oasis of calm amid the hustle and bustle of the Potsdamer Platz. It is
pleasantly light and airy, especially in the summer with plenty of greenery out-
side even though it is on the fifth floor! The modern, creative food is beautifully
presented.
➜ Taschenkrebs, Grapefruit, Basilikum und grüner Spargel. Perlhuhn von
Mieral "Dry Aged", Earl Grey Tea und Artischoke. Dessert von Rhabarber,
Yuzu, Sauerampfer und Himbeere.

❄❄ **reinstoff** (Daniel Achilles) ✗✗✗ ⊛ ⵛ 🅰🅲
Schlegelstr. 26c (Edison Höfe) ✉ *10115* Plan I: **C2**
– Ⓜ *Zinnowitzerstr.* – ℰ *(030) 30 88 12 14* – *www.reinstoff.eu* – *Closed
Sunday-Monday*
Menu 50 € (lunch)/198 € – *(Tuesday to Thursday dinner only) (booking
advisable)*
• Creative • Fashionable • Intimate •
Daniel Achilles' "Close to Home" and "Further Afield" set menus combine top-
quality fresh produce in a modern and creative manner to create some truly
excellent dishes that are served with interesting accompanying wines. The
unusual industrial style "room-in-a-room" concept continues to appeal. Reduced lunchtime menu on Fridays and Saturdays.
➜ Sepia-Flammkuchen, Bärlauchwurzeln und Pistazien. Leipziger Allerlei,
Frühlingsgemüse, Morcheln und Flusskrebse. Zitrus-Wackelpudding, Topinambur, Manzanilla und Kamille.

❄❄ **Rutz** ✗✗ ⊛ 🍃 🅰🅲
Chausseestr. 8 (1st floor) ✉ *10115* Plan I: **C2**
– Ⓜ *Oranienburger Tor* – ℰ *(030) 24 62 87 60* – *www.rutz-restaurant.de*
– *Closed Sunday-Monday*
Menu 129/169 € – Carte 70/130 € – *(dinner only)*
• Modern cuisine • Trendy •
Marco Müller's set Inspirations menu promises well-balanced, creative combina-
tions of top-quality ingredients skilfully showcasing particular flavours to give
each dish its own special character. Diners enjoy their food in the modern inte-
rior accompanied by some expert wine suggestions drawn from a fine wine list.
➜ Schafsmilch, Forellenhaut, Fichte. Ofenlauch, Neu-Müritzer Lamm und
Dashi, Landgerste. Oxalsäure "Holsteiner Blut" und roter Sauerklee, Weizen-
gras.
🍷 **Rutz Weinbar** – See restaurant listing

Tim Raue

XX 發 & AC

Rudi-Dutschke-Str. 26 ⊠ 10969 – Ⓜ Kochstr. – ℰ (030) Plan: **G2**
25 93 79 30 – www.tim-raue.com – Closed Christmas and Sunday-Tuesday lunch
Menu 48 € (lunch)/198 € – Carte 118/156 €
• Asian • Fashionable •

Tim Raue's pared down Southeast Asian cuisine uses a small number of high quality ingredients to great advantage. Sweet and savoury, mild and sharp, soft and crispy – his dishes are a riot of contrasting textures and flavours, always combined to perfection. The lunchtime menu is particularly popular.
→ Kaisergranat und Wasabi "Kanton Style". Zander, Kamebishi Soja 10y und Lauch. Dong Po Schwein, Wassermelone und Galgant.

Horváth (Sebastian Frank)

X 需 &

Paul-Lincke-Ufer 44a ⊠ 10999 – Ⓜ Schönleinstr. Plan I: **D2**
– ℰ (030) 61 28 99 92 – www.restaurant-horvath.de – Closed 5-11 February, 6-19 August and Monday-Tuesday
Menu 89/129 € – Carte 84/113 € – (dinner only) (booking advisable)
• Creative • Minimalist •

Try Horváth if you fancy some really imaginative cuisine full of interesting combinations, full-bodied flavours and intensity. The food has its own particular style, which is elaborate yet harmonious. The service is friendly and accomplished, and in good weather you can sit outside in the garden overlooking the lively street.
→ Sellerie "reif und jung" mit Hühnerbouillon und Selleriesaat. Porree und Bergkas, gedünsteter Lauch, Rauchkohlrabi. Aubergine mit "Selleriekohle", Fichtenessig, Minze.

einsunternull

XX

Hannoversche Str. 1 ⊠ 10115 – Ⓜ Oranienburger Tor Plan I: **C2**
– ℰ (030) 27 57 78 10 – www.einsunternull.com – Closed Sunday-Monday lunch
Menu 29 € (lunch)/117 € – (booking advisable)
• Creative • Design •

Take the lift down to the basement one evening here to enjoy some creative and flavoursome seasonal fare accompanied by a good selection of wines in the pared-down, minimalist-style cellar of this former brewery. Reduced lunchtime menu on the ground floor with a view of the kitchen.
→ Champignonbrot, Zwiebelgewächse und Goldleinöl. Saibling, Lauchasche und Rapsöl. Spannrippe vom Rind, saure Kartoffel und Kamille.

GOLVET

XX ≤ 需 AC

Potsdamer Str. 58 (8th floor) ⊠ 10785 Plan: **F2**
– Ⓜ Mendelsohn-Bartholdy-Park – ℰ (030) 89064222 – www.golvet.de
– Closed 5-21 March, 9-23 July and Sunday-Monday
Menu 68/104 € – Carte 52/83 € – (dinner only)
• International • Design •

GOLVET offers an impressive view over Potsdamer Platz, a stylish interior complete with open kitchen and artful, modern, pared-down cuisine made using the very best ingredients. Then of course, there's the top-quality service and excellent wine recommendations.
→ Gebeizter Wildlachs, Rhabarber, Dill. Ruppiner Lammrücken, Roscoff, Kopfsalat, getrocknete Aprikose. Opalys, Milchmädchen und Guave.

Pauly Saal

XX 發 需

Auguststr. 11 ⊠ 10117 – Ⓜ Rosenthaler Pl. – ℰ (030) Plan I: **C2**
33 00 60 70 – www.paulysaal.com – Closed Sunday-Monday
Menu 69/115 € – (booking advisable)
• Modern cuisine • Fashionable •

If you're looking for somewhere elegant yet relaxed to eat, this is it. The high-ceilinged hall in this former Jewish girls' school boasts a striking decorative rocket above the window into the kitchen and stylish Murano glass chandeliers. The food is modern with creative notes. At lunchtimes, the set menu is available from three courses.
→ Lachs, Blumenkohl, Zwiebel, Schafgarbe, Ossetra Imperial Caviar. Entrecôte, Mais, Kailan, Bärlauch. Aroniabeere, Weizengras, Vanille, Limone.

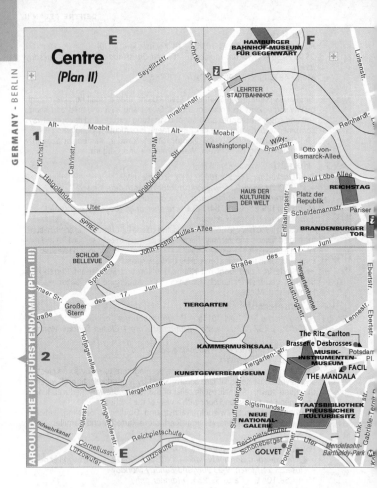

Richard

XX

Köpenicker Str. 174 (by Köpenicker Straße D2) ⌧ *10997*
– Ⓜ *Schlesisches Tor –* ✆ *(030) 49 20 72 42 – www.restaurant-richard.de*
– Closed Sunday - Monday
Menu 52/104 € – *(dinner only)*
• Modern French • Fashionable • Trendy •

Yes, this really is it, but don't be put off by the somewhat lacklustre exterior. Inside the former Köpenicker Hof, built in 1900, the fine interior has an ornate ceiling, designer lighting and artworks (the owner Hans Richard is also a painter). It provides the perfect setting for an excellent, artful and reasonably priced set menu.

→ Weißer Beelitzer Spargel mit Mandel und Joselito Schinken. Skrei von den Lofoten mit Lauchbouillon. Rhabarber Dessert mit Dulcey Schokolade.

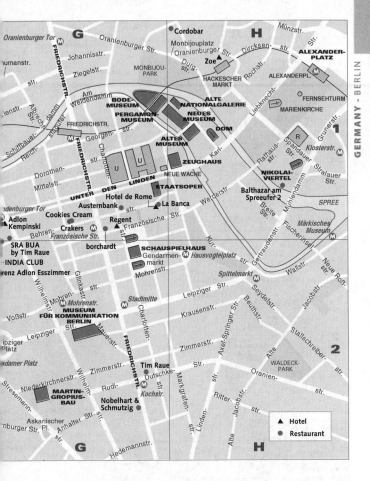

🕸 **tulus lotrek** (Maximilian Strohe)   ✗ 綴 ☂

Fichtestr. 24 ⊠ 10967 – ⓂSüdstern – ℰ (030)   Plan I: **D3**
41 95 66 87 – www.tuluslotrek.de – Closed Monday, July-August: Sunday-Monday
Menu 78/98 € – Carte 68/76 € – *(dinner only)*
• Modern cuisine • Trendy • Chic •

The USPs here are the warm and welcoming female owner and the charmingly relaxed interior with its high stuccoed ceilings, wooden floors, artworks and original wallpaper. As for the food, it's modern with an international bent, sophisticated and punchy. How about a glass of cider to wash it down?

➔ Jakobsmuschel und Seegras. Aubrac-Rind, Bibimbab, Alge, Kimchi. Mohn, Kirsche, Lorbeer.

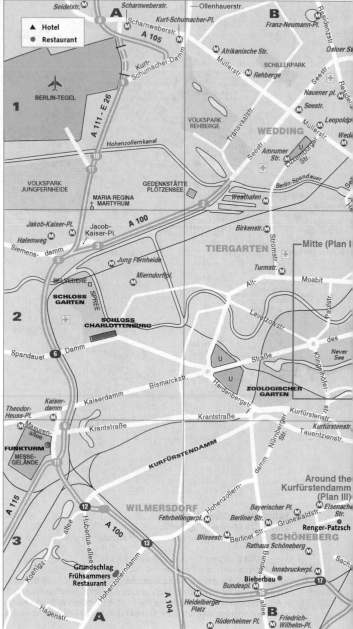

▲ Hotel
● Restaurant

Seidelstr. Ⓜ Scharnweberstr. ──Ollenhauerstr. **B**
Scharnweberstr. Ⓜ Kurt-Schumacher-Pl. Ⓜ
6 **A** Franz-Neumann-Pl. Ⓜ
A 105
Afrikanische Str. Ⓜ Ösloer Str
8 Kurt-Schumacher-Damm SCHILLERPARK
Müllerstr. Ⓜ Rehberge
1 Nauener pl. Ⓜ
✈ Seestr. Ⓜ Leopoldp Ⓜ
BERLIN-TEGEL VOLKSPARK Müllerstr. Ⓜ Wed Ⓜ
REHBERGE WEDDING
A 111 - E 26 Amrumer Ⓜ Ⓤ Luxemburger Str.
Str.
Hohenzollernkanal 10 Berlin-Spandauer
11 Westhafen Ⓜ
VOLKSPARK GEDENKSTÄTTE
JUNGFERNHEIDE PLÖTZENSEE 2
MARIA REGINA ✝ Birkenstr. Ⓜ
MARTYRUM A 100 TIERGARTEN Stromstr. ──Mitte (Plan I
Jakob-Kaiser-Pl. Ⓜ Ⓜ Jacob- Turmstr. Ⓜ
Halemweg Ⓜ Kaiser-Pl. Alt- Moabit
Siemens- damm 3 Paulstr.
5 Ⓜ Jung Fernheide Levetzowstr. des
─BELVEDERE Mierndorfpl. Ⓜ Never
SCHLOSS See
GARTEN SPREE Straße Ⓤ Klingelhöfer-
2 ✝ SCHLOSS Ⓤ
CHARLOTTENBURG Bismarckstr. Hardenbergstr. ZOOLOGISCHER
6 Damm GARTEN
Spandauer Kurfürstenstr. str
Theodor- Kaiser- Kaiserdamm Krantstraße Kurfürstenstr.
Heuss-Pl. Ⓜ damm Tauentzienstr.
8 Ⓜ
Masuren- Krantstraße
allee Ⓜ
FUNKTURM KURFÜRSTENDAMM
MESSE-
GELÄNDE 11 Around the
Kurfürstendamm
A 115 (Plan III)
12 WILMERSDORF Bayerischer Pl. Ⓜ Ⓜ Eisenache
Fehrbellingerpl. Ⓜ Berliner Str. Ⓜ Grunewaldstr. Str.
3 A 100 13 Blissestr. Ⓜ Berliner Str. SCHÖNEBERG Renger-Patzsch
Rathaus Schöneberg
Innsbruckerpl. Ⓜ Sach
Grundschlag Bieberbau ● 17
Frühsammers Bundespl. Ⓜ
Restaurant 16
A Heidelberger Bundesallee **B**
Hagenstr. Platz Ⓜ Friedrich-
A 104 Rüdenheimer Pl. Ⓜ Wilhelm-Pl. Ⓜ

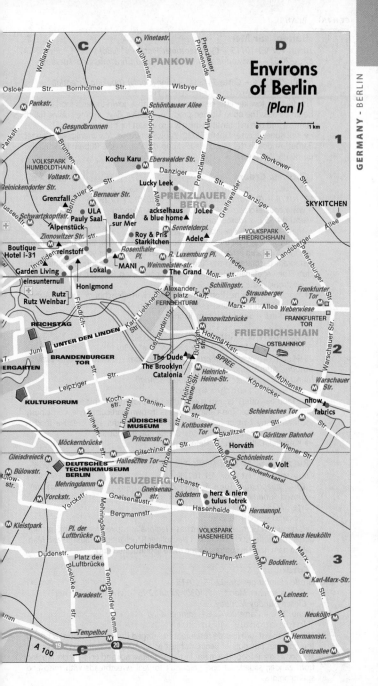

Environs of Berlin
(Plan I)

0   1 km

PANKOW

PRENZLAUER BERG

FRIEDRICHSHAIN

KREUZBERG

Vinetastr.

Prenzlauer Promenade

Wollankstr.

Osloer   Str.   Bornholmer   Str.   Wisbyer

Pankstr.

Mühlenstr.

Schönhauser Allee

Storkower   Str.

Gesundbrunnen

VOLKSPARK HUMBOLDTHAIN

Voltastr.

Brunnen

Heinickendorfer Str.

Schwartzkopffstr.

Reinickendorfer Str.

Bernauer Str.

Eberswalder Str.

Danziger

Kochu Karu

Lucky Leek

Grenzfall

ULA

Pauly Saal

Bandol sur Mer

Alpenstück

Zinnowitzer Str.

Boutique Hotel i-31

reinstoff

Garden Living

einsunternull

Honigmond

Rutz
Rutz Weinbar

Roy & Pris
Starkitchen

Lokal

MANI

Rosenthaler Pl.

Weinmeister-str.

Senefelderpl.

Adele

ackselhaus & blue home

JoLee

Greifswalder   Str.

Danziger   Str.

SKYKITCHEN

Allee

VOLKSPARK FRIEDRICHSHAIN

Landsberger

Petersburger   Str.

R. Luxemburg Pl.

Friedrich-str.

The Grand

Moll-

Schillingstr.

Karl-

Alexander-platz

FERNSEHTURM

Strausberger Pl.

Marx-

Weberwiese

Allee

Frankfurter Tor

FRANKFURTER TOR

Warschauer   Str.

REICHSTAG

Juni

UNTER DEN LINDEN

BRANDENBURGER TOR

str.

TIERGARTEN

Leipziger

KULTURFORUM

Koch-str.

Wilhelm-str.

Oranien-

Lindenstr.

JÜDISCHES MUSEUM

Prinzenstr.

Möckernbrücke

Gitschiner

Halleschesstr.

Gleisdreieck

Bülowstr.

Bülow-str.

DEUTSCHES TECHNIKMUSEUM BERLIN

Mehringdamm

Yorckstr.

Kleistpark

Yorckstr.

Gneisenaustr.

Bergmannstr.

Gerstraudenstr.

Karl-Liebknecht-

Jannowitzbrücke

Holzmarktstr.

The Dude
The Brooklyn
Catalonia

Heinrich-Heine-Str.

SPREE

Heinrich-Heine-Str.

Brücken

Moritzpl.

Horváth

Kottbusser Tor

Skalitzer   Str.

OSTBAHNHOF

Mühlenstr.

Köpenicker

Schlesisches Tor

nhow

fabrics

Görlitzer Bahnhof

Wiener Str.

Schönleinstr.

Volt

Landwehrkanal

Urbanstr.

Gneisenau-str.

Südstern

Hasenheide

herz & niere
tulus lotrek

Hermannpl.

Pl. der Luftbrücke

Columbiadamm

VOLKSPARK HASENHEIDE

Flughafen-str.

Karl-

Rathaus Neukölln

Dudenstr.

Platz der Luftbrücke

Belecke-str.

Tempelhofer Damm

Paradestr.

Boddinstr.

Hermann-

Karl-Marx-Str.

Leinestr.

Neukölln

Hermannstr.

Tempelhof

A 100

19

20

Grenzallee

277

ⓔ **Bandol sur Mer**   ✗

Torstr. 167 ✉ *10115 –* Ⓜ *Rosenthaler Platz – 𝒞 (030)*   Plan I: **C2**
67 30 20 51 – www.bandolsurmer.de – Closed Christmas and Tuesday-Wednesday
Menu 72/126 € – Carte 71/83 € – *(dinner only) (booking essential)*
• Modern French • Neighbourhood •

This friendly, low-key little restaurant is proof that down-to-earth food can also be ambitious. The open kitchen produces creative, flavoursome cuisine full of contrast and rich in intensity, which is also a feast for the eyes.
→ Kalbsbries, Erbse, Eigelb 65/30, Kapuzinerkresse, Maränenkaviar. Rouget Barbet, Andouillette, Muschelsud. Loup de Mer, weiße Rüben, Mayonnaise de Beurre Noisette.

ⓔ **Cookies Cream**   ✗ 🆔

Behrenstr. 55 (backyard off the Hotel Westin Grand)   Plan: **G1**
✉ *10178 –* Ⓜ *Französische Straße – 𝒞 (030) 27 49 29 40*
– www.cookiescream.com – Closed Sunday-Monday
Menu 44/55 € – *(dinner only)*
• Vegetarian • Trendy • Fashionable •

Finding your way here through a maze of backyards to ring the bell at the unassuming door is an adventure in itself! Up on the first floor you'll find a vibrant restaurant decorated in the "industrial" style (it was once a fashionable night club). The vegetarian cuisine, artful and sophisticated, is served to a soundtrack of electronic music.
→ Wachtelei, Brioche, Portweinschalotten, Kartoffelschaum, Trüffel. Aubergine, Mais, Bohnen, Erdnuss. Apfel, Dill, Hafer.
🕸 **Crackers** – See restaurant listing

ⓔ **Nobelhart & Schmutzig**   ✗ 🏵 ⚹ 🆔

Friedrichstr. 218 ✉ *10969 –* Ⓜ *Kochstr. – 𝒞 (030)*   Plan: **G2**
25 94 06 10 – www.nobelhartundschmutzig.com – Closed 2 weeks early January, August and Sunday-Monday
Menu 95 € – *(dinner only) (booking essential)*
• Creative • Trendy • Friendly •

This 'food bar' offers its own special mix of trendy, urban chic and relaxed but professional service. The cuisine also has its own particular style, consciously eschewing any hint of luxury or chichi. The powerful and creative food is made using predominantly regional Brandenburg produce.
→ Kartoffel, Dill. Lauch, Ei. Hefe, Fenchel.

ⓑ **Rutz Weinbar** – Restaurant Rutz   ✗ 🏵 🌿 🆔

Chausseestr. 8 (1st floor) ✉ *10115*   Plan I: **C2**
– Ⓜ *Oranienburger Tor – 𝒞 (030) 24 62 87 60 – www.rutz-restaurant.de*
– Closed Sunday-Monday
Carte 37/73 € – *(open from 4pm)*
• Country • Wine bar •

This genuinely German restaurant has a regionally inspired menu. It offers traditional specialities such as smoked Neuköllner Rauchknacker sausage and Mangalitza ham hock; in contrast to the more sophisticated Rutz.

ⓑ **Cordobar**   ✗ 🏵 🌿

Große Hamburger Str. 32 ✉ *10115*   Plan: **H1**
– Ⓜ *Hackescher Markt – 𝒞 (030) 27 58 12 15 – www.cordobar.net*
– Closed Sunday-Monday
Menu 26 € – Carte 25/42 € – *(dinner only)*
• International • Minimalist •

This minimalist, urban-style restaurant has forged itself a reputation as one of the gourmet hotspots of Berlin, not just as an Austrian/German wine bar but also for its great food. The menu includes creative hot and cold snacks ranging from zander, sauerkraut and grapefruit to veal sweetbreads with miso and spring onions.

GERMANY - BERLIN

Kochu Karu ⊛ X 🛱

Eberswalder Str. 35 ⊠ 10437 – Ⓜ Eberswalder Str.   Plan I: **C1**
– ℰ (030) 80 93 81 91 – www.kochukaru.de – Closed 13-24 August
Carte 30/43 € – *(dinner only) (booking advisable)*
• Korean • Minimalist • Neighbourhood •
This pretty little minimalist-style restaurant combines the best of Spain and Korea with passion to create ambitious, flavoursome tapas such as mackerel adobo with barley and apricots and chicory with buckwheat and wild orange. Main dishes include options such as beef ribs with red cabbage kimchi, ginko nuts and sherry jus.

Lokal ⊛ X 🛱

Linienstr. 160 ⊠ 10115 – Ⓜ Rosenthaler Platz   Plan I: **C2**
– ℰ (030) 28 44 95 00 – www.lokal-berlinmitte.de
Carte 36/53 € – *(dinner only) (booking advisable)*
• Country • Friendly •
Relaxed, friendly and pleasantly unpretentious, it is no surprise that Lokal is popular with Berliners and visitors alike. The food is fresh, flavoursome and seasonal and includes dishes such as ox cheek with swede, chicory and broccoli.

Lucky Leek ⊛ X 🛱

Kollwitzstr. 54 ⊠ 10405 – Ⓜ Senefelderplatz – ℰ (030)   Plan I: **D1**
66 40 87 10 – www.lucky-leek.com – Closed Monday-Tuesday
Menu 35/55 € – Carte 36/46 € – *(dinner only)*
• Vegan • Neighbourhood • Trendy •
Lucky Leek is a genuinely modern restaurant with a friendly, personal note. Josita Hartanto cooks vegan cuisine including vegetable consommé with potato and cress ravioli, pear and chilli risotto with tandoori cabbage and nori tempeh rolls.

🍴 SRA BUA by Tim Raue – Hotel Adlon Kempinski   XX 🕸 ⅍ 🎬

Behrenstr. 72 ⊠ 10117 – Ⓜ Brandenburger Tor – ℰ (030)   🚗
22 61 15 90 – www.srabua-berlin.de   Plan: **G1**
Menu 38/108 € – Carte 50/90 € – *(dinner only)*
• Asian • Elegant • Exotic décor •
Top-quality produce and a variety of Asian influences come together here in a range of ambitious dishes including Hokkaido seafood with tomato and Thai basil and guinea fowl tom kha gai with grilled corn – all sampled in an upmarket, elegant and minimalist yet friendly interior with attentive, charming service.

🍴 Balthazar am Spreeufer 2   XX 🛱 ⅍ 🎬 ⇔

Spreeufer 2 ⊠ 10178 – Ⓜ Märkisches Museum   Plan: **H1**
– ℰ (030) 30 88 21 56 – www.balthazar-spreeufer.de – Closed November-Easter: Sunday
Menu 20/95 € – Carte 35/51 €
• Classic cuisine • Friendly • Cosy •
This cosy, friendly restaurant offers classic cuisine. This ranges from Wiener Schnitzel with roast potatoes to redfish with pearl barley, and black salsify stew with chorizo. Its location on the River Spree makes the terrace particularly popular.

🍴 La Banca – Hotel de Rome   XX 🛱 ⅍ 🎬 ⇔ 🚗

Behrenstr. 37 ⊠ 10117 – Ⓜ Französische Str. – ℰ (030)   Plan: **G1**
46 06 09 12 01 – www.roccofortehotels.com
Menu 26 € (lunch) – Carte 31/75 €
• Mediterranean cuisine • Cosy • Design •
A casual yet classy restaurant which offers Mediterrenean cuisine made using fresh produce. There is a terrace in the beautiful interior courtyard. The lunch menu is good value for money.

ⁱ○ **The Brooklyn** – Hotel The Dude   XX
Köpenicker Str. 92 ✉ *10179 – Ⓜ Heinrich-Heine-Str.*   Plan I: **D2**
– ☎ (030) 20 21 58 20 – www.thebrooklyn.de – Closed Sunday
Carte 48/92 € – *(dinner only)*
• Grills • Cosy • Vintage •
How about a US Black Angus rib-eye steak or a chateaubriand for two? This cel-
lar restaurant with its lively New York steakhouse atmosphere offers a great
range of grilled dishes and the service is friendly, relaxed and professional.
When it's time for dessert, don't miss the New York cheesecake!

ⁱ○ **fabrics** – Hotel nhow   XX 👌 🎢 🚗
Stralauer Allee 3 ✉ *10245 – Ⓜ Warschauer Str.*   Plan I: **D2**
– ☎ (030) 2 90 29 90 – www.nhow-berlin.com – Closed Sunday
Menu 36 € – Carte 39/49 €
• Modern cuisine • Minimalist •
Cool design throughout in white, pink and a trendy green, giving a light and
airy feel. The top quality produce in the kitchen is used to create house specials
including classics such as steak Chateaubriand. Small lunchtime menu.

ⁱ○ **The Grand**   XX 🎢 ⟐
Hirtenstr. 4 ✉ *10178 – Ⓜ Alexanderplatz – ☎ (030)*   Plan I: **C2**
*27 89 09 95 55 – www.the-grand-berlin.com – Closed Saturday lunch and
Sunday lunch*
Menu 19 € *(lunch)*
– Carte 36/195 € – (August: dinner only) (bookings advisable at dinner)
• Grills • Trendy • Design •
The interior is chic with a shabby touch and the gallery tables overlooking the restau-
rant are particularly attractive. The main focus of the ambitious cuisine is steaks from the
800°C Southbend grill, which are on view in the glazed meat maturing cabinet. Reduced
lunchtime menu with good value specials. Bar and club.

ⁱ○ **INDIA CLUB**   XX 🎢 🎛
Behrensstr. 72 ✉ *10117 – Ⓜ Brandenburger Tor*   Plan: **G2**
– ☎ (030) 20 62 86 10 – www.india-club-berlin.com
Carte 39/61 € – *(dinner only)*
• Indian • Elegant •
Now you can even find authentic Indian food in Berlin! The self-styled "rustic
cuisine" from the north of India on offer here offers some delicious curries – try
the lamb shank curry – as well as original tandoori dishes such as the "maachi
tikka". The upmarket interior features dark wood and typically Indian colours
and motifs.

ⁱ○ **Alpenstück**   X 🎢 👌 ⟐
Gartenstr. 9 ✉ *10115 – Ⓜ Rosenthaler Platz – ☎ (030)*   Plan I: **C1**
21 75 16 46 – www.alpenstueck.de
Menu 35/48 € – Carte 40/48 € – *(dinner only) (booking advisable)*
• Country • Fashionable •
This relaxed and friendly restaurant uses regional produce in dishes such as
pan-fried fillet of trout with beetroot, yellow turnip and fondant potatoes. At
lunchtimes the restaurant's own bakery over the road sells fine pastries and
small snacks. In the delicatessen you can buy Maultaschen (Swabian pasta squares) and fond (caramelised meat dripping for making gravy) to take home.

ⁱ○ **Austernbank**   X 🎢 👌 🎛
Behrensstr. 42 ✉ *10117 – Ⓜ Französische Str.*   Plan: **G1**
*– ☎ (030) 7 67 75 27 24 – www.austernbank-berlin.de – Closed Sunday-
Monday*
Carte 40/112 € – *(dinner only)*
• Seafood • Historic •
What were once the vaults of the former Disconto Bank now provide an impressive restaurant setting with their high ceilings, striking pillars, lovely stone floors
and tiled walls. The open kitchen serves a fish and seafood menu including the
house speciality, oysters. There's also the Blaue Stunde smokers' bar on the first
floor and a pavement terrace.

🟡 **Brasserie Desbrosses** – Hotel The Ritz-Carlton   X 🏠 🕭 AC 🚗

Potsdamer Platz 3 ☒ 10785 – M Potsdamer Platz   Plan: **F2**
– 𝒞 (030) 3 37 77 54 02 – www.ritzcarlton.de/berlin
Carte 54/118 €
• French • Brasserie •
An eclectic group of diners come here to savour the typically French bistro
dishes on offer. The original 1875 interior comes from a brasserie in southern
Burgundy.

🟡 **Crackers** – Restaurant Cookies Cream   X AC

Friedrichstr. 158 ☒ 10178 – M Französische Straße   Plan: **G1**
– 𝒞 (030) 6 80 73 04 88 – www.crackersberlin.com
Carte 38/86 € – *(dinner only)*
• International • Trendy • Chic •
You'll find this trendy eatery one floor below Cookies Cream. Ring the bell and
the staff will lead you through the kitchen into a large and lively restaurant with
a high ceiling and dim lights. The menu offers a range of ambitious meat and
fish dishes.

🟡 **herz & niere**   X 🏠 ✉

Fichtestr. 31 ☒ 10967 – M Südstern – 𝒞 (030)   Plan I: **D3**
69 00 15 22 – www.herzundniere.berlin – Closed Monday, May-September:
Sunday-Monday
Menu 48/88 € – Carte 25/52 € – *(dinner only)*
• Country • Friendly • Cosy •
You'll find two set menus here: one focusing on offal dishes and the other vegetarian. Even if you order something in between, you won't be disappointed at
this pleasant restaurant, its "nose to tail" principle ensuring that nothing goes to
waste. The friendly front-of-house team also provide good wine suggestions.

🟡 **Roy & Pris Starkitchen**   X 🏠

Weinbergsweg 8A ☒ 10119 – M Rosenthaler Platz   Plan I: **C1**
– 𝒞 (0176) 22 01 82 45 – www.royandpris.com – Closed Saturday lunch,
Sunday lunch
Menu 38/55 € – Carte 29/40 €
• Chinese • Friendly • Minimalist •
Contemporary style, an open kitchen and a casual, friendly atmosphere await
you in this nice little restaurant on the edge of the capital's Mitte district. The
food – modern Chinese – includes a range of dim sum and a good selection of
sakes, wines and spirits.

🟡 **ULA**   X AC

Anklamer Str. 8 ☒ 10115 – M Bernauer Str. – 𝒞 (030)   Plan I: **C1**
89 37 95 70 – www.ula-berlin.de – Closed Sunday Monday
Menu 38/58 € – Carte 20/51 € – *(dinner only and Sunday lunch)*
• Japanese • Minimalist •
If you fancy some authentic Japanese cuisine, try the white miso soup with
grilled salmon, monkfish tempura or sushi here at ULA. In the same building as
the gallery of the same name, the restaurant offers a minimalist-style eatery
away from the hustle and bustle of the city.

🟡 **VOLT**   X 🏠 🕭 ♻

Paul-Lincke-Ufer 21 ☒ 10999 – M Schönleinstr.   Plan I: **D3**
– 𝒞 (030) 3 38 40 23 20 – www.restaurant-volt.de – Closed 1 week early
January, 3 weeks July-August and Sunday-Monday
Menu 51/87 € – Carte 64/72 € – *(dinner only)*
• Country • Fashionable •
Matthias Gleiß's restaurant is very popular and you can see why. With its well-
chosen industrial design features and good food – including vegetables sour-
ced from local farmers – this former electricity substation built in 1928 fits per-
fectly into Kreuzberg's lively gastro scene.

GERMANY - BERLIN

Adlon Kempinski

Plan: **G1**

Unter den Linden 77 ⊠ *10117* – Ⓜ *Brandenburger Tor*
– ℰ *(030) 2 26 10* – *www.kempinski.com/adlon*
307 rm – †270/900 € ††270/900 € – � 45 € – 78 suites
• Grand Luxury • Historic • Classic •

Situated in the capital, this imposing grand hotel, which has hosted a list of crowned heads far too long to cite here, is synonymous with glitz and glamour. Magical, luxurious ambience, plus presidential suites with limousine and butler service.

❀❀ **Lorenz Adlon Esszimmer** –⊓O SRA BUA by Tim Raue – See restaurant listing

Regent

Plan: **G1**

Charlottenstr. 49 ⊠ *10117* – Ⓜ *Französische Str.*
– ℰ *(030) 2 03 38* – *www.regenthotels.com/berlin*
156 rm – †260/495 € ††260/495 € – ⊻ 39 € – 39 suites
• Grand Luxury • Townhouse • Classic •

The guests here expect first class service and they are not disappointed. A pleasant custom is the taking of tea – English-, Russian- or Saxony-style (the hotel's own blend) – on nothing but the finest Meissen porcelain in the elegant lounge.

The Ritz-Carlton

Plan: **F2**

Potsdamer Platz 3 ⊠ *10785* – Ⓜ *Potsdamer Platz*
– ℰ *(030) 33 77 77* – *www.ritzcarlton.com*
263 rm – †295 € ††325 € – ⊻ 38 € – 40 suites
• Grand Luxury • Chain • Classic •

One of the most exclusive hotel addresses in Germany. The elegant lobby with its cantilevered marble staircase is home to a stylish lounge where guests gather for classic 'teatime' treats.

⊓O **Brasserie Desbrosses** – See restaurant listing

Hotel de Rome

Plan: **G1**

Behrenstr. 37 ⊠ *10117* – Ⓜ *Französische Str.* – ℰ *(030)*
4 60 60 90 – *www.roccofortehotels.com*
132 rm – †280/555 € ††280/555 € – ⊻ 38 € – 13 suites
• Grand Luxury • Design • Contemporary •

A luxury hotel on the Bebelplatz in the impressive framework of a building dating from 1889, formerly used by the Dresdner Bank. Today, the old strongroom is a pool.

⊓O **La Banca** – See restaurant listing

THE MANDALA

Plan: **F2**

Potsdamer Str. 3 ⊠ *10785* – Ⓜ *Potsdamer Platz*
– ℰ *(030) 5 90 05 00 00* – *www.themandala.de*
158 rm – †200/450 € ††200/450 € – ⊻ 35 € – 96 suites
• Business • Luxury • Design •

The Mandala is located on Potsdamer Platz opposite the Sony Center. The rooms, suites and apartments are spacious and luxurious in an understated way, the spa upmarket. The trendy Qiu bar serves a range of snacks and breakfast comes with home-made pastries.

❀❀ **FACIL** – See restaurant listing

Boutique Hotel i-31

Plan I: **C1**

Invalidenstr. 31 ⊠ *10115* – Ⓜ *Naturkundemuseum*
– ℰ *(030) 3 38 40 00* – *www.hotel-i31.de*
121 rm – †100/300 € ††100/300 € – ⊻ 18 €
• Business • Personalised • Contemporary •

This boutique hotel with its designer interior stands in the heart of Berlin-Mitte, still one of the trendiest parts of Berlin. The fresh, comfortable rooms – categorised as 'Pure', 'White' and 'Brown' – all come with a free mini-bar and the latest in modern technology.

nhow

Stralauer Allee 3 ✉ 10245 – Ⓜ Warschauer Str. Plan I: **D2**
– ✆ (030) 2 90 29 90 – www.nhow-berlin.com
303 rm – 🚹125/195 € 🚹🚹135/205 € – ☕ 29 € – 1 suite
• Business • Design • Minimalist •

No other hotel in Berlin combines music and lifestyle in such an unconventional and cosmopolitan manner. Clean lines and functional architecture outside; upbeat design, curved forms and young, fresh colours inside. And with its recording studio looking out over the city, it really is one of a kind!

fabrics – See restaurant listing

The Dude

Köpenicker Str. 92 ✉ 10179 – Ⓜ Heinrich-Heine-Str. Plan I: **D2**
– ✆ (030) 4 11 98 81 77 – www.thedudeberlin.com
27 rm – 🚹99/199 € 🚹🚹129/239 € – ☕ 24 €
• Townhouse • Historic • Personalised •

This is design in its purest form. The mix of historical detail (the building dates back to 1822) and modern style is reminiscent of a mansion house. If you are in search of a snack, the Deli serves sandwiches at lunchtime. Breakfast is also available.

The Brooklyn – See restaurant listing

ackselhaus & blue home

Belforter Str. 21 ✉ 10405 – Ⓜ Senefelderplatz Plan I: **D1**
– ✆ (030) 44 33 76 33 – www.ackselhaus.de
31 rm ☕ – 🚹110/170 € 🚹🚹130/300 € – 4 suites
• Townhouse • Historic • Personalised •

This establishment has a really special historical charm. It is Venetian in style with blue tones. The green inner courtyards with their lounge feel are very pretty.

Catalonia

Köpenicker Str. 80 ✉ 10178 – Ⓜ Märk. Museum Plan I: **D2**
– ✆ (030) 24 08 47 70 – www.hoteles-catalonia.com
131 rm – 🚹69/399 € 🚹🚹79/429 € – ☕ 17 €
• Chain • Contemporary • Grand luxury •

Catalonia is the so-called 'pilot project' of a Catalan hotel group in Germany. The unusual lobby design reflects the variety and changing landscape of Berlin and the landings feature some impressive graffiti. The restaurant serves a mix of Berlin and Spanish cuisine including tapas.

Garden Living

Invalidenstr. 101 ✉ 10115 – Ⓜ Zinnowitzer Straße Plan I: **C2**
– ✆ (030) 2 84 45 59 00 – www.gardenliving.de
27 rm – 🚹89/169 € 🚹🚹99/189 € – ☕ 8 €
• Townhouse • Personalised •

Part of the ethos at the Garden Living is to make you feel as if you are 'staying at home'. This is indeed the impression you get in this pretty group of three old townhouses with their generously sized and tastefully appointed apartments, each with their own small kitchen. The attractive interior courtyard or 'Green Oasis' makes the ideal place for breakfast on a lovely summer's morning.

Adele

Greifswalder Str. 227 ✉ 10405 – Ⓜ Alexanderplatz Plan I: **D1**
– ✆ (030) 44 32 43 10 – www.adele-berlin.de
13 rm – 🚹79/129 € 🚹🚹89/139 € – ☕ 14 € – 3 suites
• Townhouse • Design •

This small and very exclusive boutique hotel is furnished in Art Deco-style. It has comfortable, pretty guestrooms and a very modern breakfast room.

GERMANY - BERLIN

🏠 **Grenzfall** ☆ 🛖 ♿ 🏋 🚗

Ackerstr. 136 ✉ *13355 –* Ⓜ *Bernauer Str. –* ☏ *(030)* Plan I: **C1**
34 33 33 00 – www.hotel-grenzfall.de
37 rm – ♦63/159 € ♦♦83/179 € – ⌴ 13 €
• Townhouse • Functional • Centrally located •
The Grenzfall's attractions include a friendly welcome, a 3000m² garden and reasonable prices. The hotel, located in a quiet side street close to the site of the former Berlin wall, provides employment opportunities for the disabled. The contemporary feel also extends to the restaurant, which boasts a terrace overlooking the garden.

🏠 **Honigmond** ☆ 🏋

Tieckstr. 11 ✉ *10115 –* Ⓜ *Zinnowitzer Str. –* ☏ *(030)* Plan I: **C2**
2 84 45 50 – www.honigmond.de
36 rm – ♦99/159 € ♦♦109/199 € – ⌴ 12 €
• Historic • Classic • Personalised •
Built in 1895 this house in a quiet side street has individually-styled rooms. The Garden Hotel 350m away has a lovely inner courtyard garden. Pleasant coffee shop-cum-restaurant in a classic setting.

🏠 **MANI** ☆ ♿ 🎞

Torstr. 136 ✉ *10119 –* Ⓜ *Rosenthaler Platz –* ☏ *(030)* Plan I: **C2**
53 02 80 80 – www.amanogroup.de
63 rm – ♦75/289 € ♦♦80/294 € – ⌴ 15 €
• Boutique hotel • Contemporary •
MANI is one of Berlin's numerous stylish boutique hotels: hip, classy and fashionable. The smart rooms boast upmarket fittings and a minimalist-style decor in dark tones. The restaurant serves modern international cuisine.

🏠 **Zoe** ♿ 🎞 🚗

Große Präsidentenstr. 7 ✉ *10178* Plan: **H1**
– Ⓜ *Hackescher Markt –* ☏ *(030) 21 300 150 – www.amanogroup.de*
88 rm – ♦65/145 € ♦♦75/155 € – ⌴ 15 €
• Boutique hotel • Contemporary • Trendy •
If you are looking for a stylish hotel in Berlin's fashionable Hackescher Markt district, this is it. The epitome of urban chic with calm, dark tones, the rooms, though not enormous, are upmarket and chic, and the G&T Bar serves over 70 variations on the classic gin and tonic. Food is served on the stunning roof terrace.

AROUND THE KURFÜRSTENDAMM PLAN III

🌼 **5 - cinco by Paco Pérez** – Hotel Das Stue XxX 🍸 ♿ 🎞

Drakestr. 1 ✉ *10787 –* Ⓜ *Wittenbergplatz –* ☏ *(030)* Plan: **L2**
3 11 72 20 – www.5-cinco.com – Closed Sunday-Monday
Menu 165 € – Carte 78/140 € – *(dinner only) (booking advisable)*
• Creative • Design • Trendy •
You no longer have to make the journey to Miramar in Spain for Paco Pérez' Michelin-starred cuisine. You can now sample his upmarket creations in this modern restaurant – with 86 copper pans hanging from the centre of the ceiling – as you marvel at the intense activity in the kitchens. Choose the 'Experience Menu' or go à la carte.
➔ Thunfisch Parmentier. Taube in eigener Sauce, Oliven und Bun. Coco, Coco, Coco.

🌼 **Hugos** – Hotel InterContinental XX 🍸 ≤ ♿ 🎞 ⇕ 🚗

Budapester Str. 2 (14th floor) ✉ *10787* Plan: **L2**
– Ⓜ *Zoologischer Garten –* ☏ *(030) 26 02 12 63*
– www.hugos-restaurant.de – Closed Sunday-Monday
Menu 70 € (Vegetarian)/130 € – *(dinner only) (booking advisable)*
• Modern cuisine • Chic • Elegant •
It is true that the view from the 14th floor is fantastic but this elegant, minimalist-style restaurant is known first and foremost for its classic, modern cuisine, which is both beautifully crafted and delicious.
➔ Bretonischer Langostino, Tamarillo, Paprika, schwarzer Knoblauch. Blackmore Wagyu, gegrillte Hüfte, Tandoori, Bohnen, Staudensellerie. Kiwi und Joghurt, Sorbet, Matcha, Luftschokolade, Granola-Knuspermüsli.

GERMANY - BERLIN

🛇 Markus Semmler XX 🍴

Sächsische Str. 7 ✉ 10707 – ⓜ Hohenzollernpl. Plan: **J3**
*– ☎ (030) 89 06 82 90 – www.semmler-restaurant.de – Closed July-August
and Sunday-Tuesday*
Menu 95/185 € – Carte 102/109 € – *(dinner only) (booking essential)*
• Classic cuisine • Fashionable •

The seasonal fare on offer here relies on top-class produce, skill and flavour. Both
the interior and the front-of-house team are warm and welcoming – from time
to time the chef will bring one of the courses to your table himself. Certain
wines are served by the glass from magnums. Attractive smokers' lounge.
➜ Eismeerforelle, Radieschen, Spargel, Buttermilch-Salzzitronengranité.
Maibock, Lauch, Spargel, Waldmeister. Erdbeere, Rhabarber, fermentierter
Pfeffer.

🛇 Bieberbau (Stephan Garkisch) 🍴 🍴

Durlacher Str. 15 ✉ 10715 – ⓜ Bundesplatz – ☎ (030) Plan I: **B3**
8 53 23 90 – www.bieberbau-berlin.de – Closed Saturday-Sunday
Menu 46/66 € – *(dinner only) (booking advisable)*
• Modern cuisine • Cosy •

The atmosphere here is genuinely unique, not least thanks to Richard Bieber's
remarkable stuccowork! The chef cooks modern seasonal fare, skilfully placing
herbs and spices centre stage, while his partner oversees the charming front-of-
house team. Excellent value for money!
➜ Pulpo und Lauch, Focaccia, Paprika, Mandeln und Wildblüten. Rehrücken mit Pfifferlingen, dicken Bohnen, Gnocchi, Hagebutte und Majoran.
Erdbeeren, Mascarpone und Vogelmiere.

🕾 Colette Tim Raue X

Passauer Str. 5 ✉ 10789 – ⓜ Wittenbergplatz Plan: **L2**
– ☎ (030) 2 199 21 74 – www.brasseriecolette.de
Menu 24 € (lunch) – Carte 35/72 €
• Classic French • Brasserie •

A well-known name on the Berlin gastro scene, Colette Tim Raue has created a
friendly, modern and uncomplicated brasserie, which could easily be in Paris.
Try the paysanne pie, duck confit or lemon tart.

🕾 Jungbluth X 🍴 🛇 ⊟

Lepsius Str. 63 (by Hauptstraße B3) ✉ 12163 – ⓜ Steglitzer Rathaus
– ☎ (030) 79 78 96 05 – www.jungbluth-restaurant.de – Closed Monday
Menu 34/58 € – Carte 37/46 €
• Modern cuisine • Neighbourhood • Friendly •

The young team that runs Jungbluth have created a pleasant little restaurant
serving tasty food at reasonable prices. Try the delicious roast shoulder of beef
with cima di rapa and creamed garlic and celery.

🕾 Die Nußbaumerin X

Leibnizstr. 55 ✉ 10629 – ⓜ Adenauerpl. – ☎ (030) Plan: **J3**
50 17 80 33 – www.nussbaumerin.de – Closed Sunday and Bank Holidays
Carte 27/49 € – *(dinner only) (booking advisable)*
• Austrian • Cosy •

Here in her cosy restaurant Johanna Nußbaumer recreates a little bit of Austria
in the heart of Berlin. Specialities include breaded fried chicken, Wiener Schnitzel, sirloin steak, and a range of Austrian stews and sweet dishes. The excellent
wines also hail from her home country.

🕾 Ottenthal X 🆎

Kantstr. 153 ✉ 10623 – ⓜ Uhlandstr. – ☎ (030) Plan: **K2**
3 13 31 62 – www.ottenthal.com
Carte 34/65 € – *(dinner only) (booking advisable)*
• Austrian • Classic décor •

The typically Austrian tavern fare is a great success. In his friendly restaurant
(named after his home town in Lower Austria) chef Arthur Schneller produces
unfussy dishes including Wiener Tafelspitz (boiled rump of beef Viennese style)
and apple strudel. Good wine selection.

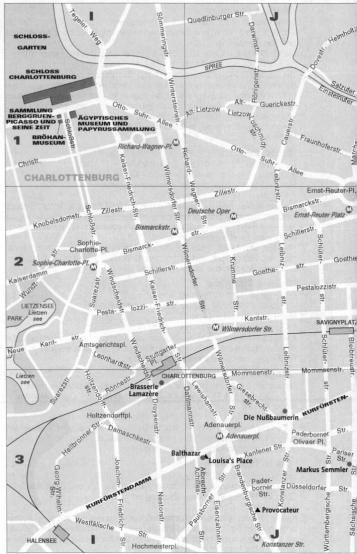

SCHLOSS-
GARTEN

SCHLOSS
CHARLOTTENBURG

SAMMLUNG
BERGGRUEN-
PICASSO UND
SEINE ZEIT

BRÖHAN-
MUSEUM

ÄGYPTISCHES
MUSEUM UND
PAPYRUSSAMMLUNG

CHARLOTTENBURG

Tegeler Weg

SCHLOSS-
GARTEN

Sömmeringstr.

Quedlinburger Str.

Darwinstr.

Helmholt-

Dovestr.

SPREE

Salzufer
Einsteinufer

Otto-
Suhr-
Allee

Alt-Lietzow

Alt-
Lietzow

Guerickestr.

Cauerstr.

Fraunhoferstr.

Richard-Wagner-Pl.

Otto-
Suhr-
Allee

Leibnizstr.

Ernst-Reuter-Pl.

Christstr.

Zillestr.

Bismarckstr.

Ernst-Reuter Platz

Knobelsdorfstr.

Schloßstr.

Zillestr.

Deutsche Oper

Schillerstr.

Sophie-
Charlotte-Pl.

Bismarck-

str.

Sophie-Charlotte-Pl.

Kaiserdamm

Schillerstr.

Goethe-

str.

Goethe

Wundt-

Pesta-

lozzi-

str.

Kantstr.

Pestalozzistr.

LIETZENSEE
PARK

Lietzen
see

Wilmersdorfer Str.

SAVIGNYPLAT.

Neue

Kant-

str.

Amtsgerichtspl.

Leonhardtstr.

Lietzen
see

CHARLOTTENBURG

Mommsenstr.

Mommsenstr.

Brasserie
Lamazère

Die Nußbaumerin

KURFÜRSTEN-

Holtzendorffstr.

Holtzendorffpl.

Damaschkestr.

Adenauerpl.

Adenauerpl.

Paderborner
Olivaer Pl.

Str.

Pariser

Str.

HALENSEE

KURFÜRSTENDAMM

Balthazar

Louisa's Place

Markus Semmler

Str.

Westfälische

Str.

Paderborner
Str.

Düsseldorfer

Str.

Provocateur

Hochmeisterpl.

Konstanzer Str.

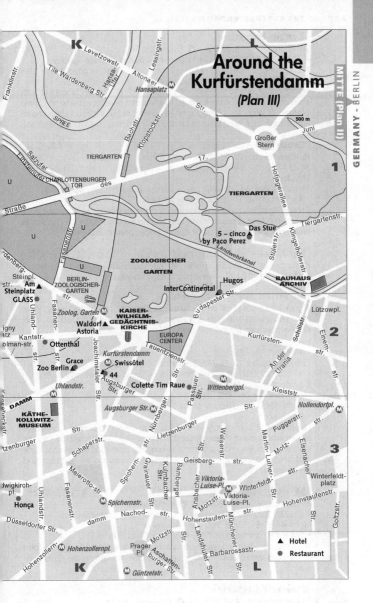

Around the Kurfürstendamm
(Plan III)

0   500 m

1

2

3

Levetzowstr.

Lessingstr.

Tile Wardenberg Str.

Hansa-Pl.

Altonaer

Hansaplatz

Franklinstr.

SPREE

Str.

Klopstockstr.

Bachstr.

Juni

Großer Stern

Großer Stern

Salzufer

Einsteinufer

CHARLOTTENBURGER TOR

TIERGARTEN

U

des

17.

TIERGARTEN

Hofjägeralle

Straße

U

U

Tiergartenstr.

Hardenberg.

Steinpl.

Steinplatz

Am Steinplatz ▲

GLASS

Fasanenstr.

U

BERLIN-ZOOLOGISCHER-GARTEN

ZOOLOGISCHER
GARTEN

5 – cinco by Paco Perez ▲

Das Stue ▲

Landwehrkanal

Stülerstr.

Klingelhöferstr.

Hugos ●

BAUHAUS ARCHIV

igny
platz

Kantstr.

olman-str.

Uhland-

Zoolog. Garten Ⓜ

Waldorf Astoria ▲

KAISER-WILHELM-GEDÄCHTNIS-KIRCHE

InterContinental ●

Budapester Str.

EUROPA CENTER

Lützowpl.

Ottenthal ●

Fasanen-

str.

Joachimstaler

Kurfürstendamm

Swissôtel Ⓜ

Tauentzienstr.

Kurfürsten-

An der Urania

Schillstr.

Einem-

str.

Grace

Zoo Berlin ▲

44 Ⓜ

Colette Tim Raue ●

Augsburger Str.

Passauer

Wittenbergpl. Ⓜ

Kleiststr.

Nollendorfpl. Ⓜ

DAMM Ⓜ

Uhlandstr.

KÄTHE-KOLLWITZ-MUSEUM

Augsburger Str.

Nürnberger

str.

Lietzenburger

Str.

Str.

Welserstr.

Str.

Martin-Luther-

Str.

Motz-

Fuggerstr.

str.

Eisenacher

Winterfeldt-platz

Hohenstaufenstr.

Str.

zenburger

Schaperstr.

Str.

Spichern-

Grainauer

Kulmbacher

Bamberger

Ansbacher

Geisberg-

str.

Motzstr.

Viktoria-Luise-Pl. Ⓜ

Viktoria-Luise-Pl.

Winterfeldt-

str.

Meierotto-str.

str.

Fasanenstr.

Spichernstr. Ⓜ

Nachod-

str.

Hohenstaufen-

str.

Münchener

Str.

Goltzstr.

dwigkirch-pl.

Hança ●

Uhlandstr.

Düsseldorfer Str.

damm

Prager
Pl.

Motzstr.

Aschaffen-burger Str.

Landshuter Str.

Barbarossastr.

Str.

Hohenzollernpl. Ⓜ

Güntzelstr. Ⓜ

Hohenzollern-

K

L

▲ Hotel
● Restaurant

GERMANY - BERLIN

Renger-Patzsch
X 🍴

Wartburgstr. 54 ✉ 10823 – Ⓜ Eisenacher Str. — Plan I: **B3**
– ℰ (030) 7 84 20 59 – www.renger-patzsch.com – Closed Sunday
Menu 30/46 € – Carte 29/43 € – *(dinner only) (booking advisable)*
• Traditional cuisine • Inn • Cosy •

Traditional, tasty and well-executed dishes such as Alsatian sauerkraut with shoulder of pork or flammekueche. The restaurant owes its name to one of the pioneers of landscape photography - a number of his black and white photos adorn the walls. A great place to eat and a very popular one. Wonderful terrace.

Grace – Hotel Zoo Berlin
XX 🍴 ⅙ AC

Kurfürstendamm 25 ✉ 10719 – Ⓜ Uhlandstr. – ℰ (030) — Plan: **K2**
88 43 77 50 70 – www.grace-berlin.de – Closed August and Sunday-Monday
Menu 69/99 € – Carte 49/114 € – *(dinner only) (booking advisable)*
• International • Chic • Design •

Combining stylish, modern design and vintage flair, Grace is a really smart place to eat. The food is modern and international and includes such delights as creamy rock shrimps with cucumber, coriander, peanuts and chilli.

Balthazar – Hotel Louisa's Place
XX 🍴 ⅙ AC ⇔

Kurfürstendamm 160 ✉ 10709 – Ⓜ Adenauerplatz — Plan: **J3**
– ℰ (030) 89 40 84 77 – www.balthazar-restaurant.de – Closed Sunday
Menu 44/95 € – Carte 37/75 € – *(dinner only)*
• International • Fashionable • Trendy •

A great little place to eat on the Ku'damm! The restaurant in the Louisa's Place Hotel serves what it refers to as 'metropolitan cuisine' – German food with a mix of influences from around the world.

Honça
XX 🍴

Ludwigkirchplatz 12 ✉ 10719 – Ⓜ Hohenzollernplatz — Plan: **K3**
– ℰ (030) 23 93 91 14 – www.honca.de – Closed 1-16 January, 20 August-4 September and Monday
Menu 25 € (lunch)/65 € (dinner)
– Carte 46/55 € – *(Tuesday to Friday dinner only)*
• Turkish • Cosy •

Diners here sit comfortably in a stylish, high-ceilinged room with attractive arched windows and pleasantly subdued decor. The food is Anatolian – try the marinated veal tenderloin with çemen (fenugreek paste) and home-made hummus. You'll also find a good-value weekend lunch menu and the Puro Lounge in the basement.

44 – Hotel Swissôtel
XX 🍴 ⅙ AC 🚗

Augsburger Str. 44 ✉ 10789 – Ⓜ Kurfürstendamm — Plan: **K2**
– ℰ (030) 2 20 10 22 88 – www.restaurant44.de – Closed Sunday
Menu 44/69 € – Carte 39/71 € – *(dinner only)*
• Swiss • Contemporary décor • Friendly •

This simple, modern and elegant restaurant serves imaginative food in the form of a tasting menu. Glass frontage and a terrace overlooking the Kurfürstendamm.

Brasserie Lamazère
X

Stuttgarter Platz 18 ✉ 10178 – Ⓜ Wilmersdorfer Str. — Plan: **I3**
– ℰ (030) 31 80 07 12 – www.lamazere.de – Closed Monday
Menu 30/46 € – Carte 42/60 € – *(dinner only) (booking advisable)*
• French • Brasserie • Neighbourhood •

You might almost be in France here in the heart of Charlottenburg at Brasserie Lamazère thanks to its charming, straightforward bistro feel and authentic, constantly changing menu of fresh and tasty seasonal fare. Try the *oeufs en cocotte* with Bayonne ham or Atlantic cod with tomato and paprika mussels.

SMALL SPELT FROM MONT VENTOUX
THE CAVIAR OF CEREALS

Grown in the purest ancestral tradition, this rustic cereal is harvested and husked with care to preserve its exceptional flavour.

Easy to digest, with a fine, crisp outer shell that gives way to a creamy interior, small spelt has a subtle taste that lends itself to a wide variety of preparations.

CARPEGNA HAM
AT THE HEART
OF ITALIAN TRADITION

Matured in the hills of Montefeltro,
Carpegna ham is made according
to traditional methods from pigs
born and bred in Italy.

As the transalpine peninsula's third
certified P.D.O., after Parma and
San Daniel, this mellow,
smooth-textured ham reveals
a combination of delicate aromas
for a journey to the heart of
Italy's finest culinary traditions.

GERMANY - BERLIN

GLASS   ✗ ᕫ

Uhlandstr. 195 ✉ *10623 –* Ⓜ *Zoologischer Garten*   Plan: **K2**
– 𝒞 (030) 54 71 08 61 – www.glassberlin.de – Closed Sunday-Monday
Menu 79/119 € – Carte 44/52 € – *(dinner only)*
• Creative • Minimalist •

The cuisine here is every bit as creative and contrasting as the interior is minimalist and modern urban. Behind the eye-catching reflective metal curtain, the kitchen staff conjure up a five- to nine-course set menu including such delights as lamb with stuffed onions, yoghurt, sumac and aubergine. Wines are also available by the glass.

Waldorf Astoria   ⛫ ᕫ ⊕ ☏ ☒ ᕫ ᴀᴄ 🅂🄰 🚗

Hardenbergstr. 28 ✉ *10623 –* Ⓜ *Zoologischer Garten*   Plan: **K2**
– 𝒞 (030) 8 14 00 00 – www.waldorfastoriaberlin.com
202 rm – 🛏200/390 € 🛏🛏200/390 € **–** ⌧ 38 € **– 30 suites**
• Grand Luxury • Elegant • Classic •

The modern, elegant interior here is designed in classic 1920s-style with perfectly judged colours and lines throughout. As befits its legendary name, it also has its own Peacock Alley restaurant serving international cuisine – a genuine piece of New York hotel tradition in Berlin! ROCA serves sandwiches and cakes.

InterContinental   ⛫ ᕫ ⊕ ☏ ☒ ᕫ ᴀᴄ 🅂🄰 🚗

Budapester Str. 2 ✉ *10787 –* Ⓜ *Zoologischer Garten*   Plan: **L2**
– 𝒞 (030) 2 60 20 – www.berlin.intercontinental.com
558 rm – 🛏220/550 € 🛏🛏240/570 € **–** ⌧ 32 € **– 44 suites**
• Business • Luxury • Classic •

The hotel offers elegant, modern guestrooms that are both spacious and upmarket (with Club InterContinental rooms and a Club Lounge on the seventh and eighth floors), a tasteful 1 000m2 spa and conference and events facilities. Eateries include Hugos, the L.A. Café and the Marlene Bar.
❀ **Hugos** – See restaurant listing

Swissôtel   ᕫ ☏ ᕫ ᴀᴄ 🅂🄰 🚗

Augsburger Str. 44 ✉ *10789 –* Ⓜ *Kurfürstendamm*   Plan: **K2**
– 𝒞 (030) 22 01 00 – www.swissotel.com/berlin
316 rm – 🛏119/399 € 🛏🛏119/399 € **–** ⌧ 16 €
• Business • Contemporary •

This modern town hotel with its glass façade welcomes its guests with a spacious atrium. It has comfortable guestrooms, including business and executive rooms.
🍴 **44** – See restaurant listing

Am Steinplatz   ⛫ ᕫ ☏ ᕫ ᴀᴄ 🅂🄰 🚗

Steinplatz 4 ✉ *10623 –* Ⓜ *Ernst-Reuter-Platz – 𝒞 (030)*   Plan: **K2**
5 54 44 40 – www.hotelsteinplatz.com
84 rm – 🛏185/295 € 🛏🛏185/295 € **–** ⌧ 35 € **– 3 suites**
• Luxury • Townhouse • Elegant •

Once Berlin's artists' hotel, today Am Steinplatz is a small, exclusive boutique hotel in the heart of Charlottenburg. The rooms are upmarket, chic and comfortable, the service attentive and personal and the interior full of period charm and high, stuccoed ceilings. Simple lunch menu, more ambitious fare in the evenings.

Das Stue   ⛫ ᕫ ⊕ ☏ ᕫ ᴀᴄ

Drakestr. 1 ✉ *10787 –* Ⓜ *Wittenbergplatz – 𝒞 (030)*   Plan: **L2**
3 11 72 20 – www.das-stue.com
78 rm – 🛏230/280 € 🛏🛏230/280 € **–** ⌧ 35 €
• Luxury • Design • Elegant •

'Stylish' is the only word that fits! In this listed 1930's building that once housed the Danish embassy the interior is a great mixture of neo-Classical and modern design. The lobby with its impressive staircases is a highlight, while rooms are individually designed; some offering a view over Berlin Zoo. Casual is both relaxed and sophisticated and offers tapas-style international dishes.
❀ **5 - cinco by Paco Pérez** – See restaurant listing

Zoo Berlin

Kurfürstendamm 25 ✉ *10179* – Ⓜ *Uhlandstr.* – ✆ *(030) 88 43 70* – *www.hotelzoo.de*

Plan: **K2**

144 rm ⌑ – †180/1500 € ††200/1500 €

• Luxury • Design • Elegant •

Well-known designer Dayna Lee has brought a bit of Berlin hotel history back to life at Zoo Berlin. She has successfully combined the elegance and class of the old hotel with a new, modern feel. The rooms are tasteful and upmarket, opulent yet functional, with all the atmosphere of a real 'grand hotel'.

‖○ **Grace** – See restaurant listing

Louisa's Place

Kurfürstendamm 160 ✉ *10709* – Ⓜ *Adenauerplatz* – ✆ *(030) 63 10 30* – *www.louisas-place.de*

Plan: **J3**

47 suites – †145/625 € ††145/625 € – ⌑ 26 €

• Business • Townhouse • Personalised •

This hotel has friendly service and offers tasteful, spacious suites with kitchens. There is also a stylish breakfast room and library.

‖○ **Balthazar** – See restaurant listing

Provocateur

Brandenburgische Str. 21 ✉ *10707* – Ⓜ *Konstanzer Str.* – ✆ *(030) 22 05 60 60* – *www.provocateur-hotel.de*

Plan: **J3**

58 rm – †150/490 € ††150/490 € – ⌑ 28 € – 2 suites

• Boutique hotel • Townhouse • Personalised •

Provocateur offers upmarket and tasteful 1920s chic. A period lift transports you up to the guestrooms which come in a range of options from "Petite" to the excellent "Terrace" and "Maison" suites. In the morning, it's breakfast à la carte, in the evenings Franco-Chinese cuisine in the Golden Phoenix plus a stylish "tempting" bar.

ENVIRONS OF BERLIN

PLAN I

AT BERLIN-GRUNEWALD

✿ Frühsammers Restaurant

Flinsberger Platz 8 ✉ *14193* – ✆ *(030) 89 73 86 28* – *www.fruehsammers.de* – *Closed Sunday-Tuesday*

Plan: **A3**

Menu 88/145 € – *(dinner only) (booking advisable)*

• Classic cuisine • Friendly •

The menu at Frühsammers, set in its red villa in the grounds of a tennis club promises aromatic cuisine full of interesting textures and contrasts made with great care using choice produce. The setting is classically elegant, the service attentive and professional.

→ Gelbflossenmakrele, Rettich, Teriyakisauce, Champignons, Koriander, Hühnerhaut. Hummer, Rhabarber, schwarzer Lauch, Dilleis. Rehbock, grüner Spargel, Grießknödel, Ochsenmark, Morcheln, Liebstöckel, Haselnuss.

⊛ **Grundschlag** – See restaurant listing

Grundschlag – Frühsammers Restaurant

Flinsberger Platz 8 ✉ *14193* – ✆ *(030) 89 73 86 28* – *www.fruehsammers.de* – *Closed Monday lunch*

Plan: **A3**

Carte 29/44 €

• Market cuisine • Cosy • Bistro •

This is the bistro alternative to the Frühsammer's gourmet restaurant. Diners here enjoy internationally influenced cuisine and popular classics served in a snug and friendly atmosphere – don't miss the wonderful selection of sardines!

SKYKITCHEN XX ⇔ ⋖ 𝆑ᷓ 🛋 ঝ 🅰 🅰 🚗

Landsberger Allee 106 (12th floor) ✉ *10369*
Plan: **D1**
– Ⓜ *Landsberger Allee* – ℰ *(030) 45 30 53 26 20* – *www.skykitchen.berlin*
– *Closed Sunday-Monday*
534 rm ⌷ – ♦94/120 € ♦♦219/245 € – 23 suites
Menu 64 € (Vegetarian)/144 €
– Carte 58/79 € – *(dinner only) (booking advisable)*
• Modern cuisine • Fashionable •

It is worth making your way out to Lichtenberg to sample the *'voyage culinaire'* on offer on the 12th floor of Andel's Hotel. The 3- to 11-course set menu showcases creative, modern cuisine full of contrasts with local and international influences. The setting is relaxed yet stylishly chic, and the view is wonderful. The SKYBAR is two floors further up.

➔ Blütenkohl, Nussbutter, Gartenkresse, Bio-Ei. Heilbutt, Stabmuschel, Sojabohne, Artischocke. Milchferkel, Spitzkraut, Gartenerbse, Holzkohleöl.

HAMBURG
HAMBURG

ponomarevvb/iStock

With a maritime role stretching back centuries, Germany's second largest city has a lively and liberal ambience. Hamburg is often described as 'The Gateway to the World', and there's certainly a visceral feel here, particularly around the big, buzzy and bustling port area. Locals enjoy a long-held reputation for their tolerance and outward looking stance, cosmopolitan to the core. Space to breathe is seen as very important in Hamburg: the city authorities have paid much attention to green spaces, and the city can proudly claim an enviable amount of parks, lakes and tree-lined canals.

There's no cathedral here (at least not a standing one, as war-destroyed St Nikolai remains a ruin), so the Town Hall acts as the central landmark. Just north of here are the Binnenalster (inner) and Aussenalster (outer) lakes. The old walls of the city, dating back over eight hundred years, are delineated by a distinct semicircle of boulevards that curve attractively in a wide arc south of the lakes. Further south from here is the port and harbour area, defined by Landungsbrücken to the west and Speicherstadt to the east. The district to the west of the centre is St Pauli, famed for its clubs and bars, particularly along the notorious Reeperbahn, which pierces the district from east to west. The contrastingly smart Altona suburb and delightful Blankenese village are west of St Pauli.

EATING OUT

Being a city immersed in water, it's no surprise to find Hamburg is a good place for fish. Though its fishing industry isn't the powerhouse of old, the city still boasts a giant trawler's worth of seafood places to eat. Eel dishes are mainstays of the traditional restaurant's menu, as is the herring stew with vegetables called Labskaus. Also unsurprisingly, considering it's the country's gateway to the world, this is somewhere that offers a vast range of international dishes. Wherever you eat, the portions are likely to be generous. There's no problem with finding somewhere early: cafés are often open at seven, with the belief that it's never too early for coffee and cake. Bakeries also believe in an early start, and the calorie content here, too, can be pretty high. Bistros and restaurants, usually open by midday, are proud of their local ingredients, so keep your eyes open for Hamburgisch on the menu. Service charges are always included in the bill, so tipping is not compulsory, although most people will round it up and possibly add five to ten per cent.

GERMANY - HAMBURG

The Table Kevin Fehling ❀❀❀ XxX 簽

Shanghaiallee 15 ⊠ 20457 – Ⓜ *HafenCity Universität* Plan I: **C2**
– ℰ (040) 22 86 74 22 – www.the-table-hamburg.de – Closed
24 December-8 January, 1-9 April, 22 July-13 August and Sunday-Monday
Menu 205 € – (dinner only) (booking essential)
• Creative • Design •

This relaxed restaurant really is one of a kind! Diners sit at a long, curved table as the chefs – a study of concentration – combine fine international ingredients to perfection before their eyes with the precision, subtlety and stunning presentation for which Kevin Fehling is famed. Excellent wine recommendations.

➔ Geflämmter Kaisergranat mit Fruchtchutney, Kalamansi, Thaicurryschaum. Wagyu Roastbeef Schaufelbraten mit Olive, Gremolata Hollandaise, Calzone. Schokoladen Canache mit Raz el Hanout Eis, Sanddorn, Safran und Avocado.

Haerlin ❀❀ – Fairmont Hotel Vier Jahreszeiten XxXxX 簽 ≼ & ⒜ ⇕

Neuer Jungfernstieg 9 ⊠ 20354 – Ⓜ *Jungfernstieg – ℰ (040)* ⌂
34 94 33 10 – www.fairmont-hvj.de – Closed1-4 January, Plan: **F2**
26 March-2 April, 9 July-5 August, 1-7 October and Sunday-Monday
Menu 145/185 € – (dinner only) (booking advisable)
• Creative French • Luxury • Elegant •

The food at Haerlin is powerful and intensely flavoured. The dishes brought to your table are creative and technically perfect, and use nothing but the very best ingredients. The culinary quality is matched by the exquisite interior where everything is of the finest quality. The view over the Inner Alster Lake adds the finishing touch.

➔ Gillardeau Auster mit grünen Erbsen und geröstetem Zwiebelsaft. Geflämmter Glattbutt mit Champignons und Zitronenthymian. Wagyu Rind aus Niedersachsen mit Liliengewächsen und Sauce béarnaise.

SE7EN OCEANS ❀ XX ≼ & ⒜

Ballindamm 40 (2nd floor) (Europa-Passage) ⊠ 20095 Plan: **G2**
– Ⓜ *Jungfernstieg – ℰ (040) 32 50 79 44 – www.se7en-oceans.de*
– Closed 5-11 February, 6-26 August and Sunday-Monday
Menu 43 € (lunch)/119 € – Carte 77/104 €
• Classic French • Chic • Design •

Ideal for escaping the crowds, this modern eatery has a great view of the Inner Alster Lake and the Jungfernstieg promenade. It offers peace and quiet in the midst of the Europa Passage shopping centre and serves classic international cuisine. The glass front opens up in the summer.

➔ Bouillabaisse, Kaisergranat, Safran. Pochiertes Seezungenfilet, Alge, Lauch. Iberico Schwein, Apfel, Zwiebel.

Tschebull ☺ XX ⇕

Mönckebergstr. 7 ⊠ 20095 – Ⓜ *Mönchebergstr.* Plan: **H2**
– ℰ (040) 32 96 47 96 – www.tschebull.de – Closed Sunday and Bank Holidays
Menu 30 € (lunch)/32 € (dinner) – Carte 36/69 € – (booking advisable)
• Austrian • Cosy •

In the centre of this exclusive shopping arcade sits a little piece of Austria, courtesy of Carinthian chef Alexander Tschebull. As you would expect, the Austrian classics, such as Tafelspitz (Viennese-style boiled beef) and Fiaker (beef) goulash are excellent, as are the more modern dishes. These include skrei cod with potato and caper champ, radish and pearl onions.

Brook ☺ X 簽

Bei den Mühren 91 ⊠ 20457 – Ⓜ *Meßberg – ℰ (040)* Plan: **G3**
37 50 31 28 – www.restaurant-brook.de – Closed Sunday-Monday
Menu 35/39 € – Carte 37/52 €
• International • Fashionable •

The most popular dishes at this relaxed modern restaurant include classics such as braised calves' cheeks, but fish fresh from the famous fish market just round the corner are also firm favourites, as is the very reasonable set lunchtime menu. It is worth coming here in the evenings too, when you can enjoy views of the illuminated warehouse district.

ⓐ **Cox**   ✗

Lange Reihe 68 ⊠ 20099 – Ⓜ Hauptbf. Nord – ℰ (040)   Plan: **H1**
*24 94 22 – www.restaurant-cox.de – Closed Saturday lunch, Sunday lunch
and Bank Holidays lunch*
Menu 35/51 € – Carte 31/48 € – *(mid July-end August: dinner only)*
• International • Bistro • Cosy •
More casual and urban than chic and elegant, Cox is a bistro in the best sense of
the word. A colourful mix of diners enjoys a varied selection of dishes including
braised lamb shanks, grass-fed beef rissoles and cod. Good value lunchtime
menu.

ⓐ **Le Plat du Jour**   ✗ 🛱 🔤

Dornbusch 4 ⊠ 20095 – Ⓜ Rathaus – ℰ (040) 32 14 14   Plan: **G3**
– www.leplatdujour.de – Closed during Christmas
Menu 35 € (dinner) – Carte 32/49 € – *(booking advisable)*
• Classic French • Bistro •
With a reputation forged largely by word of mouth, you will find the lively Le
Plat du Jour busy from lunchtime onwards. Both the interior, with its black and
white photos and closely packed tables, and the food it serves, are authentic
brasserie in style. As an alternative to the dish of the day, try the Mediterranean
French fish soup with croutons or the classic 'steak frites'.

ⓐ **Trific**   ✗

Holzbrücke 7 ⊠ 20459 – Ⓜ Rödingsmarkt – ℰ (040)   Plan: **F3**
41 91 90 46 – www.trific.de – Closed Saturday lunch, Sunday
Menu 18 € (lunch)/43 € (dinner) – Carte 35/51 € – *(booking advisable)*
• International • Fashionable • Neighbourhood •
A popular city centre address, Trific is divided over two floors. There is the light
and airy ground floor with its floor-to-ceiling windows and view of the Fleet, as
well as the basement with a bar. The food on offer is tasty and uncomplicated
and includes Holstein steak tartar with wild garlic emulsion and classic breaded
fried chicken.

🍴 **Atlantic Restaurant** – Hotel Atlantic Kempinski   XxX ≼ 🛱 🔤

An der Alster 72 ⊠ 20099 – Ⓜ Jungfernstieg – ℰ (040)   🚗
2 88 88 60 – www.kempinski.com/hamburg – Closed   Plan: **H1**
Sunday
Menu 79 € (dinner)/94 € – Carte 44/111 €
• Classic cuisine • Elegant •
The elegant restaurant of this traditional Hamburg hotel serves as a lounge for
significant numbers of the city's rich and famous. Its classic cakes are particularly
popular.

🍴 **Jahreszeiten Grill** – Fairmont Hotel Vier Jahreszeiten   XxX ≼

Neuer Jungfernstieg 9 ⊠ 20354 – Ⓜ Jungfernstieg   ⴳ 🔤 🚗
– ℰ (040) 34 94 33 02 – www.fairmont-hvj.de   Plan: **F2**
Menu 33 € (lunch) – Carte 74/116 €
• Classic French • Elegant •
This restaurant is a stylish Hamburg institution with an impressive Art Deco interior. It serves classics including smoked eel and scrambled eggs with herbs on
wholemeal bread, as well as more sophisticated fare, including codfish in a
thyme crust with chanterelle mushrooms and grilled meats. The very best ingredients are always used.

🍴 **NIKKEI NINE** – Fairmont Hotel Vier Jahreszeiten   XX

Neuer Jungfernstieg 9 ⊠ 20534 – Ⓜ Jungfernstieg   Plan: **F2**
– ℰ (040) 34943399 – www.fairmont-hvj.de – closed Sunday lunch
Menu 70/89 € – Carte 47/183 €
• Japanese • Chic • Exotic décor •
This is one of the most fashionable culinary hot spots in Hamburg! The
ambience is stylish yet warm and the food is Japanese with Peruvian influences.
Menu options include seafood toban yaki, cold soba noodles with egg, caviar
and dashi soy, wagyu steak, sushi and sashimi – all made with first-class ingre-
dients.

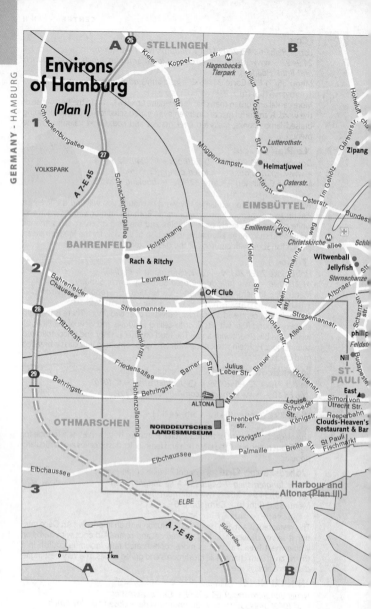

Environs of Hamburg

(Plan I)

A 26 STELLINGEN

B

Kieler Koppel-str.

Hagenbecks Tierpark

Julius Vosseler Str.

Hoheluft cha

Garner str.

1

Schnackenburgallee

27

Lutterothstr.

Zipang

VOLKSPARK

A 7-E 45

Müggenkampstr.

Heimatjuwel

Osterstr.

Osterstr.

Im Gehölz

Osterstr.

EIMSBÜTTEL

Bundess

Schnackenburgallee

Holstenkamp

Emilienstr.

Fruchta

weg

Christskirche allee

Schle

M

BAHRENFELD

Rach & Ritchy

Kieler

Doormanns

Str.

Aiken str.

Witwenball

Jellyfish

Sternschanze

Altonaer

Schanze

2

Bahrenfelder Chaussee

Leunastr.

28

Pfitznerstr.

Off Club

Stresemannstr.

Holstenstr. Allee

Stresemannstr.

philip

Feldstr

Nil

Budapeste

29

Behringstr.

Daimler str.

Friedensallee

Barner Str.

Julius Leber Str. Brauer

Holstenstr.

ST-PAULI

East

Behringstr.

Hohenzollernring

Behringstr.

Max

Louise Schroeder Str.

Simon von Utrecht Str.

OTHMARSCHEN

ALTONA

Ehrenberg str.

Königstr.

Reeperbahn

Clouds-Heaven's Restaurant & Bar

NORDDEUTSCHES LANDESMUSEUM

Königstr.

Palmaille

Breite str.

St Pauli Fischmarkt

Elbchaussee

Elbchaussee

Harbour and Altona (Plan III)

3

ELBE

A 7-E 45

Süderelbe

0   1 km

A

B

✈ HAMBURG-FUHLSBÜTTEL

GERMANY - HAMBURG

● Brechtmanns Bistro

C

● Borgweg M

D M

● Cornelia
Poletto

Sierichstr.

Barmbeker

Wiesendamm

Saarlandstr.

Barmbeck

Kellinghusenstr.

WINTERHUDE

EPPENDORF

Osterbekkanal

BARMBEK

ietto
nebar

Eppendorfer
Baum M

Klosterstern M

● Trüffelschwein

Weidestr.

Weidestr.

Dehnhalde

1

Piment

● Gallo Nero

Beethovenstr.

Hamburger Str. M

EILBECK

HOHELUFT

Hoheluftbr.

● Mittelweg

● Nippon
Zimmer-
str.

UHLENHORST

Hamburger Str.

Lerchenfeld

Wachter-
str.

Hallerstr.

● Anna Sgroi

Mundsburg M

● Eilenau

Wandsbeker
Chaussee

HAMBURGISCHES
MUSEUM FÜR
VÖLKERKUNDE

Magdalenenstr.

AUSSENALSTER

Uhlandstr.

Wartenau

● Butcher's
american
stakhouse

U U

Fontenay

Miramar
& Mare ▲

Lübecker
Str.

M

● Mirabelle

Edmund
Siemers Allee

Alsterufer

Commercial
Centre (Plan II)

● The George ▲

Sechslingsp
forte

Bürgerweide

2

FERNSEHTURM

Kennedybrücke

An der Alster

ST-GEORG

Burgstr.

Gorch Fock Wall

Lombards-
brücke

Steindamm

Lohmühlenstr.

Borgfelder Str.

Eiffestr.

BINNENALSTER

KUNSTHALLE

Berliner Tor M

Kaiser Wilhelm
Str.

Jungfernstieg

Glockengießer
Wall

HAUPT-BAHNHOF

Spaldingstr.

Heidekampsweg

Süderstr.

Holstenwall

Ludwig
Erhard Str.

St-Pauli

Ost West

Bei den
Mühren

HAMMERBROOK

Amsinckstr.

Amsinckstr.

● The Greek

Vorsetzen

VLET ▲

● Strauchs Falco

3

HAFEN

The Westin ▲

25hours
Hafen City ▲

CARLS

● Coast

● The Table
Kevin Fehling

Versmannstr.

Billhorner Brückenstr.

Norderelbe

An
Moldauhafen

▲ Hotel
● Restaurant

C

D

297

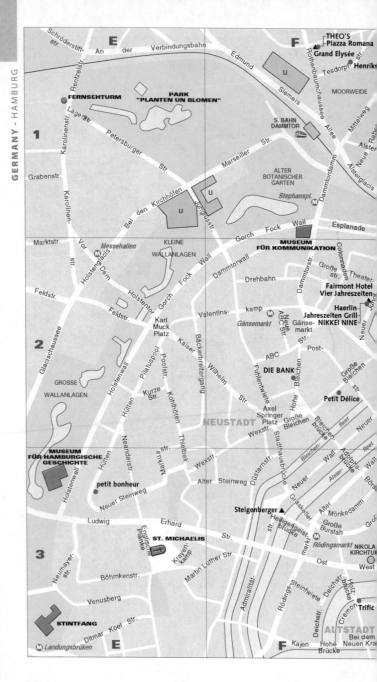

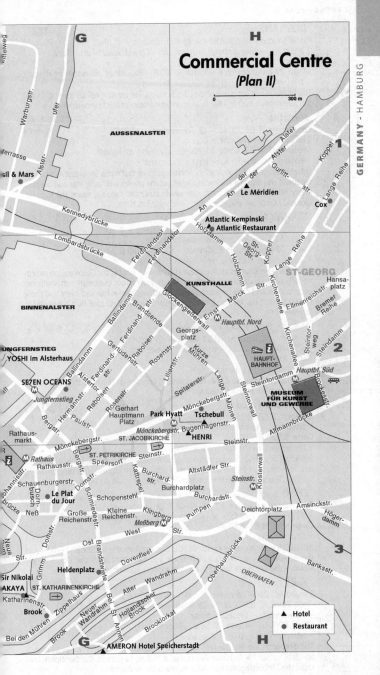

Commercial Centre
(Plan II)

0   300 m

AUSSENALSTER

▲ Le Méridien

● Cox

▲ Atlantic Kempinski
▲ Atlantic Restaurant

Kennedybrücke

Lombardsbrücke

ST-GEORG

Hansa-platz

KUNSTHALLE

Bremer Reihe

BINNENALSTER

Hauptbf. Nord

Georgs-platz

JUNGFERNSTIEG

YOSHI im Alsterhaus

HAUPT-BAHNHOF

Hauptbf. Süd

SE7EN OCEANS

Jungfernstieg

MUSEUM FÜR KUNST UND GEWERBE

Gerhart Hauptmann Platz

● Park Hyatt

● Tschebull

Rathaus-markt

Mönckebergstr.

ST. JACOBIKIRCHE

HENRI

M Rathaus
Rathausstr.

ST. PETRIKIRCHE

Speersort

Burchard-str.

Burchardplatz

Le Plat du Jour

Burchardstr.

Deichtorplatz

Höger-damm

Amsinckstr.

Heldenplatz

OBERHAFEN

Sir Nikolai

AKAYA

ST. KATHARINENKIRCHE

Banksstr.

● Brook

▲ AMERON Hotel Speicherstadt

▲	Hotel
●	Restaurant

🟡

DIE BANK   XX 🛱

Hohe Bleichen 17 ✉ *20354 –* Ⓜ *Gänsemarkt – 𝒞 (040)*   Plan: **F2**
2 38 00 30 – www.diebank-brasserie.de – Closed Sunday and Bank
Holidays
Menu 29 € (lunch)/65 € – **Carte** 42/69 € – *(bookings advisable at dinner)*
• International • Brasserie • Trendy •

This brasserie and bar is one of the city's hotspots. The banking hall on the first-floor of this former bank, built in 1897, is an impressive feature of this fashionable venue.

🟡

Henriks   XX 🛱 ᵴ 🄰🄲

Tesdorpfstr. 8 ✉ *20148 –* Ⓜ *Stephanspl. – 𝒞 (040)*   Plan: **F1**
2 88 08 42 80 – www.henriks.cc
Menu 40/130 € – **Carte** 33/100 € – *(booking essential)*
• International • Design • Elegant •

This chic designer restaurant offers ambitious cuisine that mixes Southeast Asian, Mediterranean and regional influences. Dishes include gravlax with curly kale and beetroot mayonnaise or tuna tataki steak with wasabi puree and miso soy sauce. The large terrace and lounge are always popular. Good value lunch menu.

🟡

IZAKAYA – Hotel Sir Nikolai   XX 🛱 🄰🄲 ✿

Katharinenstrasse 29 ✉ *20457 –* Ⓜ *Meßberg – 𝒞 (040)*   Plan: **G3**
29 99 66 69 – www.izakaya-restaurant.com
Menu 30 € (lunch)/85 € (dinner) – **Carte** 37/88 €
• Japanese • Elegant • Fashionable •

IZAKAYA serves authentic Japanese cuisine with what is, for Germany, an exceptionally wide range of top-quality products. How about the crispy soft-shell crab with mango and chilli lime dressing? The atmosphere is hip and lively and there is also a smart bar and an interior courtyard with a glass roof that is opened in fine weather.

🟡

Piazza Romana – Hotel Grand Elysée   XX ᵴ 🄰🄲 🚗

Rothenbaumchaussee 10 ✉ *20148 –* Ⓜ *Stephanspl.*   Plan: **F1**
– 𝒞 (040) 41 41 27 34 – www.grand-elysee.com
Carte 35/51 €
• Italian • Classic décor •

If you fancy carpaccio di vitello, a plate of linguine or tiramisu, then the Italian cuisine on offer at this restaurant is for you.

🟡

Strauchs Falco   XX 🛱

Koreastr. 2 ✉ *20354 – 𝒞 (040) 2 26 16 15 11*   Plan I: **C3**
– www.falco-hamburg.de
Carte 38/83 €
• International • Fashionable •

Strauchs Falco serves a wide range of good Mediterranean dishes, steaks and classic fare. The restaurant itself is modern in style with an open kitchen and a large terrace in summer. The tapas bar on the first floor doubles up as a café during the day.

🟡

THEO'S – Hotel Grand Elysée   XX

Rothenbaumchaussee 10 ✉ *20148 –* Ⓜ *Stephanspl.*   Plan: **F1**
– 𝒞 (040) 41 41 28 55 – www.grand-elysee.com – Closed Sunday
Carte 55/128 € – *(dinner only)*
• Steakhouse • Brasserie •

At THEO'S you can enjoy exclusive cuts of meat from the Southbend Broiler just like a New York steakhouse. Whatever you do, don't miss the Uckermärker steaks – the cattle are raised to the restaurant's specification!

🟡

VLET   XX

Sandtorkai 23/24 (entrance by Kibbelstegbrücke 1, 1st   Plan I: **C3**
floor, Block N) ✉ *20457 –* Ⓜ *Baumwall – 𝒞 (040) 3 34 75 37 50*
– www.vlet.de – Closed Sunday
Menu 69/88 € – **Carte** 49/58 € – *(dinner only)*
• Modern cuisine • Trendy •

The deliberate warehouse feel, typical of Hamburg's Speicherstadt area, makes an ideal venue for fashionable cuisine. It is best to park in the Contipark and cross the Kibbelstegbrücke bridge to reach the restaurant.

YOSHI im Alsterhaus XX 🛳 ᖚ 🔲
Plan: **G2**
Jungfernstieg 16 (Alsterhaus, 4th floor, direct Elevator, entrance Poststr. 8) ⊠ 20354 – Ⓜ *Jungfernstieg* – ℰ (040) 36 09 99 99
– www.yoshi-hamburg.de – *Closed Sunday and Bank Holidays*
Menu 26 € (weekday lunch)/95 € – Carte 34/112 €
• Japanese • Fashionable •
Christened 'Gourmet Boulevard', the fourth floor of Hamburg's upmarket Alsterhaus shopping plaza is the meeting place for enthusiasts of Japanese food and culture. The teriyaki and sushi dishes prepared by the Japanese chefs achieve a perfect marriage of the traditional and the modern. Popular roof terrace.

Basil & Mars X 🛳 🔲
Plan: **G1**
Alsterufer 1 ⊠ 20354 – ℰ (040) 41 35 35 35
– www.basilundmars.com
Menu 42 € (dinner) – Carte 41/72 €
• Modern cuisine • Trendy •
This restaurant close to the Kennedy Bridge is chic and fashionable but also pleasantly relaxed. The food prepared in the kitchens is a modern mix of regional, Mediterranean and Southeast Asian influences, such as 12-hour short ribs, grilled octopus and sashimi salad. A simpler lunchtime menu is served Monday to Friday.

CARLS X ← 🛳 ᖚ 🔲 ⇔
Plan I: **C3**
Am Kaiserkai 69 ⊠ 20457 – Ⓜ *Baumwall* – ℰ (040)
3 00 32 24 00 – www.carls-brasserie.de
Menu 42 € – Carte 41/86 €
• Country • Brasserie •
This elegant brasserie is at the New Elbe Philharmonic Hall. It serves up French cuisine with a North German slant alongside great views of the port. Savoury tarts and nibbles in the bistro; spices and other gourmet treats in the delicatessen.

Coast X 🏜 🛳 ᖚ
Plan I: **C3**
Großer Grasbrook 14 ⊠ 20457 – Ⓜ *Überseequartier*
– ℰ (040) 30 99 32 30 – www.coast-hamburg.de
Menu 63/70 € – Carte 49/80 €
• Fusion • Friendly • Fashionable •
With a great location close to the water on the Marco Polo Terrace at the edge of the Hafencity, Coast serves an interesting mix of European and Southeast Asian food and creative sushi delicacies. Downstairs in the basement you will find the Enoteca, which serves Italian cuisine. From 6pm you can park in the Unilever garage next door.

The Greek X 🔲
Plan I: **C3**
Vorsetzen 53 ⊠ 20459 – Ⓜ *Baumwall* – ℰ (040)
31 80 73 70 – www.thegreek.hamburg
Carte 38/70 €
• Greek • Fashionable •
No standard Gyros-style fare here, the three floors of this modern restaurant in the port serve upmarket, modern Greek cuisine. Dishes include shoulder of lamb with aubergine caviar, pitta bread and cardamom yoghurt and *moraitiko hilopitaki* (traditional Greek pasta with lobster). Shorter lunchtime menu.

Heldenplatz X 🔲
Plan: **G3**
Brandstwiete 46 ⊠ 20457 – Ⓜ *Meßberg* – ℰ (040)
30 37 22 50 – www.heldenplatz-restaurant.de – *Closed 24 December-12 January and Monday-Tuesday*
Menu 46/53 € – Carte 42/66 € – (dinner only)
• Modern French • Fashionable •
Great news for night owls, at Heldenplatz you will find the whole menu available until 2am! It serves options including Iberico pork with aubergines, red onions and tamarillos, followed by chocolate tart with peanuts, caramel and lemon. Relaxed, modern surroundings. Note that all the wines on offer here are sold by the glass.

GERMANY - HAMBURG

La Mirabelle ✗

Bundesstr. 15 ✉ 20146 – ⓜ Hallerstr. – ℰ (040)   Plan I: **C2**
4 10 75 85 – www.la-mirabelle-hamburg.de – Closed 1-8 January, Sunday-Monday and Bank Holidays
Menu 35 € (weekdays)/62 € – Carte 46/66 € – *(dinner only)*
• Classic French • Cosy • Family •

As the name suggests, the cuisine is French, flavoursome and without frills. Try the delicious sounding Atlantic cod with mustard sauce. Cheese lovers beware: the restaurant boasts some 50 different French cheeses!

Petit Délice ✗ 🍴 🅰🅲 ⇄

Große Bleichen 21 ✉ 20354 – ⓜ Jungfernstieg   Plan: **F2**
– ℰ (040) 34 34 70 – www.petit-delice-hamburg.de – Closed Sunday and Bank Holidays
Menu 25 € (lunch) – Carte 43/72 € – *(booking advisable)*
• Classic French • Neighbourhood •

Petit Délice serves classic cuisine with a regional influence in a warm and lively atmosphere. The menu includes roast pumpernickel with scrambled eggs and smoked eel and monkfish served with sweetheart cabbage and cucumber relish. Lovely terrace overlooking the Fleet. Traiteur next door serves simpler fare.

Fairmont Hotel Vier Jahreszeiten ⩽ 📶 🖪 ⑳ 🏯 ⓺ 🅰🅲

Neuer Jungfernstieg 9 ✉ 20354 – ⓜ Jungfernstieg   🛎 🚗
– ℰ (040) 3 49 40 – www.fairmont-hvj.de   Plan: **F2**
139 rm – †285/320 € ††315/345 € – ⌂ 39 € – 17 suites
• Grand Luxury • Traditional • Elegant •

This hotel is the very epitome of Hamburg tradition and was first established in 1897. Cleverly combining smart, fresh design and classical elegance, the rooms are both lavish and sumptuous. You can relax on the great roof terrace with a bar, take afternoon tea in the stylish Wohnhalle or enjoy a snack or cake in the trendy Condi Lounge.
❀❀ **Haerlin** • ⅈⓞ **Jahreszeiten Grill** • ⅈⓞ **NIKKEI NINE** – See restaurant listing

Atlantic Kempinski ⩽ 🏯 🖪 🅰🅲 🛎 🚗

An der Alster 72 ✉ 20099 – ⓜ Jungfernstieg – ℰ (040)   Plan: **H1**
2 88 80 – www.kempinski.com/hamburg
221 rm ⌂ – †249/469 € ††279/499 € – 33 suites
• Grand Luxury • Classic • Contemporary •

Following extensive renovation work, the Atlantic Kempinski is now even more magnificent than before. It has an elegant, classic lobby, timeless, sumptuously decorated rooms (complete with fine ebony and state-of-the-art technology) and stylish reception and conference facilities.
ⅈⓞ **Atlantic Restaurant** – See restaurant listing

Park Hyatt 🏛 🖪 ⑳ 🏯 🖪 ⓺ 🅰🅲 🛎 🚗

Bugenhagenstr. 8 (at Levantehaus) ✉ 20095   Plan: **H2**
– ⓜ Mönckebergstr. – ℰ (040) 33 32 12 34 – www.hamburg.park.hyatt.de
262 rm – †185/550 € ††225/610 € – ⌂ 34 € – 21 suites
• Grand Luxury • Chain • Contemporary •

This former Hanseatic League trading post welcomes guests on the first floor where they can make themselves comfortable in the tasteful lounge. Combining high quality and modern elegance this is a luxury hotel without equal. The Apples restaurant invites diners to watch the chef working in the show kitchen.

Grand Elysée 🏛 🖪 ⑳ 🏯 🖪 ⓺ 🅰🅲 🛎 🚗

Rothenbaumchaussee 10 ✉ 20148 – ⓜ Stephanspl.   Plan: **F1**
– ℰ (040) 41 41 20 – www.grand-elysee.com
494 rm – †170/280 € ††190/300 € – ⌂ 25 € – 17 suites
• Luxury • Classic •

The Grand Elysée is Hamburg's largest privately operated hotel. It promises elegant rooms, a spacious lobby with shop and café, a brasserie and THEO'S restaurant serving prime beef. Around the hotel you will find some 800 artworks from the family owners' personal collection. The rooms facing the garden courtyard are quiet, and those giving onto the Moorweidenpark are south facing.
ⅈⓞ **Piazza Romana** • ⅈⓞ **THEO'S** – See restaurant listing

Le Méridien
☆ ▟▄ ⋔ ◲ ⬤ ㎞ ⅏ 🚗

An der Alster 52 ✉ 20099 – ⓜ Hauptbh. Nord   Plan: **H1**
– 𝒞 (040) 21000 – www.lemeridienhamburg.com
275 rm – 🛏149/389 € 🛏🛏159/409 € – ☕ 32 € – 7 suites
• Chain • Luxury • Contemporary •
This modern hotel has an attractive, clear style extending from the brightly furnished rooms (with specially designed therapeutic beds) to the wellness area. The restaurant on the ninth floor offers a fantastic view over the Außenalster lake.

Steigenberger
☆ ▟▄ ⬤ ⋔ ◲ ㎞ ⅏ 🚗

Heiligengeistbrücke 4 ✉ 20459 – ⓜ Rödingsmarkt   Plan: **F3**
– 𝒞 (040) 36 80 60 – www.hamburg.steigenberger.de
227 rm – 🛏110/600 € 🛏🛏130/620 € – ☕ 29 € – 6 suites
• Luxury • Classic •
Right beside the Alster canal stands this well-run and elegant hotel in the shape of a ship. From the fitness area roof terrace there is a wonderful view over the city.

The Westin
☆ ≤ ▟▄ ⬤ ⋔ ◲ ㎞ 🚗

Am Platz der Deutschen Einheit 2 ✉ 20038   Plan I: **C3**
– ⓜ Baumwall – 𝒞 (040) 8 00 01 00 – www.westinhamburg.com
244 rm – 🛏220/500 € 🛏🛏220/500 € – ☕ 30 € – 39 suites
• Luxury • Trendy • Contemporary •
This hotel offers a truly spectacular location. Its futuristic superstructure set on old warehouse buildings and connected by the 'Plaza' – the Elbphilharmonie, Hamburg's latest architectural landmark. The Westin offers a magnificent view of the port and HafenCity, bright, state-of-the-art, minimalist-style rooms, a smart spa and The Saffron, which serves international cuisine.

AMERON Hotel Speicherstadt
☆ ▟▄ ⋔ ㎞ 🚗

Am Sandtorkai 4 ✉ 20457 – ⓜ Überseequartier   Plan: **G3**
– 𝒞 (040) 6 38 58 90 – www.hotel-speicherstadt.de
192 rm – 🛏149/209 € 🛏🛏149/209 € – ☕ 19 €
• Historic • Vintage •
This charming hotel is located in the middle of Hamburg's Speicherstadt district. It boasts a trendy retro decor from the 1950s with warm colours that creates a friendly and welcoming feel. The restaurant in the modern glass annexe serves Italian food.

The George
☆ ⋔ ㎞ ⅏ 🚗

Barcastr. 3 ✉ 22087 – ⓜ Lohmühlenstr. – 𝒞 (040)   Plan I: **D2**
2 80 03 00 – www.thegeorge-hotel.de
123 rm – 🛏151/268 € 🛏🛏162/279 € – ☕ 20 € – 2 suites
• Townhouse • Design • Elegant •
Elegant, British-style meets young, modern design throughout this hotel. The library, bar and rooms are decorated in muted tones with feature pictures, furnishing fabrics and wallpapers. Highlights include the roof terrace with its view over Hamburg and the garden behind the hotel. The restaurant serves Mediterranean/Italian cuisine.

Sir Nikolai
▟▄ ⋔ ◲ ㎞

Katharinenstrasse 29 ✉ 20457 – ⓜ Meßberg – 𝒞 (040)   Plan: **G3**
29 99 66 60 – www.sirhotels.com/nikolai
88 rm – 🛏145/220 € 🛏🛏150/280 € – ☕ 23 € – 6 suites
• Townhouse • Luxury • Elegant •
Located right on the Nikolaifleet canal, this initially unassuming building boasts a trendy, modern and upmarket interior and rooms that, though not exactly spacious, nevertheless verge on the luxurious. Staff will park your car for you.
🍴 **IZAKAYA** – See restaurant listing

Eilenau 🛖

Eilenau 36 ✉ *22089 –* Ⓜ *Mundsburg –* ℰ *(040)*
2 36 01 30 – www.eilenau.de   Plan I: **D2**
17 rm – 🛏99/109 € 🛏🛏119/139 €
– ⬜ 15 € – 5 suites
• Townhouse • Personalised • Elegant •

Anything but a typical city hotel, the Eilenau is housed in two carefully renovated buildings dating back to 1890. Antiques, stucco, chandeliers and old
parquet flooring mix with stylish modern furniture beneath the high ceilings. There is also a small, quiet garden where breakfast is served in the
summer.

HENRI 🛗 🛖 ⒶⒸ 🚗

Bugenhagenstr. 21 ✉ *20095 –* Ⓜ *Mönckebergstr.*
– ℰ *(040) 5 54 35 70 – www.henri-hotel.com*   Plan: **H2**
61 rm – 🛏98/237 € 🛏🛏118/257 €
– ⬜ 15 € – 4 suites
• Townhouse • Vintage • Personalised •

This former office building has been redeveloped with taste, quality and all the
modern facilities you would expect… and with a strong 1950/60s retro feel.
There are charming details such as the homely lounge, a kitchen that serves
snacks and drinks, as well as a daily 'Abendbrod' and German tea and cakes at
the weekend.

25hours Hafen City 🌱 🛖 ⅃ ⒶⒸ 🧖 🚗

Überseeallee 5 ✉ *20457 –* Ⓜ *Überseequartier*
– ℰ *(040) 2 57 77 70 – www.25hours-hotels.com*   Plan I: **C3**
170 rm – 🛏130/180 € 🛏🛏140/190 €
– ⬜ 21 €
• Townhouse • Personalised • Design •

One thing is sure, for individuality and originality you can't beat this Hamburg hotel. Bright, new design meets warm wood and stories of the sea. Old
records cover the walls in the lounge-style Vinyl Room and guests are given
a sailors' kit bag for their personal belongings in the rooftop sauna. It's no
surprise in a hotel full of seafaring references to find that all the rooms have
a cabin feel.

Miramar & Mare 🛖

Armgartstr. 20 ✉ *22087 –* Ⓜ *Uhlandstr. –* ℰ *(040)*
51 90 09 40 – www.hotelmiramar.de   Plan I: **D2**
30 rm ⬜ – 🛏95/115 € 🛏🛏130/145 €
• Boutique hotel • Personalised •

These two Art Nouveau-style houses built in 1902 and 1904 are not far from the
Alster. They offer attractive classic façades outside and tasteful, individual
design with great attention to detail inside. Both establishments offer a good,
fresh breakfast.

Piment (Wahabi Nouri) 🍽 🌿

Lehmweg 29 ✉ *20251 –* Ⓜ *Eppendorfer Baum*
– ℰ *(040) 42 93 77 88 – www.restaurant-piment.de – closed Wednesday*
and Sunday   Plan: **C1**
Menu 49/108 € – Carte 56/91 € – *(dinner only) (booking advisable)*
• Creative • Neighbourhood •

Wahabi Nouri's two set menus – 'Piment' and 'Nouri's' – are the perfect expression of his creative, sophisticated style and ambitious minimalist presentation.
These are both informed by his Moroccan roots, which he uses in a pleasingly
underplayed manner in the form of exotic spices and perfumes – more in one
menu, less in the other.
→ Fois Gras mit Tajine Aromen. Gemüse Couscous mit Safranglace. Irischer
Lammrücken, B'stilla, Kardonen, Ras el-Hanout.

GERMANY - HAMBURG

❀ **Trüffelschwein** (Kirill Kinfelt)   XX 🛱
Mühlenkamp 54 ⊠ 22303 – ⓜ *Sierichstr.*   Plan: **D1**
– ☎ (040) 69 65 64 50
– www.trueffelschwein-restaurant.de
– Closed 2-3 January, 12-18 March, 16-29 July and Sunday-Monday
Menu 89/129 €
– Carte 64/93 € – (dinner only) (booking advisable)
· Modern cuisine · Friendly ·
The cuisine is modern, elaborate and sophisticated right down to the last detail.
The attractive interior, which is warm and minimalist in style, makes a great set-
ting for this fine food.
→ Venere Reis, Frankfurter Grüne Soße, Champignons. Iberico Schwein,
Sellerie, Trüffel. Rinderschulter, Nashi Birne, Nussbutter.

❀ **Jellyfish**   X 🖾
Weidenallee 12 ⊠ 20357 – ⓜ *Christkirche*   Plan: **B2**
– ☎ (040) 4 10 54 14
– www.jellyfish-restaurant.de
Menu 74/122 € – Carte 66/83 € – *(dinner only)*
· Seafood · Fashionable ·
If you are looking for an alternative to Hamburg's established fish restaurants,
try Jellyfish. Uncomplicated, urban and minimalist, it serves ambitious food
made using excellent produce in the form of a set menu.
→ Wildgarnele, Karotte, Zimt, Reis. Zander, Lauch, Apfel, Pumpernickel, Sar-
delle. Müsli, Kaffee, Orange.

☺ **Brechtmanns Bistro**   X 🛱
Erikastr. 43 ⊠ 20251   Plan: **C1**
– ☎ (040) 41 30 58 88
– www.brechtmann-bistro.de
Carte 27/52 €
· Asian influences · Minimalist ·
Brechtmanns is an extremely popular, friendly minimalist-style bistro serving
South East Asian-inspired market-fresh cuisine including crispy tuna fish tartare
with cucumber, wasabi and sweet and sour pineapple, and boiled topside of
beef in broth with root vegetables and apple.

☺ **Heimatjuwel**   X 🛱 🖾
Stellinger Weg 47 ⊠ 20255 – ⓜ *Lutterothstr.*   Plan: **B1**
– ☎ (040) 42 10 69 89
– www.heimatjuwel.de
– Closed 1-15 January, 29 August-19 September and Sunday-Monday
Menu 37/87 € – Carte 47/58 € – *(dinner only) (booking advisable)*
· Creative · Minimalist · Rustic ·
Marcel Görke, no stranger to the Hamburg culinary scene, runs this rustic,
minimalist-style little restaurant with its friendly, informal atmosphere. It
serves creative, fully-flavoured regional cuisine that represents great value
for money. There is a very short and simple lunchtime menu. Small pavement terrace.

☺ **Zipang**   X
Eppendorfer Weg 171 ⊠ 20253 – ⓜ *Eppendorfer Baum*   Plan: **B1**
– ☎ (040) 43 28 00 32 – www.zipang.de
– Closed Sunday-Tuesday lunch, Wednesday lunch
Menu 32 € (lunch)/65 € (dinner) – Carte 32/93 €
· Japanese · Minimalist ·
The minimalist interior at Zipang has clean lines, muted colours and a smart sil-
ver sheen. This makes a perfect match for chef Toshiharu Minami's mix of tradi-
tional and modern Japanese cooking styles. The restaurant is popular with Japa-
nese diners – always a good sign.

GERMANY - HAMBURG

⁑○ **Gallo Nero**   XX 錣 ☆
Sierichstr. 46 ⊠ *22301 –* Ⓜ *Sierichstr. –* ℰ *(040)*   Plan: **C1**
27 09 22 29 – www.gallo-nero.net
Menu 39/89 € – Carte 40/70 €
• Italian • Mediterranean décor •
A restaurant, wine shop and "alimentari con cucina" with three lovely terraces, this Winterhuder institution promises authentic Italian cuisine made using top-quality produce including dishes such as burrata con datterino e culatello di Zibello and calamaretti alla griglia… all washed down with a selection of good Italian reds and some lovely Rieslings.

⁑○ **Butcher's american steakhouse**   X
Milchstr. 19 ⊠ *20148 –* ℰ *(040) 44 60 82*   Plan: **C2**
– www.butchers-steakhouse.de – Closed Saturday lunch, Sunday lunch and Bank Holidays lunch
Carte 85/178 €
• Steakhouse • Family • Cosy •
Here you can taste fine Nebraska beef that the chef presents to the table. A cosy restaurant with a decor dominated by dark wood and warm colours.

⁑○ **Cornelia Poletto**   X
Eppendorfer Landstr. 80 ⊠ *20249 –* Ⓜ *Kellenhusenstr.*   Plan: **C1**
– ℰ (040) 4 80 21 59 – www.cornelia-poletto.de – Closed Sunday-Monday and Bank Holidays
Menu 59/159 € – Carte 45/81 € – *(booking advisable)*
• Italian • Friendly • Cosy •
Cornelia Poletto (who Germans will know from the television if not from her previous restaurant) serves Italian specialities in the restaurant and sells them (spices, wine, pasta, cheese) in the shop. Booked out almost daily.

⁑○ **Poletto Winebar**   X 錣 ☆
Eppendorfer Weg 287 ⊠ *20251 –* Ⓜ *Eppendorfer Baum*   Plan: **C1**
– ℰ (040) 38 64 47 00 – www.poletto-winebar.de
Menu 32 € – Carte 32/62 € – *(bookings advisable at dinner)*
• Italian • Cosy •
This lively wine bar is definitely one of the places to be in Eppendorf. The food is flavoursome and Italian in style, including classics such as vitello tonnato and tiramisu served alongside excellent cold meats straight from the Berkel meat slicer. Great wine selection also in the adjacent wine shop.

⁑○ **Witwenball**   X 錣 ☆
Weidenallee 20 ⊠ *20357 –* Ⓜ *Christskirche – ℰ (040)*   Plan: **B2**
53 63 00 85 – www.witwenball.com – Closed Monday
Menu 35/46 € – Carte 37/57 € – *(dinner only)*
• Modern cuisine • Cosy •
Where once people danced, you will now find fresh, flavoursome fare – try the zander with cauliflower, purple curry and raisins. Good, predominantly German wines are served in a relaxed and friendly atmosphere. Lovely big marble bar.

🏠 **Mittelweg**   🛏 **P**
Mittelweg 59 ⊠ *20149 –* Ⓜ *Klosterstern – ℰ (040)*   Plan: **C1**
4 14 10 10 – www.hotel-mittelweg-hamburg.de
30 rm ⊡ – †110/135 € ††135/250 €
• Grand townhouse • Cosy •
This 1890 villa is full of turn of the century charm. Find it at the staircase, through to the stucco ceilings in the stylish breakfast room, and in the carefully selected combinations of colours, motifs and classic furniture in the bedrooms. Quiet, secluded garden.

GERMANY - HAMBURG

Le Canard nouveau   XxX ⪅ 𝄐 ⇔ P

Plan I: **C3**

Elbchaussee 139 ⊠ 22763 – Ⓜ Königstr. – ℰ (040)
88 12 95 31 – www.lecanard-hamburg.de – Closed 1-8 January and
Sunday-Monday
Menu 79/129 € (dinner) – Carte 56/89 € – *(booking advisable)*
· International · Minimalist ·

The quality of the cuisine remains excellent in this restaurant where diners enjoy creative, sophisticated and punchy food in a smart setting with a wonderful view of the port. Good business lunch available at midday.
→ Oktopus, Burrata, Erbsen, Bärlauch, Pancetta. Karree vom Salzwiesenlamm, Artischocke, gelbe Zucchini, Petersilien-Gnocchi. Valrhona Schokoladenkuchen, Mispeln, Vanilleeis.

Landhaus Scherrer (Heinz O. Wehmann)   XxX ⅋⅋ Ⓚ ⇔ P

Plan: I1

Elbchaussee 130 ⊠ 22763 – Ⓜ Königstr. – ℰ (040)
8 83 07 00 30 – www.landhausscherrer.de – Closed Sunday
Menu 37 € (lunch)/119 € – Carte 44/85 €
· Classic French · Elegant ·

Heinz O. Wehmann has been at the helm at Landhaus Scherrer since 1980. He is still serving classic cuisine in this elegant restaurant where Otto Bachmann's large erotic painting remains the decorative focus. Adding a modern note, the 600 plus wines on the wine list are presented to you on an iPad.
→ Angelschellfisch mit Schmorgurken und Hamburger Senfbutter, zweierlei Senfsamen. Graupenrisotto mit Kalbskopf, Kaisergranat und Sauce Américaine. Krosse Vierländer Ente mit Spitzkohl.

Petit Amour (Boris Kasprik)   XX 𝄐

Plan: I1

Spritzenplatz 11 ⊠ 22765 – Ⓜ Altona – ℰ (040)
30 74 65 56 – www.petitamour-hh.com – Closed end January-early
February 2 weeks, end August-early September 2 weeks and Sunday-
Monday
Menu 46 € (lunch)/140 € (dinner)
– Carte 100/156 € – *(dinner only, Thursday also lunch) (booking advisable)*
· Classic cuisine · Chic · Cosy ·

This is a very popular restaurant for a number of reasons... The upmarket design (modern and minimalist yet warm and friendly), the professional service and wine suggestions, and the unfussy, ambitious cuisine with international influences.
→ Terrine von der Foie Gras mit Steinpilzen. Hagebuttenhonig und Brioche. Steinbutt unter Kartoffelschuppen mit Vin Jaune, Lauchpüree und Pfifferlingen. Geeiste Gariguette Erdbeere mit Mandelschokolade und Tahiti-Vanille.

Nil   X 𝄐

Plan I: **B2**

Neuer Pferdemarkt 5 ⊠ 20359 – Ⓜ Feldstr. – ℰ (040)
4 39 78 23 – www.restaurant-nil.de – Closed Tuesday except in December
Menu 32/42 € – Carte 32/54 € – *(dinner only)*
· International · Neighbourhood · Friendly ·

Located in Hamburg's fashionable Schanze district, Nil is cosy, though perhaps a little cramped, and serves a range of well-cooked dishes including young goat bratwurst with lentils, parsnips and apple mustard and pan-fried skrei with baked carrots and coriander. There is an attractive garden to the rear and cookery courses next door.

philipps   X 𝄐

Plan I: **B2**

Turnerstr. 9 ⊠ 20038 – Ⓜ Feldstr. – ℰ (040)
63 73 51 08 – www.philipps-restaurant.de – Closed Sunday-Monday
Menu 38/58 € – Carte 34/55 € – *(dinner only)*
· International · Trendy · Friendly ·

Hidden away in a side street, phillips is a great place to eat. Walk down the few stairs to this friendly little restaurant with low ceilings, a relaxed atmosphere and international menu. It promises flavoursome and skilfully prepared dishes such as ox cheeks with leek champ.

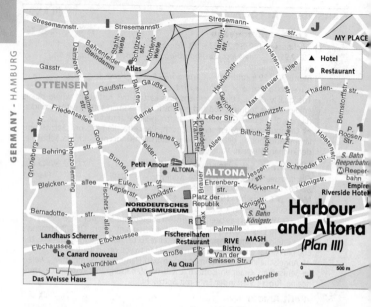

RIVE Bistro

✗ ⩽ 🛜

Van-der-Smissen Str. 1 ⊠ 22767 – Ⓜ Königstr.
Plan: **J1**
– 𝒸 (040) 3 80 59 19 – www.rive.de – Closed Monday
Menu 30 € (weekday lunch)/53 € – Carte 35/86 € – *(booking advisable)*
• Seafood • Brasserie •

Sitting right on the port, this bistro is run by the same team as Tschebull. It serves good quality, flavoursome seafood and grilled meats alongside classic dishes such as Hamburger Pannfisch and Wiener Schnitzel. In summer the wonderful terrace is a must! Hot food served throughout the day.

---

⑪○ **Fischereihafen Restaurant**

✗✗✗ ⩽ 🛜 ⭗ 🅿

Große Elbstr. 143 ⊠ 22767 – Ⓜ Königstr. – 𝒸 (040)
Plan: **J1**
38 18 16 – www.fischereihafenrestaurant.de
Menu 25 € (lunch)/75 € – Carte 35/84 € – *(booking advisable)*
• Seafood • Classic décor •

This fish restaurant overlooking the port is a veritable Hamburg institution. The service is excellent, as is the great value lunchtime menu.

---

⑪○ **East** – Hotel East

✗✗ 🛜 � 🚗

Simon-von-Utrecht-Str. 31 ⊠ 20359 – Ⓜ St. Pauli
Plan I: **B2**
– 𝒸 (040) 30 99 33 – www.east-hamburg.de
Carte 38/75 € – *(dinner only)*
• Fusion • Design • Fashionable •

The atmosphere in this former factory building draws on many styles and influences. Far Eastern charm combines skilfully with Western industrial heritage. A restaurant not to be missed.

MASH
XX 錦 ✿

Große Elbstr. 148 ⊠ 22767 – Ⓜ Königstr. – ℰ (040)
8 09 00 81 11 – www.mashsteak.de
Carte 38/83 € – *(pre-book at weekends)*
· Steakhouse · Elegant · Friendly ·

Plan: **J1**

An upmarket steak restaurant, MASH offers any number of high-quality cuts from rib-eye to NY strip and the very exclusive kobe beef. The temperature controlled wine cabinets contain over 1 500 different wines – including some excellent vintages by the glass!

Au Quai
XX ≤ 錦 Ⓟ

Große Elbstr. 145 b ⊠ 22767 – Ⓜ Königstr. – ℰ (040)
38 03 77 30 – www.au-quai.com – Closed 23 December-7 January and
Saturday lunch, Sunday
Carte 43/92 € – *(dinner only)*
· Seafood · Trendy ·

Plan: **J1**

This popular establishment is situated close to the harbour and has a terrace facing the water. The modern interior is complemented by designer items and holographs.

Clouds - Heaven's Restaurant & Bar
X ≤ 錦 Ⓚ

Reeperbahn 1 (at 23. floor der Tanzenden Türme)
⊠ 20359 – Ⓜ St. Pauli – ℰ (040) 30 99 32 80 – www.clouds-hamburg.de
– Closed Saturday lunch, Sunday lunch
Carte 40/82 € – *(booking essential)*
· French · Design ·

Plan I: **B3**

The view from Hamburg's highest restaurant is simply amazing! High above the River Elbe and St Michael's church you can choose between the ambitious French/Mediterranean cuisine (try the salt-baked turbot for two) or something from the rotisserie. One floor higher up and you will find yourself on the rooftop terrace.

Atlas
X 錦 Ⓟ

Schützenstr. 9a (entrance Phoenixhof) ⊠ 22761
– Ⓜ Altona – ℰ (040) 8 51 78 10 – www.atlas.at – Closed Saturday lunch,
Sunday dinner, Bank Holidays
Menu 19 € (weekday lunch)/45 € – Carte 18/56 €
· International · Bistro ·

Plan: **I1**

This former fish smokery is now a restaurant in a modern bistro style. Shorter menu available at lunchtimes. Pleasant ivy-covered terrace.

Das Weisse Haus
X 錦 ✿ ⊟

Neumühlen 50 ⊠ 22763 – Ⓜ Königstr. – ℰ (040)
3 90 90 16 – www.das-weisse-haus.de – Closed Monday
Menu 25 € (weekday lunch)/45 € – Carte 36/58 € – *(booking advisable)*
· International · Friendly ·

Plan: **I1**

In the little white building on the Elbpromenade your host Patrick Voelz proposes a range of international dishes alongside a now established seasonal surprise menu. The atmosphere is casual and friendly and you can sit outside too.

East
⅃ 㕷 ও Ⓚ 㡷 ⌂

Simon-von-Utrecht-Str. 31 ⊠ 20359 – Ⓜ St. Pauli
– ℰ (040) 30 99 30 – www.east-hamburg.de
120 rm – ♦129/199 € ♦♦149/309 € – ⌂ 20 € – 8 suites
· Business · Design ·

Plan I: **B2**

The design in this former iron foundry is resolutely modern and trendy. It runs from the guestrooms through to the bar-lounge and the leisure and beauty area with its professionally staffed fitness club.
① **East** – See restaurant listing

GERMANY - HAMBURG

Empire Riverside Hotel ☆ ⟨ 🏠 & 🅺 🐾 🚗

Bernhard-Nocht-Str. 97 (via Davidstraße) ✉ 20359
– **Ⓜ** *Reeperbahn* – ℰ *(040) 31 11 90* – *www.empire-riverside.de*   Plan: **J1**
327 rm – ♥129/279 € ♥♥129/279 € – ☲ 24 €
• Business • Design • Contemporary •
Famous architect David Chipperfield designed this contemporary hotel close to
the St Pauli pontoon bridges. Rooms have a view of either the river or the city as
does "20", the panoramic bar on the 20th floor. This wharf-side restaurant offers
international cuisine in a simple, contemporary setting.

MY PLACE 🚗

Lippmannstr. 5 ✉ 22769 – **Ⓜ** *Feldstr.* – ℰ *(040)*   Plan: **J1**
28 57 18 74 – *www.myplace-hamburg.de*
17 rm – ♥79/159 € ♥♥99/159 € – ☲ 5 € – 1 suite
• Townhouse • Personalised • Contemporary •
Close to the trendy Schanze district, a dedicated hostess runs a small hotel with
individually styled, charming modern rooms named after districts of Hamburg.

ELBE-WESTERN DISTRICTS   PLAN III

Süllberg - Seven Seas (Karlheinz Hauser) XxxX ⇔ 🕸 ⟨ 🖼

Süllbergsterrasse 12 (by Elbchaussee A3) ✉ 22587   & 🅺 🚗
– ℰ *(040) 8 66 25 20* – *www.suellberg-hamburg.de* – *Closed January-mid
February and Monday-Tuesday*
10 rm – ♥180/200 € ♥♥200/240 € – ☲ 19 € – 1 suite
Menu 115 € (Vegetarian)/190 € – Carte 68/88 € – *(dinner only)*
• Modern French • Luxury •
The Süllberg is a Blankenese institution and along with the Seven Seas has
become one of Hamburg's top gourmet addresses. It offers a genuinely upmarket dining experience, from the classy interior to Karlheinz Hauser's fragrant,
classic cuisine, as well as the accomplished and attentive service and expert
wine recommendations. The rooms are as attractive and stylish as the restaurant.
→ Meeresaromen "Krustentiere und Muscheln", Gurke, Mandel, schwarzer
Knoblauch. Seezunge "sous vide gegart", Blumenkohl, Yuzu, Algen-Beurre
blanc. Süß-Saure Ente, Kakao, Rote Bete, Granny Smith.
⑩ **Deck 7** – See restaurant listing

Jacobs Restaurant – Hotel Louis C. Jacob XxX 🕸 ⟨ 🖼 🅺 ⟲

Elbchaussee 401 (by Elbchaussee A3) ✉ 22609 – ℰ *(040)*   🚗
82 25 54 07 – *www.hotel-jacob.de* – *Closed Monday-Tuesday*
Menu 96/142 €
– Carte 64/116 € – *(Wednesday to Friday dinner only) (booking advisable)*
• Classic French • Chic •
Thomas Martin's food – classic, simple, free of fancy flourishes and placing great
emphasis on top-quality ingredients – is now available from an à la carte menu. The
dining experience is rounded off by the accomplished service, the stylish decor and
the magnificent lime tree shaded terrace overlooking the Elbe.
→ Eismeerforelle, Senfkörner, Rettich, Dill, Miso-Sojavinaigrette. Ganzer
Bretonischer Loup de Mer im Blätterteig gebacken. Karamellisierte Altlän-
der Apfeltarte, Crème Chantilly.

HYGGE Brasserie – Hotel Landhaus Flottbek XX 🍴 🖼 🅿

Baron-Voght-Str. 179 (by Stresemannstraße A2) ✉ 22607 – ℰ *(040)*
82 27 41 60 – *www.landhaus-flottbek.de* – *Closed Saturday lunch, Sunday
lunch*
Menu 36/48 € – Carte 36/59 €
• Country • Brasserie • Elegant •
In Danish, "hygge" describes a feeling of warmth, cosiness and wellbeing, just
the atmosphere conjured up in this chic, stylish and relaxed timber-framed restaurant with an open hearth at its centre. The food is seasonal and regional, including dishes such as cod fillet with braised cucumbers, horseradish and mash.
Trendy bar/lounge.

Weinwirtschaft Kleines Jacob – Hotel Louis C. Jacob

Elbchaussee 404 (by Elbchaussee A3) ✉ 22609 – ✆ (040) 82 25 55 10 – www.kleines-jacob.de
Menu 36 €
– Carte 37/53 € – *(dinner only and Sunday lunch) (booking advisable)*
• Classic cuisine • Wine bar • Cosy •
No wonder so many people describe Kleines Jakob as their favourite restaurant with its wine bar charm, candlelit tables and attentive service. The dishes coming out of the open kitchens include chicken fricassee vol-au-vents and rice. All the wines come from vineyards in German-speaking countries.

Deck 7 – Restaurant Süllberg - Seven Seas

Süllbergsterrasse 12 (by Elbchaussee A3) ✉ 22587 – ✆ (040) 86 62 52 77 – www.suellberg-hamburg.de – Closed January-mid February and Monday-Tuesday
Menu 30 € – Carte 28/54 €
• Country • Cosy • Elegant •
In defiance of many a passing trend, this restaurant with its smart, brown leather upholstered chairs and parquet flooring has opted for the versatility of a classic yet modern interior. In summer, eat outside with stunning views of the Elbe.

Witthüs

Elbchaussee 499a (access via Mühlenberg) (by Elbchaussee A3) ✉ 22587 – ✆ (040) 86 01 73 – www.witthues.com – Closed Monday
Menu 36/39 € – Carte 41/50 € – *(dinner only)*
• International • Friendly •
This historic farmhouse is idyllically located near the Elbe. Enjoy international cuisine and professional service in a classic, elegant setting with Nordic flair. Outdoor terrace.

Off Club

Leverkusenstr. 54 ✉ 22761 – ✆ (040) 89 01 93 33 – www.offclub.de – Closed Sunday-Monday
Plan I: **AB2**
Menu 35/77 € – Carte 37/56 € – *(dinner only) (booking advisable)*
• Modern cuisine • Fashionable •
Located in a restored factory building, Off Club has become a popular address. It boasts three separate restaurant areas where diners opt for a surprise menu or order à la carte in a relaxed setting. Whichever you choose, you will find all the dishes flavoursome, sophisticated and with a real individual note.

Rach & Ritchy

Holstenkamp 71 ✉ 22525 – ✆ (040) 89 72 61 70 – www.rach-ritchy.de – Closed Saturday lunch, Sunday-Monday and Bank Holidays lunch
Plan: **A2**
Carte 34/73 € – *(booking advisable)*
• Meats and grills • Friendly • Fashionable •
TV chef Christian Rach is now a household name. It is the second member of the duo, Richard 'Ritchy' Mayer, who does the cooking in his fashionable, modern grill restaurant. Specialities include succulent steaks from the glass-fronted maturing cabinet.

Louis C. Jacob

Elbchaussee 401 (by Elbchaussee A3) ✉ 22609 – ✆ (040) 82 25 50 – www.hotel-jacob.de
66 rm – †185/345 € ††225/385 € – ☕ 35 € – 19 suites
• Luxury • Traditional • Classic •
The management and services in this elegant hotel on the Elbe are exemplary. Equally pleasant is the classical furnishing of the rooms, some of which are as spacious as junior suites.
✿✿ **Jacobs Restaurant** • **Weinwirtschaft Kleines Jacob** – See restaurant listing

🏠 Strandhotel   ⩽ ♿ 🅿

Strandweg 13 (by Elbchaussee A3) ✉ *22587 –* ☎ *(040) 86 13 44*
– www.strandhotel-blankenese.de – Closed 25 December-18 January
14 rm – 🛏100 € 🛏🛏160/205 € – ⌚ 15 € – 1 suite
• Family • Classic •

The Elbstrand is the epitome of the lifestyle hotel. Despite its many modern features, the charm of this listed white Art Nouveau villa is omnipresent. Its high-ceilinged, stuccoed rooms match the designer furnishings to perfection. The excellent buffet breakfast comes with a lovely view of the Elbe.

🏠 Landhaus Flottbek   ♿ 🅿

Baron-Voght-Str. 179 (by Stresemannstraße A2) ✉ *22607 –* ☎ *(040)*
82 27 41 60 – www.landhaus-flottbek.de
25 rm – 🛏110/160 € 🛏🛏140/190 € – ⌚ 19 €
• Family • Cosy •

A well-run hotel consisting of several 18C farmhouses converted to create tasteful, comfortable guestrooms. Try and book one of the rooms that look out onto the lovely garden.

🍴 **HYGGE Brasserie** – See restaurant listing

MUNICH
MÜNCHEN

gameover2012/iStock

Situated in a stunning position not far north of the Alps, Munich is a cultural titan. Famously described as the 'village with a million inhabitants', its mix of German organisation and Italian lifestyle makes for a magical mix, with an enviable amount of Italian restaurants to seek out and enjoy. This cultural capital of Southern Germany boasts over forty theatres and dozens of museums; temples of culture that blend charmingly with the Bavarian love of folklore and lederhosen. Perhaps in no other world location – certainly not in Western Europe – is there such an enjoyable abundance of folk festivals and groups dedicated to playing

the local music. And there's an abundance of places to see them, too: Munich is awash with Bierhallen, Bierkeller, and Biergarten.

The heart of Munich is the Old Town, with its epicentre the Marienplatz in the south, and Residenz to the north: there are many fine historic buildings around here. Running to the east is the River Isar, flanked by fine urban thoroughfares and green areas for walks. Head north for the area dissected by the Ludwig-strasse and Leopoldstrasse – Schwabing – which is full of students as it's the University district. To the east is the English Garden, a denizen of peace. West of here, the Museums district, dominated by the Pinakothek, is characterised by bookshops, antique stores and galleries.

EATING OUT

Munich is a city in which you can eat well - especially if you're a meat-eater – and in large quantities. The local specialities are meat and potatoes, with large dollops of cabbage on the side; you won't have trouble finding roast pork and dumplings or meatloaf and don't forget the local white veal sausage, weisswurst. The meat is invariably succulent, and cabbage is often adorned with the likes of juniper berries. Potatoes, meanwhile, have a tendency to evolve into soft and buttery dumplings. And sausage? Take your pick from over 1,500 recognised species. Other specialities include Schweinshaxe (knuckle of pork) and Leberkäs (meat and offal pâté). Eating out in Munich, or anywhere in Bavaria, is an experience in itself, with the distinctive background din of laughter, singing and the clinking of mugs of Bavarian Weissbier. It's famous for the Brauereigaststätten or brewery inn; be prepared for much noise, and don't be afraid to fall into conversation with fellow diners and drinkers. The many Italian restaurants in the city provide an excellent alternative.

GERMANY - MUNICH

🏵🏵🏵 Atelier – Hotel Bayerischer Hof   XxX 🏵 AC 🚗
Promenadeplatz 2 ✉ 80333   Plan: **G2**
– Ⓜ *Marienplatz*
– ✆ *(089) 2 12 09 93 – www.bayerischerhof.de*
– *Closed Sunday-Monday*
Menu 140/190 € – *(dinner only)*
• Creative French • Elegant • Design •

With its artistic interior designed by Axel Vervoordt, this restaurant more than lives up to its name. You will find the cuisine of young and talented chef Jan Hartwig equally modern and individual in style. His tasty culinary creations are a masterpiece of balance and intensity.

→ Bretonische Sardine, Apfel, Piment d´Espelette, Parmesan und Sud aus gegrillter Sardine. Rehrücken, Rote Bete, Himbeeren, Sellerie und Pistazien. Landmilch, Essigerdbeeren, Kerbel, Vanille und Roggen.

🏵🏵 Dallmayr   XxX 🏵 AC
Dienerstr. 14 (1st floor) ✉ 80331   Plan: **G2**
– Ⓜ *Marienplatz*
– ✆ *(089) 21 35 100 – www.restaurant-dallmayr.de*
– *Closed 2 weeks 24 December-early January, 2 weeks during Easter, 3 weeks August, Sunday-Monday and Bank Holidays*
Menu 115/190 € – *(dinner only and Sunday lunch) (booking advisable)*
• Modern French • Elegant •

In the same building as the famed delicatessen, it is no surprise that the first floor restaurant prides itself on the quantity of its raw ingredients. The classically modern cuisine shuns any hint of gimmickry, centring instead on skilful craftsmanship and intense flavours. The excellent service is equally convincing.

→ Jakobsmuschel, Physalis, Cashew, Weizengras. Ente aus Challans, Topinambur, Granatapfel. Erdbeere, Miso, Kombucha, Sauerampfer.

🏵 Gourmet Restaurant Königshof – Hotel Königshof   XxxX
Karlsplatz 25 (1st floor) ✉ 80335   🏵 ⩽ AC ⇔ 🚗
– Ⓜ *Karlsplatz*   Plan: **F2**
– ✆ *(089) 66 13 60 – www.koenigshof-hotel.de*
– *Closed Sunday-Monday*
Menu 120/170 € – Carte 95/139 € – *(booking advisable)*
• Classic French • Elegant • Classic décor •

This is a classic restaurant, from the tastefully elegant interior to the professional, attentive service and the fine, fully flavoured cuisine. This is refreshingly uncomplicated and made using the very best ingredients. The window tables enjoy a good view out over the busy Stachus square.

→ Saibling leicht geräuchert, Petersilienbuttermilch, Tapioka und Kaviar. Bresse Taube, Brust, Keule, grüner Spargel und Buchweizen. Limette, Dulcey Schokolade, Banane, Kreolische Sauce und Pinienkerne.

🏵 Schuhbecks Fine Dining   XxX 🏵
Pfisterstr. 9 ✉ 80331   Plan: **H2**
– Ⓜ *Marienplatz*
– ✆ *(089) 2 16 69 01 10 – www.schuhbeck.de*
– *Closed 1-15 January, 1-20 August and Sunday-Monday*
Menu 83/116 €
• Modern cuisine • Friendly • Elegant •

Another of Alfons Schuhbeck's restaurants in the Platzl, Fine Dining promises an interior that is elegant without being overly formal and a friendly and professional front-of-house team. Culinary offerings include two seasonal set menus that are modern, harmonious, tasty and based on the finest ingredients.

→ Glasierter Schweinebauch mit Morcheln, Topfen, Malz und Kümmel. Lammrücken und Schulter mit Auberginen, Feta, Oliven. Variation von Rhabarber mit Himbeere und Kokos.

Les Deux
XX 🕸 🛖 **AC**

Maffeistr. 3a (1st Floor) ✉ 80333 – **Ⓜ** *Marienplatz*
Plan: **G2**
– 𝒞 *(089) 7 10 40 73 73 – www.lesdeux-muc.de – Closed Sunday and Bank Holidays*
Menu 48 € (weekday lunch)/110 € – Carte 71/113 € – *(booking advisable)*
• **Modern French** • **Friendly** • **Fashionable** •

"Les Deux" are Fabrice Kieffer and Johann Rappenglück and their chic designer restaurant enjoys a prime city location. The cuisine is modern yet classic, the service pleasant and friendly, the wine list attractive.
➔ Yellow Fin Thunfisch, Granny Smith Apfel, Wasabi, Rotkraut, Avocado. Zweierlei vom Limousin Lamm, Ziegenkäse, Artischocke, Tomate, Kräuterjus. Espresso, weiße Schokolade, Brombeere, Citrus.
🍴 **Brasserie** – See restaurant listing

Schwarzreiter – Hotel Vier Jahreszeiten Kempinski
XX 🕸 **AC** 🚗

Maximilianstr. 17 ✉ 80539 – **Ⓜ** *Lehel* – 𝒞 *(089)*
Plan: **H2**
21 25 21 25 – www.schwarzreiter-muenchen.de – Closed August and Sunday-Monday
Menu 92/121 € – Carte 66/88 € – *(dinner only)*
• **Modern cuisine** • **Elegant** •

Chic and upmarket without being overly formal, Schwarzreiter is this classic Munich hotel's "fine dining" restaurant. The "Young Bavarian Cuisine" served up here is sophisticated food of the very highest calibre and the friendly and professional front-of-house team will be only too pleased to provide wine recommendations.
➔ Alpenlachs, Zitrone, Meeresbohne. Gereiftes Rind, Aubergine, Kartoffel, Lauch. Pfirsich, weiße Schokolade, Anis.

Showroom
X 🛖

Lilienstr. 6 ✉ 81669 – **Ⓜ** *Isartor* – 𝒞 *(089) 44 42 90 82*
Plan I: **C3**
– *www.showroom-restaurant.de – Closed Saturday-Sunday and Bank Holidays*
Menu 115/135 € – *(dinner only) (booking essential)*
• **Creative** • **Friendly** • **Trendy** •

Showroom offers a winning formula that combines a relaxed atmosphere and creative cuisine with the emphasis on good, fresh produce. Presented in the form of a surprise menu, each dish is a perfectly judged blend of flavours served up by the professional front-of-house team who also provide excellent wine recommendations.
➔ Eigelb, Mandel, Rucola, Johannisbeere, Kaninchen. Wagyu, Heidelbeeren, Fenchel, Zimt, Rote Bete. Schokolade, Lakritze, Thymian, Rhabarber.

Le Barestovino
XX 🕸 🛖 **AC** ✿

Thierschstr. 35 ✉ 80538 – **Ⓜ** *Lehel* – 𝒞 *(089)*
Plan I: **C3**
23 70 83 55 – www.barestovino.de – Closed Sunday-Monday
Menu 37/62 € – Carte 35/52 € – *(dinner only)*
• **Classic French** • **Bistro** •

Owner Joel Bousquet runs a friendly operation here, in both the modern restaurant and the Le Bouchon wine bar. The cuisine is similarly unpretentious – it includes delicious dishes such as mi-cuit salmon with fennel and potato mash, all accompanied by French wines, making this a delightful dining experience.

Colette Tim Raue
X 🛖 ✿

Klenzestr. 72 ✉ 80469 – **Ⓜ** *Frauenhoferstraße*
Plan I: **B3**
– 𝒞 *(089) 23 00 25 55 – www.brasseriecolette.de*
Menu 26 € (lunch) – Carte 34/72 €
• **French** • **Brasserie** •

Tim Raue really has his finger on the pulse with his new culinary concept at Colette. It is as relaxed as a French brasserie, friendly with pleasantly informal service, and offers good food at great prices. The first class ingredients speak for themselves in dishes such as *boeuf bourguignon* with speck, mushrooms and shallots.

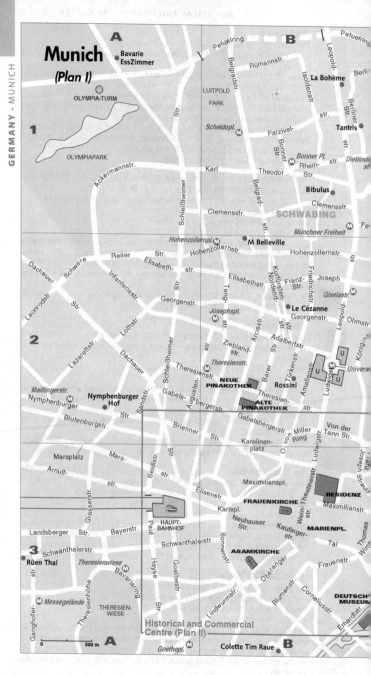

Munich
(Plan I)

A

B

Bavarie
EssZimmer

OLYMPIA-TURM

1

OLYMPIAPARK

Petuelring

Rümannstr.

La Bohème

LUITPOLD PARK

Scheidpl.

Parzival-

Tantris

Karl

Theodor Str.

Dietlinde st

Bibulus

Clemensstr.

Clemensstr.

SCHWABING

Münchner Freiheit

Hohenzollernpl.

M Belleville

Hohenzollernstr.

Reiter Str.

Hohenzollernstr.

Elisabeth- str.

Elisabethstr.

Joseph

Georgenstr.

Giselastr.

Josephspl.

Le Cézanne

Georgenstr.

Ohmstr.

2

Zieblandstr.

Adalbertstr.

Theresienstr.

NEUE PINAKOTHEK

Rossini

Nymphenburger Hof

Gabels- bergerstr.

ALTE PINAKOTHEK

Theresien- str.

Maillingerstr.

Nymphenburger

Gabelsbergerstr.

Von der Tann Str.

Blutenburgstr.

Brienner Str.

Karolinen- platz

Marsplatz

Mars-

Maximianspl.

RESIDENZ

Arnulf- str.

Elisenstr.

FRAUENKIRCHE

Maximilianstr.

Landsberger Str.

Bayerstr.

HAUPT- BAHNHOF

Karlspl.

Neuhauser Str.

MARIENPL.

Kaufinger- str.

Tal

3

Schwanthalerstr.

Rüen Thai

Theresienwiese

ASAMKIRCHE

Schwanthalerstr.

Frauenstr.

Bavariaring

DEUTSCH MUSEUM

Messegelände

THERESIEN- WIESE

Lindwurmstr.

0   500 m

A

Historical and Commercial Centre (Plan II)

Goethepl.

Colette Tim Raue

B

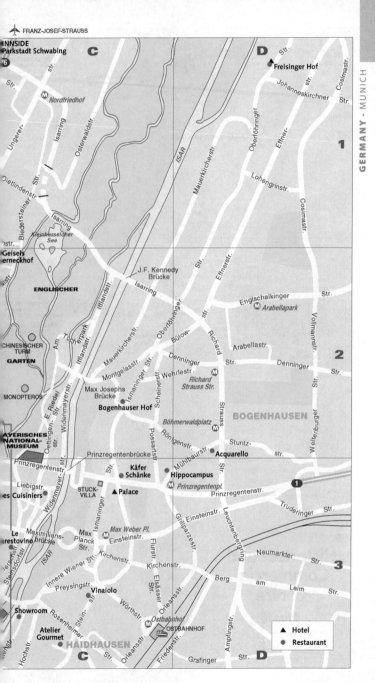

FRANZ-JOSEF-STRAUSS

C **D**

INNSIDE
Parkstadt Schwabing

▲ Freisinger Hof

Johanneskirchner Str.

Cosimastr.

Str.

Oberföhringer Str.

Effner-

Lohengrinstr.

Mauerkircherstr.

ISAR

1

Cosimastr.

Str.

Ungerer-

Str.

M Nordfriedhof

Isarring

Osterwaldstr.

Dietlindenstr.

Str.

Biedersteiner Str.

Isarring

Kleinhesseloher
See

Geibelstr.
erneckhof

str.

ENGLISCHER

J.F. Kennedy
Brücke

Isarring

Effnerstr.

Str.

Englschalkinger Str.

M Arabellapark

Vollmannstr.

Ifflandstr.

CHINESISCHER
TURM

GARTEN

Am Tucherpark

Ifflandstr.

Oberföhringer str.

Bülow-

Richard

Arabellastr.

MONOPTEROS

E. Riedel

Str.

Oettingen-

Mauerkircherstr.

Montgelasstr.

Ismaninger Str.

Scheinerstr.

Denninger Str.

Denninger Str.

Str.

M

Richard
Strauss Str.

Wehrlestr.

2

BOGENHAUSEN

Welfenburger

BAYERISCHES
NATIONAL-
MUSEUM

Widenmayerstr.

str.

Max Josephs
Brücke

▲ Bogenhauser Hof

Böhmerwaldplatz

M

Stuntz-

Possartstr.

Röntgenstr.

Strauss

str.

Prinzregentenstr.

Prinzregentenbrücke

Mühlbaurstr.

● Acquarello

Liebigstr.

es Cuisiniers ●

Str.

● Käfer
Schänke

STUCK-
VILLA

Hippocampus ●

M Prinzregentenpl.

Prinzregentenstr.

1

▲ Palace

Ismaninger str.

Widenmayerstr.

Max
Planck
Str.

M Max Weber Pl.

Einsteinstr.

Einsteinstr.

Prinzregentenstr.

Truderinger Str.

Le
restovino ●

Maximilians-
brücke

ISAR

Steinsdorfstr.

Innere Wiener Str.

Kirchenstr.

Kirchenstr.

Flurstr.

Elsässer
Str.

Gillparzerstr.

Leuchtenbergring

Neumarkter Str.

3

Preysingstr.

● Vinaiolo

Steinstr.

Wörthstr.

Orleansstr.

Berg am Laim Str.

Ampfingstr.

● Showroom

Rosenheimer

Atelier
Gourmet

M Ostbahnhof

OSTBAHNHOF

HAIDHAUSEN

Hochstr.

Str.

Orleansstr.

Friedenstr.

Grafinger Str.

C **D**

▲	Hotel
●	Restaurant

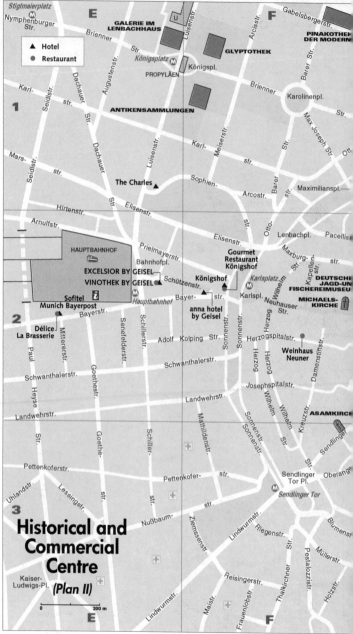

GERMANY - MUNICH

Legend

▲ Hotel
● Restaurant

Labels on map:

Stiglmaierplatz
Nymphenburger Str.
GALERIE IM LENBACHHAUS
GLYPTOTHEK
Königsplatz
PROPYLÄEN
ANTIKENSAMMLUNGEN
Gabelsbergerstr.
PINAKOTHEK DER MODERN
Brienner Str.
Karolinenpl.
Karl-str.
Seidlstr.
Dachauer Str.
Augustenstr.
Luisenstr.
Meiserstr.
Barer Str.
Max-Joseph-Str.
Mars-str.
Seidlstr.
Dachauer Str.
Sophien-str.
Arcostr.
Maximilianspl.
The Charles ▲
Hirtenstr.
Arnulfstr.
Elisenstr.
Elisenstr.
Lenbachpl.
Pacellis
HAUPTBAHNHOF
Prielmayerstr.
Bahnhofpl.
Gourmet Restaurant Königshof
Maxburg-str.
DEUTSCHE JAGD-UN FISCHEREIMUSEU
EXCELSIOR BY GEISEL
VINOTHEK BY GEISEL
Schützenstr.
Königshof
Karlsplatz
Sofitel Munich Bayerpost
Hauptbahnhof
Bayer-str.
Karlspl.
Neuhauser Str.
MICHAELS-KIRCHE
Délice La Brasserie
Bayerstr.
anna hotel by Geisel
Sonnenstr.
Herzogspitalstr.
Weinhaus Neuner
Paul-Heyse-str.
Mittererstr.
Senefelderstr.
Schillerstr.
Adolf Kolping Str.
Herzog Wilhelm Str.
Damenstiftstr.
Schwanthalerstr.
Schwanthalerstr.
Josephspitalstr.
ASAMKIRCH
Landwehrstr.
Landwehrstr.
Goethestr.
Schiller-str.
Mathildenstr.
Kreuzstr.
Sendlinger Str.
Str.
Pettenkoferstr.
Pettenkofer-str.
Sendlinger Tor Pl.
Oberange
Uhlandstr.
Lessingstr.
Sendlinger Tor
Historical and Commercial Centre *(Plan II)*

Kaiser-Ludwigs-Pl.
Nußbaum-str.
Ziemssenstr.
Lindwurmstr.
Pliegenstr.
Blumenst
Müllerstr.
Reisingerstr.
Maistr.
Frauenlobstr.
Thalkirchner Str.
Pestalozzistr.
Holzstr.

0 — 200 m

320

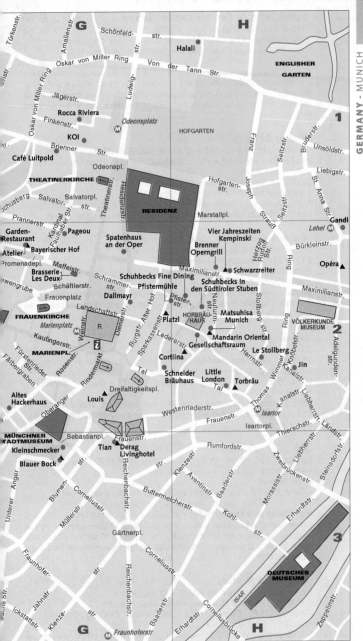

ENGLISHER GARTEN

Halali

Schönfeld-str.

Oskar von Miller Ring

Von der Tann Str.

Türkenstr.

Amalienstr.

Ludwigstr.

G

H

Jägerstr.

Rocca Riviera

Finkenstr.

KOI

Odeonsplatz

HOFGARTEN

Franz

Seitzstr.

Bruderstr.

Unsöldstr.

1

Brienner

Str.

Café Luitpold

Odeonspl.

THEATINERKIRCHE

Liebigstr.

St. Anna Str.

Salvatorstr.

Salvatorpl.

RESIDENZ

Marstallpl.

Hofgarten-str.

Joseph

Gandl

Lehel M

Prannerstr.

Kardinal Faulhaber Str.

Theatinerstr.

Residenzstr.

Pageou

Straub

Bürkleinstr.

Garden-Restaurant

Spatenhaus an der Oper

Vier Jahreszeiten Kempinski

Herzog Rudolf Str.

Ring

Opéra

Atelier

Bayerischer Hof

Brenner Operngrill

Schwarzreiter

Promenadepl.

Maffeistr.

Brasserie Les Deux

Schrammer-str.

Maximilianstr.

Maximilianstr.

Löwengrube

Schäftlerstr.

Schuhbecks Fine Dining

Pfisterstr.

Schuhbecks in den Südtiroler Stuben

Stollbergstr.

Neuturmstr.

Frauenplatz

Dallmayr

Pfistermühle

Matsuhisa Munich

VÖLKERKUNDE MUSEUM

Adelgunden-str.

FRAUENKIRCHE

Landschaftstr.

Alter Hof

Platzl

HOFBRÄU-HAUS

Marienplatz

Dienerstr.

Weinstr.

R

Burgstr.

Sparkassenstr.

Ledererstr.

Mandarin Oriental

Gesellschaftsraum

Le Stollberg

Herrnstr.

Wimmer

Knöbelstr.

Kanalstr.

Jin

Kaufingerstr.

MARIENPL.

i

Rindermarkt

Cortina

Tal

Schneider Bräuhaus

Little London

Torbräu

Thomas

Isartor

2

Fürstenrieder Str.

Rosenstr.

Färbergraben

Tal

Westenriederstr.

Frauenstr.

Liebherrstr.

Landstr.

Altes Hackerhaus

Oberanger

Louis

Dreifaltigkeitspl.

Isartorpl.

Thierschstr.

Steinsdorfstr.

MÜNCHNER STADTMUSEUM

Kleinschmecker

Blauer Bock

Sebastianpl.

Frauenstr.

Tian

Derag Livinghotel

Rumfordstr.

Reichenbachstr.

Klenzestr.

Aventinstr.

Morassistr.

Zweibrückenstr.

Erhardtstr.

Unterer Anger

Blumenstr.

Corneliusstr.

Müllerstr.

Buttermelcherstr.

Baaderstr.

Kohl-str.

3

Fraunhoferstr.

Gärtnerpl.

Corneliusstr.

DEUTSCHES MUSEUM

Jahnstr.

Reichenbachstr.

Baaderstr.

Erhardtstr.

Corneliusbrücke

ISAR

Zeppelinstr.

Ickstattstr.

Klenzestr.

G

Fraunhoferstr.

Corneliusbrücke

H

GERMANY - MUNICH

Schuhbecks in den Südtiroler Stuben ⅩⅩⅩ 🏵 🍴 🆔 ⇔

Platzl 6 ⊠ 80331 – Ⓜ Isartor – ℰ (089) 2 16 69 00 Plan: **H2**
– www.schuhbeck.de – Closed 1 week early January and Sunday
Menu 39 € (weekday lunch)/89 € – *(booking advisable)*
• Country • Rustic • Elegant •
You will find a new culinary concept here as Bavarian delicacies meet Italian specialities in this decidedly elegant restaurant. The motto is 'share and enjoy' and rather than the classic menu sequence, diners are free to order starters or mains as they wish. Also available at the Platzl: ice cream, chocolate, spices and wine.

Blauer Bock – Hotel Blauer Bock ⅩⅩ 🍴 🚗

Sebastiansplatz 9 ⊠ 80331 – Ⓜ Marienplatz – ℰ (089) Plan: **G3**
45 22 23 33 – www.restaurant-blauerbock.de – Closed Sunday-Monday and Bank Holidays
Menu 22 € (lunch)/74 € (dinner) – Carte 48/110 €
• International • Chic • Fashionable •
A chic, modern restaurant with clean lines. It offers an appealing French and regional menu including pan-fried ducks' liver and braised calves' cheeks.

Garden-Restaurant – Hotel Bayerischer Hof ⅩⅩ 🍴 🆔 🚗

Promenadeplatz 2 ⊠ 80333 – Ⓜ Marienplatz – ℰ (089) Plan: **G2**
2 12 09 93 – www.bayerischerhof.de
Menu 38 € (lunch)/78 € – Carte 50/77 € – *(booking advisable)*
• International • Friendly • Design •
Belgian designer Axel Vervoordt has given this restaurant a very particular look. The industrial-style conservatory design creates a setting reminiscent of an artist's studio.

Halali ⅩⅩ

Schönfeldstr. 22 ⊠ 80539 – Ⓜ Odeonsplatz – ℰ (089) Plan: **H1**
28 59 09 – www.restaurant-halali.de – Closed Saturday lunch, Sunday and Bank Holidays; October-Christmas: Saturday lunch, Sunday lunch
Menu 29 € (weekday lunch)/69 € – Carte 41/77 € – *(booking advisable)*
• Classic cuisine • Cosy •
The sophisticated restaurant in this 19C guesthouse has almost become an institution already. The dark wood panelling and lovely decoration has created a cosy atmosphere.

Jin ⅩⅩ 🍴 ⇔

Kanalstr. 14 ⊠ 80538 – Ⓜ Isartor – ℰ (089) 21 94 99 70 Plan: **H2**
– www.restaurant-jin.de – Closed Monday
Menu 66/96 €
– Carte 43/69 € – *(July-September: Tuesday to Friday dinner only)*
• Asian • Minimalist • Elegant •
Highlights at Jin are the upmarket, minimalist-style Southeast Asian interior and the flavoursome pan-Asian cuisine with its distinct Chinese edge, as well as Japanese and European influences. Try the carpaccio of salmon with ponzu sauce, ginger and seaweed or the Charolais rib-eye steak with wok-fried vegetables and chilli.

Matsuhisa Munich – Hotel Mandarin Oriental ⅩⅩ 🆔

Neuturmstr. 1 (1st floor) ⊠ 80331 – Ⓜ Isartor Plan: **H2**
– ℰ (089) 2 90 98 18 75 – www.mandarinoriental.com
Menu 95/125 € – Carte 50/132 € – *(dinner only) (booking advisable)*
• Asian • Fashionable •
This elegant, minimalist-style restaurant on the first floor offers Asian cuisine from Nobu Matsuhisa. His dishes are simple yet sophisticated, the produce good and fresh, and you can rely on the presence of classics such as black cod.

GERMANY - MUNICH

Nymphenburger Hof   XX 斧

Nymphenburger Str. 24 ✉ *80335 –* Ⓜ *Maillingerstr.*   Plan I: **A2**
– ℰ (089) 1 23 38 30 – www.nymphenburgerhof.de – Closed Sunday-Monday and Bank Holidays
Menu 29 € (weekday lunch)/65 € – Carte 55/74 € – *(booking advisable)*
• International • Friendly •

The Austrian inspired cuisine tastes just as good on the lovely terrace as it does in the friendly restaurant. Live piano music is also played on some evenings.

Pageou   XX 斧

Kardinal-Faulhaber-Str. 10 (1st floor) ✉ *80333*   Plan: **G2**
– Ⓜ *Marienplatz – ℰ (089) 24 23 13 10 – www.pageou.de – Closed Sunday-Monday and Bank Holidays*
Menu 47 € (lunch)/121 € (dinner) – Carte 69/88 € – *(booking advisable)*
• Mediterranean cuisine • Cosy •

Behind the magnificent historical façade, Ali Güngörmüs (previously chef at Le Canard Nouveau in Hamburg) serves Mediterranean cuisine with north African influences in the relaxed atmosphere of the tasteful interior. Quiet, attractive terrace in the courtyard. Business lunch menu.

Pfistermühle – Hotel Platzl   XX 斧 🚗

Pfisterstr. 4 ✉ *80331 –* Ⓜ *Marienplatz – ℰ (089)*   Plan: **G2**
23 70 38 65 – www.pfistermuehle.de – Closed Sunday
Menu 54/75 € (dinner) – Carte 46/63 €
• Country • Rustic • Cosy •

A separate entrance leads into the former ducal mill (1573) where you can sample regional fare in a stylish Bavarian setting (including a lovely vaulted ceiling). Try dishes such as braised calves' cheeks with parsnip puree, creamy savoy cabbage and dried fruit sauce.

Rocca Riviera   XX 斧 ✿

Wittelsbacherplatz 2 ✉ *80331 –* Ⓜ *Odeonsplatz*   Plan: **G1**
– ℰ (089) 28 72 44 21 – www.roccariviera.com – Closed Saturday lunch, Sunday
Menu 55/86 € – Carte 33/73 €
• Mediterranean cuisine • Fashionable • Chic •

Rocca Riviera is a relaxed and stylish restaurant with a pleasant atmosphere not far from the Odeonsplatz. It serves Mediterranean-French fusion cuisine on a sharing plate basis, as well as meat and fish from the charcoal grill.

Tian   XX 斧 �&ㅤ🆎

Frauenstr. 4 ✉ *80469 –* Ⓜ *Isartor – ℰ (089)*   Plan: **G3**
8 85 65 67 12 – www.taste-tian.com – Closed Sunday-Monday lunch and Bank Holidays
Menu 21 € (lunch)/95 € (dinner) – Carte 53/62 €
• Vegetarian • Fashionable •

Right on the Viktualienmarkt you will find the first Tian spin-off restaurant in Germany serving a range of refined and skilfully executed vegetarian dishes. There is also a trendy bar with a pretty interior courtyard. Reduced lunchtime menu.

Weinhaus Neuner   X 斝

Herzogspitalstr. 8 ✉ *80331 –* Ⓜ *Karlsplatz – ℰ (089)*   Plan: **F2**
2 60 39 54 – www.weinhaus-neuner.de
Carte 39/52 €
• Traditional cuisine • Traditional décor •

With its cross-vaulted ceiling, herringbone parquet and wood panelling, this old restaurant has lost nothing of its traditional charm. The food is just what you would expect from an upmarket Munich restaurant – try the flaky pastry crust chicken fricassee pie.

323

GERMANY - MUNICH

Altes Hackerhaus   X 𝄞 ㎉ ✿

Sendlinger Str. 14 ⊠ 80331 – **Ⓜ** *Marienplatz –* ☏ *(089)*   Plan: **G2**
2 60 50 26 – www.hackerhaus.de
Carte 21/51 €
• Country • Cosy • Romantic •
A very cared-for and well-run rustic restaurant where Bavarian delicacies are served in warm and homely rooms. There is a beautiful covered interior courtyard.

Brasserie – Restaurant Les Deux   X ⅋ 𝄞

Maffeistr. 3a ⊠ 80333 – **Ⓜ** *Marienplatz –* ☏ *(089)*   Plan: **G2**
7 10 40 73 73 – www.lesdeux-muc.de – Closed Sunday and Bank Holidays
Carte 28/53 € – *(booking advisable)*
• International • Bistro • Brasserie •
If you like a modern, lively bistro atmosphere, you'll enjoy the seasonal, international dishes including gnocchi with asparagus and black tiger prawns on offer on the ground floor of Les Deux. Or perhaps you'd prefer one of the "old" or "new" classics: mini burger à la Johann or beef tartare with imperial caviar for example?

Brenner Operngrill   X 𝄞

Maximilianstr. 15 ⊠ 80539 – **Ⓜ** *Lehel –* ☏ *(089)*   Plan: **H2**
4 52 28 80 – www.brennergrill.de
Carte 23/60 €
• Grills • Trendy •
A place to see and be seen... The bar, café and restaurant housed in this impressive hall with its high-vaulted ceiling (once the stables of this great residence) are a hot item on the Munich culinary scene. Homemade pasta, as well as meat and fish served hot from the open grill in the centre of the room.

Cafe Luitpold   X 𝄞 ㎉

Brienner Str. 11 ⊠ 80333 – **Ⓜ** *Odeonsplatz –* ☏ *(089)*   Plan: **G1**
2 42 87 50 – www.cafe-luitpold.de – Closed Sunday dinner and Monday dinner except Bank Holidays
Carte 32/58 €
• Traditional cuisine • Friendly • Traditional décor •
Guests can sit in the lively coffee house atmosphere of Cafe Luitpold and enjoy its good, fresh cuisine. There is also a museum on the first floor from which you can see right into the bakery – make sure you try the tarts, pralines and other delicacies!

Les Cuisiniers   X 𝄞

Reitmorstr. 21 ⊠ 80538 – **Ⓜ** *Lehel –* ☏ *(089)*   Plan I: **C3**
23 70 98 90 – www.lescuisiniers.de – Closed Saturday lunch, Sunday and Bank Holidays
Menu 25 € (lunch)/98 € (dinner) – Carte 27/69 € – *(booking advisable)*
• Classic French • Bistro •
Les Cuisiniers is a really pretty, lively bistro. It offers fresh and uncomplicated French fare that is chalked up on a blackboard and presented to diners at their tables. Tagescafé next door is run by the same team.

Délice La Brasserie – Hotel Sofitel Munich Bayerpost   X 𝄞 ㅎ

Bayerstr. 12 ⊠ 80335 – **Ⓜ** *Hauptbahnhof –* ☏ *(089)*   ㎉ 🚗
5 99 48 29 62 – www.delice-la-brasserie.com   Plan: **E2**
Carte 37/78 €
• French • Brasserie • Minimalist •
With its smart decor and incredibly high ceilings, Délice La Brasserie strikes a perfect balance between casual urban eatery and historic setting. The international cuisine has a distinct French flavour.

Gandl

X 🏠

St.-Anna-Platz 1 ✉ 80538 – Ⓜ Lehel – 𝒞 (089)
Plan: **H1**
29 16 25 25 – www.gandl.de – Closed Sunday and Monday dinner
Menu 25 € (weekday lunch)/60 € (dinner) – Carte 36/51 €
• Classic cuisine • Cosy • Bistro •
Gandl is located in a former colonial goods store, which has retained some of its old shelving and still sells one or two items. The food ranges from classic French to international. If you are here in summer don't miss the terrace overlooking the square.

Gesellschaftsraum

X 🏠

Bräuhausstr. 8 ✉ 80331 – Ⓜ Isartor – 𝒞 (089)
Plan: **H2**
55 07 77 93 – www.der-gesellschaftsraum.de – Closed Saturday lunch and Sunday
Menu 23 € (lunch)/88 € (dinner)
• Creative • Trendy • Fashionable •
If you like things casual, urban and trendy, you will find the atmosphere in this restaurant in the centre of the old town to your taste. The food is creative, modern and ambitious, and the service is pleasantly relaxed.

Kleinschmecker

X 🏠

Sebastiansplatz 3 ✉ 80331 – Ⓜ Marienplatz – 𝒞 (089)
Plan: **G3**
26 94 91 20 – www.restaurant-kleinschmecker.de – Closed 1-15 January, Sunday and Bank Holidays
Menu 59/85 € – Carte 47/65 €
• Creative • Fashionable •
This friendly, fashionable restaurant close to the Viktualienmarkt is pleasantly informal. The food is creative and sensitively combines good, fresh produce and pleasing tastes. Additional midday menu at lunchtimes.

KOI

X 🏠 ⅄ 🅰

Wittelsbacherplatz 1 ✉ 80333 – Ⓜ Odeonsplatz
Plan: **G1**
– 𝒞 (089) 89 08 19 26 – www.koi-restaurant.de – Closed during Christmas, Sunday and Bank Holidays lunch
Menu 68/95 € – Carte 36/80 € – (booking advisable)
• Japanese • Friendly • Bistro •
You can look forward to an interesting mix of visual and culinary styles on the two floors at Koi. The kitchens produce a combination of Japanese and European cuisine, including sushi and Robata-grilled meats, all based on fresh produce.

Little London

X 🏠

Tal 31 ✉ 80331 – Ⓜ Marienplatz – 𝒞 (089) 22 23 94 70
Plan: **H2**
– www.little-london.de – Closed August: Sunday-Monday
Carte 35/69 € – (dinner only)
• Grills • Friendly •
This lively steakhouse at the Isartor is fronted by a large, classic bar with a great selection of gins and whiskeys and makes a great place to enjoy some top-quality meat. The Nebraska steaks, but also the roast topside of veal and shoulder of lamb, are in particular demand.

Schneider Bräuhaus

X 🏠 ⅄ ✿

Tal 7 ✉ 80331 – Ⓜ Isartor – 𝒞 (089) 2 90 13 80
Plan: **G2**
– www.schneider-brauhaus.de
Carte 19/40 €
• Country • Cosy •
This Bavarian hostelry is like something out of a picture book. People from Munich come here for the 'Kronfleisch' or skirt of beef – just one of the many specialities from the restaurant's own butchery. Squeezing together in the rustic dining areas is also traditional!

Spatenhaus an der Oper

Residenzstr. 12 ✉ 80333 – Ⓜ Marienplatz – ✆ (089) 2 90 70 60 – www.kuffler.de Plan: G2
Carte 28/59 €
• Country • Traditional décor •

The attractive rooms in this townhouse, opposite the Bavarian State Opera, exude rural charm. On the ground floor the food is local; on the first-floor the menu is international.

Le Stollberg

Stollbergstr. 2 ✉ 80539 – Ⓜ Isartor – ✆ (089) 24 24 34 50 – www.lestollberg.de – Closed Sunday Plan: H2
Menu 45 € – Carte 42/61 € – *(booking advisable)*
• Classic cuisine • Friendly • Elegant •

After spells at several good restaurants, the charming Anette Huber has started her own venture with this modern restaurant. The classic, French and seasonal cuisine includes offerings such as calves' kidneys in red wine sauce with mashed potato. Good value lunch. Open throughout the day on Saturdays.

VINOTHEK BY GEISEL - Hotel EXCELSIOR BY GEISEL

Schützenstr. 11 ✉ 80335 – Ⓜ Hauptbahnhof – ✆ (089) 5 51 37 71 40 – www.excelsior-hotel.de – Closed Sunday lunch Plan: E2
Menu 20 € (lunch)/45 € – Carte 31/58 €
• Country • Rustic •

Diners here eat in a friendly rustic atmosphere under a lovely vaulted ceiling. The excellent wine list is accompanied by a menu of Mediterranean-inspired food. This includes selected fish in bouillabaisse broth with artichokes, celery and rouille crostini, as well as pasta dishes and classics such as roast beef with sautéed potatoes.

Mandarin Oriental

Neuturmstr. 1 ✉ 80331 – Ⓜ Isartor – ✆ (089) 29 09 80 – www.mandarinoriental.com/munich Plan: H2
67 rm – †575/895 € ††575/895 € – ☕ 44 € – 6 suites
• Grand Luxury • Historic • Classic •

This neo-Renaissance style palace is now a luxury hotel with an international reputation and one of Germany's most select addresses. A byword for exclusive accommodation and premier service, it guarantees the very highest standards – not least when it come to breakfast! The roof-top pool with its view of the Alps is the icing on the cake.

Matsuhisa Munich – See restaurant listing

Bayerischer Hof

Promenadeplatz 2 ✉ 80333 – Ⓜ Marienplatz – ✆ (089) 2 12 00 – www.bayerischerhof.de Plan: G2
319 rm – †315/395 € ††395/590 € – ☕ 41 € – 21 suites
• Grand Luxury • Traditional • Classic •

This grand hotel set in a magnificent palace was first opened in 1841. The rooms are exclusively designed in six different styles. The Blue Spa restaurant with its small menu looks out over Munich to the Alps beyond. Other restaurants include Trader Vic's, which serves Polynesian food.

✿✿✿ **Atelier** • **Garden-Restaurant** – See restaurant listing

The Charles

Sophienstr. 28 ✉ 80333 – Ⓜ Hauptbahnhof – ✆ (089) 5 44 55 50 – www.roccofortehotels.com/hotels-and-resorts/the-charles-ho Plan: E1
136 rm – †270/860 € ††270/860 € – ☕ 41 € – 24 suites
• Grand Luxury • Elegant • Contemporary •

This lovely hotel close to the Old Botanical Gardens exudes luxury with its elegant, minimalist-style decor, upmarket spa and every conceivable type of service. The suites with a view of the city are wonderful.

Königshof

Karlsplatz 25 ✉ *80335 – Ⓜ Karlsplatz – ✆ (089) 55 13 60 – www.koenigshof-hotel.de* Plan: **F2**

87 rm – †310 € ††360 € – ☕ 35 € – 8 suites

• Luxury • Traditional • Elegant •

The Geisel family have a long history in the hotel trade stretching back to 1900. It has reached its pinnacle in this classic, luxury hotel in a choice location on the Karlsplatz. The professional front of house team are always on hand to guide and advise.

✿ **Gourmet Restaurant Königshof** – See restaurant listing

Sofitel Munich Bayerpost

Bayerstr. 12 ✉ *80335 – Ⓜ Hauptbahnhof – ✆ (089) 59 94 80 – www.sofitel-munich.com* Plan: **E2**

386 rm – †240/580 € ††240/580 € – ☕ 38 € – 10 suites

• Chain • Luxury • Design •

Modern architecture and contemporary design have been incorporated into this imposing listed building dating from the latter part of the 19C with great success as you can see for yourself both in the upmarket spa and the numerous events facilities.

Délice La Brasserie – See restaurant listing

Vier Jahreszeiten Kempinski

Maximilianstr. 17 ✉ *80539 – Ⓜ Lehel – ✆ (089) 2 12 50 – www.kempinski.com/vierjahreszeiten* Plan: **H2**

230 rm – †250/600 € ††350/800 € – ☕ 42 € – 67 suites

• Luxury • Traditional • Classic •

This classic Munich grand hotel dates back to 1858. It has the sort of historic charm you don't often find, though it is not without the modern conveniences required to make it comfortable and homely. Tagesbar, facing onto Maximilianstraße, serves international fare.

✿ **Schwarzreiter** – See restaurant listing

Derag Livinghotel

Frauenstr. 4 ✉ *80469 – Ⓜ Fraunhoferstr. – ✆ (089) 8 85 65 60 – www.deraghotels.de* Plan: **G3**

83 rm – †189/209 € ††208/230 € – ☕ 21 €

• Business • Design • Functional •

The Livinghotel enjoys a great central location on the ever-lively Viktualienmarkt. It offers upmarket designer rooms equipped with state-of-the-art technology and 'Öl-Vital®' beds, as well as apartments that are perfect for long-stay guests. The free mini-bar, Nespresso machine and Wi-Fi are nice touches. The Tian restaurant serves vegetarian and vegan cuisine.

anna hotel by Geisel

Schützenstr. 1 ✉ *80335 – Ⓜ Karlsplatz (Stachus) – ✆ (089) 5 99 94 0 – www.annahotel.de* Plan: **F2**

69 rm – †185/330 € ††185/330 € – ☕ 22 € – 6 suites

• Business • Contemporary •

This modern hotel on the busy Stachus square attracts a crowd that is young, or at least young at heart! If you would like a panoramic view, ask for one of the rooms on the top floor. The rooms in the unassuming annexe next door are equally chic. The bistro and popular bar serve a range of European and Asian dishes.

Cortiina

Ledererstr. 8 ✉ *80331 – Ⓜ Isartor – ✆ (089) 2 42 24 90 – www.cortiina.com* Plan: **H2**

70 rm – †149/409 € ††189/449 € – ☕ 25 € – 5 suites

• Townhouse • Business • Elegant •

The interior of this hotel in its improbable but nonetheless central location comes as something of a surprise. It has beautiful materials including wood, slate and Jura marble, which are combined perfectly with natural colours. Some of the guestrooms are spacious and include their own kitchenette.

GERMANY - MUNICH

EXCELSIOR BY GEISEL

Schützenstr. 11 ⊠ *80335* – 🚇 *Hauptbahnhof* – ☏ *(089)*   Plan: **E2**
55 13 70 – *www.excelsior-hotel.de*
115 rm – ♦160/350 € ♦♦185/385 € – �).22 €
• Business • Classic •

The Geisel family really invests in its businesses as you can see here at the Excelsior, sister hotel to the Königshof (which is where you will find the leisure area). The attractive rooms are comfortable, the breakfast is great and the location is central.

║○ **VINOTHEK BY GEISEL** – See restaurant listing

Louis

Viktualienmarkt 6 ⊠ *80331* – 🚇 *Marienplatz* – ☏ *(089)*   Plan: **G2**
41 11 90 80 – *www.louis-hotel.com*
72 rm – ♦159/399 € ♦♦209/529 € – �).29 €
• Townhouse • Elegant • Design •

With a superb location in the Viktualienmarkt – where the excellent ingredients for breakfast come from – the Louis offers both modern design and comfort, alongside additional services such as shoe cleaning and daily newspapers. In summer, the Japanese cuisine on offer at Emiko can be enjoyed on the roof terrace facing the courtyard.

Platzl

Sparkassenstr. 10 ⊠ *80331* – 🚇 *Marienplatz* – ☏ *(089)*   Plan: **G2**
23 70 30 – *www.platzl.de*
166 rm – ♦185/545 € ♦♦195/595 € – �).29 € – 1 suite
• Traditional • Cosy •

Set in the middle of the Old Town, the Platzl certainly has a certain charm. This is thanks in no small part to its attractive, contemporary, comfortable rooms and the attractive leisure area in the style of Ludwig II's Moorish Pavilion.

║○ **Pfistermühle** – See restaurant listing

Blauer Bock

Sebastiansplatz 9 ⊠ *80331* – 🚇 *Marienplatz* – ☏ *(089)*   Plan: **G3**
45 22 23 33 – *www.hotelblauerbock.de*
67 rm �) – ♦49/152 € ♦♦93/206 € – 5 suites
• Family • Business • Contemporary •

Just a stone's throw from the Viktualienmarkt, this smart, well-appointed hotel offers rooms decorated in a variety of different styles. Note that those giving onto the interior courtyard are a little quieter.

║○ **Blauer Bock** – See restaurant listing

Opéra

St.-Anna-Str. 10 ⊠ *80538* – 🚇 *Lehel* – ☏ *(089)*   Plan: **H2**
21 04 94 0 – *www.hotel-opera.de*
25 rm �) – ♦150/290 € ♦♦170/310 € – 3 suites
• Grand townhouse • Personalised • Classic •

If you are looking for something special, this little jewel of a hotel close to the Opera offers individually designed rooms furnished with antique pieces but also some modern accents. In the summer you can take breakfast in the delightful interior courtyard.

Torbräu

Tal 41 ⊠ *80331* – 🚇 *Isartor* – ☏ *(089) 24 23 40*   Plan: **H2**
– *www.torbraeu.de*
87 rm �) – ♦155/230 € ♦♦225/325 € – 3 suites
• Traditional • Classic •

The oldest hotel in Munich, Torbräu has been in business since 1490. Now a smart, family-run property it is constantly being upgraded and modernised. Attractive and bright breakfast room on the first floor. Bavarian and Mediterranean food served in the Schapeau.

GERMANY - MUNICH

❀❀ **Tantris** XxxX 🕮 🎧 🍴 ✧ **P**
Plan: **B1**
Johann-Fichte-Str. 7 ✉ *80805*
– 🚇 *Dietlindenstr. –* ☏ *(089) 3 61 95 90 – www.tantris.de*
– Closed 2 weeks early January, Sunday-Monday and Bank Holidays
Menu 95 € (lunch)/215 €
– Carte 126/178 € – (booking advisable)
• Classic French • Vintage •

Tantris is quite simply THE place to eat with its near legendary 1970s-style and Hans Haas' sublime, product-based classic cuisine. The cult setting and fine dining are accompanied by a well-practised, friendly and professional front-of-house team, as well as good wine recommendations.

→ Huchenfilet, Kopfsalat-Erbsenpüree, Fregola Sarda und Räucheraal-crème. Rehrücken mit Spitzkraut und Morcheln. Kokosnuss Panna Cotta mit Thaimango und Zitroneneis.

❀❀ **EssZimmer** XxX 🕮 ♿ 🕮 🚗
Plan: **A1**
Am Olympiapark 1 (3th floor, elevator) (at BMW Welt)
✉ *80809 –* ☏ *(089) 3 58 99 18 14 – www.esszimmer-muenchen.de*
– Closed 2 weeks January, August, Sunday-Monday and Bank Holidays
Menu 115/190 € – *(dinner only) (booking advisable)*
• Modern French • Chic • Cosy •

There is a double pleasure on offer at EssZimmer: a view of the impressive shipping hall at BMW Welt with its smart exhibition pieces, as well as the chance to enjoy Bobby Bräuer's delicate cuisine. Dine in the elegant, modern setting with a choice of two set menus. Free parking.

→ Wolfsbarsch, Petersilienwurzel, Tamarinde, Sesam. Taube aus Anjou, Kaper, Limone, Tomate, Bäckerinkartoffel. Rhabarber, weiße Schokolade, Waldmeister, Mandel.

🍴○ **Bavarie** – See restaurant listing

❀❀ **Geisels Werneckhof** XX 🕮 🕮
Plan: **C2**
Werneckstr. 11 ✉ *80802*
– 🚇 *Münchner Freiheit –* ☏ *(089) 38 87 95 68*
– www.geisels-werneckhof.de
– Closed 24 December-4 January, end July-mid August and Sunday-Monday
Menu 135/180 €
– Carte 94/145 € – (dinner only) (booking essential)
• Creative • Cosy • Traditional décor •

The cuisine prepared by Tohru Nakamura is anything but "off the peg". The finesse and fluency with which he combines top-quality produce, classic principles and Japanese influences to create elegant, creative dishes is genuinely impressive and clearly bear his inimitable signature.

→ Langoustine, Imperial Kaviar, Auster und Topinambur. Lamm, Olive, Apfel, Radieschen und Dill. Nussecke, Traube und Kumquat.

❀ **Acquarello** (Mario Gamba) XxX 🎧 🕮
Plan: **D2**
Mühlbaurstr. 36 ✉ *81677*
– 🚇 *Böhmerwaldplatz –* ☏ *(089) 4 70 48 48 – www.acquarello.com*
– Closed Saturday lunch, Sunday lunch and Bank Holidays lunch
Menu 49 € (weekday lunch)/119 €
– Carte 82/108 €
• Mediterranean cuisine • Friendly • Mediterranean décor •

Whether Mario Gamba's cuisine is Italian with a French influence or French with Italian roots is largely irrelevant when it comes to tasting his delicious dishes made from only the finest quality ingredients. Mario has now been joined by his son, Massimiliano, who assists his father as part of the excellent front-of-house team.

→ Vitello Tonnato, Thunfischcrème, Kapern, Saisonsalate. Ravioli, Walnuss, Ricotta, Parmesan-Sabayon. Rinderschmorbraten von Fassona, Barolosauce, Sellerie.

Freisinger Hof – Hotel Freisinger Hof   XX 🛋 ✿ 🚗

Oberföhringer Str. 189 ⊠ 81925 – 𝒞 (089) 95 23 02   Plan: **D1**
– www.freisinger-hof.de – Closed 28 December-9January
Menu 38/65 € (dinner) – Carte 31/64 €
• Country • Inn •

This is just what you imagine a traditional Bavarian restaurant to be like. Dating back to 1875, it stands just outside the city gates and serves typical Bavarian and Austrian cuisine. Dishes include Krosser saddle of suckling pig, and Vienna-style beef boiled in broth.

La Bohème   X 🛋 🚗

Leopoldstr. 180 ⊠ 80804 – Ⓜ Dietlindenstr. – 𝒞 (089)   Plan: **B1**
23 76 23 23 – www.boheme-schwabing.de – Closed August: Monday-Tuesday
Menu 49/79 € (dinner) – Carte 26/76 €
• Market cuisine • Fashionable • Trendy •

La Bohème offers a trendy urban setting in which to enjoy its modern cuisine. The ambitious evening menu – try the sea bass with bouillabaisse vegetables and pearl barley risotto – gives way to simpler lunchtime offerings. The restaurant serves brunch on Sundays, and also organises occasional magic shows and musical evenings.

Le Cézanne   X

Konradstr. 1 ⊠ 80801 – Ⓜ Giselastr. – 𝒞 (089) 39 18 05   Plan: **B2**
– www.le-cezanne.de – Closed during Easter, 3 weeks early August and Monday
Menu 45 € – Carte 25/61 € – *(dinner only) (booking advisable)*
• French • Family • Friendly •

In this friendly corner restaurant the chef cooks dishes from his French homeland. You can choose from the blackboard or the small menu of classic dishes. In summer, enjoy your meal outdoors or by the open, glass façade.

M Belleville   X 🛋

Fallmerayerstr. 16 ⊠ 80796 – Ⓜ Hohenzollernpl.   Plan: **B2**
– 𝒞 (089) 30 74 76 11 – www.m-belleville.com – Closed Saturday lunch, Sunday-Monday and Bank Holidays
Menu 37 € – Carte 32/53 €
• Classic French • Bistro • Brasserie •

A little bit of Paris in Munich, this charming, lively bistro offers some excellent food. The young, relaxed front-of-house team serves such delights as *rôti de porc* with mash and calves' cheeks in braised in red wine, followed perhaps by a classic *riz au lait caramel* for dessert. You will also find some rare natural wines and regular live music.

Bogenhauser Hof   XXX 🛋 ✿

Ismaninger Str. 85 ⊠ 81675 – Ⓜ Böhmerwaldplatz   Plan: **C2**
– 𝒞 (089) 98 55 86 – www.bogenhauser-hof.de – Closed 24 December-7 January, Sunday and Bank Holidays
Menu 88 € – Carte 47/80 €
• Classic cuisine • Traditional décor • Cosy •

This elegant yet comfortable Restaurant, housed in a building dating back to 1825, serves classic cuisine prepared using the finest ingredients, which explains why it has so many regulars. It also has a leafy garden complete with mature chestnut trees.

Bibulus   XX 🛋

Siegfriedstr. 11 ⊠ 80803 – Ⓜ Münchner Freiheit   Plan: **B1**
– 𝒞 (089) 39 64 47 – www.bibulus-ristorante.de – Closed Saturday lunch and Sunday
Menu 14 € (weekday lunch)/89 € – Carte 39/64 €
• Italian • Elegant •

It says something when a restaurant is popular with the locals, and the people of Schwabing clearly appreciate the uncomplicated and flavoursome Italian food. It is especially nice outside in the little square under the plane trees. Charming service.

GERMANY - MUNICH

Hippocampus   XX 🍴

Mühlbaurstr. 5 ✉ 81677 – Ⓜ Prinzregentenplatz — Plan: **C3**
– ℰ (089) 47 58 55 – www.hippocampus-restaurant.de – Closed Saturday lunch
Menu 50/59 € – Carte 51/62 € – *(booking advisable)*
• Italian • Elegant •

Hippocampus offers friendly service, an informal atmosphere and ambitious Italian cuisine. Beautiful fixtures and fittings help create the elegant yet warm and welcoming interior.

Käfer Schänke   XX 💰 🍴 ⇔

Prinzregentenstr. 73 (1st floor) ✉ 81675 — Plan: **C3**
– Ⓜ Prinzregentenplatz – ℰ (089) 4168247 – www.feinkost-kaefer.de
– Closed Sunday and Bank Holidays
Menu 40 € (lunch)/99 € – Carte 59/91 € – *(booking advisable)*
• International • Cosy •

The name "Käfer" has become synonymous with Munich's restaurant scene. The presence of a delicatessen under the same roof as this cosy restaurant guarantees the top-class ingredients, used to make its popular classics. There are also a number of stylish function rooms for special occasions.

Acetaia   X 💰 🍴

Nymphenburger Str. 215 (by A2) ✉ 80639 – ℰ (089) 13 92 90 77
– www.restaurant-acetaia.de – Closed Saturday lunch
Menu 29 € (lunch)/100 € – Carte 47/71 €
• Italian • Cosy •

Serving Italian cuisine in a comfortable Art Nouveau setting, Acetaia takes its name from the aged balsamic vinegar you will find on sale here. Walkers will enjoy a stroll along the Nymphenburger Canal to the palace with its lovely grounds.

Vinaiolo   X

Steinstr. 42 ✉ 81667 – Ⓜ Ostbahnhof – ℰ (089) — Plan: **C3**
48 95 03 56 – www.vinaiolo.de – Closed Saturday lunch
Menu 29 € (weekday lunch)/55 €
– Carte 45/65 € – *(bookings advisable at dinner)*
• Italian • Cosy • Friendly •

Sample a taste of the 'dolce vita' in this restaurant. The service exudes southern charm, the food could not be better, even in Italy, and the lunchtime menu is very reasonably priced. The image of authentic Italy is completed by fixtures and fittings from an old grocer's shop in Trieste.

Atelier Gourmet   X 🍴

Rablstr. 37 ✉ 81669 – Ⓜ Ostbahnhof – ℰ (089) — Plan: **C3**
48 72 20 – www.ateliergourmet.de – Closed Sunday
Menu 42/86 € – Carte 49/59 € – *(dinner only) (booking advisable)*
• Classic French • Bistro •

Small, intimate, lively and popular, Atelier Gourmet is quite simply a great little restaurant. The food is fresh, delicious and good value for money thanks to chef Bousquet. It is served in a casual, friendly atmosphere with efficient service and good wine recommendations from the female owner. Try the capon and duck crépinette.

Bavarie – Restaurant Esszimmer   X 🍴 ৬ 📖 ⇔ 🚗

Am Olympiapark 1 (2nd floor, elevator) (at BMW Welt) — Plan: **A1**
✉ 80809 – ℰ (089) 3 58 99 18 18 – www.feinkost-kaefer.de
– Closed 2 weeks January, August, Sunday dinner and Bank Holidays dinner
Menu 35/42 € – Carte 38/52 €
• International • Bistro • Fashionable •

Grounded in the principles of regionality and sustainability, the Bavarie concept on offer here creates a combination of Bavarian and French cuisine based on local produce. Dishes include goose liver crème brûlée and Gutshof Polting lamb. The terrace offers views of the Olympia Park and Tower.

Rüen Thai

Kazmairstr. 58 ✉ 80339 – Ⓜ Messegelände – ✆ (089) 50 32 39 – www.rueen-thai.de – Closed 29 July-19 August Plan: **A3**

Menu 49/99 €

– Carte 29/56 € – *(Thursday to Sunday and Bank Holidays: dinner only)*

• Thai • Family • Bourgeois •

True to his roots, Anuchit Chetha has dedicated himself to the cuisine of southern Thailand, preparing a range of dishes including gung pla and nüe san kua, as well as a finger food menu. In addition to specialising in interesting spice combinations, he is also passionate about wine – the restaurant boasts a cellar containing a number of real rarities.

Palace

Trogerstr. 21 ✉ 81675 – Ⓜ Prinzregentenplatz – ✆ (089) 41 97 10 – www.hotel-muenchen-palace.de Plan: **C3**

70 rm – 🛉185/380 € 🛉🛉225/475 € – ☕ 33 € – 4 suites

• Traditional • Classic • Elegant •

This tasteful, impeccably run hotel includes many musicians amongst its regulars. The natural tones and parquet floors combine to create a warm and friendly atmosphere. Pleasant garden and roof terrace. This restaurant serves classic international cuisine.

INNSIDE Parkstadt Schwabing

Mies-van-der-Rohe-Str. 10 ✉ 80807 – Ⓜ Nordfriedhof – ✆ (089) 35 40 80 – www.melia.com/de/hotels/deutschland/munich Plan: **C1**

160 rm – 🛉99/499 € 🛉🛉99/499 € – ☕ 22 €

• Business • Functional •

Designed by famous architect Helmut Jahn, this hotel enjoys a convenient location close to the striking Highlight Towers. The whole building is beautifully light, with clean modern lines. This bistro-style restaurant decorated with its modern white interior serves international cuisine.

Freisinger Hof

Oberföhringer Str. 191 ✉ 81925 – ✆ (089) 95 23 02 – www.freisinger-hof.de – Closed 28 December - 9 January Plan: **D1**

51 rm ☕ – 🛉135/569 € 🛉🛉169/769 €

• Country house • Cosy •

The hotel annexe which has been added to this historical inn offers comfortable country-style rooms. The small lobby is bright and welcoming. Enjoy tasty regional food in this cosy inn dating from 1875. Boiled beef and other classic Austrian dishes served.

Freisinger Hof – See restaurant listing

ATHENS

GREECE
ELLÁDA

Mlenny/iStock

ATHENS
ATHÍNA

tanukiphoto/iStock

ATHENS IN...

→ **ONE DAY**
Acropolis (Parthenon), Agora and Temple of Hephaestus, Plaka.

→ **TWO DAYS**
Kolonaki, National Archaeological Museum, Filopappou Hill.

→ **THREE DAYS**
Monastiraki flea-market (Sunday), Benaki Museum, Technopolis, National Gardens, Lykavittos Hill.

Inventing democracy, the theatre and the Olympic Games... and planting the seeds of philosophy and Western Civilisation – Athens was central to all of these, a city that became a byword for glory and learning, a place whose golden reputation could inspire such awe that centuries later just the mention of its name was enough to turn people misty-eyed. It's a magical place, built upon eight hills and plains, with a history stretching back at least 3,000 years. Its short but highly productive golden age resulted in the architectural glory of The Acropolis, while the likes of Plato, Aristotle and Socrates were in the business of changing the mindset of society.

The Acropolis still dominates Athens and can be seen peeking through alleyways and turnings all over the city. Beneath it lies a teeming metropolis, part urban melting pot, part über-buzzy neighbourhood. Plaka, below the Acropolis, is the old quarter, and the most visited, a mixture of great charm and cheap gift shops. North and west, Monastiraki and Psiri have become trendy zones; to the east, Syntagma and Kolonaki are notably modern and smart, home to the Greek parliament and the famous. The most northerly districts of central Athens are Omonia and Exarcheia, distinguished by their rugged appearance and steeped in history; much of the life in these parts is centred round the polytechnic and the central marketplace.

EATING OUT

In recent times, a smart wave of restaurants has hit the city and, with many chefs training abroad before returning home, this is a good time to eat out in the shadow of The Acropolis. If you want the full experience, dine with the locals rather than the tourists and make your reservation for late evening, as Greeks rarely go out for dinner before 10pm. The trend towards a more eclectic restaurant scene now means that you can find everything from classical French and Italian cuisine to Asian and Moroccan dishes, and even sushi.

Modern tavernas offer good attention to detail, but this doesn't mean they're replacing the wonderfully traditional favourites. These older tavernas, along with mezedopoleia, are the backbone of Greek dining, and most visitors wouldn't think their trip was complete without eating in one; often the waiter will just tell you what's cooking that day - and you're usually very welcome to go into the kitchen and make your selection. Greece is a country where it is customary to tip good service; ten per cent is the normal rate.

❀❀ **Spondi** XxX 🏠 🏤 AC ⇔ P

5 Pyronos, off Varnava Sq, Pangrati ⊠ 116 36 – ℰ (210) Plan: **D3**
7564 021 – www.spondi.gr – Closed Easter
Menu 73/136 € – Carte 95/132 € – (dinner only)
• French • Romantic • Elegant •
A discreet, intimate restaurant with two delightful courtyards and two charming
dining rooms – one built from reclaimed bricks in the style of a vaulted cellar.
Top quality seasonal ingredients are used in imaginative, deftly executed, stunningly presented modern French dishes. Greek, French and Italian wines feature
on an impressive list.
→ Crab, turnip, acacia honey and tarragon. Sea bream and spring vegetables with cockles and pickled fennel. Cheesecake, caramelised apricot and
raisins.

❀❀ **Funky Gourmet** (Georgianna Chiliadaki and Nikos Roussos) XX

13 Paramythias St and Salaminos, Keramikos ⊠ 104 35 AC ⇔
– Ⓜ Keramikós – ℰ (210) 5242 727 Plan: **A2**
– www.funkygourmet.com – Closed August, Sunday and Monday
Menu 150 € – (dinner only) (booking essential) (tasting menu only)
• Creative • Minimalist • Intimate •
A charming neoclassical house in downtown Athens, set off the main tourist
track. The minimalist first floor dining room is decorated in black, white and
grey. Wonderfully well-crafted, innovative dishes feature unusual but well-
thought-through combinations, and many display playful, theatrical elements.
→ Greek bottarga tartlet with white chocolate. 'Greek Salad'. Chocolate
bomb.

❀ **Hytra** XX ≤ AC

Onassis Cultural Centre (6th Floor), 107-109 Syngrou Ave C3 (Southwest:
2.5 km) ⊠ 11745 – ℰ (021) 7707 1118 – www.hytra.gr – Closed Easter
Carte 67/73 € – (dinner only)
• Modern cuisine • Design • Fashionable •
Take the express lift up to the 6th floor of the striking Onassis Cultural Centre;
here you'll find a sultry restaurant looking out over Syngrou. Classic Greek recipes are executed in a refined modern manner – for something a little different
try the cocktail pairings. They also offer a bistro menu at the bar.
→ Squid and salsify spaghetti, rock samphire, basil and mushroom dashi.
Pork with carrot purée and sea buckthorn. Honey-infused yoghurt with
camomile, walnuts and bee pollen.

☺ **Athiri** X 🏤

15 Plateon ⊠ 104 35 – Ⓜ Keramikós – ℰ (210) Plan: **A2**
3462 983 – www.athirirestaurant.gr – Closed 2 weeks August, 1 week
Easter, 1-5 January, Sunday dinner in winter and Monday
Menu 38 € – Carte 24/39 €
• Greek • Neighbourhood •
In winter, sit inside, surrounded by blue, white and grey hues; in summer, head
out to the courtyard and well-spaced tables surrounded by lush green plants.
Local, seasonal ingredients are simply prepared in order to reveal their natural
flavours. Dishes are generous, good value and have creative touches.

☺ **Nolan** X 🏤 AC

31-33 Voulis St ⊠ 105 57 – Ⓜ Syntagma – ℰ (210) Plan: **C3**
3243545 – www.nolanrestaurant.gr – Closed 12-19 August,
25 December and Sunday
Carte 28/40 €
• Fusion • Fashionable • Minimalist •
This small, contemporary bistro stands out from the other restaurants in this
busy neighbourhood. The young chef has Greek, German and Asian roots and
his cooking fuses influences from all three countries along with many other
international flavours. Dishes provide plenty of appeal and are great for sharing.

Oikeîo
⚔ 🛋 AC

15 Ploutarhou St ⊠ 106 75 – Ⓜ Evangelismos
Plan: **D2**
– ℰ (210) 7259 216 – Closed 25-26 December and 3 days Easter
Carte 16/28 €

• Greek • Rustic • Traditional décor •

A sweet little restaurant in a chic neighbourhood, with tables on two different levels, as well as outside. The décor is traditional and the place has a warm, cosy feel. Menus offer great value family-style dishes made with fresh ingredients and feature the likes of sardines, moussaka and octopus in vinegar.

GB Roof Garden – Grande Bretagne Hotel
XxX 🏵 🛋 🛋 AC

1 Vas Georgiou A, Constitution Sq ⊠ 105 64
Plan: **C2**
– Ⓜ Syntagma – ℰ (210) 3330 766 – www.gbroofgarden.gr
Carte 38/135 € – (booking essential)

• Mediterranean cuisine • Fashionable • Elegant •

Set on the 8th floor of the Grande Bretagne hotel, this elegant rooftop restaurant offers spectacular views across Syntagma Square towards The Acropolis. Sunny, modern Mediterranean cooking uses fresh ingredients and is accompanied by an extensive wine list. Service is smooth and efficient.

Electra Roof Garden – Electra Palace Hotel
XxX 🛋 🛋 AC

18-20 Nikodimou St ⊠ 105 57 – Ⓜ Syntagma – ℰ (210)
Plan: **C3**
3370 000 – www.electrahotels.gr
Menu 35 € – Carte 30/54 € – (dinner only)

• Mediterranean cuisine • Romantic • Elegant •

Set on the top floor of the Electra Palace hotel, this superbly located restaurant offers unrivalled views of The Acropolis and downtown Athens. Well-made dishes are a mix of traditional Greek and more international flavours.

Première – Athenaeum InterContinental Hotel
XxX 🏵 🛋 AC 🚗

89-93 Syngrou Ave (9th floor) (Southwest: 2.5 km) ⊠ 117 45 – ℰ (210)
9206 981 – www.intercontinental.com/athens – Closed Sunday and Monday
Menu 65/80 € – Carte 61/87 € – (dinner only)

• Mediterranean cuisine • Friendly • Minimalist •

Start with a drink in the cocktail bar then head through to the elegant restaurant or out onto the terrace to take in views of The Acropolis. Top quality produce features in carefully crafted, delicate Mediterranean dishes.

2 Mazi
XX 🛋 AC

48 Nikis St ⊠ 105 58 – Ⓜ Syntagma – ℰ (210) 3222 839
Plan: **C3**
– www.2mazi.gr – Closed Easter
Menu 70 € – Carte 37/55 €

• Greek • Trendy • Historic •

Mazi means 'together' and within this neoclassical building you'll find a modern dining room offering a menu inspired by fresh Greek ingredients and Cretan herbs and vegetables. They also offer a good selection of local wines by the glass.

Cookoovaya
XX 🛋 ♿ AC

2A Chatzigianni Mexi St ⊠ 115 28 – Ⓜ Evangelismos
Plan: **D2**
– ℰ (210) 723 5005 – www.cookoovaya.gr – Closed Easter and 2 weeks August
Carte 34/70 € – (booking advisable)

• Greek • Friendly • Fashionable •

Five of the city's leading chefs have come together to open this bustling restaurant, where rustic, homely cooking is the order of the day and generous dishes are designed for sharing. The homemade pies from the wood-oven are a hit.

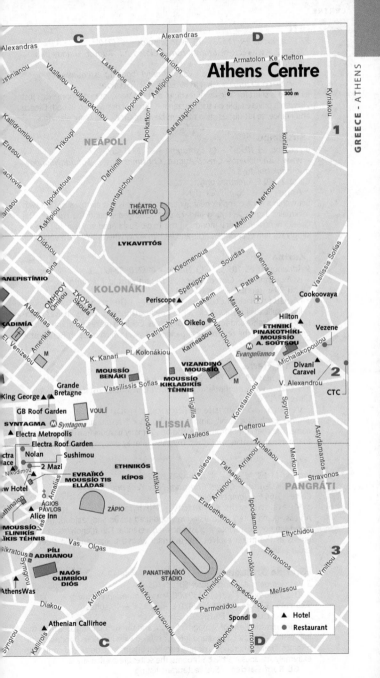

Athens Centre

0   300 m

C   Alexandras   **D**

Alexandras

Armatolon Ke Klefton

Justinianou

Vasileiou Voulgaroktonou

Laskareos

Fanarioton

Kallidromiou

Ippokratous

Apokafkon

Asklipiou

Sarantapichou

Koniari

Kyriakou

Eresou

Trikoupi

NEÁPOLI

Dafnimili

Melinas   Merkouri

Zachovis

Ippokratous

Sarantapichou

1

arilaou

Asklipiou

THÉATRO LIKAVITOÚ

Didotou

LYKAVITTÓS

Sina

Kleomenous

Souidias

Gennadiou

Vasilissis Sofias

ANEPISTÍMIO

KOLONÁKI

Spetsippou

ΟΜΗΡΟΥ
Omírou   ΣΚΟΥΦΑ
Skoufa

Periscope ▲

Ioakeim

I. Patera

Cookoovaya

Akadimias

Tsakalof

Patriarchou

Oikeío

Ploutarchou

Marasli

Hilton ▲

Solonos

Karneadou

ETHNIKÍ PINAKOTHÍKI-MOUSSÍO A. SOÚTSOU

Vezene

KADIMÍA

Amerikis

El. Venizelou

K. Kanari

Pl. Kolonákiou

Evangelismos

Michalakopoulou

Divani Caravel

M

VIZANDINÓ MOUSSÍO

V. Alexandrou

2

MOUSSÍO BENÁKI

Grande Bretagne

MOUSSÍO KIKLADIKÍS TÉHNIS

M

CTC

King George ▲

Vassilissis Sofias

Konstantinou

GB Roof Garden

VOULÍ

Rigillis

ILISSIÁ

SYNTAGMA Ⓜ Syntagma

Irodou

Vasileos

Defterou

Spyrou

Astydamantos

▲ Electra Metropolis

Electra Roof Garden

ectra
lace

Nolan   Sushimou

2 Mazi

Vasileos

Patsaniou

Archelaou

Merkouri

Stravonos

Nikodimou

ETHNIKÓS KÍPOS

Arrianou

PANGRÁTI

w Hotel

EVRAÏKÓ MOUSSÍO TIS ELLÁDAS

Attikou

Arrianou

Ippodamou

athinaiou

ÁGIOS PAVLOS

Amalias

ZÁPIO

Eratosthenous

Alice Inn

Eftichidou

MOUSSÍO ELINIKÍS LIKIS TÉHNIS

Vas. Olgas

Proklou

Efftanoros

Ymittou

3

sikratous

PÍLI ADRIANOU

Effranoros

Symgrou

NAÓS OLIMBÍOU DIÓS

PANATHINAÏKÓ STADIO

Archimidous

Empedokleous

Melissou

AthensWas

Diakou

Ardittou

Markou Mousourou

Parmenidou

Spondi ●

| ▲ | Hotel |
| ● | Restaurant |

Symgrou

Athenian Callirhoe ▲

Kallirois

C

Stiponos

Parmenidou

Pyrronos

D

CTC

⑩ XX AC ✧

27 Diocharous ⊠ *11528 –* Ⓜ *Evangelismos – ℰ (210)*　　Plan: **D2**
722 8812 – www.ctc-restaurant.com – Closed July-August, Sunday and
Monday
Menu 65 € – Carte 61/76 € – *(dinner only) (booking essential)*
• Modern cuisine • Intimate • Fashionable •
Its name is short for "the art of feeding" and the sleek, intimate room seats just
28, with a private table on the mezzanine. The chef has worked in both Greece
and France, so his dishes are a modern blend of Greek and Gallic elements.

Sushimou

⑩ X AC

6 Skoufou ⊠ *105 57 –* Ⓜ *Syntagma – ℰ (211) 4078457*　　Plan: **C3**
– www.sushimou.gr – Closed August, Christmas, Easter, Saturday-Sunday
and bank holidays
Carte 25/40 € – *(dinner only)*
• Asian • Bistro • Trendy •
Set within a large complex near Syntagma Square is this narrow sushi bar with
minimalist Japanese styling and 12 seats arranged around the counter. The
Greek chef spent several months at the Tokyo Sushi Academy learning the art;
simply tell him your preferences and let him know when you've had enough.

Kuzina

⑩ X 🛖 AC

9 Adrianou St ⊠ *105 55 –* Ⓜ *Thissio – ℰ (210) 3240 133*　　Plan: **B3**
– www.kuzina.gr – Closed Easter, 25 December and 1 January
Menu 20 € (dinner) – Carte 28/64 €
• Mediterranean cuisine • Friendly • Bistro •
A lively split-level restaurant in a busy pedestrianised street; its shelves cram-
med with alcohol and homemade preserves. Cooking makes good use of local
produce. Sit on the terrace for a panoramic view which takes in Hephaestus
Temple.

Mama Tierra

⑩ X 🛖 AC

84 Akadimias ⊠ *106 78 –* Ⓜ *Omonia – ℰ (211)*　　Plan: **B2**
411 4420 – www.mamatierra.gr – Closed Christmas, Easter and Sunday
Carte 13/17 €
• Vegetarian • Simple • Neighbourhood •
'Mother Earth' is a small, simple neighbourhood restaurant befitting of her
name. The chef comes from India and brings many flavours from his homeland
to the international vegan dishes. They also offer a takeaway service.

Vezene

⑩ X 🛖 AC

Vrasida 11 ⊠ *115 28 – ℰ (210) 723 2002*　　Plan: **D2**
– www.vezene.gr – Closed Christmas-New Year and Sunday
Carte 25/64 € – *(dinner only)*
• Meats and grills • Friendly • Minimalist •
An easy-going eatery specialising in wood-fired steaks and seafood. The dark
wood interior opens into a glass-enclosed veranda. The friendly team guide
guests as the menu evolves. Try the mini Wagyu burger and the sliced-to-
order salumi.

Grande Bretagne

≤ 🖾 🕲 🕸 🗻 ⛱ & AC 🔱 🎾

3 Vas Georgiou A, Constitution Sq ⊠ *105 64*　　Plan: **C2**
– Ⓜ *Syntagma – ℰ (210) 3330 000 – www.grandebretagne.gr*
320 rm – ❢250/420 € ❢❢250/420 € – ☲ 33 € – 46 suites
• Grand Luxury • Palace • Elegant •
Take in fantastic views of Syntagma Square and the surrounding area from this
impressive 19C hotel. The grand interior is filled with luxurious handmade furnishings. Opulent bedrooms display excellent attention to detail and come with
extremely spacious marble bathrooms; the suites are particularly striking.
⑩ **GB Roof Garden** – See restaurant listing

Athenaeum InterContinental

89-93 Syngrou Ave (Southwest: 2.5 km) ✉ *117 45*
– ☏ (210) 9206 000 – www.intercontinental.com/athens – Closed
1 January-8 January and Easter
553 rm – 🛏210/340 € 🛏🛏210/340 € – ☲ 33 € – 61 suites
• Grand Luxury • Business • Modern •
A corporate hotel with impressive meeting spaces, a business centre and jewellery and gift shops. The owner is one of the world's top 5 modern art collectors. Bedrooms are spacious and well-equipped; the Club floors offer dedicated services. Eat in the lounge-bar, the casual restaurant or more formal Première.
⑩ **Première** – See restaurant listing

Hilton

46 Vasilissis Sofias Ave ✉ *115 28* – Ⓜ *Evangelismos*   Plan: D2
– ☏ (210) 7281 000 – www.hiltonathens.gr
506 rm – 🛏225/395 € 🛏🛏225/638 € – ☲ 45 €
• Chain • Business • Modern •
One of the biggest hotels in Athens comes with a great fitness centre and spa, along with a huge lobby boasting a bookshop and a hairdresser. Modern bedrooms have balconies and sea or mountain outlooks. The restaurants serve Greek and international dishes – rooftop 'Galaxy' offers sea and Acropolis views.

King George

3 Vas Georgiou A, Syntagma Sq ✉ *105 64*   Plan: C2
– Ⓜ Syntagma – ☏ (210) 3222 210 – www.kinggeorgeathens.com
102 rm – 🛏270/450 € 🛏🛏270/450 € – ☲ 28 € – 13 suites
• Palace • Grand Luxury • Classic •
A luxuriously converted 1930s mansion set in Syntagma Square. Bedrooms have an elegant, classical style and come with smart marble bathrooms. The rooftop Penthouse Suite boasts a veranda and a stunning private pool with panoramic city and Acropolis views. Dine informally in the fashionable loungebar or head to the 7th floor Tudor Hall for a greater sense of occasion.

Divani Caravel

2 Vas Alexandrou Ave ✉ *161 21* – Ⓜ *Evelangismos*   Plan: D2
– ☏ (210) 7207 000 – www.divanis.com
471 rm – 🛏250/500 € 🛏🛏250/530 € – ☲ 29 € – 44 suites
• Business • Luxury • Classic •
Pass through the marble lobby with its impressive chandelier and up to the elegant bedrooms which combine classic charm with mod cons. Take in breathtaking views of The Acropolis and Lykavittos Hill from the rooftop pool, then head to the all-day café-restaurant or chic Brown's for modern Mediterranean fare.

Electra Palace

18-20 Nikodimou St ✉ *105 57* – Ⓜ *Syntagma – ☏ (210)*   Plan: C3
3370 000 – www.electrahotels.gr
155 rm ☲ – 🛏120/175 € 🛏🛏130/225 € – 11 suites
• Luxury • Classic •
An attractive hotel on a peaceful city street in the Plaka district. Its classical façade conceals an elegantly furnished interior; head up to the rooftop pool for fantastic panoramic views over downtown Athens and towards The Acropolis. The two restaurants serve traditional Greek and international fare.
⑩ **Electra Roof Garden** – See restaurant listing

Electra Metropolis

15 Mitropoleos ✉ *105 57* – Ⓜ *Syntagma – ☏ (214)*   Plan: C2
1006200 – www.electrahotels.gr
216 rm ☲ – 🛏175/190 € 🛏🛏200/395 €
• Business • Luxury • Modern •
The interior of the Electra Metropolis is surprisingly spacious considering its central location and the light-filled atrium is 9 floors high! Modern bedrooms come in warm tones and the Suites have balconies with stunning Acropolis views. Look out over the city from the top floor bar or Roof Garden restaurant.

Radisson Blu Park H. Athens

10 Alexandras Ave ⊠ *106 82 –* Ⓜ *Victoria –* ☏ *(210)*
8894 500 – www.radissonblu.com/hotel-athens   Plan: **B1**
153 rm ☲ – **♦**110/170 € **♦♦**120/250 €
• Business • Chain • Contemporary •

It's been in the family since 1976 and its elegant tree trunk pillars and colour-changing leaves are inspired by the park opposite. Contemporary bedrooms come in browns and greens and most have park views. The Asian restaurant overlooks The Acropolis and moves up to the rooftop to serve BBQ and pasta dishes in summer. Casual Gallo Nero offers Tuscan-inspired fare.

Athenian Callirhoe

32 Kallirois Ave and Petmeza ⊠ *117 43 –* Ⓜ *Syngrou-Fix*   Plan: **C3**
– ☏ *(210) 9215 353 – www.tac.gr*
84 rm ☲ – **♦**90/145 € **♦♦**95/205 €
• Business • Modern •

This contemporary hotel sits between two main Avenues and has an elegant lobby filled with smart design furniture. Its comfortable bedrooms come with wooden furnishings and some have balconies and jacuzzis. The 8th floor roof garden restaurant offers international dishes and a panoramic view.

AthensWas

5 Dionysiou Areopagitou St ⊠ *117 42 –* Ⓜ *Acropolis*   Plan: **C3**
– ☏ *(210) 924 9954 – www.athenswas.gr*
21 rm ☲ – **♦**175/215 € **♦♦**230/330 €
• Townhouse • Grand luxury • Design •

This stylishly understated hotel sits on a pedestrianised street in a historic part of the city and its ethos is one of relaxation. Dine on modern Mediterranean dishes on the roof terrace. The best bedrooms have large balconies with great views of The Acropolis – no other hotel is this close to the citadel!

New Hotel

16 Filellinon St ⊠ *105 57 –* Ⓜ *Syntagma –* ☏ *(210)*   Plan: **C3**
327 3000 – www.yeshotels.gr
79 rm ☲ – **♦**185/265 € **♦♦**210/295 €
• Business • Traditional • Design •

A quirky, contemporary hotel designed by the Campana brothers. The lobby walls feature wood reclaimed from old furniture and bedsteads, and the minimalist bedrooms showcase furnishings made from recycled materials. Organic ingredients feature in Mediterranean dishes in the all-day restaurant.

Periscope

22 Haritos St ⊠ *106 75 –* Ⓜ *Evangelismos –* ☏ *(210)*   Plan: **D2**
7297 200 – www.yeshotels.gr
22 rm ☲ – **♦**140/215 € **♦♦**160/475 €
• Business • Modern • Minimalist •

An elegant residential district is home to this small hotel decorated in shades of grey. Minimalist bedrooms come with balconies and large aerial photos of Athens – some on the ceiling. The stylish bar features Mini Cooper seating.

Acropolis Hill

7 Mousson St ⊠ *117 42 –* Ⓜ *Singrou-Fix –* ☏ *(210)*   Plan: **B3**
9235 151 – www.acropolishill.gr
37 rm ☲ – **♦**60/130 € **♦♦**65/160 €
• Traditional • Business • Contemporary •

A traditional-looking hotel set close to the Philopappos Monument. It has a nice outdoor pool and a contemporary, boutique style interior. Bedrooms are simple and practical; those at the front have balconies and Acropolis views.

Hermes ⚏

19 Apollonos St ✉ *105 57 –* Ⓜ *Syntagma –* ☎ *(210)*   Plan: **B3**
3235 514 – www.hermeshotel.gr
45 rm ⌲ **–** 🛏100/130 € 🛏🛏110/180 €
• Family • Functional •

A compact, modern hotel located between Monastiraki and Syntagma Square. Bedrooms are bright and simply furnished; the family rooms have two bedrooms and two bathrooms. Buffet breakfasts are served in the first floor restaurant.

Alice Inn ⚏

9 Tsatsou St ✉ *105 58 –* Ⓜ *Syntagma –* ☎ *(210)*   Plan: **C3**
3237139 – www.aliceinnathens.com
4 rm – 🛏50/185 € 🛏🛏50/185 € **–** ⌲ 5 €
• Boutique hotel • Townhouse • Personalised •

This private house sits on a quiet street in the heart of Plaka and has been transformed into a boutique guesthouse with four uniquely designed, apartment-style bedrooms. You can prepare your own meals in the communal kitchen.

ENVIRONS OF ATHENS

AT HALANDRI   Northeast : 11 km by Vas. Sofias

❀

Botrini's *(Ettore Botrini)*   ✕✕✕ 🏠 ⚏

24b Vasileos Georgiou ✉ *152 33 –* Ⓜ *Halandri –* ☎ *(210) 6857323*
– www.botrinis.com – Closed 24-31 December, 5-9 April, Sunday and Monday
Menu 75 € – Carte 69/86 € – *(dinner only)*
• Mediterranean   cuisine • Design • Contemporary décor •

A converted school in a quiet suburb – now a passionately run restaurant with an ultra-modern interior, a sleek glass-fronted kitchen and verdant terraces. Appealing modern menus feature local produce in creative, attractively presented dishes. Many of the oils, salamis and wines are produced by the family.
➜ Beef carpaccio, pear, gorgonzola and mushrooms. Duck with beetroot and kumquat. Wild strawberries with vanilla, port and meringue.

AT MAROUSSI   Northeast : 12.5 km by Vas. Sofias

🍴

Aneton ✕ ⚏

Stratigou Lekka 19 ✉ *151 22 –* Ⓜ *Maroussi –* ☎ *(210) 8066 700*
– www.aneton.gr – Closed August, 25 December, 1 January and Easter
Menu 30/35 € – Carte 28/59 € – *(booking essential)*
• Greek • Friendly • Intimate •

It's worth travelling into the smart city suburbs to seek out this appealing neighbourhood restaurant. Menus follow the seasons; in summer they have a Mediterranean base and some Middle Eastern spicing, while in winter, hearty stews and casseroles feature. The hands-on owner really brings the place to life.

AT KIFISSIA   Northeast : 15 km by Vas. Sofias

Kefalari Suites ⚏ ⅍

1 Pendelis and Kolokotroni St, Kefalari ✉ *145 62 –* Ⓜ *Kifissia –* ☎ *(210)*
6233 333 – www.yeshotels.gr
13 rm ⌲ **–** 🛏145/180 € 🛏🛏165/200 € **–** 1 suite
• Townhouse • Elegant • Cosy •

A cosy 19C villa in a smart residential area. Elegantly furnished bedrooms come with kitchenettes and are themed around everything from Jaipur to the sea. Have breakfast on the veranda, then take in the view from the rooftop jacuzzi.

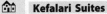

Semiramis ⚒ ᵇ̥ ⌂ 🏊 🅐🅒 ↳ 🔧 🚗

48 Charilaou Trikoupi St, Kefalari ✉ 145 62
– ⓜ *Kifissia* – ℰ *(210) 6284 400* – *www.yeshotels.gr*
51 rm ☲ – †165/200 € ††185/220 € – 1 suite
• Business • Design • Minimalist •

A bold design hotel set on the main plaza of a leafy suburb. Pinks and greens feature inside and out and are complemented by curvaceous modern furnishings. Minimalist bedrooms boast hi-tech facilities and balconies, and there's a quirky pool and sun terrace. Nolita serves modern Italian dishes and cocktails.

AT VOULIAGMENI South : 18 km by Singrou

Divani Apollon Palace & Thalasso ⚒ < 🛏 ᵇ̥ ⚙ ⌂ 🏊 🖼 ✕ 🅐🅒 ↳ 🔧 🚗

10 Ag Nikolaou and Iliou St (Kavouri) off
Athinas ✉ 166 71
– ℰ *(210) 8911 100* – *www.divaniapollonhotel.com*
280 rm ☲ – †420/560 € ††460/600 € – 7 suites
• Palace • Luxury • Classic •

A chic resort with a particularly impressive spa and thalassotherapy centre, two outdoor swimming pools and an underground walkway to a private beach. Luxurious bedrooms boast balconies and gulf views. Dine on fresh seafood in beachside Mythos, global cuisine in Anemos or all-day snacks in the coffee lounge.

Apollon Suites 🅐🅒 ↳ 🚗

11 Nikolaou St ✉ 166 71
– ℰ *(210) 8911 100* – *www.divanis.com* – *Closed November-April*
56 rm ☲ – †135/220 € ††155/450 €
• Luxury • Contemporary • Elegant •

The peaceful annexe of the Divani Apollon Palace shares its facilities but has a more intimate atmosphere. Spacious bedrooms come with hand-picked fabrics and terraces (some with sea views). Room service and concierges are available 24/7.

Margi ⚒ ᵇ̥ ⌂ 🏊 🅐🅒 ↳ 🔧 🅿

11 Litous St ✉ 166 71
– ℰ *(210) 8929 000* – *www.themargi.gr*
89 rm ☲ – †130/350 € ††150/720 € – 8 suites
• Traditional • Personalised • Mediterranean •

A stylish hotel on the peninsula, close to the beach. The lobby has a Mediterranean feel, bedrooms are furnished in a modern colonial style and offer sea or forest views from their balconies. The sun loungers are beautifully arranged in and around the pool. Cooking uses produce from their nearby farm.

AT PIRAEUS Southwest: 8 km by Singrou

❀ Varoulko Seaside (Lefteris Lazarou) XX 🔔 🅐🅒 ⇄

Akti Koumoundourou, 54-56 Mikrolimano Marina (Southeast: 1.5 km by coastal road) ✉ *185 33*
– ⓜ *Piraeus* – ℰ *(210) 522 8400* – *www.varoulko.gr* – *Closed Easter, Christmas and New Year*
Menu 60 €
– Carte 42/59 € – *(booking essential)*
• Seafood • Classic décor • Friendly •

Varoulko sits in a great spot in Mikrolimano Marina – the chef's old neighbourhood. Watch the yachts glide by from the maritime-themed dining room which opens onto the water. Greek and Mediterranean dishes feature organic vegetables, Cretan olive oil and the freshest seafood; squid and octopus feature highly.
→ Sea bass carpaccio. Grouper with celeriac cream and chorizo. White chocolate mousse, hazelnut chocolate cream and peach sorbet.

Papaioannou   ✗ 🍴 AC

Akti Koumoundourou 42, Mikrolimano Marina (Southeast: 1.5 km by coastal road) ✉ *185 33 –* Ⓜ *Piraeus –* ☎ *(210) 4225 059 – Closed 24-25 and 31 December, Easter and Sunday dinner*
Carte 38/108 €
• Seafood • Traditional décor • Family •

A traditional seafood restaurant where diners select the type, weight and cooking style of their fish. Shrimp, mussels and crayfish come 'saganaki' style – in tomato sauce with feta cheese. Menus evolve as more fresh produce arrives.

Piraeus Theoxenia   🍴 ⛴ AC ⇄ 🏊 🚗

23 Karaoli and Dimitriou St ✉ *185 31 –* Ⓜ *Piraeus –* ☎ *(210) 4112 550 – www.theoxeniapalace.com*
77 rm ⌂ – 🛏105/190 € 🛏🛏105/190 € – 1 suite
• Business • Luxury • Contemporary •

The Theoxenia is set in the heart of town, close to the bustling local markets and the harbour. The large marble lobby opens onto a classical restaurant which serves global dishes with Mediterranean influences. Spacious bedrooms combine traditional and modern styles and the business centre is well-equipped.

● BUDAPEST

HUNGARY
MAGYARORSZÁG

focusstock/iStock

BUDAPEST
BUDAPEST

jon chica parada/iStock

BUDAPEST IN...

➡ **ONE DAY**
Royal Palace, the Parliament Building, a trip on the Danube.

➡ **TWO DAYS**
Gellert Baths, a stroll down Váci utca, a concert at the State Opera House.

➡ **THREE DAYS**
Museum of Applied Arts, Margaret Island, coffee and cake at Gerbeaud.

No one knows quite where the Hungarian language came from: it's not quite Slavic, not quite Turkic, and its closest relatives appear to be in Finland and Siberia. In much the same way, Hungary's capital is a bit of an enigma. A lot of what you see is not as old as it appears. Classical and Gothic buildings are mostly neoclassical and neo-Gothic, and the fabled baroque of the city is of a more recent vintage than in other European capitals. That's because Budapest's frequent invaders and conquerors, from all compass points of the map, left little but rubble behind them when they left; the grand look of today took shape for the most part no earlier than the mid-19C.

It's still a beautiful place to look at, with hilly Buda keeping watch – via eight great bridges – over sprawling Pest on the other side of the lilting, bending Danube. These were formerly two separate towns, united in 1873 to form a capital city. It enjoyed its heyday around that time, a magnificent city that was the hub of the Austro-Hungarian Empire. Defeats in two world wars and fifty years behind the Iron Curtain put paid to the glory, but battered Budapest is used to rising from the ashes and now it's Europe's most earthily beautiful capital, particularly when winter mists rise from the river to shroud it in a thick white cloak. In summer the days can swelter, and the spas are definitely worth a visit.

EATING OUT

The city is most famous for its coffee houses so, before you start investigating restaurants, find time to tuck into a cream cake with a double espresso in, say, the Ruszwurm on Castle Hill, the city's oldest, and possibly cosiest, café. In tourist areas, it's not difficult to locate goulash on your menu, and you never have to travel far to find beans, dumplings and cabbage in profusion. Having said that, Budapest's culinary scene has moved on apace since the fall of communism, and Hungarian chefs have become much more inventive with their use of local, seasonal produce. Pest is where you'll find most choice but even in Buda there are plenty of worthy restaurants. Lots of locals like to eat sausage on the run and if you fancy the idea, buy a pocket knife. Sunday brunch is popular in Budapest, especially at the best hotels. Your restaurant bill might well include a service charge; don't feel obliged to pay it, as tipping is entirely at your own discretion – though you may find the persistence of the little folk groups that pop up in many restaurants hard to resist.

HUNGARY - BUDAPEST

✨✨ **Onyx**   XxX ͣ **AC**

Vörösmarty tér 7-8 ✉ 1051 – **Ⓜ** Vörösmarty tér   Plan: **E2**
– ℰ (30) 508 0622 – www.onyxrestaurant.hu – Closed 2 weeks
January, 3 weeks August, Tuesday and Wednesday lunch, Sunday and
Monday
Menu 19900/29900 HUF – (booking essential) (tasting menu only)
• Modern cuisine • Elegant • Intimate •
In the city's heart is this glitzy restaurant where you sit on gilt chairs, under
sparkling chandeliers, surrounded by onyx adornments. Passionate, highly skil-
led cooking keeps classic Hungarian flavours to the fore but also has interesting
modern twists. Dishes are precisely prepared and intensely flavoured.
➙ Goose liver, pistachio and green apple. Lamb terrine, artichoke and spi-
nach. Cottage cheese, apricot and lavender.

✨ **Costes**   XxX ͣ **AC**

Ráday utca 4 ✉ 1092 – **Ⓜ** Kálvin tér – ℰ (1) 219 0696   Plan: **F3**
– www.costes.hu – Closed Christmas, Monday and Tuesday
Menu 26500/37500 HUF – Carte 21000/24600 HUF – (dinner only) (booking essential)
• Modern cuisine • Design • Elegant •
A sophisticated restaurant with immaculately dressed tables, run by a confident,
experienced service team. The talented chef uses modern techniques and a
deft touch to produce accomplished, innovative dishes with clear flavours.
Most diners choose the 4-7 course set menus and their interesting wine pairings.
➙ Matyó pasta filled with butternut and sage. Pike with corn and spring
onion. 'Bling' - black cherry, vanilla cream and gingerbread.

✨ **Borkonyha Winekitchen**   XX ͣ 🍽 **AC**

Sas utca 3 ✉ 1051 – **Ⓜ** Bajcsy-Zsilinszky út – ℰ (1)   Plan: **E2**
266 0835 – www.borkonyha.hu – Closed Sunday and bank holidays
Carte 8250/14850 HUF – (booking essential)
• Modern cuisine • Fashionable • Friendly •
A bustling wine-orientated restaurant close to the Basilica. The fortnightly menu
features well-executed dishes with an elaborate modern style and subtle Hungarian influences. Top ingredients are sourced from the surrounding countries.
48 of the 200 wines are offered by the glass; many are from local producers.
➙ Rillettes of rabbit with sausage crumbs. Saddle of lamb with duck
liver pâté. Chocolate with orange flowers and apricot.

✨ **Costes Downtown** – Prestige Hotel   XX ☿ **AC**

Vigyázó Ferenc utca 5 ✉ 1051 – **Ⓜ** Vörösmarty tér   Plan: **E1**
– ℰ (1) 920 1015 – www.costesdowntown.hu
Menu 6900 HUF (weekday lunch)/22000 HUF – Carte 7900/20700 HUF
• Modern cuisine • Fashionable • Contemporary décor •
The more informal sister to Costes sits within the Prestige hotel and has chic
bistro styling and a friendly atmosphere; ask to be seated in one of the booths.
Refined modern dishes follow the seasons and feature excellent texture and fla-
vour combinations. They offer a good value business lunch.
➙ Quail with sorrel and redcurrant. Pan-fried John Dory with endive and
grapefruit. Rum Baba.

⊙ **Petrus**   XX 🍽 **AC** ↺

Ferent tér 2-3 ✉ 1094 – **Ⓜ** Klinikák – ℰ (1) 951 2597   Plan I: **B2**
– www.petrusrestaurant.hu – Closed 2 weeks August, 24-26 December,
Sunday and Monday
Menu 8490 HUF – Carte 6570/11470 HUF
• Classic French • Bistro • Neighbourhood •
A friendly neighbourhood bistro where Budapest meets Paris – both in the
décor and the food. The chef-owner's passion is obvious and the cooking is rustic and authentic, with bold flavours and a homely touch. If you're after something a little different, ask to dine in the old Citroën 2CV!

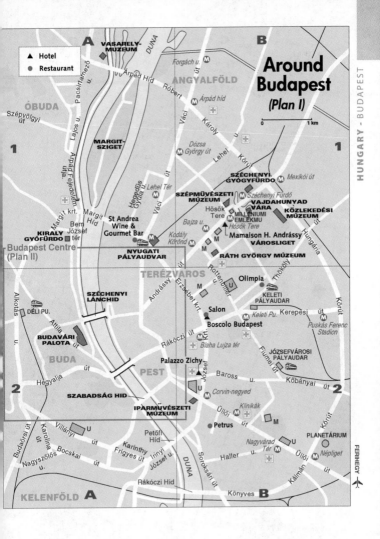

Fricska

X AC
Plan: F1

Dob utca 56-58 ✉ *1073 –* Ⓜ *Oktogon –* ✆ *(1) 951 8821
– www.fricska.eu – Closed Sunday and Monday*
Menu 2650 HUF (weekday lunch) – Carte 7250/10750 HUF – *(bookings advisable at dinner)*

· Modern cuisine · Bistro · Contemporary décor ·

The subtitle 'gastropub' is misleading, as this is a contemporary cellar bistro with crisp white décor and a laid-back vibe. The blackboard menu offers appealingly unadorned dishes with Hungarian, French and Italian influences. The home-made pastas are a highlight and the weekday lunch menu is a steal.

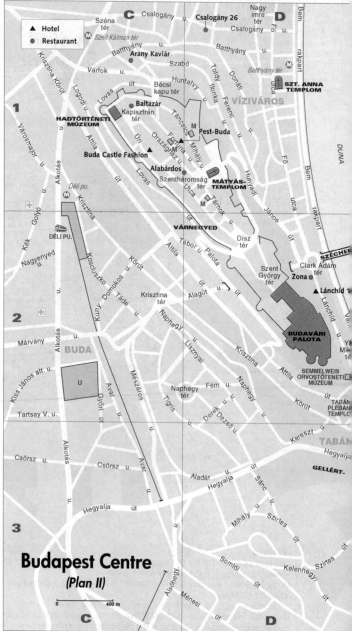

Budapest Centre
(Plan II)

0 — 400 m

HUNGARY - BUDAPEST

Stand 25   X AK

Hold utca 13 ✉ *1054 –* Ⓜ *Arany János utca – ℰ (30)*   Plan: **E1**
961 3262 – www.stand25.hu – Closed Christmas, Easter, Sunday, dinner Monday-Thursday and bank holidays
Menu 4900/8500 HUF
• Traditional cuisine • Simple • Bistro •

In the heart of the striking downtown market hall is this new age bistro: a fusion of steel, neon, wood and slate. Classic menus list fresh, rustic, well-executed dishes; the chefs' signatures – goulash and potato casserole – are mainstays. Half of the tables can be booked and half are set aside for walk-ins.

Salon – Boscolo Budapest Hotel   XxX AK

Erzsébet krt. 9-11 ✉ *1073 –* Ⓜ *Blaha Lujza tér – ℰ (1)*   Plan I: **B2**
886 6191 – www.boscolohotels.com – Closed 2 weeks August, Sunday and Monday
Menu 15900/24000 HUF – Carte 9300/16500 HUF – *(dinner only) (booking advisable)*
• Hungarian • Classic décor • Luxury •

A stunning baroque salon behind glass doors in a luxurious hotel; admire the ornate gilding and impressive painted ceiling as you dine. Extensive menus use the best local ingredients to create attractively presented modern interpretations of Hungarian classics; the 7 course tasting menu is a highlight.

Baraka   XxX AK

Dorottya utca 6 ✉ *1051 –* Ⓜ *Vörösmarty tér – ℰ (1)*   Plan: **E2**
200 0817 – www.barakarestaurant.hu – Closed 24-25 December and Sunday
Menu 27900 HUF – Carte 15700/32900 HUF – *(dinner only)*
• Modern cuisine • Elegant • Intimate •

To the front is a beautiful cocktail bar with a cosy lounge and to the rear is an intimate black and white dining room. Every table has a view of the open kitchen, where the chefs prepare creative modern dishes with Asian touches.

Babel   XX 🕸 AK

Piarista Köz 2 ✉ *1052 –* Ⓜ *Ferenciek ter – ℰ (70)*   Plan: **E2**
6000 800 – www.babel-budapest.hu – Closed 21 January-6 February, 12-28 August, Sunday and Monday
Menu 29900 HUF – Carte 12800/26200 HUF – *(dinner only) (booking essential)*
• Modern cuisine • Elegant • Design •

It's all about tradition at this intimate restaurant, where brick walls, parquet floors and a striking concrete ceiling contrast with stylish modern furnishings. Creative, complex cooking is inspired by the Austro-Hungarian Empire; texture and temperature play their part and dishes are beautifully presented.

Aszú   XX 🛋 AK

Sas utca 4 ✉ *1051 –* Ⓜ *Bajcsy-Zsilinszky út – ℰ (1)*   Plan: **E2**
328 0360 – www.aszuetterem.hu
Carte 7550/14000 HUF
• Hungarian • Elegant • Design •

As its name suggests, this restaurant celebrates Tokaj and its wines. The cooking showcases updated Hungarian classics, and the striking room features an ornate mirrored wall, a golden-hued vaulted ceiling and handcrafted wooden carvings.

Fausto's   XX AK ⇔

Dohány utca 5 ✉ *1072 –* Ⓜ *Astoria – ℰ (30) 589 1813*   Plan: **F2**
– www.fausto.hu – Closed Christmas, Sunday and bank holidays
Carte 13800/19950 HUF – *(booking essential)*
• Italian • Cosy • Intimate •

Expect a friendly welcome at this personally run eatery. Dine on sophisticated modern Italian dishes at linen-laid tables in the restaurant or on simpler, more classically based fare in the laid-back, wood-furnished osteria; the daily home-made pasta is a hit. Good quality Hungarian and Italian wines feature.

iO **Nobu Budapest** – Kempinski H. Corvinus XX ⚅ 🎬 ⟷
Erzsébet tér 7-8 ⊠ *1051 –* Ⓜ *Deák Ferenc tér –* 𝒞 *(1)* Plan: **E2**
429 4242 – www.noburestaurants.com
Menu 5000 HUF (lunch) – Carte 7380/14120 HUF
• Japanese • Minimalist • Fashionable •

A minimalist restaurant in a stylish hotel, with well-spaced wooden tables, Japanese lanterns, fretwork screens and an open kitchen. Numerous menus offer a huge array of Japanese-inspired dishes; some come with matching wine flights.

iO **St. Andrea Wine & Gourmet Bar** XX 🍴 🎐 ⚅ 🎬 ⟷
Bajcsy-Zsilinszky utca 78 ⊠ *1055* Plan I: **A1**
– Ⓜ *Nyugati pályaudvar –* 𝒞 *(1) 269 0130 – www.standreaborbar.hu*
– Closed Christmas, Easter, Saturday lunch, Sunday and bank holidays
Menu 3200/22000 HUF – Carte 4600/15000 HUF
• Modern cuisine • Elegant • Wine bar •

A stylish bar-cum-restaurant with wine-themed décor; owned by a small boutique winery. Well-presented, creative dishes are designed to match their wines – some of which aren't sold anywhere else in the world!

iO **Tigris** XX 🍴 🎬 ⟷
Mérleg utca 10 ⊠ *1051 –* Ⓜ *Bajcsy-Zsilinszky út –* 𝒞 *(1)* Plan: **E2**
317 3715 – www.tigrisrestaurant.hu – Closed 1 week
August, 24 December and Sunday
Carte 11250/16700 HUF – *(booking essential at dinner)*
• Hungarian • Traditional décor • Neighbourhood •

A traditional bistro in a historic building designed by a Hungarian architect; it exudes a luxurious feel. Classic dishes have an appealing, earthy quality and feature foie gras specialities. The wine list champions up-and-coming producers.

iO **Bock Bisztró Pest** X 🍴 🎬
Erzsébet krt. 43-49 ⊠ *1073 –* Ⓜ *Oktogon –* 𝒞 *(1)* Plan: **F1**
321 0340 – www.bockbisztro.hu – Closed bank holidays
Menu 3200 HUF (weekday lunch) – Carte 6400/11200 HUF – *(booking essential)*
• Hungarian • Bistro • Rustic •

A busy, buzzy bistro; its shelves packed with wine. Choose something from the à la carte or try one of the blackboard specials – the friendly, knowledgeable staff will guide you. Cooking is gutsy and traditional with a modern twist.

iO **Mák** X 🍴 🎬
Vigyázó Ferenc utca 4 ⊠ *1051 –* Ⓜ *Vörösmarty tér* Plan: **E1**
– 𝒞 *(30) 723 9383 – www.mak.hu – Closed 1 week summer, Sunday and Monday*
Menu 4275 HUF (weekday lunch)/18000 HUF – Carte 11700/14850 HUF – *(bookings advisable at dinner)*
• Modern cuisine • Bistro • Rustic •

A rustic restaurant with whitewashed brick walls, semi-vaulted ceilings and a relaxed feel: its name means 'poppy seed'. The talented young chef prepares creative dishes which play with different texture and flavour combinations.

iO **Olimpia** X 🎬 ⬜
Alpár utca 5 ⊠ *1076 –* Ⓜ *Keleti pályaudvar –* 𝒞 *(1)* Plan I: **B2**
321 0680 – www.alparutca5.hu – Closed August, Christmas, Saturday lunch, Sunday and Monday
Menu 2990/9900 HUF
• Modern cuisine • Neighbourhood • Friendly •

The local area might be uninspiring but as you step over the threshold of this bright basement restaurant, all is forgotten. Fresh, light cooking is unfussy at lunch and more complex in the evening; dinner is a surprise menu served at 7pm.

HUNGARY - BUDAPEST

Four Seasons Gresham Palace

Szechenyi István tér 5-6 ✉ *1051* – Ⓜ *Vörösmarty tér*
– ☏ *(1) 268 6000* – *www.fourseasons.com/budapest*   Plan: **E2**
179 rm ☲ – ♦110809/200367 HUF ♦♦110809/200367 HUF – 18 suites
· Grand Luxury · Palace · Art déco ·

A beautifully renovated art nouveau building constructed in 1906 for the Gresham Life Assurance Company. It boasts a stunning lobby with a mosaic floor and a stained glass cupola, along with an impressive rooftop spa and superb river views. Elegant bedrooms are the ultimate in luxury. The chic brasserie offers a mix of international, Hungarian and rotisserie dishes.

Corinthia Budapest

Erzsébet krt 43-49 ✉ *1073* – Ⓜ *Oktogon* – ☏ *(1)*   Plan: **F1**
479 4000 – *www.corinthia.com/budapest*
413 rm – ♦70000/150000 HUF ♦♦70000/150000 HUF – ☲ 8700 HUF
– 28 suites
· Grand Luxury · Historic · Classic ·

A superbly restored and comprehensively equipped hotel with a splendid 19C façade and a spectacular atrium, where a marble staircase leads to a rococo-style ballroom. There's a stunning pool and spa, several shops and a patisserie. The Brasserie offers international cuisine, intimate Rickshaw serves wide-ranging Asian dishes, and Caviar & Bull offers modern fare.

Kempinski H. Corvinus

Erzsébet tér 7-8 ✉ *1051* – Ⓜ *Deák Ferenc tér* – ☏ *(1)*   Plan: **E2**
429 3777 – *www.kempinski.com/budapest*
349 rm – ♦52000/93000 HUF ♦♦115000/155000 HUF – ☲ 9900 HUF
– 18 suites
· Business · Luxury · Elegant ·

A stylish, well-equipped hotel with a striking lobby, lounge and bar; overlooking a central square and named after the charismatic 15C king, Matthias Corvinus. Spacious bedrooms feature Empire-style furniture and boast excellent facilities. The bistro serves modern Hungarian and Viennese cuisine.
⑩ **Nobu Budapest** – See restaurant listing

Aria

Hercegprímás utca 5 ✉ *1051* – Ⓜ *Bajcsy-Zsilinszky út*   Plan: **E2**
– ☏ *(1) 445 4055* – *www.ariahotelbudapest.com*
49 rm ☲ – ♦80000/213200 HUF ♦♦80000/213200 HUF – 4 suites
· Luxury · Spa and wellness · Personalised ·

An 1870s building houses this luxurious hotel, which boasts a stunning glass-enclosed courtyard with views of the sky above. Chic, spacious bedrooms are set in 4 wings and each is themed around a style of music – classical, jazz, opera or contemporary. Modern Hungarian dishes feature in the restaurant. In summer, have a drink in the rooftop bar and take in the view.

Ritz-Carlton

Erzsébet tér 9-10 ✉ *1051* – Ⓜ *Deák Ferenc tér* – ☏ *(1)*   Plan: **E2**
429 5500 – *www.ritzcarlton.com*
200 rm – ♦109700/150000 HUF ♦♦109700/208300 HUF – ☲ 9600 HUF
– 30 suites
· Luxury · Elegant · Contemporary ·

Opened in 1918, this grand former insurance office and police HQ is now a luxurious hotel with plenty of original features and an understated feel. Have afternoon tea beneath a beautiful stained glass cupola and drinks amongst doric columns. The stylish brasserie serves Hungarian dishes with a modern twist.

HUNGARY - BUDAPEST

Boscolo Budapest

Erzsébet krt 9-11 ☒ 1073 – Ⓜ Blaha Lujza tér – 𝒞 (1)
Plan I: **B2**
886 6111 – www.boscolohotels.com
185 rm – ♛41600/132500 HUF ♛♛50000/213000 HUF – ☲ 8000 HUF
– 7 suites
• Grand Luxury • Historic • Modern •
A stunning building constructed in 1891 and set around an impressive five-floor Italian Renaissance style atrium. A feeling of luxury pervades: vast bedrooms have silk wallpapers, chandeliers and marble bathrooms, and there's an unusual ice-house style spa. The striking all-day café is the place to go in the city for coffee and cake, while the salon serves modern fare.
⊯○ **Salon** – See restaurant listing

Prestige

Vigyázó Ferenc utca 5 ☒ 1051 – Ⓜ Vörösmarty tér
Plan: **E1**
– 𝒞 (1) 920 1000 – www.prestigehotelbudapest.com
85 rm ☲ – ♛51450/91000 HUF ♛♛57500/97100 HUF – 13 suites
• Luxury • Elegant • Personalised •
In the heart of the city centre you'll find this 19C townhouse designed by neoclassical architect Jozsef Hild. Most of the refined, elegant bedrooms are set around a central atrium; they differ in size and colour but all are equally well-equipped with the likes of coffee machines, bathrobes and spa bags.
❁ **Costes Downtown** – See restaurant listing

Buddha-Bar Klotild Palace

Váci utca 34 ☒ 1052 – Ⓜ Ferenciek ter – 𝒞 (1)
Plan: **E2**
799 7300 – www.buddhabarhotel.hu
102 rm – ♛43000/160000 HUF ♛♛43000/200000 HUF – ☲ 7800 HUF
• Luxury • Modern • Themed •
A chic, glitzy hotel occupying a palace built for Princess Klotild of the Habsburg family. It has an Oriental theme, with a Zen garden and bedrooms featuring crimson fabrics, intimate lighting and state-of-the-art facilities. The opulent Buddha-Bar with its marble staircase and huge gold Buddha serves a mix of Asian dishes, while stylish Baalbek serves Levantine cuisine.

Iberostar Grand H. Budapest

Október 6 utka 26 ☒ 1051 – Ⓜ Arány Janos utca
Plan: **E1**
– 𝒞 (1) 354 3050 – www.iberostar.com
50 rm – ♛36160/89930 HUF ♛♛36160/89930 HUF – ☲ 6100 HUF
• Chain • Modern • Personalised •
A classic-looking hotel with a contrastingly modern interior. The lobby-lounge features padded silver chairs on a black marble floor, while bright bedrooms come with good facilities, boldly patterned furnishings and a Spanish edge. Enjoy global dishes on the pretty terrace, overlooking the stunning Grand Bank.

Casati

Paulay Ede utca 31 ☒ 1078 – Ⓜ Opera – 𝒞 (1)
Plan: **F1**
343 1198 – www.casatibudapesthotel.com
25 rm ☲ – ♛18300/57900 HUF ♛♛21350/61000 HUF
• Townhouse • Personalised • Contemporary •
An 18C townhouse with an Italian Renaissance style façade. The glass-roofed breakfast room features an old well and the Tuk Tuk Bar is reminiscent of 1920's Shanghai. Bedrooms come in four styles: elegant, bohemian, natural and minimalist.

K + K Opera

Révay utca 24 ☒ 1064 – Ⓜ Opera – 𝒞 (1) 269 0222
Plan: **F1**
– www.kkhotels.com
200 rm ☲ – ♛24000/61000 HUF ♛♛24000/61000 HUF – 2 suites
• Business • Modern • Functional •
A friendly hotel on a quiet side street behind the Opera House, close to the smart shops of Andrássy Avenue. Uniform bedrooms are comfortable and up-to-date. The cool lounge-bar serves a range of snacks; breakfasts are comprehensive.

359

HUNGARY - BUDAPEST

La Prima Fashion
Piarista utca 6 ✉ *1052* – Ⓜ *Ferenciek ter* – ℰ *(1)*   Plan: **E2**
799 0088 – *www.laprimahotelbudapest.com*
80 rm ⌂ – ▮28000/82000 HUF ▮▮31500/175500 HUF
• Business • Modern • Design •

A simple, modern hotel located near Elizabeth Bridge. A beige and turquoise colour scheme runs throughout. The small lobby-lounge has deep padded armchairs; bedrooms have velour bedheads, bold feature walls and TVs set into large mirrors.

Mamaison H. Andrássy
Munkácsy Mihály utca 5-7 ✉ *1063* – Ⓜ *Bajza utca*   Plan I: **B1**
– ℰ (1) 462 2100 – www.mamaison.com
68 rm – ▮27500/78700 HUF ▮▮27500/78700 HUF – ⌂ 4800 HUF – 5 suites
• Business • Townhouse • Design •

A classical 1937 Bauhaus building in a superb location on the elegant main street. The modern lobby-lounge features pillars of stainless steel filigree. Light, spacious bedrooms have good facilities and most come with balconies. The stylish monochrome restaurant offers modern international dishes.

Moments
Andrássy utca 8 ✉ *1061* – Ⓜ *Opera* – ℰ *(1) 611 7000*   Plan: **F1**
– www.hotelmomentsbudapest.hu
99 rm ⌂ – ▮36550/68000 HUF ▮▮39650/68000 HUF – 2 suites
• Townhouse • Modern • Centrally located •

Not far from the State Opera, on the bustling Andrássy Avenue, is this 19C townhouse. Original inlaid floors and an impressive decorative ceiling remain. Bedrooms are sleek and modern with a subtle art deco style; the suite has a balcony and Basilica views. Dine in the brasserie or on the pavement terrace.

Palazzo Zichy
Lőrinc pap tér 2 ✉ *1088* – Ⓜ *Kálvin tér* – ℰ *(1)*   Plan I: **B2**
235 4000 – *www.hotel-palazzo-zichy.hu*
80 rm ⌂ – ▮30650/60000 HUF ▮▮30650/71000 HUF
• Business • Historic building • Modern •

A beautiful rococo-style building with an impressive 1899 façade; once home to the writer Count Zichy. The glass-roofed atrium has a striking modern design. Bedrooms are generously sized and well-equipped, with a cool, minimalist style.

Parlament
Kálmán Imre utca 19 ✉ *1054* – Ⓜ *Arany János utca*   Plan: **E1**
– ℰ (1) 374 6000 – www.parlament-hotel.hu
65 rm ⌂ – ▮27150 HUF ▮▮30200 HUF
• Townhouse • Business • Modern •

The chic, stylish interior of this well-run boutique hotel is a complete contrast to its classical 19C façade. The splendid open-plan atrium hosts an unusual display and free drinks are available in the lounge. Bedrooms are contemporary.

Bohem Art
Molnár utca 35 ✉ *1056* – Ⓜ *Kálvin tér* – ℰ *(1)*   Plan: **F3**
327 9020 – *www.bohemarthotel.hu*
60 rm ⌂ – ▮18000/48500 HUF ▮▮21000/51500 HUF
• Townhouse • Modern • Design •

A trendy hotel in a bohemian area of the city, run by a hip, friendly team. Stylish bedrooms have large screen prints and are furnished in white; the standard rooms are fairly compact. Modern Hungarian art features throughout.

12 Revay
Révay utca 12 ✉ *1065* – Ⓜ *Opera* – ℰ *(1) 909 1212*   Plan: **F1**
– www.12revayhotel.com
53 rm – ▮19430/57985 HUF ▮▮21850/60400 HUF – ⌂ 2428 HUF – 3 suites
• Business • Modern • Functional •

12 Revay is a bright, modern hotel ideally situated between the Basilica and the Opera House. Uniform bedrooms feature large black and white prints of the city's monuments; the 3 apartments have small kitchenettes and wonderful views.

HUNGARY - BUDAPEST

Alabárdos   XxX 😋 🍴 🍷 ⟷

Orszaghaz Utca 2 ✉ 1014 – Ⓜ Széll Kármán tér   Plan: **D1**
– ℰ (1) 356 0851 – www.alabardos.hu – Closed 25-26 December and Sunday
Menu 13900/21000 HUF – Carte 12700/14700 HUF – *(dinner only and Saturday lunch) (booking essential)*
• Hungarian • Elegant • Intimate •

Set in a series of 15C buildings opposite the castle and named after its guards, this professionally run restaurant has stood here for over 50 years. It's formal yet atmospheric, with subtle modern touches and a delightful terrace. Cooking is rich and flavourful and features classic dishes with a modern edge.

Arany Kaviár   XxX 😋 🍷

Ostrom utca 19 ✉ 1015 – Ⓜ Széll Kálmán tér – ℰ (1)   Plan: **C1**
201 6737 – www.aranykaviar.hu – Closed 24-26 December, 20 August, Monday and bank holidays
Menu 4900 HUF (weekday lunch)/15250 HUF – Carte 9800/27500 HUF
• Russian • Intimate • Elegant •

Choose between an opulent, richly appointed room and a larger, more modern extension which opens onto the garden. French and Russian influences guide the creative, ambitious cooking; Hungarian and Siberian caviar is a speciality.

Csalogány 26   XX 🍷

Csalogány utca 26 ✉ 1015 – Ⓜ Batthyány tér – ℰ (1)   Plan: **D1**
201 7892 – www.csalogany26.hu – Closed 2 weeks summer, 2 weeks winter, Sunday, Monday and bank holidays
Menu 2500/16000 HUF – Carte 7200/11900 HUF – *(booking advisable)*
• Modern cuisine • Bistro • Friendly •

A homely neighbourhood restaurant with a simple bistro style. The passionate father and son team prepare tasty dishes in a modern manner. Choose from the à la carte, the daily blackboard or, at dinner, an 8 course tasting menu.

Baltazár   X ⟷ 🍷 🍷

Orszagház utca 31 ✉ 1014 – Ⓜ Széll Kálmán tér   Plan: **C1**
– ℰ (1) 300 7050 – www.baltazarbudapest.com
11 rm ⌧ – 🛏47766/61413 HUF 🛏🛏71650/85287 HUF
Carte 6500/17240 HUF
• Meats and grills • Design • Bistro •

A hidden gem, tucked away to the north of the Old Town, away from the crowds. Sit on the pretty terrace or head into the striking bistro, where stage spotlights illuminate boldly painted concrete walls. Cooking focuses on Hungarian classics and meats from the Josper grill. Its bedrooms are also ultra-modern.

Tanti   X 🍷 🍷

Apor Vilmos tér 11-12 (West: 4.25 km by Hegyalja and Jagelló utca) ✉ 1124 – ℰ (20) 243 1565 – www.tanti.hu – Closed 15-23 August and Sunday
Menu 4700 HUF (weekday lunch)/18000 HUF – Carte 7400/12800 HUF
• Modern cuisine • Minimalist • Neighbourhood •

'Auntie' is located in the corner of a pleasant little shopping mall and comes with an appealing terrace. It's light, bright and simply kitted out and offers a concise menu of attractive dishes. Well-chosen native wines accompany.

Vendéglő a KisBíróhoz   X 😋 🍷 ⅃ 🍷 🅿

Szarvas Gábor utca 8/d (Northwest: 3.5 km by Attila utca, Kristina Körut and Szilágyi Erzsébet off Kutvölgyi utca) ✉ 1125 – ℰ (1) 376 6044 – www.vendegloakisbirohoz.hu – Closed Monday and bank holidays
Menu 11700 HUF – Carte 6200/11100 HUF
• Hungarian • Bistro • Neighbourhood •

A contemporary glass and wood building with a large terrace, in a peaceful suburban location. Wine takes centre stage: staff will recommend a match for your dish from the extensive list. Cooking is hearty and classical with a modern edge.

Zona   X ⌂ ⚏

Lánchíd utca 7-9 ✉ *1013 – ☎ (30) 422 5981*   Plan: **D2**
– www.zonabudapest.com
Menu 3590 HUF (weekday lunch) – Carte 7100/11800 HUF
• Modern cuisine • Design • Trendy •

A contemporary restaurant with floor to ceiling windows overlooking the river and a huge shelving unit packed with wines. Gold glass balls illuminate sleek wooden tables. Modern dishes follow the seasons and arrive smartly presented.

Buda Castle Fashion   ⚏ ⌂

Úri utca 39 ✉ *1014 – ⓜ Széll Kálmán tér – ☎ (1)*   Plan: **C1**
224 7900 – www.budacastlehotel.eu
20 rm ⌂ – †20000/38000 HUF ††24500/45000 HUF – 5 suites
• Townhouse • Functional • Modern •

A lovely 15C merchant's house on a quiet street in the heart of Old Buda; a former HQ of the Hungarian Hunting Association. Bedrooms are spacious, comfy and pleasantly modern. There's also a delightfully peaceful courtyard terrace.

Lánchíd 19   ⚘ ≤ & ⚏ ⌂ ⚑

Lánchíd utca 19 ✉ *1013 – ☎ (1) 419 1900*   Plan: **D2**
– www.lanchid19hotel.hu
48 rm – †30000/45650 HUF ††30000/117000 HUF – ☲ 4000 HUF
• Business • Design • Modern •

A stylish hotel overlooking the river and castle, and featuring a glass-floored lounge looking down to the ruins of a 14C water tower. Bedrooms boast designer chairs, feature walls and modern facilities; those to the front have impressive views. The mezzanine restaurant offers an international menu.

Pest-Buda   ⚘ ⚏ ⌂

Fortuna utca 3 ✉ *1014 – ⓜ Széll Kálmán tér – ☎ (1)*   Plan: **C1**
800 9213 – www.pest-buda.com
11 rm – †39500/51650 HUF ††39500/51650 HUF – ☲ 3050 HUF
• Inn • Historic • Contemporary •

The oldest hotel in Hungary dates from 1696 and sits in a charming cobbled street in the Old Town. Bedrooms are furnished in a contemporary country style and have smart travertine-tiled bathrooms. Sit on red leather banquettes in the vaulted bistro, where gingham-covered tables spill out onto the terrace.

Republic of IRELAND
ÉIRE

Warchi/iStock

DUBLIN
BAILE ÁTHA CLIATH

gianliguori/iStock

DUBLIN IN...

➜ **ONE DAY**
Trinity College, Grafton Street,
St Stephen's Green, Merrion Square,
Temple Bar.

➜ **TWO DAYS**
Christ Church Cathedral, Dublin
Castle, Chester Beatty Library, the
quayside.

➜ **THREE DAYS**
O'Connell Street, Parnell Square,
Dublin Writers' Museum, DART train
to the coast.

For somewhere touted as the finest Georgian city in the British Isles, Dublin enjoys a very young image. When the 'Celtic Tiger' roared to prominence in the 1990s, Ireland's old capital took on a youthful expression, and for the first time revelled in the epithets 'chic' and 'trendy'. Nowadays it's not just the bastion of Guinness drinkers and those here for the 'craic', but a twenty-first century city with smart restaurants, grand new hotels, modern architecture and impressive galleries. Its handsome squares and façades took shape 250 years ago, designed by the finest architects of the time. Since then, it's gone through uprising, civil war and independence

from Britain, and now holds a strong fascination for foreign visitors.

The city can be pretty well divided into three. Southeast of the river is the classiest, defined by the glorious Trinity College, St Stephen's Green, and Grafton Street's smart shops. Just west of here is the second area, dominated by Dublin Castle and Christ Church Cathedral – ancient buildings abound, but it doesn't quite match the sleek aura of the city's Georgian quarter. Across the Liffey, the northern section was the last part to be developed and, although it lacks the glamour of its southern neighbours, it does boast the city's grandest avenue, O'Connell Street, and its most celebrated theatres.

EATING OUT

It's still possible to indulge in Irish stew but nowadays you can also dine on everything from tacos and Thai to Malaysian and Middle Eastern cuisine, particularly in the Temple Bar area. The city makes the most of its bay proximity, so seafood features highly, with smoked salmon and oysters the favourites; the latter washed down with a pint of Guinness. Meat is particularly tasty in Ireland, due to the healthy livestock and a wet climate, and Irish beef is world famous for its fulsome flavour. However, there's never been a better time to be a vegetarian in Dublin, as every type of veg from spinach to seaweed now features, and chefs insist on the best seasonal produce, cooked for just the right amount of time to savour all the taste and goodness. Dinner here is usually served until about 10pm, though many global and city centre restaurants stay open later. If you make your main meal at lunchtime, you'll pay considerably less than in the evening: the menus are often similar, but the bill in the middle of the day will probably be about half the price.

IRELAND - DUBLIN

🏵🏵   **Patrick Guilbaud** (Guillaume Lebrun)   XxxX 🏠 ᴰ 🖩 ⟷ 🅑
21 Upper Merrion St ⊠ D2 – 𝒞 (01) 6764192   Plan: **F3**
– www.restaurantpatrickguilbaud.ie
– Closed 17 and 30 March, 25-31 December, Sunday, Monday and bank
holidays
Menu 60/120 € – (booking essential)
• Modern French • Elegant • Luxury •

A truly sumptuous restaurant in an elegant Georgian house; the eponymous
owner has run it for over 35 years. Accomplished, original cooking uses luxurious ingredients and mixes classical French cooking with modern techniques.
Dishes are well-crafted and visually stunning with a superb balance of textures
and flavours.
→ Blue lobster ravioli with coconut-scented lobster cream, toasted
almonds and curry dressing. Wicklow lamb glazed in coriander mojo
with shiitake, cauliflower and lamb jus. Guanaja chocolate and peanut parfait.

🏵   **Chapter One** (Ross Lewis)   XxX 🖩 ⟷ 🅑
The Dublin Writers Museum, 18-19 Parnell Sq ⊠ D1   Plan: **E1**
– 𝒞 (01) 8732266 – www.chapteronerestaurant.com – Closed 2 weeks
August, 2 weeks Christmas, Sunday, Monday and bank holidays
Menu 40/75 € – (booking essential)
• Modern cuisine • Intimate • Design •

Good old-fashioned Irish hospitality meets with modern Irish cooking in this stylish basement restaurant beneath the Writers Museum. The series of interconnecting rooms have an understated elegance and striking bespoke art hangs
on the walls. Boldly flavoured dishes showcase produce from local artisan producers.
→ Charred mackerel with Clarinbridge oysters, apple and lovage. Wild turbot, walnut crust and poached pear with kohlrabi. Flavours & textures of
Irish milk and honey.

🏵   **L'Ecrivain** (Derry Clarke)   XxX 🍽 🖩 ⟷ 🅑
109a Lower Baggot St ⊠ D2 – 𝒞 (01) 6611919   Plan: **F3**
– www.lecrivain.com – Closed Sunday and bank holidays
Menu 35/75 € – (dinner only and lunch Thursday-Friday) (booking essential)
• Modern cuisine • Fashionable • Design •

A well-regarded restaurant with an attractive terrace, a glitzy bar and a private dining room which screens live kitchen action. The refined, balanced
menu has a classical foundation whilst also displaying touches of modernity; the ingredients used are superlative. Service is structured yet has personality.
→ Seared foie gras with rhubarb, pickled rose petals, parfait and pain
d'épices. Aged Irish lamb with wild garlic, potato mousse and parmesan
gnocchi with lamb jus. Chocolate praline, chocolate moelleux, praline
mousse and hazelnut ice.

🏵   **Greenhouse** (Mickael Viljanen)   XxX 🖩
Dawson St ⊠ D2 – 𝒞 (01) 676 7015   Plan: **E3**
– www.thegreenhouserestaurant.ie – Closed 2 weeks July, 2 weeks
Christmas, Sunday and Monday
Menu 33 € (weekday lunch)/95 €
• Modern cuisine • Elegant • Fashionable •

Stylish restaurant with turquoise banquettes and smooth service. Menus
include a good value set lunch, midweek set and tasting menus and a 5
course 'Surprise' on Friday and Saturday evenings. Accomplished, classically
based cooking has stimulating flavour combinations and creative modern
overtones.
→ Foie gras royale with walnut, apple and smoked eel. Veal rump and
sweetbreads with wild garlic, broad beans and roasting juices. Caramel custard tart with vanilla, sherry raisins and macadamia nuts.

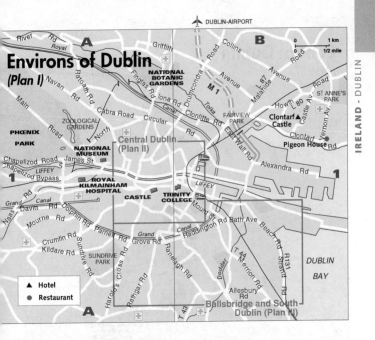

Pichet ⓒ XX 🅰🄲 🕸
14-15 Trinity St ✉ D2 – 𝒞 (01) 6771060
Plan: **E2**
– www.pichet.ie – Closed 25 December and 1 January
Menu 28 € (lunch and early dinner)/50 €
– Carte 28/53 € – (booking essential)
• Classic French • Fashionable • Brasserie •
You can't miss the bright red signs and blue and white striped canopies of this
buzzy brasserie – and its checkerboard flooring makes it equally striking inside.
Have breakfast or snacks at the bar or classic French dishes in the main room. A
good selection of wines are available by the glass or pichet.

Delahunt ⓒ X & ✿
39 Camden Street Lower ✉ D2 – 𝒞 (01) 5984880
Plan: **D3**
– www.delahunt.ie – Closed 15 August-1 September, Sunday and Monday
Menu 23 € (weekday lunch)/42 €
– Carte 34/44 € – (dinner only and lunch Thursday-Saturday) (booking
essential)
• Modern cuisine • Bistro • Fashionable •
An old Victorian grocer's shop mentioned in James Joyce's 'Ulysses'; the clerk's
snug is now a glass-enclosed private dining room. Precisely executed, flavoursome dishes are modern takes on time-honoured recipes. Lunch offers two
choices per course and dinner, four; they also serve snacks in the upstairs bar.

369

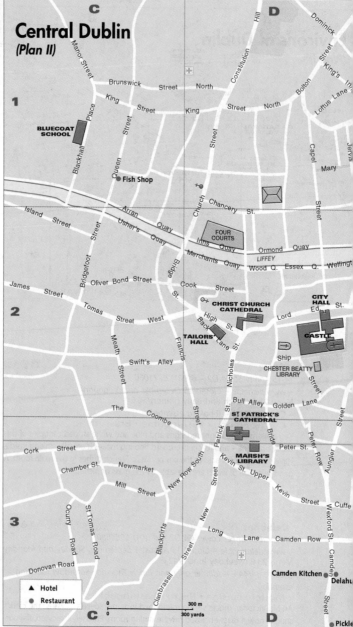

Central Dublin
(Plan II)

BLUECOAT SCHOOL

● Fish Shop

Brunswick Street North

King Street

King Street North

Manor Street

Blackhall Place

Queen Street

Constitution Hill

Dominick Street

King's Inns

Bolton Street

Loftus Lane

Capel Street

Mary Street

Jervis

Island Street

Bridgefoot Street

Usher's Quay

Arran Quay

Church St.

Chancery St.

FOUR COURTS

Inns Quay

Merchants Quay

Ormond Quay

LIFFEY

Wood Q. Essex Q. Wellingt

Oliver Bond Street

James Street

Tomas Street West

Meath Street

Swift's Alley

Cook Street

Bridge St.

Francis Street

CHRIST CHURCH CATHEDRAL

High St.

Back Lane

TAILORS' HALL

Lord Ed St.

CITY HALL

CASTLE

Ship St.

CHESTER BEATTY LIBRARY

Nicholas Street

Bull Alley

Golden Lane

The Coombe

St PATRICK'S CATHEDRAL

Patrick Street

Bride Street

MARSH'S LIBRARY

Peter St.

Peter's Row

Aungier Street

Cork Street

Chamber St.

Newmarket

Mill Street

New Row South

Kevin St. Upper

Kevin Street

Cuffe Street

Wexford St.

Ocurry Road

St Tomas Road

Blackpitts

New Street

Long Lane

Camden Row

Camden Street

Donovan Road

Clanbrassil Street

● Camden Kitchen ● Delahu

● Pickle

▲ Hotel
● Restaurant

0 ——— 300 m
0 ——— 300 yards

370

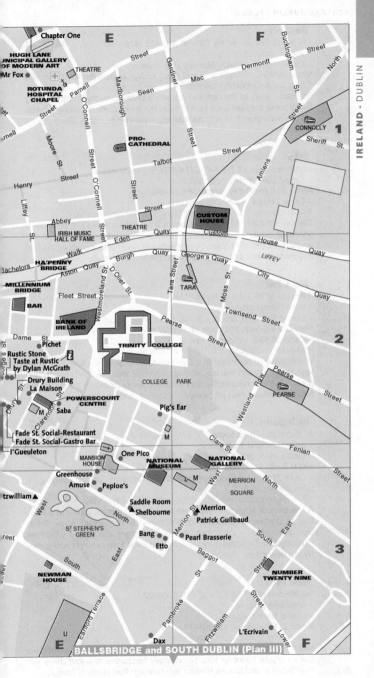

BALLSBRIDGE and SOUTH DUBLIN (Plan III)

IRELAND - DUBLIN

Bastible ✗

111 South Circular Rd ✉ *D8* – ☎ *(01) 473 7409* Plan III : **G1**
– www.bastible.com
– Closed Sunday dinner, Monday and Tuesday
Menu 38/45 € – *(dinner only and lunch Friday-Sunday) (booking essential)*
• Modern cuisine • Simple • Neighbourhood •

The name refers to the cast iron pot which once sat on the hearth of every family home; they still use it here to make the bread. Modern cooking showcases one main ingredient with minimal accompaniments; menus offer 3 choices per course.

Etto ✗

18 Merrion Row ✉ *D2* – ☎ *(01) 6788872* – *www.etto.ie* Plan: **E3**
– Closed Sunday and bank holidays
Menu 28 € (weekday lunch)/28 € (weekdays)
– Carte 29/44 € – *(booking essential)*
• Mediterranean cuisine • Rustic • Neighbourhood •

The name of this rustic restaurant means 'little' and it is totally apt! Blackboards announce the daily wines and the lunchtime 'soup and sandwich' special. Flavoursome dishes rely on good ingredients and have Italian influences; the chef understands natural flavours and follows the 'less is more' approach.

Pig's Ear ✗ ↔

4 Nassau St ✉ *D2* – ☎ *(01) 6703865* Plan: **E2**
– www.thepigsear.ie
– Closed first week January, Sunday and bank holidays
Menu 22 € (lunch and early dinner)/27 €
– Carte 28/48 € – *(booking essential)*
• Modern cuisine • Bistro • Friendly •

Well-established restaurant in a Georgian townhouse overlooking Trinity College. Floors one and two are bustling bistro-style areas filled with mirrors and porcine-themed memorabilia; floor three is a private room with a Scandinavian feel. Good value menus list hearty dishes with a modern edge.

Richmond ✗

43 Richmond Street South – ☎ *(01) 4788783* Plan: **G1**
– www.richmondrestaurant.ie
– Closed Monday
Menu 23/33 €
– Carte 31/48 € – *(dinner only and brunch Saturday-Sunday) (booking advisable)*
• Modern cuisine • Neighbourhood • Friendly •

A real gem of a neighbourhood restaurant with a rustic look and a lively feel; sit upstairs for a more sedate experience. The vibrant, gutsy dishes change regularly – apart from the Dexter burger and rib-eye which are mainstays; on Tuesdays they serve a good value tasting menu where they try out new ideas.

One Pico ✗✗✗ 🅰🅲 ↔ 🕃

5-6 Molesworth Pl ✉ *D2* – ☎ *(01) 6760300* Plan: **E3**
– www.onepico.com
– Closed bank holidays
Menu 25 € (weekday lunch)/49 €
• Modern cuisine • Elegant •

Stylish modern restaurant tucked away on a side street; a well-regarded place that's a regular haunt for MPs. Sit on comfy banquettes or velour chairs, surrounded by muted colours. Modern Irish cooking offers plenty of flavour.

⫶○

Amuse   XX 🅰🄲
Plan: **E3**
22 Dawson St ⊠ D2
– ☏ (01) 639 4889 – www.amuse.ie – Closed 2 weeks Christmas-New Year,
last week July, first week August, Sunday and Monday
Menu 29 € (weekday lunch)/65 € – (booking advisable)
• Modern cuisine • Friendly •
Modern, understated décor provides the perfect backdrop for the intricate,
innovative cooking. Dishes showcase Asian ingredients – including kombu and
yuzu; which are artfully arranged according to their flavours and textures.

⫶○

Bang   XX 🅰🄲 ✿ 🕸
Plan: **E3**
11 Merrion Row ⊠ D2
– ☏ (01) 4004229 – www.bangrestaurant.com – Closed Christmas and
bank holidays
Menu 25 € (early dinner)/50 € – Carte 40/63 € – (dinner only)
• Modern cuisine • Bistro • Fashionable •
Stylish restaurant with an intimate powder blue basement, a bright mezzanine
level and a small, elegant room above. There are good value pre-theatre menus,
a more elaborate à la carte and tasting menus showcasing top Irish produce.

⫶○

Dax   XX 🅰🄲
Plan: **E3**
23 Pembroke St Upper ⊠ D2
– ☏ (01) 6761494 – www.dax.ie – Closed 25 December-4 January, 7-
14 August, Saturday lunch, Sunday and Monday
Menu 32 € (weekday lunch)/39 € – Carte 47/68 € – (booking essential)
• French • Bistro • Classic décor •
Clubby restaurant in the cellar of a Georgian townhouse near Fitzwilliam
Square. Tried-and-tested French dishes use top Irish produce and flavours are
clearly defined. The Surprise Menu best showcases the kitchen's talent.

⫶○

Fade St. Social - Restaurant   XX ᴴ ✿ 🕸 ⓥ
Plan: **E2**
4-6 Fade St ⊠ D2
– ☏ (01) 604 0066 – www.fadestsocial.com – Closed 25-26 December and
1 January.
Menu 35 € (lunch and early dinner)
– Carte 33/88 € – (dinner only and lunch Thursday-Saturday)
• Modern cuisine • Brasserie • Fashionable •
Have cocktails on the terrace then head for the big, modern brasserie. Dishes
use Irish ingredients but have a Mediterranean feel; they specialise in sharing
and wood-fired dishes, and use large cuts of meat such as chateaubriand.

⫶○

Mr Fox   XX 🍴 🕸
Plan: **E1**
38 Parnell Sq. West ⊠ D1
– ☏ (01) 8747778 – www.mrfox.ie – Closed Sunday, Monday and bank
holidays
Menu 22 € (weekdays) – Carte 33/48 €
• Modern cuisine • Intimate • Neighbourhood •
In the basement of a striking Georgian house you'll find this light-hearted restaurant with a lovely tiled floor and a small terrace. The charming team present
tasty international dishes, some of which have a playful touch.

⫶○

Pearl Brasserie   XX 🅰🄲 🕸
Plan: **F3**
20 Merrion St Upper ⊠ D2
– ☏ (01) 6613572 – www.pearl-brasserie.com – Closed 25 December and
Sunday
Menu 25 € (lunch) – Carte 44/66 €
• Classic French • Brasserie •
Formal basement restaurant with a small bar-lounge and two surprisingly airy
dining rooms; sit in a stylish booth in one of the old coal bunkers. Intriguing
modern dishes have a classical base and Mediterranean and Asian influences.

Peploe's

XX 点 M 图

16 St Stephen's Grn. ⊠ D2
Plan: **E3**
– ℰ (01) 6763144 – www.peploes.com – *Closed 25-26 December, Good
Friday and lunch bank holidays*
Menu 32 € (lunch) – Carte 41/65 € – *(booking essential)*
• Mediterranean cuisine • Cosy • Brasserie •
Atmospheric cellar restaurant – formerly a bank vault – named after the artist.
The comfy room has a warm, clubby feel and a large mural depicts the owner.
The well-drilled team present Mediterranean dishes and an Old World wine list.

Saddle Room - Shelbourne Hotel

XX 点 M ⇔

27 St Stephen's Grn. ⊠ D2
Plan: **E3**
– ℰ (01) 6634500 – www.shelbournedining.ie
Menu 23 € (weekday lunch)/45 € – Carte 40/85 €
• Meats and grills • Elegant • Fashionable •
Renowned restaurant with a history as long as that of the hotel in which it
stands. The warm, inviting room features intimate gold booths and a crustacea
counter. The menu offers classic dishes and grills.

Suesey Street

XX 帚 M ⇔

26 Fitzwilliam Pl ⊠ D2
Plan: **H1**
– ℰ (01) 669 4600 – www.sueseystreet.ie – *Closed 25-30 December,
Saturday lunch, Sunday and Monday*
Menu 25 € (weekday dinner)/48 € – Carte 44/58 €
• Modern cuisine • Intimate • Cosy •
An intimate restaurant with sumptuous, eye-catching décor, set in the base-
ment of a Georgian townhouse; sit on the superb courtyard terrace. Refined,
modern cooking brings out the best in home-grown Irish ingredients.

Camden Kitchen

X

3a Camden Mkt, Grantham St ⊠ D8
Plan: **D3**
– ℰ (01) 4760125 – www.camdenkitchen.ie – *Closed 24-26 December,
Sunday and Monday*
Menu 24/27 € – Carte 28/50 €
• Classic cuisine • Bistro • Neighbourhood •
A simple, modern, neighbourhood bistro set over two floors; watch the owner
cooking in the open kitchen. Tasty dishes use good quality Irish ingredients pre-
pared in classic combinations. Service is relaxed and friendly.

Drury Buildings

X 帚 ⇔ 图

52-55 Drury St ⊠ D2
Plan: **E2**
– ℰ (01) 960 2095 – www.drurybuildings.com – *Closed 25-26 December*
Menu 24/28 € – Carte 30/53 €
• Italian • Trendy • Brasserie •
A hip, laid-back 'New York loft': its impressive terrace has a retractable roof and
reclaimed furniture features in the stylish cocktail bar, which offers cicchetti and
sharing boards. The airy restaurant serves rustic Italian dishes.

Fade St. Social - Gastro Bar

X 帚 点

4-6 Fade St ⊠ D2
Plan: **E2**
– ℰ (01) 604 0066 – www.fadestreetsocial.com – *Closed 25-26 December
and 1 January*
Menu 30 € (early dinner)
– Carte 24/35 € – *(dinner only and lunch Saturday-Sunday) (booking
essential)*
• International • Fashionable • Tapas bar •
Buzzy restaurant with an almost frenzied feel. It's all about a diverse range of
original, interesting small plates, from a bacon and cabbage burger to a lobster
hotdog. Eat at the kitchen counter or on leather-cushioned 'saddle' benches.

Fish Shop
X &
6 Queen St ⊠ D7 – ℰ (01) 430 8594 – www.fish-shop.ie
Plan: **C1**
– Closed Sunday-Tuesday and bank holidays
Menu 39/55 € – (dinner only) (booking advisable) (tasting menu only)
• Seafood • Rustic • Friendly •
A very informal little restaurant where they serve a daily changing seafood menu which is written up on the tiled wall. Great tasting, supremely fresh, unfussy dishes could be prepared raw or roasted on the wood-fired oven.

l'Gueuleton
X 🛖 &
1 Fade St ⊠ D2 – ℰ (01) 6753708
Plan: **E2**
– www.lgueuleton.com – Closed 25-26 December
Menu 29/38 € – Carte 39/52 €
• Classic French • Bistro • Rustic •
Rustic restaurant with beamed ceilings, Gallic furnishings, a shabby-chic bistro feel and a large pavement terrace. Flavoursome cooking features good value, French country classics which rely on local, seasonal produce. Service is friendly.

Locks
X ✪
1 Windsor Terr ⊠ D8 – ℰ (01) 416 3655
Plan III : **G1**
– www.locksrestaurant.ie – Closed Sunday dinner and Monday
Menu 30/35 € (weekday dinner)
– Carte 36/55 € – (dinner only and lunch Friday-Sunday) (booking essential)
• Modern cuisine • Bistro • Neighbourhood •
Locals love this restaurant overlooking the canal – downstairs it's buzzy, while upstairs is more intimate, and the personable team add to the feel. Natural flavours are to the fore and dishes are given subtle modern touches; for the best value menus come early in the week or before 7pm.

La Maison
X 🛖 🅰🅲
15 Castlemarket ⊠ D2 – ℰ (01) 672 7258
Plan: **E2**
– www.lamaisonrestaurant.ie – Closed 25-27 December and 1-2 January
Menu 22 € (weekday dinner) – Carte 21/56 €
• Classic French • Bistro • Cosy •
Sweet little French bistro with tables on the pavement and original posters advertising French products. The experienced, Breton-born chef-owner offers carefully prepared, seasonal Gallic classics, brought to the table by a personable team.

Osteria Lucio
X 🛖 & 🅰🅲
The Malting Tower, Clanwilliam Terr ⊠ D2 – ℰ (01)
Plan: **H1**
662 4198 – www.osterialucio.com – Closed 25-29 December and bank holiday Mondays
Menu 23 € (early dinner) – Carte 25/54 €
• Italian • Intimate • Osteria •
Set under the railway arches and run by two experienced chefs. Robust, rustic dishes showcase local produce, alongside ingredients imported from Italy; sit by the bar to watch pizzas being cooked in the wood-oven.

Pickle
X 🅰🅲 🍽
43 Camden St ⊠ D2 – ℰ (01) 555 7755
Plan: **D3**
– www.picklerestaurant.com – Closed Monday and lunch Saturday-Sunday
Menu 50 € – Carte 25/56 €
• Indian • Fashionable • Neighbourhood •
It might not look much from the outside but inside the place really comes alive. Spices are lined up on the kitchen counter and dishes are fresh and vibrant; the lamb curry with bone marrow is divine. Try a Tiffin Box for lunch.

IRELAND - DUBLIN

Rustic Stone ✗ 🎨 & 🄼

17 South Great George's St ✉ *D2 –* ✆ *(01) 707 9596*   Plan: **E2**
– www.rusticstone.ie – Closed 25-26 December and 1 January
Menu 30/40 € – Carte 33/63 €
• Modern cuisine • Fashionable • Friendly •

Split-level restaurant offering something a little different. Good quality ingredients are cooked simply to retain their natural flavours and menus focus on healthy and special dietary options; some arrive on a sizzling stone.

Saba ✗ & 🄼

26-28 Clarendon St ✉ *D2 –* ✆ *(01) 679 2000*   Plan: **E2**
– www.sabadublin.com – Closed 25-26 December
Menu 14 € (weekday lunch)/35 € – Carte 19/47 €
• Thai • Fashionable • Simple •

Trendy, buzzy restaurant and cocktail bar. Simple, stylish rooms have refectory tables, banquettes and amusing photos. Fresh, visual, authentic cooking is from an all-Thai team, with a few Vietnamese dishes and some fusion cooking too.

Taste at Rustic by Dylan McGrath ✗

17 South Great George's St (2nd Floor) ✉ *D2 –* ✆ *(01)*   Plan: **E2**
*526 7701 – www.tasteatrustic.com – Closed 25-26 December, 1 January,
Sunday and Monday*
Menu 45/55 € – Carte 34/120 € – *(dinner only) (booking advisable)*
• Asian • Rustic •

Dylan McGrath's love of Japanese cuisine inspires dishes which explore the five tastes; sweet, salt, bitter, umami and sour. Ingredients are top-notch and flavours, bold and masculine. Personable staff are happy to recommend dishes.

Shelbourne 🖼️ 🌐 🍷 🔲 & 🄼 🛁 🚗

27 St Stephen's Grn. ✉ *D2 –* ✆ *(01) 6634500*   Plan: **E3**
– www.theshelbourne.ie
265 rm – 🛏259/750 € 🛏🛏259/750 € – ☲ 29 € – 19 suites
• Grand Luxury • Classic • Elegant •

A famed hotel dating from 1824, overlooking St Stephen's Green; this is where the 1922 Irish Constitution was signed. It has classical architecture, elegant guest areas, luxurious bedrooms and even a tiny museum. The lounge and bars are the places to go for afternoon tea and drinks.
🍽 **Saddle Room** – See restaurant listing

Merrion 🍽 🛏 🖼 🔲 & 🄼 🛁 🚗

Upper Merrion St ✉ *D2 –* ✆ *(01) 6030600*   Plan: **F3**
– www.merrionhotel.com
142 rm – 🛏505/635 € 🛏🛏525/656 € – ☲ 29 € – 10 suites
• Townhouse • Luxury • Classic •

A Georgian façade conceals a luxury hotel and a compact spa with an impressive pool. Opulent drawing rooms are filled with antique furniture and fine artwork – enjoy 'Art Afternoon Tea' with a view of the formal parterre garden. Stylish bedrooms have a classic, understated feel and smart marble bathrooms. Dine from an accessible menu in the barrel-ceilinged bar.

Fitzwilliam 🍽 🖼 🄼 🛁 🚗

St Stephen's Grn ✉ *D2 –* ✆ *(01) 478 70 00*   Plan: **E3**
– www.fitzwilliamhotel.com
139 rm – 🛏200/495 € 🛏🛏220/509 € – ☲ 22 € – 3 suites
• Business • Modern •

Stylish, modern hotel set around an impressive roof garden. Contemporary bedrooms display striking bold colours and good facilities; most overlook the roof garden and the best have views over St Stephen's Green. The bright first floor brasserie offers original Mediterranean-influenced menus.

⌂ **Number 31**
31 Leeson Cl. ⊠ *D2 –* ℰ *(01) 6765011*
Plan: **H1**
– www.number31.ie
21 rm � *–* ♦120/220 € ♦♦160/300 €
· Townhouse · Design ·

A very quirky, individual property: it's classically styled around the 1960s and features a striking sunken lounge. Most of the stylish bedrooms are found in the Georgian house across the terraced garden.

BALLSBRIDGE **PLAN III**

↑○ **Chop House**
2 Shelbourne Rd ⊠ *D4 –* ℰ *(01) 6602390*
Plan: **J1**
– www.thechophouse.ie – Closed Saturday lunch
Menu 35 € – Carte 31/55 €
· Meats and grills · Pub · Neighbourhood ·

Imposing pub close to the stadium, with a small side terrace, a dark bar and a bright, airy conservatory. The relaxed lunchtime menu is followed by more ambitious dishes in the evening, when the kitchen really comes into its own.

↑○ **Old Spot**
14 Bath Ave ⊠ *D4 –* ℰ *(01) 660 5599*
Plan: **J1**
– www.theoldspot.ie – Closed 25-26 December and Good Friday
Menu 22 € (weekdays)/45 € – Carte 28/55 €
· Traditional cuisine · Pub · Friendly ·

The appealing bar has a stencilled maple-wood floor and a great selection of snacks and bottled craft beers, while the relaxed, characterful restaurant filled with vintage posters serves pub classics with a modern edge.

🏠🏠 **InterContinental Dublin**
Simmonscourt Rd. ⊠ *D4 –* ℰ *(01) 665 4000*
Plan: **J2**
– www.intercontinental.com/dublin
197 rm *–* ♦285/550 € ♦♦285/550 € – � 28 € – 58 suites
· Luxury · Business · Classic ·

Imposing hotel bordering the RDS Arena. Elegant guest areas, state-of-the-art meeting rooms and impressive ballrooms boast ornate décor, antique furnishings and Irish artwork. Spacious, classical bedrooms have marble bathrooms and plenty of extras. A wide-ranging menu is served in the bright, airy restaurant.

🏠🏠 **Dylan**
Eastmoreland Pl ⊠ *D4 –* ℰ *(01) 6603000*
Plan: **H1**
– www.dylan.ie – Closed 24-26 December
44 rm � *–* ♦250/450 € ♦♦350/550 €
· Townhouse · Design · Contemporary ·

An old Victorian nurses' home with a sympathetically styled extension and a funky, boutique interior. Tasteful, individually decorated bedrooms offer a host of extras; those in the original building are the most spacious. The stylish restaurant offers a menu of modern Mediterranean dishes and comes complete with a zinc-topped bar and a smartly furnished terrace.

⌂ **Ariel House**
50-54 Lansdowne Rd ⊠ *D4 –* ℰ *(01) 668 5512*
Plan: **J1**
– www.ariel-house.net – Closed 22 December-4 January
37 rm � *–* ♦99/250 € ♦♦99/290 €
· Townhouse · Luxury · Classic ·

Close to the Aviva Stadium and a DART station; a personally run Victorian townhouse with comfy guest areas and antique furnishings. Warmly decorated bedrooms have modern facilities and smart bathrooms – some feature four-posters.

Pembroke Townhouse

88 Pembroke Rd ✉ *D4 – ✆ (01) 66 00 277* Plan: **H1**
– www.pembroketownhouse.ie – Closed 2 weeks Christmas-New Year
48 rm – †99/350 € ††99/375 € – ☕ 15 €

• Townhouse • Traditional • Classic •

Friendly, traditionally styled hotel set in 3 Georgian houses. Small lounge with honesty bar and pantry. Sunny breakfast room offering homemade bread, cakes and biscuits. Variously sized, neutrally hued bedrooms; go for a duplex room.

ENVIRONS OF DUBLIN

AT BLACKROCK Southeast : 7.5 km by R 118

Heron & Grey (Damien Grey)

Blackrock Market, 19a Main St – ✆ (01) 212 3676
– www.heronandgrey.com – Closed 2 weeks late August, 2 weeks Christmas-New Year and Sunday dinner-Wednesday
Menu 63 € – *(dinner only and Sunday lunch) (booking essential) (tasting menu only)*

• Modern cuisine • Friendly • Intimate •

A homely, candlelit restaurant in a bohemian suburban market; it's personally run by Heron – who leads the service – and Grey, who heads the kitchen. Irish ingredients feature in intensely flavoured dishes which are full of contrasting textures and tastes. The set 5 course dinner menu changes every 2 weeks.
➜ Langoustine with seawater and fennel. Dashi, scallop and pak choi. Yuzu with nasturtium and amaretto.

AT CLONTARF Northeast : 5.5 km by R105

Pigeon House

11b Vernon Ave (East : 1km by Clontarf Rd on Vernon Ave (R808)) ✉ *D3 – ✆ (01) 8057567 – www.pigeonhouse.ie – Closed 25-26 December* Plan: **B1**
Menu 27 € (dinner) – Carte 30/47 €

• Modern cuisine • Neighbourhood • Bistro •

Slickly run neighbourhood bistro that's open for breakfast, lunch and dinner. It's just off the coast road in an up-and-coming area and has a lovely front terrace and a lively feel. Cooking is modern and assured. The bar counter is laden with freshly baked goodies and dishes are full of flavour.

Fishbone

324 Clontarf Rd (East : 1.5 km on Clontarf Rd) ✉ *D3 – ✆ (01) 536 9066*
– www.fishbone.ie – Closed 25-26 December
Menu 18 € (weekday lunch)/38 € – Carte 29/57 €

• Seafood • Neighbourhood •

A friendly little restaurant opposite the Bull Bridge, with a cocktail bar at its centre and a glass-enclosed kitchen to the rear. Prime seafood from the plancha and charcoal grill is accompanied by tasty house sauces.

Clontarf Castle

Castle Ave. ✉ *D3 – ✆ (01) 833 2321* Plan: **B1**
– www.clontarfcastle.ie
111 rm ☕ – †200/400 € ††220/420 €

• Business • Historic building • Historic •

A historic castle dating back to 1172, with sympathetic Victorian extensions; well-located in a quiet residential area close to the city. Contemporary bedrooms are decorated with bold, warm colours and many have four-poster beds. The restaurant offers local meats and seafood in a medieval ambience.

AT DONNYBROOK

Mulberry Garden

XX

Mulberry Ln (off Donnybrook Rd) ✉ *D4 –* ✆ *(01) 269 3300 – www.mulberrygarden.ie – Closed Sunday-Wednesday* Plan: **H2**

Menu 49 € – *(dinner only) (booking essential)*

• Modern cuisine • Cosy • Intimate •

Delightful restaurant hidden away in the city suburbs; its interesting L-shaped dining room set around a small courtyard terrace. Choice of two dishes per course on the weekly menu; original modern cooking relies on tasty local produce.

AT DUNDRUM South : 7.5 km by R 117

Ananda

XX

Sandyford Rd, Dundrum Town Centre ✉ *D14 –* ✆ *(01) 296 0099 – www.anandarestaurant.ie – Closed 25-26 December*

Menu 20/28 € – Carte 33/67 € – *(dinner only and lunch Friday-Sunday)*

• Indian • Exotic décor • Fashionable •

Its name means 'bliss' and it's a welcome escape from the bustle of the shopping centre. The stylish interior encompasses a smart cocktail bar, attractive fretwork and vibrant art. Accomplished Indian cooking is modern and original.

AT FOXROCK Southeast : 13 km by N 11

Bistro One

XX

3 Brighton Rd ✉ *D18 –* ✆ *(01) 289 7711 – www.bistro-one.ie – Closed 25 December-3 January, 3 April, Sunday and Monday*

Menu 29 € (weekdays) – Carte 27/57 € – *(booking essential)*

• Traditional cuisine • Neighbourhood •

Long-standing neighbourhood bistro above a parade of shops; run by a father-daughter team and a real hit with the locals. Good value daily menus list a range of Irish and Italian dishes. They produce their own Tuscan olive oil.

AT RANELAGH

Forest & Marcy

X

126 Leeson St Upper ✉ *D4 –* ✆ *(01) 660 2480 – www.forestandmarcy.ie – Closed 24 December-10 January, 22 August-5 September and Monday-Tuesday* Plan: **H1**

Menu 45 €

– Carte 36/48 € – *(dinner only and lunch Friday-Saturday) (booking essential)*

• Modern cuisine • Fashionable • Wine bar •

There's a lively buzz to this lovely little wine kitchen with high-level seating. Precisely prepared, original dishes burst with flavour; many are prepared at the counter and the chefs themselves often present and explain what's on the plate. All of the carefully chosen wines are available by the glass.

Forest Avenue

X

8 Sussex Terr. ✉ *D4 –* ✆ *(01) 667 8337 – www.forestavenuerestaurant.ie – Closed last 2 weeks August, 25 December-10 January, 11-16 April, Sunday-Tuesday and lunch Wednesday* Plan: **H1**

Menu 32 € (weekday lunch)/60 € – *(booking essential)*

• Modern cuisine • Neighbourhood • Rustic •

This rustic neighbourhood restaurant is named after a street in Queens and has a fitting 'NY' vibe. Elaborately presented tasting plates are full of originality and each dish combines many different flavours.

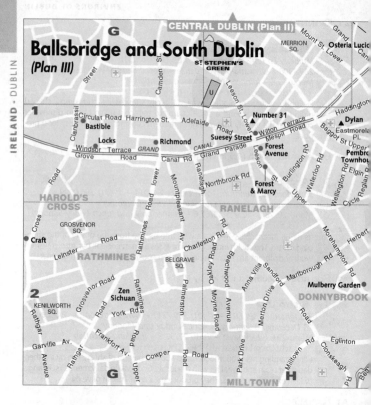

Ballsbridge and South Dublin
(Plan III)

CENTRAL DUBLIN (Plan II)

AT RATHMINES

†⃝ **Zen Sichuan** XX 🔸 AC

89 Upper Rathmines Rd ⊠ D6 – ℰ (01) 4979428   Plan: **G2**
– www.zensichuan.com – Closed 25-27 December
Menu 28 € – Carte 18/35 € – (dinner only and Friday lunch)
• Chinese • Elegant • Friendly •

Long-standing family-run restaurant, unusually set in an old church hall. At the centre of the elegant interior is a huge sun embellished with gold leaf. Imaginative Chinese cooking centres around Cantonese and spicy Sichuan cuisine.

AT SANDYFORD   South : 10 km by R 117 off R 825

†⃝ **China Sichuan** XX 🔊 🔸 AC

The Forum, Ballymoss Rd. ⊠ D18 – ℰ (01) 293 5100
– www.china-sichuan.ie – Closed 25-27 December, Good Friday, lunch Saturday and bank holidays
Menu 16 € (weekday lunch)/35 € – Carte 26/57 €
• Chinese • Fashionable • Classic décor •

A smart interior is well-matched by creative menus, where Irish produce features in tasty Cantonese classics and some Sichuan specialities. It was established in 1979 and is now run by the third generation of the family.

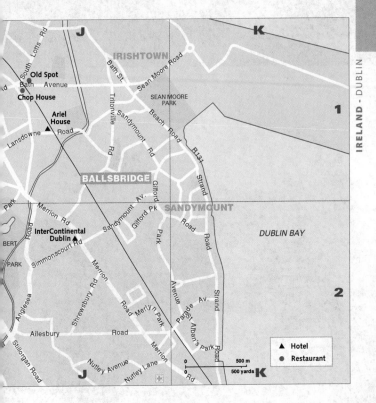

AT TERENURE

🍷 **Craft**   ✗ ⅖ ⑩
208 Harold's Cross Rd ✉ D6W – ℰ (01) 497 8632   Plan: **G2**
– www.craftrestaurant.ie – Closed 1 week Christmas-New Year, Sunday
dinner, Monday and Tuesday
Menu 27 € (early dinner)
– Carte 24/45 € – (dinner only and lunch Friday-Sunday)
• Modern cuisine • Neighbourhood • Bistro •
A busy southern suburb plays host to this neighbourhood bistro. Concise
menus evolve with seasonal availability and the lunch and early evening
menus really are a steal. Dishes are modern and creative with vibrant colours
and fresh, natural flavours. Sweet service from a local team completes the experience.

Milan

ROME

ITALY
ITALIA

MasterLu/iStock

ROME
ROMA

ROMAOSLO/iStock

ROME IN...

→ **ONE DAY**
   Capitol, Forum, Colosseum, Pantheon, Trevi Fountain, Spanish Steps.

→ **TWO DAYS**
   Via Condotti, Piazza Navona and surrounding churches, Capitoline museums.

→ **THREE DAYS**
   A day on the west bank of the Tiber at Trastevere, Vatican City.

Rome wasn't built in a day, and, when visiting, it's pretty hard to do it justice in less than three. The Italian capital is richly layered in Imperial, Renaissance, baroque and modern architecture, and its broad piazzas, hooting traffic and cobbled thoroughfares all lend their part to the heady fare: a theatrical stage cradled within seven famous hills. Being Eternal, Rome never ceases to feel like a lively, living city, while at the same time a scintillating monument to Renaissance power and an epic centre of antiquity. Nowhere else offers such a wealth of classical remains; set alongside palaces and churches, and bathed in the

soft, golden light for which it is famous. When Augustus became the first Emperor of Rome, he could hardly have imagined the impact his city's language, laws and calendar would have upon the world.

The River Tiber snakes its way north to south through the heart of Rome. On its west bank lies the characterful and 'independent' neighbourhood of Trastevere, while north of here is Vatican City. Over the river the Piazza di Spagna area to the north has Rome's smartest shopping streets, while the southern boundary is marked by the Aventine and Celian hills, the latter overlooking the Colosseum. Esquiline's teeming quarter is just to the east of the city's heart; that honour goes to The Capitol, which gave its name to the concept of a 'capital' city.

EATING OUT

Despite being Italy's capital, Rome largely favours a local, traditional cuisine, typically found in an unpretentious trattoria or osteria. Although not far from the sea, the city doesn't go in much for fish, and food is often connected to the rural, pastoral life with products coming from the surrounding Lazio hills, which also produce good wines. Pasta, of course, is not to be missed, and lamb is favoured among meats for the main course. So too, the 'quinto quarto': a long-established way of indicating those parts of the beef (tail, tripe, liver, spleen, lungs, heart, kidney) left over after the best bits had gone to the richest families. For international cuisine combined with a more refined setting, head for the elegant hotels: very few other areas of Italy have such an increasing number of good quality restaurants within a hotel setting. Locals like to dine later in Rome than say, Milan, with 1pm, or 8pm the very earliest you'd dream of appearing for lunch or dinner. In the tourist hotspots, owners are, of course, only too pleased to open that bit earlier.

ITALY - ROME

Il Pagliaccio (Anthony Genovese)   XxX 錄 AC

via dei Banchi Vecchi 129/a ⊠ *00186 –* ℰ *06 68809595*   Plan: **E2**
– www.ristoranteilpagliaccio.com – Closed 3 weeks in August, 25 January-
8 February, Sunday, Tuesday lunch and Monday
Menu 75 € (lunch)/170 € – Carte 85/145 € – *(booking advisable)*
• Creative • Elegant • Luxury •

This restaurant strikes a modern note in the heart of Renaissance Rome. The cuisine is modern and innovative, reinterpreting traditional dishes with a contemporary twist.
→ "L'Omaggio", spaghetti mediterranei e stoccafisso. "L'Insolito", anatra laccata e prugne. Passione, sale e caramello.

Imàgo – Hotel Hassler   XxxX AC

piazza Trinità dei Monti 6 ⊠ *00187 –* Ⓜ *Spagna*   Plan: **F1**
– ℰ *06 69934726 – www.imagorestaurant.com – Closed 2 weeks in*
January
Menu 120/160 € – Carte 99/157 € – *(dinner only)*
• Modern cuisine • Luxury • Friendly •

The chef's career can be seen through the dishes that arrive at the table – they combine Asian produce with Mediterranean concepts, and often display daring combinations of flavours. The cooking might provide contrasts but the enchanting view of the Eternal City offered by the large windows will appeal to all.
→ Risotto alla marinara, cozze e black lime. Petto di anatra in stile tandoori. Dolce mozzarella di bufala.

Pipero   XxX ら AC

corso Vittorio Emanuele 246 ⊠ *00186 –* ℰ *0668139022*   Plan: **E3**
– www.piperoroma.com – Closed Sunday
Menu 110/140 €
– Carte 90/110 € – *(dinner only in August) (booking advisable)*
• Creative • Elegant • Romantic •

This establishment long-favoured by food enthusiasts in the capital has moved to new premises. Alessandro Pipero now presides over an elegant, stylish contemporary restaurant opposite the Chiesa Nuova, with a mezzanine area for guests wanting a bit more privacy. In the kitchen, Luciano Monosilio uses just a few ingredients to create seemingly simple dishes which are nonetheless full of character.
→ Linguina, ostrica e paprika affumicata. Rombo, alghe e lattuga. Zafferano, cardamomo e liquirizia.

Acquolina (Alessandro Narducci) – The First Luxury Art Hotel Roma

via del Vantaggio 14 – Ⓜ *Spagna –* ℰ *06 3200655*   XxX 錄 ら AC
– www.acquolinaristorante.it – Closed 13-21 August and   Plan: **B2**
Sunday
Menu 95/130 € – Carte 85/105 € – *(dinner only)*
• Seafood • Minimalist • Intimate •

Acquolina moved from the suburban district of Fleming to this more refined central setting, where you'll find original artwork, paintings and sculptures on display. Here, the chef creates fish-based dishes inspired by Mediterranean traditions – these are accompanied by an excellent wine selection.
→ A qualcuno piace crudo: pesci, molluschi e crostacei. Mare e monti: spaghettone, ricci e 'nduja. Polpo alla Luciana... al contrario.

Il Convivio-Troiani (Angelo Troiani)   XxX 錄 AC ⇔

vicolo dei Soldati 31 ⊠ *00186 –* ℰ *06 6869432*   Plan: **E2**
– www.ilconviviotroiani.com – Closed 1 week in August, 24-26 December
and Sunday
Menu 110/150 € – Carte 81/140 € – *(dinner only)*
• Modern cuisine • Elegant • Chic •

This elegant restaurant is in the heart of the historic centre. Amid a decor of frescoes, paintings and modern minimalism, enjoy quintessential Italian cuisine. Choose from risottos and pasta, as well as a selection of specialities from the Lazio region.
→ Amatriciana de Il Convivio. Spalla di vitella "alla fornara", mostarda di capperi, midollo e liquirizia. Tiramisù de Il Convivio.

ITALY - ROME

Enoteca al Parlamento Achilli ⟨⟩ XX 🏵 🕭 AC

via dei Prefetti 15 ✉ *00186 –* Ⓜ *Spagna*
Plan: **F2**
– ℰ 06 86761422 – www.enotecalparlamento.com – Closed 14-31 August, Sunday and bank holidays
Menu 100/150 € – Carte 82/110 €
• Creative • Elegant •

Although little suggests from the outside that this city centre building houses a restaurant, the elegant wine bar leads to two successive dining rooms furnished in wood. The cuisine is highly individual, based on striking contrasts and bold presentation, making it perfect for those looking for a change from traditional fare. Some tables are reserved for bistro dining, where the food is simpler and more regional in style.
→ Ravioli cacio e pepe con consommé di guanciale. Coniglio, spuma di ostriche. Banana, caviale e cioccolato bianco.

Glass Hostaria (Cristina Bowerman) ⟨⟩ XX 🏵 AC

vicolo del Cinque 58 ✉ *00153 – ℰ 06 58335903*
Plan: **E3**
– www.glasshostaria.it – Closed 2-24 July, 8-31 January and Monday
Menu 90/140 € – Carte 64/116 € – *(dinner only)*
• Creative • Design • Fashionable •

Situated in the heart of Trastevere, this restaurant boasts an ultra-modern design with an interesting play of light. The excellent cuisine also features highly modern touches.
→ Bottoncini ripieni di lampascione, brodo di pecorino e miele, nocciole tostate e midollo. Sella di coniglio, lattuga, pomodoro, pinoli, uvetta e liquirizia. Piselli e fragola.

Per Me Giulio Terrinoni ⟨⟩ XX 🕭 ᴔ AC

vicolo del Malpasso 9 ✉ *00186 – ℰ 06 6877365*
Plan: **E3**
– www.giulioterrinoni.it – Closed 10 days in August
Menu 80/130 € – Carte 78/146 € – *(number of covers limited, pre-book)*
• Creative • Contemporary décor • Intimate •

This intimate and minimalist-style restaurant situated in a narrow street crossing Via Giulia was opened in late 2015 by chef Terrinoni. He has created an imaginative menu that is balanced and full of flavour. Renowned for his excellent fish specialities, the chef is just as skilful in his preparation of meat. The new lunchtime formula offers either a classic menu or a selection of reasonably priced tapas-style options.
→ Linguine ai frutti di mare, salsa harissa e gelato al pomodoro. Zuppa di pesce, molluschi e crostacei. Orient Express, sablè di anacardi, confettura di pompelmo e gelato al caffè.

Felice a Testaccio ⟨⟩ X AC

via Mastrogiorgio 29 ✉ *00153 – ℰ 06 5746800*
Plan: **B3**
– www.feliceatestaccio.com – Closed 1 week in August
Carte 32/48 € – *(booking advisable)*
• Friendly • Traditional décor •

The simple, family, trattoria-style atmosphere of Felice a Testaccio is so popular that it is now almost essential to book ahead for a table. Make sure you try the legendary roast lamb with potatoes, as well as the *cacio e pepe* tonnarelli pasta and the tiramisù. Without a doubt, one of the standard-bearers of Latium cuisine.

Le Jardin de Russie – Hotel De Russie ⟨⟩ XXXXX 🍴 🕭 ᴔ AC

via del Babuino 9 ✉ *00187 –* Ⓜ *Piazzale Flaminio*
Plan: **F1**
– ℰ 06 32888870 – www.roccofortehotels.com/it/hotel-de-russie
Menu 40 € (weekday lunch)/58 € – Carte 68/146 €
• Mediterranean cuisine • Luxury • Chic •

Despite its French name, this restaurant serves decidedly Italian cuisine with a creative and contemporary flavour. At lunchtime, an extensive buffet offers an alternative to the à la carte. Brunch is available on Saturdays and Sundays.

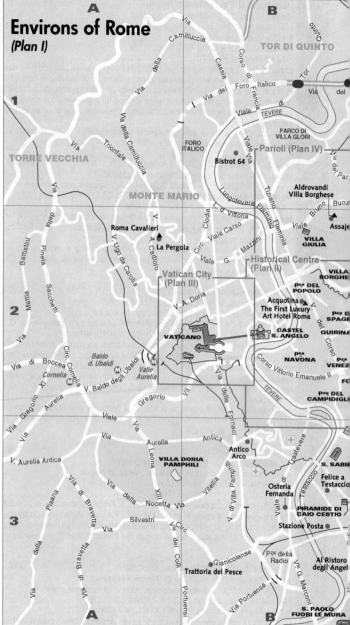

Environs of Rome
(Plan I)

TOR DI QUINTO

Via Camilluccia

Corso di Francia

Cassia

Via del Foro Italico

Via del

Viale *TEVERE*

PARCO DI VILLA GLORI

FORO ITALICO

Bistrot 64

Parioli (Plan IV)

Viale Via

Lungotevere Flaminio

Via dei Par.

TORRE VECCHIA

Via Trionfale

Via della Camilluccia

Aldrovandi Villa Borghese

Bruno Buoz

MONTE MARIO

Viale Clodia

d. Vittoria

Tiziano

Flaminia

Mazzini

Viale

Assaje

VILLA GIULIA

Battistini

Pineta

Sacchetti

Roma Cavalieri

V. Cadlolo

V.

La Pergola

Circ. Viale Carso

Viale G.

Historical Centre (Plan II)

VILLA BORGHE

Via

Mattia

V. Ugo de Carolis

Vatican City (Plan III)

V. A. Doria

P.za DEL POPOLO

P.za D SPAGN

QUIRINA

Via

di

Via di Boccea

Circ. Cornelia

Baldo d. Ubaldi

VATICANO

Acquolina
The First Luxury Art Hotel Roma

del Corso

Cornelia

V. Baldo degli Ubaldi

Valle Aurelia

CASTEL S. ANGELO

Corso Vittorio Emanuele II

P.za NAVONA

P.za VENEZ

Via Gregorio XI

Aurelia

Gregorio

Via delle Fornaci

TEVERE

P.za DEL CAMPIDIGLI

FO

Viale

V. Aurelia Antica

Via

Aurelia

Antica

Antico Arco

S. SABI

Leona

VILLA DORIA PAMPHILI

V. di Villa Pampil

Vitellia

Osteria Fernanda

Via di Trastevere

Testacc

Felice a Testaccio

V. di Bravetta

Via della

Nocetta

Via

V. Circ. dei Colli

Silvestri

PIRAMIDE DI CAIO CESTIO

Stazione Posta

Via

Via di Bravetta

Via

della

Pisana

Trattoria del Pesce

Gianicolense

P.za della Radio

Via Portuense

Via G. Marconi

Al Ristoro degli Angel

S. PAOLO FUORI LE MURA

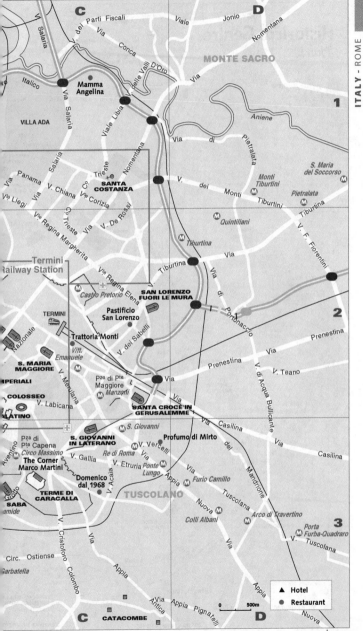

C

Via Salaria

del Parti Fiscali Via

Via Italico

Conca Viale

Viale Valli D'Oro

D

Viale Jonio

Nomentana

MONTE SACRO

Mamma Angelina

VILLA ADA

Via Salaria

Viale Libia

Nomentana

Aniene

Via di Pietralata

1

S. Maria del Soccorso

V^le Liegi

Via Panama

Via Salaria

V. Chiana

C^o Trieste

V^le Corizia

Trieste

SANTA COSTANZA

V. De Rossi

Nomentana

V. dei Monti

Monti Tiburtini

Tiburtini

Pietralata

Tiburtina

V^le Regina Margherita

Via Trieste

Termini Railway Station

V^le Regina Elena

Tiburtina

Via

Quintiliani

V. F. Fiorentini

Tiburtina

2

Castro Pretorio

SAN LORENZO FUORI LE MURA

Via di Portonaccio

TERMINI

Pastificio San Lorenzo

Via dei Sabelli

Prenestina

Trattoria Monti

V^le Nazionale

Vitt. Emanuele

Prenestina

Via

V. di Acqua Bullicante

V. Teano

S. MARIA MAGGIORE

Via Merulana

P^za di P^ta Maggiore

Manzoni

Via

IMPERIALI

COLOSSEO

V. Labicana

SANTA CROCE IN GERUSALEMME

Casilina

PALATINO

S. Giovanni

Profumo di Mirto

Via del

Via

Casilina

Aventino

P^za di P^ta Capena

Circo Massimo

The Corner Marco Martini

S. GIOVANNI IN LATERANO

Re di Roma

V. Gallia

V. Vercelli

V. Etruria

Ponte Lungo

Via Appia

Furio Camillo

Mandrione

TERME DI CARACALLA

Domenico dal 1968

V. Acaia

TUSCOLANO

Via

Tuscolana

Arco di Travertino

SABA

amide

Nuova

Colli Albani

Tuscolana

Porta Furba-Quadraro

V. Tuscolana

3

Circ. Ostiense

Garbatella

V. Cristoforo Colombo

Via Appia

Via Antica

Appia

Appia Pignatelli

Appia

Nuova

▲	Hotel
●	Restaurant

0   500m

C **CATACOMBE**

D

CIAMPINO ✈

389

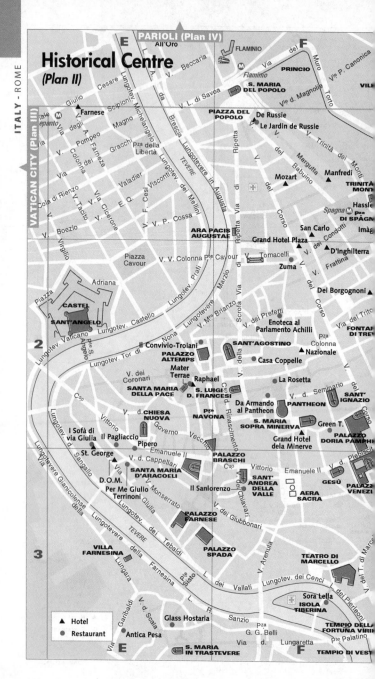

Historical Centre
(Plan II)

VATICAN CITY (Plan III)

All'Oro

FLAMINIO

PRINCIO

Flaminio

S. MARIA DEL POPOLO

PIAZZA DEL POPOLO

De Russie

Le Jardin de Russie

Mozart

Manfredi

TRINITÀ MONT

Hassle

Spagna M pza DI SPAGN

San Carlo

Imâg

Grand Hotel Plaza

D'Inghilterra

ARA PACIS AUGUSTAE

Tomacelli

Zuma

Piazza Cavour

Dei Borgognoni

CASTEL SANT'ANGELO

Adriana

V. dei Prefetti

Enoteca al Parlamento Achilli

FONTAN DI TRE

Pza Colonna

Nazionale

Il Convivio-Troiani

SANT'AGOSTINO

PALAZZO ALTEMPS

Mater Terrae

Casa Coppelle

Raphael

SANTA MARIA DELLA PACE

S. LUIGI D. FRANCESI

La Rosetta

V. d. Seminario

SANT' IGNAZIO

Da Armando al Pantheon

PANTHEON

CHIESA NUOVA

S. MARIA SOPRA MINERVA

Green T.

I Sofà di via Giulia

Il Pagliaccio

PALAZZO DORIA PAMPRH

Pipero

St. George

Grand Hotel dela Minerve

PALAZZO BRASCHI

D.O.M.

SANTA MARIA D'ARACOELI

SANT' ANDREA DELLA VALLE

GESÙ

Per Me Giulio Terrinoni

Il Sanlorenzo

PALAZZ VENEZI

AERA SACRA

PALAZZO FARNESE

VILLA FARNESINA

PALAZZO SPADA

TEATRO DI MARCELLO

Sora Lella

ISOLA TIBERINA

TEMPIO DELLA FORTUNA VIRIL

Glass Hostaria

Antica Pesa

S. MARIA IN TRASTEVERE

TEMPIO DI VEST

▲ Hotel
● Restaurant

390

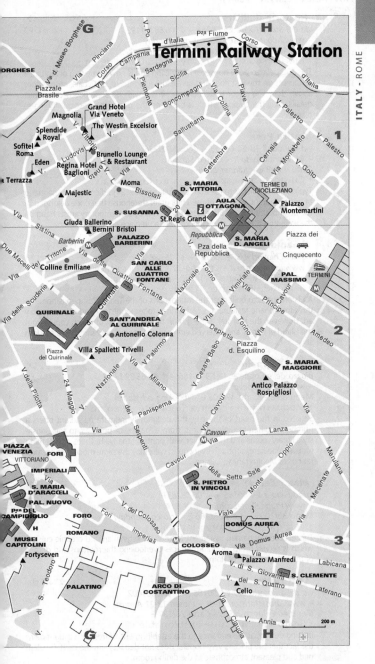

Termini Railway Station

ORGHESE

Piazzale
Brasile

BORGHESE

Via d. Museo Borghese • G

Via Pinciana

V. Po

Pza Fiume

d'Italia Corso Corso d'Italia

Via Piemonte

Campania

Sardegna

V. Sicilia

Boncompagni

Via Collina

Via Plave

V. Palestro

Sallustiana

▲ Magnolia **Grand Hotel**
Via Veneto

Splendide ▲ **The Westin Excelsior**
Royal ▲

Sofitel ▲
Roma

Eden ▲

▲ Terrazza

V.

Ludovisi

Vittorio

V.

Orlando

Brunello Lounge
& Restaurant

Regina Hotel
Baglioni

● Moma

Bissolati

▲ Majestic

S. MARIA
D. VITTORIA

AULA
OTTAGONA

S. SUSANNA

St.Regis Grand

V. 20

TERME DI
DIOCLEZIANO

▲ **Palazzo**
Montemartini

V.

M

Via Sistina

Due Macelli del Tritone

Via

Via

Barberini

Giuda Ballerino
● Bernini Bristol

PALAZZO
BARBERINI

Barberini
M

Via delle Quattro Fontane

SAN CARLO
ALLE
QUATTRO
FONTANE

V. Quattro Fontane

Colline Emiliane ●

Via delle Scuderie

QUIRINALE

V. Quirinale

SANT'ANDREA
AL QUIRINALE

● Antonello Colonna

Piazza
del Quirinale

Villa Spalletti Trivelli ▲

V. della Pilotta

V. 24 Maggio

Via Nazionale

Via V. Palermo

V. dei Milano

V. Panisperna

Via

Settembre

Cernaia

Via Montebello

V. Goito

V. Palestro

Piazza dei

Cinquecento

Repubblica

Pza della
Repubblica

S. MARIA
D. ANGELI

TERMINI
M

PAL.
MASSIMO

M

Viminale Via

Via Cavour

Nazionale Torino

Via A. V. dei V. Torino

Depretis

Principe

Amedeo

Piazza
d. Esquilino

V. Cesare Balbo

Via Cavour

S. MARIA
MAGGIORE

Via

Antico Palazzo
Rospigliosi

Via

V. dei Serpenti

Via

Cavour
M Via

G. Lanza

Cavour

V. delle Sette Sale

Monte

Oppio

Merulana

Mecenate

PIAZZA
VENEZIA

FORI
VITTORIANO

Via

IMPERIALI

S. MARIA
D'ARACŒLI

PAL. NUOVO

Pza DEL
CAMPIDIGLIO H

MUSEI
CAPITOLINI

Fortyseven ●

Via di S. Teodoro

FORO
ROMANO

PALATINO

V. di S.

Fori Imperiali

S. PIETRO
IN VINCOLI

Viale

DOMUS AUREA

COLOSSEO
M

Aroma ●

Via Domus Aurea

▲ **Palazzo Manfredi**

ARCO DI
COSTANTINO

V. di S. Giovanni

Celio ▲ dei S. Quattro

in

S. CLEMENTE

Laterano

Labicana

V. Claudia

V. Annia

0   200 m

G   H

391

ITALY - ROME

Hostaria dell'Orso
XxxX 88 🏿 ⇔

via dei Soldati 25/c ✉ *00186* – ☎ *06 68301192*   Plan: **E-F2**
– *www.hdo.it* – *Closed August and Sunday*
Carte 46/85 € – *(dinner only) (booking advisable)*
• Modern cuisine • Luxury • Traditional décor •
This 15C palazzo once housed a historic inn and is now home to a piano bar, a restaurant on the first floor and an exclusive nightclub, La Cabala, on the floor above that. The decor is deliberately simple with no superfluous decorative details, as is the cuisine, which is based on the use of the best quality ingredients.

Antica Pesa
XxX 88 🏿 🏿

via Garibaldi 18 ✉ *00153* – ☎ *06 5809236*   Plan: **E3**
– *www.anticapesa.it* – *Closed Sunday*
Carte 49/88 € – *(dinner only)*
• Cuisine from Lazio • Elegant • Cosy •
Typical Roman dishes made from carefully selected ingredients grace the menu of this restaurant, which is housed in a grain storehouse that once belonged to the neighbouring Papal State. Large paintings by contemporary artists hang on the walls and there is a small lounge with a fireplace near the entrance.

Il Sanlorenzo
XxX 88 🏿 ⇔

via dei Chiavari 4/5 ✉ *00186* – ☎ *06 6865097*   Plan: **F3**
– *www.ilsanlorenzo.it* – *Closed 6-30 August, lunch Monday and Saturday*
Menu 85/100 € – Carte 78/147 € – *(booking advisable)*
• Seafood • Elegant • Trendy •
A historic palazzo built over the foundations of the Teatro Pompeo is home to this atmospheric restaurant, which brings together history and contemporary art. However, the real star is the fish on the menu, most of which comes from the island of Ponza, and is served either raw or cooked very simply in a modern style.

Casa Coppelle
XX 88 ⅙ 🏿 ⇔

piazza delle Coppelle 49 ✉ *00186* – ☎ *06 68 89 17 07*   Plan: **F2**
– *www.casacoppelle.com*
Menu 85 € – Carte 49/108 € – *(booking advisable)*
• Mediterranean cuisine • Intimate • Elegant •
Situated in the heart of the city, this delightfully intimate restaurant offers a number of different dining rooms, from a 'gallery of portraits' to the British-style library rooms and the 'herbier' with prints on the walls. There is something for everyone here, although every guest will enjoy the same modern reinterpretations of Mediterranean cuisine.

Mater Terrae – Hotel Raphaël
XX 🏿 🏿

largo Febo 2 ✉ *00186* – ☎ *06 682831*   Plan: **E2**
– *www.raphaelhotel.com*
Menu 80/100 € – Carte 56/86 € – *(closed Monday)*
• Vegetarian • Luxury • Intimate •
This evocatively named restaurant focuses on vegetarian and organic cuisine, which is served on its stunning terraces overlooking the rooftops and domes of the historic centre of Rome.

La Rosetta
XX 🏿 🏿

via della Rosetta 8/9 ✉ *00186* – ☎ *06 6861002*   Plan: **F2**
– *www.larosettaristorante.it* – *Closed 12-21 August*
Menu 40 € (lunch)/89 € – Carte 78/187 €
• Seafood • Intimate • Fashionable •
Inviting display, at the entrance to the establishment, of fresh fish caught daily; the fact that the place is very popular does not detract from the carefully planned and pleasant atmosphere in the dining room.

ITALY - ROME

I Sofà di Via Giulia – Hotel Indigo Rome St. George   XX 🏤 ё
via Giulia 62 ✉ 00186 – ☎ 06 68661846   AK
– www.isofadiviagiulia.com   Plan: **E2**
Carte 53/81 €
• Modern cuisine • Contemporary décor • Luxury •
Regional cuisine with a modern twist, and an impressive wine list that more
than meets the high standards of this restaurant. Lively, designer-style decor,
as well as a delightful roof garden for summer dining with panoramic views of
the city centre as a backdrop.

Sora Lella   XX AK
via di Ponte Quattro Capi 16 (Tiber Island) ✉ 00186   Plan: **F3**
*– ☎ 06 6861601 – www.trattoriasoralella.it – Closed 15-22 August and
Tuesday*
Menu 45 € – Carte 34/72 €
• Roman • Traditional décor • Friendly •
Son and grandchildren of the famous late "Sora Lella", perpetuate in a dignified
way the tradition both in the warmth of the welcome and in the typical Roman
elements of the offer.

Zuma   XX 🏤 ё AK
via della Fontanella di Borghese 48 ✉ 00186   Plan: **F2**
*– Ⓜ Spagna – ☎ 06 99266622 – www.zumarestaurant.com – Closed 14-
21 August*
Menu 31 € (weekday lunch)/145 € – Carte 40/205 € – *(booking advisable)*
• Fusion • Fashionable • Trendy •
An international chain dedicated to contemporary Japanese food, Zuma has
chosen the fourth and fifth floors (with a terrace) of Palazzo Fendi for its first
Italian restaurant. The striking and decidedly fashionable cuisine consists of a
delicious sushi corner, the robata grill and a selection of modern and creative
dishes. A huge success ever since it opened.

Da Armando al Pantheon   X AK
salita dè Crescenzi 31 – Ⓜ Spagna – ☎ 06 68803034   Plan: **F2**
*– www.armandoalpantheon.it – Closed August, Saturday dinner and
Sunday*
Carte 33/57 € – *(number of covers limited, pre-book)*
• Roman • Family • Friendly •
Just a few metres from the Pantheon, this small family-run restaurant has been
delighting locals and visitors for years with its traditional cuisine. Booking ahead
is essential if you want to be sure of a table.

Green T.   X AK ⇔
Via del Piè di Marmo 28 ✉ 00186 – ☎ 06 679 8628   Plan: **F2**
– www.green-tea.it – Closed 1 week in August and Sunday
Menu 10 € (lunch)/18 € – Carte 26/77 €
• Chinese • Minimalist • Friendly •
Owner Yan introduces tea lovers to the 'Tao of Tea' (an introduction and tasting
of this ancient beverage) in this original restaurant situated on four floors of a
building not far from the Pantheon. Asian cuisine takes pride of place on the
menu.

Hassler   £å 🏤 ё AK ŝÅ
piazza Trinità dei Monti 6 ✉ 00187 – Ⓜ Spagna   Plan: **F1**
– ☎ 06 699340 – www.hotelhasslerroma.com
92 rm – †295/505 € ††380/640 € – ☑ 38 € – 13 suites
• Grand Luxury • Historic • Elegant •
Superbly located at the top of the Spanish Steps, this hotel combines tradition,
prestige and elegance. The height of splendour is reached in the magnificent
suite that occupies the whole of the eighth floor. It has a private lift, additional
accommodation for security staff, two panoramic terraces, modern furnishings
and all the latest technology.
❀ **Imàgo** – See restaurant listing

De Russie

via del Babuino 9 ⊠ *00187* – **Ⓜ** *Flaminio*

Plan: **F1**

– ℰ *06 328881 – www.roccofortehotels.com/hotel-de-russie*

121 rm – ♦405/705 € ♦♦525/910 € – ⌴ 40 € – 25 suites

• Grand Luxury • Historic • Personalised •

One of the best in Rome, this hotel occupying a building designed by Valadier in the early 19C boasts a light, harmonious decor. Elegant guestrooms, as well as the Popolo and Picasso suites, which were completely refurbished in spring 2016: these two private apartments are decorated with original art works and antiques. The hotel's 'secret garden' is planted with rose bushes and jasmine.

🍴 **Le Jardin de Russie** – See restaurant listing

Grand Hotel Plaza

via del Corso 126 ⊠ *00186* – **Ⓜ** *Spagna* – ℰ *06 67495*

Plan: **F2**

– *www.grandhotelplaza.com*

183 rm – ♦250/350 € ♦♦300/450 € – ⌴ 25 € – 10 suites

• Grand Luxury • Palace • Personalised •

This hotel boasts huge, stunning, late-19C lounges decorated in Art Nouveau-style with coffered ceilings and a profusion of marble, frescoes and glass. The guestrooms are also furnished in period style, as is the atmospheric dining room. Panoramic terrace with a Champagne bar.

Grand Hotel de la Minerve

piazza della Minerva 69 ⊠ *00186* – ℰ *06 695201*

Plan: **F2**

– *www.grandhoteldelaminerve.com*

135 rm – ♦230/470 € ♦♦280/520 € – ⌴ 35 € – 4 suites

• Luxury • Historic • Elegant •

An historic building surrounded by ancient monuments. Elegant atmosphere and an imaginative menu of traditional cuisine. Attractive views from the terrace.

D'Inghilterra

via Bocca di Leone 14 ⊠ *00187* – ℰ *06 699811*

Plan: **F2**

– *www.starhotels.it*

81 rm ⌴ – ♦270/340 € ♦♦270/600 € – 7 suites

• Historic building • Grand Luxury • Personalised •

A haven for tourists from around the world since as early as the 17C, this hotel has the charming ambience of an elegant private house with delightful, individually-styled guestrooms. Find elegant lounges, an atmospheric bar, and a restaurant serving simple, classic cuisine at lunchtime and more elaborate, ambitious fare in the evening.

The First Luxury Art Hotel Roma

via del Vantaggio 14 ⊠ *00186* – **Ⓜ** *Flaminio*

Plan: **B2**

– ℰ *06 45617070 – www.thefirsthotel.com*

13 rm – ♦355/700 € ♦♦355/700 € – ⌴ 30 € – 16 suites

• Luxury • Business • Design •

This elegant 19C palazzo features refined guestrooms and panoramic terraces overlooking the rooftops of the city centre. The interior decor is light and modern with contemporary artwork on display.

❀ **Acquolina** – See restaurant listing

Indigo Rome St. George

via Giulia 62 ⊠ *00186* – ℰ *06 686611*

Plan: **E2**

– *www.hotelindigo.com/romestgeorge*

64 rm – ♦260/380 € ♦♦320/560 € – ⌴ 29 €

• Boutique hotel • Traditional • Design •

This boutique, designer-style hotel is in one of the most beautiful streets in Rome. It offers an elegant ambience and luxurious furnishings in its public areas and spacious guestrooms.

🍴 **I Sofà di Via Giulia** – See restaurant listing

Raphaël
largo Febo 2 ✉ *00186* – ☎ *06 682831*
– *www.raphaelhotel.com*
Plan: **E2**
49 rm ☲ – **♦**150/480 € **♦♦**200/530 € – 1 suite
• Boutique hotel • Luxury • Romantic •
With its collection of porcelain, antiquarian artefacts and sculptures by famous artists, the entrance to this hotel resembles a museum. The guestrooms are modern in style. The menu in the attractive restaurant with a panoramic terrace focuses mainly on Italian cuisine, along with some French dishes.
‖○ **Mater Terrae** – See restaurant listing

Dei Borgognoni
via del Bufalo 126 ✉ *00187* – ⓜ *Spagna*
– ☎ *06 69941505* – *www.hotelborgognoni.it*
Plan: **F2**
51 rm ☲ – **♦**180/230 € **♦♦**190/285 €
• Traditional • Luxury • Contemporary •
Occupying a 19C palazzo, this elegant hotel's spacious, modern public rooms and comfortable guestrooms combine both traditional and modern features.

D.O.M.
via Giulia 131 ✉ *00186 Roma* – ☎ *06 6832144*
– *www.domhotelroma.com*
Plan: **E3**
14 rm ☲ – **♦**280/600 € **♦♦**280/600 € – 4 suites
• Luxury • Traditional • Modern •
The initials of this hotel stand for Deo Optimo Maximo. The 17C palazzo combines decor from the adjacent church with contemporary furnishings, subtle colours and three works by Andy Warhol. Terrace bar on the top floor.

Grand Hotel del Gianicolo
viale delle Mura Gianicolensi 107 ✉ *00152*
– ⓜ *Cipro Musei Vaticani* – ☎ *06 58333405* – *www.grandhotelgianicolo.it*
Plan: **B3**
48 rm ☲ – **♦**90/380 € **♦♦**110/410 €
• Traditional • Business • Classic •
A stylish hotel on the Gianicolo offering comfortable guestrooms and elegant public areas. You also have the illusion of being a guest in a smart country house, thanks to the beautiful outdoor pool – an unusual sight in Rome. Contemporary cuisine is served in the Corte degli Archi.

Nazionale
piazza Montecitorio 131 ✉ *00186* – ☎ *06 695001*
– *www.hotelnazionale.it*
Plan: **F2**
102 rm ☲ – **♦**150/220 € **♦♦**160/310 € – 1 suite
• Traditional • Luxury • Elegant •
Overlooking Piazza di Montecitorio, this hotel occupies an 18C building with elegant public areas and guestrooms furnished in different styles. In this city so often crowded with visitors, the fact that the restaurant is open non-stop from noon until 7pm will appeal, as will the delicious Mediterranean cuisine.

Piranesi-Palazzo Nainer
via del Babuino 196 ✉ *00187* – ⓜ *Flaminio*
– ☎ *06 328041* – *www.hotelpiranesi.com*
Plan: **F1**
32 rm – **♦**125/160 € **♦♦**145/235 €
• Traditional • Luxury • Classic •
The lobby, guestrooms and corridors of this hotel are decorated with marble, elegant furnishings and an unusual exhibition of old fabrics. The hotel also boasts a roof garden and sun terrace.

Manfredi Suite in Rome
via Margutta 61 ✉ *00187* – ⓜ *Spagna* – ☎ *06 3207676*
– *www.hotelmanfredi.it*
Plan: **F1**
21 rm ☲ – **♦**119/240 € **♦♦**120/330 € – 1 suite
• Inn • Traditional • Modern •
Housed on the third floor of a palazzo on the famous Via Margutta. Elegant, individually furnished guestrooms, all of which boast the latest in modern facilities. Excellent international breakfast of natural products, including yoghurt and homemade pastries.

🏨 **Mozart** ⓀⒸ
via dei Greci 23/b ✉ *00187* Plan: **F1**
– Ⓜ *Spagna*
– 𝒞 *06 36001915* – *www.hotelmozart.com*
78 rm ☷ – ♦99/299 € ♦♦109/309 €
• Traditional • Family • Cosy •

Housed in a 19C palazzo, this hotel boasts elegant public areas and guestrooms in the same refined style. The Vivaldi Luxury Rooms annexe situated just a stone's throw from the hotel offers slightly larger, modern rooms, as well as its own breakfast room.

🏨 **Fontanella Borghese** ⓀⒸ
largo Fontanella Borghese 84 ✉ *00186* Plan: **F2**
– Ⓜ *Spagna*
– 𝒞 *06 68809504* – *www.fontanellaborghese.com*
29 rm ☷ – ♦90/180 € ♦♦130/260 €
• Family • Inn • Classic •

In a central yet peaceful location, on the 2nd and 3rd floors of a historical building looking out over Palazzo Borghese, is this distinguished and refined hotel with classy finishings.

🏨 **San Carlo** ⓀⒸ
via Delle Carrozze 92/93 ✉ *00187* Plan: **F1**
– Ⓜ *Spagna*
– 𝒞 *06 6784548* – *www.hotelsancarloroma.com*
50 rm ☷ – ♦80/130 € ♦♦100/240 €
• Traditional • Cosy • Centrally located •

This inviting hotel is parallel to Via Condotti. It offers pleasant guestrooms and a charming breakfast terrace, which is particularly delightful in the summer months.

ST-PETER'S BASILICA (Vatican City and Monte Mario) **PLAN III**

❀❀❀ **La Pergola** – Hotel Rome Cavalieri ХхХхХ ⌘ ≤ 🏠 ᬵ Ⓚ ⟷ 🅿
via Cadlolo 101 ✉ *00136* Plan: **A2**
– 𝒞 *06 35092152* – *www.romecavalieri.it*
– *Closed 3 weeks in August, January, Sunday and Monday*
Menu 130/245 € – Carte 135/227 € – *(dinner only) (booking essential)*
• Modern cuisine • Luxury • Romantic •

This superb restaurant is suspended above the Eternal City in the magnificent setting of a panoramic roof garden. Mediterranean cuisine (chef Heinz Beck's constant passion), a systematic search for the best quality ingredients, and an added dose of creativity all come together in La Pergola. The restaurant's success speaks for itself.

→ Pinzimonio 2017. Piccione ai profumi di sottobosco. Come un cannolo siciliano.

❀ **Enoteca la Torre** – Hotel Villa Laetitia ХхХ ⌘ 🏠 Ⓚ
lungotevere delle Armi 22/23 ✉ *00195* Plan: **L2**
– Ⓜ *Lepanto*
– 𝒞 *0645668304* – *www.enotecalatorreroma.com*
– *Closed 10 days in August, Monday lunch and Sunday*
Menu 60 € *(weekday lunch)*/130 € – Carte 80/130 €
• Modern cuisine • Liberty • Romantic •

This restaurant has a distinctly refined and elegant look. The antique furniture, flowers, columns and stucco all contribute to an Art Nouveau feel that would not be out of place in Paris. The cuisine celebrates creativity with excellent results.

→ Risotto al limone di Amalfi, tartufi di mare, asparagi e yogurt di bufala. Piccione marinato alla soja, sedano rapa e chutney di pomodoro del piennolo. Crostatina meringata al limone, tamarindo e wasabi.

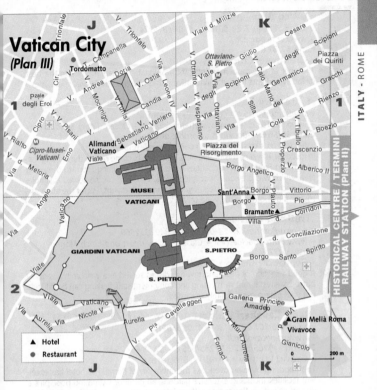

Vatican City
(Plan III)

Tordomatto

Alimandi Vaticano ▲

MUSEI VATICANI

GIARDINI VATICANI

PIAZZA S.PIETRO

S. PIETRO

Sant'Anna ▲
Bramante ▲

▲Gran Melià Roma
Vivavoce

▲ Hotel
● Restaurant

0   200 m

💮 **Tordomatto** (Adriano Baldassarre)   XX ⅓ 🅰 ✿
via Pietro Giannone 24 ⊠ 00195 – 𝒞 06 69352895   Plan: **J1**
– www.tordomattoroma.com – Closed lunch Monday and Tuesday
Menu 65/120 € – Carte 75/125 € – *(booking advisable)*
• Modern cuisine • Fashionable • Minimalist •
A minimalist-style restaurant with contemporary decor and the option of eating
at a bar in the kitchen. The dishes are full of character, demonstrating the skilful
expertise of the chef. Herbs in pots behind the windows add an attractive
touch.
➔ Patate, senape nera, latte di capra e burro affumicato. Animelle, pinzimonio, aglio e curcuma. Pesca, vino e mandorle.

🍽 **Vivavoce** – Hotel Gran Melià Roma   XxxX 🛒 ⅓ 🅰
via del Gianicolo 3 ⊠ 00165 – 𝒞 06925901   Plan: **K2**
– www.ristorantevivavoce.com – Closed January and Sunday
Menu 70/95 € – Carte 66/98 € – *(dinner only)*
• Mediterranean cuisine • Elegant • Classic décor •
This restaurant in the Eternal City serves beautifully prepared gourmet dishes
inspired by the flavours of the Amalfi Coast.

Antico Arco   XX 🏵 🔠 ⇔
piazzale Aurelio 7 ✉ *00152 –* 📞 *06 5815274*   Plan: **B3**
– www.anticoarco.it
Carte 57/87 €
• Creative • Chic • Cosy •
The chef at this modern, bright and fashionable restaurant selects the best Italian ingredients to create innovative dishes based on traditional specialities.

Settembrini   X 🏵 🚬 🔠 ⇔
via Settembrini 25 ✉ *00195 –* Ⓜ *Lepanto*   Plan: **B2**
– 📞 *06 97610325 – www.viasettembrini.com – Closed dinner Sunday*
Carte 30/56 € – *(bookings advisable at dinner)*
• Modern cuisine • Bistro • Minimalist •
In just over 10 years, this fashionable bistro has become one of the leading restaurants in Rome. Recent changes have moved the dining room to the living area, which was previously occupied by the café. The cuisine served is simple, fresh and contemporary in feel. If you like unusual settings, ask for the table surrounded by bottles in the wine cellar.

Trattoria del Pesce   X 🔠
via Folco Portinari 27 ✉ *00186 –* 📞 *349 3352560*   Plan: **B3**
– www.trattoriadelpesce.it – Closed 14-20 August and lunch Monday
Carte 31/77 €
• Seafood • Bistro • Family •
A good selection of fresh and raw fish dishes served in a welcoming, vaguely bistro-style restaurant with young and competent staff. Parking can be difficult, but your patience is definitely rewarded!

Rome Cavalieri Waldorf Astoria   🏖 ⇐ 🛌 🕍 🛎 🏊 ⚒ 🖼
via Cadlolo 101 ✉ *00136 –* 📞 *06 35091*   🍴 🔠 ⇔ 🚗
– www.romecavalieri.it   Plan: **A2**
345 rm – ✝265/565 € ✝✝265/565 € – ☲ 38 € – 25 suites
• Grand Luxury • Chain • Elegant •
This imposing building overlooks the entire city of Rome. The hotel has excellent facilities, including extensive gardens, an outdoor swimming pool, plus a fine art collection. Restaurant with an informal atmosphere by the edge of the swimming pool for dining with live music.
🕸🕸🕸 **La Pergola** – See restaurant listing

Gran Melià Roma   🏖 🏊 🛌 🕍 🍴 ⚒ 🔠 🎿 🚗
via del Gianicolo 3 ✉ *00165 –* 📞 *06925901*   Plan: **K2**
– www.granmeliarome.com
116 rm – ✝375/575 € ✝✝450/750 € – ☲ 36 € – 8 suites
• Luxury • Chain • Modern •
This hotel boasts a truly historic setting in an old monastery on the site of the villa that once belonged to Nero's mother, Agrippina. There is an elegant, modern feel to the public areas and guestrooms, some of which feature designer bathtubs that can be seen from the bed. A superb address with a charming atmosphere and an excellent choice of facilities.
🕸 **Vivavoce** – See restaurant listing

Villa Laetitia   🛌 🕍 🔠
lungotevere delle Armi 22/23 ✉ *00195 –* Ⓜ *Lepanto*   Plan: **L2**
– 📞 *06 3226776 – www.villalaetitia.com*
21 rm ☲ – ✝90/180 € ✝✝99/400 €
• Historic building • Luxury • Romantic •
Enjoying a charming location on the banks of the Tiber, this delightful Art Nouveau villa welcomes its guests as if they were visiting a private home - and what a home! The elegant and individual guestrooms all bear the stamp of the famous designer, Anna Fendi.
🕸 **Enoteca la Torre** – See restaurant listing

ITALY - ROME

🏨 Farnese   AC P

via Alessandro Farnese 30 ✉ *00192 –* Ⓜ *Lepanto*   Plan: **E1**
– ℰ 06 3212553 – www.hotelfarnese.com
23 rm ☲ **– ♦**120/220 € **♦♦**160/380 €
• Traditional • Elegant •

Decorated in period style, this hotel has elegant rooms and an attractive lobby housing a 17C polychrome marble frontal. Fine views of St Peter's from the terrace.

🏨 Alimandi Vaticano   AC 🚗

viale Vaticano 99 ✉ *00165 –* Ⓜ *Cipro – ℰ 06 39745562*   Plan: **J1**
– www.alimandi.com
24 rm – ♦100/250 € **♦♦**100/250 € **– ☲** 15 €
• Traditional • Elegant •

This pleasant hotel enjoys an excellent location directly opposite the Vatican Museums. The marble and wood decor in the well-appointed guestrooms adds to their elegant atmosphere.

🏨 Bramante   AC

vicolo delle Palline 24 ✉ *00193*   Plan: **K2**
– Ⓜ *Ottaviano-San Pietro – ℰ 06 68806426 – www.hotelbramante.com*
16 rm ☲ **– ♦**100/150 € **♦♦**140/200 €
• Historic • Elegant •

This historic hotel is situated in the heart of the typical, pedestrianised Borgo district. The oldest sections date back to the 15C.

🏨 Sant'Anna   AC

borgo Pio 133 ✉ *00193 –* Ⓜ *Ottaviano-San Pietro*   Plan: **K1-2**
– ℰ 06 68 80 16 02 – www.hotelsantanna.com
20 rm ☲ **– ♦**120/200 € **♦♦**150/250 €
• Traditional • Historic •

An original coffered ceiling and pleasant interior courtyard add a decorative touch to this small, welcoming hotel occupying a 16C building a short distance from St Peter's.

PARIOLI   **PLAN IV**

✿ Assaje – Hotel Aldrovandi Villa Borghese   XxXX 🍴 & AC P

via Ulisse Aldrovandi 15 – Ⓜ *Policlinico – ℰ 06 3223993*   Plan: **B2**
– www.aldrovandi.com
Menu 110/140 € – Carte 80/119 €
• Modern cuisine • Mediterranean décor • Luxury •

Assaje means "abundance" in the Neapolitan dialect and the focus of this restaurant is on Mediterranean cuisine. The menu offers imaginative, modern dishes alongside more traditional, classic fare with a range of fish and meat options available.
→ Tagliolini al limone con burrata, gamberi rossi crudi, asparagi di mare e foglia d'ostrica. Maialino da latte porchettato con scorzonera, scalogno al Porto e senape rustica. Paccheri di ananas con cremoso all'anice stellato, gelato di fior di latte e amarene.

✿ Metamorfosi (Roy Caceres)   XxX AC ⇔

via Giovanni Antonelli 30/32 ✉ *00197 – ℰ 06 8076839*   Plan: **M1**
– www.metamorfosiroma.it – Closed lunch Saturday and Sunday
Menu 100/130 € – Carte 80/121 € – *(dinner only in August)*
• Creative • Elegant • Cosy •

With its clean lines and minimalist style, the room respects contemporary architecture, but the colours recall the warmth of earth and nature. When it comes to the cooking, the eclectic style of the Colombian chef results in continual re-inventions of gastronomic traditions. In summary: a constant metamorphosis!
→ Anti-paste. Anguilla di Comacchio, farro franto e carpione gelato. Yuzu (agrume giapponese), mandorla e camomilla.

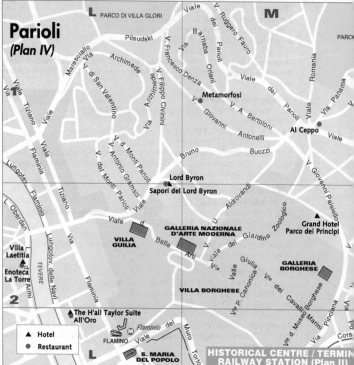

Parioli
(Plan IV)

HISTORICAL CENTRE / TERMINI
RAILWAY STATION (Plan II)

▲ Hotel
● Restaurant

❀ **All'Oro** (Riccardo Di Giacinto) – Hotel The H'All Tailor Suite XX ❀
via Giuseppe Pisanelli 25 ✉ *00196* – ✆ *06 97996907* ♿ 🅰️ ✿
– www.ristorantealloro.it Plan: **L2**
Menu 78/130 €
– Carte 80/118 € – *(dinner only except Saturday and Sunday)*
• Creative • Design • Intimate •

Having been closed for several months, Riccardo and Ramona have now reopened their restaurant, endowing it with a brand-new decor and atmosphere. One of the dining rooms is decorated in a modern, pleasantly sophisticated New York style, while the other is vaguely English in feel. The menu continues to focus on creative cuisine with the occasional regional influence.
➜ "Susci" di fassona, tartufo, parmigiano e aceto balsamico. Pollo alla cacciatora. Latte e miele.

❀ **Bistrot 64** X 🅰️
via Guglielmo Calderini 64 ✉ *00196* – ✆ *06 3235531* Plan: **B1**
– www.bistrot64.it – Closed 15 days in August, 1 week in January and Tuesday
Menu 40/90 €
– Carte 57/82 € – *(dinner only except Friday, Saturday and Sunday) (booking advisable)*
• Mediterranean cuisine • Bistro • Fashionable •

This restaurant boasts the attractive, informal decor of a bistro combined with surprisingly creative and imaginative cuisine. Courteous and attentive service.
➜ Spaghetto di patate, burro e alici. Spigola all black. Marrone (semifreddo all'aglio nero).

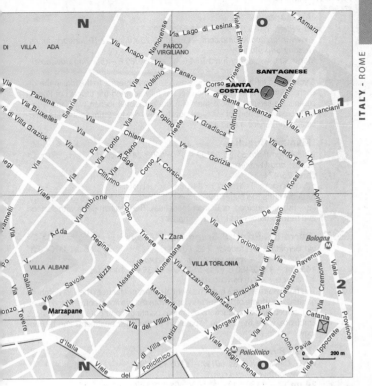

‖○ **Sapori del Lord Byron** – Hotel Lord Byron   XxxX Ⓐ ✿
via G. De Notaris 5 ✉ *00197* – ℰ *06 3220404*   Plan: **L-M1**
– *www.lordbyronhotel.com* – *Closed Sunday*
Carte 48/74 € – *(dinner only)*
• Italian • Luxury • Classic décor •
Mirror-covered walls, dark octagonal tables and fine marble decor all add to the
delightful Art Deco style of this restaurant. The food consists of delicious specialities from all over Italy, magnificently reinterpreted by the creative chef.

‖○ **Al Ceppo**   XX ✿ Ⓐ ✿
via Panama 2 ✉ *00198* – ℰ *06 8551379*   Plan: **M1**
– *www.ristorantealceppo.it* – *Closed 10-25 August, Saturday lunch June-*
September, Monday lunch rest of the year
Menu 25 € (weekday lunch) – Carte 42/76 €
• Mediterranean cuisine • Elegant • Traditional décor •
Elegant bistro-style wood panelling welcomes guests to this rustic yet elegant
restaurant which serves Mediterranean cuisine reinterpreted with a contemporary twist. Specialities include grilled fish and meat dishes prepared in front of
guests in the dining room.

ITALY - ROME

🍽️ **Marzapane** ✕✕ 🅰🅒

via Velletri 39 ✉ *00198 –* ☎ *06 6478 1692*   Plan: **N2**
*– www.marzapaneroma.com – Closed 10-25 August, 2-10 January, lunch
Tuesday and Monday*
Menu 30 € (weekday lunch)/84 € – Carte 50/89 € – *(booking advisable)*
• Creative • Classic décor • Cosy •

A young and informal atmosphere with skill and expertise to the fore in the kitchen. Originally from Spain, the chef has fully adopted the flavours of Roman cuisine. He serves classic dishes with the occasional Iberian twist and a few more creative options of excellent quality. Weekday lunchtime dishes are simpler and the service is quicker.

🍽️ **Mamma Angelina** ✕ 🏯 🏠 🅰🅒

viale Arrigo Boito 65 ✉ *00199 –* ☎ *06 8608928 – Closed*   Plan: **C1**
August and Wednesday
Carte 26/47 €
• Seafood • Trattoria • Neighbourhood •

After the antipasto buffet, the cuisine in this restaurant follows two distinct styles – fish and seafood, or Roman specialities. The paccheri pasta with seafood and fresh tomatoes sits in both camps!

🏨 **Parco dei Principi Grand Hotel & Spa** 🌳 ≤ 🛎️ 🐾 🔟

via Gerolamo Frescobaldi 5 ✉ *00198*   ♨ 🛏️ 🔲 🅰🅒 🛜 ♻ 🚗
– ☎ *06 854421 – www.parcodeiprincipi.com*   Plan: **M2**
165 rm – †350/460 € ††450/650 € – ☕ 35 € – 14 suites
• Palace • Grand luxury •

This hotel is situated in a quiet, residential district not far from the Villa Borghese gardens. The dome of St Peter's is visible from the top floor rooms. Wood panelling, carpets and reproductions of famous paintings contribute to the luxurious ambience, while the 2,000m² spa offers all the latest treatments and technology.

🏨 **Lord Byron** 🐾 🅰🅒

via G. De Notaris 5 ✉ *00197 –* ☎ *06 3220404*   Plan: **L-M1**
– www.lordbyronhotel.com
24 rm ☕ – †190/540 € ††200/560 € – 8 suites
• Luxury • Boutique hotel • Art déco •

Situated just a few metres from the greenery of the Villa Borghese gardens, this elegant aristocratic hotel is adorned with Art Deco features. The guestrooms and public areas have been carefully decorated with fabrics and furniture that bring out the original character of the building.
🍽️ **Sapori del Lord Byron** – See restaurant listing

🏨 **Aldrovandi Villa Borghese** 🌳 🛎️ 🔟 ♨ 🛏️ 🔲 🅰🅒 ♻ 🅿

via Ulisse Aldrovandi 15 ✉ *00197 –* Ⓜ *Policlinico*   Plan: **B2**
– ☎ *06 3223993 – www.aldrovandi.com*
91 rm – †204/1920 € ††204/1920 € – ☕ 28 € – 12 suites
• Luxury • Palace • Classic •

Off the beaten track, yet exclusive, this hotel situated in a smart district a stone's throw from the Villa Borghese boasts classic rooms and modern facilities.
✳️ **Assaje** – See restaurant listing

🏨 **The H'All Tailor Suite** 🅰🅒 🅿

via Giuseppe Pisanelli 23 ✉ *00186 –* Ⓜ *Lepanto*   Plan: **L2**
– ☎ *06 32110128 – www.thehallroma.com*
14 rm ☕ – †220/600 € ††270/720 € – 1 suite
• Boutique hotel • Design •

A small, personalised and beautifully kept hotel, fully dedicated to offering its guests a "tailor-made" experience. Comfortable rooms with a modern yet warm decor, plus delicious gourmet breakfasts designed and created by the owner-chef – a great way to start your day!
✳️ **All'Oro** – See restaurant listing

ITALY - ROME

La Terrazza – Hotel Eden   XxxX 錢 ≤ 🅰️ ✿
Plan: **G1**

via Ludovisi 49 ✉ 00187
– Ⓜ *Barberini*
– ☎ *06 47812752 – www.dorchestercollection.com – Closed 7-21 August,*
17-31 January and Tuesday
Menu 145/220 €
– Carte 141/210 € – *(dinner only) (booking advisable)*
• Modern cuisine • Luxury • Elegant •

In addition to its new luxurious and elegant look, this restaurant boasts two major attractions – the spectacular terrace overlooking the historic centre of Rome and the restaurant's superbly talented chef Ciervo who, since the reopening, has dedicated himself totally and with even more enthusiasm to his modern, beautifully presented and delicious cuisine.
→ Calamarata (pasta secca) con coulis di pomodori e acciughe. Stracotto di manzo con asparagi e funghi. Fondente e pistacchio.

Magnolia – Grand Hotel Via Veneto   XxxX 錢 ⅙ 🅰️
Plan: **OU**

via Sicilia 24 ✉ 00187
– Ⓜ *Barberini*
– ☎ *06 487881 – www.magnoliarestaurant.it – Closed August*
Menu 90/105 €
– Carte 82/150 € – *(dinner only) (booking advisable)*
• Creative • Luxury • Elegant •

Having made your way through a tunnel of black marble, water and changing lights, you come to a superb cloister-style courtyard, which offers the perfect setting for alfresco dining in fine weather. The chef here creates modern and inventive cuisine. Dishes are presented in the form of paintings and strike a truly innovative note – culinary works of art available either à la carte or on a tasting menu.
→ Tortello racing con ricotta, pomodoro e parmigiano. Merluzzo carbonaro, spugnole, crema di carota e aneto. Sinfonia, frutto della passione, peperoncino, cioccolato, caramello, arancia e carota, fave di cacao e gelato allo zucchero di palma.

Aroma – Hotel Palazzo Manfredi   XxX 錢 ≤ 錢 🅰️
Plan: **H3**

via Labicana 125 ✉ 00184
– Ⓜ *Colosseo*
– ☎ *06 97615109 – www.aromarestaurant.it*
Menu 115/240 €
– Carte 113/204 € – *(bookings advisable at dinner)*
• Creative • Luxury • Romantic •

The terrace offers breathtaking views of Ancient Rome, from the Colosseum to the dome of St Peter's, while the name of this restaurant pays tribute to both the city and to the aromas provided by the creative and imaginative Mediterranean cuisine served here.
→ Busiate con gamberoni rossi, pesto di pomodori Pachino confit e mandorle. Filetti di mupa ai tre colori (giallo, rosso e verde), calamaretti spillo e gel di scorzonera. Sfera di cocco con cuore di albicocca su crumble al cioccolato bianco.

Antonello Colonna   XxX 錢 🅰️
Plan: **G2**

scalinata di via Milano 9/a ✉ 00184
– Ⓜ *Termini*
– ☎ *06 47822641 – www.antonellocolonna.it – Closed August, Sunday and Monday*
Menu 95 € – Carte 80/118 € – *(dinner only) (booking advisable)*
• Creative • Contemporary décor • Elegant •

This open-plan, glass-walled restaurant is within the imposing Palazzo delle Esposizioni. It serves inventive cuisine inspired by traditional dishes, which will please the most discerning guests.
→ Negativo di carbonara. Maialino croccante, patate affumicate e mostarda di frutta. Diplomatico: crema e cioccolato con caramello al sale.

ITALY - ROME

The Corner Marco Martini
XX ⇔ 🏠 AC

viale Aventino 121 ✉ *00186 -* 𝒞 *06 45597350* — Plan: **C3**
*- www.marcomartinichef.com - Closed 14-21 Agosto, 7-14 January, lunch
Saturday and Sunday*
11 rm – 🛏100/230 € – 🛏🛏100/230 € – ☐ 6 €
Menu 60/200 € – Carte 61/81 € – *(booking advisable)*
• Creative • Trendy • Bistro •

Chef Martini and his team create modern and imaginative cuisine in this restaurant which boasts a winter garden-style dining room with a contemporary feel as well as a terrace-cum-lounge for aperitifs and snacks, dominated by a life-size marble Superman. The gourmet menu is also available at lunchtime if you book ahead.
→ Ravioli al vapore, pollo e brodo di patate. Merluzzo, patanegra e arancia amara. Cioccolato affumicato, scorzanera e vermouth.

Stazione di Posta
X 🏠 AC 🅿

largo Dino Frisullo snc ✉ *00153 –* Ⓜ *Piramide* — Plan: **B3**
- 𝒞 *06 5743548 - www.stazionediposta.eu - Closed Tuesday*
Menu 28 € (lunch)/100 €
- Carte 62/88 € - (dinner only in July and August)
• Creative • Trendy • Friendly •

Part of the 'Città dell' Altra Economia' housed in an old abattoir, this restaurant has an exciting and lively ambience thanks to its open-plan layout and post-industrial feel. The imaginative cuisine is created by a new chef and his young dynamic team. There is also a cocktail bar and simpler options available at lunchtime.
→ Spaghetti all'aglio nero, anemoni di mare e mandorle. Manzo alla cenere con carote e insalata. Dolce bianco.

Domenico dal 1968
X 🏠 AC

via Satrico 21 ✉ *00183 –* 𝒞 *06 70494602* — Plan: **C3**
*- www.domenicodal1968.it - Closed 3 weeks in August, Sunday dinner
and Monday*
Carte 35/51 €
• Roman • Simple • Family •

It's well worth heading off the usual tourist trail to experience this authentic Roman trattoria, where you can try specialities such as fish broth with broccoli and local tripe. The restaurant also serves a selection of fish-based dishes which vary according to market availability.

Profumo di Mirto
X AC

viale Amelia 8/a ✉ *00181 –* 𝒞 *06 786206* — Plan: **C3**
- www.profumodimirto.it - Closed August and Monday
Menu 22 € (weekdays)/45 € – Carte 27/80 €
• Seafood • Family • Friendly •

The cuisine at this restaurant pays tribute to its owners' native Sardinia, in addition to other typical Mediterranean fare. There's a focus on fish and seafood reinterpreted in delicious, home-style dishes, including specialities such as ravioli with sea bass, prawns cooked in Vernaccia di Oristano and *seadas* fritters.

Al Ristoro degli Angeli
X 🏠 AC

via Luigi Orlando 2 ✉ *00154 –* 𝒞 *06 51436020* — Plan: **B3**
- www.ristorodegliangeli.it - Closed Sunday
Carte 28/56 € – *(dinner only)*
• Roman • Vintage • Simple •

Situated in the Garbatella district, this restaurant with a bistro feel is decorated with vintage tables, chairs and lighting. The menu focuses on dishes from Lazio, such as *spaghetti cacio e pepe* (with a cheese and black pepper sauce) in a crunchy parmesan wafer, although vegetable and fish options are also available.

ITALY - ROME

Giuda Ballerino! – Hotel Bernini Bristol   XxX 舒 斎 AC

piazza Barberini 23 ✉ *00187 –* Ⓜ *Barberini*   Plan: **G2**
– ☏ *06 42010469 – www.giudaballerino.com – Closed 2 weeks in January and Sunday*
Menu 35 € (lunch)/110 € – Carte 87/139 € – *(dinner only)*
• **Modern cuisine** • **Elegant** • **Contemporary décor** •
The kitchen opens into the dining room in this restaurant on the 8th floor of the historic Hotel Bernini, where large windows provide magnificent views of Rome. This is the elegant setting for Guida Ballerino's modern restaurant, which is decorated with icons from some of the chef's favourite comics strips, such as Dylan Dog. Creative cuisine and an excellent wine list.

La Terrasse – Hotel Sofitel Rome Villa Borghese   XxX 舒 斎 AC ⇔

via Lombardia 47 ✉ *00187 –* Ⓜ *Barberini –* ☏ *06 478022944*
– www.laterrasseroma.com
Menu 28 € (weekday lunch)/80 €
– Carte 69/128 € – (bookings advisable at dinner)
• **Modern cuisine** • **Chic** • **Fashionable** •
As its name suggests, the jewel in the crown of this restaurant is the splendid terrace that offers panoramic views of the city. The cuisine, however, is equal to the view with imaginative Mediterranean dishes featured on the menu, as well as a simpler choice of fare available at lunchtime.

Brunello Lounge & Restaurant – Regina Hotel Baglioni

via Vittorio Veneto 72 ✉ *00187 –* Ⓜ *Barberini*   XX 舒 AC ⇔
– ☏ *06 421111 – www.baglionihotels.com*   Plan: **G1**
Menu 70/80 € – Carte 58/122 € – *(booking advisable)*
• **Modern cuisine** • **Intimate** • **Elegant** •
This warm, elegant restaurant has a faintly Oriental feel. It provides the perfect setting to enjoy superb Mediterranean cuisine, as well as international dishes that will appeal to foreign visitors to the capital.

Colline Emiliane   X AC ⇔

via degli Avignonesi 22 ✉ *00187 –* Ⓜ *Barberini*   Plan: **G2**
– ☏ *06 4817538 – Closed August, Sunday dinner and Monday*
Carte 32/64 € – *(booking advisable)*
• **Emilian** • **Trattoria** •
Just a stone's throw from Piazza Barberini, this simple, friendly, family-run restaurant has just a few tables arranged close together. It serves typical dishes from the Emilia region, including fresh pasta stretched by hand in the traditional way.

Moma   X AC

via San Basilio 42/43 ✉ *00186 –* Ⓜ *Barberini*   Plan: **G1**
– ☏ *0642011798 – www.ristorantemoma.it – Closed Sunday*
Menu 55 € – Carte 43/74 €
• **Modern cuisine** • **Trendy** • **Minimalist** •
The versatile nature of this bar-cum-bistro and restaurant makes it well worth a visit. At lunchtime, the ambience is busy and lively, while in the evening the restaurant becomes more intimate and atmospheric. Attractive modern cuisine with some imaginative dishes on the menu.

Osteria Fernanda   X AC

via Crescenzo Del Monte 18/24 ✉ *00186*   Plan: **B3**
– ☏ *06 5894333 – www.osteriafernanda.com – Closed 13-20 August, 1 week in February, Saturday lunch and Sunday*
Menu 39/65 € – Carte 42/70 €
• **Creative** • **Minimalist** • **Neighbourhood** •
In the district famous for its Porta Portese market, this restaurant run by two talented business partners is definitely worth a visit. One of the partners manages the front of house, while the other shows real passion in his creative cuisine made from locally sourced ingredients, as well as produce from further afield.

Pastificio San Lorenzo

X AC

via Tiburtina 196 ⊠ 00186 – 𝒞 *06 97273519*   Plan: **C2**
– www.pastificiosanlorenzo.com – Closed in July, August and Sunday
Menu 12/45 €
– Carte 36/58 € – (bookings advisable at dinner) (bar lunch)
• Modern cuisine • Colourful • Friendly •
The name of this modern restaurant with an international feel hints at its origins. An old industrial building once home to a pasta factory, the site subsequently became a centre for artists – right in the middle of the San Lorenzo university area – and it has retained the lively ambience despite being away from the city's main tourist sites. The food doesn't disappoint with its intriguing blend of regional flavours and modern influences.

Trattoria Monti

X AC

via di San Vito 13/a ⊠ 00185 – Ⓜ *Cavour*   Plan: **C2**
– 𝒞 *06 4466573 – Closed August, 24 December-*
3 January, Sunday dinner and Monday
Carte 33/51 € *– (booking advisable)*
• Cuisine from the Marches • Traditional décor • Family •
As a result of renovation work completed a few years ago, this trattoria is resolutely contemporary in style with wooden chairs, copper piping and low-hanging lamps. Specialities include dishes from Lazio and the Marches, the owner's birthplace.

Eden

✿ ≤ ʃ⊕ & AC sⓐ P

via Ludovisi 49 ⊠ 00187 – Ⓜ *Barberini –* 𝒞 *06 478121*   Plan: **G1**
– www.dorchestercollection.com
80 rm – †630/905 € ††730/1145 € – � 45 € – 18 suites
• Grand Luxury • Palace • Elegant •
Following 18 months of major restoration work, this historic Roman hotel now offers its guests more splendour and glamour than ever. Its stylish appeal remains, while the plain former decor has been replaced by luxurious marble and the exclusive feel that the Dorchester Collection requires from its hotels. New features include the extensive menu at the elegantly beautiful Giardino restaurant with its selection of classic dishes, vegetarian and vegan options, charcuterie and pizzas.
❀ **La Terrazza** – See restaurant listing

The Westin Excelsior Rome

ʃ⊕ ⊕ ⋒ ▨ & AC sⓐ ⊜

via Vittorio Veneto 125 ⊠ 00187 – Ⓜ *Barberini*   Plan: **G1**
– 𝒞 *06 47081 – www.restaurantdoney.com*
284 rm – †350/450 € ††500/1050 € – ⊇ 35 € – 32 suites
• Grand Luxury • Spa and wellness • Traditional •
Spoil yourself with a stay in the royal suite (the largest in Europe) or choose one of the luxurious guestrooms, where elegant and comfortable furnishings are complemented by the very latest technology. The "dolce vita" at its best!

Grand Hotel Via Veneto

✿ ʃ⊕ ⊕ ⋒ & AC sⓐ

via Vittorio Veneto 155 ⊠ 00187 – Ⓜ *Barberini*   Plan: **J3**
– 𝒞 *06 487881 – www.ghvv.it*
105 rm – †255/850 € ††315/970 € – ⊇ 33 € – 11 suites
• Grand Luxury • Spa and wellness • Modern •
Situated on one of Rome's most famous streets, this hotel offers luxury in the true sense of the word, with superb, retro-style guestrooms and a collection of more than 500 original paintings on display. A love of Italian flavours and traditions is clearly evident in the cuisine served in this restaurant. This restaurant serves Italian and international cuisine, as well as a good choice of cocktails.
❀ **Magnolia** – See restaurant listing

ITALY - ROME

Regina Hotel Baglioni

via Vittorio Veneto 72 ✉ *00187* – Ⓜ *Barberini*
– ☏ *06 421111 – www.baglionihotels.com*
Plan: **G1**
117 rm – ♦285/500 € ♦♦285/500 € – ⌂ 33 € – 10 suites
• Historic • Luxury • Elegant •
A historic hotel in an Art Nouveau-style building, with an elegant interior decor of stuccowork, period furniture and an imposing bronze and marble staircase. The only concessions to the modern day are the levels of comfort and facilities, as well as the superb guestrooms, some of which are decorated in a contemporary designer style.
⭑◯ **Brunello Lounge & Restaurant** – See restaurant listing

Splendide Royal

via di porta Pinciana 14 ✉ *00187* – Ⓜ *Barberini*
– ☏ *06 421689 – www.splendideroyal.com*
Plan: **G1**
60 rm ⌂ – ♦250/2500 € ♦♦250/2500 € – 9 suites
• Luxury • Historic • Elegant •
Gilded stucco, damask fabrics and sumptuous antique furnishings combine to make this Baroque hotel perfect for those looking for a change from the ubiquitous minimalist style. This ambience of classic luxury continues in the guestrooms, which are decorated in shades of periwinkle blue, golden yellow and cardinal red.

Bernini Bristol

piazza Barberini 23 ✉ *00187* – Ⓜ *Barberini*
– ☏ *06 488931 – www.sinahotels.com*
Plan: **J3**
117 rm – ♦380/470 € ♦♦600/660 € – ⌂ 33 € – 10 suites
• Luxury • Elegant • Personalised •
This elegant hotel is an integral part of the famous Piazza Barberini. It has guestrooms decorated either in classic or contemporary style (those with panoramic views on the upper floors are recommended). Enjoy a light à la carte menu in the 'Giuda Ballerino A pranzo' restaurant.
⭑◯ **Giuda Ballerino!** – See restaurant listing

Majestic

via Vittorio Veneto 50 ✉ *00187* – Ⓜ *Barberini*
– ☏ *06 421441 – www.hotelmajestic.com*
Plan: **G1**
94 rm – ♦190/465 € ♦♦315/720 € – ⌂ 30 € – 4 suites
• Historic • Luxury • Elegant •
Film-buffs may recognise the backdrop to the famous Italian movie 'La Dolce Vita' at this hotel, which was opened in the late 19C. The Majestic remains one of the bastions of luxury accommodation on the Via Veneto, with its antique furniture, tapestries and frescoes, nowadays accompanied by modern comforts and facilities.

Palazzo Montemartini

largo Giovanni Montemartini 20 ✉ *00186 Roma*
– Ⓜ *Termini* – ☏ *06 45661 – www.palazzomontemartini.com*
Plan: **H1**
82 rm ⌂ – ♦180/600 € ♦♦200/650 € – 4 suites
• Luxury • Spa and wellness • Elegant •
The theme of water links this hotel in an aristocratic 19C palazzo with the Roman Baths of Diocletian next door. The hotel's modern interior decor is bright, functional and minimalist.

Sofitel Rome Villa Borghese

via Lombardia 47 ✉ *00187* – Ⓜ *Barberini*
– ☏ *06 478021 – www.sofitel.com*
Plan: **G1**
78 rm ⌂ – ♦715 € ♦♦935 € – 3 suites
• Boutique hotel • Palace • Elegant •
The neo-Classical style dominates in this hotel just a stone's throw from the cosmopolitan Via Veneto. Superb guestrooms and elegant public areas. Situated on the top floor, the panoramic restaurant with its Lounge Bar boasts romantic views of the Villa Medici.
⭑◯ **La Terrasse** – See restaurant listing

Fortyseven

via Luigi Petroselli 47 ✉ *00186 –* ☎ *06 6787816*
– www.fortysevenhotel.com
Plan: **G3**

59 rm ☲ – ♦200/500 € ♦♦200/500 € – 2 suites
• Traditional • Luxury • Personalised •
The name of this hotel housed in an austere 1930s palazzo refers to the number of the street which leads down to the Teatro di Marcello. Each of the five floors here is dedicated to a 20C Italian artist (Greco, Quagliata, Mastroianni, Modigliani and Guccione) and the hotel is adorned with a collection of paintings, sculptures and lithographs.

Palazzo Manfredi

via Labicana 125 ✉ *00184 –* Ⓜ *Colosseo*
– ☎ *06 77591380 – www.palazzomanfredi.com*
Plan: **H3**

14 rm ☲ – ♦350/700 € ♦♦350/700 € – 2 suites
• Luxury • Historic • Modern •
The elegant rooms and superb suites of this hotel overlook the Colosseum and the Domus Aurea. Without a doubt the hotel's most striking feature is its delightful roof-garden terrace, which is perfect for a relaxing breakfast or romantic dinner.

✿ **Aroma** – See restaurant listing

Villa Spalletti Trivelli

via Piacenza 4 ✉ *00184 –* ☎ *0648907934*
– www.villaspallettitrivelli.com
Plan: **J4**

14 rm ☲ – ♦390/625 € ♦♦390/625 € – 4 suites
• Luxury • Traditional • Historic •
Just a stone's throw from the Quirinale, at the top of the hill, this residence overlooks its gardens and the quiet streets that surround it. It has beautiful public areas, including an impressive library, and guestrooms furnished with antiques.

Celio

via dei Santi Quattro 35/c ✉ *00184 –* Ⓜ *Colosseo*
– ☎ *06 70495333 – www.hotelcelio.com*
Plan: **H3**

19 rm ☲ – ♦130/195 € ♦♦170/280 € – 1 suite
• Family • Traditional • Personalised •
This hotel opposite the Colosseum has floors decorated with artistic mosaics in its public spaces and elegant guestrooms alike. Careful attention to detail is evident in the latter, where the carpets add a touch of warmth to the decor. A hammam and relaxation area are also available.

Antico Palazzo Rospigliosi

via Liberiana 21 ✉ *00185 –* Ⓜ *Cavour*
– ☎ *06 48930495 – www.hotelrospigliosi.com*
Plan: **G2**

39 rm ☲ – ♦115/165 € ♦♦149/220 €
• Historic • Traditional • Classic •
This 16C mansion has retained much of its period elegance in its large lounges, as well as in the fine detail of its beautiful bedrooms. The cloister-garden, with its bubbling fountain and splendid 17C chapel, is particularly delightful.

MILAN
MILANO

da-kuk/iStock

MILAN IN...

→ **ONE DAY**
Duomo, Leonardo da Vinci's 'The Last Supper' (remember to book first), Brera, Navigli.

→ **TWO DAYS**
Pinacoteca Brera, Castello Sforzesco, Parco Sempione, Museo del Novecento, a night at La Scala.

→ **THREE DAYS**
Giardini Pubblici and its museums, trendy Savona district.

If it's the romantic charm of places like Venice, Florence or Rome you're looking for, then best avoid Milan. If you're hankering for a permanent panorama of Renaissance chapels, palazzi, shimmering canals and bastions of fine art, then you're in the wrong place. What Milan does is relentless fashion, churned out with oodles of attitude and style. Italy's second largest city is constantly reinventing itself, and when Milan does a makeover, it invariably does it with flair and panache. That's not to say that Italy's capital of fast money and fast fashion doesn't have an eye for its past. The centrepiece of the whole city is the

magnificent gleaming white Duomo, which took five hundred years to complete, while up la via a little way, La Scala is quite simply the world's most famous opera house. But this is a city known primarily for its sleek and modern towers, many housing the very latest threads from the very latest fashion gurus.

Just north of Milan's centre lies Brera, with its much prized old-world charm, and Quadrilatero d'Oro, with no little new-world glitz; the popular Giardini Pubblici are a little further north east from here. South of the centre is the Navigli quarter, home to rejuvenated Middle Age canals, while to the west are the green lungs of the Parco Sempione. For those into art or fashion, the trendy Savona district is also a must.

EATING OUT

For a taste of Italy's regional cuisines, Milan is a great place to be. The city is often the goal of those leaving their home regions in the south or centre of the country; many open trattoria or restaurants, with the result that Milan offers a wide range of provincial menus. Excellent fish restaurants, inspired by recipes from the south, are a big draw despite the fact that the city is a long way from the sea. Going beyond the local borders, the emphasis on really good food continues and the quality of internationally diverse places to eat is better in Milan than just about anywhere else in Italy, including Rome. You'd expect avant-garde eating destinations to be the thing in this city of fashion and style, and you'd be right: there are some top-notch cutting-edge restaurants, thanks to Milan's famous tendency to reshape and experiment as it goes. For those who want to try out the local gastronomic traditions, risotto allo zafferano is not to be missed, nor is the cotoletta alla Milanese (veal cutlet) or the casoeula (a winter special made with pork and cabbage).

411

ITALY - MILAN

✿✿ ✿✿

Seta by Antonio Guida – Hotel Mandarin Oriental Milano

via Monte di Pietà 18 ⊠ 20121   XxxX 網 斎 ᦒ AC
– 𝕄 *Montenapoleone – ℰ 02 87318897*   Plan: **G1**
– *www.mandarinoriental.com – Closed 5-26 August, 1°-8 January,*
Saturday lunch and Sunday
Menu 65 € (weekday lunch)/190 € – Carte 91/171 € – *(booking advisable)*
• Creative • Design • Luxury •

Although this modern restaurant in the Mandarin Oriental hotel is highly elegant, if you are lucky enough to eat here in fine weather you will want to
enjoy your dinner in the charming inner courtyard of this historic palazzo.
Supervised by Antonio Guida, the kitchen team here produce delicious, highly
creative and elegant dishes, which are among the best in Milan. The exotic desserts are of the same excellent quality.
➜ Riso in cagnone con verdure, maccagno (formaggio) e polvere di lam-
pone. Triglia avvolta in foglia di bieta, salsa di granciporro e conchiglie di
mare. Bitter, pompelmo, cioccolato bianco e ciliegia.

✿✿ ✿✿

Vun – Hotel Park Hyatt Milano

via Silvio Pellico 3 ⊠ 20121 – 𝕄 *Duomo*   XxxX 網 ᦒ AC ⇔
– *ℰ 02 88211234 – www.ristorante-vun.it – Closed August, 2 weeks in*   Plan: **G2**
December, Sunday and Monday
Menu 150 € – Carte 92/120 € – *(dinner only) (booking advisable)*
• Modern cuisine • Elegant • Fashionable •

In this elegant and cosmopolitan restaurant decorated in neutral colours and
adorned with drapery, Neapolitan chef Andrea Aprea serves the best of traditional Italian cuisine and a few dishes with the immediately recognisable character
of his native city.
➜ Riso carnaroli riserva, nord... e sud. Baccalà, pizzaiola disidratata e olive
verdi. Caprese... dolce salato.

✿✿

Il Ristorante Trussardi alla Scala   XxxX 網 ᦒ AC

piazza della Scala 5 (palazzo Trussardi) ⊠ 20121   Plan: **G1**
– 𝕄 *Duomo – ℰ 02 80688201 – www.trussardiallascala.com*
– *Closed 2 weeks in August, 2 weeks December-January, Saturday lunch*
and Sunday
Menu 140/150 € – Carte 80/178 € – *(booking advisable)*
• Modern cuisine • Luxury •

Combinations which are surprising but never overly bold or excessive, a
careful choice of ingredients, and the use of seasonal produce are the hallmarks of this restaurant which specialises in gourmet reintrepretations of
traditional Italian cuisine. The setting in a palazzo facing the Piazza della
Scala is an added bonus.
➜ Patate e caviale Trussardi. Piccione al barbecue, Porto e fichi. Mandorla
e carote.
⋔○ **Café Trussardi** – See restaurant listing

✿✿

Armani – Armani Hotel Milano   XxX ⇐ ᦒ AC ⇔

via Manzoni 31 ⊠ 20121 – 𝕄 *Montenapoleone*   Plan: **G1**
– *ℰ 02 8883 8888 – www.armanihotelmilano.com – Closed 5-27August,*
1°-8 January, Sunday and Monday
Menu 150/200 € – Carte 86/162 € – *(dinner only) (booking advisable)*
• Modern cuisine • Luxury • Design •

This exclusive, designer-style restaurant has checkerboard-style flooring and
floor-to-ceiling glass windows offering superb views of Milan. The menu features excellent Italian cuisine alongside international dishes inspired by the
Umami philosophy, which focuses on the fifth sense.
➜ Risotto mantecato, crescione, ragù di rane e porri, cialda all'olio.
Vitello alla milanese, rape cotte e crude, salsa maltese. Cioccolato cremoso alla gianduia, biscotto alla nocciola, infusione di arancia e
senape.

ITALY - MILAN

Felix Lo Basso – Hotel Townhouse Duomo   XxX ⟨ ⇱ ᳖ 🆑

piazza Duomo 21 (5° piano) ✉ *20122* – Ⓜ *Duomo*   Plan: **G2**
– ☏ 02 49528914 – www.felixlobassorestaurant.it – Closed 13-27 August,
1-8 January, Saturday lunch and Sunday
Menu 140/170 € – Carte 106/147 €
• Creative • Contemporary décor • Elegant •

Puglian chef Felice Lo Basso's premises offer breathtaking views of the Duomo. He continues to prove his talent with his recognised trademark of light, creative and colourful cuisine, which is often playful and always focuses on the use of top-quality Italian ingredients.
→ Tortelli di basilico farciti con ricotta di bufala e 'nduja, scampo e acqua di pomodoro. Agnello pugliese in tre passaggi. Chicco cremoso con cuore al caffè e tapioca al cacao croccante.

Tokuyoshi   XX ᳖ 🆑

via San Calocero 3 ✉ *20123* – Ⓜ *Sant'Ambrogio*   Plan: **F3**
– ☏ 0284254626 – www.ristorantetokuyoshi.com – Closed 3 weeks in August, 2 weeks in January and Monday
Menu 90/135 € – Carte 74/134 € – *(dinner only except Sunday)*
• Creative • Minimalist • Trendy •

Mention creative cuisine in Milan and Yoji Tokuyoshi immediately comes to mind. With typical Japanese humility and precision, this chef has been serving imaginative cuisine in his eponymous restaurant for the past couple of years. His original dishes full of decisive flavours take diners on a culinary voyage around his native Japan and adopted home of Italy, the country that has nurtured his professional development.
→ Spaghetti omaggio a Noto. Maialino da latte perso nella foresta. Cemento e terra (dessert).

Savini   XxX ⌘ ᳖ 🆑

galleria Vittorio Emanuele II ✉ *20121* – Ⓜ *Duomo*   Plan: **G2**
– ☏ 02 72003433 – www.savinimilano.it – Closed 3 weeks in August, 1-7 January, Saturday lunch and Sunday
Menu 95/50 € – Carte 85/132 €
• Creative • Luxury • Chic •

The entrance to this restaurant is through the Caffè Savini, which offers a selection of Italy's most famous dishes. A lift takes diners to the first floor, where the gourmet restaurant has been delighting guests with its mix of Milanese favourites and more creative fare since 1867.

Bulgari-Il Ristorante – Hotel Bulgari   XxX ⟨ ⇱ ᳖ 🆑 🚗

via privata Fratelli Gabba 7/b ✉ *20121*   Plan: **G1**
– Ⓜ Montenapoleone – ☏ 02 8058051 – www.bulgarihotels.com
Menu 42 €, 65/150 € – Carte 73/121 € – *(booking advisable) (bar lunch)*
• Modern cuisine • Fashionable • Minimalist •

Overlooking an unexpected yet beautiful garden, this attractive restaurant boasts the same exclusive style as the rest of the hotel. The cuisine showcases top quality Italian produce in dishes that are modern and contemporary in flavour.

Don Carlos – Grand Hotel et de Milan   XxX 🆑

via Manzoni 29 ✉ *20121* – Ⓜ *Montenapoleone*   Plan: **G1**
– ☏ 02 72314640 – www.ristorantedoncarlos.it – Closed August
Menu 75/90 €
– Carte 80/119 € – (dinner only) (number of covers limited, pre-book)
• Modern cuisine • Romantic • Vintage •

The tribute paid to Verdi by the Grand Hotel is accompanied in the small Don Carlos dining rooms by a homage to Italian and Milanese cuisine. Amid a setting of sketches, pictures and paintings dedicated to the world of opera, this restaurant is a favourite with music-lovers who come here after attending a performance in La Scala opera house nearby. Also perfect for a romantic dinner.

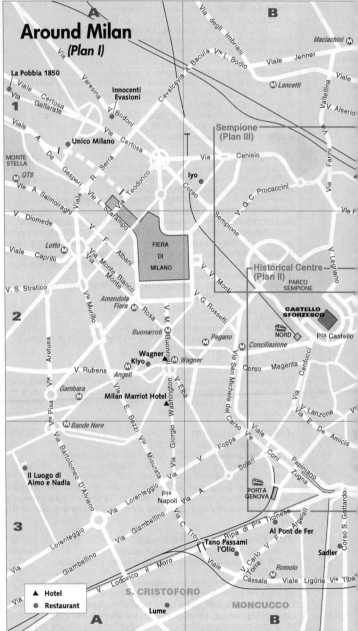

Around Milan
(Plan I)

La Pobbia 1850

Innocenti Evasioni

Unico Milano

MONTE STELLA

QT8

Lotto

Caprilli

V. S. Stratico

Iyo

Sempione
(Plan III)

FIERA DI MILANO

Amendola Fiera

Buonarroti

Wagner
Kiyo

Angeli

Milan Marriot Hotel

Bande Nere

Il Luogo di Aimo e Nadia

Historical Centre
(Plan II)

PARCO SEMPIONE

CASTELLO SFORZESCO

NORD

Pza Castello

Conciliazione

Pagano

Wagner

Magenta

Pza Napoli

Lorenteggio

Giambellino

Giambellino

PORTA GENOVA

Tano Passami l'Olio

Al Pont de Fer

Sadler

Romolo

S. CRISTOFORO

MONCUCCO

Lume

▲ Hotel
● Restaurant

Maciachini

Lancetti

V. Alserio

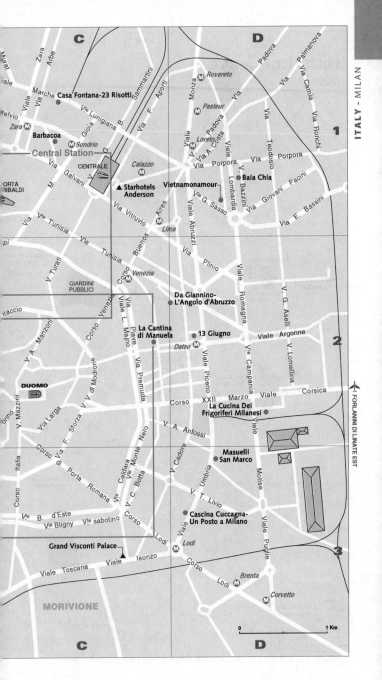

Padova

Via Palmanova

Via Camla

Via Ronchi

Rovereto

Monza

Pasteur

C

Zara

Arbe

Viale

Marche **Casa Fontana-23 Risotti**

Sammartini

Via F. Aporti

Via Padova

Via Teodosio

Via Porpora

Via Giovani Pacini

Via E. Bassini

Vle Lunigiana

Gioia

elvio

Barbacoa

● Sondrio

Zara Ⓜ

Central Station

Via A. Costa

Loreto

Via Porpora

Baia Chia ●

Via Bazzini

ORTA
RIBALDI

CENTRALE

Caiazzo

▲ **Starhotels
Anderson**

Via Galvani

Via Vitruvio

Via Ares

Vietnamonamour

Vle G. Sasso

Via Lombardia

Via Abruzzi

Via

Viale

Via Plinio

Viale Romagna

V. G. Aselli

V. Lomellina

Corsica

Viale

Lima Ⓜ

Via Turati

Vle Tunisia

Vle Tunisia

Corso

Venezia

Via Venezia

**GIARDINI
PUBBLICI**

itaccio

Corso Venezia

Viale L. Majno

**Da Giannino-
L'Angolo d'Abruzzo** ●

Via Premuda

**La Cantina
di Manuela** ●

● **13 Giugno**

Dateo Ⓜ

DUOMO
⊞

V. Mazzini

Via Larga

Via F. Sforza

V. di Modrone

Via Piceno

Viale Campania

XXII Marzo

Corso

**La Cucina Dei
Frigoriferi Milanesi** ●

Vle Caldara

Vle Monte Nero

V. A. Anfossi

**Masuelli
San Marco** ●

V. Cadore

Molise

V. T. Livio

V. Umbria

Corso di Porta Romana

V. C. Botta

**Cascina Cuccagna-
Un Posto a Milano** ●

Viale Puglie

Vle B. d'Este

Vle Bligny

Vle sabotino

Corso

Lodi

Lodi Ⓜ

Grand Visconti Palace ▲

Viale Isonzo

Viale Toscana

Corso

Lodi

Brenta

MORIVIONE

Corvetto Ⓜ

C

D

1

2

3

⚞ FORLANINI DI LINATE EST

0   1 Km

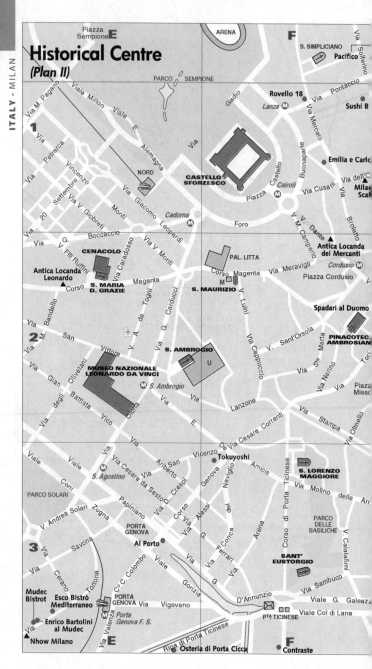

Historical Centre
(Plan II)

Piazza Sempione **E**

ARENA

F

S. SIMPLICIANO
Pacifico

PARCO SEMPIONE

Via M. Pagano
Viale Milton
Viale E.

Rovello 18
Lanza Ⓜ

Sushi B

1

Via Petrarca
Vincenzo
Via 20 Settembre
Via V. Gioberti

Via Giacomo Leopardi

Alemagna

NORD

CASTELLO SFORZESCO

Cadorna Ⓜ

Piazza

Cairoli Ⓜ

Emilia e Carlo

Via dell'O

Milan
Scal

Via Cusani

Bonaparte

Castello

Via
Montil

Foro

V. V. Dante

V. M. Campero

Brolet

Via
Boccaccio
V. Flli Ruffini

CENACOLO

Via Caradosso

PAL. LITTA

Antica Locanda
dei Mercanti

Cordusio Ⓜ

Antica Locanda
Leonardo

Corso

**S. MARIA
D. GRAZIE**

Magenta

Corso Magenta

Via Meravigli

Piazza Cordusio

Via V. Monti

Ⓜ

S. MAURIZIO

V. Luini

Via Carducci

V. A. de Togni

Spadari al Duomo

**PINACOTEC.
AMBROSIAN**

Via Sant'Orsola

2

Via Bandello
M.
Via
San

Vittore

Via G.

Ste Marta

Via Ste

Via Nerino

Tor

S. AMBROGIO

Piazz
Miss

Gian
degli

Oliveta
Battista

**MUSEO NAZIONALE
LEONARDO DA VINCI**

U

V. Cappuccio

Ⓜ S. Ambrogio

Via

Ottona

Lanzone

Via E.

Via

Stampa

Via Olmetto

Vico

Via

De Via Cesare Correnti

Vicenzo

Tokuyoshi

Amicis

**S. LORENZO
MAGGIORE**

Via Cesare da Sesto
Via
Ariberto San
Genova
Naviglio

Via Molino
delle
Arr

 Ⓜ
S. Agostino

Q. Crespi

Corso
di
Porta
Ticinese

PARCO SOLARI

Coni

Papiniano

Corso
Via Alessi

PARCO
DELLE
BASILICHE

V. Andrea Solari
Zugna

Via G.

V. Calatafimi

3

Via
Cerano

Savona

**PORTA
GENOVA**

Al Porto

Via

**SANT'
EUSTORGIO**

Tortona

C.so C. Colombo

Viale

Ferrari

Via
Conca

Arena

Via Sambuco

Gorizia

Viale G. Galeaz

Mudec
Bistrot

Esco Bistrô
Mediterraneo

**PORTA
GENOVA** Via

Vigevano

D'Annunzio

PTA TICINESE

Viale Col di Lana

**Enrico Bartolini
al Mudec**

Via Valenza

Porta
Genova F. S.

Nhow Milano

E

Ripa di Porta Ticinese

Osteria di Porta Cicca

F

Contraste

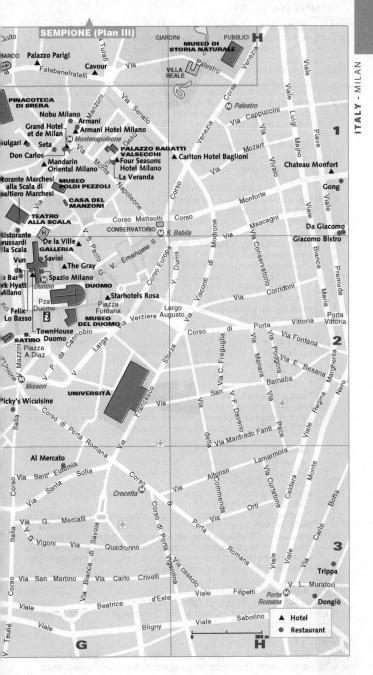

SEMPIONE (Plan III)

Golfo
MARCO
Palazzo Parigi ▲
Fatebenefratelli
Cavour ▲
Via Turati
GIARDINI PUBBLICI
MUSEO DI STORIA NATURALE
VILLA REALE
Palestro Via
Venezia
Viale

PINACOTECA DI BRERA
Nobu Milano ●
Grand Hotel ▲ et de Milan
Armani ▲
Armani Hotel Milano ▲
Bulgari ● Seta ●
Don Carlos ●
Mandarin ▲ Oriental Milano
Ristorante Marchesi alla Scala di Gualtiero Marchesi
MUSEO POLDI PEZZOLI
CASA DEL MANZONI
PALAZZO BAGATTI VALSECCHI
Four Seasons Hotel Milano ▲
La Veranda ●
Carlton Hotel Baglioni ▲
Chateau Monfort ▲
Gong ●
Via Manzoni
Via Senato
Montenapoleone
Gesù
Monte Napoleone
Corso Venezia
Via Cappuccini
Via Mozart
M Palestro
Luigi Maino
Plave
Vivaio
Viale

TEATRO ALLA SCALA
Ristorante Trussardi alla Scala
Vun ●
GALLERIA
Savini ●
The Gray ▲
Corso Matteotti Corso
CONSERVATORIO
M S. Babila
Monforte
Mascagni
Da Giacomo ●
Giacomo Bistro ●
Via Bianca
Premuda
Maria

Park Hyatt Milano
Bar
Spazio Milano ●
Duomo
DUOMO
Pza Duomo
Felix Lo Basso ●
DUOMO
Starhotels Rosa ▲
Piazza Fontana
MUSEO DEL DUOMO
C. V. Emanuele II
Corso Europa
V. Durini
Largo Augusto
Via Visconti di Modrone
Via Conservatorio
Corridoni
Porta Vittoria
Via

TownHouse Duomo ▲
S. SATIRO
Piazza A.Diaz
M Missori
"l'Unione"
V. Mazzini
Larga
V. P. da Cannobio
Via Verziere
Corso di Porta Romana
Storza
Largo Augusto
Corso Porta Vittoria
Via C. Freguglia
Via Podgora
Via Manara
Via E. Besana
Via Fontana
Margherita
Nero

Via Teulié
Italia
Corso
UNIVERSITÀ
Vicky's Wicuisine ●
Corso di Porta Romana
Via
San Francesco
Via della
V. F. Daverio
Barnaba
Via Manfredo Fanti
Pace
Viale Regina
Caldara
Monte
Botta

Al Mercato ●
Via Sant' Eufemia
Via Santa Sofia
Crocetta M
Via G. Mercalli
V. G. Vigoni
Via
Quadronno
Via Bianca di Savoia
Corso di Porta Vigentina
Corso M
Alfonso
Via Commenda
Via Orti
Via Curtatone
Lamarmora

Italia
Corso
Via San Martino
Via Carlo Crivelli
Beatrice
d'Este
Viale
Bligny
Viale
Via cassolo
Viale Filipetti
Porta Romana M
Sabotino
Viale
Porta Romana
V. L. Muratori
Trippa ●
Dongiò ●
Viale
Via Carlo
Viale

0 — 300 m

▲ Hotel
● Restaurant

G
H

Ristorante Marchesi alla Scala di Gualtiero Marchesi

via Filodrammatici 2 ⊠ *20121 –* Ⓜ *Duomo*   XxX ⅋ 🄰🄲
– ℰ *02 72094338 – www.marchesi.it – Closed 5-*   Plan: **G1**
26 August, 1°-7 January, Saturday lunch and Sunday
Menu 49 € (weekdays)/180 € – Carte 64/173 € – *(booking advisable)*
• **Modern cuisine • Classic décor •**
Housed within the La Scala opera house, this restaurant with a café and tea-room offers a careful mix of classic columns, modern paintings and designer-style furniture. Fine cuisine presented in a simple yet elegant style, with acclaimed post-theatre service.

Mio Bar – Hotel Park Hyatt Milano   XxX 🞧 ⅋ 🄰🄲

via Tommaso Grossi 1 – ℰ *02 88211234*   Plan: **G2**
– www.milan.park.hyatt.com
Carte 64/84 €
• **Modern cuisine • Trendy • Luxury •**
This welcoming and lively bar in the prestigious Park Hyatt Milan hotel is open from six in the morning until 1 am, serving a small selection of representative à la carte dishes, as well as an "Assaggi" menu just before dinner.

Rubacuori by Venissa – Hotel Château Monfort   XxX 🄰🄲 ⟷

corso Concordia 1 ⊠ *20129 –* ℰ *02 776761*
– www.hotelchateaumonfort.com
Menu 21 € (lunch) – Carte 40/110 € – *(booking advisable) (bar lunch)*
• **Modern cuisine • Luxury • Romantic •**
A feast for the eyes and the taste buds, this small intimate restaurant with a warm, friendly ambience serves imaginative cuisine. Restricted menu and faster service at lunchtime.

La Veranda – Hotel Milano Four Seasons   XxX 🞕 🞧 🄰🄲 ⟷ 🚗

via Gesù 6/8 ⊠ *20121 –* Ⓜ *Montenapoleone*   Plan: **G1**
– ℰ *02 77081478 – www.fourseasons.com/milan*
Menu 95/125 € – Carte 63/162 €
• **Classic cuisine • Luxury • Traditional décor •**
Younger guests will have no problem choosing a dish at this restaurant, thanks to its special children's menu. Other diners can enjoy Mediterranean cuisine and a wide selection of vegetarian specialities as they admire views of the cloisters, which are visible through the large windows of the modern dining room.

Sushi B   XxX 🞧 🄰🄲

via Fiori Chiari 1/A ⊠ *20121 –* ℰ *02 89092640*   Plan: **F1**
– www.sushi-b.it – Closed 5-20 August, 24 December-9 January,
Sunday and Monday
Menu 30 € (lunch)/130 € – Carte 61/133 € – *(bar lunch)*
• **Japanese • Minimalist • Elegant •**
This new, glamorous and extremely elegant restaurant has a minimalist decor that is decidedly Japanese in feel. There is an attractive bar at the entrance for pre-dinner drinks, while the actual restaurant is on the first floor. This offers well-spaced tables and the option of eating at the teppanyaki bar, where a glass window separates the guests from the kitchen. Delightful vertical garden that brightens up the outdoor summer dining area.

Emilia e Carlo   XX 🞓 🄰🄲

via Sacchi 8 ⊠ *20121 –* Ⓜ *Cairoli –* ℰ *02 875948*   Plan: **F1**
– www.emiliaecarlo.it – Closed August, Christmas Holidays, Saturday lunch and Sunday
Carte 52/80 €
• **Modern cuisine • Rustic •**
Housed in an early 19C palazzo, this trattoria has a rustic feel with arches and wooden beams. Creative contemporary cuisine, and a fine choice of wines.

ITALY - MILAN

Da Giacomo

XX AC

Plan: **H1**

via P. Sottocorno 6 ✉ *20129 – ✆ 02 76023313*
– www.giacomoristorante.com
Carte 53/132 €

• Seafood • Friendly • Neighbourhood •

This old Milanese trattoria dates from the early 20C. Seafood enthusiasts will be delighted by the numerous fish specialities on offer. The menu also includes a few meat dishes, as well as Alba truffles, Caesars' mushrooms and cep mushrooms in season.

Giacomo Bistrot

XX AC

Plan: **H1**

via P. Sottocorno 6 ✉ *20129 – ✆ 0276022653*
– www.giacomobistrot.com
Carte 57/100 €

• Classic cuisine • Bistro •

This restaurant, which stays open until late at night, boasts tables set close together in French-bistro style, while its shelves of leather-bound volumes evoke the distinctly British ambience of a traditional bookshop. The menu features meat dishes, game, oysters and truffles (in season).

Nobu Milano

XX AC ⇔

Plan: **G1**

via Pisoni 1 ✉ *20121 – Ⓜ Montenapoleone*
– ✆ 02 62312645 – www.armanirestaurants.com – Closed 13-20 August and Sunday lunch
Carte 58/105 €

• Fusion • Minimalist • Design •

The pure minimalist lines of this restaurant with numerous branches dotted around the world are not only typical of the Armani style but also distinctly Japanese in feel. Fusion cuisine takes pride of place with a hint of South American influence.

Al Porto

XX AC

Plan: **E3**

piazzale Generale Cantore ✉ *20123*
– Ⓜ Porta Genova FS – ✆ 02 89407425 – www.alportomilano.it
– Closed August, 24 December-4 January, Monday lunch and Sunday
Carte 50/80 €

• Seafood • Classic décor • Cosy •

There is a definite maritime flavour to this restaurant, which occupies the old 19C Porta Genova toll house. Always busy, Al Porto specialises exclusively in fresh fish dishes, including raw fish.

Wicky's - Wicuisine

XX & AC ⇔

Plan: **G2**

corso Italia 6 ✉ *20123 – Ⓜ Missori – ✆ 02 89093781*
– www.wicuisine.it – Closed August, 25 December-1° January, Monday lunch, Saturday lunch and Sunday
Carte 59/171 € *– (booking advisable)*

• Japanese • Design • Minimalist •

This elegant, designer-style restaurant features colours and lights that evoke the night sky. This is the best place to try Kaiseki cuisine – genuine Japanese dishes made with Mediterranean ingredients and expert technique learnt by the owner-chef in Japan.

Café Trussardi – Il Ristorante Trussardi alla Scala

X & AC

Plan: **G1**

piazza della Scala 5 ✉ *20121 – Ⓜ Duomo*
– ✆ 02 80688295 – www.cafetrussardi.com – Closed 2 weeks in August, 2 weeks in December-January and Sunday
Carte 39/93 €

• Mediterranean cuisine • Fashionable • Trendy •

If you are looking for a quick, simple meal with a minimum of fuss, then this is the place for you. There is a lively, cosmopolitan ambience and a menu focusing on delicious Mediterranean flavours.

ITALY - MILAN

ⅼ⃝ Masuelli San Marco X AC

viale Umbria 80 ⊠ 20135 – Ⓜ Lodi TIBB — Plan: **D3**
– ℰ 02 55184138 – www.masuellitrattoria.it – Closed 25 August-
9 September, 26-30 December, 1-7 January, Monday lunch and Sunday
Menu 22 € (weekday lunch) – Carte 39/71 €
• Lombardian • Vintage • Inn •

A rustic atmosphere with a luxurious feel in a typical trattoria, with the same management since 1921; cuisine strongly linked to traditional Lombardy and Piedmont recipes.

ⅼ⃝ Al Mercato X & AC

via Sant'Eufemia 16 ⊠ 20121 – Ⓜ Missori — Plan: **G3**
– ℰ 02 87237167 – www.al-mercato.it – Closed August
Menu 50/100 €
– Carte 52/132 € – (dinner only) (number of covers limited, pre-book)
• Modern cuisine • Bistro • Intimate •

An original and modern concept ; the tiny, intimate and well-furnished dining room serves as a backdrop for gourmet cuisine in the evening and a more restricted menu at lunchtime. In another part of the restaurant, the lively Burger Bar (no reservations; the queue can be long) offers various tasty snacks, including the inevitable hamburger.

ⅼ⃝ Rovello 18 X 🍸 AC

via Tivoli 2 ang. Corso Garibaldi ⊠ 20123 – Ⓜ Lanza — Plan: **F1**
– ℰ 02 72093709 – www.rovello18.it – Closed 3 weeks in August, Sunday
lunch and Saturday
Carte 39/78 €
• Italian • Vintage • Traditional décor •

This restaurant has kept its original name and is situated just 300m from its old premises. Nothing else has changed and the ambience is still attractively retro, managing to be both informal and elegant at the same time. The cuisine is Italian in style, with fish and excellent meat dishes on the menu, as well as a carefully selected wine list.

ⅼ⃝ Spazio Milano X AC

galleria Vittorio Emanuele II (3° piano del Mercato del — Plan: **G2**
Duomo) ⊠ 20123 – Ⓜ Duomo – ℰ 02 878400
– www.nikoromitoformazione.it – Closed 14-31 August
Carte 39/62 € – *(booking advisable)*
• Creative • Design •

This restaurant on the top floor of the Mercato del Duomo acts as a training ground for youngsters from the cookery school run by Romito (3-star Michelin restaurant in Abruzzo); although you would never guess from the food that these chefs are beginners. Three rooms offer views of the kitchen, Galleria and cathedral respectively and the food made from top quality produce is full of flavour.

🏨 Armani Hotel Milano ≤ ⅼ⃝ 🛋 & AC ⅼ⃝

via Manzoni 31 ⊠ 20123 – Ⓜ Montenapoleone — Plan: **G1**
– ℰ 02 8883 8888 – www.armanihotelmilano.com
95 rm – ♦500/1500 € ♦♦500/1500 € – ♻ 40 € – 32 suites
• Grand Luxury • Boutique hotel • Minimalist •

This luxury hotel is housed in an austere building dating from 1937, typical of the Armani style. It is run by a 'lifestyle manager' who offers a warm welcome to guests. Luxurious 1,000 m² spa and very spacious guestrooms.
❀ **Armani** – See restaurant listing

🏨 Bulgari ⅼ⃝ ⅼ⃝ 🏊 🛋 📺 & AC ⅼ⃝ 🚗

via privata Fratelli Gabba 7/b ⊠ 20121 — Plan: **G1**
– Ⓜ Montenapoleone – ℰ 02 8058051 – www.bulgarihotels.com
49 rm – ♦800/950 € ♦♦800/950 € – ♻ 40 € – 9 suites
• Boutique hotel • Grand Luxury • Design •

Owned by the famous jewellery company, this luxury hotel is decorated in warm colours with fine materials gracing the guestrooms. The hotel boasts one of the best spas in the city with a hammam whose green glass decor evokes an emerald.
ⅼ⃝ **Bulgari-Il Ristorante** – See restaurant listing

Carlton Hotel Baglioni ✿ Ŀ5 ᴊ 🅰 ᴊ ⌾
via Senato 5 ⊠ *20121 –* Ⓜ *San Babila –* ℰ *02 77077*   Plan: **H1**
– www.baglionihotels.com
87 rm – ♦350/825 € ♦♦350/825 € – ☲ 36 €
• Luxury • Traditional • Elegant •
Celebrities and well-known personalities are among the guests who have stayed in this splendid hotel, which describes itself as 'home from home'. It provides luxury in a warm, family atmosphere. Antique pieces and original works of art grace the public areas, while the guestrooms offer stucco decor and modern technology.

Château Monfort Ŀ5 ⌾ 🔲 ᴊ 🅰 ᴊ
corso Concordia 1 ⊠ *20129 –* ℰ *02 776761*   Plan: **H1**
– www.hotelchateaumonfort.com
77 rm – ♦290/990 € ♦♦290/990 € – ☲ 26 €
• Grand Luxury • Boutique hotel • Romantic •
Discreet elegance in a superb Art Nouveau-style palazzo designed by Paolo Mezzanotte. The guestrooms have a chic, glamorous feel – the opera inspired rooms are delightful – and there is also a small spa to relax in.
‖⌾ **Rubacuori by Venissa** – See restaurant listing

Four Seasons Hotel Milano ⇔ Ŀ5 ⌾ ♒ 🔲 ᴊ 🅰 ᴊ ⌾
via Gesù 6/8 ⊠ *20121 –* Ⓜ *Montenapoleone*   Plan: **G1**
– ℰ *02 77088 – www.fourseasons.com/milan*
93 rm – ♦575/1300 € ♦♦575/1300 € – ☲ 38 € – 25 suites
• Grand Luxury • Luxury • Classic •
This evocative hotel has achieved a perfect balance between the original architectural features of the 15C monastery in which it is housed and its elegant contemporary design. Don't be surprised by the highly modern technology available in the superb guestrooms that occupy the former monks' cells.
‖⌾ **La Veranda** – See restaurant listing

Grand Hotel et de Milan ✿ Ŀ5 ᴊ 🅰 ᴊ
via Manzoni 29 ⊠ *20121 –* Ⓜ *Montenapoleone*   Plan: **G1**
– ℰ *02 723141 – www.grandhoteletdemilan.it*
87 rm – ♦402/1444 € ♦♦430/1472 € – 7 suites
• Grand Luxury • Historic building • Historic •
This hotel opened over 150 years ago. Big names in the field of music, theatre and politics have stayed in its elegant rooms that are full of charm. Bright restaurant dedicated to the great tenor, who recorded his first record in this hotel.
‖⌾ **Don Carlos** – See restaurant listing

Mandarin Oriental Milano ✿ Ŀ5 ♒ 🔲 ᴊ 🅰 ᴊ
via Andegari 9 ⊠ *20121 Milano –* Ⓜ *Montenapoleone*   Plan: **G1**
– ℰ *02 87318888 – www.mandarinoriental.com*
104 rm – ♦590/1350 € ♦♦590/1350 € – ☲ 35 € – 21 suites
• Grand Luxury • Historic building • Design •
This luxury hotel comprises of four different buildings, offering excellent levels of service and a quality of design in the guestrooms that few other city-centre hotels can equal. The same is true of the swimming pool situated in the hotel's delightful spa. If you are looking for a simple meal, the Mandarin Bar & Bistrot offers a wide selection of delicious Italian dishes, as well as a choice of sandwiches and salads.
❀❀ **Seta by Antonio Guida** – See restaurant listing

Park Hyatt Milano Ŀ5 ᴊ 🅰 ᴊ
via Tommaso Grossi 1 ⊠ *20121 –* Ⓜ *Duomo*   Plan: **G2**
– ℰ *02 88211234 – www.milan.park.hyatt.com*
90 rm – ♦560/1700 € ♦♦560/1700 € – ☲ 40 € – 16 suites
• Luxury • Grand Luxury • Modern •
Housed in a palazzo dating from 1870, this contemporary-style hotel boasts the best of modern comforts, including spacious guestrooms and equally large bathrooms. Travertine marble covers the building and a splendid work of art by Anish Kapoor "Untitled 2013" can be admired in the lobby.
❀❀ **Vun** • ‖⌾ **Mio Bar** – See restaurant listing

Starhotels Rosa Grand
piazza Fontana 3 ✉ *20122* – Ⓜ *Duomo* – ℰ *02 88311* Plan: **G2**
– *www.starhotels.com*
326 rm ☲ – †170/790 € ††180/800 € – 4 suites
• Palace • Modern • Design •
Situated in the centre of Milan, this hotel is arranged around a central courtyard, the simple, square shape of which is echoed in its stylish decor. Although all the rooms are elegant and comfortable, only a few offer views of the Duomo spires.

The Gray
via San Raffaele 6 ✉ *20121* – Ⓜ *Duomo* Plan: **G2**
– ℰ *02 7208951* – *www.sinahotels.com* – *Closed August*
19 rm – †500 € ††550/900 € – ☲ 33 € – 2 suites
• Boutique hotel • Traditional • Personalised •
All the rooms in this delightful hotel are different – some are on two levels, while three boast views of the Galleria. But despite its name, there is nothing grey about this property! The hotel's Le Noir restaurant serves Mediterranean cuisine in a subdued and intimate ambience.

Milano Scala
via dell'Orso 7 ✉ *20121* – Ⓜ *Cairoli* – ℰ *02 870961* Plan: **F1**
– *www.hotelmilanoscala.it* – *Closed 12-26 August and 2 weeks Christmas Holidays*
56 rm ☲ – †170/590 € ††210/640 € – 6 suites
• Boutique hotel • Traditional • Personalised •
Opened in 2010, this charming hotel prides itself on its ecologically sustainable ethos. The public areas have a stylish ambience and the restaurant serves original "green" dishes made from fresh ingredients sourced from producers in the Parco del Ticino and grown in the hotel's own vegetable garden (on the hotel roof). The fully renovated Sky Terrace Bar Milano Scala makes a fascinating location for an aperitif with 360° views of the city (open to hotel guests and non-resident alike).

Townhouse Duomo
via Silvio Pellico 2 ✉ *20121* – Ⓜ *Duomo* Plan: **G2**
– ℰ *02 45397600* – *www.townhousehotels.com*
14 rm – †400/2500 € ††400/2500 € – ☲ 30 €
• Luxury • Historic • Centrally located •
The main attractions of this luxury hotel are its views of Milan cathedral and the splendid Piazza Duomo. These can be enjoyed from the luxurious guestrooms (all on the third floor), which have been designed by different architects, as well as from the small breakfast terrace on the first floor, from where the centuries-old spires appear close at hand.
❀ **Felix Lo Basso** – See restaurant listing

Cavour
via Fatebenefratelli 21 ✉ *20121* – Ⓜ *Turati* Plan: **G1**
– ℰ *02 620001* – *www.hotelcavour.it* – *Closed 7-25 August*
121 rm ☲ – †115/600 € ††126/800 € – 7 suites
• Traditional • Classic •
This simple yet elegant hotel not far from the city's main cultural sights is decorated with high quality materials, from the floors to the wood panelling. The restaurant serves reasonably priced brasserie-style dishes from 11am-7pm.

Grand Visconti Palace
viale Isonzo 14 ✉ *20135* – Ⓜ *Lodi TIBB* – ℰ *02 540341* Plan: **C3**
– *www.grandviscontipalace.com*
162 rm ☲ – †100/1000 € ††100/1000 € – 10 suites
• Palace • Business • Industrial •
A large old industrial mill has been converted to house this elegant grand hotel with a welcoming well-being centre, conference rooms and a delightful garden. Make sure you try the Quinto Piano restaurant, which delights guests with its refined and imaginative cuisine made with real care and attention.

Nhow Milano

via Tortona 35 ✉ *20144*
– ✆ *02 4898861 – www.nhow-hotels.com*
245 rm – ♦110/700 € ♦♦110/700 € – ☲ 28 € – 1 suite
• Luxury • Design •

Plan: E3

This designer-style hotel located in a former industrial district has plenty of charm, and acts as a permanent showcase for artistic and stylistic excellence. Eclectic guestrooms offer impeccable standards of comfort.

Spadari al Duomo

via Spadari 11 ✉ *20123*
– Ⓜ *Duomo*
– ✆ *02 72002371 – www.spadarihotel.com*
– *Closed 22-27 December*
39 rm ☲ – ♦120/250 € ♦♦180/500 € – 1 suite
• Traditional • Modern • Contemporary •

Plan: F2

The Spadari is a modern, centrally located hotel that pays discreet tribute to the world of art thanks to its owners, who are enthusiastic art collectors. Note the fireplace by Giò Pomodoro in the lobby and the unique furnishings and assiduous play of light in the decor. Some rooms have views of the Duomo's spires, while others have small balconies.

De la Ville

via Hoepli 6 ✉ *20121*
– Ⓜ *Duomo*
– ✆ *02 8791311 – www.sinahotels.com*
107 rm ☲ – ♦440/460 € ♦♦470/490 € – 1 suite
• Traditional • Elegant • Personalised •

Plan: G2

Although some rooms in this hotel have a contemporary feel, others are decorated in an Old English style, a decor which is repeated in the public rooms with their wood panelling, open fireplace and prints of horses and fox hunting. Relaxing swimming pool on the roof with a glass ceiling through which you can admire the spires of the Duomo.

Antica Locanda dei Mercanti

via San Tomaso 6 ✉ *20121*
– Ⓜ *Cordusio*
– ✆ *02 8054080 – www.locanda.it*
12 rm ☲ – ♦205/295 € ♦♦205/295 € – 3 suites
• Manor house • Boutique hotel • Romantic •

Plan: F2

A small, cosy hotel, simple and elegant in style, and furnished with antique furniture. Many of the light and spacious guestrooms have a small terrace.

CENTRAL STATION - VITTORIA

PLAN III

Alice-Eataly Smeraldo (Viviana Varese)

piazza XXV Aprile 10 ✉ *20123*
– Ⓜ *Porta Garibaldi FS*
– ✆ *02 49497340 – www.aliceristorante.it*
– *Closed Sunday*
Menu 47 € (lunch)/150 €
– Carte 74/148 € – *(booking advisable)*
• Creative • Design • Fashionable •

Plan: L2

In 2014, the famous Teatro Smeraldo in Milan became the setting for a large Eataly complex, in which the Alice restaurant is certainly one of the highlights. The attractive designer-style decor makes the perfect backdrop for the imaginative cuisine that includes a number of fish dishes.

➔ "Superspaghettino" con brodo affumicato, julienne di calamaro, vongole, polvere di tarallo e limone. Ossobuco al barbecue con diaframma scottato, tartare di fassone, cipollotto, maionese di senape e neve all'aceto. Rivisitazione della pastiera napoletana.

Berton
XxX ఈ ఆ AC

via Mike Bongiorno 13 ✉ *20123* – Ⓜ *Gioia* — Plan: **L1**
– ✆ 02 67075801 – www.ristoranteberton.com – Closed 2 weeks in August,
Christmas Holidays, Saturday and Monday lunch, Sunday
Menu 120 €, 110/135 € – Carte 82/188 €
• Creative • Design • Minimalist •

Light, modern and minimalist in style, the restaurant decor echoes the cuisine
served here, which uses just a few ingredients to create original and beautifully
presented dishes.
→ Risotto alla pizzaiola con acqua di mozzarella. Brodo di prosciutto crudo,
merluzzo sfogliato, pane al prezzemolo e rapanelli. Uovo di yogurt e
mango.

Joia (Pietro Leemann)
XxX ఈ AC ⇔

via Panfilo Castaldi 18 ✉ *20124* – Ⓜ *Repubblica* — Plan: **M2**
– ✆ 02 29522124 – www.joia.it – Closed 14-20 August, 24 December-
7 January, Sunday
Menu 40 € (weekday lunch)/120 € – Carte 68/106 €
• Vegetarian • Minimalist • Chic •

The dishes always let you sense their essence, in their colour, taste, texture and
presentation. To quote the chef, they are a "summary of research, where the
ingredients of Mediterranean cuisine meet with the cultures of the world; a
natural choice, without meat – a philosophy where nature is welcomed and respected". You'll be lulled by sweet, melodious background music, in this pure,
minimalist setting.
→ Ombelico del mondo (risotto con finferli, pomodoro e pepe del Sarawak, profumo di rose). Sotto una coltre tenue (sentori di bosco, cuore di
zucchine e melissa, ricotta affumicata, salvia croccante... e altro ancora,
sotto un soffice manto). Gong (spuma vaporosa di latte con croccante e
frutti di bosco).

La Cucina Dei Frigoriferi Milanesi
X 🍽 ఈ

via Piranesi 10 ✉ *20121* – *✆ 02 3966 6784* — Plan: **D2**
– www.lacucinadeifrigoriferimilanesi.it – Closed Saturday lunch and
Sunday
Menu 14 € (weekday lunch) – Carte 33/43 €
• Modern cuisine • Contemporary décor •

An interesting location in the artistic-cultural setting of the Frigoriferi Milanesi
industrial complex for this restaurant with a modern feel both in its decor and
its cuisine. The restaurant offers an "unstructured" menu, which instead of dividing the courses into the traditional antipasti, starters and main courses, consists of different dishes which can be selected however guests prefer.

Dongiò
X AC

via Corio 3 ✉ *20135* – Ⓜ *Porta Romana* — Plan: **H3**
– ✆ 02 5511372 – Closed 3 weeks in August, Saturday
lunch and Sunday
Carte 25/45 € – *(booking advisable)*
• Calabrian • Family • Rustic •

A taste of Calabria in Milan. This family-run restaurant is simply furnished and
always busy – a typical traditional trattoria of the type that is more and more
difficult to find. The house speciality is *spaghettoni alla tamarro* (with a sausage
and tomato sauce), while the menu also features fresh pasta, 'nduja sausage
and the ever-present peperoncino.

Da Giannino-L'Angolo d'Abruzzo
X AC

via Pilo 20 ✉ *20129* – Ⓜ *Porta Venezia* — Plan: **D2**
– ✆ 02 29406526
Carte 29/38 €
• Cuisine from Abruzzo • Traditional décor • Friendly •

A warm welcome combined with a simple but lively atmosphere and typical
dishes from the Abruzzo region make this a popular place to eat. Generous portions and excellent roast dishes.

ITALY - MILAN

Serendib
X AC

via Pontida 2 ✉ 20121 – Ⓜ *Moscova –* ℰ *02 6592139* — Plan: **K2**
– www.serendib.it
Menu 13/25 € – Carte 23/57 € – *(dinner only)*
• Indian • Simple • Oriental décor •

Serendib, the old name for Sri Lanka, means "to make happy" – an ambitious promise, but one which this restaurant manages to keep! True to its origins, the tempting menu focuses on Indian and Sri Lankan cuisine.

Trippa
X 斧 AC

Via Giorgio Vasari, 3 ✉ 20135 – Ⓜ *Porta Romana* — Plan: **H3**
– ℰ 327 668 7908 – www.trippamilano.it – Closed 2 weeks in August and Sunday
Carte 32/52 € – *(dinner only) (booking advisable)*
• Italian • Trattoria • Vintage •

Simple, informal and with a slightly retro feel, this restaurant serves a range of dishes from all over Italy, including the tripe which gives the restaurant its name. Unfussy and uncomplicated, the cuisine prepared by the skilful young chef using top-quality ingredients makes this one of the best trattorias in Italy. House specialities include Milanese risotto with grilled marrow, *vitello tonnato* and, of course, the ever-present tripe!

Acanto – Hotel Principe di Savoia
XXxX AC ⬦

piazza della Repubblica 17 ✉ 20124 – Ⓜ *Repubblica* — Plan: **M2**
– ℰ 02 62302026 – www.dorchestercollection.com – Closed 8-23 August
Menu 35 € (weekday lunch)/90 € – Carte 72/157 € – *(bar lunch)*
• Modern cuisine • Luxury • Chic •

Large elegant spaces full of light characterise this modern restaurant which pampers its guests with excellent, attentive service and classic contemporary-style cuisine. There's an original "La Tavolozza dello Chef" formula at lunchtime, which offers a choice of dishes combining a starter with a main course and a side dish.

Terrazza Gallia – Excelsior Hotel Gallia
XXxX 斧 & AC ⬦

piazza Duca d'Aosta 9 – Ⓜ *Centrale FS* — Plan: **M1**
– ℰ 0267853514 – www.terrazzagallia.com
Menu 40 € (weekdays)/105 € – Carte 59/166 €
• Creative • Luxury • Contemporary décor •

Run by two experienced brothers from Naples, this splendid terrace restaurant is reserved for the Milanese tradition of the aperitif in the evening and for lunches of creative, colourful cuisine at midday. The dining room is decorated in contemporary-style, as is the rest of this splendid hotel.

Daniel
XxX 斧 & AC

via Castelfidardo 7, angolo via San Marco ✉ 20121 — Plan: **L2**
– ℰ 02 63793837 – www.danielcanzian.com – Closed 3 weeks in August, Saturday lunch and Sunday
Menu 60/80 € – Carte 52/90 €
• Italian • Contemporary décor • Elegant •

One of the first things to strike you in this restaurant is the open-view kitchen, where the young friendly chef happily interacts with diners. His menu focuses on traditional Italian classics, as well as a few more inventive offerings, all of which are prepared using the very best ingredients. Simpler fare available at lunchtime.

Barbacoa
XX 斧 & AC ⬦

via delle Abbadesse 30 ✉ 20123 – Ⓜ *Zara* — Plan: **C1**
– ℰ 02 6883883 – www.barbacoa.it
Menu 29/48 € – Carte 40/75 € – *(dinner only except Sunday)*
• International • Minimalist • Cosy •

The first European restaurant of a Brazilian chain, Barbacoa is a true celebration of meat. Beef takes pride of place, although chicken, pork and lamb also feature on the menu. The traditional caipirinha, a cocktail based on cane sugar and lime, continues the Brazilian theme, while mixed salads and exotic fruit desserts complete the picture.

ITALY - MILAN

Gong
XX 爺 ⅙ AK

corso Concordia 8 ✉ *20123 –* ✆ *02 76023873*
Plan: **H1**
– www.gongmilano.it – Closed 14-19 August and Monday lunch
Menu 85 € – Carte 37/130 €
• Chinese • Minimalist • Elegant •
Guglielmo and Keisuke delight their guests with their constantly evolving menu which features Italian and Japanese cuisine, as well as Chinese specialities, internationally influenced dishes and plenty of other tempting delicacies.

Il Liberty
XX AK

viale Monte Grappa 6 ✉ *20124 –* ✆ *02 29011439*
Plan: **L2**
– www.il-liberty.it – Closed 12-19 August, 1°-7 January, Saturday lunch and Sunday
Menu 18 € (weekday lunch)/75 €
– Carte 48/72 € – (number of covers limited, pre-book)
• Creative • Cosy • Friendly •
Occupying an Art Nouveau-style palazzo, this small restaurant with two rooms and a loft area has a friendly, welcoming atmosphere. The menu includes a selection of fish and meat dishes, with a choice of simpler and more reasonably priced options at lunchtime.

Pacifico
XX AK

via Moscova 29 ✉ *20123 –* Ⓜ *Moscova*
Plan: **F1**
– ✆ *02 8724 4737 – www.wearepacifico.com – Closed 7-21 August*
Menu 25 € (lunch)/70 € – Carte 47/99 € – *(booking advisable)*
• Peruvian • Bistro • Elegant •
Cosmopolitan Milan has warmly embraced this lively restaurant, which acts as an ambassador for Peruvian cuisine with the occasional Asian influence. There is an excellent choice of ceviche – raw fish or seafood dishes marinated in lemon and flavoured with spices such as chilli pepper and coriander – which are a typical speciality of Latin American countries along the Pacific coast.

Trattoria Trombetta
XX 斎 ⅙ AK

largo Bellintani 1 ✉ *20123 –* Ⓜ *Porta Venezia*
Plan: **M2**
– ✆ *02 35941975 – www.trattoriatrombetta.eu – Closed Monday*
Carte 41/69 € – *(dinner only except Sunday)*
• Modern cuisine • Neighbourhood • Friendly •
A typical modern Milanese trattoria with a relaxed atmosphere. The dishes focus on Lombardy and, in a broader sense, Italy, with particular attention paid to the use of seasonal produce. Brunch is served on Sundays alongside a more concise menu.

13 Giugno
XX AK ⟺

via Goldoni 44 ang.via Uberti 5 ✉ *20129*
Plan: **D2**
– ✆ *02 719654 – www.ristorante13giugno.it*
Carte 57/175 €
• Sicilian • Colourful • Mediterranean décor •
This lively restaurant boasts a charming winter garden. Pasta with sea urchins, aubergine caponata, stuffed sardines and couscous are just some of the Sicilian specialities on the menu.

Vietnamonamour
X ⇦ 斎 AK

via A. Pestalozza 7 ✉ *20131 –* Ⓜ *Piola*
Plan: **D1**
– ✆ *02 70634614 – www.vietnamonamour.com – Closed Monday lunch and Sunday*
4 rm 🖃 *–* ♊70/140 € ♊♊90/200 €
Menu 25 € – Carte 24/45 € – *(booking advisable)*
• Vietnamese • Exotic décor • Romantic •
This restaurant would certainly have been appreciated by the French writer Marguerite Duras, who would have rediscovered the ambience of her native Vietnam here. If you're not familiar with Vietnamese dishes, don't be put off by the menu – everything will be clearly explained when you order and you're sure to fall under the spell of this fascinating country.

ITALY - MILAN

Baia Chia   X AC ⇔

Plan: **D1**

via Bazzini 37 ⊠ *20131* – Ⓜ *Piola* – ☎ *02 2361131*
– www.ristorantesardobaiachia.it – Closed 7-24 August, Christmas
Holidays
Carte 30/49 €
• Sardinian • Family •
This pleasant restaurant with a family atmosphere is divided into two small
dining rooms, plus a veranda which can also be used in winter. Excellent fish
dishes and Sardinian specialities on the menu. Many of the wines also come
from Sardinia.

La Cantina di Manuela   X 🏵 🏠 AC

Plan: **C2**

via Carlo Poerio 3 ⊠ *20129* – ☎ *02 76318892*
– www.lacantinadimanuela.it
Carte 32/50 € – *(booking advisable)*
• Modern cuisine • Bistro • Colourful •
The dining room in this young, dynamic restaurant is surrounded by bottles of
wine. Elaborate dishes feature on the menu, with antipasti available in the evening. At lunchtime these are replaced by various salads aimed at a business
clientele in a hurry.

Casa Fontana-23 Risotti   X AC

Plan: **C1**

piazza Carbonari 5 ⊠ *20125* – Ⓜ *Sondrio*
– ☎ 02 6704710 – www.23risotti.it – Closed 2 weeks in August, 1°-
12 January, Monday and Saturday lunch in summer
Carte 42/69 €
• Lombardian • Traditional décor • Cosy •
Despite the obligatory 25min wait for your food, this restaurant is well worth a
visit for its excellent risottos. Attractive pictures of rice fields on the walls.

Pisacco   X AC

Plan: **L2**

via Solferino 48 ⊠ *20121* – Ⓜ *Moscova*
– ☎ 02 91765472 – www.pisacco.it – Closed 12-19 August and Monday
Menu 14 € (weekday lunch) – Carte 41/63 €
• Modern cuisine • Trendy • Colourful •
A modern and informal restaurant with attentive service and reasonable prices.
Excellent selection of creative dishes, as well as some reinterpretations of classic
favourites, such as polenta and baccalà (salted cod) and Caesar salad.

Un Posto a Milano-Cascina Cuccagna   X 🏠 AC

Plan: **D3**

via Cuccagna 2 ⊠ *20121 Milano* – ☎ *02 5457785*
– www.unpostoamilano.it – Closed Monday
Menu 15 € (weekday lunch)/25 € – Carte 35/60 €
• Classic cuisine • Country house • Traditional décor •
Occupying an old restored farmhouse in urban Milan, the Cascina Cuccagna is
both a restaurant and a cultural centre. It is surrounded by greenery, providing a
delightful oasis in the city. At lunchtime, choose from a copious and reasonably
priced buffet. The evening menu is more elaborate but still offers good value for
money.

Principe di Savoia   🖪 🌐 🏵 🗏 AC 🏊

Plan: **M2**

piazza della Repubblica 17 ⊠ *20124* – Ⓜ *Repubblica*
– ☎ 02 62301 – www.dorchestercollection.com
257 rm – †255/960 € ††285/990 € – ☐ 45 € – 44 suites
• Grand Luxury • Palace • Elegant •
Overlooking Piazza della Repubblica, this majestic white building dating from
the 19C is an imposing sight. With a truly international atmosphere, this luxury
hotel boasts superb guestrooms, a well-equipped fitness area and a wellbeing
centre. Perfect for a relaxing stay.
🍽 **Acanto** – See restaurant listing

ITALY - MILAN

Excelsior Hotel Gallia

piazza Duca d'Aosta 9 ✉ *20124 –* Ⓜ *Centrale FS*
Plan: M1
– ℰ 02 67851 – www.excelsiorhotelgallia.com
182 rm – ♜300/1100 € ♜♜300/1100 € – ☲ 40 € – 53 suites
• Grand Luxury • Modern •
Now boasting a fully restored exterior, the Excelsior Gallia successfully combines the elegance of an early 20C historic building with a contemporary design that is typical of Milan. It has a mix of chrome and marble that comes together to striking effect. Top class leisure options, including a splendid spa where modern facilities and a luxury brand of cosmetics set the scene for moments of sheer indulgence and relaxation.
⍙ **Terrazza Gallia** – See restaurant listing

Palazzo Parigi

corso di Porta Nuova 1 ✉ *20121 – ℰ 02625625*
Plan: G1
– www.palazzoparigi.com
61 rm – ♜500/1250 € ♜♜500/1250 € – ☲ 40 € – 27 suites
• Grand Luxury • Elegant •
This extraordinary palazzo has been renovated to provide the highest level of luxury accommodation. It features carefully chosen elegant furnishings, precious marble, plenty of natural light and stunning views of the city from the top floor guestrooms.

The Westin Palace

piazza della Repubblica 20 ✉ *20124 –* Ⓜ *Repubblica*
Plan: M2
– ℰ 02 63361 – www.westinpalacemilan.it
227 rm – ♜90/2499 € ♜♜90/2499 € – ☲ 40 € – 5 suites
• Palace • Luxury • Grand luxury •
The Milanese apotheosis of the Imperial style – a luxury hotel with sober, austere decor. Some of the rooms have views of the Duomo, while all guests can enjoy the roof terrace in summer. Recently refurbished and just as elegant as ever, the restaurant now also offers a private dining area. Mediterranean dishes dominate the menu.

Starhotels Anderson

piazza Luigi di Savoia 20 ✉ *20124 –* Ⓜ *Centrale FS*
Plan: C1
– ℰ 02 6690141 – www.starhotels.com
106 rm – ♜109/950 € ♜♜119/950 € – ☲ 20 €
• Palace • Business • Design •
This hotel has a warm, designer-style atmosphere, with fashionable and intimate public rooms and welcoming guestrooms offering all the usual comforts of a hotel of this standard. The elegant lounge is home to a small restaurant (open only in the evenings) which serves contemporary-style cuisine.

FIERAMILANOCITY - SEMPIONE - NAVIGLI (viale Fulvio Testi, Niguarda, viale Fermi, viale Certosa, corso Sempione, piazza Carlo Magno, via Monte Rosa, San Siro, via Novara, via Washington, Ripa di porta Ticinese, Corso S. Gottardo)
PLAN I

Enrico Bartolini al Mudec

via Tortona 56 ✉ *20123 –* Ⓜ *Porta Genova*
Plan: E3
– ℰ 02 84293701 – www.enricobartolini.net – Closed 2 weeks in August, Monday lunch and Sunday
Menu 110/160 € – Carte 95/265 €
• Creative • Contemporary décor • Trendy •
This elegant, contemporary-style restaurant on the third floor of the Museo delle Culture offers an original location and attentive, solicitous service. The apparent simplicity of the menu sets the tone for a concert of dishes which feature extraordinary soloists backed by choirs of ingredients and variations on the same theme, all arranged across several courses which are striking for their imaginative quality. The conductor of this culinary orchestra is young Bartolini, poised and composed on the outside yet full of passion and energy within.
➜ Bottoni di olio e lime con salsa cacciucco e polpo arrosto. Animelle di vitello glassate con carciofi, menta e liquirizia. Crema bruciata con mirtilli ghiacciati, amarene e meringhe.

ITALY - MILAN

🌼 🌼 **Il Luogo di Aimo e Nadia** (Alessandro Negrini e Fabio Pisani)

via Montecuccoli 6 ⊠ *20147* – 🚇 *Primaticcio*   XxX 🏠 🎹 ⇔

– 📞 02 416886 – www.aimoenadia.com   Plan: **A3**

– Closed August, 1-8 January, Saturday lunch and Sunday

Menu 45 € (weekday lunch)/150 €

– Carte 87/181 €

• Creative • Design •

Although Aimo and Nadia are no longer at the helm of this restaurant, their style of cuisine is echoed by two excellent chefs. They have maintained the restaurant's tradition of creating Italian regional dishes with a modern twist. The focus has always been on top-quality ingredients (even before it was fashionable), making this restaurant in Via Montecuccoli one of the cradles of this culinary ethos. This is now kept alive through exciting, memorable cuisine created by two fine chefs.

→ Tagliolini semola e crescione con aglio orsino, peperoncino e guazzetto di frutti di mare. Anguilla caramellata alla birra doppio malto con cecina e marmellata di limoni. Notebook: crema bruciata, arance amare e sanguinelle, mango e liquirizia calabrese.

🌼 **Contraste** (Matias Perdomo)   XxX 🏠 🎐 🎹

via Meda 2 ⊠ *20123* – 📞 *02 49536597*   Plan: **F3**

– www.contrastemilano.it

– Closed 2 weeks in August, 1°-10 January, Tuesday from 12 September to 15 Juin, Sunday rest of the year

Menu 90/130 € – *(dinner only except Sunday) (booking advisable) (tasting menu only)*

• Modern cuisine • Elegant • Historic •

Glittering red silicon chandeliers hover above diners at this restaurant, which is decorated here and there with Art Nouveau touches. The cuisine is traditional yet reinterpreted in presentation and appearance, offering contrasting flavours that leave guests impressed and delighted.

→ Tortelli di risotto allo zafferano. Carpaccio di manzo, foie gras. Tarte Tatin rivisitata.

🌼 **Lume**   XxX 🏠 🎐 �& 🎹 🅿

via Watt 37 ⊠ *20123* – 📞 *02 80888624*   Plan: **B3**

– www.lumemilano.com

– Closed 14-26 August, 10 days in January, Sunday dinner and Monday

Menu 40 € (weekday lunch), 120/150 €

– Carte 78/237 €

• Modern cuisine • Design • Minimalist •

The name of this restaurant situated in an industrial setting evokes the importance of light in the premises, which boasts large windows overlooking an internal garden. The cuisine revolves around the personality of the chef, Luigi Taglienti. He creates elegant, modern and inventive dishes with influences from Lombardy and his native Liguria.

→ Ravioli di faraona alla cacciatora. Musetto di vitello allo spumante. Tartufo nero, tiramisù.

🌼 **Sadler**   XxX 🏠 🎹 ⇔

via Ascanio Sforza 77 ⊠ *20141* – 🚇 *Romolo*   Plan: **B3**

– 📞 02 58104451 – www.sadler.it

– Closed 2 weeks in August, 1 week in January and Sunday

Menu 80 € (weekdays)/130 € – Carte 78/158 € – *(dinner only)*

• Creative • Elegant •

Overlooking the Naviglio canal on the outskirts of the city, this restaurant focuses all its attention on its cuisine, which features traditional recipes reinterpreted with a contemporary flavour. Fish is the speciality here, although there is also a vegetarian menu. The children's options are designed to introduce the younger generation to gourmet dining.

→ Gnocchi rossi e neri farciti di pesto con gamberi marinati e cardi. Padellata di crostacei con verdure alla griglia e spuma al dragoncello. Varietà di cioccolato in differenti forme e sapori.

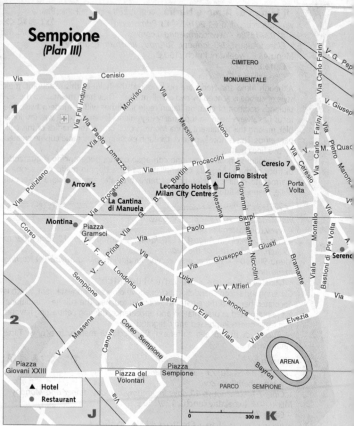

Sempione
(Plan III)

▲ Hotel
● Restaurant

0   300 m

☆ **Innocenti Evasioni** (Arrigoni e Picco)   XX 🕸 🍴 🛋 🆔 🔄

via privata della Bindellina ✉ *20155*   Plan: **A1**
– Ⓜ *Portello*
– 📞 *02 33001882 – www.innocentievasioni.com*
– *Closed 6-31 August, 1°-10 January and Sunday*
Menu 49/73 €
– Carte 52/73 € – *(dinner only) (booking advisable)*
• Creative • Fashionable •
This pleasant establishment, with large windows facing the garden, offers classic cuisine reinterpreted with imagination. Enjoyable outdoor summer dining.
➜ Spaghetti di Gragnano al pesto di nocciole e foglie di sedano, capperi e limone. Polipo rosolato, patata affumicata, cime di rapa, pomodoro e pane croccante alla cipolla. Sfera di cioccolato, lamponi alle tre consistenze e cioccolata calda.

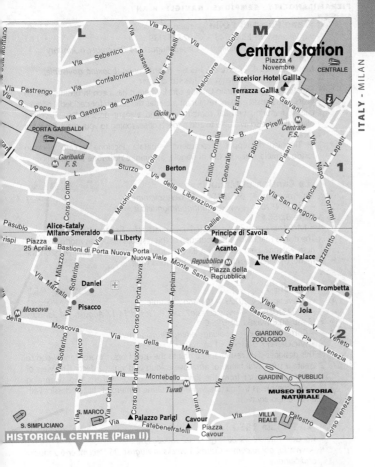

Iyo

XX 🏯 🏠 AC

Plan: **B1**

via Piero della Francesca 74 ⊠ 20154
– Ⓜ *Gerusalemme*
– 𝒞 *02 45476898 – www.iyo.it – Closed 2 weeks in August, Christmas Holidays, Monday and Tuesday lunch*
Menu 95 € – Carte 36/112 € – *(booking advisable)*
• Japanese • Minimalist • Design •

The presence of international chefs from Italy and Japan in this restaurant ensures that Iyo's distinctive culinary style is kept alive. The cuisine served here is always original, creative and inspired by Japan, and looks towards the future. The wine list is also excellent, with its selection of around 800 wines and a good choice of sake, with different varieties to accompany different dishes.

→ Ika somen: crudo di calamaro sfrangiato, caviale, verdure croccanti, uovo di quaglia. Gin dara: carbonaro nero d'Alaska in salsa di miso. Sfera di meringa al lime, mousse al cioccolato, sorbetto, composta di mela verde e menta.

ITALY - MILAN

Tano Passami l'Olio (Gaetano Simonato) XX 🏧
via Villoresi, 16 ✉ *20143* – ☎ *02 8394139* Plan: **B3**
*– www.tanopassamilolio.it – Closed August, 24 December-6 January
and Sunday*
Menu 85/125 € – Carte 95/145 € – *(dinner only) (booking advisable)*
• **Creative** • **Elegant** • **Classic décor** •
Situated near the Naviglio Grande canal, where it has been in business for 20
years. This classic, elegant restaurant provides the setting for decidedly original
cuisine featuring unusual combinations and elegant presentation. Excellent
olive oils are also available to add a touch of seasoning to your meal. Smoking
room.
➜ Tiramisù di seppia, mascarpone e patata. Piccione laccato nel suo
fondo e miele d'acacia. Gel di fragola, asparagi e riduzione al balsamico.

La Cantina di Manuela XX 🏠 ⅄ 🏧
via Procaccini 41 ✉ *20154* – Ⓜ *Gerusalemme* Plan: **J1**
– ☎ 02 3452034 – www.lacantinadimanuela.it
Carte 32/56 €
• **Modern cuisine** • **Neighbourhood** • **Friendly** •
The dishes that made the reputation of this restaurant, such as *risotto alla Milanese*, Fassone beef cheek in a Barolo sauce, and tiramisu, are always on the
menu. Updated traditional cuisine and good wine.

Ceresio 7 XxX ≤ 🏠 🏧
via Ceresio 7 ✉ *20123* – Ⓜ *Monumentale* Plan: **K1**
– ☎ 0231039221 – www.ceresio7.com – Closed 14-17 August, 1-4 January
Menu 40 € (weekdays)/95 €
– Carte 67/116 € – (bookings advisable at dinner)
• **Modern cuisine** • **Design** • **Trendy** •
This designer-style restaurant combines the use of brass, marble and wood to
create a successful blend of attractive colours and vintage decor. The view of
Milan (even better from the long outdoor terrace with its two swimming
pools) completes the picture, while the cuisine reinterprets Italian classics with
a contemporary twist.

La Pobbia 1850 XxX 🏠 ⅄ 🏧 ⇔
via Gallarate 92 ✉ *20151* – ☎ *02 38006641* Plan: **A1**
*– www.lapobbia.com – Closed 3 weeks in August, 26 December-6 January
and Sunday*
Menu 25/35 € – Carte 42/75 €
• **Lombardian** • **Elegant** • **Family** •
Housed in an old but elegant farmhouse, this restaurant is named after the
poplar trees growing alongside the road, which ran through open countryside
until as recently as the late 19C. Milanese cuisine and specialities from Lombardy take pride of place, with just a few options (almost all meat dishes) on
the menu. A new attractive outdoor dining area has recently been opened in
the garden.

Unico Milano XxX ≤ ⅄ 🏧
via Achille Papa 30, palazzo World Join Center Plan: **A1**
✉ *20149* – Ⓜ *Portello* – ☎ *02 39214847 – www.unicorestaurant.it*
– Closed Saturday lunch
Menu 25 € (weekday lunch)/140 € – Carte 75/126 €
• **Creative** • **Elegant** • **Design** •
From the 20th floor of the WJC Tower – home to the only restaurant offering
views of the city's entire skyline – Milan resembles a plastic model. The cuisine
served by the new chef here is creative in style.

Arrow's

XX

via A. Mantegna 17/19 ✉ 20154 – Ⓜ Gerusalemme – ✆ 02 341533 – www.ristorantearrows.it – Closed 3 weeks in August, Monday lunch and Sunday

Plan: **J1**

Menu 25 € (weekday lunch) – Carte 33/77 €

• Seafood • Family • Cosy •

Packed, even at midday, the atmosphere becomes cosier in the evening but the seafood cuisine, prepared according to tradition, remains the same.

Bistrot Leonardo – Leonardo Hotels Milan City Centre

XX

via Messina 10 ✉ 20154 – Ⓜ Cenisio – ✆ 02 318170 – www.fedegroup.it

Plan: **K1**

Carte 35/55 €

• Classic cuisine • Bistro • Elegant •

Bistrot Leonardo demonstrates real passion for local cuisine, and is always attentive to comments and requests from its refined and demanding guests.

Osteria di Porta Cicca

X

ripa di Porta Ticinese 51 ✉ 20143 – Ⓜ Porta Genova – ✆ 02 8372763 – www.osteriadiportacicca.com – Closed 14-21 August and Monday

Plan: **E3**

Menu 35/55 €

– Carte 44/85 € – *(dinner only except Sunday) (booking advisable)*

• Modern cuisine • Romantic • Cosy •

A welcoming, intimate ambience with a hint of Provence in an attractive canal side setting. The only sign of a traditional osteria is in the name – the cuisine is modern and innovative in style.

Esco Bistrò Mediterraneo

X

via Tortona 26 ✉ 20123 – Ⓜ Porta Genova – ✆ 028358144 – www.escobistromediterraneo.it – Closed 13-26 August, Saturday lunch and Sunday

Plan: **E3**

Menu 14 € (weekday lunch)/50 € – Carte 24/55 €

• Mediterranean cuisine • Trendy • Friendly •

This modern restaurant is informal and welcoming. Your first impression is that of finding yourself in an architect's studio, as a guest of the owner. However, this is just a preamble to the main event – that of savouring the delicious cuisine made by the talented chef. He manages to combine the use of top-quality ingredients with expert and innovative techniques.

Kiyo

X

via Carlo Ravizza 4 ✉ 20121 – Ⓜ Wagner – ✆ 02 4814295 – www.kiyo.it

Plan: **A2**

Menu 19 € (weekday lunch)/55 € – Carte 33/79 €

• Japanese • Chic • Minimalist •

The manager of this restaurant is Italian and the chef Japanese (the name kiyo means limpid and pure). Enjoy typical Japanese dishes followed by a choice of delicious European desserts in the wood-furnished dining rooms.

Mudec Bistrot

X

via Tortona 56 ✉ 20123 – Ⓜ Porta Genova – ✆ 02 84293706 – www.enricobartolini.net

Plan: **E3**

Menu 8/29 €

– Carte 29/52 € – *(lunch only except Thursday and Saturday)*

• Italian • Bistro •

A more basic version of chef Bartolini's cuisine is served at his ground-floor restaurant in the same museum. Open for breakfast, it serves mainly classic and seasonal dishes at lunchtime.

Al Pont de Ferr

X AC

Ripa di Porta Ticinese 55 ✉ 20143
Plan: **B3**
– Ⓜ Porta Genova FS – ✆ 02 89406277 – www.pontdeferr.it – Closed 24 December-6 January
Menu 20 € (weekday lunch)/75 € – Carte 36/90 €
• Creative • Osteria • Trendy •
This rustic osteria is situated near an old wrought-iron bridge alongside an artificial canal designed and built in 1179. This was initially used to irrigate the surrounding fields and is now frequented by boats. The cuisine is seasonal with an equal emphasis on fish and meat dishes.

Trattoria Montina

X 🏡 AC

via Procaccini 54 ✉ 20154 – Ⓜ Gerusalemme
Plan: **J2**
– ✆ 02 3490498 – www.trattoriamontina.it – Closed Easter, 5-27 August, 25 December-3 January, Monday lunch and Sunday
Carte 33/58 €
• Traditional cuisine • Friendly • Cosy •
Nice bistro atmosphere, tables close together, defused lighting in the evening in an establishment managed by twin brothers; seasonal national and Milanese dishes.

Leonardo Hotels Milan City Centre

&. AC 🛴 🚙

via Messina 10 ✉ 20154 – Ⓜ Cenisio – ✆ 02 318170
Plan: **K1**
– www.leonardo-hotels.com
122 rm ☲ – †109/360 € ††129/380 € – 8 suites
• Luxury • Business • Elegant •
In a district buzzing with shops and businesses, this hotel remains a solid choice amid the accommodation options in Milan. This is partly thanks to its management team who offer elegant, comfortable rooms and modern facilities.
ⓘⓄ **Bistrot Leonardo** – See restaurant listing

Milan Marriott Hotel

🍴 🛴 AC 🛴

via Washington 66 ✉ 20146 – Ⓜ Wagner
Plan: **A2**
– ✆ 02 48521 – www.milanmarriotthotel.com
321 rm – †105/400 € ††125/420 €
• Chain • Contemporary •
Not far from the bustling Corso Vercelli, this hotel combines a modern exterior with a more traditional interior decor. Functional guestrooms. Enjoy regional dishes and Mediterranean cuisine in the La Brasserie de Milan restaurant.

Wagner

AC

via Buonarroti 13 ✉ 20149 – Ⓜ Wagner
Plan: **A2**
– ✆ 02 463151 – www.hotelwagnermilano.it – Closed 12-19 August
49 rm ☲ – †80/699 € ††90/699 €
• Business • Traditional •
This hotel, next to the eponymous metro station, has attractive rooms with marble and modern furnishings.

Antica Locanda Leonardo

🛗 AC

corso Magenta 78 ✉ 20123 – Ⓜ Conciliazione
Plan: **E2**
– ✆ 02 48014197 – www.anticalocandaleonardo.com – Closed 6-19 August
17 rm ☲ – †85/380 € ††120/400 €
• Family • Cosy •
The luxury atmosphere combines with the family-style welcome in a hotel which overlooks a small inner courtyard, in an ideal location near the place where Leonardo da Vinci's painting of the "Last Supper" is housed.

LUXEMBOURG

LUXEMBOURG
LËTZEBUERG

SerrNovik/iStock

LUXEMBOURG
LËTZEBUERG

Xantana/iStock

Luxembourg may be small but it's perfectly formed. Standing high above two rivers on a sandstone bluff, its commanding position over sheer gorges may be a boon to modern visitors, but down the centuries that very setting has rendered it the subject of conquest on many occasions. Its eye-catching geography makes it a city of distinctive districts, linked by spectacular bridges spanning lush green valleys.

The absolute heart of the city is the old town, its most prominent landmarks the cathedral spires and the city squares with their elegant pastel façades – an ideal backdrop to the 'café culture' and a

worthy recipient of UNESCO World Heritage Status. Winding its way deep below to the south west is the river Pétrusse, which has its confluence with the river Alzette in the south east. Follow the Chemin de la Corniche, past the old city walls and along the Alzette's narrow valley to discover the ruins of The Bock, the city's first castle, and the Casemates, a labyrinth of rocky 17C and 18C underground defences. Directly to the south of the old town is the railway station quarter, while down at river level to the east is the altogether more attractive Grund district, whose northerly neighbours are Clausen and Pfaffenthal. Up in the north east, connected by the grand sounding Pont Grand-Duchesse Charlotte, is Kirchberg Plateau, a modern hub of activity for the EU.

EATING OUT

The taste buds of Luxembourg have been very much influenced by French classical cuisine, particularly around and about the Old Town, an area that becomes a smart open-air terrace in summer. Look out for the local speciality Judd mat Gaardebounen, smoked neck of pork with broad beans. The centre of town is an eclectic place to eat as it runs the gauntlet from fast-style pizzeria to expense account restaurants favoured by businessmen. A good bet for atmosphere is the Grund, which offers a wide variety of restaurants and price ranges, and is certainly the area that boasts the most popular cafés and pubs. A few trendy places have sprouted over recent times near the Casemates, and these too are proving to be pretty hot with the younger crowd. A service charge is included in your bill but if you want to tip, ten per cent is reasonable. The Grand Duchy produces its own white and sparkling wines on the borders of the Moselle. Over the last decade it has produced some interesting varieties but you'll rarely find these abroad, as they're eagerly snapped up by the locals.

Mosconi (Ilario Mosconi) $\quad$ XxxX 館 중 ✿

13 rue Münster ⊠ 2160 – 𝒞 54 69 94 – www.mosconi.lu $\quad$ Plan: **D1**
– closed 1 week Easter, last 3 weeks August, 24 December-early January,
Bank Holidays, Saturday lunch, Sunday and Monday
Menu 50 € (lunch) – Carte 99/139 €
• Italian • Elegant • Luxury •

Ilario and Simonetta Mosconi are an enthusiastic couple that proudly pay homage to the gastronomic traditions of Italy. Their Italian cuisine is as full of flair as it is steeped in flavours. The secret of their success no doubt lies in the infinite care and attention they devote to choosing their suppliers.
→ Maltagliata aux jaunes d'œufs, ragout de cabri et crème de menthe. Veau Sanato à la milanaise, asperge verte et jus de veau à la crème de truffe blanche. Caramel à la sicilienne.

Clairefontaine (Arnaud Magnier) $\quad$ XxxX 館 AC ✿ P

9 place de Clairefontaine ⊠ 1341 – 𝒞 46 22 11 $\quad$ Plan: **D1**
– www.restaurantclairefontaine.lu – closed 1 week Easter, last
2 weeks August-first week September, Christmas-New Year, first week
January, Bank Holidays, Saturday and Sunday
Menu 57 € (lunch)/104 € – Carte 86/120 €
• Creative French • Elegant •

This attractive restaurant with a terrace stands on an elegant square. It has traditional decor with old wooden panelling and contemporary furnishings. Creative, modern cuisine and astute wine pairings.
→ Déclinaison de thon rouge. Ris de veau cuit à l'unilatéral, purée de petits pois et fricassée de girolles. Soufflé chaud au Grand Marnier et ses madeleines à l'orange.

La Cristallerie – Hôtel Le Place d'Armes $\quad$ XxX AC 🥢

18 place d'Armes (1ˢᵗ floor) ⊠ 1136 – 𝒞 274 73 74 21 $\quad$ Plan: **C1**
– www.hotel-leplacedarmes.com – closed 22 July-20 August, 26-
30 December, 11-19 February, Saturday lunch, Sunday and Monday
Menu 78/228 € – Carte 175/208 €
• Modern French • Classic décor • Elegant •

In terms of decor, this crystal glassworks is the epitome of stylish, classical elegance. The chef amply demonstrates how subtle touches of creativity can enhance fine ingredients. His well-balanced creations feature the occasional Asian influence.
→ King crabe juste tiédi au caviar et cœur de cocotier. Hampe de bœuf grillée au feu de bois, anguille fumée et échalote noire. Cheese cake aux fruits rouges.

La Bergamote $\quad$ X

2 place de Nancy ⊠ 2212 – 𝒞 26 44 03 79 $\quad$ Plan: **A3**
– www.labergamote.lu – closed 1 week Easter, last 2 weeks August, late
December, Bank Holidays, Saturday lunch, Sunday and Monday
Menu 30 € (lunch)/37 € – Carte 47/65 €
• Modern cuisine • Trendy • Friendly •

Have you ever actually tasted bergamot? The subtle, fresh taste of this small citrus fruit is a recurring ingredient in Philippe Bridard's sun-drenched cuisine. Vitello tonnato, roast sea bream and shrimp polenta, without forgetting a few modern, French touches...

Kamakura $\quad$ X ✿

4 rue Münster ⊠ 2160 – 𝒞 47 06 04 – www.kamakura.lu $\quad$ Plan: **D1**
– closed 2 weeks Easter, last 2 weeks August-early September, late
December-early January, Bank Holidays, Saturday lunch and Sunday
Menu 12 € (lunch), 36/55 € – Carte 39/69 €
• Japanese • Minimalist •

The minimalist design of this Japanese restaurant has made no concessions to the West. It is named after the former capital of the Land of the Rising Sun and embodies the essence of Japanese cooking: understated, low-key presentation and virtuoso preparation. Kamakura celebrates its 30th anniversary in 2018!

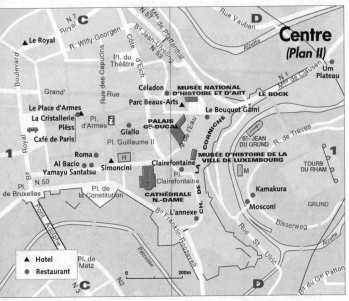

‖○ **Le Bouquet Garni**　　　　　　　XX 🖼 ✿ 🍽 (dinner)

Plan: **D1**

32 rue de l'Eau ✉ 1449 – 𝒞 26 20 06 20
– www.lebouquetgarni.lu – closed Bank Holidays, Sunday and Monday
Menu 30 € (lunch)/50 €
· Classic French · Romantic · Rustic ·

As the establishment's name suggests, the dishes are steeped in the aroma of French cuisine. The chef demonstrates his talent by the quality, sophistication and generosity of his recipes. The dining room, both elegant and rustic, provides the perfect backdrop to the menu.

‖○ **Schéiss**　　　　　　　　　　　XX 🖼 & ✿ 🅿

Plan: **A2**

142 Val Sainte-Croix ✉ 1370 – 𝒞 24 61 82
– www.scheiss.lu – closed Bank Holidays, Sunday and Monday
Menu 29 € (lunch), 56/78 € – Carte 51/75 €
· Modern cuisine · Design ·

Despite the elegant minimalist interior, you need have no fear of the usual hefty bill associated with such decor. Enjoy delicious, contemporary cuisine that is steeped in simplicity.

‖○ **Giallo**　　　　　　　　　　　　XX 🖼 🆒 ✿

Plan: **3E1**

24 rue du Curé ✉ 1368 – 𝒞 26 20 00 27
– www.giallo.lu – closed Monday dinner and Sunday
Menu 18 € (lunch) – Carte 46/70 € – (open until 11pm)
· Italian · Design ·

The two-storey water feature is one of the most striking elements of this handsome modern interior, setting the scene for the oh so stylish Giallo. The establishment is also rich in culinary ambition, backed up by first-class produce, which is perhaps unsurprising when the aim is to serve authentic Italian cuisine.

441

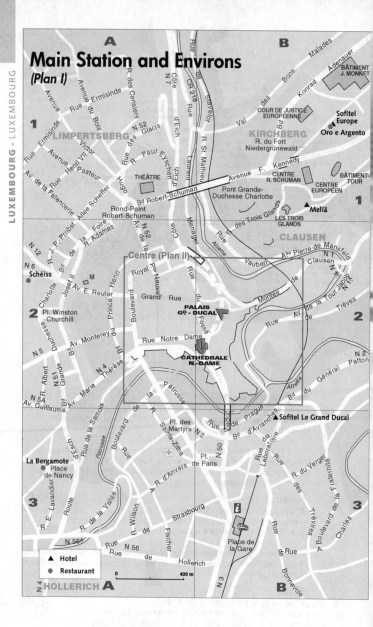

Main Station and Environs
(Plan I)

A **B**

Malades

Adenauer

BÂTIMENT
J. MONNET

Avenue Ermisinde

Rue Ermisinde

Rue du Bois

Côte N7

CR 218

Rue d'Elch

Rue Staveloi

Val des Bons

Konrad

1

LIMPERTSBERG

Victor

Avenue Henri VII

Rue Paul-Eyschen

R. St. Mathieu

COUR DE JUSTICE
EUROPÉENNE

KIRCHBERG
R. du Fort
Niedergrünewald

Sofitel
Europe

Oro e Argento

Rue Ermisinde

Avenue Henri Pasteur

Av. de la Faïencerie

Rue des Cerisiers

R. des Glacis

Hugo

Allée Scheffer

THÉÂTRE

B^d Robert-Schuman

Laurent Elch

Avenue F. Kennedy

CENTRE
R. SCHUMAN

CENTRE
EUROPÉEN

BÂTIMENT-
TOUR

1

Rond-Point
Robert-Schuman

Pont Grande-
Duchesse Charlotte

Meliä

LES TROIS
GLANDS

R. des Trois Glands

N 12

J. P.-Probst

R. de la Foire

R. Adames

Av. de la

N 52

Côte

Menager

Rue Alzette

Vauban

A^{ée} Pierre-de-Mansfeld

N 1

CLAUSEN

de Clausen

N 6

Schéiss

B^d Charlotte

Josef II

Av. E. Reuter

Prince Henri

Boulevard

Royal

R^{te} du Fossé

P^{te} Neuve

Grand' Rue

PALAIS
G^d - DUCAL

Montée

Av. de la Tour Jacob

de Trèves

2

Pl. Winston
Churchill

Duchesse

Rue Notre Dame

Rue

CATHÉDRALE
N.-DAME

N 2

Gén^{al} Patton

N 5

Av. Monterey

B^d Marie-Thérèse

N 4

Rue de la Pétrusse

Alzette

B^d du Général Patton

N 5A

R. Albert

B^d Grande

N 51

Av. Guillaume

Boulevard de la Semois

Pl. des
Martyrs

N 2

Viaduc

B^d de Prague

B^d d'Avranches

▲ Sofitel Le Grand Ducal

La Bergamote

Place
de Nancy

Pétrusse

R. d'Anvers

Pl.
de Paris

Rue du Laboratoire

R. du Verger

Boulevard de la Fraternité

3

R. E. Lavandier

Route

R. de la Vallée

Rue Wilson

Strasbourg

ℹ

Rue des Trévires

Rue A. Charles

3

N 56A

Rue Fischer

Rue de

Hollerich

Place de
la Gare

Rue de Rue

Bonnevoie

N 4

HOLLERICH **A**

N 3

B

▲ Hotel
● Restaurant

0 ——— 400 m

Centre (Plan II)

442

Plëss – Hôtel Le Place d'Armes

XX 🔲

18 place d'Armes ✉ 1136 – ℰ 274 73 74 11 — Plan: **C1**
– www.hotel-leplacedarmes.com
Menu 44 € (lunch)/56 € – Carte 53/78 €
• Classic cuisine • Brasserie •

Plëss means 'square' in Luxembourgish – an obvious reference to the Place d'Armes, which is where this lovely contemporary brasserie is located, right in the heart of town. Inside, it has a glamorous, urban atmosphere.

Roma

XX 🔲 ⇔

5 rue Louvigny ✉ 1946 – ℰ 22 36 92 – www.roma.lu — Plan: **C1**
– closed Sunday dinner and Monday
Carte approx. 55 €
• Italian • Friendly •

The Roma, Luxembourg's original Italian restaurant, specialises in homemade pasta, ultra fresh ingredients and, more unusually, themed festivals; all of which have enabled it to become a firm favourite with the locals. There is a popular range of daily specials.

Al Bacio

X 🔲

24 rue Notre-Dame ✉ 2240 – ℰ 27 99 48 81 – closed — Plan: **C1**
last 2 weeks August, late December-early January, Bank Holidays, Monday dinner, Tuesday dinner and Sunday
Menu 15 € (lunch)/42 €
• Italian • Trendy • Simple •

Presto, presto! The characteristic liveliness associated with Italian towns forms the backdrop to this popular restaurant. The regulars return for the authentic, super fresh cuisine. Who could resist such a delicious Italian kiss (bacio)?

L'annexe

X 🔲

7 rue du Saint Esprit ✉ 1475 – ℰ 26 26 25 07 — Plan: **E2**
– www.lannexe.lu – closed 24 December-1 January, Saturday lunch and Sunday
Menu 23 € (lunch), 33/50 € – Carte 36/58 €
• Market cuisine • Friendly • Contemporary décor •

Set in a lively, friendly district, this annex specialises in good wholesome victuals that any self-respecting brasserie would be proud of. The chef's traditional brasserie dishes, occasionally more sophisticated, are as mouth-watering as they are generous. Lovely terrace.

Café de Paris – Hôtel Le Place d'Armes

X 🔲 🚗

16 place d'Armes ✉ 1136 – ℰ 26 20 37 70 — Plan: **C1**
– www.hotel-leplacedarmes.com – closed Sunday dinner and Monday dinner in winter
Menu 35 € – Carte 34/54 €
• Regional cuisine • Bistro • Intimate •

A lively ambience and cosy décor set the scene in this inviting bistro. The chefs work with the best of Luxembourg's country produce to create fine, flavoursome dishes.

Céladon

X ⇔

1 rue du Nord ✉ 2229 – ℰ 47 49 34 – www.thai.lu — Plan: **C1**
– closed Bank Holidays, Saturday lunch and Sunday
Menu 45/57 € – Carte 43/56 €
• Thai • Intimate •

Lovers of Thai cuisine won't be disappointed by the fresh produce and authentic Asian flavours of Céladon. Vegetarians will no doubt be in seventh heaven with the range that is on offer.

⊩◯ **Yamayu Santatsu**   ✗ ⇔

26 rue Notre-Dame ⊠ 2240 – ℰ 46 12 49 – closed last   Plan: **C1**
week July-first 2 weeks August, late December-early January, Bank
Holidays, Sunday and Monday
Menu 16 € (lunch), 34/61 € – Carte 22/61 €
• Japanese • Minimalist •

Yamayu Santatsu's sushi is fully equal to that of Tokyo, explaining the establishment's popularity by gourmets who know how to appreciate the subtlety of Japanese cuisine. It has understated decor and private rooms for business meetings.

🏨 **Le Place d'Armes**   ᴵ⌂ Ⓜ ᵴᴬ 🚘

18 place d'Armes ⊠ 1136 – ℰ 27 47 37   Plan: **C1**
– www.hotel-leplacedarmes.com
21 rm – ♦270/570 € ♦♦270/570 € – ⟺ 26 € – 7 suites
• Grand Luxury • Historic • Elegant •

Although on the liveliest square in the town centre, this establishment is a real haven of peace. This former townhouse has been given a complete makeover. It exudes charm and an old Luxembourg atmosphere without feeling stuffy. A must.

❀ **La Cristallerie** • ⊩◯ **Plëss** • ⊩◯ **Café de Paris** – See restaurant listing

🏨 **Le Royal**   ✿ ᴵ⌂ ⊛ 🛎 🏊 & Ⓜ ᵴᴬ 🚘

12 boulevard Royal ⊠ 2449 – ℰ 241 61 61   Plan: **C1**
– www.leroyalluxembourg.com
190 rm – ♦180/400 € ♦♦180/400 € – ⟺ 31 € – 20 suites
• Grand Luxury • Business • Classic •

Nothing in this hotel is left to chance, to such an extent that a king would feel perfectly at home! Guests are waited on hand and foot by an army of staff that are available day and night. It is ideally located in the city's 'Wall Street' neighbourhood.

🏨 **Sofitel Le Grand Ducal**   ✿ ≤ ᴵ⌂ & Ⓜ

40 boulevard d'Avranches ⊠ 1160 – ℰ 24 87 71   Plan: **B3**
– www.sofitel.com
126 rm ⟺ – ♦180/253 € ♦♦180/253 € – 2 suites
• Business • Luxury •

This Sofitel offers everything you would expect from a top class, international hotel. The plush, understated ambience is offset by an interior that combines designer details with luxurious comfort. It also has a view over the town and the lush gardens of the Pétrusse Valley (from the bathtub in some rooms).

🏨 **Parc Beaux-Arts**   ✿ Ⓜ 🚘

1 rue Sigefroi ⊠ 2536 – ℰ 26 86 76   Plan: **D1**
– www.goeres-group.com
11 rm ⟺ – ♦170/495 € ♦♦190/515 € – 11 suites
• Historic • Luxury • Elegant •

This delightful hotel stands right next door to the Museum of Art and History and the Grand Ducal Palace, with whom it shares a taste for beauty and refinement. Each individually appointed spacious room has its own distinctive character. For lovers of sophisticated art de vivre!

🏨 **Simoncini**   Ⓜ

6 rue Notre-Dame ⊠ 2240 – ℰ 22 28 44   Plan: **C1**
– www.hotelsimoncini.lu
35 rm ⟺ – ♦160/190 € ♦♦180/240 €
• Business • Townhouse • Design •

This fashionable establishment, which is half hotel, half art gallery, is something of a wild card in Luxembourg's traditional hotel landscape. Well located right in the centre, it is ideal for a city trip and has a public car park nearby.

LUXEMBOURG - LUXEMBOURG

Mamma Bianca XX 🥢 & AC

33 avenue J.F. Kennedy (Ellipse Kirchberg 2) ⊠ 1855 Kirchberg
– ✆ 27 04 54 – www.mammabianca.lu – closed late December-early
January, Bank Holidays, Saturday and Sunday
Menu 22 € (lunch)/37 € – Carte 41/70 €
· Italian · Trendy ·
Mamma mia – what a restaurant! A spacious interior done up in a trendy, designer style, bordering on a lounge ambience. The menu features Italian classics. The chef rustles up dishes full of generous flavours and devoid of unnecessary frills. A delicious Bib Gourmand!

Bick Stuff X

95 rue de Clausen ⊠ 1342 Clausen – ✆ 26 09 47 31 – www.bickstuff.lu
– closed week after Pentecost, 2 weeks in August, late December, Thursday
dinner, Saturday lunch, Sunday dinner and Monday
Menu 23 € (lunch), 36/46 € – Carte 42/71 €
· Home cooking · Classic décor ·
A family-run establishment where you will instantly feel at home. Bick is a local word which literally means 'beak' in English but loosely translates as 'food'. Owners Virginie and Denis Laissy have the same goal: to serve good food in a relaxed atmosphere. Chef Denis rustles up reassuring classical recipes, adding his own distinctive touch. We recommend the set menu.

🍽️ Oro e Argento – Hôtel Sofitel Europe XXX AC P

Plan: B1
6 rue du Fort Niedergrünewald (European Centre)
⊠ 2015 Kirchberg – ✆ 43 77 68 70 – www.sofitel.com – closed 31 July-
1 September and Saturday lunch
Menu 47 € (lunch), 77/80 € – Carte 54/80 €
· Italian · Intimate ·
An attractive Italian restaurant in a luxury hotel. Contemporary cuisine is served to a backdrop of plush decor with a Venetian touch. Intimate atmosphere and stylish service.

🍽️ Um Plateau X 🍸 🥢 ✿ 🍴

Plan: D1
6 Plateau Altmünster ⊠ 1123 Clausen – ✆ 26 47 84 26
– www.umplateau.lu – closed Saturday lunch and Sunday
Menu 24 € (lunch) – Carte 39/66 €
· Modern cuisine · Chic ·
Diners appreciate the smart lounge ambience and cosy interior of this restaurant. After a glass of wine in the lively bar, treat yourself to a meal in which fine produce takes pride of place. Authentic flavours and painstaking preparations are the hallmarks of this establishment.

🏨 Sofitel Europe ♨ ₤₃ & AC 🛁 🚗

Plan: B1
4 rue du Fort Niedergrünewald (European Centre)
⊠ 2015 Kirchberg – ✆ 43 77 61 – www.sofitel.com
105 rm – †129/480 € ††157/508 € – ⊡ 28 € – 4 suites
· Business · Grand Luxury · Contemporary ·
A bold, oval shaped hotel at the heart of the European Institutions district, with a central atrium and spacious, extremely comfortable guestrooms. The service is attentive and friendly, as you would expect from this upmarket chain.
🍽️ **Oro e Argento** – See restaurant listing

🏨 Meliã ❄ ♨ ≤ ₤₃ 🏠 & AC 🛁

Plan: B1
1 Park Dräi Eechelen ⊠ 1499 Kirchberg – ✆ 27 33 31
– www.melia-luxembourg.com
160 rm ⊡ – †95/550 € ††100/570 € – 1 suite
· Business · Functional ·
The first hotel of this Spanish chain in Benelux, located next to the conference centre. Rooms are stylish, comfortable and functional. Lovely view of the city.

AMSTERDAM

● Rotterdam

NETHERLANDS
NEDERLAND

AleksandarGeorgiev/iStock

AMSTERDAM
AMSTERDAM

AndreyKrav/iStock

AMSTERDAM IN...

→ **ONE DAY**
   A trip on a canal boat,
   Rijksmuseum, Anne Frank
   Museum, Van Gogh Museum.

→ **TWO DAYS**
   Begijnhof, shopping in the
   '9 Straatjes', Vondelpark,
   evening in a brown café.

→ **THREE DAYS**
   The Jordaan, Plantage
   and Entrepotdok, red light
   district.

Once visited, never forgotten; that's Amsterdam's great claim to fame. Its endearing horseshoe shape – defined by 17C canals cut to drain land for a growing population – allied to finely detailed gabled houses, has produced a compact city centre of aesthetically splendid symmetry and matchless consistency. Exploring the city on foot or by bike is the real joy here and visitors rarely need to jump on a tram or bus.

'The world's biggest small city' displays a host of distinctive characteristics, ranging from the world-famous red light district to the cosy and convivial brown cafés, from the wonderful art galleries

and museums to the quirky shops, and the medieval churches to the tree-lined waterways with their pretty bridges. There's the feel of a northern Venice, but without the hallowed and revered atmosphere. It exists on a human scale, small enough to walk from one end to the other. Those who might moan that it's just too small should stroll along to the former derelict docklands on the east side and contemplate the shiny new apartments giving the water-front a sleek, 21C feel. Most people who come here, though, are just happy to cosy up to old Amsterdam's sleepy, relaxed vibe. No European city does snug bars better: this is the place to go for cats kipping on beat-up chairs and candles flickering on wax-encrusted tables…

EATING OUT

Amsterdam is a vibrant and multi-cultural city and, as such, has a wide proliferation of restaurants offering a varied choice of cuisines, where you can eat well without paying too much. Head for an eetcafe and you'll get a satisfying three course meal at a reasonable price. The Dutch consider the evening to be the time to eat your main meal, so some restaurants shut at lunchtime. Aside from the eetcafe, you can top up your middle-of-day fuel levels with simple, home-cooked meals and local beers at a bruin (brown) café, or for something lighter, a café specialising in coffee and cake. If you wish to try local specialities, number one on the hit list could be rijsttafel or 'rice table', as the Dutch have imported much from their former colonies of Indonesia. Fresh raw herring from local waters is another nutritious local favourite, as are apple pies and pancakes of the sweet persuasion; often enjoyed with a hot chocolate. Restaurants are never too big but are certainly atmospheric and busy, so it's worth making reservations.

Librije's Zusje Amsterdam – Hotel Waldorf Astoria ✿✿ XxxX

Herengracht 542 ⊠ 1017 CG – ✆ (0 20) 718 46 43   AC ✿ ⊞
– www.librijeszusje.com   Plan: **G3**
– closed 27 and 28 April, 30 July-21 August, 1-18 January, Sunday and
Monday
Menu 102/150 €
– Carte 80/124 € – *(dinner only except Friday and Saturday)*
• Creative • Luxury • Elegant •

Extraordinarily beautiful and classy! This refined, classic restaurant offers a true
fine dining experience. The food is elegant, with a unique interplay of textures
and tastes that is spot on, creating a wonderful harmony where every bite surprises. Definitely worth a visit!
➜ Makreel met venkelsap en schelvislever. Rode mul met pompoenboter
en cacao. Avocadosorbet met appel, komkommer en yoghurt.

&Moshik (Moshik Roth) ✿✿ XxX AC ✿

Oosterdokskade 5 ⊠ 1011 AD – ✆ (0 20) 260 20 94   Plan: **H1**
– www.samhoudplaces.com
– closed Monday and Tuesday
Menu 65 € (lunch)/170 €
– Carte 111/191 € – *(dinner only except Friday and Saturday)*
• Creative • Design •

Moshik Roth invites you on an adventure. This fashionable establishment will
take you from one pleasant surprise to the next. The chef knows how to combine inventiveness with refinement for a fantastic flavour experience, extracting
the best from top-quality ingredients with absolute precision.
➜ Carpaccio van coquilles met tomaat, watermeloen en druiven. Tarbot
met risotto van zwarte rijst, salpicon van kreeft en schaaldieren. Millefeuille
met een piña coladacrème.

Bord'Eau – Hotel de l'Europe ✿ XxxX 舘 ≤ 斎 AC ✿ ⊞ P

Nieuwe Doelenstraat 2 ⊠ 1012 CP – ✆ (0 20) 531 16 19   Plan: **G2**
– www.bordeau.nl
– closed 5-28 August, 1-16 January, Saturday lunch, Sunday and Monday
Menu 48 € (lunch), 128/176 €
– Carte 114/194 €
• Creative • Elegant • Chic •

This luxurious restaurant is a real gem, where guests can feast their eyes on the
stylish interior, as well as the delicacies that are served here. The cooking style is
original and worldly, and always maintains a good balance between the
intense, contrasting flavours. The cheese selection may well be the best in the
country.
➜ Rode mul met jus 'à la becasse', artisjok barigoule en toast. Gelakte
anjouduif met dimsum van koolrabi en de boutjes, shiitake en salmis
saus. Roomijs van donkere chocolade, koffie en Roquefort.

Bridges – Hotel Sofitel The Grand ✿ XxX 舘 斎 & AC ✿ ⊞

O.Z. Voorburgwal 197 ⊠ 1012 EX – ✆ (0 20) 555 35 60   Plan: **G2**
– www.bridgesrestaurant.nl
– closed Monday lunch
Menu 30 € (lunch)/89 €
– Carte 55/82 €
• Seafood • Elegant •

The dishes on offer in this beautiful fish restaurant combine refinement, surprise, originality and quality, and are worthy of the utmost praise. Overall,
good quality, reasonably priced cuisine.
➜ Gamba in kataïfi met pata negra, bospeen, mandarijn en ras-el-hanout-
roomijsje. Krokante rode mul en langoustine met lardo, Waldorf ravioli en
beurre blanc. Sticky toffee cake met appel en calavadosroom.

The Duchess ✿ XxX AC
Spuistraat 172 ⊠ 1012 VT – ℰ (0 20) 811 33 22 Plan: **F2**
– www.the-duchess.com
Carte 60/85 € – *(open until 11pm)*
• Mediterranean cuisine • Chic • Elegant •

The grandeur of this former ticket office is impressive. This is a magnificent venue, where the use of dark marble and the Belle Époque atmosphere lend The Duchess real flair. The beautiful Molteni kitchen turns out generous, classic dishes. Where else would you find such a delicious, traditional beef Wellington?
→ Kreeft en koningskrab met avocado en tomaat. Runderhaas Wellington. Tartelette Tropézienne met oranjebloesembrioche, vanilleschuimpje en geroosterde amandelen.

Vinkeles ✿ – Hotel The Dylan XxX
Keizersgracht 384 ⊠ 1016 GB – ℰ (0 20) 530 20 10 Plan: **F2**
– www.vinkeles.com
– closed 29 July-14 August, 24-26 December, 1-16 January, Sunday and Monday
Menu 130 €
– Carte 74/146 € – *(dinner only)*
• Creative • Friendly • Elegant •

The original features of this 18C bakery make Vinkeles a special place to eat, especially in combination with the stylish interior. The food deserves the highest praise, as the creative chef succeeds in bringing excitement and nuance to the plate, while never losing sight of natural flavours.
→ Geglaceerde kalfszwezerik met ossenstaartbouillon, fregola en groene tomaat. Wilde zeebaars met serranoham, radijs en pijlinktvis. Rabarber met macadamianoten, havermout en vlierbloesem.

The White Room ✿ – NH Grand Hotel Krasnapolsky XxX & AC 🚗
Dam 9 ⊠ 1012 JS – ℰ (020) 554 94 54 Plan: **L1**
– www.restaurantthewhiteroom.com
– closed 17 July-15 August, 2-17 January, Tuesday lunch, Wednesday lunch, Sunday and Monday
Menu 33 € (lunch), 65/105 € – Carte 87/96 €
– *(set menu only at weekends)*
• Modern cuisine • Classic décor • Elegant •

You can imagine yourself as an Austrian prince or princess in this white and gold dining room, which dates from 1885 and magnificently combines classical elegance with modern furnishings. Citrus flavours and exotic spices are combined in a creative interplay. The chef is a strong technician and understands what refinement really means.
→ Amsterdams tuintje : groentenpalet met kruiden en specerijen. Tarbot met bloemkool, lardo di colonnata en beurre noisette. Perzik met room, ras-el-hanout en citroen.

Vermeer ✿ – Hotel NH Barbizon Palace XxX & AC ⇔ 🚗 P
Prins Hendrikkade 59 ⊠ 1012 AD – ℰ (0 20) 556 48 85 Plan: **G1**
– www.restaurantvermeer.nl
– closed 22 July-13 August and Sunday
Menu 65/85 € – *(dinner only)*
• Organic • Design • Elegant •

The simple design makes this beautiful restaurant a relaxed spot. Chef Naylor offers food with a personal touch, with generous use of produce from his own vegetable garden, located on the hotel roof. His dishes are well thought through and inventive, creating delicious contrasts and harmonies for an intense flavour experience.
→ Met appel en zurkel gemarineerde makreel, komkommer, yoghurt en avocado. Gebraden lamsrug met knoflook en munt, gebakken artisjok en walnootjus. Slaatje van aardbeien met agavelikeur en chiboustcrème met limoen.

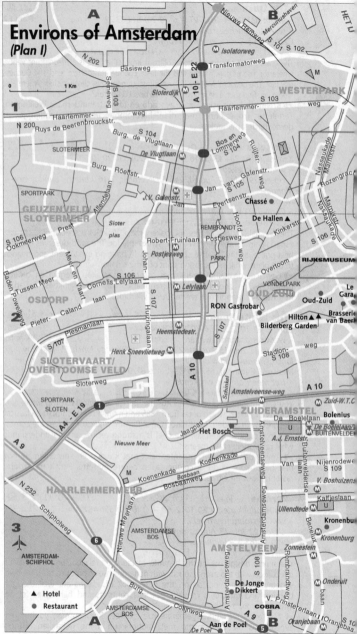

Environs of Amsterdam
(Plan I)

0   1 Km

▲ Hotel
● Restaurant

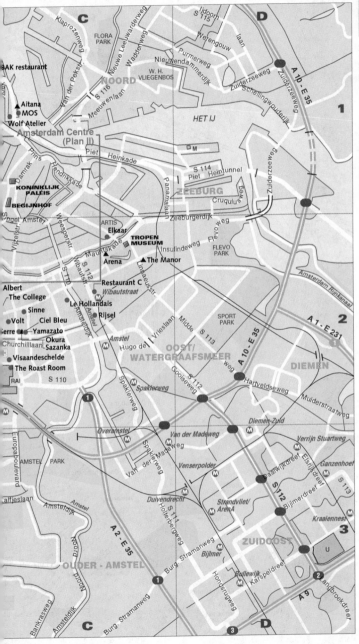

C

Klaprozenweg

FLORA PARK

BAK restaurant

NOORD

W. H. VLIEGENBOS

Nieuwe Leeuwarderweg

Waddenweg

Van de Pekstr.

S 116

Meeuwenlaan

Aitana
MOS
Wolf Atelier

Amsterdam Centre (Plan II)

Prins Hendrikkade

Piet Heinkade

Damrak

KONINKLIJK PALEIS

BEGIJNHOF

Singel Amstel

Vijzelstr.

Weesperstr.

Wibautstr.

S 112

S 110

ARTIS

Elkaar

Mauritskade

TROPEN MUSEUM

Arena

The Manor

Linnaeusstr.

Restaurant C

Wibautstraat

Albert

The College

Sinne

Volt   Ciel Bleu

Serre   Yamazato

Churchilllaan   Okura
Sazanka

Visaandeschelde

The Roast Room

RAI   S 110

Le Hollandais

Rijsel

Amstel

Amsteldijk

Amstel

Hugo de   Vrieslaan   Midde   S 113

OOST/ WATERGRAAFSMEER

SPORT PARK

Gooiseweg

A 10 - E 35

Hartveldseweg

DIEMEN

Muiderstraatweg

Spaklerweg

Spaklerweg

S 112

Overamstel

Van der Madeweg

Diemen-Zuid

Verrijn Stuartweg

Elsrijkdreef

Ganzenhoef

S 113

AMSTEL PARK

Van der Madeweg

Venserpolder

Daalwijkdreef

S 112

Bijlmerdreef

altjeslaan   Amstel

Amsteldijk

Duivendrecht

S 111

Holtebregweg

Strandvliet/ ArenA

Kraaiennest

U

Europaboulevard

A 2 - E 35

OUDER - AMSTEL

Bankraasweg

Amsteldijk   Noord   Brug

Burg. Stramanweg

Burg. Stramanweg

Bijlmer

Hondsrugweg

ZUIDOOST

Bullewijk   Karspeldreef

A 9

Gaasperdreef

HET IJ

M

Piet Heintunnel

S 114

ZEEBURG

Panamalaan

Zeeburgerdijk

Cruquius

FLEVO PARK

Insulindeweg

Flevoweg

Amsterdam Rijnkanaal

A 1 - E 231

A 10 - E 35

Purmerweg

Wingerdgouw

laan

Zuiderzeeweg

Schellingwoudedijk

Zuiderzeeweg

A 10 - E 35

1

2

3

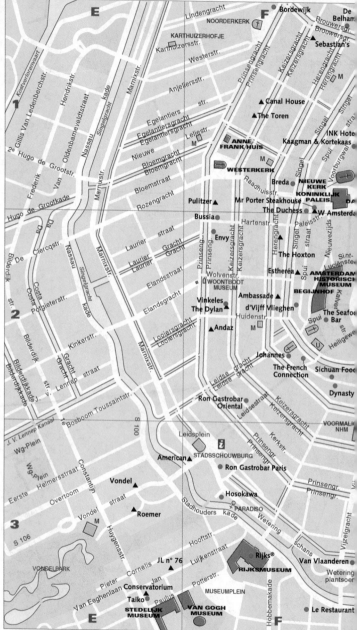

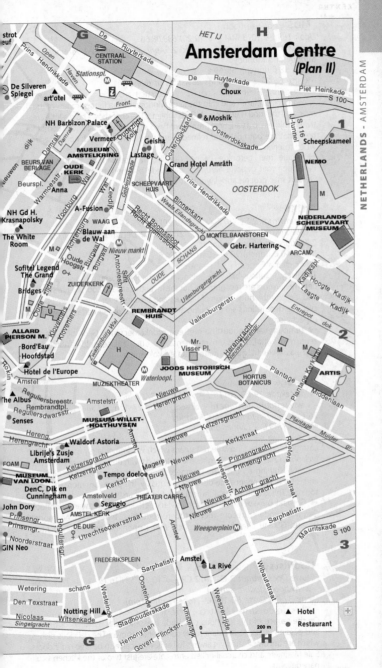

Amsterdam Centre
(Plan II)

HET IJ

De Ruyterkade
Open Haven Front
Prins Hendrikkade
CENTRAAL STATION
Stationspl.
De Ruyterkade
Piet Heinkade
S 100
Choux
S 116
IJ-tunnel
Scheepskameel
1
NEMO
M
strot
euf
De Silveren Spiegel
art'otel
NH Barbizon Palace
Vermeer
Geisha
Lastage
Oosterdokskade
Oosterdoksstraat
&Moshik
Oude Zijds Kolk
Grand Hotel Amrâth
Prins Hendrikkade
OOSTERDOK
NEDERLANDS SCHEEPVAART MUSEUM
MUSEUM AMSTELKRING
OUDE KERK
SCHEEPVAART HUIS
Anna
A-Fusion
NH Gd H. Krasnapolsky
WAAG
Blauw aan de Wal
The White Room
Nieuw markt
Waals Eilandsgracht
Binnenkant
Recht Boomssloot
Recht Boomssloot
MONTELBAANSTOREN
Gebr. Hartering
ARCAM
Kadijksplein
Hoogte Kadijk
Laagte Kadijk
Entrepot dok
M
M
2
ARTIS
Sofitel Legend The Grand
ZUIDERKERK
Sint Antoniesbreestr.
OUDE SCHANS
Uilenburgergracht
Bridges
M
REMBRANDT HUIS
Valkenburgerstr.
ALLARD PIERSON M.
Herengracht
Nieuwe Herengr.
Bord'Eau
Hoofdstad
Mr. Visser Pl.
M
M
Hotel de l'Europe
H
JOODS HISTORISCH MUSEUM
Amstel
MUZIEKTHEATER
Waterlooplein
HORTUS BOTANICUS
Plantage Middenlaan
Plantage Kerklaan
The Albus
Reguliersbreestr.
Rembrandtpl.
Reguliersdwarsstr.
Senses
Amstelstr.
Nieuwe Herengracht
Keizersgracht
Kerkstraat
Plantage Muidergracht
Roeters
Hereng.
Herengracht
Waldorf Astoria
MUSEUM WILLET-HOLTHUYSEN
Nieuwe Keizersgracht
Librije's Zusje Amsterdam
FOAM
MUSEUM VAN LOON
DenC, Dik en Cunningham
Keizersgracht
Kerkstr.
Tempo doeloe
Magere Brug
Nieuwe Prinsengracht
Prinsengracht
Nieuwe Achter gracht
Achter gracht
Weesperstr.
Nieuwe
John Dory
Prinsengr.
Prinsengr.
Segugio
Amstelveld
THEATER CARRÉ
Nieuwe
Sarphatistr.
Noorderstraat
GIN Neo
AMSTEL KERK
DE DUIF
Utrechtsedwarsstraat
Amstel
Weesperplein M
Mauritskade
S 100
3
FREDERIKSPLEIN
Sarphatistr.
Amstel
La Rivé
Wibautstraat
Wetering schans
Den Texstraat
Westeinde
Oosteinde
Amsterdam
Weesperzijde
Nicolaas Witsenkade
Notting Hill
Stadhouderskade
Nicolaas Singelgracht
Hemonylaan
Govert Flinckstr.

▲ Hotel
● Restaurant

0   200 m

G   H

455

MOS (Egon van Hoof)
%%% XX 🏠 ✿

IJdok 185 ✉ 1013 MM – ℰ (0 20) 638 08 66   Plan: **G1**
– www.mosamsterdam.nl – closed 27 April, 31 December-1 January,
Sunday and Monday
Menu 38 € (lunch), 55/69 €
– Carte 66/82 € – (bookings advisable at dinner)
• Creative French • Trendy • Fashionable •

The interior is relaxed and chic, the large windows offer a fantastic view of the IJ
river, and the food is delicious. MOS is sublime. The chef shows how a little creativity conjures up a variety of prominent flavours, producing balanced combinations that are both rich and refined. Guests are advised to ask about parking
when reserving.
→ Slaatje met gerookte paling, pastilles van takuan en zwarte sesam.
Parelhoen met gepofte aardpeer, gebrande pruimen en macadamiasausje.
Dessert met groene appel, yoghurt en verbena.

RIJKS®
XX 🏠 🕭 🚗

Museumstraat 2 ✉ 1077 XX – ℰ (0 20) 674 75 55   Plan: **F3**
– www.rijksrestaurant.nl – closed 27 April, 31 December lunch, 1 and
2 January and Sunday dinner
Menu 40 € (lunch)/70 € – Carte 42/54 €
• Modern French • Brasserie •

This lively, luxurious brasserie belonging to the Rijksmuseum is a surefire winner. The flavours are recognizable but the inventive style of cooking is a surprise
and, despite the huge range of flavours and textures, everything is well-balanced. The descriptions are intriguing and exciting and dishes certainly live up to
expectations.
→ Tempura van langoustine met een rodekerriecrème. Gegrilde kalfszwezerik met witlof, appel en rammenas. Es buah : ijsgekoelde fruitcocktail
met passievrucht, guave, mata-mata en kokosnoot.

Lastage (Rogier van Dam)
X 🅰

Geldersekade 29 ✉ 1011 EJ – ℰ (0 20) 737 08 11   Plan: **G1**
– www.restaurantlastage.nl – closed 26 and 27 April, 23 July-12 August,
26 December-4 January and Monday
Menu 47/89 € – (dinner only)
• Creative • Friendly • Bistro •

Lastage is an appealing little restaurant which will immediately make you feel
welcome. Chef Van Dam delights the taste buds with dishes that are full of personality. Nothing on the plate is unnecessary – every ingredient adds interest
and is there to enhance the dish. For the quality, the prices are more than reasonable. This is a little establishment with big flavours!
→ Gerookt buikspek met asperges, rivierkreeft, kropsla en zwarte knoflook.
Gegrilde runderentrecote met kardoen, rode biet, bloedworst en moriel-
jessaus. Gâteau chaud van chocolade met karnemelk- en passievruchten-
roomijs.

Hoofdstad – Hotel de l'Europe
XX 🏠 🅰

Nieuwe Doelenstraat 2 ✉ 1012 CP – ℰ (0 20) 531 16 19   Plan: **G2**
– www.hoofdstadbrasserie.nl
Menu 37 € – Carte 60/102 € – (open until 11pm)
• Classic cuisine • Bistro • Friendly •

On the terrace of this luxurious canal-side brasserie, with its views of bridges
and passing boats, Amsterdam really comes into its own. The delicious dishes,
which are uncomplicated yet always full of flavour, can also be enjoyed indoors.
Sole Meunière and charcoal-grilled entrecote are just two of the kitchen's culinary delights.

Van Vlaanderen
XX 😊 AK ⇔

Weteringschans 175 ✉ *1017 XD – 𝒞 (0 20) 622 82 92* — Plan: **F3**
– www.restaurant-vanvlaanderen.nl – closed 27 December-3 January,
Saturday lunch, Sunday and Monday
Menu 30 € (lunch), 37/60 € – Carte 53/75 €
• Modern cuisine • Classic décor •

Van Vlaanderen has long been recognised as the place to go for the good things in life. It has a pleasant location in the centre of Amsterdam with its own jetty on the patio. The restaurant's success lies in attentive service and a young, spirited team whose enthusiasm is evident in the modern, original versions of the classic dishes served here.

A-Fusion
X

Zeedijk 130 ✉ *1012 BC – 𝒞 (0 20) 330 40 68* — Plan: **G1**
– www.a-fusion.nl
Menu 18 € (lunch), 34/45 € – Carte 23/41 € – *(open until 11pm)*
• Asian • Brasserie • Bistro •

A fusion of Chinese and Japanese cuisine in the heart of Amsterdam's Chinatown. This restaurant boasts a grill, a sushi bar and a wok kitchen. Be sure to try the prawn dim sum, the beef with black pepper sauce and the oysters with ginger. Alternatively, give the cooks carte blanche to come up with some surprising choices.

Bistrot Neuf
X 🕸 AK

Haarlemmerstraat 9 ✉ *1013 EH – 𝒞 (0 20) 400 32 10* — Plan: **G1**
– www.bistrotneuf.nl
Menu 23 € (lunch), 34/50 € – Carte 28/59 €
• Classic cuisine • Lyonnaise bistro • Friendly •

With its clean, modern design, this relaxed bistro is ideally located in a lively area of Amsterdam. Traditional French dishes exhibit original Amsterdam flair and are impeccably cooked to bring out the true flavours of the ingredients. Efficient service.

Ron Gastrobar Paris
X

Kleine-Gartmanplantsoen 11a ✉ *1017 RP – 𝒞 (0 20)* — Plan: **K2**
496 19 43 – www.rongastrobarparis.nl
Menu 27 € (lunch)/37 € – Carte approx. 42 €
• Classic French • Bistro •

The dulcet tones of French chansonniers ring out in this interior reminiscent of 1950s Paris. This big bistro is yet another wonderful creation by Ron Blaauw; his high standards are evident in the food, which features dishes prepared according to old recipes and presented with a modern twist.

Scheepskameel
X 😊

Kattenburgerstraat 7 ✉ *1018 JA – 𝒞 (0 20) 337 96 80* — Plan: **M1**
– www.scheepskameel.nl – closed 23 December-1 January, Sunday and
Monday
Menu 35 € – Carte 29/51 € – *(dinner only)*
• Traditional cuisine • Brasserie • Trendy •

Scheepskameel is a lively, relaxed establishment, providing honest, straightforward food. Everything here starts with top-quality ingredients, prepared without fuss and beautifully seasoned. The wine list is comprised entirely of German wines and accompanies the food perfectly.

Tempo doeloe
X AK

Utrechtsestraat 75 ✉ *1017 VJ – 𝒞 (0 20) 625 67 18* — Plan: **G3**
– www.tempodoeloerestaurant.nl – closed 27 April, 25, 26 and
31 December-1 January and Sunday
Menu 35/75 € – Carte 35/63 € – *(dinner only)*
• Indonesian • Traditional décor • Exotic décor •

Regular diners at Tempo doeloe or 'Times Gone By' find it difficult to hide their enthusiasm when they visit this restaurant. They know that an Indonesian feast like no other in Amsterdam awaits them. The food here is authentically Indonesian, with no concessions to Western tastes. Selamat makan!

La Rive – Hotel Amstel XxxX ≤ 😤 🖾 ⇔ 🏖 **P**

Prof. Tulpplein 1 ⊠ 1018 GX – 𝒞 (0 20) 520 32 64 Plan: **H3**
– www.restaurantlarive.com – closed 2-21 January
Menu 90/125 € – Carte 110/159 € – *(dinner only)*
• Modern French • Chic • Elegant •
On entering this refined establishment, guests will immediately sense its rich history, although it is the Amstel that really steals the show here, thanks to the wonderful location on the riverbank. This is a classic restaurant, where the chef also works with the latest trends, taking inspiration from Asia and playing with the acidity balance of his food.

De Silveren Spiegel XxX 😤 ⇔

Kattengat 4 ⊠ 1012 SZ – 𝒞 (0 20) 624 65 89 Plan: **L1**
– www.desilverenspiegel.com – closed Sunday
Menu 50/78 € – Carte approx. 70 € – *(dinner only)*
• Modern French • Historic • Friendly •
The authentic interior of these two buildings with stepped gables, dating back to 1614, has stood the test of time, retaining features such as a warm open hearth with matching tiles. In stark contrast with the decor, the food is modern down to the last detail. The young chef works mainly with Dutch ingredients and has a well-deserved reputation.

MOMO XX & 🖾

Hobbemastraat 1 ⊠ 1071 XZ – 𝒞 (0 20) 671 74 74 Plan: **F3**
– www.momo-amsterdam.com
Menu 65/99 € – Carte 55/117 € – *(open until 11pm) (bar lunch)*
• Asian influences • Trendy • Brasserie •
MOMO is still one of the city's hotspots, with fusion cuisine in a fashionable setting. Bento (Japanese lunch box) at lunchtime and a menu designed for sharing in the evening.

Taiko – Hotel Conservatorium XX & 🖾

Van Baerlestraat 27 ⊠ 1071 AN – 𝒞 (0 20) 570 00 00 Plan: **E3**
– www.conservatoriumhotel.com – closed Sunday
Menu 85/115 € – Carte 50/165 € – *(dinner only)*
• Asian influences • Elegant • Intimate •
Taiko is an atmospheric, cosmopolitan restaurant and deliciously trendy. The establishment serves a contemporary take on Asian cuisine. It is beautifully presented, diverse and pure in flavour.

Anna XX 🖾

Warmoesstraat 111 ⊠ 1012 JA – 𝒞 (0 20) 428 11 11 Plan: **G1**
– www.restaurantanna.nl – closed 26 December
Menu 37/60 € – Carte 35/63 € – *(dinner only)*
• Modern cuisine • Fashionable • Trendy •
Diners will find Anna a lively spot. The restaurant is located in the heart of the red light district, and the cosmopolitan venue also offers an infectiously relaxed atmosphere. The diverse range of balanced dishes is similarly exciting, while the set menu is always an attractive option.

Blauw aan de Wal XX 🏵 😤 🖾 ⇔

O.Z. Achterburgwal 99 ⊠ 1012 DD – 𝒞 (0 20) 330 22 57 Plan: **G2**
– www.blauwaandewal.com – closed Sunday
Menu 39/68 € – *(dinner only until 11pm) (tasting menu only)*
• Market cuisine • Rustic • Friendly •
A popular restaurant at the end of a cul-de-sac in the lively red light district. Discreet décor, simple and tasty modern cuisine, good wine selection and a shady terrace.

🕯️ **Bordewijk** XX � AC
Noordermarkt 7 ✉ *1015 MV –* ℰ *(0 20) 624 38 99* Plan: **F1**
– www.bordewijk.nl – closed Sunday and Monday
Menu 40 € – Carte 38/67 € – *(dinner only)*
• Modern cuisine • Friendly • Trendy •
A popular restaurant due to its modern menu with inventive touches and its
minimalist decor comprising bare floorboards, Formica tables and designer
chairs. It has a noisy atmosphere when busy.

🕯️ **Bussia** XX ⇔
Reestraat 28 ✉ *1016 DN –* ℰ *(0 20) 627 87 94* Plan: **F2**
– www.bussia.nl – closed Tuesday lunch, Wednesday lunch and Monday
Menu 36 € (lunch), 46/79 € – Carte 55/69 €
• Italian • Intimate • Trendy •
A restrained yet stylish modern restaurant that conjures up Italian cuisine with a
French influence. This is accompanied by an impressive choice of fine Italian
wines presented by the female owner. As a bonus, the open kitchen enables
you to look behind the scenes.

🕯️ **DenC, Dik en Cunningham** XX AC ⇔
Kerkstraat 377 ✉ *1017 HW –* ℰ *(0 20) 422 27 66* Plan: **G3**
– www.restaurantdenc.nl – closed Sunday
Menu 37/65 € – Carte 46/65 € – *(dinner only)*
• Creative French • Bistro • Classic décor •
The deer heads on the walls of this contemporary restaurant hint at chef Dik's
hunter-family upbringing and, unsurprisingly, his cooking puts the spotlight
firmly on game. The menu offers good value for money. Sommelier Cunningham's choice of wines make a good match.

🕯️ **Dynasty** XX � AC ⇔
Reguliersdwarsstraat 30 ✉ *1017 BM –* ℰ *(0 20)* Plan: **F2**
626 84 00 – www.fer.nl – closed 27 December-31 January and Tuesday
Menu 45/68 € – Carte 38/69 € – *(dinner only until 11pm)*
• Chinese • Elegant • Exotic décor •
A pleasant, long-standing restaurant featuring cuisine from around Asia. The
trendy, exotic décor is warm and colourful. There's a lovely terrace at the back
and service is attentive.

🕯️ **Hosokawa** XX AC ⇔
Max Euweplein 22 ✉ *1017 MB –* ℰ *(0 20) 638 80 86* Plan: **F3**
– www.hosokawa.nl – closed 27 April, 31 December and 1 January
Menu 50/95 € – Carte 36/161 € – *(dinner only)*
• Teppanyaki • Fashionable • Design •
Experienced chef Hiromichi Hosokawa has mastered Japanese cuisine down to
the fine details. In 1992 he opened this smart restaurant, where he continues to
prepare traditional teppanyaki, robatayaki and sushi dishes. Characteristic Japanese precision, finesse and full flavours are part and parcel of the experience.

🕯️ **Johannes** XX �
Herengracht 413 ✉ *1017 BP –* ℰ *(0 20) 626 95 03* Plan: **F2**
*– www.restaurantjohannes.nl – closed 27 April, 31 December and
1 January*
Menu 53 € – Carte approx. 60 € – *(dinner only)*
• International • Rustic • Trendy •
Take your place in the pleasant dining room or on the terrace, and let Johannes
surprise you. All you have to do is choose the number of courses, then sit back
and enjoy balanced dishes. These often feature bold and unusual combinations
and techniques, as well as distinctive flavours blended together in delicious harmony.

John Dory

XX

Prinsengracht 999 ✉ *1017 KM – ✆ (0 20) 622 90 44* Plan: **K3**
– www.johndory.nl – closed 31 December-1 January, Sunday and Monday
Menu 35/85 € – *(dinner only except Friday, Saturday and last Sunday of the month) (tasting menu only)*

• Modern French • Friendly • Intimate •

Lovers of *vistronomie* should head for this storehouse building dating back to 1680, which is more spacious upstairs than in the lively room on the ground floor. North Sea delicacies shine through here in modern creations which bring out the best of fresh produce. Select your three to eight courses and let Dory's refinement surprise you.

Mr Porter Steakhouse – Hotel W Amsterdam

XX

Spuistraat 175 ✉ *1012 VN – ✆ (0 20) 811 33 99* Plan: **K1**
– www.wamsterdam.com
Menu 28 € (lunch) – Carte 47/86 €

• Meats and grills • Design • Trendy •

This trendy brasserie is a beautiful reflection of dazzling Amsterdam, with a terrace that includes a magnificent city view. The meat in the aging cabinets leaves no room for doubt as to the house speciality. The chef puts an original twist on international ingredients, with special side dishes to pep up the entire experience.

Segugio

XX

Utrechtsestraat 96 ✉ *1017 VS – ✆ (0 20) 330 15 03* Plan: **G3**
– www.segugio.nl – closed 27 April, 24, 25 and 31 December-1 January and Sunday
Menu 45/58 € – Carte 47/63 € – *(dinner only)*

• Italian • Intimate • Friendly •

This establishment with three modern dining rooms on several levels features sunny Italian cuisine made right before your eyes. Good selection of Italian wines.

Senses – Hotel The Albus

XX

Vijzelstraat 45 ✉ *1017 HE – ✆ (0 20) 530 62 66* Plan: **K2**
– www.sensesrestaurant.nl – closed 27 April, 25 and 26 December
Menu 29 € (lunch) – Carte 39/46 €

• Modern cuisine • Intimate • Bistro •

Lars Bertelsen is bursting with creativity, as guests will notice in the presentation, diverse textures and sometimes surprising flavour combinations in his food. The chef is also highly talented, as proven by the entire experience at Senses.

d'Vijff Vlieghen

XX

Spuistraat 294 (via Vlieghendesteeg 1) ✉ *1012 VX* Plan: **F2**
– ✆ (0 20) 530 40 60 – www.vijffvlieghen.nl – closed 27 April, 6-19 August, 24 December-5 January
Menu 47/116 € 🍷 – Carte 51/80 € – *(dinner only)*

• Traditional cuisine • Historic • Rustic •

The classic dishes on offer at these charming 17C premises are all prepared with typical Dutch products. Various attractive, country-style dining rooms where original Rembrandt sketches decorate the walls.

Envy

X

Prinsengracht 381 ✉ *1016 HL – ✆ (0 20) 344 64 07* Plan: **F2**
– www.envy.nl
Carte 30/55 € – *(dinner only except Friday, Saturday and Sunday)*

• Mediterranean cuisine • Fashionable • Brasserie •

Looking for a place to eat in trendy surroundings? Then head for this stylish trattoria, where the menu offers a beautiful range of creative recipes in tapas-style portions and the combination of subtle and pronounced flavours adds overall depth to the dishes. Note that the number of tables available for advance booking is very limited.

NETHERLANDS - AMSTERDAM

Wolf Atelier
Westerdoksplein 20 ✉ *1013 AZ* – ✆ *(0 20) 344 64 28* Plan: **G1**
– www.wolfatelier.nl – closed 25 December, 1 January and Sunday
Menu 35 € (lunch), 43/75 € – Carte approx. 47 €
• **Modern French** • **Contemporary décor** • **Design** •
Michael Wolf plays with flavours and modern combinations, offering diners the opportunity to test them out (as well as a choice of regular dishes), then refines them to retain their best features. The name Atelier is therefore particularly appropriate in this trendy, industrial-style restaurant, which is located on an old railway bridge with a beautiful view of the IJ.

BAK
Van Diemenstraat 408 ✉ *1013 CR* – ✆ *(0 20) 737 25 53* Plan: **C1**
– www.bakrestaurant.nl – closed 27 April, 25 July-7 August, 26 December, Monday and Tuesday
Menu 50/75 € – *(dinner only except Saturday and Sunday) (tasting menu only)*
• **Vegetarian** • **Vintage** • **Friendly** •
Responsibly produced, respectfully cultivated ingredients are like gold dust, and that is what it takes to create dazzling dishes. The chef here produces particularly convincing vegetarian combinations, while also using a little wild meat and fish from time to time. Make sure you ask for a table at the window, where you will have a lovely view of the IJ.

De Belhamel
Brouwersgracht 60 ✉ *1013 GX* – ✆ *(0 20) 622 10 95* Plan: **F1**
– www.belhamel.nl
Menu 35/45 € – Carte 45/57 €
• **Classic cuisine** • **Friendly** • **Bistro** •
This art nouveau style restaurant is located at the confluence of two canals and has a delightful terrace overlooking the water. Influences from France and Italy combine to deliver tasty dishes with clearly defined flavours.

Breda
Singel 210 ✉ *1016 AB* – ✆ *(0 20) 622 52 33* Plan: **J1**
– www.breda-amsterdam.com – closed 27 April, 26 December and 1 January
Menu 30 € (lunch), 50/80 € – *(surprise menu only)*
• **Modern cuisine** • **Brasserie** •
Welcome to Breda: dazzling, a touch retro, and luxurious too, but above all a place for delicious food. Choose from surprise menus featuring a range of inventive dishes created by the chef. International, varied and tasty.

Choux
De Ruyterkade 128 ✉ *1011 AC* – ✆ *(020) 210 30 90* Plan: **M1**
– www.choux.nl – closed 30 July-6 August, 25 December-2 January, Monday dinner, Saturday lunch and Sunday
Menu 30 € (lunch), 37/60 € – Carte approx. 38 €
• **Modern French** • **Fashionable** • **Trendy** •
Giving prominence to vegetables may not always be the obvious choice, but at this trendy restaurant it works beautifully. The continually surprising ingredients, creative preparations and intense flavours ensure complete fulfilment, taking diners on a wonderful voyage of discovery.

The French Connection
Singel 460 ✉ *1017 AW* – ✆ *(0 20) 737 30 51* Plan: **K2**
– www.tfcrestaurant.nl
Menu 39/69 € – Carte 38/44 € – *(dinner only)*
• **Creative French** • **Friendly** • **Intimate** •
France is clearly the theme here, from the rustic interior to the Gallic menu. The experienced chef serves up tasty dishes which deliver a creative take on classic French recipes, while also demonstrating refined precision and offering great value for money.

Gebr. Hartering   X ✧

Peperstraat 10hs ⊠ *1011 TL –* ☏ *(0 20) 421 06 99*   Plan: **M2**
– www.gebr-hartering.nl
Menu 55/80 € – Carte 50/65 € – *(dinner only)*
• French • Bistro • Rustic •

Niek and Paul Hartering share a love of ingredients. This cheerful venue proposes a short menu, which changes regularly, as the fusion cuisine depends on the
ingredients at their best on the day. Flavours don't lie.

Geisha   X AC ✧

Prins Hendrikkade 106a ⊠ *1011 AJ –* ☏ *(0 20) 626 24 10*   Plan: **G1**
– www.restaurantgeisha.nl – closed 27 April, 25 and 31 December,
1 January and Sunday
Menu 33/55 € – Carte 26/74 € – *(dinner only)*
• Asian • Exotic décor • Fashionable •

This trendy Geisha spoils guests with the delicacies of Southeast Asia. The traditional precision and freshness are certainly part of the deal, and are supplemented with more innovative dishes. You can also enjoy hors-d'oeuvres-style
options at the bar, accompanied by a choice of delicious cocktails.

GIN Neo   X 🛋 AC

Noorderstraat 19 ⊠ *1017 TR –* ☏ *(0 20) 428 36 32*   Plan: **J1**
– www.ginamsterdam.com
Menu 35/50 € – Carte 39/46 € – *(dinner only)*
• Fusion • Trendy • Neighbourhood •

The cuisine at this relaxed restaurant might best be described as Asian/French/
Mediterranean, or fusion, in short. Expect a blend of flavours, largely created
from Dutch ingredients, to complete the journey. An exciting mix.

Kaagman & Kortekaas   X

Sint Nicolaasstraat 43 ⊠ *1012 NJ –* ☏ *(0 20) 233 65 44*   Plan: **J1**
– www.kaagmanenkortekaas.nl – closed Sunday and Monday
Menu 44/60 € – *(dinner only) (booking essential)*
• Market cuisine • Friendly • Trendy •

Giel Kaagman and Bram Kortekaas focus on quality in their informal bistro. The
chef likes to work with game and poultry, making his own charcuterie and terrines. These are cleverly worked into dishes that present an up-to-date take on
traditional flavours.

Ron Gastrobar Oriental   X AC ✧

Kerkstraat 23 ⊠ *1017 GA –* ☏ *(0 20) 223 53 52*   Plan: **F2**
– www.rongastrobaroriental.nl – closed 27 April, 31 December and
1 January
Carte 32/62 € – *(dinner only until 11pm) (booking advisable)*
• Chinese • Oriental décor • Trendy •

Subtle lighting, Asian decor and natural materials set the mood at this stylish
restaurant, while a renowned bartender shakes cocktails at the extensive bar.
Full of flavour, the delicious dishes offer a contemporary take on traditional Chinese cuisine.

The Seafood Bar   X 🛋 AC

Spui 15 ⊠ *1012 WX –* ☏ *(0 20) 233 74 52*   Plan: **K2**
– www.theseafoodbar.com
Carte 28/109 €
• Brasserie • Contemporary décor •

You will not be surprised to find that this trendy establishment is a mecca for
lovers of seafood. The delicacies glisten on the display counters and look
mouthwatering on the plate, prepared with the minimum of fuss. The extensive
array of fresh ingredients guarantees a superb meal.

NETHERLANDS - AMSTERDAM

❌ Sichuan Food   ✗ 🎴 ⇔

Reguliersdwarsstraat 35 ✉ *1017 BK – ℰ (0 20) 626 93 27*
– www.sichuanfood.nl – closed 31 December
Menu 33/73 € – Carte 32/93 € – *(dinner only)*
Plan: **F2**

• Chinese • Classic décor • Simple •

Do not be deceived by the old-fashioned interior. The cuisine of Sichuan is prepared here as it should be, with subtle and powerful flavours which complement one another beautifully, combined in traditional dishes. Peking duck takes pride of place as the house speciality.

🏠 Amstel   ≤ 🛁 ⅏ 🖥 🎴 🛎 🚗

Prof. Tulpplein 1 ✉ *1018 GX – ℰ (0 20) 622 60 60*
– www.amsterdam.intercontinental.com
63 rm ☐ – †350/650 € ††350/650 € – **16 suites**
Plan: **H3**

• Grand Luxury • Historic • Personalised •

A veritable haven of luxury and good taste in this grand hotel on the banks of the Amstel. The vast rooms are decorated with stylish furnishings and attention to detail. Service is efficient and they offer every conceivable facility.
❌ **La Rive** – See restaurant listing

🏠 Sofitel Legend The Grand   ✿ 🛥 🚪 🛁 ⅏ 🖥 ⅊ 🎴 🛎 🚗

O.Z. Voorburgwal 197 ✉ *1012 EX – ℰ (0 20) 555 31 11*
– www.sofitel-legend-thegrand.com
177 rm – †320/580 € ††350/610 € – ☐ 38 € – **29 suites**
Plan: **G2**

• Grand townhouse • Grand Luxury •

This magnificent building, where William of Orange once stayed, oozes historic grandeur. The guestrooms and public spaces breathe luxury and French elegance – and there is even a butler service. Le Petit Bistro will delight fans of bistro cuisine with its many classic favourites.
✿ **Bridges** – See restaurant listing

🏠 Andaz   ✿ 🛥 🚪 🛁 ⊕ ⅏ ⅊ 🎴 🛎 🚗

Prinsengracht 587 ✉ *1016 HT – ℰ (0 20) 523 12 34*
– www.amsterdam.prinsengracht.andaz.com
117 rm – †335/495 € ††335/495 € – ☐ 30 € – **5 suites**
Plan: **F2**

• Grand Luxury • Design •

Top designer Marcel Wanders converted this former city library into a magnificent designer-style hotel. Guests can experience true luxury and find peace in stylish bedrooms with fish-themed decor. The personal welcome and attention complete the experience at Andaz.

🏠 Conservatorium   ✿ 🛁 ⊕ ⅏ 🖥 ⅊ 🎴 🛎

Van Baerlestraat 27 ✉ *1071 AN – ℰ (0 20) 570 00 00*
– www.conservatoriumhotel.com
129 rm ☐ – †400/700 € ††400/700 € – **7 suites**
Plan: **E3**

• Grand townhouse • Historic • Grand luxury •

The Conservatorium is one of Amsterdam's finest hotels. Neither expense nor effort was spared in the renovation of this neo-Classical jewel that dates back to the end of the 19C. Excellent service, with staff at hand to meet your every need. Pure, unadulterated luxury.
❌ **Taiko** – See restaurant listing

🏠 Hotel de l'Europe   ≤ 🛁 ⊕ ⅏ 🖥 ⅊ 🎴 🛎 🅿

Nieuwe Doelenstraat 2 ✉ *1012 CP – ℰ (0 20) 531 17 77*
– www.deleurope.com
88 rm – †399/699 € ††399/799 € – ☐ 38 € – **23 suites**
Plan: **G2**

• Business • Luxury • Elegant •

This luxury hotel, which dates back to the end of the 19C, offers a chic combination of charm and tradition. The rooms are elegant and the junior suites were inspired by the Dutch School. Views of the canals.
✿ **Bord'Eau** • ⊕ **Hoofdstad** – See restaurant listing

Waldorf Astoria

Herengracht 542 ⊠ 1017 CG – 𝒞 (0 20) 718 46 00
Plan: **G3**
– www.waldorfastoria.com/amsterdam
93 rm – ♥345/895 € ♥♥345/895 € – ⊡ 38 € – 11 suites
• Grand Luxury • Palace • Elegant •
Six canal houses from the 17C have been transformed into a luxury hotel with stylish decor, marble bathrooms and staff who are ever attentive to guests' needs. The views add to the appeal, with the front rooms overlooking the Herengracht and those to the rear overlooking the beautiful courtyard. Wonderful!
❀❀ **Librije's Zusje Amsterdam** – See restaurant listing

art'otel

Prins Hendrikkade 33 ⊠ 1012 TM – 𝒞 (0 20) 719 72 00
Plan: **G1**
– www.artotelamsterdam.com
107 rm ⊡ – ♥259/699 € ♥♥259/699 €
• Business • Chain • Trendy •
From the exhibition in the cellar to the creations in the corridors and bedrooms, art is the theme of this modern hotel. It also exhibits a good grasp of the art of indulgence, from the luxury and comfort of the bedrooms to the exquisite care provided in the wellness suite. All this with the backdrop of beautiful works of art.

Grand Hotel Amrâth

Prins Hendrikkade 108 ⊠ 1011 AK – 𝒞 (0 20) 552 00 00
Plan: **G1**
– www.amrathamsterdam.com
165 rm – ♥180/450 € ♥♥250/499 € – ⊡ 25 € – 9 suites
• Historic • Chain • Art déco •
The monumental staircase in this imposing Art Nouveau hotel will be your stairway to heaven as you won't want for anything here. The location is nice and central, the rooms are comfortable and the service is very personal and attentive. In the restaurant, you will find a hint of retro in the decor and an international flavour on your plate.

NH Grand Hotel Krasnapolsky

Dam 9 ⊠ 1012 JS – 𝒞 (0 20) 554 91 11
Plan: **G1**
– www.nh-collection.com
451 rm – ♥229/599 € ♥♥229/599 € – ⊡ 30 € – 2 suites
• Luxury • Classic •
Monuments should be cherished – that is why this historic grand hotel dating back to 1855 has been fully renovated. Business people and holidaymakers alike will appreciate the modern luxury and the more classic features. Breakfast in the winter garden and dinner in the stylish Grand Café complete the experience.
❀ **The White Room** – See restaurant listing

Pulitzer

Prinsengracht 315 ⊠ 1016 GZ – 𝒞 (0 20) 523 52 35
Plan: **F1**
– www.pulitzeramsterdam.com
225 rm – ♥350/600 € ♥♥350/600 € – ⊡ 28 € – 9 suites
• Chain • Luxury • Historic •
Characterful complex of no less than 25 houses (17C and 18C), set around a beautifully kept garden. The rooms have been tastefully redecorated and the artwork in the communal areas creates a pleasant ambience. Luxury brasserie Jansz is a trendy spot for tasty contemporary dishes at any time of day.

W Amsterdam

Spuistraat 175 ⊠ 1012 VN – 𝒞 (0 20) 811 25 00
Plan: **K1**
– www.wamsterdam.com
238 rm – ♥350/500 € ♥♥400/550 € – ⊡ 35 €
• Luxury • Townhouse • Design •
The adventure begins with check-in on the sixth floor, where guests will discover the beautiful view of the city. W Amsterdam is situated in an old post office and a bank, which now form a magnificent unified venue. Dutch designers have taken it in hand, coupling trendiness with pure luxury and adding stunning features like the rooftop swimming.
⬙○ **Mr Porter Steakhouse** – See restaurant listing

Ambassade

🏠 ⬅ 🅰🅲

Herengracht 341 ⊠ 1016 AZ – ℰ (0 20) 555 02 22
– www.ambassade-hotel.nl
Plan: **F2**
54 rm – ♦185/315 € ♦♦185/325 € – ⬚ 20 € – 3 suites
• Historic building • Luxury • Elegant •
The CoBrA collection and the books in the library signed by authors who have stayed here all testify to the artistic style of this hotel. It is just perfect for art loving Amsterdam!

Canal House

🍴 🅰🅲 🔱

Keizersgracht 148 ⊠ 1015 CX – ℰ (0 20) 622 51 82
– www.canalhouse.nl
Plan: **F1**
23 rm ⬚ – ♦295/800 € ♦♦295/800 €
• Townhouse • Luxury • Unique •
Canal House is synonymous with luxury and is set alongside one of Amsterdam's canals. Take your pick from guestrooms ranging in category from 'good' to 'better' to 'best', the ultimate treat! The modern character of the rooms fits in perfectly with the historic ambience of this hotel.

The Dylan

🎧 🅰🅲 🔱

Keizersgracht 384 ⊠ 1016 GB – ℰ (0 20) 530 20 10
– www.dylanamsterdam.com
Plan: **F2**
40 rm – ♦295/350 € ♦♦325/495 € – ⬚ 28 €
• Business • Grand Luxury • Design •
Discover the intimate harmony of this 17C boutique hotel with its surprising designer decor. Magnificent guestrooms and personal service make this one of the city's special addresses.
❀ **Vinkeles** – See restaurant listing

Estheréa

🅰🅲 🔱 🚕

Singel 305 ⊠ 1012 WJ – ℰ (0 20) 624 51 46
– www.estherea.nl
Plan: **F2**
91 rm – ♦100/500 € ♦♦100/500 € – ⬚ 18 € – 2 suites
• Historic building • Traditional • Elegant •
The Estheréa is a beautiful, elegant hotel full of charm. Its warm, classic interior clad in red velvet will tempt you in, and its excellent breakfasts will win you over completely.

Aitana

🏠 🌿 ⬅ 🎧 ⚙ 🅰🅲 🔱 🚕

IJdok 6 ⊠ 1013 MM – ℰ (0 20) 891 48 00
– www.room-matehotels.com
Plan: **C1**
285 rm – ♦279/409 € ♦♦279/409 € – ⬚ 19 €
• Chain • Modern • Design •
Aitana is a handsome design hotel on the IJ, and quite an exceptional one too! Lots of light and minimalist designs in the themed rooms and suites create a relaxed 'Zen-like' feel. Breakfast is served until noon, allowing guests a lazy morning in the comfortable beds. A nice extra touch: the hotel has its own marina.

American

🏠 🎧 ⚙ 🅰🅲 🔱

Leidsekade 97 ⊠ 1017 PN – ℰ (0 20) 556 30 00
– www.hampshire-hotels.com/american
Plan: **F3**
175 rm – ♦140/500 € ♦♦140/500 € – ⬚ 20 €
• Historic • Palace • Classic •
This historic building immediately grabs your attention, with its imposing façade that exudes a certain dignity, and its very characterful, comfortable interior. Café Americain offers fine cuisine in a stylish Art Deco room with a magnificent ceiling.

NETHERLANDS - AMSTERDAM

INK 👁 ⌂ 👤 🅰🅺

Nieuwezijds Voorburgwal 67 ✉ *1012 RE –* ☎ *(0 20)*   Plan: **K1**
627 59 00 – www.ink-hotel-amsterdam.com
149 rm – ♦150/350 € ♦♦200/400 € – ☕ 25 € – 1 suite
• Townhouse • Business • Contemporary •

Full of charm and character, this modern hotel owes its name to the rich history of the building. Housed in the former home of the newspaper De Tijd, the hotel boasts decor that is reminiscent of that past, with maps of Amsterdam prominently featured on the walls. Another good story is in the making here.

NH Barbizon Palace 👁 ⌂ 🕸 👤 🅰🅺 🎿 🚗

Prins Hendrikkade 59 ✉ *1012 AD –* ☎ *(0 20) 556 45 64*   Plan: **G1**
– www.nh-hotels.com
271 rm – ♦200/300 € ♦♦200/300 € – ☕ 30 € – 3 suites
• Grand townhouse • Chain • Elegant •

This elegant property directly opposite the station has a hint of 17C charm. Renovations are taking place to upgrade the traditional comfort. The famous Amsterdam canals await discovery from the private jetty. At Bar Mar-Dique discover dishes prepared in a modern bistro style, with a penchant for vegetables.
❀ **Vermeer** – See restaurant listing

Notting Hill 👁 🅰🅺 🚗

Westeinde 26 ✉ *1017 ZP –* ☎ *(0 20) 523 10 30*   Plan: **G3**
– www.hotelnottinghill.nl
71 rm – ♦150/400 € ♦♦150/400 € – ☕ 24 €
• Boutique hotel • Luxury • Contemporary •

A boutique hotel equipped with every type of modern comfort. The rooms not only look sumptuous, they are also finished with top quality materials. The hotel's car park is handy in this location in the city centre. Enjoy international cuisine to a backdrop of designer decor in the restaurant.

The Toren 🛏 🅰🅺

Keizersgracht 164 ✉ *1015 CZ –* ☎ *(0 20) 622 63 52*   Plan: **F1**
– www.thetoren.nl
40 rm – ♦100/200 € ♦♦200/300 € – ☕ 14 €
• Townhouse • Traditional • Elegant •

This romantic boutique hotel can be found just a few steps away from the Anne Frank House. The breakfast room is elegant and the bedrooms are decorated in a warm, neo-Baroque style. The three garden suites will ensure a memorable stay.

The Albus 🅰🅺

Vijzelstraat 49 ✉ *1017 HE –* ☎ *(0 20) 530 62 00*   Plan: **G2**
– www.albushotel.com
75 rm – ♦129/269 € ♦♦129/269 € – ☕ 19 €
• Townhouse • Business • Trendy •

Smart, superb, stunning: every one of the guestrooms in this design hotel is fresh and modern, leading to rave reviews. Visitors are in the hands of a highly motivated team who are happy to explain the eco-friendly aspects of The Albus.
🍴 **Senses** – See restaurant listing

De Hallen 👁 👤 🅰🅺 🎿 🚗

Bellamyplein 47 ✉ *1053 AT –* ☎ *(0 20) 820 86 70*   Plan: **B2**
– www.hoteldehallen.com
57 rm – ♦120/200 € ♦♦120/200 € – ☕ 20 €
• Historic • Townhouse • Design •

The tram depot near Amsterdam's Foodhallen has been converted into a contemporary hotel. You will discover a combination of retro, industrial, trendy and Scandinavian design elements, all of which result in a warm and charming hotel.

The Hoxton
Herengracht 255 ✉ *1016 BJ* – ℰ *(0 20) 888 55 55*
Plan: **K2**
– www.thehoxton.com
111 rm ⌂ – **♦**89/299 € **♦♦**99/529 €
• Historic • Business • Cosy •
The sign outside is tiny, so you might be surprised to step inside The Hoxton and discover a bustling, homely living room. The cosy feel reaches as far as the bedrooms, where vintage and modern elements intertwine. In the restaurant guests can enjoy an à la carte breakfast in the morning and contemporary cuisine later in the day.

JL n° 76
Jan Luijkenstraat 76 ✉ *1071 CT* – ℰ *(0 20) 348 55 55*
Plan: **F3**
– www.hoteljlno76.com
39 rm – **♦**120/200 € **♦♦**120/200 € – ⌂ 20 €
• Manor house • Luxury • Elegant •
On Jan Luijkenstraat two 18C townhouses have been converted to form this pleasant boutique hotel. The rooms are modern, stylish and peaceful, despite the hotel's location in the bustling, fashionable museum quarter. The restaurant offers a choice from a concise contemporary menu.

Roemer
Roemer Visscherstraat 10 ✉ *1054 EX* – ℰ *(0 20)*
Plan: **E3**
589 08 00 – www.hotelroemer.com
37 rm – **♦**120/200 € **♦♦**120/200 € – ⌂ 20 €
• Business • Townhouse • Design •
An attractive hotel with an elegant, designer-style interior, in an early 20C townhouse situated close to the Vondelpark. Modern interior, immaculate rooms and breakfast served in the garden in summer.

Vondel
Vondelstraat 26 ✉ *1054 GD* – ℰ *(0 20) 612 01 20*
Plan: **E3**
– www.hotelvondel.com
83 rm – **♦**120/200 € **♦♦**120/200 € – ⌂ 20 €
• Boutique hotel • Business • Modern •
This boutique hotel was created out of seven 1900s houses. Communal areas, bedrooms and conference room in a decidedly contemporary style. Breakfasts on the stylish patio when the weather is good. Hip, stylish bistro serving local and international cuisine.

Sebastian's
Keizersgracht 15 ✉ *1055 CC* – ℰ *(0 20) 423 23 42*
Plan: **F1**
– www.hotelsebastians.nl
33 rm – **♦**81/189 € **♦♦**95/252 € – ⌂ 14 €
• Boutique hotel • Traditional • Elegant •
A boutique hotel with an adventurous, yet warm colour scheme. Its convenient location on the Keizersgracht canal, close to the Jordaan area, will suit business travellers and night-owls alike. Trendy bar.

SOUTH and WEST QUARTERS

✿✿ Ciel Bleu – Hotel Okura, 23rd floor
XxxX ⅏ ≤ ⅄ ✿ ⅏ **P**
Ferdinand Bolstraat 333 ✉ *1072 LH* – ℰ *(0 20)*
Plan: **C2**
678 74 50 – www.cielbleu.nl
– closed 5-20 August, 31 December-8 January and Sunday
Menu 135/160 €
– Carte 135/194 € – (dinner only)
• Creative • Elegant •
At Ciel Bleu visitors can expect a spectacle: the view of the city is fantastic and the modern elegance of the decor is a feast for the eyes. The technically accomplished chef reveals his true character, producing an astonishing variety of international cuisine, surprising in its creativity and unexpected combinations of flavours.
➜ Koningskrab met kaviaar, roomijs van beurre blanc en gezouten citroen. Dorset lam met polenta, groene asperges en Foyotsaus. Banaan met gianduja, pinda en bruine rum.

NETHERLANDS - AMSTERDAM

Yamazato – Hotel Okura   XxX 🕸 🆉 ⇔ 🍴 🅿

Ferdinand Bolstraat 333 ✉ 1072 LH   Plan: C2
– 𝒞 (0 20) 678 74 50
– www.yamazato.nl
– closed 16-28 July
Menu 40 € (lunch), 85/115 €
– Carte 37/157 € – (dinner only except Saturday and Sunday)
• Japanese • Minimalist • Chic •

The intimate, spartan interior and view of the Japanese garden produce a Zen feel. Ladies in kimonos bring authentic kaiseki dishes to the table, showcasing the subtlety and technical accomplishment of Japanese cuisine. This place honours tradition, as visitors will also discover when ordering a simple bento box lunch.

→ Omakase en nigiri sushi. Tempura van kreeft. Shabu shabu, dunne plakjes entrecote en groenten in een bouillon.

RON Gastrobar (Ron Blaauw)   XX 🌿 🆉 ⇔ 🍴

Sophialaan 55 ✉ 1075 BP   Plan: B2
– 𝒞 (0 20) 496 19 43
– www.rongastrobar.nl
– closed 27 April, 31 December-1 January
Carte approx. 60 €
• Creative French • Fashionable • Trendy •

Ron Blaauw returns to basics here, creating cuisine that is pure and prepared with quality ingredients. This urban gastro-bar combines a hip, lively ambience with top class cuisine without the frills. It also means little formality but original, delicious food and sensational flavours. Phenomenal value for money, which is also reflected in the wine list.

→ Gebakken ganzenlever met gemarineerde bietjes, krenten in madeira en parmezaanschuim. Barbecue spare ribs met huisgemaakte sambal. Surprise ei.

Bolenius (Luc Kusters)   XX 🕸 🌿 ⇔

George Gershwinlaan 30 ✉ 1082 MT   Plan: B2
– 𝒞 (0 20) 404 44 11
– www.bolenius-restaurant.nl
– closed 4-20 August, 26 December-2 January, Bank Holidays and Sunday
Menu 35 € (lunch), 75/99 €
– Carte 66/105 €
• Creative • Design •

At Bolenius you will discover how sleek Scandinavian design can be – and this is reflected in the meticulous presentation of the dishes. The chef is a creative soul who likes to experiment and provoke reactions. Vegetables play an important role in this exciting culinary experience, which really explores the power of natural flavours.

→ Langoustine met komkommer, kardemom en ui. Kamperlam met aubergine, ansjovis en groene kruiden. Limburgse vlaai.

Sazanka – Hotel Okura   XX 🆉 🍴 🅿

Ferdinand Bolstraat 333 ✉ 1072 LH   Plan: C2
– 𝒞 (0 20) 678 74 50
– www.okura.nl
– closed 29 July-5 August
Menu 83/115 € – Carte 52/111 € – (dinner only)
• Teppanyaki • Oriental décor • Friendly •

Sazanka takes you on an adventure to Japan. The sober interior and waitresses dressed in kimonos set the tone; then enters the chef, who proudly takes his place behind the teppan-yaki grill. He confidently demonstrates his skills and uses excellent ingredients to create flavours which provide contrast but are always well balanced. What a show!

→ Gegrilde oesters met yuzuboter. Teppanyaki van zeebaars in zeezoutkorst met prei. Sukiyakirol van wagyurund en tamago saus.

❀ **Le Restaurant** (Jan de Wit)　　　　　　　　　　　　X 🆔

Frans Halsstraat 26H ✉ *1072 BR – ℰ (0 20) 379 22 07* 　Plan: **K3**
– www.lerestaurant.nl – closed 23 April-7 May, 14 July-5 August,
23 December-7 January, Sunday and Monday
Menu 60/88 € – *(dinner only) (number of covers limited, pre-book) (tasting menu only)*
• Market cuisine • Bistro •

Jan de Wit's Le Restaurant has moved to a cosy building with a bistro feel. His formula for success remains the same: a simple but spectacular menu. The best of market produce is prepared without too much fuss and plated up in its authentic form to convince diners with its powerful flavours. The price-pleasure ratio is spot on.
→ Gemarineerde makreel met mosseltjes, baba ganouch en crisps. Coquilles, rauw en gebakken met scheermesjes, zwarte knoflook, waterkers en dille. Gebraden runderschouder met peterseliewortel, spitskool en een tijm-en biersausje.

❀ **Sinne** (Alexander Ioannou)　　　　　　　　　　　　X 🆔

Ceintuurbaan 342 ✉ *1072 GP – ℰ (0 20) 682 72 90* 　Plan: **C2**
– www.restaurantsinne.nl – closed Monday and Tuesday
Menu 39/87 € – *(dinner only except Sunday) (booking essential)*
• Modern cuisine • Trendy •

The open kitchen at the back of this warm and friendly restaurant is reminiscent of a theatre scene. While chef Ioannou plays the lead role, the top quality produce steals the show in the form of modern, meticulously prepared dishes. Attentive service from hostess Suzanne, as well as reasonable prices.
→ Zachtgegaarde kabeljauw met groene kerrie, krokante rijst, limefingers en een kokossausje. Black Angus op de barbecue met seizoensgroenten en eigen jus. Ganache van witte chocolade met bonbon van kokos en passievruchtsorbet.

⊕ **Le Garage**　　　　　　　　　　　　　　　　XX 🆔 ⇔ 🍴

Ruysdaelstraat 54 ✉ *1071 XE – ℰ (0 20) 679 71 76* 　Plan: **B2**
– www.restaurantlegarage.nl – closed Saturday lunch and Sunday lunch
Menu 30 € 🍷 (lunch), 37/48 € – Carte 46/75 €
• French • Fashionable •

Smart restaurant with a luxury brasserie interior where guests can choose from an appealing set menu and an extensive à la carte. Both are founded on quality ingredients and prepared in a French style, with a touch of creativity. At En Pluche, the lively neighbouring establishment, the dishes are slightly simpler but no less sublime.

⊕ **Brasserie van Baerle**　　　　　　　　　　　XX ⊞ 🎁 ⇔

Van Baerlestraat 158 ✉ *1071 BG – ℰ (0 20) 679 15 32* 　Plan: **B2**
– www.brasserievanbaerle.nl – closed 27 April, 25, 26 and 31 December-1 January, Monday lunch and Saturday lunch
Menu 30 € (lunch)/37 € – Carte 48/60 €
• Classic cuisine • Vintage •

This retro brasserie attracts regular customers, mainly from the local area because of its appealing menu, tasty steak tartare and well-matched wines. Courtyard terrace.

⊕ **Serre** – Hotel Okura　　　　　　　　　　　XX 🆔 🍴 🅿

Ferdinand Bolstraat 333 ✉ *1072 LH – ℰ (0 20)* 　Plan: **C2**
678 74 50 – www.okura.nl – closed 12-23 February
Menu 37/40 € – Carte 48/69 €
• Modern cuisine • Brasserie •

Like Okura's other restaurants, quality is the focus of this chic brasserie, with its magnificent canal-side terrace. Excellent ingredients go into the international cuisine served here. The chef selects techniques from diverse cuisines, unifying them in straightforwardly delicious dishes.

Elkaar

X 🛱 🗚

Alexanderplein 6 ✉ 1018 CG – ℰ (0 20) 330 75 59   Plan: **C2**
– www.etenbijelkaar.nl – closed 27 April, 25 December-7 January, Sunday and Monday
Menu 30 € (lunch), 37/55 € – Carte 46/55 €
• Modern French • Family •

If you are looking for a relaxed meal out together, this friendly establishment with a pleasant summer terrace is a great option. The set menu is a good choice, offering a selection from the à la carte menu. The chef combines quality ingredients in a contemporary manner, creating beautiful flavours without overcomplicating things.

Le Hollandais

X 🛱 🗚 ⇔

Amsteldijk 41 ✉ 1074 HV – ℰ (0 20) 679 12 48   Plan: **C2**
– www.lehollandais.nl – closed 27 April, 14 August-3 September, Sunday and Monday
Menu 37/43 € – Carte 43/58 € – *(dinner only)*
• Classic cuisine • Vintage •

Feeling a little nostalgic? Then this is the place for you, as Le Hollandais really turns the clock back. The dining hall is reminiscent of the 1970s and the chef still serves up generous dishes with rich flavours, just like the old days. You will experience classic French cuisine the way it is meant to taste.

Oud-Zuid

X 🛱 ⇔

Johannes Verhulststraat 64 ✉ 1071 NH – ℰ (0 20)   Plan: **B2**
676 60 58 – www.restaurantoudzuid.nl – closed 27 April, 25, 26 and 31 December-1 January
Menu 28 € (lunch)/37 € – Carte 45/63 €
• Classic cuisine • Brasserie •

This characterful restaurant with a brasserie-style dining room presents traditional dishes with a modern touch. For music lovers, Oud-Zuid is less than a 10 min walk from the Concertgebouw.

Rijsel

X 🕸

Marcusstraat 52b ✉ 1091 TK – ℰ (0 20) 463 21 42   Plan: **G3**
– www.rijsel.com – closed 30 July-12 August and Sunday
Menu 35/55 € – Carte 30/83 € – *(dinner only) (booking essential)*
• Traditional cuisine • Simple •

Rijsel's simple interior resembles a classroom, and the restaurant happens to share its entrance with a school. In the open kitchen you can see the master at work preparing his delicious French cuisine. He has an excellent knowledge of ingredients and his traditional dishes also include a nod to Flemish food.

Het Bosch

XX ⩽ 🛱 🅿

Jollenpad 10 ✉ 1081 KC – ℰ (0 20) 644 58 00   Plan: **B3**
– www.hetbosch.com – closed 23 December-7 January and Sunday
Menu 45 € (lunch), 50/65 € – Carte 47/71 €
• Modern French • Fashionable • Trendy •

From this contemporary restaurant diners enjoy a breath-taking view of the Nieuwe Meer marina. In this dream location the chef entertains diners with lavish, up-to-date dishes prepared with real know-how. In summer Het Bosch Waterfront serves cocktails and barbecue dishes.

The Roast Room

XX 🛱 ⇔

Europaplein 2 ✉ 1078 GZ – ℰ (0 20) 723 96 14   Plan: **C2**
– www.theroastroom.nl – closed 26 and 27 April, Saturday lunch and Sunday lunch
Menu 35 € (lunch), 50/85 € – Carte 54/76 € – *(open until 11.30pm)*
• Meats and grills • Trendy • Fashionable •

An impressive steakhouse. Glass, steel and meat are the dominant features of the Roast Bar (brasserie on the ground floor) and the Rotisserie (restaurant upstairs). See the meat hanging ready to cook, smell it on the grill and taste the results when it has been cooked to perfection. Excellent side dishes complete the picture.

NETHERLANDS - AMSTERDAM

Restaurant C   XX 🍴 ✿

Wibautstraat 125 ✉ *1091 GL – ℰ (0 20) 210 30 11*   Plan: **G3**
– www.c.amsterdam
– closed 1 January
Menu 29 € (lunch)/45 € – Carte 37/47 €
• Creative French • Trendy • Chic •

The contemporary, chic Restaurant Celsius is a dazzling spot, especially the kitchen bar. The reference to degrees emphasises the precision the chefs strive for, because that is what makes the difference between good food and delicious cuisine. Creativity in the combination of strong flavours and textures makes C a top choice.

Visaandeschelde   XX 🍴 🆔 🥢 (dinner)

Scheldeplein 4 ✉ *1078 GR – ℰ (0 20) 675 15 83*   Plan: **C2**
– www.visaandeschelde.nl
– closed 27 April, 31 December-1 January, Saturday lunch and Sunday lunch
Menu 35 € (lunch), 45/75 € – Carte 55/90 € – (open until 11pm)
• Seafood • Traditional décor •

Set opposite the RAI congress centre, this restaurant is popular with Amsterdammers for its dishes full of the flavours of the sea, its contemporary brasserie décor and its lively atmosphere.

Volt   X 🍴

Ferdinand Bolstraat 178 ✉ *1072 LT – ℰ (0 20) 471 55 44*   Plan: **F3**
– www.restaurantvolt.nl
– closed 27 April and 1 January
Carte 30/41 € – (dinner only except Saturday and Sunday)
• Modern French • Bistro • Simple •

Certain elements of the austere decor at Volt are reminiscent of the lamp shop previously housed here. This is still a vibrant location, but now the excitement comes in the form of flavours. The chef produces classic cuisine as it should be, as well as a very good wine and beer list.

Okura   🍸 🍷 ⅃ð 🛎 🏦 🍽 ₺ 🆔 🐎 🚗

Ferdinand Bolstraat 333 ✉ *1072 LH – ℰ (0 20)*   Plan: **C2**
678 71 11 – www.okura.nl
291 rm – 🛏205/470 € 🛏🛏205/470 € – ☲ 30 € – 9 suites
• Palace • Personalised • Elegant •

A stay in this international luxury hotel is a real experience. Guests are received with great respect and enjoy thoroughly personal service. The bedrooms are simply magnificent, with a beautiful view of the city thrown in, and the same goes for the facilities. Okura is a Valhalla for foodies, a treat from morning to night.
✿✿ **Ciel Bleu** • ✿ **Yamazato** • ✿ **Sazanka** • 🍴 **Serre** – See restaurant listing

Hilton   🍸 🍷 🍽 ⅃ð 🏦 ₺ 🆔 🏩 🅿

Apollolaan 138 ✉ *1077 BG – ℰ (0 20) 710 60 00*   Plan: **B2**
– www.amsterdam.hilton.com
271 rm – 🛏199/399 € 🛏🛏199/399 € – ☲ 28 € – 4 suites
• Chain • Townhouse • Elegant •

This hotel is known for John Lennon and Yoko Ono's 1969 "bed-in" protest against the Vietnam War. Having found their beds and enjoyed the outstanding comfort characteristic of this hotel chain, guests might consider following their example. Visitors who are here on business can expect excellent meeting facilities.

Bilderberg Garden

Dijsselhofplantsoen 7 ✉ 1077 BJ – ✆ (0 20) 570 56 00 – www.bilderberg.nl/hotels/garden-hotel Plan: **B2**

124 rm – 🛉119/359 € 🛉🛉119/359 € – ☕ 24 € – 2 suites

• Business • Elegant •

The elegant ambience of the public spaces and the care and attention focused on comfort in the bedrooms will be appreciated by every guest at this hotel. Valet parking and the excellent meeting facilities will appeal to business travellers. The De Kersentuin restaurant is an added attraction.

Chassé

Chasséstraat 62 ✉ 1057 JJ – ✆ (0 20) 238 23 00 – www.chassehotel.com Plan: **E2**

47 rm – 🛉115/175 € 🛉🛉115/175 € – ☕ 15 €

• Boutique hotel • Family • Elegant •

The former Chassé church, in a quiet part of Amsterdam-Zuid, has made way for this thoroughly modern hotel offering the comforts expected by the guests of today. In addition to the hotel, Chassé also has its own dance studios.

The College

Roelof Hartstraat 1 ✉ 1071 VE – ✆ (0 20) 571 15 11 – www.thecollegehotel.com Plan: **C2**

40 rm – 🛉119/390 € 🛉🛉119/470 € – ☕ 20 €

• Historic • Grand Luxury • Elegant •

In this 19C school building, The College gives promising students the chance to gain experience, and they do so with conviction - their enthusiasm ensuring that guests lack nothing. Stay in stylish rooms where authentic elements provide a touch of distinction. The bar-lounge is open for a bite to eat at any time of the day.

Albert

Albert Cuypstraat 6 ✉ 1072 CT – ✆ (0 20) 305 30 20 – www.siralberthotel.com Plan: **C2**

87 rm – 🛉160/425 € 🛉🛉160/425 € – ☕ 24 € – 3 suites

• Townhouse • Luxury • Design •

Sir Albert receives you with open arms in this boutique hotel where his spirit is kept alive through subtle touches, such as notes on the mirrors and works of art. Design and luxury rule supreme in all the rooms, which are decorated mainly in black and white. This top quality address is situated in De Pijp, a residential district of Amsterdam.

Arena

's-Gravesandestraat 51 ✉ 1092 AA – ✆ (0 20) 850 24 00 – www.hotelarena.nl Plan: **C2**

116 rm – 🛉89/229 € 🛉🛉89/229 € – ☕ 20 €

• Historic • Townhouse • Trendy •

This historic building dating back to 1890 was once an orphanage; today it is an ultra-trendy hotel. Three beautiful staircases and other authentic features remain as reminders of the past, but Arena combines these with modern comfort and smart design. The restaurant is also thoroughly contemporary.

The Manor

Linnaeusstraat 89 ✉ 1093 EK – ✆ (0 20) 700 84 00 – www.hampshirehotelmanoramsterdam.com Plan: **C2**

125 rm – 🛉120/350 € 🛉🛉135/350 € – ☕ 15 €

• Grand townhouse • Chain • Modern •

A former civic hospital that has been transformed into a delightful place to stay. This is thanks to its carefully maintained historic character and the harmonious use of modern, trendy materials. Every comfort is provided for your stay, and you can easily explore the city from the tram that stops nearby.

Aan de Poel (Stefan van Sprang)   XXXX 88 ⪦ 斎 ᴬᴼ ⇔ 🐂

Handweg 1 ⊠ 1185 TS Amstelveen – ℰ (0 20) 345 17 63   Plan: **B3**
*– www.aandepoel.nl – closed 27 April, 29 July-13 August, 27 December-
8 January, Saturday lunch, Sunday and Monday*
Menu 50 € (lunch), 68/99 € – Carte 72/128 €
• Creative • Trendy •
A successful marriage of technical skill and brilliant produce ensures that every
dish is a feast for the senses. Here, contemporary cuisine can be savoured in one
of its most beautiful and tasteful forms. What's more, this restaurant benefits
from a superb lakeside setting, a chic and sophisticated designer interior and a
skilled sommelier.
→ Geroosterde kreeft met kerrie en macadamia. Gebakken tarbot met crispy ansjovis, dragon en aardappel. Geblazen suikerbal met bramen en
lavendel.

De Jonge Dikkert   XX 斎 ⇔ 🅿

Amsterdamseweg 104a ⊠ 1182 HG Amstelveen   Plan: **B3**
*– ℰ (0 20) 643 33 33 – www.jongedikkert.nl – closed 3 weeks in August,
24 and 31 December-5 January, Saturday lunch and Sunday lunch*
Menu 34 € (lunch), 36/70 € – Carte 47/57 €
• Regional cuisine • Trendy • Inn •
This timber windmill dating back to the 17C feels nice and cosy thanks to the
contemporary interior. Indulge yourself in this fantastic setting, which is equalled by the superb cuisine featuring local ingredients, beautifully crafted dishes,
and modern techniques and combinations. A strong Bib Gourmand.

Kronenburg   XX 斎 ⪢ ᴬᴼ ⇔ 🅿

Prof. E.M. Meijerslaan 6 ⊠ 1183 AV Amstelveen   Plan: **B3**
*– ℰ (0 20) 345 54 89 – www.restaurant-kronenburg.nl – closed 27 April,
24 July-6 August, Saturday lunch and Sunday*
Menu 29/42 € – Carte 30/45 €
• Mediterranean cuisine • Trendy • Fashionable •
An oasis in the Kronenburg business quarter on the edge of a lake in a verdant
setting. Dine on the terrace or behind the glass façade in a modern, bright interior that is positively sparkling. The dishes have a Mediterranean flair and are
inspired by French cuisine.

ROTTERDAM
ROTTERDAM

DutchScenery/iStock

ROTTERDAM IN...

→ **ONE DAY**
Blaak area including Kijk-Kubus and Boompjestorens, Oude Haven, Museum Boijmans Van Beuningen.

→ **TWO DAYS**
More Museumpark, Delfshaven, take in the view from Euromast, cruise along the Nieuwe Maas.

→ **THREE DAYS**
Kop Van Zuid, a show at the Luxor Theatre.

Rotterdam trades on its earthy appeal, on a rough and ready grittiness that ties in with its status as the largest seaport in the world; it handles 350 million tonnes of goods a year, with over half of all the freight that is heading into Europe passing through it. Flattened during the Second World War, Rotterdam was rebuilt on a grand scale, jettisoning the idea of streets full of terraced houses in favour of a modern cityscape of concrete and glass, and there are few places in the world that have such an eclectic range of buildings to keep you entertained (or bewildered): try the Euromast Space Tower, the Groothandelsgebouw

(which translates as 'wholesale building'), the 'Cube Houses' or the fabulous sounding Boompjestorens for size. The city is located on the Nieuwe Maas but is centred around a maze of other rivers – most importantly the Rhine and the Maas – and is only a few dozen kilometres inland from the North Sea. It spills over both banks, and is linked by tunnels, bridges and the metro; the most stunning connection across the water is the modern Erasmusbridge, whose graceful, angular lines of silver tubing have earned it the nickname 'The Swan', and whose sleek design has come to embody the Rotterdam of the new millennium. It's mirrored on the southern banks by the development of the previously rundown Kop Van Zuid area into a sleek, modern zone.

EATING OUT

Rotterdam is a hot place for dining, in the literal and metaphorical sense. There are lots of places to tuck into the flavours of Holland's colonial past, in particular the spicy delicacies of Indonesia and Surinam. The long east/west stretch of Oude and Nieuwe Binnenweg is not only handy for many of the sights, it's also chock-full of good cafés, café-bars and restaurants, and the canal district of Oudehaven has introduced to the city a good selection of places to eat while taking in the relaxed vibe. Along the waterfront, various warehouses have been transformed into mega-restaurants, particularly around the Noordereiland isle in the middle of the river, while in Kop Van Zuid, the Wilhelminapier Quay offers quality restaurants and tasty views too. Many establishments are closed at lunchtime, except business restaurants and those that set a high gastronomic standard and like to show it off in the middle of the day as well as in the evening. The bill includes a service charge, so tipping is optional: round up the total if you're pleased with the service.

❀ ❀ **Parkheuvel** (Erik van Loo) XxxX 舘 ≤ 斎 ✿ **P**
Heuvellaan 21 ⊠ *3016 GL – ℰ (0 10) 436 05 30* Plan: **E3**
– www.parkheuvel.nl
– closed 1-3 April, 27 April, 10 May, 20-22 May, 30 July-21 August,
27 December-9 January, 11-15 February, Saturday lunch, Monday and
Tuesday
Menu 58 € (lunch), 80/140 €
– Carte 88/132 €
• Creative • Elegant •

The elegant Parkheuvel, beautifully situated beside the river Maas, is a big name in Dutch gastronomy. It received its first Michelin Star in 1990 – and Erik van Loo upholds this tradition with cuisine that's well-crafted, meticulously prepared and has a natural generosity. His signature dishes are must-tries!
→ Kikkerboutjes met kalfszwezerik en komkommergazpacho. Gepocheerde kalfshaas met bundelzwammen. Banaan met chocoladecrumble, bruine suiker en advocaat.

❀ ❀ **Fred** (Fred Mustert) XxxX 舘 **AC** 彭 (dinner)
Honingerdijk 263 ⊠ *3063 AM – ℰ (0 10) 212 01 10* Plan: **C2**
– www.restaurantfred.nl
– closed 30 July-12 August, 25 December-1 January, Saturday lunch and
Sunday
Menu 48 € (lunch)/137 €
– Carte 85/108 €
• Creative French • Elegant •

'Less is more' is Fred's philosophy. The decor is contemporary and elegant; stunning because of its class and simplicity. And the dishes? They are refined, well considered creations, where every ingredient has a function. Fred Mustert delivers a personalised experience, where everything matches.
→ Gebakken langoustines met meloen, bleekselderij en komkommer. Zeetong met truffel en fregola. Gekaramelliseerde banaan met pinda, chocolade en hazelnootroomijs.

❀ ❀ **FG - François Geurds** XxX 舘 **AC** ✿ 彭
Katshoek 37B ⊠ *3032 AE – ℰ (0 10) 425 05 20* Plan: **B2**
– www.fgrestaurant.nl
– closed 1-17 January, Sunday and Monday
Menu 45 € (lunch), 125/185 €
– Carte 114/162 €
• Creative • Fashionable • Chic •

François Geurds has a clear vision and he brings it to life in this restaurant, which is urban, trendy and original. The chef adopts a style that is very detailed, sometimes even playful, but always keeps his focus on the flavours of his high quality ingredients and sauces. FG could easily stand for Fantastically Good!
→ Oester met rabarber en ganzenlever. Piepkuiken met langoustine en truffel. Macadamia met vanilleroomijs.

❀ **Amarone** (Gert Blom) XxX 舘 **AC**
Meent 72a ⊠ *3011 JN – ℰ (0 10) 414 84 87* Plan: **F1**
– www.restaurantamarone.nl
– closed 23 July-12 August, 1-4 January, Bank Holidays, Saturday
lunch and Sunday
Menu 38 € (lunch), 65/85 €
– Carte 75/95 €
• Modern French • Chic •

This fashionable city restaurant emanates the same elegance and superior quality as the fine wine from which it takes its name. Inventive cuisine made from the best ingredients.
→ Krokante kalfszwezerik met aardpeer en artisjok. Op de huid gebakken zeebaars, rode-uiencompote en in ganzenvet gegaarde aardappel. Sinaasappel met tonkamousse en sorbet van citroen en limoncello.

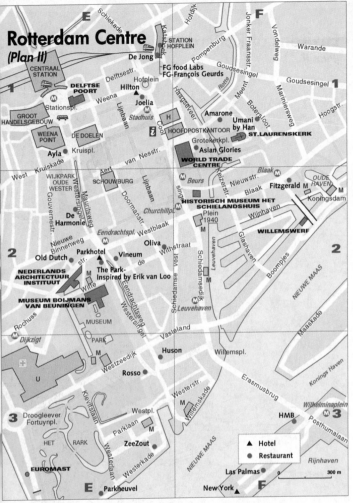

Rotterdam Centre
(Plan II)

Plan: **F2**

✿ Fitzgerald

XxX 舘 斎 ✿

Gelderseplein 49 ✉ *3011 WZ –* ✆ *(0 10) 268 70 10
– www.restaurantfitzgerald.nl – closed 27 April, 22 July-5 August,
27 December-5 January, Saturday lunch, Sunday and Monday*
Menu 30 € (lunch), 43/80 € – Carte 61/100 €

• Modern French • Elegant •

Italian marble combined with design and vintage features, big windows and a beautiful
enclosed garden all lend Fitzgerald a special allure. The modern, sometimes surprising
twists the chef gives his dishes take them to a higher level and create a fantastic
exchange of flavours. The sommelier complements this with excellent wines.
→ Gebrande langoustines met spitskoolkimchi, citrus en grijze garnalen.
Skrei op matchavelouté, zoetzure radijs en mosterd. Mango met gepofte
boekweit, schapenyoghurt en pannacotta.

477

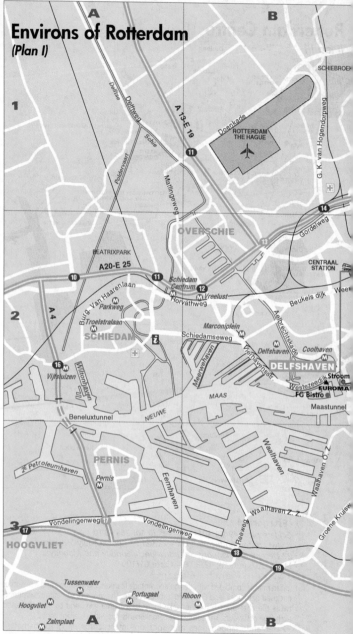

Environs of Rotterdam
(Plan I)

SCHIEBROEK

Delftse

Delftweg

Schie

Poldervaart

A 13-E 19

Doenkade

ROTTERDAM
THE HAGUE

G. K. van Hogendorpweg

Matlingeweg

OVERSCHIE

Gordelweg

CENTRAAL
STATION

BEATRIXPARK

A20-E 25

13

Schiedam
Centrum

Vreelust

Weer

Beukels dijk

Horváthweg

Burg. Van Haarenlaan

Parkweg

Marconiplein

Schiedamseweg

Aelbrechtskade

Coolhaven

Troelstralaan

SCHIEDAM

Delfshaven

DELFSHAVEN

Verhaevenstr.

Stroom
EUROMA

Vijfsluizen

Wilonhaven

Meerwehaven

Westzeedijk

FG Bistro

Maastunnel

MAAS

Beneluxtunnel

NIEUWE

Waalhaven

Waalhaven O. Z.

PERNIS

Petroleumhaven

Pernis

Eernhaven

Waalhaven Z. Z.

Reeweg

Groene Kruisw.

Vondelingenweg

Vondelingenweg

HOOGVLIET

Tussenwater

Portugaal

Rhoon

Hoogvliet

Zalmplaat

A

B

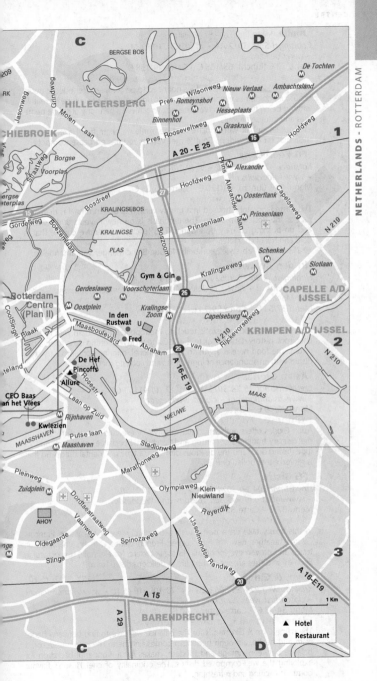

C

D

BERGSE BOS

De Tochten

209

RK

Grindweg

Jasonweg

HILLEGERSBERG

Wilsonweg Nieuw Verlaat Ambachtsland

CHIEBROEK

Molen Laan

Pres. Romeynshof

Binnenhof Hesseplaats

Straatweg

Borgse

Voorplas

Bosdreef

Pres. Rooseveltweg

Graskruid

A 20 - E 25

16

1

Hoofdweg

erse
terplas

15

Gordelweg

Boezemlaan

KRALINGSEBOS

27

Hoofdweg

Prins Alexander

Alexander

Oosterflank

Capelseweg

KRALINGSE

Boszoom

Prinsenlaan

Prins Alexanderlaan

Prinsenlaan

N 219

PLAS

Schenkel

Kralingseweg

Gym & Gin

26

Siotiaan

CAPELLE A/D
IJSSEL

Rotterdam-
Centre
(Plan II)

Gerdesiaweg

Voorschoterlaan

Oostplein

Kralingse
Zoom

Capelseburg

Rijckevorselweg

KRIMPEN A/D IJSSEL

Coolsingel

Blaak

Maasboulevard

In den
Rustwat

U

Capelseburg

N 210

N 210

steland

Fred

Abraham

25

van

De Hef

Pincoffs

Rosestr.

16-E 19

MAAS

CEO Baas
an het Vlees

Allure

Laan op Zuid

NIEUWE

Rijnhaven

24

Kwiezien

Putse laan

MAASHAVEN

Maashaven

Stadionweg

Pleinweg

Marathonweg

Zuidplein

Olympiaweg

Klein
Nieuwland

AHOY

Dordsestraatweg

Reyerdijk

Oldegaarde

Vaanweg

Spinozaweg

IJsselmondse Randweg

nge

Slinge

3

A 16-E19

A 15

20

A 16-E-19

A 29

BARENDRECHT

C

D

0   1 Km

▲ Hotel
● Restaurant

479

ఔ **Joelia** (Mario Ridder) – Hotel Hilton ✗✗✗ ✿ ✿
Coolsingel 5 ✉ *3012 AA* – ✆ *(0 10) 710 80 34* Plan: **E1**
– www.joelia.eu
Menu 33 € (lunch), 63/165 € – Carte 99/158 €
• Creative French • Design • Trendy •
Joelia proves that refinement does not need to be complex. Her eclectic decor beautifully combines vintage and design to unique effect. Her cuisine is creative without being fussy, and serves one aim: to achieve a harmony of subtle perfumes and intense flavours.
➜ Gouden gebak van brioche met ganzenlever en truffel. Hazenrug met rode biet en knolselderij. Soufflé met vanille, roomijs en bessencompote.

ఔ **FG Food Labs** ✗ ✿
Katshoek 41 ✉ *3032 AE* – ✆ *(0 10) 425 05 20* Plan: **E1**
– www.fgfoodlabs.nl
Menu 43 € (lunch), 70/120 € – Carte 55/83 €
• Creative • Fashionable •
This 'taste laboratory' housed in a trendy version of a train tunnel is definitely part of the Rotterdam scene. The emphasis is on new flavours and textures and on pushing culinary boundaries. This results in inventive cuisine that is bold and full of character.
➜ Nitro vijzel 'lab style'. Porkbelly 48 uur. Blanc-manger van amandelen.

ఴ **In den Rustwat** ✗✗✗ ✿ 🅰🅲 ✿
Honingerdijk 96 ✉ *3062 NX* – ✆ *(0 10) 413 41 10* Plan: **C2**
– www.idrw.nl – closed 15 July-6 August, 31 December-8 January, Sunday and Monday
Menu 37/53 € – Carte 59/74 €
• Modern cuisine • Intimate •
In den Rustwat adds an exotic touch to metropolitan Rotterdam with its thatched roof, history dating back to the 16C and an idyllic setting close to an arboretum. The food here is anything but traditional, offering contemporary-style dishes with an abundance of ingredients and cooking methods.

ఴ **Asian Glories** ✗✗ 🅰🅲 ✿
Leeuwenstraat 15 ✉ *3011 AL* – ✆ *(0 10) 411 71 07* Plan: **F1**
– www.asianglories.nl – closed Wednesday
Menu 30/49 € – Carte 32/51 €
• Chinese • Family •
Asian Glories offers authentic, high quality Chinese cuisine, which focuses on the culinary traditions of Canton and Szechuan. Specialities on the menu include Peking duck and the delicious dim sum, a type of Oriental dumpling that is served either boiled or fried.

ఴ **FG Bistro** ✗✗ ≤
Lloydstraat 204 ✉ *3024 EA* – ✆ *(0 10) 747 01 50* Plan: **B3**
– www.fgbistro.nl – closed Tuesday and Wednesday
Menu 37 € – Carte 32/60 €
• French • Luxury • Bistro •
In this luxury take on a bistro, with a beautiful view of the water, François Geurds breathes new life into clichéd French dishes with his characteristic touch and proven eye for detail. His steak tartare, for example, is spectacular. Even Asian dishes are served up here in delicious bistro form.

ఴ **Gym & Gin** ✗✗ ✿ 🅰🅲 ✿ 🅿
Kralingseweg 224 ✉ *3062 CG* – ✆ *(0 10) 210 45 10 – www.gymandgin.nl*
– closed first week August
Menu 34/43 € – Carte approx. 40 €
• International • Vintage • Trendy •
The name Gym & Gin stands for the balance we have to find between hedonism and health, although hedonism comes first here. The colourful decor, a balance between vintage and modern, makes for a wonderful backdrop for exploring the well-composed dishes. The originality of chef Huson's flavour bombs is exciting and refreshing.

Huson
XX 🏠 🄰🄲 ⇔

Scheepstimmermanslaan 14 ⊠ *3011 BS – ℰ (0 10)* Plan: **E3**
413 03 71 – www.huson.nl – closed Saturday lunch and Sunday dinner after 7.30pm
Menu 33 € 🍷 (lunch), 35/65 € – Carte 44/54 €
• Modern cuisine • Friendly • Vintage •
Huson is a trendy establishment where a lively industriousness always prevails. Here guests' mouths will water at the marvellous pairing of creativity with international ingredients in small dishes which are as subtle as they are exuberant. The chef is a dab hand at beautifully balancing fullness of flavour with freshness, as his signature dishes show.

The Park - Inspired by Erik van Loo – Parkhotel
XX ⭘
🄰🄲 ⇔ 🄿

Westersingel 70 ⊠ *3015 LB – ℰ (0 10) 440 81 65*
– www.thepark.nl – closed Saturday lunch and Sunday Plan: **E2**
lunch
Menu 29 € (lunch), 36/53 € – Carte 40/61 €
• Modern cuisine • Trendy •
The food at this blue-tinted luxury brasserie doesn't lie: they understand the meaning of taste here. The dishes are creatively inspired and beautifully composed. Every dish is perfectly seasoned and fits into the complete picture. So it makes sense when you hear that The Park is inspired by Erik van Loo, the chef of Michelin star establishment Parkheuvel.

Ayla
X 🏠

Kruisplein 153 ⊠ *3014 DD – ℰ (0 10) 254 00 05* Plan: **E1**
– www.ayla.nl
Menu 15 € (lunch), 25/48 € – Carte approx. 40 € – *(open until 11.30pm)*
• Mediterranean cuisine • Tapas bar • Mediterranean décor •
The air is sultry, Mediterranean scents quietly fill the room. Welcome to Ayla, where guests can enjoy the international atmosphere all day long. This is a relaxed spot where experienced chefs put all their skill into enhancing southern European flavours. Not unnecessarily complicated, but simply delicious.

Kwiezien
X 🏠 🄰🄲

Delistraat 20 ⊠ *3072 ZK – ℰ (0 10) 215 14 40* Plan: **C2**
– www.kwiezien.nl – closed 25 and 26 December, 1 January and Monday
Menu 33/45 € – *(dinner only)*
• Market cuisine • Family •
Sit back and enjoy the tempting range of dishes which this cosy restaurant has put together. Karin and Remco work exclusively with fresh ingredients and are constantly in search of inspiring combinations. The rich palette of flavours they create is sometimes daring but they always pull it off.

Umami by Han
X

Binnenrotte 140 ⊠ *3011 HC – ℰ (0 10) 433 31 39* Plan: **F1**
– www.umami-restaurant.com – closed 31 December
Menu 26/30 € – Carte approx. 18 € – *(dinner only) (booking advisable)*
• Asian • Fashionable •
The trendy, modern interior with bright colours immediately catches the eye, but the trump card of this restaurant is its rock solid concept… a range of Asian dishes with a French twist from which you can choose your heart's desire. A wonderful journey of discovery at amazing prices!

Old Dutch
XXX 🏠 ⇔ 🍴 🄿

Rochussenstraat 20 ⊠ *3015 EK – ℰ (0 10) 436 03 44* Plan: **E2**
– www.olddutch.net – closed Bank Holidays, Saturday and Sunday
Menu 40 € (lunch), 53/63 € – Carte 55/93 €
• Classic French • Classic décor •
With its serving staff decked out in suits and bow ties, this traditional restaurant with an incredibly spacious terrace has the atmosphere of a gentlemen's club. Familiar produce is given a fresh twist. Meat is even sliced at your table.

Allure
XX ≤ 🏠 AC

Cargadoorskade 107 ⊠ 3071 AW – ℰ (0 10) 486 65 29   Plan: **C2**
– www.restaurant-allure.nl – closed 26 December-4 January and Monday
Menu 25 € (lunch), 39/60 € – Carte 46/55 €
• Market cuisine • Design •

The journey starts with a purple-tinted design interior which fits beautifully with the fantastic view of the marina. Then comes the champagne trolley, the top-quality ingredients worked into modern French dishes with an international twist, and finally the well-stocked cheese trolley. Allure fully lives up to its name.

De Harmonie 23
XX ⇔

Westersingel 95 ⊠ 3015 LC – ℰ (0 10) 436 36 10   Plan: **E2**
– www.deharmonierotterdam.nl – closed 27 December-9 January, Bank Holidays, Sunday and Monday
Menu 45/99 € – Carte 55/85 €
• Creative • Elegant • Trendy •

The magnificent restored interior of De Harmonie 23 adds power to the ambition of chef Somer. His creativity is beautifully expressed here, making the name of his restaurant a reality, with authenticity and honesty combining to exciting effect. The extensive new tasting menu allows diners to truly discover his cuisine.

HMB
XX ≤ 🏠 ⇔

Holland Amerika Kade 104 ⊠ 3072 MC – ℰ (0 10)   Plan: **F3**
760 06 20 – www.hmb-restaurant.nl – closed 23 April-1 May, 31 July-14 August, 28 December-10 January, Saturday lunch, Sunday and Monday
Menu 38 € (lunch), 57/77 € – Carte 43/61 € – (booking advisable)
• International • Fashionable •

HMB stands for hummingbird, and in keeping with its name, the interior of this restaurant is elegantly playful. The large windows also provide a stunning view of the Rotterdam skyline. The delicious, beautifully presented dishes are prepared with care and attention using ingredients from different international culinary traditions.

Las Palmas
XX 🏠 ⇔

Wilhelminakade 330 ⊠ 3072 AR – ℰ (0 10) 234 51 22   Plan: **F3**
– www.restaurantlaspalmas.nl – closed Saturday lunch
Menu 26 € (lunch), 40/90 € – Carte 62/81 €
• Classic cuisine • Brasserie •

There's always plenty going on at Herman den Blijker's brasserie, which is styled as a loft. You get a sneak preview before your meal arrives: meats age in special cabinets, the shellfish is on display and the open kitchen is on a raised platform. Dishes are recognisable and produce is fresh. The lunch menu is great.

Vineum
XX 🍷 🏠 ⇔

Eendrachtsweg 23 ⊠ 3012 LB – ℰ (010) 720 09 66   Plan: **E2**
– www.vineum.nl – closed 27 April, 16-28 July, 22-27 October, 25 and 26 December, 31 December-1 January, 26 February-3 March, Saturday lunch and Sunday
Menu 33 € (lunch), 35/55 € – Carte 28/76 €
• Modern French • Friendly • Wine bar •

The wine list is the heart and soul of this restaurant with a pleasant city garden at the back. The variety and quality of the wines is truly remarkable, supported by cuisine that showcases excellent ingredients. The experienced chef brings freshness to the plate, using produce at its best.

Zeezout
XX 🏠 AC

Westerkade 11b ⊠ 3016 CL – ℰ (0 10) 436 50 49   Plan: **E3**
– www.restaurantzeezout.nl – closed Sunday lunch and Monday
Menu 43/69 € – Carte 57/65 €
• Seafood • Design •

Fish, fish and more fish. In the shipping quarter of one of the most important port cities in the world diners can enjoy the best the water has to offer. Their pure flavours seduce time and again, with dishes such as the salt-crusted sea bream topping the list. The stylishly decorated dining room also offers a view of the River Maas.

Rosso

X AC

Plan: **E3**

Van Vollenhovenstraat 15 (access via Westerlijk Handelsterrein) ⊠ *3016 BE –* ℰ *(0 10) 225 07 05 – www.rossorotterdam.nl – closed Sunday*
Menu 46/75 € – Carte 40/56 € – *(dinner only)*
• Fusion • Fashionable • Trendy •

Shades of red lend colour to the relaxed and intimate interior of this trendy restaurant. It offers fine wines and a menu that you can put together as you please, choosing from a variety of small dishes prepared with top quality produce. Excellent food and an enjoyable ambience.

C.E.O baas van het vlees

X 🛱 ♢

Plan: **C2**

Sumatraweg 1 ⊠ *3072 ZP –* ℰ *(0 10) 290 94 54 – www.ceobaasvanhetvlees.nl – closed Monday*
Menu 40 € – Carte 41/82 € – *(dinner only until 11pm)*
• Meats and grills • Contemporary décor • Bistro •

A lively bistro where prime quality American meat takes pride of place on the menu. All you have to decide is how you would like your meat cooked and whether you would like French fries and homemade mayonnaise as part of your meal.

De Hef

X AC

Plan: **D2**

Stieltjesplein 2 ⊠ *3071 JT –* ℰ *(010) 485 15 35 – www.restaurantdehef.nl – closed 29 July-21 August, 1-15 January, Sunday and Monday*
Menu 38 € – *(dinner only)*
• Creative • Intimate • Friendly •

Opposite the De Hef railway bridge, hostess Saskia and chef Martin have converted this former café into a lively bistro. The fact that it achieved popularity so quickly is down to a very attractive set menu. The experienced chef's creative dishes elevate simple flavours.

De Jong

X 🛱

Plan: **E1**

Raampoortstraat 38 ⊠ *3032 –* ℰ *(010) 465 79 55 – www.restaurantdejong.nl – closed Monday and Tuesday*
Menu 45 € – *(dinner only)*
• Organic • Neighbourhood •

Chef Jim de Jong loves vegetables and herbs. He grows them himself and is inventive in preparing them, always placing their natural flavours front and centre. In this old train tunnel, decorated in vintage style, he shows diners how surprising and delicious organic cuisine can be. Eating at De Jong is an adventure every time.

Oliva

X 🛱 AC ♢

Plan: **E2**

Witte de Withstraat 15a ⊠ *3012 BK –* ℰ *(0 10) 412 14 13 – www.restaurantoliva.nl – closed 25 December-1 January*
Menu 34/44 € – Carte 35/55 € – *(dinner only)*
• Italian • Bistro •

Enjoy down-to-earth Italian cuisine in this delightful trattoria. The menu changes daily and the dishes are made from ingredients imported straight from Italy. Authentic and delicious.

Hilton

🏢 ♨ ⅙ ₺ AC ⅏ ☂ 🚗

Plan: **E1**

Weena 10 ⊠ *3012 CM –* ℰ *(0 10) 710 80 00 – www.rotterdam.hilton.com*
246 rm – ♦149/269 € ♦♦149/269 € – ☳ 25 € – 8 suites
• Chain • Design •

Guests are received in a spacious, bright lobby and shown to a bedroom that combines comfort, warmth and minimalism. This fixture in the hotel scene has not stood still, instead keeping everything fresh and up-to-date. The city centre is all around you, but go straight to Roots restaurant to discover regional delicacies.
❀ **Joelia** – See restaurant listing

Pincoffs

⁂ ♨ **P**

Stieltjesstraat 34 ✉ *3071 JX –* ✆ *(0 10) 297 45 00*   Plan: **C2**
– www.hotelpincoffs.nl – closed 1-16 August
16 rm – ♦120/150 € ♦♦155/195 € – ⟳ 18 € – 1 suite
• Historic • Trendy • Modern •

This trendy renovated customs office is the place to be for visitors wanting to explore the city and indulge in a little pampering. Bulgari accessories in the bathroom, your favourite music on the Bluetooth sound system and impeccable, friendly service all add to the appeal.

Parkhotel

≤ ♺ ♨ ⁂ ♨ **P**

Westersingel 70 ✉ *3015 LB –* ✆ *(0 10) 436 36 11*   Plan: **E2**
– www.bilderberg.nl
187 rm – ♦89/129 € ♦♦99/249 € – ⟳ 25 € – 2 suites
• Business • Modern •

A contemporary hotel with a history dating back to 1922, situated in the heart of modern Rotterdam. The two tower blocks built in the 1980s offer panoramic views of the 'Architectural Capital of the Netherlands'.

⊛ **The Park - Inspired by Erik van Loo** – See restaurant listing

New York

⚒ ≤ ♿ ⁂ ♨ ⟲

Koninginnenhoofd 1 (Wilhelminapier) ✉ *3072 AD*   Plan: **F3**
– ✆ *(0 10) 439 05 00 – www.hotelnewyork.nl*
72 rm – ♦♦110/325 € – ⟳ 19 €
• Traditional • Vintage •

Stay at the New York hotel and experience the excitement of the fortune-seekers who came to buy their tickets here for the ocean crossing to New York. The whole place radiates character and dynamic energy, from the elegant rooms to the large restaurant, which has a pleasant, lively ambience.

Stroom

⚒ ♺ ⁂ ♨

Lloydstraat 1 ✉ *3024 EA –* ✆ *(0 10) 221 40 60*   Plan: **B2**
– www.stroomrotterdam.nl
18 rm – ♦109/129 € ♦♦129/159 € – ⟳ 18 € – 3 suites
• Townhouse • Functional • Design •

Once energy was generated in this former power station, today it houses a boutique hotel. The interior has a rather austere design, but the personal approach of the managers brings warmth to the place. The effect is truly electric.

OSLO

NORWAY
NORGE

konstantin32/iStock

OSLO
OSLO

LeoPatrizi/iStock

OSLO IN...

→ **ONE DAY**
Aker Brygge, Karl Johans Gate, Oslo Opera House.

→ **TWO DAYS**
Akershus, Astrup Fearnley Museum, ferry trip to Bygdøy.

→ **THREE DAYS**
Vigeland Park, Holmenkollen Ski Jump, Grunerlokka, Munch Museum.

Oslo has a lot going for it – and one slight downside: it's one of the world's most expensive cities. It also ranks high when it comes to its standard of living, however, and its position at the head of Oslofjord, surrounded by steep forested hills, is hard to match for drama and beauty.

It's a charmingly compact place to stroll round, particularly in the summer, when the daylight hours practically abolish the night and, although it may lack the urban cool of some other Scandinavian cities, it boasts its fair share of trendy clubs and a raft of Michelin Stars. There's a real raft, too: Thor Hyerdahl's famous Kon-Tiki – one of the star turns in a city that loves its museums.

Oslo's uncluttered feel is enhanced by parks and wide streets and, in the winter, there are times when you feel you have the whole place to yourself. Drift into the city by boat and land at the smart harbour of Aker Brygge; to the west lies the charming Bygdøy peninsula, home to museums permeated with the smell of the sea. Northwest is Frogner, with its famous sculpture park, the place where locals hang out on long summer days. The centre of town, the commercial hub, is Karl Johans Gate, bounded at one end by the Royal Palace and at the other by the Cathedral, while further east lie two trendy multi-cultural areas, Grunerlokka and Grønland, the former also home to the Edvard Munch Museum.

EATING OUT

Oslo has a very vibrant dining scene, albeit one that is somewhat expensive, particularly if you drink wine. The cooking can be quite classical and refined but there are plenty of restaurants offering more innovative menus too. What is in no doubt is the quality of the produce used, whether that's the ever-popular game or the superlative shellfish, which comes from very cold water, giving it a clean, fresh flavour. Classic Norwegian dishes often include fruit, such as lingonberries with venison. Lunch is not a major affair; most prefer just a snack or sandwich at midday while making dinner the main event of the day. You'll find most diners are seated by 7pm and are offered a 6, 7 or 8 course menu which they can reduce at their will, with a paired wine menu alongside. It doesn't have to be expensive, though. Look out for konditoris (bakeries) where you can pick up sandwiches and pastries, and kafeterias which serve substantial meals at reasonable prices. Service is a strength; staff are generally very polite, speak English and are fully versed in the menu.

NORWAY - OSLO

Maaemo (Esben Holmboe Bang)   XxX 🅰️ ⇔
Schweigaardsgate 15B (entrance via staircase) ✉️ *0191*   Plan: **D2**
– 🚇 Grønland – ℰ 22 17 99 69 – www.maaemo.no
– Closed 15-31 July, 23 December-8 January, 28 March-3 April, 16-18 May and Sunday-Tuesday
Menu 2800 NOK – (dinner only and lunch Friday-Saturday) (booking essential) (tasting menu only)
• Modern cuisine • Design • Fashionable •

Maaemo means 'Mother Earth' and this striking restaurant is all about connecting with nature. Service is perfectly choreographed and dishes are brought down from the mezzanine feature kitchen and finished at the table by the chefs themselves. Innovative, intricate cooking awakens the senses with sublime flavour combinations – some dishes take several days to construct.
→ Oyster emulsion with mussels and dill. Reindeer with preserved plum sauce and artichokes. Brown butter ice cream, molasses and roasted hazelnuts.

Statholdergaarden (Bent Stiansen)   XxX 🐝 ⇔
Rådhusgata 11 (entrance on Kirkegata) ✉️ *0151*   Plan: **C3**
– 🚇 Stortinget – ℰ 22 41 88 00 – www.statholdergaarden.no
– Closed 15 July-6 August, 23 December-3 January, 25 March-3 April, Sunday and bank holidays
Menu 975 NOK – Carte 925/1080 NOK – (dinner only) (booking essential)
• Classic cuisine • Intimate • Elegant •

A charming 17C house in the city's heart. Three elegant rooms feature an array of antiques and curios, and have wonderfully ornate stucco ceilings hung with chandeliers. Expertly rendered classical cooking uses seasonal Norwegian ingredients in familiar combinations. Service is well-versed and willing.
→ Halibut with artichoke, sorrel, barley and lime sauce. Veal, sweetbreads, celeriac and morels. Norwegian raspberry, champagne and rose.
⏍O **Statholderens Mat og Vin Kjeller** – See restaurant listing

Galt (Bjørn Svensson)   XX
Frognerveien 12B ✉️ *0263 – ℰ (47) 48514886*   Plan: **A2**
– www.galt.no
– Closed 23 December-3 January, 31 March-3 April, Sunday and Monday
Menu 795 NOK – Carte 530/650 NOK – (dinner only)
• Modern cuisine • Rustic • Chic •

The friends who previously ran Fauna and Oscarsgate have created this warm, intimate restaurant with an appealingly rustic feel. The set menu of 6 courses is nicely balanced, flavour combinations have been well thought through, and the contrast in textures is a particular strength.
→ Langoustine, watercress emulsion and fermented leeks. Halibut, onion and lovage. Oat ice cream, praline and crystallised chocolate.

Kontrast (Mikael Svensson)   XX & 🅰️ ⇔
Maridalsveien 15 ✉️ *0178 – ℰ 21 60 01 01*   Plan: **D1**
– www.restaurant-kontrast.no
– Closed Christmas, New Year, Easter, 17 May, Sunday and Monday
Menu 950/1450 NOK – Carte 555/615 NOK – (dinner only)
• Scandinavian • Design • Fashionable •

A modern restaurant with a stark, semi-industrial feel created by a concrete floor, exposed pipework and an open kitchen. Seasonal, organic Norwegian produce is used to create refined, original, full-flavoured dishes whose apparent simplicity often masks their complex nature. The service is well-paced.
→ Tomatoes with pineapple weed gel and tagetes oil. Pork with elm seeds and Holtefjell XO cheese. Strawberries and meadowsweet.

restauranteik
XX AC ⇔

Clarion Collection H. Savoy - Universitetsgata 11 — Plan: **C2**
✉ *0164* – Ⓜ *National Theatret* – ℰ *22 36 07 10* – *www.restauranteik.no*
– Closed July, Easter, Christmas, Sunday and Monday
Menu 395 NOK *– (dinner only) (tasting menu only)*
• **Modern cuisine** • **Fashionable** • **Brasserie** •

A contemporary L-shaped dining room set within a hotel close to the National Gallery. It's minimalist in style, with colourful artwork, an open kitchen and a glass-walled wine cellar. The weekly 3-5 course set menu comprises inventive international cuisine. Service is efficient and the atmosphere is friendly.

Smalhans
X ⇔

Ullevålsveien 43 ✉ *0171* – ℰ *22 69 60 00* — Plan: **C1**
– www.smalhans.no – Closed 3 weeks July, Easter, Christmas and Monday
Menu 450 NOK (dinner) – Carte 320/490 NOK
• **Traditional cuisine** • **Neighbourhood** • **Simple** •

A sweet neighbourhood café with friendly staff and an urban feel. Coffee and homemade cakes are served in the morning, with a short selection of dishes including soup and a burger on offer between 12pm and 4pm. A daily hot dish is available from 4-6pm, while set menus and sharing plates are served at dinner.

À L'aise
XxX 🏵 AC ⇔

Essendrops gate 6 ✉ *0368* – Ⓜ *Majorstuen* — Plan: **A1**
– ℰ 210 55 700 – www.alaise.no – Closed 15 July-8 August, 9-17 April,
Sunday and Monday
Menu 595 NOK (lunch) – Carte 895/1070 NOK *– (booking advisable)*
• **Modern cuisine** • **Intimate** • **Elegant** •

This elegant, sophisticated restaurant is run by an engaging, knowledgeable team. The experienced chef is something of a Francophile: expect refined Gallic dishes packed with flavour and crafted from French and Norwegian produce.

Feinschmecker
XxX 🏵 AC ⇔

Balchens gate 5 ✉ *0265* – ℰ *22 12 93 80* — Plan: **A2**
– www.feinschmecker.no – Closed 3 weeks summer, Christmas, Easter and
Sunday
Menu 845 NOK – Carte 760/1015 NOK *– (dinner only)*
• **Traditional cuisine** • **Classic décor** • **Neighbourhood** •

This long-standing restaurant has a cosy, welcoming atmosphere and a loyal local following, and is run by a charming team. The well-presented dishes are classically based, with French influences. Wine pairings are available.

Festningen
XX 🏵 ⬚ 🏡 ढ AC ⇔

Myntgata 9 ✉ *0151* – ℰ *22 83 31 00* — Plan: **C3**
– www.festningenrestaurant.no – Closed 23 December-5 January, Easter
and Sunday
Menu 315/595 NOK – Carte 615/855 NOK
• **Modern cuisine** • **Brasserie** • **Fashionable** •

A smart, contemporary brasserie with a terrace and lovely views over the water to Aker Brygge; it was once a prison and its name means 'fortress'. The experienced kitchen create unfussy, attractively presented modern Nordic dishes using fresh local produce. The impressive wine list is strong on burgundy.

BA 53
XX 🏡 AC ⇔

Bygdoy Allé 53 ✉ *0265* – ℰ *21 42 05 90* — Plan: **A2**
– www.ba53.no – Closed July, Christmas, Easter and Sunday
Carte 380/540 NOK *– (dinner only)*
• **Modern cuisine** • **Fashionable** • **Neighbourhood** •

A moody cocktail bar combines with a relaxed, softly lit brasserie to create this stylish neighbourhood hotspot. Menus offer a mix of Nordic classics and more modern dishes; four per person is ample.

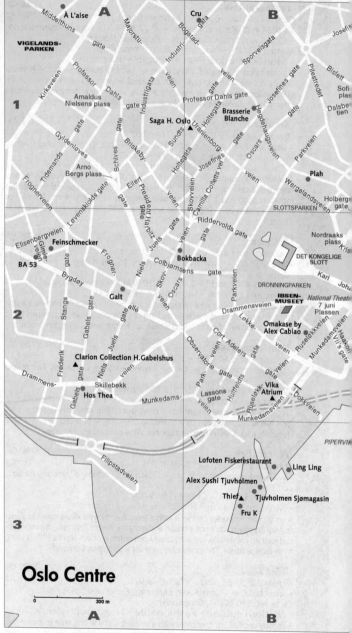

Oslo Centre

0 — 300 m

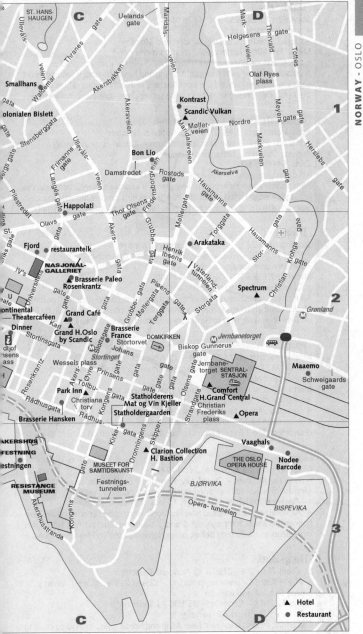

Bokbacka

XX ⇔

Skovveien 15 ✉ 0257 – ✆ 41 26 01 44 – www.bokbacka.no – Closed Christmas, Easter, Sunday and Monday Plan: **A2**

Menu 795 NOK – *(dinner only) (tasting menu only)*

• Modern cuisine • Fashionable • Neighbourhood •

A unique 'food bar' with clean, light styling and fun, idiosyncratic features; most seats are arranged around the open kitchen, with only 4 other tables. Many of the theatrically presented dishes on the set omakase-style menu have a story.

Brasserie Paleo - Hotel Rosenkrantz

XX ♿ AC ⇔

Rosenkrantz gate 1 ✉ 0159 – Ⓜ National Theatrer – ✆ 23 31 55 80 – www.brasseriepaleo.no – Closed early July-early August, Christmas, Easter and Sunday Plan: **C2**

Carte 545/595 NOK

• Scandinavian • Design • Brasserie •

With a name which reflects its philosophy, and a contemporary urban style, this is not your typical hotel restaurant. Watch the chefs prepare attractive modern Scandinavian dishes in the open kitchen. Service is professional and friendly.

Dinner

XX AC ⇔

Stortingsgata 22 ✉ 0161 – Ⓜ National Theatret – ✆ 23 10 04 66 – www.dinner.no – Closed 24 December-1 January and Sunday lunch Plan: **C2**

Menu 399/529 NOK – Carte 325/475 NOK

• Chinese • Design • Elegant •

An intimate restaurant on the central square, close to the National Theatre. A black frosted glass façade masks a smart split-level interior. The kitchen focuses on Sichuan cuisine, with some artfully presented dim sum at lunch.

Fjord

XX AC

Kristian Augusts gt. 11 ✉ 0164 – Ⓜ National Theatret – ✆ 22 98 21 50 – www.restaurantfjord.no – Closed Christmas, Easter, Sunday and Monday Plan: **C2**

Menu 445/695 NOK – *(dinner only) (booking essential) (tasting menu only)*

• Seafood • Design • Fashionable •

A contemporary restaurant opposite the National Gallery. Inside it's dimly lit, with an open kitchen, unusual cobalt blue walls and buffalo horns set into the chandeliers. The 3-6 course menu offers flavoursome seafood dishes.

Fru K - Thief Hotel

XX ♿ AC ⇔ 🚗

Landgangen 1 ✉ 0252 – ✆ 24 00 40 40 – www.thethief.com – Closed July, Christmas, Easter, Sunday and Monday Plan: **B3**

Menu 895 NOK – *(dinner only) (tasting menu only)*

• Modern cuisine • Design • Fashionable •

A chic hotel restaurant named after Fru Krogh, who tended animals on the Tjuvholmen peninsula long ago. Set 5 and 7 course menus use fine Norwegian ingredients to create tasty dishes; prime Norwegian seafood features highly.

Happolati

XX 🏖

St. Olavs Plass 2 ✉ 0165 – Ⓜ National Theatret – ✆ 47 97 80 87 – www.happolati.no – Closed 23 December-3 January, Easter, Sunday and Monday Plan: **C1**

Menu 525 NOK – Carte 385/455 NOK – *(dinner only)*

• Asian • Design • Friendly •

This bright, modish restaurant fuses Asian and Nordic styles; its assured cooking uses good quality ingredients and many dishes are designed for sharing. Tightly packed tables and friendly service add to the vibrant ambience.

Hos Thea   XX

Gabels gate 11 ✉ *0272 – ℰ 22 44 68 74*   Plan: **A2**
– www.hosthea.no – Closed July, 24-26 December and 29 March-2 April
Carte 610/690 NOK – *(dinner only)*
• Italian • Family • Neighbourhood •

A small, well-established restaurant in a charming residential area. It's decorated in natural hues and hung with beautiful oils. Menus offer a concise selection of Mediterranean dishes; start with the delicious homemade bread.

Ling Ling   XX < 余 AC ⇄

Stranden 30 ✉ *0250 – ℰ 24 13 38 00*   Plan: **B3**
– www.lingling.hakkasan.com/oslo – Closed 24-27 December, 1 January and Sunday
Menu 298/988 NOK – Carte 375/880 NOK
• Cantonese • Fashionable •

This more casual sister to Hakkasan offers an abbreviated menu of its signature Cantonese dishes but made using Norwegian produce. It has a great marina location, a cool lounge-bar and a terrific rooftop bar and terrace come summer.

Nodee Barcode   XX 余 AC ⇄

Dronning Eufemais gate 28 ✉ *0191*   Plan: **D3**
– Ⓜ Jernbanetorget – ℰ 22 93 34 50 – www.nodee.no
– Closed 23 December-1 January and Sunday lunch
Menu 340/645 NOK – Carte 260/525 NOK
• Asian • Fashionable • Trendy •

A moody, elegant restaurant serving an all-encompassing Asian menu featuring dim sum, sushi and dishes cooked on the Robata grill – crispy Peking duck is their speciality. There's a bar and terrace on the 13th floor and on the 14th floor is Nodee Sky, with its appealing set menu and city views.

Plah   XX 䀻 余 AC ⇄

Hegdehaugsveien 22 ✉ *0167 – ℰ 22 56 43 00*   Plan: **B1**
– www.plah.no – Closed 2 weeks July, Christmas, Easter and Sunday
Menu 595/795 NOK – *(dinner only) (tasting menu only)*
• Thai • Neighbourhood • Friendly •

Norwegian ingredients blend with Thai flavours at this well-run restaurant. Choose between two tasting menus: the 'Journey Through Thailand' or the 'Journey Through The Jungle' (vegetarian). Dishes are eye-catching, imaginative and full of flavour. Their neighbouring bar serves traditional Thai street food.

Theatercaféen – Continental Hotel   XX 䀻 & AC ⇄

Stortingsgaten 24-26 ✉ *0117 – Ⓜ National Theatret*   Plan: **C2**
– ℰ 22 82 40 50 – www.theatercafeen.no – Closed Christmas-New Year
Menu 395 NOK (lunch) – Carte 550/950 NOK
• Traditional cuisine • Luxury • Romantic •

A prestigious Oslo institution in a grand hotel, this charming Viennese 'grand café' comes with pillars, black banquettes and art nouveau lighting. Fresh cakes and elaborate lunchtime sandwiches make way for ambitious dinners.

Tjuvholmen Sjømagasinet   XX 䀻 余 AC ⇄

Tjuvholmen Allé 14 ✉ *0251 – ℰ 23 89 77 77*   Plan: **B3**
– www.sjomagasinet.no – Closed Christmas, Easter, Sunday and bank holidays
Menu 355/675 NOK – Carte 585/795 NOK
• Seafood • Fashionable • Brasserie •

A vast restaurant with three dining rooms, a crab and lobster tank, a superb terrace and a wet fish shop. Its name means 'sea store' and menus are fittingly seafood based. Shellfish is from the nearby dock – the langoustines are fantastic.

⅃○ **Brasserie Blanche**   🗙 🏠 𝗔𝗖 ✛
Josefinesgate 23 ✉ *0352 –* ℰ *23 20 13 10*   Plan: **B1**
– www.blanche.no – Closed 9-31 July, 23-26 December and Monday
Menu 525 NOK – Carte 340/625 NOK – *(dinner only)*
• French • Cosy • Brasserie •
A cosy French restaurant housed in an 18C building which was originally a
stable and later spent time as a garage and an interior furnishings store. It has
a small front terrace, a bar decorated with wine boxes and a wall made of corks.
The chef is a Francophile and creates flavoursome classic French dishes.

⅃○ **Omakase by Alex Cabiao**   🗙
Ruseløkkveien 3, 1st floor ✉ *0251 –* ℰ *4568 5022*   Plan: **B2**
*– www.omakaseoslo.no – Closed Christmas, Easter, Sunday and bank
holidays*
Menu 1350 NOK – *(dinner only)*
• Sushi • Design •
A three-sided counter with seats for 15 and two sittings per evening. The fish
and shellfish come largely from Norwegian waters and the rice is American. The
no-choice menu offers around 18 servings of Edomae-style sushi, although
there can be surprises, like reindeer; some wine pairings are equally original.

⅃○ **Alex Sushi Tjuvholmen**   🗙 🏠
Strandpromenaden 11 ✉ *0252 –* ℰ *22 43 99 99*   Plan: **B3**
– www.alexsushi.no – Closed Easter, Christmas and Sunday
Menu 545/995 NOK (dinner) – Carte lunch 270/645 NOK
• Sushi • Simple • Neighbourhood •
This simple neighbourhood restaurant sits in a fantastic harbourside spot
and boasts a lovely heated terrace. The knowledgeable chefs skilfully pre-
pare sushi, sashimi and nigiri at lunch, followed by 3 set menus at dinner.

⅃○ **Arakataka**   🗙 𝗔𝗖 ✛
Mariboes gate 7 ✉ *0183 –* Ⓜ *Stortinget*   Plan: **D2**
– ℰ *23 32 83 00 – www.arakataka.no – Closed July, Christmas-New
Year and Easter*
Menu 575 NOK – Carte 405/510 NOK – *(dinner only) (booking advisable)*
• Norwegian • Fashionable • Friendly •
A smart glass-fronted restaurant with a central food bar, an open kitchen and a
buzzy atmosphere. Choose from a concise menu of seasonal Norwegian small
plates – they recommend 3 savoury dishes plus a dessert per person.

⅃○ **Bon Lio**   🗙
Fredensborgveien 42 ✉ *0171 –* ℰ *46 77 72 12*   Plan: **C1**
– www.bonlio.no – Closed Christmas, Easter, July, Sunday and Monday
Menu 795 NOK – *(dinner only) (booking essential) (surprise menu only)*
• Modern cuisine • Simple • Cosy •
A lively, fun gastro-bar in a characterful 200 year old cottage. The Norwegian
owner grew up in Mallorca and showcases local and imported ingredients in a
surprise 12-17 course tapas-style menu. Spanish beers and wines accompany.

⅃○ **Brasserie France**   🗙 🏠 𝗔𝗖 ✛
Øvre Slottsgate 16 ✉ *0157 –* Ⓜ *Stortinget*   Plan: **C2**
– ℰ *23 10 01 65 – www.brasseriefrance.no – Closed Easter, 23 December-
2 January, Sunday and lunch Monday*
Menu 395/550 NOK – Carte 435/700 NOK
• French • Brasserie • Traditional décor •
This lively Gallic brasserie in a pedestrianised shopping street has two private
dining rooms. Brasserie classics range from bouillabaisse to steak frites; for des-
sert, choose from the 'eat-as-much-as-you-like' pastry trolley.

Brasserie Hansken 🍴 ✿

Akersgate 2 ✉ *0158 –* Ⓜ *Stortinget –* ☎ *22 42 60 88* Plan: **C2**
– www.brasseriehansken.no – Closed 1 week Easter, 1 week Christmas,
Monday in July and Sunday
Menu 545/645 NOK – Carte 485/815 NOK
• Modern cuisine • Family • Brasserie •
A delightfully traditional brasserie, centrally located by City Hall, with various
charming dining areas and a fantastic terrace. Classical cooking follows the sea-
sons and mixes French and Scandic influences; seafood is a speciality.

Cru 🍴 🍸

Ingelbrecht, Knudssøns gate 1 ✉ *0365 –* Ⓜ *Majorstuen* Plan: **B1**
– ☎ *23 98 98 98 – www.cru.no – Closed 2 July-4 August, 22 December-*
4 January, Easter and Sunday
Menu 395 NOK – Carte 480/560 NOK – *(dinner only)*
• Norwegian • Wine bar • Trendy •
Upstairs, in the rustic restaurant, they serve a set 4 course menu with inventive
British touches and 4 optional extra courses; while downstairs, in the wine bar,
you can enjoy everything from nibbles to a full meal from the à la carte.

Grand Café – Grand H.Oslo by Scandic 🍴 🍸 🍽 🅰🅺 ✿

Karl Johans Gate 31 ✉ *0159 –* Ⓜ *Stortinget* Plan: **C2**
– ☎ *98 18 20 00 – www.grandcafeoslo.no – Closed Easter and Christmas*
Carte 425/585 NOK
• Modern cuisine • Classic décor • Vintage •
This iconic restaurant dates from 1874; look out for the colourful mural depicting past regulars including Edvard Munch and Henrik Ibsen. The concise
menu lists flavour-filled Nordic and international dishes. The cellar wine bar
opens Tues-Sat and offers snacks, charcuterie and over 1,500 bottles of wine.

Kolonialen Bislett 🍴 🍸 🅰🅺

Sofiesgate 16 ✉ *0170 –* ☎ *901 15 098* Plan: **C1**
– www.kolonialenbislett.no – Closed last 3 weeks July, Sunday and bank
holidays
Carte 350/560 NOK – *(booking essential at dinner)*
• Modern cuisine • Brasserie • Neighbourhood •
Close to the stadium you'll find this cosy, modern bistro – previously a grocer's
shop for nearly 80 years. The concise, keenly priced menu lists oysters, cured
meats and wholesome Norwegian classics that have been brought up-to-date.

Lofoten Fiskerestaurant 🍴 ≤ 🍸 ✿

Stranden 75 ✉ *0250 –* ☎ *22 83 08 08* Plan: **B3**
– www.lofotenfiskerestaurant.no – Closed Christmas
Menu 550 NOK – Carte 615/735 NOK
• Seafood • Brasserie • Simple •
A traditional fjord-side restaurant hung with bright modern artwork and offering lovely views from its large windows and sizeable terrace. Watch as fresh,
simply cooked fish and shellfish are prepared in the semi-open kitchen.

Statholderens Mat og Vin Kjeller – Statholdergaarden 🍴

Rådhusgate 11 (entrance from Kirkegata) ✉ *0151* Plan: **C3**
– Ⓜ *Stortinget –* ☎ *22 41 88 00 – www.statholdergaarden.no – Closed*
July, 22 December-3 January, Sunday and bank holidays
Menu 650 NOK – Carte 715/940 NOK – *(dinner only) (booking essential)*
• Norwegian • Rustic • Simple •
The informal sister of Statholdergaarden – set over three rooms in the old vaults
beneath it. One wall of the large entranceway is filled with wine bottles. Choose
from a huge array of small plates or go for the 10 course tasting menu.

Vaaghals ✗ 🍴 & 🕱 ↻

Dronning Eufemias gate 8 ⊠ 0151 – Ⓜ Jernbanetorget   Plan: **D3**
– ℰ 92 07 09 99 – www.vaaghals.com – Closed last 3 weeks July,
22 December-3 January, Easter and Sunday
Menu 695 NOK (dinner) – Carte 490/570 NOK
· Scandinavian · Brasserie · Fashionable ·
A bright, contemporary restaurant with an open kitchen and a terrace; located
on the ground floor of one of the modern 'barcode' buildings. Scandinavian
menus feature dry-aged meat; many of the dinner dishes are designed for sharing.

Continental ✿ ⅃⌀ & 🕱 🖳 🚗

Stortingsgaten 24-26 ⊠ 0117 – Ⓜ National Theatret   Plan: **C2**
– ℰ 22 82 40 00 – www.hotelcontinental.no – Closed Christmas-New Year
155 rm ⌂ – †1995/3995 NOK ††2495/4500 NOK – 2 suites
· Grand Luxury · Traditional · Classic ·
A classic hotel situated by the National Theatre and run by the 4th generation of
the family, who ensure the service remains personal. Bedrooms are stylish and
contemporary – the corner suites have balconies and views of the Royal Palace.
Dine in the grand café or from an inventive daily menu in Annen Etage.
🍴 **Theatercaféen** – See restaurant listing

Grand H.Oslo by Scandic ✿ ⅃⌀ 🕮 🍴 ⃝ & 🕱 🖳 🚗

Karl Johans Gate 31 ⊠ 0159 – Ⓜ Stortinget   Plan: **C2**
– ℰ 23 21 20 00 – www.grand.no
274 rm ⌂ – †2080/3085 NOK ††2280/3280 NOK – 5 suites
· Grand Luxury · Historic · Elegant ·
An imposing, centrally located hotel built in 1874; the guest areas and grand
ballrooms reflect this. Bedrooms are charming: some are modern, some are
feminine and others are in a belle époque style. Dine on international fare in
elegant Palmen or Nordic-inspired cooking in the Grand Café.

Clarion Collection H. Bastion ⅃⌀ ⃝ 🖳

Skippergata 5-7 ⊠ 0152 – Ⓜ Jernbanetorget   Plan: **C3**
– ℰ 22 47 77 00 – www.choicehotels.no – Closed Christmas-New Year and
23 March-3 April
99 rm ⌂ – †840/2935 NOK ††990/3235 NOK – 5 suites
· Business · Modern · Personalised ·
Two unassuming buildings house this boutique business hotel. The lounge has
an English country house feel and an unusual collection of pictures and antiques are displayed throughout. Go for one of the newer, more characterful
bedrooms. The small restaurant offers a complimentary one course supper.

Clarion Collection H. Gabelshus ❦ ⅃⌀ ⃝ 🖳 🅿

Gabelsgate 16 ⊠ 0272 – ℰ 23 27 65 00   Plan: **A2**
– www.nordicchoicehotels.no – Closed Easter and Christmas
114 rm ⌂ – †800/2240 NOK ††940/2780 NOK – 1 suite
· Traditional · Business · Classic ·
A beautiful ivy-covered house with a peaceful atmosphere, located in a smart
residential neighbourhood. Charming bedrooms are a pleasing mix of traditional and designer styles. The classical wood-furnished lounge offers a complimentary one course supper in the evening.

Comfort H. Grand Central ✿ ⅃⌀ & 🕱

Jernbanetorget 1 ⊠ 0154 – Ⓜ Jernbanetorget   Plan: **D2**
– ℰ 22 98 28 00 – www.comfortgrandcentral.no
170 rm ⌂ – †1420/1949 NOK ††1610/2249 NOK
· Chain · Business · Personalised ·
A great choice for businesspeople, this delightful hotel has a superb location
above the main train station. Many of the soundproofed bedrooms have been
individually styled and boast coordinating fabrics and colour schemes, as well
as feature bathrooms. The restaurant offers a menu of simple Italian dishes.

Opera 🏠🏠🏠

Dronning Eufemias gate 4 ✉ 0191 – Ⓜ Jernbanetorget
– ☏ 24 10 30 00 – www.thonhotels.no/opera – Closed Christmas and New Year

Plan: **D2**

480 rm ☲ – †1145/2705 NOK ††1395/3055 NOK – 2 suites

• Business • Modern • Personalised •

Set on the doorstep of the National Library and the Opera House, this imposing hotel has a subtle theatrical theme both in its décor and the naming of its rooms. Bedrooms come in warm colours; ask for one at the front with a balcony. The Scala restaurant uses Norwegian produce in international recipes.

Rosenkrantz 🏠🏠🏠

Rosenkrantz gate 1 ✉ 0159 – Ⓜ National Theatret
– ☏ 23 31 55 00 – www.thonhotels.no

Plan: **C2**

151 rm ☲ – †1395/3195 NOK ††1695/3495 NOK – 8 suites

• Business • Chain • Personalised •

Located in the city centre and perfect for the business traveller. The brightly styled 8th floor guest lounge has complimentary drinks, snacks and light meals. Functional bedrooms come with Smart TVs and modern bathrooms.

⑩ **Brasserie Paleo** – See restaurant listing

Thief 🏠🏠🏠

Landgangen 1 ✉ 0252 – ☏ 24 00 40 00
– www.thethief.com

Plan: **B3**

116 rm ☲ – †2790/5000 NOK ††2990/5500 NOK – 9 suites

• Luxury • Contemporary • Themed •

A smart hotel with a superb spa, located on a huge development on Thief Island. Works from global artists – including Andy Warhol – feature throughout. Facilities are state-of-the-art and a tablet controls all of the technology in the bedrooms. Dine on international dishes in Foodbar, which moves to the rooftop in summer, or seafood-focused tasting menus in Fru K.

⑩ **Fru K** – See restaurant listing

Park Inn 🏠🏠

Ovre Slottsgate 2c ✉ 0157 – Ⓜ Stortinget
– ☏ 22 40 01 00 – www.parkinn.com/hotel-oslo

Plan: **C2**

118 rm ☲ – †995/3295 NOK ††1095/3395 NOK

• Business • Chain • Minimalist •

A converted apartment block near Karl Johans Gate. Inside it's bright and modern with pleasant guest areas. Good-sized, functional bedrooms have pale wood furniture and modern lighting; the top floor rooms have balconies.

Saga H. Oslo 🏠🏠

Eilert Sundstgate 39 ✉ 0259 – ☏ 22 55 44 90
– www.sagahoteloslo.no – Closed Christmas and Easter

Plan: **B1**

47 rm ☲ – †995/2895 NOK ††1395/3495 NOK

• Townhouse • Historic • Personalised •

A late Victorian townhouse with a smart, contemporary interior, set in a quiet city suburb. Most of the bedrooms are spacious: they have bold feature walls, modern facilities – including coffee machines – and small but stylish shower rooms. There's a Japanese restaurant in the basement.

Scandic Vulkan 🏠

Maridalsveien 13 ✉ 0178 – ☏ 21 05 71 00
– www.scandichotels.com/vulkan – Closed Christmas and Easter

Plan: **D1**

149 rm ☲ – †800/1800 NOK ††990/2200 NOK

• Business • Chain • Design •

A designer hotel set on the site of a former silver mine, next to a great food market. Modern bedrooms have bold feature walls and good facilities; the external-facing rooms have full-length windows. The bright, semi industrial style restaurant offers Italian-inspired dishes – in summer they only serve pizza.

Spectrum &

Brugata 7 ✉ *0186 –* Ⓜ *Grønland –* ✆ *23 36 27 00*   Plan: **D2**
– www.thonhotels.no/spectrum – Closed Christmas
187 rm ☲ – **†**1575/2095 NOK **††**1750/2695 NOK
• Business • Chain • Personalised •

This unassuming looking hotel sits on a pedestrianised shopping street, not far from the station. Bright, bold colours feature in a funky interior and it has all the facilities a modern traveller needs; go for a larger Business Room.

Vika Atrium &⅃ 🚗

Munkedamsveien 45 ✉ *0250 –* Ⓜ *National Theatret*   Plan: **B2**
– ✆ *22 83 33 00 – www.thonhotels.no*
103 rm ☲ – **†**999/2045 NOK **††**1195/2695 NOK
• Business • Chain • Functional •

This busy business hotel is just minutes from Aker Brygge's harbourside shops and restaurants, in a block containing a large conference centre; some of the contemporary bedrooms overlook the atrium. Breakfasts feature organic produce.

WARSAW ●

● Cracow

POLAND
POLSKA

Velishchuk/iStock

WARSAW
WARSZAWA

fotorince/iStock

WARSAW IN...

→ **ONE DAY**
Royal Castle, Warsaw History Museum, National Museum, Lazienki Park.

→ **TWO DAYS**
Monument to the Ghetto Heroes, Saxon Gardens, concert at Grand Theatre or Philharmonic Hall.

→ **THREE DAYS**
The Royal Route, Marshal Street, Solidarity Avenue, Wilanow.

When UNESCO added Warsaw to its World Heritage list, it was a fitting seal of approval for its inspired rebuild, after eighty per cent of the city was destroyed during World War II. Using plans of the old city, architects painstakingly rebuilt the shattered capital throughout the 1950s, until it became an admirable mirror image of its former self. Now grey communist era apartment blocks sit beside pretty, pastel-coloured aristocratic buildings, their architecture ranging from Gothic to baroque, rococo to secession.

Nestling against the River Vistula, the Old Town was established at the end of the 13C, around what is now the Royal Castle, and a

century later the New Town, to the north, began to take shape. To the south of the Old Town runs 'The Royal Route', so named because, from the late middle ages, wealthy citizens built summer residences with lush gardens along these rural thoroughfares. Continue southwards and you're in Lazienki Park with its palaces and pavilions, while to the west lie the more commercial areas of Marshal Street and Solidarity Avenue, once the commercial heart of the city. The northwest of Warsaw was traditionally the Jewish district, until it was destroyed during the war; today it has been redeveloped with housing estates and the sobering Monument to the Ghetto Heroes.

EATING OUT

The centuries-old traditional cuisine of Warsaw was influenced by neighbouring Russia, Ukraine and Germany, while Jewish dishes were also added to the mix. Over the years there has been a growing sophistication to the cooking and a lighter, more contemporary style has become evident, with time-honoured classics - such as the ubiquitous pierogi (dumplings with various fillings) and the ever-popular breaded pork dish 'bigos' - having been updated with flair. These are accompanied, of course, by chilled Polish vodka, which covers a bewildering range of styles. Warsaw also has a more global side, with everything from stalls selling falafel to restaurants serving Vietnamese, and a large Italian business community has ensured there are a good number of Italian restaurants too. Stylised settings are popular, such as a burghers' houses or vaulted cellars; wherever you eat, check that VAT has been included within the prices (it's not always) and add a ten per cent tip. If it's value for money you're after, head for a Milk Bar, a low priced cafeteria selling traditional dairy-based food.

Atelier Amaro (Wojciech Amaro) ✿　　　　　XxX & 函 ↳ 🅿

ul. Agrykola 1 ⊠ 00 460 – ℰ (22) 6285747　　　　　Plan I: **B2**
*– www.atelieramaro.pl – Closed 25 December-6 January, Easter, 30 July-
16 August, Sunday and bank holidays*
Menu 290/380 PLN – *(dinner only) (booking essential) (tasting menu only)*
· Modern cuisine · Design · Elegant ·

An eco-style building on the edge of the park houses this intimate restaurant
with its glass teardrops and tiled concrete sculptures. The menu is described
as 'Nature's Calendar' and showcases foraged herbs and flowers. Ambitious,
innovative dishes are full of colour and the Polish spirit matches are a must.
→ Wild strawberry, tomato and mustard. Turbot with whitecurrants and
black trumpet mushrooms. Gooseberry, raspberry and elderflower.

Senses (Andrea Camastra) ✿　　　　　　　　　XxX 函 ↩

ul. Bielanska 12 ⊠ 00 085 – Ⓜ Ratusz – ℰ (22)　　　　Plan: **C1**
*331 9697 – www.sensesrestaurant.pl – Closed Easter, last 2 weeks August,
23 December-7 January and Sunday*
Menu 290/550 PLN – *(dinner only) (booking essential) (tasting menu only)*
· Modern cuisine · Elegant · Romantic ·

As with the historic building in which it is housed, this formal restaurant con-
nects tradition with modernity. Of the 3 set menus, most opt for the 7 course
dinner to best experience cooking that is innovative, creative and at times
theatrical, but also underpinned by classic Polish flavours.
→ Sea trout with red caviar, horseradish, lemon and apricot. King crab
goulash with culatello. Raspberries, yoghurt, cherries and rose honey.

Brasserie Warszawska ✿　　　　　　　　　　XX 綴 函 ↳ ↩

ul. Górnosląska 24 ⊠ 00 484 – ℰ (22) 628 94 23　　　　Plan I: **B2**
*– www.brasseriewarszawska.pl – Closed 24-26 December, 1 January, 1-
2 April and Sunday*
Menu 35/150 PLN – Carte 95/205 PLN
· Modern cuisine · Brasserie · Vintage ·

A smart brasserie with a zinc-topped bar, a black and white tiled floor, and cari-
catures of its regulars on the walls. Modern European dishes are executed with
care and passion. Meats come from their own butcher's shop and mature steaks
are a feature, with a choice of cuts from Poland, Ireland and Australia.

Alewino ✿　　　　　　　　　　　　　　　　X 綴 斎 函

ul. Mokotowska 48 ⊠ 00 543 – ℰ (22) 628 38 30　　　　Plan: **D2**
*– www.alewino.pl – Closed 24 December-5 January, Easter, Monday lunch
and Sunday*
Carte 80/135 PLN – *(booking essential at dinner)*
· Polish ·

Alewino started life as a wine shop before developing into a rustic, modern
wine-bar-cum-restaurant. Choose a spot in one of 4 cosy rooms or in the garden. Menus might be concise but the portions are generous, with classic Polish
recipes reworked in a modern manner. Over 250 wines accompany.

Butchery and Wine ✿　　　　　　　　　　　X 綴 斎 ↳

ul. Zurawia 22 ⊠ 00 515 – Ⓜ Centrum – ℰ (22)　　　　Plan: **D2**
5023118 – www.butcheryandwine.pl – Closed Christmas and Easter
Carte 60/240 PLN – *(booking essential)*
· Meats and grills · Friendly · Trendy ·

A keenly run modern bistro in a long, narrow room. The name says it all: staff
wear butcher's aprons, there's a diagram of cuts above the kitchen pass and
the emphasis is on offal and meat – particularly beef – which is served on wooden boards. Wines from around the world provide the perfect match.

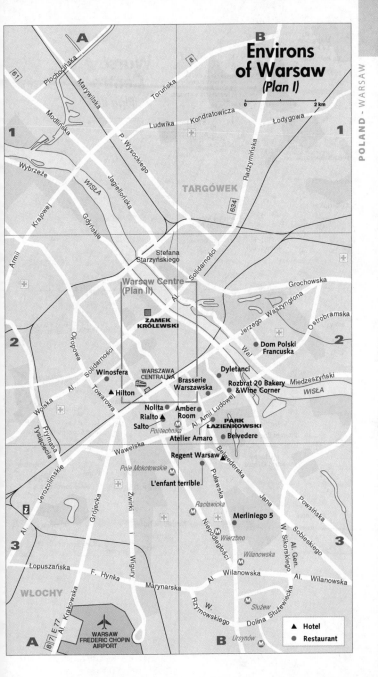

Environs of Warsaw
(Plan I)

0   2 km

TARGÓWEK

Stefana Starzyńskiego

Warsaw Centre
(Plan II)

ZAMEK KRÓLEWSKI

● Dom Polski Francuska

● Winosfera

WARSZAWA CENTRALNA

● Dyletanci

▲ Hilton

Brasserie Warszawska

Rozbrat 20 Bakery & Wine Corner

Nolita ●

Amber Room

Rialto ▲

PARK ŁAZIENKOWSKI

Salto

Politechnika

Atelier Amaro ● ● Belvedere

● Regent Warsaw

Pole Mokotowskie Ⓜ

L'enfant terrible

Raclawicka Ⓜ

Ⓜ ● Merliniego 5

Wierzbno

Wilanowska

Ⓜ Wilanowska

Al. Wilanowska

WŁOCHY

Ⓜ Służew

Łopuszańska

F. Hynka

Marynarska

Dolina Służewiecka

WARSAW FREDERIC CHOPIN AIRPORT

Ursynów

▲ Hotel
● Restaurant

507

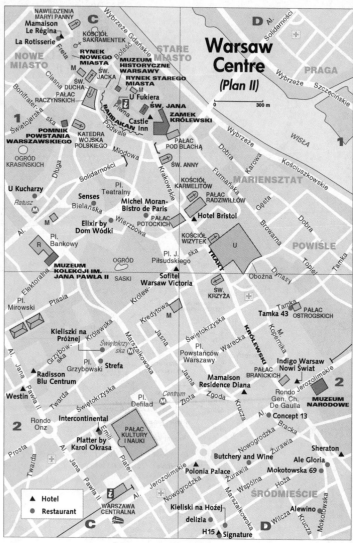

Warsaw Centre
(Plan II)

0   300 m

NAWIEDZENIA MARYI PANNY
Mamaison
Le Régina
La Rotisserie

NOWE MIASTO

KOŚCIÓŁ SAKRAMENTEK
RYNEK NOWEGO MIASTA
MUZEUM HISTORYCZNE WARSAWY
RYNEK STAREGO MIASTA

STARE MIASTO
PRAGA

ŚW. JACKA
ŚW. DUCHA
PAŁAC RACZYŃSKICH
U Fukiera

BARBAKAN
Castle Inn
ŚW. JANA
ZAMEK KRÓLEWSKI

POMNIK POWSTANIA WARSZAWSKIEGO
KATEDRA WOJSKA POLSKIEGO
Podwale

OGRÓD KRASIŃSKICH
Długa

PAŁAC POD BLACHĄ

ŚW. ANNY

WISŁA

Miodowa
Solidarności

U Kucharzy
Ratusz

Pl. Teatralny
Senses
Bielańska
Michel Moran-Bistro de Paris
Elixir by Dom Wódki

KOŚCIÓŁ KARMELITÓW
PAŁAC RADZIWIŁŁÓW
Hotel Bristol

MARIENSZTAT

Wierzbowa
PAŁAC POTOCKICH
KOŚCIÓŁ WIZYTEK

POWIŚLE

Pl. Bankowy
R
MUZEUM KOLEKCJI IM. JANA PAWŁA II
OGRÓD SASKI
Pl. J. Piłsudskiego
Sofitel Warsaw Victoria
ŚW. KRZYŻA

Pl. Mirowski
Ptasia
Królew-
Kredytowa

PAŁAC OSTROGSKICH
Tamka 43
Tamka

Kieliszki na Próżnej
Królewska
Świętokrzyska
Jasna
Świętokrzyska
Pl. Powstańców Warszawy
Warecka

KRÓLEWSKI

Indigo Warsaw Nowi Świat

Grzybow-
ska
Pl. Grzybowski
Strefa
Marszałkowska
Jasna

PAŁAC BRANICKICH
Mamaison Residence Diana
Rondo Gen. Ch. De Gaulla

MUZEUM NARODOWE

Radisson Blu Centrum
Westin

Twarda
Świętokrzyska
Pl. Defilad
Złota
Zgoda

Concept 13

Intercontinental
Rondo Onz

PAŁAC KULTURY I NAUKI

Nowogrodzka
Bracka

Sheraton
Ale Gloria

Platter by Karol Okrasa
Emili

Butchery and Wine
Żurawia
Mokotowska 69

Prosta
Twarda

Jerozolimskie
Polonia Palace
Nowogrodzka
Wspólna
Hoża

ŚRÓDMIEŚCIE

WARSZAWA CENTRALNA

Kieliski na Hożej
delizia
Alewino

▲ Hotel
● Restaurant

H15 ▲ Signature

508

POLAND - WARSAW

Kieliszki na Próżnej ✗ 🕸 😊 👍 🅼 ⑭

ul. Próżna 12 ✉ *00 107 –* Ⓜ *Świętokrzyska –* ✆ *(501)* Plan: **C2**
764 674 – www.kieliszkinaproznej.pl – Closed Christmas and Sunday
Menu 35 PLN (weekday lunch) – Carte 65/145 PLN – *(booking advisable)*
• Modern cuisine • Design • Wine bar •
A huge rack of glasses welcomes you into a parquet-floored room with a striking black & white wildlife mural and zinc ducting. Small growers feature on the 220-strong wine list and all wines are available by the glass. A concise menu offers light, modern interpretations of Polish classics; lunch is a steal.

Amber Room XxxX 🕸 😊 👍 ⇔ 🅿

al Ujazdowskie 13 ✉ *00 567 –* ✆ *(22) 523 66 64* Plan I: **B2**
– www.amberroom.pl – Closed Easter, 24-25 December, 1 January,
6 January, 31 May and 11 November.
Menu 64 PLN (lunch) – Carte 125/255 PLN
• Modern cuisine • Chic • Intimate •
A grand dining room in an attractive villa; home to the exclusive 'Round Table of Warsaw'. Modern cooking uses top ingredients and has original touches. Service is attentive and well-paced, and there's a great selection of Krug champagne.

Belvedere XxX 😊 🅰 👍 ⇔ 🅿

Lazienki Park, ul Agrykoli 1 (Entry from ul Parkowa St) Plan I: **B2**
✉ *00 460 –* ✆ *(22) 55 86 701 – www.belvedere.com.pl – Closed*
23 December-3 January
Menu 70/290 PLN – Carte 115/205 PLN – *(booking essential)*
• Modern cuisine • Chic • Romantic •
An impressive Victorian orangery in Lazienki Park; large arched windows keep it light, despite it being packed with shrubs and trees. Dishes are classic in both style and presentation. Smartly uniformed staff provide formal service.

Michel Moran - Bistro de Paris XxX 😊 🅰 👍 ⇔

Pl. Pilsudskiego 9 ✉ *00 078 –* Ⓜ *Ratusz –* ✆ *(22)* Plan: **C1**
826 01 07 – www.restaurantbistrodeparis.com – Closed Easter, Christmas,
Sunday and bank holidays
Menu 85 PLN (weekday lunch)/130 PLN – Carte 155/235 PLN
• French • Elegant • Chic •
A smart, marble-floored restaurant at the rear of the Opera House, with striking columns and colourful glass panels. The large menu offers reworked Polish and French dishes, with produce imported from France; the 'Classics' are a hit.

Platter by Karol Okrasa – InterContinental Hotel XxX 🅰 👍

ul. Emilii Plater 49 ✉ *00 125 –* Ⓜ *Centrum –* ✆ *(22)* 🛏
328 8730 – www.platter.pl – Closed August, Saturday Plan: **C2**
lunch and Sunday
Menu 270/330 PLN – Carte 140/250 PLN
• Modern cuisine • Chic • Intimate •
A first floor hotel restaurant with smart red and black décor. Menus change with the seasons and offer modern Polish dishes and European classics. Cooking is refined, sophisticated and flavoursome, and relies on native ingredients.

AleGloria XX 😊 🅰 👍 ⇔

pl. Trzech Krzyzy 3 ✉ *00 535 –* ✆ *(22) 584 70 80* Plan: **D2**
– www.alegloria.pl – Closed Easter, 24-25 December and 31 December
Carte 100/210 PLN
• Polish • Traditional décor • Intimate •
Steep steps lead down from a boutique shopping arcade to a spacious restaurant made up of several charming interconnecting rooms and furnished in white. Hearty, homemade Polish classics are served by a smartly attired team.

POLAND · WARSAW

ⅈ○ **Concept 13** XX 🏠 ⅙ 🅼 ↳ ✿

Vitkac (5th Floor), ul. Bracka 9 ✉ 00 501 – Ⓜ Centrum Plan: **D2**
– 𝒞 (22) 3107373 – www.likusrestauracje.pl – Closed Sunday dinner
and bank holidays
Menu 60/190 PLN – Carte 140/180 PLN
• Modern cuisine • Design • Fashionable •

A vast restaurant on top of a chic department store, with black furnishings, a glass-walled kitchen and a smart terrace. Dishes are modern, appealing and well-presented. They also have a wine bar and an impressive deli on the floor below.

ⅈ○ **Dom Polski Francuska** XX 🏠 🅼 ↳ ✿

ul. Francuska 11 ✉ 03 906 – 𝒞 (22) 616 24 32 Plan I: **B2**
– www.restauracjadompolski.pl – Closed 24 December
Menu 40 PLN (weekday lunch) – Carte 75/165 PLN
• Polish • Classic décor • Elegant •

A Mediterranean-style villa with attractive gardens and a lovely terrace, set in a smart residential area. Various small rooms are set over two floors. Extensive menus offer refined yet hearty dishes; duck and goose are the specialities.

ⅈ○ **Mokotowska 69** XX 🅼

ul. Mokotowska 69 ✉ 02 530 – 𝒞 (22) 628 73 84 Plan: **D2**
– www.mokotowska69.pl – Closed Christmas and Easter
Carte 100/190 PLN – (bookings advisable at dinner)
• International • Traditional décor • Romantic •

This unusual circular building has a cosy, romantic atmosphere and the welcoming team make you feel well-looked-after. Menus focus on seafood and prime quality American Black Angus, Scottish Aberdeen Angus and Japanese Kobe steaks.

ⅈ○ **Nolita** XX 🅼 ↳

ul. Wilcza 46 ✉ 00 679 – 𝒞 (22) 29 20 424 Plan I: **A2**
– www.nolita.pl – Closed 2 weeks August, Christmas-New Year, Easter,
Saturday lunch, Sunday and bank holidays
Menu 89 PLN (weekday lunch) – Carte 165/210 PLN – (booking essential)
• Modern cuisine • Design • Intimate •

Whitewashed stone and black window blinds are matched inside by a smart monochrome theme, where an open kitchen takes centre stage. Bold, modern dishes feature many flavours and take their influences from across the globe.

ⅈ○ **La Rotisserie** – Mamaison Le Régina Hotel XX 🏠 ⅙ 🅼 ↳

ul. Koscielna 12 ✉ 00 218 – 𝒞 (22) 531 60 00 Plan: **C1**
– www.mamaison.com/leregina – Closed 24 December
Menu 90/200 PLN – Carte 140/195 PLN – (booking essential)
• Modern cuisine • Chic • Intimate •

A small but stylish hotel restaurant with an arched ceiling and an intimate feel. Refined modern dishes have Polish origins and arrive attractively presented. When the weather's right, the courtyard is the place to be.

ⅈ○ **Salto** – Rialto Hotel XX ⅙ 🅼

ul. Wilcza 73 ✉ 00 670 – Ⓜ Politechnika – 𝒞 (22) Plan I: **A2**
584 87 00 – www.rialto.pl
Menu 260 PLN – Carte 115/200 PLN
• Modern cuisine • Intimate • Brasserie •

This plainly decorated dining room sits within an attractive suburban hotel. The chef hails from Argentina and is a fan of all things modern, so you'll find gels, meats cooked in a waterbath and some unusual flavour combinations.

ⅈ○ **Signature** – H15 Hotel XX ⅙ 🅼

ul. Poznańska 15 ✉ 00 680 – Ⓜ Politechnika – 𝒞 (22) Plan: **D2**
553 87 55 – www.signaturerestaurant.pl – Closed Christmas-New
Year, Easter, 1-3 May and lunch Saturday-Sunday
Menu 48/120 PLN – Carte 82/210 PLN
• Modern cuisine • Intimate • Bistro •

Black and white photos of old Hollywood Stars hang against white, pink and green walls in this striking hotel restaurant. Cooking is a modern take on traditional Polish recipes and the playful puddings are particularly memorable.

ıO **Strefa** XX 舒 AK

ul. Próżna 9 ✉ *00 107 –* Ⓜ *Świętokrzyska –* ☏ *(22)* Plan: **C2**
255 0850 – www.restauracjastrefa.pl – Closed 25 December and 1 January
Menu 35 PLN (weekday lunch) – Carte 95/185 PLN
• Modern cuisine • Elegant • Intimate •

Sit in the small bar, the neutrally hued restaurant or out on the delightful terrace
in the shadow of the church. Modern cooking has a traditional Polish heart – the
pierogi in particular are a must-try. Service is professional.

ıO **Tamka 43** XX ㅎ AK ⇔

ul. Tamka 43 (1st Floor) ✉ *00 355 –* Ⓜ *Świętokrzyska* Plan: **D2**
– ☏ *(22) 441 62 34 – www.tamka43.pl – Closed Christmas and Easter*
Menu 59 PLN (weekday lunch) – Carte 105/170 PLN
• Modern cuisine • Design • Fashionable •

Opposite the Chopin Museum, in the building where his archives are kept, is
this first floor restaurant with bare brick walls, steel girders and suede-covered
pillars. Dishes are original; some are inspired by Chopin's favourite meals!

ıO **U Fukiera** XX 舒 AK ⇔ ⇕

Rynek Starego Miasta 27 ✉ *00 272 –* ☏ *(22) 831 10 13* Plan: **C1**
– www.ufukiera.pl – Closed 24-25 and 31 December
Menu 105/170 PLN – Carte 90/205 PLN
• Polish • Traditional décor • Elegant •

An immaculately kept house in the heart of the Old Town, overlooking a historic
cobbled square. The fiercely traditional interior comprises several intimate,
homely rooms, including a 17C vaulted cellar. Cooking is hearty and classical.

ıO **U Kucharzy** XX 舒 ⇔

Państwowego Muzeum Archeologicznego, ul. Długa 52 Plan: **C1**
✉ *00 238 –* Ⓜ *Ratusz –* ☏ *(22) 826 79 36 – www.gessler.pl – Closed*
Christmas, Easter, 31 December and Saturday-Sunday lunch
Menu 25/190 PLN – Carte 65/170 PLN
• Traditional cuisine • Historic • Traditional décor •

'The Cook' is located in a 16C former arsenal and two of the original cannons sit
in its large inner courtyard. The day's ingredients are on display in the open kitchen and the chef comes to the table to carve your meat himself.

ıO **delizia** X 舒 AK ⇕

ul. Hoża 58-60 (entrance on ul. Poznańskiej) ✉ *00 682* Plan: **D2**
– Ⓜ *Centrum –* ☏ *(22) 622 66 65 – www.delizia.com.pl – Closed*
Christmas, Easter, 1-3 May, Sunday and bank holidays
Carte 130/155 PLN – *(bookings advisable at dinner)*
• Italian • Neighbourhood • Friendly •

An unassuming neighbourhood restaurant where fresh flowers sit on chunky
tables. It's owned by friends and run with the care of a family business. Menus
are concise, with pasta a speciality; fish and cheeses are imported from Italy.

ıO **Dyletanci** X 錦 AK

ul. Rozbrat 44A ✉ *00 415 –* ☏ *(69) 2887 234* Plan I: **B2**
– www.dyletanci.pl – Closed Christmas, Easter and Sunday
Menu 35 PLN (lunch) – Carte 110/155 PLN
• Modern cuisine • Friendly • Wine bar •

The brainchild of an experienced chef and a wine importer, Dyletanci has a welcoming modern bistro style and walls laden with wines sourced from across the
globe. Seasonal ingredients are prepared in a contemporary manner.

ıO **ELIXIR by Dom Wódki** X 舒 AK ⇔

ul. Wierzbowa 9-11 ✉ *00 094 –* Ⓜ *Ratusz –* ☏ *(22)* Plan: **C1**
828 22 11 – www.restauracjaelixir.pl – Closed Christmas, New Year and
Easter
Menu 39/195 PLN – Carte 95/160 PLN
• Polish • Wine bar • Fashionable •

A smart, very fashionable bar and restaurant is the setting for this marriage of
modern Polish cuisine and top quality vodkas. The likes of local herring, dumplings and beef tartare are paired with over 500 vodkas from around the world.

POLAND - WARSAW

POLAND - WARSAW

Kieliski na Hożej   X AC

ul. Hoża 41 ✉ 00 681 – ℰ (22) 4042109   Plan: **D2**
– www.kieliszkinahozej.pl – Closed Christmas, Easter and Sunday
Menu 39 PLN (lunch) – Carte 125/180 PLN – *(booking advisable)*
• Modern cuisine • Wine bar • Friendly •
A young team welcomes you into this warm restaurant, where the chef pulls together his overseas experiences to create dishes with Nordic, French and Polish elements. Over 230 wines – imported directly – are available by the glass.

L'enfant terrible   X AC

ul. Sandomierska 13 (entrance on Rejtana St.)   Plan I: **B3**
✉ 02 567 – Ⓜ Pol Mokotowskie – ℰ (22) 119 57 05 – www.eterrible.pl
– Closed Christmas, New Year, Easter, lunch Saturday-Monday and Sunday dinner
Menu 80 PLN (lunch)/85 PLN – Carte 170/190 PLN
• Modern cuisine • Neighbourhood • Romantic •
This delightfully rustic restaurant is owned by a self-taught chef, who picks up the day's produce on his 40km drive into work. The atmosphere is welcoming and dishes are modern and well-presented; the sourdough bread is fantastic.

Merliniego 5   X 🛱 AC ⇔

ul. Merliniego 5 ✉ 02 511 – ℰ (22) 6460810   Plan I: **B3**
– www.merliniego5.pl – Closed 25 December and Easter Sunday
Carte 90/190 PLN – *(booking essential at dinner)*
• Traditional cuisine • Bistro • Neighbourhood •
A passionately run bistro in the suburbs; have lunch downstairs and dinner upstairs. Wide-ranging menus offer carefully prepared European classics. Meat lovers can choose from a great range of steaks – there's even a steak tasting menu!

Rozbrat 20 Bakery & Wine Corner   X 🏵 🛱 ⇔

ul. Rozbrat 20 ✉ 00 447 – ℰ (22) 416 6266   Plan I: **B2**
– www.rozbrat20.com.pl – Closed 25-26 December, 1 November and Sunday
Menu 35 PLN (weekday lunch) – Carte 75/170 PLN
• Polish • Friendly • Bistro •
A café-cum-bakery-cum-wine-shop with a friendly neighbourhood vibe; the rear room houses the 200 wines featured on their list. Breads are a highlight and they open for breakfast every day. The young chef has a creative touch.

Winosfera   X 🛱 ዿ ⇔ ✿

ul. Chlodna 31 ✉ 00 867 – ℰ (22) 526 25 00   Plan I: **A2**
– www.winosfera.pl – Closed Christmas, Easter, Sunday and bank holidays
Menu 39 PLN (weekday lunch) – Carte 95/185 PLN
• Modern cuisine • Design • Trendy •
Winosfera sits within an old factory – it retains its industrial feel and, in a nod to the famed cinema which once stood here, comes with a screening room for private events. Modern European menus cover Italy, France and Poland.

InterContinental   ✿ Ⅰ₅ ⊕ 🛖 ዿ AC ⇔ 🛠 🚗

ul. Emilii Plater 49 ✉ 00 125 – Ⓜ Centrum – ℰ (22)   Plan: **C2**
328 8888 – www.warsaw.intercontinental.com
414 rm ☑ – †550/1900 PLN ††750/2000 PLN – 21 suites
• Grand Luxury • Business • Modern •
A striking high-rise hotel in a central location. Smart guest areas include a modern lounge and a clubby bar; bedrooms are large and contemporary. The impressive health and leisure club on the 43rd and 44th floors boasts fantastic views. Informal buffet lunches are served in Downtown, with steaks a speciality in the evening; Platter offers more refined, modern cooking.
🍴○ **Platter by Karol Okrasa** – See restaurant listing

POLAND - WARSAW

Hilton ✿ ⟨ 🖪 ⊕ ⋔ 🔲 ₺ 🕅 ₩ 🎿 🚗
ul. Grzybowska 63 ✉ 00 844 – ✆ (22) 356 55 55   Plan I: **A2**
– www.warsaw.hilton.com
314 rm – †799/1129 PLN ††799/1620 PLN – 🖵 95 PLN – 10 suites
• Business • Chain • Modern •
A large, corporate hotel in the business district. The bright atrium houses shops and a lounge-bar; extensive business and leisure facilities include a smart club lounge, a casino and the city's largest event space. Bedrooms are modern and well-equipped. The informal restaurant offers an international menu.

Hotel Bristol ✿ 🖪 ⋔ 🔲 ₺ 🕅 ₩ 🎿
ul. Krakowskie Przedmiescie 42-44 ✉ 00-325 – ✆ (22)   Plan: **D1**
551 10 00 – www.hotelbristol.pl
206 rm 🖵 – †675/1295 PLN ††785/1405 PLN – 38 suites
• Grand Luxury • Historic • Classic •
Built in 1901 and set next to the Presidential Palace, this grand, art deco hotel boasts an elegant marble-floored reception and an impressive columned bar. Luxurious bedrooms have a high level of facilities. Unwind in the wine bar or on the terrace. The smart restaurant offers a modern Polish menu.

Regent Warsaw ✿ ⟨ 🖪 ⊕ ⋔ 🔲 ₺ 🕅 ₩ 🎿 🚗
ul. Belwederska 23 ✉ 00 761 – ✆ (22) 558 12 34   Plan I: **B3**
– www.regent-warsaw.com
246 rm – †410/995 PLN ††475/1050 PLN – 🖵 92 PLN – 19 suites
• Luxury • Business • Modern •
A contemporary hotel close to a large park, featuring an impressive open-plan lobby and a glass-roofed lounge-bar. Spacious bedrooms boast top quality furniture, smart bathrooms and a host of cleverly concealed facilities. Split-level Venti Tre offers an extensive Mediterranean menu and wood-fired specialities.

Sheraton ✿ 🖪 ⋔ ₺ 🕅 ₩ 🎿 🚗
ul. Boleslawa Prusa 2 ✉ 00 493 – ✆ (22) 450 6100   Plan: **D2**
– www.sheraton.pl
350 rm – †305/1575 PLN ††305/1575 PLN – 🖵 108 PLN – 15 suites
• Luxury • Business • Classic •
A spacious hotel on the historic Three Cross Square, with a large open-plan lobby, a smart ballroom, and good conference and leisure facilities. Bedrooms are well-equipped; the top floor Club Rooms are the most contemporary. InAzia offers dishes from China, Thailand, Indonesia, Singapore and Vietnam.

Sofitel Warsaw Victoria ✿ 🖪 ⋔ 🔲 ₺ 🕅 ₩ 🎿 🚗
ul. Królewska 11 ✉ 00 065 – Ⓜ Świętokrzyska – ✆ (22)   Plan: **C1**
657 80 11 – www.sofitel-victoria-warsaw.com
359 rm 🖵 – †350/950 PLN ††400/990 PLN – 53 suites
• Business • Luxury • Contemporary •
This smart hotel sits by Pilsudski Square, overlooking the Saxon Gardens. Unwind in the lovely spa or the reflective-ceilinged pool. Contemporary guest areas pay homage to the 1970s with geometric designs, and bedrooms are bold, sleek and well-equipped. The delightful brasserie mixes Polish and French cuisine.

Mamaison Le Régina ⋔ ₺ 🕅 ₩ 🎿
ul. Koscielna 12 ✉ 00 218 – ✆ (22) 531 60 00   Plan: **C1**
– www.mamaisonleregina.com
61 rm – †430/1090 PLN ††430/1090 PLN – 🖵 100 PLN – 3 suites
• Luxury • Family • Design •
A charming boutique hotel with a small wellness facility; housed in a neo-18C building on a peaceful cobbled street near the castle. The décor is cool and understated, with a Mediterranean feel. Subtle design features include room numbers projected onto the floor and hand-painted frescoes on the bedheads.
⊕ **La Rotisserie** – See restaurant listing

POLAND - WARSAW

H15 ♿ 🖾 🍴 ☕

ul. Poznańska 15 ☒ 00 680 – ⓜ Politechnika – ℰ (22)   Plan: **D2**
553 87 00 – www.h15ab.com
47 rm – ♦290/780 PLN ♦♦310/780 PLN – 🖾 65 PLN – 30 suites
• Townhouse • Luxury • Contemporary •
This extended townhouse, built around a glass quadrangle, was once the Russian Embassy and was later occupied by the Germans during WWII. Most bedrooms are large, bespoke-furnished suites with small kitchenettes and marble-floored bathrooms.
🍴 **Signature** – See restaurant listing

Indigo Warsaw Nowy Świat ⚶ Ⅰઠ ⋔ ⅍ 🖾 ⅍ 🄿

Smolna 40 ☒ 00 375 – ℰ (22) 418 8952   Plan: **D2**
– www.indigowarsaw.com
60 rm 🖾 – ♦450/1200 PLN ♦♦525/1275 PLN – 1 suite
• Historic building • Luxury • Modern •
A chandelier comprising 900 coloured glass balls hangs down from the ceiling of this superbly located building dating from 1903. It's set around an inner courtyard and the corridors are lined with art, including several modern versions of da Vinci's 'Lady with an Ermine'. Jewish cooking has a Polish accent.

Polonia Palace ⚶ Ⅰઠ ⋔ ⅍ 🖾 ⅍ ⅍

al. Jerozolimskie 45 ☒ 00 692 – ⓜ Centrum – ℰ (22)   Plan: **D2**
318 2800 – www.poloniapalace.com
206 rm – ♦275/760 PLN ♦♦275/870 PLN – 🖾 80 PLN – 3 suites
• Business • Family • Contemporary •
A striking hotel dating from 1913, set on a busy central street. The elegant interior has a lovely glass-roofed lobby, a popular lounge-bar and a beautifully ornate gilded ballroom. Modern, well-equipped bedrooms come in browns and creams. The restaurant offers a large menu of Polish and European cuisine.

Radisson Blu Centrum ⚶ Ⅰઠ ⋔ 🖵 ⅍ 🖾 ⅍ ⅍ ☕

ul. Grzybowska 24 ☒ 00 132 – ⓜ Świętokrzyska   Plan: **C2**
– ℰ (22) 321 88 22 – www.radissonblu.com/hotel-warsaw
311 rm – ♦280/2050 PLN ♦♦300/2050 PLN – 🖾 104 PLN – 18 suites
• Business • Modern • Design •
A glass-fronted hotel in the business district, boasting state-of-the-art conference facilities and a well-equipped leisure centre. Smart bedrooms come in a choice of 'Maritime', 'Scandinavian' or 'Italian' themes. The all-day brasserie offers modern interpretations of Polish and Mediterranean dishes.

Westin ⚶ ≤ Ⅰઠ ⋔ ⅍ 🖾 ⅍ ⅍ ☕

al. Jana Pawla II 21 ☒ 00 854 – ⓜ Świętokrzyska   Plan: **C2**
– ℰ (22) 450 80 00 – www.westin.pl
365 rm – ♦270/1458 PLN ♦♦270/1458 PLN – 🖾 106 PLN – 15 suites
• Luxury • Business • Modern •
An eye-catching modern building on a busy street, featuring a soaring atrium with glass lifts and a wide choice of conference and events rooms. Smart, contemporary bedrooms have good facilities; the top floor Club Rooms are the best. Worldwide ingredients meet Eastern recipes in the restaurant.

Rialto Ⅰઠ ⋔ ⅍ 🖾 ⅍ ⅍ 🄿

ul. Wilcza 73 ☒ 00 670 – ⓜ Politechnika – ℰ (22)   Plan I: **A2**
584 87 00 – www.rialto.pl
44 rm – ♦300/950 PLN ♦♦340/1480 PLN – 🖾 80 PLN – 11 suites
• Business • Townhouse • Art déco •
This delightfully converted townhouse dates back to 1906 and its sympathetically refurbished interior still boasts original art deco and art nouveau features. Elegant bedrooms come with a host of facilities and boast beautiful marble-floored bathrooms. There's also a smart bar, a small gym and a sauna.
🍴 **Salto** – See restaurant listing

Mamaison Residence Diana

ul Chmielna 13a ✉ 00 021 – Ⓜ Centrum – ✆ (22) 505 9100 – www.mamaison.com – Closed Christmas and Easter Plan: **D2**

46 rm – †425/708 PLN ††425/708 PLN – ☕ 57 PLN – 8 suites

• Townhouse • Business • Cosy •

A cosy hotel set in a quiet courtyard off a busy central shopping street; it has a spacious lounge and a smart bar furnished in black wood. Large, modern bedrooms have small kitchen areas and good facilities; some are duplex or have jacuzzis. The Italian restaurant specialises in traditional Neapolitan pizzas.

Castle Inn

Plac Zamkowy, ul Swietojanska 2 ✉ 00 288 – ✆ (22) 4250100 – www.castleinn.pl Plan: **C1**

22 rm – †300/400 PLN ††300/600 PLN – ☕ 35 PLN

• Family • Townhouse • Historic •

A small 16C property on a cobbled street in the heart of the Old Town, just a stone's throw from the castle. Bedrooms are unique; designed by local artists, they range from bohemian to contemporary and come with quirky touches.

CRACOW
KRAKÓW

martin-dm/iStock

CRACOW IN...

→ **ONE DAY**
St Mary's Church, Cloth Hall, Wawel, main building of National Museum.

→ **TWO DAYS**
Kazimierz, Oskar Schindler's Factory, 'Footsteps of Pope Jean Paul II' tour.

→ **THREE DAYS**
Auschwitz-Birkenau, Wieliczka salt mine.

Cracow was deservedly included in the very first UNESCO World Heritage List. Unlike much of Poland, this beautiful old city – the country's capital from the 11C to the 17C – was spared Second World War destruction because the German Governor had his HQ here. So Cracow is still able to boast a hugely imposing market square – the biggest medieval square in Europe – and a hill that's crowned not just with a castle, but a cathedral too. Not far away there's even a glorious chapel made of salt, one hundred metres under the ground.

Cracow is a city famous for its links with Judaism and its Royal Route, but also for its cultural inheritance. During the Renaissance,

it became a centre of new ideas that drew the most outstanding writers, thinkers and musicians of the day. It has thousands of architectural monuments and millions of artefacts displayed in its museums and churches; but it's a modern city too, with an eye on the 21C. The heart and soul of Cracow is its old quarter, which received its charter in 1257. It's dominated by the Market Square and almost completely encircled by the Planty gardens. A short way to the south, briefly interrupted by the curving streets of the Okol neighbourhood, is Wawel Hill, and further south from here is the characterful Jewish quarter of Kazimierz. The smart residential areas of Piasek and Nowy Swiat are to the west.

EATING OUT

Even during the communist era, Cracow had a reputation as a good place to eat. In the 1990s, hundreds of new restaurants opened their doors, often in pretty locations with medieval or Renaissance interiors or in intimate cellars. Many Poles go misty-eyed at the thought of bigos on a cold winter's day; it's a game, sausage and cabbage stew that comes with sauerkraut, onion, potatoes, herbs and spices, and is reputed to get better with reheating on successive days. Pierogi is another favourite: crescent-shaped dumplings which come in either savoury or sweet style. Barszcz is a lemon and garlic flavoured beetroot soup that's invariably good value, while in Kazimierz, specialities include Jewish dumplings filled with onion, cheese and potatoes and Berdytchov soup, which imaginatively mixes honey and cinnamon with beef. There are plenty of restaurants specialising in French, Greek, Vietnamese, Middle Eastern, Indian, Italian and Mexican food too. Most restaurants don't close until around midnight and there's no pressure to rush your drinks and leave.

517

POLAND - CRACOW

⬦○ **Copernicus** – Copernicus Hotel ⠀⠀⠀⠀⠀XxX ⅋ 🅰 ↳
ul. Kanonicza 16 ✉ *31 002* – ✆ *(12) 424 34 21* ⠀⠀⠀⠀Plan: **E3**
– www.copernicus.hotel.com.pl
Menu 160/340 PLN – Carte lunch 135/190 PLN – *(booking essential)*
• Modern cuisine • Intimate • Elegant •
Set off the atrium of a charming hotel; an intimate split-level restaurant of less than 10 tables, boasting an ornate hand-painted Renaissance ceiling. 5, 7 and 12 course menus offer well-crafted Polish and European dishes.

⬦○ **Trzy Rybki** – Stary Hotel ⠀⠀⠀⠀⠀XxX ⅋ & 🅰 ↳ ⟷
ul. Szczepanska 5 ✉ *31 011* – ✆ *(12) 384 08 06* ⠀⠀⠀⠀Plan: **E1**
– www.stary.hotel.com.pl/en/restaurants/trzy-rybki/
Menu 160/320 PLN – *(tasting menu only)*
• Modern cuisine • Elegant • Design •
Thick stone walls give this stylish restaurant in the Stary hotel's basement plenty of character. A glass-fronted case stretching along one wall displays an impressive collection of wines. Well-prepared dishes have subtle Italian leanings.

⬦○ **Albertina** ⠀⠀⠀⠀⠀⠀⠀⠀⠀⠀⠀⠀⠀⠀XX ⅋ 🅰
ul. Dominikańska 3 ✉ *31 043* – ✆ *(012) 333 4110* ⠀⠀⠀Plan: **F2**
– www.albertinarestaurant.pl – Closed 24-25 December, 1 April and 1 November
Menu 80 PLN (lunch) – Carte 120/180 PLN
• Modern cuisine • Design • Chic •
A sophisticated modern restaurant with a basement wine bar. Menus show the chef's passion for hunting and fishing – venison is a speciality and they offer lobster and oyster menus. Eye-catching dishes capture the ingredients' true flavours.

⬦○ **Amarylis** – Queen Hotel ⠀⠀⠀⠀⠀⠀⠀⠀XX & 🅰 ↳
ul. Józefa Dietla 60 ✉ *31 039* – ✆ *(12) 433 33 06* ⠀⠀Plan: **F3**
– www.queenhotel.pl
Carte 110/140 PLN
• Modern cuisine • Design • Intimate •
Head down to the hotel's basement and sit in either a traditional brick room or a more modern space furnished in black and white. Cooking mixes Polish and global influences and dishes are well-presented and full of flavour.

⬦○ **Corse** ⠀⠀⠀⠀⠀⠀⠀⠀⠀⠀⠀⠀⠀⠀⠀⠀⠀⠀XX ↳
ul Poselska 24 ✉ *31 002* – ✆ *(12) 421 62 73* ⠀⠀⠀⠀Plan: **F2**
– www.corserestaurant.pl – Closed 24-25 December and Easter
Carte 65/200 PLN
• Mediterranean cuisine • Traditional décor • Bistro •
A nautically-themed restaurant featuring model ships, paintings of clippers and old ships' lamps. Good-sized menus offer Mediterranean-influenced dishes which use Polish produce; they specialise in seafood but offer more besides.

⬦○ **Cyrano de Bergerac** ⠀⠀⠀⠀⠀⠀⠀XX 🏠 🅰 ↳
ul Slawkowska 26 ✉ *31 014* – ✆ *(12) 411 72 88* ⠀⠀Plan: **E1**
– www.cyranodebergerac.pl – Closed Christmas, Easter and 1 November
Carte 105/265 PLN – *(booking essential at dinner)*
• Polish • Intimate • Rustic •
An atmospheric restaurant in the barrel-ceilinged cellars of a 17C townhouse. Tapestries, antiques and old implements fill the room, and there's a lovely enclosed rear terrace. Polish ingredients are showcased in refined French dishes.

⬦○ **Jarema** ⠀⠀⠀⠀⠀⠀⠀⠀⠀⠀⠀⠀⠀⠀⠀⠀XX 🏠 🅰 ↳
Pl. Matejki 5 ✉ *31 157* – ✆ *(12) 429 36 69* ⠀⠀⠀⠀Plan: **F1**
– www.jarema.pl
Menu 35/60 PLN – Carte 50/148 PLN
• Traditional cuisine • Traditional décor • Vintage •
A charming restaurant with a homely feel. Hunting trophies fill the walls and there's live violin and piano music every night. Family recipes are handed down through the generations and focus on dishes from the east of the country.

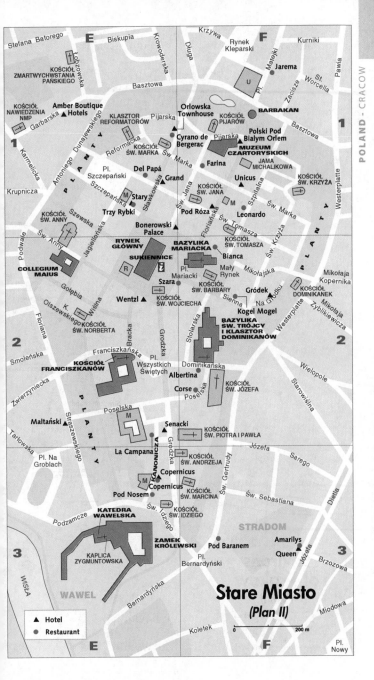

Stefana Batorego

Biskupia

Krzywa

Kurniki

E

F

Rynek
Kleparski

Matejki

St Worcella

Pawia

Jarema

U

KOŚCIÓŁ
ZMARTWYCHWSTANIA
PAŃSKIEGO

Basztowa

Krowoderska

Długa

Pl.

Zacisze

KOŚCIÓŁ
NAWIEDZENIA
NMP

Amber Boutique
▲ Hotels

Garbarska

Orlowska
Townhouse

KLASZTOR
REFORMATORÓW

Pijarska

Pijarska

KOŚCIÓŁ
PIJARÓW

BARBAKAN

Basztowa

1

Karmelicka

Antoniego

Reformacka

Dunajewskiego

Cyrano de
Bergerac

KOŚCIÓŁ
ŚW. MARKA

Św. Marka

Farina

Polski Pod
Bialym Orlem

MUZEUM
CZARTORYSKICH

JAMA
MICHALIKOWA

1

Westerplatte

Krupnicza

Pl.
Szczepański

Del Papá

Szczepańska

Grand

Szewska

Szczepańska

Trzy Rybki

M Stary

Św. Jana

Św. Jana

KOŚCIÓŁ
ŚW. JANA

Pod Róża

M

Unicus

Florianska

Leonardo

Św. Tomasza

Św. Marka

KOŚCIÓŁ
ŚW. KRZYŻA

KOŚCIÓŁ
ŚW. ANNY

Św. Anny

Bonerowski
Palace

Jagiellońska

RYNEK
GŁÓWNY

BAZYLIKA
MARIACKA

KOŚCIÓŁ
ŚW. TOMASZA

P L A N T Y

Podwale

SUKIENNICE

R

Bianca

Mały
Rynek

Mikołajska

Mikołaja
Kopernika

COLLEGIUM
MAIUS

Gołębia

Olszewskiego

Wiślna

KOŚCIÓŁ
ŚW. NORBERTA

Wentzl ▲

Pl.
Mariacki

KOŚCIÓŁ
ŚW. WOJCIECHA

Szara

KOŚCIÓŁ
ŚW. BARBARY

Sienna

Gródek

Kogel Mogel

Na Gródku

KOŚCIÓŁ
DOMINIKANEK

Mikołaja

Zyblikiewicza

2

Floriana

Smoleńska

Bracka

Grodzka

BAZYLIKA
SW. TRÓJCY
I KLASZTOR
DOMINIKANÓW

Stolarska

Westerplatte

2

Zwierzyniecka

Franciszkańska

KOŚCIÓŁ
FRANCISZKANÓW

P L A N T Y

Pl.
Wszystkich
Świętych

Albertina

Corse

Dominikańska

Poselska

KOŚCIÓŁ
ŚW. JÓZEFA

Wielopole

Starowiślna

Tarłowska

Maltański

Straszewskiego

Poselska

Pl. Na
Groblach

La Campana

Senacki ▲

KANONICZA

Grodzka

KOŚCIÓŁ
ŚW. PIOTRA I PAWŁA

KOŚCIÓŁ
ŚW. ANDRZEJA

Św. Gertrudy

Józefa

Sarego

M Copernicus

Copernicus

KOŚCIÓŁ
ŚW. MARCINA

Św. Sebastiana

Dietla

Pod Nosem

Podzamcze

KATEDRA
WAWELSKA

Św. Idziego

KOŚCIÓŁ
ŚW. IDZIEGO

STRADOM

WISŁA

KAPLICA
ZYGMUNTOWSKA

ZAMEK
KRÓLEWSKI

Pod Baranem

Pl.
Bernardyński

Amarylis

Queen

Józefa

Brzozowa

3

3

WAWEL

Bernardyńska

Stare Miasto

(Plan II)

Miodowa

▲ Hotel
● Restaurant

Koletek

0   200 m

E

F

Pl.
Nowy

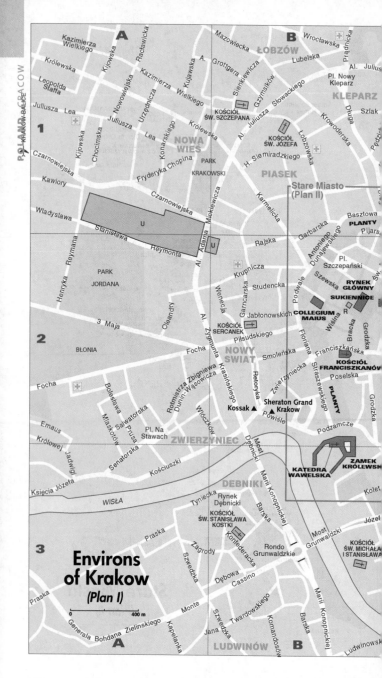

Environs of Krakow
(Plan I)

0 ──── 400 m

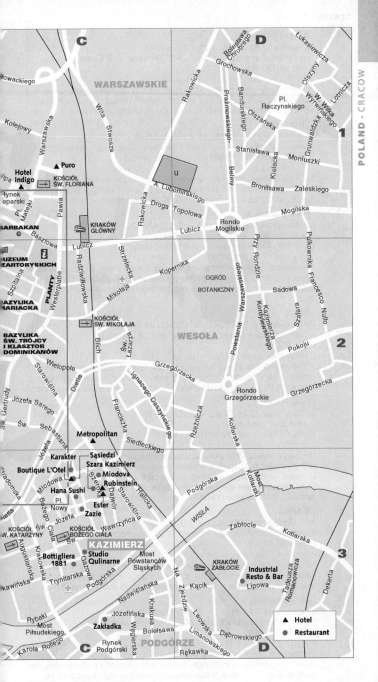

C D

Łukasiewicza

WARSZAWSKIE

Bolesława Chrobrego
Grochowska

Rakowicka

W. Wilka Wyrwińskiego
Lotnicza

Olszyny

Pl. Raczynskiego

Prazmowskiego
Bandurskiego
Olszańska

1

Nowackiego

Kolejowy

Warszawska

Wita Stwosza

Kolejowy

▲ Puro

Hotel Indigo

KOŚCIÓŁ ŚW. FLORIANA

lipa

Rynek Kleparski

Pl. Matejki

BARBAKAN

Pawia

Basztowa

Stanisława
Beliny

Kielecka

Moniuszki

Grunwaldzka

Bronisława Zaleskiego

A. Lubomirskiego

KRAKÓW GŁÓWNY

Droga Topolowa

Rakowicka

Lubicz

Rondo Mogilskie

Mogilska

MUZEUM CZARTORYSKICH

Szpitalna

PLANTY
Westerplatte

Radziwiłłowska

Strzelecka

Lubicz

Kopernika

OGRÓD BOTANICZNY

Przy Rondzie

Pułkownika Francesco Nullo

BAZYLIKA MARIACKA

BAZYLIKA ŚW. TRÓJCY I KLASZTOR DOMINIKANÓW

Mikołaja

KOŚCIÓŁ ŚW. MIKOŁAJA

Blich

Św. Łazarza

WESOŁA

Sadowa

Kazimierza Królewskiego

Szafera

2

Wielopole

Dietla

Powstania Warszawskiego

Pokoju

Św. Gertrudy

Józefa Sarego

Św. Sebastiana

Starowiślna

Franciszka

Ignacego Daszyńskiego

Grzegórzecka

Rondo Grzegórzeckie

Grzegórzecka

Siedleckiego

Rzeźnicza

Kotlarska

Metropolitan ▲

Karakter ▲
Boutique L'Otel ▲

Sąsiedzi
Szara Kazimierz
Miodova ●

Miodowa

Hana Sushi ▲

Szara

Dajwór

Halicka

Starowiślna

Podgórska

Most Kotlarski

Rubinstein ▲

Pl. Nowy

Ester ●
Zazie ●

Józefa

Św. Ciała

Wawrzyńca

WISŁA

Zabłocie

Kotlarska

3

KOŚCIÓŁ ŚW. KATARZYNY

KOŚCIÓŁ BOŻEGO CIAŁA

KAZIMIERZ

Augustiańska

Krakowska

Gazowa

Św. Wawrzyńca

Most Powstańców Śląskich

KRAKÓW ZABŁOCIE

Industrial Resto & Bar ●

Bottigliera 1881 ●

Studio Qulinarne ●

Trynitarska

Podgórska

Nadwiślańska

Na Zjeździe

Kącik

Lipowa

Tadeusza Romanowicza

Dekerta

Rybaki

Most Piłsudskiego

Józefińska

Krakusa

Lwowska

Dąbrowskiego

Limanowskiego

Zakładka ●

Bolesława

Węgierska

PODGÓRZE

Karola Rollego

Rynek Podgórski

Rę
kawka

C D

▲	Hotel
●	Restaurant

Kogel Mogel

XX 🏠 AC 🍴

ul. Sienna 12 ✉ *31 041 –* ✆ *(12) 426 49 68*

Plan: **F2**

– www.kogel-mogel.pl – Closed 24-25 December and Easter

Carte 80/150 PLN

• Polish • Brasserie • Fashionable •

A smart, lively brasserie; the wine room with its original painted ceiling is a popular spot, as is the enclosed terrace. Extensive menus offer refined, modern versions of classic Polish and Cracovian dishes. Live music is a feature.

Leonardo

XX AC ⟷

ul. Szpitalna 20-22 ✉ *31 024 –* ✆ *(12) 429 6850*

Plan: **F1**

– www.leonardo.com.pl – Closed Christmas, Easter and 1 November

Carte 80/175 PLN – *(booking essential at dinner)*

• Classic cuisine • Intimate • Classic décor •

Set in the basement of a small shopping mall, Leonardo pays homage to da Vinci, with reproduction etchings and an ornithopter on display. Menus take inspiration from France and Italy; cooking is hearty yet refined and uses prime ingredients.

Pod Baranem

XX AC 🍴

ul. Sw. Gertrudy 21 ✉ *31 049 –* ✆ *(12) 429 40 22*

Plan: **F3**

– www.podbaranem.com – Closed Christmas and Easter

Carte 70/170 PLN – *(booking essential at dinner)*

• Polish • Neighbourhood • Family •

A traditional family-run restaurant set over 5 rooms, with rug-covered stone floors, homely furnishings and contemporary artwork by Edward Dwurnik. The large menu offers classic Polish cuisine; sharing dishes must be ordered in advance.

Szara

XX 🏠 🍴

Rynek Glówny 6 ✉ *31 042 –* ✆ *(12) 421 66 69*

Plan: **E/F2**

– www.szara.pl – Closed 1 November and 24 December

Carte 95/165 PLN

• International • Brasserie • Classic décor •

A well-regarded family-run restaurant on the Grand Square, featuring a lovely terrace, a hand-painted Gothic ceiling and a pleasant brasserie atmosphere. Menus mix Polish, French and Swedish classics; cooking is authentic and hearty.

Pod Nosem

X 🏠 ⟷

ul. Kanonicza 22 ✉ *31 002 –* ✆ *(12) 376 00 14*

Plan: **E3**

– www.podnosem.com

Menu 69 PLN (weekday lunch) – Carte 90/150 PLN

• Polish • Cosy • Romantic •

The bright ground floor of this characterful medieval-style restaurant is hung with tapestries and the white wooden banquettes have tapestry seat cushions to match; while downstairs, amongst the brick and stone, it's more dimly lit. Classic Polish recipes are given appealing modern updates. Above the restaurant are 3 richly furnished suites with prices to match.

Bianca

X 🏠

Plac Mariacki 2 ✉ *31 042 –* ✆ *(12) 422 18 71*

Plan: **F2**

– www.biancaristorante.pl – Closed 24-25 December and Easter

Carte 70/140 PLN

• Italian • Bistro • Intimate •

Sit on the small terrace opposite St Mary's Basilica and watch the world go by. Classical menus cover all regions of Italy and the pastas and ragus are freshly made; be sure to try the delicious saltimbocca with its sharp, lemony tang.

La Campana

X 🏠 🍴

ul. Kanonicza 7 ✉ *31 000 –* ✆ *(12) 430 22 32*

Plan: **E2**

– www.lacampana.pl – Closed 24-25 December and Easter

Carte 80/135 PLN

• Italian • Cosy • Rustic •

Discreetly set under an archway, with a charming country interior featuring pine dressers and an olive branch frieze; it also boasts a beautiful walled garden. The wide-ranging Italian menu features imported produce – the hams are a hit.

POLAND - CRACOW

Del Papá
X 🍴 📻 ⟆
ul. Św. Tomasza 6 ✉ *31 014* – ℰ *(12) 421 83 43*   Plan: **E1**
– *www.delpapa.pl* – *Closed 24-26 December*
Carte 70/95 PLN
• Italian • Bistro • Friendly •
A simple Italian trattoria: dine in the bistro-style room, the characterful Italian 'street' or on the partially covered rear terrace. Wide-ranging menus echo the seasons and pasta is a highlight – pick your variety, sauce and portion size.

Farina
X 📻 ⟆
ul. Sw. Marka 16 ✉ *31 018* – ℰ *(12) 422 16 80*   Plan: **F1**
– *www.farina.com.pl* – *Closed Christmas*
Carte 80/230 PLN
• Seafood • Cosy • Friendly •
A pretty little restaurant set over three rooms; all of them cosy and candlelit but each with its own character. Seafood is the speciality, with fish arriving from France several times a week and then cooked whole over salt and herbs.

Grand
🍴 ⅃ᴓ 🛖 ᵭ 📻 ⟆
ul. Slawkowska 5/7 ✉ *31 014* – ℰ *(12) 424 08 00*   Plan: **E1**
– *www.grand.pl*
65 rm ⌿ – 🛏410/1075 PLN 🛏🛏475/1200 PLN – 9 suites
• Traditional • Luxury • Historic •
Once Duke Czartoryski's palace; now the city's oldest hotel. The classic façade masks a columned lobby and rooms filled with gold leaf, stained glass and antiques. Bedrooms are spacious and the suites are vast, opulent and impressively furnished. The Piano brasserie comes adorned with sheet music.

Sheraton Grand Krakow
🍴 ≪ ⅃ᴓ 🛖 🔲 ᵭ 📻 ⟆ 🛁 🚗
ul. Powisle 7 ✉ *31 101* – ℰ *(12) 662 10 00*   Plan I: **B2**
– *www.sheratongrandkrakow.com*
232 rm ⌿ – 🛏535/1350 PLN 🛏🛏620/1440 PLN – 3 suites
• Luxury • Business • Modern •
A well-located international hotel with an impressive glass-roofed atrium and extensive event space. Bedrooms are luxuriously appointed and well-equipped – and some boast river and castle views. Olive offers a popular global menu and Polish specialities, while the sports bar serves a range of pub-style dishes. Start your evening with a drink in the rooftop lounge-bar.

Copernicus
⅃ᴓ 🛖 🔲 ᵭ 📻 ⟆
ul. Kanonicza 16 ✉ *31 002* – ℰ *(12) 424 34 00*   Plan: **E3**
– *www.hotel.com.pl*
29 rm – 🛏700/900 PLN 🛏🛏800/1100 PLN – ⌿ 70 PLN – 4 suites
• Luxury • Grand townhouse • Personalised •
An elegant townhouse in the castle's shadow, on one of the city's oldest streets. The central atrium has a lounge and a small patio for breakfast or light lunch. Luxurious beamed bedrooms boast handmade furniture and excellent comforts. There's an intimate pool in the medieval cellars and a lovely rooftop terrace.
 Copernicus – See restaurant listing

Stary
⅃ᴓ 🛖 🔲 ᵭ 📻 ⟆ 🛁
ul. Szczepanska 5 ✉ *31 011* – ℰ *(12) 384 08 08*   Plan: **E1**
– *www.stary.hotel.com.pl*
78 rm ⌿ – 🛏490/950 PLN 🛏🛏590/1100 PLN – 7 suites
• Luxury • Townhouse • Design •
Behind a traditional townhouse façade, dramatic modern glass and steel structures blend cleverly with 15C features. The contemporary bar and rooftop terrace sit alongside original brick and stonework. Stylish bedrooms boast handmade furniture, impressive marble bathrooms and state-of-the-art lighting.
🍴 **Trzy Rybki** – See restaurant listing

Bonerowski Palace ☆ 🕸 🏧 ⇔ 🕍
ul. Św. Jana 1 ✉ *31 013* – ✆ *(12) 374 13 00* — Plan: **E1**
– *www.palacbonerowski.pl*
16 rm – †600/2000 PLN †† 650/2200 PLN – 65 PLN – 3 suites
• Palace • Historic • Personalised •
A former palace, superbly located on the main square and featuring medieval portals, ornate ceilings, restored polychrome décor and the largest Swarovski chandelier in Europe. Large, antique-furnished bedrooms and chic suites come with marble bathrooms. The restaurant focuses on steaks and fish.

Kossak ☆ < 🛗 🕸 ᵹ 🏧 ⇔ 🕍
Plac Kossaka 1 ✉ *31 106* – ✆ *(12) 379 59 00* — Plan I: **B2**
– *www.hotelkossak.pl*
60 rm – †750/800 PLN ††800/860 PLN – 5 suites
• Business • Modern • Contemporary •
A contemporary business hotel named after the famous Polish painter and offering views over the river towards the castle. Each of its well-equipped, modern bedrooms features a piece of Kossak's art; opt for one of the comfortable corner suites. The ground floor restaurant offers Polish specialities, while the 7th floor café and terrace serves a modern international menu.

Pod Róza ☆ 🛗 🕸 🏧 ⇔ 🕍
ul. Florianska 14 ✉ *31 021* – ✆ *(12) 424 33 00* — Plan: **F1**
– *www.podroza.hotel.com.pl*
57 rm – †400/650 PLN ††450/720 PLN – 60 PLN – 4 suites
• Historic • Traditional • Design •
A discreet entrance leads to a surprisingly large glass-covered courtyard, complete with a modern Polish restaurant and a laid-back Italian trattoria. Classically appointed bedrooms feature silhouette artwork and modern bathrooms; many have jacuzzis. The fourth floor rooms are cosiest and boast city skyline panoramas – the top floor fitness suite shares the view.

Gródek ☆ 🕸 ᵹ 🏧 ⇔
ul. Na Gródku 4 ✉ *31 028* – ✆ *(12) 431 90 30* — Plan: **F2**
– *www.donimirski.com*
23 rm – †520/650 PLN ††650/850 PLN
• Historic • Townhouse • Elegant •
This homely townhouse is hidden in a quiet side street close to the square. Unwind in the wood-panelled library bar or grab a seat on the roof terrace. Bedrooms come with good facilities; they vary in size and each has its own character. The restaurant offers a concise selection of Polish favourites.

Hotel Indigo ☆ 🛗 🕸 ᵹ 🏧 ⇔ 🕍
ul.Filipa 18 ✉ *31 150* – ✆ *(12) 300 3030* — Plan I: **C1**
– *www.hotelindigo.com/krakowfg*
56 rm – †399/999 PLN ††399/999 PLN
• Boutique hotel • Grand townhouse • Design •
This converted tenement building sits alongside the Old Kleparz food market, in an area once populated by artists. Art throughout the ages leads the hotel's theme; bedrooms have stylish, eye-catching designs and are inspired by Poland's greatest painters. Updated Polish classics are served in the brasserie.

Polski Pod Bialym Orlem ᵹ ⇔ 🕍
ul. Pijarska 17 ✉ *31 015* – ✆ *(12) 422 11 44* — Plan: **F1**
– *www.donimirski.com*
60 rm – †410/450 PLN ††530/730 PLN
• Historic • Townhouse • Classic •
A traditional hotel overlooking the city walls and owned by the family of the Czartoryski Princes. The cosy brick bar dates from the 16C and individually styled bedrooms feature tapestries and etchings which reflect the city's heritage. The small restaurant and courtyard terrace offers an international menu.

🏠 Puro ✿ ⅗ 🎬 ♿ 🏋 🚗

ul. Ogrodowa 10 ✉ *31 155 –* ℰ *(12) 314 2100*
Plan I: **C1**
– www.purohotel.pl
138 rm – 🛏300/600 PLN 🛏🛏300/600 PLN – ⊊ 50 PLN – 6 suites
• Boutique hotel • Chain • Personalised •
Colour-changing lights illuminate the modern façade and the spacious lobby is decked out with vintage furnishings. Up-to-date bedrooms feature yellow Chesterfield-style headboards, tablet-operated controls and glass bathroom walls decorated with frosted flowers. The restaurant serves an international menu.

🏠 Queen ⅗ 🎬 ♿ 🏋

ul. Józefa Dietla 60 ✉ *31 039 –* ℰ *(12) 433 33 33*
Plan: **F3**
– www.queenhotel.pl
31 rm ⊊ **–** 🛏350/700 PLN 🛏🛏400/750 PLN
• Business • Design • Contemporary •
This chic boutique hotel sits between the old market square and Kazimierz. Charming bedrooms come in brown and silver and feature the latest mod cons; go for a Deluxe, which comes with a balcony affording garden and castle views.
🍴 **Amarylis** – See restaurant listing

🏠 Unicus ✿ ⅗ 🎬 ♿ 🏋

ul Sw. Marka 20 ✉ *31 020 –* ℰ *(12) 433 71 11*
Plan: **F1**
– www.hotelunicus.pl
35 rm ⊊ **–** 🛏390/730 PLN 🛏🛏450/1020 PLN
• Business • Townhouse • Modern •
A stylish boutique hotel converted from a row of old tenement houses. Well-appointed bedrooms range in colour from green to gold and boast state-of-the-art shower rooms; the Double Deluxes, overlooking Florianska Street, are the best. The bright, barrel-ceilinged basement restaurant serves a modern menu.

🏠 Wentzl ⩽ 🎬 ♿

Rynek Glówny 19 ✉ *31 008 –* ℰ *(12) 430 26 64*
Plan: **E2**
– www.wentzl.pl
18 rm – 🛏450/860 PLN 🛏🛏460/870 PLN – ⊊ 60 PLN
• Grand townhouse • Historic • Personalised •
A 15C tenement house offering fantastic views over the market square towards St Mary's Basilica. Individually furnished bedrooms feature antiques and interesting art; ask for one with a balcony overlooking the Square.

🏠 Amber Boutique Hotels 🛎 🏋 ⅗ 🎬 ♿ 🏋

ul. Garbarska 8-10 ✉ *31 131 –* ℰ *(12) 421 06 06*
Plan: **E1**
– www.hotel-amber.pl
38 rm ⊊ **–** 🛏299/544 PLN 🛏🛏359/559 PLN
• Townhouse • Traditional • Modern •
Two traditional townhouses in a residential street, with smart breakfast and fitness rooms. Well-equipped contemporary bedrooms come with complimentary cherry vodka: the 'Design' rooms have feature walls and display local artists' work.

🏠 Maltanski ♿ 🅿

ul. Straszewskiego 14 ✉ *31 101 –* ℰ *(12) 431 00 10*
Plan: **E2**
– www.donimirski.com
16 rm ⊊ **–** 🛏510/590 PLN 🛏🛏590/650 PLN
• Townhouse • Traditional • Cosy •
A lovely little hotel by the Planty, named after its previous owners, The Knights of Malta. With the castle and square just a stroll away, it makes a great base for exploring. Some of the charming, traditional bedrooms come with patios.

⌂ **Orlowska Townhouse** 　　　　　　　　　　　　　ᴀᴄ 4⟋

ul. Slawkowska 26 ✉ *31 014 –* ☏ *(12) 429 54 45* 　　　　Plan: **E1**
– www.orlowskatownhouse.com – Closed 23-26 December and 1-2 April
5 rm – ♥540/640 PLN ♥♥570/640 PLN – � 38 PLN
• Historic • Townhouse • Personalised •

A 17C townhouse on a peaceful central street. Spacious apartment-style bedrooms have small kitchenettes and modern bathrooms, and are furnished in themes including 'Art Deco', 'Poets' and 'Boudoir'. Breakfast trays can be delivered.

⌂ **Senacki** 　　　　　　　　　　　　　　　　　　ᴙ 4⟋

ul. Grodzka 51 ✉ *31 001 –* ☏ *(12) 422 76 86* 　　　　　　Plan: **E2**
– www.hotelsenacki.pl
20 rm ⊑ – ♥750/800 PLN ♥♥800/1200 PLN
• Townhouse • Traditional • Personalised •

A smart hotel with an ornate stone façade, set opposite a 17C church on the Royal Way. Bedrooms are bright and modern – those on the upper floors have rooftop views. Buffet breakfasts take place in the hugely atmospheric 13C cellar.

---

at KAZIMIERZ 　　　　　　　　　　　　　　　　　　**PLAN I**

⊛ **Zazie** 　　　　　　　　　　　　　　　　　　　X ᴀᴄ

ul. Józefa 34 ✉ *31 056 –* ☏ *(757) 250 885* 　　　　　Plan: **C3**
– www.zaziebistro.pl – Closed 24-25 December and Easter
Menu 29 PLN (weekday lunch) – Carte 60/80 PLN – *(booking essential at dinner)*
• French • Bistro • Cosy •

You'll find this bistro in a corner spot on a pleasant square. Inside it has a lively vibe; ask for a table in the attractive cellar, with its pleasing mix of French memorabilia and brick and stone walls. Great value Gallic dishes range from quiches and gratins to roast duck and beef Bourguignon.

⮐O **Studio Qulinarne** 　　　　　　　　　　XX 🕸 🏠 ᴀᴄ 4⟋

ul. Gazowa 4 ✉ *31 060 –* ☏ *(12) 430 69 14* 　　　　　Plan: **C3**
– www.studioqulinarne.pl – Closed Christmas, Easter, 1 January and Sunday
Menu 150/215 PLN – *(dinner only) (booking advisable) (surprise menu only)*
• Modern cuisine • Intimate • Elegant •

A passionately run, restyled bus garage with folding glass doors, a cocktail bar and an intimate enclosed terrace. The airy interior features exposed timbers, unusual lighting and black linen. Choose 3, 5 or 7 'surprise' dishes with a playful, innovative edge. The wine list offers a rich, diverse selection.

⮐O **Szara Kazimierz** 　　　　　　　　　　　　　XX 🏠 4⟋

ul. Szeroka 39 ✉ *31 042 –* ☏ *(12) 429 12 19* 　　　　Plan: **C3**
– www.szarakazimierz.pl – Closed 24-25 December
Carte 90/135 PLN
• Polish • Brasserie • Neighbourhood •

A friendly brasserie in a pleasant spot on the square. Sit out the front, on the enclosed rear terrace, or inside, surrounded by photos of Gaultier models. Menus reflect the owners' heritage by mixing Polish and Swedish classics.

⮐O **Bottiglieria 1881** 　　　　　　　　　　　　　　X 🕸

ul. Bochenska 5 ✉ *31 061 –* ☏ *(660) 66 17 56* 　　　　Plan: **C3**
– www.1881.com.pl – Closed Christmas-New Year, Easter, Sunday and Monday
Carte 130/140 PLN
• Creative • Wine bar • Design •

This century old cellar is found in the Jewish district. Old wine boxes decorate the room, hand-crafted wood and stone feature and the large cave offers over 100 different wines. The menu is a concise collection of modern dishes.

⫯◯ **Hana Sushi** ✗
Kupa 12 ✉ *31 057 –* ✆ *(608) 576 255*
– www.hanasushi.pl – Closed Monday
Carte 60/140 PLN
• Japanese • Simple • Neighbourhood •
This simple Japanese-style restaurant has made a real impact in the city. The chef-owner is a Sushi Master who trained in Tokyo and the sushi is prepared with finesse. They also serve some Korean dishes like ramen and bibimbap.

⫯◯ **Karakter** ✗
Brzozowa 17 ✉ *31 050 –* ✆ *(795) 818 123 – Closed 24-*
25 December, Easter and Monday lunch
Menu 30 PLN (weekday lunch) – Carte 60/100 PLN – *(booking essential at dinner)*
• Modern cuisine • Rustic • Simple •
Karakter is a lively spot, with loud music, cocktails and a minimalist feel. The charming young team serve an extensive menu with a focus on offal; horse meat tartare is one of their signatures. Refined cooking blends many different flavours.

⫯◯ **Miodova** ✗ 🛋 🈸 ⇔
ul. Szeroka 3 ✉ *31 053 –* ✆ *(12) 432 5083*
– www.miodova.pl – Closed 24-25 December
Carte 95/120 PLN
• Polish • Friendly • Fashionable •
In a cobbled square in the busy Jewish district you'll find 'Honey', an ultra-modern restaurant set over 3 floors. It's a comfortable place, with sofa-style banquettes and colourful cushions. Regional specialities are given modern twists.

⫯◯ **Sąsiedzi** – Boutique L'Otel ✗ 🏨 🈸 ⇔
ul. Miodowa 25 ✉ *31 055 –* ✆ *(12) 654 83 53*
– www.oberza.pl – Closed 23-26 December, Easter and 1 November
Carte 65/140 PLN
• Polish • Intimate • Neighbourhood •
With its relaxed, welcoming atmosphere and delightful team, its name, 'Neighbourhood', sums it up well. Dine on the small terrace or in one of several charming cellar rooms. Honest, good value cooking uses old Polish recipes.

🏙 **Metropolitan** ✿ 🛋 ♿ 🈸 ↳ 🔊
ul Berka Joselewicza 19 ✉ *31 031 –* ✆ *(12) 442 75 00*
– www.hotelmetropolitan.pl
59 rm ⌷ – ♦249/855 PLN ♦♦289/895 PLN
• Historic building • Modern • Contemporary •
A converted 19C townhouse with a smart lobby and a lounge centred around a bar. Bold, modern décor features throughout; bedrooms come in neutral hues, with a high level of facilities. The laid-back restaurant serves modern Polish dishes and Argentinian beef. In summer, have breakfast in the walled courtyard.

🏠 **Rubinstein** ✿ 🏙 🈸 ↳ 🔊
ul. Szeroka 12 ✉ *31 053 –* ✆ *(12) 384 00 00*
– www.rubinstein.pl
28 rm ⌷ – ♦270/430 PLN ♦♦390/560 PLN
• Historic • Townhouse • Personalised •
This pair of restored townhouses are joined by a bright, glass-roofed restaurant and named after Helena Rubinstein, who lived nearby. Well-equipped, characterful bedrooms come with luxurious marble and alabaster bathrooms. It's located in a pleasant square and the roof terrace affords panoramic city views.

POLAND - CRACOW

POLAND - CRACOW

⌂ **Boutique L'Otel**   AC ⇜
ul. Miodowa 25 ✉ 31 055 – ℰ (12) 633 34 44   Plan: **C3**
– www.aparthotel.oberza.pl – Closed Christmas
18 rm ⌑ – ❗129/379 PLN ❗❗149/599 PLN
• Townhouse • Historic • Design •
This delightful former tenement house sits in the heart of Kazimierz. An impressive staircase leads up to individually styled bedrooms which follow themes such as 'Art Deco' and 'Boutique'; top floor 'Crystal' is popular.
⇋ **Sąsiedzi** – See restaurant listing

⌂ **Ester**   ✿ 斺 & AC ⇜ ⽧
ul. Szeroka 20 ✉ 31 053 – ℰ (12) 429 11 88   Plan: **C3**
– www.hotel-ester.krakow.pl
32 rm ⌑ – ❗250/590 PLN ❗❗280/850 PLN
• Townhouse • Historic • Personalised •
A cosy little hotel overlooking a pleasant square in the Jewish quarter, opposite the synagogue. Both the guest areas and the comfortable, colour-themed bedrooms are traditionally furnished; the latter boast both baths and showers. The simple café and terrace serves a mix of classic Polish and Jewish dishes.

at PODGÓRZE   PLAN I

⇋ **Zakladka**   X 斺 AC ⇜ ⟳
ul. Józefińska 2 ✉ 30 529 – ℰ (12) 442 74 42   Plan: **C3**
– www.zakladkabistro.pl – Closed 24-25 December
Menu 40 PLN (weekday lunch) – Carte 65/125 PLN
• French • Bistro • Neighbourhood •
Zakladka is set over a footbridge in an old tenement building, and run by a well-known local chef. With chequered floors and red banquettes, the characterful front rooms have a classic bistro feel; the French dishes are equally traditional.

at ZABLOCIE   PLAN I

⇋ **Industrial Resto & Bar**   X 斺 AC 🅿
ul. Lipowa 4a ✉ 33332 – ℰ (12) 263 8626   Plan: **D3**
– www.restoindustrial.pl – Closed Christmas, 1 January, Easter and Monday
Carte 65/130 PLN
• International • Rustic • Fashionable •
Housed in an old electronics factory in the former industrial heartland, this vast, funky restaurant doubles as an art gallery. Hearty, flavoursome dishes have an element of refinement and take their influences from across the world.

LISBON

SeanPavonePhoto/iStock

LISBON
LISBOA

LeoPatrizi/iStock

Sitting on the north bank of the River Tagus, beneath huge open skies and surrounded by seven hills, Lisbon boasts an atmosphere that few cities can match. An enchanting walk around the streets has an old-time ambience all of its own, matched only by a jaunt on the trams and funiculars that run up and down the steep hills. At first sight Lisbon is all flaky palaces, meandering alleyways and castellated horizon quarried from medieval stone; but there's a 21C element, too. Slinky new developments line the riverside, linking the old and new in a glorious jumble which spills down the slopes to the water's edge. The views of the water from various vantage points all over Lisbon and the vistas of the 'Straw Sea' – so

named because of the golden reflections of the sun – reach out to visitors, along with the sounds of fado, the city's alluring folk music, which conjures up a melancholic yearning.

The compact heart of the city is the Baixa, a flat, 18C grid of streets flanked by the hills. To the west is the elegant commercial district of Chiado and the funky hilltop Bairro Alto, while immediately to the east is Alfama, a tightly packed former Moorish quarter with kasbah-like qualities. North of here is the working-class neighbourhood of Graça and way out west lies the spacious riverside suburb of Belém, while up the river to the east can be found the ultra-modern Parque das Nações.

EATING OUT

Lisboetas love their local agricultural produce and the cuisine of the region can be characterised by its honesty and simplicity. The city has an age-old maritime tradition and there are a number of fishing ports nearby, so ocean-fresh fish and seafood features in a range of dishes. One thing the locals love in particular is bacalhau (cod), and it's said that in Lisbon, there's a different way to prepare it for every day of the year: it may come oven-baked, slow-cooked or cooked in milk, and it can be served wrapped in cabbage, with tocino belly pork or in a myriad of other ways. While eating in either a humble tasca, a casa de pasto or a restaurante, other specialities to keep an eye out for are clams cooked with garlic and coriander, traditional beef, chicken and sausage stew with vegetables and rice, bean casserole with tocino belly pork, and lamprey eel with rice. Enjoy them with a vinho verde, the wine of the region. A service charge will be included on your bill but it's customary to leave a tip of about ten per cent.

OLD LISBON (Alfama, Castelo de São Jorge, Rossio, Baixa, Chiado, Bairro Alto) **PLAN II**

🕸🕸 **Belcanto** (José Avillez) XxX 🕸 AC
Largo de São Carlos 10 ⊠ 1200-410 – Ⓜ Baixa-Chiado Plan: **E2**
– 𝒫 213 42 06 07 – www.belcanto.pt – Closed 18 January-2 February, 1-16 August, Sunday and Monday
Menu 145/165 € – Carte 95/115 €
• Creative • Contemporary décor •
This restaurant is located in the city's Bairro Alto, a district popular with tourists. Once through the front door you will enjoy one of the best gourmet experiences in Portugal, thanks to the cuisine of outstanding chef José Avillez. In the attractive dining room, renovated in a classically elegant style, the superb menus are of the utmost creativity and a demonstration of the very highest level of culinary skill.
→ Cozido à portuguesa. Mergulho no mar, robalo com algas e bivalves. Tangerina.

🕸 **Alma** (Henrique Sá Pessoa) XX
Anchieta 15 ⊠ 1200-023 – Ⓜ Baixa-Chiado Plan: **E2**
– 𝒫 213 47 06 50 – www.almalisboa.pt – Closed Monday
Menu 80/100 € – Carte 55/75 €
• Creative • Contemporary décor •
An attractive restaurant in the heart of the Chiado district. It occupies an 18C house that was once a warehouse for the famous Bertrand bookshop, the oldest in the world. The modern interior is one of striking contrasts and provides the backdrop for seasonal à la carte options and interesting set menus that encompass traditional, international and more innovative dishes.
→ Polvo assado, romesco, casca de batata, alcaparras e paprika fumada. Leitão confitado, puré de batata doce, pak choi e suco de laranja. Bomba de chocolate e caramelo salgado com sorvete de avelã.

🅝🅞 **Tágide** XxX ≤ AC
Largo da Academia Nacional de Belas Artes 18-20 Plan: **E2**
⊠ *1200-005 – Ⓜ Baixa-Chiado – 𝒫 213 40 40 10*
– www.restaurantetagide.com – Closed 7 days January and Sunday
Menu 60/80 € – Carte 40/65 €
• Modern cuisine • Classic décor •
Climb a few steps to Tágide's elegant dining room embellished with spider lamps and attractive azulejo tilework. Updated traditional cuisine and a tapas bar at the entrance.

🅝🅞 **Ad Lib** – Hotel Sofitel Lisbon Liberdade XX 🍴 ⅋ AC 🚗
Av. da Liberdade 127 ⊠ 1269-038 – Ⓜ Avenida Plan: **E1**
– 𝒫 213 22 83 50 – www.restauranteadlib.pt
Menu 44/70 € – Carte 37/67 € – (bar lunch)
• Modern cuisine • Contemporary décor •
A restaurant with a classic-contemporary feel and lots of personality. The cuisine here combines French and Portuguese cooking with more elaborate dishes served in the evening.

🅝🅞 **O Faz Figura** XX ≤ 🍴 AC
Rua do Paraíso 15-B ⊠ 1100-396 – 𝒫 218 86 89 81 Plan: I: **C3**
– www.fazfigura.com – Closed Monday lunch
Carte 32/55 €
• Modern cuisine • Trendy •
Next to the National Pantheon (Santa Engrácia church), near Alfama. A well-organised operation with classic facilities, in an elegant setting, and traditional cuisine with a creative touch.

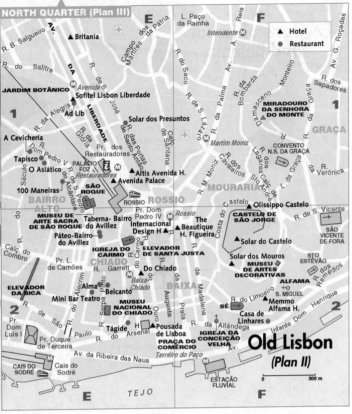

NORTH QUARTER (Plan III)

Old Lisbon (Plan II)

▲ Hotel
● Restaurant

---

†O **Solar dos Presuntos**   XX ⏛ & 🆔 🚗

Plan: **E1**

Rua das Portas de Santo Antão 150 ✉ 1150-269
– Ⓜ Avenida – 𝒞 213 42 42 53 – www.solardospresuntos.com – Closed
7 days Christmas, 21 days August, Sunday and bank holidays
Carte 33/57 €

· Traditional cuisine · Trendy ·

A culinary icon in the city which has been satisfying discerning palates for over
40 years. Extensive and traditional à la carte menu with a focus on high-quality
ingredients, in particular rice, fish and seafood.

†O **O Asiático**   X 🍽 🆔

Plan: **E1**

Rua da Rosa 317 ✉ 1250-083 – 𝒞 211 31 93 69
– www.oasiatico.com
Carte 34/40 €

· Asian · Fashionable ·

India, Thailand, China and Japan are all represented by this chef who has lived
in Asia and who creates attractive fusion cuisine based around Portuguese
ingredients which are perfect for sharing.

535

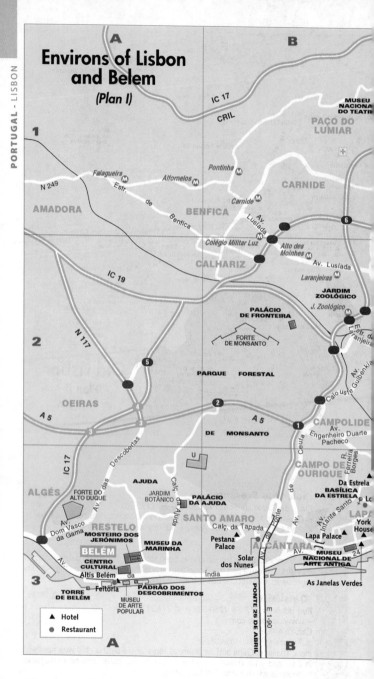

Environs of Lisbon and Belem
(Plan I)

▲ Hotel
● Restaurant

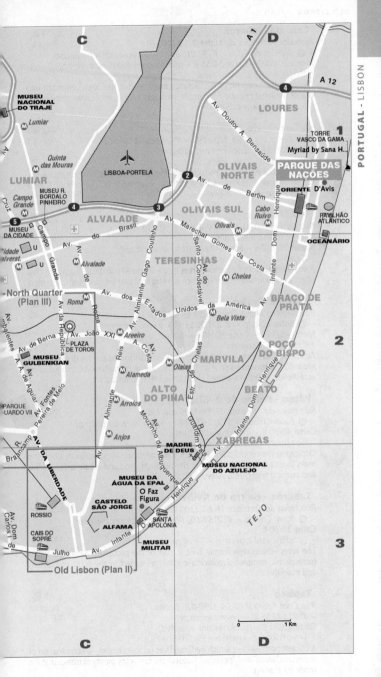

C · D

A 1

A 12

④ LOURES

Av. Doutor A. Bensaúde

TORRE VASCO DA GAMA

Myriad by Sana H...

MUSEU NACIONAL DO TRAJE

Ⓜ Lumiar

Quinta das Mouras

LISBOA-PORTELA

② Av. de Berlim

PARQUE DAS NAÇÕES

ORIENTE D'Avis

OLIVAIS NORTE

LUMIAR

MUSEU R. BORDALO PINHEIRO ④

Campo Cruz

Ⓜ ALVALADE ③ OLIVAIS SUL

Cabo Ruivo Ⓜ

PAVILHÃO ATLÂNTICO

Ⓜ Olivais

Dom

⑤ MUSEU DA CIDADE

Brasil

OCEANÁRIO

do

Av. Marechal Gomes da Costa

"idade niverst. Ⓤ

Ⓜ Alvalade

Grande

Av. de

TERESINHAS

Av. do Santo Condestável

Infante

Ⓜ Chelas

BRAÇO DE PRATA

North Quarter (Plan III)

Av. dos Estados

Av. da República

Roma

Ⓜ Roma

Av. Almirante Gago Coutinho

Unidos da América

Bela Vista

Henrique

mbientes Av. A. de Berna

Av. João XXI

Ⓜ Areeiro

A. Costa

Ⓜ Chelas

POÇO DO BISPO

MUSEU GULBENKIAN

PLAZA DE TOROS

Av. Fontes Pereira de Melo

Reis

Ⓜ Alameda

ALTO DO PINA

MARVILA

Ⓜ Olaias

Estr. de Chelas

BEATO

PARQUE EUARDO VII

R. Braancamp

AV. DA LIBERDADE

Almirante

Ⓜ Arrolos

Av. Mouzinho de Albuquerque

Guilhim Pais

Dom

Infante

Henrique

ROSSIO

Av. Dom Carlos I

Ⓜ Anjos

MADRE DE DEUS

XABREGAS

MUSEU NACIONAL DO AZULEJO

MUSEU DA ÁGUA DA EPAL

O Faz Figura

CASTELO SÃO JORGE

SANTA APOLÓNIA

CAIS DO SODRÉ

ALFAMA

D. Julho

Infante

MUSEU MILITAR

T E J O

Old Lisbon (Plan II)

0 1 Km

C · D

ⓣⓄ **Casa de Linhares** X AC
Beco dos Armazéns do Linho 2 ✉ *1100-037* Plan: **F2**
– Ⓜ *Terreiro do Paço –* 𝒸 *91 018 8118 – www.casadelinhares.com*
Menu 60/65 € – Carte 34/55 € – *(dinner only) (booking essential)*
• Portuguese • Regional décor •
This restaurant occupies a Renaissance mansion that has been converted into
one of the most popular *Fado* music venues in Lisbon. Impressive menu of tra-
ditional Portuguese cuisine.

ⓣⓄ **A Cevicheria** X AC
Dom Pedro V 129 ✉ *1200-093 –* 𝒸 *218 03 88 15* Plan: **E1**
Carte 20/30 € – *(bookings not accepted)*
• Peruvian • Fashionable •
Peruvian cooking with a Portuguese edge. The setting is tight on space but
highly original, including a huge octopus hanging from the ceiling! There's
always a queue to get in here.

ⓣⓄ **100 Maneiras** X AC
Rua do Teixeira 35 ✉ *1200-459 –* 𝒸 *91 030 7575* Plan: **E1**
– www.100maneiras.com
Menu 70/110 € – *(dinner only) (tasting menu only)*
• Creative • Traditional décor •
A small restaurant in a narrow street in the Bairro Alto district. The young chef
offers a creative tasting menu, which is fresh, light and imaginatively presented.

ⓣⓄ **Mini Bar Teatro** X 🏠 ⅙ AC
Rúa António Maria Cardoso 58 ✉ *1200-027* Plan: **E2**
– Ⓜ *Baixa-Chiado –* 𝒸 *211 30 53 93 – www.minibar.pt*
Menu 45/55 € – Carte 30/40 € – *(dinner only)*
• Creative • Bistro •
An informal, enticing and relaxed eatery in the Bairro Alto theatre district. Diners
are in for a pleasant surprise as the dishes on the menu have been created by
José Avillez – Michelin-starred chef at the Belcanto restaurant.

ⓣⓄ **Páteo - Bairro do Avillez** X AC
Rua Nova da Trindade 18 ✉ *1200-466 Lisboa* Plan: **E2**
– Ⓜ *Baixa-Chiado –* 𝒸 *215 83 02 90 – www.bairrodoavillez.pt*
Carte 40/60 € – *(booking advisable)*
• Seafood • Mediterranean décor •
Occupying the central patio of an attractive gastronomic complex in which the
main thread is the high quality of the products used and where delicious fish
and seafood take centre stage.

ⓣⓄ **Taberna - Bairro do Avillez** X AC
Rua Nova da Trindade 18 ✉ *1200-466* Plan: **E2**
– Ⓜ *Baixa-Chiado –* 𝒸 *215 83 02 90 – www.bairrodoavillez.pt*
Carte 20/30 €
• Traditional cuisine • Tavern •
The tavern-charcuterie format here is part of the successful Bairro do Avillez
gastronomic complex. Traditional cuisine presented in the form of petiscos
and main dishes.

ⓣⓄ **Tapisco** X AC
Rua Dom Pedro V 80 ✉ *1250-026 Lisboa* Plan: **E1**
– 𝒸 *213 42 06 81 – www.tapisco.pt*
Carte 20/30 € – *(bookings not accepted)*
• Traditional cuisine • Fashionable •
A contemporary eatery which perfectly lives up to its name – a combination of
the words "tapas" and "petiscos". Guests here can enjoy plenty of dishes that are
made for sharing.

Avenida Palace

Rua 1° de Dezembro 123 ⊠ 1200-359
Plan: **E1**
– **Ⓜ** Restauradores – ☏ 213 21 81 00 – www.hotelavenidapalace.pt
66 rm ⌷ – †177/219 € ††217/256 € – 16 suites
• Business • Classic •

An elegant, prestigious building dating from 1892. This hotel has a magnificent lounge area, a delightful English-style bar and well-maintained, classical-style guestrooms.

Pousada de Lisboa

Praça do Comércio 31 ⊠ 1100-148
Plan: **E2**
– **Ⓜ** Terreiro do Paço – ☏ 210 407 640 – www.pestana.com
88 rm ⌷ – †235/605 € ††235/605 € – 2 suites
• Historic building • Historic •

Located in the tourist heart of the city, the property is part of a series of buildings that are listed, national monuments. Attractive lounge furnished with antiques, comfortable guestrooms combining the traditional and the contemporary, as well as a brick-vaulted restaurant offering a modern à la carte menu.

Altis Avenida H.

Rua 1° de Dezembro 120 ⊠ 1200-360
Plan: **E1**
– **Ⓜ** Restauradores – ☏ 210 44 00 00 – www.altishotels.com
68 rm ⌷ – †160/250 € ††180/270 € – 2 suites
• Townhouse • Cosy •

The hotel's major selling point is its location on the main square, the Praça dos Restauradores. Contemporary guestrooms of differing sizes, some with a small terrace and many with views of the city. The elegant panoramic restaurant is on the seventh floor.

The Beautique H. Figueira

Praça da Figueira 16 ⊠ 1100-241 – **Ⓜ** Rossio
Plan: **F2**
– ☏ 210 49 29 40 – www.thebeautiquehotels.com
50 rm ⌷ – †116/420 € ††185/485 €
• Chain • Design •

This hotel occupies a completely remodelled building, which now boasts a distinct designer look. The intimately styled guestrooms (some with a shower, others a bathtub) are superbly appointed. Enjoy traditional Portuguese cuisine in the hotel restaurant.

Britania

Rua Rodrigues Sampaio 17 ⊠ 1150-278 – **Ⓜ** Avenida
Plan: **E1**
– ☏ 213 15 50 16 – www.heritage.pt
33 rm – †130/450 € ††143/450 € – ⌷ 14 €
• Townhouse • Art déco •

A unique property designed by the famous Portuguese architect Cassiano Branco. Stylish lounge-bar and meticulous bedrooms showcasing the spirit of the Art Deco period.

Do Chiado

Rua Nova do Almada 114 ⊠ 1200-290
Plan: **E2**
– **Ⓜ** Baixa-Chiado – ☏ 213 25 61 00 – www.hoteldochiado.pt
39 rm ⌷ – †120/240 € ††150/300 €
• Townhouse • Functional •

A hotel with well-appointed guestrooms in the heart of the Chiado district. Those on the seventh floor have private balconies with splendid views of the city.

Internacional Design H.

Rua da Betesga 3 ⊠ 1100-090 – **Ⓜ** Rossio
Plan: **E2**
– ☏ 213 24 09 90 – www.idesignhotel.com
55 rm ⌷ – †100/450 € ††110/460 €
• Townhouse • Design •

A hotel with a unique look and designer decor that that will definitely turn guests' heads thanks to its fun and colourful guestrooms spread across four floors, each with their own style: urban, tribe, zen and pop. The eclectic restaurant offers a choice of contemporary cuisine.

PORTUGAL - LISBON

Olissippo Castelo ⟨⟨ ⟨ 点 Ⅶ

Rua Costa do Castelo 120 ☒ *1100-179 –* Ⓜ *Rossio*   Plan: **F1-2**
– ☏ *218 82 01 90 – www.olissippohotels.com*
24 rm � *–* ⬥250/280 € ⬥⬥280/300 €
• Family • Classic •
Located on a hill next to the San Jorge castle, part of this hotel is built up against the castle ramparts. Very comfortable guestrooms, a dozen of which have their own garden terrace and magnificent views.

Sofitel Lisbon Liberdade 坊 点 Ⅶ 紐 ⌂

Av. da Liberdade 127 ☒ *1269-038 –* Ⓜ *Avenida*   Plan: **E1**
– ☏ *213 22 83 00 – www.sofitel-lisboa.com*
151 rm *–* ⬥180/500 € ⬥⬥180/500 € *–* ⊾ 25 € *– 12 suites*
• Business • Design •
A good location on one of the city's most prestigious and centrally located avenues. Comfortable public areas with decor that combines the traditional and contemporary. Friendly service throughout.
⫍○ **Ad Lib** – See restaurant listing

Solar do Castelo ⟅ Ⅶ

Rua das Cozinhas 2 ☒ *1100-181 –* ☏ *218 80 60 50*   Plan: **F2**
– www.heritage.pt
20 rm *–* ⬥162/450 € ⬥⬥176/450 € *–* ⊾ 14 €
• Historic • Trendy •
This hotel partially occupies a small 18C palace. It boasts a pretty paved patio with peacocks and a tiny ceramics museum. The classic yet contemporary guestrooms include seven personalised rooms in the palace itself and these offer greater comfort.

Memmo Alfama H. ⟨⟨ ⬛ Ⅶ

Travessa das Merceeiras 27 ☒ *1100-348*   Plan: **F2**
– ☏ *210 49 56 60 – www.memmohotels.com*
42 rm ⊾ *–* ⬥190/450 € ⬥⬥190/450 €
• Townhouse • Design •
Modern, truly unique and with a great location in the heart of the Alfama district, where it occupies three inter-connected buildings. Make sure you spend time enjoying the idyllic views from its sun terraces.

Solar dos Mouros ⟅ ⟨ Ⅶ

Rua do Milagre de Santo António 6 ☒ *1100-351*   Plan: **F2**
– ☏ *218 85 49 40 – www.solardosmouroslisboa.com*
13 rm ⊾ *–* ⬥199/599 € ⬥⬥219/619 €
• Historic • Modern •
A traditional-looking hotel with original decor, a somewhat irregular layout and modern furnishings. Some of the colourful guestrooms enjoy excellent views.

NORTH QUARTER (Av. da Liberdade, Parque Eduardo VII, Museu Gulbenkian)   **PLAN III**

✿ Eleven (Joachim Koerper) XxxX 器 ⟨ 点 Ⅶ ⟷

Rua Marquês de Fronteira ☒ *1070-051*   Plan: **G2**
– Ⓜ *São Sebastião*
– ☏ *213 86 22 11 – www.restauranteleven.com*
– Closed Sunday
Menu 94/175 € *–* Carte 84/135 €
• Creative • Elegant •
Housed in a designer-style building above the Amália Rodrigues gardens, this light, airy and modern restaurant boasts splendid views of the Eduardo VII park and the city. Creative gourmet cuisine features on the menu.
→ Barra de ouro, foie gras de pato, laranja, rum e soja. Lavagante, massa fresca e espargos. Soufflé de maracujá com gelado de banana.

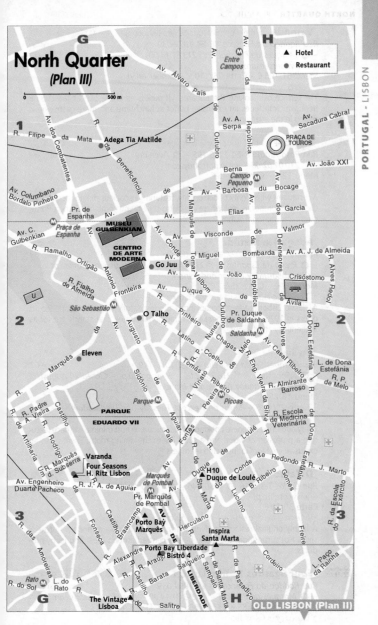

North Quarter
(Plan III)

▲ Hotel
● Restaurant

0   500 m

PORTUGAL - LISBON

G   H

Av. Álvaro Pais

Entre
Campos

Av. 5 de Outubro

Av. A. Serpa

Av. Sacadura Cabral

R. Filipe da Mata

Av. dos Combatentes

R. da Beneficência

● Adega Tia Matilde

Av. da República

PRAÇA DE
TOUROS

Av. João XXI

Av. Columbano Bordalo Pinheiro

Berna

Campo
Pequeno

Av. Barbosa du Bocage

Av. Sacadura Cabral

Pr. de Espanha

Av.

Av. Marquês de

Elias

dos

Garcia

Av. C. Gulbenkian

Praça de Espanha

MUSEU
GULBENKIAN

Av. Conde de Valbom

Visconde

Valmor

R. Ramalho Ortigão

CENTRO
DE ARTE
MODERNA

de

Bombarda

Av. A. J. de Almeida

R. Alves Redol

R. Fialho de Almeida

António

● Go Juu

Miguel

de

de

República

Crisóstomo

R. Augusto

Fronteira

Av. Duque

João

Av. de Ávila

São Sebastião

● O Talho

Pinheiro

Pr. Duque
de Saldanha

de Dona Estefânia

U

R. Latino

Nunes

Saldanha

● Eleven

Marquês

Sidónio

de

R. Tomás o Ribeiro

Chagas

R. de Melo

Av. Casal Ribeiro

L. de Dona
Estefânia

R. P.
de Melo

R. Padre de A. Vieira

Castilho

R. Rodrigo da Fonseca

R. Viriato

R. Eng. Vieira da Silva

R. Almirante Barroso

Parque

Pereira

● Picoas

PARQUE
EDUARDO VII

Aguiar

R. Fontes

R. Loulé

R. Escola
de Medicina
Veterinária

R. Artilharia 1

U R. Marquês d. Subserra

Varanda
Four Seasons
▲ H. Ritz Lisbon

Marquês
de Pombal

Duque
de Sta Marta

● H10
▲ Duque de Loulé

Conde de

R. B. Ribeiro

Redondo

R. J. Marto

R. da Escola do Exército

Av. Engenheiro Duarte Pacheco

R. J. A. de Aguiar

Pr. Marquês
de Pombal

Luciano

R. Estefânia

Castilho

Braancamp

▲ Porto Bay
Marquês

Herculano

● Inspira
Santa Marta

Freire

R. das Amoreiras

Alexandre

R. Araújo

Salgueiro

L. do
Rato

R. Castilho

Barata

Sampaio

de Passadiço

L. Paço
da Rainha

Rato

R. do Sol

▲ Porto Bay Liberdade
● Bistrô 4

R. de Santa Marta

Cordeiro

The Vintage ▲
Lisboa

do

Salitre

LIBERDADE

OLD LISBON (Plan II)

541

PORTUGAL - LISBON

⫯○ **Varanda** – Hotel Four Seasons H. Ritz Lisbon 🗙🗙🗙 ⌂ ≤ 🛒 🅰🅲
Rua Rodrigo da Fonseca 88 ✉ *1099-039* 🚗
– 🅜 *Marquês de Pombal* – 𝒞 *213 81 14 00* Plan: **G3**
– *www.fourseasons.com*
Menu 61/105 € – Carte 75/110 € – *(dinner only)*
• Modern cuisine • Elegant •
The terrace overlooking the Eduardo VII park is as impressive as the cuisine here, which includes an extensive buffet at lunchtime and more gastronomic dining in the evening.

⫯○ **Bistrô 4** – Hotel Porto Bay Liberdade 🗙🗙 ⌂ 🛒
Rua Rosa Araújo 8 ✉ *1250-195* – 🅜 *Avenida* Plan: **G3**
– 𝒞 *210 01 57 00* – *www.portobay.com*
Menu 22 € – Carte 35/45 €
• French • Bistro •
A restaurant with plenty of personality, featuring a spacious dining room with a classic-contemporary feel, where the bistro-style menu combines French, Portuguese and seasonal dishes.

⫯○ **Adega Tia Matilde** 🗙 🅰🅲 ⌖ 🚗
Rua da Beneficéncia 77 ✉ *1600-017* Plan: **G1**
– 🅜 *Praça de Espanha* – 𝒞 *217 97 21 72* – *www.adegatiamatilde.pt*
– *Closed Saturday dinner and Sunday*
Menu 22 € – Carte 35/52 €
• Traditional cuisine • Family •
A classic Lisbon address occupying a modest family house that opened its doors in 1926. The focus here is on traditional cuisine that stands out for its authenticity and flavour.

⫯○ **Go Juu** 🗙 🅰🅲
Rua Marqués Sá da Bandeira 46 ✉ *1050-149* Plan: **G2**
– 🅜 *S.Sebastião* – 𝒞 *218 28 07 04* – *www.gojuu.pt* – *Closed 20 August-3 September, Sunday dinner and Monday*
Menu 18/25 €
– Carte 25/45 € – *(lunch only except Tuesday and Wednesday)*
• Japanese • Design •
Enjoy authentic Japanese cooking in this unique, almost minimalist space featuring a profusion of wood and a sushi bar in the dining room. There's also an exclusive area for Go Juu's club members.

⫯○ **O Talho** 🗙 🅰🅲
Rua Carlos Testa 18 ✉ *1050-046* – 𝒞 *213 15 41 05* Plan: **G2**
– *www.otalho.pt*
Carte 30/50 €
• Meats and grills • Fashionable •
A highly original restaurant given that access to it is via a modern butcher's shop. Not surprisingly, the menu here is centred around meat and its by-products.

🏨 **Four Seasons H. Ritz Lisbon** ≤ 🕍 🕘 🖥 ⅚ 🅰🅲 🔱 🚗
Rua Rodrigo da Fonseca 88 ✉ *1099-039* Plan: **G3**
– 🅜 *Marquês de Pombal* – 𝒞 *213 81 14 00* – *www.fourseasons.com*
241 rm – ▯505/685 € ▯▯505/685 € – 🍽 41 € – 41 suites
• Luxury • Classic •
Experience true pleasure at this luxury hotel where the contemporary look of the building contrasts with the incredibly bright and classically elegant interior. Spacious lounge areas, highly comfortable guestrooms, and an impressive array of beauty treatments.
⫯○ **Varanda** – See restaurant listing

H10 Duque de Loulé 🕌 🛎 ⭐ 🅰️

Avenida Duque de Loulé 81-83 ✉ *1050-088*   Plan: **H3**
– ⓜ Marqués de Pombal – ☎ 213 18 20 00 – www.h10hotels.com
89 rm – 🛏120/250 € 🛏🛏130/260 € – ☕ 21 € – 5 suites
• Traditional • Contemporary •

A hotel with lots of personality, occupying a former convent, from which it has retained the original façade. The splendid interior comes as a delightful surprise with its mix of modernity and traditional Portuguese styling. The focus in the restaurant is very much on native cuisine.

Inspira Santa Marta 🕌 🛎 ⭐ 🅰️

Rua Santa Marta 48 ✉ *1150-297 – ⓜ Avenida*   Plan: **H3**
– ☎ 210 44 09 00 – www.inspirahotels.com
89 rm ☕ – 🛏120/250 € 🛏🛏150/300 €
• Townhouse • Modern •

This environmentally sustainable hotel boasts guestrooms designed according to the principles of Feng Shui, while at the same time combining excellent facilities and comfort. The informal restaurant offers à la carte dining which is complemented by several set menus at lunchtime.

Porto Bay Liberdade 🛎 ⭐ 🅰️

Rua Rosa Araújo 8 ✉ *1250-195 – ⓜ Avenida*   Plan: **G3**
– ☎ 210 01 57 00 – www.portobay.com
95 rm ☕ – 🛏200/300 € 🛏🛏300/500 € – 3 suites
• Townhouse • Contemporary •

Occupying a restored palace with a delightful classical façade and a contrasting contemporary-style interior. Facilities here include an attractive lobby, classic-contemporary guestrooms, an interior terrace-patio offering café service, plus a stylish rooftop bar.
⑩ **Bistrô 4** – See restaurant listing

Porto Bay Marquês 🕌 🛎 ⭐

Rua Duque de Palmela 32 ✉ *1250-098*   Plan: **G3**
– ☎ 210 40 20 00 – www.portobay.pt
50 rm ☕ – 🛏150/250 € 🛏🛏150/250 € – 22 suites
• Business • Contemporary •

A comfortable hotel offering extensive services and facilities, including a welcoming lobby, contemporary bedrooms, a rooftop sun terrace, plus a multi-purpose restaurant offering authentic Italian cuisine.

The Vintage Lisboa 🕌 🛎 ⭐ 🅰️

Rua Rodrigo da Fonseca 2 ✉ *1250-191 – ⓜ Rato*   Plan: **G3**
– ☎ 210 40 54 00 – www.nauhotels.com
53 rm ☕ – 🛏150/500 € 🛏🛏150/500 € – 3 suites
• Townhouse • Contemporary •

Strong attention to detail has resulted in a look that is both personalised and welcoming. The guestrooms are classic yet contemporary in style with top quality fixtures and furnishings. The multi-function restaurant is the setting for breakfast, lunch and dinner.

PARQUE DAS NAÇÕES   PLAN I

🍽 D'Avis   🍴 🌿 ⭐

Av. D. João II-1 (Parque das Nações) ✉ *1990-083*   Plan: **D1**
– ☎ 218 68 13 54 – Closed Sunday and bank holidays
Carte 20/30 €
• Cuisine from Alentejo • Rustic •

This oasis of rusticity imbued with the spirit of the Alentejo region is in the very modern setting of the Expo '98 site. The counter at the entrance sells regional products, while the two cosy dining rooms are decorated with a variety of traditional and antique objects. Highly authentic Alentejo cuisine.

Myriad by Sana H. ⚐ ≼ 𝄞 🛜 📺 ⬚ 🅰 🖧 ✆ 🚗

Cais das Naus, Lote 2.21.01 (Parque das Naçoes)   Plan: **D1**
✉ *1990-173 –* ⓜ *Oriente –* ☎ *211 10 76 00 – www.myriad.pt*
186 rm – ♦170/240 € ♦♦240/270 € – ☱ 30 €
• Business • Modern •

A hotel with a striking look, next to the Vasco de Gama tower. The interior showcases high-level design and functionality with every guestroom overlooking the river and the impressive terrace. The restaurant offers both Portuguese and international cuisine.

WEST   PLAN I

❀ ### Loco (Alexandre Silva)   XX 🅰

Rua dos Navegantes 53 ✉ *1250-731 –* ⓜ *Rato*   Plan: **B3**
– ☎ *213 95 18 61 – www.loco.pt – Closed 3-19 June, 11-27 November,*
Sunday and Monday
Menu 80/90 € – *(dinner only) (booking advisable) (tasting menu only)*
• Modern cuisine • Fashionable •

Located next to the Basílica da Estrela, Loco has just the one dining room with a surprising design and views of the kitchen. Alexandre Silva, famous for winning the first *Top Chef de Portugal* competition, showcases his cuisine via two enticing and creative tasting menus, which make full use of locally sourced ingredients.

→ Carapau com molho de pato e malagueta. Lingua de vitela com molho de mão de vaca e muscatel. Espargos brancos com café e cardamomo.

😀 ### Solar dos Nunes   X 🅰

Rua dos Lusíadas 68-72 ✉ *1300-372 –* ☎ *213 64 73 59*   Plan: **B3**
– www.solardosnunes.pt – Closed Sunday
Carte 30/40 €
• Traditional cuisine • Rustic •

This welcoming restaurant stands out for the magnificent mosaic-style floor in the main dining room and its walls covered with appreciative newspaper and magazine reviews. Impressive fish display, as well as a live seafood tank. Traditional Portuguese menu and an excellent wine list.

Lapa Palace ⚐ ⊱ ≼ 🗘 𝄞 ⌧ 🛜 ⬚ 🅰 🖧 🚗

Rua do Pau da Bandeira 4 ✉ *1249-021 –* ⓜ *Rato*   Plan: **B3**
– ☎ *213 94 94 94 – www.olissippohotels.com*
102 rm ☱ – ♦300/450 € ♦♦300/450 € – 7 suites
• Grand Luxury • Classic •

A luxurious 19C palace standing on one of the seven hills overlooking Lisbon and boasting stunning views of the Tagus estuary. The elegant and bright restaurant serves pleasantly updated traditional cuisine. The perfect setting for an unforgettable stay!

Pestana Palace ⚐ ⊱ 🗘 𝄞 ⌧ 🛜 ⬚ 🅰 🖧 🚗

Rua Jau 54 ✉ *1300-314 –* ☎ *213 61 56 00*   Plan: **B3**
– www.pestana.com
176 rm ☱ – ♦381/472 € ♦♦402/494 € – 18 suites
• Palace • Classic •

A delightful 19C palace decorated in keeping with its period, including sumptuous lounges, guestrooms high on detail, and surroundings that resemble a botanic garden. The restaurant, which features a private dining area in the former kitchen, offers simple lunches and more elaborate dining in the evening.

Da Estrela ⚐ 🅰 🖧 🚗

Rua Saraiva de Carvalho 35 ✉ *1250-242 –* ⓜ *Rato*   Plan: **B3**
– ☎ *211 90 01 00 – www.hoteldaestrela.com*
13 rm ☱ – ♦120/229 € ♦♦130/244 € – 6 suites
• Townhouse • Modern •

The hotel's original decor evokes the spirit of the former school that once occupied the building. Hence the combination of old blackboards, tables and coat racks alongside designer furniture. The multi-function restaurant is used for all three meal services.

As Janelas Verdes
♿ ἐ
Rua das Janelas Verdes 47 ✉ *1200-690*
Plan: **B3**
– ℰ 213 96 81 43 – www.heritage.pt
29 rm – ♦143/450 € ♦♦157/450 € – ☲ 14 €
• Traditional • Classic •
This hotel partially occupies an 18C house that is also home to the National Museum of Ancient Art. The hotel has a delightful mix of classic romanticism, warmth, history and personality.

York House
♉ ⓜ ⓢ
Rua das Janelas Verdes 32 ✉ *1200-691*
Plan: **B3**
– ℰ 213 96 24 35 – www.yorkhouselisboa.com
33 rm – ♦100/180 € ♦♦100/180 € – ☲ 20 €
• Historic • Contemporary •
This hotel housed in a 17C Carmelite convent has retained much of its original character. Its renovated interior offers modern comfort and decor. It has two types of guestrooms available, one contemporary and the other more classic in design. The restaurant is striking for its old glazed tiles.

BELÉM
PLAN I

★
Feitoria – Hotel Altis Belém
XXX 🍴 🌿 🛎 ⓜ ☕
Doca do Bom Sucesso ✉ *1400-038 – ℰ 210 40 02 08*
Plan: **A3**
– www.restaurantefeitoria.com – Closed 2-16 January, Sunday and Monday
Menu 80/135 € – Carte 70/95 € – *(dinner only)*
• Modern cuisine • Contemporary décor •
A restaurant of a very high standard, featuring a bar for a pre-dinner drink and a dining room arranged in a contemporary style. The chef offers creative, modern cuisine steeped in tradition, with a focus on high quality products and top-notch presentation.
→ Carabinero do Algarve. Peixe fresco da lota de Peniche, arroz de bivalves e salicornia. Frutos do bosque e gelado de leitelho de ovelha.

Altis Belém
♉ ≼ 🛁 ⓜ 🖥 🛎 ⓜ ⓢ ☕
Doca do Bom Sucesso ✉ *1400-038 – ℰ 210 40 02 00*
Plan: **A3**
– www.altishotels.com
45 rm ☲ – ♦150/240 € ♦♦170/260 € – 5 suites
• Chain • Design •
Luxury and modernity in equal measure! Facilities here include a rooftop chill-out zone, minimalist café and spacious guestrooms, all decorated around the theme of the country's age of discoveries and its cultural exchanges. Enjoy cuisine with a contemporary flair in the bright and elegant restaurant.
★ **Feitoria** – See restaurant listing

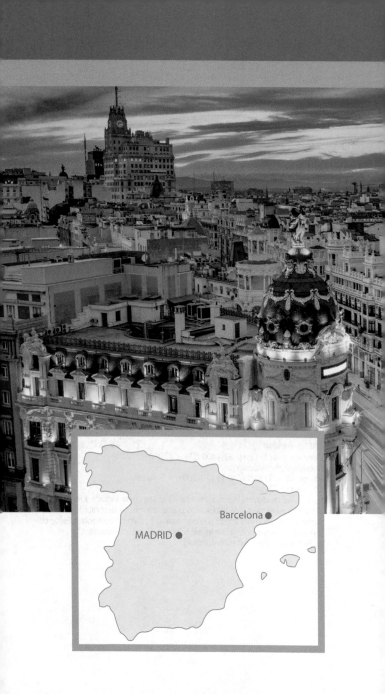

Barcelona ●

MADRID ●

SPAIN
ESPAÑA

RudyBalasko/iStock

MADRID
MADRID

benedek/iStock

MADRID IN...

→ **ONE DAY**
Puerta del Sol, Plaza Mayor,
Palacio Real, Museo del Prado.

→ **TWO DAYS**
Museo Thyssen-Bornemisza,
Retiro, Gran Vía, tapas at a
traditional taberna.

→ **THREE DAYS**
Chueca, Malasaña, Centro de Arte
Reina Sofía.

The renaissance of Madrid has seen it develop as a big player on the world cultural stage, attracting more international music, theatre and dance than it would have dreamed of a few decades ago. The nightlife in Spain's proud capital is second to none and the superb art museums which make up the city's 'golden triangle' have all undergone thrilling reinvention in recent years. This is a city that might think it has some catching up to do: it was only made the capital in 1561 on the whim of ruler, Felipe II. But its position was crucial: slap bang in the middle of the Iberian Peninsula. Ruled by Habsburgs and Bourbons, it soon made a mark in Europe, and the contemporary big wigs of Madrid are now having the same effect – this time with a 21C twist.

The central heart of Madrid is compact, defined by the teeming Habsburg hubs of Puerta del Sol and Plaza Mayor, and the mighty Palacio Real – the biggest official royal residence in the world, with a bewildering three thousand rooms. East of here are the grand squares, fountains and fine museums of the Bourbon District, with its easterly boundary, the Retiro park. West of the historical centre are the capacious green acres of Casa de Campo, while the affluent, regimented grid streets of Salamanca are to the east. Modern Madrid is just to the north, embodied in the grand north-south boulevard Paseo de la Castellana.

EATING OUT

Madrileños know how to pace themselves. Breakfast is around 8am, lunch 2pm or 3pm, the afternoon begins at 5pm and dinner won't be until 10pm or 11pm. Madrid is the European capital which has best managed to absorb the regional cuisine of the country, largely due to massive internal migration to the city, and it claims to have highest number of bars and restaurants per capita than anywhere else in the world. If you want to tuck into local specialities, you'll find them everywhere around the city. Callos a la Madrileña is Madrid-style tripe, dating back to 1559, while sopas de ajo (garlic soup) is a favourite on cold winter days. Another popular soup (also a main course) is cocido Madrileño, hearty and aromatic and comprised of chickpeas, meat, tocino belly pork, potatoes and vegetables, slowly cooked in a rich broth. To experience the real Madrid dining ambience, get to a traditional taberna in the heart of the old neighbourhood: these are distinguished by a large clock, a carved wooden bar with a zinc counter, wine flasks, marble-topped tables and ceramic tiles.

SPAIN - MADRID

La Terraza del Casino (Paco Roncero) XxxX 🏨 🛋 🎬 ⇔

Alcalá 15-3° ⊠ 28014 – ⓜ Sevilla – ℰ 91 532 12 75 Plan: **G2**
– www.casinodemadrid.es – Closed August, Sunday, Monday and bank holidays
Menu 69/138 € – Carte 80/100 €
• Creative • Elegant •

Elegant and unique, and accessed via an impressive 19C staircase leading to a contemporary space on the top floor. The famous chef Paco Roncero showcases his full gastronomic experience that starts in the English bar, continues in his workshop and is completed in the dining room. Impressive array of olive oils.
➜ Canelón de piel de leche con setas, trufa y foie-gras. Lenguado a la meunière. Tarta de zanahoria con queso fresco y canela.

El Club Allard XxxX 🏨 🎬 ⇔

Ferraz 2 ⊠ 28008 – ⓜ Plaza España – ℰ 915 59 09 39 Plan: **E1**
– www.elcluballard.com – Closed 5-28 August, Sunday and Monday
Menu 115/145 € – Carte 98/107 €
• Creative • Classic décor •

This respected restaurant occupies a listed Modernist building dating back to 1908, although you won't find any trace of this on the outside. In the elegant interior, showcasing a mix of classic and contemporary decor, Dominican chef María Marte conjures up outstandingly creative cuisine that is a fusion of Spanish cooking and a wide range of Latin American ingredients.
➜ Arroz del Mar. Rodaballo con pil-pil de arbequina ahumada y codium. Cremoso de chocolate.

DSTAgE (Diego Guerrero) XX 🎬 ⇔

Regueros 8 ⊠ 28004 – ⓜ Alonso Martínez Plan: **G1**
– ℰ 917 02 15 86 – www.dstageconcept.com – Closed Holy Week, 1-15 August, Saturday and Sunday
Menu 90/148 € – (booking essential) (tasting menu only)
• Creative • Trendy •

This restaurant has an urban and industrial look and a relaxed feel that reflects the personality of the chef. The name is an acronym of his core philosophy: 'Days to Smell Taste Amaze Grow & Enjoy'. Discover cuisine that brings disparate cultures, ingredients and flavours together from Spain, Mexico and Japan.
➜ Aguacate asado, mole y masato. Merluza al natural , proteína y angula. Maíz.

Cebo – Hotel Urban XxX 🗴 🎬 ⇔ 🍴

Carrera de San Jerónimo 34 ⊠ 28014 – ⓜ Sevilla Plan: **G2**
– ℰ 917 87 77 70 – www.cebomadrid.com – Closed August, Sunday and Monday
Menu 55/80 € – Carte 54/73 €
• Creative • Design •

A meticulously appointed modern space with a hint of designer decor plus a splendid bar where dishes are completed in front of guests. The bold and creative cuisine here is a clear declaration of intent for what will be a gastronomic experience that is impressively centred around a unique fusion of cooking from Madrid and Catalonia.
➜ "Calçots" y fresa albina. Chipirón "black andaluza". Chocoratafía.

La Candela Restò (Samy Ali Rando) XX 🎬

Amnistía 10 ⊠ 28013 – ⓜ Ópera – ℰ 911 73 98 88 Plan: **E2**
– www.lacandelaresto.com – Closed Sunday dinner, Monday and Tuesday lunch
Menu 57/92 € – (tasting menu only)
• Creative • Friendly •

An impressive, original and bold restaurant that is a faithful representation of the places in which the chef has lived. The highly unusual dining room with its retro-vintage ambience is the setting for innovative cuisine that is a perfect combination of different culinary cultures from around the world.
➜ Solo salmón. Susto del chipirón: chorizo semicurado, curry negro y coco. Candy eléctrico.

SPAIN - MADRID

Atlantik Corner
X AC

Ventura de la Vega 11 ⊠ 28014 – ⓜ Sevilla
Plan: **G2**
– ℰ 910 71 72 45 – www.atlantikcorner.com – Closed Monday
Menu 15/45 € – Carte 25/40 €
• Market cuisine • Fashionable •

An interesting option with a relaxed bistro-style atmosphere in which the cuisine has a global and Atlantic focus. The basis of its à la carte is Galician and Portuguese, though with a nod to Brazilian, Mexican and Moroccan cooking.

Barra Atlántica
X AC

Gravina 17 ⊠ 28004 – ⓜ Chueca – ℰ 619 15 57 94
Plan: **G1**
– www.barratlantica.com – Closed 24 December-3 January, 21 days
August, Sunday dinner and Monday
Menu 30/50 € – Carte 28/43 €
• Galician • Bistro •

The flavours of the Atlantic, high-quality products and modern presentation are to the fore in this simply furnished restaurant where the emphasis is on small dishes that are mainly prepared using authentic Galician ingredients. Two enticing set menus are also available here.

Gofio by Cícero Canary
X AC

Lope de Vega 9 ⊠ 28014 – ⓜ Antón Martin – Closed Monday and Tuesday
Plan: **G3**
– ℰ 915 99 44 04 – www.gofiomadrid.com – Closed Monday and Tuesday
except bank holidays and the day before bank holidays
Menu 30/60 € – Carte 25/35 €
• Regional cuisine • Bistro •

A homage to the cuisine of the Canary Islands in this modest bistro that recreates the culinary flavours of the islands in a modern yet informal way, with a focus on high levels of technical skill and reasonable prices. The main difference between the menus here is the number of courses that feature on them.

Triciclo
X AC

Santa María 28 ⊠ 28014 – ⓜ Antón Martin
Plan: **G3**
– ℰ 910 24 47 98 – www.eltriciclo.es – Closed 15 days January, 15 days
July and Sunday
Carte 48/69 €
• Creative • Bistro •

A restaurant that is on everyone's lips! Triciclo's simplicity is compensated for by a high degree of culinary expertise. This is showcased in well-prepared and attractively presented dishes that encompass personal and traditional, as well as Oriental and fusion influences.

La Lonja del Mar
XxX 🛆 & AC ↔

pl. de Oriente 6 ⊠ 28013 – ⓜ Ópera – ℰ 915 41 33 33
Plan: **E2**
– www.lalonjadelmar.com
Menu 35/100 € – Carte 45/70 €
• Seafood • Design •

Located opposite the royal palace, this impressive restaurant offers fish and seafood of a superb quality, backed up by the splendid designer decor of Nacho García de Vinuesa.

Alabaster
XxX & AC ↔

Montalbán 9 ⊠ 28014 – ⓜ Retiro – ℰ 915 12 11 31
Plan: **H2**
– www.restaurantealabaster.com – Closed Holy Week, 21 days August and
Sunday
Menu 50/80 € – Carte 40/50 €
• Modern cuisine • Trendy •

A gastro-bar with a contemporary interior featuring designer detail and a predominantly white colour scheme. It offers updated traditional cuisine that is devoted to Galician ingredients.

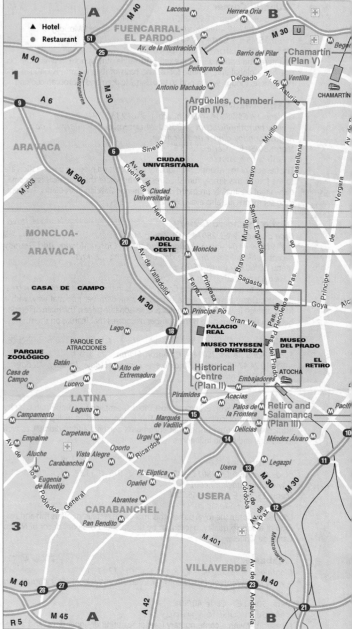

Environs of Madrid
(Plan I)

0   2 km

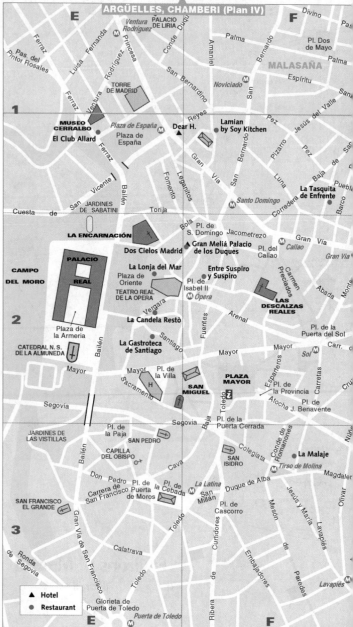

ARGÜELLES, CHAMBERI (Plan IV)

E

F

Divino

Ventura Rodríguez

PALACIO DE LIRIA

Palma

Pl. Dos de Mayo

Pas

Ferraz

Luisa Fernanda

Princesa

Conde Duque

Amaniel

Bernardo

Palma

Pas. del Pintor Rosales

Ventura Rodríguez

San Bernardino

MALASAÑA

Espíritu

Ferraz

TORRE DE MADRID

Noviciado

San

Pez

Jesús del Valle

San

1

MUSEO CERRALBO

Plaza de España

Reyes

Lamian by Soy Kitchen

Pez

Baja

Pueble

El Club Allard

Plaza de España

Dear H.

Gran

San Bernardo

Pizarro

Pez

de

Ferraz

Vía

San

Luna

La Tasquita de Enfrente

Barco

San Vicente

Bailén

Fomento

Leganitos

Santo Domingo

Corredera

Cuesta

de

San

JARDINES DE SABATINI

Torija

Bola

Pl. de S. Domingo

Jacometrezo

Gran Vía

LA ENCARNACIÓN

Gran Meliá Palacio de los Duques

Pl. del Callao

Callao

Gran Vía

2

CAMPO DEL MORO

PALACIO REAL

Dos Cielos Madrid

La Lonja del Mar

Plaza de Oriente

Entre Suspiro y Suspiro

Pl. de Isabel II

Carmen

Preciados

Abada

Monte

TEATRO REAL DE LA OPERA

Ópera

LAS DESCALZAS REALES

Plaza de la Armería

La Candela Restò

Vergara

Arenal

Pl. de la Puerta del Sol

CATEDRAL N. S. DE LA ALMUNEDA

Bailén

La Gastroteca de Santiago

Santiago

Fuentes

Mayor

Mayor

Sol

Carr.

Mayor

Mayor

Pl. de la Villa

SAN MIGUEL

PLAZA MAYOR

Esparteros

Pl. de la Provincia

Carretas

Segovia

Sacramento

H

Toledo

Atocha

Pl. de J. Benavente

Cru

Segovia

Pl. de la Puerta Cerrada

3

JARDINES DE LAS VISTILLAS

Pl. de la Paja

SAN PEDRO

Bailén

Cava

Baja

Colegiata

SAN ISIDRO

Conde de Romanones

La Malaje

Tirso de Molina

Magdale

CAPILLA DEL OBISPO

Don Pedro

Carrera de San Francisco

Pl. de Puerta de Moros

Pl. de la Cebada

La Latina

San Millán

Duque de Alba

Jesús y María

Olivar

SAN FRANCISCO EL GRANDE

Gran Vía de San Francisco

Toledo

Pl. de Cascorro

Mesón

Lavapiés

Ronda de Segovia

Calatrava

Curtidores

de

Embajadores

Paredes

Lavapiés

▲ Hotel

● Restaurant

Ribera

E

Glorieta de Puerta de Toledo

Puerta de Toledo

F

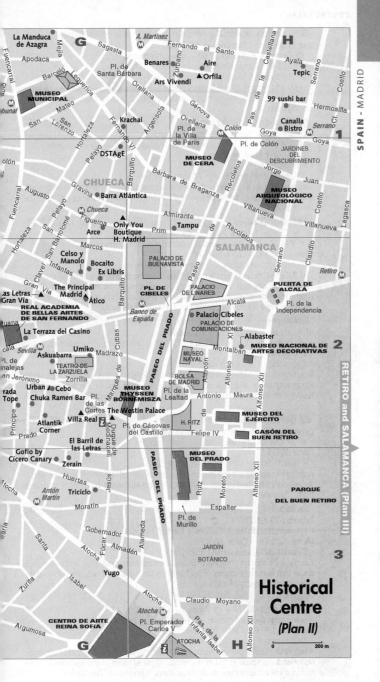

G

La Manduca
de Azagra
Apodaca
Mejía
Sagasta
A. Martínez
Fernando el Santo
H
de la Castellana
Ayala
Fuencarral
Barceló
Leguerica
Pl. de
Santa Bárbara
Benares
Zurbano
Aire
Tepic
Serrano
Coello
MUSEO
MUNICIPAL
Mateo
Orellana
Ars Vivendi
▲ Orfila
bunal
San
San Lorenzo
Hortaleza
Fernando VI
Krachai
Génova
Orellana
99 sushi bar
Hermosilla
Argensola
Pl. de
la Villa
de París
Colón
Goya
Canalla
Bistro
Serrano
olón
Pelayo
DSTAgE
Barquillo
Bárbara de Braganza
Goya
Goya
Fuencarral
Augusto
Gravina
● Barra Atlántica
CHUECA
MUSEO
DE CERA
Recoletos
Pl. de Colón
JARDINES
DEL
DESCUBRIMIENTO
Jorge
Juan
San Bartolomé
Pelayo
Chueca
Almirante
MUSEO
ARQUEOLÓGICO
NACIONAL
Hortaleza
Clavel
Figueroa
Arce
Only You
Boutique
H. Madrid
Prim
● Tampu
Villanueva
de
Recoletos
Coello
Villanueva
Lagasca
Infantas
Marcos
SALAMANCA
Celso y
Manolo
Bocaito
Ex Libris
PALACIO DE
BUENAVISTA
Paseo
Serrano
Claudio
Retiro
Gran Vía
The Principal
Madrid
Ático
PL. DE
CIBELES
PALACIO
DE LINARES
PUERTA DE
ALCALÁ
as Letras ▲
Gran Vía
REAL ACADEMIA
DE BELLAS ARTES
DE SAN FERNANDO
Banco de
España
Palacio Cibeles
Alcalá
Pl. de la
Independencia
uana
La Terraza del Casino
Barquillo
PALACIO DE
COMUNICACIONES
cala
Sevilla
Askuabarra
Umiko
Madrazo
Marqués de Cubas
MUSEO
NAVAL
Alabaster
Montalbán
MUSEO NACIONAL DE
ARTES DECORATIVAS
2
Pl. de
nalejas
an Jerónimo
TEATRO DE
LA ZARZUELA
Zorrilla
Alcalá
Alfonso XII
rada
Tope
Urban Cebo
Chuka Ramen Bar
Pl.
de las
Cortes
MUSEO
THYSSEN
BORNEMISZA
BOLSA
DE MADRID
Pl. de la
Lealtad
Antonio
Maura
MUSEO DEL
EJÉRCITO
ríncipe
Atlantik
Corner
Villa Real
The Westin Palace
de
Prado
El Barril de
las Letras
Duque de Medinaceli
Pl. de Cánovas
del Castillo
H. RITZ
Felipe IV
CASÓN DEL
BUEN RETIRO
Gofio by
Cícero Canary
Zeraín
Huertas
Jesús
MUSEO
DEL PRADO
Moreto
PARQUE
DEL BUEN RETIRO
tocha
Antón
Martín
Triciclo
Moratín
PASEO DEL PRADO
Espalter
Ruiz
Alfonso XII
Gobernador
Almadén
Pl. de
Murillo
Santa
Atocha
Fúcar
Alameda
JARDÍN
BOTÁNICO
3
Zurita
Isabel
Yugo
Argumosa
CENTRO DE ARTE
REINA SOFÍA
Atocha
Pl. Emperador
Carlos V
ATOCHA
Claudio Moyano
Pas. de la Infanta Isabel
Alfonso XII

**Historical
Centre**
(Plan II)

0   200 m

G   H

🍴 **Dos Cielos Madrid** – Hotel Gran Meliá Palacio de los Duques

cuesta de Santo Domingo 5 ✉ *28005*   XxX 🛬 & 🅰️ ⇔
– Ⓜ *Ópera* – 𝒞 *915 41 67 00* – *www.melia.com*   Plan: **F2**
Menu 75 € – Carte 70/90 €
• Creative • Elegant •
The Madrid outpost of the famous Torres twins, occupying the stables of a luxurious palace. Tasting menu plus a contemporary à la carte based around seasonal ingredients.

🍴 **La Manduca de Azagra**   XxX 🅰️

Sagasta 14 ✉ *28004* – Ⓜ *Alonso Martínez*   Plan: **G1**
– 𝒞 *915 91 01 12* – *www.lamanducadeazagra.com* – *Closed August,*
Sunday and bank holidays
Carte 34/54 €
• Traditional cuisine • Minimalist •
This spacious, well-located restaurant is decorated in minimalist style with particular attention paid to the design and lighting. The menu focuses on high quality produce.

🍴 **Palacio Cibeles**   XxX 🛬 & 🅰️

pl. de Cibeles 1-6º ✉ *28014* – Ⓜ *Banco de España*   Plan: **H2**
– 𝒞 *915 23 14 54* – *www.adolfo-palaciodecibeles.com*
Menu 39/55 € – Carte 50/70 €
• Traditional cuisine • Contemporary décor •
The Palacio Cibeles enjoys a marvellous location on the sixth floor of the city's emblematic city hall (Ayuntamiento). In addition to the modern-style dining room, the restaurant has two attractive terraces where guests can dine or simply enjoy a drink. The cooking is of a traditional flavour.

🍴 **Ático** – Hotel The Principal Madrid   XX & 🍽

Marqués de Valdeiglesias 1 ✉ *28004*   Plan: **G2**
– Ⓜ *Banco de España* – 𝒞 *915 21 87 43* – *www.restauranteatico.es*
Carte 40/55 €
• Creative • Bourgeois •
Boasting its own individual charm inside the Hotel Principal, with its classic-contemporary decor and impressive views of the city's skyline. Ático is under the tutelage of renowned chef Ramón Freixa, with a focus on relaxed modern cuisine.

🍴 **El Barril de las Letras**   XX & 🅰️

Cervantes 28 ✉ *28014* – Ⓜ *Antón Martín*   Plan: **G3**
– 𝒞 *91 186 36 32* – *www.barrildelasletras.com*
Carte 45/55 €
• Traditional cuisine • Friendly •
A delightful restaurant laid out on different levels with striking tiled floors and a superb fish and seafood display cabinet. The kitchen is open here non-stop from 12 noon.

🍴 **Ex Libris**   XX 🅰️ ⇔

Infantas 29 ✉ *28004* – Ⓜ *Chueca* – 𝒞 *915 21 28 28*   Plan: **G2**
– *www.restauranteexlibris.com* – *Closed August*
Menu 12/55 € – Carte 30/45 €
• Traditional cuisine • Elegant •
A restaurant with an attractively maintained contemporary style and an original decor that features pictures of "ex libris" on the walls. Well-prepared up-to-date cuisine and a variety of menus.

🍴 **Yugo**   X 🅰️

San Blas 4 ✉ *28014* – Ⓜ *Atocha* – 𝒞 *914 44 90 34*   Plan: **G3**
– *www.yugothebunker.com* – *Closed Sunday and Monday*
Menu 85/110 € – Carte 70/135 €
• Japanese • Exotic décor •
A highly unusual Japanese restaurant decorated with typical objects from their homeland alongside recycled materials. Another room in the basement, available for the exclusive use of club members, is known as "The Bunker".

Arce
X AC ⇔

Augusto Figueroa 32 ⊠ 28004 – Ⓜ Chueca   Plan: **G1**
– ℰ 915 22 04 40 – www.restaurantearce.com – Closed 17-25 April,
15 days August, Monday and Tuesday
Menu 80 € – Carte 45/62 €
• Classic cuisine • Classic décor •
A family-run business that prides itself on doing things well, hence the classic cuisine with a focus on quality ingredients and lots of flavour. Extensive à la carte, set menus and the option of half-*raciones*.

Askuabarra
X AC

Arlabán 7 ⊠ 28014 – Ⓜ Sevilla – ℰ 915 93 75 07   Plan: **G2**
– www.askuabarra.com – Closed Sunday dinner in October-May, Sunday
in June-September and Monday
Carte 35/58 €
• Market cuisine • Rustic •
Run by two brothers who have grown up in this profession, hence the value they attach to the use of top-quality products. A modern take on seasonal cuisine, including the house speciality – steak tartare.

Chuka Ramen Bar
X AC

Echegaray 9 ⊠ 28014 – Ⓜ Sevilla – ℰ 640 65 13 46   Plan: **G2**
– www.chukaramenbar.com – Closed August, Sunday, Monday and
Tuesday lunch
Carte 26/37 €
• Japanese • Oriental décor •
A bar where the menu features a fusion of Chinese and Japanese cooking. It includes legendary dishes such as the noodle-based ramen and other more popular street food-style recipes.

Entre Suspiro y Suspiro
X AC ⇔

Caños del Peral 3 ⊠ 28013 – Ⓜ Ópera   Plan: **F2**
– ℰ 915 42 06 44 – www.entresuspiroysuspiro.com – Closed Sunday
Carte 29/49 €
• Mexican • Friendly •
A good option for those looking to try Mexican cuisine. Behind the discreet façade you will discover a bright, colourful restaurant. It has a bar at the entrance, dining rooms spread across two floors and an impressive collection of tequilas!

La Gastroteca de Santiago
X 🛱 AC

pl. Santiago 1 ⊠ 28013 – Ⓜ Ópera – ℰ 915 48 07 07   Plan: **E2**
– www.lagastrotecadesantiago.es – Closed 15-31 August, Sunday dinner
and Monday
Carte 40/65 €
• Modern cuisine • Cosy •
A small, cosy restaurant with two large windows and modern decor. Friendly staff, contemporary cuisine and a kitchen that is partially visible to diners.

Krachai
X AC

Fernando VI-11 ⊠ 28004 – Ⓜ Alonso Martínez   Plan: **G1**
– ℰ 918 33 65 56 – www.krachai.es – Closed 20 days August and Sunday
dinner
Menu 14/35 € – Carte 25/55 €
• Thai • Oriental décor •
The Krachai is split between two dining rooms, each with attractive lighting and a contemporary feel. The Thai cuisine on offer is listed on the menu according to the way it is prepared.

SPAIN - MADRID

Lamian by Soy Kitchen X AC

pl. Mostenses 4 ⊠ 28015 – Ⓜ Plaza de España — Plan: **F1**
– ℰ 910 39 22 31 – www.lamianconcept.com – Closed Monday
Menu 30 € – Carte 25/40 €
• Fusion • Bistro •
Named after a type of Chinese noodle, this restaurant is the perfect place to try ramen and a menu featuring an interesting fusion of Spanish and Oriental cuisine.

La Malaje X AC

Relatores 20 ⊠ 28012 – Ⓜ Tirso de Molina — Plan: **F3**
– ℰ 910 81 30 31 – www.lamalaje.es – Closed Holy Week, 7-27 August, Sunday dinner and Monday
Menu 48 € – Carte 35/50 €
• Andalusian • Bistro •
A restaurant with a tapas section and an original, Mediterranean-inspired dining room, the latter looking onto an attractive internal patio. Andalucian dishes with a contemporary flourish.

Tampu X AC

Prim 13 ⊠ 28004 – Ⓜ Chueca – ℰ 91 564 19 13 — Plan: **H1**
– www.tampurestaurante.com – Closed Sunday dinner and Monday
Menu 16 € – Carte 30/45 €
• Peruvian • Design •
A mix of slate, wood and wicker, plus a Quechua name that is in reference to old lodgings built along the Inca Trail. Classic Peruvian cuisine, including ceviches, raw fish tiraditos, and potato-based causas.

La Tasquita de Enfrente X AC

Ballesta 6 ⊠ 28004 – Ⓜ Gran Vía – ℰ 91 532 54 49 — Plan: **F1**
– www.latasquitadeenfrente.com – Closed August and Sunday
Menu 77 € – Carte 45/70 € – (booking essential)
• International • Family •
An informal eatery with the benefit of a very loyal clientele. Its French-inspired cuisine with a contemporary touch is based around products of the highest quality.

Umiko X AC

Los Madrazo 18 ⊠ 28014 – Ⓜ Sevilla – ℰ 914 93 87 06 — Plan: **G2**
– www.umiko.es – Closed Sunday
Carte 35/55 €
• Japanese • Minimalist •
A fun and different Asian restaurant whose aim is to combine traditional Japanese cuisine with the more traditional cooking of Madrid. The finishing touches to most of the dishes are added at the bar.

Zerain X AC ⇔

Quevedo 3 ⊠ 28014 – Ⓜ Antón Martín — Plan: **G3**
– ℰ 914 29 79 09 – www.restaurante-vasco-zerain-sidreria.es – Closed August and Sunday dinner
Menu 32/57 € – Carte 28/59 €
• Basque • Rustic •
This Basque cider bar is in the heart of Madrid's literary quarter. It has two floors with a welcoming atmosphere and large barrels on display. A typical steakhouse with a focus on grilled meats.

Bocaito

Libertad 6 ⊠ 28004 – Ⓜ Chueca – ℰ 915 32 12 19 — Plan: **G2**
– www.bocaito.com – Closed 15 days August and Sunday dinner
Tapa 5 € **Ración** approx. 12 €
• Traditional cuisine • Regional décor •
A family-run restaurant split between two adjoining and inter-connecting buildings. Enjoy a mix of traditional Castilian and Andalucian cooking in its rustic-style dining rooms.

SPAIN - MADRID

Celso y Manolo
♀/ ᴀᴄ
Libertad 1 ⊠ 28004 – Ⓜ Gran Vía – ℰ 915 31 80 79
– www.celsoymanolo.es
Plan: **G2**
Ración approx. 12 €
• Traditional cuisine • Neighbourhood •
A young and informal eatery occupying the site of an old tavern. Extensive ración based menu with an emphasis on natural and organic ingredients.

Prada a Tope
♀/ ᴀᴄ
Príncipe 11 ⊠ 28012 – Ⓜ Sevilla – ℰ 914 29 59 21
– www.pradaatope.es – Closed 31 July-14 August
Plan: **G2**
Tapa 6 € **Ración** approx. 12 €
• Traditional cuisine • Rustic •
Roast peppers with ventresca tuna, morcilla from León, empanada pasties and chestnuts in syrup all feature in this restaurant full of personality where you can discover the typical cooking of the Bierzo region.

The Westin Palace Madrid
✿ ℔ ⅍ ᴀᴄ 🛁 ⇕ 🚗
pl. de las Cortes 7 ⊠ 28014 – Ⓜ Sevilla
– ℰ 913 60 80 00 – www.westinpalacemadrid.com
Plan: **G2**
470 rm – ♦300/850 € ♦♦300/850 € – 51 suites
• Luxury • Classic •
An elegant, historic hotel that is a quintessential symbol of the Belle Époque period, with a stunning lounge crowned by an Art Nouveau dome, and sumptuous guestrooms, some classic in style, others more contemporary. Choose from a menu of international cuisine in the La Rotonda restaurant.

Gran Meliá Palacio de los Duques
℔ ⅍ ᴀᴄ 🛁
cuesta de Santo Domingo 5 ⊠ 28005 – Ⓜ Ópera
– ℰ 915 41 67 00 – www.melia.com
Plan: **F2**
180 rm – ♦250/450 € ♦♦250/450 € – ⊊ 35 €
• Historic building • Elegant •
Located just a few metres from the royal theatre, this 19C palace is themed around the artist Velázquez. Various multi-purpose public and private spaces (Red Level), contemporary guestrooms offering high levels of comfort, plus idyllic views from the rooftop terrace.
🕯O **Dos Cielos Madrid** – See restaurant listing

Urban
℔ ⌇ ⅍ ᴀᴄ 🛁 🚗
Carrera de San Jerónimo 34 ⊠ 28014 – Ⓜ Sevilla
– ℰ 917 87 77 70 – www.hotelurban.com
Plan: **G2**
96 rm – ♦175/350 € ♦♦175/350 € – ⊊ 29 €
• Chain • Design •
A perfect place to feel the pulse of the city with its cutting-edge look and special relationship with art, highlighted by the many original works on display throughout the hotel and even in its own museum. Classic-contemporary guestrooms high on decorative detail.
❀ **Cebo** – See restaurant listing

Villa Real
✿ ⅍ ᴀᴄ 🛁 🚗
pl. de las Cortes 10 ⊠ 28014 – Ⓜ Sevilla
– ℰ 914 20 37 67 – www.hotelvillareal.com
Plan: **G2**
115 rm – ♦150/475 € ♦♦175/475 € – ⊊ 23 € – 17 suites
• Chain • Personalised •
This hotel displays a valuable collection of Greek and Roman art in many of its public areas. The comfortable guestrooms are attractively decorated with mahogany furniture. The informal restaurant with an abundance of natural light serves cuisine with an international flavour.

SPAIN - MADRID

☆☆☆ Dear H. ☆ ⊐ & 🗚 ⚱ ⇌
Gran Vía 80 ✉ *28013*   Plan: **E1**
– Ⓜ *Plaza de España*
– ☎ *914 12 32 00* – *www.dearhotelmadrid.com*
162 rm – 🛏100/400 € 🛏🛏100/400 € – ☲ 19 €
• Boutique hotel • Classic •

Occupying a neo-Classical building in a superb location on the Gran Vía – Madrid's equivalent of Broadway. Comfortable, classically furnished guestrooms, fusion-style cuisine and, above all, superb views from its rooftop terrace.

☆☆☆ Las Letras Gran Vía ☆ ⌶₆ & 🗚 ⚱
Gran Vía 11 ✉ *28013*   Plan: **G2**
– Ⓜ *Gran Vía*
– ☎ *915 23 79 80* – *www.iberostar.com*
109 rm – 🛏135/640 € 🛏🛏135/640 € – ☲ 20 €
• Business • Classic •

The hotel's restored façade contrasts sharply with the colourful and contemporary interior. The guestrooms showcase New York-style design, including intimate lighting and even poems on the walls. The modern restaurant, which almost merges into the lounge-bar, offers à la carte choices and set menus with an emphasis on traditional cuisine.

☆☆☆ Only You Boutique H. Madrid ☆ & 🗚 ⚱ ⇌
Barquillo 21 ✉ *28004*   Plan: **G1**
– Ⓜ *Chueca*
– ☎ *910 05 22 22* – *www.onlyyouhotels.com*
125 rm ☲ – 🛏180/350 € 🛏🛏200/380 €
• Business • Design •

A charming hotel occupying a restored 19C palace in the heart of the Chueca district. Considerable work on the inside has resulted in a modern interior featuring myriad decorative details. It has welcoming guest areas, very well-equipped bedrooms, and a pleasant restaurant.

☆☆☆ The Principal Madrid ⌶₆ & 🗚 ⚱ ⇌
Marqués de Valdeiglesias 1 ✉ *28004*   Plan: **G2**
– Ⓜ *Banco de España*
– ☎ *915 21 87 43* – *www.theprincipalmadridhotel.com*
76 rm – 🛏220/450 € 🛏🛏220/450 € – ☲ 29 € – 4 suites
• Boutique hotel • Elegant •

Occupying one of the first buildings constructed along Gran Vía, next to the emblematic Metrópolis, with the reception on the sixth floor. Guestrooms with varying views, all contemporary in design. The rooftop terrace is a particular highlight.
⃛○ **Ático** – See restaurant listing

RETIRO – SALAMANCA   **PLAN III**

❁❁ Ramón Freixa Madrid – Hotel Único Madrid XxxX ⅋ 🗚 ⇌
Claudio Coello 67 ✉ *28001*
– Ⓜ *Serrano*   Plan: **I1**
– ☎ *917 81 82 62* – *www.ramonfreixamadrid.com* – *Closed Christmas, Holy Week, August, Sunday, Monday and bank holidays*
Menu 140/165 € – Carte 90/135 €
• Creative • Design •

A magical contradiction between traditional and cutting-edge cuisine is the culinary philosophy of Ramón Freixa, a Catalan chef who showcases flavours and classic combinations alongside plenty of creativity. His elegant dining room is connected to a glass-fronted pavilion which is perfect for a pre- or post-dinner drink.
→ El estudio del tomate 2018. Micro menú de liebre y trufa. Albaricoque, sésamo y amargos.

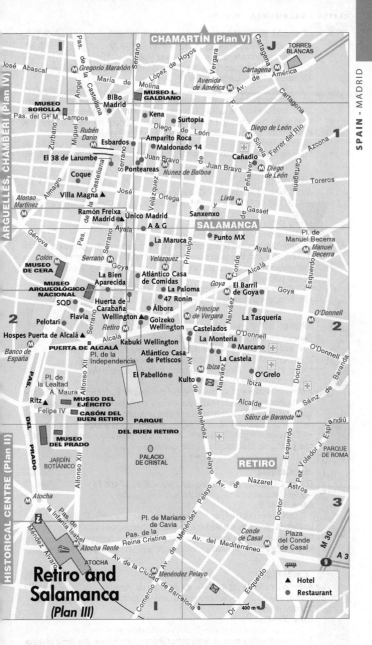

Retiro and Salamanca
(Plan III)

▲ Hotel
● Restaurant

0   400 m

SPAIN - MADRID

❀ **Kabuki Wellington** (Ricardo Sanz) – Hotel Wellington   XxX ✿

Velázquez 6 ✉ *28001 –* Ⓜ *Retiro –* ☏ *915 77 78 77*   �&. Ⓐⓒ
– www.restaurantekabuki.com – Closed Holy   Plan: I2
Week, 21 days August, Saturday lunch, Sunday and bank holidays
Menu 93/150 € – Carte 65/130 €
• Japanese • Design •

An emblematic restaurant reflecting the gastronomic connection between
Japan and the Mediterranean. Elegant dining room on two levels plus an enticing sushi bar offering a fusion of Japanese culinary culture, the very best
local products, and a mastery of cutting, slicing and exquisite textures.
➔ Usuzukuri de toro (ventresca de atún) con pan y tomate. Costilla de
buey de wagyu con salsa teriyaki. Falso yokan de manzana verde con lichis.

❀ **Álbora**   XX Ⓐⓒ

Jorge Juan 33 ✉ *28001 –* Ⓜ *Velázquez*   Plan: I2
– ☏ *917 81 61 97 – www.restaurantealbora.com – Closed August and*
Sunday
Menu 58/85 € – Carte 50/70 €
• Modern cuisine • Design •

An attractive modern setting with two distinct sections: the gastro-bar on the
ground floor and the gastronomic restaurant upstairs. Enjoy high level cuisine
that makes full use of seasonal ingredients, with some dishes available in smaller half portions.
➔ Tallarín y fondo de calamar. Cabezada ibérica y fondo de pimiento mor-
rón. Brioche caramelizado y helado de leche.

❀ **Punto MX** (Roberto Ruiz)   XX Ⓐⓒ

General Pardiñas 40 ✉ *28001 –* Ⓜ *Goya*   Plan: J2
– ☏ *914 02 22 26 – www.puntomx.es – Closed 23-31 December, 2-*
6 January, 27-31 March, 12-31 August, Sunday and Monday
Menu 65/110 € – *(booking essential) (tasting menu only)*
• Mexican • Minimalist •

A Mexican restaurant that steers clear of stereotypes. Both the decor and cuisine
are thoroughly modern. Traditional recipes are bolstered by a contemporary
technical approach while at the same time adapting to local tastes. Highly interesting combination of Mexican ingredients and others sourced from Spain.
➔ Carabinero y guajillo. Quesadilla de flor de calabaza rellena de huitlaco-
che y salsa de chile morita. Postre cítrico.

🅐 **La Castela**   X ᴅ. Ⓐⓒ

Doctor Castelo 22 ✉ *28009 –* Ⓜ *Ibiza –* ☏ *91 574 00 15*   Plan: J2
– www.lacastela.com – closed August and Sunday dinner
Carte 28/40 €
• Traditional cuisine • Traditional décor •

La Castela continues the tradition of Madrid's historic taverns. Choose from the
lively tapas bar or the simply furnished dining room where you can enjoy cooking with a traditional flavour, including an impressive choice of daily specials.

🅐 **Castelados**   X Ⓐⓒ

Antonio Acuña 18 ✉ *28009 –* Ⓜ *Principe de Vergara*   Plan: J2
– ☏ *910 51 56 25 – www.castelados.com – Closed 15 days August and*
Sunday dinner
Carte 30/40 €
• Traditional cuisine • Traditional décor •

A restaurant with a relaxed, lively atmosphere which follows the same philosophy as its nearby older sibling, La Castela. Traditional cooking based around
excellent raw ingredients and interesting daily suggestions that include impressive fresh fish dishes.

SPAIN - MADRID

La Maruca   X 🍴 🅰🅲 ⇄

Velázquez 54 ☒ 28001 – Ⓜ Velázquez – 𝒞 917 81 49 69   Plan: I2
– www.restaurantelamaruca.com
Carte 25/40 €
• Traditional cuisine • Friendly •

A bright, casual and contemporary restaurant offering high standard, traditional cuisine. There is a predominance of typical and very reasonably priced Cantabrian dishes.

La Montería   X 🅰🅲

Lope de Rueda 35 ☒ 28009 – Ⓜ Ibiza – 𝒞 915 74 18 12   Plan: J2
– www.lamonteria.es – Closed Sunday dinner
Menu 42/46 € – Carte approx. 35 €
• Traditional cuisine • Simple •

This family-run business has a bar and intimate dining room, which are both contemporary in feel. The chef creates updated traditional cuisine including game dishes. Don't leave without trying the monterías (stuffed mussels)!

La Tasquería   X 🅰🅲

Duque de Sesto 48 ☒ 28009 – Ⓜ Goya   Plan: J2
– 𝒞 914 51 10 00 – www.latasqueria.com – Closed 10 days January,
21 days August and Sunday dinner
Menu 39 € – Carte 24/35 €
• Spanish • Bistro •

A new-generation tavern (*tasca*) that combines an urban, industrial look with modern, meticulously prepared dishes. There is a particular emphasis on high-quality offal dishes (veal, lamb, pork) served as half-raciones.

Tepic   X 🍴 🅰🅲

Ayala 14 ☒ 28001 – Ⓜ Goya – 𝒞 915 22 08 50   Plan II : H1
– www.tepic.es – Closed Sunday dinner
Menu 31 € – Carte 30/40 €
• Mexican • Rustic •

A Mexican restaurant with its very own character, featuring a rustic yet contemporary space defined by a profusion of wood and a predominance of varying tones of white. High quality cuisine from their homeland alongside an interesting menu of beers, tequila and mezcal.

🍽️ **A y G**   XxX 🅰🅲 ⇄

Ayala 27 ☒ 28001 – Ⓜ Goya – 𝒞 917 02 62 62   Plan: I1-2
– www.aygmadrid.com – Closed Sunday dinner
Menu 45/69 € – Carte 40/65 €
• Peruvian • Minimalist •

A restaurant with an urban feel, offering Peruvian cuisine with Japanese touches, in addition to several signature dishes such "ají de gallina", "ceviche del amor" and "beso de moza".

🍽️ **Goizeko Wellington** – Hotel Wellington   XxX 🅰🅲 ⇄

Villanueva 34 ☒ 28001 – Ⓜ Retiro – 𝒞 915 77 01 38   Plan: I2
– www.goizekogaztelupe.com – Closed Sunday
Menu 85/120 € – Carte 52/74 €
• Modern cuisine • Classic décor •

The contemporary-classic dining room and the two private rooms have been exquisitely designed. The cuisine on offer is a fusion of traditional, international and creative cooking, and is enriched with a few Japanese dishes.

🍽️ **Sanxenxo**   XxX 🍴 🅰🅲 ⇄

José Ortega y Gasset 40 ☒ 28006 – Ⓜ Núñez de Balboa   Plan: J1
– 𝒞 915 77 82 72 – www.sanxenxo.es – Closed Holy Week, 1-15 August
and Sunday dinner
Menu 50/120 € – Carte 45/65 €
• Seafood • Classic décor •

This restaurant serves traditional Galician cuisine based on quality fish and seafood. Covering two floors, the superb dining rooms are decorated with a profusion of granite and wood.

SPAIN - MADRID

Amparito Roca

XX & AC

Juan Bravo 12 ✉ *28006 –* Ⓜ *Núñez de Balboa*   Plan: I1
– ℰ 913 48 33 04 – www.restauranteamparitoroca.com – Closed Sunday
Menu 49/65 € – Carte 41/55 €
• Traditional cuisine • Cosy •
A restaurant that takes its name from a famous pasodoble, where the focus is on honest cuisine that flies the flag for the very best ingredients. A classic-contemporary dining room with some surprising decorative details.

BiBo Madrid

XX 🏵 & AC ⇨

paseo de la Castellana 52 ✉ *28046*   Plan: I1
– Ⓜ *Gregorio Marañón – ℰ 918 05 25 56 – www.grupodanigarcia.com*
Carte 31/51 €
• Modern cuisine • Bistro •
The magic of southern Spain is transported to this restaurant. The striking, light design inspired by the entrance gateway to the Málaga Fair provides the backdrop for the more informal cuisine of award-winning chef Dani García.

La Bien Aparecida

XX 🏠 AC

Jorge Juan 8 ✉ *28001 – ℰ 911 59 39 39*   Plan: I2
– www.restaurantelabienaparecida.com – Closed 14-27 August
Menu 70 € – Carte 45/67 €
• Traditional cuisine • Fashionable •
Named after the patron saint of Cantabria, this restaurant is laid out on two floors with different atmospheres. Updated traditional cuisine featuring fine textures and strong flavours.

Cañadío

XX 🏠 AC ⇨

Conde de Peñalver 86 ✉ *28005 –* Ⓜ *Diego de León*   Plan: J1
– ℰ 912 81 91 92 – www.restaurantecanadio.com – Closed August and Sunday dinner
Carte 32/52 €
• Traditional cuisine • Friendly •
The name will ring a bell with those familiar with Santander, given the location of this, the original Cañadio restaurant, on one of the city's most famous squares. Café-bar for tapas, two contemporary dining rooms, and well-prepared traditional cuisine.

47 Ronin

XX 🏠 & AC

Jorge Juan 38 ✉ *28001 –* Ⓜ *Velázquez*   Plan: I2
– ℰ 913 48 50 34 – www.47-ronin.es – Closed 1-4 January, 30 July-22 August and Monday
Menu 77/110 € – Carte 40/55 €
• Japanese • Oriental décor •
Creative Japanese cuisine featuring modern techniques, fine textures and an enticing adaptation of Japanese recipes to Spanish ingredients, to produce dishes that are impressive on the eye.

Esbardos

XX & AC

Maldonado 4 ✉ *28006 –* Ⓜ *Núñez de Balboa*   Plan: I1
– ℰ 914 35 08 68 – www.restauranteesbardos.com – Closed Holy Week, August and Sunday dinner
Menu 50/65 € – Carte 35/55 €
• Asturian • Traditional décor •
Esbardos takes its name from an Asturian word meaning 'bear cub', which is appropriate given that the owners own another restaurant called El Oso (The Bear). Typical Asturian cuisine based around top quality products and traditional stews.

O grelo
XX 🆔 ⇔
Plan: **J2**

Menorca 39 ✉ *28009 –* Ⓜ *Ibiza –* ☎ *914 09 72 04*
– www.restauranteogrelo.com – Closed Sunday dinner
Carte 35/70 €
• Galician • Classic décor •
Experience the excellence of traditional Galician cuisine at this restaurant serving a huge variety of seafood. Having undergone gradual renovation, O grelo has a more modern look, which includes a reasonably popular gastro-bar, a main dining room and three private sections.

Huerta de Carabaña
XX 🆔
Plan: **I2**

Lagasca 32 ✉ *28001 –* Ⓜ *Serrano –* ☎ *910 83 00 07*
– www.huertadecarabana.es – Closed Sunday dinner
Carte 50/70 €
• Traditional cuisine • Contemporary décor •
A traditional culinary dominion where the very best fresh vegetables from Carabaña, 50km outside of Madrid, reign supreme. Choose between the bistro-style dining room and a second room offering more gastronomic fare.

Kena
XX 🆔
Plan: **I1**

Diego de León 11 ✉ *28006 –* Ⓜ *Núñez de Balboa*
– ☎ *917 25 96 48 – www.kenadeluisarevalo.com – Closed 13-21 August,*
Sunday and Monday in August and Sunday dinner the rest of the year
Menu 30/70 € – Carte 40/55 €
• Peruvian • Contemporary décor •
An enticing sushi bar, TV screens showing the team at work in the kitchen and a chill-out zone add to the designer feel of this restaurant that is keen to showcase the best of Japanese fusion cuisine.

Maldonado 14
XX 🆔
Plan: **I1**

Maldonado 14 ✉ *28006 –* Ⓜ *Núñez de Balboa*
– ☎ *914 35 50 45 – www.maldonado14.com – Closed Holy Week, 5-*
27 August, Sunday and bank holidays dinner
Menu 37 € – Carte 35/60 €
• Traditional cuisine • Classic décor •
A single dining room on two levels, both featuring classic decor, quality furnishings and wood floors. The à la carte menu has a traditional feel and includes delicious homely desserts, such as the outstanding apple tart.

99 sushi bar
XX 🆔 ⇔
Plan II : **H1**

Hermosilla 4 ✉ *28001 –* Ⓜ *Serrano –* ☎ *914 31 27 15*
– www.99sushibar.com – Closed 1-25 August, Sunday and bank holidays
Menu 80 € – Carte 42/65 €
• Japanese • Minimalist •
A good restaurant in which to discover the flavours and textures of Japanese cuisine. There is a small bar where sushi is prepared in front of diners, an attractive glass-fronted wine cellar, and a modern dining room featuring typical Japanese decor and furnishings.

El Pabellón
XX 🍴 ⅊ 🆔
Plan: **I2**

paseo de Panamá (Parque de El Retiro) ✉ *28009*
– Ⓜ *Ibiza –* ☎ *918 27 52 75 – www.floridaretiro.com – Closed Monday*
Carte 35/50 €
• Modern cuisine • Contemporary décor •
The gastronomic dining option within the historic and now completely transformed Florida Retiro venue. The meticulous cuisine here encompasses traditional recipes, including rice dishes, as well as more contemporary cooking options.

SPAIN - MADRID

‡○ **La Paloma**   XX 🕼 🎜

Jorge Juan 39 ✉ 28001 – Ⓜ Príncipe de Vergara   Plan: I2
– 𝒞 915 76 86 92 – www.lapalomarestaurante.es – Closed Holy Week,
August, Sunday, Monday dinner and bank holidays
Menu 45 € – Carte 47/71 €
• Classic cuisine • Classic décor •

A professionally run restaurant in an intimate setting. The extensive menu brings together classic and traditional dishes alongside a selection of daily suggestions and set menus. Signature dishes here include sea urchin, carpaccio of liver and stuffed pigeon.

‡○ **Ponteareas**   XX ⅋ 🎜

Claudio Coello 96 ✉ 28005 – Ⓜ Núñez de Balboa   Plan: I1
– 𝒞 915 75 58 73 – www.grupoportonovo.es – Closed August, Sunday
dinner and bank holidays dinner
Menu 49 € – Carte 45/65 €
• Galician • Contemporary décor •

This restaurant with a modern decor offers a tapas bar and an attractive dining room overlooking a garden. Traditional cuisine with Galician roots, as well as good quality fish dishes.

‡○ **Surtopía**   XX 🎜

Núñez de Balboa 106 ✉ 28006 – Ⓜ Núñez de Balboa   Plan: I1
– 𝒞 915 63 03 64 – www.surtopia.es – Closed Holy Week, 21 days August,
Sunday and Monday
Menu 35/45 € – Carte 36/55 €
• Andalusian • Contemporary décor •

A restaurant with a modern ambience that translates to the cuisine, featuring the aromas and flavours of Andalucia and showcasing contemporary techniques and interesting innovative touches.

‡○ **El 38 de Larumbe**   XX 🕼 ⅋ 🎜 ⇔

paseo de la Castellana 38 ✉ 28006 – Ⓜ Rubén Darío   Plan: I1
– 𝒞 915 75 11 12 – www.larumbe.com – Closed 15 days August, Sunday
dinner and bank holidays dinner
Menu 58 € – Carte 45/60 €
• Modern cuisine • Classic décor •

This restaurant has two highly distinct dining areas – one has a gastro-bar feel, and the other has a more refined setting for à la carte dining. Updated traditional cuisine with the option of ordering half-raciones.

‡○ **Atlántico Casa de Comidas**   X 🎜

Velázquez 31 ✉ 28001 – Ⓜ Velázquez – 𝒞 914 35 63 16   Plan: I2
– www.atlanticocasadecomidas.es – Closed Sunday dinner
Menu 28/50 € – Carte 31/48 €
• Galician • Friendly •

An attractive maritime decor provides the backdrop for Pontevedra chef Pepe Solla, who conjures up traditional and more contemporary dishes that are firmly embedded in Galician culinary culture.

‡○ **Canalla Bistro**   X ⅋ 🎜 ⇔

Goya 5 (Platea Madrid) ✉ 28001 – Ⓜ Serrano   Plan II : H1
– 𝒞 915 77 00 25 – www.plateamadrid.com
Carte 35/45 €
• Modern cuisine • Contemporary décor •

At this bistro, discover the informal cuisine of Valencian chef Ricard Camarena who is keen to leave his stamp on the city via his highly urban cooking. His dishes are perfect for sharing.

SPAIN - MADRID

Flavia
X AC

Gil de Santivañes 2 ✉ *28001 –* Ⓜ *Colón*   Plan: I2
– ☏ 914 93 90 51 – www.flaviamadrid.com
Menu 17 € – Carte 27/46 €
• Italian • Mediterranean décor •

A modern, urban trattoria laid out on several floors. Good traditional Italian cuisine, always prepared using original ingredients from their homeland.

Kulto
X AC

Ibiza 4 ✉ *28009 –* Ⓜ *Ibiza – ☏ 911 73 30 53*   Plan: J2
– www.kulto.es – Closed Tuesday
Carte 43/62 €
• Modern cuisine • Friendly •

This restaurant is pleasant, modern and bright and just a stone's throw from the Retiro park. Contemporary cuisine that showcases seasonal ingredients and a fusion of international flavours and influences.

Marcano
X AC

Doctor Castelo 31 ✉ *28009 –* Ⓜ *Ibiza – ☏ 914 09 36 42*   Plan: J2
– www.restaurantemarcano.com – Closed Holy Week and Sunday except December
Carte 45/75 €
• International • Simple •

The cooking here focuses on well-defined flavours. This is demonstrated by the range of traditional and international dishes, the latter with a European and Asian twist.

Pelotari
X AC ⇔

Recoletos 3 ✉ *28001 –* Ⓜ *Colón – ☏ 915 78 24 97*   Plan: I2
– www.pelotari-asador.com – Closed Sunday
Menu 40/67 € – Carte 35/60 €
• Basque • Rustic •

This typical Basque eatery specialising in roasted meats is run by its owners, with one in the kitchen and the other front of house. There are four regional style dining rooms, two of which can be used as private rooms.

SQD
X & AC ⇔

Villanueva 2 ✉ *28001 –* Ⓜ *Banco de España*   Plan: I2
– ☏ 914 35 30 71 – www.familiasescude.es – Closed Holy Week, 3-21 August, Christmas, Sunday dinner, Monday and Tuesday dinner
Menu 20/65 € – Carte 50/70 €
• Meats and grills • Friendly •

A modern bistro located next to the Museo Arqueológico Nacional. The house speciality is the superb matured beef sourced from either Galicia or France.

Atlántico Casa de Petiscos
9/ 🍴 AC

Menéndez Pelayo 11 ✉ *28009 –* Ⓜ *Ibiza*   Plan: J2
– ☏ 91 435 28 19 – www.atlanticocasadecomidas.es
Tapa 4 € **Ración** approx. 12 €
• Traditional cuisine • Friendly •

A gastrobar with high chairs and tables where diners can enjoy typical Galician-style tapas (*petiscos*), including sandwiches of different sizes. A simply furnished yet welcoming setting in which to enjoy dishes for sharing.

El Barril de Goya
9/ 🍴 AC

Goya 86 ✉ *28009 –* Ⓜ *Goya – ☏ 915 78 39 98*   Plan: J2
– www.elbarrildegoya.com – Closed Sunday dinner
Tapa 6 € **Ración** approx. 14 €
• Seafood • Traditional décor •

A highly renowned seafood restaurant thanks to the extraordinary quality of its ingredients. Away from the sea, its marvellous sliced Iberian ham is equally delicious.

Ritz
⌂ ⅃ᴃ ᵹ ⒜ᴄ ⚿
pl. de la Lealtad 5 ✉ *28014 –* Ⓜ *Banco de España* Plan: **I2**
– ℰ *917 01 67 67 – www.mandarinoriental.com*
132 rm – ♦275/620 € ♦♦275/620 € – ☲ 35 € – 30 suites
• Grand Luxury • Elegant •
This internationally prestigious hotel occupies a palatial property from the early
20C. It features beautiful public spaces and sumptuously decorated guestrooms. In the Goya restaurant, endowed with its own inimitable personality,
enjoy well-prepared dishes based around a concept that is classical in style.

Villa Magna
⌂ ⅃ᴃ ᵹ ⒜ᴄ ⚿ ⇔
paseo de la Castellana 22 ✉ *28046 –* Ⓜ *Rubén Darío* Plan: **I1**
– ℰ *915 87 12 34 – www.hotelvillamagna.com*
150 rm – ♦660/860 € ♦♦760/860 € – ☲ 42 € – 18 suites
• Luxury • Classic •
This magnificent hotel boasts a classically elegant lounge area and various categories of
guestroom, with the suites on the top floor enjoying the added bonus of a terrace. The
enticing food choices include lighter lunch options, one gastronomic restaurant, and
another dedicated to a mix of Cantonese and Oriental cuisine.

Hospes Puerta de Alcalá
⌂ ⅃ᴃ ⊕ ᵹ ⒜ᴄ ⚿
pl. de la Independencia 3 ✉ *28001 –* Ⓜ *Retiro* Plan: **I2**
– ℰ *914 32 29 11 – www.hospes.com*
37 rm – ♦185/1000 € ♦♦215/1000 € – 5 suites
• Luxury • Contemporary •
A hotel occupying a building dating back to 1883 with a reception located at the old
carriage entrance, two meeting rooms and modern guestrooms, most overlooking the
Puerta de Alcalá. In the restaurant, choose from a selection of raciones, a daily set menu,
and a bonafide Cocido Madrileño stew served in three parts.

Único Madrid
⅃ᴃ ᵹ ⒜ᴄ ⚿ ⇔
Claudio Coello 67 ✉ *28001 –* Ⓜ *Serrano* Plan: **I1**
– ℰ *917 81 01 73 – www.unicohotelmadrid.com*
43 rm – ♦220/450 € ♦♦220/450 € – ☲ 26 € – 1 suite
• Luxury • Contemporary •
Behind the attractive classical façade, guests will discover a designer-inspired
entrance hall, an elegant public area with several small lounges, and comfor-
table guestrooms, all featuring a combination of classic and avant-garde decor.
A chauffeur-driven service is also available to help you explore the city.
❀❀ **Ramón Freixa Madrid** – See restaurant listing

Wellington
⅃ᴃ ⅃ ᵹ ⒜ᴄ ⚿ ⇔
Velázquez 8 ✉ *28001 –* Ⓜ *Retiro –* ℰ *915 75 44 00* Plan: **I2**
– www.hotel-wellington.com
226 rm – ♦165/220 € ♦♦165/220 € – ☲ 36 € – 26 suites
• Luxury • Classic •
Luxury and tradition go hand-in-hand in this truly emblematic hotel – one that
is used by many bullfighters during the city's San Isidro festival. Classically elegant public spaces, a busy English-style bar, plus fully equipped bedrooms.
❀ **Kabuki Wellington** • ⇲○ **Goizeko Wellington** – See restaurant listing

---

ARGÜELLES **PLAN IV**

El Barril de Argüelles
XX ⒜ᴄ
Andrés Mellado 69 ✉ *28015 –* Ⓜ *Islas Filipinas* Plan: **K2**
– ℰ *915 44 36 15 – www.restauranteelbarrildearguelles.com*
Carte 40/60 €
• Seafood • Classic décor •
A bar with enticing seafood counters precedes the classic yet contemporary
dining room decorated with a maritime theme. The specialities here are shell-
fish and octopus, although savoury rice dishes and delicious homemade stews
also feature on the menu.

El Barril de Argüelles

Andrés Mellado 69 ✉ *28015*
Plan: **K2**

– Ⓜ *Islas Filipinas*
– ☎ *915 44 36 15 – www.grupo-oter.com*
Tapa 10 € **Ración** approx. 20 €
• Seafood • Classic décor •
This impressive seafood restaurant has an elegant layout and extremely popular bar. Superb fish and seafood, including octopus and delicious Andalucian-style fresh fish, is served.

CHAMBERÍ   PLAN IV

Coque (Mario Sandoval)

Marqués de Riscal 11 ✉ *28010*
Plan III : **I1**

– Ⓜ *Rubén Darío*
– ☎ *916 04 02 02 – www.restaurantecoque.com*
– *Closed 23 December-2 January, August, Sunday and Monday*
Menu 130/180 € – *(tasting menu only)*
• Creative • Design •
The Sandoval brothers have landed in the Spanish capital ready to create a stir! Their cuisine goes much further that what you see on the plate, dissecting the culinary experience into five distinct areas (cocktail bar, wine cellar, kitchen, dining room and a dessert/post-dinner zone), each of which is designed to surprise and elicit different emotions.
➜ Txaka con caldo de congrio, dados de pil-pil de bacalao y perlas de Txacolí. T-bone de toro bravo con rebozuelos y su estofado trufado. Chocolates especiados con sal ahumada, helado de naranja y romero.

Santceloni – Hotel Hesperia Madrid

paseo de la Castellana 57 ✉ *28046*
Plan: **L2**

– Ⓜ *Gregorio Marañón*
– ☎ *912 10 88 40 – www.restaurantesantceloni.com*
– *Closed Holy Week, August, Saturday lunch, Sunday and bank holidays*
Menu 175 €
– Carte 122/152 €
• Creative • Elegant •
Elegance, comfort and good service are the perfect cocktail for a culinary experience that you won't forget in a hurry. In the completely glass-fronted kitchen chef Óscar Velasco creates traditional and international dishes that showcase plenty of creativity. Extensive wine cellar.
➜ Caballa flambeada, caviar y jalea de manzana. Lubina, tomate confitado, pimiento rojo, avellana y sésamo. Panacota de hinojo, aguacate y limón.

La Cabra

Francisco de Rojas 2 ✉ *28010*
Plan: **L3**

– Ⓜ *Bilbao*
– ☎ *914 45 77 50 – www.restaurantelacabra.com*
– *Closed 1-6 January, Holy Week, August and Sunday*
Menu 50/121 €
– Carte 45/60 €
• Creative • Contemporary décor •
A restaurant in which modernity and creativity go hand in hand. The gastrobar at the entrance, where guests can choose from a reduced menu, leads to the main dining room, which is much more focused on highly interesting gastronomic dishes chosen from several memorable menus. There is also an attractive wine cellar that diners can visit.
➜ Salsifí de trufa y piel de leche. Cigalas flambeadas, tapioca, comté y tamarillo de árbol. Yuzu, zanahoria y cilantro.

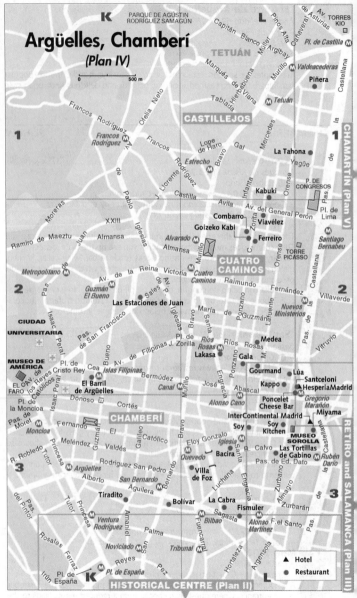

Argüelles, Chamberí
(Plan IV)

0   500 m

PARQUE DE AGUSTÍN
RODRÍGUEZ SAMAGÚN

TETUÁN

CASTILLEJOS

CUATRO CAMINOS

CIUDAD
UNIVERSITARIA

MUSEO DE AMÉRICA

EL FARO

Pl. de la Moncloa

CHAMBERÍ

MUSEO SOROLLA

CHAMARTÍN (Plan V)

RETIRO and SALAMANCA (Plan III)

HISTORICAL CENTRE (Plan II)

▲ Hotel
● Restaurant

570

SPAIN - MADRID

✿ **Lúa** (Manuel Domínguez)   XX 🔠 ⇄
Plan: **L2**
Eduardo Dato 5 ⊠ *28003 –* Ⓜ *Rubén Darío*
– ℰ *913 95 28 53 – www.restaurantelua.com – Closed Sunday*
Menu 65 € – *(tasting menu only)*
• Modern cuisine • Cosy •
Lúa has two completely different ambiences. One a gastrobar at the entrance
serving an à la carte of half and full *raciones*, the other a more gastronomic set-
ting on the lower level. Here, guests can enjoy contemporary cuisine with a
strong Galician influence focused around an impressive tasting menu.
→ Arroz verde con apio de carabinero. Corvina con salsa de callos y alca-
chofas. Manzana y limonada.

🌚 **Bacira**   X 🔠 ⇄
Plan: **L3**
Castillo 16 ⊠ *28010 –* Ⓜ *Iglesia –* ℰ *918 66 40 30*
– www.bacira.es – Closed 24 December-2 January, Sunday dinner and
Monday
Carte 30/44 € – *(booking advisable)*
• Fusion • Vintage •
Occupying an attractive vintage setting and run by its three young owner-chefs.
Fresh fusion-style cooking with a mix of Mediterranean, Oriental and Japanese
dishes made for sharing and served in an informal atmosphere.

🌚 **Gala**   X 🔠 ⇄
Plan: **L2**
Espronceda 14 ⊠ *28003 –* Ⓜ *Alonso Cano*
– ℰ *914 42 22 44 – www.restaurantegala.com – Closed 15 days August,*
Sunday and Monday dinner
Menu 35 € – Carte 30/45 €
• Modern cuisine • Intimate •
A small but long-established restaurant with a single contemporary dining
room. The market-inspired cooking has been brought bang up-to-date. It is sup-
ported by different set menus and interesting day-long gastronomic events
with a variety of themes. Make sure you try the sirloin steak tartare.

🌚 **Las Tortillas de Gabino**   X 🔠 ⇄
Plan: **L3**
Rafael Calvo 20 ⊠ *28010 –* Ⓜ *Rubén Darío*
– ℰ *91 319 75 05 – www.lastortillasdegabino.com – Closed Holy Week,*
15 days August, Sunday and bank holidays
Carte 30/48 €
• Traditional cuisine • Cosy •
A restaurant with two modern dining rooms decorated with wood panelling, as
well as a separate private dining section. Its seasonally inspired, seasonal menu
is complemented by a superb selection of tortillas that changes throughout the
year. The trufada, Velazqueña and pulpo are particular favourites here.

🍴 **Benares**   XxX 🛋 🔠 ⇄
Plan II : **H1**
Zurbano 5 ⊠ *28010 –* Ⓜ *Alonso Martínez*
– ℰ *913 19 87 16 – www.benaresmadrid.com – Closed 6-22 August and*
Sunday dinner
Menu 45/65 € – Carte 48/62 €
• Indian • Classic décor •
Benares follows in the footsteps of its London namesake with its restaurant and
cocktail bar. Updated Indian cuisine, an excellent wine cellar, and a charming
terrace on an inner patio.

🍴 **Ars Vivendi**   XX 🔠 ⇄
Plan II : **H1**
Zurbano 6 ⊠ *28010 –* Ⓜ *Alonso Martínez*
– ℰ *913 10 31 71 – www.restaurantearsvivendi.com – Closed Sunday*
dinner and Monday
Menu 35/70 € – Carte 47/54 €
• Italian • Cosy •
The life and soul of this restaurant is provided by the couple that own it, with
the husband working front-of-house and his wife in charge of the kitchen. Deli-
cious, Italian inspired cuisine that is both creative and attractively presented.
The homemade pasta is a feast for the senses!

SPAIN - MADRID

Las Estaciones de Juan

XX 🛱 🔤 ⇔
Plan: **K2**

paseo San Francisco de Sales 41 ✉ *28003*
– Ⓜ *Guzmán el Bueno* – 🕿 *915 98 86 66*
– *www.lascuatroestacionesdejuan.com*
Menu 33/50 € – Carte 40/56 €

• Traditional cuisine • Classic décor •

A solid performer preparing traditional cuisine with well-prepared ingredients in an impeccable setting combining the traditional and modern. One of the signature dishes is fillet of T-bone steak.

Gourmand

XX 🔤
Plan: **L2**

Bretón de los Herreros 39 ✉ *28003* – Ⓜ *Alonso Cano*
– 🕿 *915 45 84 48* – *www.restaurantegourmand.com* – *Closed Sunday dinner and Monday*
Menu 35/46 € – Carte 45/60 €

• Belgian • Cosy •

Authentic Belgian cuisine showcasing interesting creative touches. Its mussel specialities and the skate with capers and black butter are particularly worth trying. Superb beer menu.

Lakasa

XX 🛱 🕭 🔤
Plan: **L2**

pl. del Descubridor Diego de Ordás 1 ✉ *28003*
– Ⓜ *Rios Rosas* – 🕿 *915 33 87 15* – *www.lakasa.es* – *Closed Holy Week and Sunday*
Carte 38/60 €

• Traditional cuisine • Fashionable •

A restaurant enjoying lots of popularity thanks to its gastrobar and main dining room serving market-fresh cooking and daily recommendations. Every dish can also be served as a half-*ración*.

Soy Kitchen

XX 🔤 ⇔
Plan: **L3**

Zurbano 59 ✉ *28010* – Ⓜ *Gregorio Marañón*
– 🕿 *913 19 25 51* – *www.soykitchen.es* – *Closed 15 days August and Sunday dinner*
Menu 45/65 €

• Fusion • Trendy •

The chef here, who hails from Beijing, creates unique dishes that combine Asian (Chinese, Korean, Japanese etc) and Spanish and Peruvian cooking. Dishes full of colour and flavour.

Aire

X 🕭 🔤
Plan II : **H1**

Orfila 7 ✉ *28010* – Ⓜ *Alonso Martínez*
– 🕿 *911 70 42 28* – *www.airerestaurante.com* – *Closed 20 days August and Sunday dinner*
Menu 65 € – Carte 38/56 €

• Classic cuisine • Contemporary décor •

This charming, bistro-style restaurant is the first stage of a unique project. Everything revolves around poultry here (chicken, pigeon, pheasant, goose, partridge etc).

Bolívar

X 🔤
Plan: **K3**

Manuela Malasaña 28 ✉ *28004* – Ⓜ *San Bernardo*
– 🕿 *914 45 12 74* – *www.restaurantebolivar.com* – *Closed 6 August-1 September and Sunday*
Menu 20/38 € – Carte 36/44 €

• Traditional cuisine • Family •

A small restaurant in the bohemian Malasaña district in which the single dining room is divided into two sections with a modern feel. Traditional cuisine inspired by the seasons.

SPAIN - MADRID

Fismuler
X & AC
Sagasta 29 ⊠ *28005*

– Ⓜ *Alonso Martínez* – 𝒞 *918 27 75 81* – *www.fismuler.com*
– *Closed 31 December-6 January, Holy Week, 15 days August and Sunday*
Carte 35/47 €
• Traditional cuisine • Fashionable •
Gastronomy meets interior design in this restaurant with an austere retro-industrial feel. Despite this, the service and ambience are relaxed, with a menu that features pleasantly updated traditional cuisine.

Kappo
X AC
Bretón de los Herreros 54 ⊠ *28003*

Plan: **L2**

– Ⓜ *Gregorio Marañón* – 𝒞 *910 42 00 66* – *www.kappo.es*
– *Closed Holy Week, 21 days August, Sunday and Monday*
Menu 54/65 € – *(tasting menu only)*
• Japanese • Fashionable •
An intimate, contemporary address with an enticing sushi bar as its main focus. Diners order from a single yet extensive menu of modern Japanese cuisine.

Medea
X AC
Ríos Rosas 45 ⊠ *28003*

Plan: **L2**

– Ⓜ *Ríos Rosas* – 𝒞 *910 81 97 71* – *www.medearestaurante.com*
– *Closed Holy Week, 25 days August, Sunday dinner and Monday*
Menu 50/65 € – *(tasting menu only)*
• Modern cuisine • Simple •
Don't be deceived by first impressions as the simplicity of this restaurant is compensated by the modern, creative cooking in which Asian flavours and fusion details come to the fore.

Miyama
X AC
paseo de la Castellana 45 ⊠ *28046*

Plan: **L3**

– Ⓜ *Gregorio Marañón* – 𝒞 *913 91 00 26* – *www.restaurantemiyama.com*
– *Closed August, Sunday and bank holidays*
Menu 28/90 € – Carte 40/65 €
• Japanese • Contemporary décor •
A Japanese restaurant that is hugely popular in the city, including with Japanese visitors. An extensive sushi bar and simply laid tables share space in the single dining area. High quality, traditional Japanese cuisine.

Soy
X AC
Viriato 58 ⊠ *28010*

Plan: **L3**

– Ⓜ *Iglesia* – 𝒞 *914 45 74 47* – *www.soypedroespina.com*
– *Closed 15 days August, Saturday lunch, Sunday and Monday dinner*
Menu 65 € – Carte 45/60 € – *(booking essential)*
• Japanese • Simple •
This restaurant is simple, intimate and contemporary in style – the perfect setting for the delicious, traditional Japanese cuisine served here. It is not so easy to find, as there is no sign on the building!

Tiradito
X 🏠 AC
Conde Duque 13 ⊠ *28015*

Plan: **K3**

– Ⓜ *San Bernardo* – 𝒞 *915 41 78 76* – *www.tiradito.es*
– *Closed 7 days August, Sunday dinner and Monday*
Menu 35/65 € – Carte 36/58 €
• Peruvian • Trendy •
A young and easy-going restaurant serving 100% traditional Peruvian cuisine. Dishes on the menu include ceviches, tiraditos, picoteos and tapas criollas.

🍴 **Villa de Foz** ✗ ᴀᴄ

Gonzálo de Córdoba 10 ⊠ 28010
Plan: **L3**
– 🚇 *Bilbao*
– 📞 *914 46 89 93 – www.villadefoz.es*
– *Closed August, Sunday dinner and Monday*
Menu 20/60 € – Carte 30/50 €
• Galician • Simple •
A long-established restaurant with two dining rooms, both combining classic and contemporary decor. The traditional Galician menu is embellished with a number of rice and seafood dishes.

🍴 **Poncelet Cheese Bar** ⼬/ ᴋ ᴀᴄ

José Abascal 61 ⊠ 28003
Plan: **L2**
– 🚇 *Gregorio Marañón*
– 📞 *91 399 25 50 – www.ponceletcheesebar.es*
– *Closed Sunday dinner and Monday*
Tapa 5 € **Ración** approx. 14 €
• Cheese, fondue and raclette • Design •
An innovative designer space where cheese is king, with a menu featuring 150 options if you include the cheese plates, fondues and raclettes. However, dishes without cheese are still available!

🏨 **InterContinental Madrid** ⼬ ᴸⱴ ᴋ ᴀᴄ ⼫ ⛟

paseo de la Castellana 49 ⊠ 28046
Plan: **L3**
– 🚇 *Gregorio Marañón*
– 📞 *917 00 73 00 – www.madrid.intercontinental.com*
269 rm – ▮180/280 € ▮▮180/280 € – ⛵ 32 € – 33 suites
• Grand Luxury • Classic •
A luxury hotel with a classically elegant entrance hall crowned by a cupola and embellished with a profusion of marble, a pleasant inner patio-terrace, and guestrooms that stand out for their high levels of comfort. In the restaurant adjoining the entrance hall-bar, the focus is on an attractive international menu, with an impressive brunch on Sundays.

🏨 **Hesperia Madrid** ⼬ ᴸⱴ ᴋ ᴀᴄ ⼫ ⛟

paseo de la Castellana 57 ⊠ 28046
Plan: **L2**
– 🚇 *Gregorio Marañón*
– 📞 *912 10 88 00 – www.hesperia-madrid.com*
139 rm ⛵ – ▮159/259 € ▮▮169/259 € – 32 suites
• Luxury • Elegant •
This chain hotel enjoys a superb location on the city's main avenue in a central business and shopping district. It offers a large choice of elegantly classical guestrooms and lounges. There is also a variety of dining options including one restaurant focusing on the flavours of the Mediterranean, and another on Japanese cooking.
❀❀ **Santceloni** – See restaurant listing

🏨 **Orfila** ⼬ ᴀᴄ ⼫ ⛟

Orfila 6 ⊠ 28010
Plan II : **H1**
– 🚇 *Alonso Martínez*
– 📞 *917 02 77 70 – www.hotelorfila.com*
– *Closed August*
32 rm – ▮255/400 € ▮▮255/500 € – ⛵ 30 € – 12 suites
• Luxury • Elegant •
This delightfully charming small palace built in the 19C occupies a quiet street in a central location. It has elegant guestrooms embellished with period furniture. The restaurant has a classic air and serves traditional cuisine as impressive as its welcoming terrace.

☘ **Kabuki**   XX & 🅐🅒

Plan: **L1**

av. Presidente Carmona 2 ⊠ 28020
– Ⓜ Santiago Bernabeu – ℰ 914 17 64 15 – www.grupokabuki.com
– Closed Holy Week, 6-28 August, Saturday lunch, Sunday and bank holidays
Carte 65/92 €

• Japanese • Minimalist •

A Japanese restaurant with a simple minimalist look that deliberately shifts the focus to the cooking created here. You're best advised to go with the daily recommendations which you can enjoy in the same way as a traditional Omakase (chef's choice) menu. Booking ahead is recommended as it is always full.
➜ Tartar de toro con angulas. Costillas de buey en teriyaki. Cremoso de yuzu.

🕽 **Combarro**   XxX 🍴 🅐🅒 ⇔

Plan: **L2**

Reina Mercedes 12 ⊠ 28020 – Ⓜ Nuevos Ministerios
– ℰ 915 54 77 84 – www.combarro.com – Closed Holy Week, 1-15 August and Sunday dinner
Menu 50/120 € – Carte 45/60 €

• Seafood • Classic décor •

Galician cuisine with an emphasis on fresh quality produce, including live fish tanks. Public bar, dining on the first floor and a number of rooms in the basement. Classic and elegant in style.

🕽 **Ferreiro**   XX 🅐🅒 ⇔

Plan: **L2**

Comandante Zorita 32 ⊠ 28020 – Ⓜ Alvarado
– ℰ 915 53 93 42 – www.restauranteferreiro.com
Menu 36/60 € – Carte 38/58 €

• Traditional cuisine • Classic décor •

Classic-contemporary dining rooms act as a backdrop for traditional cuisine with strong Asturian roots in this restaurant. Extensive menu that is supplemented by a good choice of specials.

🕽 **Goizeko Kabi**   XX 🍴 🅐🅒

Plan: **L2**

Comandante Zorita 37 ⊠ 28020 – Ⓜ Alvarado
– ℰ 915 33 01 85 – www.goizeko-gaztelupe.com – Closed Sunday dinner
Menu 55/70 € – Carte 45/70 €

• Basque • Contemporary décor •

A classic restaurant which has been given a new contemporary feel. Traditional Basque cuisine, with the option of choosing half-raciones from the menu.

🕽 **Piñera**   XX 🅐🅒 ⇔ 🚗

Plan: **L1**

Rosario Pino 12 ⊠ 28020 – Ⓜ Valdeacederas
– ℰ 914 25 14 25 – www.restaurantepinera.com – Closed 21 days August and Sunday
Menu 45/75 € – Carte 45/70 €

• Traditional cuisine • Contemporary décor •

Owner-chef Carlos Posadas has given this restaurant a new feel, with two very different dining rooms. Traditional cuisine with a modern twist.

🕽 **La Tahona**   XX 🍴 🅐🅒 ⇔

Plan: **L1**

Capitán Haya 21 (beside) ⊠ 28020 – Ⓜ Cuzco
– ℰ 915 55 04 41 – www.asadordearanda.com – Closed 1-26 August and Sunday dinner
Menu 35/50 € – Carte 30/55 €

• Meats and grills • Classic décor •

Part of the El Asador de Aranda chain. La Tahona's dining rooms have a medieval Castillian ambience with a wood fire at the entrance taking pride of place. The suckling lamb (lechazo) is the star dish here!

‖○ **Viavélez**   XX AC

av. General Perón 10 ⊠ 28020 – ⓜ *Santiago Bernabeu*   Plan: **L2**
*– ℰ 915 79 95 39 – www.restauranteviavelez.com – Closed August, Sunday
and Monday lunch in summer, Sunday dinner and Monday the rest of the
year*
Menu 19/58 € – Carte 35/60 €
• Creative • Trendy •

Viavélez boasts a stylish tapas bar plus a modern dining room in the basement
where you can enjoy creative dishes that remain faithful to Asturian cuisine. The
taberna does not close for holidays.

❀❀❀ **DiverXO** (David Muñoz) – Hotel NH Collection Eurobuilding   XxX

Padre Damián 23 ⊠ 28036 – ⓜ *Cuzco – ℰ 915 70 07 66*   AC ⌂
– www.diverxo.com – Closed Holy Week, 21 days   Plan: **M2**
August, Sunday and Monday
Menu 195/250 € – *(booking essential) (tasting menu only)*
• Creative • Design •

This restaurant is an exciting and groundbreaking culinary wonderland, and a
journey into the highly personal world of this chef. To a backdrop of stunning
modern design, enjoy world cuisine that will challenge your palate, intensifying
sensations and reaching its apogee in presentation worthy of the finest canvas.
→ Cocido Pho vietnamita de chuleta de vaca roja gallega madurada con guisantes del Maresme y ali oli de humo. Spicy bolognesa de carabineros con gamba
roja atemperada, rocoto, hojas de curry, mostaza picante y dulce japonesa. Petit
suisse de fresas silvestres, mascarpone de leche de oveja requemada, pimienta
rosa, flores, aceite de oliva y crema helada de galanga-lima.

❀ **A'Barra**   XxxX 🕸 & AC ⇔

Del Pinar 15 ⊠ 28014 – ⓜ *Gregorio Marañón*   Plan: **M3**
*– ℰ 910 21 00 61 – www.restauranteabarra.com – Closed Holy
Week, August and Sunday*
Menu 55/105 € – Carte 60/85 €
• Traditional cuisine • Design •

Both the decor, featuring a profusion of high-quality wood, and the spacious
layout come as a pleasant surprise. Choose between the calm setting of the
dining room and a large circular bar, which is more geared towards show cooking. Elaborate, modern cuisine with an emphasis on choice ingredients.
→ Puerro, caviar y anguila ahumada. Pichón , mole, maíz y café. Yemas
avainilladas y bergamota.

❀ **Gaytán** (Javier Aranda)   XX & AC

Príncipe de Vergara 205 (beside) ⊠ 28002   Plan: **M3**
– ⓜ *Concha Espina – ℰ 913 48 50 30 – www.chefjavieraranda.com
– Closed 5 days Christmas, Holy Week, August, Sunday and Monday*
Menu 50/121 € – *(tasting menu only)*
• Modern cuisine • Minimalist •

This gastronomic restaurant has been designed to cause a stir. The minimalist
interior decor is unexpected, dominated by the presence of original columns
and a large open kitchen, which is the epicentre of activity here. Its different
tasting menus demonstrate an interesting creativity.
→ Guisantes, raíz de perejil y regaliz. Despiece de cordero lechal. Cala-
mansi, pistacho y lima negra.

‖○ **Lágrimas Negras** – Hotel Puerta América   XxX 🕸 🏠 AC ⇔ ⌂

av. de América 41 ⊠ 28002 – ⓜ *Cartagena*   Plan: **N3**
– ℰ 917 44 54 05 – www.hotelpuertaamerica.com
Carte 45/60 €
• Modern cuisine • Design •

Part of a designer hotel, this restaurant boasts a contemporary look, including
high ceilings and large windows, plus direct access to the terrace. Contemporary cuisine of a very high standard.

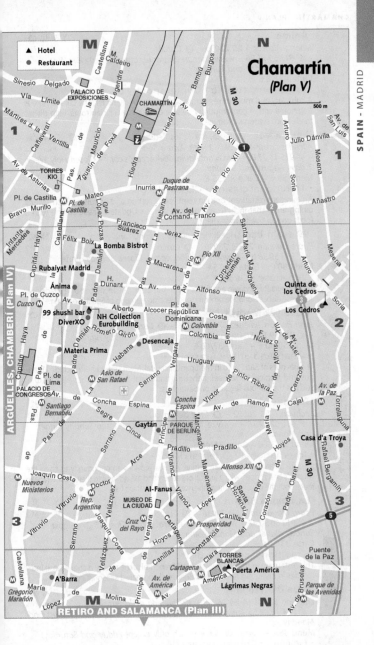

Chamartín
(Plan V)

0 500 m

▲ Hotel
● Restaurant

PALACIO DE EXPOSICIONES

CHAMARTÍN

Sinesio Delgado
Vía Límite
Mártires d. la Ventilla
Cañaveral
Av. de Asturias
TORRES KIO
Pl. de Castilla
Bravo Murillo
Infanta Mercedes
Capitán Haya
Félix Boix
La Bomba Bistrot
Rubaiyat Madrid
Ánima
Pl. de Cuzco
Cuzco
99 shushi bar
DiverXO
NH Collection Eurobuilding
Desencaja
Materia Prima
Asío de San Rafael
PALACIO DE CONGRESOS
Santiago Bernabéu
Gaytán
PARQUE DE BERLÍN
Joaquín Costa
Nuevos Ministerios
Rep. Argentina
Al-Fanus
MUSEO DE LA CIUDAD
Cruz del Rayo
Prosperidad
Castellana
María Gregorio Marañón
A'Barra

M. Caldeiro
Castellana
Legendre
Mauricio
Agustín de Foxá
Hiedra
Bambú
Burgos
Av. de Pío XII
Av. de Pío XII
M 30
Av. de San Luis
Arturo
Julio Dánvila
Mesena
Soria
Añastro
Duque de Pastrana
Inurria
Av. del Comand. Franco
Francisco Suárez
Jerez
La Habana
Santa María Magdalena
Mesena
de Macarena
Pío XII
Torpedero Tucumán
Arturo
Soria
H. Dunant
Av. de Alfonso XIII
Quinta de los Cedros
Los Cedros
Alberto Alcocer
Pl. de la República Dominicana
Costa Rica
F. Núñez
Av. de Aster
Cerezos
Colombia
Colombia
Serrano
Uruguay
la Pintor Ribera
Av. de la Paz
Torrelaguna
Habana
Vergara
Victor
Av. de Ramón y Cajal
María
Concha
Espina
Concha Espina
Casa d'a Troya
Serrano
Cinca
Príncipe
Marcenado
Pradillo
Pradillo
Hoyos
M 30
Rafael Bergantín
Arce
Viranoz
Alfonso XIII
Doctor
Velázquez
Viranoz
López
de
Santa Hortensia
Rey
Padre Claret
Corazón
Canillas
Joaquín Costa
Vitruvio
Joaquín Costa
Hoyos
del
Constancia
Puente de la Paz
Cartagena
Clara
TORRES BLANCAS
Puerta América
Lágrimas Negras
Av. de América
Av. de Bruselas
Parque de las Avenidas
Molina
Príncipe
Av. de América

ⅱ○ **Ánima** XX & 🎧 ⇔

Alberto Alcocer 5 ✉ *28036* – Ⓜ *Cuzco* Plan: **M2**
– ℰ 913 59 73 86 – www.animarestaurante.com – Closed Holy Week,
August, Saturday and Sunday
Carte 43/58 €
• Traditional cuisine • Contemporary décor •
A light, airy and modern restaurant with plenty of character. The cuisine here is
traditional with a contemporary twist and distinctly Galician roots, with dishes
made from seasonal produce.

ⅱ○ **Los Cedros** – Hotel Quinta de los Cedros XX 🎧 🎧 🚗

Allendesalazar 4 ✉ *28043* – Ⓜ *Arturo Soria* Plan: **N2**
– ℰ 915 15 22 00 – www.hotelquintadeloscedros.com – Closed Holy Week,
7 days August and Sunday
Menu 39 € – Carte 35/55 €
• Traditional cuisine • Classic décor •
An excellent restaurant both in terms of its setting and its cuisine, with several
dining areas that include an attractive terrace. Updated classic cuisine with a
focus on top quality ingredients.

ⅱ○ **99 sushi bar** – Hotel NH Collection Eurobuilding XX 🎧

Padre Damián 23 ✉ *28036* – Ⓜ *Cuzco* Plan: **M2**
– ℰ 913 59 38 01 – www.99sushibar.com – Closed Sunday dinner
Menu 80 € – Carte 60/75 €
• Japanese • Design •
This restaurant is modern and full of decorative detail. The menu combines traditional
Japanese dishes alongside other recipes blending elements of Spanish cooking.

ⅱ○ **Rubaiyat Madrid** XX 🎧 🎧 & 🎧 ⇔

Juan Ramón Jiménez 37 ✉ *28036* – Ⓜ *Cuzco* Plan: **M2**
– ℰ 91 359 10 00 – www.rubaiyat.es – Closed Sunday dinner
Menu 50/90 € – Carte 37/60 €
• Meats and grills • Brasserie •
The flavours of São Paulo in the Spanish capital. Meat served here includes Bran-
gus and tropical Kobe beef, although traditional Brazilian dishes also feature,
such as the famous feijoada on Saturdays.

ⅱ○ **Alfanus** X 🎧

Pechuán 6 ✉ *28002* – Ⓜ *Cruz del Rayo* Plan: **M3**
– ℰ 915 62 77 18 – www.restaurantealfanus.es – Closed Sunday dinner
and Monday dinner
Menu 21/33 € – Carte 31/46 €
• International • Oriental décor •
If you're unfamiliar with Syrian cuisine, Alfanus provides an opportunity to enjoy the
country's best recipes, which are full of subtlety and always loyal to their Mediterranean
roots. Both the decor and the ambience have an Arabian feel.

ⅱ○ **La Bomba Bistrot** X 🎧 🎧

Pedro Muguruza 5 ✉ *28036* – Ⓜ *Cuzco* Plan: **M2**
– ℰ 913 50 30 47 – www.labombabistrot.com – Closed 3-27 August,
Sunday dinner and Monday dinner
Carte 33/50 €
• Traditional cuisine • Bistro •
This restaurant in the style of a typical French bistro is run by a chef whose inte-
rest lies in inventing new dishes. Beautifully prepared seasonal cuisine.

ⅱ○ **Casa d'a Troya** X 🎧

Emiliano Barral 14 ✉ *28043* – Ⓜ *Avenida de la Paz* Plan: **N3**
– ℰ 914 16 44 55 – www.casadatroya.es – Closed Holy Week, August and
Monday
Menu 38 € – Carte 30/45 € – *(lunch only except Friday and Saturday)*
• Galician • Contemporary décor •
A long-established family restaurant which has recently been updated by the
latest generation at the helm. Simple, modestly presented Galician cuisine and
generous raciones.

⫟○ **Desencaja** ✗ ⒶⒸ
Plan: **M2**
paseo de la Habana 84 ✉ *28036 –* Ⓜ *Colombia*
– ℰ *914 57 56 68 – www.dsncaja.com – Closed Holy Week, August,*
Sunday dinner and Monday dinner
Menu 20/52 € – Carte 36/65 €
• Traditional cuisine • Contemporary décor •
A restaurant which is constantly changing while also managing to retain its
identity, and always looking to meet the culinary needs of its guests. The
menu changes according to market availability, including a few interesting
game dishes.

⫟○ **Materia Prima** ✗ 🏠 ⒶⒸ
Plan: **M2**
Doctor Fleming 7 ✉ *28036 –* Ⓜ *Santiago Bernabeu*
– ℰ *913 44 01 77 – www.materia-prima.es – Closed Sunday dinner*
Carte 35/55 €
• Traditional cuisine • Traditional décor •
A unique culinary concept where products are displayed as they would be in a
market, which customers then buy at market rates, before being prepared at a
fixed price. Materia Prima's range of fish options is particularly superb.

🏨🏨 **NH Collection Eurobuilding** 🛗 💪 🌐 ⛑ ⒶⒸ ♨ 🚗
Plan: **M2**
Padre Damián 23 ✉ *28036 –* Ⓜ *Cuzco*
– ℰ *913 53 73 00 – www.nh-hotels.com*
412 rm – 🛏135/195 € 🛏🛏135/195 € – 🍴 20 €
• Business • Contemporary •
This hotel has a spectacular lobby featuring a high-tech LED inspired barrel-
vaulted ceiling that doubles as the biggest multimedia screen in Europe! Over-
all, the facilities are spacious with well-equipped contemporary-style guest-
rooms, a plethora of meeting rooms and myriad lounge areas. The interesting
culinary options add an extra dimension.
❀❀❀ **DiverXO** • ⫟○ **99 sushi bar** – See restaurant listing

🏨🏨 **Puerta América** 🛗 🖥 💪 ⒶⒸ ♨ 🚗
Plan: **N3**
av. de América 41 ✉ *28002 –* Ⓜ *Cartagena*
– ℰ *917 44 54 00 – www.hotelpuertamerica.com*
301 rm – 🛏140/550 € 🛏🛏140/550 € – 🍴 22 € – 14 suites
• Business • Design •
This colourful and cosmopolitan hotel has a distinct design feel with each of its
floors reflecting the creativity of a renowned architect or famous interior designer. Highly original guestrooms with an attractive fitness and well-being space
on the top floor.
⫟○ **Lágrimas Negras** – See restaurant listing

🏨🏨 **Quinta de los Cedros** ⒶⒸ ♨ 🚗
Plan: **N2**
Allendesalazar 4 ✉ *28043 –* Ⓜ *Arturo Soria*
– ℰ *915 15 22 00 – www.hotelquintadeloscedros.com*
32 rm – 🛏100/165 € 🛏🛏129/185 € – 🍴 15 €
• Traditional • Elegant •
This attractive and surprising modern hotel is surrounded by gardens in the
style of a Tuscan villa. Comfortable guestrooms, including some with a terrace
and others in bungalow style.
⫟○ **Los Cedros** – See restaurant listing

PARQUE FERIAL PLAN I

🏨 **Globales Acis y Galatea** 🍴 🛗 ⒶⒸ 🅿
Plan: **D1**
Galatea 6 ✉ *28042 –* Ⓜ *Canillejas –* ℰ *917 43 49 01*
– www.hotelesglobales.com
26 rm 🍴 – 🛏70/150 € 🛏🛏80/335 €
• Business • Elegant •
This hotel located in a residential district offers classic-contemporary guestrooms, three of which have their own terrace. The rooftop solarium and trans-
fers to the IFEMA exhibition centre and the airport are also available to guests.

BARCELONA
BARCELONA

MasterLu/iStock

BARCELONA IN...

→ **ONE DAY**
Catedral de Santa Eulalia, Las Ramblas, La Pedrera, Museu Picasso, Sagrada Familia.

→ **TWO DAYS**
Montjuïc, Parc Güell, Nou Camp Stadium, Barceloneta Waterfront, Tibidabo.

→ **THREE DAYS**
Barri Gotic and Palau de la Música Catalana, Via Laietana, Sitges.

It can't be overestimated how important Catalonia is to the locals of Barcelona: pride in their region of Spain runs deep in the blood. Barcelona loves to mix the traditional with the avant-garde, and this exuberant opening of arms has seen it grow into a pulsating city for visitors. Its rash of theatres, museums and concert halls is unmatched by most other European cities, and many artists and architects, including Picasso, Miró, Dalí, Gaudí and Subirachs, have chosen to live here.

The 19C was a golden period in the city's artistic development, with the growth of the great Catalan Modernism movement, but it

was knocked back on its heels after the Spanish Civil War and the rise to power of the dictator Franco, who destroyed hopes for an independent Catalonia. After his death, democracy came to Spain and since then, Barcelona has relished its position as the capital of a restored autonomous region. Go up on the Montjuïc to get a great overview of the city below. Barcelona's atmospheric Old Town is near the harbour and reaches into the teeming streets of the Gothic Quarter, while the newer area is north of this; its elegant avenues in grid formation making up Eixample. The coastal quarter of Barcelona has been transformed with the development of trendy Barceloneta. For many, though, the epicentre of this bubbling city is Las Ramblas, scything through the centre of town.

EATING OUT

Barcelona has long had a good gastronomic tradition, and geographically it's been more influenced by France and Italy than other Spanish regions. But these days the sensual enjoyment of food has become something of a mainstream religion here. The city has hundreds of tapas bars; a type of cuisine which is very refreshing knocked back with a draught beer. The city's location brings together produce from the land and the sea, with a firm emphasis on seasonality and quality produce. This explains why there are myriad markets in the city, all in great locations. Specialities to look out for include pantumaca: slices of toasted bread with tomato and olive oil; escalivada, which is made with roasted vegetables; esqueixada, a typically Catalan salad, and crema Catalana, a light custard. One little known facet of Barcelona life is its exquisite chocolate and sweet shops. Two stand out: Fargas, in the Barri Gothic, is the city's most famous chocolate shop, while Cacao Sampaka is the most elegant chocolate store you could ever wish to find.

Caelis (Romain Fornell) – Hotel Ohla Barcelona   XXX ఉ AC

Via Laietana 49 ✉ *08003 –* Ⓜ *Urquinaona*   Plan: **F1**
*– ℰ 935 10 12 05 – www.caelis.com – Closed Sunday, Monday and
Tuesday lunch*
Menu 87/132 € – Carte 65/95 €
• Creative • Elegant •
Elegant, contemporary and with an open kitchen surrounded by a bar where
guests can also enjoy the cuisine on offer here. The award-winning French
chef showcases his creative talents via several menus, from which you can also
choose single, individually priced dishes.
→ El huevo de Xavier Frauca a la trufa negra en su nido. Caviar, buey de
mar y coliflor en emulsión. Haba de cacao crujiente con sopa de pasión.

Koy Shunka (Hideki Matsuhisa)   XX ఉ AC

Copons 7 ✉ *08002 –* Ⓜ *Urquinaona – ℰ 934 12 79 39*   Plan: **F1**
*– www.koyshunka.com – Closed Christmas, Holy Week, August, Sunday
dinner and Monday*
Menu 89/132 € – Carte 60/90 €
• Japanese • Contemporary décor •
If you enjoy Japanese cuisine and the spectacle of superb nigiri and sushi prepared in front of you, then Koy Shunka is the place for you. There is an open-
view kitchen standing in the middle of one of the dining rooms. The passionate
chef is known for preparing Japanese dishes with a creative touch, which he
manages to cleverly combine with the cuisine and products of the Mediterranean.
→ Nigiri de anguila del Delta del Ebro. Ikegime de bogavante. Cacao y
coco.

Dos Palillos   ଚ/ ⌂ AC ⇔

Elisabets 9 ✉ *08001 –* Ⓜ *Catalunya – ℰ 933 04 05 13*   Plan: **E2**
*– www.dospalillos.com – Closed 24 December-8 January, 6-27 August,
Sunday, Monday, Tuesday lunch and Wednesday lunch*
Tapa 8 € – Menu 80 € – Carte 38/54 €
• Asian • Contemporary décor •
A highly original dining option both for its unique "show cooking" concept and
its culinary philosophy. This is centred on the fusion of Oriental cuisine and typically Spanish products. There are two counters for dining, one at the entrance
(no reservations taken and only for à la carte dining), and another further inside,
which has a more gastronomic focus with its tasting menus.
→ Nigiri de sepia con caviar oscietra. Toro laqueado con raviolis de
yamaimo y mentaiko. Kakigori de piel de yuzu.

Fonda España – Hotel España   XX ఉ AC

Sant Pau 9 ✉ *08001 –* Ⓜ *Liceu – ℰ 935 50 00 00*   Plan: **F2**
– www.hotelespanya.com – Closed Sunday dinner
Menu 27/75 € – Carte 36/56 € – *(dinner only August)*
• Traditional cuisine • Cosy •
This charming address is in a listed building with high ceilings, Modernist decor
and beautiful mosaics created by the renowned Barcelona architect Domènech
i Montaner. Updated traditional cuisine.

Senyor Parellada   XX AC

L'Argenteria 37 ✉ *08003 –* Ⓜ *Jaume I*   Plan: **G2**
– ℰ 933 10 50 94 – www.senyorparellada.com
Menu 18 € – Carte 25/45 €
• Regional cuisine • Cosy •
An attractive restaurant with a classic-cum-colonial style and various dining
rooms in which time seems to have stood still. The highlights are the authentic
Catalan cuisine and the small patio with an impressive glass roof.

Torre d'Alta Mar
XxX ≤ AC
passeig Joan de Borbó 88 ✉ *08039* – Ⓜ *Barceloneta*
*– 𝄂 932 21 00 07 – www.torredealtamar.com – Closed 24-27 December,
13-17 August, Sunday lunch and Monday lunch*
Menu 39/96 € – Carte 70/92 €
Plan: **H3**
• Modern cuisine • Classic décor •
A restaurant whose outstanding feature is its location on top of a 75m-high metal tower. Highly contemporary glass-fronted circular dining room with superb views of the sea, port and city. Traditional à la carte menu featuring contemporary touches.

Bravo 24 – Hotel W Barcelona
XX 🛋 ⚃ AC ⟷
pl. de la Rosa dels Vents 1 (Moll De Llevant) ✉ *08039*
– 𝄂 932 95 26 36 – www.carlesabellan.com
Menu 90/130 € – Carte 60/80 €
Plan: **C3**
• Traditional cuisine • Fashionable •
Located on the mezzanine of the W hotel in Barcelona, Bravo 24 has a resolutely contemporary feel, in which wood takes pride of place, plus an attractive summer terrace. Traditionally inspired cuisine enhanced by contemporary touches, as well as an impressive array of raciones!

El Cercle
XX ⚃ AC ⟷
dels Arcs 5-1º ✉ *08002* – Ⓜ *Liceu* – 𝄂 *936 24 48 10*
– www.elcerclerestaurant.com
Menu 28/50 € – Carte 30/48 €
Plan: **F2**
• Classic cuisine • Classic décor •
This restaurant is housed in the Reial Cercle Arstístic. It offers different types of cuisine in different dining areas. These range from Japanese specialities to modern Catalan fare.

Elx
XX ≤ 🛋 ⚃ AC
Moll d'Espanya 5-Maremagnum, Local 9 ✉ *08039*
– Ⓜ Drassanes – 𝄂 932 25 81 17 – www.elxrestaurant.com
Carte 40/57 €
Plan: **G3**
• Traditional cuisine • Trendy •
A restaurant graced with views of the fishing port. Modern dining room and an attractive terrace, where the focus is on fish and a good selection of savoury rice dishes.

Dos Pebrots
X ⚃ AC
Doctor Dou 19 ✉ *08001* – Ⓜ *Catalunya*
*– 𝄂 938 53 95 98 – www.dospebrots.com – Closed January, 1 week
August, Monday and Tuesday*
Carte 35/50 € – *(dinner only except Friday, Saturday and Sunday)*
Plan: **E2**
• Mediterranean cuisine • Neighbourhood •
Dos Pebrots combines its informal character with a unique concept which focuses on minutely researched cooking that narrates the evolution of Mediterranean gastronomy.

Estimar
X AC
Sant Antoni dels Sombrerers 3 ✉ *08003* – Ⓜ *Jaume I*
*– 𝄂 932 68 91 97 – www.restaurantestimar.com – Closed 23 December-
9 January, 14 August-4 September, Sunday and Monday lunch*
Carte 75/95 €
Plan: **G2**
• Seafood • Mediterranean décor •
An intimate restaurant that is somewhat tucked away but which has received many plaudits thanks to the passion for the sea shown by the Gotanegra family and chef Rafa Zafra. Grilled dishes and high-quality products are to the fore here.

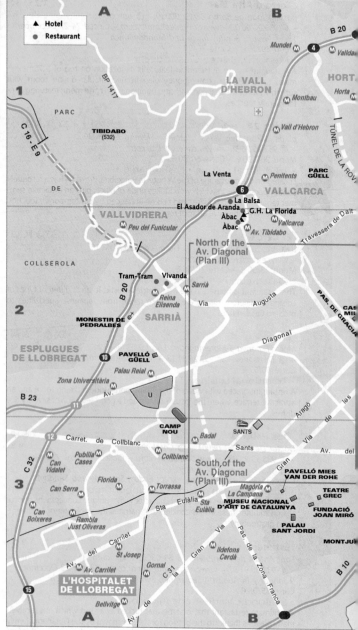

A

B

▲ Hotel
● Restaurant

C 16 - E 9

PARC

TIBIDABO
(532)

BP 1417

DE

VALLVIDRERA

Peu del Funicular ⓜ

COLLSEROLA

B 20

MONESTIR DE
PEDRALBES

ESPLUGUES
DE LLOBREGAT

10

PAVELLÓ
GÜELL

Palau Reial

Zona Universitària ⓜ

B 23

Av.

U

11

12

Carret. de Collblanc

CAMP
NOU

C 32

Can
Vidalet

Publilla ⓜ
Cases

Florida ⓜ

Collblanc

Sants

Can Serra ⓜ

Torrassa ⓜ

Sta
Eulàlia

Sta
Eulàlia

Can
Boixeres

Rambla
Just Oliveras

Carrilet

Av.
del

Carrilet

St Josep

Av. Carrilet

Gornal

C 31

Ildefons
Cerdà

15

L'HOSPITALET
DE LLOBREGAT

Bellvitge ⓜ

Av.

de

A

B 20

Mundet ⓜ **4** ⓜ Valldau

LA VALL
D'HEBRON

Montbau ⓜ

HORT

Horta ⓜ

Vall d'Hebron ⓜ

TÚNEL DE LA ROV

Penitents ⓜ

PARC
GÜELL

La Venta ●

6

VALLCARCA

● La Balsa

El Asador de Aranda ●

G.H. La Florida

Àbac ▲

Àbac ●

ⓜ Vallcarca

Av. Tibidabo

Travessera de Dalt

North of the
Av. Diagonal
(Plan III)

Vivanda ●

Tram-Tram ●

Sarrià ⓜ

Reina
Elisenda ⓜ

Via

Augusta

PAS. DE GRÀCIA

CAS
MIL

SARRIÀ

Diagonal

las

Aragó

de

Badal ⓜ

SANTS

Via

Sants

Av.

del

South of the
Av. Diagonal
(Plan III)

Magòria ⓜ
La Campana ●

Gran

PAVELLÓ MIES
VAN DER ROHE

TEATRE
GREC

MUSEU NACIONAL
D'ART DE CATALUNYA

FUNDACIÓ
JOAN MIRÓ

PALAU
SANT JORDI

MONTJU

Via

Gran

Pas de la Zona Franca

B 10

B

EL PRAT-BARCELONA ✈

Environs of Barcelona
(Plan I)

0   1 km

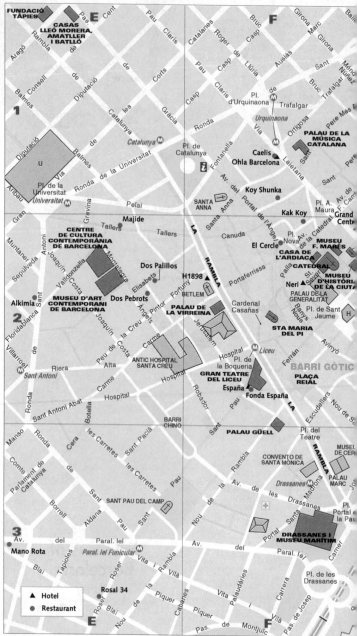

E

FUNDACIÓ TÀPIES

CASAS LLEÓ MORERA, AMATLLER I BATLLÓ

F

Pl. d'Urquinaona

PALAU DE LA MÚSICA CATALANA

Caelis
Ohla Barcelona

Pl. de Catalunya

Koy Shunka

SANTA ANNA

Kak Koy

Pl. A. Maura

Grand Cent

MUSEU F. MARÈS

CENTRE DE CULTURA CONTEMPORÀNIA DE BARCELONA

Majide

El Cercle

Pl. Nova

CASA DE L'ARDIACA

CATEDRAL

MUSEU D'HISTÒRIA DE LA CIUTA

Dos Palillos

H1898

Alkimia

MUSEU D'ART CONTEMPORANI DE BARCELONA

Dos Pebrots

PALAU DE LA VIRREINA

BETLEM

Neri

PALAU DE LA GENERALITAT

Pl. de Sant Jaume

Cardenal Casañas

STA MARIA DEL PI

ANTIC HOSPITAL SANTA CREU

Pl. de la Boqueria

GRAN TEATRE DEL LICEU

BARRI GÒTIC

Liceu

España

PLAÇA REIAL

Fonda España

BARRI CHINO

PALAU GÜELL

Pl. del Teatre

MUSEU DE CER

CONVENTO DE SANTA MONICA

Drassanes

PALAU MARC

SANT PAU DEL CAMP

Pl. Portal la Pau

Mano Rota

DRASSANES I MUSEU MARÍTIM

Rosal 34

Pl. de les Drassanes

▲ Hotel
● Restaurant

1

2

3

E

F

586

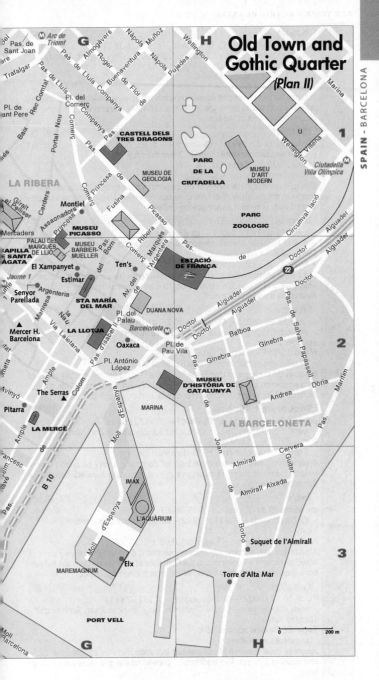

Old Town and Gothic Quarter
(Plan II)

Pas. de Sant Joan
Arc de Triomf
Trafalgar
Almogàvers
Nàpols
Muñoz
Wellington
Marina

Pl. de Sant Pere
Pas. de Lluís Companys
Pas. de Lluís Companys
Roger
Buenaventura
Nàpols
Pujades

Pl. del Comerç
Comerç
Compañys
Wellington
Villena

Baix
Portal Nou
Comerç
U

Rec Comtal
Pas. de Lluís

CASTELL DELS TRES DRAGONS

PARC DE LA CIUTADELLA

MUSEU D'ART MODERN

LA RIBERA

Giralt el Pellisser
Carders
Princesa
Comerç
Fusina
Picasso
Ciutadella Villa Olímpica

Montiel
Assaonadors
Princesa

MUSEU DE GEOLOGIA

PARC ZOOLOGIC

Mercaders
MUSEU PICASSO

Ribera
Marquès
Pas.

Circumval·lació
Aiguader

PALAU DEL MARQUÈS DE LLIÓ
MUSEU BARBIER-MUELLER
Pas. del Born
Comerç
Marquès de l'Argentera

Doctor
Aiguader

CAPILLA DE SANTA ÀGATA

El Xampanyet
Ten's

ESTACIÓ DE FRANCA

Doctor

Jaume 1
Estimar

Argenteria

Via Laietana
Manresa
Nau
Av. del
de

Aiguader
Aiguader

Senyor Parellada

STA MARÍA DEL MAR

Pl. del Palau
DUANA NOVA

Doctor

Doctor

Pas. de Salvat Papasseit

Mercer H. Barcelona

LA LLOTJA

Pl. d'Isabel
Barceloneta

Balboa

Ginebra

Oaxaca

Pl. Antónío López

Ginebra

Dòria

Marítim

Avinyó

Colom

Pl. de Pau Vila

Pas.

LA BARCELONETA

Pitarra

The Serras

MARINA

MUSEU D'HISTÒRIA DE CATALUNYA

Andrea

Pas.

LA MERCÉ

Joan

Cervera

Gúiter

Francesc

Almirall

B 10

de

Almirall
Aixada

IMAX

Borbó

L'AQUÁRIUM

Suquet de l'Almirall

Elx

Torre d'Alta Mar

MAREMAGNUM

Moll

PORT VELL

Moll Barcelona

0   200 m

587

Majide

X ᗢ AC

Tallers 48 ⊠ *08001 –* Ⓜ *Universitat –* 𝒞 *930 16 37 81*   Plan: **E2**
– www.majide.es – Closed 7 days Christmas, 21 days August, Sunday dinner and Monday lunch
Menu 16/65 € – Carte 30/45 €
• Japanese • Simple •
A Japanese restaurant that follows the path of the award-winning Koy Shunka, which is part of the same group. As the kitchen is completely open view, we recommend a seat at the bar.

Montiel

X AC ⇔

Flassaders 19 ⊠ *08003 –* Ⓜ *Jaume I –* 𝒞 *932 68 37 29*   Plan: **G1**
– www.restaurantmontiel.com – Closed Tuesday
Menu 30/70 € – Carte 41/71 €
• Modern cuisine • Simple •
This gastronomic restaurant is in the bohemian Born district. It surprises guests thanks to the creativity of its tasting menus, which are always meticulously presented and come with a wine pairing option.

Oaxaca

X ᗢ & AC

Pla del Palau 19 ⊠ *08002 –* Ⓜ *Barceloneta*   Plan: **G2**
– 𝒞 *933 19 00 64 – www.oaxacacuinamexicana.com*
Menu 48 € – Carte 35/55 €
• Mexican • Fashionable •
Discover authentic Mexican cuisine in a restaurant with a modern and informal ambience, which nonetheless manages to retain a typical flavour of Mexico. The mezcalería is well worth a visit!

Pitarra

X AC ⇔

Avinyó 56 ⊠ *08002 –* Ⓜ *Liceu –* 𝒞 *933 01 16 47*   Plan: **G2**
– www.restaurantpitarra.cat – Closed 6-26 August, Sunday and bank holidays dinner
Menu 15/55 € – Carte 33/50 €
• Traditional cuisine • Traditional décor •
It was in these premises that Frederic Soler, a leading figure from the world of Catalan theatre, once had his watchmaker's shop. Dining rooms with an old-fashioned feel, including two rooms for private parties. Traditional cuisine.

Suquet de l'Almirall

X ᗢ & AC

passeig Joan de Borbó 65 ⊠ *08003 –* 𝒞 *932 21 62 33*   Plan: **H3**
– www.suquetdelalmirall.com – Closed Sunday dinner and Monday
Menu 22/37 € – Carte 30/50 €
• Traditional cuisine • Traditional décor •
A restaurant boasting a maritime inspired decor and a very pleasant outdoor terrace. Extensive menu of traditional cuisine, including a varied selection of fish and rice dishes.

Ten's

X ᗢ & AC

av. Marqués de l'Argentera 11 ⊠ *08003*   Plan: **G2**
– Ⓜ *Barceloneta –* 𝒞 *933 19 22 22 – www.tensbarcelona.com*
Menu 48/62 € – Carte 22/36 €
• Modern cuisine • Fashionable •
A gastro-bar with a thoroughly modern look that is dominated by varying tones of white. Its concise menu, overseen by the TV chef Jordi Cruz, features tapas and half portions. These cleverly combine traditional and more cutting-edge cuisine.

Kak Koy

9/ AC

Ripoll 16 ⊠ *08002 –* Ⓜ *Urquinaona –* 𝒞 *933 02 84 14*   Plan: **F2**
– www.kakkoy.com – Closed Christmas, Holy Week, August, Sunday and Tuesday lunch
Tapa 6 € **Ración** approx. 15 €
• Japanese • Cosy •
Japanese cuisine with a Mediterranean influence that has adopted the tapas and *raciones* concept. The traditional Japanese robata grill takes centre stage here.

Rosal 34

Roser 34 ⊠ 08004 – Ⓜ Paral.lel – ℰ 933 24 90 46
Plan: **E3**
– www.rosal34.com – Closed 5-19 September, Sunday and Monday lunch
Tapa 5 € **Ración** approx. 12 €
• Creative • Rustic •
Rosal 34 is located in an old family wine cellar, where the rustic stonework blends in with the contemporary decor. Seasonal dishes plus interesting tapas with a creative touch.

El Xampanyet

Montcada 22 ⊠ 08003 – Ⓜ Jaume I – ℰ 933 19 70 03
Plan: **G2**
– Closed 15 days January, Holy Week, August, Sunday dinner and Monday
Tapa 2 € **Ración** approx. 10 €
• Traditional cuisine • Traditional décor •
This old tavern with a long-standing family tradition is decorated with typical azulejo tiles. Varied selection of tapas with an emphasis on cured meats and high-quality canned products.

W Barcelona

pl. de la Rosa dels Vents 1 (Moll De Llevant) ⊠ 08039
Plan: **C3**
– ℰ 932 95 28 00 – www.w-barcelona.com
406 rm – ♦299/1025 € ♦♦299/1025 € – ⊈ 22 € – 67 suites
• Business • Design •
This hotel designed by Ricardo Bofill is located in the city's port area. It comprises of two glass buildings: one a cube, the other a huge sail rising impressively above the Mediterranean. It has extensive spa facilities. The contemporary looking gastronomic restaurant offers an à la carte menu based around high quality products.
⫶○ **Bravo 24** – See restaurant listing

H1898

La Rambla 109 ⊠ 08002 – Ⓜ Catalunya
Plan: **F2**
– ℰ 935 52 95 52 – www.hotel1898.com
166 rm – ♦180/600 € ♦♦180/600 € – ⊈ 24 € – 3 suites
• Chain • Historic •
The decor in this hotel occupying the former Tabacos de Filipinas headquarters is a mix of the traditional and contemporary. Spa area, guestrooms offering the very best amenities, plus a rooftop solarium with views of the city. This resolutely contemporary restaurant offers an à la carte menu of international dishes.

Mercer H. Barcelona

Lledó 7 ⊠ 08002 – Ⓜ Jaume I – ℰ 933 10 74 80
Plan: **G2**
– www.mercerbarcelona.com
27 rm ⊈ – ♦400/1010 € ♦♦400/1010 € – 1 suite
• Palace • Historic •
A hotel with lots of history, occupying a palace remodelled by Rafael Moneo but which has retained vestiges of the past, including walls from the Roman city of Barcino. Plenty of artistic detail, superb guestrooms and an attractive rooftop sun terrace.

The Serras

Passeig de Colom 9 ⊠ 08002 – Ⓜ Drassanes
Plan: **G2**
– ℰ 931 69 18 68 – www.hoteltheserrasbarcelona.com
28 rm ⊈ – ♦250/450 € ♦♦350/550 €
• Luxury • Elegant •
Luxury, practicality and pure lines at this hotel opposite the gigantic Prawn designed by Javier Mariscal. It offers well-equipped guestrooms, a sun terrace on the roof with superb views of the port, and an informal restaurant.

SPAIN - BARCELONA

España 🏠🏠🏠   ♿ 🅰🅒 🕸

Sant Pau 9 ✉ *08001 –* Ⓜ *Liceu*   Plan: **F2**
– 🕿 935 50 00 00 – www.hotelespanya.com
83 rm – ♦140/315 € ♦♦140/315 € – ⊊ 17 €
• Chain • Cosy •

Located right in the heart of the old quarter and easy to find since it occupies a 19C building next to the Liceu. Pleasant lounge area with some historical details, plus comfortable, albeit rather small guestrooms with a contemporary design.

Ⓐ **Fonda España** – See restaurant listing

Grand H. Central 🏠🏠🏠   🛁 ⊼ ♿ 🅰🅒 🕸

Via Laietana 30 ✉ *08003 –* Ⓜ *Jaume I*   Plan: **F2**
– 🕿 932 95 79 00 – www.grandhotelcentral.com
140 rm – ♦210/751 € ♦♦210/751 € – ⊊ 26 € – 7 suites
• Traditional • Contemporary •

A hotel with a contemporary look and welcoming facilities. Here, guests will find bedrooms with lots of attention to detail, and interesting public spaces such as the rooftop Sky Bar, with a chill-out zone and panoramic pool, the modern City Bar, and the multi-functional Gallery.

Neri 🏠🏠🏠   ❀ ♿ 🅰🅒

Sant Sever 5 ✉ *08002 –* Ⓜ *Liceu*   Plan: **F2**
– 🕿 933 04 06 55 – www.hotelneri.com
21 rm – ♦300/600 € ♦♦300/600 € – ⊊ 27 € – 1 suite
• Historic • Modern •

Located just a few steps from the cathedral in an impressive setting and occupying two historic buildings, one a medieval palace whose origins date back to the 12C. Here, you will find guestrooms high on detail, an attractive rooftop terrace, plus a stylish restaurant.

Ohla Barcelona 🏠🏠🏠   🛁 ♿ 🅰🅒 🕸

Via Laietana 49 ✉ *08003 –* Ⓜ *Urquinaona*   Plan: **F1**
– 🕿 933 41 50 50 – www.ohlabarcelona.com
74 rm ⊊ **–** ♦230/460 € ♦♦230/460 €
• Boutique hotel • Contemporary •

Located in the heart of the city, behind a fine neo-Classical façade adorned with unique eye sculptures by the artist Frederic Amat, this hotel is a great choice for visitors to the city. Contemporary bedrooms featuring designer detail, plus a roof terrace with impressive views and an attractive chill-out bar.

❀ **Caelis** – See restaurant listing

SOUTH of AV. DIAGONAL   PLAN III

❀❀❀   **Lasarte** – Hotel Monument H.   XxxX 🕸 ♿ 🅰🅒 ⇔ 🍷
Mallorca 259 ✉ *08008 –* Ⓜ *Passeig de Gràcia*   Plan: **K2**
– 🕿 934 45 32 42 – www.restaurantlasarte.com
– Closed 1-9 January, Holy Week, 21 days August, Sunday, Monday and bank holidays
Menu 195/225 € – Carte 105/145 €
• Creative • Design •

This impeccable contemporary-style restaurant is constantly changing and has the personal stamp of Martín Berasategui and his team. The original and imaginative cuisine bears the innovative hallmark of the chef, whose creativity is evident in the à la carte options and tasting menus alike.

➔ Cigala y colinabo, dado de consomé de jarrete y limón. Pichón a la brasa, picadita cítrica de alcaparras, oliva negra, salsa ahumada de zanahoria. Crema helada de mandarina con Maria Luisa, gelée de naranja y perlas de limón.

SPAIN - BARCELONA

Moments – Hotel Mandarin Oriental Barcelona · XxxX ⇔ & 🖭

passeig de Gràcia 38-40 ⊠ *08007*
Plan: **K2**
– Ⓜ *Passeig de Gràcia* – ℰ *931 51 87 81* – *www.mandarinoriental.com*
– *Closed 14-30 January, 30 August-13 September, Sunday and Monday*
Menu 77/171 € – Carte 105/130 €
• Creative • Design •
Accessed via the hotel lobby, Moments stands out for its design, including a private chef's table. Trained in the famous Sant Pau restaurant, Raül Balam conjures up top-notch creative cuisine, which respects flavours, showcases textures and is able to reinterpret tradition through contemporary eyes.
→ Arroz caldoso de colas de gamba, homenaje a los pescadores de Sant Pol de Mar. Pluma de cerdo ibérico con bizcocho de avellanas, garbanzos y orejones de melocotón. Banana split 2.0.

Disfrutar · XX & 🖭

Villarroel 163 ⊠ *08036* – Ⓜ *Hospital Clinic*
Plan: **J2**
– ℰ *933 48 68 96* – *www.disfrutarbarcelona.com* – *Closed 24 December-8 January, 3-12 March, 6-21 August, Saturday and Sunday*
Menu 110/180 € – *(tasting menu only)*
• Creative • Design •
Creativity, high technical skill, fantasy and good taste are the hallmarks of the three chefs here. They conjure up a true gastronomic experience via several tasting menus in a simple, contemporary space with an open-view kitchen. The name of the restaurant, which translates as 'enjoy', says it all!
→ Panchino relleno de caviar y crema agria. Secuencia de suquet. Elaboraciones de pistacho.

Enigma · XxX ⇔ & 🖭

Sepúlveda 38-40 ⊠ *08015* – Ⓜ *Plaza España*
Plan: **J3**
– *www.enigmaconcept.es* – *Closed 2 weeks Christmas, Holy Week, 3 weeks August, Sunday and Monday*
Menu 220 € – *(dinner only except Saturday) (booking essential) (tasting menu only)*
• Creative • Design •
A truly incomparable restaurant with a modular layout and ground-breaking design that is aiming to become the gastronomic standard-bearer for the "El Barri" group under the helm of Albert Adrià. Enigma offers a dining experience in seven zones or rooms, culminating in "41º" at the end of the meal. Online bookings open.
→ Gamba atemperada con jugo de sus cabezas. Espardenya fileteada con gel de su piel. Praliné de avellanas con maíz liofilizado.

Angle · XxX & 🖭 ⇔ 🚗

Aragó 214 ⊠ *08011* – Ⓜ *Universitat*
Plan: **K2**
– ℰ *932 16 77 77* – *www.anglebarcelona.com*
Menu 50/100 € – *(tasting menu only)*
• Modern cuisine • Minimalist •
Located on the first floor of the Hotel Cram, Angle has a minimalist look dominated by the presence of large white curtains. The creative cooking here demonstrates a high level of technical skill and is influenced by the very best seasonal products. This is in keeping with the philosophy of chef Jordi Cruz who brings inspiration to every dish.
→ Yema de huevo curada en agua de mar con selección de ibéricos. Pintada glaseada con foie-gras, berenjena y ajo negro. Helado de plátano caramelizado con bizcochito de jengibre y chocolate especiado.

Cinc Sentits (Jordi Artal) · XxX 🖭

Aribau 58 ⊠ *08011* – Ⓜ *Universitat* – ℰ *933 23 94 90*
Plan: **K2**
– *www.cincsentits.com* – *Closed 15 days August, Sunday, Monday and bank holidays*
Menu 100/120 € – *(tasting menu only)*
• Creative • Minimalist •
The stylish setting and layout is matched by a truly unique minimalist look, with a predominance of dark tones. You won't find à la carte dishes here as the focus is on enticing set menus that change frequently. Inventive cuisine centred on select Catalan ingredients.
→ Patata a la sal, verduras y mayonesa de atún. Foie-gras caramelizado sobre cama de trinxat. Espárrago en texturas con estragón, limón y avellanas.

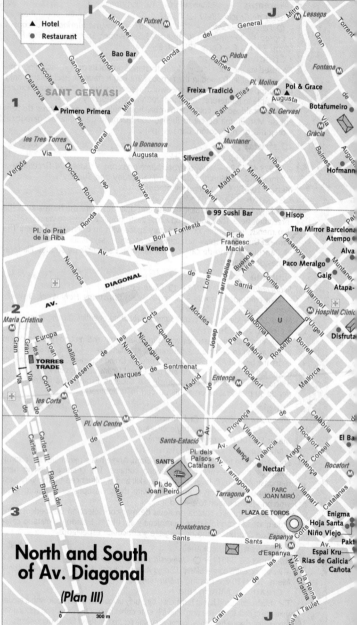

**North and South
of Av. Diagonal**

(Plan III)

0   300 m

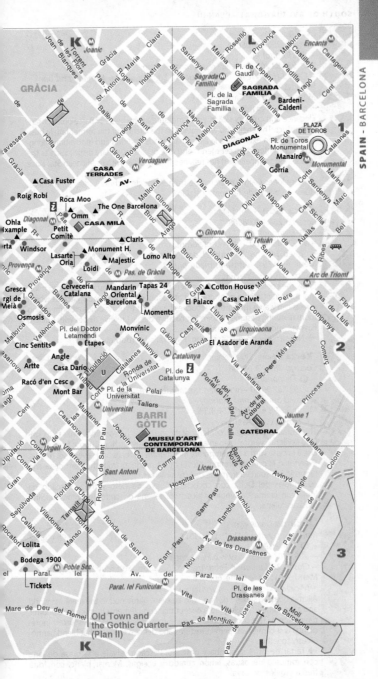

GRÀCIA

Joanic

Joan Blanques

de les Flors

Torrent

Gràcia

Maria

Roger

Antoni

Industria

Claret

Sardenya

Marina

Rosselló

Provença

Mallorca

Encants

Castillejos

Cartagena

Pl. de Gaudí

Sagrada Família

SAGRADA FAMILIA

Padilla

Cent

Aragó

de

l'Olla

Travessera

de Gràcia

Pas.

St. Antoni

de

Bailén

Córsega

sant

Girona

Rosselló

Provença

Joan

Nápols

Flor

Mallorca

València

Sardenya

Sicilia

Aragó

Pl. de la Sagrada Família

SAGRADA FAMILIA

DIAGONAL

Bardeni-Caldeni

Marina

Manairó

PLAZA DE TOROS

Pl. de Toros Monumental

Catalanes

1

Verdaguer

CASA TERRADES

AV.

▲ Casa Fuster

Roig Robí

Roca Moo

The One Barcelona

Omm

Petit Comitè

CASA MILÀ

Ohla Eixample

Diagonal

Rda

Pta

Windsor

Lasarte Oria

Loidi

▲ Monument H.

▲ Majestic

▲ Claris

Lomo Alto

Pas. de Gràcia

Girona

Bruc

Girona

Bailén

Roger

Consell

Diputació

Nápols

Caspe

Sardenya

Girona

Tetuán

de

Sant

Joan

Via

Ausias

Ali

Ribes

Arc de Triomf

Gorria

Corts

Sicilia

Monumental

Marina

Marc

Bel

Manairó

Cresca

rgi de Meià

Osmosis

Cinc Sentits

Artte

Racó d'en Cesc

Mont Bar

Angle

Casa Dario

Cerveceria Catalana

Granados

Balmes

València

Mallorca

Provença

Aragó

Mandarin Oriental Barcelona

Tapas 24

Moments

El Palace

Lluria

Ausias

Casp

Claris

Tapas 24

▲ Cotton House

Casa Calvet

St.

de

Urquinaona

El Asador de Aranda

Gran

Pau

Pere

Marc

Pas. de Lluis

Companys

Pl. del Doctor Letamendi

Monvínic

Etapes

Catalanes

Ronda de la Universitat

Gràcia

Catalunya

Ronda

Pl. de Catalunya

2

Casanova

Muntaner

Comte

Urgell

Villarroel

Diputació

Gran Via

Cent

Aragó

Pl. de la Universitat

Universitat

Casanova

Joaquín

Costa

Corts

Pelai

Tallers

BARRI GÒTIC

La

Av. del Àngel

Portal de l'Àngel

Palla

Av. de la Catedral

CATEDRAL

St. Pere Més Baix

Via Laietana

Princesa

Jaume 1

Via Laietana

Comerç

Lolita

Bodega 1900

Tickets

Rocafort

Calàbria

Viladomat

Manso

Comte

Borrell

Tamarit

Urgell

Floridablanca

Ronda

de

Sant

Pau

Sant Antoni

Carme

Hospital

Sant Pau

Ronda de Sant Pau

Nou de la Rambla

Poble Sec

Paral.

lel

Av.

del

Paral.

lel

Paral. lel Funicular

Vita

MUSEU D'ART CONTEMPORANI DE BARCELONA

Liceu

Sant Pau

La Rambla

Av. de les Drassanes

Drassanes

Ferràn

Avinyó

Ample

Pas.

Colom

3

Sepúlveda

Mare de Deu del Remei

Old Town and the Gothic Quarter (Plan II)

K

Pl. de les Drassanes

Pas. de Josep

Moll de Barcelona

Vita

i

Vila

Pas. de Montjuïc

L

❀ **Gaig** (Carles Gaig)　　　　　　　　　　XxX 舘 ᠖ ⅍ ⇔
Còrsega 200 ✉ *08036*　　　　　　　　　　　　Plan: **J2**
– ⓜ *Hospital Clinic*
– ☎ *934 53 20 20 – www.restaurantgaig.com*
– *Closed Holy Week, 10 days August, Sunday dinner, Monday and bank holidays dinner*
Menu 68/120 € – Carte 65/90 €
• Modern cuisine • Elegant •
Elegance and culinary skill in equal measure in the heart of Barcelona's Ensanche district. The chef, who was trained in the kitchen of the former family business, offers an extensive à la carte that blends tradition and innovation, alongside highly interesting set menus and one or two legendary dishes such as the famous Gaig cannelloni. It has retained its love affair with its Michelin Star since 1993!
→ Canelones Gaig con crema de trufa. Arroz de pichón y setas de Burdeos. Nuestra versión de la crema catalana.

❀ **Roca Moo** – Hotel Omm　　　　　　　XxX 舘 ᠖ ⅍ 荐
Rosselló 265 ✉ *08008*　　　　　　　　　　　Plan: **K1**
– ⓜ *Diagonal*
– ☎ *934 45 40 00 – www.hotelomm.com*
– *Closed 14 days January, 21 days August, Sunday* and Monday
Menu 49/175 € – *(tasting menu only)*
• Creative • Trendy •
Enjoy the cooking of the Roca brothers to the full in this large, urban and informal restaurant with a cosmopolitan atmosphere, an open-view kitchen where guests can watch the finishing touches being put to dishes, plus a bright dining room featuring designer-inspired decorative detail. Creative dishes with marked flavours and original presentation.
→ Nuestro huerto mediterráneo. Raya rallada. Todo el olivo.

❀ **Xerta** – Hotel Ohla Eixample　　　　　XxX ᠖ ⅍ 🚗
Corsega 289 ✉ *08008*　　　　　　　　　　　Plan: **K1-2**
– ⓜ *Diagonal*
– ☎ *937 37 90 80 – www.xertarestaurant.com*
– *Closed Sunday and Monday*
Menu 35/98 € – Carte 56/85 €
• Creative • Design •
This restaurant is elegant, contemporary and oozes personality thanks to its striking skylights, vertical garden and large open-view kitchen. Choose from a concise à la carte with a contemporary Mediterranean focus and several set menus. Everything is centred around the very best products from the Ebro delta and fantastic fish sourced from the daily fish market.
→ Angulas del Delta con cocochas, huevo de pato y trufa. Pescado de lonja con crema de hinojo y alcachofa rellena de crema de marisco. Simbiosis catalana.

❀ **Alkimia** (Jordi Vilà)　　　　　　　　　　XX 舘 ᠖ ⅍
Ronda San Antoni 41, 1º ✉ *08011*　　　　　Plan II: **E2**
– ⓜ *Universitat*
– ☎ *932 07 61 15 – www.alkimia.cat*
– *Closed 22 January-4 February, 13-26 August, Saturday and Sunday*
Menu 98/155 € – Carte 60/90 €
• Modern cuisine • Design •
Alkimia boasts a striking design, with an avant-garde nod to the maritime world and a brand-new "unplugged" concept that complements its main gastronomic dining room. The contemporary cuisine (based around locally sourced ingredients) is sublime, with perfect textures and defined flavours that blend harmoniously together.
→ Tartar de cigalas, gamba y pescado. Pescado salvaje a la brasa de leña con romesco de ostras, limón curado y acelgas. Menjar blanc, con fruta fresca y gelée de cava.

Nectari (Jordi Esteve) XX AC ⇔

València 28 ⊠ *08015 –* Ⓜ *Tarragona –* ℰ *932 26 87 18*   Plan: **J3**
– www.nectari.es – Closed 15 days August and Sunday
Menu 35/75 € – Carte 55/85 €
• Modern cuisine • Classic décor •
A cosy setting for this completely family-run operation with two small contemporary-style dining rooms and one private area. The owner-chef has put together a menu with a marked Mediterranean bias, enhanced by pleasing creative and innovative touches.
→ Arroz meloso de crustáceos con aire de lima. San Pedro con puerros infusionados y espárragos trigueros. Coulant de chocolate con sorbete cítrico.

Pakta XX & AC

Lleida 5 ⊠ *08004 –* Ⓜ *Espanya –* ℰ *936 24 01 77*   Plan: **J3**
– www.pakta.es – Closed Christmas, Holy Week, 3 weeks August, Sunday and Monday
Carte 45/70 € – *(dinner only except Saturday) (booking essential)*
• Peruvian • Design •
A colourful, contemporary and informal restaurant that evokes Peruvian culture. This is evident both in its name (that means 'together' or 'union' in the Quechua language) and its decor with walls and ceilings adorned with striking fabrics. However, the cuisine is very much Japanese, showcasing lots of technical prowess and meticulous presentation. Bookings need to be made online.
→ Ceviche clásico. Salmonete con escabeche nikkei de ají amarillo. Humita.

Hoja Santa (Paco Méndez) ✗ & AC

av. Mistral 54 ⊠ *08015 –* Ⓜ *Espanya –* ℰ *933 48 21 94*   Plan: **J3**
– www.hojasanta.es – Closed 24 December-15 January, 15-23 April, 13-26 August, Tuesday except April-October, Sunday and Monday
Menu 120/140 €
– Carte 56/84 € – (dinner only except Sunday November-March and Saturday)
• Mexican • Design •
Guests can enjoy fine Mexican cuisine at this restaurant named after an indigenous bush. The ambience is relaxed and contemporary, featuring decor made up of ethnic and colonial details. The enticing combination of flavours and, above all, spicy dishes adapted to a European palate, ensure a thoroughly enjoyable experience.
→ Nube de tequila y naranja sangrita. Mole encacahuatado con pichón madurado ocho días. Ecosistema de cacao.

Tickets ⁹/ & AC

av. del Paral.lel 164 ⊠ *08015 –* Ⓜ *Espanya*   Plan: **K3**
– www.ticketsbar.es – Closed 24 December-16 January, Holy Week, 13-28 August, Sunday and Monday
Tapa 12 € – *(dinner only except Saturday) (booking essential)*
• Creative • Friendly •
A unique restaurant with lots of colour and several bar counters. The innovative cuisine on offer here, prepared in front of diners, plays homage to the legendary dishes that were once created at El Bulli. Bookings can only be made via its website.
→ Gamba marinada a la sal helada. Ostra con salsa de kétchup. El cheesecake de Tickets.

Casa Calvet XxX & AC ⇔

Casp 48 ⊠ *08010 –* Ⓜ *Urquinaona –* ℰ *934 12 40 12*   Plan: **L2**
– www.casacalvet.es – Closed Sunday dinner and bank holidays
Menu 38/68 € – Carte 49/68 €
• Traditional cuisine • Elegant •
This restaurant occupies a Modernist building designed by Gaudí. It once served as a textile factory and the offices have been converted into private dining rooms. A mix of classic Catalan dishes for à la carte dining alongside good set menus.

SPAIN - BARCELONA

Petit Comitè
XxX & AC ⟷

passatge de la Concepció 13 ⊠ *08007 –* Ⓜ *Diagonal*   Plan: **K2**
– ℰ 936 33 76 27 – www.petitcomite.cat – Closed 21 days August
Menu 52 € – Carte 35/60 €
• Regional cuisine • Design •
This contemporary restaurant is decorated with lots of dishes. The focus is on
local cuisine prepared using Spanish ingredients, including enticing themed
daily specials.

Racó d'en Cesc
XxX ৪৪ 🍽 & AC ⟷

Diputació 201 ⊠ *08011 –* Ⓜ *Universitat*   Plan: **K2**
– ℰ 934 51 60 02 – www.elracodencesc.com – Closed Holy Week, August,
Sunday and bank holidays
Menu 40 € – Carte 40/53 €
• Modern cuisine • Classic décor •
A restaurant with a small terrace, a bistro-style section and a classic dining room,
with a different creative Catalan menu in each. A wide choice of craft beers is
also available.

Rías de Galicia
XxX ৪৪ 🍽 AC

Lleida 7 ⊠ *08004 –* Ⓜ *Espanya – ℰ 934 24 81 52*   Plan: **J3**
– www.riasdegalicia.com
Carte 65/80 €
• Seafood • Classic décor •
Goose barnacles, lamprey, oysters and tuna are among the many culinary treasures from the Atlantic and Mediterranean on offer here. The wine cellar is
home to some impressive labels and vintages.

Windsor
XxX ৪৪ 🍽 & AC ⟷ 🚗

Còrsega 286 ⊠ *08008 –* Ⓜ *Diagonal – ℰ 932 37 75 88*   Plan: **K2**
– www.restaurantwindsor.com – Closed 6-10 December, 1-10 January,
Holy Week, 5-27 August and Sunday
Menu 30/99 € – Carte 50/74 €
• Modern cuisine • Classic décor •
This restaurant, with its updated classic decor, is enhanced by an exquisite ter-
race and several dining rooms that allow for different configurations. Contem-
porary Catalan cuisine.

Asador de Aranda
XX & AC ⟷

Londres 94 ⊠ *08036 –* Ⓜ *Hospital Clínic*   Plan: **L2**
– ℰ 934 14 67 90 – www.asadordearanda.com
Menu 42/60 € – Carte 38/55 €
• Meats and grills • Traditional décor •
This spacious restaurant is decorated in Castilian style with a wood oven in full
view of the dining room. Cooking is traditional, with a particular focus on roast
dishes.

Atempo – Hotel The Mirror Barcelona
XX & AC

Còrsega 255 ⊠ *08036 –* Ⓜ *Provença – ℰ 932 02 86 85*   Plan: **J2**
– www.atemporestaurant.com – Closed Sunday dinner and Monday
Carte 32/45 €
• International • Contemporary décor •
This new bistro, with its black and white decor reminiscent of The Great Gatsby,
is the new vintage-style offering by chef Jordi Cruz. International and Mediterranean cuisine with an innovative touch.

Casa Darío
XX & AC ⟷

Consell de Cent 256 ⊠ *08011 –* Ⓜ *Universitat*   Plan: **K2**
– ℰ 934 53 31 35 – www.casadario.com – Closed 15 days August, Sunday
dinner and Monday
Menu 35 € – Carte 40/75 €
• Galician • Classic décor •
A well-established restaurant with a good reputation for the quality of its ingre-
dients. The restaurant has a private bar, three dining rooms and three private
rooms. Galician dishes and seafood are the house specialities.

Gorría
XX 🕮 ⇄
Plan: **L1**

Diputació 421 ✉ *08013 –* Ⓜ *Monumental*
– ☎ *932 45 11 64 – www.restaurantegorria.com*
– Closed Holy Week, August, Sunday, Monday dinner and bank holidays
dinner
Carte 45/65 €

• Basque • Rustic •

A well-established Basque restaurant with rustic style decor. The excellent menu is complemented by an extensive wine list. Service is attentive.

Loidi
XX & 🕮 🚗
Plan: **K2**

Mallorca 248 ✉ *08008 –* Ⓜ *Passeig de Gràcia*
– ☎ *934 92 92 92 – www.loidi.com – Closed 21 days August,*
Sunday in July, Sunday dinner and bank holidays dinner the rest of the
year
Menu 29/55 € – *(tasting menu only)*

• Modern cuisine • Friendly •

In this restaurant, the innovative cuisine on offer is light, fast and reasonably priced. Several menus are available, all created under the tutelage of famous chef Martín Berasategui.

Manairó
XX & 🕮
Plan: **L1**

Diputació 424 ✉ *08013 –* Ⓜ *Monumental*
– ☎ *932 31 00 57 – www.jordiherrera.es – Closed 1-7 January, Sunday and*
bank holidays
Menu 90 € – Carte 56/78 €

• Creative • Contemporary décor •

A unique restaurant, both in terms of its modern decor and intimate lighting. Contemporary, meticulously presented cuisine with its roots in Catalan cooking.

Monvínic
XX 🕸 & 🕮 ⇄
Plan: **K2**

Diputació 249 ✉ *08007 –* Ⓜ *Catalunya*
– ☎ *932 72 61 87 – www.monvinic.com – Closed August, Saturday lunch,*
Sunday and Monday lunch
Menu 20/75 € – Carte 50/70 €

• Modern cuisine • Wine bar •

This restaurant impresses through its contemporary design and philosophy, with everything revolving around the world of wine. A modern take on traditional cuisine, as well as a splendid wine cellar.

Oria – Hotel Monument H.
XX 🕮
Plan: **K2**

passeig de Gràcia 75 ✉ *08008 –* Ⓜ *Passeig de Gràcia*
– ☎ *935 48 20 33 – www.monument-hotel.com*
Menu 40 € – Carte 55/75 €

• Modern cuisine • Design •

Spacious, modern and opening onto the lobby of the hotel, Oria offers updated traditional cooking and a unique "Menú a medida", a menu which can be tailored to your specific budget from 40 euros upwards.

Alvart
X 🕮
Plan: **J2**

Aribau 141 ✉ *08036 –* Ⓜ *Diagonal –* ☎ *934 30 57 58*
– www.alvart.es – Closed Sunday and Monday
Menu 24/66 € – *(tasting menu only)*

• Creative • Contemporary décor •

Through his menus, Àlvar Ayuso, one of Catalonia's most promising young chefs, showcases his culinary philosophy which fully embraces his own personality. His cuisine is based around contemporary, seasonal cooking with the occasional Nordic influence visible in his pickled dishes. The setting and decor are as meticulous as the cuisine.

Artte   X &. AC

Muntaner 83C ✉ *08011 –* Ⓜ *Universitat*   Plan: **K2**
– ℰ 934 54 90 48 – www.artte.es – Closed August, Sunday and Monday
Carte 24/47 €

• Mediterranean cuisine • Design •

An unusual bistro that takes its inspiration from the tea rooms of China. Enjoy an artistic-cum-gastronomic experience that extols the virtues of raw, natural foods and vegetarian dishes.

El Bar   X 🍽 AC

Calabria 118 ✉ *08015 –* Ⓜ *Rocafort – ℰ 934 26 03 82*   Plan: **J3**
– www.elbarbarcelona.com – Closed Sunday dinner and Monday
Menu 22 € – Carte 33/53 €

• Catalan • Tapas bar •

A restaurant that lives up to its name more in terms of its size and simple decor rather than its menu which is both extensive and consistent in quality. Choose from a wide variety of tapas plus a choice of more elaborate dishes.

Espai Kru   X AC ⇄

Lleida 7 ✉ *08004 –* Ⓜ *Espanya – ℰ 934 23 45 70*   Plan: **J3**
– www.espaikru.com – Closed Sunday dinner and Monday
Menu 100 € – Carte 35/60 €

• International • Fashionable •

Located on the first floor of a building, Espai Kru boasts an impressive appearance enhanced by its single space featuring an open-view kitchen, private dining room and cocktail bar. Extensive international and fusion menu, featuring both raw and cooked ingredients.

Etapes   X 🍽 AC ⇄

Enrique Granados 10 ✉ *08007 – ℰ 933 23 69 14*   Plan: **K2**
– www.etapes.cat – Closed Saturday lunch and Sunday lunch
Menu 16/60 € – Carte 40/60 €

• Modern cuisine • Simple •

A restaurant with an informal, contemporary look and an elongated dining room in which iron, wood and glass provide the decorative backdrop. Cuisine with a contemporary edge but with its roots in traditional cooking.

Gresca   X AC

Provença 230 ✉ *08036 –* Ⓜ *Diagonal – ℰ 934 51 61 93*   Plan: **K2**
– www.gresca.net – Closed 7 days Christmas, Holy Week, 15 days August, Saturday lunch and Sunday
Menu 21/65 € – Carte 35/65 €

• Modern cuisine • Family •

Much talked about in Barcelona thanks to its relaxed atmosphere and friendly service. Find attractive contemporary cuisine including enticing set menus.

Lomo Alto   X &. AC

Aragó 283-285 ✉ *08007 –* Ⓜ *Passeig de Gràcia*   Plan: **K2**
– ℰ 935 19 30 00 – www.lomoalto.barcelona – Closed 6-19 August
Menu 40/125 € – Carte 40/70 €

• Meats and grills • Friendly •

A mecca for meat-lovers laid out on two floors (Lomo Bajo and Lomo Alto) with impressive vaulted windows. The mature beef is sourced from old Iberian breeds and cooked on the grill.

Mano Rota   X AC ⇄

Creus dels Molers 4 ✉ *08004 –* Ⓜ *Poble Sec*   Plan II : **E3**
– ℰ 931 64 80 41 – www.manorota.com – Closed 31 December-7 January, Saturday lunch and Sunday
Menu 60 € – Carte 33/48 €

• Modern cuisine • Neighbourhood •

Mano Rota boasts an industrial feel and champions a specific concept: a restaurant with a bar. Its interesting menu includes traditional and contemporary recipes, as well as international dishes from Peru and Japan.

SPAIN - BARCELONA

Osmosis ✗ AC

Aribau 100 ⊠ 08036 – Ⓜ Diagonal – ℰ 934 54 52 01 Plan: **K2**
– www.restauranteosmosis.com – Closed 24-29 December and Sunday
Menu 25/68 € – *(tasting menu only)*
• Modern cuisine • Contemporary décor •
A restaurant with a pleasant, modern ambience arranged over two floors. The contemporary tasting menu, available in both long and short formats, is created using seasonal, market-fresh ingredients.

Sergi de Meià ✗ ꜛ AC

Aribau 106 ⊠ 08036 – Ⓜ Diagonal – ℰ 931 25 57 10 Plan: **K2**
– www.restaurantsergidemeia.cat – Closed Sunday and Monday
Menu 23/68 € – Carte 40/70 €
• Regional cuisine • Simple •
The owner-chef unashamedly promotes 100% Catalan cuisine. He rediscovers the flavours of yesteryear and always focuses on organic and locally sourced products.

Bodega 1900 ☙/ 🍴 AC

Tamarit 91 ⊠ 08015 – Ⓜ Poble Sec – ℰ 933 25 26 59 Plan: **K3**
– www.bodega1900.com – Closed Christmas, Holy Week, 3 weeks August, Sunday and Monday
Ración approx. 8 €
• Traditional cuisine • Neighbourhood •
This restaurant has all the charm of an old-fashioned grocery store. The small menu features grilled dishes, Iberian specialities and homemade preserves, all of excellent quality.

Mont Bar ☙/ 🍴 🍴 ꜛ AC ⇔

Diputació 220 ⊠ 08011 – Ⓜ Universitat Plan: **K2**
– ℰ 933 23 95 90 – www.montbar.com – Closed 24-26 December and 10-25 January
Tapa 7 € **Ración** approx. 17 €
• Traditional cuisine • Bistro •
This charming and unusual gastro-bar serves traditional cuisine prepared using top quality ingredients. Friendly and professional service.

Atapa-it ☙/ AC

Muntaner 146 ⊠ 08036 – Ⓜ Hospital Clínic Plan: **J2**
– ℰ 934 52 07 82 – www.atapait.com – Closed 15 days August, Sunday dinner, Monday lunch and bank holidays
Tapa 4.50 € **Ración** approx. 13 €
• Regional cuisine • Bistro •
Contemporary-style restaurant with a small bar and two dining rooms, both with an informal feel. It serves modern tapas and small dishes that change depending on market availability.

Cañota ☙/ 🍴 AC

Lleida 7 ⊠ 08002 – Ⓜ Espanya – ℰ 933 25 91 71 Plan: **J3**
– www.casadetapas.com – Closed Sunday dinner and Monday
Tapa 5 € **Ración** approx. 14 €
• Traditional cuisine • Friendly •
A friendly and relaxed ambience in which to enjoy creative cuisine with its roots firmly in tradition but without closing the door to flavours from elsewhere. Almost every dish here has been designed for sharing.

Cervecería Catalana ☙/ 🍴 AC

Mallorca 236 ⊠ 08008 – Ⓜ Diagonal – ℰ 932 16 03 68 Plan: **K2**
Tapa 4 € **Ración** approx. 7 €
• Traditional cuisine • Contemporary décor •
This popular local pub, decorated with racks full of bottles, serves a comprehensive choice of top quality tapas.

Lolita
Tamarit 104 ✉ *08015 –* Ⓜ *Poble Sec –* ☏ *934 24 52 31*   Plan: **K3**
– www.lolitataperia.com – Closed December, Sunday and Monday
Tapa 7 € *– (dinner only except Friday and Saturday)*
• Traditional cuisine • Neighbourhood •
Situated close to the city's exhibition site, this restaurant stands out for its personalised decor. Traditional tapas created using top quality ingredients.

Niño Viejo
av. Mistral 54 ✉ *08015 –* Ⓜ *Poble Sec –* ☏ *933 48 21 94*   Plan: **J3**
– www.ninoviejo.es – Closed 24 December-15 January, 15-23 April,
7-27 August, Tuesday November-24 December and January-March,
Sunday and Monday
Tapa 5 € **Ración** approx. 15 € *– (dinner only except Thursday, Friday and Saturday)*
• Mexican • Exotic décor •
Unusual, lively, colourful and informal – this taco bar with an ethnic feel serves delicious homemade tacos, antojitos and spicy salsas. High quality Mexican cuisine.

Paco Meralgo
Muntaner 171 ✉ *08036 –* Ⓜ *Hospital Clínic*   Plan: **J2**
– ☏ *934 30 90 27 – www.restaurantpacomeralgo.com*
Tapa 5 € **Ración** approx. 11 €
• Traditional cuisine • Mediterranean décor •
The Paco Meralgo has two bars and two separate entrances, although its most impressive feature is its display cabinets filled with fresh, varied, top quality seafood. A private room is also available.

Tapas 24
Diputació 269 ✉ *08007 –* Ⓜ *Passeig de Gràcia*   Plan: **K2**
– ☏ *934 88 09 77 – www.carlesabellan.com*
Tapa 7 € **Ración** approx. 17 €
• Traditional cuisine • Friendly •
A fun tapas restaurant with a long bar where you can see the kitchen team at work, and where renowned chef Carles Abellan pays homage to traditional Catalan cuisine. Don't miss the 'Bikini Comerç 24' sandwich!

Mandarin Oriental Barcelona
passeig de Gràcia 38-40 ✉ *08007*   Plan: **K2**
– Ⓜ *Passeig de Gràcia –* ☏ *931 51 88 88 – www.mandarinoriental.com*
120 rm – †425/725 € ††425/725 € – ⊑ 45 € – 29 suites
• Luxury • Design •
Experience a fusion of luxury, relaxation and pleasure in a building that once served as a bank. Today, the designer interior is highly innovative and cosmopolitan in feel. It features guestrooms offering high levels of comfort, excellent dining options in the lobby, an attractive patio-terrace, and a laid-back rooftop terrace with great views of the city.
❀❀ **Moments** – See restaurant listing

El Palace
Gran Via de les Corts Catalanes 668 ✉ *08010*   Plan: **L2**
– Ⓜ *Urquinaona –* ☏ *935 10 11 30 – www.hotelpalacebarcelona.com*
120 rm – †290/575 € ††290/575 € – ⊑ 29 € – 17 suites
• Luxury • Classic •
This emblematic hotel occupies a historic building that has been restored to re-create the essence of the golden years of the 1920s. Distinguished lounges and superbly equipped guestrooms, the majority of which are classically elegant in feel with some bathrooms inspired by Roman baths!

SPAIN - BARCELONA

Claris
Pau Claris 150 ⊠ *08009* – Ⓜ *Passeig de Gràcia*
– ℰ 934 87 62 62 – www.hotelclaris.com
Plan: **K2**
84 rm ⊡ – ♦250/715 € ♦♦250/715 € – 40 suites
• Traditional • Modern •
This elegant, stately hotel occupies the former Vedruna Palace. It offers a perfect fusion of tradition, cutting-edge design and technology. Impressive archaeological collection. The restaurant of the rooftop offers spectacular views of central Barcelona.

Majestic
passeig de Gràcia 68 ⊠ *08007* – Ⓜ *Passeig de Gràcia*
– ℰ 934 88 17 11 – www.hotelmajestic.es
Plan: **K2**
272 rm – ♦224/800 € ♦♦224/800 € – ⊡ 37 € – 40 suites
• Traditional • Classic •
The Majestic is superbly located and boasts an impressive rooftop terrace with a snack bar and delightful views. It combines excellent service with classic guestrooms offering high levels of comfort. The more functional restaurant alternates between a set menu and à la carte dining in the evening.

Monument H.
passeig de Gràcia 75 ⊠ *08008* – Ⓜ *Passeig de Gràcia*
– ℰ 935 48 20 00 – www.monument-hotel.com
Plan: **K2**
60 rm – ♦291/523 € ♦♦291/523 € – ⊡ 34 € – 24 suites
• Grand Luxury • Contemporary •
Occupying an attractive pre-Modernist building with an enviable location just a few metres from Gaudí's famous La Pedrera building. The impressive interior design features a large lobby with a cocktail bar within it, and guestrooms offering high levels of comfort.
❀❀❀ **Lasarte** • ❍ **Oria** – See restaurant listing

Cotton House
Gran Vía de les Corts Catalanes 670 ⊠ *08010*
– Ⓜ Urquinaona – ℰ 934 50 50 45 – www.hotelcottonhouse.com
Plan: **L2**
83 rm – ♦300/600 € ♦♦300/600 € – ⊡ 28 € – 3 suites
• Chain • Elegant •
As its name suggests, this imposing late-19C building was once the headquarters of the Fundación Textil Algodonera (cotton foundation). Full of character, the hotel offers beautifully kept rooms, albeit some a little on the small side, and creative cuisine based on traditional and international dishes.

The One Barcelona
Provença 277 ⊠ *08037* – Ⓜ *Diagonal* – ℰ *932 14 20 70*
– www.hotelstheone.com
Plan: **K1**
84 rm ⊡ – ♦340/380 € ♦♦340/380 € – 5 suites
• Luxury • Design •
Urban luxury next to the area of the city known as the Quadrat d'Or of Modernism in which marble from Jordan, the finest-quality woods and designer details combine with timeless classic elegance. Enjoy an impressive culinary experience in the Somni restaurant, which has its own separate access.

The Mirror Barcelona
Córsega 255 ⊠ *08036* – Ⓜ *Provença* – ℰ *932 02 86 86*
– www.themirrorbarcelona.com
Plan: **J2**
63 rm ⊡ – ♦108/454 € ♦♦126/472 €
• Business • Design •
The most striking aspect of this hotel is its design, which will appeal to guests keen on this type of minimalist decor. Everything is dominated by mirrors, the colour white and the use of simple, clean lines.
❍ **Atempo** – See restaurant listing

Ohla Eixample

🛏 🗂 ♿ 🅰 ⛨ 🚗

Corsega 289-291 ✉ *08008 –* Ⓜ *Diagonal*   Plan: **K1-2**
– 𝒞 937 37 79 77 – www.ohlaeixample.com
94 rm ⛱ *–* 🛏205/370 € 🛏🛏205/370 €
• Business • Industrial •

A modern hotel with an industrial aesthetic and a surprising façade, which is even more striking at night thanks to an impressive play of light. Designer inspired guestrooms, an interior terrace and an attractive rooftop and chill-out zone on the roof add to its appeal.

⚜ **Xerta** – See restaurant listing

Omm

🛏 ⓟ 🗂 ♿ 🅰 ⛨ 🚗

Rosselló 265 ✉ *08008 –* Ⓜ *Diagonal – 𝒞 934 45 40 00*   Plan: **K1**
– www.hotelomm.com
87 rm *–* 🛏215/490 € 🛏🛏215/490 € *–* ⛱ *27 € –* 4 suites
• Business • Design •

This urban, cutting-edge hotel boasts a spacious lounge area, contemporary bedrooms, and a bar open all day for drinks and informal dining. Other options here include the Ommsession Club with a live DJ, and the rooftop bar with its superb views of the city.

⚜ **Roca Moo** – See restaurant listing

SANT MARTÍ   PLAN I

❀❀ **Enoteca** – Hotel Arts   ✗✗✗ ❀ ☂ 🅰 🚗

Marina 19 ✉ *08005 –* Ⓜ *Ciutadella-Vila Olímpica*   Plan: **C2**
– 𝒞 934 83 81 08 – www.hotelartsbarcelona.com – Closed 2-17 December, 4-19 March, Sunday and Monday
Menu 175 € – Carte 105/133 €
• Modern cuisine • Mediterranean décor •

A bright, fresh look with a penchant for varying tones of white that encapsulates the essence of the Mediterranean. This restaurant, which is under the baton of chef Paco Pérez, enhances the flavours of the Catalan coast with delicate international touches and the occasional nod to Asian fusion cooking.

→ Lenguado meunière, cremoso de patata, azahar, almendra y polos cítricos. Solomillo de wagyu, su jugo, caviar de verduras, chirivía y trufa de verano. Torrija, frutos rojos, miel y merengue.

❀❀ **Dos Cielos** (Sergio y Javier Torres) – Hotel Meliá Barcelona Sky

Pere IV-272, Planta 24 ✉ *08005*   ✗✗✗ ❀ ≤ ☂ ♿ 🅰 ⇆ 🚗
– Ⓜ *Poblenou – 𝒞 933 67 20 70 – www.doscielos.com*   Plan: **D2**
– Closed January, Sunday and Monday
Menu 85 € – Carte 75/100 € – *(dinner only June-15 September)*
• Modern cuisine • Design •

If you are looking for a restaurant with a view it is hard to find a better one, thanks to the bird's eye view of the city's skyline. In this designer setting, the media-savvy Torres brothers offer market-inspired cuisine. It stands out as a result of the successful fusion of top-quality ingredients and refined presentation.

→ Ensalada de tomates de invierno, capellanes y encurtidos. Cabrito a la brasa con crema suave de ajos, salsifí y brotes. Plátano de Canarias, cinco especias y lácteos.

🍴 **Arola** – Hotel Arts   ✗✗ ❀ ≤ ☂ 🅰 ⇆ 🚗

Marina 19 ✉ *08005 –* Ⓜ *Ciutadella-Vila Olímpica*   Plan: **C2**
– 𝒞 934 83 80 90 – www.hotelartsbarcelona.com – Closed 8 January-7 February, Tuesday and Wednesday
Carte 59/108 €
• Creative • Trendy •

Modern, urban and informal, including live music sessions with a DJ. Savour a creative tapas- and ración-based menu either in the dining room or on the chill-out terrace.

⭑○ **Els Pescadors**   XX 🍴 AC
pl. Prim 1 ✉ 08005   Plan: **D2**
– Ⓜ Poblenou
– ✆ 932 25 20 18 – www.elspescadors.com – Closed 22 December-
4 January
Carte 40/74 €
• Seafood • Trendy •
This restaurant has three dining rooms, one in early-20C café style and two with
more modern decor. A generous menu based on fish and seafood with rice
dishes and cod to the fore.

⭑○ **Ají**   X AC 👶 AC
Marina 19 ✉ 08005   Plan: **C2**
– Ⓜ Ciutadella-Vila Olímpica
– ✆ 935 11 97 67 – www.restaurantaji.com – Closed 1-15 January, Sunday
and Monday
Menu 21/45 € – Carte 32/51 €
• Peruvian • Bistro •
The name, which translates as "chilli pepper" in Peruvian Spanish and "taste" in
Japanese, gives us a good insight into the culinary intentions of this restaurant.
Japanese cuisine with a focus on well-defined textures and flavours.

🏨🏨 **Arts**   👗 ≤ 🛁 🕥 🍴 👶 AC 🛁 🚗
Marina 19 ✉ 08005   Plan: **C2**
– Ⓜ Ciutadella-Vila Olímpica
– ✆ 932 21 10 00 – www.hotelartsbarcelona.com
397 rm – †325/535 € ††325/535 € – 86 suites
• Luxury • Design •
Superb in every respect. Occupying one of two glass-fronted towers at the
Olympic port, the hotel's many selling points include its magnificent views and
a stunning, spacious interior including intimate public areas and top-notch
guestrooms with good attention to detail. Extensive lounges adorned with
works of art and exquisite dining options complete the picture.
❀❀ **Enoteca** • ⭑○ **Arola** – See restaurant listing

🏨🏨 **Meliá Barcelona Sky**   👗 ≤ 🛁 🕥 👶 AC 🛁 🚗
Pere IV-272 ✉ 08005   Plan: **D2**
– Ⓜ Poblenou
– ✆ 933 67 20 70 – www.meliahotels.com
249 rm – †150/200 € ††175/225 € – ⊡ 22 € – 9 suites
• Business • Design •
The Meliá's main selling points are its modern, designer inspired lobby, lounge
bar, and contemporary bedrooms, most enjoying splendid views. The good
dining options on offer are complemented by the uniquely decorated restaurant in the lobby with a menu focusing on light and traditional cuisine.
❀❀ **Dos Cielos** – See restaurant listing

NORTH of AV. DIAGONAL   **PLAN III**

❀❀❀ **ABaC** – Hotel ABaC   XxxX 🍴 🍴 AC ✧ 🚗
av. del Tibidabo 1 ✉ 08022   Plan I: **B2**
– Ⓜ Av. Tibidabo
– ✆ 933 19 66 00 – www.abacrestaurant.com
Menu 140/170 € – (tasting menu only)
• Creative • Design •
Discover the unique culinary vision of the bold, media-friendly chef Jordi Cruz
who has raised technical skill, creativity and gastronomic perfection to even
higher levels. His dishes tell stories that are complex yet at the same time
intelligent and understandable, and which evolve in line with seasonal products.
→ Bullabesa de gamba infusionada. Carnes de cordero lechal, asadas, cura-
das y desecadas con compota de ajos. Camomila, leche y barquillo con
toques cítricos y suavemente especiados.

SPAIN - BARCELONA

Via Veneto
XxxX 🕸 AC ⇔

Ganduxer 10 ✉ *08021 –* Ⓜ *Hospital Clínic* Plan: I2
– ℰ 932 00 72 44 – www.viavenetorestaurant.com – Closed August,
Saturday lunch and Sunday
Menu 80/165 € – Carte 75/104 €
• Classic cuisine • Classic décor •
A famous property in attractive Belle Epoque-style with a dining room laid out
on several levels and a number of private dining areas. Impressively updated
classic menu with game in season and interesting tasting menus. Its wine cellar,
featuring around 1 800 labels, is one of the best in Spain.
→ Gamba roja con lima, zanahoria y calabaza. Salmonetes de roca con su
consomé a la soja coreana y hojas de cebolla de Figueres. Manzana de
Girona en texturas con helado y bizcocho de yogur persa.

Hofmann
XxX & AC ⇔

La Granada del Penedès 14-16 ✉ *08006 –* Ⓜ *Diagonal* Plan: J1
– ℰ 932 18 71 65 – www.hofmann-bcn.com – Closed Christmas, Holy
Week, August, Saturday lunch, Sunday and bank holidays
Menu 75/95 € – Carte 52/73 €
• Modern cuisine • Classic décor •
The word gastronomy reflects the great passion of May Hofmann, the founder-
chef who set the guidelines to be followed in one of the country's most influen-
tial restaurant schools. Her daughter Silvia and the current students continue
her work, producing cuisine that is full of creativity.
→ Canelón de ternera con crema trufada y crujiente de parmesano. Rodaballo con toque de brasa, espárragos, royal y su jugo. Crujientes templados
de vainilla con uvas pasas.

Hisop (Oriol Ivern)
XX AC

passatge de Marimon 9 ✉ *08021 –* Ⓜ *Hospital Clínic* Plan: J2
– ℰ 932 41 32 33 – www.hisop.com – Closed 1-8 January, Saturday lunch,
Sunday and bank holidays
Menu 33/92 € – Carte 50/65 €
• Creative • Minimalist •
Because of its size, this modern restaurant offers guests an intimate dining
experience. Enjoy fresh and creative dishes based around traditional recipes in
the minimalist dining room. Everything is prepared with locally sourced and
seasonal products brought together to produce some interesting combinations.
→ Gambas de Palamós con bearnesa. Arroz de pichón con cítricos. Crema
catalana de rebozuelos con pino.

Freixa Tradició
XxX AC

Sant Elies 22 ✉ *08006 –* Ⓜ *Plaça Molina* Plan: J1
– ℰ 932 09 75 59 – www.freixatradicio.com – Closed Holy Week, 21 days
August, Sunday dinner and Monday
Menu 25/50 € – Carte 34/49 €
• Regional cuisine • Design •
Run by the couple that own it, Freixa Tradició has developed into one of the
city's gastronomic institutions since it opened over 30 years ago. In the minima-
list-style dining room you can savour delicious and well-prepared traditional
Catalan cuisine created using a whole host of seasonal ingredients.

Vivanda
X 🍽 & AC ⇔

Major de Sarrià 134 ✉ *08017 –* Ⓜ *Reina Elisenda* Plan I: A2
– ℰ 932 03 19 18 – www.vivanda.cat – Closed Sunday dinner and Monday
Carte 25/37 €
• Traditional cuisine • Cosy •
A unique restaurant offering a traditional menu centred around small dishes
(slightly larger than half raciones) advertised as *platos del mes* (dishes of the
month). Attractive tree-shaded terrace and a modern interior combining stan-
dard tables for restaurant dining and bar tables for tapas.

SPAIN - BARCELONA

Botafumeiro

XxX 🆎 ⇔
Plan: **J1**

Gran de Gràcia 81 ⊠ *08012 –* Ⓜ *Fontana*
– ℰ 932 18 42 30 – www.botafumeiro.es
Carte 50/80 €
• Seafood • Classic décor •

Botafumeiro opened its doors in 1975, hence its status as one of Barcelona's premier seafood restaurants. Galician products are to the fore, along with big cuts of meat and a variety of platters.

Roig Robí

XxX 🛱 🆎 ⇔
Plan: **K1**

Sèneca 20 ⊠ *08006 –* Ⓜ *Diagonal – ℰ 932 18 92 22*
– www.roigrobi.com – Closed 1-7 January, 6-28 August, Saturday lunch and Sunday
Menu 33/66 € – Carte 50/65 €
• Regional cuisine • Classic décor •

A pleasant restaurant in a classic setting that includes a winter garden style dining room laid out around a patio-garden. Traditional Catalan à la carte dining, set menus and an extensive wine list.

Tram-Tram

XxX 🛱 🆎 ⇔
Plan I: **A2**

Major de Sarrià 121 ⊠ *08017 –* Ⓜ *Reina Elisenda*
– ℰ 932 04 85 18 – www.tram-tram.com – Closed Holy Week, 15 days August, Sunday, Monday lunch and Tuesday lunch August, Sunday dinner, Monday and Tuesday dinner the rest of the year
Menu 29 € – Carte 40/60 €
• Modern cuisine • Family •

A classically furnished restaurant, the name of which pays homage to this old form of transport. Updated traditional cuisine with the occasional international influence, and the option of ordering one of the set menus.

La Balsa

XX 🛱 �でよ 🆎
Plan I: **B1**

Infanta Isabel 4 ⊠ *08022 – ℰ 932 11 50 48*
– www.labalsarestaurant.com – Closed August, Sunday dinner and Monday
Menu 20/68 € – Carte 32/55 €
• Mediterranean cuisine • Cosy •

A classic address whose renovation has transformed it into a small architectural jewel nestled amid a haven of peace and quiet. Good Mediterranean cooking with a focus on quality products, which you can also enjoy on La Balsa's charming outdoor terraces.

Asador de Aranda

XX 🛱 🆎 ⇔ 🅿
Plan I: **B1-2**

av. del Tibidabo 31 ⊠ *08022 – ℰ 934 17 01 15*
– www.asadordearanda.com – Closed Sunday dinner
Menu 40/60 € – Carte 35/50 €
• Meats and grills • Cosy •

This restaurant occupies the incomparable Casa Roviralta, a Modernist building also known as El Frare Blanc. The culinary focus here is on typical Castilian cuisine, with a house speciality of roast lamb cooked in a clay oven.

99 sushi bar

XX 🆎 ⇔
Plan: **J2**

Tenor Viñas 4 ⊠ *08002 –* Ⓜ *Muntaner*
– ℰ 936 39 62 17 – www.99sushibar.com – Closed August and Sunday
Menu 88 € – Carte 55/75 €
• Japanese • Design •

High-quality Japanese cuisine in keeping with other restaurants in the chain. Eat at the bar if there's space so you can enjoy the preparation of the attractive cuisine here at close quarters.

Silvestre

Ⅹ ΑΚ ⇔

Santaló 101 ✉ *08021 –* Ⓜ *Muntaner –* ☏ *630 59 36 76*   Plan: **J1**
– www.restaurante-silvestre.com – Closed Holy Week, 15 days August,
Saturday dinner July-August, Saturday lunch, Sunday and bank holidays
Menu 25/60 € – Carte 30/45 €

• Traditional cuisine • Cosy •

This restaurant is cosy and welcoming with various private dining areas that add an intimate feel. Traditional and international cuisine, including appealing fixed menus and the option of half-racions for every dish. Try the pig's trotters filled with cep mushrooms, or the Catalan sausage (butifarra) with port wine... delicious!

La Venta

Ⅹ ≤ ⌂ ΑΚ ⇔

pl. Dr. Andreu ✉ *08035 –* ☏ *932 12 64 55*   Plan I: **B1**
– www.laventarestaurant.com – Closed Sunday August and Sunday dinner
the rest of the year
Menu 28/57 € – Carte 32/54 €

• Catalan • Traditional décor •

A not-to-be-missed experience given its location in the terminus of the Tramvia Blau tram, with its delightful views of the rooftops of Barcelona. A mix of traditional, Catalan and Mediterranean cuisine.

Bao Bar

♈/ ΑΚ

Arimón 48 ✉ *08022 –* ☏ *932 12 30 47*   Plan: **I1**
– www.baobar.barcelona – Closed August, Sunday dinner and Monday
Tapa 5 € **Ración** approx. 10 €

• Asian • Friendly •

One of famous chef Paco Pérez's more informal dining options. Here, you can enjoy dishes made for sharing as well as delicious Baos – steamed buns from Asia with a choice of highly original fillings.

Bardeni-Caldeni

♈/ ΑΚ

Valencia 454 ✉ *08013 –* Ⓜ *Sagrada Familia*   Plan: **L1**
– ☏ *932 32 58 11 – www.bardeni.es – Closed August, Sunday and Monday*
Ración approx. 15 €

• Meats and grills • Design •

A restaurant in which meat is very much centre stage. The ambience is that of an old butcher's shop, enhanced by the exclusive chef's table.

Casa Fuster

⇪ ⅃ 占 ΑΚ ⅍

passeig de Gràcia 132 ✉ *08008 –* Ⓜ *Diagonal*   Plan: **K1**
– ☏ *932 55 30 00 – www.hotelcasafuster.com*
85 rm – ♦176/600 € ♦♦176/600 € – ⊡ 30 € – 20 suites

• Luxury • Design •

A hotel occupying an impressively Modernist-style property with facilities that include the Café Vienés with live jazz, top-notch guestrooms, and a panoramic bar on the rooftop terrace. Boasting views of the city's most elegant avenue, the restaurant offers à la carte dining, complemented by an interesting choice of set menus.

G.H. La Florida

⇪ ⊗ ≤ ⌂ ⅃ ⅃ ⊡ 占 ΑΚ ⅍ ⊜

carret. Vallvidrera al Tibidabo 83-93 ✉ *08035*   Plan I: **B2**
– ☏ *932 59 30 00 – www.hotellaflorida.com*
62 rm – ♦180/350 € ♦♦200/400 € – ⊡ 28 € – 8 suites

• Luxury • Design •

Find charm and avant-garde design on the top of Tibidabo hill, with an interior created by famous designers and delightful terraces built on different levels. Its biggest attraction is without doubt the spectacular view of the city from both the hotel and restaurant.

ABaC 🔳 🚗

av. del Tibidabo 1 ⊠ *08022 –* Ⓜ *Av. Tibidabo*
– ℰ 933 19 66 00 – www.abacbarcelona.com
15 rm � – ♦230/653 € ♦♦252/679 €

Plan I: **B2**

• Luxury • Modern •
Enjoy a stay in superb, highly contemporary guestrooms featuring the latest smart technology and even chromotherapy in the bathrooms. Some spa services are also available.
✿✿✿ **ABaC** – See restaurant listing

Primero Primera 🔳 ⌁ ὼ 🔳 🚗

Doctor Carulla 25-29 ⊠ *08017 –* Ⓜ *Tres Torres*
– ℰ 934 17 56 00 – www.primeroprimera.com
25 rm – ♦155/330 € ♦♦165/350 € – ⊊ 17 € – 5 suites

Plan: **I1**

• Traditional • Elegant •
This hotel is in a residential district with access via a wide, carriage-style entrance. Attractive spiral staircase leading to eclectic guestrooms, with those under the eaves the preferred choice.

Pol & Grace ὼ 🔳 ὼ 🚗

Guillen Tell 49 ⊠ *08006 –* Ⓜ *Plaça Molina*
– ℰ 934 15 40 00 – www.polgracehotel.es
61 rm – ♦70/180 € ♦♦85/215 € – ⊊ 12 €

Plan: **J1**

• Townhouse • Functional •
A functional, urban and trendy hotel to the north of the Passeig de Gràcia that tells its own story from the origins of its name to the different themes found on each of the hotel's floors.

AT SANTA COLOMA de GRAMENET

✿ Lluerna (Víctor Quintillà) XX ὼ 🔳 ⟷

Pallaresa 104 ⊠ *08921 Santa Coloma de Gramenet –* Ⓜ *Santa Coloma*
*– ℰ 933 91 08 20 – www.lluernarestaurant.com – Closed 26 March-2 April,
6-27 August, Sunday and Monday*
Menu 40/75 € – Carte 45/69 €

• Modern cuisine • Design •
A restaurant with a modern decor in which the kitchen, "hidden" behind three glass doors, is as much the centre of attraction as the dining room. The cuisine on offer, an updated take on traditional cooking, is focused where possible around locally sourced products but without completely turning its back on ingredients and influences from elsewhere. Interesting selection of tasting menus.
➜ Rabo de cerdo duroc con cohombros. Pichón de la familia Tatje asado y alcachofa rellena. Crema de arroz con leche y toffee.

✿ Ca n'Armengol XX 🔳 ⟷ 🚗

Prat de La Riba 1 ⊠ *08921 Santa Coloma de Gramenet*
– Ⓜ *Santa Coloma – ℰ 933 91 68 55 – www.canarmengol.net – Closed
Holy Week, 2 weeks August, Sunday dinner, Monday and Tuesday dinner*
Menu 12/33 € – Carte 30/50 €

• Traditional cuisine • Classic décor •
A family-run restaurant with a classic ambience. There are two entrances: one directly through to the old bar, where customers can dine from the set menu, and the other to the dining rooms and private section reserved for à la carte dining. Traditionally based cuisine with the option of half-raciones (portions).

STOCKHOLM

Gothenburg

Malmö

SWEDEN
SVERIGE

STOCKHOLM
STOCKHOLM

adisa/iStock

Stockholm is the place to go for clean air, big skies and handsome architecture. And water. One of the great beauties of the city is the amount of water that runs through and around it; it's built on 14 islands, and looks out on 24,000 of them. An astounding two-thirds of the area within the city limits is made up of water, parks and woodland, and there are dozens of little bridges to cross to get from one part of town to another. It's little wonder Swedes appear so calm and relaxed.

It's in Stockholm that the salty waters of the Baltic meet head-on the fresh waters of Lake Mälaren, reflecting the broad boulevards

and elegant buildings that shimmer along their edge. Domes, spires and turrets dot a skyline that in the summertime never truly darkens. The heart of the city is the Old Town, Gamla Stan, full of alleyways and lanes little changed from their medieval origins. Just to the north is the modern centre, Norrmalm: a buzzing quarter of shopping malls, restaurants and bars. East of Gamla Stan you reach the small island of Skeppsholmen, which boasts fine views of the waterfront; directly north from here is Östermalm, an area full of grand residences, while southeast you'll find the lovely park island of Djurgården. South and west of Gamla Stan are the two areas where Stockholmers particularly like to hang out, the trendy (and hilly) Södermalm, and Kungsholmen.

EATING OUT

Everyone thinks that eating out in Stockholm is invariably expensive, but with a little forward planning it doesn't have to be. In the middle of the day, most restaurants and cafés offer very good value set menus. Keep in mind that, unlike in Southern Europe, the Swedes like to eat quite early, so lunch can often begin at around 11am and dinner may start from 6pm. Picking wild food is a birthright of Swedes, and there's no law to stop you going into forest or field to pick blueberries, cloudberries, cranberries, strawberries, mushrooms and the like. This love of outdoor, natural fare means that Stockholmers have a special bond with menus which relate to the seasons: keep your eyes open for restaurants that feature husmanskost (traditional Swedish dishes), along with huge buffet-style smörgåsbords. These days, however, you might find that your classic meatball, dumpling, herring or gravlax dish comes with a modern twist.

611

SWEDEN · STOCKHOLM

❀❀❀ **Frantzén** (Björn Frantzén) XxX 🅰🅲

Klara Norra Kyrkogata 26 ✉ *111 22* – Ⓜ *T-Centralen* Plan: **B2**
– ℰ *(08) 20 85 80* – www.restaurantfrantzen.com
– *Closed mid June-mid July, 2 weeks Christmas-New Year and Sunday-Tuesday*
Menu 3000 SEK – *(dinner only and lunch Friday-Saturday) (booking essential) (tasting menu only)*
· Modern cuisine · Design · Fashionable ·
A unique restaurant set over 3 floors of a 19C property; ring the doorbell, enjoy an aperitif in the living room and have the day's luxurious ingredients explained. A beautiful wood counter borders the sleek kitchen and the chefs present, finish and explain the flavour-packed dishes personally. Cooking is modern and creative but also uses classic techniques.
→ Liquorice roasted calves' sweetbread. French toast 'Grand Tradition 2008'. Preserved blueberries, meringue, pepper and buffalo milk ice cream.

❀ **Operakällaren** XxXxX 🕸 ⟳

Operahuset, Karl XII's Torg ✉ *111 86* Plan: **C2**
– Ⓜ *Kungsträdgården* – ℰ *(08) 676 58 01* – www.operakallaren.se
– *Closed 23 December -15 January, July, midsummer, Sunday and Monday*
Menu 1050/1550 SEK – *(dinner only) (booking advisable)*
· Classic cuisine · Luxury · Historic ·
Sweden's most opulent restaurant sits within the historic Opera House, and the stunning, high-ceilinged room boasts original gilt panelling decorated with frescoes and carvings. Carefully constructed dishes are underpinned by classic techniques. The wine list boasts extensive vintages of the world's great wines.
→ Spider crab ravioli, parsley emulsion and crab velouté. Butter-baked sole with truffle and lobster. Blackcurrant bavarois and sorrel ice cream.

❀ **Esperanto** (Sayan Isaksson) XxX 🅰🅲

Kungstensgatan 2 (1st Floor) ✉ *114 25* Plan: **B1**
– Ⓜ *Tekniska Högskolan* – ℰ *(08) 696 23 23*
– www.esperantorestaurant.se
– *Closed July, Christmas, Easter and Sunday-Tuesday*
Menu 1450/1900 SEK – *(dinner only) (tasting menu only)*
· Creative · Fashionable · Design ·
Esperanto is a language that crosses frontiers, as does this restaurant's food. Passionately prepared, original Swedish and Asian dishes have a theatrical element, which is fitting seeing as it's located in a 1920s theatre. The modern room has a silver vaulted ceiling and all tables face the open kitchen.
→ Oyster with sugar snap peas and blossoms. Guinea fowl egg, autumn vegetables and goat's milk yoghurt. Sunchoke pancake, maple butter and frozen milk.

❀ **Gastrologik** (Jacob Holmström and Anton Bjuhr) XX 🕸

Artillerigatan 14 ✉ *114 51* – Ⓜ *Östermalmstorg* Plan: **C2**
– ℰ *(08) 66 23 060* – www.gastrologik.se
– *Closed Christmas-New Year, midsummer weekend, Sunday and Monday*
Menu 1595 SEK – *(dinner only) (booking essential) (surprise menu only)*
· World cuisine · Intimate · Design ·
This intimate restaurant is owned by two accomplished young chefs. Cooking is innovative, flavours are pure and each main ingredient is allowed to shine. Dishes rely on the latest seasonal ingredients to arrive at the door, so are constantly evolving; the menu isn't presented to you until the end of the meal.
→ Grilled langoustine and potato pancake with herbs. Roasted quail with miso and truffle butter. Wild camomile with sorrel ice cream and rhubarb.

✿ **Ekstedt** (Niklas Ekstedt) 🍴 🎋 ㄟ

Humlegårdsgatan 17 ✉ *114 46* – Ⓜ *Östermalmstorg* Plan: **C1**
– 𝒞 (08) 611 1210 – www.ekstedt.nu – Closed 24, 25 and 31 December,
midsummer, Sunday and Monday
Menu 890/1090 SEK *– (dinner only) (booking essential) (tasting menu only)*
• Meats and grills • Design • Friendly •
An unassuming façade hides a very relaxed, friendly, yet professionally run brasserie, where ingredients are cooked in a wood-burning oven, over a fire-pit or
smoked through a chimney using birch wood. Dishes are inventive but well-
balanced – they are given their finishing touches at the stone bar.
→ Blackened leeks with vendace roe and charcoal-smoked cream. Pike-
perch, chanterelles and peas. Wood-fired honey cake with raspberries.

✿ **Mathias Dahlgren-Matbaren** – Grand Hotel 🍴 ㄟ 🎴

Södra Blasieholmshamnen 6 ✉ *103 27* Plan: **C2**
– Ⓜ Kungsträdgården – 𝒞 (08) 679 35 00 – www.mdghs.com
– Closed 13 July-6 August, 22 December-7 January, Saturday lunch and Sunday
Carte 475/835 SEK *– (booking advisable)*
• Modern cuisine • Fashionable • Design •
This popular hotel restaurant is both fun and charmingly run. The open kitchen speciali-
ses in flavoursome, well-balanced dishes from an appealing menu divided into the hea-
dings 'From our country', 'From other countries' or 'From the plant world'. They keep
some seats at the counter for those who haven't booked.
→ Squid with trout roe, artichoke and soy. Chargrilled pork, truffle, cabbage and hazelnuts. Yuzu sabayon with Swedish berries and sponge cake.

✿ **Agrikultur** (Filip Fastén) 🍴

Roslagsgatan 43 (Northwest : 2.5 km. by Birger Jarlsgatan) ✉ *113 54*
– 𝒞 (08) 15 02 02 – www.agrikultur.se – Closed 5 weeks midsummer,
2 weeks Christmas-New Year and Sunday-Monday
Menu 795 SEK *– (dinner only) (booking essential) (tasting menu only)*
• Modern cuisine • Cosy • Neighbourhood •
A lovely little restaurant with a certain homespun charm. The passionate young team
deliver a 5 course menu which follows a local, seasonal and sustainable ethos. Creative
cooking sees modernised Swedish classics prepared using some more traditional
methods and the Aga and wood-burning oven play a key part.
→ Fish stock, fava beans and char. Langoustine and truffle. Apple, cardamom and maple syrup pie.

✿ **Imouto** 🍴 🎴

Kungstensgatan 2 (1st Floor) ✉ *114 25* Plan: **B1**
– Ⓜ Tekniska Högskolan – 𝒞 (08) 696 23 23 – www.imouto.se – Closed
July, Christmas, Easter and Sunday-Tuesday
Menu 1200 SEK *– (dinner only) (booking essential)*
• Sushi • Intimate • Simple •
Its name means 'little sister' and you'll find this 9-seater sushi counter in the cor-
ner of Esperanto restaurant. Only an omakase menu is offered, with hot and
cold dishes served before the sushi; the rice is from Japan but the fish is mainly
from Swedish waters. There are two sittings on Fridays and Saturdays.
→ Soy-glazed langoustine. Turbot with wild garlic oil. Pike-perch sushi.

✿ **Sushi Sho** (Carl Ishizaki) 🍴

Upplandsgatan 45 ✉ *113 28* – Ⓜ *Odenplan – 𝒞 (08)* Plan: **A1**
30 30 30 – www.sushisho.se – Closed Christmas, New Year, July,
midsummer, Sunday and Monday
Menu 695 SEK *– (dinner only and Saturday lunch) (booking essential)*
(surprise menu only)
• Japanese • Neighbourhood • Friendly •
With its white tiled walls and compact counter seating the room couldn't be
simpler, but the food is sublime. Meals are served omakase-style, with the chef
deciding what's best each day and dishes arriving as they're ready. Top quality
seafood from local waters features alongside some great egg recipes.
→ Seared halibut skirt with bonito vinegar. Herring with akazu shari. Soy-
cured egg yolk with tuna, toasted rice and okra.

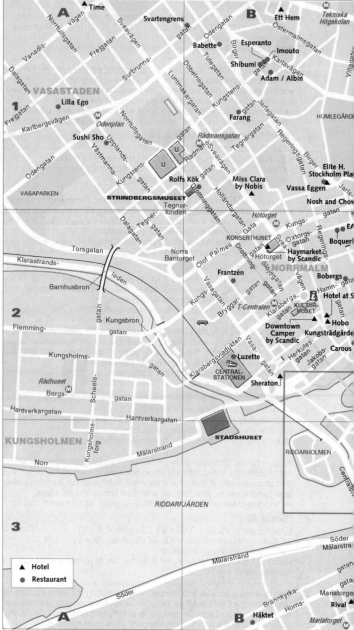

A ▲ Time

B ▲ Ett Hem

◎ Tekniska
Högskolan

Norrtullsgatan

Vanadis-gatan

Sveavägen

Svartengrens-gatan

Odengatan

Östermalmsgatan

Freigatan

Surbrunnsgatan

Babette

Tulegatan

Birger

Esperanto
Shibumi

Imouto

Villag

Dalagatan

Döbelnsgatan

Luntmakargatan

Karlavägen

Adam / Albin

VASASTADEN

Karlbergsvägen

Lilla Ego

1

Freigatan

Odengatan

◎ Odenplan

Norrtullsgatan

Kungstens-gatan

Jarlsgatan

HUMLEGÅRD

Farang

Sushi Sho

Västmanna-gatan

Upplands-gatan

Kungstens-gatan

Rådmansgatan

Sveavägen

Tegnérgatan

Birger

VASAPARKEN

Kungs-gatan

U

U

Rolfs Kök

Miss Clara
by Nobis ▲

STRINDBERGSMUSEET

Rådmansgatan

Hollandargatan

Drottninggatan

Elite H.
Stockholm Pla

Vassa Eggen ▲

Jarls

Tegnér-lunden

Nosh and Chov

Hötorget

gatan

Torsgatan

Dalagatan

◎ Kungs-

KONSERTHUSET

Sveavägen

Oxtorgs-gatan

Regerings-

EA

Klarastrands-

Norra
Bantorget

Olof Palmes gata

Drottninggatan

Hötorget

Haymarket
by Scandic

Boqueri

Barnhusbron

leden

Vasagatan

Sköfgatan

NORRMALM

Bobergs

Kungs-gatan

Bryggar-gatan

Hamn- gatan

Frantzén

2

Flemming-gatan

Kungsbron-gatan

Klarabergs-gatan

Hotel at S ▲

T-Centralen

◎ T-Centralen

KULTUR-HUSET

Hobo ▲

Kungsholms-

Scheele-

Downtown
Camper
by Scandic

Kungsträdgårde

Rådhuset

Bergs-gatan

gatan

Klarabergsviadukten

Vasagatan

Luzette ●

Herkules-gatan

Jakobs-gatan

Carous

Hantverkargatan

Hantverkargatan

CENTRAL-STATIONEN

Sheraton

Centralb

KUNGSHOLMEN

Kungsholms-torg

STADSHUSET

Norr

Mälarstrand

RIDDARHOLMEN

RIDDARFJÄRDEN

3

Söder
Mälarstra

Mälarstrand

gatan

Söder

Brännkyrka-

Horns-

gata

Mariatorge

Rival ▲

A

B ▲ Häktet

Mariatorge
◎

▲	Hotel
●	Restaurant

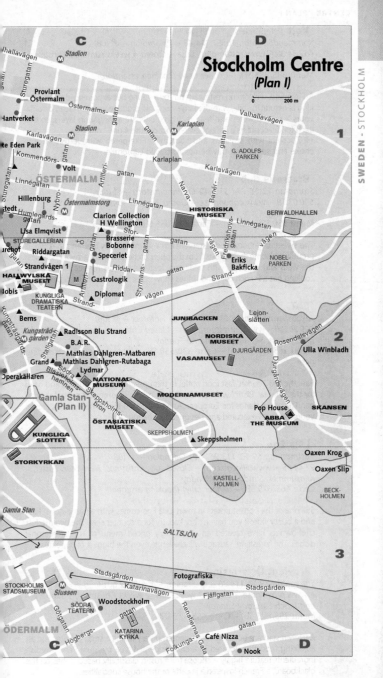

Stockholm Centre
(Plan I)

0   200 m

C

Stadion

Proviant
Östermalm

Hantverket

Östermalms-

gatan

Stadion

Karlavägen

Kommendörs-

te Eden Park

Volt

ÖSTERMALM

Hillenburg

Östermalmstorg

tedt

Humlegårds-
gatan

Lisa Elmqvist

STUREGALLERIAN

urehof   Riddargatan

Strandvägen 1

HALLWYLSKA
MUSEET

lobis

KUNGLIGA
DRAMATISKA
TEATERN

Berns

Radisson Blu Strand

B.A.R.

Mathias Dahlgren-Matbaren

Grand   Mathias Dahlgren-Rutabaga

Lydmar

Operakällaren   NATIONAL-
MUSEUM

Gamla Stan
(Plan II)

KUNGLIGA
SLOTTET

STORKYRKAN

Gamla Stan

D

Valhallavägen

Karlaplan

Karlaplan

G. ADOLFS-
PARKEN

Karlavägen

HISTORISKA
MUSEET

BERWALDHALLEN

Linnégatan

Clarion Collection
H Wellington

Stor-
Brasserie
Bobonne

Speceriet

Riddar-

gatan

Eriks
Bakficka

NOBEL-
PARKEN

Gastrologik

Diplomat

Strand-

JUNIBACKEN

Lejons-
slätten

NORDISKA
MUSEET

DJURGÅRDEN

Rosendalsvägen

Ulla Winbladh

VASAMUSEET

MODERNAMUSEET

ÖSTASIATISKA
MUSEET

SKEPPSHOLMEN

Skeppsholmen

Pop House

ABBA
THE MUSEUM

SKANSEN

Oaxen Krog

Oaxen Slip

BECK-
HOLMEN

KASTELL-
HOLMEN

SALTSJÖN

Fotografiska

STOCKHOLMS
STADSMUSEUM

Slussen

SÖDRA
TEATERN

Woodstockholm

ÖDERMALM

Högbergs-

Stadsgården

Katarinavägen

Fjällgatan

KATARINA
KYRKAN

Folkunga-

Stadsgården

gatan

Café Nizza

Nook

1

2

3

❀ **Volt** (Peter Andersson and Fredrik Johnsson) ✗
Kommendörsgatan 16 ⊠ *114 48 –* Ⓜ *Stadion –* ℰ *(08)*   Plan: **C1**
662 34 00 – www.restaurangvolt.se – Closed 4 weeks summer, Christmas,
New Year and Sunday-Monday
Menu 685/885 SEK – *(dinner only) (booking essential)*
• Creative • Intimate • Neighbourhood •
An intimate, welcoming restaurant run by a young but experienced team. Coo-
king is natural in style, with the largely organic produce yielding clear, bold fla-
vours – natural wines also feature. Ingredients are arranged in layers, so that
each forkful contains a little of everything; choose 4 or 6 courses.
→ Zucchini with scallions and sour milk. Pike-perch with Jerusalem artichoke and seaweed. Strawberries with wild camomile.

⊕ **Brasserie Bobonne** ✗
Storgatan 12 ⊠ *114 51 –* Ⓜ *Östermalmstorg –* ℰ *(08)*   Plan: **C1**
660 03 18 – www.bobonne.se – Closed 4 weeks summer, Christmas
and Sunday
Menu 550 SEK *(dinner)* – Carte 320/655 SEK
• French • Cosy • Bistro •
This sweet neighbourhood restaurant has a warm, homely feel, and the owners
proudly welcome their guests from the open kitchen. Modern artwork hangs on
the walls and contrasts with traditional features such as mosaic tiling. Classic
cooking has a French core and dishes show obvious care in their preparation.

⊕ **EAT** ✗ 🍴 &
Jakobsbergsgatan 15 ⊠ *111 44 –* Ⓜ *Hötorget –* ℰ *(08)*   Plan: **B2**
509 20300 – www.eatrestaurant.se – Closed Christmas-New Year, mid July-
mid August, Saturday lunch and Sunday
Menu 265 SEK *(lunch)* – Carte 330/550 SEK – *(bookings advisable at din-*
ner)
• Asian • Brasserie • Fashionable •
Pass the EAT 'Market' fast food outlet in this upmarket shopping mall and head
for the Oriental 'Bistro' with its rich, moody colour scheme and central cocktail
bar. The name stands for 'European Asian Taste' and the Chinese dishes are flavoursome, well-executed and designed for sharing.

⊕ **Lilla Ego** ✗ ⇔
Västmannag 69 ⊠ *113 26 –* Ⓜ *Odenplan –* ℰ *(08)*   Plan: **A1**
27 44 55 – www.lillaego.com – Closed July, Christmas, New Year, Easter,
midsummer, Sunday and Monday
Carte 465/675 SEK – *(dinner only) (booking essential)*
• Modern cuisine • Bistro • Friendly •
Still one of the hottest tickets in town, Lilla Ego comes with a pared-down look
and a buzzy vibe; if you haven't booked, try for a counter seat. The two modest
chef-owners have created an appealingly priced menu of robust seasonal
dishes. The 'wrestling' sausage will challenge even the biggest of appetites.

⊕ **Proviant Östermalm** ✗ 🍴 &
Sturegatan 19 ⊠ *114 36 –* Ⓜ *Stadion –* ℰ *(08) 22 60 50*   Plan: **C1**
– www.proviant.se – Closed 3 weeks July, 2 weeks Christmas, 1 January
and lunch Saturday-Sunday
Menu 295/625 SEK – Carte 455/625 SEK
• Swedish • Bistro • Intimate •
A lively restaurant boasting smart, contemporary décor, a small counter and an
adjoining foodstore; located in a chic residential area by Sture Park. Swedish
ingredients feature highly – choose from rustic, classically based dishes on the
blackboard, a French-inspired à la carte or the house specialities.

Rolfs Kök 🕸 ※

Tegnérgatan 41 ⊠ 111 61 – Ⓜ Rådmansgatan — Plan: **B1**
– 𝒞 (08) 10 16 96 – www.rolfskok.se – Closed July, 24-25 and
31 December, 1 January, midsummer and lunch Saturday-Sunday
Menu 148 SEK (lunch) – Carte dinner 505/665 SEK – (booking essential)
• Modern cuisine • Bistro • Rustic •

A popular, buzzy restaurant in a lively commercial district, run by a passionate
chef-owner. The contemporary interior was designed by famous Swedish
artists; sit at the counter to watch the chefs in action. Dishes include homely
Swedish classics and blackboard specials – every dish has a wine match.

Shibumi ※ 🆔

Kungstensgatan 2 ⊠ 114 25 – Ⓜ Tekniska Högskolan — Plan: **B1**
– 𝒞 (08) 696 23 10 – www.shibumi.se – Closed Christmas, New
Year, Easter, midsummer, Sunday and Monday
Carte 225/405 SEK – (dinner only) (booking advisable)
• Japanese • Minimalist • Fashionable •

This moody, modern restaurant is based on a Japanese izakaya. It's open until
late and comes with an underground buzz – and not just because it's in a basement. The menu offers authentic dishes designed for sharing; some with a
slightly Westernised edge. The daily changing cocktail list is worth a look.

Bobergs 🕸🕸🕸 ⅊ 🆔

NK Department Store (4th floor), Hamngatan 18-20 — Plan: **B2**
⊠ 111 47 – Ⓜ Kungsträdgården – 𝒞 (08) 762 8161
– www.bobergsmatsal.se – Closed July-mid August, Christmas-New Year,
Sunday and bank holidays
Menu 345 SEK – Carte 395/765 SEK – (lunch only) (booking advisable)
• Modern cuisine • Elegant • Classic décor •

Head past the canteen in this historic department store to the elegant birch-
panelled room and ask for a river view. Choose the set business lunch or from
the seasonal à la carte; classic cooking mixes French and Swedish influences.

AG 🕸🕸 🕸 🆔

Kronobergsgatan 37 (2nd Floor), Kungsholmen (via Flemminggatan A2)
⊠ 112 33 – Ⓜ Fridhemsplan – 𝒞 (08) 410 681 00
– www.restaurangag.se – Closed July, 24-25 and 31 December,
1 January and Sunday
Carte 425/805 SEK – (dinner only)
• Meats and grills • Rustic • Fashionable •

An industrial, New York style eatery on the 2nd floor of an old silver factory.
Swedish, American and Scottish beef is displayed in huge cabinets and you choose your accompaniments. Expect a great wine list and smooth service.

Farang 🕸🕸 ⅊ 🆔

Tulegatan 7 ⊠ 113 53 – Ⓜ Rådmansgatan – 𝒞 (08) — Plan: **B1**
673 74 00 – www.farang.se – Closed July, Christmas, Sunday and Monday
Menu 245/695 SEK – Carte 410/655 SEK
• South East Asian • Minimalist • Fashionable •

The unusual front door harks back to its Stockholm Electric Company days, and
behind it lies a stylish restaurant and bar – the former sits in the old machine
hall. Zingy, aromatic dishes focus on Southeast Asia and are full of colour.

Hantverket 🕸🕸 🕸 🆔

Sturegatan 15 ⊠ 114 36 – Ⓜ Stadion – 𝒞 (08) — Plan: **C1**
121 321 60 – www.restauranghantverket.se – Closed 3 weeks July,
Christmas, Saturday lunch and Sunday
Menu 295 SEK (lunch) – Carte 300/525 SEK – (booking advisable)
• Modern cuisine • Rustic • Fashionable •

Exposed ducting contrasts with chunky tables and leafy plants at this buzzy restaurant. It has a cool lounge-bar, counter seats and a mix of raised and regular
tables. Cooking has an artisanal Swedish heart and service is bright and breezy.

Hillenberg   XX

Humlegårdsgatan 14 ⊠ 114 34 – Ⓜ Östermalmstorg   Plan: **C1**
– ℰ (08) 519 421 53 – www.hillenberg.se – Closed Christmas and Sunday
Carte 365/860 SEK
• Modern cuisine • Design • Brasserie •
There's a marble bar on each side of this bright, modern restaurant, where the
designer's eye for detail is evident. The food reflects the surroundings by being
fresh, contemporary, colourful and free from unnecessary frills.

Nosh and Chow   XX & 🝙 ⇦

Norrlandsgatan 24 ⊠ 111 43 – Ⓜ Hötorget – ℰ (08)   Plan: **B2**
503 389 60 – www.noshandchow.se – Closed Easter, 24 December,
1 January, midsummer and Sunday
Menu 295/450 SEK – Carte 345/785 SEK
• International • Brasserie • Fashionable •
This former bank has been transformed into a glitzy cocktail bar and brasserie
which displays a smart mix of New York and New England styling. Filling dishes
blend French, American and Swedish influences with other global flavours.

Strandvägen 1   XX 🝙 🝙

Strandvägen 1 ⊠ 114 51 – Ⓜ Kungsträdgården   Plan: **C2**
– ℰ (08) 663 80 00 – www.strandvagen1.se – Closed 24 December
Carte 425/765 SEK
• International • Design • Elegant •
Sit on the terrace of this modern bistro-style restaurant – a former bank – and
watch the boats bobbing up and down in the harbour. Seasonal menus offer
generously proportioned, globally inspired dishes with bold flavours.

Vassa Eggen – Elite H. Stockholm Plaza   XX 🝙

Birger Jarlsgatan 29 ⊠ 103 95 – Ⓜ Östermalmstorg   Plan: **B1**
– ℰ (08) 21 61 69 – www.vassaeggen.com – Closed midsummer,
Christmas, Saturday lunch and Sunday
Menu 695 SEK – Carte 495/1000 SEK
• Meats and grills • Fashionable • Rustic •
A pleasant bar leads through to a dimly lit hotel dining room where bold art-
work hangs on the walls. Hearty Swedish cooking relies on age-old recipes,
with a particular focus on meat; whole beasts are butchered and hung on-site.

Adam / Albin   X & 🝙

Rådmansgatan 16 ⊠ 114 25 – Ⓜ Tekniska Högskolan   Plan: **B1**
– ℰ (08) 411 5535 – www.adamalbin.se – Closed Christmas, Sunday, bank
holidays and restricted opening in summer
Menu 895 SEK – (dinner only) (booking essential)
• Modern cuisine • Intimate • Neighbourhood •
Owners Adam and Albin have stamped their mark on this charming restaurant,
which comes with Italian marble clad walls and a mix of individual and communal tables. Snacks are followed by a 4 course menu, where refined, eye-catching
dishes blend the ethos of a Scandic kitchen with Asian flavours.

Babette   X 🝙

Roslagsgatan 6 ⊠ 113 55 – Ⓜ Tekniska Högskolan   Plan: **B1**
– ℰ (08) 5090 2224 – www.babette.se – Closed 24-26, 31 December and
18-25 June
Carte 295/415 SEK – (dinner only)
• Modern cuisine • Neighbourhood • Bistro •
You'll feel at home in this modern neighbourhood bistro. Cooking is rustic and
unfussy and the daily selection of small plates and pizzas makes dining flexible.
They limit their bookings so that they can accommodate walk-ins.

🍴○ **B.A.R.** X AC
Blasieholmsgatan 4a ✉ *111 48 –* Ⓜ *Kungsträdgården* Plan: **C2**
– 𝒞 (08) 611 53 35 – www.restaurangbar.se – Closed Christmas-New Year,
Saturday lunch and Sunday
Carte 345/585 SEK
• Seafood • Brasserie • Fashionable •
This bright, buzzy restaurant is just a cast away from the waterfront and has a
semi-industrial fish-market style. Choose your seafood from the fridge or the
tank, along with a cooking style, a sauce and one of their interesting sides.

🍴○ **Boqueria** X 🛋 ⅃
Jakobsbergsgatan 17 ✉ *111 44 –* Ⓜ *Hötorget – 𝒞 (08)* Plan: **B2**
307400 – www.boqueria.se – Closed 24-25 December, 1 January and
midsummer
Menu 145 SEK (weekday lunch) – Carte 370/995 SEK
• Spanish • Tapas bar • Fashionable •
A vibrant, bustling tapas restaurant with high-level seating, located in a smart
mall. Appealing menus offer tapas and a range of authentic dishes for two or
more to share. Sangria and pintxos can be enjoyed in their nearby bar.

🍴○ **Carousel** X 🛋 ⅃ AC
Gustav Adolfs Torg 20 ✉ *111 53 –* Ⓜ *Kungsträdgården* Plan: **B2**
– 𝒞 (08) 10 27 57 – www.restaurantcarousel.se – Closed Christmas,
midsummer and Sunday
Carte 425/765 SEK
• Swedish • Classic décor • Historic •
Start with a drink under the impressive original ceiling in the bar then sit near
the carousel or out on the terrace. The experienced chefs carefully prepare fla-
voursome dishes which follow the seasons and have classic Swedish roots.

🍴○ **Eriks Bakficka** X
Fredrikshovsgatan 4 ✉ *115 23 – 𝒞 (08) 660 15 99* Plan: **D2**
– www.eriks.se – Closed July, Christmas, Easter, Saturday lunch and
Sunday
Carte 445/780 SEK
• Swedish • Bistro •
Set in a residential area close to Djurgårdsbron Bridge and a favourite with the
locals. The bistro-style interior has wood panelling and marble-topped tables.
Simple, unpretentious cooking features Swedish classics and a 'dish of the day'.

🍴○ **Lisa Elmqvist** X
Humlesgårdsgatan 1 ✉ *114 39 –* Ⓜ *Östermalmstorg* Plan: **C1**
– 𝒞 (08) 553 40410 – www.lisaelmqvist.se – Closed 24 December,
midsummer, Sunday and bank holidays
Carte 425/1190 SEK
• Seafood • Family • Bistro •
While the original 19C market hall is being restored, this established family-run
restaurant is operating from the temporary marketplace next door. Top quality
seafood from the day's catch features in unfussy, satisfying combinations.

🍴○ **Luzette** X 🛋 ⅃ AC
Centralstationen, Centralplan 25 ✉ *111 20* Plan: **B2**
– Ⓜ *T-Centralen – 𝒞 (08) 519 316 00 – www.luzette.se*
Carte 425/715 SEK
• Swedish • Brasserie • Design •
A modern brasserie in the Central train station, inspired by the grand restau-
rants of old; its name means 'light' and refers to the 1920s luminaire designed
by Peter Behrens. Swedish menus include weekend brunches and rotisserie
specials.

⫯○ **Mathias Dahlgren-Rutabaga** – Grand Hotel   ✗ ✿ ᵭ 🅰

Södra Blasieholmshamnen 6 ✉ *103 27*   Plan: **C2**
– ⓜ *Kungsträdgården* – ℰ *(08) 679 35 84 – www.mdghs.se – Closed
22 December-7 January, 13 July-6 August and Sunday*
Menu 795 SEK – Carte 260/375 SEK – *(dinner only) (booking essential)*
• Vegetarian • Simple • Fashionable •

A light, bright restaurant offering something one doesn't usually find in grand
hotels – vegetarian cuisine. The sharing plates come with flavours from across
the world; the 'Taste of Rutabaga' menu best showcases the kitchen's range.

⫯○ **Speceriet**   ✗ 🅰

Artillerigatan 14 ✉ *114 51* – ⓜ *Östermalmstorg*   Plan: **C2**
– ℰ *(08) 662 30 60 – www.speceriet.se – Closed July-August, Christmas-
New Year, midsummer, Saturday lunch, Sunday-Monday and bank
holidays*
Carte 375/575 SEK
• Classic cuisine • Simple •

The more casual addendum to the Gastrologik restaurant will get you in the
mood for sharing. Sit at communal tables and choose from three main dishes
at lunchtime and a wider selection of mix and match dishes at dinner.

⫯○ **Sturehof**   ✗ ✿ 🍴 ᵭ 🅰 ⇄

Stureplan 2 ✉ *114 46* – ⓜ *Östermalmstorg* – ℰ *(08)*   Plan: **C2**
440 57 30 – www.sturehof.com
Carte 290/915 SEK
• Seafood • Brasserie • Fashionable •

This bustling city institution dates back over a century and is a wonderful mix of
the traditional and the modern. It boasts a buzzing terrace, several marble-topped bars and a superb food court. Classic menus focus on seafood.

⫯○ **Svartengrens**   ✗

Tulegatan 24 ✉ *113 53* – ⓜ *Tekniska Högskolan*   Plan: **B1**
– ℰ *(08) 612 65 50 – www.svartengrens.se – Closed midsummer
and Christmas*
Menu 725 SEK – Carte 315/845 SEK – *(dinner only)*
• Meats and grills • Friendly • Neighbourhood •

The eponymous chef-owner has created a modern bistro specialising in sustainable meat and veg from producers in the archipelago. Along with smoking
and pickling, the dry-ageing is done in-house, and the cuts change daily.

🏨 **Grand**   ⚘ ≤ 🛗 🛎 🛖 🖼 ᵭ ♨ ⇊

Södra Blasieholmshamnen 6 ✉ *103 27*   Plan: **C2**
– ⓜ *Kungsträdgården* – ℰ *(08) 679 35 00 – www.grandhotel.se*
278 rm ☲ – †3600/4200 SEK ††4900/5800 SEK – 34 suites
• Luxury • Historic building • Elegant •

The Grand certainly lives up to its name with its Corinthian columns, handsome
panelled bar and impressive spa. Classical bedrooms have marble-decked bathrooms and those at the front have great views over the water to the Old Town.
Dining choices include Verandan with its harbour outlook and smörgåsbords,
lively Matbaren and vegetarian restaurant Rutabaga.

   ❀ **Mathias Dahlgren-Matbaren** – See restaurant listing

🏨 **Hotel at Six**   ⚘ ≤ 🛗 ♨ ᵭ 🅰 🛖 ⇊

Brunkebergstorg 6 ✉ *111 51* – ⓜ *Kungsträdgården*   Plan: **B2**
– ℰ *(08) 57882800 – www.hotelatsix.com*
340 rm – †1700/2400 SEK ††1700/2400 SEK – ☲ 175 SEK – 1 suite
• Business • Design • Contemporary •

With its laid-back vibe, bold colour scheme, contemporary art collection and
14m long cocktail bar and 'listening lounge', its cool interior couldn't be more
of a contrast to its unassuming façade. Bedrooms are monochrome; those on
the top floors have panoramic windows. The modern brasserie serves global
fare.

Nobis ☆ ╚ 🕸 & 🛁 🚗

Norrmalmstorg 2-4 ⊠ 111 86 – Ⓜ Östermalmstorg   Plan: **C2**
– 𝒞 (08) 614 10 00 – www.nobishotel.com
201 rm – †1890/2290 SEK ††2290/2990 SEK – ⌸ 175 SEK – 1 suite
• Historic • Design • Personalised •

It started life as two Royal Palaces and later became a bank (the famous 'Stockholm Syndrome' robbery took place here); now it's a smart hotel with two internal courtyards and spacious bedrooms with clean lines, African wood furnishings and marble bathrooms. Dine on refined Italian cuisine in Caina or more rustic, wholesome dishes in Bakfica, with its pavement terrace.

Sheraton ☆ ╚ 🕸 & 🄰🄲 🛁 🚗

Tegelbacken 6 ⊠ 101 23 – Ⓜ T-Centralen – 𝒞 (08)   Plan: **B2**
412 36 02 – www.sheratonstockholm.com
465 rm – †1395/5185 SEK ††1395/5185 SEK – ⌸ 259 SEK – 29 suites
• Business • Chain • Modern •

This was the first Sheraton to open in Europe, back in 1971, and its unassuming concrete façade is now a listed feature. Bedrooms are smart, spacious and understated, and some overlook Lake Mälaren or the Old Town. The lively restaurant offers international buffet lunches and traditional Swedish dinners.

Berns ╚ 🛁

Näckströmsgatan 8, Berzelii Park ⊠ 111 47   Plan: **C2**
– Ⓜ Kungsträdgården – 𝒞 (08) 566 322 00 – www.berns.se
82 rm – †1100/3300 SEK ††1200/3500 SEK – ⌸ 195 SEK – 6 suites
• Historic building • Boutique hotel • Design •

In 1863 Heinrich Robert Berns opened Stockholm's biggest concert and party hall on this site and, continuing that tradition, events are a big part of this hotel's business. Bedrooms are modern and some have seating areas or balconies. The stunning rococo ballroom offers an extensive Asian fusion menu.

Diplomat ☆ ╚ 🕸 🛁

Strandvägen 7C ⊠ 114 56 – Ⓜ Kungsträdgården   Plan: **C2**
– 𝒞 (08) 459 68 00 – www.diplomathotel.com
130 rm ⌸ – †2550/3950 SEK ††2850/4650 SEK – 3 suites
• Traditional • Luxury • Elegant •

Early 20C charm combines with modern furnishings in this art nouveau hotel. Take the old cage lift up to the cosy library, which leads through to a sweet little cocktail bar. Elegant bedrooms come in pastel hues and some have harbour views. T Bar (the old tea salon) serves Scandinavian-inspired brasserie dishes.

Downtown Camper by Scandic ☆ 🕥 🕸 🝫 & 🄰🄲 🛁

Brunkebergstorg 9 ⊠ 111 51 – Ⓜ Kungsträdgården   Plan: **B2**
– 𝒞 (08) 51726300 – www.scandichotels.com/downtowncamper
494 rm ⌸ – †1700/2300 SEK ††2150/3000 SEK – 20 suites
• Business • Industrial • Eco-friendly •

This unique hotel has an outside living theme: guest areas have urban-chic styling and eco-friendly bedrooms bring the outdoors indoors courtesy of window seats and natural materials. Creatively styled conference rooms come with games, each floor has a table tennis table and bikes, skateboards and kayaks are available for hire. The brasserie offers comforting fare.

Elite Eden Park ╚ 🕸 & 🄰🄲 🚗

Sturegatan 22 ⊠ 114 36 – Ⓜ Östermalmstorg – 𝒞 (08)   Plan: **C1**
5556 2700 – www.elite.se
124 rm ⌸ – †1300/3300 SEK ††1500/3500 SEK – 1 suite
• Business • Contemporary • Modern •

A smart hotel in a converted office block, designed with the business traveller in mind. Stylish bedrooms boast comfy beds and large showers – some rooms overlook the park and some have small balconies. Choose from an Asian-inspired menu in Miss Voon or traditional British pub dishes in The Bishops Arms.

Haymarket by Scandic
Hötorget 13-15 ⊠ *111 57 –* Ⓜ *Hötorget –* ℱ *(08)*   Plan: **B2**
517 267 00 – www.scandichotels.com/haymarket
401 rm 🖳 – ♛1600/2800 SEK ♛♛1700/3200 SEK – 7 suites
• Business • Historic building • Art déco •
Built in the 1900s, this former department store sits overlooking the Square, just across from the Concert Hall. Swedish-born Greta Garbo once worked here and the décor, particularly in the bedrooms, gives a nod to the art deco style. There's a small movie theatre, a healthy café-cum-bistro, a European restaurant and an American bar which hosts jazz at weekends.

Miss Clara by Nobis
Sveavägen 48 ⊠ *111 34 –* Ⓜ *Hötorget –* ℱ *(08)*   Plan: **B1**
440 67 00 – www.missclarahotel.com
90 rm – ♛1590/2790 SEK ♛♛1690/3190 SEK – 🖳 169 SEK – 2 suites
• Business • Modern • Personalised •
A fashionable hotel in a great location; it used to be a girls' school and its name is that of the former principal. Surprisingly quiet, dark wood bedrooms have good facilities. The atmospheric brasserie offers an international menu with an Italian slant and some classic Swedish specialities.

Radisson Blu Strand
Nybrokajen 9 box 16396 ⊠ *103 27*   Plan: **C2**
– Ⓜ *Kungsträdgården –* ℱ *(08) 506 640 00*
– www.radissonblu.com/strandhotel-stockholm
160 rm – ♛1295/2695 SEK ♛♛1395/3395 SEK – 🖳 170 SEK – 11 suites
• Business • Historic building • Contemporary •
This imposing hotel part-dates from the 1912 Olympics and sits in a lively water-side spot overlooking Nybroviken. Bedrooms are a mix of traditional and modern styles; the Tower Suite boasts a roof terrace with stunning city views. Enjoy a mix of local and global dishes in the airy atrium restaurant.

Ett Hem
Sköldungagatan 2 ⊠ *114 27 –* Ⓜ *Tekniska Högskolan*   Plan: **B1**
– ℱ *(08) 20 05 90 – www.etthem.se*
12 rm 🖳 – ♛3920/4900 SEK ♛♛4720/5900 SEK
• Luxury • Design • Classic •
A charming Arts and Crafts townhouse built as a private residence in 1910. It's elegant, understated and makes good use of wood; its name means 'home' and that's exactly how it feels. Bedroom No.6 features an old chimney and No.1 has a four-poster and a huge marble bath. Modern set menus use top seasonal produce and are served in the kitchen, library and orangery.

Lydmar
Södra Blasieholmshamnen 2 ⊠ *111 48*   Plan: **C2**
– Ⓜ *Kungsträdgården –* ℱ *(08) 22 31 60 – www.lydmar.com*
46 rm 🖳 – ♛2700/3800 SEK ♛♛3100/5200 SEK – 6 suites
• Townhouse • Personalised • Design •
Superbly located across the water from the Palace is this charming townhouse; formerly the store for the neighbouring museum's archives. It has a relaxed yet funky vibe and regularly changing contemporary artwork – and the roof terrace with its water feature is a delightful spot come summer. The attractive restaurant offers a modern European brasserie menu.

Elite H. Stockholm Plaza
Birger Jarlsgatan 29 ⊠ *103 95 –* Ⓜ *Östermalmstorg*   Plan: **B1**
– ℱ *(08) 566 220 00 – www.elite.se*
143 rm 🖳 – ♛1290/2890 SEK ♛♛1690/3290 SEK – 12 suites
• Business • Chain • Contemporary •
The smaller sister of the Elite Eden Park is this attractive, centrally located building with a façade dating from 1884. Bright fabrics stand out against neutral walls in the compact modern bedrooms; go for one of the corner suites.
🍴 **Vassa Eggen** – See restaurant listing

Hobo
⚒ ⅙ 🎬 ⚒

Brunkebergstorg 4 ⊠ *111 51* – ⓜ *Kungsträdgården*   Plan: **B2**
– 𝒞 (08) 57882700 – www.hobo.se
201 rm – ♦900/1700 SEK ♦♦1900/2200 SEK – ⚏ 120 SEK
• Boutique hotel • Unique • Design •

With eco-inspired décor and quirky design features, Hobo offers something a little different. The ground floor exhibits local businesses' work and houses a laid-back bar-lounge serving modern menus. Cleverly designed bedrooms come with headboards that transform into desks and peg board walls hung with gadgets.

Kungsträdgården
⚒ ⅃ 🐱 🎬

Västra Trädgårdsgatan 11B ⊠ *11153*   Plan: **B2**
– ⓜ Kungsträdgården – 𝒞 (08) 440 6650 – www.hotelkungstradgarden.se
94 rm ⚏ – ♦1450/2950 SEK ♦♦1750/3250 SEK
• Townhouse • Historic • Personalised •

Overlooking the park of the same name is this part-18C building with a classical façade and attractive original features. Bedrooms are individually furnished in a Gustavian-style – it's worth paying the extra for a bigger room. A concise menu of French-inspired dishes is served in the covered courtyard.

Riddargatan
⚒

Riddargatan 14 ⊠ *114 35* – ⓜ *Östermalmstorg*   Plan: **C2**
– 𝒞 (08) 555 730 00 – www.ligula.se
78 rm ⚏ – ♦995/2995 SEK ♦♦1195/3195 SEK – 4 suites
• Business • Modern • Personalised •

This smart former office block is situated close to the shops and restaurants, and feels very much like a home-from-home. The newer bedrooms have bold designs and modern wet rooms. The contemporary breakfast room doubles as a lively bar.

Time
🐱 ⅙ ⚒ ⚗

Vanadisvägen 12 ⊠ *113 46* – ⓜ *Odenplan – 𝒞 (08)*   Plan: **A1**
54 54 73 00 – www.timehotel.se
144 rm ⚏ – ♦1850/2150 SEK ♦♦2050/2550 SEK
• Business • Modern • Personalised •

This purpose-built business hotel sits in a smart residential area on the edge of town and is run by a friendly, hands-on team. Bedrooms are bright, airy and of a good size; Superiors have Juliet balconies and Studios offer long-term lets.

Clarion Collection H. Wellington
🐱 ⅙ ⚗

Storgatan 6 ⊠ *114 51* – ⓜ *Östermalmstorg – 𝒞 (08)*   Plan: **C1**
667 09 10 – www.wellington.se – Closed 22 December-4 January
61 rm ⚏ – ♦820/2420 SEK ♦♦1420/3220 SEK – 1 suite
• Business • Townhouse • Traditional •

Set in a former office block, this centrally located hotel makes an ideal base for shopping and sightseeing. Simple bedrooms feature bright fabrics and those on the top floor have city views. Buffet dinners are included in the price.

AT GAMLA STAN (OLD STOCKHOLM)   PLAN II

Kagges
✗

Lilla Nygatan 21 ⊠ *111 28* – ⓜ *Gamla Stan*   Plan: **F1**
– www.kagges.com – Closed January, midsummer and Monday-Tuesday
Menu 495 SEK – Carte 420/505 SEK – *(dinner only) (booking essential)*
• Swedish • Fashionable • Cosy •

Two enthusiastic friends run this cosy restaurant with a lively buzz. Ask for a seat at the counter to watch the team prepare constantly evolving seasonal small plates with plenty of colour and a Swedish heart. 4 plates per person is about right or go for the 4 course Chef's Choice of the Day menu.

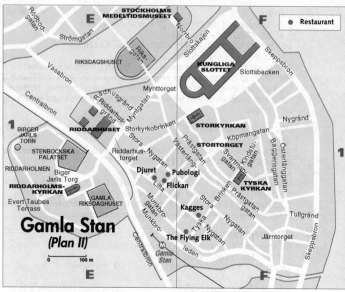

Gamla Stan
(Plan II)

🍴 **Djuret**   XxX 🏛
Lilla Nygatan 5 ⊠ 111 28 – Ⓜ Gamla Stan – ℰ (08)   Plan: E1
506 400 84 – www.djuret.se – Closed July, Christmas and Sunday
Menu 595 SEK – *(dinner only) (booking essential) (tasting menu only)*
• Meats and grills • Rustic • Neighbourhood •
Various rooms make up this atmospheric restaurant, including one part-built into the city walls and looking into the impressive wine cellar. Monthly set menus are formed around 3 key ingredients; masculine cooking has big, bold flavours.

🍴 **Pubologi**   XX 🏛
Stora Nygatan 20 ⊠ 111 27 – Ⓜ Gamla Stan – ℰ (08)   Plan: E1
506 400 86 – www.pubologi.se – Closed July, Christmas, Sunday and Monday
Menu 650 SEK – *(dinner only) (booking advisable) (tasting menu only)*
• Swedish • Cosy • Neighbourhood •
Book a window table at this charming modern bistro for views out over the cobbled street. The 5 course set menu offers refined, rustic dishes; flavours are strong and punchy and seasonality is key. The wine list is impressive.

🍴 **Flickan**   X 🆔
Yxsmedsgränd 12 ⊠ 111 28 – Ⓜ Gamla Stan – ℰ (08)   Plan: E1
506 40080 – www.restaurangflickan.se – Closed July, Christmas and Sunday-Wednesday
Menu 850 SEK – *(dinner only) (booking essential) (tasting menu only)*
• Modern cuisine • Fashionable • Intimate •
Pass through the busy bar to this small 16-seater restaurant, where you'll be greeted by a welcoming team. The 13 course set menu keeps Swedish produce to the fore, and modern dishes have the occasional Asian or South American twist.

‖○ **The Flying Elk** ✗
Mälartorget 15 ✉ *111 27* – ⓜ *Gamla Stan* Plan: **F1**
– ℰ (08) 20 85 83 – www.theflyingelk.se
– Closed 24-25, 31 December, 1 January and midsummer
Carte 475/750 SEK – (dinner only and lunch Saturday and Sunday)
• Modern cuisine • Inn • Friendly •
A good night out is guaranteed at this lively corner spot, which is modelled on a
British pub and has several different bars. Choose from bar snacks, pub dishes
with a twist or a popular tasting menu of refined modern classics.

AT DJURGÅRDEN PLAN I

🌼🌼 **Oaxen Krog** (Magnus Ek) ✗✗ 🏵 ≤ 🐧
Beckholmsvägen 26 (off Djurgårdsvägen) ✉ *115 21* Plan: **D3**
– ℰ (08) 551 531 05 – www.oaxen.com
– Closed Christmas-New Year, Easter, midsummer, Sunday and Monday
Menu 1900/2100 SEK – (dinner only) (booking essential)
• Creative • Design • Friendly •
This rebuilt boat shed sits in a delightful waterside location. Diners are led
through a door in Oaxen Slip into an oak-furnished room with a slightly nautical
feel. Beautifully constructed New Nordic dishes are allied to nature and the sea-
sons – they're delicate and balanced but also offer depth of flavour.
➜ Fermented and pickled vegetables with ox marrow. Duck, forest
capers, fennel seeds and oak moss. Rhubarb with celery sorbet and fresh
herbs.

🏵 **Ulla Winbladh** ✗✗ 🏵 🐧
Rosendalsvägen 8 ✉ *115 21* Plan: **D2**
– ℰ (08) 534 897 01 – www.ullawinbladh.se
– Closed 24-25 December
Menu 595 SEK – Carte 440/660 SEK – (booking essential)
• Swedish • Classic décor • Cosy •
Ulla Winbladh was originally built as a steam bakery for the 1897 Stockholm
World Fair and is set in charming parkland beside the Skansen open-air
museum. Sit on the terrace or in the older, more characterful part of the buil-
ding. Hearty Swedish dishes include sweet and sour herring and fish roe.

🏵 **Oaxen Slip** ✗ 🏵 🐧 🐧
Beckholmsvägen 26 (off Djurgårdsvägen) ✉ *115 21* Plan: **D3**
– ℰ (08) 551 53105 – www.oaxen.com
– Closed Christmas
Carte 410/665 SEK
• Traditional cuisine • Bistro •
A bright, bustling bistro next to the old slipway; try for a spot on the delightful
terrace. Light floods the room and boats hang from the girders in a nod to the
local shipbuilding industry. The food is wholesome and heartening and features
plenty of seafood – whole fish dishes are a speciality.

 Pop House 🏵 🐧 🐧 ▦
Djurgårdsvägen 68 ✉ *115 21* Plan: **D2**
– ℰ (08) 502 541 40 – www.pophouse.se
49 rm 🖵 – 🛏1195/3095 SEK 🛏🛏1295/3295 SEK – 2 suites
• Boutique hotel • Personalised • Minimalist •
Pop House is ideally placed for visitors to the parks and museums of Djurgården. Bypass the queues waiting to enter 'ABBA The Museum', and head up to
one of the spacious, simply furnished bedrooms; most have balconies with
pleasant views. The small lounge, bar and restaurant are open-plan.

🏨 **Skeppsholmen**   🕏 🦢 ⇐ 🍴 ℟⑥ ✖ ⅗ ௸ ᴬᶜ ♨ ✪ **P**

Gröna Gången 1 ✉ *111 49 –* ℰ *(08) 407 23 00*   Plan: **D2**
– www.hotelskeppsholmen.se
78 rm ⌂ *–* †*1495/2995 SEK* ††*1495/2995 SEK –* 1 *suite*
• Historic • Design • Personalised •

This 17C hotel is perfect for a peaceful stay close to the city. It's set on a small island beside a beautiful park and was built by the king in 1699 for his soldiers (the conference room was once the officers' mess). White bedrooms have a minimalist style and sea or park views. Menus feature Swedish recipes.

😊 **Bar Agrikultur**   ✗

Skånegatan 79 (by Folkungagatan and Nytorgsgatan) ✉ *116 35*
– Ⓜ *Medborgarplatsen*
– www.baragrikultur.se
– Closed Christmas-New Year and midsummer
Carte 340/435 SEK – (dinner only) (bookings not accepted)
• Swedish • Cosy • Neighbourhood •

The trendy Södermalm district is home to this intimate wine bar. The constantly changing blackboard menu lists fresh, tasty small plates which showcase the region's produce. The three stainless steel tanks contain home-distilled gin – flavours are changed regularly using various herbs, oils or fruits.

😊 **Nook**   ✗

Åsögatan 176 ✉ *116 32 –* Ⓜ *Medborgarplatsen*   Plan: **D3**
– ℰ *(08) 702 1222 – www.nookrestaurang.se*
– Closed July, Christmas, Sunday and Monday
Menu 380/430 SEK – (dinner only) (booking advisable)
• Modern cuisine • Intimate • Friendly •

This modern restaurant offers great value. Drop into the bar for Asian-influenced snacks or head to the intimately lit dining room with its checkerboard floor for one of two set menus. Creative cooking blends Swedish ingredients with Korean influences; order 3 days ahead for the suckling pig feast.

🍴○ **Fotografiska**   ✗✗ ⇐ ⅗ ᴬᶜ

Stadsgårdshamnen 22 ✉ *116 45 –* Ⓜ *Slussen –* ℰ *(08)*   Plan: **D3**
50 900 500 – www.fotografiska.se
– Closed July, 25 December, midsummer and Sunday
Menu 540 SEK – Carte 400/440 SEK – (dinner only)
• Country • Rustic • Design •

Take in lovely water views from the photography museum. From the room to the food, there's a green ethos, courtesy of reclaimed wood and ethical produce. Fresh, flavoursome dishes are largely vegetarian; go for 1 cold, 2 warm and 1 sweet.

🍴○ **Café Nizza**   ✗ 🌳 ᴬᶜ

Åsögatan 171 ✉ *116 32 –* Ⓜ *Medborgarplatsen*   Plan: **D3**
– ℰ *(08) 640 99 50 – www.cafenizza.se*
– Closed 24-26 December, 1 January and midsummer
Menu 595 SEK – (dinner only) (booking essential) (tasting menu only)
• Swedish • Bistro • Neighbourhood •

Drop in for a drink and some bar snacks or a 4 course set menu of unfussy, flavoursome dishes with a mix of Swedish and French influences. The small room has chequerboard flooring, a granite-topped bar and a bustling Parisian feel.

🍴 **Häktet**   X 🏠 ⇔

Hornsgatan 82 ✉ *118 21 –* Ⓜ *Zinkensdamn –* ✆ *(08)*   Plan: **B3**
84 59 10 – www.haktet.se – Closed 24 and 31 December, 1 January,
midsummer and Sunday
Carte 395/600 SEK – *(dinner only)*
• Modern cuisine • Bistro • Simple •
From 1781-1872 this was a debtors' prison. It has a characterful courtyard terrace and three bars – one in the style of a speakeasy, with a secret door. The simple bistro at the back serves classic Swedish dishes with a modern edge.

🍴 **Woodstockholm**   X 🏠 ⇔

Mosebacke Torg 9 ✉ *116 46 –* Ⓜ *Slussen –* ✆ *(08)*   Plan: **C3**
36 93 99 – www.woodstockholm.com – Closed Christmas, Sunday and
Monday
Menu 565 SEK – Carte 525/620 SEK – *(dinner only and lunch Friday)*
• Modern cuisine • Bistro • Neighbourhood •
A chef-turned-furniture-maker owns this neighbourhood restaurant overlooking the park. Cooking follows a theme which changes every 2 months and dishes are simple yet full of flavour. In summer, the private room opens as a wine bar.

🏠 **Rival**   ⇪ 🕭 🏛

Mariatorget 3 ✉ *118 91 –* Ⓜ *Mariatorget –* ✆ *(08)*   Plan: **B3**
545 789 00 – www.rival.se
99 rm ⬒ – ♦1195/2595 SEK ♦♦1695/4195 SEK – 2 suites
• Boutique hotel • Business • Personalised •
The location is delightful: opposite a beautiful square with gardens and a fountain. It's owned by ABBA's Benny Andersson and the stylish bedrooms come with Swedish movie themes and murals of famous scenes; the 700-seater art deco theatre also hosts regular events and shows. Dine on global dishes either in the bistro or on the balcony; the café is popular for snacks.

AT ARLANDA AIRPORT Northwest : 40 km by Sveavägen and E 4

🏠 **Clarion H. Arlanda Airport**   ⇪ 🛁 🕭 ⬛ 🛗 🏛

Tornvägen 2, Sky City (at Terminals 4-5, 1st floor above street level)
✉ *190 45 –* ✆ *(08) 444 18 00 – www.choice.se/clarion/arlandaairport.se*
414 rm ⬒ – ♦990/2900 SEK ♦♦1200/3100 SEK – 13 suites
• Business • Modern • Eco-friendly •
A sleek, corporate hotel next to Terminals 4 and 5, with sound eco-credentials – they even make honey from their own hives. Relax in the large 'Living Room' lounge area or in the outside pool, then have dinner in the bistro which offers a mix of international and Swedish dishes along with runway views.

ENVIRONS OF STOCKHOLM

AT NORRTULL North : 2 km by Sveavägen (at beginning of E4)

🏠 **Stallmästaregården**   ⇪ 🍴 🏛 🅿

Nortull ✉ *113 47 –* ✆ *(08) 610 13 00 – www.stallmastaregarden.se*
– Closed 23-30 December
49 rm ⬒ – ♦1995/3120 SEK ♦♦1995/3120 SEK – 3 suites
• Inn • Historic building • Cosy •
You can enjoy beautiful views over the water to the Royal Park from this brightly painted inn, which dates from the 17C. It comprises several buildings set around a garden courtyard. Cosy bedrooms have a classic style and Oriental touches. Modern Swedish cuisine is influenced by classic Tore Wretman recipes.

AT **LADUGÅRDSGÄRDET** East : 3 km by Strandvägen

Villa Källhagen   🌿 🐕 ⇐ 🛋 🏛 AC ⚙ P

Djurgårdsbrunnsvägen 10 ✉ 115 27
– ℰ (08) 665 03 00 – www.kallhagen.se
36 rm 🛏 – ♦1295/2795 SEK ♦♦1495/2995 SEK – 3 suites
• Traditional • Business • Minimalist •
This well-run hotel is a popular place for functions, but with its tranquil
waterside location, it's a hit with leisure guests too. Bedrooms feature four
different colour schemes – inspired by the seasons – and have park or water
views. The modern Swedish menu has a classic edge and comes with wine
pairings.

AT **FJÄDERHOLMARNA ISLAND** East: 25 minutes by boat from Sodermalm,
or 5 minutes from Nacka Strand

🍴 **Fjäderholmarnas Krog**   XX ⇐ 🌳 ⅙

Stora Fjäderholmen ✉ 111 15
– ℰ (08) 7188 33 55 – www.fjaderholmarnaskrog.se
– Closed 29 September-23 November and 22 December-26 April
Menu 330/545 SEK
– Carte 415/715 SEK – (booking essential)
• Seafood • Friendly • Rustic •
The location is idyllic and on a sunny day nothing beats a spot on the ter-
race watching the ships glide through the archipelago. The airy interior has
a boathouse feel. Classic seafood dishes are replaced by a buffet table at
Christmas.

AT **ÄLVSJÖ** Southwest : 11 km by Hornsgaten and E20/E4

❁ **Aloë** (Niclas Jönsson and Daniel Höglander)   XX

Svartlösavägen 52 ✉ 125 33
– ℰ (08) 556 361 68 – www.aloerestaurant.se
– Closed Sunday-Tuesday
Menu 1600 SEK – (dinner only) (booking essential) (surprise menu only)
• Creative • Rustic • Intimate •
Unusually hidden in an old suburban supermarket, this warm, welcoming
restaurant is run by two talented chefs. Snacks at the kitchen counter are
followed by a locally-influenced surprise menu with a seafood bias. Creative
dishes stimulate the senses with their intense flavours and original combi-
nations.
➔ Langoustine, fermented beans and gochujang. Aged pork loin, apple
and vin jaune. "Forêt-Noire" with shiso

AT **LILLA ESSINGEN** West : 5.5 km by Norr Mälarstrand

🍴 **Lux Dag för Dag**   XX ⇐ 🌳 ⅙ AC

Primusgatan 116 ✉ 112 67
– ℰ (08) 619 01 90 – www.luxdagfordag.se
– Closed 23 December-7 January, 16 July-16 August, Saturday lunch,
Sunday and Monday
Menu 580 SEK (dinner)
– Carte 325/725 SEK
• Modern cuisine • Brasserie • Neighbourhood •
A bright, modern, brasserie-style restaurant in an old waterside Electrolux
factory dating back to 1916. Generously proportioned dishes might look
modern but they have a traditional base; sourcing Swedish ingredients is
paramount.

Bockholmen   XX ≤ 🏠 ⇔ 🅿

Bockholmsvägen ⊠ 170 78 – Ⓜ Bergshamra – ℰ (08) 624 22 00
– www.bockholmen.com – Closed 22 December-10 January, midsummer,
lunch October-April and Monday
Carte 425/625 SEK – *(booking essential)*
• Swedish • Traditional décor • Country house •

With charming terraces leading down to the water, and an outside bar, this 19C
summer house is the perfect place to relax on a summer's day. It's set on a tiny
island, so opening times vary. Wide-ranging menus include weekend brunch.

AT **EDSVICKEN** Northwest : 8 km by Sveavägen and E 18 towards Norrtälje

Ulriksdals Wärdshus   XX ≤ 🍴 ⇔ 🅿

Ulriksdals Slottspark (Northwest: 8 km by Sveavägen and E 18 towards
Norrtälje then take first junction for Ulriksdals Slott) ⊠ 170 79
– Ⓜ Bergshamra – ℰ (08) 85 08 15 – www.ulriksdalswardshus.se – Closed
Sunday dinner
Menu 470 SEK (weekday lunch)/945 SEK – Carte 475/830 SEK – *(booking*
essential)
• Traditional cuisine • Inn • Romantic •

A charming 19C wood-built inn located on the edge of a woodland; start with
drinks on the terrace overlooking the lake. Every table in the New England style
room has an outlook over the attractive gardens and there's a characterful wine
cellar. Classic Swedish dishes are supplemented by a smörgåsbord at lunch.

GOTHENBURG
GÖTEBORG

clagge/iStock

Gothenburg is considered to be one of Sweden's friendliest towns, a throwback to its days as a leading trading centre. This is a compact, pretty city whose roots go back four hundred years. It has trams, broad avenues and canals and its centre is boisterous but never feels tourist heavy or overcrowded. Gothenburgers take life at a more leisurely pace than their Stockholm cousins over on the east coast. The mighty shipyards that once dominated the shoreline are now quiet; go to the centre, though, and you find the good-time ambience of Avenyn, a vivacious thoroughfare full of places in which to shop, eat and drink. But for those still itching for a feel of

the heavy industry that once defined the place, there's a Volvo museum sparkling with chrome and shiny steel.

The Old Town is the historic heart of the city: its tight grid of streets has grand façades and a fascinating waterfront. Just west is the Vasastan quarter, full of fine National Romantic buildings. Further west again is Haga, an old working-class district which has been gentrified, its cobbled streets sprawling with trendy cafes and boutiques. Adjacent to Haga is the district of Linné, a vibrant area with its elegantly tall 19th century Dutch-inspired buildings. As this is a maritime town, down along the quayside is as good a place to get your bearings as any.

EATING OUT

Gothenburg's oldest food market is called Feskekörka or 'Fish Church'. It does indeed look like a place of worship but its pews are stalls of oysters, prawns and salmon, and where you might expect to find an organ loft, you'll find a restaurant instead. Food – and in particular the piscine variety – is a big reason for visiting Gothenburg. Its restaurants have earned a plethora of Michelin Stars, which are dotted all over the compact city. If you're after something a little simpler, head for one of the typical Swedish Konditoris (cafés) – two of the best are Brogyllen and Ahlströms. If you're visiting between December and April, try the traditional cardamom-spiced buns known as 'semla'. The 19C covered food markets, Stora Saluhallen at Kungstorget and Saluhallen Briggen at Nordhemsgatan in Linnestaden, are worth a visit. Also in Kungstorget is the city's most traditional beer hall, Ölhallen 7:an; there are only 6 others in town. Gothenburgers also like the traditional food pairing 'SOS', where herring and cheese are washed down with schnapps.

SWEDEN - GOTHENBURG

Upper House – Upper House Hotel   XxxX 畿 ≤ 玉 瓼

Gothia Towers (25th Floor), Mässans gata 24 ✉ *402 26*   Plan: **D3**
– 𝒞 (031) 708 82 00 – www.upperhouse.se
– Closed 10 July-7 August, 23-25 December, Sunday and Monday
Menu 995/1400 SEK – *(dinner only) (booking essential) (tasting menu only)*
• Creative • Elegant • Chic •

Look out from the 25th floor over 360° of twinkling city lights. Start with snacks in the plush bar then watch your bread being cooked over a hot stone. Two set menus offers elaborate, visually pleasing, flavourful dishes made with an abundance of local ingredients. Service is attentive and professional.
→ Quail egg, lemon and dried bleak roe. Courgette flower with sweetbreads and tomato. Cinnamon madeleine with apple butter.

Thörnströms Kök (Håkan Thörnström)   XxX 畿 玉 ⇔

Teknologgatan 3 ✉ *411 32 – 𝒞 (031) 16 20 66*
– www.thornstromskok.com
– Closed 7 July-14 August, 22 December-3 January, Easter and Sunday
Menu 675 SEK – Carte 695/755 SEK – *(dinner only) (booking essential)*
• Classic cuisine • Neighbourhood • Romantic •

An elegant, long-standing restaurant with a stunning wine cave; set in a quiet residential area and run by a welcoming, knowledgeable team. There's a good choice of menus, including 4 different tasting options. Precise, confident, classically based cooking uses top quality produce to create pronounced flavours.
→ Sweetbreads, salsify and morels. Poached turbot with burnt broccoli. Variations of blackberry, roasted wheat, lovage and rapeseed oil.

28+   XxX 畿 玉 ⇔

Götabergsgatan 28 ✉ *411 34 – 𝒞 (031) 20 21 61*
– www.28plus.se
– Closed 1 July-21 August, Christmas, New Year, Sunday, Monday and bank holidays
Menu 895 SEK – Carte 595/675 SEK – *(dinner only)*
• Modern cuisine • Romantic • Intimate •

This passionately run basement restaurant has been a Gothenburg institution for over 30 years. Modern cooking showcases prime seasonal ingredients, skilfully blending French and Swedish influences to create intricate, flavourful dishes. There's an exceptional cheese selection and an outstanding wine list.
→ Scallop, bacon, peas and caviar. Lemon sole with ramsons and asparagus beurre blanc. Blueberry sorbet with whipped cream cheese.

SK Mat & Människor (Stefan Karlsson)   XX 玉 玉

Johannebergsgatan 24 ✉ *412 55 – 𝒞 (031) 812 580*
– www.skmat.se
– Closed 5 weeks summer, Christmas, Sunday and bank holidays
Menu 595 SEK – Carte 535/560 SEK – *(dinner only) (booking essential)*
• Modern cuisine • Design • Neighbourhood •

The main focal point of this buzzy restaurant is the 360° open kitchen; not only can you watch the chefs at work but they also deliver your food. The effort put into sourcing and the reverence with which ingredients are treated is commendable and dishes are exciting and packed with flavour.
→ Chanterelles with egg custard. Lamb, carrots, wild pepper, spring onion and lamb jus. Strawberries with violet ice cream and strawberry curd.

Koka ❌ 🆑

Viktoriagatan 12 ✉ *411 25 –* ✆ *(031) 701 79 79* Plan: **B3**
– www.restaurangkoka.se – Closed July, Christmas and Sunday
Menu 480/880 SEK – *(dinner only) (tasting menu only)*
• Modern cuisine • Design • Neighbourhood •

An understatedly elegant room with wooden planks on the floors and walls and wooden furniture to match. Choose 3, 5 or 7 courses from the daily set menu; dishes are light and refreshingly playful in their approach and fish features highly. Well-chosen wines and smooth service complete the picture.
➔ Mackerel, rhubarb and beetroot. Lamb, marigold and shellfish salt. Strawberries with marjoram and mustard.

Bhoga (Gustav Knutsson) ❌

Norra Hamngatan 10 ✉ *411 14 –* ✆ *(031) 13 80 18* Plan: **B2**
– www.bhoga.se – Closed 1 week Christmas, 1 week August, Sunday and Monday
Menu 600/900 SEK – *(dinner only) (tasting menu only)*
• Creative • Design • Fashionable •

A chic, contemporary restaurant with an elegant feel, which is passionately run by two well-travelled friends and their charmingly attentive team. Top quality seasonal ingredients are used in imaginative ways, creating provocative yet harmonious texture and flavour combinations. Wine pairings are original.
➔ Mackerel with green strawberries and blackcurrant leaves. Smoked turbot, turnips and gooseberries. Beach Rose sorbet, red berries and cream.

Familjen ❌ 🏛 🌳 🆑

Arkivgatan 7 ✉ *411 34 –* ✆ *(031) 20 79 79* Plan: **C3**
– www.restaurangfamiljen.se – Closed Christmas and Sunday
Menu 375/475 SEK – Carte 340/500 SEK – *(dinner only) (booking essential)*
• Scandinavian • Design • Neighbourhood •

A lively, friendly eatery divided into three parts: a bar with bench seating and an open kitchen; a bright red room with a characterful cellar and a glass wine cave; and a superb wrap-around terrace. Cooking is good value and portions are generous. There's an appealing wine, beer and cocktail list too.

Project ❌ 🌳 ⇔

Södra vägen 45 ✉ *412 54 –* ✆ *(031) 18 18 58* Plan: **C3**
– www.projectgbg.com – Closed Christmas and Sunday-Tuesday
Menu 525/725 SEK – Carte 450/535 SEK – *(dinner only) (booking essential)*
• Modern cuisine • Neighbourhood • Fashionable •

A young couple and their charming service team run this cosy little bistro. Creative dishes are Swedish at heart and full of flavour; the delicious bread takes 5 days to make and the homemade butter, 2 days. Flexible menus allow diners to tailor their experience and provide the opportunity for sharing.

Somm ❌ 🏛 🆑 ⇔

Lorensbergsgatan 8 ✉ *411 36 –* ✆ *(031) 28 28 40* Plan: **C3**
– www.somm.se – Closed July, Christmas and midsummer
Menu 425 SEK – Carte 520/625 SEK – *(dinner only)*
• Modern cuisine • Rustic • Cosy •

A simply but warmly decorated neighbourhood bistro with contemporary artwork and a cosy, friendly feel. Quality seasonal ingredients are used to create tasty modern dishes, which feature on an à la carte and various tasting menus. The wine list offers great choice and the service is charming and professional.

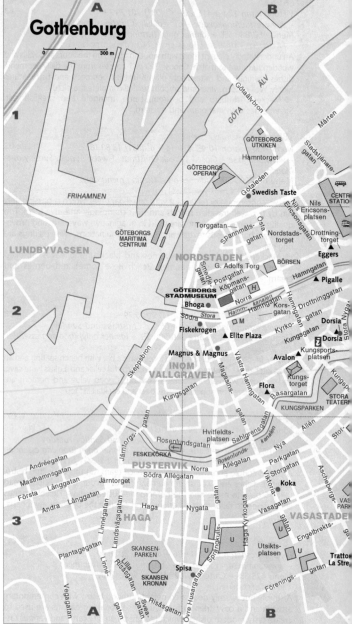

Gothenburg

0 _____ 300 m

A **B**

1

GÖTA ÄLV

GÖTA

Götaälvbron

Mårten

Stadstjänare-gatan

GÖTEBORGS UTKIKEN

Hamntorget

CENTRA STATIO

GÖTEBORGS OPERAN

Götaleden

Swedish Taste

Nils Ericssons-platsen

Nils Ericssonsgatan

FRIHAMNEN

Torggatan

Östra gatan

Spannmåls-gatan

Nordstads-torget

Drottning-torget

GÖTEBORGS MARITIMA CENTRUM

LUNDBYVASSEN

NORDSTADEN

BÖRSEN

Eggers

2

G. Adolfs Torg

Smedje-gatan

Postgatan

Köpmans-gatan

Hamngatan

Pigalle

GÖTEBORGS STADMUSEUM

Bhoga

Norra Hamn-gatan

H

Hamngatan

Hamngatan

kanalen

Korsgatan

Drottninggatan

Kyrko-gatan

Dorsia

Södra Stora

Fiskekrogen

Elite Plaza

M

Kungsgatan

Dorsia

Stora Nyga

Magnus & Magnus

Västra Hamngatan

Magnus-gatan

Avalon

Kungsports-platsen

Kungsp

Skeppsbron

Flora

Kungs-torget

INOM VALLGRAVEN

Basargatan

STORA TEATER

Kungsgatan

KUNGSPARKEN

Kungsp

Järntorgs-gatan

Hvitfeldts-platsen

Sahlgrensgatan

Allén

Stor

Rosenlundsgatan

kanalen

Andréegatan

FESKEKÖRKA

Nya

Parkgatan

Ascheberg

Masthamnsgatan

PUSTERVIK

Norra

Rosenlunds-Allégatan

Storgatan

VAS PARK

Första

Långgatan

Järntorget

Södra Allégatan

gatan

Viktoria-

Vasagatan

Koka

Andra

Långgatan

Haga

Nygata

Haga Kyrkogata

Viktoria-

VASASTADE

3

Linnégatan

Plantagegatan

Landsvägsgatan

HAGA

Sprängkulls-

U

U

Utsikts-platsen

Engelbrekts-

Tratto La Stre

Lilla Risåsgatan

SKANSEN-PARKEN

Spisa

U

Förenings-gatan

Linné-

Svea-

Risåsgatan

SKANSEN KRONAN

Övre Husargatan

Vegagatan

gatan

A **B**

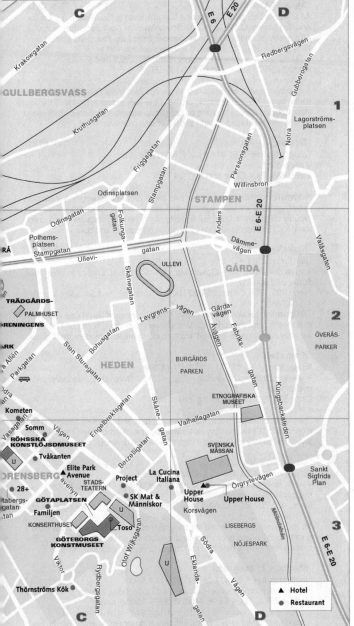

C

D

E 6
E 20
E 6

Krakowgatan

Redbergsvägen

Gubberogatan

GULLBERGSVASS

1

Lagorströms-
platsen

Kruthusgatan

Notra

Friggagatan

Stampgatan

Perssonsgatan

Odinsplatsen

Willinsbron

STAMPEN

E 6-E 20

Odinsgatan

Anders

Folkunga-
gatan

Dämme-
vägen

Valåsgatan

RÅ

Polhems-
platsen
Stampgatan

Ullevi-

gatan

 ULLEVI

GÅRDA

Skånegatan

TRÄDGÅRDS-
PALMHUSET

Levgrens-

vägen

Gårda-
vägen

Fabriks-

2

ÖVERÅS-
PARKER

RENINGENS

ARK

a Allén

Parkgatan

Bohusgatan

Sten Sturegatan

Åvägen

BURGÅRDS

PARKEN

gatan

Kungsbackaleden

Södra
an

HEDEN

Skåne-

gatan

Engelbrektsgatan

ETNOGRAFISKA
MUSEET

Kometen

Valhallagatan

Vägen

Somm

Vasagatan

RÖHSSKA
KONSTLÖJSDMUSEET

Tvåkanten

Berzeliigatan

SVENSKA
MÄSSAN

Sankt
Sigfrids
Plan

U

RENSBERG

Elite Park
Avenue

Project

La Cucina
Italiana

Örgrytevägen

28+

tabergs-
gatan
tan

STADS-
TEATERN

GÖTAPLATSEN

SK Mat &
Människor

Upper
House

Upper House

Korsvägen

Familjen

KONSERTHUSET

U

Toso

LISEBERGS

NÖJESPARK

GÖTEBORGS
KONSTMUSEET

Olof Wijksgatan

Viktor

Rydbergsgatan

U

Eklanda-

Södra

Vägen

Mölndalsån

E 6-E 20

3

Thörnströms Kök

▲ Hotel
● Restaurant

C

D

635

Sjömagasinet   XxX 錄 ≤ 斋 & ✿ **P**

Adolf Edelsvärds gata 5, Klippans Kulturreservat 5 (Southwest: 3.5 km by
Andréeg taking Kiel-Klippan exit (Stena Line), or boat from Rosenlund.
Also evenings and weekends in summer from Lilla Bommens Hamn)
✉ 414 51 – ℰ (031) 775 59 20 – www.sjomagasinet.se
– *Closed 23 December-10 January, Saturday lunch and Sunday*
Menu 595/925 SEK – Carte 745/1165 SEK
• Swedish • Rustic • Traditional décor •

A charming split-level restaurant in an old East India Company warehouse
dating from 1775; ask for a table on the upper floor to take in the lovely harbour
view. Cooking offers a pleasing mix of classic and modern dishes; lunch sees a
concise version of the à la carte and a 3 course set menu.

Dorsia – Dorsia Hotel   XX 錄 斋 **AC** ✿

Trädgårdsgatan 6 ✉ *411 08* – ℰ *(031) 790 10 00*   Plan: **B2**
– *www.dorsia.se*
Menu 385 SEK – Carte 600/800 SEK
• Modern cuisine • Exotic décor • Romantic •

A dramatic hotel dining room split over two levels, with striking flower arrange-
ments, gloriously quirky lighting, and belle époque oil paintings hanging
proudly on the walls. Local fish features highly and puddings are worth saving
room for. The impressive wine list is rich in burgundies and clarets.

Fiskekrogen   XX 錄 **AC** ✿

Lilla Torget 1 ✉ *411 18* – ℰ *(031) 10 10 05*   Plan: **B2**
– *www.fiskekrogen.se* – *Closed mid July-mid August, Christmas, New Year,*
Easter and Sunday
Menu 495 SEK – Carte 525/800 SEK – *(dinner only and Saturday lunch)*
• Seafood • Elegant • Classic décor •

This charming restaurant is set within a 1920s columned Grand Café and showcases top quality seafood in classical dishes; the seafood buffet on Friday and
Saturday is impressive. 'Bifångst' offers a tasting menu of modern small plates.

Kometen   XX 斋

Vasagatan 58 ✉ *411 37* – ℰ *(031) 137988*   Plan: **C2**
– *www.restaurangkometen.se* – *Closed 23-27 December, 1 January and*
midsummer
Carte 335/790 SEK – *(booking essential)*
• Swedish • Traditional décor • Neighbourhood •

The oldest restaurant in town has a classic façade and a homely, traditional feel;
it opened in 1934 and is now part-owned by celebrated chef Leif Mannerström.
Sweden's culinary traditions are kept alive here in generous, tasty dishes.

La Cucina Italiana   X 斋

Skånegatan 33 ✉ *412 52* – ℰ *(031) 166 307*   Plan: **C3**
– *www.lacucinaitaliana.nu* – *Closed 2 weeks July, Christmas, Easter,*
midsummer, Sunday-Monday
Menu 400/700 SEK – Carte 430/620 SEK – *(dinner only) (booking essential)*
• Italian • Intimate • Neighbourhood •

An enthusiastically run restaurant consisting of 6 tables. Choose between the à
la carte, a daily fixed price menu and a 6 course surprise tasting 'journey'. The
chef-owner regularly travels to Italy to buy cheeses, meats and wines.

Magnus & Magnus   X 斋

Magasinsgatan 8 ✉ *411 18* – ℰ *(031) 13 30 00*   Plan: **B2**
– *www.magnusmagnus.se* – *Closed 24-25 December, Sunday and Monday*
Menu 495/745 SEK – Carte 440/555 SEK – *(dinner only)*
• Modern cuisine • Fashionable • Neighbourhood •

A trendy restaurant with a warm, intimate atmosphere, a central bar, an open
kitchen and a bright, well-informed team. Modern Nordic cooking has the occasional Asian twist; most diners plump for the set 4 course menu.

Spisa

X & AC

Övre Husargatan 3 ⊠ 411 22 – ℰ (031) 3860610   Plan: **B3**
– www.spisamatbar.se – Closed dinner Monday and lunch Saturday and Sunday
Menu 295/495 SEK – Carte 305/445 SEK
• Mediterranean cuisine • Fashionable • Neighbourhood •

A contemporary restaurant set in an up-and-coming area a short walk from the city centre and frequented by a lively, sociable crowd. The menu offers tasty sharing plates with French, Spanish and Italian origins. Try a cocktail too.

Toso

X AC

Götaplatsen ⊠ 412 56 – ℰ (031) 787 98 00   Plan: **C3**
– www.toso.nu – Closed Christmas, 1 January and bank holidays
Carte 355/550 SEK – (dinner only)
• Asian • Bistro • Exotic décor •

There's something for everyone at this modern Asian restaurant, where terracotta warriors stand guard and loud music pumps through the air. Dishes mix Chinese and Japanese influences; start with some of the tempting small plates.

Trattoria La Strega

X 斎

Aschebergsgatan 23B ⊠ 411 27 – ℰ (031) 18 15 01   Plan: **B3**
– www.trattorialastrega.se – Closed July, 24 December-6 January and Monday
Menu 600 SEK – Carte 320/530 SEK – (dinner only) (booking essential)
• Italian • Friendly • Bistro •

A lively little trattoria in a quiet residential area; run by a charming owner. Sit at a candlelit table to enjoy authentic, boldly flavoured Italian cooking and well-chosen wines. Signature dishes include pasta with King crab ragout.

Tvåkanten

X 斎 斎 ⇔

Kungsportsavenyn 27 ⊠ 411 36 – ℰ (031) 18 21 15   Plan: **C3**
– www.tvakanten.se – Closed Christmas, Easter, midsummer and bank holidays
Menu 645 SEK (dinner) – Carte 395/705 SEK
• Traditional cuisine • Brasserie • Neighbourhood •

With its welcoming hum and friendly team, it's no wonder this long-standing family-run restaurant is always busy. The dimly-lit, brick-walled dining room is the place to eat. Homely lunches are followed by more ambitious dinners.

vRÅ

X & AC

Clarion Hotel Post, Drottningtorget 10 ⊠ 411 03   Plan: **C2**
– ℰ (031) 61 90 60 – www.restaurangvra.se – Closed 12 July-12 August, Christmas, Sunday and Monday
Menu 495/1050 SEK – Carte 335/545 SEK – (dinner only)
• Japanese • Fashionable • Simple •

A modern hotel restaurant run by an attentive, knowledgeable team. Their tagline is 'Swedish ingredients, Japanese flavours' and the produce is top quality. Choose the 8 course set menu or a menu with 3 core dishes which you can add to.

Elite Park Avenue

⇧ ≼ ₤ᵒ 祝 AC ᏚᎯ ⇔

Kungsportsavenyn 36-38 ⊠ 400 15 – ℰ (031) 727 1076   Plan: **C3**
– www.parkavenuecafe.se
317 rm ⊡ – †1050/2350 SEK ††1250/2750 SEK – 9 suites
• Business • Traditional • Modern •

Set in a lively location close to many museums and galleries, the Elite Park Avenue is a popular place for conferences. The interior is stylish and the bedrooms are spacious and well-equipped – the rooftop suites come with balconies. Dine in the English pub or on French or Swedish dishes in the bistro.

Elite Plaza

Västra Hamngatan 3 ✉ *402 22 –* ✆ *(031) 720 40 40*   Plan: **B2**
– www.elite.se – Closed 22-26 December
127 rm ⌑ *–* ♦1200/2900 SEK ♦♦1400/3900 SEK *– 3 suites*
• Traditional • Business • Modern •
This elegant building dates back to the 19C and features ornate ceilings and a Venetian-style sitting room. Bedrooms seamlessly blend the classic and the modern and the service is welcoming and personalised. The restaurant sits within a glass-enclosed courtyard and mixes French and Scandinavian influences.

Upper House

Gothia Towers, Mässans gata 24 ✉ *402 26 –* ✆ *(031)*   Plan: **D3**
708 82 00 – www.upperhouse.se
53 rm ⌑ *–* ♦2890/5390 SEK ♦♦2890/5390 SEK *– 1 suite*
• Luxury • Business • Modern •
Set at the top of one of the Gothia Towers; take in the dramatic view from the terrace or from the lovely three-storey spa. Spacious bedrooms are filled with top electronic equipment and Scandic art – the duplex suites are sublime.
❀ **Upper House** – See restaurant listing

Avalon

Kungstorget 9 ✉ *411 17 –* ✆ *(031) 751 02 00*   Plan: **B2**
– www.avalonhotel.se
101 rm ⌑ *–* ♦1245/2445 SEK ♦♦1445/2745 SEK *– 3 suites*
• Business • Boutique hotel • Design •
A boutique hotel in a great location near the shops, theatres and river. Designer bedrooms have the latest mod cons and come with stylish bathrooms; the penthouse suites have balconies. Relax in the rooftop pool then head for the all-day bistro, which opens onto the piazza and serves international cuisine.

Dorsia

Trädgårdsgatan 8 ✉ *411 08 –* ✆ *(031) 790 10 00*   Plan: **B2**
– www.dorsia.se
37 rm ⌑ *–* ♦2000 SEK ♦♦2600/7000 SEK
• Townhouse • Luxury • Art déco •
Exuberant, eccentric, seductive and possibly a little decadent, this townhouse hotel comes with a theatrical belle époque style, where art from the owner's personal collection, fine fabrics and rich colours add to the joie de vivre. The restaurant is equally vibrant and the atmosphere suitably relaxed. The Salon is set to serve gourmet dinners as of Spring 2018.
⊓O **Dorsia** – See restaurant listing

Eggers

Drottningtorget 2-4 ✉ *411 03 –* ✆ *(031) 3334440*   Plan: **B2**
– www.hoteleggers.se – Closed 22-27 December
69 rm ⌑ *–* ♦995/2190 SEK ♦♦1220/3325 SEK
• Traditional • Luxury • Elegant •
An elegant railway hotel that opened in 1859 with electricity and a telephone in every room. The warm, welcoming interior features old wrought iron, stained glass and period furnishings. The characterful restaurant still has its original wallpaper and offers Swedish and French favourites.

Pigalle

Södra Hamngatan 2A ✉ *411 06 –* ✆ *(031) 802921*   Plan: **B2**
– www.hotelpigalle.se
60 rm ⌑ *–* ♦1000/1700 SEK ♦♦1700/2600 SEK *– 1 suite*
• Townhouse • Family • Vintage •
A top-hatted manager will welcome you to the reception-cum-welcome-bar of this quirky hotel, which is set within the walls of a historic building. The décor is bold and eclectic, with dramatic features and plenty of personality. In the restaurant you can choose to sit at proper tables or on comfy sofas.

Flora

Plan: **B2**

Grönsaksgatan 2 ✉ *411 17 – ☎ (031) 13 86 16*
– www.hotelflora.se – Closed 22 December- 2 January
70 rm ⌂ – ♦1120/1720 SEK ♦♦1450/1970 SEK
• Family • Business • Design •

This well-located Victorian mid-terrace is nicely run and has a relaxed, funky feel.
Bedrooms benefit from high ceilings; ask for one of the newer, designer rooms.
The bar-lounge is a popular spot and doubles as the breakfast room.

ENVIRONS OF GOTHENBURG

AT ERIKSBERG West : 6 km by Götaälvbron and Lundbyleden, or boat from
Rosenlund

Villan

Sjöportsgatan 2 ✉ *417 64 – ☎ (031) 725 77 77 – www.hotelvillan.com*
26 rm ⌂ – ♦1100/1600 SEK ♦♦1300/2000 SEK
• Traditional • Family • Cosy •

A characterful wood-clad, family-run house; once home to a shipbuilding manager and later floated over to this location. The stylish interior has smart, clean
lines. Contemporary bedrooms boast good mod cons – No.31 has a sauna and
a TV in the bathroom. The first floor restaurant overlooks the river.

AT LANDVETTER AIRPORT East : 30 km by Rd 40

Landvetter Airport Hotel

Flygets Hotellväg ✉ *438 13 – ☎ (031) 97 75 50*
– www.landvetterairporthotel.com
187 rm ⌂ – ♦1595 SEK ♦♦1695/2495 SEK – 1 suite
• Business • Family • Design •

A family-run hotel located just minutes from the airport terminal. The light,
open interior has a calm air and a fresh Scandic style, and bedrooms have an
unfussy retro feel. The informal restaurant offers a mix of Swedish and global
dishes, along with a BBQ and grill menu at dinner.

Malmö
MALMÖ

Allard1/iStock

MALMÖ IN...

→ **ONE DAY**
Lilla Torg and the Form/Design Centre, Western Harbour.

→ **TWO DAYS**
Modern Museum, Contemporary Art Exhibition at the Konsthall.

→ **THREE DAYS**
Skt Petri Church, an evening at the Malmö Opera.

Malmö was founded in the 13C under Danish rule and it wasn't until 1658 that it entered Swedish possession and subsequently established itself as one of the world's biggest shipyards. The building of the 8km long Øresund Bridge in 2000 reconnected the city with Denmark and a year later, the Turning Torso apartment block was built in the old shipyard district, opening up the city to the waterfront. Once an industrial hub, this 'city of knowledge' has impressively green credentials: buses run on natural gas and there are 400km of bike lanes. There's plenty of green space too; you can picnic in Kungsparken or Slottsparken, sit by the lakes in Pildammsparken or pet the farm animals in 'Folkets'.

At the heart of this vibrant city lie three squares: Gustav Adolfs Torg, Stortorget and Lilla Torg, connected by a pedestrianised shopping street. You'll find some of Malmö's oldest buildings in Lilla Torg, along with bustling open-air brasseries; to the west is Scandinavia's oldest surviving Renaissance castle and its beautiful gardens – and beyond that, the 2km Ribersborg Beach with its open-air baths. North is Gamla Väster with its charming houses and galleries, while south is Davidshall, filled with designer boutiques and chic eateries. Further south is Möllevångstorget, home to a throng of reasonably priced Asian and Middle Eastern shops.

EATING OUT

The gloriously fertile region of Skåne puts a wealth of top quality produce on Malmö's doorstep. Dishes rich in dairy and meat – perhaps a little meatier than expected given its waterside proximity – are staple fare and wild herbs and foraged ingredients are the order of the day; wild garlic, asparagus, potatoes and rhubarb are all celebrated here. The locals eat early, so don't be surprised if you're one of just a handful of diners at 1pm or 8pm. The popular social phenomenon 'fika' is a tradition observed by most, preferably several times a day, and involves the drinking of coffee accompanied by something sweet; usually cake or cinnamon buns. Hot meals are popular midday – look out for the great value dagens lunch, which often offers the dish of the day plus salad, bread and water for under 100kr – or for lunch on the run, grab a tunnbrödsrull (sausage and mashed potato in a wrap) from a Korv kiosk. Local delicacies include äggakaka (thick pancakes and bacon), wallenbergare (minced veal patties with mashed potato and peas), marinated herring, eel and goose.

❀❀ **Vollmers** (Mats Vollmer) XX 🔣 ⟷
Tegelgårdsgatan 5 ✉ *211 33 –* ℰ *(040) 57 97 50* Plan II : **E2**
– www.vollmers.nu – Closed 3 weeks January and Sunday
Menu 950/1350 SEK – *(dinner only) (booking essential) (tasting menu only)*
• Creative • Elegant • Intimate •

An intimate restaurant with charming, professional service, set in a pretty 19C townhouse. The talented Mats Vollmer showcases some of the area's finest seasonal ingredients in set 4, 6 or 8 course menus of intricate and elaborate modern dishes, which are innovative, perfectly balanced and full of flavour.
→ Nettle soup with lumpfish roe and green tomatoes. Lamb with spring onions and potato. Strawberry, violet and cream.

❀ **SAV** (Sven Jensen and Alexander Fohlin) XX ⟺ **P**
Vindåkravägen 3, Tygelsjö (South 10.5 km by Trelleborgsvägen E22/E6)
✉ *21875 –* ℰ *(072) 022 85 20 – www.savrestaurang.nu – Closed 23 December-9 January, 21-24 February, 28-31 March, 22 June-31 July and Sunday-Tuesday*
Menu 565/795 SEK – *(dinner only) (booking essential) (surprise menu only)*
• Creative • Cosy • Rustic •

Flickering candles and crackling fires provide a warm welcome at this charming 19C farmhouse. The two young chefs pick many of the ingredients and explain their surprise menu personally. Dishes belie their apparent simplicity – inspired combinations of tastes, textures and temperatures all play their part.
→ Sugar beet, goat's cheese and truffle. Pork with glazed parsley root and gooseberry. Fermented apple, pine syrup and apple sorbet.

❀ **Bloom in the Park** XX 🌭 ⅋ 🔣
Pildammsvägen 17 ✉ *214 66 –* ℰ *(040) 793 63* Plan I: **B2**
– www.bloominthepark.se – Closed 24 December, Easter, Sunday and bank holidays
Menu 695 SEK – *(dinner only) (booking advisable) (surprise menu only)*
• Creative • Design • Chic •

A delightful lakeside lodge with a waterside terrace for drinks, run by an ebullient owner. There is no written menu or wine list; instead, the kitchen prepares a balanced set meal of modern dishes with international influences, which are accompanied by thoughtfully paired wines.
→ Cod, wasabi, peas and grapefruit. Variations of lamb with cabbage, truffle and walnuts. Chocolate, Sichuan pepper, passion fruit and white chocolate.

❀ **Sture** (Karim Khouani) XX
Adelgatan 13 ✉ *21122 –* ℰ *40 12 12 53* Plan II : **E1**
– www.restaurantsture.com – Closed July, 21-31 December and Sunday
Menu 950/1195 SEK – *(dinner only) (tasting menu only)*
• French • Friendly • Neighbourhood •

In 2016, accomplished chef Karim Khouani brought his exciting blend of French and Scandic cooking from the country into the centre of the city, reinvigorating this culinary institution. Top quality ingredients are used to create inventive, well-balanced and sublimely flavoured dishes.
→ Foie gras with passion fruit and nuts. Turbot with lettuce and chicken stock. Apricot soufflé with vanilla.

🈁 **Bastard** X 🌭 🔣
Mäster Johansgatan 11 ✉ *211 21 –* ℰ *(040) 12 13 18* Plan II : **E1**
– www.bastardrestaurant.se – Closed Christmas, New Year, Easter, midsummer, Sunday and Monday
Carte 285/365 SEK – *(dinner only) (booking advisable)*
• Modern cuisine • Simple • Trendy •

Popular with the locals, this is a bustling venue with an edgy, urban vibe. Stylewise, schoolroom meets old-fashioned butcher's, with vintage wood furniture, tiled walls, moody lighting and an open kitchen. Small plates offer nose-to-tail eating with bold, earthy flavours; start with a 'Bastard Plank' to share.

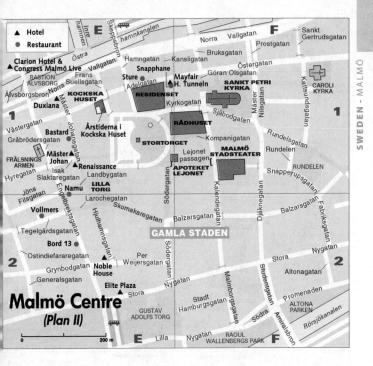

Malmö Centre
(Plan II)

- ▲ Hotel
- ● Restaurant

0 — 200 m

Namu   X 🛋 AC
Landbygatan 5 ☒ 21134 – ℰ (040) 12 14 90   Plan II : E1/2
*– www.namu.nu – Closed Christmas, 31 December-1 January, Sunday and
Monday*
Menu 395/595 SEK (dinner) – Carte 355/550 SEK
· Korean · Friendly · Simple ·

Colourful, zingy food from a past Swedish MasterChef winner blends authentic
Korean flavours with a modern Scandinavian touch. Dishes are satisfying – particularly the fortifying ramen – and desserts are more than an afterthought. Cookbooks line the shelves and friendly service adds to the lively atmosphere.

Årstiderna i Kockska Huset   XxX 🛋 ✿
Frans Suellsgatan 3 ☒ 211 22 – ℰ (040) 23 09 10   Plan II : E1
*– www.arstiderna.se – Closed July, Easter, 24-26 December, Saturday
lunch, Sunday and bank holidays*
Menu 525 SEK (dinner) – Carte 485/905 SEK
· Traditional cuisine · Elegant · Historic ·

Set in softly lit, vaulted cellars, this elegant, formal restaurant is a city institution.
Classic cooking proves a match for its surroundings, with local, seasonal ingredients proudly used to create traditional Swedish dishes.

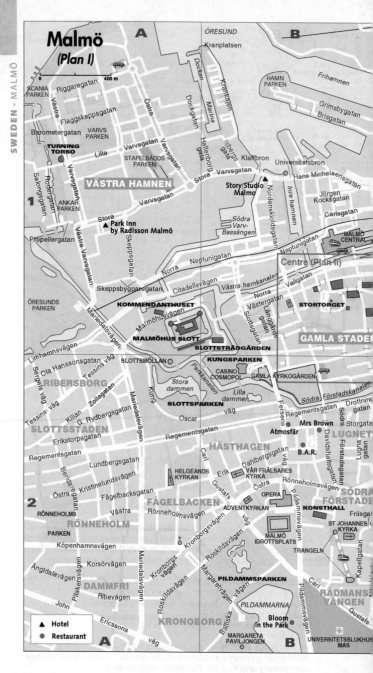

Malmö
(Plan I)

ÖRESUND

B

SWEDEN - MALMÖ

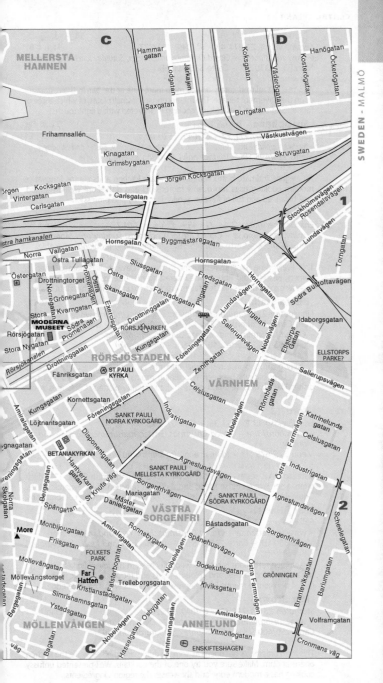

MELLERSTA HAMNEN

Hammargatan
Lodgatan
Jårkajen
Saxgatan
Koksgatan
Väderögatan
Hanögatan
Kosterögatan
Öckerögatan

Frihamnsallén
Borrgatan
Västkustvägen

Kinagatan
Grimsbygatan
Skruvgatan

Jörgen Kocksgatan

Örgen
Kocksgatan
Vintergatan
Carlsgatan

Carlsgatan
Stockholmsvägen
Rosendalsvägen
Lundavägen
Torngatan

Östra hamkanalen
Hornsgatan
Byggmästaregatan

Norra Vallgatan
Hornsgatan
Östra Tullagatan
Slussgatan
Fredsgatan
Hornsgatan

Östergatan
Drottningtorget
Östra Promenaden
Östra
Skansgatan
Förstadsgatan
Piltgatan
Södra Bulltoftavägen

Norregatan
Grönegatan
Kvarngatan
Exercisgatan
Drottninggatan
Lundavägen
Vårgatan
Nobelvägen
Sallerupsvägen
Idaborgsgatan
Ellstorps Gatan

Stora
MODERNA MUSEET
Södra Promenaden
RÖRSJÖPARKEN
Kungsgatan
Föreningsgatan

Rörsjögatan
Stora Nygatan
ELLSTORPS PARKE?

Rörsjökanalen
Drottninggatan
RÖRSJÖSTADEN
Zenithgatan
Sallerupsvägen

Fänriksgatan
ST PAULI KYRKA
VÄRNHEM

Celsiusgatan

Kungsgatan
Kornettsgatan
Föreningsgatan
Industrigatan
Nobelvägen
Römblads gatan
Katrinelunds gatan

Amiralsgatan
Löjtnantsgatan
Disponentgatan
SANKT PAULI NORRA KYRKOGÅRD
Farmvägen
Celsiusgatan

gnagatan
BETANIAKYRKAN
Hantverkaregatan
Östra Industrigatan

reningsgatan
Bergsgatan
St Knuts väg
Agneslundsvägen
SANKT PAULI MELLESTA KYRKOGÅRD
Östra Industrigatan

Norra Skolgatan
Spångatan
Sorgenfrivägen
Mariagatan
Mäster Danielsgatan
SANKT PAULI SÖDRA KYRKOGÅRD
Agneslundsvägen
Scheelegatan

More
Monbijougatan
VÄSTRA SORGENFRI
Amiralsgatan
Ronnebygatan
Spånehusvägen
Sorgenfrivägen

Friisgatan
FOLKETS PARK
Nobelvägen
Båstadsgatan
Östra Farmvägen
GRÖNINGEN
Branteviksgatan
Bariumgatan

Mollevångsgatan
Möllevångstorget
Far i Hatten
Falsterbogatan
Bodekullsgatan
Kiviksgatan

Bergsgatan
Simrishamnsgatan
Kristianstadsgatan
Trelleborgsgatan
Amiralsgatan
Volframgatan

stadsgatan
Ystadsgatan
MÖLLENVÄNGEN
Nobelvägen
Hasselgatan
Lantmannagatan
Osbygatan
ANNELUND
Vitmöllegatan
Cronmans väg

väg
Bagatan
ENSKIFTESHAGEN

C
D

1
2

C
D

🍴 **Atmosfär**   XX 🍴 ६ 🅰 ⇔

Fersens väg 4 ✉ *211 42* – ✆ *(040) 12 50 77*   Plan I: **B2**
– www.atmosfar.com – Closed Christmas, midsummer, Saturday lunch and Sunday
Menu 125/330 SEK – Carte 335/490 SEK
• Swedish • Neighbourhood •

A formal yet relaxed eatery on the main road; dine at the bar, in the restaurant or on the pavement terrace. The menu consists of small plates, of which three or four should suffice. Fresh Skåne cooking is delivered with a light touch.

🍴 **Snapphane** – Mayfair Hotel Tunneln   XX 🅰 ☜

Adelgatan 4 ✉ *211 22* – ✆ *(040) 15 01 00*   Plan II: **E1**
– www.snapphane.nu – Closed 22-26 December, 1 January, Easter and Sunday
Menu 225/495 SEK – *(dinner only) (booking essential)*
• Modern cuisine • Trendy • Intimate •

An elegant, intimate bistro with an open-plan kitchen at its centre. Innovative modern cooking uses top quality ingredients and dishes are well-presented, well-balanced and full of flavour. Service is friendly and professional.

🍴 **B.A.R.**   X 🍴 ⇔

Erik Dahlbersgatan 3 ✉ *211 48* – ✆ *(040) 17 01 75*   Plan I: **B2**
– www.barmalmo.se – Closed Easter, Christmas, Sunday and Monday
Menu 400 SEK – Carte 335/445 SEK – *(dinner only) (booking advisable)*
• Modern cuisine • Wine bar • Neighbourhood •

This lively wine-bar-cum-restaurant in trendy Davidshall is named after its owners, Besnick And Robert. The interesting menu tends towards the experimental; expect dishes like Jerusalem artichoke ice cream with hazelnut mayo.

🍴 **Bistro Stella**   X ⇔

Linnégatan 25, Limhamn (Southwest: 7 km by Limhamnsvägen: bus 4 from Central station) ✉ *216 12* – ✆ *(040) 15 60 40 – www.bistrostella.se – Closed Christmas, midsummer, Sunday and Monday*
Menu 395 SEK – Carte 240/635 SEK – *(dinner only)*
• Modern cuisine • Neighbourhood • Pub •

A lively gastropub in a residential area not far from the Øresund Bridge. Its bright, cosy bar sits between two dining rooms and its menu features pub dishes like burgers, fish and chips and charcuterie platters. Cooking is rustic and tasty.

🍴 **Bord 13**   X

Engelbrektsg 13 ✉ *211 33* – ✆ *(042) 58788*   Plan II: **E2**
– www.bord13.se – Closed Christmas, Easter, midsummer, Sunday and Monday
Menu 375/675 SEK – *(dinner only) (tasting menu only)*
• Creative • Wine bar • Friendly •

Sister to B.A.R. restaurant, is the bright, spacious and stylish 'Table 13', which offers a set 3 or 6 course menu and a diverse selection of biodynamic wines. Original Nordic cooking has some interesting texture and flavour combinations.

🍴 **Far i Hatten**   X 🍴

Folkets Park ✉ *21437* – ✆ *(040) 615 36 51*   Plan I: **C2**
– www.farihatten.se – Closed Christmas, New Year and midsummer
Menu 350 SEK – Carte 235/375 SEK – *(dinner only and lunch June-August)*
• Swedish • Rustic • Friendly •

This unique restaurant is set in a wooden chalet in the lovely Folkets Park and has a cosy, informal feel, and colourful lights and regular live music in the summer. 4 or 6 course menus list well-presented classics with a creative edge.

🍴 **Mrs Brown**   X 🍴 ६ 🅰

Storgatan 26 ✉ *211 42* – ✆ *(040) 97 22 50*   Plan I: **B2**
– www.mrsbrown.se – Closed Easter, 24 December and Sunday
Carte 250/400 SEK – *(dinner only and Saturday lunch)*
• Traditional cuisine • Wine bar • Trendy •

This retro brasserie's bar opens at 3pm for drinks and nibbles, while the kitchen opens at 6pm. Make sure you try one of the cocktails. Well-presented unfussy cooking has a modern edge and showcases the region's ingredients.

Clarion H. and Congress Malmö Live

Dag Hammarskjölds Torg 2 ✉ *211 18 –* ☎ *(040) 207500*
– www.clarionlive.se
444 rm ⌂ – **†**980/2580 SEK **††**980/2580 SEK – 2 suites
• Business • Modern • Functional •

Plan II : **E1**

The city's second tallest building affords a superb 360° view of the city; choose a bedroom on an upper floor for a view of the Øresund Bridge and Denmark. Kitchen & Table's eclectic menu combines American classics and international influences and you can enjoy a cocktail in the adjoining Skybar. The Ground floor houses an informal Mexican-themed restaurant and bar.

Elite Plaza

Gustav Adolfs torg 49 ✉ *211 39 –* ☎ *(040) 66 44 871*
– www.elite.se
116 rm ⌂ – **†**977/2372 SEK **††**1100/2712 SEK – 1 suite
• Business • Chain • Modern •

Plan II : **E2**

Behind the wonderful period façade is a smart, up-to-date corporate hotel. Modern bedrooms are a good size: the best look onto a pretty square; the quietest overlook the inner courtyard. The British-themed bar has a pleasant pavement terrace.

Mäster Johan

Mäster Johangatan 13 ✉ *211 21 –* ☎ *(040) 664 64 00*
– www.masterjohan.se – Closed Christmas
68 rm ⌂ – **†**900/2000 SEK **††**1400/2500 SEK – 10 suites
• Business • Modern • Personalised •

Plan II : **E1**

A centrally located hotel, just off the main square, with a relaxed and peaceful air. Stylish, well-proportioned bedrooms have luxurious touches. Enjoy a locally sourced organic breakfast under the atrium's glass roof.

Renaissance

Mäster Johansgatan 15 ✉ *211 21 –* ☎ *(040) 248 500*
– www.renaissancemalmo.se
128 rm ⌂ – **†**995/2195 SEK **††**1046/2345 SEK – 1 suite
• Business • Chain • Modern •

Plan II : **E1**

A smart hotel on the site of the city's original food market: beamed ceilings and iron columns bring character to the modern interior. Bright, well-equipped bedrooms are quiet considering the hotel's location. There's a colourful bar and a simply furnished restaurant; modern dishes are created using local produce.

Story Studio Malmo

Tyfongatan 1 ✉ *211 19 –* ☎ *(040) 616 52 00*
– www.storyhotels.com – Closed 23-25 December
95 rm ⌂ – **†**790/2190 SEK **††**790/2190 SEK
• Chain • Business • Personalised •

Plan I : **B1**

The modern, well-equipped bedrooms of this hotel are situated on the top 5 floors of a 14 storey building next to the old port, and feature floor to ceiling windows. The ground floor eatery offers French cuisine, while the rooftop restaurant serves Asian dishes accompanied by beautiful city and harbour views.

Duxiana

Mäster Johansgatan 1 ✉ *211 21 –* ☎ *(040) 60 77 000*
– www.malmo.hotelduxiana.com
22 rm – **†**900/2315 SEK **††**1130/2315 SEK – ⌂ 70 SEK
• Townhouse • Design • Contemporary •

Plan II : **E1**

A well-located boutique hotel; owned by the Dux bed company, who unusually use part of the lobby to showcase their products! Chic, contemporary bedrooms range from compact singles to elegant junior suites with a bath in the room. Staff are friendly and professional. Modern Swedish dishes are served at lunch.

Mayfair H. Tunneln

Adelgatan 4 ⊠ *211 22 –* ℰ *(040) 10 16 20* Plan II : **E1**
– www.mayfairhotel.se
81 rm ⌸ – **†**800/1900 SEK **††**900/2200 SEK
• Townhouse • Historic • Personalised •

An imposing early 17C property steeped in history. Some of the homely, spotlessly kept bedrooms have spa baths. Breakfast is served in the impressive vaulted cellars dating back to 1307 and you can enjoy a complimentary coffee in the classical lounge. Snapphane showcases the latest local, organic ingredients.
⊩○ **Snapphane** – See restaurant listing

More

Norra Skolgatan 24 ⊠ *214 22 –* ℰ *(040) 655 10 00* Plan I: **C2**
– www.themorehotel.com
68 rm ⌸ – **†**895/1695 SEK **††**1095/2695 SEK
• Townhouse • Business • Modern •

A striking aparthotel converted from a late 19C chocolate factory. The studios are modern and extremely spacious, with kitchenettes, sofa beds and light loft-style living areas. They are let on a nightly basis but are ideal for longer stays.

Park Inn by Radisson Malmö

Sjömansgatan 2 ⊠ *211 19 –* ℰ *(040) 628 6000* Plan I: **A1**
– www.parkinn.com/hotel-malmo
231 rm ⌸ – **†**795/1395 SEK **††**795/1395 SEK
• Chain • Functional • Modern •

A good value hotel, well-situated on the Western Harbour beside the World Trade Centre and the Västra Hamnen waterfront. Bedrooms are spacious and well-equipped; the business rooms on the higher floors come with robes and have better views. The Bar & Grill offers easy dining.

Noble House

Per Weijersgatan 6 ⊠ *21134 –* ℰ *(040) 664 30 00* Plan II : **E2**
– www.hotelnoblehouse.se
137 rm ⌸ – **†**795/1550 SEK **††**895/1750 SEK – 2 suites
• Business • Family • Functional •

A centrally located hotel, close to the bus station. Classically furnished, well-equipped bedrooms offer good value for money; ask for a room on one of the upper floors. There's a cosy lounge and a modern restaurant which serves traditional Swedish dishes.

SWITZERLAND
SUISSE, SCHWEIZ, SVIZZERA

AleksandarGeorgiev/iStock

BERN
BERNE

LeeYiuTung/IStock

To look at Bern, you'd never believe it to be a capital city. Small and beautifully proportioned, it sits sedately on a spur at a point where the River Aare curves gracefully back on itself. The little city is the best preserved medieval centre north of the Alps – a fact recognised by UNESCO when it awarded Bern World Heritage status – and the layout of the streets has barely changed since the Duke of Zahringen chose the superbly defended site to found the city over 800 years ago. Most of the buildings date from between the 14 and 16C – when Bern was at the height of its power – and the cluster of

cobbled lanes, surrounded by ornate sandstone arcaded buildings and numerous fountains and wells, give it the feel of a delightfully overgrown village. (Albert Einstein felt so secure here that while ostensibly employed as a clerk in the Bern patent office he managed to find the time to work out his Theory of Relativity.)

The Old Town stretches eastwards over a narrow peninsula, and is surrounded by the arcing River Aare. The eastern limit of the Old Town is the Nydeggbrücke bridge, while the western end is marked out by the Käfigturm tower, once a city gate and prison. On the southern side of the Aare lies the small Kirchenfeld quarter, which houses some impressive museums, while the capital's famous brown bears are back over the river via the Nydeggbrücke.

EATING OUT

Bern is a great place to sit and enjoy a meal. Pride of place must go to the good range of alfresco venues in the squares of the Old Town – popular spots to enjoy coffee and cake. Hiding away in the arcades are many delightful dining choices; some of the best for location alone are in vaulted cellars that breathe historic ambience. If you want to feel what a real Swiss restaurant is like, head for a traditional rustic eatery complete with cow-bells and sample the local dishes like the Berner Platte – a heaving plate of hot and cold meats, served with beans and sauerkraut – or treberwurst, a sausage poached with fermented grape skins. There's no shortage of international restaurants either, and along with Germany, France and Italy also have their country's cuisine well represented here – it's not difficult to go from rösti to risotto. And, of course, there's always cheese – this is the birthplace of raclette - and tempting chocolates waiting in the wings. A fifteen percent service charge is always added but it's customary to round the bill up.

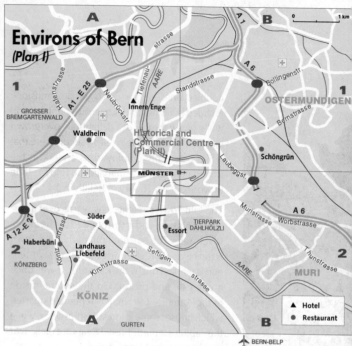

Environs of Bern
(Plan I)

GROSSER
BREMGARTENWALD

A 1

Halenstrasse

A1 - E 25

Neubrückstr.

Tiefenaustrasse

AARE

Standstrasse

Innere/Enge ▲

Waldheim ●

**Historical and
Commercial Centre
(Plan II)**

MÜNSTER 🏛

Laubeggstr.

Schöngrün ●

B

A 1

0   1 km

🏥

Bollingenstr.

OSTERMUNDIGEN **1**

Bernstrasse

Muristrasse

A 6

Worbstrasse

Süder ●

Essort ●

TIERPARK
DÄHLHÖLZLI

Haberbüni ▲

Landhaus
Liebefeld ▲

KÖNIZBERG

Könizstrasse

A 12 - E 27

Kirchstrasse

Seftigen-
strasse

AARE

Thunstrasse

MURI **2**

KÖNIZ

A

GURTEN

B

▲ Hotel
● Restaurant

✈ BERN-BELP

HISTORICAL AND COMMERCIAL CENTRE   PLAN II

❀ **Meridiano** – Hotel Allegro   XxX 🍴 ≤ 🌳 AC ⇔ 🚗
Kornhausstr. 3 ⊠ 3000 – ℰ 031 339 52 45   Plan: **D1**
– www.allegro-hotel.ch – Closed Saturday lunch and Sunday-Monday
Menu 88 CHF (lunch)/165 CHF – Carte 101/125 CHF
· Modern cuisine · Fashionable · Trendy ·
This elegant restaurant with its wonderful view and stunning terrace is absolutely *the* place to eat in Bern. The food is modern and sophisticated, fully-flavoured and intense, and made with top-quality Swiss ingredients.
➔ Bio-Freilandei, Roggen-Sauerteigbrotcreme, Nussbutter, Bärlauch. Holzen Kalb², Béarnaise, gebratener Spargel, Zwiebel. Ziegenfrischkäse "Pia Mattmann", Walliser Sanddorn, Schafgarbe, Gantrisch 5 Korn.

😊 **Kirchenfeld**   X 🌳 ⇔
Thunstr. 5 ⊠ 3005 – ℰ 031 351 02 78   Plan: **E2**
– www.kirchenfeld.ch – Closed Sunday-Monday
Menu 36/78 CHF – Carte 48/85 CHF – *(booking advisable)*
· Traditional cuisine · Brasserie ·
Eating in this loud and lively restaurant is great fun! Try the flavoursome zander fish served on Mediterranean couscous and one of the sweets, which include lemon tart and chocolate cake, displayed on the dessert trolley. At lunchtimes the restaurant is full of business people who swear by the daily set menu.

milles sens - les goûts du monde ✗ 🅰️🅲

Spitalgasse 38 (Schweizerhofpassage, 1st floor) ✉ *3011* Plan: **C2**
– 𝒞 031 329 29 29 – www.millesens.ch – Closed end July-early August and Saturday-Sunday; September-April: Saturday lunch, Sunday
Menu 69/120 CHF (dinner) – Carte 66/98 CHF
• International • Fashionable •

If you are looking for a lively, modern restaurant, this minimalist-style establishment is for you. The mouthwatering menu promises Aargau chicken tagine, Gurten highland beef duo, and exotic Thai green vegetable curry. At midday there is also an interesting business lunch menu.

🍽️ VUE – Hotel Bellevue Palace ✗✗✗ 🕸️ ⪡ 🛋️

Kochergasse 3 ✉ *3011 – 𝒞 031 320 45 45* Plan: **D2**
– www.bellevue-palace.ch/vue
Menu 68 CHF (weekday lunch)/158 CHF – Carte 79/112 CHF
• Modern cuisine • Classic décor •

Ambitious, contemporary seasonal cuisine with traditional roots is served in this tastefully decorated setting. The terrace affords magnificent views over the Aare.

🍽️ Casa Novo ✗✗ 🛋️ ⟳

Läuferplatz 6 ✉ *3011 – 𝒞 031 992 44 44* Plan: **F1**
– www.casa-novo.ch – Closed 24 December-8 January and Saturday lunch, Sunday-Monday
Menu 65 CHF (lunch)/107 CHF – Carte 69/105 CHF
• Mediterranean cuisine • Friendly •

The great location on the River Aare means that the terrace is a real highlight here. The seasonal Mediterranean food on offer includes meagre with crustacean emulsion, beluga lentils and ratatouille as well Swiss classics such as hand-chopped steak tartare. There is also a wine shop and you'll find the Klösterli car park just over the river.

🍽️ Jack's Brasserie – Hotel Schweizerhof ✗✗ 🕸️ ⛓️ 🅰️🅲

Bahnhofplatz 11 ✉ *3001 – 𝒞 031 326 80 80* Plan: **C1**
– www.schweizerhof-bern.ch
Menu 57 CHF (weekday lunch)/120 CHF – Carte 68/110 CHF
• Classic cuisine • Brasserie •

The restaurant at the Schweizerhof provides an elegant setting, with its decor, pretty alcoves, parquet flooring and stylish lighting. The menu features typical brasserie-style fare, alongside a number of popular classics including the Wiener schnitzel.

🍽️ Bellevue Bar – Hotel Bellevue Palace ✗ 🛋️ ⛓️

Kochergasse 3 ✉ *3011 – 𝒞 031 320 45 45* Plan: **D2**
– www.bellevue-palace.ch
Carte 54/113 CHF
• International • Traditional décor •

The sedate charm of this long established grand hotel also extends into the restaurant. Diners, many of whom have travelled from far and wide to get here, can choose from an international menu.

🍽️ Brasserie Obstberg ✗ 🛋️ ⟳

Bantigerstr. 18 ✉ *3006 – 𝒞 031 352 04 40* Plan: **F2**
– www.brasserie-obstberg.ch – Closed Saturday lunch, Sunday
Menu 49 CHF (weekdays)/79 CHF – Carte 54/85 CHF
• Classic cuisine • Brasserie •

Diners have been coming to Brasserie Obstberg for over 100 years. Today they eat in the lovely, 1930s-style brasserie with its wonderful terrace shaded by mature sweet chestnut trees. The food is fresh and classically French with Swiss influences from the braised lamb shank to the sautéed zander.

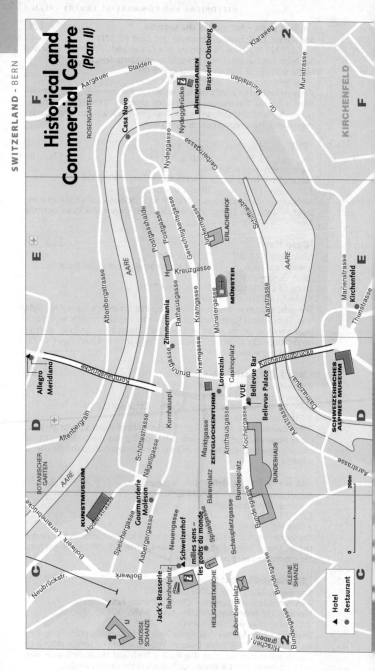

Historical and Commercial Centre *(Plan II)*

Gourmanderie Moléson

Aarbergergasse 24 ✉ 3011 – ✆ 031 311 44 63 Plan: **C1**
– www.moleson-bern.ch – Closed Christmas-New Year and Saturday lunch, Sunday
Menu 59/86 CHF – Carte 52/95 CHF
• Classic French • Brasserie •

Established in 1865, the Moléson is a lively restaurant located in the centre of Bern. It serves a range of traditional-style dishes from Alsatian flammekueche to multi-course meals.

Lorenzini

Hotelgasse 10 ✉ 3011 – ✆ 031 318 50 67 Plan: **D2**
– www.lorenzini.ch
Carte 44/90 CHF
• Italian • Friendly •

This attractive Italian restaurant located in the pedestrian zone is tastefully decorated with original paintings. It boasts a formal restaurant on the first floor and a bar, bistro and attractive interior courtyard at ground level.

Zimmermania

Brunngasse 19 ✉ 3011 – ✆ 031 311 15 42 Plan: **D1**
– www.zimmermania.ch – Closed 9 July-6 August and Sunday-Monday; June-September: Saturday lunch
Menu 65 CHF – Carte 44/95 CHF
• Classic French • Traditional décor •

A restaurant as far back as the 19C, today this charming, picture-postcard bistro caters for fans of traditional cuisine. It offers classics such as calf's head vinaigrette, entrecôte Café de Paris and slow cooked stews.

Bellevue Palace

Kochergasse 3 ✉ 3011 – ✆ 031 320 45 45 Plan: **D2**
– www.bellevue-palace.ch
128 rm – †400/440 CHF ††560/640 CHF – ☕ 40 CHF – 28 suites
• Grand Luxury • Classic •

This exclusive hotel - established in 1913 and sited in the heart of Bern - offers elegant conference facilities and first-class guestrooms and suites; all in a truly unique atmosphere. There's a modern gym with sauna. The comfortable Bellevue Bar serves international cuisine.

VUE • **Bellevue Bar** – See restaurant listing

Schweizerhof

Bahnhofplatz 11 ✉ 3001 – ✆ 031 326 80 80 Plan: **C1**
– www.schweizerhof-bern.ch
99 rm – †359/419 CHF ††459/519 CHF – ☕ 25 CHF – 5 suites
• Luxury • Elegant •

Behind the beautifully restored historic façade lies a happy marriage of modern and classic chic, which not only looks beautiful but provides all the latest technology for business guests. Those in search of charm will love Jack's Brasserie.

Jack's Brasserie – See restaurant listing

Allegro

Kornhausstr. 3 ✉ 3013 – ✆ 031 339 55 00 Plan: **D1**
– www.allegro-hotel.ch
167 rm – †190/270 CHF ††200/300 CHF – ☕ 26 CHF – 4 suites
• Business • Contemporary •

This lifestyle hotel is ideal for conferences and events, as well as individual guests. Modern rooms in different categories, plus a beautiful penthouse floor with its own lounge. One of the restaurants, Il Giardino, serves Italian food.

✿ **Meridiano** – See restaurant listing

SWITZERLAND - BERN

Landhaus Liebefeld   XX ⇔ 🏠 🛋 ㅚ ✿ **P**

Schwarzenburgstr. 134 – ℰ *031 971 07 58*   Plan: **A2**
– www.landhaus-liebefeld.ch – Closed Sunday
6 rm 🖙 – 🛉180/221 CHF 🛉🛉290/356 CHF
Menu 95/135 CHF – Carte 61/119 CHF – *(booking advisable)*
• Classic French • Elegant •

Anywhere you can eat this well in such pleasant surroundings as this former
1671 sheriff's house is bound to attract plenty of regulars. Try the fish soup
– they've been making it from the same recipe for 25 years! The Gaststube
serves simpler fare including meatloaf and German noodle dishes. And if
you fancy staying the night, the individually designed rooms are pretty
and well furnished.

Essort   XX 🏠 ✿

Jubiläumstr. 97 ✉ *3000* – ℰ *031 368 11 11*   Plan: **A2**
– www.essort.ch – Closed 1 week early January, 2 weeks early October,
during Christmas
Menu 68/105 CHF – Carte 63/88 CHF
• International • Friendly •

In the former US embassy the Lüthi family runs a modern restaurant. It produces international fare in its open kitchen, which is inspired by the owners' countless trips abroad. In summer, dine alfresco at one of the lovely tables laid outside under the mature trees.

Schöngrün   XX 🏠 ㅚ ✿

Monument im Fruchtland 1 (near Paul Klee Centre)   Plan: **B1**
✉ *3006* – ℰ *031 359 02 90* – *www.restaurants-schoengruen.ch* – *closed*
24-31 December and Sunday dinner-Tuesday
Menu 38 CHF (lunch)/140 CHF – Carte 53/101 CHF – *(booking advisable)*
• Creative • Fashionable •

Next to the Zentrum Paul Klee, Schöngrün serves seasonal, modern cuisine with
an evening menu including a vegetarian option. Housed in a modern, glazed
summer-house-style annexe to a period villa, it also boasts a pretty garden terrace. The bistro serves lunchtime snacks. Accessible by bus (n° 12) from the
main railway station.

Haberbüni   X 🏠 🏠 **P**

Könizstr. 175 – ℰ *031 972 56 55* – *www.haberbueni.ch*   Plan: **A2**
– Closed Saturday lunch and Sunday
Menu 61 CHF (lunch)/110 CHF (dinner)
– Carte 61/89 CHF – (booking advisable)
• Modern cuisine • Bourgeois • Cosy •

This warm and welcoming restaurant set in the loft of a large renovated farmhouse or Büni offers ambitious contemporary cuisine and a fine selection of
wines. Shorter midday menu and good business lunch options.

Süder   X 🏠 **P**

Weissensteinstr. 61 ✉ *3007* – ℰ *031 371 57 67*   Plan: **A2**
– www.restaurant-sueder.ch – Closed 1-10 January, 2 weeks July and
Saturday lunch, Sunday-Monday
Menu 67 CHF (dinner)/89 CHF – Carte 51/85 CHF
• Swiss • Bourgeois •

This down-to-earth corner restaurant with its lovely wood panelling has many
regulars. They are attracted by the good, honest, fresh Swiss cooking, such as
the veal ragout. In the summer it is no surprise that the tables in the garden
are particularly popular.

Waldheim

☒ 🛱

Waldheimstr. 40 ☒ 3012 – ℰ 031 305 24 24
– www.waldheim-bern.ch – Closed Saturday lunch, Sunday-Monday
Menu 56 CHF – Carte 41/90 CHF
• Traditional cuisine • Neighbourhood •

This pretty restaurant is panelled in light wood and located in a quiet residential area. It boasts a healthy number of regulars thanks to the fresh Swiss cuisine (try the marinated leg of lamb, spit-roasted to a perfect pink) and the friendly service.

Innere Enge

✿ ⊗ ੯ 🎴 ॐ P

Engestr. 54 ☒ 3012 – ℰ 031 309 61 11
– www.innere-enge.ch
26 rm – ♥180/240 CHF ♥♥220/280 CHF – ☲ 28 CHF
• Country house • Personalised •

Passionate about jazz, your hosts have created this unique hotel-cum-jazz-venue. Many of the rooms are named after famous musicians and decorated with original artefacts. The basement houses a jazz club. Josephine's Brasserie and the historic Park Pavilion offer views over the city.

GENEVA
GENEVE

Onfokus/iStock

GENEVA IN...

→ **ONE DAY**
St Peter's Cathedral, Maison Tavel, Jet d'Eau, Reformation Wall.

→ **TWO DAYS**
MAMCO (the Art & History Museum), a lakeside stroll, a trip to Carouge.

→ **THREE DAYS**
A day in Paquis, including time relaxing at the Bains des Paquis.

In just about every detail except efficiency, Geneva exudes a distinctly Latin feel. It boasts a proud cosmopolitanism, courtesy of a whole swathe of international organisations (dealing with just about every human concern), and of the fact that roughly one in three residents is non-Swiss. Its renowned savoir-vivre challenges that of swishy Zurich, and along with its manicured city parks, it boasts the world's tallest fountain and the world's longest bench. It enjoys cultural ties with Paris and is often called 'the twenty-first arrondissement' – it's also almost entirely surrounded by France.

The River Rhône snakes through the centre, dividing the city into the southern left bank - the Old Town – and the northern right bank – the 'international quarter' (home to the largest UN office outside New York). The east is strung around the sparkling shores of Europe's largest alpine lake, while the Jura Mountains dominate the right bank, and the Alps form a backdrop to the left bank. Geneva is renowned for its orderliness: the Reformation was born here under the austere preachings of Calvin, and the city has provided sanctuary for religious dissidents, revolutionaries and elopers for at least five centuries. Nowadays, new arrivals tend to be of a more conservative persuasion, as they go their elegant way balancing international affairs alongside la belle vie.

EATING OUT

With the number of international organisations that have set up camp here, this is a place that takes a lot of feeding, so you'll find over 1,000 dining establishments in and around the city. If you're looking for elegance, head to a restaurant overlooking the lake; if your tastes are for home-cooked Sardinian fare, make tracks for the charming Italianate suburb of Carouge; and if you fancy something with an international accent, trendy Paquis has it all at a fair price and on a truly global scale, from Mexican to Moroccan and Jordanian to

Japanese. The Old Town, packed with delightful brasseries and alpine-style chalets, is the place for Swiss staples: you can't go wrong here if you're after a fondue, rustic longeole (pork sausage with cumin and fennel) or a hearty papet vaudois (cream and leek casserole); for a bit of extra atmosphere, head downstairs to a candlelit, vaulted cellar. Although restaurants include a fifteen per cent service charge, it's customary to either round up the bill or give the waiter a five to ten per cent tip.

SWITZERLAND - GENEVA (GENÈVE)

Le Chat Botté – Hôtel Beau Rivage   XXxX 🕸 ≤ 🎿 ♻ 🚗

Quai du Mont-Blanc 13 ⊠ 1201 – ℰ 022 716 69 20   Plan: **F3**
– www.beau-rivage.ch – Closed 24 March-7 April, 21 July-
4 August and Saturday-Sunday
Menu 60 CHF (weekday lunch)/220 CHF
– Carte 128/198 CHF – *(booking advisable)*
• Modern French • Elegant • Luxury •

This appealingly named restaurant ('Puss in Boots') serves contemporary-style
cuisine with traditional roots, using culinary techniques that create harmonious
flavours. The food is complemented by the expert work of the sommelier, who
skilfully guides guests through the impressive wine list.
➔ Bonbon de truffe de la Drôme, risotto de céleri. Œuf de ferme, noir et
croustillant, cèpes et mokka. Morille blonde farcie, petits pois et lard du
Valais.

Il Lago – Four Seasons Hôtel des Bergues   XXxX 🕸 🍴 & 🎿

Quai des Bergues 33 ⊠ 1201 – ℰ 022 908 71 10   Plan: **F3**
– www.fourseasons.com/geneva
Menu 78 CHF (lunch)/130 CHF – Carte 108/187 CHF – *(booking essential)*
• Italian • Classic décor • Elegant •

Offering a taste of Italy on Lake Geneva, this restaurant combines decorative
features such as pilasters and paintings with elegant Italian cuisine which is
light, subtle and fragant. A delightful dining experience!
➔ Langoustines avec haricots coco et consommé d´oignons. Cabri laqué
au banyuls, céleri rave rôti et pomme verte. Ananas rôtis aux saveurs exotiques et crumble.

Bayview – Hôtel Président Wilson   XXX 🕸 ≤ & 🎿 🚗

Quai Wilson 47 ⊠ 1211 – ℰ 022 906 65 52   Plan: **F2**
– www.hotelpresidentwilson.com – Closed 1-14 January, 16-24 April,
30 July-26 August and Sunday-Monday
Menu 68 CHF (lunch)/170 CHF – Carte 107/215 CHF
• Modern French • Design • Elegant •

With its chic, carefully designed decor and large bay windows facing the lake,
this restaurant provides the ideal setting to enjoy the elegant cuisine. French
classics are reinterpreted with creativity and subtlety, and the carefully produced dishes are chic and contemporary.
➔ Médaillon de langoustine à l'orange sanguine, croustillant de moules de
bouchot. Agneau de lait des Pyrénées à la sarriette pied, asperges du
Domaine de Roques-Hautes et Kumquat. Millefeuille à la crème diplomate,
sauce chocolat, caramel à la fleur de sel.

Côté Square – Hôtel Bristol   XxX 🎿

Rue du Mont-Blanc 10 ⊠ 1201 – ℰ 022 716 57 58   Plan: **F3**
– www.bristol.ch – Closed 1-7 January, 30 March-8 April and Saturday-
Sunday
Menu 55 CHF (weekday lunch)/90 CHF – Carte 77/98 CHF
• French • Cosy •

This restaurant has a classic elegance. Wood panelling and paintings add an
aristocratic air, enhanced by the occasional notes emanating from the attractive
black piano near the bar. On tables covered with immaculate white cloths,
enjoy delicious dishes showcasing a variety of textures and flavours.

Le Jardin – Hôtel Le Richemond   XxX 🍴 & 🎿

Rue Adhémar-Fabri 8 ⊠ 1201 – ℰ 022 715 71 00   Plan: **F3**
– www.dorchestercollection.com – Closed Saturday lunch and Sunday,
except season
Menu 49 CHF (weekday lunch)/120 CHF – Carte 91/123 CHF
• Modern French • Elegant • Cosy •

This restaurant is situated in the Le Richemond hotel, facing the lake. It serves
French cuisine with contemporary flavours and a focus on produce from the
region. The terrace is a must in fine weather.

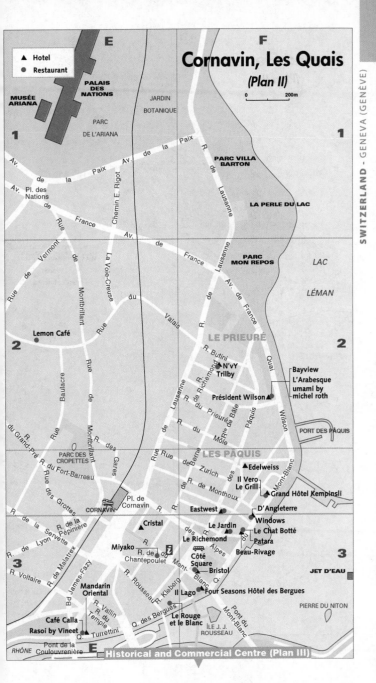

Cornavin, Les Quais
(Plan II)

0   200m

▲ Hotel
● Restaurant

MUSÉE ARIANA

PALAIS DES NATIONS

JARDIN BOTANIQUE

PARC DE L'ARIANA

Av. de la Paix

R. de la Paix

PARC VILLA BARTON

LA PERLE DU LAC

Av. Pl. des Nations

Rue de France

Chemin E. Rigot

La Voie-Creuse

Av. de France

R. de Lausanne

PARC MON REPOS

Av. de France

LAC

LÉMAN

Rue de Vermont

Rue de Montbrillant

Rue du Valais

LE PRIEURÉ

R. Butini

▲ N'vY
Trilby

Quai Wilson

Bayview
L'Arabesque
umami by michel roth

Lemon Café

Rue de Montbrillant

Rue de

R. de Richemond

R. de du Prieuré

R. du Môle

R. de Bâle

R. de Paquis

Président Wilson ▲

PORT DES PÂQUIS

Baulacre

PARC DES CROPETTES

Rue des Gares

Rue de Berne

Rue de Zurich

LES PÂQUIS

▲ Edelweiss

R. du Grand-Pré

R. du Fort-Barreau

R. de Monthoux

Il Vero
Le Grill ●

Mont-Blanc

● Grand Hôtel Kempinski

R. de la Servette

R. des Grottes

Pl. de Cornavin

CORNAVIN

Eastwest ●

● D'Angleterre

R. de Lyon

R. de la Pépinière

● Cristal

Le Jardin ●

Windows
● Le Chat Botté

R. de Malatrex

Miyako ●

R. de Chantepoulet

Le Richemond ●

Patara
Beau-Rivage

R. des Alpes

R. du Mont-Blanc

Côté Square ●
● Bristol

JET D'EAU

Bd James-Fazy

Mandarin Oriental ▲

R. Vallin

R. du Temple

R. Rousseau

R. Kléberg

Il Lago ●
● Four Seasons Hôtel des Bergues

PIERRE DU NITON

Café Calla ●
Rasoi by Vineet ●

Q. Turrettini

Pont de la Coulouvrenière

RHÔNE

Q. des Bergues

Le Rouge et le Blanc ●

ÎLE J. J. ROUSSEAU

Pont du Mont-Blanc

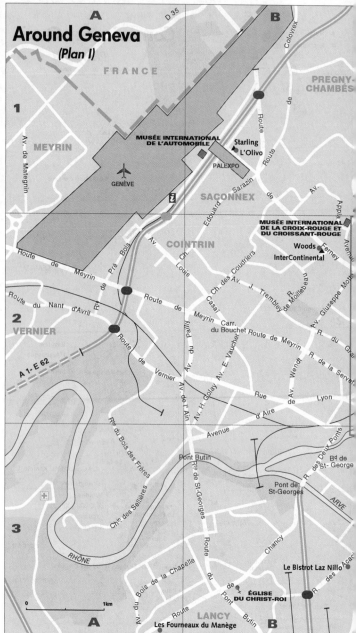

SWITZERLAND - GENEVA (GENÈVE)

Around Geneva
(Plan I)

A   D 35

B   Colovrex

FRANCE

PREGNY-CHAMBÉS

1

MEYRIN

Route de

Av. de Mategnin

MUSÉE INTERNATIONAL DE L'AUTOMOBILE

Route de

Starling
▲ L'Olivo

PALEXPO

✈ GENÈVE

🛈

SACONNEX

Edouard Sarazin

Av.

Appia Avenue

MUSÉE INTERNATIONAL DE LA CROIX-ROUGE ET DU CROISSANT-ROUGE

COINTRIN

Ch. des Coudriers

Woods ●
InterContinental

Ferney

Route de Meyrin

Pré Bois

Av. Louis

Casai

Ch. des

Av. J. Trembley

R. de Mollebeau

R. du Grand

2

VERNIER

Route du Nant d'Avril

Route de

Meyrin

Carr. du Bouchet

Route de Meyrin

Av. Giuseppe Motta

A 1- E 62

Rte de

Av. du Pailly

Av. H. Golay

Av. E. Vaucher

Av. Wendt

R. de la Servet

Route de Vernier

Av. de l'Ain

Rue

de

Lyon

d' Aire

Rte du Bois des Frères

Avenue

3

Ch. des Sellières

✚

Pont Butin

Rte de St-Georges

R. des Deux Ponts

Bd de St- George

Pont de St-Georges

ARVE

RHÔNE

Route du

Chancy

Le Bistrot Laz Nillo ●

R. des Acaci

Av. du Bois de la Chapelle

Route

de

Pont

ÉGLISE DU CHRIST-ROI ●

0   1km

A

LANCY

Les Fourneaux du Manège ●

Route

Butin

B

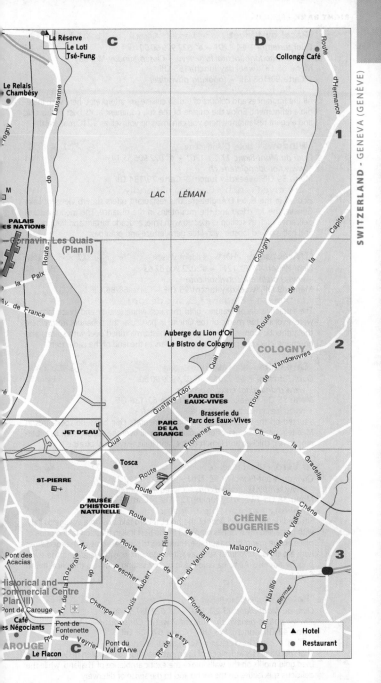

La Réserve
Le Loti
Tsé-Fung

C

D

Route d'Hermance

Collonge Café

Le Relais
Chambésy

Lausanne

de

regny

M

LAC   LÉMAN

Capite

1

**PALAIS
ES NATIONS**

Cornavin, Les Quais
(Plan II)

la   Paix

Route

v. de France

Cologny

de

la

Route

2

Auberge du Lion d'Or
Le Bistro de Cologny

COLOGNY

Quai

Gustave-Ador

Route   de   Vandœuvres

é

**PARC DES
EAUX-VIVES**

Brasserie du
Parc des Eaux-Vives

**PARC
DE LA
GRANGE**

Frontenex

Ch.   de   la   Gradelle

JET D'EAU

Quai

de

Tosca

Route

Route

de

Chêne

ST-PIERRE

**MUSÉE
D'HISTOIRE
NATURELLE**

Route

de

Route du Vallon

**CHÊNE
BOUGERIES**

3

Pont des
Acacias

Av.   de   la   Roseraie

de

Route

Av. Peschier

Champel

Ch. Rieu

de

Malagnou

Av. Louis Aubert

Ch. du Velours

Florissant

Naville

Seymaz

Ch.

istorical and
ommercial Centre
Plan (II)

ont de Carouge

Café
es Négociants

Pont de
Fontenette

de

Veyrier

AROUGE

C

R^{te}

R^{te} de Vessy

Pont du
Val d'Arve

D

▲	Hotel
●	Restaurant

Le Flacon

Ⅺ○ **Rasoi by Vineet** – Hôtel Mandarin Oriental   XxX & 📺 ✿ 🚗
Quai turrettini 1 ✉ *1201* – ℰ *022 909 00 00*   Plan: **E3**
– *www.mandarinoriental.fr/geneva* – *Closed Sunday-Monday*
Menu 65 CHF (weekday lunch)/155 CHF
– Carte 98/168 CHF – *(booking advisable)*
• Indian • Cosy •

All the fragrances and colours of Indian cuisine are interpreted here with incredible refinement. Enjoy the cuisine of the sub-continent at its best in this chic and elegant restaurant where you can imagine yourself as a 21C maharaja!

Ⅺ○ **Windows** – Hôtel D'Angleterre   XxX 🕷 ⩽ 📺
Quai du Mont-Blanc 17 ✉ *1201* – ℰ *022 906 55 14*   Plan: **F3**
– *www.hoteldangleterre.ch*
Menu 59 CHF (weekday lunch) – Carte 79/134 CHF
• Creative French • Elegant • Friendly •

Housed in the Hôtel D'Angleterre, this restaurant offers superb views of Lake Geneva, the Jet d'Eau and the mountains in the distance. The menu features delicacies such as scallop carpaccio with lime, avocado tartare and fleur de sel, and half a baked lobster with little gem lettuce and potatoes.

Ⅺ○ **L'Arabesque** – Hôtel Président Wilson   XX ⩽ & 📺 🚗
Quai Wilson 47 ✉ *1211* – ℰ *022 906 67 63*   Plan: **F2**
– *www.hotelpresidentwilson.com*
Menu 49 CHF (weekday lunch)/95 CHF – Carte 68/86 CHF
• Lebanese • Elegant • Exotic décor •

The attractive decor features gold mosaics, white leather and black lacquerware, evoking the magic of the Orient; in particular the Lebanon, from where the authentic aromas of dishes such as bastorma (dried beef with spices) and houmous (chickpea purée) transport diners to the land of the cedar tree!

Ⅺ○ **Café Calla** – Hôtel Mandarin Oriental   XX ⩽ & 📺 ✿ 🚗
Quai Turrettini 1 ✉ *1201* – ℰ *022 909 00 00*   Plan: **E3**
– *www.mandarinoriental.fr/geneva*
Menu 55 CHF (weekday lunch) – Carte 62/138 CHF
• Mediterranean cuisine • Elegant •

Situated on the lakeside, the Mandarin Oriental's chic brasserie specialises in Mediterranean flavours, offering dishes from all over the region, such as aubergine caviar, chicken and lemon tagine, and Italian-style veal picatta.

Ⅺ○ **Il Vero** – Grand Hôtel Kempinski   XX ⩽ 🍴 & 📺 🚗
Quai du Mont-Blanc 19 ✉ *1201* – ℰ *022 908 92 20*   Plan: **F3**
– *www.kempinski-geneva.com* – *Closed 1-7 January*
Menu 38 CHF (weekday lunch)/129 CHF – Carte 73/135 CHF
• Italian • Fashionable • Design •

Situated on the second floor of the hotel, Il Vero takes us on a voyage to Italy, with pasta and meat dishes prepared in the best Italian tradition taking pride of place on the menu. It's no surprise, therefore, to see that some of the specialities here are Italian favourites such as *vitello tonnato*, *bucatini verdi* and the ever-popular tiramisu. All to be enjoyed in a cosy setting with real theatrical Italian flavour.

Ⅺ○ **Patara** – Hôtel Beau-Rivage   XX ⩽ 🍴 📺 🚗
Quai du Mont-Blanc 13 ✉ *1201* – ℰ *022 731 55 66*   Plan: **F3**
– *www.patara-geneva.ch* – *Closed 2 weeks Christmas-New Year*
Menu 42 CHF (lunch)/125 CHF – Carte 62/108 CHF
• Thai • Exotic décor • Romantic •

Thai specialities served in one of the most beautiful luxury hotels in Geneva. Stylised gold motifs on the walls evoke the exotic ambience of Thailand, while the delicious specialities on the menu add to the sense of discovery.

Trilby – Hôtel N'vY　　　　　XX ঙ 🅰 🚗
Rue de Richemont 18 ⊠ 1202 – ℰ 022 544 66 66　Plan: F2
– www.hotelnvygeneva.com
Menu 70 CHF – Carte 49/95 CHF
• International • Fashionable • Elegant •
You might want to doff your own trilby as you enter this elegant and welcoming restaurant. The speciality is the outstanding beef, whether it is Scottish (Black Angus), Japanese (Wagyu Kobe) or Swiss (Simmental), accompanied by a choice of original sauces.

Woods – Hôtel InterContinental　　XX ≤ 🈐 ঙ 🅰 🚗
Chemin du Petit-Saconnex 7 ⊠ 1209 – ℰ 022 919 39 39　Plan: B2
– geneva-intercontinental.com
Menu 59 CHF (weekday lunch)/68 CHF – Carte 75/117 CHF
• Modern cuisine • Friendly • Romantic •
The name of this restaurant refers to its decor, which serves as an elegant backdrop for the natural Mediterranean cuisine served here, which is full of flavour and made from top-quality produce. The contemporary ambience chimes perfectly with the atmosphere of the InterContinental to which the restaurant belongs.

Eastwest – Hôtel Eastwest　　　X 🈐 🅰 ⇔
Rue des Pâquis 6 ⊠ 1201 – ℰ 022 708 17 07　Plan: F3
– www.eastwesthotel.ch
Menu 39/117 CHF – Carte 63/86 CHF – *(booking advisable)*
• Modern cuisine • Design • Cosy •
Eastwest avoids the rather formal menus of the nearby hotels to offer a more relaxed style of cuisine where a hint of Asia is evident in the dishes. Well-prepared fare, as well as a range of snack options, makes this restaurant a good choice.

Le Grill – Grand Hôtel Kempinski　　X ≤ ঙ 🅰 ⇔ 🚗
Quai du Mont-Blanc 19 ⊠ 1201 – ℰ 022 908 92 24　Plan: F3
– www.kempinski.com/geneva
Menu 38 CHF (weekday lunch)/45 CHF – Carte 84/118 CHF
• Meats and grills • Fashionable • Friendly •
A chic and original restaurant. It offers views of Lake Geneva, as well as of the kitchens, rotisserie and cold rooms where the splendid cuts of meat are stored (300g Parisian entrecôte, beef fillet, rack of lamb, etc). The meat is cooked to perfection and the set menu works well.

Lemon Café　　　　　　X 🈐 ⇔
Rue du Vidollet 4 ⊠ 1202 – ℰ 022 733 60 24　Plan: E2
– www.lemon-cafe.ch – Closed 1-7 January and 23 July-5 August,
24-31 December and Saturday-Sunday
Menu 50 CHF – Carte 52/90 CHF
• Modern French • Simple • Bistro •
At this restaurant the chef delights guests with his travel-inspired dishes. Just some of the options are cod ceviche with a Peruvian flavour, pork spare ribs cooked for 12 hours and served with Maxim's potatoes, and lemon cheesecake.

Miyako　　　　　　　X ⇔
Rue Chantepoulet 11 ⊠ 1201 – ℰ 022 738 01 20　Plan: E3
– www.miyako.ch – Closed Sunday
Menu 108 CHF – Carte 67/100 CHF
• Japanese • Simple •
This aptly named restaurant (Miyako is the Japanese for heart) plunges you into the heart of Japan. It has tatami flooring, teppanyaki cuisine, fresh fish and attentive service. Arigato!

○|○ **Le Rouge et le Blanc** ✗ 淼 AC

Quai des Bergues 27 ✉ *1201 – ℰ 022 731 15 50* Plan: **E3**
– www.lerougeblanc.ch – Closed Sunday
Carte 67/78 CHF – *(dinner only) (booking advisable)*
• Traditional cuisine • Wine bar • Friendly •
A good wine selection, rib of beef as the house speciality (for two or three people), plates of tapas that vary according to market availability, and a relaxed and convivial atmosphere. This restaurant makes a good choice for an enjoyable meal out. Open evenings only.

○|○ **umami by michel roth** – Hôtel Président Wilson ✗ ≤ 戋 AC

Quai Wilson 47 ✉ *1211 – ℰ 022 906 64 52* ⇔
– www.hotelpresidentwilson.com – Closed October-May Plan: **F2**
and Sunday dinner
Menu 59 CHF (lunch) – Carte 66/116 CHF
• Japanese • Exotic décor • Fashionable •
Dine at this restaurant and you will soon realise that there is far more to Japanese cuisine than sushi and sashimi. Creativity is very much to the fore, with the occasional French influence thrown in for good measure. The maki rolls sautéed with foie gras, green apple and ginger are a delicious combination.

🏨🏨🏨 **Beau-Rivage** ≤ 戋 AC 洨 ⇔

Quai du Mont-Blanc 13 ✉ *1201 – ℰ 022 716 66 66* Plan: **F3**
– www.beau-rivage.ch
95 rm – ♦510/2890 CHF ♦♦510/2890 CHF – ⌗ 47 CHF – 15 suites
• Grand Luxury • Family • Grand luxury •
The legendary Beau-Rivage still boasts many of the features of its glorious past (columns and pilasters, marble and stucco decor, objets d'art etc) but manages to avoid wallowing in nostalgia. This is thanks to modern touches such as cutting-edge high-tech equipment and superb duplex suites introduced by the fifth generation of the family. All in all, an exceptional place to stay.
❀ **Le Chat Botté** • ○|○ **Patara** – See restaurant listing

🏨🏨🏨 **Four Seasons Hôtel des Bergues** ❀ ≤ 戋 ⊕ 洨 ▣ 戋 AC

Quai des Bergues 33 ✉ *1201 – ℰ 022 908 70 00* 洨 ⇔
– www.fourseasons.com/geneva Plan: **F3**
85 rm – ♦735/1250 CHF ♦♦735/1250 CHF – ⌗ 55 CHF – 20 suites
• Palace • Historic • Grand luxury •
With a lovely location at the point where the River Rhone rises from the clear waters of Lake Geneva, this was the first of the great Geneva hotels (1834). It is the very essence of the grand hotel with excellent service and splendid decor (period furniture, marble, fine fabrics, etc). All in all, a superb, luxurious experience.
❀ **Il Lago** – See restaurant listing

🏨🏨🏨 **Grand Hôtel Kempinski** ≤ 戋 ⊕ 洨 ▣ 戋 AC 洨 ⇔

Quai du Mont-Blanc 19 ✉ *1201 – ℰ 022 908 90 81* Plan: **F3**
– www.kempinski.com/geneva
379 rm – ♦424/1500 CHF ♦♦490/1500 CHF – ⌗ 50 CHF – 33 suites
• Grand Luxury • Classic • Elegant •
This contemporary hotel that looks out over the famous fountain and across Lake Geneva offers a wide range of services. The interior is modern but muted. It is full of bars and restaurants, meeting rooms, banqueting suites and shops – offering all the facilities you could ever need!
○|○ **Le Grill** • ○|○ **Il Vero** – See restaurant listing

🏨🏨🏨 **Mandarin Oriental** ≤ 戋 ⊕ 洨 戋 AC 洨 ⇔

Quai Turrettini 1 ✉ *1201 – ℰ 022 909 00 00* Plan: **E3**
– www.mandarinoriental.fr/geneva
189 rm – ♦495/655 CHF ♦♦495/655 CHF – ⌗ 54 CHF – 20 suites
• Luxury • Art déco • Elegant •
Shimmering fabrics, precious woods and marble panelling all contribute to the Art Deco style of this luxurious hotel on the banks of the Rhone. On the seventh floor, the suites have their own private terrace with views of the entire city. Highly comfortable, extremely chic and infinitely elegant.
○|○ **Rasoi by Vineet** • ○|○ **Café Calla** – See restaurant listing

Président Wilson ⬩ 🄻🌐🛁🏊🎿📻🛗🛎️

Quai Wilson 47 ✉ 1211 – ☎ 022 906 66 66   Plan: **F2**
– www.hotelpresidentwilson.com
180 rm – 🛏850/1500 CHF 🛏🛏850/1500 CHF – ☕ 47 CHF – 48 suites
• Grand Luxury • Elegant •
A large, modern building on the waterfront, the Président Wilson offers every conceivable comfort. This includes wonderful architectural spaces, beautiful materials, a panoramic pool and a range of restaurants. From the upper floors on the Lake Geneva side, the city pales into insignificance before the wonderful green or snow covered scenery beyond.
❀ **Bayview** • ⌾ **L'Arabesque** • ⌾ **umami by michel roth** – See restaurant listing

D'Angleterre ⬩ 🄻🛁📻🛗

Quai du Mont-Blanc 17 ✉ 1201 – ☎ 022 906 55 55   Plan: **F3**
– www.hoteldangleterre.ch
45 rm – 🛏410/800 CHF 🛏🛏410/800 CHF – ☕ 48 CHF
• Luxury • Townhouse • Classic •
Is it the stone façade reminiscent of Haussmann's Paris that gives the Hotel D'Angleterre its very particular character? Or perhaps the muted London club style of its lounges? Or even the carefully chosen decor (classic, Venetian, design, etc.) in each of its individually furnished rooms? Whatever the answer, this hotel is without a doubt the epitome of elegance.
⌾ **Windows** – See restaurant listing

InterContinental ⬩ 🍴🄻🌐🛁🏊🛗🛎️

Chemin du Petit-Saconnex 7 ✉ 1209 – ☎ 022 919 39 39   Plan: **B2**
– www.intercontinental-geneva.ch
333 rm – 🛏250/1500 CHF 🛏🛏250/1500 CHF – ☕ 46 CHF – 49 suites
• Chain • Luxury • Elegant •
Just behind the United Nations, this hotel perfect for business travellers is housed in the highest building in the city. Spacious, contemporary-style guestrooms with views of the Jura or the lake and there's a superb spa, a cocktail bar and an elegance that is evident right down to the last detail. Quite simply exceptional!
⌾ **Woods** – See restaurant listing

Le Richemond ⬩ 🄻📻🛗🛎️

Rue Adhémar-Fabri 8 ✉ 1201 – ☎ 022 715 70 00   Plan: **F3**
– www.dorchestercollection.com
109 rm – 🛏525/890 CHF 🛏🛏525/890 CHF – ☕ 47 CHF – 10 suites
• Luxury • Historic • Personalised •
Opened in 1863, Le Richemond provides the perfect combination of late-19C European style and the international taste of the modern day. Its original rotunda-style lobby and wrought iron balconies look out over the city; these contrast with the luxuriously remodelled areas that are full of refined understatement.
⌾ **Le Jardin** – See restaurant listing

N'vY ⬩ 🍴🄻📻🛎️

Rue de Richemont 18 ✉ 1202 – ☎ 022 544 66 66   Plan: **F2**
– www.hotelnvygeneva.com
153 rm – 🛏200/670 CHF 🛏🛏200/670 CHF – ☕ 30 CHF – 1 suite
• Business • Luxury • Design •
This hotel has enjoyed a major facelift and the result is explosive. Find arty design, super trendy, hi-tech fittings wherever you look, and bright guestrooms that owe as much to the writer Jack Kerouac as to street art. The N'vY will take your breath away!
⌾ **Trilby** – See restaurant listing

Bristol ⓘ ⓘ ⓘ ⓘ

Rue du Mont-Blanc 10 ⊠ 1201 – 𝒞 022 716 57 00   Plan: **F3**
– www.bristol.ch
110 rm – 🛇290/600 CHF 🛇🛇290/600 CHF – ⬒ 38 CHF – 1 suite
• Business • Functional •

A smart hotel with very comfortable guestrooms decorated in an unfussy, classic style. After a hard day's work, take some time to relax in the basement fitness centre which also has a sauna, hammam and jacuzzi.

🍴○ **Côté Square** – See restaurant listing

Eastwest ⓘ ⓘ ⓘ ⓘ

Rue des Pâquis 6 ⊠ 1201 – 𝒞 022 708 17 17   Plan: **F3**
– www.eastwesthotel.ch
41 rm – 🛇218/435 CHF 🛇🛇218/435 CHF – ⬒ 32 CHF – 3 suites
• Townhouse • Contemporary • Cosy •

This pleasant, impeccable hotel is firmly up to date in style with its contemporary furniture, dark tones, occasional splash of colour and open-plan bathrooms. Extremely central location not far from the banks of the river.

🍴○ **Eastwest** – See restaurant listing

Edelweiss ⓘ ⓘ

Place de la Navigation 2 ⊠ 1201 – 𝒞 022 544 51 51   Plan: **F3**
– www.hoteledelweissgeneva.com
42 rm – 🛇150/460 CHF 🛇🛇150/460 CHF – ⬒ 18 CHF
• Business • Cosy • Alpine •

Named after the famous Swiss flower (known as the immortal flower of the snow), this hotel has the typical ambience of a welcoming Swiss chalet. Light wood dominates in the guestrooms, while the restaurant boasts a real ski resort atmosphere, with its live music (every night) and cheese specialities on the menu.

Cristal ⓘ ⓘ ⓘ

Rue Pradier 4 ⊠ 1201 – 𝒞 022 716 12 21   Plan: **E3**
– www.fassbindhotels.ch
78 rm – 🛇110/270 CHF 🛇🛇140/300 CHF – ⬒ 19 CHF
• Business • Design • Minimalist •

A stone's throw from the train station, this Cristal shines brightly. This is firstly thanks to its commitment to the environment, as witnessed by its solar panels and heating supplied by water circulation and airflow. And secondly, by its bright, designer layout dominated by silver and glass.

LEFT BANK   **PLAN III**

⌘ La Bottega (Francesco Gasbarro) ⓧⓧ ⓘ ⓘ ⓘ ⓘ

Rue de La Corraterie 21 – 𝒞 022 736 10 00   Plan: **G2**
– www.labottegatrattoria.com
– Closed 23 December-9 January, 1 week Easter, 2 weeks early August and Saturday-Sunday
Menu 55 CHF (weekday lunch)/123 CHF
– Carte 90/120 CHF – (booking advisable)
• Italian • Friendly • Neighbourhood •

There isn't a menu at La Bottega, just a whole heap of inspiration! The chef here presents a re-worked version of Italian cuisine with the help of top-quality Swiss ingredients. The modern, delicious dishes come full of surprises to delight guests.

➜ Truite de la mer, chèvre et maïs. Cappelleti de crabe et burrata, choufleur et citronelle. Passion de chocolat et framboise.

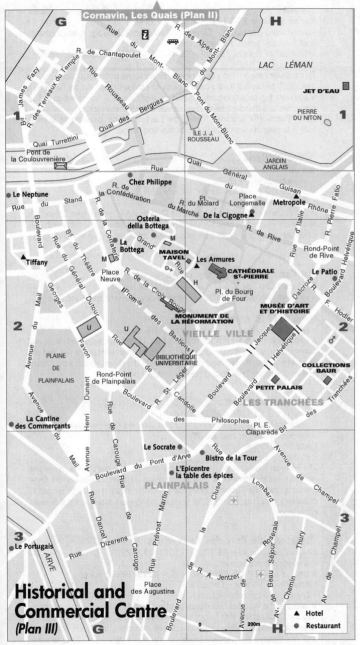

Cornavin, Les Quais (Plan II)

G H

Rue du Mont-Blanc
R. des Alpes Mont-Blanc
R. de Chantepoulet
B⁴ James Fazy
R. des Terreaux du Temple
Rue
Rousseau
Quai des Bergues
Quai du Mont-Blanc
Pont du Mont-Blanc
LAC LÉMAN
JET D'EAU
PIERRE DU NITON

1

Quai Turrettini
Pont de la Coulouvrenière
ÎLE J. J. ROUSSEAU
Quai Général du
JARDIN ANGLAIS

Chez Philippe
Le Neptune
Rue du Stand
R. de la Confédération
Pl. du Molard
Place Longemalle
Metropole
Rhône
Guisan
R. Pierre Fatio
R. du Marché
De la Cigogne
R. de Rive
Rue d'Italie
R. Pierre

Osteria della Bottega
La Bottega
Grand'
MAISON TAVEL
Les Armures
CATHÉDRALE ST-PIERRE
Le Patio
Rond-Point de Rive
Boulevard Helvétique

Tiffany
Boulevard du Théâtre
R. du Général Dufour
Place Neuve
R. de la Croix Rouge
Pl. du Bourg de Four
MUSÉE D'ART ET D'HISTOIRE
Dalcroze R.
F. Hodler

2

Avenue du Mail
B⁴ Georges Favon
MONUMENT DE LA RÉFORMATION
VIEILLE VILLE
Boulevard Jacques Helvétique
COLLECTIONS BAUR

PLAINE DE PLAINPALAIS
BIBLIOTHÈQUE UNIVERSITAIRE
Rond-Point de Plainpalais
Boulevard
R. St-Léger
Boulevard
PETIT PALAIS
LES TRANCHÉES
des Tranchées

La Cantine des Commercants
Avenue Henri
Rue de Carouge
R. Candolle
des Philosophes
Pl. E. Claparède Bd

Le Socrate
Bistro de la Tour
Rue d'Arve
Avenue de Champel

Boulevard du Pont d'Arve
L'Epicentre la table des épices
PLAINPALAIS
Lombard
Avenue de la Cluse

Rue de Carouge
Rue Dancet
Rue Dizerens
Rue Prévost Martin
Beau Séjour
la Roseraie
Thury
Av. de Champei

3

Le Portugais
ARVE
R. A. Jentzer
Place des Augustins
Avenue
Av. de
Chemin
Av. de

Historical and Commercial Centre
(Plan III)

G H

0   200m

▲ Hotel
● Restaurant

671

❀ **Tosca** XX AC

Rue de la Mairie 8 ⊠ 1207 – ℰ 022 707 14 44 Plan I: **C3**
*– www.tosca-geneva.ch – Closed 23 December-7 January, 1 week Easter
and Saturday lunch, Sunday-Monday,*
Menu 55 CHF (lunch)/130 CHF – Carte 70/105 CHF – *(booking advisable)*
• Tuscan • Chic •

This popular new addition to Geneva's dining scene does not disappoint! The
beautifully presented Italian cuisine (with an obvious emphasis on Tuscany) is
made from top-quality ingredients and is full of flavour. A fine selection of Tuscan wines and friendly, professional service complete the picture.
➜ La Panzanella toscane. Tortelli de tourteaux, son bouillon et sucrine.
Sole à la plancha, agrumes et sauce aux coquillages.

☺ **Chez Philippe** XX 舒 余 & AC

Rue du Rhône 8 ⊠ 1204 – ℰ 022 316 16 16 Plan: **G1**
– www.chezphilippe.ch
Menu 39 CHF (weekday lunch) – Carte 33/179 CHF
• Meats and grills • Friendly •

Philippe Chevrier, from the Domaine de Châteauvieux, is the brains behind this
restaurant inspired by New York steakhouses. Top-quality Swiss meat with delicious seasoning and vegetables ensures that this venture is a resounding success.

☺ **La Cantine des Commerçants** X 余 &

Boulevard Carl Vogt 29 ⊠ 1205 – ℰ 022 328 16 70 Plan: **G2**
*– www.lacantine.ch – Closed Christmas-early January and Sunday-
Monday*
Menu 36/65 CHF (dinner) – Carte 60/71 CHF
• Modern French • Design • Fashionable •

A neo-bistro in the old abattoir district of the city, characterised by white and
bright green walls, retro decor and a large counter where you can sit and eat.
The varied menu is very much in keeping with the times: risotto with prawns
and wild herbs, grilled fish and pan-fried fillet of beef.

☺ **Osteria della Bottega** X 舒

Grand Rue 3 ⊠ 1204 – ℰ 022 810 84 51 Plan: **G2**
*– www.osteriadellabottega.com – Closed 2 weeks Christmas-New Year,
3 weeks July-August and Sunday*
Carte 56/82 CHF
• Italian • Friendly • Simple •

The Bottegas have created a new member of the family, the Osteria. In keeping
with its nearby gastronomic sibling, Francesco Gasbarro celebrates the finest
products from the Tuscan countryside which he incorporates into recipes of
disarming simplicity. A successful venture made even more so by the reasonable prices.

🅞 **Brasserie du Parc des Eaux-Vives** XX ⇦ ⪡ 余 & ✿

82 Quai Gustave Ador ⊠ 1207 – ℰ 022 849 75 75 Plan: **D2**
– www.parcdeseauxvives.ch
5 rm – ✝350/480 CHF ✝✝350/480 CHF – ⌑ 29 CHF – 2 suites
Menu 39 CHF (lunch) – Carte 73/97 CHF
• Modern French • Classic décor • Friendly •

Situated in the Parc des Eaux-Vives, this beautiful classic-style restaurant occupies a magical setting with long green lawns running down to the lake. The à la
carte menu features dishes such as octopus with citrus fruit, local pork chops
and veal kidneys in a mustard sauce. Guestrooms with a view of the lake add
to the appeal.

‖○ **De la Cigogne** – Hôtel De la Cigogne　　　　XX 錦 斎 AC ⇔
Place Longemalle 17 ✉ *1204*　　　　　　　　Plan: **H1**
– ℰ *022 818 40 40* – www.relaischateaux.com/cigogne
– *Closed Christmas-New Year and Saturday lunch, Sunday*
Menu 65/125 CHF – Carte 86/122 CHF
• Modern French • Elegant • Friendly •
Trained in some top-notch restaurants, the chef at De la Cigogne creates fine
French cuisine, which is full of flavour and always beautifully presented. Enjoy
a glass of fine wine (there is an impressive list of Swiss labels) with your meal
and don't miss the terrace in sunny weather.

‖○ **Le Portugais**　　　　　　　　　　　　　　XX AC
Boulevard du Pont d'Arve 59 ✉ *1205*　　　　Plan: **G3**
– ℰ *022 329 40 98* – www.leportugais.ch
– *Closed 2 weeks mid April and Sunday-Monday*
Menu 46 CHF (lunch)/59 CHF – Carte 47/85 CHF
• Portuguese • Simple • Neighbourhood •
Many Portuguese have left their mark on history, including famous explorers
such as Vasco de Gama and Magellan. However, the only exploring you will be
doing in this restaurant is of the culinary variety. Enjoy a choice of excellent fish
cooked by an enthusiastic chef and accompanied by good local wine. Friendly,
rustic ambience. Obrigado!

‖○ **Bistro de la Tour**　　　　　　　　　　　　X AC
Boulevard de la Tour 2 ✉ *1205*　　　　　　Plan: **H3**
– ℰ *022 321 97 66* – www.bistrodelatour.ch
– *Closed 24 December-5 January, 15 July-15 August and Saturday-Sunday*
Menu 29 CHF – Carte 58/97 CHF
• World cuisine • Neighbourhood • Intimate •
Seasonal produce is the hallmark of the Bistro de la Tour, situated on the boule-
vard of the same name. The menu focuses on fresh ingredients, which change
regularly, with flavoursome dishes that include the occasional surprise. Friendly
and welcoming owner.

‖○ **L'Epicentre, la table des épices**　　　　　　X 斎
Rue Prévost-Martin 25 ✉ *1205*　　　　　　Plan: **G3**
– ℰ *022 328 14 70* – www.lepicentre.ch
– *Closed 23 December-8 January, mid July-mid August and Saturday-Sunday*
Menu 104 CHF (weekdays)/127 CHF – Carte 68/103 CHF
• Creative • Exotic décor • Simple •
The two chefs at this aptly named restaurant (table des épices means spice
table) create fragrant and well-balanced dishes that are full of flavour. They
select one or two spices from the 300 varieties that they have bought either in
Geneva or abroad as the foundation for the dish. The excellent wine list features
mainly natural wines.

‖○ **Le Neptune**　　　　　　　　　　　　　　　X 斎
Rue de la Coulouvrenière 38 ✉ *1204*　　　　Plan: **G1**
– ℰ *022 320 15 05* – www.leneptune.ch – *Closed Bank Holidays*
Menu 39 CHF (weekday lunch)/99 CHF – Carte 69/78 CHF
• Modern cuisine • Design • Friendly •
Situated in a quiet district on the left bank, this restaurant is run by a chef who is
a keen promoter of Alpine cuisine. He carefully selects his suppliers himself,
choosing only organic produce and creating dishes that are innovative as well
as delicious. In fine weather, enjoy alfresco dining on the small terrace in the
inner courtyard.

Le Patio   X

Boulevard Helvétique 19 ✉ *1207* – ☎ *022 736 66 75*   Plan: **H2**
*– www.lepatio-restaurant.ch – Closed 2 weeks Christmas-New Year and
Sunday*
Menu 45 CHF (lunch) – Carte 47/177 CHF
• Creative French • Friendly • Bistro •

Philippe Chevrier (chef at the Domaine de Châteauvieux in Satigny) has chosen an original concept here: cuisine that is almost exclusively based on lobster and beef. The menu includes dishes such as lobster tartare and oxtail parmentier, which are fresh, delicious and full of flavour. A highly enjoyable dining experience!

Le Socrate   X 🔲 AC

Rue Micheli-du-Crest 6 ✉ *1205*   Plan: **H3**
– ☎ 022 320 16 77 – www.lesocrate.ch
– Closed Saturday lunch, Sunday
Carte 46/70 CHF
• Traditional cuisine • Vintage • Friendly •

A bistro with a delightfully retro dining room adorned with old posters. Sample simple, honest and delicious dishes at tables set close together. A place where good food and conversation are to the fore, in an atmosphere that a certain Greek philosopher would have appreciated!

Metropole   ✿ ≤ Ló AC ♨

Quai Général-Guisan 34 ✉ *1204*   Plan: **H1**
– ☎ 022 318 32 00 – www.metropole.ch
118 rm – †330/850 CHF ††350/850 CHF – ☲ 42 CHF – 9 suites
• Historic • Business • Elegant •

This imposing hotel that dates from 1854 is an integral part of Geneva's history. Situated between Lake Geneva and the rue du Rhône (one of the city's most famous shopping streets), the hotel boasts comfortable, tastefully decorated rooms. An excellent choice.

Les Armures   ✿ ⌖ AC

Rue du Puits-Saint-Pierre 1 ✉ *1204*   Plan: **H2**
– ☎ 022 310 91 72 – www.hotel-les-armures.ch
32 rm – †425/525 CHF ††695/720 CHF – ☲ 40 CHF
• Traditional • Historic • Contemporary •

Situated in the heart of the old town, this 17C residence has a certain charm. It has old stone walls and wooden beams, as well as some superb painted ceilings. It is also intimate, romantic and resolutely contemporary in style. Offering a completely different atmosphere, the restaurant is an authentic tavern serving raclettes and fondues.

De la Cigogne   AC ♨

Place Longemalle 17 ✉ *1204*   Plan: **H1**
– ☎ 022 818 40 40 – www.relaischateaux.com/cigogne
46 rm ☲ – †300/580 CHF ††405/705 CHF – 6 suites
• Luxury • Townhouse • Historic •

A cosy, luxurious hotel decorated with pretty prints, antique furniture, paintings and carpets, all of which create a chic, delicate and classic ambience. The sense of comfort and well-being makes it very difficult to leave.
🕪 **De la Cigogne** – See restaurant listing

Tiffany   ✿ Ló 🕸 AC ♨

Rue de l'Arquebuse 20 ✉ *1204*   Plan: **G2**
– ☎ 022 708 16 16 – www.tiffanyhotel.ch
65 rm – †180/315 CHF ††198/415 CHF – ☲ 29 CHF
• Traditional • Contemporary • Cosy •

This small, stylish Belle Époque hotel is situated on the edge of the Old Town. It offers Art Nouveau decor in its lobby and restaurant and Art Deco furnishings in its guestrooms. Pleasant ambience and friendly welcome.

Domaine de Châteauvieux (Philippe Chevrier)   ⅩⅩⅩⅩ ⇦ 🍸

Chemin de Châteauvieux 16 (West: 10 km)   ⅅ ⟨ 🍴 🅿️ ⇧ 🅿️
– ℰ 022 753 15 11 – www.chateauvieux.ch
– *Closed 2 weeks Christmas-New Year, 1 week during Easter, 2 weeks end July-early August and Sunday-Monday*
13 rm ⌂ – ♥230/350 CHF ♥♥285/400 CHF
Menu 96 CHF (weekday lunch)/290 CHF
– Carte 180/239 CHF – *(booking advisable)*
• Creative • Rustic • Inn •

Off the beaten track, standing above the Geneva countryside and its vineyards, this large traditional house teeming with cachet and individual charm cultivates a true sense of excellence! A culinary technician as much as he is an artist, Philippe Chevrier follows a unique path to unearth truly natural flavours that reconnect with the basics. Delightful rooms for those wishing to stay the night.

➜ Jambonnettes de cuisses de grenouilles sautées, mousseline d'artichauts aux olives noires. Encornet farci, fondue de poireaux aux huîtres « Rouméagous n°3 », émulsion à la cardamome. Bécasse rôtie à la broche, salsifis, jus de cuisson réduit à la truffe noire du Tricastin.

Auberge du Lion d'Or (Thomas Byrne et Gilles Dupont)

Place Pierre-Gautier 5 – ℰ 022 736 44 32   ⅩⅩⅩⅩ 🍸 ⟨ 🍴 ⅗ 🎦 ⇧
– www.dupont-byrne.ch   Plan: **D2**
– *Closed 24 December-16 January and Saturday-Sunday*
Menu 78 CHF (weekday lunch)/210 CHF
– Carte 128/176 CHF
• Modern cuisine • Elegant • Chic •

Two heads are often better than one and the two chefs at this restaurant certainly combine their talents to good effect. They offer an excellent choice of produce, original flavour combinations and cuisine that is full of flavour. Not to mention a romantic view of the lake. A great dining option!

➜ Tarshimi de thon rouge Albacore, salade d'algues. Printanière de homard, confit de citron jaune et olives Taggiasca. Filet d'omble chevalier aux morilles et vin jaune du Jura.

🍽 **Le Bistro de Cologny** – See restaurant listing

Tsé Fung – Hôtel La Réserve   ⅩⅩⅩ 🍸 ⟨ 🍴 ⅗ 🎦 ⇧ 🚗

Route de Lausanne 301 – ℰ 022 959 59 59   Plan: **C1**
– www.tsefung.ch
Menu 78 CHF (lunch)/188 CHF
– Carte 68/284 CHF
• Chinese • Exotic décor •

Cantonese - and Chinese cooking in general - can count on Frank Xu to act as its gastronomic ambassador here. His culinary creations are authentic and delicious in equal measure, meticulously prepared with the very best ingredients. His desserts in particular will live long in the memory. Pleasant view of the garden and lake.

➜ Rouleaux de riz rouge aux crevettes. Filet de Black Cod braisé en cocotte, ail et gingembre. Canard laqué à la pékinoise en deux services.

La Chaumière by Serge Labrosse-La Table du 7 – Restaurant

La Chaumière by Serge Labrosse-Côté Jardin   ⅩⅩ ⇧ 🅿️ 🍴
Chemin de la Fondelle 16 (via Route du Pont Butin B3) – ℰ 022 784 30 66
– www.lachaumiere.ch – *Closed mid june-mid September and Sunday-Monday*
Menu 115/155 CHF – *(dinner only)*
• Modern French • Cosy •

Serge Labrosse's new acquisition is all the enticement you'll need to head out of the city. In this bright and airy restaurant, enjoy a surprise menu featuring 5, 6 or 7 courses. Fine cuisine prepared using the very best ingredients.

➜ St. Pierre, pois, chorizo. Côtelette d'agneau, carotte. Variation fraise.

SWITZERLAND - GENEVA (GENÈVE)

❀ **Le Cigalon** (Jean-Marc Bessire)   XX 斎 **P**

Route d'Ambilly 39 (South-East: 5 km by Route de Chêne D3)
– ✆ 022 349 97 33 – www.le-cigalon.ch
– Closed 2 weeks end December-early January, Easter, 3 weeks mid July-
early August and Sunday-Monday
Menu 54 CHF (weekday lunch)/150 CHF – Carte 95/122 CHF
• Seafood • Elegant • Romantic •

Judging by the fresh fish on the menu, you would be forgiven for thinking that
the Breton coast lies just outside the doors of this restaurant. Le Cigalon has
specialised in seafood for over 20 years, with delicacies such as fish soup, scallops and monkfish from Roscoff all featuring on the menu. Table d'hôte meals
for five guests are also available.
→ Ormeaux d'ores à la plancha. Ceviche de thon, mariné minute, racine de
coriandre. Pavé de bar de ligne cuit sur écailles.

❀ **Le Flacon**   X 斎 ⴹ **AK** ⟷

Rue Vautier 45 – ✆ 022 342 15 20 – www.leflacon.ch   Plan: **C3**
– Closed Saturday lunch and Sunday-Monday
Menu 75 CHF (lunch)/120 CHF – Carte 90/108 CHF
• Modern cuisine • Design •

An enchanting restaurant where the young chef, only just in his 30s, creates
delicious cuisine from his open-view kitchen. He demonstrates a fine command
of flavour and ingredient combinations, as well as a real eye for detail in his
beautifully presented dishes.
→ Asperges de Roques-Hautes, citron confit, poutargue et lard blanc.
Volaille du Nant d'Avril, risotto de blette et mousseline de pomme ratte.
Mangue Nam Dok Mai, glace yaourt et lait d'amande.

⬡ **Le Bistrot Le Lion d'Or**   X 品 斎 ⟷

Rue Ancienne 53 – ✆ 022 342 18 13 – www.lebistrot.ch   Plan: **C3**
– Closed Christmas-New Year and Sunday
Menu 40 CHF (lunch)/58 CHF – Carte 50/79 CHF
• Classic French • Bistro •

The team from Bistrot Laz Nillo has taken over the restaurant in this hotel dating
from 1750. In a light, relaxed atmosphere, they create delicious French dishes
full of flavour, such as the chicken salad with lime, rice vinegar and bird's eye
chilli pepper. Pleasant terrace in a tranquil setting.

⬡ **Collonge Café**   X 斎 ⴹ ⟷ **P**

Chemin du Château-de-Bellerive 3 – ✆ 022 777 12 45   Plan: **D1**
– www.collonge-cafe.ch – Closed Christmas-New Year and Sunday dinner-
Monday; October-May: Monday
Menu 38 CHF (weekday lunch) – Carte 56/99 CHF
• Italian • Friendly • Bistro •

This village inn is now run by Angelo and Viviana Citiulo, previously of La Close-
rie in Cologny. The couple add just a hint of contemporary style to their Italian
dishes, with great results, while the attractive prices certainly pose a challenge
to the restaurant's competitors!

🍴 **Le Loti** – Hôtel La Réserve   XxX 品 < 🛏 斎 **AK** ⟷ 🚗

Route de Lausanne 301 – ✆ 022 959 59 59   Plan: **C1**
– www.lareserve.ch – Closed Sunday
Menu 55 CHF (lunch)/148 CHF – Carte 96/156 CHF
• Mediterranean cuisine • Elegant • Intimate •

Named after the travel writer Pierre Loti, this restaurant, with its warm tones and
exotic influences, evokes a fascination with other lands. The menu features
dishes such as truffle risotto, veal chops, rum baba and chocolate fondant.

⊪◯ **La Chaumière by Serge Labrosse** XX 🏠 & 🅿

Chemin de la Fondelle 16 (via Route du Pont Butin B3) – ☏ 022 784 30 66
– www.lachaumiere.ch – Closed April-September: Sunday dinner-Monday;
October-March: Sunday-Monday
Menu 36 CHF (weekday lunch)/85 CHF – Carte 60/92 CHF
• French • Inn • Cosy •

Parmesan sablé biscuit with multicoloured fresh and cooked tomatoes, burrata and basil, and supreme of roast chicken with herb butter, girolle mushrooms, broad beans and summer truffle are just two of the dishes that you can enjoy in this pleasant, lively restaurant offering classic French bistro cuisine.
❀ **La Chaumière by Serge Labrosse-La Table du 7** – See restaurant listing

⊪◯ **Les Fourneaux du Manège** XX 🖰 🏠 ✛

Route de Chancy 127 – ☏ 022 870 03 90 Plan: **A3**
– www.fourneauxdumanege.ch – Closed 22 December-9 January, 30 July-
13 August
Menu 54 CHF (weekday lunch)/118 CHF
– Carte 62/121 CHF – (dinner only and Sunday lunch)
• Traditional cuisine • Cosy • Inn •

In this attractive 19C building in the centre of Onex, you will enjoy a warm welcome from a dynamic team. They work mainly with regional produce, in particular the famous fish from Lake Geneva: pike, the salmon-like fera, char and perch. It is all served with great enthusiasm in the dining room or on the terrace.

⊪◯ **L'Olivo** – Hôtel Starling XX 🏠 & 🛗 ✛ 🅿

Route François-Peyrot 34 – ☏ 022 747 04 00 Plan: **B1**
– www.shgeneva.com – Closed Christmas-New Year, Saturday-Sunday and
Bank Holidays
Menu 55 CHF (weekday lunch)/95 CHF – Carte 73/97 CHF
• Italian • Cosy • Mediterranean décor •

A pleasant restaurant near the airport, with a large terrace shaded by olive trees. The flavours of Italy dominate the menu, which features specialities such as pasta, risotto, gnocchi with sweet chestnuts, and veal escalopes in Milanese sauce.

⊪◯ **Café des Négociants** X 🕸 🏠 ✛

Rue de la Filature 29 – ☏ 022 300 31 30 Plan: **C3**
– www.negociants.ch – Closed January-November: Sunday
Menu 31 CHF (lunch)/80 CHF – Carte 45/79 CHF – (booking advisable)
• Classic cuisine • Bistro • Friendly •

This retro-style bistro offers all the pleasures of flavoursome, seasonal cuisine and a wine cellar of gargantuan proportions, accompanied by excellent advice. This combination has more than proved its worth: the restaurant is often fully booked.

⊪◯ **Le Bistro de Cologny** – Restaurant Auberge du Lion d'Or X

Place Pierre-Gautier 5 – ☏ 022 736 57 80 ⬷ 🏠 & 🛗
– www.dupont-byrne.ch – Closed 24 December- Plan: **D2**
9 January
Carte 72/119 CHF
• Traditional cuisine • Bistro • Inn •

Echoing the success of the gourmet Lion d'Or restaurant, this bistro annexe is much more than an add on, offering delicious dishes such as sole from Brittany and veal fillet with cep mushrooms. The stunning views from the terrace allow diners to make the most of the 'bistronomic' set menu at weekends.

Le Relais de Chambésy

X ⌂ **P**

Place de Chambésy 8 – ℰ 022 758 11 05
Plan: **C1**
– www.relaisdechambesy.ch – Closed Sunday
Menu 72 CHF – Carte 64/95 CHF

• Classic French • Rustic • Friendly •

Situated in a quiet village, this old coaching inn continues its tradition of hospitality on the outskirts of Geneva. Classic French cuisine, as well as an attractive terrace surrounded by greenery.

La Réserve

⌂ ⌘ ⌐ ⌂ ⌂ ⌂ ⌂ ⌂ ⌂ ⌂ ⌂ ⌂ ⌂ ⌂ ⌂

Route de Lausanne 301 ✉ 1293 – ℰ 022 959 59 59
Plan: **C1**
– www.lareserve.ch

103 rm � – †790 CHF ††790 CHF – 29 suites

• Grand Luxury • Elegant • Cosy •

This luxury hotel is a true sanctuary of beauty! Designer Jacques Garcia has used fine materials and dark colours to create guestrooms with an exotic atmosphere and a style that brings to mind an African lodge. It has a superb spa, access to the lake, a boat available for guests – everything seems possible here. Three restaurants offer a vast selection of flavours.

❀ **Tsé Fung** • ⅢO **Le Loti** – See restaurant listing

Starling

⌂ ⌂ ⌂ ⌂ ⌂ ⌂ **P**

Route François-Peyrot 34 – ℰ 022 747 04 00
Plan: **B1**
– www.shgeneva.com

496 rm – †180/540 CHF ††180/540 CHF – ⊆ 39 CHF – 2 suites

• Business • Chain • Functional •

Situated near the airport and Palexpo, this hotel is worthy of the A380, with almost 500 rooms used mainly by business travellers and conference guests. Despite its size, the hotel is anything but impersonal, with an attentive staff and numerous leisure facilities (fitness room, well-being centre, restaurants, etc.).

ⅢO **L'Olivo** – See restaurant listing

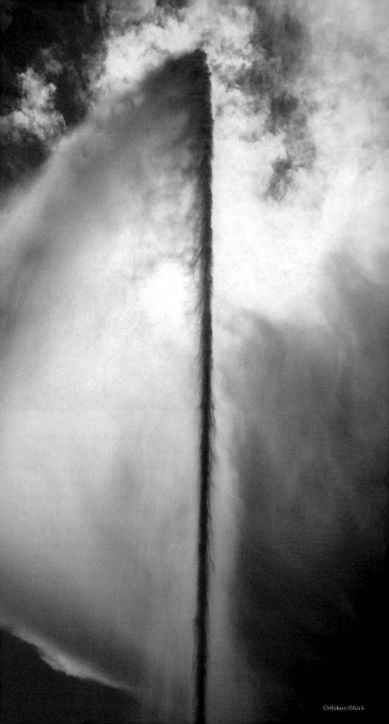

ZURICH
ZÜRICH

Juergen Sack/iStock

ZURICH IN...

→ **ONE DAY**
Old Town, Bahnhofstrasse, Zurich West, Grossmünster.

→ **TWO DAYS**
Watch chessplayers on Lindenhof, see Chagall's windows at Fraumünster, Kunsthaus, Cabaret Voltaire, Café Odeon.

→ **THREE DAYS**
Utoquai, Zürichhorn Park, night at the Opera House.

Zurich has a lot of things going for it. A lot of history (2,000 years' worth), a lot of water (two rivers and a huge lake), a lot of beauty and, let's face it, a lot of wealth. It's an important financial and commercial centre, and has a well-earned reputation for good living and a rich cultural life. The place strikes a nice balance – it's large enough to boast some world-class facilities but small enough to hold onto its charm and old-world ambience. The window-shopping here sets it apart from many other European cities – from tiny boutiques and specialist emporiums to a shopping boulevard that's famed across the globe. Although it's not Switzerland's political capital, it's the spiritual one because of its

pulsing arts scene: for those who might think the Swiss a bit staid, think again – this is where the nihilistic, anti-art Dada movement began. The attractive Lake Zurich flows northwards into the city, which forms a pleasingly symmetrical arc around it. From the lake, the river Limmat bisects Zurich: on its west bank lies the Old Town, the medieval hub, where the stylishly vibrant Bahnhofstrasse shopping street follows the line of the old city walls. Across the Limmat on the east side is the magnificent twin-towered Grossmünster, while just beyond is the charmingly historic district of Niederdorf and way down south, is the city's largest green space, the Zürichhorn Park.

EATING OUT

Zurich stands out in Switzerland (along with Geneva) for its top-class restaurants serving international cuisine. Zurich, though, takes the prize when it comes to trendy, cutting-edge places to dine, whether restaurant or bar, whether along the lakeside or in the converted loft of an old factory. In the middle of the day, most locals go for the cheaper daily lunchtime menus, saving themselves for the glories of the evening. The city is host to many traditional, long-standing Italian restaurants, but if you want to try something

'totally Zurcher', you can't do any better than tackle geschnetzeltes with rösti: sliced veal fried in butter, simmered with onions and mushrooms, with a dash of white wine and cream, served with hash brown potatoes. A good place for simple restaurants and bars is Niederdorf, while Zurich West is coming on strong with its twenty-first century zeitgeist diners. It's customary to round up a small bill or leave up to ten percent on a larger one.

Florhof – Hotel Florhof   XX 🛋 & ⇔
Florhofgasse 4 ✉ *8001 –* ✆ *044 250 26 26*   Plan: **D2**
*– www.hotelflorhof.ch – Closed 24 December-8 January and Saturday
lunch, Sunday-Monday*
Menu 51 CHF (lunch)/125 CHF – Carte 55/104 CHF
• Mediterranean cuisine • Cosy •
Fancy some flambéed tuna fish sashimi or pan-fried fillet of zander with peas,
carrots and a ginger, coriander and macadamia nut gremolata? Try for a table
on the lovely terrace – a little corner of peace and quiet in the heart of Zürich.

Stapferstube da Rizzo   XX 🛋 🅿
Culmannstr. 45 ✉ *8006 –* ✆ *044 350 11 00*   Plan: **D1**
– www.stapferstube.com – Closed Sunday
Menu 26/98 CHF – Carte 55/114 CHF
• Italian • Rustic •
Southern Italian Giovanni Rizzo has been calling the shots here at Stapferstube,
a well-known Zürich eatery, for some time. As a result, the cooking has a strong
Italian feel, as evidenced by the delicious pan-fried squid with garlic, herbs and
chilli. The food is served in a friendly, rustic setting and outdoors in summer.
Conveniently, the restaurant has its own car park.

Drei Stuben   X 🛋 ⇔
Beckenhofstr. 5 ✉ *8006 –* ✆ *044 350 33 00*   Plan: **C1**
*– www.dreistuben-zuerich.ch – Closed during Christmas and Saturday
lunch, Sunday*
Menu 65/89 CHF – Carte 57/108 CHF
• Traditional cuisine • Rustic •
The floors, ceilings and walls here are all done out in rustic wood, lending a
comfortable, cosy atmosphere to this restaurant – just what you would expect
from a local hostelry with a 300-year-old tradition of serving food. There is also a
lovely garden with mature trees. You are offered ambitious, traditional yet contemporary international food.

⫯◯ Bianchi   XX 🛋 🆔
Limmatquai 82 ✉ *8001 –* ✆ *044 262 98 44*   Plan: **D2**
– www.ristorante-bianchi.ch
Carte 58/103 CHF – *(booking advisable)*
• Seafood • Fashionable •
This bright, modern restaurant is located in a quiet spot on the banks of the
River Limmat. It serves Mediterranean cuisine and diners are invited to take
their pick from the fish and shellfish on offer at the generous buffet.

⫯◯ Conti   XX
Dufourstr. 1 ✉ *8008 –* ✆ *044 251 06 66*   Plan: **D3**
– www.bindella.ch – Closed 4 weeks mid July-mid August
Menu 38 CHF (weekday lunch)/68 CHF – Carte 58/120 CHF
• Italian • Mediterranean décor •
This restaurant is set immediately next to the opera. You'll find an interior of
classical dignity with a lovely high stucco ceiling, an exhibition of paintings,
and Italian cuisine.

⫯◯ Haus zum Rüden   XX & 🆔 ⇔
Limmatquai 42 (1st Floor) ✉ *8001 –* ✆ *044 261 95 66*   Plan: **D2**
*– www.hauszumrueden.ch – Closed 24 December-2 January and Saturday
lunch, Sunday-Monday*
Menu 36/145 CHF – Carte 67/118 CHF
• Modern cuisine • Elegant •
This guild house on the Münsterbrücke bridge dates back to 1348, as does the
unique 11m-wide wooden barrel-vaulted ceiling in the Gothic Room. It serves
Mediterranean crossover cuisine with Southeast Asian and North African influences. The modern Rüden Bar (complete with terrace) also serves a small selection of food.

Environs of Zurich
(Plan I)

0   1 Km

ZÜRICH-KLOTTEN

B

• Rias

KLOTTEN

Glattalstrasse

A

Flughofstrasse

Glattalstrasse

1

Katzenrüti-strasse

Glattalstrasse

A1 - E - 60

Kasnadelstrasse

GLATTBRUGG

Flughofstr.

Schaffhauserstr.

A 50

Klotenerstr.

Wallisellerstr.

Wallisellerstr.

1

▲ Kameha Grand Zürich
YOU

Schaffhauserstr.

Thurgauerstrasse

WALLISELLEN

Weststr.

Weststrasse

Wehntalerstrasse

Hagenholzstr.

A1- E 60- E 41

Binzmühlestr.

Regensbergstr.

Wallisellenstrasse

Ueberland

strasse

Glaubtenstr.

KÄFERBERG

Wehntalerstrasse

Bucheggstrasse

Schaffhauserstr.

Winterthurerstrasse

Dübendorfstrasse

2

Emil

Klöti

Strasse

Peterstrasse

Nordstr.

Rotbuchstr.

Winterthurstr.

ZÜRICHBERG

2

Limmattalstrasse

Hardturmstr.

Limmat

Simquai

Rigiblick
Bistro

ZOO
ZÜRICH

A3

Pfingstweidstr.

25Hours
Zürich West

▲ Renaissance
Tower Hotel

Schaffhauserstr.

Winterthurstr.

R 21

• mesa

CLOUDS Kitchen •

Da Angela •

Gustav •

25hours

Langstrasse ▲

SCHWEIZERISCHES
LANDESMUSEUM

Historical and
Commercial Centre
(Plan II)

ADLISBERG

Caduff's
Wine Loft •

Badenerstr.

Nachtjäger •

Café Boy •

EquiTable im
Sankt Meinrad •

Le Chef Metas •
Restaurant

▲ Plattenhof

Asylstrasse

Bergstr.

Saltz •
The Restaurant
The Dolder Grand

Gustrasse

Helvetia ▲

KUNSTHAUS

Talstr.

Rämistr.

Sonnenberg •

Birmensdorferstr.

B2 Boutique Hotel
+ Spa ▲

Weststr.

3

Maison Manesse •

▲ Alden Luxury
Suite Hotel

Seestr.

Bellevuestr.

Witikonerstr.

Forchstr.

3

Schweighofstr.

RIETBERGMUSEUM

Razzia •

Mutschellenstr.

Mythenquai

Riviera •

• Blaue Ente

Zollikerstr.

Forchstr.

FRIESENBERG

Sihl

A 3

Mythenquai

ZÜRICHSEE

B

ZOLLIKON

▲ Hotel
• Restaurant

683

SWITZERLAND - ZURICH

†○ **Kronenhalle** XX 🖾 ⟷
Rämistr. 4 ✉ *8001* – ℰ *044 262 99 00* Plan: **D3**
– *www.kronenhalle.com*
Carte 62/140 CHF – *(booking advisable)*
• Traditional cuisine • Classic décor •
This building, constructed in 1862, is a Zurich institution, and is located on Belle-vue Square. Be sure to take a look at the art collection put together over a period of decades. The atmosphere is traditional, as is the cooking.

†○ **Quaglinos** – Hotel Europe XX
Dufourstr. 4 ✉ *8008* – ℰ *043 456 86 86* Plan: **D3**
– *www.europehotel.ch* – *Closed 21-26 December*
Carte 65/135 CHF
• Classic French • Bistro •
A lively and authentic Quaglinos brasserie based on the tried and tested bistro formula. It offers typical French savoir vivre and, of course, classic French cuisine including duck foie gras and 'Café de Paris' entrecote.

†○ **Razzia** XX 🖼
Seefeldstr. 82 ✉ *8008* – ℰ *044 296 70 70* Plan I: **B3**
– *www.razzia-zuerich.ch* – *Closed Saturday lunch, Sunday*
Menu 45 CHF (lunch)/100 CHF – Carte 54/116 CHF – *(booking advisable)*
• International • Trendy • Brasserie •
One of the city's culinary hotspots, it is set in a former cinema. The small tables in this stylish high-ceilinged restaurant with its attractive stucco work are highly coveted. Menu offerings range from Thai beef salad to misoyaki black cod and Wiener Schnitzel.

†○ **Il Gattopardo** – Hotel Rössli X
Rössligasse 7 ✉ *8001* – ℰ *079 605 01 08* Plan: **D3**
– *www.ilgattopardo.ch* – *Closed Sunday*
Menu 89/150 CHF – Carte 57/115 CHF – *(dinner only)*
• Italian • Family •
Located on the first floor of the Hotel Rössli, this charming family-run restaurant is decorated with lovely blue and white terracotta tiles. Try the 'spaghetti mafiosi' or the *branzino al sale grosso* (sea bass cooked in salt). Specialities inclu-de truffles in winter and asparagus in the spring.

†○ **Oepfelchammer** X 🖼
Rindermarkt 12 (1st floor) ✉ *8001* – ℰ *044 251 23 36* Plan: **D2**
– *www.oepfelchammer.ch* – *Closed 15 July-13 August, 23 December-7 January, Sunday-Monday and Bank Holidays*
Menu 69/92 CHF – Carte 65/81 CHF
• Traditional cuisine • Rustic • Wine bar •
The oldest remaining wine tavern in Zürich dating back to the 14C, Oepfelc-hammer once played host to 19C Swiss poet Gottfried Keller. In keeping with the quaint rustic charm, it serves traditional Swiss fare. Don't be afraid to try your hand at the famed "beam challenge"!

†○ **DU THÉÂTRE** X 🖼
Dufourstr. 20 ✉ *8008* – ℰ *044 251 48 44* Plan: **D3**
– *www.du-theatre.ch* – *Closed 1 week Christmas-New Year and Saturday lunch, Sunday*
Carte 57/99 CHF
• Traditional cuisine • Fashionable • Bistro •
Established in 1890, this fashionable restaurant full of historic charm is located close to the Zürich Opera. It offers traditional and Southeast Asian cuisine ran-ging from beef tartare to chicken teriyaki with poached egg and mushrooms, as well as 'Sashimi Du Théâtre'. Smaller lunchtime menu.

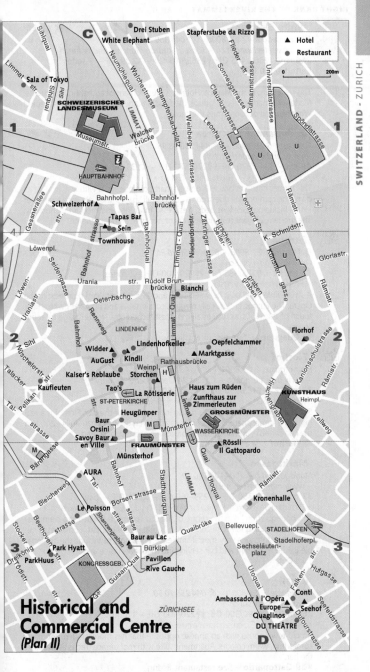

Drei Stuben

White Elephant

Stapferstube da Rizzo

▲ Hotel
● Restaurant

0   200m

C   D

Sala of Tokyo

SCHWEIZERISCHES
LANDESMUSEUM

1   U   U   1

Museumstr.

HAUPTBAHNHOF

Bahnhofpl.   Bahnhof-
brücke

Schweizerhof ▲

Tapas Bar
Sein
Townhouse

Löwenpl.

Urania   str.   Rudolf Brun-
brücke   Bianchi

Oetenbachg.

LINDENHOF   Oepfelchammer   Florhof

2   2

Widder ▲   Lindenhofkeller   ▲ Marktgasse
AuGust   Kindli
Kaiser's Reblaube   Weinpl.   Rathausbrücke
Storchen   H
Kaufleuten   Tao's   La Rôtisserie
ST-PETERKIRCHE   Haus zum Rüden   KUNSTHAUS
Zunfthaus zur   Heimpl.
Heugümper   Zimmerleuten
GROSSMÜNSTER
Baur   WASSERKIRCHE
Orsini   M   Münsterbr.
Savoy Baur   Rössli
en Ville   FRAUMÜNSTER   Il Gattopardo
Münsterhof

M

AURA

Bleicherweg   Kronenhalle

Le Poisson   Bellevuepl.   STADELHOFEN

3   Park Hyatt   Sechseläuten-   Stadelhoferpl.   3
ParkHuus   Baur au Lac   platz
KONGRESSGEB.   Bürklipl.
Pavillon
Rive Gauche

Conti
Historical and   Ambassador à l'Opéra   Seehof
Commercial Centre   ZÜRICHSEE   Europe ▲   Quaglinos
(Plan II)   C   DU THÉÂTRE   D

SWITZERLAND - ZURICH

White Elephant

Neumühlequai 42 ⊠ *8006 – ℰ 044 360 73 22*
Plan: **C1**
– www.whiteelephant.ch – Closed Saturday lunch, Sunday lunch
266 rm – ♦365/495 CHF ♦♦365/495 CHF – ⊆ 39 CHF – 9 suites
Carte 64/110 CHF
• Thai • Exotic décor •
This restaurant in the Marriott Hotel is a must for fans of authentic Thai cuisine. Made with market fresh produce, the food is authentic and authentically spicy! Whatever you do, don't miss the curries.

Ambassador à l'Opéra

Falkenstr. 6 ⊠ *8008 – ℰ 044 258 98 98*
Plan: **D3**
– www.ambassadorhotel.ch
45 rm – ♦240/370 CHF ♦♦270/570 CHF – ⊆ 33 CHF
• Townhouse • Elegant • Cosy •
This former patrician house is now a smart boutique hotel with a style all of its own. The comfortable guestrooms come in all shapes and sizes with a range of extras including excellent beds, Nespresso machines and modern technology. The modern, elegant restaurant is decorated with an opera theme.

Europe

Dufourstr. 4 ⊠ *8008 – ℰ 043 456 86 86*
Plan: **D3**
– www.europehotel.ch
39 rm ⊆ – ♦185/385 CHF ♦♦220/700 CHF – 2 suites
• Historic • Townhouse • Cosy •
A stylish little hotel built between 1898 and 1900 and situated right next to the Opera. The Europe is classically elegant, comfortable and upmarket with a little touch of the 1950s, as well as all the latest technology. No surcharge for room service.
🍴 **Quaglinos** – See restaurant listing

Florhof

Florhofgasse 4 ⊠ *8001 – ℰ 044 250 26 26*
Plan: **D2**
– www.hotelflorhof.ch – Closed 24 December-2 January
32 rm ⊆ – ♦185/290 CHF ♦♦300/360 CHF
• Townhouse • Elegant • Personalised •
Set in a lovely 18C nobleman's house in the centre of the city, Florhof is a real gem. The atmosphere is pleasantly casual, everything is beautifully kept, and the comfortable, upmarket rooms promise a great night's sleep.
🍴 **Florhof** – See restaurant listing

Marktgasse

Marktgasse 17 – ℰ 044 266 10 10
Plan: **D2**
– www.marktgassehotel.ch
37 rm – ♦199/350 CHF ♦♦259/460 CHF – ⊆ 21 CHF – 2 suites
• Boutique hotel • Historic building • Contemporary •
This boutique hotel is in the centre of the Old Town. It is housed in a centuries-old listed building full of historical details that give the smart, upmarket, mini-malist-style interior a very special ambience. Food options include the fashiona-ble Baltho restaurant and bar serving international cuisine and the Delish Café Take-Out.

Rössli

Rössligasse 7 ⊠ *8001 – ℰ 044 256 70 50*
Plan: **D3**
– www.hotelroessli.ch
26 rm ⊆ – ♦190/300 CHF ♦♦220/400 CHF – 1 suite
• Historic • Contemporary •
An old town house with an annexe opposite that has more modern rooms in comforting, warm colours. Apartment suite with roof terrace. Tapas available in the bar.
🍴 **Il Gattopardo** – See restaurant listing

SWITZERLAND - ZURICH

⌂ **Seehof**

Seehofstr. 11 ⊠ *8008* – ☎ *044 254 57 57*   Plan: **D3**
– www.seehof.ch – Closed 24-27 December
19 rm ⌧ – ♦180/300 CHF ♦♦220/390 CHF – 1 suite
• Business • Contemporary •

Seehof sits in an excellent central location, tucked away behind the Opera. It has charming rooms with a sea-faring note. Prettily decorated in welcoming blues and whites, they are simple, modern and very comfortable. There's also the Japanese restaurant SAKU.

LEFT BANK OF THE RIVER LIMMAT   PLAN II

❀ **Pavillon** – Hotel Baur au Lac   XxX 錄 ৬ 瓲 ☞

Talstr. 1 ⊠ *8001* – ☎ *044 220 50 22*   Plan: **C3**
– www.aupavillon.ch – Closed 15-26 February, 8-22 October and Saturday lunch, Sunday, Bank Holidays
Menu 98 CHF (lunch)/205 CHF – Carte 134/228 CHF
• Classic French • Elegant • Friendly •

Star architect Pierre-Yves Rochon designed this elegant restaurant. The almost 360° glazed rotunda with its garden and lake views is wonderful. Exquisite classic cuisine prepared by Laurent Eperon, with dishes that include roast sea bass with Périgord truffles.

→ Bouillabaisse, Rouille, Knoblauchchips. Taube aus der Vendée, Entenleber, Koriander, Sellerie, Rettich. Wild geangelter Steinbutt, Kardamom, Beurre blanc, Kaviar, Frühlingsgemüse.

❀ **Sein** (Martin Surbeck)   XX 霜 瓲 ⟷

Schützengasse 5 ⊠ *8001* – ☎ *044 221 10 65*   Plan: **C1**
– www.zuerichsein.ch – Closed 24 December-3 January, 16 March-8 April, 16 July-5 August, Saturday-Sunday and Bank Holidays; mid November-December: Saturday lunch, Sunday
Menu 84 CHF (lunch)/175 CHF – Carte 91/151 CHF
• Modern cuisine • Design • Elegant •

You will find a modern note here, not only in the elegant, minimalist-style decor but also in the classic cuisine – made from high quality ingredients without any unnecessary frills. There is also a vegetarian menu. The floor-to-ceiling windows in the restaurant provide an interesting view of the main shopping street outside.

→ Geschüttelte Tomatenconsommé mit Basilikumschaum. Störcarpaccio auf Kartoffelstock mit Kaviar und Sauerrahmsauce. Geschmortes Toggenburger "KalbsMüsli", in Öl pochierte Karotten und Vin Jaune-Sauce.
🝑 **Tapas Bar** – See restaurant listing

☺ **AuGust** – Hotel Widder   X 霜

Rennweg 7 ⊠ *8001* – ☎ *044 224 28 28*   Plan: **C2**
– www.au-gust.ch
Carte 47/122 CHF
• Meats and grills • Brasserie •

Diners here enjoy fresh, flavoursome cuisine in a charming, classic brasserie setting. Dishes include some excellent terrines and sausages – try the meatloaf or a dish of venison goulash. Parties of six and over should book.

☺ **Kaufleuten**   X 霜 ⟷

Pelikanplatz ⊠ *8001* – ☎ *044 225 33 33*   Plan: **C2**
– www.kaufleuten.ch – Closed Sunday lunch
Carte 44/97 CHF – (booking advisable)
• Market cuisine • Brasserie •

This lively brasserie located in the fashionable venue of the same name is much in demand, not least thanks to its good food. Try the duck ravioli with leek salad or the veal cutlet – sliced for you at your table – before moving on to the bar or club.

687

Tapas Bar – Restaurant Sein ⚄ 🗶 ☲ 🆎

Schützengasse 5 ⊠ 8001 – ℰ 044 221 10 65   Plan: **C1**
– www.zuerichsein.ch – Closed 24 December-3 January, 26 March-8 April,
16 July-5 August, Saturday-Sunday and Bank Holidays; mid November-
December: Saturday lunch, Sunday
Menu 35 CHF – Carte 28/78 CHF
• Modern cuisine • Tapas bar •
This friendly, modern restaurant boasts a light and airy interior and tapas-style
food. Try the ravioli with rosemary butter or the Pilze mit Kakaoerde und Mimolette (a mushroom speciality).

Baur – Hotel Savoy Baur en Ville ⅋ XxX 🖗 🆎

Poststr. 12 (at Paradeplatz) ⊠ 8001 – ℰ 044 215 25 25   Plan: **C2**
– www.savoy-zuerich.ch – Closed Saturday-Sunday
Menu 72 CHF (weekday lunch) – Carte 74/146 CHF
• Classic French • Elegant • Classic décor •
This restaurant has a stylish, elegant feel that is perfect for its classic French cuisine. Details such as the unusual rock crystal chandeliers together with the
luxury fittings and smart table settings set the scene.

Rive Gauche – Hotel Baur au Lac ⅋ XX 🖗 🆎 🅿

Talstr. 1 ⊠ 8001 – ℰ 044 220 50 60 – www.agauche.ch   Plan: **C3**
– Closed 16 July-13 August
Carte 66/180 CHF
• Classic cuisine • Cosy •
A 'brasserie de luxe', Rive Gauche offers chic, stylish design, attentive and
accomplished service and modern cuisine with an attractive bar to boot. Menu
offerings range from octopus carpaccio and vegan ravioli to steak and the
Wagyu beefburger.

Heugümper ⅋ XX 🖗 🖗 🆎 ⇔

Waaggasse 4 ⊠ 8001 – ℰ 044 211 16 60   Plan: **C2**
– www.heuguemper.ch – Closed 23 December-6 January, 16 July-
17 August and Saturday lunch, Sunday, January-September: Saturday-
Sunday
Menu 49 CHF (lunch)/120 CHF (dinner) – Carte 74/105 CHF
• Modern cuisine • Elegant • Romantic •
This venerable townhouse in the heart of Zürich serves international food with a
Southeast Asian twist in its smart modern interior. Small lunchtime menu.

Kaiser's Reblaube ⅋ XX 🖗

Glockengasse 7 ⊠ 8001 – ℰ 044 221 21 20   Plan: **C2**
– www.kaisers-reblaube.ch – Closed 23 July-13 August, January-October:
Saturday lunch, Sunday-Monday; November-December: Saturday lunch,
Sunday
Menu 58 CHF (lunch)/120 CHF – Carte 55/104 CHF
• Classic cuisine • Rustic • Cosy •
Enjoy modern cooking with a traditional influence in this house that was built in
1260 along a small, narrow alley. Comfortable little restaurant on the first-floor
and a wine bar on the ground floor.

Kindli – Hotel Kindli ⅋ XX 🖗

Pfalzgasse 1 ⊠ 8001 – ℰ 043 888 76 78 – www.kindli.ch   Plan: **C2**
– Closed Sunday and Bank Holidays
Carte 67/116 CHF – *(booking advisable)*
• Classic French • Inn •
The restaurant's charming character comes in part from its wonderful old wood
panelling and the bistro-style, communal arrangement of its beautifully laid
tables.

iIO **La Rôtisserie** – Hotel Storchen   XX ⪡ 🛋 ᕖ 🚗

Weinplatz 2 (access via Storchengasse 16) ⊠ *8001*   Plan: **C2**
– ℰ 044 227 27 27 – www.storchen.ch
Carte 72/117 CHF
• Classic French • Classic décor • Intimate •
The classically traditional Rôtisserie boasts a lovely high-ceilinged dining room
with large arched windows and an elegant atmosphere and serves French cui-
sine with Swiss influences. Try the veal ravioli with sage foam, the zander Café
de Paris or the woodland game. The lovely terrace looks over the River Limmat.

iIO **Lindenhofkeller**   XX 錦 🛋

Pfalzgasse 4 ⊠ *8001 – ℰ 044 211 70 71*   Plan: **C2**
*– www.lindenhofkeller.ch – Closed 3 weeks end July-August, 1 week
Christmas, Saturday-Sunday and Bank Holidays*
Menu 69 CHF (lunch)/145 CHF
– Carte 67/141 CHF – (bookings advisable at dinner)
• Classic cuisine • Elegant • Romantic •
With its homely romantic touch, this elegant cellar restaurant with wine lounge
fits harmoniously into the contemplative Old Town scene. Classic cooking with
modern elements.

iIO **Orsini** – Hotel Savoy Baur en Ville   XX 🛋 🎴

Poststr. 12 (at Paradeplatz) ⊠ *8001 – ℰ 044 215 25 25* Plan: **C2**
– www.savoy-zuerich.ch
Menu 72 CHF (lunch) – Carte 69/146 CHF – *(booking advisable)*
• Italian • Elegant • Classic décor •
This elegant restaurant has been serving classic Italian cuisine for over 30 years.
The sumptuous poppy design on the carpet, repeated in the filigree motif in the
oil paintings on the walls, adds a special touch.

iIO **ParkHuus** – Hotel Park Hyatt   XX 錦 🛋 🎴 🚗

Beethoven Str. 21 ⊠ *8002 – ℰ 043 883 10 75*   Plan: **C3**
– www.zurich.park.hyatt.ch – Closed Saturday lunch, Sunday lunch
Carte 67/120 CHF
• Modern cuisine • Fashionable •
The restaurant here is every bit as contemporary and international as the hotel
and the modern dishes that emerge from the show kitchen are made using
good Swiss produce. There is also an impressive glazed wine cellar accessible
via a spiral staircase.

iIO **Le Poisson**   XX 🎴 🅿

Claridenstr. 30 ⊠ *8022 – ℰ 044 286 22 22*   Plan: **C3**
– www.lepoisson.ch – Closed Saturday lunch, Sunday lunch
Menu 58 CHF (dinner) – Carte 68/114 CHF
• Seafood • Classic décor •
It is all about fish and seafood here with menu options ranging from sea bass to
bouillabaisse and lobster claws. Diners in the tasteful interior can look forward
to house classics but should also take a look at some of the kitchen team's new
dishes.

iIO **Tao's**   XX 錦 ✿

Augustinergasse 3 ⊠ *8001 – ℰ 044 448 11 22*   Plan: **C2**
– www.taos-zurich.ch – Closed Sunday
Carte 58/140 CHF
• Fusion • Exotic décor • Elegant •
A touch of the exotic in the middle of Zurich! Elegant upstairs, a little more infor-
mal on the ground floor. Smokers can use Tao's Lounge Bar that offers a Euro-
Asian menu. Grilled meats.

‖○ **AURA** ✗ ⅙ 🆎 ⇔

Bleicherweg 5 ✉ *8001 –* ☏ *044 448 11 44*   Plan: **C3**
– www.aura-zurich.ch – Closed Sunday
Carte 58/159 CHF
• Meats and grills • Trendy • Design •

A stylishly urban restaurant, a top-flight events venue, a lounge or a club? AURA is a little bit of each, but above all the place to be for lovers of modern crossover cuisine with a weakness for grilled food – just watch the chefs at work! Located on Paradeplatz in the old stock exchange building.

‖○ **Münsterhof** ✗ 🆎

Münsterhof 6 ✉ *8001 –* ☏ *044 262 33 00*   Plan: **C2**
– www.mhof.ch – Closed Sunday, November-March: Sunday, Monday dinner
Menu 35 CHF (weekday lunch) – Carte 59/101 CHF – *(booking advisable)*
• Classic cuisine • Rustic • Friendly •

Set in a historic 11C building, Münsterhof offers a rustic dining room on the ground floor and something a little more elegant upstairs. The menus are the same and include homemade tortellini with veal and Lake Zurich bouillabaisse, not to mention an excellent steak tartare.

‖○ **Sala of Tokyo** ✗ 🍴 🆎 ⇔

Limmatstr. 29 ✉ *8005 –* ☏ *044 271 52 90*   Plan: **C1**
– www.sala-of-tokyo.ch – Closed 3 weeks July-August, 2 weeks Christmas-New Year
Menu 72/195 CHF – Carte 62/128 CHF
• Japanese • Friendly • Exotic décor •

The go-to Japanese restaurant in Zürich since 1981, Sala of Tokyo retains its own individual style using top-quality produce to create authentic flavoursome cuisine. Try the excellent Kobe and Toro beef dishes, the *nabemono* stews and, of course, the sushi.

🏨 **Baur au Lac** 🚗 ᵫ ⅙ 🆎 🏊 🛎

Talstr. 1 ✉ *8001 –* ☏ *044 220 50 20*   Plan: **C3**
– www.bauraulac.ch
119 rm – ♦570/870 CHF ♦♦680/1200 CHF – ⊊ 49 CHF – 18 suites
• Grand Luxury • Elegant • Personalised •

Guests have been coming to this magnificent grand hotel since 1844. Today they appreciate the high standards throughout, from the stylish lobby via the upmarket, elegant rooms and excellent service to the gorgeous garden facing the lake.
❀ **Pavillon** • ‖○ **Rive Gauche** – See restaurant listing

🏨 **Savoy Baur en Ville** ⅙ 🆎 🏊 🛎

Poststr. 12 (at Paradeplatz) ✉ *8001 –* ☏ *044 215 25 25*   Plan: **C2**
– www.savoy-zuerich.ch
95 rm ⊊ – ♦400/820 CHF ♦♦690/820 CHF – 9 suites
• Luxury • Classic • Elegant •

The building of this wonderful hotel in 1838 laid the foundations of a long and lasting hotel tradition. Offering first class service in a made-to-measure interior, the upmarket restaurant features unusual Brazilian rock crystal chandeliers and fine table settings. Live piano music in the bar.
‖○ **Orsini** • ‖○ **Baur** – See restaurant listing

🏨 **Widder** ᵫ 🆎 🏊 🛎

Rennweg 7 ✉ *8001 –* ☏ *044 224 25 26*   Plan: **C2**
– www.widderhotel.com
42 rm ⊊ – ♦470/820 CHF ♦♦470/820 CHF – 7 suites
• Luxury • Design • Historic •

Swiss architect Tilla Theus has successfully combined old and new in these nine beautifully restored townhouses in the old city. Historic detail is combined with some lovely one-off decorative pieces. The service is excellent and the Wirtschaft zur Schtund serves tasty Flammkuchen.
❀ **AuGust** – See restaurant listing

Park Hyatt

Beethoven Str. 21 ✉ *8002*
– ☎ *043 883 12 34*
– *www.zurich.park.hyatt.ch*
139 rm – ♦490/1120 CHF ♦♦560/1190 CHF – ☲ 43 CHF – 4 suites
• Luxury • Business • Contemporary •
The Park Hyatt has a large, elegant hall and a lobby area with an entrance to the striking Onyx Bar. It features stylish, modern rooms with lots of space, and a tasteful little spa. The elegant ParkHuus has a show kitchen and a glazed wine cellar on two floors.
🍴 **ParkHuus** – See restaurant listing

Plan: **C3**

Schweizerhof

Bahnhofplatz 7 ✉ *8021*
– ☎ *044 218 88 88*
– *www.hotelschweizerhof.com*
90 rm ☲ – ♦245/660 CHF ♦♦390/725 CHF – 9 suites
• Luxury • Business • Classic •
Established in the 19C, this city hotel with its imposing façade stands at the entrance to the pedestrian zone and is just a few steps from the railway station. It offers excellent service with lots of extras and some particularly comfortable junior suites. Snacks in the Café Gourmet.

Plan: **C1**

Storchen

Weinplatz 2 (access via Storchengasse 16) ✉ *8001*
– ☎ *044 227 27 27*
– *www.storchen.ch*
66 rm ☲ – ♦390/580 CHF ♦♦430/880 CHF – 2 suites
• Traditional • Elegant • Contemporary •
Storchen is one of the oldest hotels in the city (first appearing in the records in 1357) and enjoys a wonderful location on the banks of the Limmat with the Old Town on its doorstep. Try one of the large suites complete with private terrace. The service is attentive, the breakfast excellent, and the barcum-lounge is chic.
🍴 **La Rôtisserie** – See restaurant listing

Plan: **C2**

Kindli

Pfalzgasse 1 ✉ *8001*
– ☎ *043 888 76 78*
– *www.kindli.ch*
20 rm ☲ – ♦240/340 CHF ♦♦340/480 CHF
• Historic • Cosy • Personalised •
Established over 500 years ago as a hostel for pilgrims, Kindli is now a charming boutique hotel with genuine allure and comfortable, individually designed rooms that will appeal to business guests and tourists alike. It also offers a number of upmarket apartments.
🍴 **Kindli** – See restaurant listing

Plan: **C2**

Townhouse

Schützengasse 7 (5th floor) ✉ *8001*
– ☎ *044 200 95 95*
– *www.townhouse.ch*
25 rm – ♦160/355 CHF ♦♦190/395 CHF – ☲ 21 CHF
• Townhouse • Contemporary • Cosy •
The Townhouse is an exclusive hotel in an almost perfect location – just a few steps from the famed Bahnhofstrasse. The furniture and wallpaper will delight enthusiasts of the English style. Breakfast is served in your room or in the bar on the ground floor.

Plan: **C1**

SWITZERLAND - ZURICH

❀❀ **The Restaurant** – Hotel The Dolder Grand   XxXX ❀ ⇔ 🏠 🖪 🔠
Kurhausstr. 65 ✉ *8032*   ⬦ 🚗
– ℰ *044 456 60 00* – *www.thedoldergrand.com*   Plan: **B3**
– *Closed 18 February-5 March, 22 July-13 August and Saturday lunch,*
Sunday-Monday
Menu 98 CHF (weekday lunch)/298 CHF
– Carte 146/242 CHF – *(booking advisable)*
• Creative • Luxury • Elegant •

Intense cuisine presented in well-matched, creative combinations with top quality products combined with skill and flair. The lunchtime taster menu offers guests the chance
to sample an interesting cross-section of dishes from the main menu. Stylish decor
inside and a stunning terrace with a fantastic view outside.
➜ Jakobsmuschel mit Erdnuss, Dill und Kaviar. Bergkartoffel mit Spinat, Ei
und weissem Trüffel. Reh mit Gartenkräutern, Sonnenblumenkernen und
Angostura.

❀❀ **Ecco Zürich** – Hotel Atlantis by Giardino   XxX 🏠 ♿ 🖪 ⬦ 🚗
Döltschiweg 234 (by Birmensdorferstrasse A3) ✉ *8055*
– ℰ *044 456 55 55* – *www.ecco-restaurant.ch*
– *Closed 1-23 January, 23 July-14 August and Sunday-Monday*
Menu 150/235 CHF – *(dinner only and Sunday lunch) (booking essential)*
• Creative • Design • Elegant •

This creative concept is already well known from the Ecco restaurants in
Ascona and St. Moritz, but here Stefan Heilemann brings his own personal
touch. He cooks innovative food with fine, intelligent contrasts and great
depth. The interior is genuinely elegant, while the service is friendly and
professional.
➜ Alaska Königskrabbe, Wintersalate, Yuzu. Mieral Perlhuhn, Kohlrabi, Peri-
gordtrüffel. Felchlin Schokolade „Cru Cuba 72%", Sauerkirsche, Tonka-
bohne.

❀ **Rigiblick**   XxX ⇔ ☟ ⇐ 🏠 ♿ 🚗
Germaniastr. 99 ✉ *8044*   Plan: **B2**
– ℰ *043 255 15 70* – *www.restaurantrigiblick.ch*
– *Closed 2 weeks February, mid July-mid August and Sunday-Monday*
7 rm ⛄ – 🛏220/350 CHF 🛏🛏250/450 CHF
Menu 105/185 CHF – *(dinner only) (booking advisable)*
• Modern cuisine • Elegant • Intimate •

In this smart residential district overlooking Zürich, the amazing view alone is a
great draw, though it is more than matched by the attractive modern interior
and sophisticated cuisine. The food, which includes vegetarian options, is
made using local organic products. Those who wish to stay longer will appreciate the pretty apartments.
➜ Felchen, Mandel, Broccoli und Nussbutter. Bresse Ei, Blumenkohl und
Schnittlauch beurre blanc. Cheesecake, Rotweinbuttereis.
🍽 **Bistro** – See restaurant listing

❀ **mesa**   XX ❀ 🏠 ♿ 🖪
Weinbergstr. 75 ✉ *8006*   Plan: **A2**
– ℰ *043 321 75 75* – *www.mesa-restaurant.ch*
– *Closed 24 December-14 January, 15 July-15 August and Saturday lunch,*
Sunday-Monday
Menu 75 CHF (lunch)/135 CHF – *(booking advisable)*
• Modern cuisine • Minimalist • Elegant •

Tasteful and pleasantly unpretentious, mesa boasts a friendly atmosphere, great
service and excellent, produce-based food that is tasty and full of contrast. Wine
lovers will be pleased to hear that even the rare wines on offer here are available by the glass.
➜ Brüggli Saibling mit Miso, Gurke, Ingwer. Kalbfleisch-Tortelloni, Kalbsjus,
saisonales Gemüse. Königs-Taube mit Risotto, Schlossbergkäse, Birne.

£3 **YOU** – Hotel Kameha Grand Zürich   XX 斎 M 🚗

Dufaux-Str. 1 – ℰ 044 525 50 00   Plan: **B1**
– www.kamehagrandzuerich.com – Closed 17 December-8 January,
25 February-5 March, 25 March-9 April, 15 July-13 August and Sunday-
Monday
Menu 109/170 CHF
– Carte 121/154 CHF – (dinner only) (booking advisable)
• Modern cuisine • Exotic décor • Fashionable •
YOU boasts a smart, minimalist-style, Far Eastern interior that gives it a genui-
nely unusual atmosphere. The food coming out of the kitchens is modern, crea-
tive, beautifully presented and based on high-quality produce.
→ Weisser Spargel mit Bio-Ei, Kaviar, Brunnenkresse. Geschmorter Ostsee-
Aal mit Randen "Süss-Sauer", Spinatsalat und Meerrettich. Kondensmilch
mit Trauben, Karamell und Felchlin-Schokolade.

£3 **EquiTable im Sankt Meinrad**   X 斎

Stauffacherstr. 163 ⊠ 8004 – ℰ 043 534 82 77   Plan: **A3**
– www.equi-table.ch – Closed 1 week early January, mid July-mid August
and Sunday-Monday
Menu 120/180 CHF – *(dinner only) (booking advisable)*
• Modern cuisine • Fashionable •
Just as Sankt Meinrad's parent company deals only in fair trade and organic products, so its kitchen team under Fabian Fuchs uses nothing but the best ingredients in its modern cuisine. The whole experience is rounded off by the
friendly service and informal atmosphere.
→ Saibling, Rande, Gurke. Milchkuhfilet, Spargel, Mandel, Morchel, Urdin-
kelgras. Weisse Schokolade, Rhabarber.

£3 **Maison Manesse**   X 錦 斎

Hopfenstr. 2 ⊠ 8045 – ℰ 044 462 01 01   Plan: **A3**
– www.maisonmanesse.ch – Closed Christmas-New Year and Sunday-
Monday
Menu 60/130 CHF – *(dinner only) (booking advisable)*
• Creative • Rustic • Family •
If you like relaxed dining, you will enjoy this friendly, informal restaurant and its
excellent, creative cuisine prepared using top-quality produce. A must for wine
lovers, the 1 200 bottles on its wine list include a number of rarities and old vintages. Much reduced lunchtime menu.
→ Lobster, Barbe di Frate, Kapern. Kalbsschulter, Cime di Rape, Brot-
espuma. Banane, Rhabarber, Zitronengras.

🙂 **Da Angela**   XX 斎 & 🅿

Hohlstr. 449 ⊠ 8048 – ℰ 044 492 29 31   Plan: **A3**
– www.daangela.ch – Closed 24 December-7 January, end July-early
August and Sunday
Carte 59/120 CHF – *(booking advisable)*
• Italian • Traditional décor •
It's no wonder that this long-established restaurant with its traditional charm is
so popular. It serves really good classic Italian cuisine including home-made
pasta – try the cappelletti Angela – and the ever popular ossobuco.

🙂 **Rias**   XX 斎

Gerbegasse 6 – ℰ 044 814 26 52 – www.rias.ch   Plan: **B1**
– Closed Saturday-Sunday and Bank Holidays
Menu 65/95 CHF – Carte 53/118 CHF
• Country • Fashionable •
Rias promises good cuisine, as well as an attractive modern interior with menu
options including octopus carpaccio or Grosi's veal burger with potato mash.
Wines by the glass. Reduced lunchtime menu.

Café Boy ✗ ☆

Kochstr. 2 ✉ *8004 – ✆ 044 240 40 24* Plan: **A3**
– www.cafeboy.ch – Closed 2 weeks end December and Saturday-Sunday
Menu 69 CHF (weekday dinner) – Carte 59/93 CHF
• Traditional cuisine • Bistro •

Once home to left-wing political activists, Café Boy is now a simple, lively bistro serving fresh, traditional cuisine. There is a passion for wine as you can see from the extensive selection. Simpler lunchtime menu.

Hide & Seek – Hotel Atlantis by Giardino ✗ ☆ ᪮ 🎬 ↔ 🚗

Döltschiweg 234 (by Birmensdorferstrasse A3) ✉ *8055 – ✆ 044 456 55 55*
– www.atlantisbygiardino.ch
Menu 49 CHF (lunch) – Carte 65/114 CHF – *(Sunday lunch: brunch only)*
• International • Chic • Fashionable •

This restaurant with a fusion theme offers a mix of modern European, Middle Eastern and Southeast Asian cuisine and design. The menu includes Thai fishcakes and zander with black quinoa, vanilla carrots and orange *beurre blanc.*

Nachtjäger ✗ ☆

Badenerstr. 310 ✉ *8004 – ✆ 043 931 77 90* Plan: **A3**
– www.nachtjaeger.ch – Closed 24 December-2 January, 17 July-
20 August, Sunday-Monday and Bank Holidays
Carte 62/70 CHF – *(dinner only)*
• Market cuisine • Cosy •

This charming little restaurant serves a little outside the city centre serves "comfort food" – fresh, unfussy cuisine that is highly prized by its guests. The flavoursome fare chalked up on the blackboard includes veal and wheat beer pie, and shin of beef with chickpeas and paprika.

Sonnenberg ✗✗✗ ⅜ ⪪ ☆ ᪮ 🎬 ↔ 🅿

Hitzigweg 15 ✉ *8032 – ✆ 044 266 97 97* Plan: **B3**
– www.sonnenberg-zh.ch – Closed 1-8 January
Menu 69 CHF – Carte 79/159 CHF – *(booking advisable)*
• Classic French • Chic •

Sonnenberg's elevated location above Zürich provides a wonderful view over the city and lake. The cuisine includes various Sonnenberg specials including traditional Swiss veal chops and boiled beef as well as Piedmont gnocchi with king crab and the classic ossobuco. The terrace is truly idyllic.

Blaue Ente ✗✗ ☆ ᪮ 🎬 ↔

Seefeldstr. 223 ✉ *8008 – ✆ 044 388 68 40* Plan: **B3**
– www.blaue-ente.ch – Closed Saturday lunch, Sunday and Bank Holidays
Menu 27 CHF – Carte 56/93 CHF – *(booking advisable)*
• Country • Trendy • Friendly •

Historic industrial architecture outside and a trendy and lively atmosphere (and some fine old machinery) inside. The service is attentive and straightforward while the flavoursome food is made using local produce. The flour even comes from the restaurant's own mill next door. There is a more ambitious evening menu.

Caduff's Wine Loft ✗✗ ⅜ ☆

Kanzleistr. 126 ✉ *8004 – ✆ 044 240 22 55* Plan: **A3**
– www.wineloft.ch – Closed 24 December-4 January, Saturday lunch and Sunday
Menu 30 CHF (weekday lunch)/130 CHF
– Carte 72/124 CHF – *(bookings advisable at dinner)*
• Classic French • Trendy • Neighbourhood •

This former engineering works serves good seasonal cuisine including pheasant terrine with black chanterelle mushrooms and pistachios, followed perhaps by a good raw-milk cheese. The walk-in wine cellar boasts over 2 000 different bottles!

SWITZERLAND - ZURICH

⫯◯ **Le Chef Metas Restaurant**   XX 🖼
Kanonengasse 29 ⊠ *8004 – ☏ 044 240 41 00*   Plan: **A3**
– www.restaurant-lechef.ch – Closed 2 weeks end December, 3 weeks July-August and Sunday-Monday
Menu 81 CHF – Carte 39/101 CHF
• International • Cosy •
Le Chef manages to be modern yet warm and welcoming thanks to its combination of clean, straight lines, warm wood and purple tones. Meta Hiltebrand offers a range of delicious dishes including roast tomato soup and beef fillet stroganoff.

⫯◯ **CLOUDS Kitchen**   XX ≤ 🖼 ⇔
Maagplatz 5 (at Prime Tower, 35th floor) ⊠ *8005*   Plan: **A3**
– ☏ 044 404 30 00 – www.clouds.ch
Menu 39 CHF (lunch)/120 CHF – Carte 47/117 CHF – *(booking essential)*
• International • Chic • Elegant •
One of Zürich's culinary hotspots, CLOUDS boasts stunning views of the city. But it's not just the spectacle outside that deserves attention. The interesting mix of Mediterranean, Southeast Asian and classic cuisine includes lobster cocktail, slow cooked pork belly and Japanese sea bass with pak choi. Meanwhile Bistro serves simpler fare.

⫯◯ **Gustav**   XX 🕸 🏠 占 🖼
Gustav-Gull-Platz 5 – ☏ 044 250 65 00   Plan: **A3**
– www.gustav-zuerich.ch – Closed Saturday lunch, Sunday
Menu 95/165 CHF – Carte 89/108 CHF
• Italian • Design • Fashionable •
Set in an apartment block right next to the main railway station, this elegant restaurant also boasts a café, a bar and a lovely interior courtyard. The Italian food on offer includes turbot and calamari *alla romana* and boned shoulder of veal with polenta.

⫯◯ **R21**   XX ⇔ 🕸 ≤ 🏠 占 🔥 🚗
Orellistr. 21 ⊠ *8044 – ☏ 044 268 35 35*   Plan: **B2**
– www.sorellhotels.com/zuerichberg/
66 rm ⌂ – ♦215/355 CHF ♦♦325/505 CHF   Carte 54/101 CHF
• Swiss • Fashionable •
Situated in an attractive, exposed location above Zurich, this restaurant in the Zürichberg Hotel boasts an interesting menu and a simple, modern interior. Enjoy a front row seat as the chefs go about their business in the very impressive show kitchen. Sunday brunch.

⫯◯ **Saltz** – Hotel The Dolder Grand   XX ≤ 🏠 占 🖼 🚗
Kurhausstr. 65 ⊠ *8032 – ☏ 044 456 60 00*   Plan: **B3**
– www.thedoldergrand.com
Menu 54 CHF – Carte 89/167 CHF
• International • Fashionable • Friendly •
The original, modern design takes Switzerland as its theme while the international food concentrates on the essentials. The menu includes burrata with datterini tomatoes, hamachi sashimi, sea bass baked in a salt crust or, if you prefer, a dish of *Zürcher Geschnetzeltes* – veal strips in a cream and white wine sauce.

⫯◯ **Bistro** – Restaurant Rigiblick   X 🕸 ≤ 🏠 占 🚗
Germaniastr. 99 ⊠ *8044 – ☏ 043 255 15 70*   Plan: **B2**
– www.restaurantrigiblick.ch – Closed 20 December-4 January and Monday
Menu 59/75 CHF – Carte 58/104 CHF
• Modern cuisine • Bistro • Fashionable •
The friendly alternative to Rigiblick offers a relaxed bistro ambience and regional fare using seasonal produce. This includes wild boar stew with red cabbage, spätzli and caramelised chestnuts. The great terrace has a view over the city.

🟡○ **Riviera**   X 🍴 ⇔
Dufourstr. 161 ☒ 8008 – 𝒞 044 422 04 26   Plan: **B3**
*– www.enoteca-riviera.ch – Closed 1-10 January, 24 July-14 August and Saturday
lunch, Sunday-Monday; October-December: Saturday lunch, Sunday*
Menu 33/78 CHF (dinner) – Carte 58/86 CHF
• Italian • Rustic •
Riviera boasts a charming rustic interior complete with green wood panelling.
The food is authentic Italian and includes home-made pasta and ossobuco.
Smaller lunchtime menu. There is also a wine shop.

🏨🏨🏨 **The Dolder Grand**   🦢 ≤ 🛏 ♨ 🐎 🔲 ✗ ⬡ & 🅰 🈑
Kurhausstr. 65 ☒ 8032 – 𝒞 044 456 60 00   Plan: **B3**
– www.thedoldergrand.com
175 rm – ♦540/740 CHF ♦♦750/1150 CHF – ☲ 48 CHF – 12 suites
• Grand Luxury • Spa and wellness • Contemporary •
Architect Norman Foster has transformed the *grande dame* of the Zürich hotel
world into a state-of-the-art address; its elegance and luxury culminating in the
Maestro suite. There is also a very elegant spa and some wonderful views from
the rooms and terraces. The display of paintings and sculpture is another highlight.
❀❀ **The Restaurant** • 🟡○ **Saltz** – See restaurant listing

🏨🏨🏨 **Atlantis by Giardino**   🦢 🛏 ♨ 🐎 🔲 ⬡ & 🅰 🈑 🚗
Döltschiweg 234 (by Birmensdorferstrasse A3) ☒ 8055 – 𝒞 044 456 55 55
– www.atlantisbygiardino.ch
80 rm ☲ – ♦430/875 CHF ♦♦430/875 CHF – 15 suites
• Luxury • Townhouse • Design •
First opened in 1970, the Atlantis today is a picture of luxury and elegance. You
will appreciate the attentive, personal service just as much as the upmarket
interior and, of course, the magnificent rural location.
❀❀ **Ecco Zürich** • ⊛ **Hide & Seek** – See restaurant listing

🏨🏨🏨 **Renaissance Tower Hotel**   💈 ≤ 🛏 ♨ & 🅰 🈑 🚗
Turbinenstr. 20 ☒ 8005 – 𝒞 044 630 30 30   Plan: **A2**
– www.renaissancezurichtower.com
300 rm – ♦259/309 CHF ♦♦259/309 CHF – 11 suites
• Business • Contemporary •
The reception area with its smart, minimalist design and contrasting light and
dark hues sets the "urban lifestyle" tone which can be seen throughout the
hotel, from the bedrooms to the restaurant and the lobby bar. The Executive
Club Lounge and 24hr health club and fitness suite on the top floor offer magnificent views.

🏨🏨 **B2 Boutique Hotel+Spa**   🛏 & 🅰 🚗
Brandschenkenstr. 152 ☒ 8002 – 𝒞 044 567 67 67   Plan: **A3**
– www.b2boutiquehotels.com
60 rm ☲ – ♦315/560 CHF ♦♦365/610 CHF – 8 suites
• Historic • Boutique hotel • Design •
This listed building dating from 1866 – part of Zürich's brewing history – is now
a stylish urban designer hotel. It features a library containing 33 000 books and
chandeliers made from Hürlimann beer bottles and serves a range of light
meals including a cheese selection and burgers. The thermal spa with rooftop
pool comes at an additional cost.

🏨🏨🏨 **Kameha Grand Zürich**   💈 🛏 ♨ & 🅰 🈑 🚗
Dufaux-Str. 1 – 𝒞 044 525 50 00   Plan: **B1**
– www.kamehagrandzuerich.com
224 rm – ♦169/2000 CHF ♦♦169/2000 CHF – ☲ 39 CHF – 21 suites
• Business • Luxury • Design •
A genuinely unusual lifestyle hotel in the centre of the Glattpark. The Kameha
boasts a striking façade, an imposing lobby (including a smart bar), tasteful
upmarket design and attentive but straightforward service. L'Unico offers Italian
cuisine in an impressive interior.
❀ **YOU** – See restaurant listing

Alden Luxury Suite Hotel ⚐ 🅰
Splügenstr. 2 ✉ *8002* – ☎ *044 289 99 99* Plan: **A3**
– www.alden.ch
22 suites – 🛏450/1200 CHF 🛏🛏450/1200 CHF – ⯊ 39 CHF
• Luxury • Design •
This smart villa built in 1895 boasts a classy interior, pleasant all-round service and charmingly elegant upmarket suites – the loft suites complete with roof terraces are the icing on the cake! The restaurant serves regional classics, burgers and sandwiches in a modern setting (one of the dining rooms has a lovely stucco ceiling).

25hours Langstrasse ⚐ 🛁 🕸 🅰 🚗
Langstr. 150 ✉ *8004* – ☎ *044 576 50 00* Plan: **A2**
– www.25hours-hotels.com
170 rm – 🛏340/390 CHF 🛏🛏340/390 CHF – ⯊ 32 CHF
• Townhouse • Design •
Anything but 'off the peg', 25hours has a refreshingly unconventional look courtesy of Werner Aisslinger. The interior cleverly reflects the character of the surrounding district with its contrasting red lights and banks. It offers real designer chic from the rooms via the lobby and Cinchona Bar to the Neni restaurant. This serves Israeli/Middle Eastern cuisine and dishes from the Josper grill.

25Hours Zürich West ⚐ 🕸 🅰 🚗
Pfingstweidstr. 102 ✉ *8005* – ☎ *044 577 25 25* Plan: **A2**
– www.25hours-hotels.com
126 rm – 🛏150/300 CHF 🛏🛏150/300 CHF – ⯊ 25 CHF
• Business • Design •
This modern business hotel, in the city's fast-growing development area, is designer Alfredo Häberli's homage to the city of Zurich. The rooms, which come in Silver, Gold and Platinum categories, are brightly coloured, curvaceous and very urban. NENI offers a minimalist feel and Israeli/Oriental cuisine.

Helvetia ⚐
Stauffacherquai 1 ✉ *8004* – ☎ *044 297 99 99* Plan: **A3**
– www.hotel-helvetia.ch
37 rm ⯊ – 🛏165/285 CHF 🛏🛏185/345 CHF – 1 suite
• Townhouse • Cosy • Contemporary •
A nice little boutique hotel right on the River Sihl, the Helvetia offers charming rooms with a mix of Art Nouveau and modern features. Both the popular, lively bar and the restaurant above it with its warm wooden floor and panelling are friendly and welcoming.

Plattenhof ⚐ 🅰
Plattenstr. 26 ✉ *8032* – ☎ *044 251 19 10* Plan: **B3**
– www.plattenhof.ch
37 rm ⯊ – 🛏155/335 CHF 🛏🛏195/365 CHF
• Business • Design • Minimalist •
This hotel is in a residential quarter on the edge of the city centre. Find distinctly personal service and functional rooms in a modern, plain, designer style. Sento has a bistro atmosphere and serves Italian cuisine.

UNITED KINGDOM
UNITED KINGDOM

A. Wiewiora/Caiaimages/Photononstop

LONDON

LONDON

coldsnowstorm/iStock

LONDON IN...

→ **ONE DAY**
British Museum, Tower of London, St Paul's Cathedral, Tate Modern.

→ **TWO / THREE DAYS**
National Gallery, London Eye, Natural History Museum, visit a theatre.

→ **THREE DAYS**
Science Museum, Victoria and Albert Museum, National Portrait Gallery.

The term 'world city' could have been invented for London. Time zones radiate from Greenwich, global finances zap round the Square Mile and its international restaurants are the equal of anywhere on earth. A stunning diversity of population is testament to the city's famed tolerance; different lifestyles and languages are as much a part of the London scene as cockneys and black cabs. London grew over time in a pretty haphazard way, swallowing up surrounding villages, but retaining an enviable acreage of green 'lungs': a comforting 30 per cent of London's area is made up of open space.

The drama of the city is reflected in its history. From Roman settlement to banking centre to capital of a 19C empire, the city's pulse has never missed a beat; it's no surprise that a dazzling array of theatres, restaurants, museums, markets and art galleries populate its streets. London's piecemeal character has endowed it with distinctly different areas, often breathing down each other's necks. North of Piccadilly lie the playgrounds of Soho and Mayfair, while south is the gentleman's clubland of St James's. On the other side of town are Clerkenwell and Southwark, artisan areas that have been scrubbed down and freshened up. The cool sophistication of Kensington and Knightsbridge is to the west, while a more touristy aesthetic is found in the heaving piazza zone of Covent Garden.

EATING OUT

London is one of the food capitals of the world, where you can eat everything from Turkish to Thai and Polish to Peruvian. Those wishing to sample classic British dishes also have more choice these days as more and more chefs are rediscovering home-grown ingredients, regional classics and traditional recipes. Eating in the capital can be pricey, so check out good value pre- and post-theatre menus, or try lunch at one of the many eateries that drop their prices, but not their standards, in the middle of the day. "Would I were in an alehouse in London! I would give all my fame for a pot of ale and safety", says Shakespeare's Henry V. Samuel Johnson agreed, waxing lyrical upon the happiness produced by a good tavern or inn. Pubs are often open these days from 11am to 11pm (and beyond), so this particular love now knows no bounds, and any tourist is welcome to come along and enjoy the romance. It's not just the cooking that has improved in pubs but wine too; woe betide any establishment in this city that can't distinguish its Gamay from its Grenache.

RESTAURANTS - ALPHABETICAL LIST

MAYFAIR

Alain Ducasse at The Dorchester – Dorchester Hotel

Park Ln ⊠ *W1K 1QA*   XxXxX 舘 &. 風 ⇔ 1♡ 🚗
– Ⓜ *Hyde Park Corner* – ℰ *(020) 76298866*   Plan: **G4**
– www.alainducasse-dorchester.com
– *Closed 3 weeks August, first week January, 26-30 December, Easter,
Saturday lunch, Sunday and Monday*
Menu £ 65/105 – *(booking essential)*
• French • Elegant • Luxury
Elegance, luxury and attention to detail are the hallmarks of Alain Ducasse's
London outpost, where the atmosphere is warm and relaxed. The kitchen uses
the best seasonal produce, whether British or French, to create visually striking,
refined modern dishes. The 'Table Lumière' with its shimmering curtain affords
an opulent, semi-private dining experience.
➔ Dorset crab, celeriac and caviar. Dry aged beef, artichoke and bone mar-
row. 'Baba like in Monte Carlo'.

The Araki (Mitsuhiro Araki)   XX 風 ⇔

12 New Burlington St ⊠ *W1S 3BF* – Ⓜ *Oxford Circus*   Plan: **H3**
– ℰ *(020) 7287 2481* – www.the-araki.com
– *Closed August, Christmas-first week January and Monday*
Menu £ 300 – *(dinner only) (booking essential) (tasting menu only)*
• Japanese • Intimate • Minimalist •
Behind the beautiful 9-seater cypress counter stands Mitsuhiro Araki, one of
Japan's great Sushi Masters. He closed his Three Star sushi restaurant in Tokyo
to move to London for a fresh challenge, which included using largely European
fish. He has spent time adjusting his Edomae methods and techniques and the
results are extraordinary.
➔ Cornish squid with albino caviar. Salmon roe with seaweed. Japanese
rice cake with red bean paste and macadamia.

Hélène Darroze at The Connaught – Connaught Hotel

Carlos Pl. ⊠ *W1K 2AL* – Ⓜ *Bond Street* – ℰ *(020)*   XxxX 舘 風 ⇔
71078880 – www.the-connaught.co.uk   Plan: **G3**
Menu £ 52/95 – *(booking essential)*
• Modern cuisine • Luxury • Elegant •
From a Solitaire board of 13 marbles, each bearing the name of an ingredient, you choose 5, 7 or 9 (courses); this highlights the quality of produce
used. The cooking is lighter these days yet still with the occasional unexpected flavour. The warm service ensures the wood-panelled room never feels
too formal.
➔ Norfolk lobster with almond, peach, mint and bottarga. Duck with beetroot, cherry and buckwheat. Strawberry, vanilla, thyme and olive oil.

Sketch (The Lecture Room & Library)   XxxX 舘 風 1♡

9 Conduit St (1st floor) ⊠ *W1S 2XG* – Ⓜ *Oxford Circus*   Plan: **H3**
– ℰ *(020) 76594500* – www.sketch.london
– *Closed 25 December, 1 January, 2 weeks late August-early September,
Sunday, Monday and lunch Tuesday-Thursday.*
Menu £ 35/120
– Carte £ 110/143 – *(booking essential)*
• French • Luxury • Elegant •
Mourad Mazouz and Pierre Gagnaire's 18C funhouse is awash with colour,
energy and vim and the luxurious 'Lecture Room & Library' provides the
ideal setting for the sophisticated French cooking. Relax and enjoy artfully
presented, elaborate dishes that provide many varieties of flavours and tex-
tures.
➔ Perfume of the Earth. Wild turbot on the bone with plankton butter and
broccoli. Pierre Gagnaire's 'grand dessert'

Le Gavroche (Michel Roux Jnr)   XxxX ಟಿ ᴀᴄ ⟷

43 Upper Brook St ✉ *W1K 7QR*   Plan: **G3**
– Ⓜ *Marble Arch*
– ✆ *(020) 74080881 – www.le-gavroche.co.uk*
– *Closed 2 weeks Christmas, Saturday lunch, Tuesday lunch, Sunday, Monday and bank holidays*
Menu £ 67/160
– Carte £ 67/197 – *(booking essential)*
• French • Intimate • Luxury •

Classical, rich and indulgent French cuisine is the draw at Michel Roux's renowned London institution. The large, smart basement room has a clubby, masculine feel; service is formal and structured but also has charm.
→ Lobster mousse with champagne and caviar butter sauce. Loin and cheek of Dingley Dell pork with heritage beetroots and confit lemon. Bitter chocolate and praline with gold leaf.

Greenhouse   XxX ಟಿ ᴀᴄ ⟷

27a Hay's Mews ✉ *W1J 5NY*   Plan: **G4**
– Ⓜ *Hyde Park Corner*
– ✆ *(020) 74993331 – www.greenhouserestaurant.co.uk*
– *Closed Saturday lunch, Sunday and bank holidays*
Menu £ 40/100
• Creative • Fashionable • Elegant •

Chef Arnaud Bignon's cooking is confident, balanced and innovative and uses the best from Europe's larder; his dishes exude an exhilarating freshness. The breadth and depth of the wine list is astounding. This is a discreet, sleek and contemporary restaurant with well-judged service.
→ Native lobster with Green Chartreuse, rhubarb and puntarella. Welsh lamb with aubergine, gomasio, harissa and soya. Garrigue honey with gavotte biscuit and Greek yoghurt.

Umu   XxX ಟಿ ᴀᴄ

14-16 Bruton Pl. ✉ *W1J 6LX*   Plan: **H3**
– Ⓜ *Bond Street*
– ✆ *(020) 74998881 – www.umurestaurant.com*
– *Closed Christmas, New Year, Easter, Sunday and bank holidays*
Menu £ 45/155 – Carte £ 46/151
• Japanese • Fashionable • Design •

Stylish, discreet interior using natural materials, with central sushi bar. Extensive choice of Japanese dishes; choose one of the seasonal kaiseki menus for the full experience. Over 160 different labels of sake.
→ Sake-steamed abalone sunomono. Charcoal-grilled quail with sake kasu egg and sansho pepper. Gariguette strawberry, sakura mousse and yomogi.

Fera at Claridge's – Claridge's Hotel   XxxX ಟಿ & ᴀᴄ ⟷ ⑩

Brook St ✉ *W1K 4HR*   Plan: **G3**
– Ⓜ *Bond Street*
– ✆ *(020) 7107 8888 – www.feraatclaridges.co.uk*
Menu £ 42 (lunch)/110
– Carte £ 61/83 – *(booking advisable)*
• Creative British • Elegant • Luxury •

Elegant without stuffiness, this is one of the most striking rooms in the capital and the attentive, personable service is a good match to the setting. There's an impressive purity and originality to the seasonal ingredients, and dishes are deftly executed and wonderfully balanced, with layers of texture and flavour. Tasting menus only, Thurs-Sat.
→ White asparagus with veal sweetbread, curd and smoked egg. Belted Galloway beef with globe artichoke, tomato and sea greens. Chocolate and sweet clover mousse with goat's cheese and apricot.

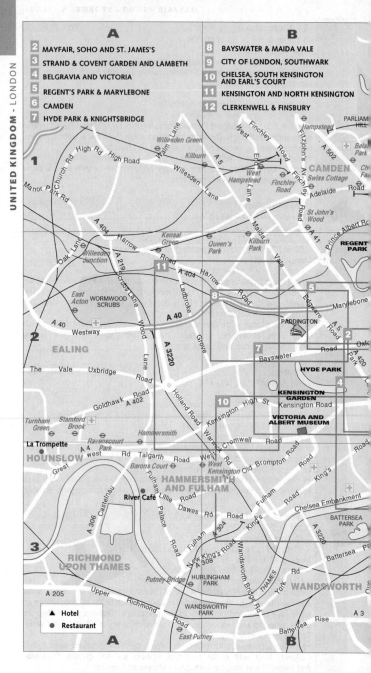

A

2 MAYFAIR, SOHO AND ST. JAMES'S

3 STRAND & COVENT GARDEN AND LAMBETH

4 BELGRAVIA AND VICTORIA

5 REGENT'S PARK & MARYLEBONE

6 CAMDEN

7 HYDE PARK & KNIGHTSBRIDGE

B

8 BAYSWATER & MAIDA VALE

9 CITY OF LONDON, SOUTHWARK

10 CHELSEA, SOUTH KENSINGTON AND EARL'S COURT

11 KENSINGTON AND NORTH KENSINGTON

12 CLERKENWELL & FINSBURY

▲ Hotel
● Restaurant

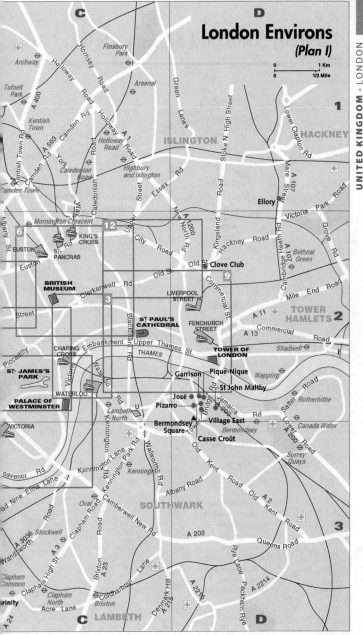

London Environs
(Plan I)

0		1 Km
0		1/2 Mile

Archway

Finsbury Park

Tufnell Park

Arsenal

HACKNEY

Kentish Town

Camden Rd

Holloway Road

A 1

Green Lanes

Stoke N. High Street

Lower Clapton Rd

York

Caledonian Road

Highbury and Islington

ISLINGTON

Ellory

Victoria Park Road

A 107 Mare Street

A 107 Cambridge Heath Rd

Grove Rd

Camden Town

Mornington Crescent

Upper Street

City Road

New North Rd

A 1200

Kingsland Road

Hackney Road

Bethnal Green

6 EUSTON

ST-PANCRAS

KING'S CROSS

12

Old St

Clove Club

Mile End Road

BRITISH MUSEUM

Clerkenwell Rd

Old Street

Commercial St

9

LIVERPOOL STREET

A 11

TOWER HAMLETS

3

St PAUL'S CATHEDRAL

FENCHURCH STREET

Commercial

A 13

Road

Street

Blackfriars Rd

Upper Thames St.

CHARING CROSS

Embankment

TOWER OF LONDON

Shadwell

THAMES

Garrison

Pique-Nique

Wapping

St John Maltby

Salter Road

Rotherhithe

St-JAMES'S PARK

Piccadilly

Victoria

Waterloo

WATERLOO

Waterloo Rd

José

Pizarro

Tower Bridge Rd

A 200

Jamaica Rd

Village East

Lower Road A 200

Canada Water

PALACE OF WESTMINSTER

VICTORIA

Lambeth North

Bermondsey Square

Casse Croût

Bermondsey

Surrey Quays

osvenor Rd

Nine Elms Lane

Kennington Lane

Kennington Park Rd

Walworth Rd

Old

Kent

Road

A 2

Kent

Road

Grosvenor Rd

A 3036 Stockwell

Wandsworth

A 3

Clapham Road

Camberwell New Rd

Oval

Kennington

Albany Road

SOUTHWARK

A 202

Rye Lane

Queens Road

Clapham Common

Clapham High St.

Brixton A 23

Coldharbour Lane

A 202

A 216

A 22a

Peckham Rye

A 2214

rinity

A 24

Clapham North Acre Lane

Brixton

Denmark Hill

A 215

LAMBETH

C

D

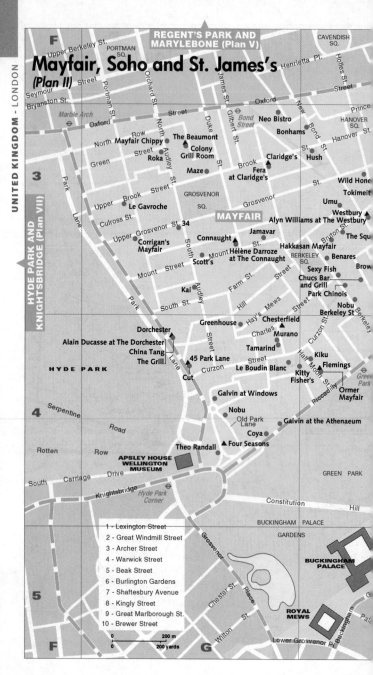

REGENT'S PARK AND
MARYLEBONE (Plan V)

CAVENDISH
SQ.

Mayfair, Soho and St. James's
(Plan II)

Upper Berkeley St.
PORTMAN
SQ.

Henrietta Pl.

Holles St.

Seymour

Bryanston St.

Marble Arch

Oxford

Street

Oxford

Orchard St.

Street

James St.

Gilbert St.

Prince

HANOVER
SQ.

Hanover St.

Duke St.

Bond Street

Neo Bistro

New

Bond St.

Bonhams

North
Row

Mayfair Chippy

The Beaumont

North
Audley
Street

Colony
Grill Room

Green
Street

Roka

Maze

Brook
St.

Claridge's

St.
James's

Hush

Fera
at Claridge's

Wild Hone

GROSVENOR
SQ.

Grosvenor

St.

Tokimeit

Umu

Upper
Brook
Street

Le Gavroche

Westbury

Culross St.

34

MAYFAIR

Alyn Williams at The Westbury

Brton St.

The Squ

Upper
Grosvenor St.

Connaught

Jamavar

Corrigan's
Mayfair

South

Scott's

Mount

Hélène Darroze
at The Connaught

Hakkasan Mayfair

BERKELEY
SQ.

Benares

Brow

Mount
Street

Farm St.

Sexy Fish

Chucs Bar
and Grill

Park
Lane

Kai

South St.

Park Chinois

Nobu
Berkeley St

Berkeley

Park
Lane

Greenhouse

Hay's Mews

Chesterfield

Curzon
Street

HYDE PARK

Dorchester

Charles

Murano

Alain Ducasse at The Dorchester

China Tang

45 Park Lane

Tamarind

Half Moon St.

Kiku

Flemings

Green
Park

The Grill

Cut

Curzon

Street

Le Boudin Blanc

Kitty
Fisher's

Ormer
Mayfair

Piccadilly

Galvin at Windows

Serpentine

Road

Nobu

Old Park
Lane

Galvin at the Athenaeum

Rotten

Row

Coya

South

Carriage

Drive

Theo Randall

APSLEY HOUSE
WELLINGTON
MUSEUM

Four Seasons

GREEN PARK

Knightsbridge

Hyde Park
Corner

Constitution

Hill

BUCKINGHAM PALACE
GARDENS

Grosvenor

Chester St.

BUCKINGHAM
PALACE

Place

Wilton
St.

ROYAL
MEWS

Lower Grosvenor Pl.

Buckingham

1 - Lexington Street
2 - Great Windmill Street
3 - Archer Street
4 - Warwick Street
5 - Beak Street
6 - Burlington Gardens
7 - Shaftesbury Avenue
8 - Kingly Street
9 - Great Marlborough St.
10 - Brewer Street

0   200 m
0   200 yards

712

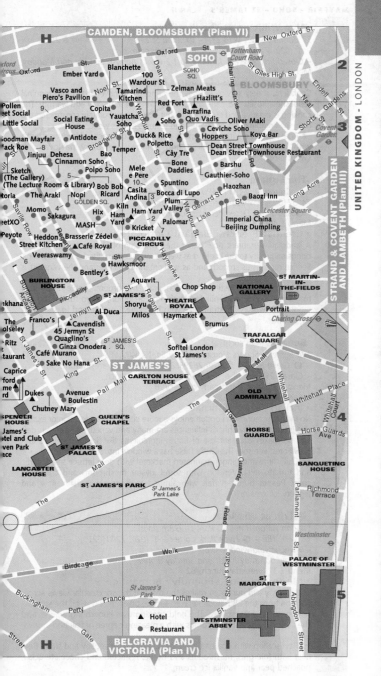

New Oxford St.

Oxford St.

SOHO
SQ.

SOHO

Tottenham
Court Road

Charing Cross

St. Giles High St.

BLOOMSBURY

Endell

Neal

Oxford St.
Oxford
Circus

Ember Yard
Vasco and
Piero's Pavilion

Blanchette
Wardour St
Tamarind
Kitchen

Dean St.

Noel St.

100

Zelman Meats

Red Fort

Hazlitt's

Shorts
Gardens
St.

Covent
Garden

Oliver Maki

Pollen
eet Social

Little Social

oodman Mayfair
ack Roe

Copita

Social Eating
House

Antidote

Dehesa

9

Broadwick St.

Yauatcha
Soho

Duck& Rice

Polpetto

Barrafina

Soho

Quo Vadis

Wardour St.

Ceviche Soho

Hoppers

Koya Bar

—8

Jinjuu

Bao

Cinnamon Soho

Temper

Câ/y Tre

Dean Street Townhouse
Dean Street Townhouse Restaurant

Barshu

Sketch
(The Gallery)
(The Lecture Room & Library)

Polpo Soho

5

Mele
e Pere

Bone
Daddies

Gauthier-Soho

toria

The Araki

Nopi

Bob Bob
Ricard

10

Casita
Andina

Spuntino

Bocca di Lupo

Haozhan

Long Acre

Baozi Inn

GOLDEN SQ.

3

Plum
Valley

Leicester Square

etXO

Momo

Sakagura

Kiln

Ham
Yard

Wardour St.

Gerrard St.

Imperial China

Peyote

MASH

2

Lisle St.

Beijing Dumpling

Heddon
Street Kitchen

Brasserie Zédel

Kricket

Palomar

6

▲ Café Royal

PICCADILLY
CIRCUS

Veeraswamy

Hawksmoor

Bentley's

Aquavit

Haymarket

Chop Shop

NATIONAL
GALLERY

St. MARTIN-
IN-
THE-FIELDS

BURLINGTON
HOUSE

Piccadilly

St. JAMES'S

Regent St.

THEATRE
ROYAL

Portrait

nkhana

Al Duca

Jermyn St.

Shoryu

Charing Cross

The
olseley

Franco's

Cavendish
45 Jermyn St
Quaglino's
Ginza Onodera

Milos

Haymarket

Brumus

TRAFALGAR
SQUARE

Ritz

St. JAMES'S
SQ.

Café Murano

taurant

Sake No Hana

ST. JAMES'S

King St.

Sofitel London
St James's

Caprice
ford
me
rd

Dukes

Avenue
Boulestin

Pall Mall

CARLTON HOUSE
TERRACE

The Mall

Whitehall

OLD
ADMIRALTY

Whitehall Place
Whitehall
Court

SPENCER
HOUSE

Chutney Mary

QUEEN'S
CHAPEL

Horse

HORSE
GUARDS

Horse Guards
Ave

James's
otel and Club
ven Park
ace

ST. JAMES'S
PALACE

BANQUETING
HOUSE

LANCASTER
HOUSE

The Mall

ST. JAMES'S PARK

St. James's
Park Lake

Guards Road

Richmond
Terrace

Parliament St.

Birdcage

Walk

Westminster
St.

PALACE OF
WESTMINSTER

Buckingham

St James's
Park

France

Petty

Tothill St.

Storey's Gate

St.

ST.
MARGARET'S

Abingdon St.

Street

Gate

▲ Hotel
● Restaurant

WESTMINSTER
ABBEY

Street

Alyn Williams at The Westbury – Westbury Hotel   XxxX

37 Conduit St ⊠ *W1S 2YF* – ⓜ *Bond Street*   🍸 ⑂ 🔟 ⇄ ⓥ
– 𝒞 (020) 71836426 – www.alynwilliams.com   Plan: **H3**
– Closed first 2 weeks January, last 2 weeks August, Sunday and Monday
Menu £ 30/80
• Modern cuisine • Design • Elegant •
Confident, cheery service ensures the atmosphere never strays into terminal seriousness; rosewood panelling and a striking wine display add warmth. The cooking is creative and even playful, but however elaborately constructed the dish, the combinations of flavours and textures always work.
→ Roast lobster with guacamole and green gazpacho. Herdwick lamb with preserved green walnut and borage. Strawberry pavlova with sweet cicely.

The Square   XxxX 🍸 🔟 ⇄ ⓥ

6-10 Bruton St. ⊠ *W1J 6PU* – ⓜ *Green Park* – 𝒞 *(020)*   Plan: **H3**
74957100 – www.squarerestaurant.com
– Closed 24-26 December and Sunday
Menu £ 40/105
• Creative French • Elegant • Intimate •
A landmark restaurant now under the ownership of Marlon Abela. The chef brings originality to the cooking as well as more unusual flavour combinations. Service remains as smooth and as well-organised as ever and the wine list is now even longer.
→ Marinated langoustine sandwich with mushroom, apple and coral mayonnaise. Pyrenean milk-fed lamb, Roscoff onion, Tokyo turnip and tarragon. Jura whisky chestnut cake with buckwheat praline and toasted malt ice cream.

Benares (Atul Kochhar)   XxX 🍸 🔟 ⇄ ⓥ

12a Berkeley Square House, Berkeley Sq. ⊠ *W1J 6BS*   Plan: **H3**
– ⓜ Green Park – 𝒞 (020) 76298886 – www.benaresrestaurant.com
– Closed 25 December, 1 January and Sunday lunch
Menu £ 25 (lunch and early dinner)/98
– Carte £ 52/68
• Indian • Chic • Intimate •
No Indian restaurant in London enjoys a more commanding location or expansive interior. Atul Kochhar's influences are many and varied; his spicing is deft and he makes excellent use of British ingredients like Scottish scallops and New Forest venison. The Chef's Table has a window into the kitchen.
→ Chilli, lime and ginger marinated mackerel with gem lettuce salad, garlic and tomato raita. Venison with sorrel, oyster mushrooms and chocolate curry. Peanut butter parfait with almond cake, cumin marshmallow and jaggery ice cream.

Galvin at Windows   XxX ⩽ ⑂ 🔟

London Hilton Hotel, 22 Park Ln (28th floor)   Plan: **G4**
⊠ *W1K 1BE* – ⓜ *Hyde Park Corner* – 𝒞 *(020) 72084021*
– www.galvinatwindows.com
– Closed Saturday lunch and Sunday dinner
Menu £ 37 (weekday lunch)/82
• Modern cuisine • Friendly • Romantic •
The cleverly laid out room makes the most of the spectacular views across London from the 28th floor. Relaxed service takes the edge off the somewhat corporate atmosphere. The bold cooking uses superb ingredients and the classically based food comes with a pleasing degree of flair and innovation.
→ Raw scallop with nori emulsion, blood orange, sweet soy and shiso. Beef fillet with foie gras, mushrooms and truffle. Pistachio and chocolate éclair, poached pear and vanilla ice cream.

Kai   XxX 器 W ⇔ |♡

65 South Audley St ⊠ W1K 2QU – ⓜ *Hyde Park Corner*   Plan: **G3**
– ☎ *(020) 74938988 – www.kaimayfair.co.uk*
– Closed 25-26 December and 1 January
Carte £ 44/199 *– (booking essential)*
• Chinese • Intimate • Chic •

There are a few classics on the menu but Chef Alex Chow's strengths are his modern creations and re-workings of Chinese recipes. His dishes have real depth, use superb produce and are wonderfully balanced. The interior is unashamedly glitzy and the service team anticipate their customers' needs well.
→ Pork belly open bao and char siew with BBQ glaze, crispy bao and pickled cucumber. Roasted Chilean sea bass with sweet lime, chilli and lemongrass sambal. 'Chocolate does grow on trees'.

Murano (Angela Hartnett)   XxX ċ W

20 Queen St ⊠ W1J 5PP – ⓜ *Green Park –* ☎ *(020)*   Plan: **G4**
74951127 – www.muranolondon.com
– Closed Christmas and Sunday
Menu £ 33/70
• Italian • Fashionable • Elegant •

Angela Hartnett's Italian-influenced cooking exhibits an appealing lightness of touch, with assured combinations of flavours, borne out of confidence in the ingredients. This is a stylish, elegant room run by a well-organised, professional and friendly team who put their customers at ease.
→ Manzo di pozza with ricotta, broad beans, spring onion and hazelnuts. Hake, crab and ginger raviolo with savoy cabbage, baby leek and ginger velouté. Honey panna cotta with macadamia clusters and brown bread ice cream.

Tamarind   XxX W |♡

20 Queen St. ⊠ W1J 5PR – ⓜ *Green Park –* ☎ *(020)*   Plan: **G4**
76293561 – www.tamarindrestaurant.com
– Closed 25-26 December and 1 January
Menu £ 25 (weekday lunch)/75 *–* Carte £ 37/66
• Indian • Chic • Exotic décor •

Makes the best use of its basement location through smoked mirrors, gilded columns and a somewhat exclusive feel. The appealing northern Indian food is mostly traditionally based; kebabs and curries are the specialities, the tandoor is used to good effect and don't miss the carefully judged vegetable dishes.
→ Pudhina chops with dried mint and tomato & coriander chutney. Murgh tikka masala with dried fenugreek leaves. Mango kulfi.

Bonhams   XX 器 ċ W

101 New Bond St (lower ground floor) (For dinner   Plan: **H3**
entrance via Haunch of Venison Yard off Brook St) ⊠ W1S 1SR
– ⓜ *Bond Street –* ☎ *(020) 7468 5868 – www.bonhamsrestaurant.com*
– Closed 2 weeks Christmas, 2 weeks mid August, Saturday, Sunday,
dinner Monday-Tuesday and bank holidays
Menu £ 60 (dinner) *–* Carte £ 47/59 *– (booking advisable)*
• Modern cuisine • Minimalist • Intimate •

Established in 1793, Bonhams is now one of the world's largest fine art and antique auctioneers. Its restaurant is bright, modern and professionally run. Dishes are elegant and delicate and there is real clarity to the flavours. The wine list has also been very thoughtfully compiled by Bonhams' own wine department.
→ Scallops, smoked roe, peas and endive. Lamb with ratatouille, olive and anchovy. Chocolate sabayon tart with vanilla ice cream and sour cherry.

Gymkhana

XX AC ⇔ ☺ ⑩

42 Albemarle St ✉ W1S 4JH

Plan: **H3**

– Ⓜ Green Park
– ✆ (020) 3011 5900 – www.gymkhanalondon.com
– Closed 1-3 January, 25-27 December and Sunday
Menu £ 25 (weekday lunch)/80
– Carte £ 25/71 – (booking essential)
• Indian • Intimate • Fashionable •

If you enjoy Trishna then you'll love Karam Sethi's Gymkhana – that's if you can get a table. Inspired by Colonial India's gymkhana clubs, the interior is full of wonderful detail and plenty of wry touches; ask to sit downstairs. The North Indian dishes have a wonderful richness and depth of flavour.
➔ Dosa, Chettinad duck and coconut. Wild muntjac biryani with pomegranate and mint raita. Mango kheer.

Hakkasan Mayfair

XX ⅋ & AC ⇔ ⑩

17 Bruton St ✉ W1J 6QB

Plan: **H3**

– Ⓜ Green Park
– ✆ (020) 79071888 – www.hakkasan.com
– Closed 24-25 December
Menu £ 38 (lunch and early dinner)/128
– Carte £ 37/110 – (booking essential)
• Chinese • Minimalist • Trendy •

If coming for lunchtime dim sum then sit on the ground floor; for dinner ask for a table in the moodily lit and altogether sexier basement. The Cantonese cuisine uses top quality produce and can be delicate one minute; robust the next. There are also specialities specific to this branch.
➔ Supreme dim sum platter. Black pepper rib-eye beef with merlot. Banana and caramel délice.

Jamavar

XX AC ⇔ ☺ ⑩

8 Mount St ✉ W1K 3NF

Plan: **G3**

– Ⓜ Bond Street
– ✆ (020) 7499 1800 – www.jamavarrestaurants.com
– Closed 25 December, 1 January and Sunday
Menu £ 25 (lunch and early dinner)
– Carte £ 34/54 – (booking essential at dinner)
• Indian • Exotic décor • Elegant •

Leela Palaces & Resorts are behind this smartly dressed Indian restaurant. The menus, including vegetarian, look to all parts of India, although there's a bias towards the north. The 'small plates' section includes jewels like Malabar prawns, and kid goat shami kebab; from the tandoor the stone bass tikka is a must; and biryanis are also good.
➔ Malabar prawns with turmeric, onion and curry leaves. Tulsi chicken tikka with sweet basil, pickled radish and raita. Port-poached pear with chocolate and pink peppercorn kulfi.

Pollen Street Social (Jason Atherton)

XX ⅋ AC ⇔ ⑩

8-10 Pollen St ✉ W1S 1NQ

Plan: **H3**

– Ⓜ Oxford Circus
– ✆ (020) 7290 7600 – www.pollenstreetsocial.com
– Closed Sunday and bank holidays
Menu £ 37 (lunch)
– Carte £ 62/87 – (booking essential)
• Creative • Fashionable • Elegant •

The restaurant where it all started for Jason Atherton when he went solo. Top quality British produce lies at the heart of the menu and the innovative dishes are prepared with great care and no little skill. The room has plenty of buzz, helped along by the 'dessert bar' and views of the kitchen pass.
➔ Pine-smoked quail, 'English breakfast'. Loin & braised shoulder of lamb hotpot with spiced tomato and mint sauce. Bitter chocolate pavé, olive biscuit and olive oil ice cream.

UNITED KINGDOM - LONDON

Veeraswamy
XX 🏧 ⇔ 🐿 🍷

Plan: **H3**

Victory House, 99 Regent St (Entrance on Swallow St.)
✉ W1B 4RS – ⓜ Piccadilly Circus – ☎ (020) 77341401
– www.veeraswamy.com
Menu £ 34 (lunch and early dinner)/45 – Carte £ 33/75
• Indian • Design • Historic •

It may have opened in 1926 but this celebrated Indian restaurant just keeps getting better and better! The classic dishes from across the country are prepared with considerable care by a very professional kitchen. The room is awash with colour and it's run with great charm and enormous pride.
➜ Tandoori green prawns. Hyderabadi lamb biryani. Coconut and palm sugar crème brûlée.

Cut – 45 Park Lane Hotel
XxX ⅋ 🏧

Plan: **G4**

45 Park Ln ✉ W1K 1PN – ⓜ Hyde Park Corner
– ☎ (020) 7493 4545 – www.dorchestercollection.com
Menu £ 45 (weekday lunch) – Carte £ 55/185 – *(booking essential)*
• Meats and grills • Design • Chic •

The first European venture from Wolfgang Puck, the US-based Austrian celebrity chef, is this very slick, stylish and sexy room where glamorous people come to eat meat. The not-inexpensive steaks are cooked over hardwood and charcoal and finished off in a broiler.

Park Chinois
XxX 🏧 ⇔

Plan: **H3**

17 Berkeley St ✉ W1J 8EA – ⓜ Green Park – ☎ (020)
3327 8888 – www.parkchinois.com – *Closed 25 December*
Menu £ 30 (lunch) – Carte £ 37/107 – *(booking essential)*
• Chinese • Exotic décor •

Old fashioned glamour, strikingly rich surroundings and live music combine to great effect at this sumptuously decorated restaurant. The menu traverses the length of China, with dim sum at lunchtimes and afternoon tea at weekends.

Scott's
XxX 🏧 ⇔ 🍷

Plan: **G3**

20 Mount St ✉ W1K 2HE – ⓜ Bond Street – ☎ (020)
74957309 – www.scotts-restaurant.com – *Closed 25-26 December*
Carte £ 37/83
• Seafood • Fashionable • Chic •

Scott's is proof that a restaurant can have a long, proud history and still be fashionable, glamorous and relevant. It has a terrific clubby atmosphere and if you're in a two then the counter is a great spot. The choice of prime quality fish and shellfish is impressive.

China Tang – Dorchester Hotel
XxX ⅋ 🏧 ⇔

Plan: **G4**

Park Ln ✉ W1K 1QA – ⓜ Hyde Park Corner – ☎ (020)
76299988 – www.chinatanglondon.co.uk – *Closed 24-25 December*
Menu £ 30 (lunch) – Carte £ 28/79
• Chinese • Fashionable • Elegant •

Sir David Tang's atmospheric, art deco-inspired Chinese restaurant, downstairs at The Dorchester, is always abuzz with activity. Be sure to see the terrific bar, before sharing the traditional Cantonese specialities.

Corrigan's Mayfair
XxX ⅋ 🏧 ⇔

Plan: **G3**

28 Upper Grosvenor St. ✉ W1K 7EH – ⓜ Marble Arch
– ☎ (020) 74999943 – www.corrigansmayfair.com – Closed 25-30 December, Saturday lunch and bank holidays
Menu £ 28 (weekday lunch) – Carte £ 48/81
• Modern British • Elegant •

Richard Corrigan's flagship celebrates British and Irish cooking, with game a speciality. The room is comfortable, clubby and quite glamorous and feels as though it has been around for years.

The Grill – Dorchester Hotel

XxX 📽 & AC

Park Ln ✉ *W1K 1QA* – 🚇 *Hyde Park Corner* – ✆ *(020)*
Plan: **G4**
7317 6531 – www.dorchestercollection.com
Menu £ 40 (weekday lunch) – Carte £ 38/87 – *(booking advisable)*
• French • Elegant • Design •

The Grill is relaxed yet formal, with an open kitchen and a striking, hand-blown Murano glass chandelier as its centrepiece. Grill favourites sit alongside modern day classics on the menu; sharing dishes are a good choice, as are the speciality soufflés. Service is smooth and highly professional.

Sartoria

XxX 🀫 & AC ⇄

20 Savile Row ✉ *W1S 3PR* – 🚇 *Oxford Circus* – ✆ *(020)*
Plan: **H3**
*75347000 – www.sartoria-restaurant.co.uk – Closed 25-
26 December, Saturday lunch, Sunday except lunch September-June and
bank holidays*
Menu £ 27 (weekday lunch) – Carte £ 38/61
• Italian • Chic • Elegant •

A long-standing feature on Savile Row but now looking much more dapper. Francesco Mazzei, formerly of L'Anima, hooked up with D&D to take the reins and the place now feels more energised. There are hints of Calabria but the menu covers all Italian regions and keeps things fairly classical.

34

XxX AC ⇄

34 Grosvenor Sq (entrance on South Audley St)
Plan: **G3**
✉ *W1K 2HD* – 🚇 *Marble Arch* – ✆ *(020) 3350 3434*
*– www.34-restaurant.co.uk – Closed 25-26 December, dinner 24 December
and lunch 1 January*
Menu £ 28 (weekdays) – Carte £ 34/60
• Meats and grills • Brasserie • Fashionable •

A wonderful mix of art deco styling and Edwardian warmth makes it feel like a glamorous brasserie. A parrilla grill is used for fish, game and beef – choose from Scottish dry-aged, US prime, organic Argentinian and Australian Wagyu.

Colony Grill Room – The Beaumont Hotel

XX & AC

Brown Hart Gdns. ✉ *W1K 6TF* – 🚇 *Bond Street*
Plan: **G3**
– ✆ (020) 7499 9499 – www.colonygrillroom.com
Carte £ 28/68 – *(booking essential)*
• Traditional British • Brasserie • Fashionable •

Based on 1920s London and New York grill restaurants, The Beaumont's Colony Grill comes with leather booths, striking age-of-speed art deco murals and clever lighting. By making the room and style of service so defiantly old fashioned, Chris Corbin and Jeremy King have created somewhere effortlessly chic.

Momo

XX 🀫 AC

25 Heddon St. ✉ *W1B 4BH* – 🚇 *Oxford Circus*
Plan: **H3**
– ✆ (020) 7434 4040 – www.momoresto.com – Closed 25 December
Menu £ 19 (weekday lunch) – Carte £ 29/81
• Moroccan • Exotic décor • Intimate •

An authentic Moroccan atmosphere comes courtesy of the antiques, kilim rugs, Berber artwork, bright fabrics and lanterns – you'll feel you're eating near the souk. Go for the classic dishes: zaalouk, briouats, pigeon pastilla, and tagines with mountains of fluffy couscous.

Sketch (The Gallery)

XX AC

9 Conduit St ✉ *W1S 2XG* – 🚇 *Oxford Circus* – ✆ *(020)*
Plan: **H3**
76594500 – www.sketch.london – Closed 25 December and 1 January
Carte £ 38/79 – *(dinner only) (booking essential)*
• Modern cuisine • Trendy • Intimate •

The striking 'Gallery' has a smart look from India Mahdavi and artwork from David Shrigley. At dinner the room transmogrifies from art gallery to fashionable restaurant, with a menu that mixes the classic, the modern and the esoteric.

Bentley's
XX 🆎 ⇔

11-15 Swallow St. ✉ *W1B 4DG –* Ⓜ *Piccadilly Circus* — Plan: **H3**
– 𝒞 (020) 77344756 – www.bentleys.org – Closed 25 December, 1 January,
Saturday lunch and Sunday
Menu £ 25 (weekday lunch) – Carte £ 35/72
• Seafood • Traditional décor • Classic décor •
This hundred year old seafood institution comes in two parts: upstairs is the
more formal and smartly dressed Grill, with seafood classics and grilled meats;
on the ground floor is the Oyster Bar which is more fun and does a good fish
pie.

Black Roe
XX 🆎 ⇔

4 Mill St ✉ *W1S 2AX –* Ⓜ *Oxford Circus – 𝒞 (020)* — Plan: **H3**
3794 8448 – www.blackroe.com
Carte £ 26/66
• World cuisine • Trendy • Neighbourhood •
Poke, made famous in Hawaii, is the star here. You can choose traditional ahi
over the sushi rice or something more original like scallop and octopus. Other
options include dishes with assorted Pacific Rim influences, along with others
cooked on the Kiawe wood grill.

Chucs Bar and Grill
XX 🌲 🆎

30b Dover St. ✉ *W1S 4NB –* Ⓜ *Green Park – 𝒞 (020)* — Plan: **H3**
3763 2013 – www.chucsrestaurant.com – Closed 25-26 and dinner 24 and
31 December, 1 January and bank holidays
Carte £ 40/71 – (booking essential)
• Italian • Elegant • Cosy •
Like the shop to which it's attached, Chucs caters for those who summer on the
Riviera and are not afraid of showing it. It's decked out like a yacht and the con-
cise but not inexpensive menu offers classic Mediterranean dishes.

Coya
XX 🆎 ⇔

118 Piccadilly ✉ *W1J 7NW –* Ⓜ *Hyde Park Corner* — Plan: **G4**
– 𝒞 (020) 7042 7118 – www.coyarestaurant.com – Closed 24-26 December
and 1 January
Menu £ 31 (weekday lunch) – Carte £ 27/66 – (booking advisable)
• Peruvian • Friendly • Fashionable •
A lively, loud and enthusiastically run basement restaurant that celebrates all
things Peruvian, from the people behind Zuma and Roka. Try their ceviche
and their skewers, as well as their pisco sours in the fun bar.

Galvin at the Athenaeum
XX 🆎 🐧

Athenaeum Hotel,116 Piccadilly ✉ *W1J 7BJ* — Plan: **G4**
– Ⓜ *Hyde Park Corner – 𝒞 (020) 7640 3333 – www.athenaeumhotel.com*
Menu £ 25 – Carte £ 22/48
• Modern cuisine • Brasserie • Contemporary décor •
The ground-floor restaurant of the Athenaeum hotel is now run by the Galvin
brothers. Forget the name tags and the turgid music – this is a keenly run
room with good food. The ingredients are mostly British but the best dishes
are the French ones, like cassoulet and Floating Island.

Goodman Mayfair
XX 🆎

26 Maddox St ✉ *W1S 1QH –* Ⓜ *Oxford Circus* — Plan: **H3**
– 𝒞 (020) 7499 3776 – www.goodmanrestaurants.com – Closed Sunday
and bank holidays
Carte £ 28/89 – (booking essential)
• Meats and grills • Brasserie • Classic décor •
A worthy attempt at recreating a New York steakhouse; all leather and wood
and macho swagger. Beef is dry or wet-aged in-house and comes with a choice
of four sauces; rib-eye the speciality.

UNITED KINGDOM - LONDON

Hawksmoor

XX 🕸 & AC 🗺

5a Air St ⊠ W1J 0AD – ⓜ Piccadilly Circus – ℰ (020)   Plan: **H3**
7406 3980 – www.thehawksmoor.com – Closed 24-26 December
Menu £ 28 (lunch and early dinner) – Carte £ 23/58 – *(booking advisable)*
• **Meats and grills** • **Fashionable** • **Vintage** •

The best of the Hawksmoors is large, boisterous and has an appealing art deco feel. Expect top quality, 35-day aged Longhorn beef but also great seafood, much of which is charcoal grilled. The delightful staff are well organised.

Heddon Street Kitchen

XX 🚡 & AC ⇔

3-9 Heddon St ⊠ W1B 4BE – ⓜ Oxford Circus   Plan: **H3**
– ℰ (020) 7592 1212 – www.gordonramsayrestaurants.com – Closed
25 December
Menu £ 23 (lunch and early dinner) – Carte £ 26/63
• **Modern cuisine** • **Brasserie** • **Trendy** •

Gordon Ramsay's follow up to Bread Street is spread over two floors and is all about all-day dining: breakfast covers all tastes, there's weekend brunch, and an à la carte offering an appealing range of European dishes executed with palpable care.

Hush

XX 🚡 & AC ⇔

8 Lancashire Ct., Brook St. ⊠ W1S 1EY – ⓜ Bond Street   Plan: **H3**
– ℰ (020) 76591500 – www.hush.co.uk – Closed 25 December and
1 January
Carte £ 27/64 – *(booking essential)*
• **Modern cuisine** • **Fashionable** • **Brasserie** •

If there's warmth in the air then tables on the large courtyard terrace are the first to go. The ground floor serves brasserie classics prepared with care; there's a stylish cocktail bar upstairs, along with smart private dining rooms.

Kiku

XX & AC ⇔

17 Half Moon St. ⊠ W1J 7BE – ⓜ Green Park   Plan: **H4**
– ℰ (020) 74994208 – www.kikurestaurant.co.uk – Closed 25-
27 December, 1 January and lunch Sunday and bank holidays
Menu £ 26 (weekday lunch) – Carte £ 37/125
• **Japanese** • **Neighbourhood** • **Simple** •

For over 35 years this earnestly run, authentically styled, family owned restaurant has been providing every style of Japanese cuisine to its homesick Japanese customers, from shabu shabu to sukiyaki, yakitori to teriyaki.

Maze

XX 🕸 & AC ⇔

London Marriott Hotel Grosvenor Square, 10-13   Plan: **G3**
Grosvenor Sq ⊠ W1K 6JP – ⓜ Bond Street – ℰ (020) 71070000
– www.gordonramsayrestaurants.com
Menu £ 30 (weekday lunch) – Carte £ 33/53
• **Modern cuisine** • **Fashionable** • **Design** •

This Gordon Ramsay restaurant still offers a glamorous night out, thanks to its great cocktails, effervescent atmosphere and small plates of Asian-influenced food. Three or four dishes per person is about the going rate.

Nobu

XX ⩤ & AC ⇔ 🕸

Metropolitan by COMO Hotel, 19 Old Park Ln   Plan: **G4**
⊠ W1Y 1LB – ⓜ Hyde Park Corner – ℰ (020) 74474747
– www.noburestaurants.com
Menu £ 33 (lunch) – Carte £ 24/73 – *(booking essential)*
• **Japanese** • **Fashionable** • **Minimalist** •

Nobu restaurants are now all over the world but this was Europe's first and opened in 1997. It retains a certain exclusivity and is buzzy and fun. The menu is an innovative blend of Japanese cuisine with South American influences.

io **Nobu Berkeley St** XX AC ⑩

15 Berkeley St. ⊠ *W1J 8DY* – Ⓜ *Green Park* – ℰ *(020)* Plan: **H3**
72909222 – *www.noburestaurants.com* – *Closed 25 December and Sunday lunch except December*
Menu £ 33 (lunch) – Carte £ 30/92 – *(booking essential)*
• Japanese • Fashionable • Trendy •
This branch of the glamorous chain is more of a party animal than its elder sibling at The Metropolitan. Start with cocktails then head upstairs for Japanese food with South American influences; try dishes from the wood-fired oven.

io **Ormer Mayfair** – Flemings Hotel XX ও AC ⇔ ⑩

7-12 Half Moon St ⊠ *W1J 7BH* – Ⓜ *Green Park* Plan: **F4**
– ℰ *(020) 7016 5601* – *www.flemings-mayfair.co.uk* – *Closed Sunday and lunch Monday*
Menu £ 30 (lunch) – Carte £ 50/70
• Modern British • Traditional décor • Intimate •
Run in partnership with Shaun Rankin, chef-owner of Ormer in Jersey. The Channel Islands provide much of the produce in the carefully crafted dishes. The restaurant may suffer a little from its hotel basement location but it is run with care and enthusiasm.

io **Roka** XX 🎐 AC

30 North Audley St ⊠ *W1K 6HP* – Ⓜ *Bond Street* Plan: **G3**
– ℰ *(020) 7305 5644* – *www.rokarestaurant.com* – *Closed Christmas-New Year*
Carte £ 24/99
• Japanese • Elegant • Fashionable •
London's third Roka ventured into the rarefied surroundings of Mayfair and the restaurant's seductive looks are a good fit. All the favourites from their modern Japanese repertoire are here, with the robata grill taking centre stage.

io **Sakagura** XX 🎐 AC

8 Heddon St ⊠ *W1B 4BS* – Ⓜ *Oxford Circus* – ℰ *(020)* Plan: **H3**
3405 7230 – *www.sakaguralondon.com* – *Closed 25 December*
Menu £ 30/80 – Carte £ 27/55
• Japanese • Exotic décor • Contemporary décor •
A contemporary styled Japanese restaurant part owned by the Japan Centre, a sake and Gekkeikan, a sake manufacturer. Along with an impressive drinks list is an extensive menu covering a variety of styles; highlights include the skewers cooked on the robata charcoal grill.

io **Sexy Fish** XX AC ⇔

Berkeley Sq. ⊠ *W1J 6BR* – Ⓜ *Green Park* – ℰ *(020)* Plan: **H3**
3764 2000 – *www.sexyfish.com* – *Closed 25-26 December*
Menu £ 36 (weekday lunch) – Carte £ 34/147
• Seafood • Design • Elegant •
Everyone will have an opinion about the name but what's indisputable is that this is a very good looking restaurant, with works by Frank Gehry and Damien Hirst, and a stunning ceiling by Michael Roberts. The fish comes with various Asian influences but don't ignore the meat dishes like the beef rib skewers.

io **StreetXO** XX

15 Old Burlington St ⊠ *W1S 2JL* – Ⓜ *Oxford Circus* Plan: **H3**
– ℰ *(020) 3096 7555* – *www.streetxo.com* – *Closed 22-26 December*
Menu £ 25/90 – Carte £ 38/54
• Creative • Trendy • Design •
The menu at Madrid chef David Muñoz's London outpost is inspired by European, Asian and even South American cuisines. Dishes are characterised by explosions of colour and a riot of different flavours, techniques and textures. The quasi-industrial feel of the basement room adds to the moody, noisy atmosphere.

🏠 **Theo Randall**   XX 🅰️ ⇔ 🕤 📶

InterContinental London Park Lane, 1 Hamilton Pl, Park   Plan: **G4**
Ln ✉ *W1J 7QY* – Ⓜ *Hyde Park Corner* – ☎ *(020) 73188747*
– www.theorandall.com – Closed Christmas, Easter, Saturday lunch,
Sunday dinner and bank holidays
Menu £ 29 (weekdays)/33 – Carte £ 34/65
· Italian · Classic décor · Chic ·

A lighter, less formal look to the room was unveiled in 2016 to celebrate Theo's 10 years at the InterContinental. The lack of windows and the corporate nature of the hotel have never helped but at least there is now greater synergy between the room and the rustic Italian fare, made with prime ingredients.

🏠 **Tokimeitë**   XX 🅰️ ⇔

23 Conduit St ✉ *W1S 2XS* – Ⓜ *Oxford Circus* – ☎ *(020)*   Plan: **H3**
3826 4411 – www.tokimeite.com – Closed 25 December, 1-3 January and
Sunday
Carte £ 28/143
· Japanese · Chic · Intimate ·

Yoshihiro Murata, one of Japan's most celebrated chefs, teamed up with the Zen-Noh group to open this good looking, intimate restaurant on two floors. Their aim is to promote Wagyu beef in Europe, so it's understandably the star of the show.

🏠 **Wild Honey**   XX 🅰️ 🕤

12 St George St. ✉ *W1S 2FB* – Ⓜ *Oxford Circus*   Plan: **H3**
– ☎ (020) 7758 9160 – www.wildhoneyrestaurant.co.uk – Closed 25-
26 December, 1 January, Sunday and bank holidays except Good Friday
Menu £ 35 (lunch and early dinner)/35 – Carte £ 33/55
· Modern cuisine · Design · Intimate ·

The elegant wood panelling and ornate plasterwork may say 'classic Mayfair institution' but the personable service team keep the atmosphere enjoyably easy-going. The kitchen uses quality British ingredients and a French base but is not afraid of the occasional international flavour.

🏠 **Le Boudin Blanc**   X 🏵️ 🍴 🅰️ ⇔

5 Trebeck St ✉ *W1J 7LT* – Ⓜ *Green Park* – ☎ *(020)*   Plan: **G4**
74993292 – www.boudinblanc.co.uk – Closed 24-26 December and
1 January
Menu £ 19 (lunch) – Carte £ 28/55
· French · Rustic · Neighbourhood ·

Appealing, lively French bistro in Shepherd Market, spread over two floors. Satisfying French classics and country cooking are the draws, along with authentic Gallic service. Good value lunch menu.

🏠 **Little Social**   X ⅺ 🅰️ ⇔ 📶

5 Pollen St ✉ *W1S 1NE* – Ⓜ *Oxford Circus* – ☎ *(020)*   Plan: **H3**
7870 3730 – www.littlesocial.co.uk – Closed Sunday and bank holidays
Menu £ 21 (weekday lunch) – Carte £ 37/56 – *(booking essential)*
· French · Bistro · Fashionable ·

Jason Atherton's lively French bistro, opposite his Pollen Street Social restaurant, has a clubby feel and an appealing, deliberately worn look. Service is breezy and capable and the food is mostly classic with the odd modern twist.

🏠 **Kitty Fisher's**   X

10 Shepherd Mkt ✉ *W1J 7QF* – Ⓜ *Green Park*   Plan: **H4**
– ☎ (0203) 302 1661 – www.kittyfishers.com – Closed Christmas, New
Year, Easter, Sunday and bank holidays
Menu £ 30 (weekday lunch) – Carte £ 30/63 – *(booking essential)*
· Modern cuisine · Bistro · Cosy ·

Warm, intimate and unpretentious restaurant – the star of the show is the wood grill which gives the dishes added depth. Named after an 18C courtesan, presumably in honour of the profession for which Shepherd Market was once known.

UNITED KINGDOM - LONDON

Mayfair Chippy

14 North Audley St ⊠ *W1K 6WE –* Ⓜ *Marble Arch* Plan: **G3**
– 𝒞 (020) 7741 2233 – www.eatbrit.com – Closed 25 December and 1 January
Carte £ 21/38
• Fish and chips • Vintage • Traditional décor •
There are chippies, and there is the Mayfair Chippy. Here you can get cocktails,
wine, oysters, starters and dessert but, most significantly, the 'Mayfair Classic'
– fried cod or haddock with chips, tartar sauce, mushy peas and curry sauce.

Neo Bistro

11 Woodstock St ⊠ *W1C 2AE –* Ⓜ *Bond Street* Plan: **G3**
– 𝒞 (020) 7499 9427 – www.neobistro.co.uk – Closed Christmas, Sunday,
Monday and lunch Tuesday
Menu £ 42 (dinner) – Carte £ 31/37
• Modern British • Rustic • Intimate •
A rustic two floored former pub which offers a tasting menu alongside its con-
cise and ever-evolving à la carte. The easy-eating, vividly coloured dishes are
not only aesthetically pleasing but also packed with flavour.

Peyote

13 Cork St ⊠ *W1S 3NS –* Ⓜ *Green Park – 𝒞 (020)* Plan: **H3**
7409 1300 – www.peyoterestaurant.com – Closed Saturday lunch and
Sunday
Menu £ 25 (weekday lunch) – Carte £ 32/63 – *(booking essential)*
• Mexican • Trendy • Design •
From the people behind Zuma and Roka comes a 'refined interpretation of
Mexican cuisine' at this fun, glamorous spot. There's an exhilarating freshness
to the well-judged dishes; don't miss the great guacamole or the cactus salad.

Claridge's

Brook St ⊠ *W1K 4HR –* Ⓜ *Bond Street – 𝒞 (020)* Plan: **G3**
76298860 – www.claridges.co.uk
197 rm – †£ 480/1140 ††£ 480/1140 – ⌑ £ 34 – 62 suites
• Grand Luxury • Historic • Classic •
Claridge's has a long, illustrious history dating back to 1812 and this iconic and
very British hotel has been a favourite of the royal family over generations. Its
most striking decorative feature is its art deco. The hotel also moves with the
times, with its modern restaurant Fera proving a perfect fit.
❀ **Fera at Claridge's** – See restaurant listing

Connaught

Carlos Pl. ⊠ *W1K 2AL –* Ⓜ *Bond Street – 𝒞 (020)* Plan: **G3**
74997070 – www.the-connaught.co.uk
121 rm – †£ 540/990 ††£ 630/1110 – ⌑ £ 38 – 25 suites
• Grand Luxury • Townhouse • Classic •
One of London's most famous hotels, the Connaught offers effortless serenity
and exclusivity and an elegant British feel. All the luxurious bedrooms come
with large marble bathrooms and butler service; some overlook a small oriental
garden, others look down onto mews houses. Refined French cooking in Hélène
Darroze; eclectic dishes in relaxed, all-day Jean-Georges.
❀❀ **Hélène Darroze at The Connaught** – See restaurant listing

Dorchester

Park Ln ⊠ *W1K 1QA –* Ⓜ *Hyde Park Corner – 𝒞 (020)* Plan: **G4**
76298888 – www.dorchestercollection.com
250 rm – †£ 410/895 ††£ 480/1085 – ⌑ £ 34 – 51 suites
• Grand Luxury • Classic •
One of the capital's iconic properties offering every possible facility and exemplary levels of service. The striking marbled and pillared promenade provides an
elegant backdrop for afternoon tea. Bedrooms are eminently comfortable;
some overlook Hyde Park. The Grill is for all things British; Alain Ducasse waves
Le Tricolore; China Tang celebrates the cuisine of the Orient.
❀❀❀ **Alain Ducasse at The Dorchester** • ⅰ○ **The Grill** • ⅰ○ **China
Tang** – See restaurant listing

Four Seasons

Hamilton Pl, Park Ln ⊠ *W1J 7DR*
Plan: **AL4**
– Ⓜ *Hyde Park Corner* – ℰ *(020) 7499 0888*
– *www.fourseasons.com/london*
193 rm – ♦£ 480/930 ♦♦£ 480/930 – ☲ £ 30 – 33 suites
• Grand Luxury • Business • Modern •

It raised the bar for luxury hotels: a striking red and black lobby sets the scene, while the spacious, sumptuous and serenely coloured bedrooms have a rich, contemporary look and boast every conceivable comfort. Italian influenced menu in Amaranto, with its outdoor terrace. Great views from the stunning rooftop spa.

The Beaumont

Brown Hart Gdns ⊠ *W1K 6TF* – Ⓜ *Bond Street*
Plan: **G3**
– ℰ *(020) 7499 1001* – *www.thebeaumont.com*
73 rm ☲ – ♦£ 395/825 ♦♦£ 395/825 – 10 suites
• Luxury • Art déco • Personalised •

From a 1926 former garage, restaurateurs Chris Corbin and Jeremy King fashioned their first hotel; art deco inspired, it's stunning, stylish and exudes understated luxury. The attention to detail is exemplary, from the undeniably masculine bedrooms to the lively, cool cocktail bar and busy brasserie.

⑩ **Colony Grill Room** – See restaurant listing

45 Park Lane

45 Park Ln ⊠ *W1K 1PN* – Ⓜ *Hyde Park Corner*
Plan: **G4**
– ℰ *(020) 7493 4545* – *www.45parklane.com*
46 rm – ♦£ 495/695 ♦♦£ 495/695 – ☲ £ 32 – 10 suites
• Luxury • Townhouse • Modern •

It was the original site of the Playboy Club and used to be a car showroom, before being reborn as The Dorchester's sister hotel. The bedrooms, all with views over Hyde Park, are wonderfully sensual and the marble bathrooms are beautiful.

⑩ **Cut** – See restaurant listing

Brown's

33 Albemarle St ⊠ *W1S 4BP* – Ⓜ *Green Park* – ℰ *(020)*
Plan: **H3**
7493 6020 – *www.roccofortehotels.com*
115 rm – ♦£ 500/1000 ♦♦£ 500/1000 – ☲ £ 36 – 33 suites
• Luxury • Traditional • Classic •

Opened in 1837 by James Brown, Lord Byron's butler. This urbane and very British hotel with an illustrious past offers a swish bar with Terence Donovan prints, bedrooms in neutral hues and a classic English sitting room for afternoon tea.

Westbury

Bond St ⊠ *W1S 2YF* – Ⓜ *Bond Street* – ℰ *(020)*
Plan: **H3**
76297755 – *www.westburymayfair.com*
225 rm ☲ – ♦£ 300/529 ♦♦£ 300/529 – 13 suites
• Business • Luxury • Modern •

As stylish now as when it opened in the 1950s. Smart, comfortable bedrooms with terrific art deco inspired suites. Elegant, iconic Polo bar and bright, fresh sushi bar. All the exclusive brands are outside the front door.

❀ **Alyn Williams at The Westbury** – See restaurant listing

Chesterfield

35 Charles St ⊠ *W1J 5EB* – Ⓜ *Green Park* – ℰ *(020)*
Plan: **G4**
74912622 – *www.chesterfieldmayfair.com*
107 rm ☲ – ♦£ 195/390 ♦♦£ 220/510 – 4 suites
• Townhouse • Traditional • Classic •

There's an assuredly English feel to this Georgian house. The discreet lobby leads to a clubby bar and wood panelled library. Individually decorated bedrooms, with some antique pieces. Intimate and pretty restaurant.

🏛️ **Flemings**   ⅃⅋ 🔶 AC

7-12 Half Moon St ✉ *W1J 7BH* – Ⓜ *Green Park*   Plan: **F4**
– ☏ (020) 7499 0000 – www.flemings-mayfair.co.uk
129 rm – †£ 228/276 ††£ 282/456 – ☛ £ 27 – 10 suites
• Townhouse • Contemporary •
Made up of a series of conjoined townhouses, this hotel was re-launched in 2016 following a comprehensive refit. Bedrooms are very pleasantly decorated and the keen team provide charming and attentive service.
🍽️ **Ormer Mayfair** – See restaurant listing

Soho

❀ **Yauatcha Soho**   XX AC

15 Broadwick St ✉ *W1F 0DL*   Plan: **I3**
– Ⓜ Tottenham Court Road – ☏ (020) 74948888 – www.yauatcha.com
– Closed 25 December
Menu £ 30 (lunch) – Carte £ 29/67
• Chinese • Design • Trendy •
It's been here almost 15 years but still manages to feel fresh and contemporary, with its bright ground floor and moody basement, featuring low banquettes, an aquarium bar and a star-lit ceiling. Dishes are colourful with strong flavours and excellent texture contrasts; dim sum is the highlight – try the venison puff.
→ Venison puff. Stir-fried rib-eye beef. Raspberry délice.

❀ **Barrafina**   X AC

26-27 Dean St ✉ *W1D 3LL* – Ⓜ *Tottenham Court Road*   Plan: **I3**
– ☏ (020) 7440 1456 – www.barrafina.co.uk – Closed bank holidays
Carte £ 18/44 – *(bookings not accepted)*
• Spanish • Tapas bar • Fashionable •
In 2016 the original Barrafina moved to this brighter, roomier site fashioned out of what was previously a part of Quo Vadis restaurant. Dishes burst with flavour – do order some dishes from the blackboard specials – the staff are fun and the L-shaped counter fills up quickly, so be prepared to wait.
→ Pluma Iberica with confit potatoes. Rump of milk-fed lamb. Santiago tart.

❀ **Social Eating House**   X AC

58 Poland St ✉ *W1F 7NR* – Ⓜ *Oxford Circus* – ☏ *(020)*   Plan: **H3**
79933251 – www.socialeatinghouse.com – Closed Christmas, Sunday and bank holidays
Menu £ 27 (lunch and early dinner) – Carte £ 39/56 – *(booking advisable)*
• Modern cuisine • Fashionable • Brasserie •
There's something of a Brooklyn vibe to this Jason Atherton restaurant, with its bare brick and raw plastered walls and its speakeasy bar upstairs. It's great fun, very busy and gloriously unstuffy; the menu is an eminently good read, with the best dishes being the simplest ones.
→ Scorched mackerel and tartare with pickled walnuts, apple and chicory. Roast rack of lamb, braised neck, baby gem, cured lamb and rocket. Caramelised milk and brown sugar tart with ginger wine and fromage frais sorbet.

🏛️ **Brasserie Zédel**   XX AC

20 Sherwood St ✉ *W1F 7ED* – Ⓜ *Piccadilly Circus*   Plan: **H3**
– ☏ (020) 7734 4888 – www.brasseriezedel.com – Closed 25 December
Menu £ 13/20 – Carte £ 18/44 – *(booking advisable)*
• French • Brasserie •
A grand French brasserie, which is all about inclusivity and accessibility, in a bustling subterranean space restored to its original art deco glory. Expect a roll-call of classic French dishes and some very competitive prices.

Dehesa

X ॐ 🏠 AC ↔

25 Ganton St ⊠ W1F 9BP – Ⓜ Oxford Circus – 𝒞 (020)
79494170 – www.dehesa.co.uk – Closed 25 December
Carte £ 14/36

Plan: H3

• Mediterranean cuisine • Tapas bar • Fashionable •

Repeats the success of its sister restaurant, Salt Yard, by offering flavoursome and appealingly priced Spanish and Italian tapas. Busy, friendly atmosphere in appealing corner location. Terrific drinks list too.

Bao

X AC

53 Lexington St ⊠ W1F 9AS
– Ⓜ Tottenham Court Road – 𝒞 (020) 30111632 – www.baolondon.com
– Closed 23 December-3 January and Sunday
Carte £ 17/27 – (bookings not accepted)

Plan: H3

• Asian • Simple • Cosy •

There are some things in life worth queueing for – and that includes the delicious eponymous buns here at this simple, great value Taiwanese operation. The classic bao and the confit pork bao are standouts, along with 'small eats' like trotter nuggets. There's also another Bao in Windmill St.

Copita

X AC

27 D'Arblay St ⊠ W1F 8EP – Ⓜ Oxford Circus
– 𝒞 (020) 7287 7797 – www.copita.co.uk – Closed Sunday and bank holidays
Carte £ 19/32 – (bookings not accepted at dinner) (bookings not accepted)

Plan: H3

• Spanish • Tapas bar • Rustic •

Perch on one of the high stools or stay standing and get stuck into the daily menu of small, colourful and tasty dishes. Staff add to the atmosphere and everything on the Spanish wine list comes by the glass or copita.

Hoppers

X AC

49 Frith St ⊠ W1D 4SG – Ⓜ Tottenham Court Road
– 𝒞 (020) 3011 1021 – www.hopperslondon.com – Closed 25-27 December and 1-3 January.
Carte £ 15/25 – (bookings not accepted)

Plan: I3

• South Indian • Simple • Rustic •

Street food inspired by the flavours of Tamil Nadu and Sri Lanka features at this fun little spot from the Sethi family (Trishna, Gymkhana). Hoppers are bowl-shaped pancakes made from fermented rice and coconut – ideal with a creamy kari. The 'short eats' are great too, as are the prices, so expect a queue.

Kiln

X

58 Brewer St ⊠ W1F 9TL – Ⓜ Piccadilly Circus
– www.kilnsoho.com
Carte £ 14/20 – (bookings not accepted)

Plan: H3

• Thai • Simple • Cosy •

Sit at the far counter to watch chefs prepare fiery Thai food in clay pots, woks and grills. The well-priced menu includes influences from Laos, Myanmar and Yunnan – all prepared using largely British produce. The counter is for walk-ins only but parties of four can book a table downstairs.

Kricket

X AC

12 Denman St ⊠ W1D 7HH – Ⓜ Piccadilly Circus
– 𝒞 (020) 7734 5612 – www.kricket.co.uk
Carte £ 12/34 – (bookings not accepted)

Plan: I3

• Indian • Simple •

From Brixton pop-up to a permanent spot in Soho; not many Indian restaurants have a counter, an open kitchen, sharing plates and cocktails. The four well-priced dishes under each heading of 'Meat, 'Fish' and 'Veg' are made with homegrown ingredients. Bookings are only taken for groups of 4 or more at the communal tables downstairs.

tical UNITED KINGDOM - LONDON</p>

Palomar ⠀⠀X & ▥

34 Rupert St ⠀W1D 6DN – Ⓜ Piccadilly Circus ⠀Plan: I3
– ℰ (020) 7439 8777 – www.thepalomar.co.uk – Closed dinner 24-26 December
Carte £ 26/33 – (booking advisable)
• World cuisine • Trendy • Cosy •

A hip slice of modern-day Jerusalem in the heart of theatreland, with a zinc kitchen counter running back to an intimate wood-panelled dining room. Like the atmosphere, the contemporary Middle Eastern cooking is fresh and vibrant.

Polpetto ⠀⠀X ▥

11 Berwick St ⠀W1F 0PL – Ⓜ Tottenham Court Road ⠀Plan: I3
– ℰ (020) 7439 8627 – www.polpetto.co.uk – Closed Sunday
Carte £ 12/21 – (bookings not accepted at dinner)
• Italian • Simple • Rustic •

Re-opened by Russell Norman in bigger premises. The style of food is the perfect match for this relaxed environment: the small, seasonally inspired Italian dishes are uncomplicated, appealingly priced and deliver great flavours.

Quo Vadis ⠀⠀XXX ▥ ⇔ ⊡

26-29 Dean St ⠀W1D 3LL – Ⓜ Tottenham Court Road ⠀Plan: I3
– ℰ (020) 7437 9585 – www.quovadissoho.co.uk – Closed 25-26 December, 1 January, Sunday and bank holidays
Menu £ 23 – Carte £ 36/50
• Traditional British • Traditional décor • Elegant •

Annexed in 2016 to accommodate Barrafina, this Soho institution is now limited to one room – upstairs is a private members' dining club. The cooking, though, remains as robust and forthright as ever.

Gauthier - Soho ⠀⠀XXX ▥ ⇔ ⊙

21 Romilly St ⠀W1D 5AF – Ⓜ Leicester Square ⠀Plan: I3
– ℰ (020) 7494 3111 – www.gauthiersoho.co.uk – Closed Monday, Sunday and bank holidays except Good Friday
Menu £ 24/75
• French • Intimate • Neighbourhood •

Detached from the rowdier elements of Soho is this charming Georgian townhouse, with dining spread over three floors. Alex Gauthier offers assorted menus of his classically based cooking, with vegetarians particularly well looked after.

Imperial China ⠀⠀XXX ▥ ⇔

White Bear Yard, 25a Lisle St ⠀WC2H 7BA
– Ⓜ Leicester Square – ℰ (020) 7734 3388 ⠀Plan: I3
– www.imperialchina-london.com – Closed 25 December
Menu £ 20/46 – Carte £ 15/57 – (booking advisable)
• Chinese • Elegant •

Sharp service and comfortable surroundings are not the only things that set this restaurant apart: the Cantonese cooking exudes freshness and vitality, whether that's the steamed dumplings or the XO minced pork with fine beans.

Red Fort ⠀⠀XXX ▥ ⊡

77 Dean St. ⠀W1D 3SH – Ⓜ Tottenham Court Road ⠀Plan: I3
– ℰ (020) 7437 2525 – www.redfort.co.uk – Closed Sunday
Menu £ 15/49 – Carte £ 31/59 – (bookings advisable at dinner)
• Indian • Exotic décor • Chic •

A smart, stylish and professionally run Indian restaurant that has been a feature in Soho since 1983. Cooking is based on the Mughal Court and uses much UK produce such as Welsh lamb; look out for more unusual choices like rabbit.

Bob Bob Ricard

XX AC

1 Upper James St ⊠ W1F 9DF – Ⓜ *Oxford Circus*
– ℰ *(020) 31451000 – www.bobbobricard.com*

Plan: H3

Carte £ 37/90

• Modern cuisine • Vintage • Elegant •

Everyone needs a little glamour now and again and this place provides it. The room may be quite small but it sees itself as a grand salon – ask for a booth. The menu is all-encompassing – oysters and caviar to pies and burgers.

Dean Street Townhouse Restaurant – Dean Street Townhouse Hotel

69-71 Dean St. ⊠ W1D 3SE – Ⓜ *Piccadilly Circus*
– ℰ *(020) 74341775 – www.deanstreettownhouse.com*

XX 🛱 AC 🕃 🎗
Plan: I3

Menu £ 29 – Carte £ 29/44 – *(booking essential)*

• Modern British • Brasserie • Elegant •

A Georgian house that's home to a fashionable bar and restaurant which is busy from breakfast onwards. Appealingly classic British food includes some retro dishes and satisfying puddings.

Ham Yard – Ham Yard Hotel

XX 🛱 ♿ AC

1 Ham Yard, ⊠ W1D 7DT – Ⓜ *Piccadilly Circus*
– ℰ *(020) 3642 1007 – www.firmdalehotels.com*

Plan: I3

Menu £ 20 (dinner) – Carte £ 28/46

• Modern cuisine • Brasserie • Design •

An exuberantly decorated restaurant; start with a cocktail – the bitters and syrups are homemade with herbs from the hotel's roof garden. The menu moves with the seasons and the kitchen has the confidence to keep dishes simple.

Hix

XX AC ⇔ 🕃 🎗

66-70 Brewer St. ⊠ WIF 9UP – Ⓜ *Piccadilly Circus*
– ℰ *(020) 72923518 – www.hixsoho.co.uk – Closed 25-26 December*

Plan: H3

Menu £ 20 (lunch and early dinner) – Carte £ 25/68

• Traditional British • Fashionable • Trendy •

The exterior may hint at exclusivity but inside this big restaurant the atmosphere is fun, noisy and sociable. The room comes decorated with the works of eminent British artists. Expect classic British dishes and ingredients.

MASH

XX 🎋 ♿ AC ⇔ 🕃

77 Brewer St ⊠ W1F 9ZN – Ⓜ *Piccadilly Circus*
– ℰ *(020) 7734 2608 – www.mashsteak.co.uk – Closed 24-26 December and Sunday lunch*

Plan: H3

Menu £ 30 (lunch) – Carte £ 30/96

• Meats and grills • Brasserie • Fashionable •

A team from Copenhagen raised the old Titanic and restored the art deco to create this striking 'Modern American Steak House', offering Danish, Nebraskan and Uruguayan beef. A great bar and slick service add to the grown up feel.

100 Wardour St

XX AC ⇔ 🕃

100 Wardour St ⊠ W1F 0TN
– Ⓜ *Tottenham Court Road –* ℰ *(020) 7314 4000*
– www.100wardourst.com – Closed 25-26 December and Sunday-Monday

Plan: I3

Menu £ 15 (weekday dinner)/35 – Carte £ 27/59

• Modern cuisine • Contemporary décor •

D&D have reinvented the space formerly occupied by Floridita and the original Marquee Club. At night, head downstairs for cocktails, live music and a modern menu with Japanese and South American influences. In the daytime stay on the ground floor for an all-day menu, a bar and a pop-in/plug-in lounge.

Plum Valley

XX ⇔

20 Gerrard St. ⊠ W1D 6JQ – Ⓜ *Leicester Square*
– ℰ *(020) 74944366 – Closed 23-24 December*

Plan: I3

Menu £ 38 – Carte £ 19/37

• Chinese • Design •

Its striking black façade makes this modern Chinese restaurant easy to spot in Chinatown. Mostly Cantonese cooking, with occasional forays into Vietnam and Thailand; dim sum is the strength.

Tamarind Kitchen ⅩⅩ 🅰🅲

167-169 Wardour St ⊠ W1F 8WR
– Ⓜ *Tottenham Court Road* – ✆ (020) 72874243
– *www.tamarindkitchen.co.uk* – *Closed 25-26 December, 1 January*
Carte £ 21/36
• Indian • Exotic décor •

A more relaxed sister to Tamarind in Mayfair, this Indian restaurant comes with endearingly earnest service and a lively buzz. There's a nominal Northern emphasis to the fairly priced menu, with Awadhi kababs a speciality, but there are also plenty of curries and fish dishes.

Plan: **I3**

Temper ⅩⅩ 🈁 🅰🅲 ⇄

25 Broadwick St ⊠ W1F 0DF – Ⓜ *Oxford Circus*
– ✆ (020) 3879 3834 – *www.temperrestaurant.com* – *Closed 25-26 December and 1 January*
Carte £ 16/37
• Barbecue • Contemporary décor •

A fun, basement restaurant all about barbecue and meats. The beasts are cooked whole, some are also smoked in-house and there's a distinct South African flavour to the salsas that accompany them. Kick off with some tacos – they make around 1,200 of them every day.

Plan: **H3**

Vasco and Piero's Pavilion ⅩⅩ 🅰🅲 ⇄

15 Poland St ⊠ W1F 8QE – Ⓜ *Oxford Circus* – ✆ (020)
7437 8774 – *www.vascosfood.com* – *Closed Saturday lunch, Sunday and bank holidays*
Menu £ 18 (lunch and early dinner) – Carte £ 27/49 – *(booking essential at lunch)*
• Italian • Friendly • Neighbourhood •

Regulars and tourists have been flocking to this institution for over 40 years; its longevity is down to a twice daily changing menu of Umbrian-influenced dishes rather than the matter-of-fact service or simple decoration.

Plan: **H2**

Nopi Ⅹ ♿ 🅰🅲 🕼

21-22 Warwick St. ⊠ W1B 5NE – Ⓜ *Piccadilly Circus*
– ✆ (020) 74949584 – *www.nopi-restaurant.com* – *Closed bank holidays*
Carte £ 21/50
• Mediterranean cuisine • Design • Fashionable •

The bright, clean look of Yotam Ottolenghi's charmingly run all-day restaurant matches the fresh, invigorating food. The sharing plates take in the Mediterranean, the Middle East and Asia and the veggie dishes stand out.

Plan: **H3**

Antidote Ⅹ 🈁 🈂

12a Newburgh St ⊠ W1F 7RR – Ⓜ *Oxford Circus*
– ✆ (020) 7287 8488 – *www.antidotewinebar.com* – *Closed Sunday and bank holidays*
Carte £ 25/38 – *(booking advisable)*
• Modern cuisine • Intimate • Wine bar •

A cute, busy little wine bar on the ground floor offers charcuterie, cheese and mostly biodynamic and organic French wines. Upstairs is a more comfy restaurant with sharing plates of largely European dishes.

Plan: **H3**

Baozi Inn Ⅹ 🍴

25-26 Newport Court ⊠ WC2H 7JS – Ⓜ *Leicester Square*
– ✆ (020) 72876877 – *Closed 24-25 December*
Carte £ 15/22 – *(bookings not accepted)*
• Chinese • Rustic • Simple •

Buzzy, busy little place that's great for a quick bite, especially if you like pork buns, steaming bowls of noodles, a hit of Sichuan fire and plenty of beer or tea. You'll leave feeling surprisingly energised and rejuvenated.

Plan: **I3**

‖○ **Barshu**   X ⅃AC ⇔

28 Frith St. ⊠ W1D 5LF – ⓜ Leicester Square – ℰ (020)   Plan: I3
72878822 – www.barshurestaurant.co.uk – Closed 24-25 December
Carte £ 26/58 – *(booking advisable)*
• Chinese • Exotic décor •
The fiery and authentic flavours of China's Sichuan province are the draw here;
help is at hand as the menu has pictures. It's decorated with carved wood and
lanterns; downstairs is better for groups.

‖○ **Beijing Dumpling**   X ⅃AC

23 Lisle St. ⊠ WC2H 7BA – ⓜ Leicester Square   Plan: I3
– ℰ (020) 7287 6888 – Closed 24-25 December
Menu £ 18 – Carte £ 10/40
• Chinese • Neighbourhood • Simple •
This relaxed little place serves freshly prepared dumplings of both Beijing and
Shanghai styles. Although the range is not as comprehensive as the name sug-
gests, they do stand out, especially varieties of the famed Siu Lung Bao.

‖○ **Blanchette**   X ⅃AC ⇔

9 D'Arblay St ⊠ W1F 8DR – ⓜ Oxford Circus – ℰ (020)   Plan: H2
7439 8100 – www.blanchettesoho.co.uk
Menu £ 15 (lunch) – Carte £ 14/28 – *(booking essential)*
• French • Simple • Fashionable •
Run by three frères, Blanchette takes French bistro food and gives it the 'small
plates' treatment. It's named after their mother – the ox cheek Bourguignon is
her recipe. Tiles and exposed brick add to the rustic look.

‖○ **Bocca di Lupo**   X ⅃AC ⇔

12 Archer St ⊠ W1D 7BB – ⓜ Piccadilly Circus – ℰ (020)   Plan: I3
77342223 – www.boccadilupo.com – Closed 25 December and 1 January
Carte £ 26/45 – *(booking essential)*
• Italian • Tapas bar •
Atmosphere, food and service are all best when sitting at the marble counter,
watching the chefs at work. Specialities from across Italy come in large or small
sizes and are full of flavour and vitality. Try also their gelato shop opposite.

‖○ **Bone Daddies**   X ⅃AC

31 Peter St ⊠ W1F 0AR – ⓜ Piccadilly Circus – ℰ (020)   Plan: I3
7287 8581 – www.bonedaddies.com – Closed 25 December
Carte £ 17/27 – *(bookings not accepted)*
• Asian • Fashionable • Neighbourhood •
Maybe ramen is the new rock 'n' roll. The charismatic Aussie chef-owner feels
that combinations are endless when it comes to these comforting bowls. Be
ready to queue then share a table. It's a fun place, run by a hospitable bunch.

‖○ **Casita Andina**   X

31 Great Windmill St ⊠ W1D 7LP – ⓜ Piccadilly Circus   Plan: I3
– ℰ (020) 33279464 – www.andinalondon.com/casita
Carte £ 13/25
• Peruvian • Rustic •
Respect is paid to the home-style cooking of the Andes at this warmly run and
welcoming Peruvian picantería. Dishes are gluten-free and as colourful as the
surroundings of this 200 year old house.

‖○ **Cây Tre**   X ⅃AC ⅃○

42-43 Dean St ⊠ W1D 4PZ – ⓜ Tottenham Court Road   Plan: I3
– ℰ (020) 7317 9118 – www.caytresoho.co.uk
Menu £ 25/23 – Carte £ 23/32 – *(booking advisable)*
• Vietnamese • Minimalist •
Bright, sleek and bustling surroundings where Vietnamese standouts include
Cha La Lot (spicy ground pork wrapped in betel leaves), slow-cooked Mekong
catfish with a well-judged sweet and spicy sauce, and 6 versions of Pho (noodle
soup).

Ceviche Soho   X AC

17 Frith St ⊠ *W1D 4RG* – **M** *Tottenham Court Road*   Plan: I3
– ℰ (020) 7292 2040 – www.cevicheuk.com/soho
Carte £ 18/26 – *(booking essential)*
• Peruvian • Friendly • Fashionable •
Based on a Lima pisco bar, Ceviche is as loud as it is fun. First try the deliriously addictive drinks based on the Peruvian spirit pisco, and then share some thinly sliced sea bass or octopus, along with anticuchos skewers.

Cinnamon Soho   X 🏠 AC 🍸

5 Kingly St ⊠ *W1B 5PF* – **M** *Oxford Circus* – *ℰ (020)*   Plan: H3
7437 1664 – www.cinnamonsoho.com – Closed 1 January
Menu £ 15 (lunch and early dinner) – Carte £ 16/32
• Indian • Friendly • Fashionable •
Younger and more fun than its sister the Cinnamon Club. Has a great selection of classic and more modern Indian dishes like Rogan Josh shepherd's pie. High Chai in the afternoon and a pre-theatre menu that's a steal.

Duck & Rice   X AC

90 Berwick St ⊠ *W1F 0QB* – **M** *Tottenham Court Road*   Plan: I3
– ℰ (020) 3327 7888 – www.theduckandrice.com – Closed 25 December
Carte approx. £ 38
• Chinese • Intimate • Romantic •
Alan Yau is one of our most innovative restaurateurs and once again he's created something different – a converted pub with a Chinese kitchen. Beer is the thing on the ground floor; upstairs is for Chinese favourites and comforting classics.

Ember Yard   X AC ⇔

60 Berwick St ⊠ *W1F 8DX* – **M** *Oxford Circus* – *ℰ (020)*   Plan: H2
7439 8057 – www.emberyard.co.uk – Closed 25-26 December and
1 January
Carte £ 14/25 – *(booking advisable)*
• Mediterranean cuisine • Tapas bar • Fashionable •
Those familiar with the Salt Yard Group will recognise the Spanish and Italian themed menus – but their 4th fun outlet comes with a focus on cooking over charcoal or wood. There's even a seductive smokiness to some of the cocktails.

Haozhan   X AC

8 Gerrard St ⊠ *W1D 5PJ* – **M** *Leicester Square* – *ℰ (020)*   Plan: I3
74343838 – www.haozhan.co.uk – Closed 24-25 December
Menu £ 14 – Carte £ 15/43
• Chinese • Design •
Interesting fusion-style dishes, with mostly Cantonese but other Asian influences too. Specialities like jasmine ribs or wasabi prawns reveal a freshness that marks this place out from the plethora of Chinatown mediocrity.

Jinjuu   X AC

15 Kingly St ⊠ *W1B 5PS* – **M** *Oxford Circus* – *ℰ (020)*   Plan: H3
8181 8887 – www.jinjuu.com – Closed 25 December
Menu £ 17 (weekday lunch)/42 – Carte £ 29/41
• Asian • Design • Fashionable •
American-born celebrity chef Judy Joo's restaurant is a celebration of her Korean heritage. The vibrant dishes, whether Bibimbap bowls or Ssam platters, burst with flavour and are as enjoyable as the fun surroundings. There's another branch in Mayfair.

Koya Bar   X

50 Frith St ⊠ *W1D 4SQ* – **M** *Tottenham Court Road*   Plan: I3
– ℰ (020) 74949075 – www.koyabar.co.uk – Closed 24-25 December and
1 January
Carte £ 12/25 – *(bookings not accepted)*
• Japanese • Simple • Friendly •
A simple, sweet place serving authentic Udon noodles and small plates; they open early for breakfast. Counter seating means everyone has a view of the chefs; bookings aren't taken and there is often a queue, but the short wait is worth it.

UNITED KINGDOM - LONDON

Mele e Pere

X AC 🕸

46 Brewer St ⊠ W1F 9TF – ⓜ Piccadilly Circus – ☎ (020) Plan: I3
7096 2096 – www.meleepere.co.uk – Closed 25-26 December and
1 January
Menu £ 23 (lunch and early dinner) – Carte £ 23/44
• **Italian** • **Friendly** • **Neighbourhood** •
Head downstairs – the 'apples and pears'? – to a vaulted room in the style of a
homely Italian kitchen, with an appealing vermouth bar. The owner-chef has
worked in some decent London kitchens but hails from Verona so expect
gutsy Italian dishes.

Oliver Maki

X AC

33 Dean St ⊠ W1D 4PW – ⓜ Leicester Square Plan: I3
– ☎ (020) 7734 0408 – www.olivermaki.co.uk – Closed 23-30 December
Menu £ 12/65 – Carte £ 22/56
• **Japanese** • **Minimalist** • **Simple** •
A small, eagerly run corner restaurant from a group with branches in Kuwait
and Bahrain. The modern Japanese food has a more pronounced fusion element than similar types of place – not everything works but the confident kitchen uses good produce.

Polpo Soho

X AC ⇔

41 Beak St ⊠ W1F 9SB – ⓜ Oxford Circus – ☎ (020) Plan: H3
7734 4479 – www.polpo.co.uk
Menu £ 25 – Carte £ 14/28 – *(bookings not accepted at dinner)*
• **Italian** • **Tapas bar** • **Rustic** •
A fun and lively Venetian bacaro, with a stripped-down, faux-industrial look. The
small plates, from arancini and prosciutto to fritto misto and Cotechino sausage,
are so well priced that waiting for a table is worth it.

Spuntino

X AC

61 Rupert St. ⊠ W1D 7PW – ⓜ Piccadilly Circus Plan: I3
– www.spuntino.co.uk – Closed dinner 24 December, 25-26, 31 December
and 1 January
Carte £ 12/30 – *(bookings not accepted)*
• **North American** • **Rustic** •
Influenced by Downtown New York, with its no-booking policy and industrial
look. Sit at the counter and order classics like mac 'n' cheese or sliders. The
staff, who look like they could also fix your car, really add to the fun.

Zelman Meats

X

2 St Anne's Ct ⊠ W1F 0AZ – ⓜ Tottenham Court Rd Plan: I2
– ☎ (020) 7437 0566 – www.zelmanmeats.com – Closed Monday lunch
and bank holidays
Carte £ 18/49
• **Meats and grills** • **Rustic** •
Those clever Goodman people noticed a lack of affordable steakhouses and so
opened this fun, semi-industrial space. They serve three cuts of beef: sliced
picanha (from the rump), Chateaubriand, and a wonderfully smoky short rib.

Café Royal

🏛 🛗 ⊕ 🏊 🔲 🕭 AC 🧖

68 Regent St ⊠ W1B 4DY – ⓜ Piccadilly Circus Plan: H3
– ☎ (020) 7406 3333 – www.hotelcaferoyal.com
160 rm – †£ 440/600 ††£ 440/600 – ☑ £ 32 – 16 suites
• **Grand Luxury** • **Palace** • **Historic** •
One of the most famous names of the London social scene for the last 150 years
is now a luxury hotel. The bedrooms are beautiful, elegant and discreet and the
wining and dining options many and varied – they include the gloriously
rococo Oscar Wilde bar, once home to the iconic Grill Room.

Ham Yard

1 Ham Yard, ⊠ W1D 7DT – **Ⓜ** *Piccadilly Circus*
– 𝒞 (020) 3642 2000 – www.firmdalehotels.com
91 rm – 🛏️£ 260/380 🛏️🛏️£ 260/380
– 🍽️ £ 14 – 2 suites
• Luxury • Business • Elegant •

Plan: I3

This stylish hotel from the Firmdale group is set around a courtyard – a haven of tranquillity in the West End. Each of the rooms is different but all are supremely comfortable. There's also a great roof terrace, a theatre, a fully stocked library and bar... and even a bowling alley.
🍴 **Ham Yard** – See restaurant listing

Soho

4 Richmond Mews ⊠ W1D 3DH
– **Ⓜ** *Tottenham Court Road – 𝒞 (020) 7559 3000*
– www.firmdalehotels.com
96 rm – 🛏️£ 264/408 🛏️🛏️£ 264/408
– 🍽️ £ 18 – 7 suites
• Luxury • Personalised • Contemporary •

Plan: AN2

Stylish and fashionable hotel that mirrors the vibrancy of the neighbourhood. Boasts two screening rooms, a comfortable drawing room and up-to-the-minute bedrooms; some vivid, others more muted but all with hi-tech extras.

Dean Street Townhouse

69-71 Dean St. ⊠ W1D 3SE – **Ⓜ** *Piccadily Circus*
– 𝒞 (020) 74341775 – www.deanstreettownhouse.com
39 rm – 🛏️£ 200/450 🛏️🛏️£ 220/470
– 🍽️ £ 15
• Townhouse • Classic • Grand luxury •

Plan: I3

In the heart of Soho and where bedrooms range from tiny to bigger; the latter have roll-top baths in the room. All are well designed and come with a good range of extras. Cosy ground floor lounge.
🍴 **Dean Street Townhouse Restaurant** – See restaurant listing

Hazlitt's

6 Frith St ⊠ W1D 3JA – **Ⓜ** *Tottenham Court Road*
– 𝒞 (020) 74341771 – www.hazlittshotel.com
30 rm – 🛏️£ 205/235 🛏️🛏️£ 255/750
– 🍽️ £ 12 – 3 suites
• Townhouse • Traditional • Historic •

Plan: I3

Dating from 1718, the former house of essayist and critic William Hazlitt still welcomes many a writer today in its role as a charming townhouse hotel. It has plenty of character and is warmly run. No restaurant so breakfast in bed really is the only option – and who is going to object to that?

St James's

🟢 Ritz Restaurant – Ritz Hotel

150 Piccadilly ⊠ W1J 9BR – **Ⓜ** *Green Park – 𝒞 (020)*
73002370 – www.theritzlondon.com
Menu £ 52 (weekday lunch) – Carte £ 75/136
• Classic cuisine • Luxury • Historic •

Plan: H4

Thanks to the lavishness of its Louis XVI decoration, there is nowhere grander than The Ritz. The classic cuisine uses extravagant ingredients along with subtle contemporary elements to lift dishes to new heights while still respecting their heritage. The formal service is now more youthful and enthusiastic.
➔ Norfolk crab with pickled cucumber, egg yolk and oscietra caviar. Fillet of veal with wild mushrooms and smoked bone marrow. Crêpes Suzette.

Seven Park Place – St James's Hotel and Club XxX 🗚 ⇔

7-8 Park Pl ⊠ SW1A 1LS – ⓜ Green Park – ℰ (020) Plan: **H4**
73161615 – www.stjameshotelandclub.com – Closed Sunday and Monday
Menu £ 33 (weekday lunch)/71 – *(booking essential)*
• Modern cuisine • Cosy • Fashionable •
William Drabble's cooking is all about the quality of the produce, much of which
comes from the Lake District, and his confident cooking allows natural flavours
to shine. This diminutive restaurant is concealed within the hotel and divided
into two; ask for the warmer, gilded back room.
➜ Warm salad of poached native lobster tail with spring vegetables. Saddle of Lune
Valley lamb with garlic and rosemary. Passion fruit soufflé with dark chocolate sauce.

Aquavit XX ᰔ 🗚 ⇔ 🕮

St James's Market, 1 Carlton St ⊠ SW1Y 4QQ Plan: **I3**
– ⓜ Piccadilly Circus – ℰ (020) 7024 9848 – www.aquavitrestaurants.com
– Closed 24-26 December and 1 January
Menu £ 29 (lunch) – Carte £ 26/67
• Scandinavian • Brasserie • Elegant •
Unlike the original in NYC, this Aquavit comes in the form of a warmly lit,
relaxed brasserie. The Scandinavian cooking may also be less intricate but it's
still immeasurably appealing. Kick things off by heading straight to the smör-
gåsbord section and some wonderful herring or shrimp.
➜ Smoked eel with charred spring cabbage. Boned trout, dill, almond and
capers. Arctic bird's nest.

Chutney Mary XxX 🗚 ⇔ 🕅

73 St James's St ⊠ SW1A 1PH – ⓜ Green Park Plan: **H4**
– ℰ (020) 7629 6688 – www.chutneymary.com – Closed 25 December
Menu £ 28 (weekday lunch) – Carte £ 34/77
• Indian • Elegant • Design •
One of London's pioneering Indian restaurants, set in the heart of St James's.
Elegant surroundings feature bold art and Indian artefacts. Spicing is understa-
ted, classics are done well, and some regional dishes have been subtly updated.

Milos XxX ᰔ 🗚 ⇔

1 Regent St ⊠ SW1Y 4NR – ⓜ Piccadilly Circus Plan: **I3**
– ℰ (020) 7839 2080 – www.milos.ca – Closed 25 December and
1 January
Menu £ 29/49 – Carte £ 58/131
• Seafood • Elegant • Luxury •
London's branch of this international group of Greek seafood estiatorios makes
the most of the grand listed building it occupies. Choose from the impressive
display of fish flown in daily from Greek waters – and prepare for a sizeable bill.

The Wolseley XxX 🗚 ⇔ 🕅

160 Piccadilly ⊠ W1J 9EB – ⓜ Green Park – ℰ (020) Plan: **H4**
74996996 – www.thewolseley.com – Closed dinner 24 December
Carte £ 23/69 – *(booking essential)*
• Modern cuisine • Fashionable •
This feels like a grand and glamorous European coffee house, with its pillars
and high vaulted ceiling. Appealing menus offer everything from caviar to a
hotdog. It's open from early until late and boasts a large celebrity following.

Al Duca XX 🗚 🕮

4-5 Duke of York St ⊠ SW1Y 6LA – ⓜ Piccadilly Circus Plan: **H4**
– ℰ (020) 7839 3090 – www.alduca-restaurant.co.uk – Closed Easter, 25-
26 December, 1 January, Sunday and bank holidays
Menu £ 17 (dinner)/30 – Carte £ 26/45
• Italian • Friendly •
Cooking which focuses on flavour continues to draw in the regulars at this
warm and spirited Italian restaurant. Prices are keen when one considers the
central location and service is brisk and confident.

Avenue XX 🏡 ᴋ 🎔 🕅

7-9 St James's St. ✉ *SW1A 1EE –* Ⓜ *Green Park*   Plan: **H4**
– ℰ (020) 7321 2111 – www.avenue-restaurant.co.uk – Closed Sunday dinner and bank holidays
Menu £ 25 (weekdays) – Carte dinner £ 32/80
• Modern cuisine • Elegant •
Mayfair meets Manhattan at this buzzing, all-American restaurant with a light, bright interior designed by Russell Sage. Enjoy buttermilk pancakes at brunch and grain-fed USDA New York strip for dinner; cocktails add to the fun.

Brumus – Haymarket Hotel XX ᴋ 🕅 🚗

1 Suffolk Pl ✉ *SW1Y 4HX –* Ⓜ *Piccadilly Circus*   Plan: **I4**
– ℰ (020) 74704000 – www.haymarkethotel.com
Menu £ 20 – Carte £ 24/62
• Modern cuisine • Fashionable • Romantic •
Pre-theatre dining is an altogether less frenzied activity when you can actually see the theatre from your table. This is a modern, elegant space with switched-on staff. Stick to the good value set menu or the 'dish of the day'.

Cafe Murano XX 🎔 🕅

33 St. James's St ✉ *SW1A 1HD –* Ⓜ *Green Park*   Plan: **H4**
– ℰ (0203) 371 5559 – www.cafemurano.co.uk – Closed Sunday dinner
Menu £ 23 (lunch and early dinner)/23 – Carte £ 26/43 – *(booking essential)*
• Italian • Fashionable •
Angela Hartnett and her chef have created an appealing and flexible menu of delicious North Italian delicacies – the lunch menu is very good value. It's certainly no ordinary café and its popularity means pre-booking is essential.

Le Caprice XX 🍴 🕅 🕅 🕅

Arlington House, Arlington St. ✉ *SW1A 1RJ*   Plan: **H4**
– Ⓜ *Green Park – ℰ (020) 76292239 – www.le-caprice.co.uk – Closed 24-26 December*
Menu £ 25 (lunch and early dinner) – Carte £ 33/64
• Modern cuisine • Fashionable •
For over 35 years Le Caprice's effortlessly sophisticated atmosphere and surroundings have attracted a confident and urbane clientele. The kitchen is well-practised and capable and there's something for everyone on their catch-all menu.

45 Jermyn St XX 🏡 🕅 🕅

45 Jermyn St. ✉ *SW1 6DN –* Ⓜ *Piccadilly Circus*   Plan: **H4**
– ℰ (020) 72054545 – www.45jermynst.com – Closed 25-26 December
Menu £ 30 (weekday dinner) – Carte £ 24/67
• Modern British • Brasserie • Elegant •
What was Fortnum & Mason's Fountain restaurant for 60 years is now a bright, contemporary brasserie. The sodas, coupes and floats pay tribute to its past and cooking has a strong British element. Prices can be steep but, in contrast, the well-chosen wine list has very restrained mark-ups.

Franco's XX 🕅 🕅

61 Jermyn St ✉ *SW1Y 6LX –* Ⓜ *Green Park – ℰ (020)*   Plan: **H4**
74992211 – www.francoslondon.com – Closed Sunday and bank holidays
Menu £ 26/36 – Carte £ 28/66 – *(booking essential)*
• Italian • Traditional décor • Romantic •
Open from breakfast until late, with a café at the front leading into a smart, clubby restaurant. The menu covers all parts of Italy and includes a popular grill section and plenty of classics.

Game Bird – Stafford Hotel

XX 点 AC ⇔

16-18 St James's Pl. ⊠ *SW1A 1NJ –* Ⓜ *Green Park*   Plan: **H4**
– ℰ *(020) 7493 0111 – www.thestaffordlondon.com*
Menu £ 25 – Carte £ 32/72
• **Modern British** • Classic décor •

A hotel dining room is not for everyone but the warmth of the service, the discreet atmosphere and the classic British dishes prepared with care and understanding make this a worthwhile choice. Smoked and cured salmon and game are specialities.

Ginza Onodera

XX AC ⇔

15 Bury St ⊠ *SW1Y 6AL –* Ⓜ *Green Park –* ℰ *(020)*   Plan: **H4**
7839 1101 – www.onodera-group.com – Closed 25 December and
1 January
Menu £ 23 (lunch) – Carte £ 25/70
• **Japanese** • Elegant • Design •

Re-fitted and re-launched in 2017 on the site of what was Matsuri for over 20 years. A staircase leads down to the smart restaurant and the three counters: for sushi, teppanyaki and the robata grill. The emphasis is on traditional Japanese cuisine and top-end ingredients.

Quaglino's

XX AC ⇔ 🕸

16 Bury St ⊠ *SW1Y 6AJ –* Ⓜ *Green Park –* ℰ *(020)*   Plan: **H4**
79306767 – www.quaglinos-restaurant.co.uk – Closed Easter Monday and
Sunday dinner
Menu £ 23 (weekdays)/33 – Carte £ 37/68
• **Modern cuisine** • Design • Romantic •

This colourful, glamorous restaurant manages to be cavernous and cosy at the same time, with live music and a late night bar adding a certain sultriness to proceedings. The kitchen specialises in contemporary brasserie-style food.

Sake No Hana

XX AC

23 St James's ⊠ *SW1A 1HA –* Ⓜ *Green Park –* ℰ *(020)*   Plan: **H4**
7925 8988 – www.sakenohana.com – Closed 25 December and Sunday
Menu £ 31 – Carte £ 24/121
• **Japanese** • Minimalist • Fashionable •

A modern Japanese restaurant within a Grade II listed '60s edifice – and proof that you can occasionally find good food at the end of an escalator. As with the great cocktails, the menu is best enjoyed when shared with a group.

Chop Shop

X 点 AC 🕸

66 Haymarket ⊠ *SW1Y 4RF –* Ⓜ *Piccadilly Circus*   Plan: **I3**
– ℰ *(020) 7842 8501 – www.chopshopuk.com*
Menu £ 22 (lunch and early dinner)/35 – Carte £ 21/50
• **Meats and grills** • Simple • Friendly •

Spread over two floors and with an ersatz-industrial look, this lively spot could be in Manhattan's Meatpacking district. Start with a cocktail, then order 'jars', 'crocks' or 'planks' of mousses, meatballs and cheeses; then it's the main event – great steaks and chops.

Portrait

X ≤ AC 🕸

National Portrait Gallery (3rd floor), St Martin's Pl.   Plan: **I3**
⊠ *WC2H 0HE –* Ⓜ *Charing Cross –* ℰ *(020) 73122490*
– www.npg.org.uk/portraitrestaurant – Closed 24-26 December
Menu £ 32 – Carte £ 36/48 – *(lunch only and dinner Thursday-Saturday)*
(booking essential)
• **Modern cuisine** • Design •

Set on the top floor of National Portrait Gallery with rooftop local landmark views: a charming spot to dine or enjoy breakfast or afternoon tea. Carefully prepared modern European dishes; good value pre-theatre and weekend set menus.

Shoryu

9 Regent St. ✉ *SW1Y 4LR* – Ⓜ *Piccadilly Circus* – ✆ *(020) 3405 1391* – *www.shoryuramen.com* – *Closed 25 December and 1 January*

Plan: **I3**

Carte £ 15/33 – *(bookings not accepted)*

• Japanese • Simple •

Owned by the Japan Centre opposite and specialising in Hakata tonkotsu ramen. The base is a milky broth made from pork bones to which is added hosomen noodles, egg and assorted toppings. Its restorative powers are worth queuing for. There are two larger branches in Soho.

Ritz

150 Piccadilly ✉ *W1J 9BR* – Ⓜ *Green Park* – ✆ *(020) 74938181* – *www.theritzlondon.com*

Plan: **H4**

136 rm – †£ 430/1130 ††£ 430/1130 – ☕ £ 39 – 24 suites

• Grand Luxury • Classic • Grand luxury •

World famous hotel, opened in 1906 as a fine example of Louis XVI architecture and decoration. Elegant Palm Court famed for its afternoon tea. Many of the lavishly appointed and luxurious rooms and suites overlook the park.

✿ **Ritz Restaurant** – See restaurant listing

Haymarket

1 Suffolk Pl. ✉ *SW1Y 4HX* – Ⓜ *Piccadilly Circus* – ✆ *(020) 74704000* – *www.haymarkethotel.com*

Plan: **I4**

50 rm – †£ 276/648 ††£ 276/648 – ☕ £ 14 – 3 suites

• Luxury • Personalised • Contemporary •

Smart and spacious hotel in John Nash Regency building, with a stylish blend of modern and antique furnishings. Large, comfortable bedrooms in soothing colours. Impressive basement pool is often used for private parties.

Brumus – See restaurant listing

Sofitel London St James

6 Waterloo Pl. ✉ *SW1Y 4AN* – Ⓜ *Piccadilly Circus* – ✆ *(020) 77472200* – *www.sofitelstjames.com*

Plan: **AP3**

183 rm – †£ 350/663 ††£ 350/683 – ☕ £ 25 – 18 suites

• Luxury • Elegant •

Great location for this international hotel in a Grade II former bank. The triple-glazed bedrooms are immaculately kept; the spa is one of the best around. The bar is inspired by Coco Chanel; the lounge by an English rose garden. Balcon is a grand brasserie in a former banking hall.

Dukes

35 St James's Pl. ✉ *SW1A 1NY* – Ⓜ *Green Park* – ✆ *(020) 74914840* – *www.dukeshotel.com*

Plan: **AM4**

90 rm – †£ 376/540 ††£ 376/540 – ☕ £ 24 – 6 suites

• Traditional • Luxury • Classic •

The wonderfully located Dukes has been steadily updating its image over the last few years, despite being over a century old. Bedrooms are now fresh and uncluttered and the atmosphere less starchy. GBR restaurant offers an all-day menu of British dishes and also serves afternoon tea.

Stafford

16-18 St James's Pl. ✉ *SW1A 1NJ* – Ⓜ *Green Park* – ✆ *(020) 7493 0111* – *www.thestaffordlondon.com*

Plan: **H4**

104 rm – †£ 348/678 ††£ 390/720 – ☕ £ 31 – 15 suites

• Luxury • Elegant •

Styles itself as a 'country house in the city'; its bedrooms are divided between the main house, converted 18C stables and a more modern mews. The legendary American bar is certainly worth a visit.

Game Bird – See restaurant listing

St James's Hotel and Club
7-8 Park Pl. ⊠ *SW1A 1LS –* Ⓜ *Green Park –* ℰ *(020)* Plan: **H4**
73161600 – www.stjameshotelandclub.com
60 rm – †£ 295/580 ††£ 295/580 – ⌲ £ 20 – 10 suites
• Business • Modern •
1890s house, formerly a private club, in a wonderfully central yet quiet location. Modern, boutique-style interior with over 300 European works of art from the '20s to the '50s. Fine finish to the compact but well-equipped bedrooms.
❀ **Seven Park Place** – See restaurant listing

STRAND – COVENT GARDEN – LAMBETH PLAN III

STRAND AND COVENT GARDEN

❀ ### L'Atelier de Joël Robuchon Ⅹ ♿ 🅰🄲 📶
13-15 West St. ⊠ *WC2H 9NE –* Ⓜ *Leicester Square* Plan: **I3**
– ℰ *(020) 70108600 – www.joelrobuchon.co.uk – Closed 25-26 December, 1 January and August bank holiday Monday*
Menu £ 45 (lunch and early dinner) – Carte £ 64/119
• French • Elegant • Contemporary décor •
Ground floor L'Atelier, with counter dining and chefs on view; La Cuisine upstairs offers table dining in an intimate setting just a few nights a week. Assured, accomplished cooking with an emphasis on the Mediterranean; dishes are creative and well-balanced, with a pleasing simplicity to their presentation.
➔ Langoustine and truffle ravioli with savoy cabbage. Fillet of beef fillet with Malabar pepper and spring vegetables. Passion fruit soufflé with exotic fruit sorbet.

⊛ ### Cinnamon Bazaar Ⅹ 🅰🄲 ⇔
28 Maiden Ln ⊠ *WC2E 7JS –* Ⓜ *Leicester Square* Plan: **J3**
– ℰ *(020) 7395 1400 – www.cinnamon-bazaar.com*
Menu £ 16/24 – Carte £ 20/31
• Indian • Exotic décor • Friendly •
Vivek Singh's latest venture provides relaxed, all-day contemporary Indian dining in the heart of Covent Garden, with a bright, colourful interior evoking a marketplace. Menus are influenced by the trade routes of the subcontinent, with twists that encompass Afghanistan, the Punjab and the Middle East.

🅝 ### Delaunay ⅩⅩⅩ 🅰🄲 ⇔
55 Aldwych ⊠ *WC2B 4BB –* Ⓜ *Temple –* ℰ *(020)* Plan: **J3**
74998558 – www.thedelaunay.com – Closed 25 December
Carte £ 27/70 – *(booking essential)*
• Modern cuisine • Elegant • Fashionable •
The Delaunay was inspired by the grand cafés of Europe but, despite sharing the same buzz and celebrity clientele as its sibling The Wolseley, is not just a mere replica. The all-day menu is more mittel-European, with great schnitzels and wieners.

🅝 ### The Ivy ⅩⅩⅩ 🅰🄲 ⇔ 📶
9 West St ⊠ *WC2H 9NE –* Ⓜ *Leicester Square –* ℰ *(020)* Plan: **I3**
7836 4751 – www.the-ivy.co.uk – Closed 25 December
Menu £ 24 (weekday lunch) – Carte £ 31/70
• Traditional British • Fashionable • Classic décor •
This landmark restaurant has had a facelift and while the glamorous clientele remain, it now has an oval bar as its focal point. The menu offers international dishes alongside the old favourites and personable staff anticipate your every need.

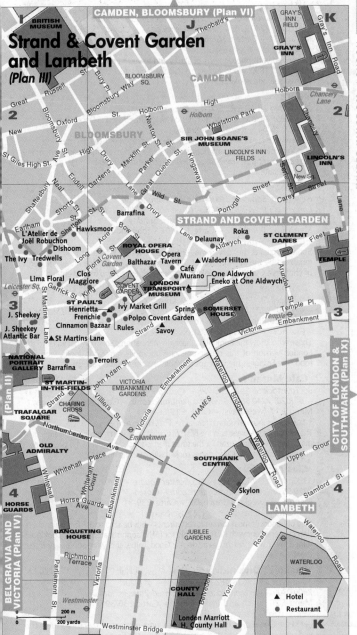

Strand & Covent Garden and Lambeth
(Plan III)

CAMDEN, BLOOMSBURY (Plan VI)

GRAY'S INN FIELD

BRITISH MUSEUM

Theobald's

GRAY'S INN

BLOOMSBURY SQ.

CAMDEN

Russell St.

Bury Pl.

Bloomsbury Way

Holborn

High

Holborn

Chancery Lane

Great

Oxford St.

New

Bloomsbury

High

BLOOMSBURY

Newton St.

Whetstone Park

SIR JOHN SOANE'S MUSEUM

LINCOLN'S INN FIELDS

LINCOLN'S INN

St Giles High St.

Shaftesbury Ave.

Neal St.

Drury

Macklin St.

Parker St.

Great Queen St.

Kingsway

New Sq.

Portugal Street

Carey

Serle St.

Earlham St.

Shorts Gardens

Endell St.

Lane

Great Wild St.

STRAND AND COVENT GARDEN

Barrafina

Drury

Lane

Delaunay

Roka

ST CLEMENT DANES

Fleet St.

L'Atelier de Joël Robuchon

Hawksmoor

Shelton St.

Bow St.

Aldwych

Dishoom

Long Acre

Floral St.

ROYAL OPERA HOUSE

Opera Tavern

Balthazar

Waldorf Hilton

TEMPLE

The Ivy

Tredwells

Covent Garden

Café Murano

One Aldwych

Eneko at One Aldwych

Lima Floral

Clos Maggiore

Garrick St.

King St.

COVENT GARDEN

LONDON TRANSPORT MUSEUM

Spring

SOMERSET HOUSE

Temple Pl.

Leicester Sq.

St Martins Ln.

ST PAUL'S

Henrietta

Ivy Market Grill

Temple

Embankment

J. Sheekey

Frenchie

Polpo Covent Garden

Strand

Cinnamon Bazaar

Rules

Savoy

Victoria

J. Sheekey Atlantic Bar

St Martins Lane

NATIONAL PORTRAIT GALLERY

Terroirs

John Adam St.

Embankment

Barrafina

ST MARTIN-IN-THE-FIELDS

VICTORIA EMBANKMENT GARDENS

Strand

CHARING CROSS

Villiers St.

Victoria

THAMES

Waterloo Bridge

TRAFALGAR SQUARE

Northumberland

Embankment

CITY OF LONDON & SOUTHWARK (Plan IX)

OLD ADMIRALTY

Ave

Upper Ground

Stamford St.

Whitehall

Whitehall Place

Whitehall Court

SOUTHBANK CENTRE

Waterloo Road

HORSE GUARDS

Horse Guards Ave

Embankment

Skylon

LAMBETH

BELGRAVIA AND VICTORIA (Plan IV)

BANQUETING HOUSE

Whitehall

JUBILEE GARDENS

Waterloo

Richmond Terrace

Road

WATERLOO

Parliament St.

Victoria

Westminster

COUNTY HALL

York Road

Belvedere

London Marriott H. County Hall

Westminster Bridge

200 m

200 yards

▲ Hotel

● Restaurant

UNITED KINGDOM - LONDON

(Plan II)

739

UNITED KINGDOM - LONDON

J.Sheekey
XX & AC

28-32 St Martin's Ct ⊠ *WC2N 4AL –* Ⓜ *Leicester Square*   Plan: I3
– ℰ *(020) 7240 2565 – www.j-sheekey.co.uk – Closed 25-26 December*
Menu £ 24 – Carte £ 36/58 – *(booking essential)*
• Seafood • Fashionable •
Festooned with photographs of actors and linked to the theatrical world since opening in 1890. Wood panels and alcove tables add famed intimacy. Accomplished seafood cooking.

Rules
XX AC ⇦

35 Maiden Ln ⊠ *WC2E 7LB –* Ⓜ *Leicester Square*   Plan: J3
– ℰ *(020) 78365314 – www.rules.co.uk – Closed 25-26 December*
Carte £ 36/64 – *(booking essential)*
• Traditional British • Traditional décor • Elegant •
London's oldest restaurant boasts a fine collection of antique cartoons, drawings and paintings. Tradition continues in the menu, specialising in game from its own estate.

Spring
XX & AC ⇦

New Wing, Somerset House, Strand (Entrance on   Plan: J3
Lancaster Pl) ⊠ *WC2R 1LA –* Ⓜ *Temple –* ℰ *(020) 3011 0115*
– www.springrestaurant.co.uk – Closed Sunday
Menu £ 32 (lunch)/32 – Carte £ 39/67 – *(booking advisable)*
• Italian • Fashionable • Elegant •
Spring occupies the 'new wing' of Somerset House that for many years was inhabited by the Inland Revenue. It's a bright, feminine space under the aegis of chef Skye Gyngell. Her cooking is Italian-influenced and ingredient-led.

Balthazar
XX & AC ⇦ 🕸

4-6 Russell St. ⊠ *WC2B 5HZ –* Ⓜ *Covent Garden*   Plan: J3
– ℰ *(020) 3301 1155 – www.balthazarlondon.com – Closed 25 December*
Menu £ 20 (lunch and early dinner) – Carte £ 31/62 – *(booking essential)*
• French • Brasserie • Classic décor •
Those who know the original Balthazar in Manhattan's SoHo district will find the London version of this classic brasserie uncannily familiar in looks, vibe and food. The Franglais menu keeps it simple and the cocktails are great.

Cafe Murano
XX AC 🕸

36 Tavistock St ⊠ *WC2E 7PB –* Ⓜ *Charing Cross*   Plan: J3
– ℰ *(020) 7240 3654 – www.cafemurano.co.uk – Closed Sunday dinner*
Menu £ 17 (weekdays) – Carte £ 19/38
• Italian • Neighbourhood • Fashionable •
The second Cafe Murano is in the heart of Covent Garden, in a space much larger than the St James's original; head for the smart marble-topped counter at the back. Appealing menu of Northern Italian dishes cooked with care and respect.

Clos Maggiore
XX 🌿 AC ⇦ 🕸

33 King St ⊠ *WC2E 8JD –* Ⓜ *Leicester Square –* ℰ *(020)*   Plan: J3
7379 9696 – www.closmaggiore.com – Closed 24-25 December
Menu £ 28 (weekday lunch)/38 – Carte £ 39/81
• French • Classic décor • Romantic •
One of London's most romantic restaurants – but be sure to ask for the enchanting conservatory with its retractable roof. The sophisticated French cooking is joined by a wine list of great depth. Good value and very popular pre/post theatre menus.

Eneko at One Aldwych – One Aldwych Hotel
XX & AC 🕸

1 Aldwych ⊠ *WC2B 4BZ –* Ⓜ *Temple –* ℰ *(020)*   Plan: J3
7300 0300 – www.eneko.london – Closed 2 weeks January
Menu £ 25 (lunch and early dinner) – Carte £ 30/39
• Basque • Design • Elegant •
Set in the One Aldwych Hotel, this stylish, ultra-modern restaurant features curved semi-private booths and a bar which seems to float above like a spaceship. Menus offer a refined reinterpretation of classic Basque dishes.

Ivy Market Grill
XX 🍴 ৬ ẩ ⇄ 🕸

1 Henrietta St ⊠ *WC2E 8PS* – ⓜ *Covent Garden*
– ☎ *(020) 3301 0200 – www.theivymarketgrill.com* Plan: **J3**
Menu £ 21 (early dinner) – Carte £ 27/61
• Traditional British • Design • Brasserie •
Mere mortals can now experience a little of that Ivy glamour by eating here at the first of their diffusion line. Breakfast, a menu of largely British classics and afternoon tea keep it busy all day. There's another branch in Chelsea.

Roka
XX ৬ ẩ 🕸

71 Aldwych ⊠ *WC2B 4HN* – ⓜ *Temple* – ☎ *(020)* Plan: **J3**
7294 7636 – www.rokarestaurant.com – Closed 25 December
Menu £ 31 (weekday lunch) – Carte £ 32/85
• Japanese • Fashionable • Design •
This is the fourth and largest Roka in the group. It shares the same stylish look, efficient service and modern Japanese food, although there are some dishes unique to this branch. Consider the tasting menu for a good all-around experience.

J.Sheekey Atlantic Bar
X 🍴 ৬

33-34 St Martin's Ct. ⊠ *WC2 4AL* – ⓜ *Leicester Square* Plan: **I3**
– ☎ *(020) 72402565 – www.j-sheekey.co.uk – Closed 25-26 December*
Carte £ 25/38 – (booking advisable)
• Seafood • Intimate •
An addendum to J. Sheekey restaurant. Sit at the bar to watch the chefs prepare the same quality seafood as next door but at slightly lower prices; fish pie and fruits de mer are the popular choices. Open all day.

Barrafina
X ẩ ⇄

10 Adelaide St ⊠ *WC2N 4HZ* – ⓜ *Charing Cross* Plan: **I3**
– ☎ *(020) 7440 1456 – www.barrafina.co.uk – Closed Christmas, New Year and bank holidays*
Carte £ 15/41 – (bookings not accepted)
• Spanish • Tapas bar • Trendy •
The second Barrafina is not just brighter than the Soho original – it's bigger too, so you can wait inside with a drink for counter seats to become available. Try more unusual tapas like ortiguillas, frit Mallorquin or the succulent meats.

Barrafina
X 🍴 ẩ ⇄

43 Drury Ln ⊠ *WC2B 5AJ* – ⓜ *Covent Garden* – ☎ *(020)* Plan: **J3**
7440 1456 – www.barrafina.co.uk – Closed bank holidays
Carte £ 28/41 – (bookings not accepted)
• Spanish • Tapas bar • Simple •
The third of the Barrafinas is tucked away at the far end of Covent Garden; arrive early or prepare to queue. Fresh, vibrantly flavoured fish and shellfish dishes are a real highlight; tortillas y huevos also feature.

Dishoom
X 🍴 ẩ

12 Upper St Martin's Ln ⊠ *WC2H 9FB* Plan: **I3**
– ⓜ *Leicester Square* – ☎ *(020) 7420 9320 – www.dishoom.com*
– *Closed 24 December dinner, 25-26 December and 1-2 January*
Carte £ 12/26 – (booking advisable)
• Indian • Trendy • Trendy •
A facsimile of a Bombay café, of the sort opened by Persian immigrants in the early 20C. Try baked roti rolls with chai, vada pav (Bombay's version of the chip butty), a curry or grilled meats. There's another branch in Shoreditch.

Frenchie
X ৬ ẩ

16 Henrietta St ⊠ *WC2E 8QH* – ⓜ *Covent Garden* Plan: **J3**
– ☎ *(020) 78364222 – www.frenchiecoventgarden.com – Closed 25-26 December and 1 January*
Menu £ 26 (weekday lunch) – Carte £ 43/58 – (booking advisable)
• Modern cuisine • Bistro • Design •
A well-run modern-day bistro – younger sister to the Paris original, which shares the name given to chef-owner Greg Marchand when he was head chef at Fifteen. The adventurous, ambitious cooking is informed by his extensive travels.

Hawksmoor

X ⅍ 🔤 ⇄ 🈳

11 Langley St ⊠ WC2H 9JG – ⓜ *Covent Garden* Plan: I3
– ℰ (020) 7420 9390 – www.thehawksmoor.com – Closed 24-26 December
Menu £ 25 (weekdays)/28 – Carte £ 25/75
• Meats and grills • Rustic • Brasserie •
Steaks from Longhorn cattle lovingly reared in North Yorkshire and dry-aged for
at least 35 days are the stars of the show. Atmospheric, bustling basement res-
taurant in former brewery cellars.

Henrietta – Henrietta Hotel

X ⅙ 🔤

14-15 Henrietta St ⊠ WC2E 8QH – ⓜ *Covent Garden* Plan: J3
– ℰ (020) 3794 5314 – www.henriettahotel.com
Carte £ 29/47 – *(booking advisable)*
• Modern cuisine • Fashionable • Friendly •
An informal, lounge-style hotel restaurant and cocktail bar. The ingredient-led
menu follows the seasons and cooking has an appealing modern style, with
well-defined yet delicate flavours. Madeleines make an excellent end to the
meal.

Lima Floral

X 🔤 ⇄ 🈳

14 Garrick St ⊠ WC2E 9BJ – ⓜ *Leicester Square* Plan: I3
*– ℰ (020) 7240 5778 – www.limalondongroup.com/floral – Closed 25-
27 December, 1-2 January and bank holiday Mondays*
Menu £ 20 (early dinner) – Carte £ 33/52
• Peruvian • Fashionable • Friendly •
This second Lima branch has a light and airy feel by day and a cosy, candlelit
vibe in the evening; regional Peruvian dishes are served alongside the more
popular causa and ceviche. Basement Pisco Bar for Peruvian tapas and Pisco
sours.

Opera Tavern

X ⅍ 🔤

23 Catherine St. ⊠ WC2B 5JS – ⓜ *Covent Garden* Plan: J3
*– ℰ (020) 7836 3680 – www.operatavern.co.uk – Closed 25 December and
1 January*
Menu £ 21 (lunch) – Carte £ 14/29
• Mediterranean cuisine • Tapas bar • Wine bar •
Another in the Salt Yard stable, this former pub has a lively ground floor and a
quieter first floor dining room. Spanish-Italian menus follow the seasons, with a
selection of flavourful small plates designed for sharing.

Polpo Covent Garden

X 🔤

6 Maiden Ln. ⊠ WC2E 7NA – ⓜ *Leicester Square* Plan: J3
– ℰ (020) 7836 8448 – www.polpo.co.uk – Closed 25-26 December
Carte £ 13/21 – *(bookings not accepted at dinner)*
• Italian • Simple • Trendy •
First Soho, then Covent Garden got a fun Venetian bacaro. The small plates are
surprisingly filling, with delights such as pizzette of white anchovy vying with
fennel and almond salad; fritto misto competing with spaghettini and meat-
balls.

Terroirs

X ⅍ 🔤

5 William IV St ⊠ WC2N 4DW – ⓜ *Charing Cross* Plan: J3
*– ℰ (020) 70360660 – www.terroirswinebar.com – Closed 25-26 December,
1 January, Sunday and bank holidays*
Carte £ 26/72
• Mediterranean cuisine • Wine bar • Simple •
Flavoursome French cooking, with extra Italian and Spanish influences and a
thoughtfully compiled wine list. Eat in the lively ground floor bistro/wine bar
or in the more intimate cellar, where they also offer some sharing dishes like
rib of beef for two.

Tredwell's

4a Upper St Martin's Ln ✉ *WC2H 9EF*
Plan: **I3**
– ⓜ *Leicester Square* – ☏ *(020) 3764 0840 – www.tredwells.com – Closed 24-26 December and 1 January*
Menu £ 30 (lunch and early dinner) – Carte £ 27/56
• Modern British • Brasserie • Fashionable •
A modern brasserie from Marcus Wareing, with an art deco feel. Cooking is best described as modern English; dishes show a degree of refinement, and a commendable amount of thought has gone into addressing allergen issues.

Savoy

Strand ✉ *WC2R 0EU* – ⓜ *Charing Cross* – ☏ *(020)*
Plan: **J3**
78364343 – www.fairmont.com/savoy
267 rm – ♦£ 420/1500 ♦♦£ 420/1500 – ⌹ £ 35 – 45 suites
• Grand Luxury • Art déco • Elegant •
One of the grande dames of London's hotel scene. Luxurious bedrooms come in Edwardian or Art Deco styles; many have magnificent views over the Thames and the stunning suites pay homage to past guests. Enjoy tea in the Thames Foyer; sip a cocktail in the iconic American Bar or elegant Beaufort bar. Dine in the famous Savoy Grill or enjoy seafood and steaks in Kaspar's.

One Aldwych

1 Aldwych ✉ *WC2B 4BZ* – ⓜ *Temple* – ☏ *(020)*
Plan: **J3**
73001000 – www.onealdwych.com
105 rm – ♦£ 324/576 ♦♦£ 324/576 – ⌹ £ 29 – 12 suites
• Grand Luxury • Modern • Elegant •
A stylish, modern hotel featuring over 400 pieces of contemporary artwork. Bedrooms are understated in style with fine linen, iPod docking stations, and fresh fruit and flowers daily. Charlie and the Chocolate Factory themed afternoon tea. Gluten and dairy-free British dishes in Indigo; Basque cooking in Eneko.
⓸○ **Eneko at One Aldwych** – See restaurant listing

Waldorf Hilton

Aldwych ✉ *WC2B 4DD* – ⓜ *Temple* – ☏ *(020)*
Plan: **J3**
7836 2400 – www.waldorf.hilton.com
298 rm – ♦£ 289/600 ♦♦£ 289/600 – ⌹ £ 25 – 12 suites
• Historic • Elegant •
Impressive curved and columned façade: an Edwardian landmark in a great location. Stylish, contemporary bedrooms in calming colours have superb bathrooms and all mod cons. Tea dances in the Grade II listed Palm Court Ballroom. Stylish 'Homage' is popular for afternoon tea and relaxed brasserie style dining.

St Martins Lane

45 St Martin's Ln ✉ *WC2N 3HX* – ⓜ *Charing Cross*
Plan: **I3**
– ☏ *(020) 7300 5500 – www.morganshotelgroup.com*
204 rm – ♦£ 219/399 ♦♦£ 219/459 – ⌹ £ 18 – 2 suites
• Luxury • Design •
The unmistakable hand of Philippe Starck is evident at this most contemporary of hotels. Unique and stylish, from the starkly modern lobby to the state-of-the-art bedrooms, which come in a blizzard of white.

Henrietta

14-15 Henrietta St ✉ *WC2E 8QH* – ⓜ *Covent Garden*
Plan: **J3**
– ☏ *(020) 3794 5313 – www.henriettahotel.com*
18 rm – ♦£ 220/500 ♦♦£ 220/500 – ⌹ £ 20
• Boutique hotel • Townhouse • Design •
Cosy boutique townhouse in the heart of Covent Garden; stylish, contemporary bedrooms offer good facilities including Bluetooth speakers and Nespresso machines. Ask for one of the quieter rooms at the back; 18, with its balcony and city views, is best. Cocktail bar and restaurant serving original modern dishes.
⓸○ **Henrietta** – See restaurant listing

LAMBETH

Skylon
XxX 🏵 ⩽ 🔟 🈂️

1 Southbank Centre, Belvedere Rd ✉ *SE1 8XX*   Plan: **J4**
– Ⓜ *Waterloo*
– 𝒞 *(020) 76547800 – www.skylon-restaurant.co.uk*
– *Closed 25 December*
Menu £ 30/35
– Carte £ 39/58
• Modern cuisine • Design • Trendy •

Ask for a window table here at the Royal Festival Hall. Informal grill-style operation on one side, a more formal and expensive restaurant on the other, with a busy cocktail bar in the middle.

London Marriott H. County Hall
🏶 ⩽ 🛁 🌐 🍽 🔟 ⴺ 🔟

Westminster Bridge Rd ✉ *SE1 7PB* – Ⓜ *Westminster*   ⛴
– 𝒞 *(020) 79285200 – www.marriott.co.uk/lonch*   Plan: **J5**
206 rm – ✝£ 260/600 ✝✝£ 260/900
– ☲ £ 17 – 5 suites
• Business • Chain • Modern •

Occupying the historic County Hall building on the banks of the River Thames. Bedrooms are spacious, stylish and modern; many enjoy river and Parliament outlooks. Impressive leisure facilities. World famous views too from wood-panelled Gillray's, which specialises in steaks.

BELGRAVIA – VICTORIA   PLAN IV

BELGRAVIA

✿✿ Marcus – Berkeley Hotel
XxxX 🏵 🔟 ⇔ 🍽

Wilton Pl ✉ *SW1X 7RL* – Ⓜ *Knightsbridge* – 𝒞 *(020)*   Plan: **G4**
72351200 – www.marcusrestaurant.com
– *Closed Sunday*
Menu £ 55/120
• Modern cuisine • Elegant • Intimate •

Marcus Wareing's flagship – now run by two long-serving protégés of the MasterChef judge – is elegant, stylish and eminently comfortable. The menu is flexible and dishes come with a refreshing lack of complication; they rely instead on excellent ingredients and accurate techniques to deliver well-defined flavours.

➜ Tropea onion with truffle, Old Winchester cheese and wild garlic. Goosnargh duck with chickweed, cauliflower and cumin. Yorkshire rhubarb, vanilla, mascarpone and pistachio.

✿ Céleste – The Lanesborough Hotel
XxxX ⴺ 🔟 🍽 🚗

Hyde Park Corner ✉ *SW1X 7TA* – Ⓜ *Hyde Park Corner*   Plan: **G4**
– 𝒞 *(020) 7259 5599 – www.lanesborough.com*
Menu £ 38 (lunch)
– Carte £ 77/107
• Creative French • Elegant • Luxury •

The Lanesborough Hotel's restaurant is dressed in opulent Regency clothes; its vast chandeliers, Wedgwood blue friezes and fluted columns giving it a luxurious, formal feel. Classic French cuisine is delivered in an original, modern style; the richness of the dishes reflecting the opulence of the décor.

➜ Pressed foie gras terrine, corn-fed chicken, mustard vinaigrette and brioche. Stone bass with globe artichoke, mussels and seaweed butter. Fudge ice cream with roast almonds, caramel and fudge sauce.

❀ **Pétrus** XxX ❀ ⅁ 🅰 ⇄ ⑩
1 Kinnerton St ⊠ SW1X 8EA – Ⓜ Knightsbridge Plan: **F5**
– ℰ (020) 75921609 – www.gordonramsayrestaurants.com/petrus
– Closed 21-27 December, 1 January and Sunday
Menu £ 38/85
• French • Elegant • Fashionable •
Gordon Ramsay's Belgravia restaurant is a sophisticated and elegant affair. The service is discreet and professional, and the cooking is rooted in classical techniques but isn't afraid of using influences from further afield. The superb wine list has Château Pétrus going back to 1928.
→ Curried Orkney scallop with egg sabayon, braised kombu and bacon. Poulet de Bresse with pancetta, foie gras, morels and leeks. 'Black Forest', Kirsch mousse and Morello cherry sorbet.

❀ **Amaya** XxX 🅰 ⇄ ⑩
Halkin Arcade, 19 Motcomb St ⊠ SW1X 8JT Plan: **F5**
– Ⓜ Knightsbridge – ℰ (020) 78231166 – www.amaya.biz
Menu £ 26 (weekday lunch) – Carte £ 34/78
• Indian • Design • Minimalist •
A decade and a half on and Amaya is still as bright and lively as ever, thanks to the buzz of excited diners and the theatre of its open kitchen. Order a selection of small dishes from the tawa, tandoor or sigri grill and finish with a curry or biryani. Dishes are aromatic, visually appealing and very satisfying.
→ Black pepper chicken tikka. Smoked chilli lamb chops. Almond and saffron crème brûlée.

❀ **Ametsa** – COMO The Halkin Hotel XxX 🅰
5 Halkin St ⊠ SW1X 7DJ – Ⓜ Hyde Park Corner Plan: **G5**
– ℰ (020) 73331234 – www.comohotels.com/thehalkin – Closed 24-26 December, lunch 31 December, Sunday and lunch Monday
Menu £ 29/110 – Carte £ 60/85
• Creative • Elegant • Fashionable •
Whilst the father and daughter team from the celebrated Arzak restaurant in San Sebastián are behind it, Ametsa has its own style. Most ingredients are sourced from within the British Isles but the flavours, combinations and colours are typically Basque and the dishes are wonderfully vibrant.
→ Scallops with hemp seeds. Sea bass 'Tamal'. Chocolate emeralds and strata.

⑩ **Zafferano** XxX 🍽 🅰 ⇄
15 Lowndes St ⊠ SW1X 9EY – Ⓜ Knightsbridge Plan: **F5**
– ℰ (020) 72355800 – www.zafferanorestaurant.com – Closed 25 December
Carte £ 37/84 – (booking essential)
• Italian • Fashionable • Neighbourhood •
The immaculately coiffured regulars continue to support this ever-expanding, long-standing and capably run Italian restaurant. They come for the reassuringly familiar, if rather steeply priced dishes from all parts of Italy.

⑩ **The Alfred Tennyson** 🌐 🍽 ⇄
10 Motcomb St ⊠ SW1X 8LA – Ⓜ Knightsbridge. Plan: **G5**
– ℰ (020) 77306074 – www.thealfredtennyson.co.uk – Closed 26 December-4 January
Carte £ 30/43 – (booking advisable)
• Modern British • Pub • Neighbourhood •
A cosy, enthusiastically run pub with a busy first-come-first-served ground floor and a more formal upstairs dining room. Classic dishes have light, modern touches; expect smoked mackerel, duck and venison alongside steaks, burgers and pies.

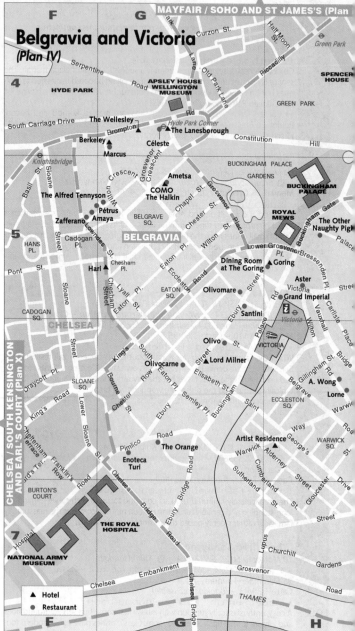

Belgravia and Victoria
(Plan IV)

UNITED KINGDOM - LONDON

HYDE PARK

Serpentine

Road

Curzon St.

Old Park Lane

Half Moon St.

Piccadilly

Green Park

SPENCER HOUSE

APSLEY HOUSE WELLINGTON MUSEUM

GREEN PARK

South Carriage Drive

Brompton

Rd

Hyde Park Corner

▲ The Lanesborough

Constitution

Hill

The Wellesley ▲

Berkeley ▲

Céleste

Marcus ▲

Knightsbridge

Basil

Sloane

Crescent

Grosvenor
Crescent

Chester St.

Grosvenor

Place

BUCKINGHAM PALACE

GARDENS

BUCKINGHAM PALACE

The Alfred Tennyson ▲

Ametsa ●

COMO
The Halkin ▲

Chapel St.

Wilton

ROYAL MEWS

Buckingham Gate

The Other Naughty Pig ●

Palace

Street

Pétrus ●

Amaya ●

Zafferano ●

Lowndes St.

Wilton Cres.

BELGRAVE SQ.

BELGRAVIA

Chester

Wilton

Lower Grosvenor

Pl.

HANS PL.

Cadogan Pl.

Pont

St.

Sloane Street

Chesham
Street

Chesham Pl.

Hari ▲

Lyall St.

EATON SQ.

Eaton Pl.

Eccleston

Road

Dining Room at The Goring ●

▲ Goring

Aster ●

Victoria

Rd

Grand Imperial ●

Victoria

VICTORIA

Lower Grosvenor

Pl.

Bressenden Pl.

Vauxhall

Carlisle Place

Olivomare ●

Santini ●

Ebury

St.

CADOGAN SQ.

CHELSEA

Sloane

Street

Eaton

King's

South
Row

Chester
St.

Bourne

St.

Ebury

Olivo ●

St.

▲ Lord Milner

Olivocarne ●

Eaton Pl.

Elisabeth St.

Semley Pl.

Buckingham

Palace

Rd

Saint

Gillingham St.

A. Wong ●

Belgrave

Lorne ●

ECCLESTON SQ.

Way

Warwi

Road

George's

WARWICK SQ.

SLOANE SQ.

Draycott Pl.

King's

Road

Lower Sloane

St.

Cheltenham
Terrace

Franklin's
Row

Burton's

Row

Pimlico

Road

The Orange ●

Enoteca Turi ●

Chelsea

Bridge

Road

Ebury
Bridge
Road

Warwick

Artist Residence ▲

Alderney

George's

Sutherland

Cumberland

St.

St.

Gloucester

Drive

Street

BURTON'S COURT

THE ROYAL HOSPITAL

Hospital

Lupus

Churchill

Grosvenor

Gardens

Road

NATIONAL ARMY MUSEUM

Chelsea

Embankment

Chelsea
Bridge

THAMES

| ▲ Hotel |
| ● Restaurant |

746

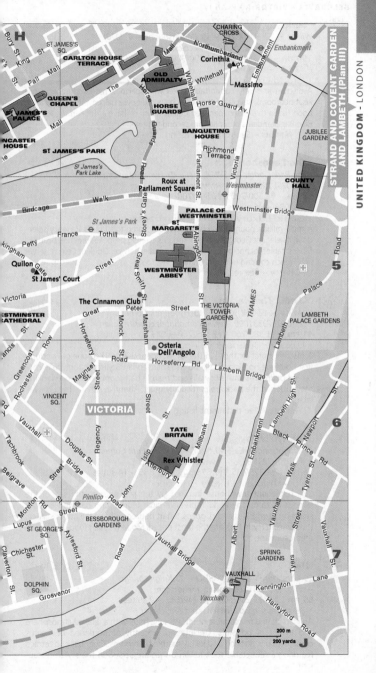

ST JAMES'S SQ.

Bury St.
St.
King
St.

Pall Mall

CARLTON HOUSE
TERRACE

CHARING
CROSS

Northumberland

Corinthia

Embankment

J

QUEEN'S
CHAPEL

's St.

Pall Mall

OLD
ADMIRALTY

The

Mall

Whitehall

Massimo

Embankment

ST JAMES'S
PALACE

LANCASTER
HOUSE

The

Mall

Horse Guards

HORSE
GUARDS

Horse Guard Av.

JUBILEE
GARDENS

ST JAMES'S PARK

St James's
Park Lake

BANQUETING
HOUSE

Richmond
Terrace

COUNTY
HALL

Guards
Road

Roux at
Parliament Square

Victoria

Westminster

Birdcage
Walk

St James's Park
Tothill
St.

France

Storey's Gate

PALACE OF
WESTMINSTER

S.T
MARGARET'S

Abingdon

Westminster Bridge

5

Road

Palace

kingham
Petty

Gate

Street

Great Smith St.

WESTMINSTER
ABBEY

LAMBETH
PALACE GARDENS

Quilon
St James' Court

Victoria

THE VICTORIA
TOWER
GARDENS

St. Margaret's

THAMES

WESTMINSTER
CATHEDRAL

The Cinnamon Club
Great

Peter
Street

Monck

Street

Lambeth

Lambeth High St.

ancis
Greencoat Pl.
Row
Rochester

Horseferry
Maunsel
St.
Street

Osteria
Dell'Angolo

Horseferry Rd

Lambeth Bridge

6

VINCENT
SQ.

Regency

Street

VICTORIA

Black

Prince

Newport

Vauxhall

St.

Tachbrook

Douglas St.

Street

Bridge

TATE
BRITAIN

Millbank

Rex Whistler

Embankment

Walk

Prince Rd

Tyers St.

Vauxhall St.

Belgrave

Street

Islip

Atterbury St.

John

Street

Vauxhall

Street

Moreton Rd
Lupus

Pimlico
Road

Street

ST GEORGE'S
SQ.

BESSBOROUGH
GARDENS

Albert

SPRING
GARDENS

Tyers

Street

7

Chichester
St.

Aylesford St.

Road

Vauxhall Bridge

Vauxhall St.

Claverton
St.

DOLPHIN
SQ.

Grosvenor

VAUXHALL

Vauxhall

Kennington

Lane

Harleyford
Road

0   200 m
0   200 yards

I

J

Berkeley

Wilton Pl ⊠ SW1X 7RL – ⓜ Knightsbridge – ✆ (020)
Plan: **G4**
72356000 – www.the-berkeley.co.uk
190 rm – †£ 330/780 ††£ 390/900
– ⊡ £ 38 – 27 suites
• Grand Luxury • Business • Elegant •
A discreet and very comfortable hotel with spacious, modern, immaculately kept bedrooms; several of the suites have their own balcony. Relax over afternoon tea in the gilded, panelled Collins Room or have a drink in the ice cool Blue Bar. Standards of service are second to none.
❀❀ **Marcus** – See restaurant listing

The Lanesborough

Hyde Park Corner ⊠ SW1X 7TA – ⓜ Hyde Park Corner
Plan: **G4**
– ✆ (020) 72595599 – www.lanesborough.com
93 rm – †£ 500/700 ††£ 500/700
.– ⊡ £ 38 – 46 suites
• Grand Luxury • Historic • Elegant •
A multi-million pound refurbishment has restored this hotel's Regency splendour; its elegant Georgian-style bedrooms offering bespoke furniture, beautiful fabrics, tablet technologies and 24 hour butler service. Opulent Céleste serves rich French cooking under its domed glass roof.
❀ **Céleste** – See restaurant listing

COMO The Halkin

5 Halkin St ⊠ SW1X 7DJ – ⓜ Hyde Park Corner
Plan: **G5**
– ✆ (020) 73331000 – www.comohotels.com/thehalkin
41 rm – †£ 385/760 ††£ 385/760 – ⊡ £ 25 – 6 suites
• Luxury • Business • Elegant •
A discreet hotel for those in the know: opened in 1991 as one of London's first boutique hotels and still looking sharp today. Stylish, thoughtfully conceived bedrooms with silk walls and marble bathrooms; those overlooking the garden at the back are particularly quiet. Attentive service; butlers available.
❀ **Ametsa** – See restaurant listing

The Wellesley

11 Knightsbridge ⊠ SW1X 7LY – ⓜ Hyde Park Corner
Plan: **G4**
– ✆ (020) 7235 3535 – www.thewellesley.co.uk
36 rm – †£ 325/445 ††£ 375/505 – ⊡ £ 35 – 14 suites
• Townhouse • Luxury • Art déco •
Stylish, elegant townhouse inspired by the jazz age, on the site of the famous Pizza on the Park. Impressive cigar lounge and bar with a super selection of whiskies and cognacs. Smart bedrooms have full butler service; those facing Hyde Park are the most prized. Modern Italian food in the discreet restaurant.

Hari

20 Chesham Pl ⊠ SW1X 8HQ – ⓜ Knightsbridge
Plan: **G5**
– ✆ (020) 7858 0100 – www.thehari.com
85 rm ⊡ – †£ 230/500 ††£ 242/512 – 9 suites
• Business • Townhouse • Modern •
An elegant and fashionable boutique-style hotel with a relaxed atmosphere and a hint of bohemia. Uncluttered, decently proportioned bedrooms come with oak flooring and lovely marble bathrooms. Cigar bar and terrace featuring a retractable roof. Italian dishes are served in the stylish restaurant.

VICTORIA

✿ **Dining Room at The Goring** – Goring Hotel XxX 🏵 � ⒶⒸ

Plan: **H5**

15 Beeston Pl ⊠ SW1W 0JW – Ⓜ Victoria – ℰ (020) 73969000 – www.thegoring.com – Closed Saturday lunch
Menu £ 35/60
• **Traditional British** • **Elegant** • **Classic décor** •

A paean to all things British and the very model of discretion and decorum – the perfect spot for those who 'like things done properly' but without the stuffiness. The menu is an appealing mix of British classics and lighter, more modern dishes, all prepared with great skill and understanding.
→ Cured sea bream with pickled lemon, iced celery and cucumber. Roast squab with Tokyo turnip, crispy leg parcel and cider vinegar sauce. Gianduja chocolate with Williams pear, caramelised hazelnut and sweet cream cheese.

✿ **Quilon** – St James' Court Hotel XxX ⒶⒸ ⇔ ⑩

Plan: **H5**

41 Buckingham Gate ⊠ SW1E 6AF – Ⓜ St James's Park – ℰ (020) 78211899 – www.quilon.co.uk – Closed 25 December
Menu £ 31/60 – Carte £ 42/57
• **Indian** • **Design** • **Elegant** •

A meal here will remind you how fresh, vibrant, colourful and healthy Indian food can be. Chef Sriram Aylur and his team focus on India's southwest coast, so the emphasis is on seafood and a lighter style of cooking. The room is stylish and comfortable and the service team, bright and enthusiastic.
→ Chargrilled scallops with pawpaw, poppy seeds and chilli relish. Panfried duck breast with coconut cream sauce. Hot vermicelli kheer with rose ice cream.

✿ **A. Wong** (Andrew Wong) X 🌅 ⒶⒸ

Plan: **H6**

70 Wilton Rd ⊠ SW1V 1DE – Ⓜ Victoria – ℰ (020) 7828 8931 – www.awong.co.uk – Closed 23 December-4 January, Sunday and lunch Monday
Menu £ 14 (weekday lunch) – Carte £ 18/42 – *(booking essential)*
• **Chinese** • **Neighbourhood** • **Neighbourhood** •

A modern Chinese restaurant with a buzzy ground floor and a sexy basement. The talented eponymous chef reinvents classic Cantonese dishes using creative, modern techniques; retaining the essence of a dish, whilst adding an impressive lightness and intensity of flavour. Service is keen, as are the prices.
→ Hong Kong egg waffle with marinated scallop salad. 'Gold Fish' dumpling with foie gras, dried pork and chive flower oil. Poached meringue with lychee granité, mango purée, orange sorbet and lotus root.

🍽 **The Cinnamon Club** XxX & ⒶⒸ ⇔ ⑩

Plan: **I5**

30-32 Great Smith St ⊠ SW1P 3BU – Ⓜ St James's Park – ℰ (020) 7222 2555 – www.cinnamonclub.com – Closed 2 April, 27 August and bank holidays
Menu £ 26 (weekday lunch) – Carte £ 35/69
• **Indian** • **Historic** • **Elegant** •

Locals and tourists, business people and politicians – this smart Indian restaurant housed in the listed former Westminster Library attracts them all. The fairly elaborate dishes arrive fully garnished and the spicing is quite subtle.

🍽 **Grand Imperial** XxX & ⒶⒸ ⇔ 🈂

Plan: **H5**

Grosvenor Hotel, 101 Buckingham Palace Rd ⊠ SW1W 0SJ – Ⓜ Victoria – ℰ (020) 7821 8898 – www.grandimperiallondon.com – Closed 25-26 December
Menu £ 16/26 – Carte £ 24/78
• **Chinese** • **Elegant** •

Grand it most certainly is, as this elegant restaurant is in the Grosvenor Hotel's former ballroom. It specialises in Cantonese cuisine, particularly the version found in Hong Kong; steaming and frying are used to great effect.

UNITED KINGDOM - LONDON

Roux at Parliament Square
Royal Institution of Chartered Surveyors, Parliament Sq.　Plan: I5
✉ SW1P 3AD – **Ⓜ** *Westminster* – *✆* (020) 73343737
– www.rouxatparliamentsquare.co.uk – Closed Christmas, Saturday,
Sunday and bank holidays
Menu £ 42 (weekday lunch)/59 – *(bookings advisable at lunch)*
• Modern cuisine • Elegant •
Light floods through the Georgian windows of this comfortable restaurant within the offices of the Royal Institute of Chartered Surveyors. Carefully crafted, elaborate and sophisticated cuisine, with some interesting flavour combinations.

Santini
29 Ebury St ✉ SW1W 0NZ – **Ⓜ** *Victoria* – *✆* (020)　Plan: G5
7730 4094 – www.santinirestaurant.com – Closed 25-26 December,
1 January dinner
Carte £ 33/81
• Italian • Fashionable • Neighbourhood •
This elegant restaurant is still pulling in the crowds over thirty years after it opened, thanks to its reliable, confident cooking and impeccable service. Classic Italian dishes have a Venetian accent and pasta's the star of the show.

Rex Whistler
Tate Britain, Millbank ✉ SW1P 4RG – **Ⓜ** *Pimlico*　Plan: I6
– ✆ (020) 78878825 – www.tate.org.uk – Closed 24-26 December
Menu £ 35 – *(lunch only)*
• Modern cuisine • Classic décor • Traditional décor •
A hidden gem, tucked away on the lower ground floor of Tate Britain; its most striking element is Whistler's restored mural, 'The Expedition in Pursuit of Rare Meats', which envelops the room. The menu is stoutly British and the remarkably priced wine list has an unrivalled 'half bottle' selection.

Aster
150 Victoria St ✉ SW1E 5LB – **Ⓜ** *Victoria* – *✆* (020)　Plan: H5
3875 5555 – www.aster-restaurant.com – Closed Sunday
Carte £ 29/58
• Modern cuisine • Contemporary décor • Fashionable •
Aster has a deli, a café, a bar and a terrace, as well the restaurant; a stylish, airy space on the first floor. The Finnish chef brings a Nordic slant to the modern French cuisine, with dishes that are light, refined and full of flavour.

Enoteca Turi
87 Pimlico Rd ✉ SW1W 8PU – **Ⓜ** *Sloane Square*　Plan: G6
– ✆ (020) 7730 3663 – www.enotecaturi.com – Closed 25-26 December,
1 January, Sunday and bank holiday lunch
Menu £ 25 (lunch) – Carte £ 31/61
• Italian • Neighbourhood •
In 2016 Putney's loss was Pimlico's gain when, after 25 years, Giuseppe and Pamela Turi had to find a new home for their Italian restaurant. They brought their warm hospitality and superb wine list with them, and the chef has introduced a broader range of influences from across the country.

Massimo – Corinthia Hotel
10 Northumberland Ave. ✉ WC2N 5AE　Plan: AQ4
*– **Ⓜ** Embankment – ✆ (020) 73213156 – www.corinthia.com/london*
– Closed Sunday
Menu £ 30 (dinner) – Carte £ 37/71
• Italian • Elegant • Fashionable •
An opulent, visually impressive restaurant in the luxurious Corinthia hotel. An all-Italian kitchen team bring their own regional influences to the menu, which offers authentic, flavourful Italian dishes including excellent pasta.

║○ **Osteria Dell' Angolo** XX 🅰️ ⇔
47 Marsham St ⊠ *SW1P 3DR* – Ⓜ *St James's Park* Plan: **I6**
– ☎ (020) 32681077 – www.osteriadellangolo.co.uk – Closed 1-4 January,
24-28 December, Easter, Saturday lunch, Sunday and bank holidays
Menu £ 23 (lunch) – Carte £ 26/47 – *(booking essential at lunch)*
• Italian • Neighbourhood • Brasserie •
At lunch, this Italian opposite the Home Office is full of bustle and men in suits; at dinner it's a little more relaxed. Staff are personable and the menu is reassuringly familiar; homemade pasta and seafood dishes are good.

║○ **Lorne** X 🕸️ 🅰️
76 Wilton Rd ⊠ *SW1V 1DE* – Ⓜ *Victoria* – ☎ *(020)* Plan: **H6**
3327 0210 – www.lornerestaurant.co.uk – Closed 1 week Christmas,
Sunday, Monday lunch and bank holiday Mondays
Menu £ 22 (lunch) – Carte £ 35/43 – *(booking essential)*
• Modern cuisine • Simple • Neighbourhood •
A small, simply furnished restaurant down a busy side street. The experienced chef understands that less is more and the modern menu is an enticing list of unfussy, well-balanced British and European dishes. Diverse wine list.

║○ **Olivo** X 🅰️
21 Eccleston St ⊠ *SW1W 9LX* – Ⓜ *Victoria* – ☎ *(020)* Plan: **G6**
77302505 – www.olivorestaurants.com – Closed lunch Saturday-Sunday
and bank holidays
Menu £ 27 (weekday lunch) – Carte £ 38/50 – *(booking essential)*
• Italian • Neighbourhood • Bistro •
A popular, pleasant and relaxed neighbourhood Italian with rough wooden floors, intimate lighting and contemporary styling. Carefully prepared, authentic and tasty dishes, with the robust flavours of Sardinia to the fore.

║○ **Olivocarne** X 🅰️
61 Elizabeth St ⊠ *SW1W 9PP* – Ⓜ *Sloane Square* Plan: **G6**
– ☎ (020) 7730 7997 – www.olivorestaurants.com
Menu £ 27 (weekday lunch) – Carte £ 39/53
• Italian • Fashionable • Neighbourhood •
Mauro Sanna seems to have this part of town sewn up! As suggested by its name, this smart, spacious restaurant focuses on meat dishes, with a selection of satisfying Sardinian specialities. Head upstairs first for a cocktail in Joe's Bar.

║○ **Olivomare** X 🍴 🅰️
10 Lower Belgrave St ⊠ *SW1W 0LJ* – Ⓜ *Victoria* Plan: **G5**
– ☎ (020) 77309022 – www.olivorestaurants.com – Closed bank holidays
Carte £ 36/49
• Seafood • Design • Neighbourhood •
Expect understated and stylish piscatorial decoration and seafood with a Sardinian base. Fortnightly changing menu, with high quality produce, much of which is available in the deli next door.

║○ **The Other Naughty Piglet** X 🕸️ ♿ 🅰️
The Other Palace, 12 Palace St ⊠ *SW1E 5JA* Plan: **H5**
– Ⓜ Victoria – ☎ (020) 7592 0322 – www.theothernaughtypiglet.co.uk
– Closed Christmas, Sunday and lunch Monday
Carte £ 25/32 – *(booking essential)*
• Modern cuisine • Simple • Neighbourhood •
A light, spacious restaurant with friendly staff and a relaxed atmosphere, set on the first floor of The Other Palace theatre. Eclectic modern small plates are designed for sharing and accompanied by an interesting list of natural wines.

🏠 **The Orange**   ⬚ ↻

37 Pimlico Rd ⊠ SW1W 8NE – Ⓜ *Sloane Square.*   Plan: **G6**
– ℰ *(020) 78819844 – www.theorange.co.uk*
Carte £ 31/41
• Modern cuisine • Friendly • Neighbourhood •
The old Orange Brewery is as charming a pub as its stucco-fronted façade sug-
gests. Try the fun bar or book a table in the more sedate upstairs room. The
menu has a Mediterranean bias; spelt or wheat-based pizzas are a speciality.
Bedrooms are stylish and comfortable.

🏨🏨 **Corinthia**   ⿻ ⅃⅁ ⊛ ⥶ ◨ ⅋ 🅐🅒 ⅍ ⌂

Whitehall Pl. ⊠ SW1A 2BD – Ⓜ *Embankment*   Plan: **AQ4**
– ℰ *(020) 7930 8181 – www.corinthia.com*
294 rm ⌑ *–* ⅋£ 570/1026 ⅋⅋£ 570/1026 *– 23 suites*
• Grand Luxury • Elegant • Contemporary •
The restored Victorian splendour of this grand, luxurious hotel cannot fail to
impress. Tasteful and immaculately finished bedrooms are some of the largest
in town; suites come with butlers. The stunning spa is over four floors. Dine on
creative British dishes in elegant Northall; opulent Massimo serves seasonal
Italian fare.
🏠 **Massimo** – See restaurant listing

🏨🏨 **Goring**   ⥶ 🅐🅒 ⅍

15 Beeston Pl ⊠ SW1W 0JW – Ⓜ *Victoria –* ℰ *(020)*   Plan: **H5**
7396 9000 – www.thegoring.com
69 rm ⌑ *–* ⅋£ 360/615 ⅋⅋£ 410/710 *– 8 suites*
• Luxury • Townhouse • Elegant •
Under the stewardship of the founder's great grandson, this landmark hotel has
been restored and renovated while maintaining its traditional atmosphere and
pervading sense of Britishness. Expect first class service and immaculate, very
comfortable bedrooms, many of which overlook the garden.
❀ **Dining Room at The Goring** – See restaurant listing

🏨🏨 **St James' Court**   ⿻ ⅃⅁ ⥶ ⅋ 🅐🅒 ⅍

45 Buckingham Gate ⊠ SW1E 6BS – Ⓜ *St James's Park*   Plan: **H5**
– ℰ *(020) 7834 6655 – www.tajhotels.com/stjamescourt*
318 rm *–* ⅋£ 315/505 ⅋⅋£ 315/505 *–* ⌑ £ 20 *– 20 suites*
• Luxury • Classic •
Built in 1897 as serviced accommodation for visiting aristocrats. Behind the
impressive Edwardian façade lies an equally elegant interior. The quietest
bedrooms overlook a courtyard. Relaxed, bright Bistro 51 comes with an international menu; Bank offers brasserie classics in a conservatory.
❀ **Quilon** – See restaurant listing

🏠 **Artist Residence**   ⿻ 🅐🅒

52 Cambridge St ⊠ SW1V 4QQ – Ⓜ *Victoria –* ℰ *(020)*   Plan: **H6**
79318946 – www.artistresidencelondon.co.uk
10 rm *–* ⅋£ 235/450 ⅋⅋£ 235/450 *–* ⌑ £ 15
• Townhouse • Personalised • Contemporary •
A converted pub made into a comfortable, quirky townhouse hotel, with stylish
bedrooms featuring mini Smeg fridges, retro telephones, reclaimed furniture
and pop art. Cool bar and sitting room beneath the busy Cambridge Street Kitchen.

🏠 **Lord Milner**   🅐🅒

111 Ebury St ⊠ SW1W 9QU – Ⓜ *Victoria –* ℰ *(020)*   Plan: **G6**
78819880 – www.lordmilner.com
11 rm *–* ⅋£ 110/160 ⅋⅋£ 145/290 *–* ⌑ £ 17
• Townhouse • Classic •
A four storey terraced house, with individually decorated bedrooms, three with
four-poster beds and all with smart marble bathrooms. Garden Suite is the best
room; it has its own patio. Breakfast served in your bedroom.

❀   **Locanda Locatelli** (Giorgio Locatelli)   XxX ॐ ᵹ 🄰🄲 ⇔

8 Seymour St. ⊠ W1H 7JZ – Ⓜ Marble Arch – ℰ (020)   Plan: **G2**
79359088 – www.locandalocatelli.com
– Closed 24-26 December and 1 January
Carte £ 38/69

• Italian • Fashionable • Elegant •

Giorgio Locatelli's Italian restaurant may be well into its second decade but it still looks as dapper as ever. The service is smooth and the room was designed with conviviality in mind. The hugely appealing menu covers all regions; unfussy presentation and superb ingredients allow natural flavours to shine.
→ Scallops with saffron. Linguine with Cornish lobster, tomato, garlic and sweet chilli. Warm apple with sultanas, Grand Marnier and yoghurt.

❀   **Texture** (Agnar Sverrisson)   XX ॐ 🄰🄲 ⇔

34 Portman St ⊠ W1H 7BY – Ⓜ Marble Arch – ℰ (020)   Plan: **G2**
72240028 – www.texture-restaurant.co.uk
– Closed first 2 weeks August, 1 week Easter, Christmas-New Year, Sunday, Monday and lunch Tuesday
Menu £ 34/95
– Carte £ 60/92

• Creative • Design • Fashionable •

Technically skilled but light and invigorating cooking from an Icelandic chef-owner, who uses ingredients from his homeland. Bright restaurant with high ceiling and popular adjoining champagne bar. Pleasant service from keen staff, ready with a smile.
→ Chargrilled Anjou pigeon with sweetcorn, shallots, bacon popcorn and red wine essence. Salted cod with Jersey Royals, avocado and romanesco. Icelandic skyr with rye bread and Yorkshire rhubarb.

❀   **Lima Fitzrovia**   X 🄰🄲

31 Rathbone Pl ⊠ W1T 1JH – Ⓜ Goodge Street   Plan: **I2**
– ℰ (020) 3002 2640 – www.limalondongroup.com/fitzrovia
– Closed 24-26 December, 1 January, Monday lunch and bank holidays
Menu £ 25 (lunch and early dinner)
– Carte £ 41/57

• Peruvian • Neighbourhood • Exotic décor •

Lima Fitzrovia is one of those restaurants that just makes you feel good about life – and that's even without the pisco sours. The Peruvian food at this informal, fun place is the ideal antidote to times of austerity: it's full of punchy, invigorating flavours and fantastically vivid colours.
→ Black bream ceviche with avocado, sweet potato and chilli. Suckling pig, chicharrón, sesame and celeriac. Elderberry with avocado mousse, 75% chocolate and rocoto pepper.

❀   **Portland**   X ॐ 🄰🄲 ⇔

113 Great Portland St ⊠ W1W 6QQ   Plan: **H2**
– Ⓜ Great Portland Street – ℰ (020) 7436 3261
– www.portlandrestaurant.co.uk
– Closed 23 December-3 January and Sunday
Menu £ 39/65
– Carte dinner £ 43/55 – (booking essential)

• Modern cuisine • Intimate • Simple •

A no-frills, pared-down restaurant that exudes honesty. One look at the menu and you know you'll eat well: it twists and turns on a daily basis and the combinations just sound right together. Dishes are crisp and unfussy but with depth and real understanding – quite something for such a young team.
→ Isle of Mull scallop, carrots, macadamia nuts and ramson. Denham Estate venison with brassica tops, burnt bread and black garlic jam. Gariguette strawberries with yoghurt sorbet, lemon curd and tarragon.

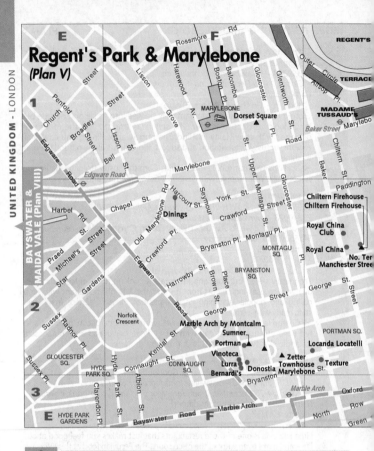

Regent's Park & Marylebone
(Plan V)

Trishna (Karam Sethi)   🍴 🆎 ⬦ ⍟

15-17 Blandford St. ⊠ *W1U 3DG –* Ⓜ *Baker Street*   Plan: **G2**
*– ℰ (020) 79355624 – www.trishnalondon.com – Closed 25-27 December
and 1-3 January*
Menu £ 35 (lunch)/70 – Carte £ 38/53
• Indian • Neighbourhood • Simple •

A double-fronted, modern Indian restaurant dressed in an elegant, understated
style. The coast of southwest India provides the influences and the food is vibrant, satisfying and executed with care – the tasting menus provide a good all-
round experience, and much thought has gone into the matching wines.
➔ Aloo tokri chaat. Seafood pilau with pink peppercorn raita. Chocolate
mousse chikki.

Clipstone   🍴 ☂ 🆎

5 Clipstone St ⊠ *W1W 6BB –* Ⓜ *Great Portland Street*   Plan: **H2**
– ℰ (020) 76370871 – www.clipstonerestaurant.co.uk – Closed Sunday dinner
Carte £ 24/38 – (booking advisable)
• Modern cuisine • Fashionable • Neighbourhood •

Another wonderful neighbourhood spot from the owners of Portland, just
around the corner. The great value sharing menu is a lesson in flavour and originality; choose one charcuterie dish, one from the seasonal vegetable-based
section, one main and a dessert. Cocktails and 'on-tap' wine add to the fun.

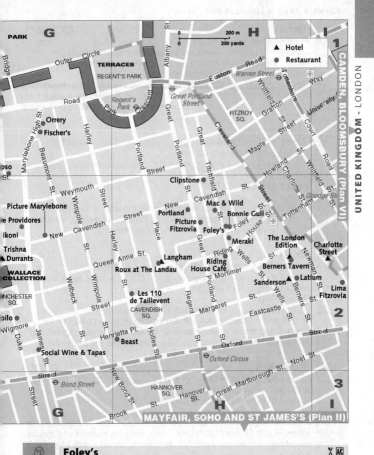

▲	Hotel
●	Restaurant

Foley's ✕ AC

Plan: **H2**

23 Foley St ⊠ W1W 6DU – ⓂGoodge Street – ℰ (020) 3137 1302 – www.foleysrestaurant.co.uk – Closed Christmas-New Year, Easter and Sunday

Carte £ 17/28 – *(booking advisable)*

• World cuisine • Neighbourhood • Friendly •

Cosy up in one of the ground floor booths or head downstairs to the engine room of this lively, well-run restaurant, with its busy open kitchen and counter seating, and its barrel-vaulted caves for six. Vibrant, original small plates reflect the international spice trail; 3 or 4 dishes will suffice.

Picture Fitzrovia ✕ AC

Plan: **H2**

110 Great Portland St. ⊠ W1W 6PQ – ⓂOxford Circus – ℰ (020) 7637 7892 – www.picturerestaurant.co.uk – Closed Sunday and bank holidays

Menu £ 22 (lunch) – Carte £ 27/33

• Modern British • Simple • Friendly •

An ex Arbutus and Wild Honey triumvirate created this cool, great value restaurant. The look may be a little stark but the delightful staff add warmth. The small plates are vibrant and colourful, and the flavours are assured.

755

Orrery

XxX 🛱 ◪ ⇔
Plan: **G1**

55 Marylebone High St ⊠ *W1U 5RB* – **Ⓜ** *Regent's Park*
– ℰ *(020) 7616 8000* – *www.orrery-restaurant.co.uk*
Menu £ 28/60 – Carte lunch £ 34/73 – *(booking essential)*
• Modern cuisine • Neighbourhood • Design •
These are actually converted stables from the 19C but, such is the elegance and style of the building, you'd never know. Featured is elaborate, modern European cooking; dishes are strong on presentation and come with the occasional twist.

Roux at The Landau – Langham Hotel

XxX ◪ ⇔ 🕭
Plan: **H2**

1c Portland Pl., Regent St. ⊠ *W1B 1JA*
– **Ⓜ** *Oxford Circus* – ℰ *(020) 76361000* – *www.rouxatthelandau.com*
– Closed Saturday lunch
Menu £ 39 – Carte £ 41/95
• French • Elegant • Design •
Grand, oval-shaped hotel restaurant run under the aegis of the Roux organisation. Classical, French-influenced cooking is the order of the day, but a lighter style of cuisine using the occasional twist is also emerging.

Beast

XX ⅙ ◪
Plan: **H2**

3 Chapel Pl ⊠ *W1G 0BG* – **Ⓜ** *Bond Street* – ℰ *(020)*
7495 1816 – *www.beastrestaurant.co.uk* – *Closed Sunday, lunch Monday-Wednesday and bank holidays*
Carte £ 49/110
• Meats and grills • Elegant • Fashionable •
An underground banquet hall with three exceedingly long tables set for communal dining. Mains include a perfectly cooked hunk of rib-eye steak and a large platter of succulent King crab. Bring a big appetite and a fat wallet.

Bernardi's

XX ◪ ⇔
Plan: **F2**

62 Seymour St ⊠ *W1H 5BN* – **Ⓜ** *Marble Arch* – ℰ *(020)*
3826 7940 – *www.bernardis.co.uk*
Menu £ 18 (weekday lunch) – Carte £ 31/56
• Italian • Neighbourhood • Fashionable •
A modern neighbourhood Italian: chic yet relaxed and with a friendly atmosphere. Pop in for breakfast, brunch, lunch, dinner or cicchetti and cocktails; everything is homemade and dishes are vibrantly flavoured, with a lightness of touch.

Berners Tavern – The London Edition Hotel

XX ⅙ ◪ ⇔
Plan: **H2**

10 Berners St ⊠ *W1T 3NP* – **Ⓜ** *Tottenham Court Road*
– ℰ *(020) 7908 7979* – *www.bernerstavern.com*
Menu £ 25 (lunch) – Carte £ 34/76
• Modern British • Brasserie • Elegant •
What was once a hotel ballroom is now a very glamorous restaurant, with every inch of wall filled with gilt-framed pictures. Jason Atherton has put together an appealing, accessible menu and the cooking is satisfying and assured.

Chiltern Firehouse – Chiltern Firehouse Hotel

XX 🛱 ◪ ⇔
Plan: **G2**

1 Chiltern St ⊠ *W1U 7PA* – **Ⓜ** *Baker Street* – ℰ *(020)*
7073 7676 – *www.chilternfirehouse.com*
Carte £ 37/74
• World cuisine • Fashionable • Design •
How appropriate – one of the hottest tickets in town is a converted fire station. The room positively bursts with energy but what makes this celebrity hangout unusual is that the food is rather good. Nuno Mendes' menu is full of vibrant North and South American dishes that are big on flavour.

110

Fischer's   XX AC

50 Marylebone High St ✉ *W1U 5HN –* Ⓜ *Baker Street*   Plan: **G1**
– ℰ (020) 7466 5501 – www.fischers.co.uk – Closed 25 December
Carte £ 23/59
• Austrian • Brasserie • Fashionable •

An Austrian café and konditorei that summons the spirit of old Vienna, from the
owners of The Wolseley et al. Open all day; breakfast is a highlight – the viennoi-
serie are great. Schnitzels are also good; upgrade to a Holstein.

110

Latium   XX AC

21 Berners St. ✉ *W1T 3LP –* Ⓜ *Oxford Circus – ℰ (020)*   Plan: **H2**
7323 9123 – www.latiumrestaurant.com – Closed 25-26 December,
1 January and Sunday lunch
Menu £ 18 (weekdays) – Carte £ 29/50
• Italian • Neighbourhood •

An Italian stalwart with warm, welcoming service, a contemporary look and a
loyal following. The menu focuses on Lazio but travels the length of Italy for
inspiration; 'fatto a casa' is their motto and fresh pasta, their speciality.

110

Lurra   XX 🍴 AC

9 Seymour Pl ✉ *W1H 5BA –* Ⓜ *Marble Arch – ℰ (020)*   Plan: **F2**
7724 4545 – www.lurra.co.uk – Closed Monday lunch and Sunday dinner
Menu £ 20 (weekday lunch) – Carte £ 31/70
• Basque • Design • Neighbourhood •

Its name means 'land' in Basque and reflects their use of the freshest produce,
cooked over a charcoal grill. Choose tasty nibbles or sharing plates like 14 year
old Galician beef, whole grilled turbot or slow-cooked shoulder of lamb.

110

Meraki   XX 🍴 & AC ⇔

80-82 Great Titchfield St ✉ *W1W 7QT*   Plan: **H2**
– Ⓜ *Goodge Street – ℰ (020) 7305 7686 – www.meraki-restaurant.com*
– Closed Sunday dinner and Christmas
Carte £ 25/60
• Greek • Fashionable • Neighbourhood •

A lively Greek restaurant from the same owners as Roka and Zuma; its name a
fitting reference to the passion put into one's work. Contemporary versions of
classic Greek dishes; much of the produce is imported from Greece, including
the wines.

110

Les 110 de Taillevent   XX 🕸 AC

16 Cavendish Sq ✉ *W1G 9DD –* Ⓜ *Oxford Circus*   Plan: **H2**
– ℰ (020) 3141 6016 – www.les-110-taillevent-london.com – Closed
25 December and 1 January
Menu £ 20 – Carte £ 31/64
• French • Elegant • Design •

Ornate high ceilings and deep green banquettes create an elegant look for this
brasserie deluxe. Dishes are firmly in the French vein and they offer 110 wines
by the glass: 4 different pairings for each dish, in 4 different price brackets.

110

The Providores   XX 🕸 AC

109 Marylebone High St. ✉ *W1U 4RX –* Ⓜ *Bond Street*   Plan: **G2**
– ℰ (020) 7935 6175 – www.theprovidores.co.uk – Closed Easter, dinner
24 and 31 December and 25-26 December
Menu £ 34 (dinner) – Carte £ 25/54
• Creative • Trendy • Romantic •

Tables and tapas are shared in the buzzing ground floor; head to the elegant,
slightly more sedate upstairs room for innovative fusion cooking, with ingredients from around the world. New Zealand wine list; charming staff.

UNITED KINGDOM - LONDON

Royal China

XX 🌁 ⑩

24-26 Baker St ⊠ W1U 7AB – Ⓜ Baker Street – ℰ (020)   Plan: **G2**
74874688 – www.royalchinagroup.co.uk – Closed 23-25 December
Menu £ 34 (lunch)/38 – Carte £ 25/100

• Chinese • Exotic décor • Family •

Barbequed meats, assorted soups and stir-fries attract plenty of large groups to this smart and always bustling Cantonese restaurant. Over 40 different types of dim sum served during the day.

Royal China Club

XX 🌁 ⑩

40-42 Baker St ⊠ W1U 7AJ – Ⓜ Baker Street – ℰ (020)   Plan: **G2**
7486 3898 – www.royalchinagroup.co.uk – Closed 25-27 December
Carte £ 35/80

• Chinese • Oriental décor • Romantic •

'The Club' is the glittering bauble in the Royal China chain but along with the luxurious feel of the room comes an appealing sense of calm. Their lunchtime dim sum is very good; at dinner try their more unusual Cantonese dishes.

Bonnie Gull

X 🏠 🌁

21a Foley St ⊠ W1W 6DS – Ⓜ Goodge Street – ℰ (020)   Plan: **H2**
7436 0921 – www.bonniegull.com – Closed 25 December-3 January
Carte £ 27/45 – (booking essential)

• Seafood • Simple • Traditional décor •

Sweet Bonnie Gull calls itself a 'seafood shack' – a reference perhaps to its modest beginnings as a pop-up. Start with something from the raw bar then go for classics like Cullen skink, Devon cock crab or fish and chips. There's another branch in Soho.

Dinings

X

22 Harcourt St. ⊠ W1H 4HH – Ⓜ Edgware Road   Plan: **F2**
– ℰ (020) 77230666 – www.dinings.co.uk – Closed Christmas
Carte £ 21/65 – (booking essential)

• Japanese • Cosy • Simple •

It's hard not to be charmed by this sweet little Japanese place, with its ground floor counter and basement tables. Its strengths lie with the more creative, contemporary dishes; sharing is recommended but prices can be steep.

Donostia

X

10 Seymour Pl ⊠ W1H 7ND – Ⓜ Marble Arch – ℰ (020)   Plan: **F2**
3620 1845 – www.donostia.co.uk – Closed Christmas, New Year and Monday lunch
Carte £ 20/43

• Basque • Tapas bar • Fashionable •

The two young owners were inspired by the food of San Sebastián to open this pintxos and tapas bar. Sit at the counter for Basque classics like cod with pil-pil sauce, chorizo from the native Kintoa pig and slow-cooked pig's cheeks.

Jikoni

X 🌁

19-21 Blandford St ⊠ W1U 3DH – Ⓜ Baker Street   Plan: **G2**
– ℰ (020) 7034 1988 – www.jikonilondon.com – Closed Saturday lunch and Sunday dinner
Menu £ 20 (weekday lunch) – Carte £ 26/45

• Indian • Elegant • Neighbourhood •

Indian tablecloths and colourful cushions create a homely feel at this idiosyncratic restaurant. Born in Kenya of Indian parents and brought up in London, chef Ravinder Bhogal takes culinary inspiration from these sources and more.

Mac & Wild

X 🌁

65 Great Titchfield St ⊠ W1W 7PS – Ⓜ Oxford Circus   Plan: **H2**
– ℰ (020) 7637 0510 – www.macandwild.com – Closed Sunday dinner
Carte £ 23/50

• Scottish • Friendly • Neighbourhood •

The owner of this 'Highland restaurant' is the son of an Ardgay butcher – it is all about their wild venison and top quality game and seafood from Scotland. Don't miss the 'wee plates' like the deliriously addictive haggis pops. There's also a choice of over 100 whiskies.

Opso

10 *Paddington St* ⊠ *W1U 5QL* – Ⓜ *Baker Street*
– ℰ *(020) 7487 5088* – *www.opso.co.uk* – *Closed 23 December-3 January*
Menu £ 15 (weekday lunch) – Carte £ 17/53
• Greek • Neighbourhood •

Plan: **G1**

A modern Greek restaurant which has proved a good fit for the neighbourhood – and not just because it's around the corner from the Hellenic Centre. It serves small sharing plates that mix the modern with the traditional.

Picture Marylebone

19 *New Cavendish St* ⊠ *W1G 9TZ* – Ⓜ *Bond Street*
– ℰ *(020) 7935 0058* – *www.picturerestaurant.co.uk* – *Closed Sunday and bank holidays*
Menu £ 22 (lunch) – Carte £ 27/33
• Modern British • Design • Friendly •

Plan: **G2**

This follow-up to Picture Fitzrovia hit the ground running. The cleverly created à la carte of flavoursome small plates lists 3 vegetable, 3 fish and 3 meat choices, followed by 3 desserts – choose one from each section.

Riding House Café

43-51 *Great Titchfield St* ⊠ *W1W 7PQ*
– Ⓜ *Oxford Circus* – ℰ *(020) 79270840* – *www.ridinghousecafe.co.uk*
– *Closed 25-26 December*
Carte £ 25/46
• Modern cuisine • Rustic • Fashionable •

Plan: **H2**

It's less a café, more a large, quirkily designed, all-day New York style brasserie and cocktail bar. The small plates have more zing than the main courses. The 'unbookable' side of the restaurant is the more fun part.

Social Wine & Tapas

39 *James St* ⊠ *W1U 1DL* – Ⓜ *Bond Street* – ℰ *(020)*
7993 3257 – *www.socialwineandtapas.com* – *Closed bank holidays*
Menu £ 16 (lunch) – Carte £ 15/34 – *(bookings not accepted)*
• Mediterranean cuisine • Neighbourhood • Trendy •

Plan: **G2**

From the Jason Atherton stable, and the name says it all. Urban styling, with wines on display; sit in the moodily lit basement. A mix of Spanish and Mediterranean dishes, with some Atherton classics too; desserts are a highlight.

Vinoteca

15 *Seymour Pl.* ⊠ *W1H 5BD* – Ⓜ *Marble Arch* – ℰ *(020)*
7724 7288 – *www.vinoteca.co.uk* – *Closed Christmas, bank holidays and Sunday dinner*
Menu £ 16 (weekday lunch) – Carte £ 22/36 – *(booking advisable)*
• Modern cuisine • Wine bar • Neighbourhood •

Plan: **F2**

A fun place with a great selection of wines, fresh flavourful cooking and enthusiastic staff. Influences from sunnier parts of Europe, along with some British dishes. Great value midweek lunch menu; try the themed monthly wine flight.

Zoilo

9 *Duke St.* ⊠ *W1U 3EG* – Ⓜ *Bond Street* – ℰ *(020)*
7486 9699 – *www.zoilo.co.uk*
Menu £ 15 (weekday lunch) – Carte £ 25/53
• Argentinian • Friendly • Wine bar •

Plan: **G2**

It's all about sharing so plonk yourself at the counter and discover Argentina's regional specialities. Typical dishes include braised pig head croquettes or grilled scallops with pork belly, and there's an appealing all-Argentinian wine list.

Portman

51 *Upper Berkeley St* ⊠ *W1H 7QW* – Ⓜ *Marble Arch.*
– ℰ *(020) 7723 8996* – *www.theportmanmarylebone.com*
Carte £ 26/46
• Modern cuisine • Pub • Friendly •

Plan: **F2**

The condemned on their way to Tyburn Tree gallows would take their last drink here. Now it's an urbane pub with a formal upstairs dining room. The ground floor is more fun for enjoying the down-to-earth menu.

Langham

1c Portland Pl, Regent St ✉ W1B 1JA Plan: **H2**
– Ⓜ *Oxford Circus*
– ✆ *(020) 76361000 – www.langhamhotels.com*
380 rm – 🚹£ 400/600 🚹🚹£ 400/600
– ☕ £ 34 – 31 suites
• Luxury • Palace • Elegant •

Was one of Europe's first purpose-built grand hotels when it opened in 1865. Now back to its best, with its famous Palm Court for afternoon tea, its stylish Artesian bar and bedrooms that are not without personality and elegance.

🍴 **Roux at The Landau** – See restaurant listing

The London Edition

10 Berners St ✉ W1T 3NP – Ⓜ Tottenham Court Road Plan: **H2**
– ✆ *(020) 7781 0000 – www.editionhotels.com/london*
173 rm – 🚹£ 295/500 🚹🚹£ 295/500
– ☕ £ 26 – 7 suites
• Business • Luxury • Design •

Formerly Berners, a classic Edwardian hotel, strikingly reborn through a partnership between Ian Schrager and Marriott – the former's influence most apparent in the stylish lobby and bar. Slick, understated rooms; the best ones have balconies.

🍴 **Berners Tavern** – See restaurant listing

Charlotte Street

15 Charlotte St ✉ W1T 1RJ – Ⓜ Goodge Street Plan: **I2**
– ✆ *(020) 78062000 – www.charlottestreethotel.co.uk*
52 rm – 🚹£ 276/396 🚹🚹£ 276/612
– ☕ £ 18 – 3 suites
• Luxury • Townhouse • Contemporary •

Stylish interior designed with a charming, understated English feel. Impeccably kept and individually decorated bedrooms. Popular in-house screening room. Colourful restaurant whose terrace spills onto Charlotte Street; grilled meats a highlight.

Chiltern Firehouse

1 Chiltern St ✉ W1U 7PA – Ⓜ Baker Street Plan: **G2**
– ✆ *(020) 7073 7676 – www.chilternfirehouse.com*
26 rm – 🚹£ 455/545 🚹🚹£ 720/950
– ☕ £ 25 – 10 suites
• Townhouse • Luxury • Contemporary •

From Chateau Marmont in LA to The Mercer in New York, André Balazs' hotels are effortlessly cool. For his London entrance, he sympathetically restored and extended a Gothic Victorian fire station. The style comes with an easy elegance; it's an oasis of calm and hardly feels like a hotel at all.

🍴 **Chiltern Firehouse** – See restaurant listing

Sanderson

50 Berners St ✉ W1T 3NG – Ⓜ Oxford Circus Plan: **H2**
– ✆ *(020) 73001400 – www.morganshotelgroup.com*
150 rm – 🚹£ 219/459 🚹🚹£ 219/459
– ☕ £ 22
• Luxury • Business • Minimalist •

Originally designed by Philippe Starck and his influence is still evident. The Purple Bar is dark and moody; the Long Bar is bright and stylish. Bedrooms are crisply decorated and come complete with all mod cons.

Zetter Townhouse Marylebone

28-30 Seymour St ⊠ *W1H 7JB* — Plan: **F2**
– Ⓜ *Marble Arch*
– ✆ *(020) 7324 4544 – www.thezettertownhouse.com*
24 rm – †£ 290/570 ††£ 290/570 – ☲ £ 14
• Townhouse • Elegant • Unique •

A stylish Georgian townhouse, with a sumptuously decorated lounge and cocktail bar and beautifully appointed bedrooms; the best features a roll-top bath on its rooftop terrace. Friendly, professional staff and impressive eco credentials.

Dorset Square

39-40 Dorset Sq ⊠ *NW1 6QN* — Plan: **F1**
– Ⓜ *Marylebone*
– ✆ *(020) 77237874 – www.dorsetsquarehotel.co.uk*
38 rm – †£ 180/234 ††£ 240/504 – ☲ £ 18
• Townhouse • Business • Contemporary •

Having reacquired this Regency townhouse, Firmdale refurbished it fully before reopening it in 2012. It has a contemporary yet intimate feel and visiting MCC members will appreciate the cricketing theme, which even extends to the cocktails in their sweet little basement brasserie.

Durrants

26-32 George St ⊠ *W1H 5BJ* — Plan: **G2**
– Ⓜ *Bond Street*
– ✆ *(020) 7935 8131 – www.durrantshotel.co.uk*
92 rm – †£ 195 ††£ 250 – ☲ £ 20 – 4 suites
• Traditional • Business • Classic •

Traditional, privately owned hotel with friendly, long-standing staff. Bedrooms are now brighter in style but still retain a certain English character. Clubby dining room for mix of British classics and lighter, European dishes.

Marble Arch by Montcalm

31 Great Cumberland Pl ⊠ *W1H 7TA* — Plan: **F2**
– Ⓜ *Marble Arch*
– ✆ *(020) 7258 0777 – www.themarblearch.co.uk*
42 rm – †£ 250/395 ††£ 265/395 – ☲ £ 20
• Townhouse • Business • Contemporary •

Bedrooms at this 5-storey Georgian townhouse come with the same high standards of stylish, contemporary design as its parent hotel opposite, the Montcalm, but are just a little more compact.

No. Ten Manchester Street

10 Manchester St ⊠ *W1U 4DG* — Plan: **G2**
– Ⓜ *Baker Street*
– ✆ *(020) 73175900 – www.tenmanchesterstreethotel.com*
44 rm – †£ 180/385 ††£ 180/385 – ☲ £ 15 – 9 suites
• Townhouse • Business • Modern •

Converted Edwardian house in an appealing, central location. A discreet entrance leads into a little lounge and an Italian-themed bistro; the semi-enclosed cigar bar is also a feature. Neat, well-kept bedrooms.

Sumner

54 Upper Berkeley St ⊠ *W1H 7QR* — Plan: **F2**
– Ⓜ *Marble Arch*
– ✆ *(020) 77232244 – www.thesumner.com*
19 rm ☲ – †£ 140/300 ††£ 140/300
• Townhouse • Business • Personalised •

Two Georgian terrace houses in a great central location. There's a stylish sitting room, a basement breakfast room and well-kept, comfortable bedrooms; the largest of which – 101 and 201 – benefit from having full-length windows.

Pied à Terre   ✕✕✕ ⊛ AC ⇔ 🍴 🍸

34 Charlotte St ✉ W1T 2NH – Ⓜ Goodge Street   Plan: **I2**
– ☎ (020) 76361178 – www.pied-a-terre.co.uk – Closed last week
December-5 January, Saturday lunch, Sunday and bank holidays
Menu £ 30/80 – (booking essential)
• Creative • Elegant • Intimate •

For over 25 years, David Moore's restaurant has stood apart in Charlotte Street,
confident in its abilities and in the loyalty of its regulars. Subtle decorative changes keep it looking fresh and vibrant, while the chef delivers refined, creative,
flavoursome cooking.
→ Scallop ceviche with hazelnut, black radish and truffle. Suckling pig with
parsnip and cider. Coconut rice pudding, sweet cheese, sake and yoghurt.

Hakkasan Hanway Place   ✕✕ ⊛ AC 🍸

8 Hanway Pl. ✉ W1T 1HD – Ⓜ Tottenham Court Road   Plan: **I2**
– ☎ (020) 79277000 – www.hakkasan.com – Closed 24-25 December
Menu £ 38/128 – Carte £ 29/98
• Chinese • Trendy • Fashionable •

There are now Hakkasans all over the world but this was the original. It has the
sensual looks, air of exclusivity and glamorous atmosphere synonymous with
the 'brand'. The exquisite Cantonese dishes are prepared with care and consistency by the large kitchen team; lunch dim sum is a highlight.
→ Dim sum platter. Grilled Chilean sea bass in honey. Chocolate and olive
oil ganache.

Kitchen Table at Bubbledogs (James Knappett)   ✕✕ AC

70 Charlotte St ✉ W1T 4QG – Ⓜ Goodge Street   Plan: **H2**
– ☎ (020) 76377770 – www.kitchentablelondon.co.uk – Closed 1-
14 January, 17 August-2 September, 23-27 December and Sunday-Tuesday
Menu £ 98 – (dinner only) (booking essential) (tasting menu only)
• Modern cuisine • Fashionable • Neighbourhood •

Fight through the crowds enjoying a curious mix of hotdogs and champagne
and head for the curtain – behind it is a counter for 19 diners. Chef-owner
James prepares a no-choice menu of around 12 dishes. The produce is exemp-
lary; the cooking has a clever creative edge; and the dishes have real depth.
→ Lobster and tomatoes with lemon verbena. Duck, cherry and turnips.
Strawberries, black pepper meringue, tarragon and milk.

The Ninth (Jun Tanaka)   ✕ AC

22 Charlotte St ✉ W1T 2NB – Ⓜ Goodge Street   Plan: **I2**
– ☎ (020) 3019 0800 – www.theninthlondon.com – Closed Christmas-New
Year, Sunday and bank holidays
Menu £ 25 (weekday lunch) – Carte £ 32/57
• Mediterranean cuisine • Brasserie • Fashionable •

Jun Tanaka's first restaurant – the ninth in which he has worked – is this neighbourhood spot with a lively downstairs and more intimate first floor. Cooking
uses classical French techniques with a spotlight on the Med; dishes look
appealing but the focus is firmly on flavour. Vegetables are a highlight.
→ Sea bass carpaccio with salsa verde and pickled kohlrabi. Chargrilled sea
bream with lemon confit, miso and fennel salad. Pain perdu with vanilla ice
cream.

Barbary   ✕ AC

16 Neal's Yard ✉ WC2H 9DP – Ⓜ Covent Garden   Plan: **I3**
– www.thebarbary.co.uk – Closed dinner 24-26 December
Carte £ 16/32 – (bookings not accepted)
• World cuisine • Tapas bar • Rustic •

A sultry, atmospheric restaurant from the team behind Palomar: a tiny place
with 24 non-bookable seats squeezed around a horseshoe-shaped, zinc-topped
counter. The menu of small sharing plates lists dishes from the former Barbary
Coast. Service is keen, as are the prices.

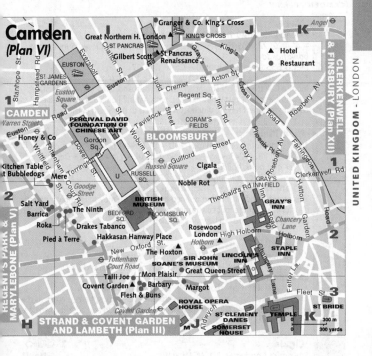

Camden
(Plan VI)

▲ Hotel
● Restaurant

CAMDEN
Warren Street

REGENT'S PARK & MARYLEBONE (Plan VI)

CLERKENWELL & FINSBURY (Plan XII)

STRAND & COVENT GARDEN AND LAMBETH (Plan III)

300 m
300 yards

Barrica
ⓧ ☂ AC
62 Goodge St ⊠ W1T 4NE – Ⓜ Goodge Street
Plan: **H2**
– ℰ (020) 7436 9448 – www.barrica.co.uk – Closed 25-31 December,
1 January, Easter, Sunday and bank holidays
Carte £ 17/36 – *(booking essential)*
• **Spanish** • **Tapas bar** • **Friendly** •
All the staff at this lively little tapas bar are Spanish, so perhaps it's national pride that makes them run it with a passion lacking in many of their competitors. When it comes to the food, authenticity is high on the agenda.

Honey & Co
ⓧ AC Ⓚ
25a Warren St ⊠ W1T 5LZ – Ⓜ Warren Street
Plan: **H1**
– ℰ (020) 73886175 – www.honeyandco.co.uk – Closed 24-26,
31 December, 1 January and Sunday
Menu £ 33 – Carte £ 25/31 – *(booking essential)*
• **World cuisine** • **Simple** • **Neighbourhood** •
The husband and wife team at this sweet little café were both Ottolenghi head chefs so expect cooking full of freshness and colour. Influences stretch beyond Israel to the wider Middle East. Open from 8am; packed at night.

Salt Yard
ⓧ ✿ AC
54 Goodge St. ⊠ W1T 4NA – Ⓜ Goodge Street
Plan: **H2**
– ℰ (020) 76370657 – www.saltyard.co.uk – Closed dinner 24 and 25,
31 December and 1 January
Carte £ 18/28
• **Mediterranean cuisine** • **Tapas bar** • **Intimate** •
A ground floor bar and buzzy basement restaurant specialising in good value plates of tasty Italian and Spanish dishes, ideal for sharing. Ingredients are top-notch; charcuterie is a speciality. Super wine list and sincere, enthusiastic staff.

763

UNITED KINGDOM - LONDON

Mere
XX ⅄ 🔟 ⟺ 🕅

74 Charlotte St ⊠ W1T 4QH – Ⓜ Goodge Street
Plan: **H1/2**
– 𝒞 (020) 7268 6565 – www.mere-restaurant.com – *Closed Sunday and bank holidays*
Menu £ 35 (weekday lunch) – Carte £ 44/67
• **Modern cuisine** • **Fashionable** • **Elegant** •

Monica Galetti's first collaboration with her husband, David, is an understatedly elegant basement restaurant flooded with natural light. Global, ingredient-led cooking features French influences with a nod to the South Pacific.

Mon Plaisir
XX 🐜

19-21 Monmouth St. ⊠ WC2H 9DD – Ⓜ Covent Garden
Plan: **I3**
– 𝒞 (020) 78367243 – www.monplaisir.co.uk – *Closed 25-26 December, Easter and bank holidays*
Menu £ 16 (weekdays)/28 – Carte £ 26/55
• **French** • **Bistro** • **Traditional décor** •

This proud French institution opened in the 1940s. Enjoy satisfyingly authentic classics in any of the four contrasting rooms, full of Gallic charm; apparently the bar was salvaged from a Lyonnais brothel.

Roka
XX ⅄ 🔟

37 Charlotte St ⊠ W1T 1RR – Ⓜ Goodge Street
Plan: **I2**
– 𝒞 (020) 7636 5228 – www.rokarestaurant.com – *Closed 25 December*
Carte £ 42/75
• **Japanese** • **Fashionable** • **Design** •

The original Roka, where people come for the lively atmosphere as much as the cooking. The kitchen takes the flavours of Japanese food and adds its own contemporary touches; try specialities from the on-view Robata grill.

Cigala
X 🛋 🔟 ⟺

54 Lamb's Conduit St. ⊠ WC1N 3LW
Plan: **J1**
– Ⓜ Russell Square – 𝒞 (020) 74051717 – www.cigala.co.uk – *Closed 25-26 December, 1 January, Easter Sunday and Monday*
Menu £ 25 (weekdays) – Carte £ 29/43 – *(booking essential)*
• **Spanish** • **Neighbourhood** • **Friendly** •

Longstanding Spanish restaurant, with a lively and convivial atmosphere, friendly and helpful service and an appealing and extensive menu of classics. The dried hams are a must and it's well worth waiting the 30 minutes for a paella.

Drakes Tabanco
X 🔟

3 Windmill St ⊠ W1T 2HY – Ⓜ Goodge Street – 𝒞 (020)
Plan: **I2**
7637 9388 – www.drakestabanco.com – *Closed Sunday and bank holidays*
Carte £ 16/37
• **Spanish** • **Simple** • **Rustic** •

Taking advantage of our newfound fondness for fino is this simple tabanco, from the people behind nearby Barrica and Copita. The small, Andalusian-inspired tapas menu uses imported produce from Spain alongside British ingredients.

Flesh & Buns
X 🔟 🐜

41 Earlham St ⊠ WC2H 9LX – Ⓜ Covent Garden
Plan: **I3**
– 𝒞 (020) 7632 9500 – www.bonedaddies.com – *Closed 24-25 December*
Menu £ 22 (lunch and early dinner)/40 – Carte £ 16/46 – *(booking advisable)*
• **Asian** • **Trendy** • **Fashionable** •

A fun, frenetic basement spot next to The Donmar. The mostly Japanese dishes are fairly priced and full of flavour; star billing goes to the gua bao bun – soft, steamed pillows of delight that sandwich your choice of meat or fish filling.

Noble Rot

51 Lamb's Conduit St ✉ *WC1N 3NB – Ⓜ Russell Square* Plan: **J1**
– ✆ (020) 7242 8963 – www.noblerot.co.uk – Closed 25-26 December and Sunday
Carte £ 30/43 – *(booking advisable)*
• Traditional British • Rustic • Wine bar •
A wine bar and restaurant from the people behind the wine magazine of the same name. Unfussy cooking comes with bold, gutsy flavours; expect fish from the Kent coast as well as classics like terrines, rillettes and home-cured meats.

Covent Garden

10 Monmouth St ✉ *WC2H 9HB – Ⓜ Covent Garden* Plan: **AP2**
– ✆ (020) 78061000 – www.firmdalehotels.com
52 rm – †£ 240/378 ††£ 240/378 – ☕ £ 18
• Luxury • Townhouse • Design •
Popular with those of a theatrical bent. Boldly designed, stylish bedrooms, with technology discreetly concealed. Boasts a very comfortable first floor oak-panelled drawing room with its own honesty bar. Easy-going menu in Brasserie Max.

Holborn

Great Queen Street

32 Great Queen St ✉ *WC2B 5AA – Ⓜ Holborn* Plan: **J2**
– ✆ (020) 72420622 – www.greatqueenstreetrestaurant.co.uk – Closed Christmas-New Year, Sunday dinner and bank holidays
Menu £ 18 (weekday lunch) – Carte £ 19/42 – *(booking essential)*
• Modern British • Rustic • Neighbourhood •
The menu is a model of British understatement and is dictated by the seasons; the cooking, confident and satisfying with laudable prices and generous portions. Lively atmosphere and enthusiastic service. Highlights include the shared dishes like the suet-crusted steak and ale pie for two.

Margot

45 Great Queen St ✉ *WC2 5AA – Ⓜ Holborn – ✆ (020) 34094777 – www.margotrestaurant.com – Closed 25 December* Plan: **J3**
Menu £ 25 (lunch and early dinner) – Carte £ 30/53
• Italian • Elegant • Fashionable •
Bucking the trend of casual eateries is this glamourous, elegant Italian, where a doorman greets you, staff sport tuxedos and the surroundings are sleek and stylish. The seasonal, regional Italian cooking has bags of flavour and a rustic edge.

Rosewood London

252 High Holborn ✉ *WC1V 7EN – Ⓜ Holborn – ✆ (020) 77818888 – www.rosewoodhotels.com/london* Plan: **J2**
306 rm ☕ – †£ 378/882 ††£ 378/882 – 44 suites
• Historic • Luxury • Elegant •
A beautiful Edwardian building that was once the HQ of Pearl Assurance. The styling is very British and the bedrooms are uncluttered and smart. Cartoonist Gerald Scarfe's work adorns the walls of his eponymous bar. A classic brasserie with a menu of British favourites occupies the former banking hall.

The Hoxton

199 - 206 High Holborn ✉ *WC1V 7BD – Ⓜ Holborn* Plan: **J2**
– ✆ (020) 7661 3000 – www.thehoxton.com
174 rm ☕ – †£ 109/229 ††£ 189/389
• Townhouse • Business • Contemporary •
When the room categories are Shoebox, Snug, Cosy and Roomy, you know you're in a hip hotel. A great location and competitive rates plus a retro-style diner, a buzzy lobby and a 'Chicken Shop' in the basement.

🕪

Gilbert Scott – St Pancras Renaissance Hotel
XX & 🎬 ⇔

Euston Rd ⊠ *NW1 2AR* – Ⓜ *King's Cross St Pancras*
Plan: **J0**
– ℰ *(020) 7278 3888* – *www.thegilbertscott.co.uk*
Menu £ 21 (lunch)
– Carte £ 28/61
· Traditional British · Brasserie · Elegant ·
Named after the architect of this Gothic masterpiece and run under the aegis of
Marcus Wareing, this restaurant has the splendour of a Grand Salon but the
buzz of a brasserie. The appealing menu showcases the best of British produce,
whilst incorporating influences from further afield.

🕪

Granger & Co. King's Cross
X 🍴 & 🎬

Stanley Building, 7 Pancras Sq. ⊠ *N1C 4AG*
Plan: **J0**
– Ⓜ *King's Cross St Pancras*
– ℰ *(020) 3058 2567* – *www.grangerandco.com*
– Closed 25 December
Carte £ 18/39
· Modern cuisine · Friendly · Neighbourhood ·
The third London outpost for Aussie chef Bill Granger is a bright, buzzing place
serving small plates, barbecue dishes, and bowls and grains, with plenty of
South East Asian flavours. Dishes are vibrant, fresh and uplifting.

🏨

St Pancras Renaissance
ﭏ ⊛ ⋔ & 🎬 � 🚗

Euston Rd ⊠ *NW1 2AR* – Ⓜ *King's Cross St Pancras*
Plan: **J0**
– ℰ *(020) 7841 3540* – *www.stpancraslondon.com*
245 rm – ♥£ 250/400 ♥♥£ 400/550 – ⊇ £ 18 – 10 suites
· Business · Historic · Elegant ·
This restored Gothic jewel was built in 1873 as the Midland Grand hotel and
reopened in 2011 under the Marriott brand. A former taxi rank is now a spacious
lobby and all-day dining is in the old booking office. Luxury suites in Chambers
wing; Barlow wing bedrooms are a little more functional.
🕪 **Gilbert Scott** – See restaurant listing

🏨

Great Northern H. London
✿ & 🎬

Pancras Rd ⊠ *N1C 4TB* – Ⓜ *King's Cross St Pancras*
Plan: **R3**
– ℰ *(020) 3388 0818* – *www.gnhlondon.com*
91 rm – ♥£ 249/299 ♥♥£ 249/379 – ⊇ £ 25 – 1 suite
· Historic building · Traditional · Contemporary ·
Built as a railway hotel in 1854 and reborn as a stylish townhouse; it's con-
nected to King's Cross' western concourse and just metres from the Eurostar
check-in. Bespoke furniture features in each of the modern bedrooms. Clas-
sic British dishes in the intimate first floor bistro; start with a drink in the
GNH bar.

❀❀

Dinner by Heston Blumenthal – Mandarin Oriental Hyde Park Hotel
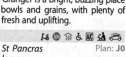

66 Knightsbridge, ⊠ *SW1X 7LA* – Ⓜ *Knightsbridge*
XxX 🕃 🎬 ⇔
– ℰ *(020) 7201 3833* – *www.dinnerbyheston.com*
Plan: **F4**
– Closed 17-31 October
Menu £ 45 (weekday lunch)
– Carte £ 58/121
· Traditional British · Design · Fashionable ·
Don't come expecting 'molecular gastronomy' – this is all about respect for, and
a wonderful renewal of, British food, with just a little playfulness thrown in. Each
one of the meticulously crafted and deceptively simple looking dishes comes
with a date relating to its historical provenance.
➔ Mandarin, chicken liver parfait and grilled bread (c.1500). Hereford rib-
eye with mushroom ketchup and triple cooked chips (c.1830). Tipsy cake
with spit-roast pineapple (c.1810).

iO **Bar Boulud** – Mandarin Oriental Hyde Park Hotel   XX & ⚫ ⇔
66 Knightsbridge ⊠ *SW1X 7LA* – ⓜ *Knightsbridge*   Plan: **F4**
– ℰ (020) 72013899 – www.mandarinoriental.com/london
Menu £ 19 (weekday lunch) – Carte £ 26/57
• French • Brasserie • Fashionable •
Daniel Boulud's London outpost is fashionable, fun and frantic. His hometown is
Lyon but he built his considerable reputation in New York, so charcuterie, sausa-
ges and burgers are the highlights.

iO **The Magazine**   XX ⇔ ⌂ & ⚫
Serpentine Sackler Gallery, West Carriage Dr, Kensington   Plan: **E4**
Gardens ⊠ *W2 2AR* – ⓜ *Lancaster Gate* – ℰ (020) 7298 7552
– www.magazine-restaurant.co.uk – Closed Monday except bank holidays
Menu £ 26/35 – Carte £ 26/40 – *(lunch only)*
• Modern cuisine • Design • Fashionable •
Designed by the late Zaha Hadid, the Serpentine Sackler Gallery comprises a
restored 1805 gunpowder store and a modern tensile extension. The Magazine
is a bright open space with an easy-to-eat menu of dishes whose influences are
largely from within Europe.

iO **Rivea** – Bulgari Hotel   XX ✾ & ⚫ ⇔
171 Knightsbridge ⊠ *SW7 1DW* – ⓜ *Knightsbridge*   Plan: **F4**
– ℰ (020) 7151 1025 – www.rivealondon.com
Menu £ 26 (lunch) – Carte £ 39/51
• Mediterranean cuisine • Design • Fashionable •
Elegant basement restaurant where blues and whites make reference to warmer climes – and also to its sister in St Tropez. Precise, unfussy cooking focuses
on the French and Italian Riviera, with an interesting range of vibrant small plates.

iO **Zuma**   XX ⚫
5 Raphael St ⊠ *SW7 1DL* – ⓜ *Knightsbridge* – ℰ (020)   Plan: **F5**
75841010 – www.zumarestaurant.com – Closed 25 December
Menu £ 76/124 – Carte £ 26/193 – *(booking essential)*
• Japanese • Fashionable •
Now a global brand but this was the original. The glamorous clientele come for
the striking surroundings, bustling atmosphere and easy-to-share food. Go for
the more modern dishes and those cooked on the robata grill.

🏯 **Mandarin Oriental Hyde Park**   ≤ ⌗ ⚑ ⍟ ▦ & ⚫ ⚿
66 Knightsbridge ⊠ *SW1X 7LA* – ⓜ *Knightsbridge*   Plan: **F4**
– ℰ (020) 72352000 – www.mandarinoriental.com/london
181 rm – ♦£ 540/1080 ♦♦£ 540/1080 – � £ 36 – 25 suites
• Grand Luxury • Historic • Contemporary •
This celebrated hotel, dating from 1889, is a London landmark; to ensure it
remains as such, improvements are constantly being made – this time to the
spacious bedrooms, many of which have views of Hyde Park. Enjoy afternoon
tea in the charming Rosebery salon or relax in the luxurious spa with its 17m
pool. Service remains as strong as ever.
✿✿ **Dinner by Heston Blumenthal** • iO **Bar Boulud** – See restaurant
listing

🏯 **Bulgari**   ⌗ ⍟ ⍟ ▦ & ⚫ ⚿
171 Knightsbridge ⊠ *SW7 1DW* – ⓜ *Knightsbridge*   Plan: **F4**
– ℰ (020) 7151 1010 – www.bulgarihotels.com/london
85 rm – ♦£ 550/835 ♦♦£ 550/835 – � £ 34 – 23 suites
• Luxury • Elegant • Design •
Impeccably tailored hotel making stunning use of materials like silver, mahogany, silk and marble. Luxurious bedrooms with sensual curves, sumptuous
bathrooms and a great spa – and there is substance behind the style. Down a
sweeping staircase to the Alain Ducasse restaurant.
iO **Rivea** – See restaurant listing

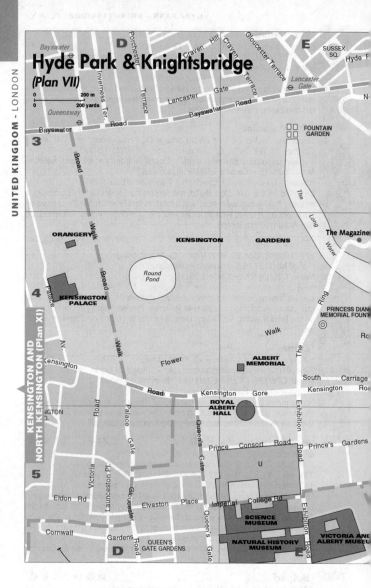

Hyde Park & Knightsbridge
(Plan VII)

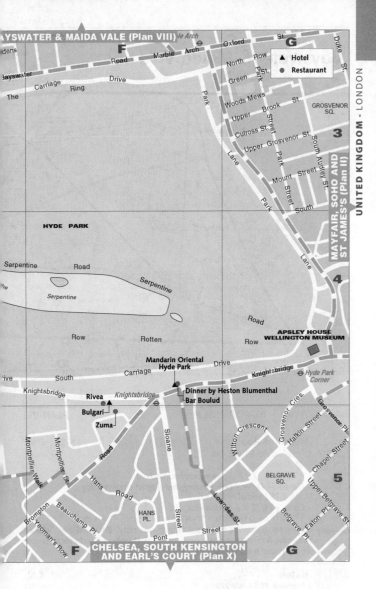

BAYSWATER & MAIDA VALE (Plan VIII)

F

G

Hotel ▲

Restaurant ●

MAYFAIR, SOHO AND ST JAMES'S (Plan II)

HYDE PARK

APSLEY HOUSE
WELLINGTON MUSEUM

Mandarin Oriental
Hyde Park

Dinner by Heston Blumenthal
Bar Boulud

Hyde Park Corner

Rivea

Bulgari

Zuma

BELGRAVE SQ.

HANS PL.

F

G

Bayswater & Maida Vale
(Plan VIII)

BAYSWATER – MAIDA VALE

PLAN VIII

Hereford Road

X ⛱ & 🅰🅲

3 Hereford Rd ⊠ W2 4AB
Plan: **C2**
– Ⓜ Bayswater
– ℰ (020) 77271144 – www.herefordroad.org
– Closed 24 December-3 January and August bank holiday
Menu £ 16 (weekday lunch)
– Carte £ 24/32 – (booking essential)
• Traditional British • Neighbourhood • Bistro •
Converted butcher's shop specialising in tasty British dishes without
frills, using first-rate, seasonal ingredients; offal a highlight. Booths for six people
are the prized seats. Friendly and relaxed feel.

Kateh

X 🅰🅲

5 Warwick Pl ⊠ W9 2PX
Plan: **D1**
– Ⓜ Warwick Avenue
– ℰ (020) 7289 3393 – www.katehrestaurant.co.uk
– Closed 25-26 December
Carte £ 21/35 – (dinner only and lunch Friday-Sunday) (booking essential)
• Mediterranean cuisine • Neighbourhood • Intimate •
Booking is imperative if you want to join the locals who have already discovered
what a little jewel they have in the form of this buzzy, busy Persian restaurant.
Authentic stews, expert chargrilling and lovely pastries and teas.

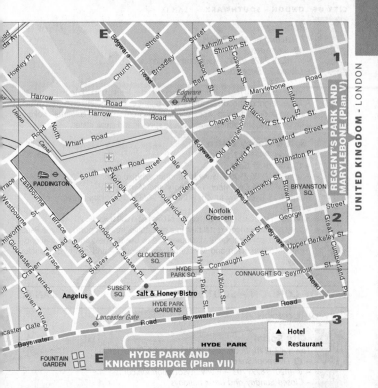

Angelus

XX & 🅰🅲 ↔
Plan: **E3**

4 Bathurst St ⊠ W2 2SD
– Ⓜ *Lancaster Gate*
– ℰ *(020) 74020083 – www.angelusrestaurant.co.uk*
– *Closed 24-25 December and 1 January*
Menu £ 23/41
– Carte £ 39/70
• **French** • **Brasserie** • **Neighbourhood** •

Hospitable owner has created an attractive French brasserie within a 19C former pub, with a warm and inclusive feel. Satisfying and honest French cooking uses seasonal British ingredients.

Marianne

XX 🅰🅲 🛇
Plan: **C2**

104a Chepstow Rd ⊠ W2 5QS
– Ⓜ *Westbourne Park*
– ℰ *(020) 3675 7750 – www.mariannerestaurant.com*
– *Closed 22 December-4 January , August bank holiday and Monday*
Menu £ 35/95 – *(dinner only and lunch Friday-Sunday) (booking essential)*
(tasting menu only)
• **French** • **Cosy** • **Intimate** •

The eponymous Marianne was a finalist on MasterChef. Her restaurant is a sweet little place with just 6 tables. Concise daily lunch menu and seasonal tasting menu; cooking is classically based but keeps things quite light.

UNITED KINGDOM - LONDON

⍩○ **Pomona's**   ✗ 🏠 ᯤ 🅰🅲
47 Hereford Rd ⊠ W2 5AH   Plan: **C2**
– Ⓜ *Bayswater*
– 𝒞 *(020) 7229 1503 – www.pomonas.co.uk*
– *Closed 25 December*
Carte £ 23/51
• World cuisine • Neighbourhood • Fashionable •
A large neighbourhood restaurant with bright décor, an airy, open feel and a
fun, laid-back Californian vibe. All-day menus offer soulful, colourful cooking
with breakfast, smoothies, salads, house specials and small plates.

⍩○ **Salt & Honey Bistro**   ✗ 🅰🅲
28 Sussex Pl ⊠ W2 2TH   Plan: **E3**
– Ⓜ *Lancaster Gate*
– 𝒞 *(020) 7706 7900 – www.saltandhoneybistro.com*
– *Closed 25-26 December, 1 January and Monday*
Menu £ 15 (weekday lunch) – Carte £ 26/39 – *(bookings advisable at
dinner)*
• Modern cuisine • Bistro • Neighbourhood •
A cosy neighbourhood restaurant in a residential area just north of Hyde Park.
Well-priced, colourful, boldly flavoured dishes use the best British ingredients;
expect Mediterranean and Middle Eastern flavours – and plenty of Manuka
honey.

CITY OF LONDON – SOUTHWARK   PLAN IX

CITY OF LONDON

❀ **City Social**   ✗✗✗ 🏠 ≤ ᯤ 🅰🅲 ⇔
Tower 42 (24th floor), 25 Old Broad St ⊠ EC2N 1HQ   Plan: **M3**
– Ⓜ *Liverpool Street*
– 𝒞 *(020) 78777703 – www.citysociallondon.com*
– *Closed Sunday and bank holidays*
Carte £ 43/68
• Modern cuisine • Elegant • Design •
Jason Atherton's dark and moody restaurant with an art deco twist, set on the
24th floor of Tower 42; the City views are impressive, especially from tables 10
and 15. The flexible menu is largely European and the cooking manages to be
both refined and robust at the same time.
➔ Yellowfin tuna tataki with cucumber salad and radish with ponzu dressing. Cornish sea bass with deep-fried oyster, cucumber, cauliflower and
oyster velouté. Hazelnut plaisir sucré with chocolate syrup, biscuit and
milk ice cream.

❀ **La Dame de Pic** – Four Seasons Hotel London at Ten Trinity Square
10 Trinity Sq ⊠ EC3N 4AJ   ✗✗ ᯤ 🅰🅲 ⇔
– Ⓜ *Tower Hill*   Plan: **N3**
– 𝒞 *(020) 3297 3790 – www.ladamedepiclondon.co.uk*
– *Closed Sunday dinner*
Menu £ 39 (weekday lunch)
– Carte £ 65/102
• Modern French • Design • Contemporary décor •
A high-ceilinged, columned room in the impressive Beaux-Arts style Four Sea-
sons Hotel at Ten Trinity Square; a charming brasserie deluxe with a spacious,
stylish feel. Pic's cuisine is feminine and highly original: firmly rooted in classic
French techniques yet delivered in a modern manner; relying on exciting fla-
vour combinations of top quality ingredients.
➔ Berlingots with smoked Pélardon cheese, wild mushrooms and Voatsi-
perifery pepper. Wild turbot with beetroot, lovage sabayon and saffron.
The white millefeuille.

Club Gascon (Pascal Aussignac)   XX ⊛ AC

57 West Smithfield ⊠ EC1A 9DS – ⓜ *Barbican*
– ℰ *(020) 76006144 – www.clubgascon.com – Closed August, Christmas-*
New Year, Saturday lunch, Sunday-Monday and bank holidays
Menu £ 45/80 – Carte £ 50/70 – *(booking essential)*
• French • Intimate • Elegant •

Plan: **L2**

The gastronomy of Gascony and France's southwest are the starting points but the assured and intensely flavoured cooking also pushes at the boundaries. Marble and huge floral displays create suitably atmospheric surroundings.
➜ Flamed duck and smoked pine with aromatic razor clams. Barbecued 'white gold' fish with maize, truffle and bacon sauce. 'Millionaire' 72% Colombian chocolate with black olive, lemon gel and thyme ice cream.

Mei Ume – Four Seasons Hotel London at Ten Trinity Square   XxX

10 Trinity Sq ⊠ EC3N 4AJ – ⓜ *Tower Hill –* ℰ *(020)*   & AC ⇔
3297 3799 – www.meiume.com – Closed Sunday
Menu £ 29 (lunch) – Carte £ 42/75
• Asian • Elegant •

Plan: **N3**

Within the impressive surroundings of the Four Seasons Hotel; an elegant, high ceilinged room with subtle Asian touches, including some beautiful themed friezes. The menu focuses on Chinese dishes but also incorporates some Japanese elements; dishes come with a pleasing refinement and a lightness of touch.

Lutyens   XxX ⊛ AC ⇔

85 Fleet St. ⊠ EC4Y 1AE – ⓜ *Blackfriars –* ℰ *(020)*
7583 8385 – www.lutyens-restaurant.com – Closed Christmas,
Saturday, Sunday and bank holidays
Menu £ 33 (weekday lunch) – Carte £ 31/61
• Modern cuisine • Elegant • Contemporary décor •

Plan: **K3**

The unmistakable influence of Sir Terence Conran: timeless and understated good looks mixed with functionality, and an appealing Anglo-French menu with plenty of classics such as Cornish lamb cassoulet and game in season.

Barbecoa   XX AC

20 New Change Passage ⊠ EC4M 9AG – ⓜ *St Paul's*
– ℰ *(020) 3005 8555 – www.barbecoa.com – Closed 25-26 December and*
1 January
Menu £ 27 (weekday lunch) – Carte £ 32/64 – *(booking essential)*
• Meats and grills • Design • Brasserie •

Plan: **L3**

Set up by Jamie Oliver, to show us what barbecuing is all about. The prime meats, butchered in-house, are just great; go for the pulled pork shoulder with cornbread on the side. By dessert you may be willing to share.

Bird of Smithfield   XX AC ⇔

26 Smithfield St ⊠ EC1A 9LB – ⓜ *Farringdon*
– ℰ *(020) 7559 5100 – www.birdofsmithfield.com*
– Closed Christmas, New Year, Sunday and bank holidays
Menu £ 18 (lunch and early dinner)
– Carte £ 28/53 – (booking essential)
• Modern cuisine • Contemporary décor • Intimate •

Plan: **L2**

Five floors of fun include a cocktail bar, lounge, rooftop terrace and small, friendly restaurant – it feels like a private members' club but without the smugness. Carefully executed classic French dishes have a subtle modern edge.

Bread Street Kitchen   XX AC

10 Bread St ⊠ EC4M 9AJ – ⓜ *St Paul's*
– ℰ *(020) 3030 4050 – www.breadstreetkitchen.com*
Carte £ 31/63 – *(booking advisable)*
• Modern cuisine • Trendy • Brasserie •

Plan: **L3**

Gordon Ramsay's take on NY loft-style dining comes with a large bar, thumping music, an open kitchen and enough zinc ducting to kit out a small industrial estate. For the food, think modern bistro dishes with an element of refinement.

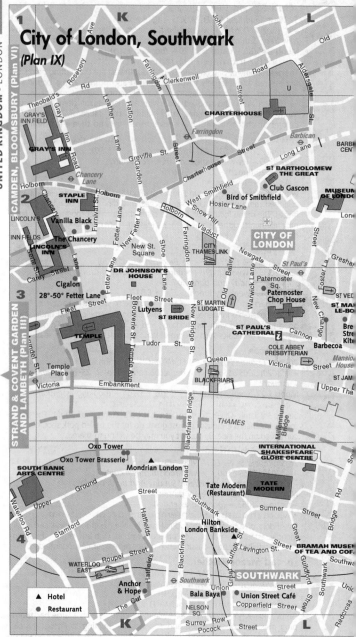

City of London, Southwark
(Plan IX)

CHARTERHOUSE

ST BARTHOLOMEW THE GREAT

Club Gascon

Bird of Smithfield

MUSEUM OF LONDON

GRAY'S INN

STAPLE INN

Vanilla Black

The Chancery

LINCOLN'S INN

CITY OF LONDON

CITY THAMESLINK

St Paul's

DR JOHNSON'S HOUSE

Cigalon

28°-50° Fetter Lane

Lutyens

Paternoster Chop House

ST BRIDE

ST MARTIN LUDGATE

ST PAUL'S CATHEDRAL

Barbecoa

TEMPLE

COLE ABBEY PRESBYTERIAN

Temple Place

BLACKFRIARS

Embankment

THAMES

Oxo Tower

Oxo Tower Brasserie

Mondrian London

INTERNATIONAL SHAKESPEARE GLOBE CENTRE

SOUTH BANK ARTS CENTRE

Tate Modern (Restaurant)

TATE MODERN

Hilton London Bankside

BRAMAH MUSEUM OF TEA AND COF.

WATERLOO EAST

SOUTHWARK

Anchor & Hope

Bala Baya

Union Street Café

▲ Hotel
● Restaurant

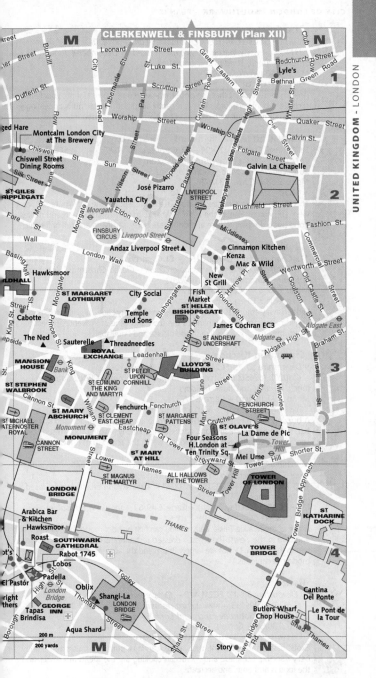

CLERKENWELL & FINSBURY (Plan XII)

Leonard Street

Luke St.

Scrutton Street

Worship Street

Worship St.

Redchurch Street

Lyle's

Quaker Street

Calvin St.

Folgate Street

Galvin La Chapelle

Montcalm London City at The Brewery

Chiswell St.

Chiswell Street Dining Rooms

Silk Street

ST GILES CRIPPLEGATE

José Pizarro

Yauatcha City

Moorgate Eldon St.

FINSBURY CIRCUS

Liverpool Street

London Wall

Andaz Liverpool Street ▲

LIVERPOOL STREET

Brushfield Street

Middlesex Street

Fashion St.

Cinnamon Kitchen

Kenza

Mac & Wild

New St Grill

Wentworth Street

Harrow Pl.

Goulston Street

Aldgate East

GUILDHALL

Hawksmoor

ST MARGARET LOTHBURY

City Social

Temple and Sons

Cabotte

The Ned

Sauterelle ▲ Threadneedles

ROYAL EXCHANGE

MANSION HOUSE ▲

Bank

ST STEPHEN WALBROOK

Cannon St.

ST MICHAEL PATERNOSTER ROYAL

Fish Market

ST HELEN BISHOPSGATE

James Cochran EC3

ST ANDREW UNDERSHAFT

Aldgate

Aldgate High St.

Braham St.

Mansell St.

Leadenhall

ST PETER UPON CORNHILL

LLOYD'S BUILDING

Street

ST EDMUND THE KING AND MARTYR

ST MARY ABCHURCH

Fenchurch

ST CLEMENT EAST CHEAP

Monument

Eastcheap

MONUMENT

CANNON STREET

ST MARGARET PATTENS

Gt Tower

FENCHURCH STREET

Friars

Minories

ST OLAVE'S

La Dame de Pic

Four Seasons H.London at Ten Trinity Sq.

Mei Ume

Tower Hill

Shorter St.

ST MARY AT HILL

Lower Thames

ST MAGNUS THE MARTYR

ALL HALLOWS BY THE TOWER

Street

Tower Hill

TOWER OF LONDON

LONDON BRIDGE

THAMES

Tower Bridge Approach

ST KATHARINE DOCK

Arabica Bar & Kitchen

Hawksmoor

Roast

SOUTHWARK CATHEDRAL

Rabot 1745

Lobos

Padella

El Pastor

Wright Brothers

Tapas Brindisa

Oblix

GEORGE INN

Aqua Shard

Shangri-La LONDON BRIDGE

London Bridge

Tooley

Thomas Street

TOWER BRIDGE

Cantina Del Ponte

Butlers Wharf Chop House

Le Pont de la Tour

Shad Thames

Borough High St.

Story

200 m

200 yards

UNITED KINGDOM - LONDON

The Chancery
XX 🎨 ⟷
9 Cursitor St ⊠ EC4A 1LL – Ⓜ *Chancery Lane –* ℰ *(020)* Plan: **K2**
78314000 – www.thechancery.co.uk – Closed 23 December-4 January,
Saturday lunch, Sunday and bank holidays
Menu £ 40 (weekdays)/65
• Modern cuisine • Chic • Neighbourhood •
An elegant restaurant that's so close to the law courts you'll assume your fellow diners are barristers, jurors or the recently acquitted. The menu is appealingly concise; dishes come with a classical backbone and bold flavours.

Chiswell Street Dining Rooms – Montcalm London City at The Brewery
XX 🛴 🎨 🐾
56 Chiswell St ⊠ EC1Y 4SA – Ⓜ *Barbican –* ℰ *(020)* Plan: **M2**
7614 0177 – www.chiswellstreetdining.com – Closed 25-
26 December, 1 January, Saturday and Sunday
Menu £ 38 – Carte £ 31/57
• Modern British • Brasserie • Design •
This Martin brothers' restaurant is set in a corner spot of the old Whitbread Brewery and comes alive in the evening, thanks to its busy bar. The menu makes good use of British produce and dishes are gutsy, satisfying and full of flavour.

Cigalon
XX 🎨 ⟷
115 Chancery Ln ⊠ WC2A 1PP – Ⓜ *Chancery Lane* Plan: **K3**
– ℰ *(020) 7242 8373 – www.cigalon.co.uk – Closed Christmas, New Year,*
Saturday, Sunday and bank holidays
Menu £ 22/37 – Carte lunch £ 29/39
• French • Elegant • Romantic •
Hidden away among the lawyers offices on Chancery Lane, this bright, high-ceilinged restaurant pays homage to the food and wine of Provence. Expect flavoursome French classics like salade niçoise and bouillabaisse.

Cinnamon Kitchen
XX 🛴 🛴 🎨 ⟷ 🌱
9 Devonshire Sq ⊠ EC2M 4YL – Ⓜ *Liverpool Street* Plan: **N2**
– ℰ *(020) 76265000 – www.cinnamon-kitchen.com – Closed Saturday*
lunch, Sunday and bank holidays
Menu £ 21 (lunch) – Carte £ 27/52
• Indian • Trendy • Minimalist •
A buzzing Indian restaurant with contemporary styling, a terrace and a trendy bar. The cooking is creative and original, with punchy flavours and arresting presentation. Meat dishes are a highlight – watch the action from the Grill Bar.

Fenchurch
XX ≼ 🎨 ⟷
Level 37, 20 Fenchurch St ⊠ EC3M 3BY Plan: **M3**
– Ⓜ *Monument –* ℰ *(0333) 772 0020 – www.skygarden.london – Closed*
25-26 December
Menu £ 35 (weekday lunch) – Carte £ 49/69 – *(booking advisable)*
• Modern cuisine • Design •
Arrive at the 'Walkie Talkie' early so you can first wander round the Sky Garden and take in the views. The smartly dressed restaurant is housed in a glass box within the atrium. Dishes are largely British and the accomplished cooking uses modern techniques.

Kenza
XX 🎨 ⟷
10 Devonshire Sq. ⊠ EC2M 4YP – Ⓜ *Liverpool Street* Plan: **N2**
– ℰ *(020) 79295533 – www.kenza-restaurant.com – Closed 24-*
25 December, Saturday lunch and bank holidays
Menu £ 30/50 – Carte £ 31/38
• Lebanese • Exotic décor • Design •
Exotic basement restaurant, with lamps, carvings, pumping music and nightly belly dancing. Lebanese and Moroccan cooking are the menu influences and the food is authentic and accurate.

New St Grill
XX 爺 帝 占 AC

16a New St ✉ *EC2M 4TR –* Ⓜ *Liverpool Street*   Plan: **N2**
– 𝒞 (020) 3503 0785 – www.newstreetgrill.com – Closed 25 December-
3 January except dinner 31 December
Menu £ 29 (weekdays) – Carte £ 30/85
• Meats and grills • Friendly • Intimate •
D&D converted an 18C warehouse to satisfy our increasing appetite for red
meat. They use Black Angus beef: grass-fed British, aged for 28 days, or corn-
fed American, aged for 40 days. Start with a drink in the Old Bengal Bar.

Sauterelle
XX 占 ⇔

The Royal Exchange, Threadneedle St ✉ *EC3V 3LR*   Plan: **M3**
– Ⓜ *Bank – 𝒞 (020) 76182480 – www.royalexchange-grandcafe.co.uk*
– Closed Christmas, Easter, Saturday, Sunday and bank holidays
Menu £ 25 (weekdays) – Carte £ 36/52
• Modern cuisine • Historic • Contemporary décor •
This D&D restaurant has an impressive location on the mezzanine floor of the
Royal Exchange, overlooking what was once the original trading floor – now a
Grand Café by day and a cocktail bar by night. Contemporary, Italian-inspired
menus.

Vanilla Black
XX AC 🕅

17-18 Tooks Ct. ✉ *EC4A 1LB –* Ⓜ *Chancery Lane*   Plan: **K2**
– 𝒞 (020) 72422622 – www.vanillablack.co.uk – Closed 2 weeks Christmas
and bank holidays
Menu £ 27 (weekday lunch)/55 – *(booking essential)*
• Vegetarian • Intimate • Romantic •
A vegetarian restaurant where real thought has gone into the creation of dishes,
which deliver an array of interesting texture and flavour contrasts. Modern techniques are subtly incorporated and while there are some original combinations,
they are well-judged.

Yauatcha City
XX 帝 占 AC ⇔

Broadgate Circle ✉ *EC2M 2QS –* Ⓜ *Liverpool Street*   Plan: **M2**
– 𝒞 (020) 38179880 – www.yauatcha.com – Closed 24 December-
3 January and bank holidays
Menu £ 29 (weekday lunch) – Carte £ 26/67
• Chinese • Fashionable •
A more corporate version of the stylish Soho original, with a couple of bars and
a terrace at both ends. All the dim sum greatest hits are on the menu but the
chefs have some work to match the high standard found in Broadwick Street.

Cabotte
X 爺 占 AC ⇔

48 Gresham St ✉ *EC2V 7AY –* Ⓜ *Bank – 𝒞 (020)*   Plan: **M3**
7600 1616 – www.cabotte.co.uk – Closed Saturday and Sunday
Carte £ 30/44 – *(booking essential)*
• French • Wine bar • Intimate •
A bistro de luxe with a stunning wine list – owned by two master sommeliers
who share a passion for the wines of Burgundy. Cooking comes with the same
regional bias and the accomplished classics are simple in style and rich in flavour.

Fish Market
X 帝 占 AC

16b New St ✉ *EC2M 4TR –* Ⓜ *Liverpool Street*   Plan: **N2**
– 𝒞 (020) 3503 0790 – www.fishmarket-restaurant.com – Closed 25-
26 December, 1 January, Sunday dinner and bank holidays
Menu £ 20 – Carte £ 29/50 – *(booking advisable)*
• Seafood • Friendly • Simple •
How to get to the seaside from Liverpool Street? Simply step into this bright fish
restaurant, in an old warehouse of the East India Company, and you'll almost
hear the seagulls. The menu is lengthy and the cooking style classic.

UNITED KINGDOM - LONDON

Hawksmoor

X ❀ AC ✧

10-12 Basinghall St ⊠ EC2V 5BQ
Plan: M3
– Ⓜ Bank – ℰ (020) 7397 8120 – www.thehawksmoor.com
– Closed 24 December-2 January, Saturday, Sunday and bank holidays
Menu £ 28 (lunch and early dinner) – Carte £ 23/63 – (booking essential)
• Meats and grills • Traditional décor • Brasserie •

Fast and furious, busy and boisterous, this handsome room is the backdrop for another testosterone filled celebration of the serious business of beef eating. Nicely aged and rested Longhorn steaks take centre-stage.

James Cochran EC3

X

19 Bevis Marks ⊠ EC3A 7JA
Plan: N3
– Ⓜ Liverpool Street – ℰ (020) 3302 0310 – www.jcochran.restaurant
– Closed Christmas, Saturday lunch, Sunday and bank holidays
Carte £ 26/46 – (booking essential at lunch)
• Modern cuisine • Simple • Contemporary décor •

A spacious, simply furnished restaurant where the eponymous chef offers original combinations of interesting ingredients in an array of gutsy, good value small plates. The 6 course evening tasting menu is available with matching wines.

José Pizarro

X 斎 ♿ AC

36 Broadgate Circle ⊠ EC2M 1QS
Plan: M2
– Ⓜ Liverpool Street – ℰ (020) 72565333 – www.josepizarro.com
– Closed Sunday
Carte £ 15/40
• Spanish • Tapas bar • Friendly •

The eponymous chef's third operation is a good fit here: it's well run, flexible and fairly priced – and that includes the wine list. The Spanish menu is nicely balanced, with the seafood dishes being the standouts.

Mac & Wild

X AC

9a Devonshire Sq ⊠ EC2M 4YN
Plan: N2
– Ⓜ Liverpool Street – ℰ (020) 7637 0510 – www.macandwild.com
– Closed Sunday
Carte £ 22/31
• Scottish • Trendy • Friendly •

Sister to the Fitzrovia original, this fun spot offers good service, good value and prime Scottish ingredients, with a focus on wild game, seafood and whisky. Dishes come with subtle contrasts and great flavours.

Paternoster Chop House

X 斎 AC

Warwick Ct., Paternoster Sq. ⊠ EC4M 7DX
Plan: L3
– Ⓜ St Paul's – ℰ (020) 70299400 – www.paternosterchophouse.co.uk
– Closed 26-30 December, 1 January, lunch Saturday and dinner Sunday
Menu £ 24 (lunch and early dinner) – Carte £ 25/63
• Traditional British • Brasserie • Trendy •

Appropriately British menu in a restaurant lying in the shadow of St Paul's Cathedral. Large, open room with full-length windows; busy bar attached. Kitchen uses thoughtfully sourced produce.

Temple and Sons

X 斎 ♿ AC

22 Old Broad St ⊠ EC2N 1HQ
Plan: M3
– Ⓜ Liverpool Street – ℰ (020) 7877 7710 – www.templeandsons.co.uk
– Closed Sunday
Carte £ 19/62
• Traditional British • Bistro • Trendy •

In a glass cube next to Tower 42 is this relaxed restaurant styled on a Victorian grocer's shop, with a bar serving home-canned cocktails, and a menu of traditional British dishes like sausage and mash and sticky toffee pudding.

28°-50° Fetter Lane

140 Fetter Ln ✉ EC4A 1BT – Ⓜ Temple – ✆ (020) 72428877 – www.2850.co.uk – Closed Saturday, Sunday and bank holidays Plan: **K3**

Menu £ 25 (weekday lunch) – Carte £ 32/53

• Modern cuisine • Wine bar • Simple •

From the owner of Texture comes this cellar wine bar and informal restaurant. The terrific wine list is thoughtfully compiled and the grills, cheeses, charcuterie and European dishes are designed to allow the wines to shine.

Jugged Hare

42 Chiswell St ✉ EC1Y 4SA – Ⓜ Barbican. – ✆ (020) 7614 0134 – www.thejuggedhare.com – Closed 25-26 December Plan: **M2**

Menu £ 25 (early dinner) – Carte £ 27/58 – *(booking essential)*

• Traditional British • Pub • Cosy •

Vegetarians may feel ill at ease – and not just because of the taxidermy. The atmospheric dining room, with its open kitchen down one side, specialises in stout British dishes, with meats from the rotisserie a highlight.

Four Seasons H. London at Ten Trinity Square

10 Trinity Sq ✉ EC3N 4AJ – Ⓜ Tower Hill – ✆ (020) 3297 9200 – www.fourseasons.com Plan: **N3**

100 rm – †£ 390/700 ††£ 390/700 – ☕ £ 24 – 7 suites

• Historic building • Grand Luxury • Elegant •

This extraordinary building, built in 1922, is the former headquarters of The Port of London Authority and boasts many original features including the impressive rotunda lounge with its domed ceiling and plaster reliefs. Classically furnished bedrooms; choose an Executive for more space and a contemporary look. Accomplished French cooking in La Dame de Pic. Asian dishes in Mei Ume.

✿ **La Dame de Pic** • **Mei Ume** – See restaurant listing

Andaz Liverpool Street

40 Liverpool St ✉ EC2M 7QN – Ⓜ Liverpool Street – ✆ (020) 79611234 – www.andazliverpoolstreet.com Plan: **M2**

267 rm – †£ 169/699 ††£ 169/699 – ☕ £ 28 – 14 suites

• Business • Luxury • Design •

A contemporary and stylish interior hides behind the classic Victorian façade. Bright and spacious bedrooms boast state-of-the-art facilities. Various dining options include a brasserie specialising in grilled meats, a compact Japanese restaurant and a traditional pub.

The Ned

27 Poultry ✉ EC2R 8AJ – Ⓜ Bank – ✆ (020) 3828 2000 – www.thened.com Plan: **M3**

252 rm – †£ 180/500 ††£ 180/500 – ☕ £ 15

• Historic building • Contemporary • Elegant •

The former Midland bank headquarters, designed and built by Sir Edward Lutyens in 1926; now a hotel and members club offering relaxed luxury and considerable style. Edwardian-style bedrooms feature rug-covered wooden floors and beautiful furniture. There are numerous restaurants housed in the vast hall; pay a visit to the former bank vaults – now a quirky bar.

Montcalm London City at The Brewery

52 Chiswell St ✉ EC1Y 4SA – Ⓜ Barbican – ✆ (020) 7614 0100 – www.themontcalmlondoncity.co.uk Plan: **M2**

236 rm ☕ – †£ 147/400 ††£ 187/500 – 7 suites

• Business • Contemporary • Historic •

The majority of the stylish, modern bedrooms are in the original part of the Whitbread Brewery, built in 1714; ask for a quieter one overlooking the courtyard, or one of the 25 found in the 4 restored Georgian townhouses across the road. Enjoy a meal in the Chiswell Street Dining Rooms or The Jugged Hare.

Chiswell Street Dining Rooms – See restaurant listing

Threadneedles 🏨 ♿ 🎨 🛁 ⟷

5 Threadneedle St. ✉ *EC2R 8AY* Plan: **M3**
– Ⓜ *Bank*
– ℰ *(020) 7657 8080 – www.hotelthreadneedles.co.uk*
74 rm – ♦£ 149/599 ♦♦£ 149/599 – ☑ £ 15
· Historic building · Business · Contemporary ·

A converted bank, dating from 1856, with a smart, boutique feel and a stunning stained-glass cupola in the lounge. Individually styled bedrooms feature Egyptian cotton sheets, iPod docks and thoughtful extras. Spacious Wheeler's with its marble, pillars and panelling specialises in grills and seafood.

BERMONDSEY

Story (Tom Sellers) 🟫 XX ♿ 🎨

199 Tooley St ✉ *SE1 2JX* Plan: **N5**
– Ⓜ *London Bridge*
– ℰ *(020) 7183 2117 – www.restaurantstory.co.uk – Closed 2 weeks Christmas-New Year, Sunday dinner and Monday lunch*
Menu £ 45 *(weekday lunch)*/120 *– (booking essential) (tasting menu only)*
· Modern cuisine · Design · Neighbourhood ·

Tom Sellers offers a 6 or 10 course lunch and a 12 course dinner menu; serving just 12 tables in what used to be a public toilet and now looks like a Nordic eco-lodge. Modern techniques and a light touch result in food with a back-to-nature feel and strong earthy flavours. Dishes are colourful, playful and easy to eat.
→ Crab with avocado and sea vegetables. Herdwick lamb with sheep's curd. Almond and dill.

José 🟫 X ♿ 🎨

104 Bermondsey St ✉ *SE1 3UB* Plan: **D2**
– Ⓜ *London Bridge*
– ℰ *(020) 7403 4902 – www.josepizarro.com – Closed 24-26 December and Sunday dinner*
Carte £ 14/28 *– (bookings not accepted)*
· Spanish · Minimalist · Tapas bar ·

Standing up while eating tapas feels so right, especially at this snug, lively bar that packs 'em in like boquerones. The vibrant dishes are intensely flavoured – five per person should suffice; go for the daily fish dishes from the blackboard. There's a great list of sherries too.

Le Pont de la Tour ⅠⓄ XxX 舘 ≤ 🌳 ♿ ⟷

36d Shad Thames, Butlers Wharf ✉ *SE1 2YE* Plan: **N4**
– Ⓜ *London Bridge*
– ℰ *(020) 74038403 – www.lepontdelatour.co.uk – Closed 1 January*
Menu £ 24/55 – Carte £ 33/62
· French · Elegant · Intimate ·

Few restaurants can beat the setting, especially when you're on the terrace with its breathtaking views of Tower Bridge. For its 25th birthday it got a top-to-toe refurbishment, resulting in a warmer looking room in which to enjoy the French-influenced cooking.

Aqua Shard ⅠⓄ XX ≤ 🎨 ⟷

Level 31, The Shard, 31 St Thomas St, ✉ *SE1 9RY* Plan: **M4**
– Ⓜ *London Bridge*
– ℰ *(020) 3011 1256 – www.aquashard.co.uk*
– Closed 25 December
Menu £ 32 *(weekday lunch)* – Carte £ 49/82 *– (booking advisable)*
· Modern cuisine · Fashionable · Design ·

The Shard's most accessible restaurant covers all bases by serving breakfast, brunch, lunch, afternoon tea and dinner. If you don't mind queuing, you can even come just for a drink. The contemporary cooking makes good use of British ingredients and comes with a degree of finesse in flavour and looks.

Oblix
XX ⪡ 🕭 🎵

Level 32, The Shard, 31 St Thomas St. ✉ *SE1 9RY* — Plan: **M4**
– **Ⓜ** *London Bridge* – 🕾 *(020) 72686700 – www.oblixrestaurant.com*
Menu £ 55 (weekday lunch) – Carte £ 30/164
• Meats and grills • Trendy • Design •

A New York grill restaurant on the 32nd floor of The Shard; window tables for two are highly prized. Meats and fish from the rotisserie, grill and Josper oven are the stars of the show; brunch in the lounge bar at weekends.

Butlers Wharf Chop House
X ⪡ 🕭 🎵

36e Shad Thames, Butlers Wharf ✉ *SE1 2YE* — Plan: **N4**
– **Ⓜ** *London Bridge* – 🕾 *(020) 7403 3403*
– *www.chophouse-restaurant.co.uk – Closed 1 January*
Menu £ 29 – Carte £ 28/69
• Traditional British • Brasserie • Simple •

Grab a table on the terrace in summer and dine in the shadow of Tower Bridge. Rustic feel to the interior; noisy and fun. The menu focuses on traditional English ingredients and dishes; grilled meats a speciality.

Cantina Del Ponte
X ⪡ 🕭

36c Shad Thames, Butlers Wharf ✉ *SE1 2YE* — Plan: **N4**
– **Ⓜ** *London Bridge* – 🕾 *(020) 74035403 – www.cantina.co.uk – Closed 26-27 December*
Menu £ 20 (weekday lunch)/23 – Carte £ 31/42
• Italian • Rustic •

This Italian stalwart offers an appealing mix of classic dishes and reliable favourites from a sensibly priced menu, in pleasant faux-rustic surroundings. Its pleasant terrace takes advantage of its riverside setting.

Casse Croûte
X

109 Bermondsey St ✉ *SE1 3XB* – **Ⓜ** *London Bridge* — Plan: **D2**
– 🕾 *(020) 7407 2140 – www.cassecroute.co.uk – Closed Sunday dinner*
Carte £ 30/36 – *(booking essential)*
• French • Bistro • Friendly •

Squeeze into this tiny bistro and you'll find yourself transported to rural France. A blackboard menu offers three choices for each course but new dishes are added as others run out. The cooking is rustic, authentic and heartening.

Pique-Nique
X 🕭 🕭

Tanner St. Park ✉ *SE1 3LD* – **Ⓜ** *London Bridge* — Plan: **D2**
– 🕾 *(020) 7403 9549 – www.pique-nique.co.uk*
Menu £ 38 – Carte £ 32/39 – *(booking essential)*
• French • Bistro • Friendly •

Set in a converted 1920s park shelter is this fun French restaurant with a focus on rotisserie-cooked Bresse chicken. Concise menu of French classics; go for the 6 course 'Menu autour du poulet de Bresse' which uses every part of the bird.

Pizarro
X 🎵 ⇔

194 Bermondsey St ✉ *SE1 3TQ* – **Ⓜ** *London Bridge* — Plan: **D2**
– 🕾 *(020) 73789455 – www.josepizarro.com – Closed 24-28 December*
Menu £ 35 – Carte £ 28/42
• Mediterranean cuisine • Neighbourhood • Simple •

José Pizarro has a refreshingly simple way of naming his establishments: after José, his tapas bar, comes Pizarro, a larger restaurant a few doors down. Go for the small plates, like prawns with piquillo peppers and jamón.

St John Maltby
X

41 Ropewalk, Maltby St ✉ *SE1 3PA* — Plan I: **D2**
– **Ⓜ** *London Bridge* – 🕾 *(020) 7553 9844 – www.stjohngroup.uk.com*
– *Closed Christmas, New Year and Sunday dinner-Tuesday*
Carte £ 31/35 – *(dinner only and lunch Friday-Sunday) (booking advisable)*
• Traditional British • Bistro • Simple •

An austere, industrial-style dining space, tucked under a railway arch in deepest Bermondsey. Cooking is tasty, satisfying and as British as John Bull and the earthy, original selection of wines are also available to take away.

⫩O ### Village East   ✗ ⓀⓀ ⇔

171-173 Bermondsey St ⊠ *SE1 3UW*   Plan: **D2**
– Ⓜ *London Bridge* – ☎ *(020) 7357 6082 – www.villageeast.co.uk – Closed 24-26 December*
Carte £ 22/50
• Modern cuisine • Trendy • Neighbourhood •
Counter dining is the focus in the main room; those celebrating can tuck themselves away in a separate bar. Cooking mixes contemporary dishes with Mediterranean-inspired plates; the confit turkey leg is the house speciality.

⫩O ### Garrison   🍴 ⓀⓀ ⇔

99-101 Bermondsey St ⊠ *SE1 3XB* – Ⓜ *London Bridge.*   Plan: **D2**
– ☎ *(020) 70899355 – www.thegarrison.co.uk – Closed 25 December*
Menu £ 24/29 – Carte £ 26/39 – *(booking essential at dinner)*
• Mediterranean cuisine • Pub • Friendly •
Known for its charming vintage look, booths and sweet-natured service, The Garrison boasts a warm, relaxed vibe. Open from breakfast until dinner, when a Mediterranean-led menu pulls in the crowds.

Shangri-La   ☆ ‹ ♨ 🗓 & ⓀⓀ ♨ 🛋

The Shard, 31 St Thomas St ⊠ *SE1 9QU*   Plan: **M4**
– Ⓜ *London Bridge* – ☎ *(020) 7234 8000 – www.shangri-la.com/london*
202 rm – ♦£ 350/725 ♦♦£ 350/875 – ☲ £ 32 – 17 suites
• Luxury • Chain • Elegant •
When your hotel occupies floors 34-52 of The Shard, you know it's going to have the wow factor. The pool is London's highest and north-facing bedrooms have the best views. An East-meets-West theme includes the restaurant's menu and afternoon tea when you have a choice of traditional English or Asian.

Bermondsey Square   & ⓀⓀ ♨

Bermondsey Sq, Tower Bridge Rd ⊠ *SE1 3UN*   Plan: **D2**
– Ⓜ *London Bridge* – ☎ *(020) 7378 2450*
– *www.bermondseysquarehotel.co.uk*
90 rm ☲ – ♦£ 150/450 ♦♦£ 160/480
• Business • Modern • Design •
Cleverly designed hotel in a regenerated square, with subtle '60s influences and a hip feel. Relaxed public areas; well-equipped bedrooms include stylish loft suites.

SOUTHWARK

Elliot's   ✗

12 Stoney St, Borough Market ⊠ *SE1 9AD*   Plan: **L4**
– Ⓜ *London Bridge* – ☎ *(020) 74037436 – www.elliotscafe.com – Closed Sunday and bank holidays*
Carte £ 25/33 – *(booking advisable)*
• Modern cuisine • Rustic • Friendly •
A lively, unpretentious café which sources its ingredients from Borough Market, in which it stands. The appealing menu is concise and the cooking is earthy, pleasingly uncomplicated and very satisfying. Try one of the sharing dishes.

Padella   ✗ ⓀⓀ

6 Southwark St, Borough Market ⊠ *SE1 1TQ*   Plan: **M4**
– Ⓜ *London Bridge* – *www.padella.co – Closed 25-26 December, Sunday dinner and bank holidays*
Carte £ 12/22 – *(bookings not accepted)*
• Italian • Bistro • Simple •
This lively little sister to Trullo offers a short, seasonal menu where hand-rolled pasta is the star of the show. Sauces and fillings are inspired by the owners' trips to Italy and prices are extremely pleasing to the pocket. Sit at the ground floor counter overlooking the open kitchen.

🍽️ ## Oxo Tower   ✗✗✗ 🍴 ⇐ 🎐 **AC** 🍷

Oxo Tower Wharf (8th floor), Barge House St   Plan: **K4**
✉ *SE1 9PH* – Ⓜ *Southwark* – ✆ *(020) 78033888 – www.oxotower.co.uk*
– Closed 25 December
Menu £ 35 (lunch) – Carte £ 38/81
• **Modern cuisine** • **Fashionable** • **Design** •
Set on top of an iconic converted factory and providing stunning views of the
Thames and beyond. Stylish, minimalist interior with huge windows. Expect
quite ambitious, mostly European, cuisine.
🍽️ **Oxo Tower Brasserie** – See restaurant listing

🍽️ ## Rabot 1745   ✗✗ 🎐 ⬩ **AC** ⇔

2-4 Bedal St, Borough Market ✉ *SE1 9AL*   Plan: **M4**
– Ⓜ *London Bridge* – ✆ *(020) 73788226 – www.rabot1745.com – Closed*
25-30 December, Sunday and Monday
Carte £ 25/43
• **Modern cuisine** • **Design** • **Fashionable** •
Want something different? How about cocoa cuisine? Rabot 1745 is from the
owners of Hotel Chocolat and is named after their estate in St Lucia. They take
the naturally bitter, spicy flavours of the bean and use them subtly in classically
based dishes. The chocolate mousse dessert is pretty good too!

🍽️ ## Roast   ✗✗ ⬩ **AC** 🍷

The Floral Hall, Borough Market ✉ *SE1 1TL*   Plan: **M4**
– Ⓜ *London Bridge* – ✆ *(020) 30066111 – www.roast-restaurant.com*
– Closed 25-26 December, 1 January and Sunday dinner
Menu £ 30 (weekdays)/38 – Carte £ 31/63 – *(booking essential)*
• **Modern British** • **Friendly** • **Fashionable** •
Known for its British food and for promoting UK producers – not surprising con-
sidering the restaurant's in the heart of Borough Market. The 'dish of the day' is
often a highlight; service is affable and there's live music at night.

🍽️ ## Union Street Café   ✗✗ ⬩ **AC** ⇔

47-51 Great Suffolk St ✉ *SE1 0BS* – Ⓜ *London Bridge*   Plan: **L4**
– ✆ *(020) 7592 7977 – www.gordonramsayrestaurants.com*
Menu £ 26 (lunch) – Carte £ 31/55
• **Italian** • **Trendy** • **Design** •
Occupying a former warehouse, this Gordon Ramsay restaurant has been busy
since day one and comes with a New York feel, a faux industrial look and a basement bar. The Italian menu keeps things simple and stays true to the classics.

🍽️ ## Arabica Bar & Kitchen   ✗ ⬩ **AC** 🍷

3 Rochester Wk. Borough Market ✉ *SE1 9AF*   Plan: **M4**
– Ⓜ *London Bridge* – ✆ *(020) 3011 5151*
– www.arabicabarandkitchen.com – Closed 25-27 December and
1 January
Menu £ 17/25 – Carte £ 21/36 – *(bookings advisable at dinner)*
• **World cuisine** • **Rustic** • **Simple** •
The owner-chef once sold mezze in Borough Market so it's no surprise he
opened his Levantine-inspired restaurant under a railway arch here. This fun,
cavernous place serves sharing plates from Egypt, Syria, Iraq, Jordan and Lebanon.

🍽️ ## Bala Baya   ✗ ⬩ **AC**

Arch 25, Old Union Yard Arches, 229 Union St   Plan: **L4**
✉ *SE1 0LR* – Ⓜ *Southwark* – ✆ *(020) 8001 7015 – www.balabaya.co.uk*
– Closed 25-26 December and Sunday dinner
Menu £ 20 (lunch) – Carte £ 22/41 – *(bookings advisable at dinner)*
• **Middle Eastern** • **Design** • **Friendly** •
A friendly, lively restaurant which celebrates the Middle Eastern heritage of its
passionate owner. Dishes are fresh, vibrant and designed for sharing and the
bright, modern interior is inspired by the Bauhaus architecture of Tel Aviv.

⁂○ **El Pastór** ✕ 🄰🄲

7a Stoney St, Borough Market ✉ *SE1 9AA* Plan: **M4**
– Ⓜ *London Bridge – www.tacoselpastor.co.uk – Closed 25-26 December,*
1-2 January and Sunday
Carte £ 12/20 – *(bookings not accepted)*
• Mexican • Trendy • Simple •
A lively, informal restaurant under the railway arches at London Bridge; inspired by the taquerias of Mexico City. Flavours are beautifully fresh, fragrant and spicy; don't miss the Taco Al Pastór after which the restaurant is named.

⁂○ **Hawksmoor** ✕ 🕭 🄰🄲 ⇄

16 Winchester Wk ✉ *SE1 9AQ –* Ⓜ *London Bridge* Plan: **M4**
– ℰ *(020) 7234 9940 – www.thehawksmoor.com – Closed 24-26 December*
and 1 January
Menu £ 25 (lunch and early dinner) – Carte £ 23/68
• Meats and grills • Brasserie • Vintage •
Hawksmoor's lively 7th branch is a stone's throw from Borough Market, and its Market Specials menu makes good use of its produce. Chargrilled, grass-fed, 35 day dry-aged British steaks are properly cooked and rested and very, very tasty.

⁂○ **Lobos** ✕ 🄰🄲

14 Borough High St ✉ *SE1 9QG –* Ⓜ *London Bridge* Plan: **M4**
– ℰ *(020) 74075361 – www.lobostapas.co.uk – Closed 25-26 December*
and 1 January
Carte £ 18/45
• Spanish • Tapas bar • Rustic •
A dimly lit, decidedly compact tapas bar under the railway arches – sit upstairs to enjoy the theatre of the open kitchen. Go for one of the speciality meat dishes like the leg of slow-roasted Castilian milk-fed lamb.

⁂○ **Oxo Tower Brasserie** ✕ ⇐ 🖼 🄰🄲

Oxo Tower Wharf (8th floor), Barge House St Plan: **K4**
✉ *SE1 9PH –* Ⓜ *Southwark –* ℰ *(020) 7803 3888 – www.oxotower.co.uk*
– Closed 25 December
Menu £ 30 (lunch) – Carte £ 27/49
• Modern cuisine • Design •
Less formal but more fun than the next-door restaurant. The open-plan kitchen produces modern, colourful and easy-to-eat dishes with influences from the Med. Great views too from the bar.

⁂○ **Tapas Brindisa** ✕ 🖼 🕚

18-20 Southwark St, Borough Market ✉ *SE1 1TJ* Plan: **M4**
– Ⓜ *London Bridge –* ℰ *(020) 73578880*
– www.brindisatapaskitchens.com
Carte £ 25/32 – *(bookings not accepted)*
• Spanish • Tapas bar •
A blueprint for many of the tapas bars that subsequently sprung up over London. It has an infectious energy and the well-priced, robust dishes include Galician-style octopus and black rice with squid; try the hand-carved Ibérico hams.

⁂○ **Tate Modern (Restaurant)** ✕ 🕭 ⇄

Switch House (9th floor), Tate Modern, Bankside Plan: **L4**
✉ *SE1 9TG –* Ⓜ *Southwark –* ℰ *(020) 7401 5621 – www.tate.org.uk*
– Closed 24-26 December
Carte £ 27/56 – *(lunch only and dinner Friday-Saturday)*
• Modern British • Design • Brasserie •
A contemporary, faux-industrial style restaurant on the ninth floor of the striking Switch House extension. Modern menus champion British ingredients; desserts are a highlight and the wine list interesting and well-priced.

UNITED KINGDOM - LONDON

⫶○ **Wright Brothers** ✗

11 Stoney St, Borough Market ✉ *SE1 9AD*   Plan: **L4**
– Ⓜ *London Bridge –* ℰ *(020) 74039554 – www.thewrightbrothers.co.uk*
– Closed bank holidays
Carte £ 28/38 *– (booking advisable)*
• Seafood • Cosy • Traditional décor •
Originally an oyster wholesaler; now offers a wide range of oysters along with porter, as well as fruits de mer, daily specials and assorted pies. It fills quickly and an air of contentment reigns.

⫶○ **Anchor & Hope** 🍽 🍴

36 The Cut ✉ *SE1 8LP –* Ⓜ *Southwark. –* ℰ *(020)*   Plan: **K4**
*79289898 – www.anchorandhopepub.co.uk – Closed Christmas-New Year,
Sunday dinner, Monday lunch and bank holidays*
Menu £ 17 *(weekday lunch) –* Carte £ 19/45 *– (bookings not accepted)*
• Modern British • Pub • Rustic •
As popular as ever thanks to its congenial feel and lived-in looks but mostly because of the appealingly seasonal menu and the gutsy, bold cooking that delivers on flavour. No reservations so be prepared to wait at the bar.

🏨 **Hilton London Bankside** ✿ 🛁 🖥 ⚹ 🅰🅲 ⚒

2-8 Great Suffolk St ✉ *SE1 0UG –* Ⓜ *Southwark*   Plan: **L4**
– ℰ *(020) 3667 5600 – www.londonbankside.hilton.com*
292 rm *–* 💷£ 270/369 💷💷£ 270/369 *–* ☕ £ 30 *–* 30 suites
• Business • Modern •
A sleek, design-led hotel with faux industrial touches; ideally situated for visiting the attractions of the South Bank. Spacious, contemporary bedrooms are furnished in a minimalist style. Impressive pool in the basement. OXBO serves a range of British dishes including meats from the Josper grill.

🏨 **Mondrian London** ✿ ⫷ 🛁 🍽 🎿 ⚹ 🅰🅲 ⚒ ✥ 🚗

20 Upper Ground ✉ *SE1 9PD –* Ⓜ *Southwark –* ℰ *(020)*   Plan: **K4**
3747 1000 – www.mondrianlondon.com
359 rm *–* 💷£ 232/515 💷💷£ 350/930 *–* ☕ £ 16 *–* 5 suites
• Business • Design • Grand luxury •
The former Sea Containers house now has slick, stylish look evoking the golden age of the transatlantic liner. Rooms come with a bright splash of colour; Suites have balconies and Superiors, a river view. Globally influenced small plates in the smart restaurant, with meat and fish from the grill & clay oven.

CHELSEA – SOUTH KENSINGTON – EARL'S COURT   PLAN X

CHELSEA

❀❀❀ **Gordon Ramsay** ✗✗✗ 🌱 🅰🅲 ⫶○

68-69 Royal Hospital Rd. ✉ *SW3 4HP*   Plan: **F7**
– Ⓜ *Sloane Square –* ℰ *(020) 73524441*
*– www.gordonramsayrestaurants.com – Closed 21-28 December, Saturday
and Sunday*
Menu £ 65/110 *– (booking essential)*
• French • Elegant • Intimate •
Gordon Ramsay's flagship restaurant is a model of composure and professionalism. The service is discreet and highly polished, yet also warm and reassuring. The cooking bridges both classical and modern schools and is executed with considerable poise, a lightness of touch and remarkable attention to detail.
➜ Pan-fried scallops with apple, walnuts, celery and cider. Poached halibut, king crab and lime with ras el hanout infused broth. Earl Grey parfait, Yorkshire rhubarb and lemon balm.

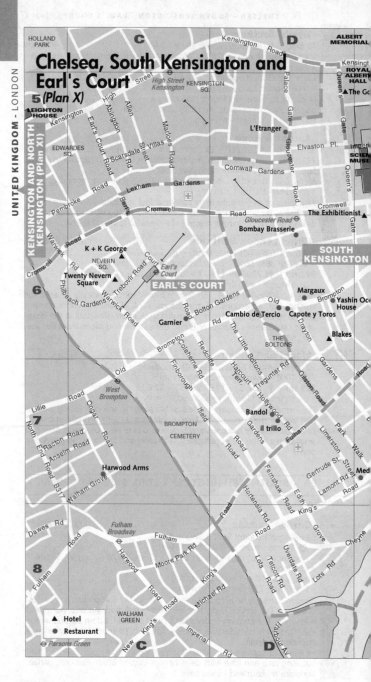

Chelsea, South Kensington and Earl's Court
(Plan X)

HOLLAND PARK

Kensington Road

ALBERT MEMORIAL

ROYAL ALBERT HALL

▲The Go

LEIGHTON HOUSE

High Street Kensington

KENSINGTON SQ.

Kensingt

L'Etranger

Elvaston Pl.

Imperi SCIEN MUSE

EDWARDES SQ.

Cornwall Gardens

Cornwall Gardens

Gardens

Cromwell Road

Road

Gloucester Road

Cromwell

The Exhibitionist ▲

Gloucester Road

Bombay Brasserie

K + K George ▲

NEVERN SQ.

Earl's Court

EARL'S COURT

SOUTH KENSINGTON

Twenty Nevern Square ▲

Margaux

Yashin Oc House

Garnier

Bolton Gardens

Cambio de Tercio

Capote y Toros

THE BOLTONS

Blakes

Brompton

Old West Brompton

BROMPTON CEMETERY

Bandol

il trillo

Harwood Arms

Med

Fulham Broadway

Fulham

King's Road

WALHAM GREEN

Parsons Green

New King's Road

Imperial Rd

▲ Hotel
● Restaurant
⊖ Parsons Green

786

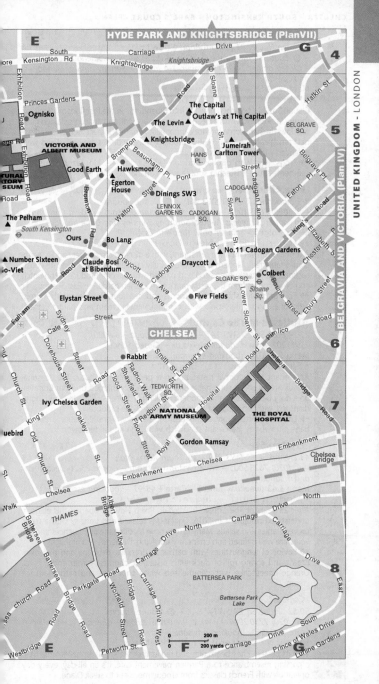

UNITED KINGDOM - LONDON

BELGRAVIA AND VICTORIA (Plan IV)

South Kensington Rd

Carriage Drive

Knightsbridge

Knightsbridge

Halkin St.

Exhibition Road

Princes Gardens

Ognisko

Sloane

Road

The Capital

The Levin ▲ ▲ Outlaw's at The Capital

BELGRAVE SQ.

5

Lane Rd

Exhibition Road

VICTORIA AND ALBERT MUSEUM

▲ Knightsbridge

Brompton

Beauchamp Pl.

HANS PL.

Jumeirah ▲ Carlton Tower

Belgrave Pl.

Eaton Pl.

Belgrave Pl.

TURAL TORY SEUM

Road

Good Earth ●

▲ Hawksmoor

Egerton House ●

Pont

Street

CADOGAN LANE

Cadogan Pl.

King's Road

● Dinings SW3

Street

Walton

LENNOX GARDENS

Sloane

CADOGAN SQ.

CADOGAN PL.

Elizabeth St.

Chesterton St.

The Pelham ▲

South Kensington ⊖

Ours ●

● Bo Lang

Brompton Rd

St.

St. ▲ No.11 Cadogan Gardens

● Colbert

▲ Number Sixteen

io-Viet

Claude Bosi at Bibendum ●

Draycott ▲

Draycott

SLOANE SQ.

Sloane Sq. ⊖

Lower Sloane St.

Bourne Street

Ebury Street

Road

Fulham

Road

Sydney

Cale

Dovehouse Street

Elystan Street ●

Sloane

Cadogan

Ave.

Ave.

● Five Fields

Pimlico Road

6

Street

CHELSEA

Street

Church St.

● Rabbit

Smith St.

St. Leonard's Terr.

TEDWORTH SQ.

Road

Chelsea

7

Ivy Chelsea Garden ●

King's

Old Church St.

Oakley

St.

Radnor Walk

Shawfield St.

Flood Street

Redburn St.

Flood Street

Hospital

NATIONAL ARMY MUSEUM

THE ROYAL HOSPITAL

Bridge

Road

uebird

● Gordon Ramsay

Royal

Embankment

Chelsea Bridge

St.

Chelsea

Chelsea

Embankment

Walk

Albert Bridge

THAMES

North

Carriage

Drive

Battersea Bridge

ea church Road

Battersea

Bridge

Parkgate Road

Albert Bridge

Carriage Drive North

Worfield Street

Carriage Drive

Carriage Drive West

BATTERSEA PARK

Battersea Park Lake

Drive

South

Drive

East

8

Westbridge

E

Petworth St.

0   200 m

0   200 yards

F

Carriage

Prince of Wales Drive

Luffine Gardens

G

ŝ ŝ **Claude Bosi at Bibendum** XxX 錄 M̄C

Michelin House, 81 Fulham Road ⊠ *SW3 6RD* Plan: **E6**
– Ⓜ *South Kensington –* ℰ *(020) 7581 5817 – www.bibendum.co.uk*
– Closed dinner 24-26 December, 2-4 January, Sunday dinner, Monday and Tuesday
Menu £ 37/85 *– (booking essential)*
• French • Elegant • Historic •
Claude Bosi has breathed new life into Bibendum, on the first floor of Michelin's former London HQ. With a clean, contemporary look and an iconic stained glass window, the handsome interior cannot fail to impress. Expect high-end traditional French cooking with creative modern touches; dishes are poised and well-balanced with bold, assured flavours.
➜ Frogs' legs with girolles and vin jaune. Somerset kid, razor clams and sea beets sauce. Pistachio soufflé with banana ice cream.

ŝ **Five Fields** (Taylor Bonnyman) XxX 錄 �& M̄C ⇔

8-9 Blacklands Terr ⊠ *SW3 2SP –* Ⓜ *Sloane Square* Plan: **F6**
– ℰ *(020) 7838 1082 – www.fivefieldsrestaurant.com – Closed Christmas-mid January, 2 weeks August, Saturday, Sunday and bank holidays*
Menu £ 65/85 *– (dinner only) (booking essential)*
• Modern cuisine • Neighbourhood • Intimate •
A formally run yet intimate restaurant, with a discreet atmosphere and a warm, comfortable feel. Modern dishes are skilfully conceived, quite elaborate constructions; attractively presented and packed with flavour. Produce is top-notch and often comes from the restaurant's own kitchen garden in East Sussex.
➜ Foie gras with shimeji mushrooms and beetroot. Roe deer with morels, artichoke and truffle. Apple with caramel, vanilla cream and panna cotta.

ŝ **Outlaw's at The Capital** – The Capital Hotel XX 錄 M̄C ⇔ I♡

22-24 Basil St. ⊠ *SW3 1AT –* Ⓜ *Knightsbridge –* ℰ *(020)* Plan: **F5**
75911202 – www.capitalhotel.co.uk – Closed Sunday
Menu £ 29/62 *– (booking essential)*
• Seafood • Intimate • Elegant •
An elegant yet informal restaurant in a personally run hotel. The seasonal menus are all about sustainable seafood, with fish shipped up from Cornwall on a daily basis. The original modern cooking is delicately flavoured and ingredient-led, with the spotlight on the freshness of the produce.
➜ Lobster risotto, orange and basil. John Dory, Porthilly sauce and cabbage. Strawberry ice cream sandwich with lime and elderflower.

ŝ **Elystan Street** (Philip Howard) XX �& M̄C ⇔

43 Elystan St ⊠ *SW3 3NT –* Ⓜ *South Kensington* Plan: **E6**
– ℰ *(020) 7628 5005 – www.elystanstreet.com – Closed 25-26 December and 1 January*
Menu £ 43 *(weekday lunch) – Carte £ 45/92 – (booking essential)*
• Modern British • Elegant • Friendly •
After 25 years at The Square in Mayfair, Philip Howard opened this elegant, understated restaurant in 2016. Cooking is relaxed and unfussy with a focus on vegetables and salads. Many dishes have Mediterranean influences and flavours are well-defined and eminently satisfying. Desserts are a highlight.
➜ Ravioli of langoustines with barbecue dressing, cabbage and pumpkin. Breast and spring roll of duck with pistachio, cherries, turnip and greens. Orange cheesecake with caramelised white chocolate and cardamom ice cream.

I○ **Colbert** XX 龠 M̄C I♡

50-52 Sloane Sq ⊠ *SW1W 8AX –* Ⓜ *Sloane Square* Plan: **G6**
– ℰ *(020) 7730 2804 – www.colbertchelsea.com – Closed 25 December*
Carte £ 21/56 *– (booking advisable)*
• French • Brasserie • Neighbourhood •
With its posters, chessboard tiles and red leather seats, Colbert bears more than a passing resemblance to a Parisian pavement café. It's an all-day, every day operation with French classics from croque monsieur to steak Diane.

Bluebird
XX 戋 🗚 ⇔

350 King's Rd. ⊠ *SW3 5UU –* Ⓜ *South Kensington*
– ✆ *(020) 75591000 – www.bluebird-restaurant.co.uk*
Carte £ 30/55
• Modern British • Design • Friendly •

Plan: **E7**

It boasts an épicerie, a café, a terrace and even a clothes shop, but the highlight is the first floor restaurant with its marble-topped horseshoe bar, bold print banquettes and abundance of foliage. A Mediterranean menu and super cocktails.

Good Earth
XX 🗚 ⑩

233 Brompton Rd. ⊠ *SW3 2EP –* Ⓜ *Knightsbridge*
– ✆ *(020) 75843658 – www.goodearthgroup.co.uk – Closed 23-31 December*
Menu £ 12 (weekday lunch) – Carte £ 26/46
• Chinese • Elegant •

Plan: **E5**

The menu might appear predictable but this long-standing Chinese has always proved a reliable choice in this area. Although there's no particular geographical bias, the cooking is carefully executed and dishes are authentic.

Hawksmoor
XX 🗚

3 Yeoman's Row ⊠ *SW3 2AL –* Ⓜ *South Kensington*
– ✆ *(020) 7590 9290 – www.thehawksmoor.com – Closed 24-26 December and 1 January*
Menu £ 28 (weekday lunch) – Carte £ 23/69
• Meats and grills • Brasserie •

Plan: **F5**

The Hawksmoor people turned to rarefied Knightsbridge for their 5th London branch. Steaks are still the star of the show but here there's also plenty of seafood. Art deco elegance and friendly service compensate for the basement site.

il trillo
XX 錢 龠 🗚

4 Hollywood Rd ⊠ *SW10 9HY –* Ⓜ *Earl's Court*
– ✆ *(020) 3602 1759 – www.iltrillo.net – Closed Monday*
Menu £ 31 – Carte £ 36/60 – (dinner only and lunch Saturday-Sunday)
• Italian • Friendly • Neighbourhood •

Plan: **D7**

The Bertuccelli family have been making wine and running a restaurant in the Tuscan Hills for over 30 years. Two of the brothers now run this smart local which showcases the produce and wine from their region. Delightful courtyard.

Ivy Chelsea Garden
XX 龠 戋 🗚

197 King's Rd ⊠ *SW3 5ED –* Ⓜ *South Kensington*
– ✆ *(020) 3301 0300 – www.theivychelseagarden.com*
Carte £ 27/61 – (booking essential)
• Traditional British • Fashionable • Intimate •

Plan: **E7**

A sophisticated restaurant with a lively atmosphere; start with a cocktail, then head down to the orangery or out to the garden. The menu covers all bases; from breakfast through to lunch, afternoon tea and dinner, with brunch at weekends.

Medlar
XX 錢 龠 🗚 ⇔

438 King's Rd ⊠ *SW10 0LJ –* Ⓜ *South Kensington*
– ✆ *(020) 73491900 – www.medlarrestaurant.co.uk – Closed 24-26 December and 1 January*
Menu £ 35/49
• Modern cuisine • Neighbourhood • Romantic •

Plan: **E7**

A charming, comfortable and very popular restaurant with a real neighbourhood feel, from two alumni of Chez Bruce. The service is engaging and unobtrusive; the kitchen uses good ingredients in dishes that deliver distinct flavours in classic combinations.

⊗ **Bandol**　　　　　　　　　　　　　　　　X ⊛ ⓐⓒ
6 Hollywood Rd ⊠ SW10 9HY – ⓜ *Earl's Court*　　　Plan: **D7**
– ℰ (020) 7351 1322 – www.barbandol.co.uk – *Closed 24-26 December and 1 January*
Menu £ 15 (weekday lunch) – Carte £ 26/57
• Provençal • Design • Intimate •
Stylishly dressed restaurant with a 100 year old olive tree evoking memories of sunny days spent on the French Riviera. Sharing plates take centre stage on the Provençal and Niçoise inspired menu; seafood is a highlight.

⊗ **Bo Lang**　　　　　　　　　　　　　　　　　X ⓐⓒ
100 Draycott Ave ⊠ SW3 3AD – ⓜ *South Kensington*　　Plan: **E6**
– ℰ (020) 7823 7887 – www.bolangrestaurant.com
Menu £ 15 (lunch) – Carte £ 30/50
• Chinese • Trendy •
It's all about dim sum at this diminutive Hakkasan wannabe. The kitchen has a deft touch but stick to the more traditional combinations; come with friends for the cocktails and to mitigate the effects of some ambitious pricing.

⊗ **Dinings SW3**　　　　　　　　　　　　　　X ⓗⓣ ⓐⓒ
Walton House, Lennox Garden Mews (off Walton St.)　　Plan: **F5**
⊠ SW3 2JH – ⓜ *Sloane Square* – ℰ (020) 7723 0666
– www.diningssw3.co.uk – *Closed 24-26, 31 December and 1 January*
Carte £ 19/65 – *(booking advisable)*
• Japanese • Intimate • Neighbourhood •
Head to the basement dining area with its closely spaced tables and brightly lit marble-topped bar – the best place to sit to enjoy the kitchen's signature sushi and sashimi, made with top quality sustainable seafood mostly from UK waters.

⊗ **Rabbit**　　　　　　　　　　　　　　　　　　　X
172 King's Rd ⊠ SW3 4UP – ⓜ *Sloane Square*　　　　Plan: **F6**
– ℰ (020) 3750 0172 – www.rabbit-restaurant.com – *Closed 22 December-2 January*
Menu £ 14 (weekday lunch)/28 – Carte £ 21/31 – *(pre-book at weekends)*
• Modern British • Rustic • Friendly •
The Gladwin brothers have followed the success of The Shed with another similarly rustic and warmly run restaurant. Share satisfying, robustly flavoured plates; game is a real highlight, particularly the rabbit dishes.

🏨 **Jumeirah Carlton Tower**　　　< ☞ ⓕⓢ ⓦ ⓡ ☒ ✕ ⓖ ⓢⓐ ⓐ
Cadogan Pl ⊠ SW1X 9PY – ⓜ *Knightsbridge* – ℰ (020)　Plan: **F5**
72351234 – www.jumeirah.com/jct
216 rm – †£ 342/835 ††£ 342/835 – ☒ £ 32 – 58 suites
• Business • Modern • Elegant •
Imposing international hotel overlooking a leafy square and just yards from all the swanky boutiques. Well-equipped rooftop health club has great views. Generously proportioned bedrooms boast every conceivable facility.

🏨 **The Capital**　　　　　　　　　　　　　ⓐⓒ ⓢⓐ ⓐ
22-24 Basil St. ⊠ SW3 1AT　　　　　　　　　　　　Plan: **F5**
– ⓜ *Knightsbridge* – ℰ (020) 75895171 – www.capitalhotel.co.uk
49 rm – †£ 265/395 ††£ 315/495 – ☒ £ 17 – 1 suite
• Luxury • Traditional • Classic •
A fine, thoroughly British hotel, known for its discreet atmosphere and its conscientious and attentive service. Comfortable, immaculately kept bedrooms are understated in style. Enjoy afternoon tea in the intimate Sitting Room.
❀ **Outlaw's at The Capital** – See restaurant listing

Draycott

26 Cadogan Gdns ✉ SW3 2RP Plan: **F6**
– Ⓜ Sloane Square – ✆ (020) 77306466 – www.draycotthotel.com
35 rm – †£ 190/240 ††£ 380/522 – ☕£ 22
• Townhouse • Luxury • Personalised •
Charming 19C house with elegant sitting room overlooking tranquil garden for afternoon tea. Bedrooms are individually decorated in a country house style and are named after writers or actors.

Egerton House

17-19 Egerton Terr ✉ SW3 2BX Plan: **F5**
– Ⓜ South Kensington – ✆ (020) 75892412
– www.egertonhousehotel.com
28 rm – †£ 295/425 ††£ 295/425 – ☕£ 29
• Townhouse • Luxury • Classic •
Compact but comfortable townhouse in a very good location, well-maintained throughout and owned by the Red Carnation group. High levels of personal service make the hotel stand out.

Knightsbridge

10 Beaufort Gdns ✉ SW3 1PT Plan: **F5**
– Ⓜ Knightsbridge – ✆ (020) 75846300 – www.knightsbridgehotel.com
44 rm – †£ 240/342 ††£ 270/366 – ☕£ 19
• Luxury • Townhouse • Personalised •
Charming and attractively furnished townhouse in a Victorian terrace, with a very stylish, discreet feel. Every bedroom is immaculately appointed and has a style all of its own; fine detailing throughout.

The Levin

28 Basil St. ✉ SW3 1AS Plan: **F5**
– Ⓜ Knightsbridge – ✆ (020) 75896286 – www.thelevinhotel.co.uk
12 rm – †£ 245/379 ††£ 245/379 – ☕£ 13
• Townhouse • Classic • Art déco •
Little sister to The Capital next door. Impressive façade, contemporary interior and comfortable bedrooms in a subtle art deco style, with marvellous champagne mini bars. Simple dishes served all day down in the basement restaurant.

No.11 Cadogan Gardens

11 Cadogan Gdns ✉ SW3 2RJ Plan: **F6**
– Ⓜ Sloane Square – ✆ (020) 7730 7000 – www.11cadogangardens.com
56 rm – †£ 295/395 ††£ 395/495 – ☕£ 24 – 7 suites
• Townhouse • Personalised • Classic •
Townhouse hotel fashioned out of four red-brick houses and exuberantly dressed in bold colours and furnishings. Theatrically decorated bedrooms vary in size from cosy to spacious. Intimate basement Italian restaurant with accomplished and ambitious cooking.

Earl's Court

K + K George

1-15 Templeton Pl ✉ SW5 9NB – Ⓜ Earl's Court Plan: **C6**
– ✆ (020) 75988700 – www.kkhotels.com
154 rm ☕ – †£ 190/280 ††£ 200/300
• Business • Modern •
In contrast to its period façade, this hotel's interior is stylish, colourful and contemporary. The hotel is on a quiet street, yet close to the Tube and has a large rear garden where you can enjoy breakfast in summer. Comfortable bar/lounge and a spacious restaurant serving a wide-ranging menu.

⌂ **Twenty Nevern Square**   **P**

20 Nevern Sq ⊠ *SW5 9PD –* Ⓜ *Earl's Court –* 🕾 *(020)*   Plan: **C6**
7565 9555 – www.mayflowercollection.com
25 rm 🖵 *–* ♟£ 75/160 ♟♟£ 85/215
• Townhouse • Luxury • Personalised •
Privately owned townhouse overlooking an attractive Victorian garden square.
It's decorated with original pieces of hand-carved Indonesian furniture; breakfast in a bright conservatory. Some bedrooms have their own terrace.

SOUTH KENSINGTON

🍴 **Bombay Brasserie**   XxxX 🄰🄲 🕅☺

Courtfield Rd. ⊠ *SW7 4QH –* Ⓜ *Gloucester Road*   Plan: **D6**
– 🕾 *(020) 73704040 – www.bombayb.co.uk – Closed 25 December*
Menu £ 27 *(weekday lunch) –* Carte £ 36/52 *– (bookings advisable at
dinner)*
• Indian • Exotic décor • Chic •
A well-run, well-established and comfortable Indian restaurant, featuring a very
smart bar and conservatory. Creative dishes sit alongside more traditional
choices on the various menus and vegetarian are well-catered for.

🍴 **Cambio de Tercio**   XX 🕭 🄰🄲 ⇔

163 Old Brompton Rd. ⊠ *SW5 0LJ*   Plan: **D6**
– Ⓜ *Gloucester Road –* 🕾 *(020) 72448970 – www.cambiodetercio.co.uk
– Closed 2 weeks December and 2 weeks August*
Menu £ 45/55 *–* Carte £ 21/69
• Spanish • Cosy • Family •
A long-standing, ever-improving Spanish restaurant. Start with small dishes like
the excellent El Bulli inspired omelette, then have the popular Pluma Iberica.
There are super sherries and a wine list to prove there is life beyond Rioja.

🍴 **L'Etranger**   XX 🕭 🄰🄲 ⇔

36 Gloucester Rd. ⊠ *SW7 4QT –* Ⓜ *Gloucester Road*   Plan: **D5**
– 🕾 *(020) 75841118 – www.etranger.co.uk*
Menu £ 25 *(weekdays)/30 –* Carte £ 30/57 *– (booking essential)*
• Modern French • Neighbourhood • Romantic •
A moody, atmospheric restaurant serving an eclectic menu which mixes French
dishes with techniques and flavours from Japanese cooking. Impressive wine
and sake lists and a great value set menu. Ask for a corner table.

🍴 **Ognisko**   XX 🕭 ⅍ ⇔ 🕾

55 Prince's Gate, Exhibition Rd ⊠ *SW7 2PN*   Plan: **E5**
– Ⓜ *South Kensington –* 🕾 *(020) 7589 0101
– www.ogniskorestaurant.co.uk – Closed 24-26 December and 1 January*
Menu £ 22 *(lunch and early dinner) –* Carte £ 27/37
• Polish • Elegant • Historic •
Ognisko Polskie – The Polish Hearth Club – was founded in 1940 in this magnifi-
cent townhouse; its elegant restaurant serves traditional dishes from across Eas-
tern Europe and the cooking is without pretence and truly from the heart.

🍴 **Ours**   XX ⅍ 🄰🄲 ⇔

264 Brompton Rd ⊠ *SW3 2AS –* Ⓜ *South Kensington*   Plan: **E6**
– 🕾 *(020) 7100 2200 – www.restaurant-ours.com – Closed 24-
28 December, Sunday and Monday*
Menu £ 45/55 *–* Carte £ 35/77 *– (dinner only and Saturday lunch) (booking advisable)*
• Modern cuisine • Fashionable • Trendy •
An immense restaurant featuring trees, a living plant wall of 1,200 flower pots
and a mezzanine level bar-lounge. The modern menu offers seasonal, ingredient-led dishes with a fresh, light style. Keen service; weekend brunches.

Yashin Ocean House

XX 🍴 ᓂ 🗚 ⇔

117-119 Old Brompton Rd ⊠ *SW7 3RN*
Plan: **D6**
– Ⓜ *Gloucester Road* – ✆ *(020) 7373 3990* – *www.yashinocean.com*
– *Closed Christmas*
Carte £ 20/86

• Japanese • Chic • Elegant •

The USP of this chic Japanese restaurant is 'head to tail' eating, although, as there's nothing for carnivores, 'fin to scale' would be more precise. Stick with specialities like the whole dry-aged sea bream for the full umami hit.

Capote y Toros

X 🕸 🍴 🗚

157 Old Brompton Road ⊠ *SW5 0LJ*
Plan: **D6**
– Ⓜ *Gloucester Road* – ✆ *(020) 73730567* – *www.cambiodetercio.co.uk*
– *Closed 2 weeks Christmas, Sunday and Monday*
Menu £ 30 – Carte £ 15/33 – *(dinner only)*

• Spanish • Tapas bar • Cosy •

Expect to queue at this compact and vividly coloured spot which celebrates sherry, tapas, ham... and bullfighting. Sherry is the star; those as yet unmoved by this most underappreciated of wines will be dazzled by the variety.

Go-Viet

X 🗚

53 Old Brompton Rd ⊠ *SW7 3JS* – Ⓜ *South Kensington*
Plan: **E6**
– ✆ *(020) 7589 6432* – *www.vietnamfood.co.uk* – *Closed 24-26 December*
Carte £ 20/74

• Vietnamese • Contemporary décor •

A Vietnamese restaurant from experienced chef Jeff Tan. Lunch concentrates on classics like pho and bun, while dinner provides a more sophisticated experience, offering interesting flavourful dishes with a distinct modern edge.

Margaux

X 🕸 🗚 ⇔

152 Old Brompton Rd ⊠ *SW5 0BE*
Plan: **D6**
– Ⓜ *Gloucester Road* – ✆ *(020) 7373 5753* – *www.barmargaux.co.uk*
– *Closed 24-26 December, 1 January and lunch August*
Menu £ 15 *(weekday lunch)* – Carte £ 32/57

• Mediterranean cuisine • Trendy • Bistro •

France and Italy are the primary influences at this modern bistro, where classics feature alongside more unusual dishes. The wine list provides a good choice of varietals and the ersatz industrial look is downtown Manhattan.

Blakes

⭧

33 Rowland Gdns ⊠ *SW7 3PF* – Ⓜ *Gloucester Road*
Plan: **D6**
– ✆ *(020) 73706701* – *www.blakeshotels.com*
45 rm – ♦£ 235/255 ♦♦£ 345/395 – �ⵏ £ 23 – 7 suites

• Luxury • Design • Contemporary •

Behind the Victorian façade is one of London's first 'boutique' hotels. Dramatic, bold and eclectic décor, with oriental influences and antiques from around the world. International dishes in the spacious ground floor restaurant.

The Pelham

⭧ 🛎 🗚

15 Cromwell Pl ⊠ *SW7 2LA*
Plan: **E6**
– Ⓜ *South Kensington* – ✆ *(020) 7589 8288*
– *www.pelhamhotel.co.uk*
52 rm – ♦£ 200/350 ♦♦£ 200/350 – ⊑ £ 15 – 2 suites

• Luxury • Townhouse • Elegant •

Great location if you're in town for museum visiting. It's a mix of English country house and city townhouse, with a panelled sitting room and library with honesty bar. Sweet and intimate basement restaurant with Mediterranean menu.

Number Sixteen

⌂⌂   ⬛ AC

16 Sumner Pl. ⊠ *SW7 3EG*   Plan: **E6**
– Ⓜ *South Kensington* – ℰ *(020) 7589 5232*
– *www.firmdalehotels.co.uk*
41 rm – †£ 180/240 ††£ 276/342 – ☕ £ 20
• Townhouse • Luxury • Elegant •

Elegant 19C townhouses in a smart neighbourhood; well-run by charming, helpful staff. Tastefully furnished lounges feature attractive modern art. First floor bedrooms benefit from large windows and balconies; basement rooms are the quietest and two have their own terrace. Airy Orangery restaurant for afternoon tea and light meals overlooking the pretty garden.

The Exhibitionist

⌂⌂   ✿ AC

8-10 Queensberry Pl ⊠ *SW7 2EA*   Plan: **E6**
– Ⓜ *South Kensington* – ℰ *(020) 7915 0000*
– *www.theexhibitionisthotel.com*
37 rm – †£ 199/599 ††£ 199/899 – ☕ £ 20 – 3 suites
• Townhouse • Design • Quirky •

A funky, design-led boutique hotel fashioned out of several 18C townhouses. The modern artwork changes every few months and the bedrooms are individually furnished – several have their own roof terrace.

The Gore

⌂⌂   ✿ AC ⛱

190 Queen's Gate ⊠ *SW7 5EX*   Plan: **D5**
– Ⓜ *Gloucester Road* – ℰ *(020) 7584 6601*
– *www.gorehotel.com*
50 rm – †£ 190/500 ††£ 190/500 – ☕ £ 18
• Townhouse • Historic • Personalised •

Idiosyncratic, hip Victorian house close to the Royal Albert Hall, whose charming lobby is covered with pictures and prints. Individually styled bedrooms have plenty of character and fun bathrooms. Bright and casual bistro.

KENSINGTON – NORTH KENSINGTON – NOTTING HILL

     PLAN XI

KENSINGTON

Kitchen W8

☸   XX AC

11-13 Abingdon Rd ⊠ *W8 6AH*   Plan: **C5**
– Ⓜ *High Street Kensington* – ℰ *(020) 79370120*
– *www.kitchenw8.com*
– *Closed 24-26 December and bank holidays*
Menu £ 28/30 – Carte £ 40/55
• Modern cuisine • Neighbourhood •

A joint venture between Rebecca Mascarenhas and Philip Howard. Not as informal as the name suggests but still refreshingly free of pomp. The cooking has depth and personality and prices are quite restrained considering the quality of the produce and the kitchen's skill.
→ Smoked eel with grilled mackerel, golden beetroots and sweet mustard. Roast rump of veal with bulgur wheat, charred lettuce, hazelnuts and shiitake. Muscovado financiers with salted peanut ice cream, bitter chocolate and banana.

Launceston Place

⑩   XXX AC ⇄

1a Launceston Pl ⊠ *W8 5RL* – Ⓜ *Gloucester Road*   Plan: **D5**
– ℰ *(020) 7937 6912* – *www.launcestonplace-restaurant.co.uk* – *Closed 25-30 December, 1 January, Tuesday lunch and Monday*
Menu £ 25/75 – *(bookings advisable at dinner)*
• Modern cuisine • Neighbourhood • Fashionable •

A favourite of many thanks to its palpable sense of neighbourhood, pretty façade and its nooks and crannies which make it ideal for trysts or tête-à-têtes. The menu is fashionably terse and the cooking is quite elaborate, with dishes big on originality and artfully presented.

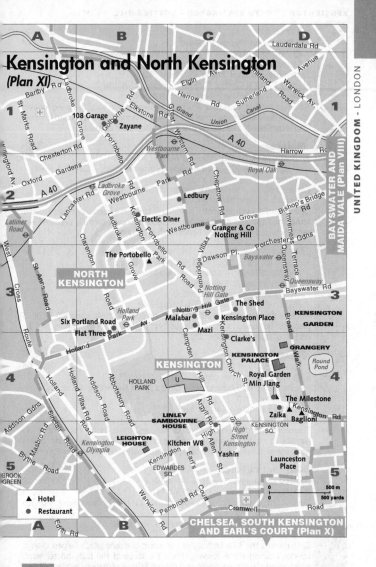

Kensington and North Kensington

(Plan XI)

BAYSWATER AND MAIDA VALE (Plan VIII)

NORTH KENSINGTON

KENSINGTON

KENSINGTON GARDEN

KENSINGTON PALACE

ORANGERY

Round Pond

HOLLAND PARK

LEIGHTON HOUSE

LINLEY SAMBOURNE HOUSE

Kensington Olympia

EDWARDES SQ.

HIGH STREET KENSINGTON

KENSINGTON SQ.

BROOK GREEN

108 Garage
Zayane
Ledbury
Electic Diner
Granger & Co Notting Hill
The Portobello
Six Portland Road
Flat Three
Malabar
The Shed
Kensington Place
Mazi
Clarke's
Royal Garden
Min Jiang
The Milestone
Zaika
Baglioni
Kitchen W8
Yashin
Launceston Place

▲ Hotel
● Restaurant

0   500 m
0   500 yards

CHELSEA, SOUTH KENSINGTON AND EARL'S COURT (Plan X)

---

110 **Min Jiang** – Royal Garden Hotel   XxX ⩽ AC ⟺
2-24 Kensington High St (10th Floor) ⊠ W8 4PT   Plan: **D4**
– Ⓜ High Street Kensington
– ☎ (020) 73611988 – www.minjiang.co.uk
Menu £ 40/80 – Carte £ 30/99

• Chinese • Elegant • Design •

The cooking at this stylish 10th floor Chinese restaurant covers all provinces, but Cantonese and Sichuanese dominate. Wood-fired Beijing duck is a speciality. The room's good looks compete with the great views of Kensington Gardens.

Clarke's
XX & 🏧 ⟳

124 Kensington Church St ⊠ W8 4BH   Plan: **C4**
– 🅜 Notting Hill Gate – 𝒞 (020) 72219225 – www.sallyclarke.com
– Closed 2 weeks August, Christmas-New Year, Sunday January-
September and bank holidays
Menu £ 27/39 – Carte £ 40/60 – *(booking advisable)*
· Modern cuisine · Neighbourhood ·

A forever popular restaurant, which has enjoyed a loyal local following for over 30 years. Sally Clarke uses only the freshest seasonal ingredients and her cooking is confidently executed with a pleasing lightness of touch.

Malabar
XX 🏧

27 Uxbridge St. ⊠ W8 7TQ – 🅜 Notting Hill Gate   Plan: **C3**
– 𝒞 (020) 77278800 – www.malabar-restaurant.co.uk – Closed 1 week
Christmas
Carte £ 18/37 – *(dinner only and lunch Saturday-Sunday)*
· Indian · Neighbourhood ·

Opened in 1983 in a residential Notting Hill street, but keeps up its appearance, remaining fresh and good-looking. Balanced menu of carefully prepared and sensibly priced Indian dishes. Buffet lunch on Sunday.

Yashin
XX 🏧

1a Argyll Rd. ⊠ W8 7DB – 🅜 High Street Kensington   Plan: **C5**
– 𝒞 (020) 79381536 – www.yashinsushi.com – Closed 24, 25 and
31 December and 1 January
Carte £ 45/89 – *(booking essential)*
· Japanese · Design · Fashionable ·

Ask for a counter seat to watch the chefs prepare the sushi; choose 8, 11 or 15 pieces, to be served together. The quality of fish is clear; tiny garnishes and the odd bit of searing add originality.

Zaika
XX 🏧 🍸

1 Kensington High St. ⊠ W8 5NP   Plan: **D4**
– 🅜 High Street Kensington – 𝒞 (020) 77956533
– www.zaikaofkensington.com – Closed 25-26 December, 1 January
and Monday lunch
Menu £ 19 (lunch) – Carte £ 32/67
· Indian · Exotic décor ·

The cooking focuses on the North of India and the influences of Mughal and Nawabi, so expect rich and fragrantly spiced dishes. The softly-lit room makes good use of its former life as a bank, with its wood-panelling and ornate ceiling.

Kensington Place
X 🏧 ⟳

201-209 Kensington Church St. ⊠ W8 7LX   Plan: **C3**
– 🅜 Notting Hill Gate – 𝒞 (020) 77273184
– www.kensingtonplace-restaurant.co.uk – Closed Sunday dinner, Monday
lunch and bank holidays
Menu £ 20 (lunch and early dinner) – Carte £ 25/52
· Seafood · Neighbourhood · Brasserie ·

2017 marked the 30th birthday of this iconic brasserie which helped change London's dining scene forever. Fish is the focus of the fairly priced menu which mixes classics like prawn cocktail and fish pie with more modern dishes.

Mazi
X 🍽

12-14 Hillgate St ⊠ W8 7SR – 🅜 Notting Hill Gate   Plan: **C3**
– 𝒞 (020) 72293794 – www.mazi.co.uk – Closed 24-25 December and 1-
2 January
Menu £ 15 (weekday lunch) – Carte £ 28/43
· Greek · Friendly · Neighbourhood ·

It's all about sharing at this simple, bright Greek restaurant where traditional recipes are given a modern twist to create vibrant, colourful and fresh tasting dishes. The garden terrace at the back is a charming spot in summer.

The Shed ✗

122 Palace Gardens Ter. ✉ *W8 4RT*   Plan: **C3**
– ⓜ Notting Hill Gate – ℰ (020) 7229 4024
– www.theshed-restaurant.com – Closed Monday lunch and Sunday
Carte £ 21/32
• Modern British • Rustic • Neighbourhood •

It's more than just a shed but does have a higgledy-piggledy charm and a healthy dose of the outdoors. One brother cooks, one manages and the third runs the farm which supplies the produce for the earthy, satisfying dishes.

Royal Garden   ✿ ⟨ ⅙ 𝔰 ⅙ 🄺 ⅗ 🄿

2-24 Kensington High St ✉ *W8 4PT*   Plan: **D4**
– ⓜ High Street Kensington – ℰ (020) 79378000
– www.royalgardenhotel.co.uk
394 rm – †£ 170/460 ††£ 210/520 – ☑ £ 25 – 17 suites
• Business • Luxury • Modern •

A tall, modern hotel with many of its rooms enjoying enviable views over the adjacent Kensington Gardens. All the modern amenities and services, with well-drilled staff. Bright, spacious Park Terrace offers an international menu as well as afternoon tea for which you're accompanied by a pianist.

⊞○ **Min Jiang** – See restaurant listing

The Milestone   ✿ ⅙ 𝔰 🄺

1-2 Kensington Ct ✉ *W8 5DL*   Plan: **D4**
– ⓜ High Street Kensington – ℰ (020) 79171000
– www.milestonehotel.com
62 rm ☑ – †£ 330/500 ††£ 450/1500 – 6 suites
• Luxury • Townhouse • Personalised •

Elegant and enthusiastically run hotel with decorative Victorian façade and a very British feel. Charming oak-panelled sitting room is popular for afternoon tea; snug bar in former stables. Meticulously decorated bedrooms offer period detail. Ambitious cooking in discreet Cheneston's restaurant.

Baglioni   ✿ ⅙ 🄺 ⅗

60 Hyde Park Gate ✉ *SW7 5BB*   Plan: **AE5**
– ⓜ High Street Kensington – ℰ (020) 73685718
– www.baglionihotels.com
67 rm ☑ – †£ 315/660 ††£ 315/660 – 15 suites
• Luxury • Personalised • Classic •

It's opposite Kensington Palace and there's no escaping the fact that this is an Italian-owned hotel. The interior is bold and ornate and comes with a certain swagger. Stylish bedrooms have a masculine feel and boast impressive facilities. Italian classics are served in the ground floor restaurant.

NORTH KENSINGTON

Ledbury (Brett Graham)   ✗✗✗ 🕸 🎍 🄺

127 Ledbury Rd. ✉ *W11 2AQ* – ⓜ *Notting Hill Gate*   Plan: **C2**
– ℰ (020) 7792 9090 – www.theledbury.com – Closed 25-26 December,
August bank holiday and lunch Monday-Tuesday
Menu £ 75/145
• Modern cuisine • Neighbourhood • Contemporary décor •

Brett Graham's husbandry skills and close relationship with his suppliers ensure the quality of the produce shines through and flavour combinations linger long in the memory. This smart yet unshowy restaurant comes with smooth and engaging service. Only a tasting menu is served at dinner on weekends.

➜ Clay-baked golden beetroot with English caviar, smoked and dried eel. Dorset Sika deer with hen-of-the-wood, pickled wild hops and smoked bone marrow. Chocolate, dark chocolate Chantilly and mint.

�

Flat Three

XX AC ⁣

120-122 Holland Park Ave ⊠ *W11 4UA*   Plan: **B3/4**
– Ⓜ *Holland Park* – ℰ *(020) 7792 8987 – www.flatthree.london – Closed
21 December-4 January, 21 August-1 September, Sunday and Monday
Carte £ 40/66 – *(dinner only and lunch Friday-Saturday)*
• Creative • Design • Minimalist •
Basement restaurant blending the cuisines of Scandinavia, Korea and Japan.
Not everything works but there's certainly ambition. They make their own soy
and miso and serve more foraged ingredients than you'll find in Ray Mears'
pocket.

Electric Diner

X ⅟ AC

191 Portobello Rd ⊠ *W11 2ED* – Ⓜ *Ladbroke Grove*   Plan: **B2**
– ℰ *(020) 7908 9696 – www.electricdiner.com – Closed 30-31 August and*
25 December
Carte £ 17/34
• Meats and grills • Rustic • Neighbourhood •
Next to the iconic Electric Cinema is this loud, brash and fun all-day operation
with an all-encompassing menu; the flavours are as big as the portions. The
long counter and red leather booths add to the authentic diner feel.

Granger and Co. Notting Hill

X ⅟ AC

175 Westbourne Grove ⊠ *W11 2SB* – Ⓜ *Bayswater*   Plan: **C2**
– ℰ *(020) 7229 9111 – www.grangerandco.com – Closed August bank*
holiday weekend and 25 December
Carte £ 19/41 – *(bookings not accepted)*
• Modern cuisine • Friendly • Fashionable •
When Bill Granger moved from sunny Sydney to cool Notting Hill he opened a
local restaurant too. He brought with him that delightful 'matey' service that
only Aussies do, his breakfast time ricotta hotcakes and a fresh, zesty menu.

108 Garage

X AC

108 Golborne Rd ⊠ *W10 5PS* – Ⓜ *Westbourne Park*   Plan: **B1**
– ℰ *(020) 8969 3769 – www.108garage.com – Closed 2 weeks August,*
2 weeks Christmas, Sunday and Monday
Menu £ 35/45 – Carte £ 28/46 – *(booking essential)*
• Modern British • Neighbourhood • Intimate •
A former garage with a utilitarian look that's more Hackney than Kensington; all
bare brick, exposed ducting and polished concrete. Sit at the counter and chat
to the affable chef; modern dishes are colourful and vibrant and change daily.

Six Portland Road

X AC

6 Portland Rd ⊠ *W11 4LA* – Ⓜ *Holland Park* – ℰ *(020)*   Plan: **B3**
7229 3130 – www.sixportlandroad.com – Closed Christmas-New Year, last
2 weeks August, Sunday dinner and Monday
Menu £ 19 *(weekday lunch)* – Carte £ 30/52
• French • Neighbourhood • Cosy •
An intimate and personally run neighbourhood restaurant owned by Oli Barker,
previously of Terroirs. The menu changes frequently and has a strong French
accent; dishes are reassuringly recognisable, skilfully constructed and very tasty.

Zayane

X AC

91 Golborne Rd ⊠ *W10 5NL* – Ⓜ *Westbourne Park*   Plan: **B1**
– ℰ *(020) 8960 1137 – www.zayanerestaurant.com – Closed 26 August-3 September*
Menu £ 25 – Carte £ 24/38
• Moroccan • Neighbourhood • Friendly •
An intimate neighbourhood restaurant owned by Casablanca-born Meryem Mortell and
evoking the sights and scents of North Africa. Carefully conceived dishes have authentic
Moroccan flavours but are cooked with modern techniques.

🏠 **The Portobello**

22 Stanley Gdns. ⊠ W11 2NG – Ⓜ Notting Hill Gate   Plan: **B3**
– ℰ (020) 77272777 – www.portobellohotel.com
21 rm � – 🛏£ 175 🛏🛏£ 180/395
· Townhouse · Luxury · Personalised ·

An attractive Victorian townhouse in an elegant terrace, with original, theatrical décor, charming staff and a home-from-home feel. Circular beds, half-testers, Victorian baths: no two bedrooms are the same.

CLERKENWELL · FINSBURY

CLERKENWELL

❀ **St John**   X AC ⇄

26 St John St ⊠ EC1M 4AY – Ⓜ Farringdon   Plan: **L2**
– ℰ (020) 7251 0848 – www.stjohnrestaurant.com
– Closed Christmas-New Year, Saturday lunch, Sunday dinner and bank holidays
Carte £ 27/61 – *(booking essential)*
· Traditional British · Simple · Brasserie ·

A glorious celebration of British fare and a champion of 'nose to tail' eating. Utilitarian surroundings and a refreshing lack of ceremony ensure the food is the focus; it's appealingly simple, full of flavour and very satisfying.
➔ Roast bone marrow with parsley salad. Pigeon and trotter pie. Dr Henderson ice cream.

❀ **Comptoir Gascon**   X AC

61-63 Charterhouse St. ⊠ EC1M 6HJ – Ⓜ Farringdon   Plan: **K2**
– ℰ (020) 7608 0851 – www.comptoirgascon.com
– Closed Christmas-New Year, Sunday, Monday and bank holidays
Menu £ 15 (weekday lunch) – Carte £ 18/34 – *(booking essential)*
· French · Bistro · Rustic ·

A buzzy, well-priced restaurant; sister to Club Gascon. Rustic and satisfying specialities from the SW of France include wine, bread, cheese and plenty of duck, with cassoulet and duck rillettes perennial favourites and the duck burger popular at lunch. There's also produce on display to take home.

🍽 **Luca**   XX 🌿 ᳮ AC

88 St. John St ⊠ EC1M 4EH – Ⓜ Farringdon – ℰ (020)   Plan: **L1**
3859 3000 – www.luca.restaurant
– Closed Sunday
Menu £ 55 – Carte £ 32/52 – *(booking essential)*
· Italian · Design · Fashionable ·

Owned by the people behind The Clove Club, but less a little sister, more a distant cousin. There's a cheery atmosphere, a bar for small plates and a frequently changing menu of Italian dishes made with quality British ingredients.

🍽 **Sosharu**   XX AC

64 Turnmill St ⊠ EC1M 5RR – Ⓜ Farringdon – ℰ (020)   Plan: **K1**
3805 2304 – www.sosharulondon.com
– Closed Sunday and bank holidays except Good Friday
Menu £ 30 (lunch and early dinner)/30 – Carte £ 28/50
· Japanese · Fashionable · Trendy ·

The seventh London restaurant from Jason Atherton and the first serving Japanese food is this bustling operation with a chic, understated style. Six small plates with a large rice pot or a 'classic' between two will do nicely.

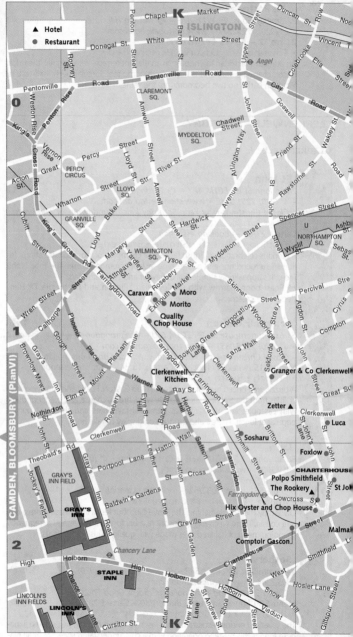

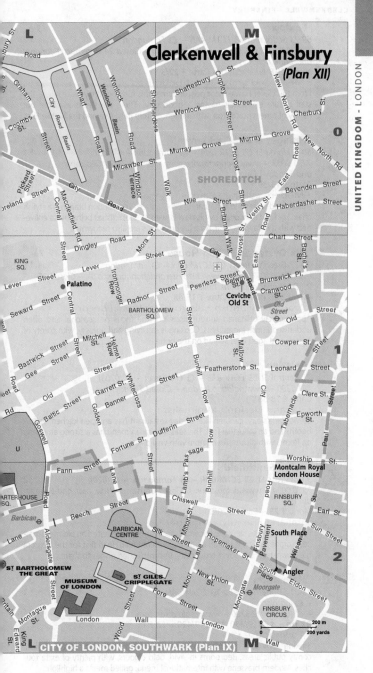

Clerkenwell & Finsbury
(Plan XII)

L

M

O

Road

Road

Graham Street

Coombs St.

Pickard Street

Ireland

Central Street

Macclesfield Rd

City Road Basin

Wharf

Wenlock Basin

Wenlock Road

City Road

Micawber St.

Windsor Terrace

Shepherdess Walk

Shaftesbury St.

Wenlock Street

Copley St.

Murray Grove

Nile Street

Britannia Walk

Provost Street

Vestry St.

City Road

New North Rd

Cherbury St.

New North Rd

East Road

SHOREDITCH

Bevenden Street

Haberdasher Street

Chart Street

Bache's St.

KING SQ.

Lever Street

Dingley Road

Lever Street

Seward Street

Central Street

Mora St.

Bath Street

Peerless Street

Street

Baldwin St.

Brunswick Pl.

Cranwood St.

Old Street ⊖ Old

Street

● Palatino

Ironmonger Row

Radnor Street

Bartholomew Street

● Ceviche Old St

BARTHOLOMEW SQ.

Mitchell St.

Helmet Row

Old Street

Street

Mallow St.

Cowper St.

Street

Bastwick Street

Gee Street

Old Street

Garrett St.

Whitecross Street

Banner Street

Bunhill Row

Featherstone St.

City Road

Leonard Street

Clere St.

Baltic Street

Golden Lane

Dufferin Street

Epworth St.

Tabernacle Street

Paul Street

Fortune St.

Lamb's Passage

Bunhill Row

Worship St.

Montcalm Royal London House ▲

Fann Street

CHARTERHOUSE SQ.

Barbican ⊖

Goswell Road

U

Aldersgate Street

Beech Street

Lane

Chiswell Street

FINSBURY SQ.

Earl St.

Sun Street

Street

St Bartholomew the Great

Museum of London

BARBICAN CENTRE

St Giles Cripplegate

Silk Street

Milton St.

Ropemaker St.

Moor Lane

New Union St.

Fore Street

Moorgate

Finsbury Pavement

South Place

South Place

Eldon Street

Wilson St.

South Place ● Angler

Moorgate ⊖

FINSBURY CIRCUS

0   200 m
0   200 yards

London Wall

Montague St.

King Edward St.

Wood Street

London Wall

London Wall

Foxlow

⚵ ৬

69-73 St John St ✉ EC1M 4AN – Ⓜ Farringdon — Plan: **L2**
– ☏ (020) 7680 2702 – www.foxlow.co.uk – Closed 24 December-1 January and bank holidays
Menu £ 18 (weekdays) – Carte £ 22/39

• Meats and grills • Neighbourhood •

From the clever Hawksmoor people comes this fun and funky place where the staff ensure everyone's having a good time. There are steaks available but plenty of other choices too, with influences from Italy, Asia and the Middle East.

Granger & Co. Clerkenwell

⚵ ৬ ⓀⒸ

50 Sekforde St ✉ EC1R 0HA – Ⓜ Farringdon – ☏ (020) — Plan: **K1**
7251 9032 – www.grangerandco.com – Closed 24-26 December and Sunday dinner
Carte £ 13/39

• Modern cuisine • Family • Elegant •

Aussie food writer and restaurateur Bill Granger's 2nd London branch is a stylish affair. His food is inspired by his travels, with the best dishes being those enlivened with the flavours of SE Asia; his breakfasts are also renowned.

Hix Oyster and Chop House

⚵ 🍴

36-37 Greenhill Rents ✉ EC1M 6BN – Ⓜ Farringdon — Plan: **L2**
– ☏ (020) 70171930 – www.hixoysterandchophouse.co.uk – Closed 25-29 December and bank holidays
Menu £ 15 (lunch) – Carte £ 15/48

• Traditional British • Bistro • Traditional décor •

Appropriately utilitarian surroundings put the focus on seasonal and often underused British ingredients. Cooking is satisfying and unfussy, with plenty of oysters and aged beef served on the bone.

Palatino

⚵ ৬ ⓀⒸ

71 Central St ✉ EC1V 8AB – Ⓜ Old Street – ☏ (0203) — Plan: **L1**
481 5300 – www.palatino.london – Closed Sunday
Carte £ 18/38

• Italian • Design • Minimalist •

Stevie Parle's airy, canteen-like, all-day restaurant has an open kitchen, yellow booths and an industrial feel. The seasonal Italian menu has a strong emphasis on Rome, with dishes like rigatoni with veal pajata.

Polpo Smithfield

⚵ 🍴 ⓀⒸ

3 Cowcross St ✉ EC1M 6DR – Ⓜ Farringdon. – ☏ (020) — Plan: **L2**
7250 0034 – www.polpo.co.uk – Closed Christmas, New Year and Sunday dinner
Menu £ 28 – Carte £ 20/30

• Italian • Friendly • Wine bar •

For his third Venetian-style bacaro, Russell Norman converted an old meat market storage facility; it has an elegantly battered feel. Head first for the Negroni bar downstairs; then over-order tasty, uncomplicated dishes to share.

Malmaison

⟨⟩ ৬ ⓀⒸ ⌂

18-21 Charterhouse Sq ✉ EC1M 6AH — Plan: **L2**
– Ⓜ Barbican
– ☏ (020) 7012 3700 – www.malmaison.com
97 rm – ✦£ 119/350 ✦✦£ 119/420 – ⌕ £ 15

• Townhouse • Modern • Personalised •

Striking early 20C red-brick building overlooking a pleasant square. Stylish, comfy public areas. Bedrooms in vivid, bold colours, with plenty of extra touches. Modern brasserie with international menu; grilled meats a highlight.

🏠 **The Rookery**   AK
12 Peters Ln, Cowcross St ⊠ *EC1M 6DS*   Plan: **L2**
– Ⓜ Farringdon
– ℰ (020) 73360931 – www.rookeryhotel.com
33 rm *– ♥£ 205/235 ♥♥£ 235/349 – ⊑ £ 12 – 3 suites*
• Townhouse • Luxury • Personalised •
A row of charmingly restored 18C houses which remain true to their roots courtesy of wood panelling, flagstone flooring, open fires and antique furnishings. Highly individual bedrooms have feature beds and Victorian bathrooms.

FINSBURY

☸ **Angler** *– South Place Hotel*   XX ❀ 斎 & AK
3 South Pl ⊠ *EC2M 2AF*   Plan: **M2**
– Ⓜ Moorgate
– ℰ (020) 32151260 – www.anglerrestaurant.com – Closed 26-30 December, Saturday lunch and Sunday
Menu £ 38 *(weekday lunch) – Carte £ 61/72 – (booking advisable)*
• Seafood • Elegant • Design •
It's built into the eaves of D&D's South Place hotel, but this 7th floor room feels very much like a stand-alone entity and is bright, elegant and intimate. Fish is the mainstay of the menu; its quality is supreme and the kitchen has a light, yet assured touch.
➔ Tartare of yellowfin tuna with avocado, wasabi and shiso. Cornish turbot with crab and Jersey Royals. Seville orange soufflé with toasted brioche ice cream and marmalade.

☺ **Morito**   X 斎
32 Exmouth Mkt ⊠ *EC1R 4QE*   Plan: **K1**
– Ⓜ Farringdon
– ℰ (020) 72787007 – www.morito.co.uk – Closed 24 December-2 January, Sunday dinner and bank holidays
Carte £ 14/29 *– (bookings not accepted at dinner)*
• Spanish • Tapas bar • Rustic •
From the owners of next door Moro comes this authentic and appealingly down to earth little tapas bar. Seven or eight dishes between two should suffice but over-ordering is easy and won't break the bank.

🍴 **Quality Chop House**   X ❀ AK ⇄
92-94 Farringdon Rd ⊠ *EC1R 3EA*   Plan: **K1**
– Ⓜ Farringdon
– ℰ (020) 7278 1452 – www.thequalitychophouse.com
– Closed 24-31 December, Sunday dinner and bank holidays
Carte £ 24/49 *– (booking advisable)*
• Traditional British • Cosy • Bistro •
In the hands of owners who respect its history, this 'progressive working class caterer' does a fine job of championing gutsy British grub; game is best but steaks from the butcher next door are also worth ordering. The terrific little wine list has lots of gems. The Grade II listed room, with its trademark booths, has been an eating house since 1869.

🍴 **Caravan**   X
11-13 Exmouth Market ⊠ *EC1R 4QD –* Ⓜ *Farringdon*   Plan: **K1**
– ℰ (020) 78338115 – www.caravanrestaurants.co.uk – Closed 25-26, 31 December and 1 January
Carte £ 18/35 *– (booking advisable)*
• World cuisine • Trendy • Neighbourhood •
A discernible Antipodean vibe pervades this casual eatery, from the laid-back charm of the service to the kitchen's confident combining of unusual flavours. Cooking is influenced by the owner's travels – hence the name.

UNITED KINGDOM - LONDON

Ceviche Old St

2 Baldwin St ✉ EC1V 9NU – Ⓜ Old Street – ✆ (020) 33279463 – www.cevicheuk.com Plan: **M1**

Menu £ 20 (weekday lunch)/50 – Carte £ 15/37

• Peruvian • Brasserie • Fashionable •

Sister to the Soho original is this buzzy Peruvian restaurant in the former Alexandra Trust Dining Rooms, built by tea magnate Sir Thomas Lipton. Start with ceviche and a pisco sour; dishes are easy to eat, vibrant and full of flavour.

Clerkenwell Kitchen

27-31 Clerkenwell Cl ✉ EC1R 0AT – Ⓜ Farringdon – ✆ (020) 71019959 – www.theclerkenwellkitchen.co.uk – Closed Christmas-New Year, Saturday, Sunday and bank holidays Plan: **K1**

Carte £ 15/28 – *(lunch only) (booking advisable)*

• Modern cuisine • Friendly • Simple •

The owner of this simple, friendly, tucked away eatery worked with Hugh Fearnley-Whittingstall and is committed to sustainability. Daily changing, well-sourced produce; fresh, flavoursome cooking.

Moro

34-36 Exmouth Mkt ✉ EC1R 4QE – Ⓜ Farringdon – ✆ (020) 78338336 – www.moro.co.uk – Closed dinner 24 December-2 January, Sunday dinner and bank holidays Plan: **K1**

Carte £ 32/42 – *(booking essential)*

• Mediterranean cuisine • Friendly • Simple •

It's the stuff of dreams – pack up your worldly goods, drive through Spain, Portugal, Morocco and the Sahara, and then back in London, open a restaurant and share your love of Moorish cuisine. The wood-fired oven and chargrill fill the air with wonderful aromas and food is vibrant and colourful.

South Place

3 South Pl ✉ EC2M 2AF – Ⓜ Moorgate – ✆ (020) 35030000 – www.southplacehotel.com Plan: **M2**

80 rm – †£ 195/350 ††£ 195/350 – ☕ £ 25 – 1 suite

• Business • Design • Contemporary •

Restaurant group D&D's first venture into the hotel business is a stylish affair; unsurprising as its interior was designed by Conran & Partners. Bedrooms are a treat for those with an eye for aesthetics and no detail has been forgotten. The ground floor hosts 3 South Place, a bustling bar and grill.

✿ **Angler** – See restaurant listing

Montcalm Royal London House

22-25 Finsbury Sq ✉ EC2A 1DX – Ⓜ Moorgate – ✆ (020) 3873 4000 – www.montcalmroyallondoncity.co.uk Plan: **M2**

253 rm – †£ 140/367 ††£ 200/552 – ☕ £ 25 – 16 suites

• Business • Luxury • Modern •

A modern business hotel overlooking Finsbury Square, stylish bedrooms come with their own aromatherapy machines and smart phones. Burdock bar features craft beers and some unique shuffleboard tables. 10th floor Aviary serves classic grill dishes and has a superb panorama of the city skyline from its terrace.

Zetter

St John's Sq, 86-88 Clerkenwell Rd. ✉ EC1M 5RJ – Ⓜ Farringdon – ✆ (020) 7324 4444 – www.thezetter.com Plan: **K1**

59 rm – †£ 113/266 ††£ 113/266 – ☕ £ 16

• Townhouse • Modern • Vintage •

A trendy and discreet converted 19C warehouse with well-equipped bedrooms that come with pleasant touches, such as Penguin paperbacks. The more idiosyncratic Zetter Townhouse across the square is used as an overflow.

CHISWICK

✿ **Hedone** (Mikael Jonsson)   XX 🅰🅲

301-303 Chiswick High Rd ✉ W4 4HH
– ⓜ Chiswick Park – ☏ (020) 8747 0377 – www.hedonerestaurant.com
– Closed 2 weeks summer, 2 weeks Christmas-New Year, Sunday and Monday
Menu £ 95/135 – (dinner only and lunch Friday-Saturday) (booking essential) (surprise menu only)
• Modern cuisine • Design • Friendly •

Mikael Jonsson, former lawyer turned chef, is not one for complacency, so his restaurant continues to evolve. The content of his surprise menus is governed entirely by what ingredients are in their prime – and it is this passion for produce which underpins the superlative and very flavoursome cooking.
➔ Devon crab with velvet crab consommé, hazelnut mayonnaise and Granny Smith apple. Hare à la royale. Vanilla millefeuille with balsamic vinegar.

✿ **La Trompette**   XX 🕾 🏠 🅰🅲 ♿

5-7 Devonshire Rd ✉ W4 2EU   Plan I: **A3**
– ⓜ Turnham Green
– ☏ (020) 87471836 – www.latrompette.co.uk
– Closed 24-26 December and 1 January
Menu £ 35 (weekday lunch)/55 – (booking essential)
• Modern British • Neighbourhood • Fashionable •

Chez Bruce's sister is a delightful neighbourhood restaurant that's now a little roomier. The service is charming and the food terrific. Dishes at lunch are quite simple but great value; the cooking at dinner is a tad more elaborate.
➔ Raw bream, bonito, shimeji, shiso cress and English wasabi. Crisp suckling pig shoulder, creamed polenta, grapes, cavolo nero and chilli. Banana soufflé with gingerbread and passion fruit ice cream.

Clapham Common

✿ **Trinity**   XX 🕾 🏠 🅰🅲

4 The Polygon ✉ SW4 0JG   Plan I: **C3**
– ⓜ Clapham Common
– ☏ (020) 76221199 – www.trinityrestaurant.co.uk
– Closed 24-30 December and 1-2 January
Menu £ 39 (lunch) – Carte £ 47/63
• Modern cuisine • Fashionable • Neighbourhood •

Adam Byatt's Trinity and Clapham Old Town are a perfect fit. This bright, warmly run and contemporary restaurant has a genuine neighbourhood feel and the cooking is sophisticated yet easy to eat. This is a kitchen at the top of its game.
➔ Tuna tartare with crab salad, avocado and pickled cucumber. Pot-roast Anjou pigeon with salt-baked celeriac and red wine salsify. Salted caramel custard tart.

FULHAM

✿ **Harwood Arms**   🍺 🕾 🅰🅲

Walham Grove ✉ SW6 1QP – ⓜ Fulham Broadway.   Plan X: **C7**
– ☏ (020) 73861847 – www.harwoodarms.com – Closed 24-27 December, 1 January and Monday lunch except bank holidays
Menu £ 36 (weekday lunch)/43 – (booking essential)
• Modern British • Pub • Neighbourhood •

Its reputation may have spread like wildfire but this remains a proper, down-to-earth pub that just happens to serve really good food. The cooking is very seasonal, proudly British, full of flavour and doesn't seem out of place in this environment. Service is suitably relaxed and friendly.
➔ Cornish crab with herbs and a muffin. Braised shoulder of venison, smoked bone marrow tart and beets. Lemon curd doughnuts with Earl Grey cream.

HAMMERSMITH

ॐ **River Café** (Ruth Rogers) XX 畿 縉 よ ⇔

Thames Wharf, Rainville Rd ⊠ *W6 9HA* Plan I: **A3**
– Ⓜ *Barons Court –* ℰ *(020) 73864200 – www.rivercafe.co.uk – Closed Christmas-New Year and Sunday dinner*
Carte £ 61/85 *– (booking essential)*
• Italian • Fashionable • Design •

It's more than 30 years since this iconic restaurant opened, and superlative ingredients are still at the centre of everything they do. Dishes come in hearty portions and are bursting with authentic Italian flavours. The on-view kitchen with its wood-fired oven dominates the stylish and buzzing riverside room.
➜ Calamari ai ferri. Wood-roasted Dover sole with marjoram, lemon and artichoke alla Romana. Chocolate Nemesis.

KEW

ॐ **The Glasshouse** XX 畿 AC

14 Station Par. ⊠ *TW9 3PZ*
– Ⓜ *Kew Gardens –* ℰ *(020) 89406777 – www.glasshouserestaurant.co.uk – Closed 24-26 December and 1 January*
Menu £ 35 *(weekday lunch)/70*
• Modern cuisine • Fashionable • Neighbourhood •

The Glasshouse is the very model of a modern neighbourhood restaurant and sits in the heart of lovely, villagey Kew. Food is confident yet unshowy – much like the locals – and comes with distinct Mediterranean flavours along with the occasional Asian hint. Service comes with the eagerness of youth.
➜ Roast duck breast with charred salsify, pickled rhubarb and samphire. Monkfish, Fowey mussels, sea beets, parsnips, blood orange and verjus sauce. Passion fruit meringue with coconut ice cream and caramelised mango.

London Fields

ॐ **Ellory** X 畿 縉 よ

Netil House, 1 Westgate St ⊠ *E8 3RL* Plan I: **D1**
– Ⓜ *London Fields –* ℰ *(020) 3095 9455 – www.ellorylondon.com – Closed 23 December-3 January*
Menu £ 30/42 *–* Carte £ 32/43 *– (dinner only and lunch Saturday-Sunday)*
• Modern cuisine • Simple • Neighbourhood •

On the ground floor of Netil House is this unpretentious, stripped back restaurant with an open kitchen and a turntable. No-frills menu of Mediterranean-influenced small plates; unfussy modern dishes are perfectly balanced and rich in flavour. Well-priced European wine list with a good selection by the glass.
➜ Chicory with walnut and Ossau-Iraty cheese. Brill with lovage and parsley root. Pear sorbet, parmesan and olive oil.

SHOREDITCH

ॐ **Clove Club** (Isaac McHale) X AC ⊗

380 Old St ⊠ *EC1V 9LT –* Ⓜ *Old Street –* ℰ *(020)* Plan I: **D2**
77296496 – www.thecloveclub.com
– Closed 2 weeks Christmas-New Year, August bank holiday, Monday lunch and Sunday
Menu £ 75/110 *–* Carte lunch £ 35/56 *– (bookings advisable at dinner) (tasting menu only)*
• Modern cuisine • Trendy •

The smart, blue-tiled open kitchen takes centre stage in this sparse room at Shoreditch Town Hall. Menus showcase expertly sourced produce in dishes that are full of originality, verve and flair – but where flavours are expertly judged and complementary; seafood is a highlight.
➜ Raw Orkney scallop with mandarin, hazelnut and Périgord truffle. Grilled red mullet with new season onions, cinnamon and curry leaf sauce. Amalfi lemonade and Kampot pepper ice cream.

❀ **Lyle's** (James Lowe) X AC
Tea Building, 56 Shoreditch High St ✉ *E1 6JJ* Plan IX : **N1**
– Ⓜ *Shoreditch High Street –* ℰ *(020) 30115911 – www.lyleslondon.com*
– Closed Sunday and bank holidays
Menu £ 55 (dinner) – Carte lunch £ 37/47 – *(set menu only at dinner)*
• Modern British • Simple •
The young chef-owner is an acolyte of Fergus Henderson and delivers similarly unadulterated flavours from seasonal British produce, albeit from a set menu at dinner. This pared-down approach extends to a room that's high on functionality, but considerable warmth comes from the keen young service team.
➔ Monkfish liver with blood orange. Red mullet with cured roe and turnip tops. Sleightlett cheese ice cream with burnt pear and goat's whey.

SPITALFIELDS

❀ **Galvin La Chapelle** XxX 🍴 ⅃ AC ⇩ 🅟🅟
35 Spital Sq ✉ *E1 6DY –* Ⓜ *Liverpool Street* Plan IX : **N2**
– ℰ *(020) 7299 0400 – www.galvinrestaurants.com*
– Closed 25-26 December and 1 January
Menu £ 35 (lunch and early dinner) – Carte £ 48/76
• French • Elegant • Elegant •
With its vaulted ceiling, arched windows and marble pillars, this restaurant remains as impressive now as when it first opened nearly a decade ago. Service is professional and the atmosphere, relaxed and unstuffy. Cooking is assured, with a classical French foundation and a sophisticated modern edge.
➔ Lasagne of Dorset crab with beurre Nantais. Tagine of Bresse pigeon with couscous and harissa sauce. Tarte Tatin with crème fraîche.

WANDSWORTH

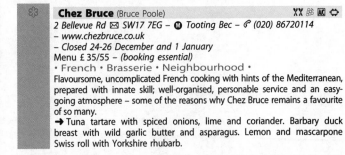

❀ **Chez Bruce** (Bruce Poole) XX 🌿 AC ⇩
2 Bellevue Rd ✉ *SW17 7EG –* Ⓜ *Tooting Bec –* ℰ *(020) 86720114*
– www.chezbruce.co.uk
– Closed 24-26 December and 1 January
Menu £ 35/55 – *(booking essential)*
• French • Brasserie • Neighbourhood •
Flavoursome, uncomplicated French cooking with hints of the Mediterranean, prepared with innate skill; well-organised, personable service and an easygoing atmosphere – some of the reasons why Chez Bruce remains a favourite of so many.
➔ Tuna tartare with spiced onions, lime and coriander. Barbary duck breast with wild garlic butter and asparagus. Lemon and mascarpone Swiss roll with Yorkshire rhubarb.

HEATHROW AIRPORT

🍴 **Mr Todiwala's Kitchen** – Hilton London Heathrow Airport Terminal 5 Hotel
Poyle Rd, Colnbrook (West : 2.5 mi by A 3113) XX AC 🅿
✉ *SL3 OFF –* ℰ *(01753) 766482 – www.hilton.com/heathrowt5 – Closed*
Christmas and Sunday
Carte £ 25/55 – *(dinner only and lunch Thursday-Saturday)*
• Indian • Friendly • Design •
Secreted within the Hilton is Cyrus Todiwala's appealingly stylish, fresh-looking restaurant. The choice ranges from street food to tandoor dishes, Goan classics to Parsee specialities; order the 'Kitchen menu' for the full experience.

Hilton London Heathrow Airport Terminal 5

Poyle Rd, Colnbrook (West : 2.5 mi by A 3113)
✉ SL3 OFF – ✆ (01753) 686860 – www.hilton.com/heathrowt5
350 rm – 🚹£ 139/345 🚹🚹£ 159/375 – 4 suites
• Business • Chain • Modern •
A feeling of light and space pervades this modern, corporate hotel. Soundproofed rooms are fitted to a good standard; the spa offers wide-ranging treatments. Open-plan Gallery for British comfort food.
Mr Todiwala's Kitchen – See restaurant listing

Sofitel

Terminal 5, Heathrow Airport ✉ TW6 2GD – Ⓜ Heathrow Terminal 5 – ✆ (020) 87575029 – www.sofitelheathrow.com
605 rm – 🚹£ 169/329 🚹🚹£ 199/359 – 27 suites
• Business • Chain • Contemporary •
Smart and well-run contemporary hotel, designed around a series of atriums, with direct access to T5. Crisply decorated, comfortable bedrooms with luxurious bathrooms. Choice of restaurant: international or classic French cuisine.

BIRMINGHAM
BIRMINGHAM

KrisKuzniar/iStock

It's hard to visualise Birmingham as an insignificant market town, but England's second city was just such a place throughout much of its history. Then came the boom times of the Industrial Revolution; the town fattening up on the back of the local iron and coal trades. In many people's minds that legacy lives on, the city seen as a rather dour place with shoddy Victorian housing, but 21C Brum has swept away much of its factory grime and polished up its civic face. Its first 'makeover' was over a century ago, when the mayor, Joseph Chamberlain, enlarged the city's boundaries to make it the second largest in the country.

Today it's feeling the benefits of a second modernist surge – a multi-million pound regeneration, typified by shopping arcades and appealing squares; it now boasts more canal miles than Venice and more trees than inhabitants. It's pretty much in the centre of England, surrounded by Stratford-on-Avon in the south and Bridgnorth and Ironbridge in the west, with Wolverhampton and Coventry in its hinterland. Former resident JRR Tolkien would be lost nowadays, with the undulating contours of the flyovers, the self-important muscle of the sporting, conference and exhibition centres – the Arena Birmingham, the ICC and the NEC – and the trendy makeover of the Bullring and the Gas Street Basin. Perhaps he would feel more at home in the elegant Jewellery Quarter further north.

EATING OUT

To the southwest of the city is Cadbury World, the UK's only purpose-built visitor centre devoted entirely to chocolate. It's located in the evocative sounding Bourneville area and staff are on hand to tell visitors the history of chocolate and how it's made, but, let's face it, most people go along to get a face full of the stuff. More conventionally, many people who come to Birmingham make for the now legendary area of Sparkbrook, Balsall Heath and Moseley, to the south of the centre. In itself that may not sound too funky, but over the last 30 years or so it's become the area known as the Balti Triangle. The balti was 'officially' discovered in Birmingham in 1976, a full-on dish of aromatic spices, fresh herbs and rich curries, and The Triangle now boasts over 50 establishments dedicated to the dish. For those after something a little more subtle, the city offers a growing number of lively and fashionable restaurants, offering assured and contemporary cuisine.

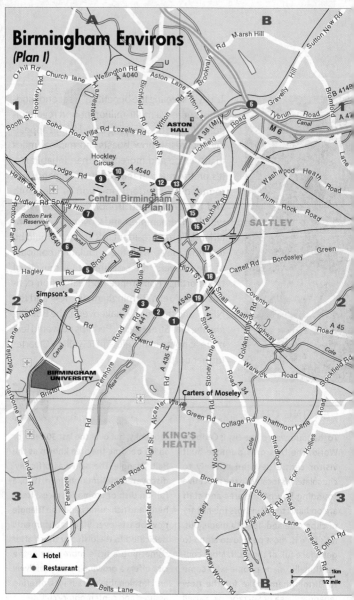

Birmingham Environs
(Plan I)

Marsh Hill

Sutton New Rd

Oxhill Rd   Church lane
Wellington Rd   A 4040
Aston Lane

Booth St.   Rookery Rd
Soho Road

Hamstead Rd
Villa Rd   Lozells Rd

Birchfield Rd
Witton Rd   Witton La.

Brookvale Rd
Gravelly   Hill

Bromford   A 4148
A 47

ASTON HALL

A 38 (M1)

M 6

Tyburn   Road
Canal

Lane

Hockley
Circus   **10**   A 4540
A 41   **9**
Lodge   Rd

Lichfield   Rd

Washwood   Heath   Road

Heath Street
Dudley   Rd   Spring Hill
7
Rotton Park
Reservoir
A4540   Canal
6
Rotton   Park   Rd
Hagley   Rd
5   Broad   St.

Bristole St.

Central Birmingham
(Plan II)

12   **13**

A 47

A 34

15
Vauxhall   Rd
16

Rock   Road

SALTLEY

17

High   St.
18   Cattell Rd
Bordesley   Green

Small   Heath   Highway
Coventry

Simpson's

Matchley Lane   Harborne

Church   Rd

A 38   A 441
Edward   Rd
3
2
1   A 4540
19

Stratford   Lane
Golden Hillock   Rd
Warwick   Road   A 34
Road   Road

A 45
Road

Cole

Stockfield   Rd

**BIRMINGHAM
UNIVERSITY**

Pershore   Rea   Rd
Bristol

Alcester   Rd

High   St.
Wake   Green   Rd
Collage Rd

Carters of Moseley

Shaftmoor Lane

Harborne La.

Linden   Rd

Pershore   Rd

Vicarage   Road

Alcester   Rd
High   St.

Wood

Brook   Lane

Cole   Stratford

Robin

Hood   Lane
Highfield   Rd
Fox

Hollies
Stratford   Otton Rd

**KING'S
HEATH**

Priory   Rd

Yardley   Wood   Rd

Bells   Lane

| ▲ Hotel |
| ● Restaurant |

0 ———— 1km
0 ———— 1/2 mile

Simpsons (Andreas Antona & Luke Tipping)   XxX ⬦ 🍴 🚭 ⅙ 🅰
20 Highfield Rd, Edgbaston ⊠ B15 3DU – ℰ (0121)
4543434 – www.simpsonsrestaurant.co.uk – Closed
Plan: **A2**
25 December, Sunday dinner and Monday
3 rm 🛏 – 🛏£ 110 🛏🛏£ 110   Menu £ 35/90
· Modern cuisine · Fashionable · Contemporary décor ·
Behind the walls of this suburban Georgian house is a sleek dining room
and three contemporary bedrooms. Cooking has a clean, Scandic style
and the visually appealing dishes are packed with flavour. Lunch sees a 2-
choice set price menu; dinner a 4-course set price menu and a tasting
option – some courses are served by the chefs. Desserts are satisfyingly traditional.
→ Cured salmon with prawns, cucumber, buttermilk and dill. Roasted lamb
chump, black garlic and sheep's curd. Speculoos biscuit with caramelised
white chocolate and coffee granité.

Adam's (Adam Stokes)   XxX ⅙ 🅰
New Oxford House, 16 Waterloo St ⊠ B2 5UG
Plan: **E2**
– ℰ (0121) 643 3745 – www.adamsrestaurant.co.uk – Closed 2 weeks
summer, Christmas-New Year, Sunday and Monday
Menu £ 38/60 – (booking essential)
· Modern cuisine · Elegant · Design ·
Enjoy a drink in the smart cocktail bar then move on to the bright, elegant
restaurant with a subtle retro feel. Choose from a concise set menu or an 8
course tasting menu: top notch produce is used in carefully prepared dishes
which have wonderfully bold complementary flavours and contrasting tex-
tures.
→ Veal sweetbread with roasted cauliflower, air-dried ham and raisins.
Goosnargh chicken with asparagus, morels and haggis. 63% dark chocolate
with salted milk and blood orange.

Purnell's (Glynn Purnell)   XxX ⅙ 🅰 ⬦
55 Cornwall St ⊠ B3 2DH – ℰ (0121) 2129799
Plan: **E2**
– www.purnellsrestaurant.com – Closed 2 weeks August, 1 week Easter,
1 week Christmas, Saturday lunch, Sunday and Monday
Menu £ 35 (weekday lunch)/90 – (tasting menu only)
· Modern cuisine · Design · Fashionable ·
Start in the comfy lounge, then head past the wine display to the vibrantly
decorated dining room. Menus range from 3 to 9 courses and some of
them offer swaps so you can try the chef's signature dishes. Sophisticated
cooking ranges from classic to Scandic in style and flavours and textures
marry perfectly.
→ Scallop with mussel chowder, potato cooked in beurre noisette and dill.
Loin of veal, confit tomato, asparagus and squid. Mango and passion fruit
with lime gel and white chocolate.

Carters of Moseley (Brad Carter)   XX ⅙ 🅰 🍸
2c St Mary's Row, Wake Green Rd ⊠ B13 9EZ
Plan: **B3**
– ℰ (0121) 449 8885 – www.cartersofmoseley.co.uk – Closed 1-
18 January, 31 July-16 August, Sunday and Monday
Menu £ 40/85 – (booking advisable) (tasting menu only)
· Modern British · Neighbourhood · Friendly ·
Lovely little neighbourhood restaurant with black ash tables and a glass-fronted
wine cabinet running down one wall. The passionate young chef continually evolves his cooking and the team are friendly and engaging. Each
dish is made up of three well-balanced key components and the flavours
are intense.
→ Skrei cod with Musselburgh leeks and buttermilk. Cornish duck
with Kyoto carrots and 5 year old soy. Black rice with kombu.

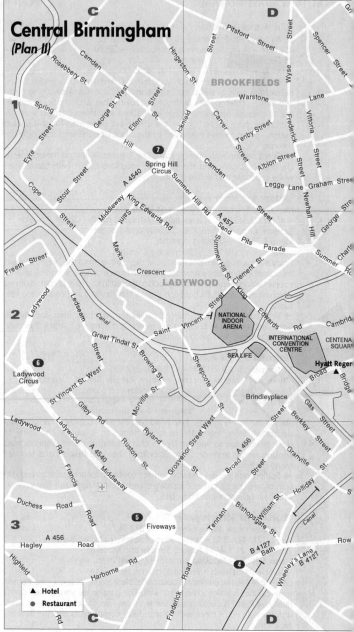

Central Birmingham
(Plan II)

Camden

Rosebbery St.

Spring

George St. West

Ellen St.

Street

Hill

Eyre Street

Stour Street

Cope

Street

7

Spring Hill
Circus

A 4540

Middleway King Edwards Rd

Saint

Marks

Freeth Street

Crescent

LADYWOOD

Ladywood

Ledsam

Canal

Great Tindal St. Browing St.

6

Ladywood
Circus

St Vincent St. West

Gilby Rd

Ladywood

A 4540

Ruston St.

Saint Vincent

Morville St.

Ryland

Grosvenor Street West

St.

Ladywood
Rd

Francis Road

Middleway

Duchess Road

Road

5

Fiveways

3

Hagley

A 456

Road

Highfield

Harborne Rd

Frederick Road

Rd

Pitsford Street

Hingeston St.

Street

Spencer Street

BROOKFIELDS

Warstone

Lane

Wyse

Camden

Carver Street

Tenby Street

Frederick Street

Vittoria Street

Icknield

Albion Street

Summer Hill Rd

Camden

Street

Legge Lane

Graham Street

Newhall Hill

George Street

A 457 Sand

Pits Parade

Summer Charles

Summer Hill St. Clement St.

Summer Rd

King

Street

**NATIONAL
INDOOR
ARENA**

Edwards Rd

Cambri

Sheepcote

**INTERNATIONAL
CONVENTION
CENTRE**

**CENTENA
SQUAR**

SEA LIFE

▲ **Hyatt Reger**

Broad

Bridge

St.

Brindleyplace

Gas Street

Berkley Street

Granville St.

A 456

Broad

Street

Holliday

Tennant

Bishopsgate St.

William St.

Canal

B 4127

Bath

Wheeley's Lane B 4127

4

Row

C

D

1

2

3

C

D

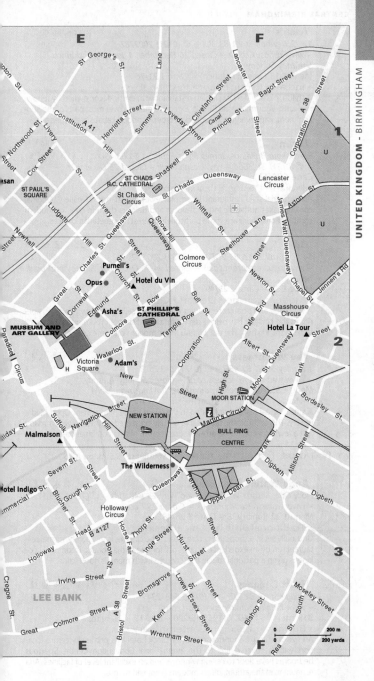

E

F

St. George's St.

Lane

Lancaster

Bagot Street

Corporation A 38 Street

1

U

Constitution A 41

Northwood St.

Livery

Cox Street

Street

Henrietta Street

Summer Lr. Loveday St.

Cleveland Street

Canal

Princip St.

Street

Lancaster Circus

U

James Watt Queensway

Aston St.

Jennen's Rd

Ludgate

Hill

St Chads Shadwell St.

ST CHADS R.C. CATHEDRAL

ST PAUL'S SQUARE

St Chads Circus

St Chads Queensway

Whittall St.

Steelhouse Lane

Street

Newhall

Street

Charles St. Queensway

Snow Hill Queensway

Colmore Circus

Newton St.

Masshouse Circus

Chapel St.

Great

Hill

Charles St.

St.

Church

Cornwall

Purnell's

Opus

Edmund

Hotel du Vin

St. Row

Bull St.

Dale End

Hotel La Tour

Street

2

Asha's

Colmore

ST PHILLIP'S CATHEDRAL

Temple Row

Street

MUSEUM AND ART GALLERY

Paradise Circus

St.

Waterloo

H

Victoria Square

Adam's

New

Corporation

High St.

Albert St. Queensway

Moor St. Queensway

Park

Bordesley St.

Street

MOOR STATION

Suffolk

Navigation

Hill

Street

NEW STATION

St. Martin's Circus

BULL RING CENTRE

Park St.

Allison Street

Digbeth

Holliday St.

Malmaison

Street

The Wilderness

Queensway

Pershore

Upper Dean St.

Digbeth

Hotel Indigo St.

Severn St.

Blucher

Gough St.

Commercial St.

Holloway Circus

Head St.

B 4127

Horse Fair

Thorp St.

Inge Street

Hurst Street

Street

3

Holloway

Bow St.

Irving Street

Bromsgrove Street

Lower Essex Street

Bishop St.

Moseley Street

LEE BANK

Cregoe St.

Great

Colmore Street

A 38 Street

Bristol St.

Kent Street

Wrentham Street

Rea St. South

E

F

0   200 m
0   200 yards

Asha's
XX & 🅰🄺 ⇔ 🕙

12-22 Newhall St ✉ *B3 3LX –* ☏ *(0121) 2002767*   Plan: **E2**
*– www.ashasuk.co.uk – Closed 26 December, 1 January and lunch
Saturday-Sunday*
Menu £ 18 (weekday lunch) – Carte £ 21/76
• Indian • Exotic décor • Fashionable •
A stylish, passionately run Indian restaurant with exotic décor; owned by renowned artiste/gourmet Asha Bhosle. Extensive menus cover most parts of the Subcontinent, with everything cooked to order. Tandoori kebabs are a speciality.

Lasan
XX 🅰🄺 🕙

3-4 Dakota Buildings, James St, St Pauls Sq ✉ *B3 1SD*   Plan: **E1**
– ☏ *(0121) 2123664 – www.lasan.co.uk – Closed 25 December*
Carte £ 30/47
• Indian • Design • Fashionable •
An industrial-style restaurant in an old Jewellery Quarter art gallery. Original cooking takes authentic Indian flavours and delivers them in creative modern combinations; there are some particularly interesting vegetarian choices.

Opus
XX & 🅰🄺 ⇔ 🕙

54 Cornwall St ✉ *B3 2DE –* ☏ *(0121) 200 2323*   Plan: **E2**
*– www.opusrestaurant.co.uk – Closed 24-26 December, Sunday and bank
holidays*
Menu £ 33 – Carte £ 23/49
• Modern cuisine • Design • Chic •
A very large and popular restaurant with floor to ceiling windows; enjoy an aperitif in the cocktail bar before dining in the stylish main room or at the chef's table in the kitchen. The daily menu offers modern brasserie dishes.

The Wilderness
X &

1 Dudley St ✉ *B5 4EG –* ☏ *(0121) 643 2673*   Plan: **F3**
– www.wearethewilderness.co.uk – Closed Sunday-Tuesday
Menu £ 35/70 – (booking advisable) (tasting menu only)
• Modern British • Simple • Intimate •
A small, casual restaurant located in the avant-garde Birmingham Open Media gallery. The enthusiastic team serve artfully presented set menus which marry just a few local and home-grown ingredients in playful combinations.

AT NATIONAL EXHIBITION CENTRE Southeast : 9,5 m. on A 45

Andy Waters
XX & 🅰🄺 🅿

Floor One, Resorts World, Pendigo Way ✉ *B40 1PU –* ☏ *(0201) 273 1238*
– www.watersrestaurant.co.uk – Closed 25 December
Menu £ 22 (lunch)/38 – Carte £ 26/48
• Traditional British • Chic • Design •
Unusually set in a shopping centre, beside the cinema, is this comfy, formal restaurant run by an experienced chef – ask for one of the booths. Traditional cooking is given a personal touch; the 2 course lunch menu is good value.

Hyatt Regency
🍴 ≤ 🛁 🏠 🖼 & 🅰🄺 🔧

2 Bridge St ✉ *B1 2JZ –* ☏ *(0121) 6431234*   Plan: **D2**
– www.birmingham.regency.hyatt.com
319 rm – ♟£ 114/220 ♟♟£ 146/220 – ☴ £ 19 – 11 suites
• Business • Luxury • Contemporary •
An eye-catching, mirror-fronted, tower block hotel in a prime city centre location, with a covered link to the International Convention Centre. Spacious bedrooms have floor to ceiling windows and an excellent level of facilities. Aria restaurant, in the atrium, offers modern European menus.

Hotel Du Vin ✿ ⅃ʒ ⊚ ⋒ AK ⅃ʌ 🚗

25 Church St ⊠ B3 2NR – 𝒞 (0121) 7943005
Plan: **E2**
– www.hotelduvin.com
66 rm ⊊ – ♦£ 99/250 – ♦♦£ 99/350
· Business · Luxury · Design ·
A characterful former eye hospital with a relaxed, shabby-chic style. Bright bedrooms are named after wine companies and estates; one suite boasts an 8 foot bed, two roll-top baths and a gym. Kick-back in the small cellar pub or comfy champagne bar; the classical bistro has a lively buzz and a French menu.

Hotel La Tour ✿ ⅃ʒ AK ⅃ʌ

Albert St ⊠ B5 5JE – 𝒞 (0121) 718 8000
Plan: **F2**
– www.hotel-latour.co.uk – Closed 23-30 December
174 rm – ♦£ 98/245 ♦♦£ 98/328 – ⊊ £ 18
· Business · Luxury · Modern ·
A striking modern building with spacious, stylish guest areas. With their media hubs and TV recording facilities, bedrooms are ideal for business travellers; Superiors come with baths which have TVs mounted above them. The informal chophouse serves an extensive menu of hearty, unfussy classics and steaks.

Malmaison ✿ ⅃ʒ ⋒ ⅃ AK ⅃ʌ

Mailbox, 1 Wharfside St ⊠ B1 1RD – 𝒞 (0121) 2465000
Plan: **E2**
– www.malmaison.com
192 rm – ♦£ 89/179 ♦♦£ 99/189 – ⊊ £ 17 – 1 suite
· Business · Luxury · Modern ·
A stylish hotel with dark, moody décor, set on the site of the old Royal Mail sorting office, next to designer clothing and homeware shops. Bedrooms are spacious and stylish; the Penny Black suite has a mini-cinema and a steam room. Dine from an accessible British menu in the bright, bustling brasserie.

Hotel Indigo ✿ < ⅃ʒ ⊚ ⋒ ⅃ AK 🚗

The Cube ⊠ B1 1PR – 𝒞 (0121) 6432010
Plan: **E3**
– www.hotelindigobirmingham.com
52 rm – ♦£ 99/200 ♦♦£ 140/210 – ⊊ £ 16
· Business · Chain · Design ·
Stylish hotel located on the top three floors of the eye-catching 'Cube' building. Both the appealingly styled guest areas and vividly decorated bedrooms come with floor to ceiling windows. A smart steakhouse serves classic dishes and boasts a champagne bar, a terrace and a view from every table.

EDINBURGH
EDINBURGH

EDINBURGH IN...

→ **ONE DAY**
Calton Hill, Royal Mile, Edinburgh Castle, New Town café, Old Town pub.

→ **TWO DAYS**
Water of Leith, Scottish National Gallery of Modern Art, Leith.

→ **THREE DAYS**
Arthur's Seat, National Museum of Scotland, Holyrood Park, Pentland Hills.

The beautiful Scottish capital is laid out on seven, formerly volcanic, hills – a contrast to the modern city, which is elegant, cool and sophisticated. It's essentially two cities in one: the medieval Old Town, huddled around and beneath the crags and battlements of the castle, and the smart Georgian terraces of the New Town, overseen by the 18C architect Robert Adam. You could also say there's now a third element to the equation: the revamped port of Leith, just two miles away.

This is a city that's been attracting tourists since the 19C; and since 1999 it's been the home of the Scottish Parliament, adding

a new dimension to its worldwide reputation. It accepts its plaudits with the same ease that it accepts an extra half million visitors at the height of summer, and its status as a UNESCO World Heritage site confirms it as a city that knows how to be both ancient and modern. In the middle is the castle, to the south is the Old Town and to the north is the New Town. There's a natural boundary to the north at the Firth of Forth, while to the south lie the rolling Pentland Hills. Unless you've had a few too many drams, it's just about impossible to get lost here, as prominent landmarks like the Castle, Arthur's Seat and Calton Hill access all areas. Bisecting the town is Princes Street, one side of which invites you to shop, the other, to sit and relax in your own space.

EATING OUT

Edinburgh enjoys a varied and interesting restaurant culture so, whatever the occasion, you should find somewhere that fits the bill. The city is said to have more restaurants per head than anywhere in the UK and they vary from lavish establishments in grand hotels to cosy little bistros; you can dine with ghosts in a basement eatery or admire the city from a rooftop table. Scotland's great larder provides much of the produce, and cooking styles range from the innovative and contemporary to the simple and traditional. There are also some good pubs to explore in the Old Town, and drinking dens also abound in Cowgate and Grassmarket. Further away, in West End, you'll find enticing late-night bars, while the stylish variety, serving cocktails, are more in order in the George Street area of the new town. If you'd rather drink something a little more special then try the 19C Cadenhead's on the Royal Mile – it's the place to go for whiskies and it sells a mindboggling range of rare distillations. The peaty flavoured Laphroaig is a highly recommended dram.

Number One – Balmoral Hotel   XxxX 🕸 & 🔠 ⑰

1 Princes St ✉ *EH2 2EQ –* 📞 *(0131) 5576727*   Plan: **G2**
– www.roccofortehotels.com – Closed 2 weeks mid-January
Menu £ 75 *– (dinner only)*
• Modern cuisine • Intimate • Elegant •
A stylish, long-standing restaurant with a chic cocktail bar, set in the basement of a grand hotel. Richly upholstered banquettes and red lacquered walls give it a plush, luxurious feel. Cooking is modern and intricate and prime Scottish ingredients are key. Service is professional and has personality.
→ The Balmoral's Tomatin smoked salmon with quail's egg, lemon and caviar. Fillet of Scottish beef with hay-cooked short rib, aubergine and bone marrow fondant. Vanilla soufflé with poached rhubarb and almond ice cream.

21212 (Paul Kitching)   XxX ⇦ & 🔠 ⇔ ⑰

3 Royal Terr ✉ *EH7 5AB –* 📞 *(0345) 2221212*   Plan: **H1**
– www.21212restaurant.co.uk – Closed 10 days January, 10 days summer, Sunday and Monday
4 rm 🛏 *–* 🛏£ 95/295 🛏🛏£ 95/295   Menu £ 32/85 *– (booking essential)*
• Creative • Elegant • Design •
Stunningly refurbished Georgian townhouse designed by William Playfair. The glass-fronted kitchen is the focal point of the stylish, high-ceilinged dining room. Cooking is skilful and innovative and features quirky combinations; '21212' reflects the number of dishes per course at lunch – at dinner it's '31313'. Some of the luxurious bedrooms overlook the Firth of Forth.
→ Crab, celeriac and caviar with scallop. Pintade, pecan and mango with cauli roots. Glazed lemon meringue with marzipan and apple nut crumble.

Galvin Brasserie De Luxe – Waldorf Astoria Edinburgh The Caledonian Hotel

Princes St ✉ *EH1 2AB –* 📞 *(0131) 222 8988*   XX & 🔠 🅿
– www.galvinrestaurants.com   Plan: **F2**
Menu £ 23 (lunch and early dinner) – Carte £ 29/65
• French • Brasserie • Chic •
It's accurately described by its name: a simply styled restaurant which looks like a brasserie of old, but with the addition of a smart shellfish counter and formal service. There's an appealing à la carte and a good value two-choice daily set selection; dishes are refined, flavoursome and of a good size.

Dogs   X

110 Hanover St (1st Floor) ✉ *EH2 1DR –* 📞 *(0131)*   Plan: **G1**
220 1208 – www.thedogsonline.co.uk – Closed 25 December and 1 January
Carte £ 12/25
• Traditional cuisine • Bistro • Rustic •
Cosy, slightly bohemian-style eatery on the first floor of a classic Georgian mid-terrace, with two high-ceilinged, shabby chic dining rooms and an appealing bar. Robust, good value comfort food is crafted from local, seasonal produce; dishes such as cock-a-leekie soup and devilled ox livers feature.

Passorn   X

23-23a Brougham Pl ✉ *EH3 9JU –* 📞 *(0131) 229 1537*   Plan: **F3**
– www.passornthai.com – Closed 25-26 December, 1-2 January, Sunday and lunch Monday
Menu £ 16 (weekday lunch) – Carte £ 24/37 *– (booking essential)*
• Thai • Friendly • Neighbourhood •
The staff are super-friendly at this extremely popular neighbourhood restaurant, whose name means 'Angel'. Authentic menus feature Thai classics and old family recipes; the seafood dishes are a highlight and presentation is first class. Spices and other ingredients are flown in from Thailand.

UNITED KINGDOM - EDINBURGH

The Scran & Scallie ⓐ 🍴 ᴖ ᴁ

1 Comely Bank Rd, Stockbridge ✉ *EH4 1DT –* ℰ *(0131)*   Plan: **E1**
332 6281 – www.scranandscallie.com – Closed 25 December
Menu £ 15 (weekday lunch) – Carte £ 24/46 – *(booking advisable)*
• Traditional British • Neighbourhood • Family •
The more casual venture from Tom Kitchin, located in a smart, village-like
suburb. It has a wood-furnished bar and a dining room which blends rustic
and contemporary décor. Extensive menus follow a 'Nature to Plate' philosophy
and focus on the classical and the local.

The Pompadour by Galvin – Waldorf Astoria Edinburgh The Caledonian Hotel ⓘ

Princes St ✉ *EH1 2AB –* ℰ *(0131) 222 8975*   XˣX ᴖ ᴁ ᵇᵍ 🕙 **P**
– www.galvinrestaurants.com   Plan: **F2**
– Closed 1-16 January, Monday and Tuesday
Menu £ 35 (early dinner)/65 – Carte £ 47/67 – *(dinner only and Saturday
lunch)*
• French • Chic • Intimate •
A grand hotel restaurant which opened in the 1920s and is modelled on a
French salon. Classic Gallic dishes showcase Scottish produce, using techniques
introduced by Escoffier, and are executed with a lightness of touch.

Rhubarb – Prestonfield Hotel ⓘ   XX ᵇ ᴖ ᴁ **P**

Priestfield Rd ✉ *EH16 5UT –* ℰ *(0131) 2251333*   Plan: **C2**
– www.prestonfield.com
Menu £ 25/38 – Carte £ 35/66
• Modern cuisine • Elegant • Chic •
Two sumptuous, richly decorated dining rooms set within a romantic 17C
country house; so named as this was the first place in Scotland where rhubarb
was grown. The concise menu lists modern dishes with some innovative touches and is accompanied by an interesting wine list, with a great selection by
the glass.

Angels with Bagpipes ⓘ   XX ᴖ

343 High St, Royal Mile ✉ *EH1 1PW –* ℰ *(0131)*   Plan: **G2**
*220 1111 – www.angelswithbagpipes.co.uk – Closed 7-23 January and 24-
28 December*
Menu £ 22 (lunch) – Carte £ 31/54
• Modern cuisine • Bistro • Design •
Small, stylish restaurant named after the wooden sculpture in St Giles Cathedral,
opposite. Dishes are more elaborate than the menu implies; modern interpretations of Scottish classics could include 'haggis, neeps and tattiesgine'.

Castle Terrace ⓘ   XX ᴖ ᴁ 🕙

33-35 Castle Terr ✉ *EH1 2EL –* ℰ *(0131) 2291222*   Plan: **F2**
*– www.castleterracerestaurant.com – Closed Christmas, New Year, 1 week
April, 1 week July, 1 week October, Sunday and Monday*
Menu £ 33/70
• Modern cuisine • Intimate • Elegant •
Set in the shadow of the castle is this bright, contemporary restaurant with
hand-painted wallpapers and a mural depicting the Edinburgh skyline. Cooking
is ambitious with a playful element. The wine list offers plenty of choice.

Cucina – G & V Royal Mile Hotel ⓘ   XX ᴖ ᴖ ᴁ

1 George IV Bridge ✉ *EH1 1AD –* ℰ *(0131) 2206666*   Plan: **G2**
– www.gandvhotel.com
Menu £ 21 (lunch) – Carte £ 29/57
• Italian • Design • Fashionable •
A buzzy mezzanine restaurant in a chic hotel, featuring red and blue glass-topped tables and striking kaleidoscope-effect blocks on the walls. Italian dishes
follow the seasons – some are classically based and others are more modern.

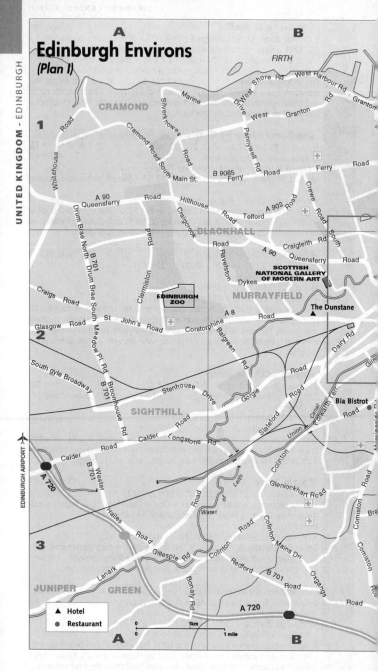

Edinburgh Environs
(Plan I)

A

B

FIRTH

CRAMOND

West Shore Rd

West Harbour Rd

Granton

Marine

West Granton Road

West Drive

Silverknowes Road

Cramond Road South Main St.

Pannywell Rd

Ferry Road

Road

1

Whitehouse Road

A 90 Queensferry Road

Hillhouse

B 9085 Ferry Road

Telford

Crewe Road

A 902

Ferry Road

Road

Craigleith Rd

Drum Brae North

B 701 Drum Brae South

Craigcrook Road

BLACKHALL

A 90 Queensferry Road

Road

Clermiston Road

Ravelston

SCOTTISH NATIONAL GALLERY OF MODERN ART

Craigs Road

St John's Road

EDINBURGH ZOO

Dykes

MURRAYFIELD

▲ The Dunstane

Glasgow Road

Meadow Pl. Rd.

Corstorphine

A 8 Road

Road

Balgreen Rd

Dairy Rd

2

South gyle Broadway

B 701 Broomhouse Rd.

Stenhouse Drive

Gorgie

Road

Road

Gilm

SIGHTHILL

Calder Road

Longstone Rd.

Slateford Road

Union Canal

Water of Leith

Bia Bistrot Road

EDINBURGH AIRPORT ✈

A 720

Calder Road

B 701 Wester

Colinton Road

Gleniockhart Road

Comiston Road

Bra

Hailes Road

Water

Colinton Road

3

Gillespie Rd.

Colinton

Redford B 701 Road

Colinton Mains Dri.

Oxgangs Road

Comiston

Lanark Road

Bonaly Rd.

Road

JUNIPER GREEN

A 720

A

▲ Hotel

● Restaurant

| 0 | | 1km |
| 0 | | 1 mile |

B

OF   FORTH

C   **D**

901

Lindsay Rd

Craighall Rd

Newhaven Rd

1

Kitchin ●   ▲ Malmaison

RINITY

Ferry   Rd   Shore ● Martin Wishart

● Norn

A 199
Seafield Rd

Seafield Road East

LEITH ✚

ROYAL BOTANIC
GARDENS

Broughton Rd

Pilrig St.

Walk

Leith

Easter   Road

Lockend Rd

Restalrig Rd

Sleigh   Drive

Restalrig   Drive

Craigentimy Rd

Portobello High St.

London

Marionville Rd

RESTALRIG
A 1140

Queen St.
York Pl.

George St.

Regent Rd

Road

Portobello

2

WAVERLEY

**ABBEY AND PALACE
OF HOLYROODHOUSE**

Holyrood Rd

Queen's   Drive

Willowbrae   Road

West   Port

CASTLE

Nicolson St.

HOLYROOD

PARK

Rd   West   Milton

Road   West

MEADOW
PARK

Melville   Drive

Queen's   Drive

DUDDINGSTON

A 6095

Edinburgh Centre
(Plan II) ✚

Grange Rd

Dalkeith

▲ Prestonfield

Grange Loan

Mayfield

Mainto St.

94 DR ▲   ● Rhubarb

▲ 23 Mayfield

Road

Duddingston

Niddrie   Mains

Peffermill

A 6106

RAID

Road

Lady Rd

Old

Craigmillar Castle Road

U

Brae

Gilmerton

Liberton

Kirk Brae

Kirkgate

Braid Burn

Hills

Drive

Liberton

Liberton Drive

Howden Liberton Gdns

Lasswade   Road

Dalkeith

✚

NORTHFIELD

Road

**CRAIGMILLAR
CASTLE**

Ferniehill Drive

The   Wisp

Millerhill   Road

3

FAIRMILEHEAD

gston Rd West   Frogston Rd East

Frogston Rd East   Hall Rd

B 701

Captain's Rd

Lasswade   Rd

B 701

Drum St

Drum St Gilmerton Rd

**DRUM
WOOD**

GILMERTON

C   **D**

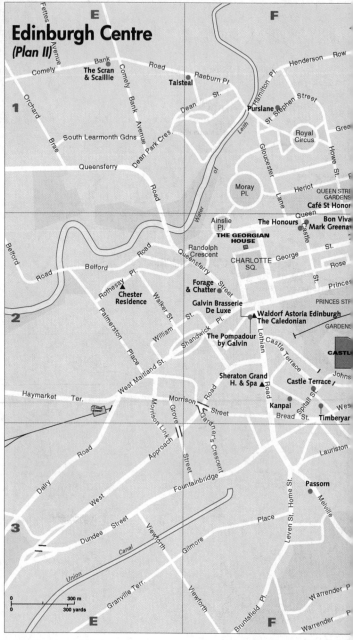

Edinburgh Centre
(Plan II)

E

Fettes Avenue

Comely Bank

Orchard Brae

Comely Bank Road

The Scran & Scaillie

Taisteal

Raeburn Pl.

South Learmonth Gdns

Dean Park Cres.

Dean St.

Queensferry Road

Water of Leith

1

F

Henderson Row

Hamilton Pl.

Purslane

St Stephen Street

Royal Circus

Green

Howe St.

Gloucester Lane

Heriot

QUEEN STRE
GARDENS

Moray Pl.

Café St Honor

E

Belford Road

Rothesay Pl.

Chester Residence

Belford Road

Walker Road

Queensferry

Randolph Crescent

Ainslie Pl.

THE GEORGIAN HOUSE

Queensferry Street

Forage & Chatter

Galvin Brasserie De Luxe

Shandwick Pl.

William St.

The Pompadour by Galvin

The Honours

Mark Greena

Castle St.

CHARLOTTE SQ.

George St.

Rose St.

Princes

PRINCES STF

Waldorf Astoria Edinburgh
The Caledonian

Lothian Road

GARDENS

Bon Viva

2

Palmerston Place

West Maitland St.

Haymarket Ter.

Morrison Link

Grove

Gardner's Crescent

Morrison Street

Sheraton Grand H. & Spa

Castle Terrace

Castle Terrace

Kanpai

Bread St.

Spitall St.

Johns

CASTLE

CASTL

West

Timberyar

Dairy Road

West

Dundee Street

Viewforth

Canal

Approach

Fountainbridge

Place

Leven St.

Home St.

Lauriston

Passorn

Melville

3

Union

Granville Terr.

Viewforth

Gilmore

Bruntsfield Pl.

Warrender P

Warrender

0 ———— 300 m
0 ———— 300 yards

E

F

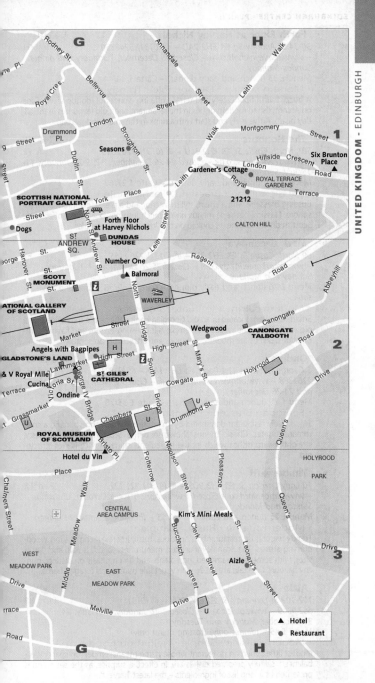

G Rodney St.
Royal Cres.
Bellevue
Drummond Pl.
Seasons
Annandale
H Walk
Leith Walk
Montgomery Street **1**
Hillside Crescent London Road
Six Brunton Place ▲
Gardener's Cottage
ROYAL TERRACE GARDENS
21212
Royal Terrace
CALTON HILL

London Street
Broughton St.
Dublin St.
Drummond Pl.
York Place
SCOTTISH NATIONAL PORTRAIT GALLERY
Dogs
St. ANDREW SQ.
North St. Andrew St.
Forth Floor at Harvey Nichols
DUNDAS HOUSE
Leith Street
York Street
George St.
Hanover St.

St. SCOTT MONUMENT
St.
NATIONAL GALLERY OF SCOTLAND
Number One ▲ **Balmoral**
North Bridge
WAVERLEY
Regent Road
Abbeyhill
Canongate

Market Street
Angels with Bagpipes
GLADSTONE'S LAND
& V Royal Mile
Cucina
Lawnmarket
George IV Bridge
H
High Street
St GILES' CATHEDRAL
South Bridge
High Street
St. Mary's St.
Wedgwood
CANONGATE TALBOOTH
Holyrood Road **2**
Holyrood Drive
U

Terrace
Victoria St.
Ondine
Cowgate
Bridge
Drummond St.
U

Grassmarket
U
ROYAL MUSEUM OF SCOTLAND
Chambers St.
U
Bristo Pl.
Nicolson Street
Queen's Drive
HOLYROOD PARK

Hotel du Vin ▲
Place
Walk
Potterrow
Pleasance

Chalmers Street
CENTRAL AREA CAMPUS
Meadow Walk
Middle Meadow Walk
Kim's Mini Meals
Buccleuch
Clerk Street
St. Leonard's St.
HOLYROOD PARK
Drive **3**

WEST MEADOW PARK
EAST MEADOW PARK
Aizle

rrace
Road
Melville Drive
Drive
U

G **H**

▲	Hotel
●	Restaurant

825

Forth Floor at Harvey Nichols XX ≤ 🛋 ⅙ 🎹 🗟 🕅

30-34 St Andrew Sq ⊠ EH2 2AD – ℰ (0131) 5248350 Plan: **G1**
*– www.harveynichols.com – Closed 25 December, 1 January and dinner
Sunday-Monday*
Menu £ 33 (lunch and early dinner) – Carte £ 34/44
• Modern cuisine • Fashionable • Trendy •
A buzzy fourth floor eatery and terrace offering wonderful rooftop views. Dine
on accomplished modern dishes in the restaurant or on old favourites in the all-
day bistro. Arrive early and start with a drink in the smart cocktail bar.

The Honours XX 🎹 🗟

58A North Castle St ⊠ EH2 3LU – ℰ (0131) 220 2513 Plan: **F2**
*– www.thehonours.co.uk – Closed 24-26 December, 1-2, 9-24 January, 11-
15 July, Sunday and Monday*
Menu £ 29 (lunch and early dinner) – Carte £ 27/67
• Classic cuisine • Brasserie • Fashionable •
Bustling brasserie with a smart, stylish interior and a pleasingly informal atmo-
sphere. Classical brasserie menus have French leanings but always offer some
Scottish dishes too; meats cooked on the Josper grill are popular.

Mark Greenaway XX ⇔ 🗟

69 North Castle St ⊠ EH2 3LJ – ℰ (0131) 226 1155 Plan: **F2**
*– www.markgreenaway.com – Closed 25-26 December, 1-2 January,
Sunday and Monday*
Menu £ 26 (lunch and early dinner) – Carte £ 42/58 – (booking advisable)
• Modern cuisine • Intimate • Romantic •
Smart restaurant located in an old Georgian bank – they store their wine in the
old vault. The well-travelled chef employs interesting texture and flavour combinations. Dishes are modern, ambitious and attractively presented.

Ondine XX ⅙ 🎹 🗟

2 George IV Bridge (1st floor) ⊠ EH1 1AD – ℰ (0131) Plan: **G2**
*2261888 – www.ondinerestaurant.co.uk – Closed 1 week early January
and 24-26 December*
Menu £ 25 (lunch and early dinner) – Carte £ 33/78
• Seafood • Brasserie • Elegant •
Smart, lively restaurant dominated by an impressive horseshoe bar and a crustacean counter. Classic menus showcase prime Scottish seafood in tasty,
straightforward dishes which let the ingredients shine. Service is well-structu-
red.

Timberyard X 🛋 ⅙ ⇔ 🗟 🕅

10 Lady Lawson St ⊠ EH3 9DS – ℰ (0131) 221 1222 Plan: **F2**
*– www.timberyard.co – Closed 1 week April, 1 week October, Christmas,
Sunday and Monday*
Menu £ 25 (lunch and early dinner)/55 – (booking essential at dinner)
• Modern cuisine • Rustic • Simple •
Trendy warehouse restaurant; its spacious, rustic interior incorporating wood-
burning stoves. The Scandic-influenced menu offers 'bites', 'small' and 'large'
sizes, with some home-smoked ingredients and an emphasis on distinct, punchy flavours. Cocktails are made with vegetable purées and foraged herbs.

Aizle X 🎹 🕅

107-109 St Leonard's St ⊠ EH8 9QY – ℰ (0131) Plan: **H3**
*662 9349 – www.aizle.co.uk – Closed 1-16 January, 2-17 July, 24-
31 December, Monday and Tuesday*
Menu £ 45 – (dinner only) (tasting menu only)
• Modern cuisine • Simple • Neighbourhood •
Modest little suburban restaurant whose name means 'ember' or 'spark'. Well-
balanced, skilfully prepared dishes are, in effect, a surprise, as the set menu is
presented as a long list of ingredients – the latest 'harvest'.

Bia Bistrot   🗙 🕼

19 Colinton Rd ⊠ EH10 5DP – ℰ (0131) 4528453   Plan: **B2**
– www.biabistrot.co.uk – Closed first week January, second week
April, second week July, second week October, Sunday and Monday
Menu £ 10 (lunch and early dinner) – Carte £ 19/38
• Classic cuisine • Neighbourhood • Bistro •
A simple, good value neighbourhood bistro with a buzzy vibe. Unfussy, flavour-
some dishes range in their influences due to the friendly owners' Irish-Scottish
and French-Spanish heritages; they are husband and wife and cook together.

Bon Vivant   🗙 🕮

55 Thistle St ⊠ EH2 1DY – ℰ (0131) 225 3275   Plan: **F1**
– www.bonvivantedinburgh.co.uk – Closed 25-26 December and 1 January
Menu £ 16 (weekday lunch) – Carte £ 25/38
• Traditional cuisine • Wine bar • Cosy •
A relaxed wine bar in the city backstreets, with a dimly lit interior, tightly packed
tables and a cheery, welcoming team. The appealing, twice daily menu has an
eclectic mix of influences; start with some of the bite-sized nibbles.

Café St Honoré   🗙

34 North West Thistle Street Ln. ⊠ EH2 1EA – ℰ (0131)   Plan: **F1**
2262211 – www.cafesthonore.com – Closed 24-26 December and 1-
2 January
Menu £ 15/24 – Carte £ 31/51 – (booking essential)
• Classic French • Bistro • Neighbourhood •
Long-standing French bistro, tucked away down a side street. The interior is
cosy, with wooden marquetry, mirrors on the walls and tightly packed tables.
Traditional Gallic menus use Scottish produce and they even smoke their own
salmon.

Forage & Chatter   🗙 🄰🄲

1A Alva St ⊠ EH2 4PH – ℰ (0131) 225 4599   Plan: **F2**
– www.forageandchatter.co.uk – Closed 24-26 December, 1-3 January,
Sunday and Monday
Menu £ 15 (weekday lunch) – Carte £ 27/41
• Modern cuisine • Friendly • Neighbourhood •
Follow the narrow staircase down to the basement, where a series of small, rus-
tic rooms and a pretty conservatory await. Appealing Scottish dishes feature
many foraged ingredients. Service is engaging and goes the extra mile.

Gardener's Cottage   🗙

1 Royal Terrace Gdns ⊠ EH7 5DX – ℰ (0131) 558 1221   Plan: **H1**
– www.thegardenerscottage.co – Closed 25-26 December and 1 January
Menu £ 50 (dinner) – Carte lunch £ 30/40 – (bookings advisable at dinner)
• Traditional cuisine • Rustic • Friendly •
This quirky little eatery was once home to a royal gardener. Two cosy, simply
furnished rooms have long communal tables. Lunch is light and dinner offers
an 8 course set menu; much of the produce comes from the kitchen garden.

Kanpai   🗙

8-10 Grindlay St ⊠ EH3 9AS – ℰ (0131) 228 1602   Plan: **F2**
– www.kanpaisushiedinburgh.co.uk – Closed Sunday and Monday
Carte £ 13/40
• Japanese • Simple • Design •
Uncluttered, modern Japanese restaurant with a smart sushi bar and cheerful
service. Colourful, elaborate dishes have clean, well-defined flavours; the menu
is designed to help novices feel confident and experts feel at home.

Kim's Mini Meals
5 Buccleuch St ⊠ *EH8 9JN –* ℰ *(0131) 6297951*   Plan: **H3**
Carte approx. £ 18 – *(booking essential at dinner)*
• Korean • Simple • Friendly •
A delightfully quirky little eatery filled with bric-a-brac and offering good value,
authentic Korean home cooking. Classic dishes like bulgogi, dolsot and jjigae
come with your choice of meat or vegetables as the main ingredient.

Purslane
33a St Stephen St ⊠ *EH3 5AH –* ℰ *(0131) 226 3500*   Plan: **F1**
*– www.purslanerestaurant.co.uk – Closed 25-26 December, 1 January and
Monday*
Menu £ 15 (lunch and early dinner)/35 – *(booking essential)*
• Modern cuisine • Neighbourhood • Rustic •
A cosy, atmospheric basement restaurant made up of just 9 tables. The young
chef-owner creates ambitious modern dishes which mix tried-and-tested flavours with modern techniques. Lunch is particularly good value.

Seasons
36 Broughton St ⊠ *EH1 3SB –* ℰ *(0131) 4669851*   Plan: **G1**
*– www.seasonstasting.co.uk – Closed 1-7 January, 24-26 December,
Monday and Tuesday*
Menu £ 19/40
• Modern cuisine • Friendly • Neighbourhood •
An enthusiastic young chef runs this modest wood-clad restaurant. A well-priced set lunch is followed by a 5 or 7 course surprise dinner menu, and cooking
is fresh and vibrant. Head downstairs if you fancy a cocktail.

Taisteal
1-3 Raeburn Pl, Stockbridge ⊠ *EH4 1HU –* ℰ *(0131)*   Plan: **F1**
332 9977 – www.taisteal.co.uk – Closed 2 weeks January and Monday
Menu £ 15 (weekdays) – Carte £ 22/37
• Modern British • Neighbourhood • Friendly •
Taisteal is Irish Gaelic for 'journey' and is the perfect name: photos from the
chef's travels line the walls and dishes have global influences, with Asian flavours to the fore. The wine list even has a sake section.

Wedgwood
267 Canongate ⊠ *EH8 8BQ –* ℰ *(0131) 5588737*   Plan: **H2**
*– www.wedgwoodtherestaurant.co.uk – Closed 1-21 January and 25-
26 December*
Menu £ 19 (lunch) – Carte dinner £ 32/52
• Modern cuisine • Friendly • Intimate •
Atmospheric bistro hidden away at the bottom of the Royal Mile. Well-presented dishes showcase produce foraged from the surrounding countryside and
feature some original, modern combinations. It's personally run by a friendly
team.

Balmoral
1 Princes St ⊠ *EH2 2EQ –* ℰ *(0131) 5562414*   Plan: **G2**
– www.roccofortehotels.com
188 rm – ♥£ 200/645 ♥♥£ 225/645 – ☲ £ 27 – 20 suites
• Grand Luxury • Palace • Classic •
Renowned Edwardian hotel which provides for the modern traveller whilst
retaining its old-fashioned charm. Bedrooms are classical with a subtle contemporary edge; JK Rowling completed the final Harry Potter book in the top suite!
Live harp music accompanies afternoon tea in the Palm Court and 'Scotch'
offers over 460 malts. Dine on up-to-date dishes or brasserie classics.
❀ **Number One** – See restaurant listing

Sheraton Grand H. & Spa

1 Festival Sq ✉ EH3 9SR – ✆ (0131) 2299131 – www.sheratonedinburgh.co.uk Plan: **F2**

269 rm – 🚶£ 160/675 🚶🚶£ 160/675 – ☕ £ 22 – 11 suites

• Grand Luxury • Business • Modern •

A spacious hotel with castle views from some rooms – an impressive four-storey glass cube houses the stunning spa. Sleek, stylish bedrooms have strong comforts, the latest mod cons and smart bathrooms with mood lighting. The casual restaurant serves an all-encompassing menu and the bar offers over 50 gins.

Waldorf Astoria Edinburgh The Caledonian

Princes St ✉ EH1 2AB – ✆ (0131) 222 8888 – www.waldorfastoriaedinburgh.com Plan: **F2**

241 rm – 🚶£ 249/619 🚶🚶£ 269/639 – ☕ £ 23 – 6 suites

• Historic • Luxury • Design •

Smart hotel in the old railway terminus: have afternoon tea on the former forecourt or cocktails where the trains once pulled in. Sumptuous modern bedrooms have excellent facilities; ask for a castle view. Unwind in the UK's first Guerlain spa, then dine in the grand French salon or luxurious brasserie.

Galvin Brasserie De Luxe • **The Pompadour by Galvin** – See restaurant listing

Prestonfield

Priestfield Rd ✉ EH16 5UT – ✆ (0131) 2257800 – www.prestonfield.com Plan: **C2**

23 rm ☕ – 🚶£ 220/395 🚶🚶£ 220/395 – 5 suites

• Luxury • Country house • Personalised •

17C country house in a pleasant rural spot, with an opulent, dimly lit interior displaying warm colours, fine furnishings and old tapestries – it's hugely atmospheric and is one of the most romantic hotels around. Luxurious bedrooms boast a high level of facilities and service is excellent.

Rhubarb – See restaurant listing

G & V Royal Mile

1 George IV Bridge ✉ EH1 1AD – ✆ (0131) 2206666 – www.gandvhotel.com Plan: **G2**

136 rm ☕ – 🚶£ 150/300 🚶🚶£ 200/400 – 7 suites

• Luxury • Design •

A striking hotel in a great central location on the historic Royal Mile. Bedrooms on the upper floors have impressive city skyline views. Bold colour schemes, stylish furnishings and clever design features can be seen throughout.

Cucina – See restaurant listing

Hotel du Vin

11 Bristo Pl ✉ EH1 1EZ – ✆ (0131) 2474900 – www.hotelduvin.com/edinburgh Plan: **G3**

47 rm ☕ – 🚶£ 195/355 🚶🚶£ 195/355

• Luxury • Design •

Boutique hotel located close to the Royal Mile, featuring unique murals and wine-themed bedrooms furnished with dark wood. Guest areas include a whisky snug and a mezzanine bar complete with glass-fronted cellars and a wine tasting room. The traditional bistro offers classic French cooking.

Chester Residence

9 Rothesay Pl ✉ EH3 7SL – ✆ (0131) 226 2075 – www.chester-residence.com – Closed 23-26 December Plan: **E2**

23 suites – 🚶£ 135/325 🚶🚶£ 145/325 – ☕ £ 12

• Townhouse • Contemporary • Personalised •

A series of peacefully located Georgian townhouses. The luxurious suites come with kitchens and state-of-the-art facilities including video entry and integrated sound systems; the Mews apartments are the best.

UNITED KINGDOM - EDINBURGH

The Dunstane   **P**
4 West Coates ⊠ *EH12 5JQ* – ℰ *(0131) 3376169*   Plan: **B2**
– *www.thedunstane.co.uk*
35 rm ⌂ – ♦£ 109/229 ♦♦£ 129/259
• Townhouse • Contemporary • Personalised •
An impressive house which used to be a training centre for the Royal Bank of Scotland. Guest areas retain original Victorian features and the smart bedrooms have designer touches; some are located across a busy road. Light snacks are served all day in the lounge.

Six Brunton Place
6 Brunton Pl ⊠ *EH7 5EG* – ℰ *(0131) 6220042*   Plan: **H1**
– *www.sixbruntonplace.com*
– *Closed 7-29 December*
4 rm ⌂ – ♦£ 89 ♦♦£ 139/199
• Townhouse • Luxury • Contemporary •
This late Georgian townhouse – run by a charming owner – was once home to Frederick Ritchie, who designed the One O'Clock Gun and Time Ball. Inside you'll find flagged floors, columns, marble fireplaces and a cantile-vered stone staircase; these contrast with contemporary furnishings and vibrant modern art.

23 Mayfield   **P**
23 Mayfield Gdns ⊠ *EH9 2BX* – ℰ *(0131) 667 5806*   Plan: **C2**
– *www.23mayfield.co.uk*
7 rm ⌂ – ♦£ 99/169 ♦♦£ 125/199
• Traditional • Classic • Personalised •
Lovingly restored Victorian house with a helpful owner, an outdoor hot tub and a rare book collection. Sumptuous bedrooms come with coordinated soft furnishings, mahogany features and luxurious bathrooms. Breakfast is extravagant.

94 DR   **P**
94 Dalkeith Rd ⊠ *EH16 5AF* – ℰ *(0131) 6629265*   Plan: **C2**
– *www.94dr.com*
– *Closed 4-18 January and 25-26 December*
6 rm ⌂ – ♦£ 90/150 ♦♦£ 100/225
• Townhouse • Personalised • Contemporary •
Charming owners welcome you to this very stylish and individual hotel in a Vic-torian terraced house. Bedrooms are well-equipped, there's a retro lounge with an honesty bar and breakfast is served in the conservatory with its decked ter-race.

LEITH   PLAN I

✤ Martin Wishart   XxX & ⃞
54 The Shore ⊠ *EH6 6RA* – ℰ *(0131) 5533557*   Plan: **C1**
– *www.martin-wishart.co.uk*
– *Closed 25 July-4 August, 25-26 December, 18-19 April, Sunday and Monday*
Menu £ 32 (weekday lunch)/85 – *(booking essential)*
• Modern cuisine • Elegant • Intimate •
This elegant, modern restaurant is becoming something of an Edinburgh insti-tution. Choose between three 6 course menus – Classic, Seafood and Vegeta-rian – and a concise à la carte. Top ingredients are used in well-judged, flavour-ful combinations; dishes are classically based but have elaborate, original touches.
➜ Orkney scallops with white asparagus, peas, broad beans and sea rosemary. Squab pigeon with short rib, potato cannelloni, cauliflower and sage sauce. Yorkshire rhubarb with vanilla cream, ginger curd and sorrel granité.

Kitchin (Tom Kitchin) XX ⚇ 🅰🅒 ⇔ 🕪

78 Commercial Quay ⊠ EH6 6LX – ℰ (0131) 5551755   Plan: **C1**
– www.thekitchin.com – Closed 23 December-13 January, 3-7 April,
31 July-4 August, 16-20 October, Sunday and Monday
Menu £ 33 (lunch) – Carte £ 70/87 – (booking essential)
• Modern cuisine • Design • Fashionable •

Set in a smart, converted whisky warehouse. 'From nature to plate' is the eponymous chef-owner's motto and the use of natural features like bark wall cover-
ings, alongside the more traditional Harris tweed, reflect his passion for using
the freshest and best quality Scottish ingredients. Refined, generously proportioned classic French dishes are packed with vivid flavours.
➔ Shellfish cannelloni with crab, celeriac, orange and Newhaven green
crab bisque. Peppered loin of Borders roe deer served with rhubarb, root
vegetable mash and red wine sauce. Warm apple tart served with Airthrey
Kerse Farm vanilla ice cream and caramel sauce.

🕪 Norn XX 🅰🅒

50-54 Henderson St ⊠ EH6 6DE – ℰ (0131) 629 2525   Plan: **C1**
– www.nornrestaurant.com – Closed 26 December-10 January, 17-
21 October, Sunday and Monday
Menu £ 40/65 – (dinner only) (booking advisable) (tasting menu only)
• Modern cuisine • Fashionable • Neighbourhood •

A young couple run this likeable modern restaurant where the chefs serve their
dishes themselves. Creative, intricate cooking showcases produce from small
Scottish suppliers along with items they have foraged.

🏠 Malmaison ⇧ ⅙ ⅚ ⚙ 🅿

1 Tower Pl ⊠ EH6 7BZ – ℰ (0131) 285 1478   Plan: **C1**
– www.malmaison.com
100 rm – ♦£ 95/245 ♦♦£ 95/245 – ⌧ £ 14
• Business • Luxury • Contemporary •

An impressive former seamen's mission located on the quayside – the first of
the Malmaison hotels. The décor is a mix of bold stripes and contrasting black
and white themes. Bedrooms are well-equipped and one has a tartan roll-top
bath! The restaurant serves grills and European fare.

MICHELIN
IS CONTINUALLY
INNOVATING
FOR SAFER, CLEANER,
MORE ECONOMICAL,
BETTER CONNECTED...
ALL-ROUND
MOBILITY.

Tyres wear more quickly on short urban journeys.

?

TRUE!

You tend to accelerate and brake more often when driving around town so your tyres work harder!
If you are stuck in traffic, keep calm and drive slowly.

Tyre pressure only affects your car's safety.

?

FALSE!

Driving with underinflated tyres (0.5 bar below recommended pressure) doesn't just impact handling and fuel consumption, it will shave 8,000 km off tyre lifespan.
Make sure you check tyre pressure about once a month and before you go on holiday or a long journey.

If you only encounter **winter weather from time to time** - sudden showers, snowfall or black ice - **one type of tyre** will do the job.
?
TRUE!
The revolutionary **MICHELIN CrossClimate** - the very first summer tyre with winter certification - is a practical solution to keep you on the road whatever the weather.

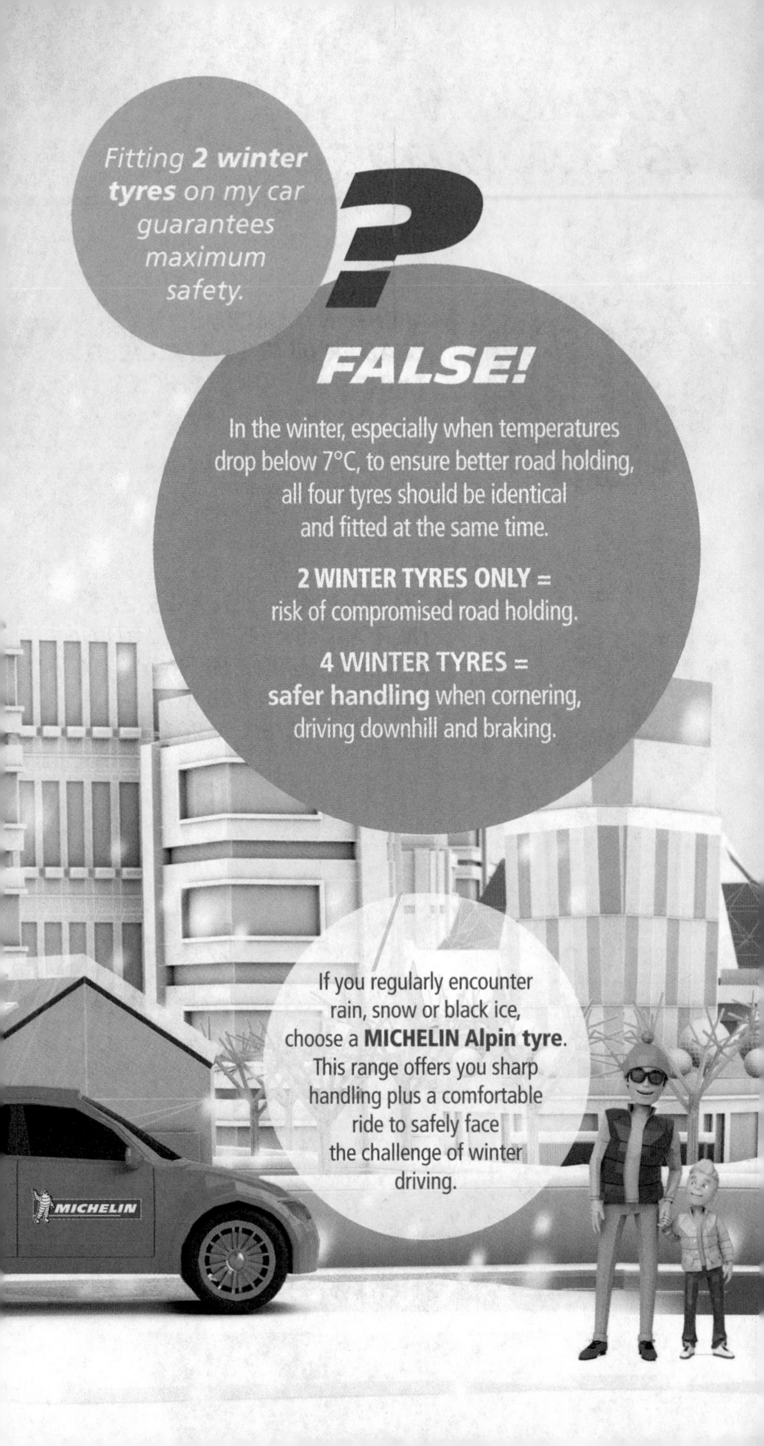
Fitting **2 winter tyres** on my car guarantees maximum safety.
?
FALSE!
In the winter, especially when temperatures drop below 7°C, to ensure better road holding, all four tyres should be identical and fitted at the same time.
2 WINTER TYRES ONLY = risk of compromised road holding.
4 WINTER TYRES = **safer handling** when cornering, driving downhill and braking.
If you regularly encounter rain, snow or black ice, choose a **MICHELIN Alpin tyre**. This range offers you sharp handling plus a comfortable ride to safely face the challenge of winter driving.
MICHELIN

MICHELIN
IS COMMITTED

► MICHELIN IS **GLOBAL LEADER IN FUEL-EFFICIENT TYRES** FOR LIGHT VEHICLES.

► **TO EDUCATE YOUNGSTERS IN ROAD SAFETY,** INCLUDING CYCLING, MICHELIN ROAD SAFETY CAMPAIGNS WERE RUN IN **16 COUNTRIES** IN 2015.

QUIZ

1 TYRES ARE BLACK SO WHY IS THE MICHELIN MAN WHITE?

Back in 1898 when the Michelin Man was first created from a stack of tyres, they were made of natural rubber, cotton and sulphur and were therefore light-coloured. The composition of tyres did not change until after the First World War when carbon black was introduced. But the Michelin Man kept his colour!

2 HOW LONG HAS MICHELIN BEEN GUIDING TRAVELLERS?

Since 1900. When the MICHELIN guide was first published at the turn of the century, it was claimed that it would last for a hundred years. It's still around today, with new editions published every year, along with online restaurant listings.

3 WHEN WAS THE "BIB GOURMAND" INTRODUCED IN THE MICHELIN GUIDE?

The symbol was created in 1997 but as early as 1954 the MICHELIN guide was recommending "good food at moderate prices". Today, it also features on the ViaMichelin website and on the Michelin Restaurants app.

If you want to enjoy a fun day out and find out more about Michelin, why not visit the l'Aventure Michelin museum and shop in Clermont-Ferrand, France:

www.laventuremichelin.com

MICHELIN
A better way forward

Europe in maps
and numbers

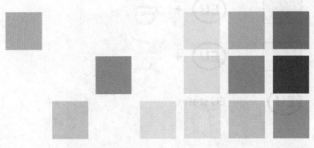

Eurozone : €

	(EU) + €
	(EU) + ¥̶
(EU)	EU states

Schengen Countries

Area of free movement between member states

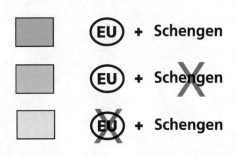

Driving in Europe

KEY

The information panels which follow give the principal motoring regulations in force when this guide was prepared for press; an explanation of the symbols is given below, together with some additional notes.

Speed restrictions in kilometres per hour applying to:

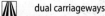

motorways

dual carriageways

single carriageways

 urban areas

 Maximum permitted level of alcohol in the bloodstream. This should not be taken as an acceptable level - it is NEVER sensible to drink and drive.

 Whether tolls are payable on m otorways and/or other parts of the road network.

Whether seatbelts are compulsory for the driver and all passengers in both front and back seats.

Whether headlights must be on at all times.

Driving in Europe

		![motorway]	![dual carriageway]	![main road]	![urban]	![alcohol]	![first aid]	![warning triangle]	![headlamp]
(A)	AUSTRIA	130	100	100	50	0,5	●	●	●
(B)	BELGIUM	120	120	90	50	0,5		●	
(CZ)	CZECHIA	130		90	50	⧗	●	●	●
(DK)	DENMARK	130		80	50	0,5		●	●
(FIN)	FINLAND	120	100	80	50	0,5		●	●
(F)	FRANCE	130	110	90	50	0,5		●	
(D)	GERMANY			100	50	0,5		●	
(GR)	GREECE	130	110	90	50	0,5		●	
(H)	HUNGARY	130	110	90	50	⧗	●	●	●
(IRL)	IRELAND	120	100	80	50	0,5		●	
(I)	ITALY	130	110	90	50	0,5		●	●
(L)	LUXEMBOURG	130		90	50	0,5		●	
(NL)	NETHERLANDS	130	100	80	50	0,5		●	
(N)	NORWAY	100	100	80	50	0,5		●	●
(PL)	POLAND	140	120	90	50	0,2		●	●
(P)	PORTUGAL	120	100	90	50	0,2		●	
(E)	SPAIN	120	100	90	50	0,5		●	
(S)	SWEDEN	110	110	90	50	0,2		●	●
(CH)	SWITZERLAND	120	100	80	50	0,5	●	●	●
(GB)	UNITED KINGDOM	112	112	96	48	0,8		●	

Compulsory ●

Distances

123: distances by road in kilometers

Time zones

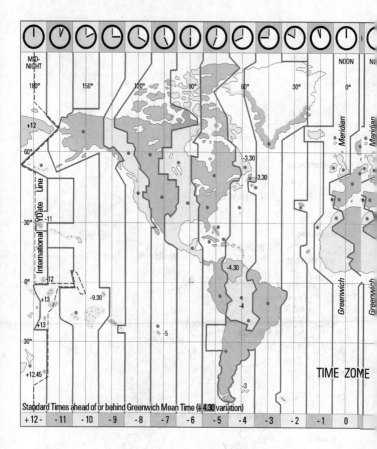

Standard Times ahead of or behind Greenwich Mean Time (+ 4.30 variation)

| + 12 - | - 11 | - 10 | - 9 | - 8 | - 7 | - 6 | - 5 | - 4 | - 3 | - 2 | - 1 | 0 |

852

Time zones

| MID-NIGHT | NOON | | 30° | 60° | 90° | 120° | 150° | 180° |
| 0° | 0° | | | | | | | |

+2 +3 +5 +7 +9 +10 +11 +12

+6 +10

+2 +8 +8.30

+3.30 +4.30 +5.45

+5.30 +6.30

+3 +9.30 +11.30

+13

+12.45

ZOME ZONES

• Area operating daylight saving time

| 0 | 0 | +1 | +2 | +3 | +4 | +5 | +6 | +7 | +8 | +9 | +10 | +11 | +12 - |

Meridian

Greenwich

International Date Line

Michelin Travel Partner
Société par actions simplifiées au capital de 11 288 880 EUR
27 Cours de l'Île Seguin - 92100 Boulogne Billancourt (France)
R.C.S. Nanterre 433 677 721

© **2018 Michelin Travel Partner** - All right reserved

Dépôt légal : 02-2018

No part of this publication may be reproduced in any form without the prior permission of the publisher.

"Based on Ordnance Survey Ireland by permission of the Government Permit No 8908 © Government of Ireland"

City plans of Bern, Geneva and Zürich:
with the permission of Federal directorate for cadastral surveys

"Based on Ordnance Survey of Great Britain with the permission
of the Controller of Her Majesty's Stationery Office, © Crown Copyright 100000247"

Printed in Italy: 02-2018

Typesetting: JOUVE, Saran (France)

Printing-binding: LEGO Print, Lavis (Italie)

Printed on paper from sustainably managed forests

Our editorial team has taken the greatest care in writing and checking the information in this guide. However, pratical information (administrative formalities, prices, addresses, telephone numbers, Internet addresses, etc) is subject to frequent change and such information should therefore be used for guidance only. It is possible that some of the information in this guide may not be accurate or exhaustive as of the date of publication. Before taking action (in particular in regard to administrative and customs regulations and procedures), you should contact the appropriate of f icial administration. We hereby accept no liability in regard to such information.